July 4-7, 2017
Prague, Czech Republic

Association for Computing Machinery

Advancing Computing as a Science & Profession

HT'17

Proceedings of the 28th ACM Conference on
Hypertext and Social Media

Sponsored by:
ACM SIGWEB

In cooperation with:
ACM SIGCHI

Supported by:
Charles University

Association for
Computing Machinery

Advancing Computing as a Science & Profession

The Association for Computing Machinery
2 Penn Plaza, Suite 701
New York, New York 10121-0701

Notice to Past Authors of ACM-Published Articles
ACM intends to create a complete electronic archive of all articles and/or other material previously published by ACM. If you have written a work that has been previously published by ACM in any journal or conference proceedings prior to 1978, or any SIG Newsletter at any time, and you do NOT want this work to appear in the ACM Digital Library, please inform permissions@acm.org, stating the title of the work, the author(s), and where and when published.

ISBN: 978-1-4503-4708-2 (Digital)

ISBN: 978-1-4503-5609-1 (Print)

Additional copies may be ordered prepaid from:

ACM Order Department
PO Box 30777
New York, NY 10087-0777, USA

Phone: 1-800-342-6626 (USA and Canada)
+1-212-626-0500 (Global)
Fax: +1-212-944-1318
E-mail: acmhelp@acm.org
Hours of Operation: 8:30 am – 4:30 pm ET

Printed in the USA

General Chairs' Welcome

It is our great pleasure to welcome you to the 2017 ACM International Conference on Hypertext and Social Media (HT 2017)! HT 2017 is held annually at locations all over the world. The last two years it has been in Canada and Cyprus. In 2017 it is held in Prague, Czech Republic on 4th – 7th July.

HT 2017 continues its long tradition of focusing on linking from both, technical and artistic perspective. This year, besides traditional tracks focusing on linking people, resources and stories, we have emphasized semantic web and linked data. This is further supported by the keynote talk on that topic. Furthermore, we have phrased the tracks so that they connect to the external communities of social media, adaptive hypermedia and recommendation, and semantic web. The whole conference program includes one tutorials, one festival, two workshops, thirty one long or short oral presentations of papers, 4 demonstrations and additional optional poster presentations of conference and workshop authors. We are happy and honored to have two keynote speakers, Kristina Lerman and Peter Mika.

Organizing a conference such as HT requires the effort and the dedication and effort of many volunteers. We are grateful to an outstanding group of colleagues for serving on the organization team for generously contributing their time and energy, including especially our Local Organization Chair and Treasurer, Anna Kotěšovcová; Program Chairs, Francesco Bonchi and Denis Helic, Workshop and Tutorial Chairs Jessica Rubart and Yeliz Yesilada; Doctoral Consortium Chairs Geert-Jan Houben and Philipp Singer; Publicity Chairs, Ladislav Peška and Simon Walk. The conference would be impossible to organize without their volunteer spirit. Throughout the entire period of conference organization, we have also benefited from advice and mentoring from the HT Steering Committee, especially the Simon Harper, Yeliz Yesilada, and Peter Brusilovsky. We want to thank all of them, especially. Finally, we want to thank the hosting university, Charles University in Prague and event management company Conforg in Prague as well as sponsors: ACM, SIGWEB, in cooperation with ACM SIGCHI.

Peter Dolog
ACM HT'17 General Chair
Aalborg University, Denmark

Peter Vojtáš
ACM HT'17 General Chair
Charles University, Czech Republic

Program Chairs' Welcome

It is our great pleasure to welcome you to the 2017 ACM International Conference on Hypertext and Social Media (HT 2017) in Prague, Czech Republic on 4th – 7th July.

HT is a top-tier ACM conference in the areas of Hypertext and Social Media. Since 1987, it has successfully brought together leading researchers and developers from the community. It is concerned with all aspects of modern hypertext research, including social media, adaptation, personalization, recommendations, user modeling, linked data and semantic web, dynamic and computed hypertext, and its application in digital humanities, as well as with interplay between those aspects such as linking stories with data or linking people with resources.

HT 2017 continues to create an outstanding technical program consisting of research and demo paper presentations. This year we organized the call for papers in four technical tracks: Social Networks and Digital Humanities (Linking people), Semantic Web and Linked Data (Linking data), Adaptive Hypertext and Recommendations (Linking resources), News and Storytelling (Linking stories). In total, we have received 69 regular paper (10 pages) submissions reviewed by a group of 86 program committee (PC) members. In the research track the PC accepted 19 regular papers (acceptance rate 27%), and 12 short-presentation papers (with the same number of pages in the proceeding as the regular ones). In addition, the conference will feature 4 demonstrations, which will appear as demo papers in the main conference proceedings. The conference keynote speakers will be Kristina Lerman and Peter Mika.

We are grateful to everyone who made this technical program possible. First of all, we would like to thank all the contributing authors who submitted their excellent work. The conference would not exist without your contributions. Secondly, we would like to acknowledge the great work done by our Track Chairs, Luca Maria Aiello, Axel Polleres, Alexander Felfernig, Charlie Hargood, and the Demonstration Chair, Martin Atzmueller.

Finally, we would like to particularly recognize the immense efforts of program committee members and external reviewers, who selected the technical program with their great expertise. We hope you enjoy the program and the opportunity to interact and collaborate with friends and colleagues from around the world.

Francesco Bonchi
ACM HT'17 Program Chair
ISI Foundation, Turin, Italy

Denis Helic
ACM HT'17 Program Chair
Graz University of Technology, Austria

Table of Contents

Keynotes

Full Papers

Demo Papers

Author Index

The 28th ACM Conference on Hypertext and Social Media

General Chairs:	Peter Dolog *(Aalborg University, Denmark)*
	Peter Vojtas *(Charles University, Prague, Czech Republic)*
Program Chairs:	Francesco Bonchi *(ISI Foundation, Turin, Italy)*
	Denis Helic *(Graz University of Technology, Austria)*
Track Chairs:	Luca Maria Aiello *(Bell Labs Cambridge, United Kingdom)*
	Axel Polleres *(Vienna University of Business and Administration, Austria)*
	Alexander Felfernig *(Graz University of Technology, Austria)*
	Charlie Hargood *(Bournemouth University, United Kingdom)*
	Martin Atzmueller *(Tilburg University, The Netherlands)*
Proceedings Chairs:	Francesco Bonchi *(ISI Foundation, Turin, Italy)*
	Peter Dolog *(Aalborg University, Denmark)*
	Denis Helic *(Graz University of Technology, Austria)*
	Peter Vojtas *(Charles University, Prague, Czech Republic)*
Local Arrangements Chair:	Anna Kotesovcova *(ConfOrg Prague, Czech Republic)*
Local Arrangements Committee:	Anna Kotesovcova *(ConfOrg Prague, Czech Republic)*
Publicity Chairs:	Simon Walk *(Stanford University, USA)*
	Ladislav Peska *(Charles University, Prague, Czech Republic)*
Treasurer & Registration Chair:	Anna Kotesovcova *(ConfOrg Prague, Czech Republic)*
Steering Committee Chair:	Yeliz Yesilada *(Middle East Techn. Univ., Northern Cyprus Campus)*
Steering Committee:	Helen Ashman *(University of South Australia, Australia)*
	Jamie Blustein *(Dalhousie University, Canada)*
	Peter Brusilovsky *(University of Pittsburgh, USA)*
	Leo Ferres *(Universidad del Desarrollo,Chile)*
	Simon Harper *(University of Manchester, United Kingdom)*
	Eelco Herder *(L3S Research Center, Germany)*
	David Millard *(University of Southampton, United Kingdom)*
	April Mosqus *(Association for Computing Machinery, USA)*
	Ethan Munson *(University of Wisconsin-Milwaukee, USA)*
	Jessica Rubart *(University of Applied Sciences Ostwestfalen-Lippe)*
Program Committee:	Harshavardhan Achrekar *(University of Massachusetts Lowell, USA)*
	Dirk Ahlers *(NTNU, Norway)*
	Luca Aiello *(Bell Labs Cambridge, United Kingdom)*
	Liliana Ardissono *(University of Turin, Italy)*
	Martin Atzmueller *(Tilburg University, The Netherlands)*
	Alejandro Bellogin *(Universidad Autonoma de Madrid, Spain)*

Additional reviewers: Yi Bu   Sarasi Lalithsena
                     Despoina Chatzakou   Shubhanshu Mishra
                     Alexander Dallmann   Thomas Niebler
                     Lisette Espín-Noboa   Christian Pölitz
                     Kalpa Gunaratna   Amon Rapp
                     Ming Jiang   Rezvaneh Rezapour
                     Johannes Jurgovsky   Fatemeh Salehi Rizi
                     Patrick Kasper   Stylianos Sergis
                     Christoph Kling   Ivan Srba
                     Michal Kompan   Bo Wang

HT 2017 Sponsors & Supporters

Sponsor: Association for Computing Machinery   sig web

In cooperation with: SIGCHI

Institutional supporter: FACULTY OF MATHEMATICS AND PHYSICS Charles University

A Meme is Not a Virus: The Role of Cognitive Heuristics in Information Diffusion*
Keynote Talk Abstract[†]

Kristina Lerman

USC Information Sciences Institute

4676 Admiralty Way, Marina del Rey, CA, 90292 USA

lerman@isi.edu

ABSTRACT

[1]The many decisions people make about what information to consume affect emerging trends, their popularity, and the diffusion of information through online social networks. Due to constraints of available time and cognitive resources, the ease of discovery strongly affects how people allocate their attention. Through empirical analysis and online experiments, I measure the impact of cognitive biases on collective attention. I show that position of information in the user interface strongly determines whether it is seen, while explicit signals about its popularity increases the likelihood of response. Accounting for these factors simplifies dynamics of information diffusion, allows for more accurate prediction of social behavior, and explains why most memes fail to spread widely online.

CCS CONCEPTS

Information systems → **Web applications**; *Social Networks* • **Networks** → Online social networks • **Human-centered computing** → HCI

KEYWORDS

Online social networks; social media; information diffusion; cognitive factors

ACM Reference format:
K. Lerman. 2017. A meme is not a virus: the role of cognitive heuristics in information diffusion. In *Proceedings of ACM Hypertext conference, Prague, Czech Republic, July 2017 (Hypertext'17)*, 1 page.

BIOGRAPHY

Kristina Lerman is Research Team Lead at the University of Southern California Information Sciences Institute and holds a joint appointment as a Research Associate Professor in the USC Computer Science Department. Trained as a physicist, she now applies network analysis and machine learning to problems in computational social science, including crowdsourcing, social network and social media analysis. Her recent work on modeling and understanding cognitive biases in social networks has been covered by the Washington Post, Wall Street Journal, and MIT Tech Review.

REFERENCES

[1] Kristina Lerman. 2016. Information Is Not a Virus, and Other Consequences of Human Cognitive Limits. *Future Internet*, **8**(2): 21+.

[2] Nathan O. Hodas and Kristina Lerman. 2014. The Simple Rules of Social Contagion. *Scientific Reports*, **4**. http://dx.doi.org/10.1038/srep04343

[3] Kristina Lerman and Tad Hogg. 2014. Leveraging position bias to improve peer recommendation. *PLoS One*, **9**(6): e98914.

[4] Greg Ver Steeg, Rumi Ghosh and Kristina Lerman. 2011. What Stops Social Epidemics. In *Proceedings of 5th International Conference on Web and Social Media*.

[5] Kristina Lerman and Rumi Ghosh. 2010. Information Contagion: an Empirical Study of the Spread of News on Digg and Twitter Social Networks. In *Proceedings of 4th International Conference on Weblogs and Social Media (ICWSM)*.

What Happened To The Semantic Web?

Keynote Talk Abstract

Peter Mika

Schibsted Diagonal 682 Barcelona Spain 08034

pmika@schibsted.com

ABSTRACT

The idea of the Semantic Web has surfaced in the literature over 20 years ago, and this area has been a major focus of academic research and standardisation for almost as long. In this talk, we look back at the history of the Semantic Web. We discuss what the original aspirations of its creators were, and what has been achieved in practice in these two decades. We also seek to find where the Semantic Web has failed and succeeded, illustrated by usage in web search, e-commerce and online media. Further, we will attempt to understand whether it makes sense to pursue at least some of these ideas in a different age, with new opportunities brought about by recent developments in Big Data, cloud computing, and Deep Learning.

KEYWORDs: Semantic Web, Linked Data, ontology

BIOGRAPHY

Peter Mika is a Senior Director of Engineering at Schibsted, working on user profiling, personalised search and recommendations for marketplace and media sites across 30 markets around the world. Previously, he was Director of Research at Yahoo Labs, based in London, UK, where he was working on the applications of semantic technology to Web search. He received his MSc and PhD in computer science (summa cum laude) from Vrije Universiteit Amsterdam. He is the author of numerous publications, as well as the book 'Social Networks and the Semantic Web' (Springer, 2007). In 2008 he has been selected as one of "AI's Ten to Watch" by the editorial board of the IEEE Intelligent Systems journal. In 2015, he received a 10 year best paper award for Ontologies are us: A unified model of social networks and semantics, originally published at ISWC 2005. He is a member of the editorial board of the Journal of Web Semantics (Elsevier). Peter is a regular speaker at both academic and technology conferences and serves on the advisory board of a number of public and private initiatives.

HT'17, July 4-7, 2017, Prague, Czech Republic.

ACM ISBN 978-1-4503-4708-2/17/07.

DOI: http://dx.doi.org/10.1145/3078714.3078751

Clarity is a Worthwhile Quality – On the Role of Task Clarity in Microtask Crowdsourcing

Ujwal Gadiraju
L3S Research Center
Leibniz Universität Hannover
Hannover, Germany
gadiraju@L3S.de

Jie Yang
Web Information Systems
Delft University of Technology
The Netherlands
j.yang-3@tudelft.nl

Alessandro Bozzon
Web Information Systems
Delft University of Technology
The Netherlands
a.bozzon@tudelft.nl

ABSTRACT

Workers of microtask crowdsourcing marketplaces strive to find a balance between the need for monetary income and the need for high reputation. Such balance is often threatened by poorly formulated tasks, as workers attempt their execution despite a sub-optimal understanding of the work to be done.

In this paper we highlight the role of *clarity* as a characterising property of tasks in crowdsourcing. We surveyed 100 workers of the CrowdFlower platform to verify the presence of issues with task clarity in crowdsourcing marketplaces, reveal how crowd workers deal with such issues, and motivate the need for mechanisms that can predict and measure task clarity. Next, we propose a novel model for task clarity based on the *goal* and *role* clarity constructs. We sampled 7.1K tasks from the Amazon mTurk marketplace, and acquired labels for task clarity from crowd workers. We show that task clarity is coherently perceived by crowd workers, and is affected by the type of the task. We then propose a set of features to capture task clarity, and use the acquired labels to train and validate a supervised machine learning model for task clarity prediction. Finally, we perform a long-term analysis of the evolution of task clarity on Amazon mTurk, and show that clarity is not a property suitable for temporal characterisation.

CCS CONCEPTS

•**Information systems** → **World Wide Web; Crowdsourcing;**

KEYWORDS

Task Clarity; Crowdsourcing; Microtasks; Crowd Workers; Goal Clarity; Role Clarity; Prediction; Performance

1 INTRODUCTION

Microtask crowdsourcing has become an appealing approach for data collection and augmentation purposes, as demonstrated by the consistent growth of crowdsourcing marketplaces such as Amazon Mechanical Turk[1] and CrowdFlower[2].

[1]http://www.mturk.com/
[2]http://www.crowdflower.com/

HT'17, July 4-7, 2017, Prague, Czech Republic.
© 2017 ACM. 978-1-4503-4708-2/17/07...$15.00
DOI: http://dx.doi.org/10.1145/3078714.3078715

Task consumption in microtask crowdsourcing platforms is mostly driven by a self-selection process, where workers meeting the required eligibility criteria select the tasks that they prefer to work on. Workers strive to maintain high reputation and performance to access more tasks, while maximizing monetary income. When discussing such a trade-off, the dominant narrative suggests that workers are more interested in obtaining their rewards, than in executing good work. We challenge this widespread opinion by focusing on an often neglected component of microtask crowdsourcing: the *clarity* of task description and instructions in terms of comprehensibility for workers.

Poor formulation of tasks has clear consequences: to compensate for a lack of alternatives in the marketplace, workers often attempt the execution of tasks despite a sub-optimal understanding of the work to be done. On the other hand, requesters are often not aware of issues with their task design, thus considering unsatisfactory work as evidence of malicious behaviour and deny rewards. As a result, crowd workers get demotivated, the overall quality of work produced decreases, and all actors lose confidence in the marketplace. Despite the intuitive importance of task *clarity* for microtask crowdsourcing, there is no clear understanding of the extent by which the lack of clarity in task description and instructions impacts worker performance, ultimately affecting the quality of work.

Research Questions and Original Contributions. This paper aims at filling this knowledge gap by contributing novel insights on the nature and importance of task clarity in microtask crowdsourcing. By combining qualitative and quantitative analysis, we seek to answer the following research questions.

> **RQ1**: What makes the specification of a task unclear to crowd workers? How do workers deal with unclear tasks?

First, we investigate if clarity is indeed a concern for workers. We designed and deployed a survey on the CrowdFlower platform, where we asked workers to describe what makes a task unclear, and to illustrate their strategies for dealing with unclear tasks. The survey involved 100 workers, and clearly highlights that workers confront unclear tasks on a regular basis.

Some workers attempt to overcome the difficulties they face with inadequate instructions, and unclear language by using external help, dictionaries or translators. Several workers tend to complete unclear tasks despite not understanding the objectives entirely.

These results demonstrate the need for methods for task clarity measurement and prediction, and shaped the formulation of the following questions.

> **RQ2:** How is the clarity of crowdsourcing tasks perceived by workers, and distributed over tasks?

Inspired by work performed in the field of organisational psychology, we consider clarity both in the context of *what* needs to be produced by the worker (*goal clarity*) and *how* such work should be performed (*role clarity*). We sampled 7.1K tasks from a 5 years worth dataset of the Amazon mTurk marketplace. Tasks were published on CrowdFlower to collect clarity assessments from workers. Results show that task clarity is coherently perceived by crowd workers, and is affected by the type of the task. We unveil a significant lack of correlation between the *clarity* and the *complexity* of tasks, thus showing that these two properties orthogonally characterise microwork tasks.

> **RQ3:** Which features can characterise the goal and role clarity of a task? Using such features, to what extent can task clarity be predicted?

We propose a set of features based on the metadata of tasks, task type, task content, and task readability to capture task clarity. We use the acquired labels to train and validate a supervised machine learning model for task clarity prediction. Our proposed model to predict task clarity on a 5-point scale achieves a mean absolute error (*MAE*) of *0.4 (SD=.003)*, indicating that task clarity can be accurately predicted.

> **RQ4:** To what extent is task clarity a macro-property of the Amazon mTurk ecosystem?

We analyzed 7.1K tasks to understand how task clarity evolves over time. We found that the overall task clarity in the marketplace fluctuates over time, albeit without a discernible pattern. We found a weak positive correlation between the average task clarity and the number of tasks deployed by requesters over time, but no significant effect of the number of tasks deployed by requesters on the magnitude of change in task clarity.

2 RELATED LITERATURE

Text readability. Readability has been defined as the sum of all elements in text that affect a reader's understanding, reading speed and level of interest in the material [11]. There has been a lot of work in the past on analyzing the readability of text, as summarized in [7]. Early works range from simple approaches that focus on the semantic and syntactic complexity of text [25], or vocabulary based approaches where semantic difficulty is operationalized by means of gathering information on the average vocabulary of a certain age or social status group [6]. More recently, authors proposed statistical language models to compute readability [8]. Other works studied the lexical richness of text by capturing the range and diversity of vocabulary in given text [29]. Several machine learning models have also been proposed to predict the readability of text [23, 31]. De Clerq et al. recently investigated the use of crowdsourcing for assessing readability [12]. The vast body of literature corresponding

to text readability has also resulted in several software packages and tools to compute readability [9, 17].

In this paper, we draw inspiration from related literature on text readability in order to construct features that aid in the prediction of task clarity on crowdsourcing platforms.

Task Clarity in Microtask Crowdsourcing. Research works in the field of microtask crowdsourcing have referred to the importance of task clarity tangentially; several authors have stressed about the positive impact of task design, clear instructions and descriptions on the quality of crowdsourced work [3, 26, 30, 34]. Grady and Lease pointed out the importance of wording and terminology in designing crowdsourcing tasks effectively [16]. Alonso and Baeza-Yates recommended providing 'clear and colloquial' instructions as an important part of task design [1]. Kittur et al. identified 'improving task design through better communication' as one of the pivotal next steps in designing efficient crowdsourcing solutions in the future [27]. The authors elaborated that task instructions are often ambiguous and incomplete, do not address boundary cases, and do not provide adequate examples. Khanna et al. studied usability barriers that were prevalent on Amazon mTurk (AMT), which prevented workers with little digital literacy skills from participating and completing work on AMT [24]. The authors showed that the task instructions, user interface, and the workers' cultural context corresponded to key usability barriers. To overcome such usability obstacles on AMT and better enable access and participation of low-income workers in India, the authors proposed the use of simplified user interfaces, simplified task instructions, and language localization. More recently, Yang et al. investigated the role of *task complexity* in worker performance, with an aim to better the understanding of task-related elements that aid or deter crowd work [37].

While the importance of task clarity has been acknowledged in the microtask crowdsourcing community, there is neither a model that describes task clarity nor a measure to quantify it. In this paper, we not only propose a model for task clarity, but we also present a means to measure it. To the best of our knowledge, this is the first work that thoroughly investigates the features that determine task clarity in microtask crowdsourcing, and provides an analysis of the evolution of task clarity.

Task Clarity in Other Domains. In the field of organizational psychology, researchers have studied how the sexual composition of groups affects the authority behavior of group leaders in cases where the task clarity is either *high* or *low* [33]. In this case, the authors defined task clarity as the degree to which the goal (i.e., the desired outcome of an activity) and the role (i.e., the activities performed by an actor during the course of a task) are clear to a group leader. In self-regulated learning, researchers have widely studied task interpretation as summarized in [32]. Hadwin proposed a model that suggests the role of the following three aspects in task interpretation and understanding; (i) implicit aspects, (ii) explicit aspects, and socio-contextual aspects [18, 19]. Recent literature regarding task interpretation in the learning field has revolved around text decoding, instructional practices or perceptions of tasks on the one hand [4, 22, 28], and socio-contextual aspects of task interpretation such as beliefs about expertise, ability, and knowledge on the other hand [5, 10].

Inspired by the modeling of task clarity in the context of authority behavior in Psychology, we model task clarity as a combination of *goal clarity* and *role clarity* (as explained in Section 4).

3 ARE CROWDSOUCRED MICROTASKS ALWAYS CLEAR?

We aim to investigate whether or not workers believe task clarity to impact their work performance (**RQ1**). We thereby deployed a survey consisting of various questions ranging from general demographics of the crowd to questions regarding their experiences while completing microtasks on crowdsourcing platforms.

3.1 Methodology

We deployed the survey on CrowdFlower[3] and gathered responses from 100 distinct crowd workers. To detect untrustworthy workers and ensure reliability of the responses received, we follow recommended guidelines for ensuring high quality results in surveys [15]. To this end, we intersperse two attention check questions within the survey. In addition, we use the filter provided by CrowdFlower to ensure the participation of only high quality workers (i.e., *level 3* crowd workers as prescribed on the CrowdFlower platform). We flagged workers who failed to pass at least one of the two attention check questions and do not consider them in our analysis.

3.2 Analysis and Findings

Worker's Experience. We found that around 36% of the workers who completed the survey earn their primary source of income through crowd work. 32.6% of the workers claim to have been contributing piecework through crowdsourcing platforms over the last 3 to 6 months. 63.2% of the workers have been doing so for the last 1 to 3 years. A small fraction of workers (3.2%) claim to have been working on microtasks for the last 3 to 5 years, while 1% of the worker population has been contributing to crowdsourced microtasks for over 5 years. During the course of this time, almost 74% of workers claim to have completed over 500 different tasks.

What factors make tasks unclear? We asked the workers to provide details regarding the factors that they believe make tasks unclear, in an open text field. The word-cloud in Figure 1a represents the responses collected from the crowd workers. Workers complained about the task instructions and descriptions being '*vague*', '*blank*', '*unclear*', '*inconsistent*', '*imprecise*', '*ambiguous*', or '*poor*'. Workers also complained about the language used; '*too many words*', '*high standard of English*', '*broken English*', '*spelling*', and so forth. Workers also pointed out that adequate examples are seldom provided by requesters. Excerpts of these responses are presented on the companion webpage[4].

Task Clarity and Influence on Performance. Around 49% of workers claimed that up to a maximum of 30% of the tasks that they worked on were unclear. 37% of workers claimed that between 31-60% of the tasks they completed lacked clarity, while 14% of the workers claimed that more than 60% of their completed tasks were unclear. We also asked the workers about the perceived influence of

---
[3]http://crowdflower.com
[4]https://sites.google.com/site/ht2017clarity/

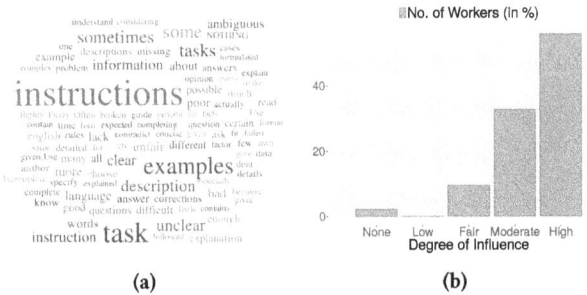

Figure 1: (a) Word-cloud representing factors cited by workers that make tasks unclear. Size of words indicate their frequency. (b) Perceived degree of influence of task clarity on performance of workers.

task clarity on their performance. Our findings are presented in the Figure 1b. A large majority of workers believe that task clarity has a quantifiable influence on their performance. We also asked workers about the frequency of encounter for tasks containing difficult words, which might have hindered their performance. Figure 2a depicts our findings, indicating that workers observed tasks which contained difficult words reasonably frequently.

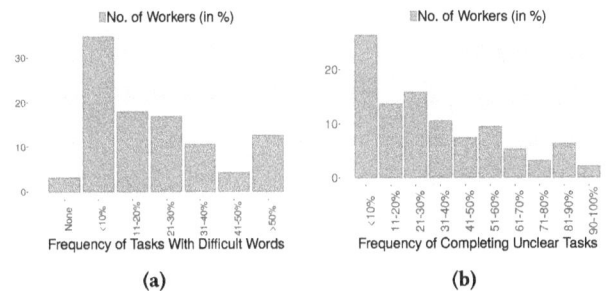

Figure 2: (a) Frequency of tasks with difficult words, and (b) frequency of workers completing unclear tasks.

How do workers deal with unclear tasks? We investigated the frequency with which workers complete tasks despite the lack of clarity. As shown in Figure 2b, we found that nearly 27% of workers complete less than 10% of the unclear tasks that they encounter.

On the other hand, another 27% of workers completed more than 50% of all the unclear tasks they come across. In addition, around 18% of workers used dictionaries or other helpful means/tools to better understand over 50% of tasks they completed. 20% of workers used translators in more than 50% of the tasks that they completed.

4 MODELING TASK CLARITY

We address **RQ2** by modelling task clarity of crowdsourced microtasks as a combination of *goal clarity* and *role clarity*. Inspired by previous work in organizational psychology [33], we define task clarity as a combination of the extent to which the desired outcome of a task is clear (goal clarity), and the extent to which the workflow or activities to be carried out are clear (role clarity).

4.1 Assessing Task Clarity

Task clarity of microtasks in a marketplace is a notion that can be quantified by human assessors by examining task metadata such as the *title*, *keywords* associated with the task, *instructions* and *description*. Since these are the main attributes that requesters use to communicate the desired outcomes of the tasks, and prescribe how crowd workers should proceed in order to realize the objectives, we argue that they play an important role in shaping crowd work.

4.2 Acquiring Task Clarity Labels

With an aim to understand the distribution of task clarity across the diverse landscape of tasks on AMT [13], we sampled 7,100 tasks that were deployed on AMT over a period of 1 year between October 2013 to September 2014. For every month spanning the year, we randomly sampled 100 tasks of each of the 6 task types proposed in previous work [14]; *content creation* (CC), *information finding* (IF), *interpretation and analysis* (IA), *verification and validation* (VV), *content access* (CA)[5] and *surveys* (SU). Next, we deployed a job[6] on CrowdFlower to acquire task clarity labels from crowd workers. We first provided detailed instructions describing task clarity, goal clarity and role clarity. An excerpt from the task overview is presented below:

"Task clarity defines the quality of a task in terms of its comprehensibility. It is a combination of two aspects; (i) goal clarity, i.e, the extent to which the objective of the task is clear, and (ii) role clarity, i.e., the extent to which the steps or activities to be carried out in the task are clear."

In each task workers were required to answer 10 questions on a 5-point Likert scale. The questions involved assessing the goal and role clarity of the corresponding task, the overall task clarity, the influence of goal and role clarity in assessing overall task clarity, clarity of title, instructions and description, the extent to which the title conveyed the task description, the extent to which the keywords conveyed the task description and goal of the task, and the quality of language in the task description. Apart from these 10 questions, workers were provided with an optional text field where they could enter comments or remarks about the AMT task they evaluated. We gathered responses to these questions for each of the 7,100 tasks from 5 distinct crowd workers. We controlled for quality by using the *highest quality* restriction on CrowdFlower, that allows only workers with a near perfect accuracy over hundreds of different tasks and varying task types. In addition, we interspersed attention check questions where workers were asked to enter alphanumeric codes that were displayed to them. In return, workers were compensated according to the hourly rate of 7.5 USD.

4.3 Perception of Task Clarity

We found that the mean task, goal and role clarity across the different tasks were nearly the same. On average, workers perceived tasks to be moderately clear (*M=3.77, SD=.53*). The same is the case with goal clarity (*M=3.76, SD=.53*) and role clarity (*M=3.76, SD=0.54*). On investigating the influence of goal and role clarity on the crowd workers in adjudicating the overall task clarity, we found that role

---

[5]Note that there were fewer than 100 tasks of the CA type in a few months during the time period considered. In those cases, we considered all available tasks.
[6]Preview available in the companion page: https://sites.google.com/site/ht2017clarity/.

clarity and goal clarity were both important in determining task clarity. On average, workers responded that goal clarity influenced their judgment of overall task clarity to an extent of 3.98/5 (*SD=.51*), and that in case of role clarity was 3.93/5 (*SD=.52*). We found that goal clarity was slightly more influential than role clarity in determining the task clarity, and this difference was statistically significant; $t(14199) = 25.28, p < .001$.

We also analyzed the relationship of task clarity with goal and role clarity respectively. We found strong positive linear relationships in both cases, as shown in Figure 3.

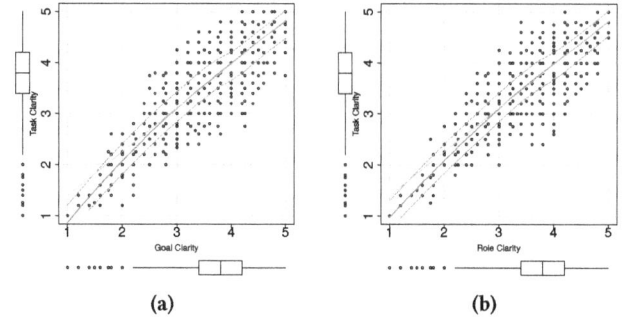

(a)   **(b)**

Figure 3: Relationship of Task Clarity with (a) Goal Clarity, and (b) Role Clarity. The trendline is represented in green, and the regression line is represented by the thick red line.

We computed Pearson's **r** between task clarity with each of goal and role clarity; $r(14998) = .85, R^2 = .72, p < .001$ and $r(14998) = .86, R^2 = .74, p < .001$. These findings indicate that it is equally important for task requesters to ensure that the objective of the task, as well as the means to achieve the desired outcome are adequately communicated to crowd workers via the task title, instructions and description, and keywords associated with the task.

4.3.1 Inter-worker Agreement. To find out whether or not task clarity is coherently perceived by workers, we verify the presence of agreement of task clarity evaluations among workers. Given the subjective nature of task clarity evaluations, we apply the SOS Hypothesis [20], which examines the extent to which individual evaluations of clarity spread around the mean clarity value per task. The SOS Hypothesis has proven to be more reliable than other inter-evaluator agreement measures such as Krippendorff's alpha, in subjective assessment tasks that involve a set of participants evaluating the same item – in our case, the same task [2]. In SOS Hypothesis, we test the magnitude of the squared relationship between the standard deviation (i.e. SOS) of the evaluations and the mean opinion score (MOS; in our case, mean clarity score), denoted by α. The value of α can then be compared with those of other subjective assessment tasks that are deemed to be more (high α) or less prone to disagreement (low α) among evaluators. Specifically, for 5-point scale evaluations, SOS Hypothesis tests a square relationship between SOS and MOS by fitting the following equation:

$$SOS(i) = -\alpha MOS(i)^2 + 6\alpha MOS(i) - 5\alpha$$

considering each task i in the evaluation pool.

Table 1: SOS Hypothesis α values for Task Clarity, Goal Clarity and Role Clarity.

Clarity	Task Clarity	Goal Clarity	Role Clarity
α	0.3166	0.3229	0.3184

Table 1 shows the α values computed for task clarity, goal clarity and role clarity. All these evaluations have a value of 0.32, which is similar to what could be obtained in other subjective assessment tasks such as smoothness of web surfing, VoIP quality, and cloud gaming quality [20]. We therefore consider it acceptable. Figure 4 shows the fitted quadratic curve against worker evaluations for individual tasks. A significant correlation could be obtained between the fitted SOS value and the actual SOS value (Pearson's $r = 0.506$, $p < .001$). In conclusion, we find that task clarity is coherently perceived by workers. The substantial evidence of workers' agreement in perceiving task clarity helps establish the mean clarity score as ground truth for modeling task clarity using objective task features, as we report in Section 5.

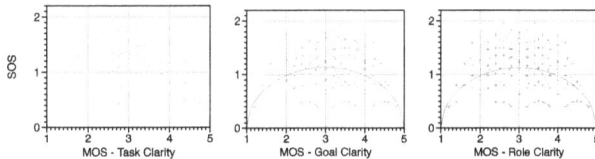

Figure 4: SOS Hypothesis plots for Task Clarity (green), Goal Clarity (red), and Role Clarity (blue). The quadratic curve depicts the fitting to worker evaluations for individual tasks.

4.3.2 Task Types and Perception of Task Clarity. We investigated the impact of task types on the perception of task clarity and the constructs of goal and role clarity. We note that Levene's test for homogeneity of variances was not violated across the different task types with respect to each of task, goal and role clarity. We conducted a one-way between workers ANOVAs to compare the effect of task types on the perception of task, goal and role clarity respectively. We found a significant effect of task type on the perception of task clarity at the $p < .01$ level, across the 6 task type conditions; $F(5,7002) = 6.176, p < .001$. Post-hoc comparisons using the Tukey HSD test indicated that the perception of task clarity in some task types was significantly poorer than others; as presented in Table 2.

Table 2: Post-hoc comparisons using the Tukey HSD test to investigate the effect of task types on *task clarity*. Comparisons resulting in significant outcomes are presented here. (* indicates $p < .05$ and ** indicates $p < .01$)

Task Type	M	SD	Comparison	Tukey HSD p-value
CA	3.75	.51	CA vs SU	0.011*
CC	3.76	.51	CA vs VV	0.004**
IA	3.74	.52	CC vs SU	0.046*
IF	3.77	.52	CC vs VV	0.020*
SU	3.82	.50	IA vs SU	0.001**
VV	3.82	.48	IA vs VV	0.001**

Table 3: Post-hoc comparisons using the Tukey HSD test to investigate the effect of task types on *goal clarity*. Comparisons resulting in significant outcomes are presented here. (* indicates $p < .05$ and ** indicates $p < .01$)

Task Type	M	SD	Comparison	Tukey HSD p-value
CA	3.76	0.52	CA vs VV	0.006**
CC	3.76	0.50	CC vs VV	0.004**
IA	3.74	0.51	IA vs SU	0.005**
IF	3.78	0.52	IA vs VV	0.001**
SU	3.82	0.51		
VV	3.83	0.50		

Table 4: Post-hoc comparisons using the Tukey HSD test to investigate the effect of task types on *role clarity*. Comparisons resulting in significant outcomes are presented here. (* indicates $p < .05$ and ** indicates $p < .01$)

Task Type	M	SD	Comparison	Tukey HSD p-value
CA	3.75	0.51	CA vs SU	0.030*
CC	3.76	0.50	CA vs VV	0.001**
IA	3.73	0.52	CC vs SU	0.048*
IF	3.78	0.51	CC vs VV	0.001**
SU	3.82	0.50	IA vs SU	0.001**
VV	3.84	0.48	IA vs VV	0.001**
			IF vs VV	0.043*

We also found a significant effect of task type on (i) the perception of goal clarity at the $p < .01$ level, across the 6 task type conditions; $F(5,7002) = 5.918, p < .001$, and (ii) the perception of role clarity at the $p < .01$ level, across the 6 task type conditions; $F(5,7002) = 8.074, p < .001$. Post-hoc comparisons using the Tukey HSD test (Tables 3 and 4) indicated that the perception of goal and role clarity in some task types was significantly poorer than others.

4.4 Task Clarity and Task Complexity

Recent work by Yang et al. modeled *task complexity* in crowd-sourcing microtasks [37]. By using the task complexity predictor proposed by the authors, we explored the relationship between task clarity and task complexity. We found no significant correlation between the two variables across the different types of 7,100 tasks in our dataset (see Figure 5a). This absence of a linear relationship between task complexity and task clarity suggests that tasks with high clarity can still be highly complex or tasks with low clarity can have low task complexity at the same time.

We analyzed the relationship between *task clarity* and *complexity* across different types of tasks, and found that there is no observable correlation between the two variables across the different types of tasks. As can be observed from Figure 3, a majority of tasks are perceived to lie within the range of moderate to high clarity. We therefore further investigated tasks with low clarity or complexity.

4.4.1 Relationship in Tasks with Low Clarity. As shown earlier, task clarity was coherently perceived by workers. We reason that tasks corresponding to a clarity rating < 3 have relatively *low* clarity. We investigated the effect of task types on the relationship between task clarity and complexity in tasks with low clarity. Using Pearson's **r**, we found a weak positive linear relationship between the two variables in information finding (IF) tasks with low clarity (see Figure 5b); *N=80*, **r**=.34. This can be explained as a

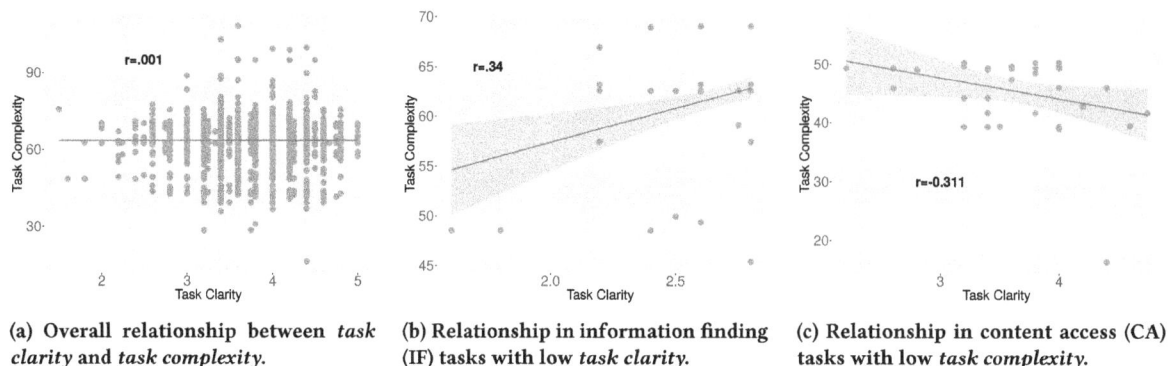

(a) Overall relationship between *task clarity* and *task complexity*.

(b) Relationship in information finding (IF) tasks with low *task clarity*.

(c) Relationship in content access (CA) tasks with low *task complexity*.

Figure 5: Relationship between *task clarity* and *complexity*.

consequence of complex workflows required to complete some IF tasks, where high task complexity is concomitant with relatively high task clarity. Accordingly, in IF tasks with low clarity, task complexity accounted for 11.56% of the variance in task clarity (the coefficient of determination, $R^2 = .1156, p<.01$). We did not find a significant relationship between the two variables in the low clarity subsets of other task types.

4.4.2 Relationship in Tasks with Low Complexity. Similarly, we consider tasks having a complexity score < 50 have relatively *low* complexity. We investigated the effect of task types on the relationship between task clarity and complexity in tasks with low complexity. Using Pearson's **r**, we found a weak negative linear relationship between the two variables in content access (CA) tasks with low complexity (see Figure 5c); $N=41$, $\mathbf{r}=.311$. Thus, in CA tasks with low complexity, task clarity accounted for 9.67% of the variance in task complexity (the coefficient of determination, $R^2 = .0967, p<.05$).

4.4.3 Discussion. The lack of linear correlation between clarity and complexity yields interesting observations. While surprising (intuitively, one might assume that a better task formulation – high clarity – would yield a lower complexity), this result is aligned with the classical theory on cognitive load, by Sweller and Chandler [35]. The theory postulates the presence of two sources of cognitive load: *intrinsic* and *extraneous*. Intrinsic cognitive load refers to the inherent difficulty in the content of presented material, which approximates task complexity in our context; extraneous cognitive load, on the other hand, refers to the organization and presentation of material, i.e. task clarity in our context. Sweller and Chandler suggest in their theory that, while the intrinsic cognitive load is unalterable, the extraneous cognitive load can either be increased because of inappropriate instructional design, or be reduced by well-structured presentation. We show that the theory can find application in microtask crowdsourcing, as tasks of similar complexity can either be of high clarity or low clarity.

When considering tasks of specific types, however, we find correlation could be established. Specifically, we find a negative correlation with content access (CA) tasks, thus suggesting that (poorly formulated) tasks asking workers to interact with on line content (e.g. watch a video, click a link) can be perceived more complex

to execute. With information finding (IF) tasks, high task complexity maps with high clarity, thus suggesting that requests for complex finding and retrieval operations can be associated with clearer instructions. These results provide further insights into the relationship between task clarity and complexity, and call for further investigation.

5 PREDICTION OF TASK CLARITY

In this section we tackle **RQ3** and propose to model task clarity based on objective features that are extractable from tasks. We envision a system that could automatically predict task clarity and thus provides feedback to requesters on task design and to workers on task selection and execution. To test the feasibility of this idea, our study starts by designing task features that are potentially predictive for task clarity; we then build a predictive model to automatically learn task clarity based on these features.

5.1 Features Sets

We explore four classes of task features, namely: *metadata features*, *task type features*, *content features*, and *readability features*. In the following we provide a brief introduction to each feature class, and refer the readers to the companion page for a full description of the feature set.

Metadata Features are the task attributes associated with the definition of tasks when they are created. Typical metadata features include the number of `initial HITs`, attributes of the descriptions about desired activities to be performed by workers (e.g., `title length` and `description length`), the required qualification of workers (e.g., worker `location` and `minimum approval rate`), the estimated execution time (i.e. `allotted time`) and `reward`. These features characterize a task from different aspects that might be correlated with task clarity. For example, we assume that a longer description could entail more efforts from the requester in explaining the task.

Task Type Features categorize a task into one of the six task types defined by [14]. They are therefore high level features that comprehensively describe what knowledge is in demand. Through previous analysis, we have observed that task type has a significant effect on the perception of task clarity. We therefore assume that task type could be indicative of task clarity in prediction.

Content Features capture the semantics of a task. These features use the high-dimensional bag of words (BOW) representation. To maximize the informativeness of the content features while minimizing the amount of noise, one-hot (i.e. binary) coding was applied to the BOW feature of task title and keywords, while TF-IDF weighting was applied to the BOW feature of task description. It has been shown by research in related domains (e.g., community Q&A systems [36]) that the use of words is indicative of the quality of task formulation, therefore we are interested in understanding the effect of language use on workers' perception of task clarity.

Readability Features are by nature correlated with task clarity: tasks with higher readability are better formulated, and are thereby expected to have a higher clarity. We experiment with several widely used readability metrics in our clarity prediction task to understand their predictive power of task clarity. These include the use of long words (`long_words`), long sentence (`words_per_sentence`), the use of `preposition`, `nominalization`, and more comprehensive readability metrics such as ARI, LIX, and in particular, `Coleman_Liau`, which approximates the U.S. grade level necessary to comprehend a piece of text.

5.2 Prediction Results

Due to the high dimension of the content features (size of vocabulary = 10,879), we apply the Lasso method, which does feature selection and regression simultaneously. We adopt 5-fold cross-validation and mean absolute error (MAE) for evaluation. Table 5 shows the prediction results. The prediction on task clarity achieves a MAE of 0.4032 (SD = 0.0031). The relatively small error compared to the scale of ground truth (i.e. 1-5) indicates that task clarity can be predicted accurately. In addition, the small standard deviation shows that the prediction is robust across different tasks. Similar results also hold for the prediction of goal clarity and role clarity, which confirms our previous observation that both are highly correlated with the overall task clarity.

Table 5: Prediction results for Task Clarity, Goal Clarity and Role Clarity, shown by $\mu \pm \sigma$.

Clarity	Task Clarity	Goal Clarity	Role Clarity
MAE	0.4032±0.0031	0.4076±0.0067	0.4008± 0.0070

Predictive Features. In the following we analyze the predictive features selected by Lasso. Table 6 shows the features with positive and negative coefficients in the Lasso model after training for task clarity prediction, i.e. features that are positively and negatively correlated with task clarity. Similar observations can be obtained for predicting goal and role clarity.

With regard to metadata features, it can be observed that longer descriptions and more keywords are positively correlated with task clarity. This suggests that more description and keywords could potentially improve the clarity of task formulation. We also observe that the increased use of images, or less use of external links could enhance task clarity. These are reasonable, since intuitively, images can help illustrate task requirements, while external links would bring in extra ambiguity to task specification in the absence of detailed explanations.

Table 6: Predictive features for task clarity prediction.

Feat. Class	Feat. w. Positive Coef.		Feat. w. Negative Coef.	
	Feature	Coef.*	Feature	Coef.*
Metadata	number_keywords	0.719	external_links	-0.598
	description_length	0.295		
	number_images	0.071		
	total_approved	0.011		
Task Type	VV	0.434	IA	-0.922
	SU	0.413		
Content	keyword: audio	2.673	keyword: id	-2.658
	keyword: transcription	1.548		
	keyword: survey	1.178		
Readability	preposition	1.748	ARI	-1.982
	GunningFogIndex	1.467	long_words	-0.671
	Coleman_Liau	0.855	syllables	-0.478
	words_per_sentence	0.620	nominalization	-0.136
	characters	0.237	pronoun	-0.104
	LIX	0.150	FleschReadingEase	-0.075
			RIX	-0.038
	(all about title)		(all about title)	

* For the sake of comparison, each value is shown with original coefficient ×10^2.

With regard to task type features, we find that tasks of type SU and VV are in general of higher clarity, while tasks of type IA are of lower clarity. This result confirms our previous findings.

With regard to content features, we observe that keyword features are more predictive than other types of content features (e.g. words in title or description). Predictive keywords include `audio`, `transcription`, `survey`, etc., which can actually characterize the majority of tasks in AMT. We therefore reason that workers' familiarity with similar tasks could enhance their perception of task clarity.

Finally, several interesting findings with regard to task readability are observed as follows. First, many types of readability scores are indicative of task clarity, indicating a strong correlation between task readability and task clarity. Second, compared with description or keyword readability, title readability is most predictive of task clarity. As an implication for requesters, putting efforts in designing better titles can improve task clarity. Third, we observe a positive correlation between task clarity and `Coleman_Liau`, which approximates the U.S. grade level necessary to comprehend the text. The increase of Coleman_Liau (i.e. more requirements on workersfi capability to comprehend the title) therefore does not lead to lower task clarity perceived by workers. The result is not surprising, given the demographic statistics of crowdworkers [13]. However, it raises questions on the suitability of this class of microtask crowdsourcing tasks for other types of working population.

On decomposing `Coleman_Liau` and exploring the effect of length of words (in terms of #letters) and length of sentences (in terms of #words), it can be observed that longer words (i.e., `long_words`) would decrease task clarity, while longer sentence (i.e., `words_per_sentence`) can enhance task clarity. This suggests that workers can generally comprehend long sentences, while the use of long words would decrease task clarity. This is consistent with our findings from **RQ1**, where workers identified difficult words as a factor that decreased task clarity and also suggested that tasks with difficult words are commonplace in the microtask crowdsourcing market. We also found a positive correlation between preposition and task clarity, in contrast to the negative correlation between syllables (or nominalization) and task clarity. These results suggest that partitioning sentences with prepositions could increase task clarity, while complicating individual words decreases task clarity.

6 EVOLUTION OF TASK CLARITY

6.1 Role of Task Types

To address **RQ4**, we investigated the evolution of task clarity over time (see Figure 6). We found that there was no monotonous trend in the overall average task clarity over time, as shown in Figure 6a. We also investigated the effect of task type on the evolution of task clarity. We found no discernible trend in the evolution of task clarity of different types of tasks over the 12 month period considered in the dataset (Figure 6b). We conducted a one-way ANOVA to compare the effect of task type on the evolution of task clarity over time. We did not find a significant effect of task type on the evolution of task clarity at the $p < .05$ level, across the 6 task type conditions; $F(5, 66) = 0.081, p = .994$.

These findings suggest that the overall task clarity in the marketplace varies over time but does not follow a clear pattern. This can be attributed to the organic influx of new task requesters every month [13]. To identify whether the experience of task requesters plays a role in the evolution of task clarity, i.e., whether individual requesters deploy tasks with increasing task clarity over time we investigated the role of requesters in the evolution of task clarity.

6.2 Role of Requesters

Recent analysis of the AMT marketplace, revealed that there is an organic growth in the number of active requesters and a constant growth in the number of new requesters (at the rate of 1,000 new requesters per month) on the platform [13]. Poor task design leading to a lack of task clarity can be attributed to inexperienced requesters. To assess the role of requesters in the evolution of task clarity, we analyzed the evolution of task clarity of different types of tasks with respect to individual requesters.

We analyzed the distribution of unique requesters corresponding to the 7.1K tasks in our dataset. We found that a few requesters deployed a large portion of tasks, as depicted by the power law relationship in Figure 6c. We also found that over 40% of the requesters exhibited an overall average task clarity of $\geq 4/5$, and in case of nearly 75% of the requesters it was found to be over 3.5/5 (as presented in Figure 6d). We considered requesters who deployed ≥ 15 tasks within the 12-month period as being experienced requesters, and analyzed the relationship between the number of tasks they deployed with the corresponding overall task clarity. Using Pearson's **r**, we found a weak positive correlation between the average task clarity and the number of tasks deployed by experienced requesters (see Figure 6e); **r**= .28. Thus, the experience of requesters (i.e., the number of tasks deployed) explains over 8% of the variance in the average task clarity of tasks deployed by the corresponding requesters; the coefficient of determination, $R^2 = 0.081$.

Considering the requesters who deployed tasks during more than 6 months in the 12-month period, we investigated the overall change in terms of average task clarity of the tasks deployed from one month to the next. We measure the overall change in task clarity for each requester using the following equation.

$$\Delta TaskClarity_r = \frac{1}{n} \sum_{i=1}^{n} (TC_{i+1} - TC_i)$$

where, TC_i represents the average task clarity of tasks deployed by a requester in the month i, n is the total number of months during which requester r deployed tasks.

Figure 6f presents our findings with respect to the overall change in task clarity corresponding to such requesters. The size of the points representing each requester depict the number of tasks deployed by that requester. We did not find a significant effect of the number of tasks deployed by requesters on the magnitude of change in task clarity.

Based on our findings, we understand that the overall task clarity in the marketplace fluctuates over time. We found a weak positive linear relationship between the number of tasks deployed by individual task requesters and the associated task clarity over time. However, we did not find evidence that the magnitude of change in task clarity is always positive in case of experienced requesters.

6.3 Top Requesters

We note that the top-3 task requesters accounted for around 67% of the tasks that were deployed between Oct'13 to Sep'14. The requesters were found to be *SpeechInk*–1,061 tasks, *AdTagger*–944 tasks, and *CastingWords*–824 tasks. The evolution of task clarity of the tasks corresponding to these requesters over time is presented in the Figure 7 below.

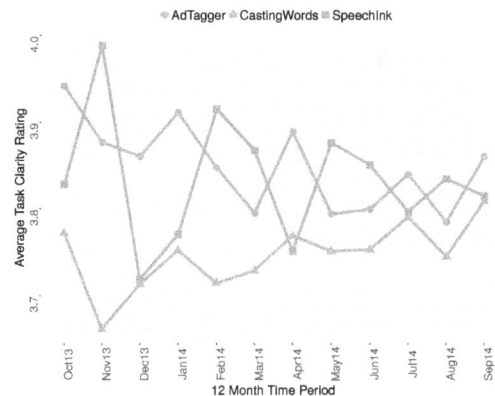

Figure 7: Top-3 task requesters w.r.t. the number of tasks deployed, and the evolution of their task clarity over time.

To understand the effect of the task requesters on the evolution of task clarity over time, we conducted a one-way between requesters ANOVA. We found a significant effect of task requesters on the evolution of task clarity across the three different requester conditions (SpeechInk, AdTagger, CastingWords) over the 12-month period; $F(2, 33) = 11.837, p < .001$. Post-hoc comparisons using the Tukey HSD test revealed that the evolution of task clarity corresponding to tasks from *SpeechInk* and *AdTagger* were significantly different in comparison to *CastingWords*.

We observe a gradual increase in the task clarity of *CastingWords* tasks over time in contrast to the other two top requesters.

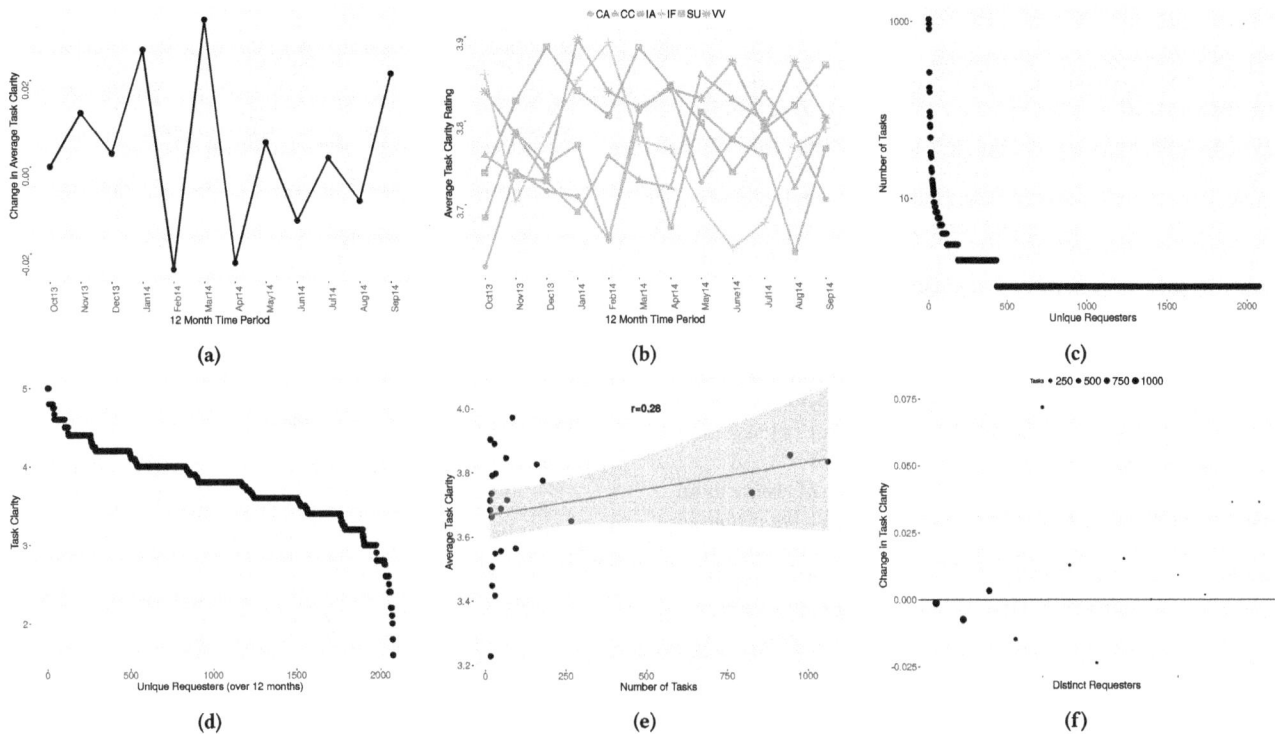

Figure 6: (a) Evolution of overall task clarity and (b) with respect to different types of tasks from Oct'13-Sep'14, (c) distribution of tasks corresponding to requesters who deployed them, (d) distribution of the average task clarity of tasks corresponding to distinct requesters across the 12 months, (e) relationship between the average task clarity and the number of tasks deployed by experienced requesters, (f) $\Delta TaskClarity$ of requesters who deployed tasks during more than 6/12 months in our dataset.

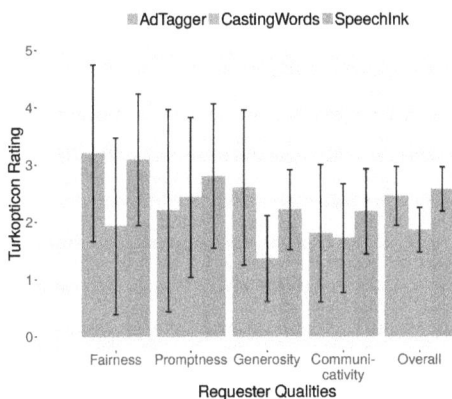

Figure 8: Average Turkopticon ratings of the top requesters from Oct'13–Sep'14.

In the context of these requesters and the time period of Oct'13-Sep'14, we explored the Turkopticon ratings [21] corresponding to the requesters. Turkopticon collects ratings from workers on the following qualities : *fairness* of a requester in approving/rejecting work, *communicativity*– the responsiveness of a requester when contacted, *generosity*– quality of pay with respect to the amount of time required for task completion, *promptness* of the requester in approving work and paying the workers. Figure 8 presents a comparison of the Turkopticon ratings of the 3 requesters for each

of the four qualities. We note that *SpeechInk* received consistently better ratings across all qualities within the given period. This coincides with the relatively higher task clarity of *SpeechInk* (*M=3.83, SD=0.47*) tasks when compared to *CastingWords* (*M=3.73, SD=0.48*) tasks over the 12 months (see Figure 7). A two-tailed T-test revealed a significant difference in the task clarity between *SpeechInk* and *CastingWords*; *t(1883)=18.43, p* < .001. We did not find ratings of tasks deployed by *AdTagger* on Turkopticon during the time period considered. However, we present a comparison based on the ratings received by *AdTagger* prior to Oct'13. Once again, in comparison to *CastingWords* we note that the higher overall quality ratings of *AdTagger* on Turkopticon coincide with the higher task clarity over the 12 months (*M=3.85, SD=0.48*); *t(1766)=25.23, p* < .001.

Through our findings it is clear that task clarity is not a global, but a local property of the AMT marketplace. It is influenced by the actors in the marketplace (i.e., tasks, requesters and workers) and fluctuates with the changing market dynamics.

7 CONCLUSIONS AND FUTURE WORK

In this paper we examined *task clarity*, an important, yet largely neglected aspect of crowdsourced microtasks. By surveying 100 workers, we found that workers confront unclear tasks on a regular basis. They deal with such tasks by either exerting extra effort to overcome the suboptimal clarity, or by executing them without a clear understanding. Poor task formulation thereby greatly hinders the progress of workers' in obtaining rewards, and in building up a good reputation.

To better understand how clarity is perceived by workers, we collected workers' assessments for 7.1K tasks sampled from a 5 years worth dataset of the AMT marketplace. With an extensive study we revealed that clarity is coherently perceived by workers, and that it varies by the task type. In addition, we found compelling evidence about the lack of direct correlation between clarity and complexity, showing the presence of a complex relationship that requires further investigation. We proposed a supervised machine learning model to predict task clarity and showed that clarity can be accurately predicted. We found that workers' perception of task clarity is most influenced by the number of keywords and title readability. Finally, through temporal analysis, we show that clarity is not a macro-property of the AMT ecosystem, but rather a local property influenced by tasks and requesters.

In conclusion, we demonstrated the importance of clarity as an explicit property of microwork crowdsourcing tasks, we proposed an automatic way to measure it, and we unveiled interesting relationships (or lack thereof) with syntactical and cognitive properties of tasks. Our findings enrich the current understanding of crowd work and bear important implications on structuring workflow. Predicting task clarity can assist workers in task selection and guide requesters in task design. In the imminent future, we will investigate the impact of task clarity in shaping market dynamics such as worker retention versus dropout rates.

Acknowledgments

This research has been supported in part by the European Commission within the H2020-ICT-2015 Programme (Analytics for Everyday Learning – AFEL project, Grant Agreement No. 687916), the Dutch national e-infrastructure with the support of SURF Cooperative, and the Social Urban Data Lab (SUDL) of the Amsterdam Institute for Advanced Metropolitan Solutions (AMS).

REFERENCES

[1] Omar Alonso and Ricardo Baeza-Yates. 2011. Design and implementation of relevance assessments using crowdsourcing. In *ECIR*. Springer, 153–164.

[2] Omar Alonso, Catherine Marshall, and Marc Najork. 2014. *Crowdsourcing a subjective labeling task: a human-centered framework to ensure reliable results.* Technical Report. MSR-TR-2014-91.

[3] Janine Berg. 2016. Income security in the on-demand economy: findings and policy lessons from a survey of crowdworkers. *Comparative Labor Law & Policy Journal* 37, 3 (2016).

[4] Hein Broekkamp, Bernadette HAM van Hout-Wolters, Gert Rijlaarsdam, and Huub van den Bergh. 2002. Importance in instructional text: teachers' and students' perceptions of task demands. *Journal of Educational Psychology* 94, 2 (2002), 260.

[5] Francisco Cano and María Cardelle-Elawar. 2004. An integrated analysis of secondary school studentsfi conceptions and beliefs about learning. *European Journal of Psychology of Education* 19, 2 (2004), 167–187.

[6] Jeanne Sternlicht Chall and Edgar Dale. 1995. *Readability revisited: The new Dale-Chall readability formula.* Brookline Books.

[7] Kevyn Collins-Thompson. 2014. Computational assessment of text readability: A survey of current and future research. *ITL-International Journal of Applied Linguistics* 165, 2 (2014), 97–135.

[8] Kevyn Collins-Thompson and James P Callan. 2004. A language modeling approach to predicting reading difficulty.. In *HLT-NAACL*. 193–200.

[9] Scott A Crossley, Kristopher Kyle, and Danielle S McNamara. 2015. The tool for the automatic analysis of text cohesion (TAACO): automatic assessment of local, global, and text cohesion. *Behavior research methods* (2015), 1–11.

[10] Tove I Dahl, Margrethe Bals, and Anne Lene Turi. 2005. Are students' beliefs about knowledge and learning associated with their reported use of learning strategies? *British journal of educational psychology* 75, 2 (2005), 257–273.

[11] Edgar Dale and Jeanne S Chall. 1949. The concept of readability. *Elementary English* 26, 1 (1949), 19–26.

[12] Orphée De Clercq, Véronique Hoste, Bart Desmet, Philip Van Oosten, Martine De Cock, and Lieve Macken. 2014. Using the crowd for readability prediction. *Natural Language Engineering* 20, 03 (2014).

[13] Djellel Eddine Difallah, Michele Catasta, Gianluca Demartini, Panagiotis G Ipeirotis, and Philippe Cudré-Mauroux. 2015. The Dynamics of Micro-Task Crowdsourcing: The Case of Amazon MTurk. In *WWW*. International World Wide Web Conferences Steering Committee, 238–247.

[14] Ujwal Gadiraju, Ricardo Kawase, and Stefan Dietze. 2014. A taxonomy of microtasks on the web. In *Hypertext*. ACM, 218–223.

[15] Ujwal Gadiraju, Ricardo Kawase, Stefan Dietze, and Gianluca Demartini. 2015. Understanding malicious behavior in crowdsourcing platforms: the case of online surveys. In *CHI*. ACM, 1631–1640.

[16] Catherine Grady and Matthew Lease. 2010. Crowdsourcing document relevance assessment with mechanical turk. In *HLT-NAACL workshop on creating speech and language data with Amazon's mechanical turk*. Association for Computational Linguistics, 172–179.

[17] Arthur C Graesser, Danielle S McNamara, Max M Louwerse, and Zhiqiang Cai. 2004. Coh-Metrix: analysis of text on cohesion and language. *Behavior research methods, instruments, & computers* 36, 2 (2004), 193–202.

[18] Allison Hadwin. 2006. Student task understanding. In *Learning and Teaching Conference. University of Victoria, Victoria, British Columbia, Canada.*

[19] AF Hadwin, M Oshige, M Miller, and P Wild. 2009. Examining student and instructor task perceptions in a complex engineering design task. In *international conference on innovation and practices in engineering design and engineering education. McMaster University, Hamilton, ON, Canada.*

[20] T Hoßfeld, Raimund Schatz, and Sebastian Egger. 2011. SOS: The MOS is not enough!. In *QoMEX*. IEEE, 131–136.

[21] Lilly C Irani and M Silberman. 2013. Turkopticon: Interrupting worker invisibility in amazon mechanical turk. In *CHI*. ACM, 611–620.

[22] Diane Lee Jamieson-Noel. 2004. *Exploring task definition as a facet of self-regulated learning.* Ph.D. Dissertation. Faculty of Education-Simon Fraser University.

[23] Rohit J Kate, Xiaoqiang Luo, Siddharth Patwardhan, Martin Franz, Radu Florian, Raymond J Mooney, Salim Roukos, and Chris Welty. 2010. Learning to predict readability using diverse linguistic features. In *ACL*. Association for Computational Linguistics, 546–554.

[24] Shashank Khanna, Aishwarya Ratan, James Davis, and William Thies. 2010. Evaluating and improving the usability of Mechanical Turk for low-income workers in India. In *DEV*. ACM, 12.

[25] J Peter Kincaid, Robert P Fishburne Jr, Richard L Rogers, and Brad S Chissom. 1975. *Derivation of new readability formulas (automated readability index, fog count and flesch reading ease formula) for navy enlisted personnel.* Technical Report. DTIC Document.

[26] Aniket Kittur, Ed H Chi, and Bongwon Suh. 2008. Crowdsourcing user studies with Mechanical Turk. In *CHI*. ACM, 453–456.

[27] Aniket Kittur, Jeffrey V Nickerson, Michael Bernstein, Elizabeth Gerber, Aaron Shaw, John Zimmerman, Matt Lease, and John Horton. 2013. The future of crowd work. In *CSCW*. ACM, 1301–1318.

[28] Lieve Luyten, Joost Lowyck, and Francis Tuerlinckx. 2001. Task perception as a mediating variable: A contribution to the validation of instructional knowledge. *British Journal of Educational Psychology* 71, 2 (2001), 203–223.

[29] David Malvern and Brian Richards. 2012. Measures of lexical richness. *The Encyclopedia of Applied Linguistics* (2012).

[30] Catherine C Marshall and Frank M Shipman. 2013. Experiences surveying the crowd: Reflections on methods, participation, and reliability. In *WebSci*. ACM, 234–243.

[31] Emily Pitler and Ani Nenkova. 2008. Revisiting readability: A unified framework for predicting text quality. In *EMNLP*. Association for Computational Linguistics, 186–195.

[32] Presentacion Rivera-Reyes. 2015. Students' task interpretation and conceptual understanding in electronics laboratory work. (2015).

[33] Libby O Ruch and Rae R Newton. 1977. Sex characteristics, task clarity, and authority. *Sex Roles* 3, 5 (1977), 479–494.

[34] Aaron D Shaw, John J Horton, and Daniel L Chen. 2011. Designing incentives for inexpert human raters. In *CSCW*. ACM, 275–284.

[35] John Sweller and Paul Chandler. 1994. Why some material is difficult to learn. *Cognition and instruction* 12, 3 (1994), 185–233.

[36] Jie Yang, Claudia Hauff, Alessandro Bozzon, and Geert-Jan Houben. 2014. Asking the right question in collaborative q&a systems. In *Hypertext*. ACM, 179–189.

[37] Jie Yang, Judith Redi, Gianluca Demartini, and Alessandro Bozzon. 2016. Modeling task complexity in crowdsourcing. In *HCOMP*. AAAI, 249–258.

Tiree Tales: A Co-operative Inquiry into the Poetics of Location-Based Narratives

David E. Millard
Web and Internet Science, University of Southampton
dem@ecs.soton.ac.uk

Charlie Hargood
Creative Technology, Bournemouth University
chargood@bournemouth.ac.uk

ABSTRACT

In a location-based story a reader's movement through physical space is translated into movement through narrative space, typically by presenting them with text fragments on a smart device triggered by location changes. Despite the increasing popularity of such systems their poetics are poorly understood, meaning limited guidance for authors, and few authoring tools. To explore these poetics we present a co-operative inquiry into the authoring of an interactive location-based narrative, 'The Isle of Brine', set on the island of Tiree. Our inquiry reveals both pragmatic and aesthetic considerations driven by the locations themselves, that affect the design of both the Story (narrative structure) and Fabula (events within the story). These include the importance of paths, bottlenecks, and junctions as a physical manifestation of calligraphic patterns, the need for coherent narrative areas, and the requirement to use evocative places and to manage thematic and tonal discord between the landscape and the narrative.

CCS CONCEPTS

• **Human-centered computing** → **Hypertext / hypermedia**;

KEYWORDS

Location-Based Narrative, Sculptural Hypertext

1 INTRODUCTION

Location-based narratives are digital stories, read on a smart device, that are aware of the user's location. Typically the stories require readers to move through a space, making new story nodes available as a result. They differ from traditional hypertext narratives in that navigation is a result of physical movement rather than link traversal, and are thus similar in their interactivity to game narratives, where narrative choices are associated with player actions. However, the location-based narratives created to date have mostly been exploratory, and little work has been undertaken to understand the poetics of location-based writing (in contrast to the body of theory on hypertext writing and poetics). Without this understanding it

is difficult to produce effective tools for creating location-based narratives, or to educate writers about the possibilities [1].

Our StoryPlaces project[2] is a collaboration between Computer Scientists and English Scholars to explore the poetics of location-based narratives. There have been a number of attempts to develop critical theory or design frameworks for digital narratives, historically in the Hypertext community [20], but as location-based systems are relatively new, the theory behind them is in its early stages; examples include attempts to explore the boundaries between storytelling and games [11], considering the user's interaction as a trajectory through complex spaces [5], or placing them on a continuum from tightly managed to emergent system [9].

In StoryPlaces we have taken a co-design approach, where domain experts (in this case English academics and authors) are brought into the design team and actively take part in decisions. One of the consequences of co-design is that the participants learn a little about each other's areas of expertise. Normally this is more important for the domain experts, as their grasp of the affordances of technology is a key factor in the design process, but it is also true of the technology experts who gain insight into the domain itself.

In our project we are the technology experts, and through our interaction with domain experts have begun to understand some of the issues around authoring interactive location-based stories, an approach that we have used successfully in the past [36]. However, it became clear that this understanding would always be deficient unless we attempted to create a story ourselves and experienced the issues first hand. We also felt that we were more likely to push the technological boundaries of what was possible (for example, by using more complex interactive structures) as we were more comfortable with those aspects of the technology, and less conscious of the negative impacts that this focus might have on the resulting text.

In short, we were likely to create a less well crafted story, but one that better demonstrated the edges of what was possible with the technology, an experience that could usefully feedback into the co-design. Our approach is thus an extension, or adjunct, to traditional co-design. It does not seek to replace the main activity of working hand-in-hand with genuine domain experts, but rather to support an oft-overlooked aspect of the process, namely educating the technologists about the domain and fostering empathy between participants in order to support the ongoing conversation.

The Tiree Tech Wave, a 'hands on making and meeting event' on the Scottish island of Tiree provided us with the opportunity of a safe space [31] where, as technology experts, we could take on the role of authors without the fear of criticism, and where the

HT '17, July 04-07, 2017, Prague, Czech Republic
© 2017 ACM. 978-1-4503-4708-2/17/07...$15.00
DOI: http://dx.doi.org/10.1145/3078714.3078716

---

[1] Authoring systems for location games (e.g. arisgames.org or silogames.org), focus on rich mechanics rather than rich narrative.
[2] storyplaces.soton.ac.uk

risk of failure was minimal. We attended the April 2016 Tech Wave, and spent five days on the island, using this time to research local history, explore geographical locations, and draft a story structure in the StoryPlaces format.

This paper contains a reflection and analysis of that experience, focusing on what we learned about writing interactive location-based stories from our time on the island. We approached the work as a *Co-operative Inquiry* a qualitative method that places emphasis on experiential reflection and analysis [30], and report the authorial process we undertook, give a brief structural description of the story we created, and present our observations and analysis of our experience.

2 BACKGROUND

Some of the earliest examples of location-based narrative systems were designed as tour guides, for example the HIPS system [10] which connected location-aware software to a knowledge base of information in order to generate personalised information pages based on current location. Many early systems focused on dealing with location inaccuracy, for example GUIDE which dynamically constructed pages with possible locations for the user to choose from [16]. More recent examples depend on more reliable location data, and the focus has moved to the experience itself, often through the use of more evocative stories, for example location sensitive historical plays [8] or tapestries of personal stories that overlay a visited space to build up a cultural picture [26].

Interactive educational tools such as 'Gaius' Day in Egnathia' [3] push the interactive elements of this kind of storytelling by giving participants goals, in the case of Gaius' Day this is in the form of exploration targets that they must identify be collecting location-based clues. The Chawton House project [35] also supports an educational experience, but in Chawton (set in the grounds of a period house) the activities themselves are non-digital (for example, for the children to act out a scene between two characters, or pause and create a short poem).

We have also seen researchers explore new ways of fusing location-based narratives with real world context. For example, in 'Viking Ghost Hunt' [25] where players hunt down the ghosts of Dublin using an augmented reality system, or 'University of Death' [11] a hybrid reality system that requires its players to adopt specific roles and behaviours and utilise real world props and clues alongside digital information.

In contrast, the narratives that we are concerned with in our research are better classed as interactive fiction with a focus on delivering an engaging story as opposed to location description or interactive play. Some, such as The 'iLand of Madeira' rely on the effectiveness of a simple mosaic of story nodes that are gradually revealed [17], while other systems like 'San Servolo, travel into the memory of an island' have more complex rules, based not just on location but other contextual factors such as weather and reader history [29].

Location-based interactive fictions are analogous to 'Walking Sims', games where readers explore virtual spaces and interact with objects triggering narrative sequences, San Servolo and Tiree even echo the first popular example 'Dear Esther' which also takes place on an island [27]. The main difference being that authors of walking sims have full control over the environment, designing both the virtual world and the narrative together, whereas location-based narratives are written to existing places and locations, and must deal with a changing environment that is beyond the control of the author. In this regard they are in the tradition of psychogeography, which seeks to challenge the traditional relationships that individuals have to place and encourages playful and exploratory behaviour[15].

Despite this prior work we still understand little about the way in which location-based stories are constructed by authors, and how they use their physical locations for narrative effect. As a counter-example it is worth considering the world of literary hypertext. Writers such as Rosenberg have contemplated the aesthetics of link types and effects [32], while others have explored the impact of textual nodes on overall coherence and experience [28], and seminal pieces, such as Michael Joyce's 'afternoon, a story' have been analysed critically [34].

Models of hypertext can be applied to location-based stories, in particular *Sculptural Hypertext* systems model all nodes as potentially available, but at any point in the interaction 'sculpt away' a number of nodes depending on the reader's state (normally derived by cumulatively applying rules that are attached to each node)[7, 37]. If location is modelled as part of the reader's state then it can be used as a factor in what is removed - effectively meaning that as the reader moves around in space different nodes become available to read. This single model has been shown to be sufficient to describe many different types of location-based narrative [24].

Therefore we could see location-based narrative authoring as similar to the authoring of sculptural hypertexts. Several authoring systems do exist for sculptural hypertext, for example StoryNexus[3] is an online system that frames these variables as *qualities*, and the rules as *consequences* - thus attempting to give a more friendly vocabulary to something that is effectively a state machine. In addition it identifies different types of qualities (such as quest, progress, or accomplishments) that help authors to understand how the system may be used. Similarly the latest version of StorySpace [22] takes the notion of guard fields (conditions attached to links) and extends them to a full sculptural hypertext system that can be authored visually.

Our long term goal is to apply these ideas to location-based systems, focusing initially on creating a poetics of location-based narrative that we can use to inform the creation of new authoring tools. This was the purpose of our co-design activity, and the motivation behind our trip to the Tiree Tech Wave was to directly experience the challenges of creating a location-based narrative, in order to develop those poetics.

3 METHODOLOGY AND EXPERIENCE

Experiential Inquiry is a qualitative approach that attempts to go beyond positivist scientific methods, especially in regard to understanding human behaviour. In Experiential Inquiry "the agent himself (sic) engages systematically in a self-directed exploration of his own experience and behaviour and attends fully to the experience and behaviour of other agents who are similarly engaged

---

[3]StoryNexus, examples like 'Fallen London': www.storynexus.com

in interaction with him" [18]. Co-operative inquiry is a specific methodology that emphasises the experiential reflection and analysis of a group of researchers working on a particular problem [30], as such it is similar to both Action Research and Ethnography but with greater emphasis on the researchers themselves, and less concern with the broader social and political contexts [14]. Co-operative Inquiry may involve working with domain experts (to co-operatively solve a problem), however it is interpreted widely, and can also mean a group of people coming together to collaboratively solve a problem, in this case two technologists (the authors) approaching the co-creation of a location-based story.

A Co-operative inquiry cycles through four phases [19]. In the first phase the researchers come together and identify the agreed area for inquiry, in the second they become co-subjects - engaging in the actions they have agreed and recording the process and outcomes, in the third they become fully immersed in the activity and elaborate on their initial superficial understanding, and in the fourth they come together after an appropriate time to share their data and analyse their experiences in order to achieve new levels of understanding.

In our work the creation of a location-based story on the island was the focus of the inquiry, and the Tech Wave the mechanism by which we came together and engaged with the task (phase one of co-operative inquiry). In total we spent five days on the island, two of which included travel, giving us three full days to develop our location-based story.

In co-operative inquiry the account itself is of high importance, and the process aims to bring out the subjective experiences of the participants, using their knowledge to interpret and make sense of what occurred rather than attempt a more objective analysis (for example, by thematic coding). Hence throughout the trip we kept a photo record of our visit and used a cross-platform app called 'Fieldtrip GB' [4] on our personal devices to record the GPS co-ordinates of likely locations and make notes in situ. We used Google Docs as a scratchpad for our story - using it to draft story nodes, store the JSON definitions required by our software, and to record a daily journal of our activities. We have reported the account of our authorial experience in Section 4 below, and our reflections in Section 6.

Our plan was to spend the first day researching the history of the island and developing the high level story concept and structure (phase two of co-operative inquiry). The second and third days would be spent scouting locations, recording GPS positions, and drafting the first versions of the story nodes (phase three of co-operative inquiry). The goal being to have a bare bones functioning story by the time we left, that could be fleshed out in the weeks following our visit.

We held three brainstorming meetings to review our records and make sense of our experience (phase four of co-operative inquiry). The first at the end of day three, the second a week after we had returned, and the third around eight weeks after the trip (at the point where the majority of the story nodes had been written). These notes were then added to the Google Doc and used as the basis for the reflection presented here.

4 AN ACCOUNT OF OUR AUTHORIAL PROCESS

On day one we began the process by discussing the key themes that we wanted to explore, the starting premise, and the sorts of narrative and sculptural structures that we might want to use. Our experience of flying to the island, especially the last leg sharing a small and ageing propeller plane with only a handful of passengers, evoked the idea of the 'professional stranger' [2], someone who brings their expertise into a foreign world. In an effort to make our story reflect our own experience of travelling to a remote island, we decided that our protagonist should be a professional visiting a foreign land in the spirit of Lovecraft's 'The Mountains of Madness'. This is a common trope that has also appeared in film's such as 'The Wicker Man', the twist being that although the stranger brings their expertise into a new place in order to apply it (typically with a sense of superiority), in the end it is the place that teaches them new things about themselves and the world.

We also discussed the structure that the story should take, and decided to base it around three acts unfolding across three separate areas of the island. Again we were informed by our own experience, as we had been advised to hire a car to travel around the island. Our structure would enable readers to drive between acts, but then walk and explore the nodes within the act. In preparation for our trip it had become clear that there were excellent local resources about the myths of the island, and our idea was to link one of these with our protagonist. As they progressed through the Acts of the story, these links would become clearer. We also discovered a rich resource in the form of Tiree Place Names [5], a website that mapped English, Gaelic and Norse place names to survey data. This inspired us to make our protagonist a surveyor, and we reasoned we could use this resource to populate a number of nodes about the island and its history.

Tonally we wanted Act 1 to be a straight account of the surveyor's work. Act 2 would begin to play with the reader's perception of the surveyor as a reliable narrator, and hint at some connection to the island. Act 3 would more obviously descend into delusion, but would reveal that connection, and present a resolution. With this rough structure in mind we visited the island's museum to search for appropriate historical stories and legends. But rather than one or two key stories, the island is replete with local legends and tales - spanning from Viking invasion to the island's role in World War II. Throughout the stories we noted key themes of Death and the Sea, as many referred to the hard life of the islanders and their symbiotic relationship with the Atlantic. Travelling around the island we were also struck by how unusually low-lying it is, as if part of the ocean itself. We therefore decided to change our plan, and have our surveyor encounter many of these stories on his travels, and to make his past connection not to one story in particular, but to some traumatic event at sea - which the stories could thematically allude to in Acts 1 and 2, and then explicitly link with in Act 3.

For the remainder of day one we used our time to expand our narrative structure. In particular adding a second parallel three act structure, that would expand the history of the surveyor and his reasons for visiting the island, and act as an interactive element in the

---

[4]Uni. of Edinburgh EDINA Project: fieldtripgb.blogs.edina.ac.uk

[5]http://http://www.tireeplacenames.org

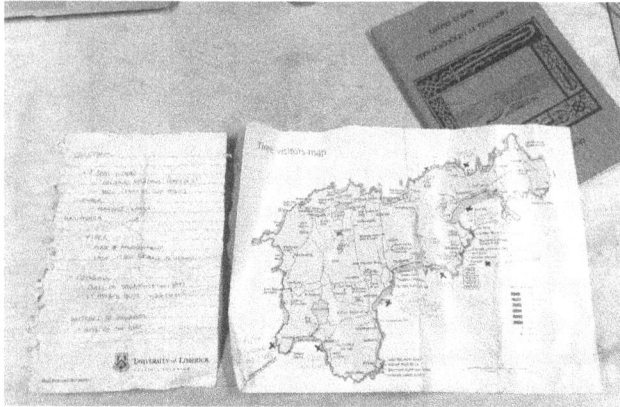

Figure 1: Map and booklet sourced from the island's museum, annotated with planning notes for the Day 2 fieldtrip

story (as readers would experience the story differently according to the juxtaposition of the Acts).

We also began to plan the location elements of the story, mapping the stories we had identified to places on the island with the help of locals attending the Tech Wave Event. Some were directly linked to the stories, but others could be linked thematically (or the locations were not known, and we could therefore take artistic license). It was also important to us that the structure of the locations matched the structure of our narrative, especially that the climax of the story should occur in a meaningful place. We created a simple written manifest of locations for each area, listing the sorts of location we would need to match our stories (an example is shown in Figure1). On the following two days we visited the areas, located appropriate starting places (where we could park), and then walked around the area using Fieldtrip GB to record location stamps, and our camera to capture a visual record of each spot. Our choice of location stamps was partly practical (was it on an effective path or route), partly logical (could you see things that were referenced in the stories), and partly aesthetic (was the location evocative of the things described in the stories).

On each day we returned to base to convert our field notes into stubs for the story (JSON objects in the Google doc). We also downloaded the names data and created a simple script to find place names in the areas we had visited. Some of these became additional locations and stubs for Act 1 and 2 of the story where the surveyor is still playing his professional role.

One of our assumptions was that it would be easy to add to a sculptural hypertext organically, and therefore we could fully develop a handful of nodes into a working story and expand it from there. In reality we had to carefully plan all the elements of the story, including all the locations, points of story revelation, and how those fitted into the high level structure, meaning that we could not simply add new nodes at a later time. As a result what we actually completed during the trip was a skeleton of the full story, including all the nodes and their locations, conditions and rules (but with actual content for only a handful of nodes, this content was then added in subsequent weeks after we had met to flesh out the story premise that we outlined while on the island).

5 OUR STORY: THE ISLE OF BRINE

Our story is called 'The Isle of Brine', the protagonist is a surveyor, sent from the mainland (for unclear reasons) to survey Tiree, replete with notes on its history and legends. As the story progresses it becomes clear that he has some other connection to the island, and that he is haunted by an event from his past. As the reader moves around the island, reality and myth become blurred, until the surveyor is forced to confront the decisions he has made to bring him there.

Previous work on Sculptural Hypertext has revealed a number of common patterns that author's use to build their narratives [13]. Our three act structure matched a pattern called *Phasing*, where a story progresses through a number of key phases and only nodes in the current phase are available - at some point reading a node triggers a change to the next phase.

Another pattern is *parallel threads* where two or more sequenced of nodes develop independently of one another (for example, following the Points of View of different characters). Each node in the thread requires the previous to have been read, but the threads are independent. Isle of Brine applies this pattern but at the level of phases. The main phases (Acts 1 to 3) follow the surveyor as he moves across the island, and develops the story of why he and the island are linked. A secondary set of phases progress backwards in time, and tell in flashback how he came to visit Tiree. This juxtaposition of phases provides an element of hypertextuality to the story, as a reader's interpretation of events will depend on their relative positions in each set of phases.

The largest phases are the ones representing the main three Acts (comprising 40 nodes, compared to 12 nodes in the secondary phases). Each Act starts with an intro phase, with a start node at a beginning location that can be reached by car, once this is read the story moves into the main phase for the Act containing nodes that can be read in any order. In both intro and main phases a node that is available regardless of location gives a brief description of the current state of the story, and some advice on how to proceed. Within each main phase there is one node that will transition the story to the next act, we used another pattern *un-locking* to ensure that this only became available once half the nodes in the act had been read.

The secondary phases are the ones that describe the events leading up to the trip to Tiree. All the nodes in the phase must be read before it changes to the next phase. Every node in all three of these secondary phases are mapped to three different locations, one in each of the areas of island used for the main phases (the three acts). This means that the nodes are available locally to the current Act whatever combination of main and secondary phases are active. Figure 2 shows a graphical version of the structure [12], in the Figure the three 'Island' phases represent the main Acts, and the three 'History' phases are secondary. Figure 3 shows how Act 1 (the 'Island 1' phase) appears on our mobile viewer.

6 ANALYSIS AND REFLECTION

This section records the outcome of the fourth phase of our cooperative inquiry, and is the result of analysis and reflection meetings held in the two months following our return from Tiree. Reflecting on our experience has led us to a number of pragmatic and

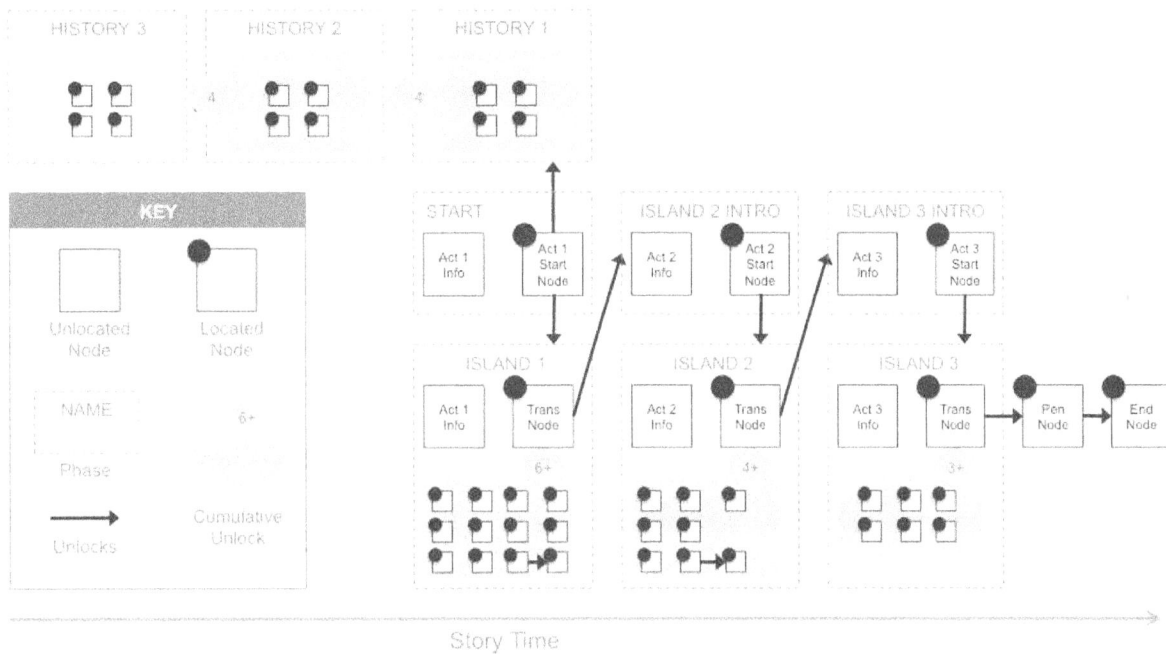

Figure 2: The sculptural structure of 'Isle of Brine'

aesthetic considerations that were part of the story design process, and has led us to consider how locations can be seen as Text in traditional narratological terms.

6.1 Pragmatic Considerations

When faced with constructing our own location-based story, it became clear that the pragmatics of the locations themselves are of paramount importance. Everything that a reader experiences in the story is done through the lens of location, and in particular the navigation of those locations, if the navigation is not practical, then there is a very real chance the reader will give up and never fully experience the story. In our story we quickly realised that, we would need the locations to reflect the transportation options open to our readers. Points of arrival and departure are especially important. This led us to have three areas, with the intention that the readers would drive between those areas and then explore locally on foot, with clear starting nodes linked to places to park.

It was also clear that the locations of the story should be meaningful in the context of that story, and probably linked to the narrative design. In our case this meant linking three areas of the island to the three main Acts of the story, thus associating navigation between those areas with tonal shifts in our narrative. This could be taken to the point where it supersedes practical concerns, e.g. one can imagine stories where the confusion and challenge of widely dispersed locations had some sort of narrative resonance with the story being told, but this should be an intentional decision by the author.

Another example of how location impacted narrative design was in Act 1, where the reader is progressing along a beach towards a headland. Given the rules it is likely that the transition node to Act 2 will appear behind them before they reach the end of the beach. Readers are then faced with the choice of when to turn around. Aware of this we ensured that the nodes at the far end of the beach contained no information that was needed to make the story coherent, but that instead were tonally consistent with Act 2 (bringing in elements of delusion), and therefore acted as a premonition of things to come, and an Easter Egg for particularly vigilant readers.

In general the accessibility of locations is an important factor. Whether because of distance to other locations, or because of local conditions. For example, when choosing locations on the beach, we were aware that the tide might make certain places inaccessible, and that time might change the shape of the sand dunes and access to the tundra behind.

Whilst many of the models of location-based narratives include open areas that can be explored in any order (Plains [24]), the reality is that paths are pre-eminent and there is a lack of genuinely open spaces in real environments. For some areas of our story this mean that despite the sculptural hypertext model we were using, the navigation began to look more like caligraphic patterns, where the readers choices are constrained just as much as when confronted with link choices [6].

Realising early on that paths and routes were essential to the navigation of the space, meant that it was important that we identified junctions and bottlenecks, as junctions were good places to situate choices and bottlenecks a good place for important nodes. It also meant that we could use the landscape to guide users rather than the digital rules of the hypertext. For example, in Act 1 the car

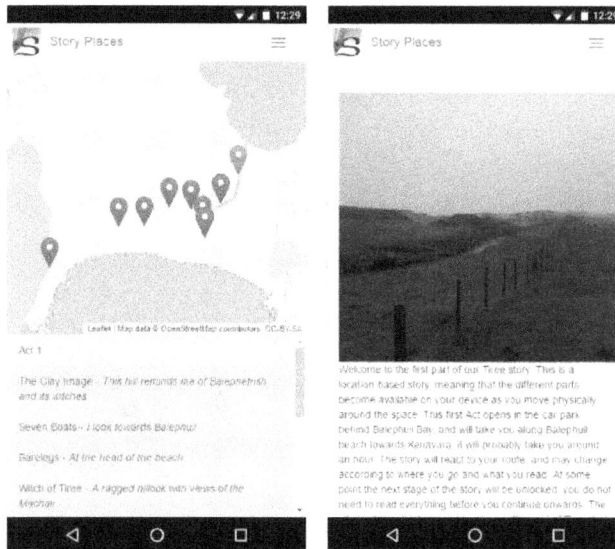

Figure 3: Screenshots of 'Isle of Brine' map screen upon start (left), and page showing the introduction node for Act 1 (right)

park is several hundred yards from the beach, where most of the nodes are located, and there is only one path. Nodes placed on that path are highly likely to be seen by the readers before the ones on the beach.

6.2 Aesthetic Considerations

An early observation was that we had naturally started writing in the first person present tense. Both of us did this unconsciously and independently. This could be because of the active and present nature of authoring in situ, or because of the discrete nature of the writing, lots of small textual nodes, which puts one in mind of writing a journal or diary (which also tend to be first-person present tense).

Something else that became clear early on was that the drama of the story needed to be matched to the dramatic landscape. The island is a striking place, and in some cases the locations made aesthetic demands of us, particularly obvious points of interest. Walkers (and thus readers) will be drawn to these spots. The author need not yield to these demands, but again that is an active choice that has consequences. A striking location that is silent may carry significant meaning.

We have already noted how the topology of the landscape (e.g. the paths and natural routes) is important to consider pragmatically, but its juxtaposition with the hypertext structures of the story also has an aesthetic affect, for example by matching our three island areas with our three main phases we associate navigation between those areas with tonal transitions in our narrative – leaning on the sense of story as journey (progress through a landscape) that is often used in game design [1].

On our second day the weather was bad, but on the third day, the weather improved considerably. It was obvious to us, contrasting

those two days, that the weather had a significant impact on our perceptions of the places. The poor weather on our first day could well explain the somewhat grim tone of our eventual story, which seemed slightly out of place when read in brilliant sunshine. Dealing with the changing aesthetics of a space (either because of weather or simple differences in time of day) is likely to be a challenge for location-based authors. The technology could potentially use these as part of its rules set, and this could get around problems of diegetic references in the text (for example, different nodes could describe a view differently depending on visibility), but it does not really help with the overall tone of the story. In some cases, readings in different contexts will be equally valuable and interesting to contrast, but in our case there was a clash between the feeling of the island on a sunny day, to the aesthetic of the story itself.

6.3 Location as Text

Many of the points that emerged from our reflection concern the practical difficulties of creating a location-based story and the relationship that those choices have with the narrative itself. We can draw comparisons between the poetic impact of this relationship and the idea of "The Medium is the Message" [23] or its similar counterpart from games design: Portnow's concept of "Mechanics as Metaphor" as reported by Locke [21]. Through location design the author can create emphasis or otherwise alter the impact of their story, not just from the use of the setting of individual locations themselves (whose impact is inherent in location aware narrative) but in the structure of their linking. There are frameworks that can help us begin to make sense of this relationship.

In the structuralist tradition of narratology a three layer view of narrative is often taken. The precise terms used vary in English, French and Russian, but a useful overview is presented by Bal in her seminal book on narratology [4]. Bal talks about three layers: *Fabula*, the events, objects, characters and their interactions; *Story*, the way in which those events are organised into a telling, rarely in a purely chronological way; and *Text*, the textual artefact in which the story is engrained. Often the model is thought of from the ground up, i.e. things happen, they are arranged into a story, and that story is written down or told. But it is just as accurate to say that the form of the text means that the story must be told in a particular sequence, and that certain events have to happen for that sequence to work. In other words, the layers are co-dependent on one another.

The Text layer can more accurately be thought of as the medium in which the story is told, for example in his 1923 work on Literature and Cinematography Shklovsky applied this model to film [33], and we can usefully follow this lead and apply it to our Location-Based Stories.

Framed in this way the pragmatic and aesthetic considerations concerning the reader's physical location in a real environment with a smart device (the Text) can be seen to impact the narrative structure (the Story), and the things that occur within that story (the Fabula). Table 1 shows a summary of our observations within this framework. (We use 'vs.' purposely to indicate that both harmony and discord are possible choices for the author. E.g. topology may give walkers navigational choices, but these may or may not translate into narrative choices for a reader).

Table 1: Aesthetic and Pragmatic Affects of Location Text on Story and Fabula

	Aesthetic Affects	Pragmatic Effects
Story	• Topology vs. hypertext structure (e.g. using landscape to establish coherent narrative areas)	• Establishing points of sensible Arrival/Departure (good places for key phase changes) • Using topology to supplement logical control of the narrative. E.g. Paths (sequences, cycles) and Junctions (choices)
Fabula	• Authorial Voice (situated and present) • Landscape points of Interest vs. narrative events of interest. • Theme/tone of the Space (which typically will change over time) vs. theme/tone of the Narrative (which typically will not)	• Diegetic references (which may become inaccurate) • Using landscape to managing the experience. E.g. choosing locations with reasonable distance for mode of travel • Using bottlenecks (e.g. for placing key events) • Identifying high cost locations (that are far away, difficult to access, or restricted; these should only be used for non-key events, and could be considered rewards for reader effort).

In the background section we mentioned the similarity of location-based narratives to walking sims, and it is interesting to reflect that our observations here – concerning building a narrative that fits the environment and parameters of a reader's visit – may also apply to walking sims, but in that case are reversed and become requirements for the construction of the environment itself. This mirroring of design rationale is something that we intend to explore in our future work.

7 CALLIGRAPHIC PATTERNS AND LANDSCAPE

In our previous work on location-based storytelling we identified patterns within the sculptural hypertext; these patterns work on the logical structure of the narrative, and ultimately shape the possible routes through the hypertext [13]. However, as mentioned in the previous section it became clear through our own authoring activity that the topology of the landscape, the natural paths and routes found within the location, also shape the possible narrative routes. Thus a location-based narrative is shaped by both logical and topographical relationships, working simultaneously on the reader.

This means that narrative structures can be both explicit within the rules of the hypertext or implicit in the layout of the location. For example, a sequence of nodes where each node has the previous node as a prerequisite (forming a Canyon [24]) will cause the reader to experience those nodes in that sequence, however, the same set of nodes arranged in an open logical structure with no prerequisites (a Plain [24]) when placed along a road will implicitly create the same linear structure due to the topology. More complex topology has more complex effects, for example the locations for Act 1 of 'Isle of Brine' (as shown in Figure 3) are set around a beach with tundra behind, to move from the beach to the tundra is possible, but requires climbing and is practical at only a few points. So while this is technically an open set of nodes the inclination to walk from the car down the beach and back again on the tundra (in a loop) will mean a very predictable linear experience for many readers (as shown in figure 4).

If sculptural patterns describe the logical structures of a location-based narrative, then we could return to Bernstein's calligraphic patterns to describe the topographical patterns through the landscape. The *Cycle* for example is a good match for the 'Isle of Brine' beach example above. "In the Cycle, the reader returns to a previously-visited node and eventually departs along a new path" [6], although there are two important differences. Firstly, that the node returned to is in the same location, but is actually a different node (the start is a welcome node in the beach car park, the end a different node in the same car park), this means that unlike a traditional hypertext where the one of the key functions of the cycle is to reinterpret the text on a second (or third or fourth) viewing, here it is a reinterpretation of the location – firstly as a point of arrival, then later of departure. Second, the overall function of the cycle in a calligraphic hypertext is often to emphasise parts of the narrative by

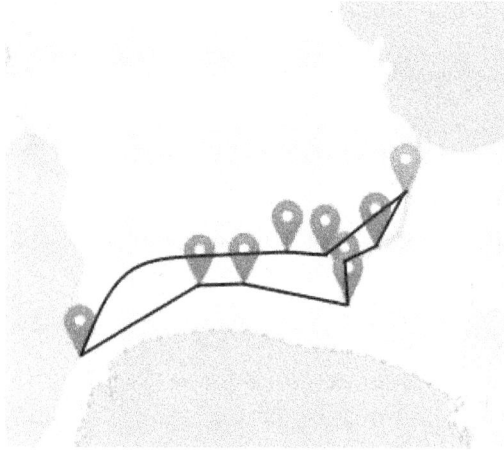

Figure 4: The locations in Act 1 are open but form a natural cycle.

encouraging this sort of re-reading and reinterpretation, while in a location-based story due to the effort of revisiting, this seems a less-likely approach (not least because of the physical effort of revisiting many nodes).

In our story we use a cycle to zone the first act of the narrative, allowing the leap to Act 2 to occur only at the root of the cycle. *Contours* are made of several cycles that interlink together, and although we do not have contours in "Isle of Brine" (they seem more likely in an urban landscape of buildings and blocks) they also seem a potentially useful way to zone a location-based story, allowing the reader to choice different paths and move between those paths, but again the emphasis is on choosing the reading order rather than on re-reading.

We also use *Neighbourhoods* to give coherence to the story, using three regions of the island to denote three distinct stages of the story. Neighbourhoods are the most obvious example of calligraphic patterns applying to location, and location is even used as an analogy in Bernstein's original definition "just as a prominent church spire shows a walker that two spots separated by long, winding streets are still in the same neighbourhood, deliberate display of commonality in a hypertext can express relationships that individual links might not emphasise." This was such a major part of our experience that in our reflection we explicitly identified the use of landscape to establish coherent narrative areas (see Table 1).

A *Sieve* is an example of a pattern that applies in both the narrative logic and the landscape. In the logic it is essentially a Delta, implemented as choices between nodes, and the subsequent unlocking of alternative nodes to take the story forward. However, it is can also be applied to junctions in the landscape, and we used it in the third Act of "Isle of Brine" where the reader can choose whether to explore the graveyard in Balinoe, or move into the village proper. Similarly a *Tangle* could potentially be implemented using a complex set of sculptural unlocking relationships to disorientate the reader, or it could be said to represent a plain, where the landscape is open, and thus any node (within a given set) could potentially be visited from any other node. We expected to use this a lot for our story, as each Act is essentially a plain, however in practice

the paths in the landscape make many of the navigational choices unlikely, turning a tangle into a de facto Contour, or in the case of our first Act a single Cycle.

Other calligraphic patterns do match the sculptural patterns. For example, a *Counterpoint* is where two voices alternate, with the reader following links between. We previously identified this in sculptural hypertext as Parallel Threads, and "Isle of Brine" uses this approach, presenting both historical and contemporary nodes (the History and Island phases respectively) presented in the same regions and sometimes sharing locations. Similarly you might see the three acts of "Isle of Brine" as *Split/Joins* (with the splits and joins happening at the transition nodes), certainly the final denouement of the story, a linear sequence of three nodes at the culmination of Act Three (Island 3), is an ultimate join that brings the readers back to a common experience whatever their wanderings to that point.

Finally some calligraphic patterns have the potential to be applied in new ways in a location-based story. *Mirrorworlds* are hypertexts with (near) symmetrical structure, but where each side of the mirror gives a different perspective. This could translate to a location-based story across a common set of locations, but where an early choice determined which version (or proportion) of the nodes were revealed. We could have done this in "Isle of Brine" with our History nodes, but ultimately wanted to decouple the progress through that part of the story from the progress the reader made across the island, hence all the History nodes map to three locations, one in each of the areas used for the main Acts of the story.

8 CONCLUSIONS

The authoring process for the creation of interactive location-based narratives is not well understood, despite the existence of many examples of the genre in the research literature, and increasing numbers of commercial examples available for smart devices. This limits the tools that can be developed, and the educational resources available for potential authors. We are currently involved in an interdisciplinary project that aims to address this problem by using co-design to explore the poetics of location-based storytelling. However, as technologists working alongside writers and English scholars we do not get the opportunity to develop our own experiential understanding of the authoring process.

In this paper we have described how we took the opportunity of a safe space, the Tiree Tech Wave, to take on the role of authors and undertake a co-operative inquiry into the authoring process. We developed our own story, 'The Isle of Brine', that was substantially more complex than the other examples developed in our research (via working with traditional authors). Our experience highlighted the complexity of author's choices, and is to our knowledge the first time that the authoring process for a location-based story has been explored independently of an evaluation of the technology of deployment.

In the co-operative inquiry method the analysis is emergent from the experience of the participants themselves and is thus rooted in their perspective, drawing from their discussions and based on the way that they rationalise and explain their own behaviour and decision making.

When physically visiting the places where the story occurred the absolute primacy of those locations for the reader experience was stark, and immediately impacted our thinking as authors. On reflection the locations had both a pragmatic and aesthetic impact on the Story and Fabula of our narrative. Whereas it might be imagined that a story can be overlaid relatively simply on a place, in fact we discovered a deeply interconnected set of decisions that show that narrative structure, location topology, and story events are co-dependent. As authors we had to develop these simultaneously in order to create a workable and coherent narrative. We also observe that the topological structure of the landscape demonstrates a number of features which may impact the resulting poetics directly, and that these features are similar in form (if not quite function) to traditional calligraphic patterns. This leads us to the conclusion that location aware narrative is a marriage between sculptural patterns at the logical level of the narrative and calligraphic patterns at the level of the landscape.

In our broader co-design work in StoryPlaces we have worked with over 45 different authors, and in all cases they struggled to appreciate the primacy of location to their reader's experience, and to understand how to address this in their own narratives. Authors are not typically game designers or technologists who might think more broadly about the process of user interaction, and their focus on the story world and the narrative structure hides the ways in which location might impact their readers. The findings expressed in Table 1 have already given us some very concrete guidance that we have been able to give to authors in subsequent co-design sessions, and will form the basis of a toolkit for authors and an associated authoring tool.

We are not in a position to judge whether 'Isle of Brine' has been successful, and a high quality text was not the aim of the activity, but our experience will feed back into the co-design process for our research informing the design of new authoring tools and training materials for writers. Our hope is that the observations reported here will inform other researchers and developers, encourage them to experience the authoring process first hand themselves, and ultimately will help them to work more effectively with writers of location-based stories, with the aim of opening up this intriguing new medium to a wider range of authors and voices.

9 ACKNOWLEDGMENTS

We would like to thank Professor Alan Dix for his help and support during the Tiree Tech Wave, our fellow participants who contributed enormously to our experience, and our colleagues on the StoryPlaces project: Mark Weal, Verity Hunt, Will Davis, James Jordan, and Phillip Hoare. This work was undertaken as part of the StoryPlaces project funded by The Leverhulme Trust (RPG-2014-388).

REFERENCES

[1] Ernest Adams. 2014. *Fundamentals of Game Design* (3rd ed.). New Riders Publishing, Thousand Oaks, CA, USA.
[2] Michael H. Agar. 1996. *The Professional Stranger : An Informal Introduction to Ethnography*. Academic Press.
[3] C Ardito, P Buono, M.F Costabile, R Lanzilotti, T. Visual Languages Pederson, and Human-Centric Computing 2007 VL HCC 2007 IEEE Symposium on. 2007. Mobile games to foster the learning of history at archaeological sites. *Visual Languages and Human-Centric Computing, 2007. VL/HCC 2007. IEEE Symposium on* (2007).
[4] Mieke Bal. 1985. *Narratology. Introduction to the theory of narrative* (2 ed.). University of Toronto Press, Toronto, Buffalo and London.
[5] Steve Benford, Gabriella Giannachi, Boriana Koleva, and Tom Rodden. 2009. From Interaction to Trajectories: Designing Coherent Journeys Through User Experiences. In *Chi2009: Proceedings of the 27th Annual Chi Conference on Human Factors in Computing Systems, Vols 1-4*. ACM Press, New York, New York, USA, 709–718. DOI:http://dx.doi.org/10.1145/1518701.1518812
[6] Mark Bernstein. 1998. Patterns of Hypertext. In *Proceedings of the Ninth ACM Conference on Hypertext and Hypermedia : Links, Objects, Time and Space—structure in Hypermedia Systems: Links, Objects, Time and Space—structure in Hypermedia Systems (HYPERTEXT '98)*. ACM, New York, NY, USA, 21–29. DOI: http://dx.doi.org/10.1145/276627.276630
[7] Mark Bernstein. 2001. Card shark and thespis: exotic tools for hypertext narrative. In *Proceedings of the twelfth ACM conference on Hypertext and Hypermedia*. http://portal.acm.org/citation.cfm?id=504216.504233
[8] M. Blythe, J. Reid, P. Wright, and E. Geelhoed. 2006. Interdisciplinary criticism: analysing the experience of riot! a location-sensitive digital narrative. *Behaviour & Information Technology* 25, 2 (2006), 127–139.
[9] Elizabeth Bonsignore, Vicki Moulder, Carman Neustaedter, Derek Hansen, Kari Kraus, and Allison Druin. 2014. Design Tactics for Authentic Interactive Fiction: Insights from Alternate Reality Game Designers. *Proceedings of the 32nd annual ACM conference on Human factors in computing systems - CHI '14* February 2016 (2014), 947–950. DOI:http://dx.doi.org/10.1145/2556288.2557245
[10] J. Broadbent and P. Marti. 1997. Location aware mobile interactive guides: usability issues. In *Proceedings of the Fourth International Conference on Hypermedia and Interactivity in Museums (ICHIM97)*. 162–172.
[11] B.S. Bunting, J. Hughes, and T. Hetland. 2012. The Player as Author: Exploring the Effects of Mobile Gaming and the Location-Aware Interface on Storytelling. *Future Internet* 4, 1 (2012), 142–160.
[12] Hargood Charlie and Millard David E. 2016. Location location location: experiences of authoring an interactive location-based narrative. In *Proceedings of the 9th International Conference on Interactive Digital Storytelling (ICIDS 2016)*.
[13] Hargood Charlie, Hunt Verity, Weal Mark, and David E. Millard. 2016. Patterns of Sculptural Hypertext in Location Based Narratives. In *Proceedings of the 27th ACM Conference on Hypertext and Social Media (HT '16)*. ACM, New York, NY, USA.
[14] Andrea Cornwall and Rachel Jewkes. 1995. What is participatory research? *Social Science & Medicine* 41, 12 (Dec. 1995), 1667–1676.
[15] Merlin Coverley. 2010. *Psychogeography*. Pocket Essentials.
[16] N Davies, K Cheverst, K Mitchell, and A Efrat. 2001. Using and determining location in a context-sensitive tour guide. *Computer* 34, 8 (2001), 35–41.
[17] Mara Dionisio, Valentina Nisi, and Jos P. Van Leeuwen. 2010. The iLand of Madeira Location Aware Multimedia Stories. In *Proceedings of the Third Joint Conference on Interactive Digital Storytelling (ICIDS'10)*. Springer-Verlag, Berlin, Heidelberg, 147–152. http://dl.acm.org/citation.cfm?id=1926497.1926521
[18] John Heron. 1971. *EXPERIENCE AND METHOD. An Inquiry into the Concept of Experiential Research*. Technical Report. Department of Educational Studies, University of Surrey, UK.
[19] J Heron and P Reason. 2006. Handbook of Action Research: Concise Paperback Edition - Google Books. *Handbook of action research* (2006).
[20] George P. Landow. 1994. What's a Critic to Do? In *Hyper / Text / Theory*, George P. Landow (Ed.). Baltimore: John Hopkins University Press, 1–48.
[21] Vince Locke. 2015. The Power of Ludonarrativity. *The Play Versus Story Divide in Game Studies: Critical Essays* (2015), 86.
[22] Bernstein Mark. 2016. Storyspace 3. In *Proceedings of the 27th ACM Conference on Hypertext and Social Media (HT '16)*. ACM, New York, NY, USA.
[23] Marshall McLuhan. 1994. *Understanding media: The extensions of man*. MIT press.
[24] David E. Millard, Charlie Hargood, Michael O. Jewell, and Mark J. Weal. 2013. Canyons, Deltas and Plains: Towards a Unified Sculptural Model of Location-based Hypertext. In *Proceedings of the 24th ACM Conference on Hypertext and Social Media (HT '13)*. ACM, New York, NY, USA, 109–118. DOI:http://dx.doi.org/10.1145/2481492.2481504
[25] K. Naliuka, T. Carrigy, N. Paterson, and M. Haahr. 2011. A narrative architecture for story-driven location-based mobile games. In *New Horizons in Web-Based Learning-ICWL 2010 Workshops*. Springer, 11–20.
[26] V. Nisi, I. Oakley, and M. Haahr. 2008. Location-aware multimedia stories: turning spaces into places. *Universidade Católica Portuguesa* (2008), 72–93.
[27] Dan Pinchbeck. 2008. Dear Esther: an interactive ghost story built using the Source engine. In *Interactive storytelling : first joint international conference on interactive digital storytelling, ICIDS 2008, Erfurt, Germany, November 26-29, 2008 : proceedings:*. Number 5334 in Lecture notes in computer science. Springer, Berlin, 51–55. http://eprints.port.ac.uk/3435/
[28] Mariusz Pisarski. 2011. New Plots for Hypertext?: Towards Poetics of a Hypertext Node. In *Proceedings of the 22Nd ACM Conference on Hypertext and Hypermedia (HT '11)*. ACM, New York, NY, USA, 313–318. DOI:http://dx.doi.org/10.1145/1995966.1996007
[29] F. Pittarello. 2011. Designing a context-aware architecture for emotionally engaging mobile storytelling. *Human-Computer Interaction–INTERACT 2011*

(2011), 144–151.

[30] Peter Reason. 1994. Three approaches to participative inquiry. In *Handbook of qualitative research*, N K Denzin and Y S Lincoln (Eds.). Thousand Oaks: Sage., 324–339.

[31] Peter Reason. 2002. Editorial Introduction: The Practice of Co-operative Inquiry. *Systemic Practice and Action Research* 15, 3 (2002), 169–176.

[32] Jim Rosenberg. 2001. And And: Conjunctive Hypertext and the Structure Acteme Juncture. In *Proceedings of the 12th ACM Conference on Hypertext and Hypermedia (HYPERTEXT '01)*. ACM, New York, NY, USA, 51–60. DOI : http://dx.doi.org/10.1145/504216.504235

[33] V Shklovsky, R R Sheldon, and I Masinovsky. 2008. Literature and Cinematography, Richard Robert Sheldon - Google Books. (2008).

[34] Jill Walker. 1999. Piecing Together and Tearing Apart: Finding the Story in Afternoon. In *Proceedings of the Tenth ACM Conference on Hypertext and Hypermedia : Returning to Our Diverse Roots: Returning to Our Diverse Roots (HYPERTEXT '99)*. ACM, New York, NY, USA, 111–117. DOI : http://dx.doi.org/10.1145/294469.

294496

[35] M.J. Weal, D. Cruickshank, D.T. Michaelides, D.E. Millard, D.C.D. Roure, K. Howland, and G. Fitzpatrick. 2007. A card based metaphor for organising pervasive educational experiences. In *Pervasive Computing and Communications Workshops, 2007. PerCom Workshops' 07. Fifth Annual IEEE International Conference on*. IEEE, 165–170.

[36] Mark J. Weal, Eva Hornecker, Don G. Cruickshank, Danius T. Michaelides, David E. Millard, John Halloran, David C. De Roure, and Geraldine Fitzpatrick. 2006. Requirements for In-Situ Authoring of Location Based Experiences. In *8th ACM International Conference on Human Computer Interaction with Mobile Devices and Services (MobileHCI 06)*. ACM Press, New York, NY, USA, 121–128. http://eprints.soton.ac.uk/262589/ Event Dates: 12th to 15th September.

[37] Mark J. Weal, David E. Millard, Danius T. Michaelides, and David C. De Roure. 2001. Building Narrative Structures Using Context Based Linking. In *In Hypertext '01. Proceddings of the Twelfth ACM conference on Hypertext, Aarhus, Denmark*. 37–38. http://eprints.soton.ac.uk/256136/

Entity-centric Data Fusion on the Web

Andreas Thalhammer
Institute AIFB, Karlsruhe Institute of Technology
andreas.thalhammer@kit.edu

Steffen Thoma
Institute AIFB, Karlsruhe Institute of Technology
steffen.thoma@kit.edu

Andreas Harth
Institute AIFB, Karlsruhe Institute of Technology
andreas.harth@kit.edu

Rudi Studer
Institute AIFB, Karlsruhe Institute of Technology
rudi.studer@kit.edu

ABSTRACT

A lot of current web pages include structured data which can directly be processed and used. Search engines, in particular, gather that structured data and provide question answering capabilities over the integrated data with an entity-centric presentation of the results. Due to the decentralized nature of the web, multiple structured data sources can provide similar information about an entity. But data from different sources may involve different vocabularies and modeling granularities, which makes integration difficult. We present an approach that identifies similar entity-specific data across sources, independent of the vocabulary and data modeling choices. We apply our method along the scenario of a trustable knowledge panel, conduct experiments in which we identify and process entity data from web sources, and compare the output to a competing system. The results underline the advantages of the presented entity-centric data fusion approach.

CCS CONCEPTS

• **Information systems → Data extraction and integration; Resource Description Framework (RDF)**;

KEYWORDS

entity-centric data fusion; data/knowledge fusion; structured data; linked data; n-ary relations; entity data fusion; data provenance

1 INTRODUCTION

Between December 2014 and December 2015 the percentage of web pages that include semantic markup has risen from 22% to 31.3% [16]. A large fraction of the structured data is based on schema.org annotations, which can be parsed to RDF [23], a graph-structured data model specified by the W3C. Government initiatives, non-profit organizations, and commercial data providers publish structured data on the web. They often use data publication features of current content management or electronic shop systems. Some organizations even provide a dedicated interface on top of their

databases following the Linked Data principles [2]. Large-scale retrieval systems (e.g., search engines) collect, clean, normalize, and integrate the data to drive user-facing functionality [10, 28].

Data from the web is heterogeneous, as pointed out in a recent paper [3], where "heterogeneity, quality and provenance" has been identified as one of the four most pressing topics concerning the Semantic Web: "It is a truism that data on the Web is extremely heterogeneous. [...] A dataset precise enough for one purpose may not be sufficiently precise for another." [3] As the data can differ in modeling granularities and can be sparse and overlapping across sources, integration on the quality level that supports fine-grained querying often requires manual curation to map the data to a canonical representation [34]. Less manual effort is involved in supporting entity-centric views of only parts of the data, as done in so-called "knowledge panels", which tolerate noisier data. The knowledge panels only contain a condensed top-k rendering of the data and use ranking to achieve high precision at k data items [28, 30]; k is often very small (10 or 20) compared to the overall available data for an entity (which can often be multiple GBs).[1] However, many knowledge panels often do not show the provenance for individual data items and doubts about correctness or notability have been pointed out [6, 14].

In this paper, we address the problem of *entity-centric data fusion*. In essence, we tackle the challenge of identifying when multiple sources make the same claim[2] about an entity in different structured ways (i.e., by using different RDF vocabularies)—which boils down to: different URIs, varying literals, and different *modeling granularities*. We leverage what could be perceived as "cross-source redundancy" by reconciling identical or similar claims while still keeping track of the respective sources and their representation of a claim.

Our approach is based on a data processing pipeline, which takes as input a set of equivalent entity identifiers and provides as output a similarity-based grouping (clustering) of RDF triples and *chains of triples* from multiple sources that describe the entity. The pipeline consists of the following steps: retrieve claims from different web sources; extract path features; perform hierarchical clustering; refine clusters; and select representatives. We provide placeholder steps around record linkage (at the start of the pipeline) and filtering/ranking (at the end), which can be implemented depending on the specific scenario. The focus of our approach is to establish

---

[1]The process of selecting the k most important data items about an entity is also called "entity summarization" [30, 31].

[2]We use the term "claim" when one or multiple sources state a concise piece of information in RDF, independent of its concrete modeling (in RDF), and the term "triple" when information is represented in a single subject-predicate-object notation.

mappings in entity-centric data while accounting for different modeling granularities. This also includes the mappings between the involved vocabulary terms and entity identifiers. The basic idea is to move back and forth between representing claims about an entity in a structured way (based on identifiers and triples) and representing claims as strings. In contrast to more traditional data integration methods (e.g., [11]), we do not directly aim at identifying contradicting information but our approach can be extended with such functionality. A straight-forward interpretation of the output of our method could be a weighting/ranking of claims about an entity in accordance to the number of sources that make it.

Generic or customized record linkage algorithms [18, 19] commonly solve the problem of establishing equality between entity identifiers. In our work, we assume that entity identifiers are already linked (as done via owl:sameAs in web data). In the past, many ontology alignment approaches relied on clean and extensively modeled ontologies without making strong use of instance data (e.g., [27]). For example, [26] mapped different modeling granularities between two extensively modeled ontologies using "complex correspondences" expressed in rules. On the web, with many different ontologies which are often inadequately modeled for ontology alignment purposes, we require a more robust method. Approaches such as [25, 29] allow for more heterogeneous input data, but do not address modeling granularities ([29] identifies "structural heterogeneity" to be addressed in future work). In fact, nowadays many sources, most prominently Wikidata [33], use n-ary relations for modeling RDF data in combination with additional context factors [13, 17], making the problem of addressing their integration more acute.

The contributions of our work are as follows:

- We present the problem of granularity-agnostic entity data fusion for graph-structured data on the web.
- We provide an entity-centric approach that enables the fusion of claims from multiple web sources without prior knowledge about the used schemas or required alignment patterns, taking into account data provenance.
- We introduce the concept of path features, a graph reconciliation model that enables easy switching between (multi-hop) paths and their string representations.
- In our experiments, we measure the effectiveness of the entity data fusion approach for entity-centric, multi-sourced claims and demonstrate superiority over a baseline established as part of the Sig.ma system in [32].

2 EXAMPLE

Figure 1 depicts our idea of a "trustable knowledge panel". The colors of the buttons implement a traffic light scheme for the trustability of the claims. By clicking on such a button, a pop up would open that provides direct reference to documents which cover the claim together with each document's representation. Amongst others, such a panel can serve two important purposes:

(1) users can verify the sources provided for a claim; and
(2) the number of sources can serve as a straight-forward justification for notability.

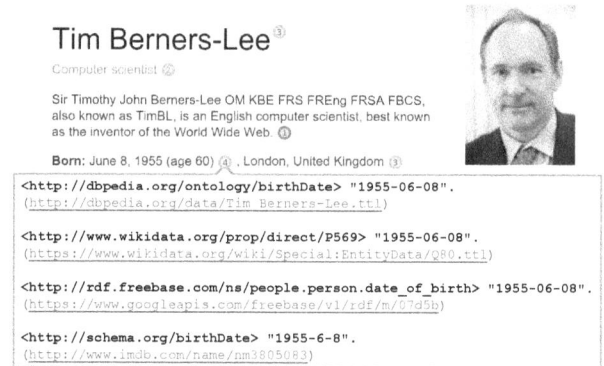

Figure 1: Mock-up of a trustable knowledge panel (based on a Google screenshot).

The trustable knowledge panel requires the integration of data from multiple sources, both on the syntactic and semantic level. The input to the panel would be a single unique identifier for an entity (e.g., http://dbepdia.org/resource/Tim_Berners-Lee). Before rendering the panel, we require to have multiple groups of claims about the same entity. The claims can be single RDF triples or multiple ones (depending on the used vocabulary, in particular modeling granularities). The claims of one group can come from different sources. Each group has a representative. The groups can be ranked via "number of sources" but other ranking methods and combinations are possible. In our work, we focus on the steps in the pipeline to reconcile and fuse the data from multiple sources. The trustable knowledge panel serves as illustration of how to apply the output of our system in a user-facing scenario.

Let us assume, we want to state that the entity "Tim Berners-Lee" (TimBL) has "Web Developer" as an occupation. The following three sets of triples transmit the claim at different levels of granularity:

(1) [ex1:TimBL ex1:occ "Web Developer"]
(2) [ex2:TimBL ex2:job ex2:webDev]
(3) [ex3:TimBL ex3:work ex3:work42],
    [ex3:work42 ex3:occ ex3:webDev],
    [ex3:work42 ex3:since "1989-03"]

In (1), only a non-clickable string would be displayed for "Web Developer". With (2) and (3), a link to ex2:webDev or ex3:webDev can be provided where potentially more information about the profession can be retrieved. However, if we also want to model "since when Tim Berners-Lee has been a Web Developer", we make use of n-ary[3] relations as shown in (3). In the example, we create an individual connecting node (ex3:work42) to combine the information that "Tim Berners-Lee has been a Web Developer since March 1989". While some vocabularies (such as schema.org[4] or the Open Graph Protocol[5]) commonly use the more coarse-grained variants of (1) and (2) in their modeling, web knowledge bases such as Freebase [4] (that has been discontinued) and Wikidata [33] enable fine-grained modeling with n-ary relations (context/qualifiers) as exemplified in (3). In general, it is the authors' decision which level of detail they

---

[2]See also Tim Berners-Lee's idea of the "Oh yeah?" button – https://www.w3.org/DesignIssues/UI.html#OhYeah.

[3]"Defining N-ary Relations on the Semantic web" – http://www.w3.org/TR/swbp-n-aryRelations
[4]schema.org – http://schema.org
[5]Open Graph Protocol – http://ogp.me/

want to address with the data they publish on the web. Our entity data fusion approach performs the complex alignment of different vocabularies and automatically moves similar claims—expressed RDF triple(s)—into the same clusters.

3 APPROACH

Our approach for entity-centric data fusion starts with a URI $u \in U$ (with U being the set of all URIs) that identifies a specific focus entity e and returns a filtered and ranked set of claims about e. Different resources can provide data for an entity, possibly under different URIs. Our approach uses a pipeline which consists of seven different processing steps that are visualized in Figure 2:

(1) Record Linkage: discover the URIs of all resources equivalent to the entity e;
(2) Data Retrieval: retrieve RDF data for each resource and its connected resources;
(3) Feature Extraction: extract a set of information compounds (that we call "path features") from RDF data;
(4) Clustering: run agglomerative hierarchical clustering on the set of path features;
(5) Cluster Merging: refine clusters by merging;
(6) Representative Selection: identify claims as cluster representatives;
(7) Filtering/Ranking: use different cluster features for filtering or ranking.

The main focus is on the steps 2 to 6 but we also provide general information on step 1 (i.e., what kind of input do we expect from the record linkage step) and step 7 (i.e., what kind of output does the pipeline produce and how can the results be used). We now describe each step of the pipeline in detail.

3.1 Record Linkage

The topic of record linkage has a long tradition in statistics and different subfields of computer science, including databases and information retrieval [22]. The main idea is to retrieve different files, entries, or identifiers that refer to the same entity (e.g., a specific person). The problem has also been explored in the (Semantic) web context [1, 18, 19]. With the use of explicit equivalence (e.g., by using schema:sameAs or owl:sameAs), the availability of a variety of algorithms (e.g., [15] for a recent work), and the availability of systems that offer record linkage as a service (e.g., sameAs.org), we regard this problem as sufficiently addressed. The record linkage approach is expected to take one URI for an entity e as input (e.g., http://dbpedia.org/resource/Tim_Berners-Lee) and then produces an extended set R of reference URIs that all refer to e, for example:

$$R = \{ \text{ ex1:TimBL, ex2:TimBL } \}$$

3.2 Data Retrieval

We assume that all structured data is available as RDF [23]. The sources either directly provide RDF in N-Triples, Turtle, RDF/XML or JSON-LD via HTTP content negotiation or provide HTML pages with embedded markup, where RDFa, Microdata, and JSON-LD are the most supported formats [16, 24]. An RDF graph is defined as follows:

Definition 3.1 (RDF Graph, RDF Triples). With the three sets of URIs U, blank nodes B, and literals L, an RDF graph G is defined as:

$$G \subseteq (U \cup B) \times U \times (U \cup B \cup L) \qquad (1)$$

The elements $t \in G$ of a graph G are called triples. The first element of a triple t is called the "subject", the second "predicate", and the third "object". URIs provide globally unique identifiers; blank nodes can be used instead of URIs if there is no URI available for an entity, or the entity's URI is unknown; and RDF literals encode data type values such as strings or integers.

For each reference URI $r \in R$ from the record linkage step, we aim to retrieve RDF data. If one of the URIs offers RDF, the crawler performs a breadth-first search around the URI (up to a certain depth d). For example, if the triple [ex2:TimBL ex2:job ex2:webDev] is contained in the retrieved dataset of ex2:TimBL, the crawler also tries to retrieve RDF data from the URI ex2:webDev. In addition, the crawler also retrieves information about the used predicates; in this case the crawler retrieves data from ex2:job. During this process, the crawler stores the complete path to the finally delivering URI (i.e., the URI that returns data with status 200 in case of redirects) for each request. That URI is used as a graph name for all retrieved corresponding triples (therefore, with the notion of named graphs – see Definition 3.2, producing quads). Cycles in the breadth-first search are resolved if the URI has already been requested in the same search around $r \in R$ or if the target URI is contained in the set R (or their respective redirect variants; i.e., cross-references in R are removed in this step). In these cases, we do not retrieve the URI a second time. The result of the data retrieval step is an RDF dataset that contains a forest of trees that each have one reference URI as a root (together with provenance information, that is, the URIs of the graphs in which the RDF triples occur). Figure 3 shows an example for such a forest.

Overall, the forest together with the provenance information forms a set of RDF graphs (i.e., an RDF dataset). An RDF dataset can cover multiple RDF graphs and is defined as follows:

Definition 3.2. [Named Graph, RDF Dataset] Let D be the set of RDF graphs and U be the set of URIs. A pair $\langle d, u \rangle \in D \times U$ is called a named graph. An RDF dataset consists of a (possibly empty) set of named graphs (with distinct names) and a default graph $d \in D$ without a name.

3.3 Feature Extraction

We produce path features from the forests in the RDF dataset D created in the data retrieval step. In the following, we consider paths in the tree from the root to a leaf. In accordance to the definition of RDF, each tree can have two types of leaves: URI nodes or literal nodes. However, leaves that are URI nodes do not provide sufficient information as the node itself is a URI that was not retrieved. The system only knows that it exists. For example, if we crawl ex2:TimBL only with depth 0 (i.e., ex2:TimBL and predicate URIs are retrieved) the system knows that the node ex2:webDev exists but we do not get the label "Web Developer" if the URI is not retrieved (i.e., it is not in the RDF Dataset D as a graph name). Therefore, we only consider paths that end with a literal node.

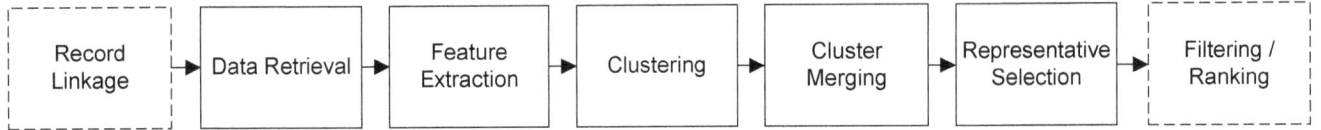

Figure 2: Overview: entity-centric data fusion.

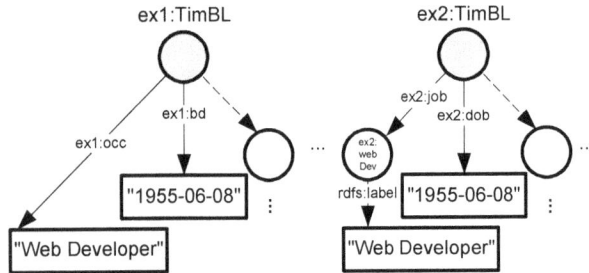

Figure 3: Output of data retrieval: an RDF dataset containing a forest of trees, each with a reference URI as a root.

Definition 3.3 (Path Feature). Let G be an RDF graph. A path feature p is a sequence of triples in G. A path feature fulfills the following three conditions:

(1) It starts with a triple $t_1 \in G$ of the retrieved graph G that has a reference URI in the subject position.
(2) It terminates with a triple $t_2 \in G$ of the retrieved graph G that has a literal in the object position.
(3) It does not contain triples that have a reference URI in the object position (to avoid loops).
(4) If it contains two consecutive triples $t_1, t_2 \in G$, the object of t_1 needs to be the subject of t_2.

Single triples that fulfill the above conditions are also path features. We refer to path features that involve multiple triples as "multi-hop" path features and to those that are constituted by only one triple as "single-hop" path features. We use the ∘–∘ symbol to denote the sequence of path features.

In our example, if we only consider the depicted claims of Figure 3, the following path features can be identified:

(1) [ex1:TimBL ex1:bd "1955-06-08"]
(2) [ex1:TimBL ex1:occ "Web Developer"]
(3) [ex2:TimBL ex2:dob "1955-06-08"]
(4) [ex2:TimBL ex2:job ex2:webDev]∘–∘
    [ex2:webDev rdfs:label "Web Developer"]

Next, we introduce a way that enables us to represent path features as linked lists of strings: we remove all URI nodes and use the rdfs:label of the predicate URIs. A predicate can also have more than one label in the same language, so that we create a representation for each. For example, ex2:job may have the additional label "profession". To take this into account, we add another string representation for the full path feature. For all text-based literals and labels we fix the language. In practice, best results can be achieved with English as vocabularies often provide labels only in that language.

We collect all string representations in a multi-valued map M:

M = [("birth date"→"1955-06-08", ⟨1⟩) ;
("occupation"→"Web Developer", ⟨2⟩) ;
("date of birth"→"1955-06-08", ⟨3⟩) ;
("occupation"→"label"→"Web Developer", ⟨4⟩) ;
("profession"→"label"→"Web Developer", ⟨4⟩)]

3.4 Clustering

We cluster path features in accordance to their string representations. At this point, a key feature of the approach—the *entity centricity*—mitigates the occurrence of ambiguities and unwanted merges. For example, the string "web" has only one reasonable meaning in the vicinity of the entity ex1:TimBL while in the whole web graph there are many different meanings for the term.

Similarity. In order to compare the string representations with each other, we use string similarity functions as they are proposed for ontology alignment [7]. For two given string representations we compare the head h^6 (i.e., the label of the first predicate) and the tail t (i.e., the label of the leaf node) of each string representation $l_i \in keySet(M)$ respectively. We compute the common result with a linear combination ($0 \leq \lambda \leq 1$):

$$\text{sim}(l_1, l_2) = \lambda \cdot \text{sim}(h(l_1), h(l_2)) + (1 - \lambda) \cdot \text{sim}(t(l_1), t(l_2)) \quad (2)$$

In our experiments we set $\lambda = 0.5$, which produced good results for the clustering. The string similarity function incorporates tokenization (*to*) and normalization steps. We distinguish between single-token and multi-token strings:

$$\text{sim}(s_1, s_2) = \begin{cases} \text{jw}(s_1, s_2) & \text{if } |to(s_1)| = 1 \\ & \& |to(s_2)| = 1 \quad (3) \\ \text{ja}(to(s_1), to(s_2)) & \text{otherwise} \end{cases}$$

Single-token strings use the Jaro-Winkler similarity metric (jw) and multi-token strings use Jaccard similarity (ja). These measures are recommended in [7] for achieving high precision. For both string similarity measures, a value of 0 means no similarity and 1 is an exact match.

Clustering. We compute a similarity matrix for all string representations as an input for agglomerative hierarchical clustering. The clustering is based on two steps: in the beginning, the linkage of all elements is computed and afterwards the clusters are formed by a cut-off. The linkage starts with clusters of size 1 and uses the

---

[6] We assume that the first predicate is commonly more descriptive than the second or third predicate with respect to the focus entity e. It has to be noted that, in some cases, the second or third predicate could make a better fit for string comparison. For example, a string representation for the n-ary "work"-relation (see Example (3) in Section 2) could be: "work"→"occupation"→"label"→"Web Developer".

similarity matrix in order to link two clusters. This is done in accordance to the smallest Euclidean distance of any two elements in the respective clusters. In the matrix, the elements are represented as column vectors. We repeat this step until all clusters are linked. The linkage is then used to determine a cut-off level that produces n or fewer clusters. Under the assumption that all resources in R provide RDF data and that each covers the same amount of information, the value of n can be set to $\left\lceil \frac{|M|}{|R|} \right\rceil$.[7] In our running example n would be $\left\lceil \frac{5}{2} \right\rceil = 3$. After the clustering, we use the map M to move back from the string representation level to the path feature level. The clusters are then represented as follows:

- **Cluster 1:** { [ex1:TimBL ex1:bd "1955-06-08"],
  [ex2:TimBL ex2:dob "1955-06-08"] }
- **Cluster 2:** { [ex1:TimBL ex1:occ "Web Developer"],
  [ex2:TimBL ex2:job ex2:webDev]○─○
  [ex2:webDev rdfs:label "Web Developer"] }
- **Cluster 3:** { [ex2:TimBL ex2:job ex2:webDev]○─○
  [ex2:webDev rdfs:label "Web Developer"] }

In accordance to the defined similarity measure, the items of Cluster 2 have a perfect match. The items of Cluster 1 have a high similarity as the literal values match perfectly and the predicates have a partial match. The most dissimilar item is Path Feature 4 with its alternative label "profession" for ex2:job. This item ends up in its own cluster (as the number of total clusters is predefined with 3, see above).

3.5 Cluster Merging

After the clustering, similar string representations of path features are in the same cluster but some information is also dispersed. For example, Cluster 2 and Cluster 3 represent similar information. The data retrieval step (see Section 3.2) also retrieves path features that include information about related entities. For example, in the case of ex1, if we also cover the birth place of the entity "Tim Berners-Lee", via [ex1:TimBL ex1:bp ex1:London] we produce a lot of path features that differ only in factual information about London. ex2 might cover similar claims and its information about London might be gathered in the same clusters as the claims from ex1. This naturally leads to many clusters that have the following shape:

```
{ [ex1:TimBL ex1:bp ex1:London]○─○
[ex1:London ex1:long "-0.127"],
[ex2:TimBL ex2:pob ex2:London]○─○
[ex2:London ex2:longitude "-0.1275"] }
```

Similar clusters would be formed about the latitude of London, its population, total area, etc. In the case of the entity "Tim Berners-Lee", another fraction of different clusters would cover claims about the MIT (e.g., number of students, founding year, etc.). A commonality among these fractions (e.g., London, MIT) of clusters is that the first triples of the contained path features are overlapping with the first triples of the path features in other clusters. The individual entity focus (in the example "Tim Berners-Lee") provides that only these first triples are relevant as—independent of the modeling

granularity—the first hop is most relevant to the entity. Therefore, we can merge clusters in which the first triples of the path features are overlapping.

In our example, the first triples of Cluster 2 and Cluster 3 are as follows:

- **Cluster 2:** { [ex1:TimBL ex1:occ "Web Developer"],
  [ex2:TimBL ex2:job ex2:webDev] }
- **Cluster 3:** { [ex2:TimBL ex2:job ex2:webDev] }

For the merging we apply the following method: if, in terms of first triples, two clusters have an equal or higher degree of overlap (estimated via Jaccard index, that has a range between 0 and 1) than a threshold ϵ,[8] the clusters are merged. Note that the criteria for merging clusters is based on structure (i.e., first triples of path features) and the measure with which we derive the clusters is string similarity.

In our example, with $\epsilon = 0.5$, Cluster 2 and Cluster 3 are merged:

Cluster 2: { [ex1:TimBL ex1:occ "Web Developer"],
[ex2:TimBL ex2:job ex2:webDev]○─○
[ex2:webDev rdfs:label "Web Developer"],
[ex2:TimBL ex2:job ex2:webDev]○─○
[ex2:webDev rdfs:label "Web Developer"] }

Clusters containing [ex1:TimBL ex1:bp ex1:London] as a first triple would also get merged. While first triples of single-hop path features such as [ex1:TimBL ex1:occ "Web Developer"] can occur only in multiple clusters if there are more labels for the predicate, multi-hop path features can generate a variety of different label-leaf combinations for their string representations and the first triple or—like in the example—the complete path feature can occur in multiple different clusters before the merging step. In our approach, the combination of path features, their clustering, and the merging of clusters can address all of these cases in a suitable manner.

3.6 Representative Selection

For each cluster, we can select two types of representatives: one general representative and one representative for each source. Both types of representatives are needed for the scenario of Figure 1: one triple to be shown in the panel and one triple per source to support the presented triple. Before we present the details of the representative selection approach, we need to define the term "source". For this we tracked the provenance of each triple in the data retrieval step (cf. Section 3.2). For a specific path feature, we take the first triple: the hostname of the delivering URI of this triple is considered as the *source* of the path feature. The complete delivering URI of a source representative may be used for a more detailed output (as exemplified in Figure 1).

Cluster representative. We consider two cases for the cluster representative:

(1) If the cluster contains only single-hop path features, return the triple that has the highest similarity (see Formula 2) to all other triples.

---

[7]R is defined as the set of all reference URIs in Section 3.1, M is defined as the multi-valued map between string representation and the respective path features in Section 3.3.

[8]The value of ϵ is flexible and can be adjusted within the range of 0 and 1.

(2) If the cluster contains only multi-hop path features or single-hop and multi-hop path features use the first triple of each multi-hop path feature and count its occurrence in the cluster. The first triple that occurs most often in the cluster is returned as the representative.

In our example, the first case returns any of the two birth-date triples (as they have equal similarity to each other) for Cluster 1. The first case enables to select the most common representation among multiple candidates. For example, Wikidata provides also "label"→"Sir Tim Berners-Lee" for the entity and the according path feature gets clustered together with the path feature represented by "label"→"Tim Berners-Lee" from Wikidata[9], IMDb, Freebase etc. The first case selects the representative that is most similar to all others and chooses the version without "Sir".

In our example, the second case returns [ex2:TimBL ex2:job ex2:webDev] as a representative for Cluster 2 (the triple occurs twice). The idea of the second case is that links to other resources (multi-hop) are always better than returning a plain string (single-hop). However, the single-hop path features in multi-hop clusters support the respective claim as a source. In addition, the second case returns a triple that occurs in most path features and, as such, the linked resource (i.e., ex2:webDev in the example) can provide most information on the claim that is described by the cluster.

For the running example, the output of the representatives would be as follows:

```
[ex1:TimBL ex1:bd "1955-06-08"],
[ex2:TimBL ex2:job ex2:webDev]
```

For both claims, the two sources ex1 and ex2 can be provided as references.

Source representative. Source representatives are selected in the same way as the cluster representative with the following restriction: it is chosen as (1) the most similar or (2) most often occurring representative from a single source (e.g., dbpedia.org) compared to all entries across sources.

3.7 Filtering / Ranking

Our approach covers the clustering of similar claims about entities. It does not address steps that can build on the gained information. In this section we provide an overview.

An important aspect, that we have not yet addressed, is the handling of contradicting information. In general, following the open-world assumption, we consider all made claims of all sources as true. If a claim is missing in one source but occurs in another, it can be true. If, in the case of persons, different sources provide different claims about spouses, employers, and even the birth dates, we consider all of them as true. However, as a general idea, we assume that claims are more likely to be true if they are made by multiple different sources.[10] In fact, the more sources support a claim, the more likely it is to be valid or important. In contrast, if a claim is made only by a single source, it is considered less likely or unimportant. The lack of (a sufficient amount of) sources and the

explanations why certain claims are provided in knowledge panels has led to criticism [6, 14]. With the presented entity data fusion approach, we can support the identification of additional sources for claims. This enables users to verify the individual sources and decide themselves whether they want to trust the claim or not. In addition, in order to enable an automatically produced trustability score, additional measures—such as PageRank [5] or knowledge-based trust [12]—can be applied on the sources for each claim.

In a similar way, additional support for the notability of claims can be estimated: the more sources support a claim about an entity, the more it can be considered as important. This is in line with the ideas of [32] that present entities in this manner (ranking claims by the number of sources that support them).

4 EXPERIMENTS

In our experiments, we evaluated our entity data fusion method relative to the Sig.ma baseline established in [32]. We compare the coverage and the number of sources with respect to the scenario of a trustable knowledge panel (see Section 1). The idea is that we do not want to compare agreement on randomly selected claims but to make sure that the evaluated claims would actually be presented to an end user. For this, we use the claims presented in the Google Knowledge Graph (GKG) panels. With regard to the size and the heterogeneity of the dataset (actual data from the web), this restriction made the task of evaluation feasible.

4.1 Dataset

The TREC entity track was last run in 2011.[11] We used the provided evaluation data from that year[12] and selected the entity names of the REF and ELC tasks. This produced 100 entities with two duplicates. Afterwards, we tried to identify the DBpedia URIs for the remaining set of 98 entities. For 18 entities (e.g, "Landfall Foundation" or "Foundation Morgan horses") we could not find according DBpedia identifiers (and also Google did not provide a graph panel for these entities). Therefore, the final set of entities contained 80 entities. This included persons, organizations, universities, places, bands, etc. The service sameAs.org then enabled the retrieval of the according Freebase identifiers (e.g., m/027bp7c – entity "Abraham Verghese") and we could then retrieve Google summaries by adding the GKG API namespace http://g.co/kg/ to these IDs, for example http://g.co/kg/m/027bp7c. We manually retrieved GKG panels by storing the respective HTML to files. In this context, we used http://google.com in English language with a clean browser history for each entity.

The list of the used entities, their DBpedia and Google identifiers, the crawled dataset, the stored Google result pages, and the output of our approach are available at http://people.aifb.kit.edu/ath/entity_data_fusion.

4.2 Baseline: Sig.ma

The Sig.ma system described in [32] provides basic functionality on entity data fusion. The approach is mostly based on string modification in order to derive a uniform representation. In particular, the provided URIs for properties and the URIs/literals for values are analyzed heuristically. The approach cannot deal with n-ary

---

[9]Wikidata provides multiple English labels for this entity.
[10]Note: In a web setting, this assumption is not necessarily correct as the sources are often not independent from each other. We discuss this matter in Section 4.6.

[11]TREC tracks – http://trec.nist.gov/tracks.html
[12]TREC entity track 2011 – http://trec.nist.gov/data/entity2011.html

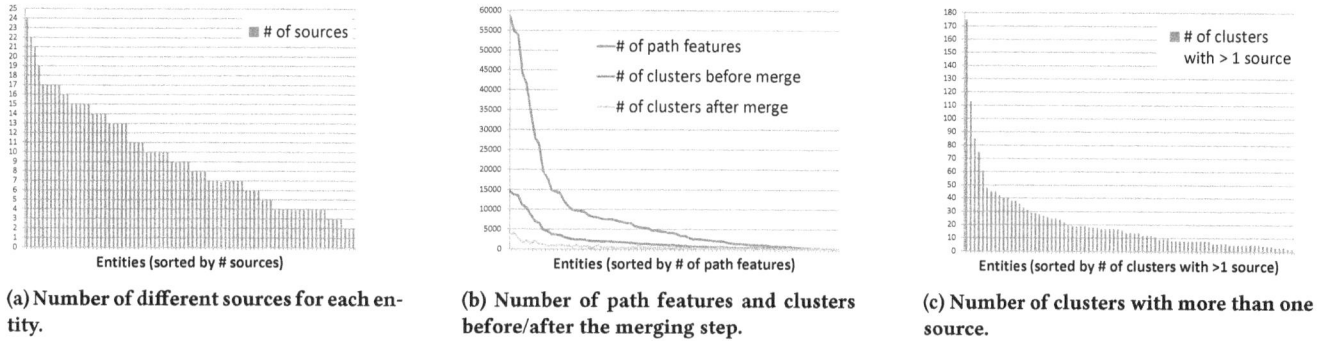

(a) Number of different sources for each entity.

(b) Number of path features and clusters before/after the merging step.

(c) Number of clusters with more than one source.

Figure 4: Different statistics on the distribution of path features, clusters, and sources. The ticks on the x-axes each represent one entity of the TREC dataset.

relations and can only rudimentary reconcile between 0-hop and 1-hop granularity levels. However, in these cases it can serve as a baseline so we re-implemented the main ideas[13] of Sig.ma by performing the following steps:

(1) We use the properties and values of triples where an identifier for an entity is involved, for example:
ex4:occupation "Web Developer"@en

(2) For URIs (in the property or object position) we use the last segment of the URI (e.g., occupation). Typical patterns such as *camelCase* and dashes/underscores are split up. Literal values are used without further modification. All strings are transformed to lower case. For the reconciliation, the Sig.ma approach does not make use of rdfs:label [32].

(3) These basic string representations are then aggregated with an exact match and by attributing their sources:
"occupation Web Developer"
(http://example4.com, http://example5.com)

4.3 Configuration

We applied the two data fusion methods on 80 entities of the TREC entity dataset. We used the sameAs.org service as a record linkage approach with the DBpedia identifiers as an input. Multiple crawls were performed in order to account for periods of unavailability of resources. The crawls happened in June 2015. The crawler operated with depth 1 and retrieved RDF data via content negotiation. After the individual crawls were completed the retrieved data was merged. Per entity, there were 2 to 24 different sources while 75% of the entities included RDF information from at least 5 sources (see Figure 4a). For our method, for each entity, we computed the similarity matrix of the English string representations of all path features. We set the parameter $\lambda = 0.5$. For this matrix, we produced the linkage and retrieved $n = \left\lceil \frac{|M|}{4} \right\rceil$ clusters for each entity. We merged all clusters at an overlap threshold of $\epsilon = 0.5$. An overview of the distribution of the numbers of path features, clusters, and merged clusters is provided in Figure 4b. All entities had more than two clusters with at least two sources and 59% of the entities had

more than 10 such clusters. An overview of this distribution is provided in Figure 4c.

4.4 Evaluation Setup

The evaluation included two steps, the matching of GKG claims to clusters of the output of the respective systems and the evaluation of the identified matches.

Step 1: Match GKG claims to clusters. For the evaluation of the quality of the results, the Google result pages and the produced output of the systems needed to be aligned. Unfortunately, although the data presented by Google is often found in Freebase (which was covered by our crawl), it was not possible to identify a sufficient number of direct links. On the one hand, this was due to the incorrect Turtle RDF output produced by Freebase. On the other hand, a lot of information covered by Freebase included n-ary relations that are presented flat in GKG panels. Therefore, starting from a GKG claim, it is difficult to determine the respective Freebase claim—especially if a variety of domains are covered (as it was the case for the TREC entities). As a consequence, we nominated two human evaluators (both experts on RDF and related technologies) and asked them to provide a manual matching. For all entities, the following was performed: For each claim that was presented in the GKG panel, they used the systems' output to identify clusters in which at least one source representative matched the information content of the GKG claim.

Step 2: Evaluation of matches. For all clusters in the output of the systems that matched a specific GKG claim, the evaluators were instructed to choose the cluster that had most correct sources (i.e., clusters where most source representatives match the information content of the GKG claim). The number of correct sources of this cluster was then documented. In the same step the evaluators kept track of the following two types of error:

Type 1 error: Number of source representatives in the best-fit cluster that did not match the GKG claim (false positives).

Type 2 error: Number of source representatives in other clusters, that also matched the information content of the GKG claim (false negatives).

---

[13] We omitted several highly customized rules of Sig.ma such as the "[...] manually-compiled list of approximately 50 preferred terms" [32].

Table 1: Results for our approach and Sig.ma: the number of produced GKG claims, GKG coverage, number of type 1 errors, number of type 2 errors, precision, recall, and f-measure at different thresholds for the number of sources. The # symbol should be read as "number of".

# sources in output:	≥ 1	≥ 2	≥ 3	≥ 4	≥ 5
Our approach:					
# GKG claims:	414	235	135	76	39
GKG coverage:	55%	31%	18%	10%	5%
# type 1 errors:	81	46	26	17	12
# type 2 errors:	146	81	43	26	16
Precision:	0.84	0.84	0.84	0.82	0.76
Recall:	0.74	0.74	0.76	0.75	0.71
F-measure:	0.78	0.79	0.80	0.78	0.74
Sig.ma:					
# GKG claims:	299	112	70	44	9
GKG coverage:	40%	15%	9%	6%	1%
# type 1 errors:	0	0	0	0	0
# type 2 errors:	304	151	92	57	34
Precision:	1.0	1.0	1.0	1.0	1.0
Recall:	0.50	0.43	0.43	0.44	0.21
F-measure:	0.66	0.60	0.60	0.61	0.35

Table 2: Statistics about the 15 most occurring predicates (with respect to the 755 claims of the GKG panels) and according statistics for the number of (true-positive) sources each system provides ($\downarrow$ min, ø avg, $\uparrow$ max).

Predicate	Count	Our approach			Sig.ma		
		$\downarrow$	ø	$\uparrow$	$\downarrow$	ø	$\uparrow$
label	80	0	3.18	7	1	3.29	7
abstract	80	0	1.74	3	0	0.99	2
founder	42	0	0.79	4	0	0.02	1
place of interest	26	0	0.00	0	0	0.00	0
location	25	0	1.28	4	0	0.24	1
subsidiary	24	0	0.13	1	0	0.04	1
phone number	24	0	0.00	0	0	0.00	0
book	23	0	0.39	1	0	0.09	1
college/uni.	22	0	0.00	0	0	0.00	0
longitude	21	0	3.24	8	1	1.90	4
latitude	21	0	3.10	8	1	1.95	4
ceo	20	0	0.35	5	0	0.10	1
alumni	18	0	0.00	0	0	0.00	0
founding date	15	0	0.93	2	0	0.80	1
founding year	15	0	2.00	6	0	0.93	2

4.5 Evaluation Results

The evaluators identified 755 claims in the GKG panels of the 80 TREC entities. In average, each GKG panel covered 9.4 claims. Table 1 respectively present the main results of our approach and Sig.ma. Our entity data fusion method produced 414 GKG claims (with a respective coverage of 55%) and, in total, 923 source representatives. The baseline Sig.ma produced 299 GKG claims (with a respective coverage of 40%). In almost all cases our approach outperforms Sig.ma by ×2 or higher with respect to the task of retrieving multiple sources per GKG claim (GKG coverage at ≥ 2,

≥ 3, etc.). Sig.ma only considers direct 1:1 matches which means that it produces a precision of 1.0 (there are no type 1 errors). As a side effect, this also implies a strongly reduced recall (which stems from the high number of type 2 errors). The recall levels of Sig.ma drop strongly when more than five sources are needed. In contrast, our approach produces high precision and recall levels and also remains stable when more sources are required (the small increases/decreases are due to the varying proportion of type 1/2 errors with respect to the respective coverage). These scores are also reflected in the respective f-measure scores where our approach outperforms Sig.ma by differences from 0.12 (≥ 1 source) up to 0.39 (≥ 5 sources). In only 22 cases out of 755, Sig.ma produced more sources than our approach. In these cases, relevant claims ended up in larger clusters that had different representatives chosen. Table 2 presents the 15 most-used predicates of the 755 GKG claims and the minimum, average, and maximum number of sources per claim for each of the two systems. It shows that there exist GKG claims (such as phone number or places of interest) that were not covered by any of the web data sources. This explains the gap between 755, the total number of GKG claims, and 414, the number of claims for which we could identify at least one source. In average, in almost all cases, our entity data fusion approach provides more sources than Sig.ma for all different claim predicates.

4.6 Discussion

The results of the experiments demonstrate the effectiveness of our entity data fusion approach. They show, that the recall is significantly improved by considering multiple granularity levels and by the approximate matching via string similarity. As a matter of fact, these factors affect the precision in a negative way, however (as the f-measure scores demonstrate) only to a point where the advantages of the improved recall have a significant overweight. In applications where precision is of ultimate importance, we would suggest an approach that utilizes direct or manually defined mappings. In the presented scenario of a trustable knowledge panel, we suggest to use our entity data fusion approach (which provides a highly improved recall).

A number of challenges that we encountered deal with the quality of Linked Data data on the web in general: not every URI is dereferenceable, not every URI provides RDF data, not all returned RDF data is in (any) correct format, not all RDF data contains information about the retrieved URI, not all RDF data contains labels, and not all RDF data contains language tags. We still made use of all these features and were able to retrieve RDF data from a number of reference URIs (up to 24) via content-negotiation and could make sufficient use of the provided data. For production environments, we would recommend the implementation of a data curation infrastructure that deals with the mentioned challenges.

RDF triples are often used in the subject-predicate-object style but, although—technically—the predicate provides a direction, every such triple also provides information about the object. Tim Berners-Lee encourages RDF creators not to put too much emphasis on the direction of RDF triples.[14] However, only few sources (DBpedia is one of them) provide information about an entity when it is in the

---

[14]Tim Berners-Lee: "Backward and Forward links in RDF just as important" – http://dig.csail.mit.edu/breadcrumbs/node/72

object position of a triple. One way to address this matter could be to perform a full web crawl and apply path feature extraction also for triples that use the entity URI in the object position.

For a variety of parameters of the method, potential extension and optimization with a gold standard is possible. One particular point is literal/object similarity: Many literals are annotated by their type. For example, a birth date like "1955-06-08" often has xsd:date as data type. Therefore, additional (or alternative) similarity measures could be defined for the most common data types. Ultimately, this could be extended towards media similarity for URIs that represent an audio file, an image, or a video.

With increased crawling depth, the number of path features grows exponentially. As we compare path features via their string representation, and we have $|M| \cdot (|M| - 1)/2$ comparisons, this leads to a significant demand for computation time. One solution that we consider in order to mitigate this effect is locality-sensitive hashing [21]. This hashing method moves similar strings to similar buckets and strongly reduces the number of candidates for traditional string comparison.

One aspect that is not addressed in this work is the question "how can we verify that the sources gathered their information *independently* from each other?" Unfortunately, for small information units, such as triples, it is often impossible to gain a deep understanding of provenance if respective information is not explicitly given; especially if the claims are commonly known and true. A related task was addressed in [9] where the authors tackle the problem of copy detection by tracking different datasets and their change over time.

5 RELATED WORK

Our approach is most related to the data fusion and presentation method of Sig.ma by Tummarello et al. [32]. Sig.ma presents a rule-based, entity-centric data fusion method embedded in the context of semantic search. As such, further components of Sig.ma include object retrieval via keyword queries, parallel data gathering, live consolidation, and presentation. The presented entity data fusion approach is strongly focused on efficiency and relies on meaningful URIs, a frequently used feature of many vocabularies and datasets. In contrast, in our approach we fully rely on rdfs:label and can also deal with multiple languages and opaque identifiers as they are used in Wikidata or schema.org (that makes strong use of blank nodes). Although n-ary relations are mentioned in [32], they are not addressed by Sig.ma. In contrast, we designed our approach to deal with claims distributed over multiple hops and enable to align sources with different modeling granularities.

Data/Knowledge fusion: Recent work of Dietze points out the main challenges of "retrieval, crawling and fusion of entity-centric data" [8]. The author mentions the issues of missing (*owl:sameAs*) links, redundancy, and quality. In our work, we extend on that and lay particular focus on modeling granularities and introduce a feasible solution for the presented challenges. In [11], Dong et al. define knowledge fusion as the problem of constructing a large knowledge base from unstructured data (like HTML tables or natural language text) with different extractors from different sources. In contrast, data fusion is defined as the processing of a source-feature matrix for each entity where the entries mark the actual values.

Our work lies between these two extremes as we deal with data for which we do not need extractors but the complexity of the data goes beyond database-like tables as we need to deal with different identifiers, vocabularies, and different modeling approaches. The work on knowledge-based trust by Dong et al. [12] is also related to our task. The authors estimate the trust-worthiness of web sources by extracting information and verifying its correctness. With this method, a trust value is computed for each web source. In contrast, we try to identify multiple occurrences of the same or similar claim. The methods complement each other and we could use the approach of Dong et al. [12] to compute the trustworthiness of the sources that we provide in our output.

Schema/Ontology alignment: The field of schema and ontology alignment has been very active in the past decade. Most relevant to our work is the approach by Suchanek et al. [29], that integrates relations, instances, and schemas. The authors use a probabilistic model to integrate each of the mentioned aspects. The approach is tested with YAGO, DBpedia, and IMDb. In contrast, in our work, we account for different granularities at the modeling level and also match claims that include more than one hop. Further, we test our approach in a real-world scenario with data from the web. The authors of [20] investigate on the problem of the large amount of different vocabularies. They state the question: "How Matchable Are Four Thousand Ontologies on the Semantic Web?" Although we do not explicitly deal with the merging of different vocabularies, our clustering approach could be used to mine complex mapping rules for vocabulary terms via patterns from different clusters (across entities) in an iterative way.

6 CONCLUSIONS

We have introduced a novel entity-centric approach for fusing claims from multiple web sources. Our approach works without any prior knowledge about the used vocabularies and just uses core features of the RDF data model. We have demonstrated two key features of the approach: the entity centricity, which enables the application of string similarity measures for clustering, and the robustness of the approach against fine- or coarse-grained RDF data modeling (via path features). In our experiments, we compared our system to the Sig.ma baseline and demonstrated that our system produces higher coverage, recall, and f-measure scores.

We also shed light on a variety of challenges that encompass the task of web-scale entity data fusion. In particular, the large number of different vocabularies, their individual modelling focus, and various issues with Linked Data quality bring additional complexity to an already computationally challenging problem.

We plan to address the use of existing mappings on the schema level based on rdfs:subClassOf, rdfs:subPropertyOf, owl:equivalentClass and owl:equivalentProperty. A strength of our current approach is that we do not need these mappings, as not many of them exist; schema.org, for example, only maps to a handful of external classes and properties. But we believe that, over time, more mappings will become available, either manually constructed or with the support of ontology alignment approaches that can handle schema diversity in arbitrary web data. In that line, we plan to extend the string-based similarity measure by a rule learning system that detects frequent vocabulary alignment patterns in the clusters and iteratively feeds this information back to the similarity measure. In the further work, we also plan to combine the presented approach with our entity summarization system LinkSUM [31].

ACKNOWLEDGMENTS

The research leading to these results has received funding from the Marie Curie International Research Staff Exchange Scheme (IRSES) of the European Union Seventh Framework Programme (FP7/2007-2013) under grant agreement no. 612551 and by the German Federal Ministry of Education and Research (BMBF) within the Software Campus project "SumOn" (grant no. 01IS12051).

REFERENCES

[1] Krisztian Balog, David Carmel, Arjen P. de Vries, Daniel M. Herzig, Peter Mika, Haggai Roitman, Ralf Schenkel, Pavel Serdyukov, and Thanh Tran Duc. 2012. The First Joint International Workshop on Entity-oriented and Semantic Search (JIWES). *SIGIR Forum* 46, 2 (2012), 87–94. DOI:http://dx.doi.org/10.1145/2422256.2422268
[2] Tim Berners-Lee. 2006. Linked Data. https://www.w3.org/DesignIssues/LinkedData.html. (2006).
[3] Abraham Bernstein, James Hendler, and Natalya Noy. 2016. A New Look at the Semantic Web. *Commun. ACM* 59, 9 (2016), 35–37. DOI:http://dx.doi.org/10.1145/2890489
[4] Kurt Bollacker, Colin Evans, Praveen Paritosh, Tim Sturge, and Jamie Taylor. 2008. Freebase: A Collaboratively Created Graph Database for Structuring Human Knowledge. In *Proceedings of the 2008 ACM SIGMOD International Conference on Management of Data*. ACM, New York, NY, USA, 1247–1250. DOI:http://dx.doi.org/10.1145/1376616.1376746
[5] Sergey Brin and Lawrence Page. 1998. The anatomy of a large-scale hypertextual Web search engine. *Computer Networks and ISDN Systems* 30, 1 (1998), 107–117. DOI:http://dx.doi.org/10.1016/S0169-7552(98)00110-X
[6] Amy Cavenaile. 2016. You probably haven't even noticed Google's sketchy quest to control the world's knowledge. https://www.washingtonpost.com/news/the-intersect/wp/2016/05/11/you. (2016).
[7] Michelle Cheatham and Pascal Hitzler. 2013. String Similarity Metrics for Ontology Alignment. In *The Semantic Web – ISWC 2013: 12th International Semantic Web Conference, Sydney, NSW, Australia, October 21-25, 2013, Proceedings, Part II*. Springer Berlin Heidelberg, Berlin, Heidelberg, 294–309. DOI:http://dx.doi.org/10.1007/978-3-642-41338-4_19
[8] Stefan Dietze. 2017. Retrieval, Crawling and Fusion of Entity-centric Data on the Web. In *Semantic Keyword-Based Search on Structured Data Sources: COST Action IC1302 Second International KEYSTONE Conference, IKC 2016, Cluj-Napoca, Romania, September 8-9, 2016, Revised Selected Papers*, Andrea Calì, Dorian Gorgan, and Martín Ugarte (Eds.). Springer International Publishing, Cham, 3–16. DOI:http://dx.doi.org/10.1007/978-3-319-53640-8_1
[9] Xin Luna Dong, Laure Berti-Equille, and Divesh Srivastava. 2009. Truth Discovery and Copying Detection in a Dynamic World. *Proc. VLDB Endow.* 2, 1 (2009), 562–573. DOI:http://dx.doi.org/10.14778/1687627.1687691
[10] Xin Luna Dong, Evgeniy Gabrilovich, Geremy Heitz, Wilko Horn, Ni Lao, Kevin Murphy, Thomas Strohmann, Shaohua Sun, and Wei Zhang. 2014. Knowledge Vault: A Web-scale Approach to Probabilistic Knowledge Fusion. In *Proceedings of the 20th ACM SIGKDD International Conference on Knowledge Discovery and Data Mining (KDD '14)*. ACM, New York, NY, USA, 601–610. DOI:http://dx.doi.org/10.1145/2623330.2623623
[11] Xin Luna Dong, Evgeniy Gabrilovich, Geremy Heitz, Wilko Horn, Kevin Murphy, Shaohua Sun, and Wei Zhang. 2014. From Data Fusion to Knowledge Fusion. *Proc. VLDB Endow.* 7, 10 (2014), 881–892. DOI:http://dx.doi.org/10.14778/2732951.2732962
[12] Xin Luna Dong, Evgeniy Gabrilovich, Kevin Murphy, Van Dang, Wilko Horn, Camillo Lugaresi, Shaohua Sun, and Wei Zhang. 2015. Knowledge-based Trust: Estimating the Trustworthiness of Web Sources. *Proc. VLDB Endow.* 8, 9 (2015), 938–949. DOI:http://dx.doi.org/10.14778/2777598.2777603
[13] Fredo Erxleben, Michael Günther, Markus Krötzsch, Julian Mendez, and Denny Vrandečić. 2014. Introducing Wikidata to the Linked Data Web. In *The Semantic Web – ISWC 2014: 13th International Semantic Web Conference, Riva del Garda, Italy, October 19-23, 2014. Proceedings, Part I*. Number 8796 in Lecture Notes in Computer Science. Springer International Publishing, 50–65. DOI:http://dx.doi.org/10.1007/978-3-319-11964-9_4
[14] Heather Ford and Mark Graham. 2016. *Code and the City*. Routledge, Chapter Semantic Cities: Coded Geopolitics and the Rise of the Semantic Web, 200–214.
[15] Anja Gruenheid, Xin Luna Dong, and Divesh Srivastava. 2014. Incremental Record Linkage. *Proc. VLDB Endow.* 7, 9 (2014), 697–708. DOI:http://dx.doi.org/10.14778/2732939.2732943
[16] Ramanathan V. Guha, Dan Brickley, and Steve MacBeth. 2015. Schema.Org: Evolution of Structured Data on the Web. *Queue* 13, 9, Article 10 (2015), 28 pages. DOI:http://dx.doi.org/10.1145/2857274.2857276
[17] Daniel Hernández, Aidan Hogan, and Markus Krötzsch. 2015. Reifying RDF: What Works Well With Wikidata?. In *Proceedings of the 11th International Workshop on Scalable Semantic Web Knowledge Base Systems (CEUR Workshop Proceedings)*, Vol. 1457. CEUR-WS.org, 32–47.
[18] Daniel M. Herzig, Peter Mika, Roi Blanco, and Thanh Tran. 2013. Federated Entity Search Using On-the-Fly Consolidation. In *The Semantic Web – ISWC 2013: 12th International Semantic Web Conference, Sydney, NSW, Australia, October 21-25, 2013, Proceedings, Part I*. Springer Berlin Heidelberg, Berlin, Heidelberg, 167–183. DOI:http://dx.doi.org/10.1007/978-3-642-41335-3_11
[19] Aidan Hogan, Andreas Harth, and Stefan Decker. 2007. Performing Object Consolidation on the Semantic Web Data Graph. In *Proceedings of 1st I3: Identity, Identifiers, Identification Workshop co-located with the 16th International World Wide Web Conference (WWW2007), Banff, Alberta, Canada*.
[20] Wei Hu, Jianfeng Chen, Hang Zhang, and Yuzhong Qu. 2011. How Matchable Are Four Thousand Ontologies on the Semantic Web. In *The Semantic Web: Research and Applications: 8th Extended Semantic Web Conference, ESWC 2011, Heraklion, Greece, May 29-June 2, 2011, Proceedings, Part I*. Springer Berlin Heidelberg, Berlin, Heidelberg, 290–304. DOI:http://dx.doi.org/10.1007/978-3-642-21034-1_20
[21] Piotr Indyk and Rajeev Motwani. 1998. Approximate Nearest Neighbors: Towards Removing the Curse of Dimensionality. In *Proceedings of the Thirtieth Annual ACM Symposium on Theory of Computing (STOC '98)*. ACM, New York, NY, USA, 604–613. DOI:http://dx.doi.org/10.1145/276698.276876
[22] Nick Koudas, Sunita Sarawagi, and Divesh Srivastava. 2006. Record Linkage: Similarity Measures and Algorithms. In *Proceedings of the 2006 ACM SIGMOD International Conference on Management of Data*. ACM, New York, NY, USA, 802–803. DOI:http://dx.doi.org/10.1145/1142473.1142599
[23] Frank Manola and Eric Miller. 2004. RDF Primer. (2004). W3C Recommendation, http://www.w3.org/TR/rdf-syntax/.
[24] Robert Meusel, Petar Petrovski, and Christian Bizer. 2014. The WebDataCommons Microdata, RDFa and Microformat Dataset Series. In *The Semantic Web – ISWC 2014: 13th International Semantic Web Conference, Riva del Garda, Italy, October 19-23, 2014. Proceedings, Part I*. Springer International Publishing, Cham, 277–292. DOI:http://dx.doi.org/10.1007/978-3-319-11964-9_18
[25] Rahul Parundekar, Craig A. Knoblock, and José Luis Ambite. 2010. *Linking and Building Ontologies of Linked Data*. Springer Berlin Heidelberg, Berlin, Heidelberg, 598–614. DOI:http://dx.doi.org/10.1007/978-3-642-17746-0_38
[26] Dominique Ritze, Christian Meilicke, Ondřej Šváb Zamazal, and Heiner Stuckenschmidt. 2009. A Pattern-based Ontology Matching Approach for Detecting Complex Correspondences. In *Proceedings of the 4th International Workshop on Ontology Matching (OM-2009) Collocated with the 8th International Semantic Web Conference (ISWC 2009) (CEUR Workshop Proceedings)*, Vol. 551. CEUR-WS.org, 25–36.
[27] Pavel Shvaiko, Jérôme Euzenat, Fausto Giunchiglia, Heiner Stuckenschmidt, Natasha Noy, and Arnon Rosenthal (Eds.). 2009. *Proceedings of the 4th International Workshop on Ontology Matching (OM-2009) Collocated with the 8th International Semantic Web Conference (ISWC 2009)*. CEUR Workshop Proceedings, Vol. 551. CEUR-WS.org.
[28] Amit Singhal. 2012. Introducing the Knowledge Graph: things, not strings. http://googleblog.blogspot.com/2012/05/introducing-knowledge-graph-things-not.html. (2012).
[29] Fabian M. Suchanek, Serge Abiteboul, and Pierre Senellart. 2011. PARIS: Probabilistic Alignment of Relations, Instances, and Schema. *Proc. VLDB Endow.* 5, 3 (2011), 157–168. DOI:http://dx.doi.org/10.14778/2078331.2078332
[30] Andreas Thalhammer. 2016. *Linked Data Entity Summarization*. Phdthesis. KIT, Fakultät für Wirtschaftswissenschaften, Karlsruhe. DOI:http://dx.doi.org/10.5445/IR/1000065395
[31] Andreas Thalhammer, Nelia Lasierra, and Achim Rettinger. 2016. LinkSUM: Using Link Analysis to Summarize Entity Data. In *Web Engineering: 16th International Conference, ICWE 2016, Lugano, Switzerland, June 6-9, 2016. Proceedings*. Lecture Notes in Computer Science, Vol. 9671. Springer International Publishing, Cham, 244–261. DOI:http://dx.doi.org/10.1007/978-3-319-38791-8_14
[32] Giovanni Tummarello, Richard Cyganiak, Michele Catasta, Szymon Danielczyk, Renaud Delbru, and Stefan Decker. 2010. Sig.ma: Live views on the Web of Data. *Web Semantics: Science, Services and Agents on the World Wide Web* 8, 4 (2010), 355–364. DOI:http://dx.doi.org/10.1016/j.websem.2010.08.003
[33] Denny Vrandečić and Markus Krötzsch. 2014. Wikidata: A Free Collaborative Knowledgebase. *Commun. ACM* 57, 10 (2014), 78–85. DOI:http://dx.doi.org/10.1145/2629489
[34] Denny Vrandečić, Varun Ratnakar, Markus Krötzsch, and Yolanda Gil. 2011. Shortipedia: Aggregating and Curating Semantic Web Data. *Web Semantics: Science, Services and Agents on the World Wide Web* 9, 3 (2011), 334–338. DOI:http://dx.doi.org/10.1016/j.websem.2011.06.006

Revisiting Hypertext Infrastructure

Claus Atzenbeck*
Hof University
Institute of Information Systems
Alfons-Goppel-Platz 1
95028, Hof, Germany
claus.atzenbeck@iisys.de

Thomas Schedel
Hof University
Institute of Information Systems
Alfons-Goppel-Platz 1
95028, Hof, Germany
thomas.schedel@iisys.de

Manolis Tzagarakis
University of Patras
Department of Economics
26504, Rion, Greece
tzagara@upatras.gr

Daniel Roßner
Hof University
Institute of Information Systems
Alfons-Goppel-Platz 1
95028, Hof, Germany
daniel.rossner@iisys.de

Lucas Mages
Hof University
Institute of Information Systems
Alfons-Goppel-Platz 1
95028, Hof, Germany
lucas.mages@hof-university.de

ABSTRACT

Specialized systems aiming at offering hypertext functionality in users' computing have been discussed since the early days of hypertext. However, with the claim to also support other structure domains than node-link structures, hypertext systems had to overcome some challenges. Researchers came up with component-based approaches and low level structure services.

Due to the raising omnipresence of the Web, research on traditional hypertext systems has been fading out over the past decade. This paper focuses again on hypertext infrastructures and goes beyond ongoing Web discussions. Based on lessons learned from well thought through previous work, we present a novel design for multi-structure supporting, general purpose hypertext systems that can be used in a series of application domains. The system provides intelligence analysis which is needed for sophisticated user support. We argue that this lets us use the hypertext system also as a visual analytics tool. Furthermore, for demonstration purposes we describe the use of the system in combination with a Web-based software engineering platform, which is part of the ongoing project ODIN.

CCS CONCEPTS

•**Human-centered computing** →**Hypertext / hypermedia;**
•**Software and its engineering** →*Software infrastructure;*

KEYWORDS

hypertext infrastructure; open hypermedia systems; CB-OHS; spatial hypertext; navigational hypertext; taxonomic hypertext; Asgard

---

*Corresponding author

HT'17, July 4-7, 2017, Prague, Czech Republic.
© 2017 Copyright held by the owner/author(s). 978-1-4503-4708-2/17/07...$15.00
DOI: http://dx.doi.org/10.1145/3078714.3078718

1 INTRODUCTION

Hypertext has been described as a "computer-based medium for thinking and communication" [17]. It has a long tradition in computer science. Vannevar Bush foresaw the rapid growth of information and the need of associations already in the 1940s. He issued the idea that people should be able to persistently store "paths" among documents that can be followed at any time later or shared with others. He was pioneering the idea that human mind should be extended by machines and called his prototypic design *Memory Extender* or short *Memex* [15]. Later in the 1960s, when computers were more widely available in academia Ted Nelson coined "the word 'hypertext' to mean a body of written or pictorial material interconnected in such a complex way that it could not conveniently be presented or represented on paper" [41]. For the first time computers have been used to augment human intellect. In the following years Nelson's strategy was to develop a hypertext system that holds all documents and its versions and called it *Xanadu* [43]. Another hypertext pioneer was Douglas Engelbart, who developed *Augment* and *NLS* [25]. He had a cooperative point of view on hypertext as systems to be used for collaborative problem solving.

The 1980s became the time of various new hypertext projects, including *KMS* [1], *Hyperties* [56], *NoteCards* [30], *Intermedia* [37], *Guide* [14], and *HyperCard* [57]. They all followed a node-link paradigm and many of them were based on monolithic system architectures. The Dexter Hypertext Reference Model [28] aimed at providing a general model at the end of the pre-Web era.

In the late 1980s and early 1990s new structure types have been addressed by hypertext scientists, such as spatial hypertext [35], taxonomic hypertext [50], or argumentation supporting structures [18]. Those differed from the node-link structures fundamentally and demanded new system functionalities and behavior.

This was the birth of various research projects that aimed to provide generalized hypertext infrastructures, so-called Open Hypermedia Systems (OHS) and later Component-based OHS (CB-OHS). Their aim is to abstract from specific structure services and enable specialized modules for the tasks at hand. Furthermore, they have the potential of interoperable services in order to support "functional aggregation of other domains" [59], for example, digital libraries and linguistic domains.

This research on hypertext infrastructures has started fading out in the early 2000s, as Tim Berners-Lee's World Wide Web [10] became dominant in science and economy. Although there were approaches in merging OHS and the Web (i. e., [12]), the Web never adopted fundamental findings from hypertext research widely. A *research gap* can be witnessed between the original hypertext infrastructure work around the year 2000 and today which has not been compensated by the growing Web.

In this paper we describe our core system architecture as a consequent next step in the development of traditional hypertext infrastructures. Our major goal was to develop a component-based system that enables support for various structure types, including spatial hypertext, taxonomic hypertext, or node-link structures. From lessons learned we have significantly changed parts of traditional paradigms such that our system includes machine intelligence and provides better support to users.

The remainder of the paper includes a brief historical perspective of hypertext infrastructures in Sect. 2 which leads to a description of our current system in Sect. 3. In Sect. 4 we will present a case scenario taken from an ongoing research project. It acts as a proof of concept for the discussed infrastructure. Finally, Sect. 5 concludes our work and provides a glimpse of future work.

2 HISTORICAL VIEW

2.1 General

The evolution of hypertext systems can be described as successive steps of abstracting and opening up parts of their architecture [46, 48]. Within each evolutionary step, such systems removed various functionalities from their core and made them identifiable, first class abstractions within their architectures. Being a first class abstraction, these functionalities could be reused and appropriately tailored to facilitate a variety of data structuring or organization problems. In the next paragraphs we outline the evolutionary steps hypermedia systems took from which their ability to address a wider range of structuring problems emerged.

2.2 Monolithic Systems

Early hypermedia systems are monolithic in their architecture (cf. Fig 1a). The term *monolithic* is used to denote that these systems do not identify or separate different layers and hence render presentation, hypertext, and storage layer as a single process. Those systems do not offer interfaces or protocols which the different layers could use to communicate. Most are based on node-link structures supporting navigation between informational units, for example, KMS [1], NoteCards [30], or Intermedia [69]. Some other monolithic systems support further structure domains, for example, argumentation support (e. g., gIBIS [19]) or spatial hypertext (e. g., VIKI [36], VKB [55], or Tinderbox [11]).

Due to their monolithic nature, these hypertext systems exhibited a number of shortcomings including:

(1) *Proprietary document formats.* In general, each monolithic hypertext system defines its own representation and storage format for hypertext documents. This requires the non-trivial task of transforming external data in order to be used [26].

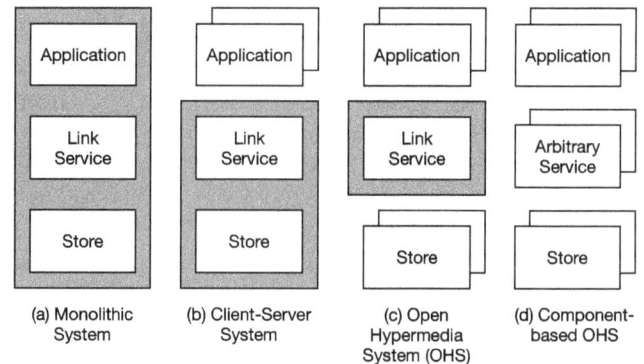

Figure 1: Hypermedia infrastructure history [67]

(2) *Embedded hypertext abstractions.* Monolithic systems emphasize embedding hypertext abstractions (such as anchors, nodes, and links) within its content and storing them as a single entity. This makes it difficult for these systems to integrate other media.

(3) *Closed set of applications.* Their monolithic nature restrict development of new services and integration of third party applications. This forces users to abandon their preferred tools.

The above issues caused that monolithic hypertext systems are considered islands that would not "talk to each other" [60]. They are steering away from Ted Nelson's vision of a *docuverse* [42] and from making hypertext functionality as natural as "copy & paste" in the everyday computing environment of users [38].

2.3 Client Server Hypertext Systems

The first move towards addressing the concerns regarding monolithic systems was to open up the application layer (cf. Fig 1b). This resulted in client-server based hypertext systems, in which an open set of applications could request hypertext functionalities from the system. In these systems applications (i. e., clients) request hypertext services from so-called link services which implement the hypertext layer by using specific system related protocols. Hence new client applications can be effortlessly developed by simply adhering to the system's protocol.

Client-server hypermedia systems can be classified as *Link Server Systems* (LSS) or *Hyperbase Management Systems* (HBMS). They differ in how they treat the storage of content. While for LSSs the data storage is handled by the application (not the hypertext system), in HBMSs it is the responsibility of the hypertext system [49]. HBMSs adopted such approach to address issues of editing problems or link integrity, whereby links still could point to data that has been deleted [20]. A notable example of a LSS is Sun's Link Service [51] while examples of HBMSs include Neptune [23], HAM [16], or DGS [54].

The World Wide Web [10] can also be considered a client-server hypertext system. However, while the WWW meets the mandatory requirement of offering an open set of applications that can communicate via a well defined protocol (namely HTTP), it has been criticized of its inability to "understand" and reason upon structural abstractions, such as anchors, nodes, and links. This makes the Web is very data (not structure) centric. Due to that the question has been raised of whether the WWW can be considered a hypertext system at all [45].

2.4 Open Hypermedia Systems – OHS

The next step for hypermedia systems was to further open up their architecture by decoupling the hypertext from the storage layer (cf. Fig 1c) as well as providing hypertext services to an even more extended set of applications, including third party applications. This development initiated the era of *Open Hypermedia Systems* (OHS). The focus of integrating third party applications was a focal point, attempting to bring hypermedia services to users' everyday computing environment [21, 63].

These efforts gave birth to systems such as Devise [29] (demonstrating the integration of Microsoft Word with an hypermedia system), HyperDisco [66] (successfully integrating XEmacs), or Microcosm [32] (integrating Microsoft Calendar, WAIS, and Gopher). There were also efforts in integration the WWW with OHS (e. g., [3, 13]).

OHSs ease the tailored integration of navigational hypertext functionality in a wide range of applications and avoid the need to design and implement large parts of the system over and over. Furthermore, standardization efforts were initiated in the context of the Open Hypermedia Systems Working Group (OHSWG) in order to support interoperability between applications and OHSs: applications integrated with one hypermedia system should be able to work with any other OHS as well. The Open Hypermedia Protocol (OHP), which specifies a standard way of communication between applications and hypermedia systems, was an outcome of these efforts [22].

The emphasis on integrating third party applications enabled OHSs to address problem areas that used to be outside the realm of hypertext. Examples include the fields of software engineering [4, 24] or ontologies [62] for which hypertext has been introduced as a useful way to organize and navigate these kind of information spaces. Despite their increasing openness regarding applications, OHSs still are systems that offer predominantly node-link structures to applications in order to facilitate navigation of information.

2.5 Component-based Open Hypermedia Systems – CB-OHS

Component-based Open Hypermedia Systems (CB-OHS) resulted from opening up the hypertext layer of OHSs (cf. Fig 1d). Several reasons led to this evolutionary step. One was that the design of the OHP turned out to be complicated [2]. Moreover, efforts were concentrated on supporting different structure paradigms within the same system, such as taxonomic or spatial hypertext as well as making their development and tailoring easier. The architecture of CB-OHS offers a hypertext layer that admits an open set of so-called *structure services*. Each of them addresses the organization problems of a particular domain, such as navigational, taxonomic, or spatial hypertext. Hence, a single CB-OHS is able to support an open set of organization problems in parallel. CB-OHSs have also reconsidered the storage layer, which is capable of storing *generalized structures*. This makes it possible to persistently store different hypertext types

at the same place. This opened the discussion on how deep structure awareness should be pushed into the system, leading to the research thread of *structural computing* [44, 47].

There are different approaches of granting openness and generality for various CB-OHS layers; examples include Callimachus [59], the Fundamental Open Hypermedia Model (FOHM) [39, 40], or Construct [68]. The latter, for example, acknowledges *any* set of services at the hypertext layer, not only services related to hypertext functionality. This is why it has been classified as a *Multiple Open Hypermedia System* [65]. FOHM instead offers only support for three domains, namely navigational, spatial, and taxonomic. However, it devises for these distinct domains a well defined, coherent, and complete logical model for the hypertext layer.

As discussed above, hypermedia systems moved from closed, monolithic systems to open, distributed and modular systems, providing rich hypertext functionalities to an open set of applications. The benefits of CB-OHS include in particular (i) easier integration of new structure services; (ii) better bridging to Web-based services; (iii) efficient tailoring existing structure services for specific problem domains; and (iv) support of diverse data sources without the need for data transformation. These advantages will be demonstrated in the following sections.

3 INFRASTRUCTURE DISCUSSION

3.1 General

The design of previous hypertext systems was based upon the following specific priorities and assumptions:

(1) They were designed primarily with node-link structures in mind. Other structure types, such as spatial hypertext or metadata support (see, e. g., Construct [68]) have been included additionally on top of that.

(2) Sophisticated hypertext systems do not offer rich applications for various structure types. (See Wiil's keynote at ACM Hypertext 2005 [64]).

(3) Even though intelligence became a huge issue for the Web community, it has never been an important part of previous hypertext infrastructures.

However, today, we would expect hypertext systems that (i) provide sophisticated, component-based, and general purpose infrastructures; (ii) support various and rich structure types for different tasks at hand; and (iii) include intelligence components to support knowledge workers.

The research prototype described in this paper provides support for the following main features that are relevant for modern hypertext infrastructures:

(1) Component-based system with support for multiple structure domains (e. g., node-link structures, spatial hypertext, taxonomic hypertext, or argumentation support structures)

(2) General purpose infrastructure to be used in various application domains or for different organization problems

(3) Intelligence components for increased user support

(4) Multiple general purpose parsers to be used for spatial hypertext structures

The overall framework is divided into three different areas with specific purposes. The names are borrowed from the Norse mythology:

Midgard includes all *application* components to which we mainly count user interfaces;

Asgard holds (partly intelligent) components that deal with *structures*, such as a spatial structure services with multiple, highly specialized parsers; and

Hel hosts a collection of *knowledge-centric* components, e. g., knowledge bases or intelligent software that is used to populate those.

The basic idea is that Asgard's components analyze structures that users created via Midgard applications. The result of this analysis is used to query relevant information from Hel knowledge bases which is then presented to the users.

The first developed Asgard component in our system was the spatial structure service. Instead of designing the overall architecture upon node-link structures (as it was the case with previous systems) the Asgard framework has been developed primarily with one of the most complex (and for machines most difficult to "understand") hypertext structures in mind. This approach appreciates the specific demands of implicit structures rather than explicit ones. As we will argue in the following, explicit structure types, such as node-link or taxonomic structures can be added easily. Those are currently under development.

Both a Hypertext System and a Visual Analytics Tool. Through Asgard and Hel the overall system reaches computational intelligence to a level not seen in previous traditional hypertext applications. This enables an iterative process of human *and* machine in which the machine learns from what the user does and the user benefits from the machine's suggestions. It can be seen as a way of intelligently navigating through knowledge provided by (i) the user's structure created in Midgard and computed in Asgard; and (ii) the machine computed knowledge existing in specialized Hel knowledge bases. As such, our system goes along with what is known as *visual analytics* and its mantra "Analyze first, Show the Important, Zoom, filter and analyze further, Details on demand." [34]. The relevance of Midgard, Asgard, and Hel for visual analytics point becomes even more obvious by a statement given by Sun et al.:

> "The combination and interaction between visual and automatic analysis methods are the key feature of visual analytics, which helps distinguish the visual analytics process from other data analysis processes. It allows for progressive refinement and evaluation of the analysis results." [58]

We argue that from this perspective our framework can be considered both a *generalized hypertext infrastructure* and a *specialized visual analytics tool.*

Figure 2 provides an overview of potential infrastructure components. The communication protocols between system components are formally described in the Asgard technical specification [61]. In the following sections we will present the three system layers individually, referring to the mentioned overview figure.

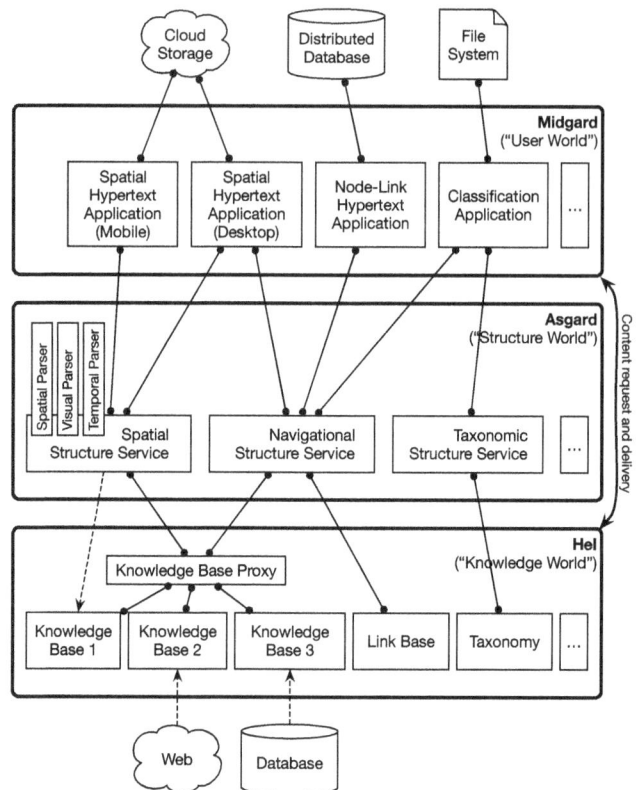

Figure 2: Infrastructure components in Midgard, Asgard, and Hel

3.2 Asgard – The Structure World

Asgard in Norse mythology is the place of the gods. In our system the name refers to the central intelligence components of the system. Those are components that deal with various kinds of structures and are aware of what is going on in the user's world. They also have access to knowledge-centric services. Asgard is the most central layer in our infrastructure. It refers to the arbitrary service layer in CB-OHSs [67] (cf. Fig. 1).

Today, Asgard provides a spatial structure service written in Java. Its structure awareness is provided by various parsers, including (i) a spatial parser that analyses the spatial arrangement or distance of objects; (ii) a visual parser that considers the visual appearance of objects; (iii) a temporal parser that computes relationships based on the sequence of user interactions; and (iv) a content parser that extracts relationships between objects based on their textual content. Those enable analyzing spatially organized information, as described in various previous work [cf. 7–9]. A novel approach was the consideration of time to foster higher accuracy in analyzed associations between informational units, which was first introduced in [6] and formally described in [52].

The spatial structure service follows a plug & play metaphor for its parsers, such that others can be connected easily. As discussed in [53] the output of the various parsers is merged and normalized such that a high accuracy of correctly found relationships between spatially arranged objects is provided.

The question remains about whether parsers (or similar components) should be treated as add-ons to structure services or rather be considered as top level Asgard components. We follow the paradigm to treat components as add-ons whenever they are specific to a *single* component, whereas software units that may be used by *several* components become native Asgard services. The mentioned parsers are highly specialized components, only used by the spatial structure service.

The spatial structure service is (as any Asgard service) purely structure aware, but does not have knowledge over the data itself. This idea is borrowed from the Dexter Hypertext Reference Model [27, 28, 31] in which the so-called "storage layer" only considers structural components, but not the data within. The latter is taken care of inside the "within-component" layer. However, contrary to Dexter our infrastructure puts responsibility of managing data to Midgard applications. As a given spatial structure can be analyzed at any given time, there is no need to persistently store the computed associations (i. e., the parsers' output). Consequently, the spatial structure service has no facilities to save structure persistently. Instead, it holds the currently computed (i. e. yet made explicit) structure only in main memory.

Other Asgard services support node-link structures (so-called navigational structures) or taxonomies. Both (currently under development) differ in important aspects to spatial structure services. The most obvious fact is that they deal with *explicit* rather than implicit structures. As such, structure needs to be stored persistently in order to follow links later or classify objects according to a given taxonomy. In our architecture this is the task of specialized services within Hel (i. e., the "knowledge world") including link bases for navigational hypertext or storage facilities for taxonomies (see Fig. 2). From there the Asgard service retrieves information required for link traversal etc. This architecture consequently separates data (responsibility in Midgard) and structure/behavior (responsibility in Asgard/Hel).

Furthermore, there are connections between Hel knowledge bases and Asgard services. They are used to retrieve relevant information and pass it to the user interface. Indicated by a dashed arrow in Fig. 2, the spatial structure service is also able to fill a knowledge base with computed associations. This lets the overall system gain from user created knowledge.

3.3 Midgard – The User World

In Norse mythology Midgard is the place where humans live. In our system it refers to frontend applications, mainly to those used by humans to interact with the system. Those applications are also responsible themselves for persistently storing their data. This may be solved by writing it into files, connecting to additional databases, using cloud storage, etc.

It is assumed that any Midgard application supports structuring tasks, for example, via node-link hypertext, spatial hypertext, or classification tools. These applications are connected to the respective Asgard structure services. A Midgard application may connect to multiple structure services. For example, as indicated in Fig. 2, the spatial hypertext desktop application connects to both the spatial and navigational structure service. By doing so, the user may use spatial structuring and creating/traversing hypertext links

within the same graphical user interface. This is what some monolithic spatial hypertext applications also can do (e. g., Tinderbox [11] or VKB [55]).

In particular spatial hypertext applications may demand a high frequency of messages being sent to or received from the spatial structure service. This is the case, for example, if during a drag operation of objects on the space the interim coordinates are communicated to Asgard. The effect that can be reached by that is astounding: while a user drags an object, suggested additional nodes coming from the Hel knowledge base fade in, smoothly reposition, or fade out. This enables the user to experiment with implicit associations in a very flexible way based on knowledge stored in Hel services. This feature is novel and unique in the context of hypertext systems. As discussed in Sect. 3.1, it shifts the overall system towards a specialized visual analytics tool that supports exploring unknown information spaces by an iterative process in which machine *and* human are involved equally.

In order to support the high frequency of messages sent between Midgard and Asgard, we developed our communication protocols to be in binary format. This is much more efficient than, for example, XML would be. Only the changes on a knowledge space are sent to Asgard. The suggested results coming from Hel are yet passed through Asgard to Midgard without further modification. However, those results do not contain content. This is natural for Asgard, as applications on this layer do not deal with content. From a Midgard perspective there are also good reasons for this:

(1) The content may be big (e. g., a picture), which would take some time to send to the GUI application. By receiving the associations of a suggested node beforehand, the GUI may calculate and indicate the positions of all suggested nodes to be placed on the screen before finishing loading their content.

(2) There may be too little space available to position all suggested nodes. For those discarded by the Midgard application no content request would be sent.

(3) During an operation (e. g., dragging a node) information from a knowledge base is added and immediately (i. e., even before the content is requested) removed again from space. In this case our approach shows higher efficiency.

Figure 2 indicates the direct connection between Midgard and Hel applications by an arrow on the right hand side.

The Midgard application is responsible for data storage, for example, a spatial hypertext, nodes of a navigational hypertext, or classified specimen. The storage itself takes place outside of our framework and depends on the application developer's decision. This could be storage facilities like (possibly distributed) file systems or databases, cloud storage, etc.

Mindspace and Mindspace2: Two Midgard Prototypes. Currently, two prototype Midgard application exist with the name of *Mindspace* (respectively *Mindspace2*), developed to demonstrate the basic concepts of the system from a user's perspective. The first prototype is written in Swift running on macOS, the latter (more sophisticated one) is written as a JavaFX application. Mindspace works as a virtual pin board allowing users to put nodes onto a 2D space. Furthermore, text can be added to nodes or visual attributes of nodes (e. g., size, shape, or color) can be changed.

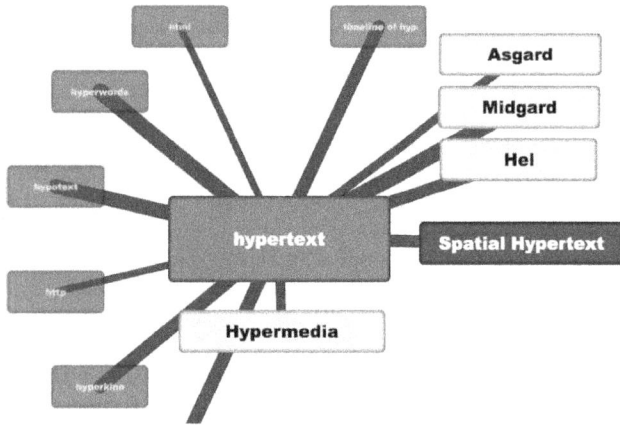

Figure 3: Hovering over a node (here: "hypertext") in Mindspace2 fades in representations of associations to suggestion nodes including the connection strengths (i. e., line thickness)

Mindspace gathers these inputs and passes them to Asgard. The spatial structure service then parses those in order to identify associations between objects and query relevant information from Hel. Asgard then sends back a set of suggestions as well as information about groupings that it has detected among the user's nodes.

The retrieved suggestion nodes are then displayed to the user. He may chose to turn some into "user nodes" by simply dragging them onto the space. Suggestion nodes may contain different data types. For example, a suggestion may contain a URI referencing a Web site, a JPEG image, etc. Currently, both Mindspace prototypes only support text or images, however, other data types may be included in the future.

Mindspace has a tight communication with Hel in order to exchanged data content as discussed above. Furthermore, it receives information about the strength between suggestion nodes and user added nodes from the knowledge base.

Hovering with the mouse over a node will show all currently known connections in Hel of this particular node to any other related node on the space. Figure 3 shows an example screenshot. The thickness of the respective lines correspond to the strength of the connection. With this information a user may get a quick overview on how current nodes are related.

In debug mode (cf. Fig. 4) additional information is displayed. This includes information about nodes' positions or their status in Midgard. In addition, this mode shows the group memberships computed by Asgard, indicated by colored borders surrounding each node. The same color indicates a membership of the same group.

Each suggestion node contains additional information that can be revealed by hovering over and clicking on the "text" icon. A result of that action can be seen in Fig. 5. Currently, only short Wikipedia excerpts are saved. However, also URIs to corresponding Wikipedia pages are available from within our system, which can be opened in a Web browser.

Finally, Mindspace currently stores its spatial hypertext persistently in files. On opening such a file, Mindspace replays the

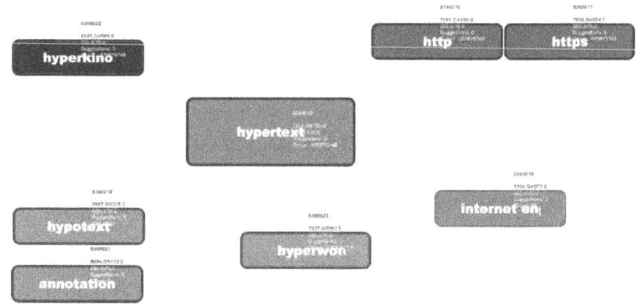

Figure 4: The debug mode (suggestions omitted) in Mindspace2 shows additional information about nodes, including their group membership (computed by Asgard and indicated by colored borders around nodes)

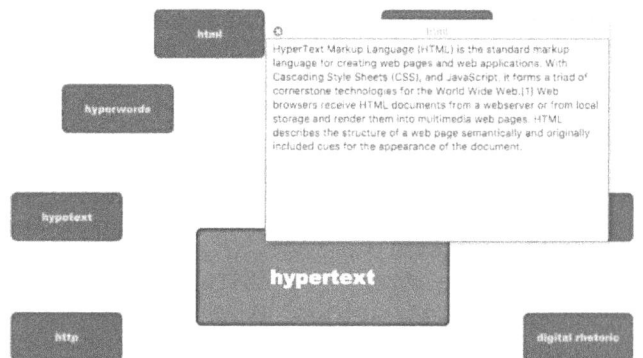

Figure 5: Viewing additional content associated with a suggestion node in Mindspace2 (in this example the related information comes from Wikipedia)

creation process and passes this information to Asgard. This enables Asgard to rebuild the interpretation of the structure, including analyzing the creation process itself (via the temporal parser). This is required, because Asgard does not persistently store computed structures (cf. Sect. 3.2).

3.4   Hel – The Knowledge World

The name Hel in Norse mythology refers to the death goddess and her realm alike. The name is related to the English word "hidden". In our terms it refers to knowledge-centric components that mostly include not yet explored information. It relies on the Asgard services to query relevant information and reveal it to the user via Midgard applications.

Previous traditional hypertext infrastructures do not deal with computer generated knowledge. This is a novel aspect of our system. Knowledge bases in Hel may be created upon various sources, depending on the target application/problem domain. This may include information from the Web (e. g., Wikipedia article or news sites), open data sites, databases with company related documents, or any other relevant source. Data and text mining methods are used to extract knowledge from these sources and store it in specific knowledge bases. Those knowledge bases may be of different type, including semantic databases or graph databases. The type depends on the requirements of the respective services, for example, the number of requests expected within a given time frame.

Knowledge bases may be also filled by knowledge extracted from user generated structures. Section 3.2 mentions spatial hypertexts as an example. Furthermore, link bases or taxonomies would be examples for Hel components, as they store (user generated) knowledge.

Figure 2 depicts also a knowledge base proxy. The reason behind is that the communication to general knowledge bases should become transparent to Asgard services. The proxy translates and distributes the queries to the available (i. e., registered) knowledge bases. The advantage is that a spatial structure service only has to implement a single interface in order to communicate with a heterogeneous set of knowledge bases, possibly each using a different query language.

Knowledge Base Implementations. Hel can be divided into three main parts: (i) the communication interface with Asgard; (ii) an interface towards Midgard; and (iii) the knowledge gathering components. Each of those components has different requirements towards the underlying structure of the databases. Changing the needs of the overall system may require modified protocols or even different databases.

Even though pure relational databases show a very good sequential search performance, they cause problems in our system. An object within the database should be able to have any number of properties, ideally without type constraints. Thus NoSQL document-based databases seem to be a good choice, as they provide a good performance and support arbitrary properties. However, representing connections between objects can be done more efficiently in graph databases.

Currently, Hel includes two implemented databases: (i) the graph database *Neo4j*[1]; and (ii) the NoSQL document database *MongoDB*[2]. The reason behind picking those two databases for implementation and demonstration was to get the best of the two worlds: while MongoDB would be used to store *documents* corresponding to any given object, Neo4j would hold the corresponding *graph* (i. e., connections between those objects). This increased the overall performance for graph-based requests. Furthermore, MongoDB overcame performance issues we had encountered by exclusively emulating documents on Neo4j's property system.

While in current protocols the functionality requirements towards Hel are intentionally very limited, more complex requests can be easily adapted. To support this, Hel offers a proxy layer described above. In its current version the proxy distributes incoming requests to all connected databases, merges all incoming replies into a single message, and returns it to Asgard.

In order to fill the knowledge bases with useful information we first targeted Wikipedia and used basic data mining methods, for example, the Seealsology tool[3], which uses ForceAtlas2 [33] for generating a graph of Wikipedia. From this graph (based on the distances between any two nodes), weights have been computed. Then, the full weighted graph has been added to the Neo4j database.

Additionally, the MongoDB database has been filled with the corresponding documents, each one representing a single Wikipedia page.

4 THE ODIN/HEIMDALL PROJECT

4.1 About the Project

In this section we describe a scenario that reflects the use of our framework in the domain of software engineering (partly still under development). It is also a proof of concept that shows that our framework is capable of working with other (in this case Web-based) services.

There are various possibilities for publishing data on the World Wide Web, but in most cases they are difficult to use. To simplify this process is the main goal of the ODIN ("Open Data Innovation") project. Its sub-project HEIMDALL focuses on an intelligent user interface. ODIN uses a Web-based platform. Instead of harvesting data from many different data sources (with all accompanying problems like different file formats or access possibilities) ODIN offers ready-to-use components for accessing, manipulating, and visualizing data. Those are called *Cubbles*; they are based on Meme Media Technology and previously known as *Webbles* [cf. 5]. Users can utilize those or publish new ones by uploading them to a public server, the so-called *Cubbles Base*. Cubbles are Web components, implemented in JavaScript and executed in the user's Web browser (which loads all required Cubbles from the Cubbles Base.) This makes Cubbles highly reusable software components.

The composition of already existing Cubbles components can be done in a classic manner, for example, by using an IDE. An alternative approach would be the use of the BDE[4] ("Browser-based Development Environment"), a Web application offering a 2D space on which Cubbles (represented as rectangles with names) can be added and connected. This eases data processing tasks in particular for non-programmers.

For example, imagine a scenario in which a researcher wants to correlate weather data and data about traffic accidents in order to publish the result on a Web page. Even though he finds appropriate data sources, he may not be able to transform the data and generate a meaningful visualization as he is not an IT expert. Assuming that the Cubbles Base already contains all required components, he would just have to add them to the work space and connect them to model the desired data flow.

4.2 Cubbles Integration in the Hypertext Infrastructure

The current implemented solution of the Cubbles Web application lacks an efficient way of finding required components. We want to support the user by proposing other relevant Cubbles. For that an Asgard service is used to analyze the user created spatial structure and matching Cubbles will then be presented to the user. Those can then be easily added and used. Figure 6 shows the BDE including some Cubbles that model the above mentioned scenario. The system suggests some further components suitable for the task at hand.

In addition to the solution of the described problem, we wanted to demonstrate how our infrastructure can easily be used for various

---

[1]https://neo4j.com/
[2]https://www.mongodb.com/
[3]http://tools.medialab.sciences-po.fr/seealsology/

[4]https://github.com/cubbles/bde

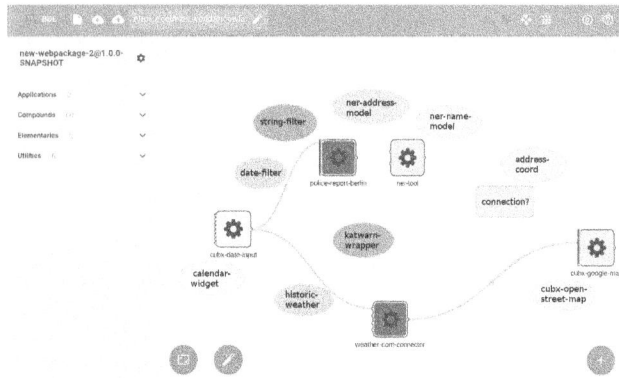

Figure 6: BDE work space with Cubbles and suggestions

scenarios. Since we use a three layer software architecture, the BDE can be seen as a Midgard implementation. Because Asgard and Hel host multiple services, there is no need to re-implement any business logic in the Midgard layer. Furthermore, there is no need for customizing, since we use generic messaging between layers [cf. 61].

The loosely coupled layers make it possible to be independent of specific programming languages, as long as they support TCP/IP communication. However, even though JavaScript is not limited to that respect, Web browsers are. We needed a solution that would work with the protocols defined in [61]. One possibility would be a Web service using simple HTTP requests, offering a second API to Asgard and Hel. This approach would ease the development of a client written in JavaScript or another language, however, using our low level protocols would become difficult. As we wanted to strictly stick to the given architecture and its layers as well as to the TCP/IP based protocols, we decided to follow a different path.

The messages between components via TCP/IP reduce messaging overhead and feature a full duplex communication between client and server. To make use of these advantages we chose to establish a connection via WebSocket[5], a protocol supported by the majority of modern Web browsers, set up on top of TCP. With WebSocket it is not necessary to define a new API connecting Midgard to the other layers; a script called "websockify"[6] translates WebSocket traffic to normal socket traffic. This shows the flexibility of low level protocols. The required JavaScript code is designed in a way to work also with any future projects. It hides the protocol behind user-friendly and generic method calls.

Besides the technical integration, it is important that Asgard and Hel are capable of handling the specific needs issued in the ODIN project. Sect. 3.2 mentions that Asgard is only aware of structure, but not of data. Thus, it does not matter whether text nodes, pictures, or Cubbles are used on the space. A big challenge, however, is building a suitable knowledge base for the Cubbles Base which holds associations between Cubbles. Those are then used to identify the relevant ones.

Cubbles are rather complex in their characteristics. They have many different properties to be considered for appropriate feature

---

[5]https://tools.ietf.org/html/rfc6455
[6]https://github.com/novnc/websockify

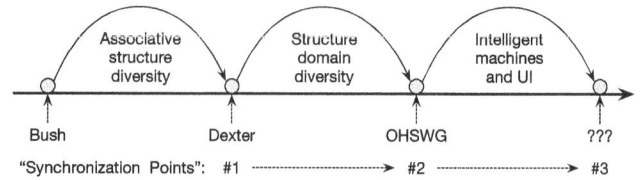

Figure 7: Synchronization points in hypertext research, extending [64]

vectors. This work has to be done for every scenario, since there is no "omniscient" knowledge base. The advantage of our architecture is the independence of Asgard regarding these project specific issues. This allows us to focus on functional integration, making use of the already existing spatial structure service. Furthermore, Asgard/Hel does not restrict the design and technical implementation of the knowledge base; as discussed in Sect. 3.4, we can pick a database that fits the requirements of the project best.

5 CONCLUSION AND FUTURE WORK

In his 2005 ACM Hypertext conference keynote Wiil addressed:

> "In order to reach the full potential of hypermedia technology support for knowledge workers, a long term community effort [...] is needed – an effort where domain experts and infrastructure experts work together to fulfill a common vision." [64]

He refers to certain "synchronization points" in hypertext research, depicted in Fig. 7. The first took place when the Dexter Hypertext Reference Model was defined, the second when the OHSWG defined protocols for open hypermedia (cf. Sect. 1 and 2). Exactly one decade after that keynote we now extend the original figure by adding machine intelligence and intelligent user interfaces to it. This defines the next (not yet named) synchronization point #3.

We argue that the infrastructure proposed in this paper is a demonstration expected for synchronization point #3, as we combine "fancy infrastructure" and "fancy applications", as suggested in [64]. Additionally, we push intelligence into the system, which is currently discussed in various fields, such as big/smart data, visual analytics, or artificial intelligence. In particular we argue that our system

(1) provides a flexible and modular infrastructure supporting various services and structure domains;
(2) is designed from the beginning with spatial hypertext in mind, the most difficult hypertext structure type to be handled by machines;
(3) includes sophisticated parsers for spatial hypertext structures that form fundamental modules for rich user interfaces; and
(4) makes heavy use of knowledge bases built by supporting intelligence components.

There are a number of issues still to be solved by future work. Those can be divided in three different categories: (i) improving or extending the infrastructure; (ii) identifying application domains and creating matching user interfaces; and (iii) designing and building up specialized knowledge bases that match the demands of the target application domains.

In more detail, the development of additional structure services (e. g., node-link or taxonomy support) needs to be finished. Also, the ODIN/HEIMDALL software needs to be completed with respect to their full feature sets. New parsers should be introduced, for example, the content parser (computing associations based on nodes' content). This opens again the question of how to prioritize various parser outputs that are running in parallel. Adaptive features may be considered to better focus on the users' needs. Research provided by the adaptive hypertext community will be of high value to this. Furthermore, we plan to provide clients for mobile devices (e. g., mobile phones or tablets). This opens the discussion of multi-structure support on multitouch devices. A still not solved question relates to security and privacy issues, which would need to be solved urgently if the system is used in productive environments.

As argued, there are a number of application domains that may benefit from the presented infrastructure. In the ODIN/HEIMDALL project we focus already on software engineering tasks. Furthermore, we consider e-learning, since linking of information as well as emerging structures (nicely to build up with spatial hypertexts) are important aspects for learners.

We are currently looking into using our system in combination with specialized user interfaces for people with dementia. First discussions with experts supports us in our assumptions that rich and intelligent structures may support those patients in their daily tasks and provide a means to physicians for diagnosing or measuring the progress of the disease.

Another area we are currently looking into is the field of "Industry 4.0". We plan to build maintenance diagnosis software on top of our infrastructure that provides linking and implicit associations (via spatial hypertext). Experts will be enabled to express their tacit knowledge at ease. We plan to enrich this with machine intelligence to further support users.

Finally, we need to spend time for identifying the best database technology for the specific knowledge bases in the context of their target application domains and tasks at hand. Furthermore, we have to identify good candidates for data sources and content processing in order to fill these knowledge bases, which depends on the respective application domain. Another important question relates to the computed associations within the knowledge bases, which directly influences the feedback proposed to the users.

As expected from a system that is as complex and rich as the proposed one, there a many open questions. It is up the scientific community to address those within the next years. There is a high potential of such systems to be used in many different contexts for the benefit of individuals and society.

ACKNOWLEDGMENTS

This work is part of the ODIN project, sub-project HEIMDALL, funded by the German Federal Ministry of Education and Research (grant ID 03PSWKPD).

REFERENCES

[1] Robert M. Akscyn, Donald L. McCracken, and Elise A. Yoder. 1988. KMS: a distributed hypermedia system for managing knowledge in organizations. *Commun.*

ACM 31, 7 (1988), 820–835. http://doi.acm.org/10.1145/48511.48513

[2] Kenneth Anderson, Richard Taylor, and E. Whitehead. 2006. A Critique of the Open Hypermedia Protocol. *Journal of Digital Information* 1, 2 (2006). https://journals.tdl.org/jodi/index.php/jodi/article/view/5

[3] Kenneth M. Anderson. 1997. Integrating Open Hypermedia Systems with the World Wide Web. In *Proceedings of the Eighth ACM Conference on Hypertext*. ACM, 157–166. http://doi.acm.org/10.1145/267437.267454

[4] Kenneth M. Anderson. 1999. Supporting software engineering with open hypermedia. *ACM Computing Surveys (CSUR)* 31, 4es (1999), 20. http://doi.acm.org/10.1145/345966.346013

[5] Oksana Arnold, Wolfgang Spickermann, Nicolas Spyratos, and Yuzuru Tanaka (Eds.). 2013. *Webble Technology. First Webble World Summit (WWS)*. Communications in Computer and Information Science, Vol. 372. Springer.

[6] Claus Atzenbeck and David L. Hicks. 2009. Integrating Time Into Spatially Represented Knowledge Structures. In *Proceedings of the International Conference on Information, Process, and Knowledge Management (eKNOW)*. IEEE Computer Society, 34–42. http://dx.doi.org/10.1109/eKNOW.2009.27

[7] Claus Atzenbeck, David L. Hicks, and Nasrullah Memon. 2008. Emergent Structure and Awareness Support for Intelligence Analysis. In *Proceedings of the 12th International Conference on Information Visualization (IV'08)*, Ebad Banissi, Liz Stuart, Mikael Jern, Gennady Andrienko, Francis T. Marchese, Nasrullah Memon, Reda Alhajj, Theodor G. Wyeld, Remo Aslak Burkhard, Georges Grinstein, Dennis Groth, Anna Ursyn, Carsten Maple, Anthony Faiola, and Brock Craft (Eds.). IEEE Computer Society, 326–332. http://dx.doi.org/10.1109/IV.2008.44

[8] Claus Atzenbeck, David L. Hicks, and Nasrullah Memon. 2011. Supporting Reasoning and Communication for Intelligence Officers. *International Journal of Networking and Virtual Organisations (IJNVO), Special Issue on Open Source Intelligence and Web Mining (OSINT-WM)* 8, 1/2 (2011). http://dx.doi.org/10.1504/IJNVO.2011.037159

[9] Claus Atzenbeck, Fatih Ozgul, and David L. Hicks. 2009. Linking and Organising Information in Law Enforcement Investigations. In *Proceedings of the 13th International Conference on Information Visualization (IV'09)*. IEEE Computer Society, 443–449. http://dx.doi.org/10.1109/IV.2009.107

[10] Tim Berners-Lee, Robert Cailliau, Ari Luotonen, Henrik Frystyk Nielsen, and Arthur Secret. 1994. The World-Wide Web. *Communication of the ACM* 37, 8 (Aug. 1994), 76–82. http://doi.acm.org/10.1145/179606.179671

[11] Mark Bernstein. 2006. *The Tinderbox Way*. Eastgate Systems.

[12] Niels Olof Bouvin. 2000. *Augmenting the Web through Open Hypermedia. The Development of the Arakne Environment, a Collaborative Open Hypermedia System for Web Augmentation*. Ph.D. Dissertation. University of Aarhus. http://www.daimi.au.dk/~bouvin/Arakne/thesis.pdf

[13] Niels Olof Bouvin. 2000. Experiences with OHP and Issues for the Future. In *Proceedings of the 6th International Workshop and 2nd International Workshop on Open Hypertext Systems and Structural Computing*. Springer, 13–22. http://www.springerlink.com/link.asp?id=du610p0bt7xnqrca

[14] P. J. Brown. 1987. Turning ideas into products: the Guide system. In *Proceedings of the ACM Conference on Hypertext*. ACM, 33–40. http://doi.acm.org/10.1145/317426.317430

[15] Vannevar Bush. 1945. As we may think. *The Atlantic Monthly* 176, 1 (7 1945), 101–108. http://www.theatlantic.com/doc/194507/bush

[16] Brad Campbell and Joseph M. Goodman. 1988. HAM: a general purpose hypertext abstract machine. *Commun. ACM* 31, 7 (1988), 856–861. http://doi.acm.org/10.1145/48511.48515

[17] Jeff Conklin. 1987. Hypertext: an introduction and survey. *Computer* 20, 9 (1987), 17–41. http://dx.doi.org/10.1109/MC.1987.1663693

[18] Jeff Conklin and Michael L. Begeman. 1987. gIBIS: a hypertext tool for team design deliberation. In *Proceedings of the ACM Conference on Hypertext*. ACM Press, 247–251. http://doi.acm.org/10.1145/317426.317444

[19] Jeff Conklin and Michael L. Begeman. 1988. gIBIS: a hypertext tool for exploratory policy discussion. In *Proceedings of the 1988 ACM Conference on Computer-Supported Cooperative Work*. ACM Press, 140–152. http://doi.acm.org/10.1145/62266.62278

[20] Hugh Davis, Wendy Hall, Ian Heath, Gary Hill, and Rob Wilkins. 1992. Towards an Integrated Information Environment with Open Hypermedia Systems. In *Proceedings of the ACM Conference on Hypertext*. ACM, 181–190. http://doi.acm.org/10.1145/168466.168522

[21] Hugh C. Davis, Simon Knight, and Wendy Hall. 1994. Light Hypermedia Link Services: A Study of Third Party Application Integration. In *Proceedings of the 1994 ACM European Conference on Hypermedia Technology*. ACM, 41–50. http://doi.acm.org/10.1145/192757.192767

[22] H. C. Davis, D. E. Millard, S. Reich, N. Bouvin, K. Grønbæk, P. J. Nürnberg, L. Sloth, U. K. Wiil, and K. Anderson. 1999. Interoperability between hypermedia systems: the standardisation work of the OHSWG. In *Proceedings of the 10th ACM Conference on Hypertext and Hypermedia*. ACM Press, 201–202. http://doi.acm.org/10.1145/294469.294904

[23] Norman Delisle and Mayer Schwartz. 1986. Neptune: a hypertext system for CAD applications. In *Proceedings of the 1986 ACM SIGMOD international conference on Management of data*. ACM Press, 132–143. http://doi.acm.org/10.1145/16894.

16867

[24] Serge Demeyer. 1996. *ZYPHER – Tailorability as a Link from Object-Oriented Software Engineering to Open Hypermedia.* Ph.D. Dissertation. Vrije University.

[25] Douglas C. Engelbart. 1962. *Augmenting Human Intellect: A Conceptual Framework.* Summary Report AFOSR-3233. Standford Research Institute. http://www.dougengelbart.org/pubs/augment-3906.html

[26] A. Fountain, W. Hall, I. Heath, and H. Davis. 1990. Microcosm: An Open Model for Hypermedia with Dynamic Linking. In *Hypertext: Concepts, Systems and Applications, Proceedings of ECHT'90,* A. Rizk, N. Streitz, and J. Andre (Eds.). Cambridge University Press, 298–311. http://eprints.soton.ac.uk/254308/

[27] Kaj Grønbæk, Jens A. Hem, Ole L. Madsen, and Lennert Sloth. 1994. Cooperative hypermedia systems: a Dexter-based architecture. *Commun. ACM* 37, 2 (1994), 64–74. http://doi.acm.org/10.1145/175235.175240

[28] Kaj Grønbæk and Randall H. Trigg. 1992. Design issues for a Dexter-based hypermedia system. In *Proceedings of the ACM Conference on Hypertext.* ACM Press, 191–200. http://doi.acm.org/10.1145/168466.168525

[29] Kaj Grønbæk and Randall H. Trigg. 1994. Design issues for a Dexter-based hypermedia system. *Commun. ACM* 37, 2 (2 1994), 40–49. http://doi.acm.org/10.1145/175235.175238

[30] Frank G. Halasz, Thomas P. Moran, and Randall H. Trigg. 1987. NoteCards in a nutshell. In *Proceedings of the SIGCHI/GI Conference on Human Factors in Computing Systems and Graphics Interface (CHI '87).* ACM Press, 45–52. http://doi.acm.org/10.1145/29933.30859

[31] Frank G. Halasz and Mayer Schwartz. 1994. The Dexter Hypertext Reference Model. *Commun. ACM* 37, 2 (2 1994), 30–39. http://doi.acm.org/10.1145/175235.175237

[32] Gary Hill and Wendy Hall. 1994. Extending the microcosm model to a distributed environment. In *Proceedings of the 1994 ACM European Conference on Hypermedia Technology.* ACM Press, 32–40. http://doi.acm.org/10.1145/192757.192763

[33] Mathieu Jacomy, Tommaso Venturini, Sebastien Heymann, and Mathieu Bastian. 2014. ForceAtlas2, a Continuous Graph Layout Algorithm for Handy Network Visualization Designed for the Gephi Software. *PLOS ONE* 9, 6 (June 2014), 1–12. http://dx.doi.org/10.1371/journal.pone.0098679

[34] Daniel Keim, Gennady Andrienko, Jean-Daniel Fekete, Carsten Görg, Jörn Kohlhammer, and Guy Melançon. 2008. Visual Analytics: Definition, Process, and Challenges. In *Information Visualization,* Andreas Kerren, JohnT. Stasko, Jean-Daniel Fekete, and Chris North (Eds.). Lecture Notes in Computer Science, Vol. 4950. Springer Berlin Heidelberg, 154–175. http://dx.doi.org/10.1007/978-3-540-70956-5_7

[35] Catherine C. Marshall, Frank G. Halasz, Russell A. Rogers, and William C. Janssen. 1991. Aquanet: a hypertext tool to hold your knowledge in place. In *Proceedings of the 3rd ACM Conference on Hypertext.* ACM Press, 261–275. http://doi.acm.org/10.1145/122974.123000

[36] Catherine C. Marshall, Frank M. Shipman, and James H. Coombs. 1994. VIKI: Spatial hypertext supporting emergent structure. In *Proceedings of the 1994 ACM European Conference on Hypermedia Technology.* ACM Press, 13–23. http://doi.acm.org/10.1145/192757.192759

[37] Norman Meyrowitz. 1986. Intermedia: The architecture and construction of an object-oriented hypemedia system and applications framework. *ACM SIGPLAN Notices* 21, 11 (1986), 186–201. http://doi.acm.org/10.1145/960112.28716

[38] Norman Meyrowitz. 1989. The missing link: why we're all doing hypertext wrong. In *The society of text: hypertext, hypermedia, and the social construction of information.* MIT Press, 107–114.

[39] David E. Millard. 2003. Discussions at the data border: from generalised hypertext to structural computing. *Journal of Network and Computer Applications* 26, 1 (2003), 95–114. http://dx.doi.org/10.1016/S1084-8045(02)00063-2

[40] Dave E. Millard, Luc Moreau, Hugh C. Davis, and Siegfried Reich. 2000. FOHM: A Fundamental Open Hypertext Model for Investigating Interoperability between Hypertext Domains. In *Proceedings of the 11th ACM Conference on Hypertext and Hypermedia.* ACM Press, 93–102. http://doi.acm.org/10.1145/336296.336334

[41] T. H. Nelson. 1965. Complex information processing: a file structure for the complex, the changing and the indeterminate. In *Proceedings of the 20th National Conference.* ACM Press, 84–100. http://doi.acm.org/10.1145/800197.806036

[42] Theodor Holm Nelson. 1982. *Literary Machines.* Mindful Press.

[43] Theodor Holm Nelson. 1999. The Unfinished Revolution and Xanadu. *Comput. Surveys* 31, 4es (Dec. 1999). http://doi.acm.org/10.1145/345966.346039

[44] Peter J. Nürnberg. 1997. *HOSS: An Environment to Support Structural Computing.* Ph.D. Dissertation. Department of Computer Science, Texas A&M University. http://cs.aue.auc.dk/~pnuern/papers/diss/

[45] Peter J. Nürnberg and Helen Ashman. 1999. What was the question? Reconciling open hypermedia and World Wide Web research. In *Proceedings of the 10th ACM Conference on Hypertext and Hypermedia.* ACM Press, 83–90. http://doi.acm.org/10.1145/294469.294492

[46] Peter J. Nürnberg, John J. Leggett, and Erich R. Schneider. 1997. As we should have thought. In *Proceedings of the 8th ACM Conference on Hypertext.* ACM Press, 96–101. http://doi.acm.org/10.1145/267437.267448

[47] Peter J. Nürnberg, John J. Leggett, Erich R. Schneider, and John L. Schnase. 1996. Hypermedia operating systems: a new paradigm for computing. In *Proceedings*

of the 7th ACM Conference on Hypertext. ACM Press, 194–202. http://doi.acm.org/10.1145/234828.234847

[48] Peter J. Nürnberg, John J. Leggett, and Uffe K. Wiil. 1998. An agenda for open hypermedia research. In *Proceedings of the 9th ACM Conference on Hypertext and Hypermedia.* ACM Press, 198–206. http://doi.acm.org/10.1145/276627.276649

[49] Kasper Østerbye and Uffe Kock Wiil. 1996. The flag taxonomy of open hypermedia systems. In *Proceedings of the 7th ACM Conference on Hypertext.* ACM Press, 129–139. http://doi.acm.org/10.1145/234828.234841

[50] H. Van Dyke Parunak. 1991. Don't link me in: Set based hypermedia for taxonomic reasoning. In *Proceedings of the 3rd Annual ACM Conference on Hypertext.* ACM Press, 233–242. http://doi.acm.org/10.1145/122974.122998

[51] Amy Pearl. 1989. Sun's Link Service: a protocol for open linking. In *Proceedings of the 2nd Annual ACM Conference on Hypertext.* ACM Press, 137–146. http://doi.acm.org/10.1145/74224.74236

[52] Thomas Schedel. 2016. *Spatio-Temporal Parsing in Spatial Hypermedia.* Ph.D. Dissertation. Aalborg University. https://opus4.kobv.de/opus4-hof/frontdoor/index/index/docId/71

[53] Thomas Schedel and Claus Atzenbeck. 2016. Spatio-Temporal Parsing in Spatial Hypermedia. In *Proceedings of the 27th ACM Conference on Hypertext and Social Media.* ACM, 149–157. http://doi.acm.org/10.1145/2914586.2914596

[54] Douglas E. Shackelford, John B. Smith, and F. Donelson Smith. 1993. The Architecture and Implementation of a Distributed Hypermedia Storage System. In *Proceedings of the Fifth ACM Conference on Hypertext.* New York, NY, USA, 1–13. http://doi.acm.org/10.1145/168750.168753

[55] Frank M. Shipman, Robert Airhart, Haowei Hsieh, Preetam Maloor, J. Michael Moore, and Divya Shah. 2001. Visual and spatial communication and task organization using the Visual Knowledge Builder. In *Proceedings of the 2001 International ACM SIGGROUP Conference on Supporting Group Work.* ACM Press, 260–269. http://doi.acm.org/10.1145/500286.500325

[56] Ben Shneiderman. 1987. User interface design for the Hyperties electronic encyclopedia (panel session). In *Proceedings of the ACM conference on Hypertext.* ACM Press, 189–194. http://doi.acm.org/10.1145/317426.317441

[57] Ted Smith and Steve Bernhardt. 1988. Expectations and experiences with Hyper-Card: a pilot study. In *Proceedings of the 6th Annual International Conference on Systems Documentation (SIGDOC '88).* ACM Press, 47–56. http://doi.acm.org/10.1145/358922.358931

[58] Guo-Dao Sun, Ying-Cai Wu, Rong-Hua Liang, and Shi-Xia Liu. 2013. A Survey of Visual Analytics Techniques and Applications: State-of-the-Art Research and Future Challenges. *Journal of Computer Science and Technology* 28, 5 (9 2013), 852–867. http://link.springer.com/article/10.1007/s11390-013-1383-8

[59] Manolis Tzagarakis, Dimitris Avramidis, Maria Kyriakopoulou, Monica M. C. Schraefel, Michalis Vaitis, and Dimitris Christodoulakis. 2003. Structuring primitives in the Callimachus component-based open hypermedia system. *Journal of Network and Computer Applications* 26, 1 (2003), 139–162. http://dx.doi.org/10.1016/S1084-8045(02)00064-4

[60] Andries van Dam. 1988. Hypertext '87: Keynote Address. *Commun. ACM* 31, 7 (July 1988), 887–895. http://doi.acm.org/10.1145/48511.48519

[61] Visual Analytics Research Group. 2017. *Asgard Core.* Technical Specification rev. f2d1ab62a824. Institute of Information Systems at Hof University.

[62] Mark J. Weal, Gareth V. Hughes, David E. Millard, and Luc Moreau. 2001. Open hypermedia as a navigational interface to ontological information spaces. In *Proceedings of the 12th ACM Conference on Hypertext and Hypermedia.* ACM Press, 227–236. http://doi.acm.org/10.1145/504216.504270

[63] E. James Whitehead. 1997. An Architectural Model for Application Integration in Open Hypermedia Environments. In *Proceedings of the Eighth ACM Conference on Hypertext.* ACM, 1–12. http://doi.acm.org/10.1145/267437.267438

[64] Uffe Kock Wiil. 2005. Hypermedia technology for knowledge workers: a vision of the future. In *Proceedings of the 16th ACM Conference on Hypertext and Hypermedia.* ACM Press, 4–6. http://doi.acm.org/10.1145/1083356.1083358

[65] Uffe K. Wiil, David L. Hicks, and Peter J. Nürnberg. 2001. Multiple open services: a New Approach to Service Provision in Open Hypermedia Systems. In *Proceedings of the 12th ACM Conference on Hypertext and Hypermedia.* ACM Press, 83–92. http://doi.acm.org/10.1145/504216.504241

[66] Uffe Kock Wiil and John J. Leggett. 1996. The HyperDisco approach to open hypermedia systems. In *Proceedings of the 7th ACM Conference on Hypertext.* ACM Press, 140–148. http://doi.acm.org/10.1145/234828.234842

[67] Uffe K. Wiil, Peter J. Nürnberg, and John J. Leggett. 1999. Hypermedia research directions. An infrastructure perspective. *Comput. Surveys* 31, 4 (12 1999). http://doi.acm.org/10.1145/345966.345971

[68] Uffe K. Wiil, Samir Tata, and David L. Hicks. 2003. Cooperation services in the Construct structural computing environment. *Journal of Network and Computer Applications* 26, 1 (2003), 115–137. http://dx.doi.org/10.1016/S1084-8045(02)00065-6

[69] Nichole Yankelovich, Bernard J. Haan, Norman K. Meyrowitz, and Steven M. Drucker. 1988. Intermedia: The Concept and the Construction of a Seamless Information Environment. *Computer* 21, 1 (1988), 81–83, 90–96. http://dx.doi.org/10.1109/2.222120

Hyperlocal Home Location Identification of Twitter Profiles

Adam Poulston
Department of Computer Science
University of Sheffield
211 Portobello
Sheffield, UK S1 4DP
ARSPoulston1@sheffield.ac.uk

Mark Stevenson
Department of Computer Science
University of Sheffield
211 Portobello
Sheffield, UK S1 4DP
mark.stevenson@sheffield.ac.uk

Kalina Bontcheva
Department of Computer Science
University of Sheffield
211 Portobello
Sheffield, UK S1 4DP
k.bontcheva@sheffield.ac.uk

ABSTRACT

Knowledge of user's location provides valuable information that can be used to build region-specific models (e.g. language used in a particular region and map-based visualisations of social media posts). Determining a user's home location presents a challenge. Current approaches make use of geo-located tweets or textual cues but are often only able to predict location to a coarse level of granularity (e.g. city level), while many applications require finer-grained (hyperlocal) predictions.

A novel approach for hyperlocal home location identification, based on clustering of geo-located tweets, is presented. A gold-standard data set for home location identification is developed by making use of indicative phrases in geo-located tweets. We find that the cluster-based approaches outperform current techniques for hyperlocal location prediction.

CCS CONCEPTS

• **Information systems** → **Data mining**; *Clustering*; • **Social and professional topics** → **Geographic characteristics**;

KEYWORDS

User geo-location, home location identification, geographic clustering, data mining

1 INTRODUCTION

Social media is becoming the information and communication channel of choice for an ever growing number of people, leading to a surge in applications (e.g. disaster response [12], hyperlocal media [28]) and methods aiming to extract information from social media (e.g. user profiling [34], opinion analysis [30], knowledge discovery [2], content recommendation [33] and event detection [43]).

In many of those cases, the ability to geo-locate users with high accuracy is needed, e.g. such as hyperlocal content recommendation [18], inference of user characteristics based on neighborhood demography [3, 29, 35] or extraction and mapping of information to aid disaster response [27]. Unfortunately, location information

within social media posts is particularly sparse, often inaccurate, and cannot be easily validated. A number of user geo-location approaches have been developed to address this problem, at varying levels of granularity, by building models based on features such as the user's social media posts [5], online behaviour [25, 26], and social network [40].

User geo-location approaches typically rely on training data, consisting of profiles labelled with *home location* information. The definition of *home* often varies from task-to-task, but generally refers to some representation a user's local area. Some approaches use fine-grained coordinate level locations but coarser-grained regions are more widely used. Profiles are usually associated with some kind of public boundary data to generate labels and the granularity of these varies between studies. For example, Mahmud et al. [25, 26] associate users with their country of residence, Chandra et al. [4], Chang et al. [5], Cheng et al. [6], Eisenstein et al. [10], Rout et al. [40] with their local city, and Kinsella et al. [23] link users to their ZIP code.

Home location is attached to profiles in various ways; commonly a profile's location field is resolved to a real-world location through the use of a gazetteer [23, 40], however this approach can be inaccurate. Other approaches to assigning home location make use of geo-located tweets. Many use a profile's first geo-located tweet, whilst others use tweets that provide information about the location associated with the profile [10, 25, 26, 39]. However, these methods are not always reliable. Some approaches take all of a profile's geo-located tweets into account by applying some form spatial average [8, 21, 22], which is likely to produce better judgements than a single tweet, but may run into problems when a user is active at multiple locations (such as work and home). For a more in-depth discussion of state-of-the-art methods and their limitations, see Section 2.

This paper proposes two novel methods that overcome some of the limitations of current methods by acknowledging that social media users are active at multiple locations, and that their most active location is likely to be their primary location (see Section 3). The first method, *Majority voting*, measures a user's activity in real world regions as defined by public boundary datasets. Four such resources are used in this paper (see Section 4.1.1). The second method works at the hyperlocal level by applying a clustering algorithm to each user's geo-located tweets, revealing centres of activity. The most populous cluster is taken as the users *home*, and its geometric median is taken as the user's *home coordinate*.

Previous methods for home location identification have not been evaluated at the hyperlocal level, limiting understanding of their accuracy for this fine-grained task. A new data set containing hyperlocal geographic information was created (Section 4). This dataset was created by identifying a set of key phrases indicating which tweets were sent from the user's home. These phrases were used to identify the home location of 1,042 Twitter users. Each tweet containing a home-indicative phrase was checked to ensure it referred to 'home' in the correct context, being removed from the dataset if not. The 'true' home location was calculated for each profile by taking the spatial average of its home-indicative tweets.

To evaluate the accuracy of state-of-the-art and newly proposed methods, we applied them to all profiles in the gold-standard dataset, comparing the predicted and 'true' locations (Section 6). Two metrics are presented; error distance (in miles) and exact match accuracy (at four granularities of UK administrative region). The results demonstrate that our clustering based approach outperforms state-of-the-art methods on the hyperlocal geo-location task, at both coordinate and region-level granularity.

2 RELATED WORK

Hecht et al. [16] report that 66% of Twitter users provide valid geographic information in the 'location' field of their profile; mostly at city level. Of the profiles that do report a location, many are accompanied with non-standard text and abbreviations, such as "kcmo-call da po po", referring to Kansas City, Missouri, and a mixture of fictional and real information, such as "Bieberville, California". In addition, less than 1% of tweets had associated geo-location information. To overcome this lack of reliable location information, approaches have been developed to geo-locate social media users based on the content of their tweets. Typically this problem is called 'user geo-location', dealing with identifying the 'home' of a user (although the exact definition of 'home' varies between studies, ranging from the coordinate (hyperlocal) level, to larger regions such as cities and states).

To carry out user geo-location, a training set of profiles with known home location is required. A method for creating this training set must have certain characteristics to be reliable. Geographic statistical units, such as output areas (a UK statistical unit), exist at various scales, with some being less than a square mile in area. As such, a method for creating a training set must be able to provide highly accurate/fine-grained location judgements. Having assigned a user a home location, some measure of 'certainty' is required (i.e. accurate to within an N mile radius), allowing profiles with low certainty to be excluded (or downgraded) from analysis.

Various approaches for generating location-labelled profiles which have been used in previous works are described below.

2.1 First tweet

The simplest possible method for identifying a user's location is to take the coordinate of their first tweet, or the tweet used to identify them in the first place. Eisenstein et al. [10] use the first geo-located tweet by each user to label profiles in their training set at the region and city level in the US, applying this to build geographic topic models. Roller et al. [39] also make use of this dataset, as well as their own created in the same fashion, applied to a method based on adaptive grids. Mahmud et al. [25, 26] use the first tweet coordinate to label the profiles in their dataset at time zone, state and city level in order to train a hierarchical ensemble of classifiers.

The first tweet method is error prone, as a single tweet provides little guarantee that a user frequents an area and is therefore unsuitable for hyperlocal home location detection. Despite this Mahmud et al. [25, 26] identify that the majority of users will rarely travel outside of their home city or state, and so if only this low granularity identification is required, first tweet has a good chance of leading to a correct assignment. Further, steps were taken by Mahmud et al. [25, 26] to identify and omit those users who frequently travel, avoiding incorrect labelling.

2.2 Location field information

Twitter provides users with the option to declare their location through a non-required free-text field. A number of methods have created training datasets based on the information included in this field. Kinsella et al. [23] predicted location at a number of levels, generating their location labels via the Yahoo GeoPlanet[1] tool, and applying this in a method based on ranking probable location labels by Kullback-Leibler divergence. Rout et al. [40] explore the use of social network features to geo-locate a set of UK Twitter users to the town/city level. Their training data was acquired by selecting profiles with an unambiguous reference to a UK town/city in the profile field. Rahimi et al. [37, 38] combine social network features with text based features to improve geo-location accuracy. Alex et al. [1] present an improved tool for parsing geo-located information in the location field and other text, and apply it to geo-locate users discussing a number of topics as well as demonstrating country-wide sentiment analysis.

Due to the fluid nature of this field it can be unreliable, with users providing incorrect, out of date or non-location information, as highlighted in Hecht et al. [16]. Han et al. [14] present a pilot study identifying that despite its noisiness, self-declared user metadata can help boost performance. In addition to accuracy issues, the task of resolving text to a point location is itself a difficult problem; there are cities called London in the UK, US, Canada and South Africa, all of which speak English as a primary or dominant language.

A limited number of profiles provide coordinate data in their location field rather than a named location. These were used to build the training dataset in Cheng et al. [6], which was used to build a model at the US region/state level based on location-specific terms within tweets. This approach would appear favourable over named locations as it avoids the place name ambiguity problem, however, it is no longer feasible, as this information was placed by an early mobile Twitter client and thus rarely appears in recent profiles.

2.3 Geometric median

Home location of each user is assigned by Compton et al. [8], Jurgens [21], Jurgens et al. [22] as a single coordinate, taken as the geometric median of their geo-located posts L (a variant of the multivariate L_1 median) given by

$$GM = \arg \min_{x \in L} \sum_{y \in L} D(x, y), \tag{1}$$

---

[1]Yahoo! GeoPlanet https://developer.yahoo.com/geo/geoplanet/

where the distance D is calculated using Vincenty's formula [42]. Median location was used to ensure robustness to outliers, such as those introduced by tweets produced while the user is on holiday abroad. In Jurgens et al. [22] an additional constraint is also applied to eliminate users with overly spread coordinates by limiting their analysis to only those profiles whose coordinates have an absolute median deviation of less than 30 km.

As opposed to using first tweet or location field information, Compton et al. [8], Jurgens [21], Jurgens et al. [22] produces judgements with the highest rigour as it takes all of a user's tweets into account in an outlier resistant fashion, and is used in conjunction with a measure of 'certainty'—median absolute deviation.

2.4 Grid based

Han et al. [13, 14] assign the users in their dataset (which covers the world) home location as a coarse representation of population centres they call 'cities'. To construct these 'cities' they take all actual cities in each 'region' (such as state or province) available in the Geonames[2] dataset, and collapse the actual cities within 50km of one another into a single point, producing 3,709 very coarse location labels. To label users the world was split into a grid containing 0.5′ by 0.5′ cells, with a tweet defined as being from a city if the cell containing it, or a surrounding cell, also contained a city. The most common city identified across a user's geo-located tweets was taken as their home location.

This method is well suited for providing coarse location labels in large countries such as the US, with sporadic yet dense areas of population, but is not well suited to smaller regions with more consistent population densities such as the UK and Europe.

2.5 Suitability for Hyperlocal Geolocation

For a home location identification method to be suitable for hyperlocal user geo-location, it needs to perform accurate coordinate-level predictions or pick potentially small regions from a list of candidates. While the first tweet method supports hyperlocal, coordinate level geo-location, it does not always identify reliably the current home location of the user. At the same time, information in the location field can only reasonably be used to geo-locate at town/city level granularity or higher, which makes these methods less suited to hyperlocal geo-location. The grid based approach in Han et al. [13, 14] reliably locates profiles, but at a granularity far above what could be called hyperlocal, and as such will not be assessed in this article. The geometric media approach of Compton et al. [8], Jurgens [21], Jurgens et al. [22] is likely to be the most reliable state-of-the-art method for hyperlocal geo-location, producing single coordinate level predictions with outlier resistance and a measure of judgement certainty.

Nevertheless, as our experiments will demonstrate, further improvements in hyperlocal geo-location are possible through the new clustering method proposed next.

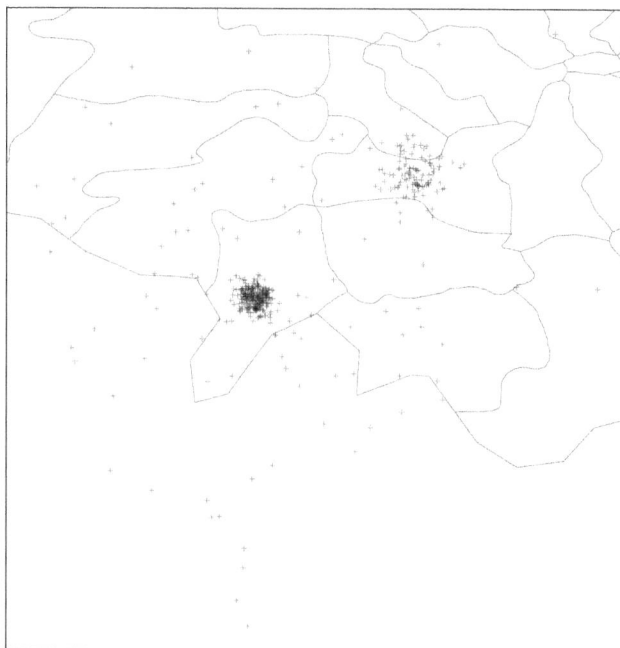

Figure 1: Example collection of unprocessed tweet coordinates.

3 OUR METHODS FOR HYPERLOCAL GEO-LOCATION

The two new methods proposed here take into account all of a user's geo-located tweets (e.g. Figure 1), in order to identify the user's home location at coordinate level. Both approaches assume that each social media user commonly posts from a limited number of locations, with the highest frequency tweeting location assumed to be the user's home (in line with human home-return patterns [20] and other user geo-location approaches [13–15]). The first method is based on majority voting across possible regions and is presented in Section 3.1, whereas the second is based on clustering of geo-located tweets (see Section 3.2).

3.1 Majority voting

User geo-location studies are typically associated with some form of public boundary data, such as states or other administrative subdivisions. We propose a method that, similarly to that presented in Han et al. [13, 14], operates in discrete space and counts points. Unlike Han et al. [13, 14], however, our method can be applied to any boundary data, at any scale.

By projecting all the coordinates of a user's tweets onto the same surface as the boundary data (county borders, for example, in the US), the boundary containing the majority of a user's tweets can be identified. Immediately putting locations into the 'boundary space' is in contrast to most of the methods described in this article that first determine home location in coordinate form. This (brute force) method is likely to be slow, as many point-in-polygon tests must be performed.

To pick the home location, the boundary containing the most tweets is chosen. The number of tweets in other boundaries to this

────────
[2]Geonames: http://geonames.org/

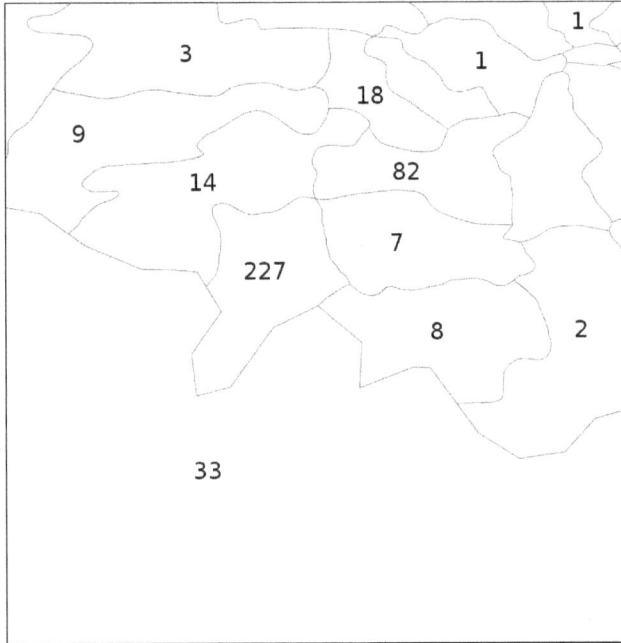

Figure 2: Example application of the majority voting method to the data in Figure 1.

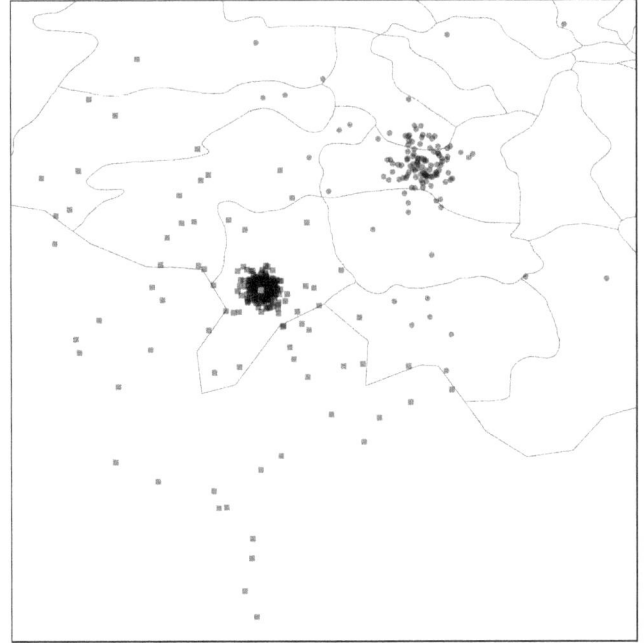

Figure 3: Example clustering of the tweet coordinates in Figure 1.

home estimate are known, and so some measure of uncertainty can be calculated, such as the proportion of tweets that reside within the home region. This allows for the elimination/downgrading of profiles with low region certainty. As such, majority voting does solve the requirements of needing to pick a region/coordinate as the home location and quantify the uncertainty around such an estimate.

Figure 2 shows an example of the majority voting method applied to the unprocessed tweet coordinates displayed in Figure 1. The region with the most tweets contains 227 examples, and is selected as the user's home.

3.2 Clustering approach

Since social media users are often active from more than one location, an approach that first clusters tweets into regions of activity prior to picking one as the home location is more promising over simply picking the geometric median of all user posts [8, 21, 22]. In particular, for users with more than one commonly posted-from location (such as a home and work location), the geometric median can sometimes pick a point in between these two locations, while a clustering approach can overcome this limitation.

In more detail, our method first clusters the coordinates of each user's geo-located posts using an algorithm such as K-means, DB-SCAN, or Gaussian mixture models (GMM) (see details below). This reveals a collection of candidate clusters for the home location. The cluster with the highest number of posts is identified and taken as the 'home cluster' and the home location coordinate is taken to be the geometric median (Equation 1) from all locations within the home cluster.

Figure 3 shows an example of the clustering approach on the data in Figure 1; two clusters are identified with cluster membership of each point presented as a square or circle (home coordinate in red). In this case the most populous cluster is the one represented by squares and the red square is taken as the user's home coordinate.

The ability of a clustering method to estimate location can be quantified by assessing the geographic size of the estimated 'home cluster'; a geographically small cluster that is dense in points will likely lead to a better estimate than a geographically large cluster with a sparse coverage of points. A measure of the size of a cluster could therefore be to take the average distance from the estimated home location to each point in the home cluster. Explicitly these distances are determined by the Haversine [41] distance, and the mean of these is taken.

In an application where the goal is to assign a given user to a region, the number of point-in-polygon tests can be greatly reduced compared to majority voting because it would be feasible to only check the points in the home cluster.

3.2.1 Clustering algorithms. Since our clustering geo-location method relies on identifying location clusters, we experimented with partitional clustering algorithms [19]. In particular, three well established clustering algorithims were experimented with (K-means, DBSCAN and Gaussian mixture models), described in the following.

   K-means K-means [24] attempts to partition a set of observations $X = \{x_1, x_2, \ldots, x_N\}$ of length N into $k \leq N$ clusters $C = \{c_1, c_2, \ldots, c_k\}$ by minimising a criterion called the 'within-cluster sum of squares' (WCSS, also known as inertia). More formally, K-means aims to find

$$\arg\min_{C} \sum_{i=1}^{k} \sum_{x \in C_i} ||x - \text{mean}(C_i)||^2. \qquad (2)$$

The K-means algorithm has three steps, first the k clusters have their centroids initialised (for example by taking k points at random from the dataset). Then the algorithm loops between assigning each point to its nearest centroid, and calculating new centroids based on the changes in the previous step. This continues until the difference between the new and previous centroids falls bellow a threshold (the centroids are stationary). K-means is sensitive to its initialised centroids, thus the algorithm is usually run multiple times with different initialisations to help ensure good clusters.

DBSCAN 'Density-based spatial clustering of applications with noise' (DBSCAN) [11] is a density-based clustering algorithm that forms clusters based on the presence of high density regions (large numbers of neighbouring points). If a point lies in a low density region (i.e. no or few nearby neighbours), the point is marked as an outlier and not included in any cluster. Unlike K-means in which clusters are always convex, DBSCAN is able to produce clusters of any shape, including rings around other clusters.

GMM A Gaussian mixture model (GMM) is a probabilistic model in which all points in the data are generated from a finite mixture of Gaussian distributions with unknown parameters [36]. Inference on the parameters of a GMM is typically approached using the expectation maximisation (EM) algorithm [9]. Having pre-specified the number of Gaussian components and initialising parameter values, the EM algorithm consists of two steps; the 'expectation' step, in which the likelihood is evaluated at the current parameter estimates, and the 'maximization' step, in which the expected likelihood from the previous step is maximised.

4 DATA

We were unable to compare different approaches to assigning home location on an existing dataset for multiple reasons. The permanence of Twitter data is a difficult issue for studies centred on the platform; Twitter does not allow Tweets to be shared in full, instead only tweet IDs can be provided. This leads to a problem in sharing datasets as large numbers of tweets are time-consuming to acquire, and many tweets and profiles are deleted over time. None of the datasets available provided high certainty gold-standard hyperlocal home location labels. Eisenstein et al. [10], Mahmud et al. [25, 26], Roller et al. [39] all used the earliest tweet in their sample for each user to label their home location and made little effort to validate these labels. Alex et al. [1], Rout et al. [40] used the profile's location field to assign gold-standard home location at the city level, which is unsuitable for assessing hyperlocal methods. Han et al. [13] assigned user's home location taking all of a user's geo-located tweets into account, but uses very coarse labels, not

comparable to hyperlocal methods. As a result, we constructed our own gold-standard dataset or profiles labelled with home location.

The Twitter public streaming API[3] was used to identify geo-located tweets within the UK, from November 2014 to July 2015. A 'gold-standard' set of profiles was created from this information by assigning 'true home location' based on implicit mentions of 'home' in geo-located tweets (discussed in Section 4.1).

UK users were chosen as the population- and city-density is much higher than in the USA, which makes the geo-location task much more challenging. Two major and distinct cities, Liverpool and Manchester, are close enough together that they would be considered one place in the scheme proposed in Han et al. [13, 14], for example.

4.1 Gold-standard home location dataset

To build the gold-standard dataset, we proposed that if a user emits a phrase referring to being 'at home' from the same location multiple times, it is their home location. A small number of phrases were collated by performing an analysis of tweets containing the word 'home'. For each tweet 3, 4 and 5-grams were calculated, and those not containing the word 'home' were discarded. The most frequent n-grams were manually inspected, and ones that seemed indicative of being 'at home' chosen.On manual inspection it was noted that some indicative tweets did not use 'home' in the correct context. Examples include; university students using 'home' to refer to their family home, and holiday-makers calling their hotel room 'home'. As such, the tweets were manually checked to ensure that the text referenced residential home.

Profiles containing geo-located tweets with one or more indicative phrase were selected from the whole collection of around 135,000 profiles, leaving 7348 (5.44%) with at least one example and 1498 (1.12%) with two or more. To improve certainty only those profiles with two or more 'at home' tweets were considered. If the coordinates of their 'at home' tweets were within a short distance of each other (taken to be 0.5 miles) we took the spatial mean of these as the 'true home location', resulting in 1048 users. After selection each profile was represented as an anonymous table row with three fields: gold standard home location, geocoded location field text (see Section 5.1), and geo-located tweet coordinates.

4.1.1 Addition of boundary data. Government bodies maintain a number of geographic datasets that split countries, or even groups of countries, into subdivisions for statistical or administrative purposes. These boundaries are used in addition to, or in conjunction with, more traditional boundaries such as states, cities, electoral regions or postal codes. Many examples exist such as the European Union's 'Nomenclature of Territorial Units for Statistics' (NUTS) [4]. This is a three layer hierarchy of subdivisions that covers all European member states, which is used to tabulate EU population statistics and inform decisions on the distribution of EU funds to avoid regional disparities in wealth, income and opportunities. The US Census Bureau [5] maintains standard geographic boundaries for

---

[3]https://dev.twitter.com/streaming/overview
[4]NUTS: http://ec.europa.eu/eurostat/web/nuts/overview/
[5]US Census Bureau: http://www.census.gov/

the entire US such as states and counties, as well as various statistical groupings/subdivisions such as 'metropolitan/micropolitan statistical areas' and 'combined statistical areas'.

Geographic data in the UK is maintained by the Office for National Statistics (ONS) [6], who provide boundary data for a wide range of geographic areas such as counties, electoral wards and civil parishes. They also provide purely statistical subdivisions, derived from distributions of population in the latest census, called 'output areas' (OA). OAs form the smallest building block in a hierarchy of subdivisions known as the 'Neighbourhood Statistics Geography' (NSG), which consists of OAs, 'Lower Layer Super Output Areas' (LSOA), and 'Middle Layer Super Output Areas' (MSOA). These units are used to present census data in a consistent fashion, as well as other statistics such as the 'Indices of Deprivation', a measure of poverty in small areas across the UK.

As described in Section 4.1, we have compiled a gold-standard collection of UK Twitter profiles labelled with home location in the coordinate form. Many analyses, however, do not deal with home location in the coordinate form directly, instead converting it to some region of lower granularity such as state, postal code or city. As such we additionally label our gold-standard with 'true home boundary' data, in particular we label each profile covered by the NSG at the OA, LSOA and MSOA level as well labelling each profile with their 'Local Authority District' (LAD), a larger region type governed by a council.

In Table 1 we present the characteristics of the NSG which consists the OA, LSOA and MSOA region types and covers England and Wales. MSOAs and LSOAs are constructed from groupings of the previous level and both are always larger than the maximum size of the previous level; to illustrate this, Figure 4 shows a 0.55 square mile MSOA, one if its component LSOAs (0.13 square miles) and an OA (0.04 square miles). The groupings are consistent in terms of population but do vary in geographic size, meaning there are more divisions in areas of high population density such as cities. LADs are excluded from the table as they are not consistent in population or geographic size. 415 LADs were used to label the gold-standard, covering all of the UK, including Northern Ireland and Scotland.

5 EXPERIMENTS

The three state-of-the-art methods for determining a user's home location (Section 2) and the two new methods proposed here (Section 2) were applied to the gold-standard dataset (Section 4).

5.1 Implementation

In order to apply the first tweet method, the first recorded geolocated tweet in our sample for each user is used as the home location coordinate, as with [10, 25, 26, 39]. The location field method was implemented using a gazetteer of unique place names extracted from OpenStreetMap[7] to identify profiles with a single reference to a city or town within the UK in their location field. Employing a gazetteer for this task aided in discarding those profiles whose location field were either clearly fictitious (e.g. '221B Baker Street', '90210' and '42 Wallaby Way, Sydney'), did not actually reference locations (e.g. 'she/they', strings of emoji), or were unclear (e.g. 'notts

_____
[6]ONS: http://www.ons.gov.uk/
[7]OpenStreetMap: https://www.openstreetmap.org/

Figure 4: Example MSOA (whole shape) with nested LSOA (shaded with horizontal line) and OA (shaded with vertical line).

ladd'). Varying levels of granularity were present in the declared location fields; ranging from street level to country. A small number of actual coordinates were also included in addition to the named location profiles. As with Hecht et al. [16], city level profiles were most prevalent followed closely by town, and as such we chose to restrict our analysis to profiles who declared a location only at these two levels, similar to Rout et al. [40], rather than higher and lower granularities. A limited number (~30%) of profiles in the gold-standard had location field resolvable to a uniquely named town or city.

The geometric median method of Compton et al. [8], Jurgens [21], Jurgens et al. [22] was applied, although Haversine distance was used instead of Vincenty for consistency across approaches (although we believe this will cause no discernible change in computed distance), and median absolute deviation of the posts was not limited in order to assess this method's performance on all users.

Majority voting was applied at the four level of granularity introduced in Section 4.1.1. Three different clustering algorithms (K-means, DBSCAN and GMM) were experimented with, using the implementations available in scikit learn [32], using default parameters. For K-means and GMM a k and n_components of 10 were used respectively.

5.2 Evaluation metrics

Two metrics that have previously been used in the user geo-location literature are used to evaluate the approaches.

'Error distance' is applied when continuous (coordinate level) predictions are made, and is the distance between the 'true home location' and the estimated home location. The mean error distance

Table 1: Characteristics of the NSG shown in terms of maximum, minimum and average population.

Geography	Total number	Min population	Max population	Average population
OA	181408	100	625	309
LSOA	34753	1000	3000	1500
MSOA	7201	5000	15000	7200

(i.e. the sum of the error distance for each profile divided by the number of profiles) is computed for each approach, and reported alongside the quantiles of the full set of error distances.

'Exact match accuracy' refers to the proportion of examples that are correctly geo-located within the correct region (e.g. the correct city, state or ZIP code), referred to in Section 4.1.1 as the 'true home boundary'.

6 RESULTS

The results of two experiments on the state-of-the-art and new methods are presented in the following. The first experiment was carried out in continuous-space, aiming to assign each user a co-ordinate home location, and comparing this to the true home co-ordinate given by the gold-standard dataset. The ability of each method to estimate this location was evaluated via the error distance, discussed in Section 6.1. The second experiment was carried out in discrete-space, aiming to assign each user a home boundary (for four boundary datasets), making a comparison with the true home boundary defined within the gold-standard. Accuracy of each method's evaluation of this was evaluated using exact match accuracy, discussed in Section 6.2.

6.1 Error distance

The distance in miles between the 'true home location' and the estimated home location for each user was calculated (referred to in the following as the 'error distance'). The set of error distances for the whole gold-standard dataset (and around 30% in the location field case) were used to quantify each method's accuracy, with summary statistics shown in Table 2. Due to the limited number of profiles with location field, we also include results for only those profiles with a valid location field so as to not penalise the method unfairly (presented in Table 3). Note that the majority vote method is not included here because it does not involve estimating a home coordinate.

First tweet produces an estimated home location to within 0.1849 miles of the 'true' home location in over half the users in our dataset (i.e. the 50th percentile (median) is 0.1849); this is in line with our hypothesis that tweets have a high probability of being produced at a user's home. However, a quarter of the cases in our dataset had home location errors over 9.8909 miles, which is a high level of error in comparison to other approaches.

As location field is applied at the city/town level, error distances up to ~5 miles are to be expected, however, a quarter of the errors calculated exceed this. On manual inspection of the profiles, it became apparent that many were poorly labelled due to unreliable information; many seemed to be residents of satellite towns or villages and declared their location as the larger nearby town or city.

Examples of this include: Mansfield to Nottingham (15 miles), Cheadle to Manchester (7 miles) and many London commuter towns. The accuracy of location field-based geolocation is therefore dependent on the proximity of the user to the centre of a town/city, which makes such methods ill-suited to hyperlocal geolocation.

As expected, the geometric median approach of Compton et al. [8], Jurgens [21], Jurgens et al. [22] produced the best results of all state-of-the-art methods, due to the method's outlier resistant nature and reliance on all tweets.

Our new three clustering methods achieved similar results to each other, being almost indistinguishable the 75th percentile of errors. K-Means does however have the largest errors of these clustering methods when applied to the full gold-standard (Table 2), but is the best performing when limited to those profiles only with location field.

6.1.1 Sources of error.
Gaussian mixture models produce the best home location judgements of the clustering methods presented, however a small number of the error distances were above one mile; which we deem as 'high' in the context of hyperlocal home location identification. In Section 3.2 we highlighted that a large 'home cluster size', calculated as the mean Haversine distance to the home coordinate from each point in the home cluster, is a potential indicator of poor home location estimates.

We investigated the effect of limiting cluster size by discarding those users where their 'home cluster size' was above one mile. Of all (1048) error distances for GMMs, 46 (4.38%) were above 1 mile and 13 (1.24%) were above 10 miles. Upon discarding profiles with home cluster size above 1 mile, 913 error distances remained, of these 16 (1.71%) had error distances above 1 mile, and 8 (0.876%) above 10 miles. Applying this limit improved the performance of the method, thus we can conclude that cluster size is a useful indicator of the quality of home location estimates.

Limiting cluster size did not reduce all errors to zero, and therefore additional sources of error are present in the method. This is likely due to the somewhat naive assumption that the area a user posts most commonly from is their home. It is likely that some users are more active at a place other than their home, such as those who use Twitter for professional purposes or are also active while at a place of leisure or study. In future work we plan to overcome this weakness by adding labelling for the identified location clusters, which will distinguish those users who post most frequently from places other than home.

6.2 Exact match accuracy

As stated in Section 4.1.1, the 'true' home location was used to determine four granularities (OA, LSOA, MSOA, LAD) of 'true' home boundary, for each user in the gold-standard. The home

Table 2: Quantiles of the set of error distances (in miles) for the 'gold-standard' dataset, calculated using home locations estimated via a number of methods (best results in bold). Under the first post method, 5% of the profiles analyzed had estimated home locations to *within* 0.0024 miles of the true location. Half of the profiles analyzed were correctly estimated to *within* 0.18 miles. Finally, 5% of the profiles analyzed had estimated home locations that were incorrect by *over* 568 miles.

Method	Percentile of the error distance					Mean
	5	25	50	75	95	
First tweet	0.0024	0.0079	0.1849	9.8909	568.8185	165.3717
Location field	0.3871	1.0463	2.5591	5.7749	30.2101	8.7826
Geometric median	0.0025	0.0057	0.009	0.0252	1.7246	1.2769
Clustering: K-means	0.0027	**0.0051**	**0.0081**	**0.0158**	**0.3079**	10.8883
Clustering: DBSCAN	0.0025	0.0054	0.0082	0.0166	0.5211	1.4055
Clustering: GMM	**0.0024**	0.0052	0.0083	0.0176	0.6168	**0.963**

Table 3: Quantiles of the set of error distances (in miles) for the profiles with a valid location field from the 'gold-standard' dataset, calculated using home locations estimated via a number of methods (best results in bold).

Method	Percentile of the error distance					Mean
	5	25	50	75	95	
First tweet	0.0023	0.0071	0.1179	7.8129	167.2743	100.780
Location field	0.3871	1.0463	2.5591	5.7749	30.2101	8.7826
Geometric median	0.0025	0.0055	0.0089	0.0224	1.0111	1.4401
Clustering: K-means	0.0029	**0.0047**	**0.0076**	**0.0139**	**0.1585**	**0.4851**
Clustering: DBSCAN	0.0027	0.0055	0.0078	0.0149	0.2438	1.4873
Clustering: GMM	**0.0025**	0.0050	0.0080	0.0142	0.2894	1.2708

location estimated by each of the coordinate methods is similarly converted to a boundary (the majority vote method already outputs boundaries), and the proportion of users from the dataset whose estimated home boundary was the same as the 'true' boundary was calculated. Note that the number of user profiles that could be included here is lower than the total number of users in the dataset because the boundary data does not cover the whole of the UK (1012 for LAD and 953 for the other granularities). These proportions of correct boundary classification are shown in Table 4.

It again becomes clear that the first tweet and location field methods are particularly inaccurate; first tweet is only able to correctly classify more than half the profiles at the lower two granularities and location field only at the lowest. The geometric median [21, 22], majority voting and clustering methods all perform well, classifying over three quarters of the profiles correctly at the highest granularity, and over 95% at the lowest granularity. As with error distance, geometric median is outperformed by clustering methods at region discrimination. In particular, GMM (the best performing clustering algorithm) correctly classifies an additional 4.2% of profiles at the highest granularity and 1.2% at the lowest.

Majority voting beats the clustering methods at the OA, LSOA and MSOA granularities by a small margin (< 3% at the highest granularity), but is narrowly beaten by K-means at the highest granularity (LAD).

7 DISCUSSION

This paper has three main contributions:

- a comparative evaluation of state-of-the-art user geo-location methods, with respect to identifying the users' home location at a hyperlocal (coordinate) level, as well as at regional level (based on four UK regional classifications at multiple granularities);
- two new methods for user geo-location, which were shown to outperform the state-of-the-art methods;
- a new gold-standard dataset for evaluation of Twitter user geo-location at hyperlocal granularity. UK users were chosen specifically since population- and city-density is much higher than in the USA, which makes the geolocation task much more challenging. For instance, Stockport is a large town in the UK, only 7 miles from Manchester, which is less than the error distance of some of the methods reported in Table 2.

Amongst the state-of-the-art methods evaluated on the new UK dataset, we found that the first tweet method is the most prone to large errors, even though around 75% of user profiles were still correctly located to within 10 miles.

Similar to previous findings [16], we demonstrated that the textual location field is unreliable for hyperlocal user geo-location, since many users tend to specify the nearest larger city as their

Table 4: Proportion of users whose estimated home boundary was equal to the true home boundary, displayed by method and boundary granularity (best results in bold).

Method	Proportion same by boundary type			
	OA	LSOA	MSOA	LAD
First tweet	0.4260	0.4732	0.5273	0.6749
Location field	0.0094	0.0219	0.1003	0.6742
Geometric median	0.7534	0.8311	0.8939	0.9625
Clustering: K-means	0.7985	0.8783	0.9328	**0.9783**
Clustering: DBSCAN	0.7912	0.8688	0.9296	0.9733
Clustering: GMM	0.7954	0.8741	0.9275	0.9733
Majority vote	**0.8279**	**0.8919**	**0.9443**	0.9763

location, instead of the more accurate smaller village or commuter town. Consequently, user geo-location based on the location field text is ill suited to hyperlocal or fine-grain region prediction, but performed well in 67% of cases on the larger LAD regions —the largest boundaries we experimented with here.

The geometric median performed the best of all state-of-the-art methods, predicting accurately at both hyperlocal and regional level at different granularity. Nevertheless, it suffers from the limitation that it does not take into account cases where users post often from multiple, distinct locations.

Our newly proposed clustering methods outperformed all state-of-the-art methods, with a particularly strong lead over the first tweet and location field-based approaches. Amongst the three clustering algorithms evaluated, Gaussian Mixture Models achieved the best results at both hyperlocal and region based user geo-location. Majority voting marginally outperforms the clustering approaches at region prediction, but suffers from the drawback that it must be used in conjunction with boundary data. While such data is readily available in the UK, this may not always be the case for other countries.

Similar to the first tweet and the geometric median methods, our newly proposed approaches rely on geo-located tweets (which make up only 1.24% of all tweets [31]). This limits their applicability to only a small fraction of all Twitter users, but nevertheless, our methods are useful for unsupervised generation of high accuracy home location information, which can then be used as training data for user geo-location models.

7.1 Future work

Our current approach rests on the assumption that a user's most posted-from location is their home, and while this assumption appears to work for most users in practice, it is highly likely that some users post more commonly from an alternate location such as their place of work, study or the homes of friends/family (leading to incorrect location labels under the current scheme). To help overcome this drawback, we would like to expand our method in future work to evaluate user's active locations beyond 'home'. Identification of additional 'location types' will be carried out by incorporating the textual cues and meta-data in tweets in addition to coordinate data. For the problem of differentiating 'home' and

'work' locations the proportion of tweets at each location in and out of canonical work hours will be investigated (building on the work in Cho et al. [7]). Additionally the nature of the geography at the predicted locations could be assessed, for example a prediction in a known residential area may more likely be correct than a predominately industrial area.

8 WIDER CONSIDERATIONS

Knowledge of a user's location can be used for a range of purposes including those with social benefit, such as to aid disaster response [27], track disease outbreaks, reduce bias in demographic analysis by balancing user characteristics [3, 29, 35] and perform geographically linked opinion analysis [17]. However, there is also potential for misuse. When processing the data for the work described here we took care to ensure that geolocation data was processed separately from other information about the user and, as an extra precaution, we have not made the data publicly available.

The findings here highlight that accurate estimates of some Twitter user's home location can be made using geo-location history and publicly available tools. In addition, we found that some Twitter users state they are 'at home' in geo-located tweets, implicitly revealing their residential location. This work further highlights the need for users of social media platforms such as Twitter to be aware of the implications of sharing the information they make available in their posts. In particular, when choosing privacy settings or attaching geo-location information to their posts, users should be aware that they may be revealing their location to variety of actors and that inferences can be drawn from this information as it builds up over time.

REFERENCES

[1] B. Alex, C.A. Llewellyn, C. Grover, J. Oberlander, and R. Tobin. 2016. Homing in on Twitter users: Evaluating an enhanced geoparser for user profile locations. In *Proceedings of 10th Language Resources and Evaluation Conference.*
[2] Albert Bifet and Eibe Frank. 2010. Sentiment knowledge discovery in twitter streaming data. In *International Conference on Discovery Science.* Springer, 1–15.
[3] Su Lin Blodgett, Lisa Green, and Brendan O'Connor. 2016. Demographic Dialectal Variation in Social Media: A Case Study of African-American English. In *Proceedings of the 2016 Conference on Empirical Methods in Natural Language Processing.* Association for Computational Linguistics, Austin, Texas, 1119–1130.
[4] Swarup Chandra, Latifur Khan, and Fahad Bin Muhaya. 2011. Estimating twitter user location using social interactions–a content based approach. In *Privacy, Security, Risk and Trust (PASSAT) and 2011 IEEE Third Inernational Conference on*

Social Computing (SocialCom), 2011 IEEE Third International Conference on. IEEE, 838–843.

[5] Hau-wen Chang, Dongwon Lee, Mohammed Eltaher, and Jeongkyu Lee. 2012. @ Phillies Tweeting from Philly? Predicting Twitter user locations with spatial word usage. In *Proceedings of the 2012 International Conference on Advances in Social Networks Analysis and Mining (ASONAM 2012)*. IEEE Computer Society, 111–118.

[6] Zhiyuan Cheng, James Caverlee, and Kyumin Lee. 2010. You are where you tweet: a content-based approach to geo-locating twitter users. In *Proceedings of the 19th ACM international conference on Information and knowledge management*. ACM, 759–768.

[7] Eunjoon Cho, Seth A Myers, and Jure Leskovec. 2011. Friendship and mobility: user movement in location-based social networks. In *Proceedings of the 17th ACM SIGKDD international conference on Knowledge discovery and data mining*. ACM, 1082–1090.

[8] Ryan Compton, David Jurgens, and David Allen. 2014. Geotagging one hundred million twitter accounts with total variation minimization. In *Big Data (Big Data), 2014 IEEE International Conference on*. IEEE, 393–401.

[9] Arthur P Dempster, Nan M Laird, and Donald B Rubin. 1977. Maximum likelihood from incomplete data via the EM algorithm. *Journal of the royal statistical society. Series B (methodological)* (1977), 1–38.

[10] Jacob Eisenstein, Brendan O'Connor, Noah A Smith, and Eric P Xing. 2010. A latent variable model for geographic lexical variation. In *Proceedings of the 2010 Conference on Empirical Methods in Natural Language Processing*. Association for Computational Linguistics, 1277–1287.

[11] Martin Ester, Hans-Peter Kriegel, Jörg Sander, Xiaowei Xu, and others. 1996. A density-based algorithm for discovering clusters in large spatial databases with noise.. In *Kdd*, Vol. 96. 226–231.

[12] Michael F. Goodchild and J. Alan Glennon. 2010. Crowdsourcing geographic information for disaster response: a research frontier. *International Journal of Digital Earth* 3, 3 (2010), 231–241.

[13] Bo Han, Paul Cook, and Timothy Baldwin. 2012. Geolocation prediction in social media data by finding location indicative words. *Proceedings of COLING 2012: Technical Papers* (2012), 1045–1062.

[14] Bo Han, Paul Cook, and Timothy Baldwin. 2014. Text-based Twitter user geolocation prediction. *Journal of Artificial Intelligence Research* (2014), 451–500.

[15] Bo Han, Afshin Rahimi, Leon Derczynski, and Timothy Baldwin. 2016. Twitter Geolocation Prediction Shared Task of the 2016 Workshop on Noisy User-generated Text. In *Proceedings of the W-NUT Workshop*.

[16] Brent Hecht, Lichan Hong, Bongwon Suh, and Ed H Chi. 2011. Tweets from Justin Bieber's heart: the dynamics of the location field in user profiles. In *Proceedings of the SIGCHI Conference on Human Factors in Computing Systems*. ACM, 237–246.

[17] Bahareh Rahmanzadeh Heravi and Ihab Salawdeh. 2015. Tweet location detection. In *Computation + Journalism Symposium*.

[18] Yuheng Hu, Shelly D. Farnham, and Andrés Monroy-Hernández. 2013. Whoo.Ly: Facilitating Information Seeking for Hyperlocal Communities Using Social Media. In *Proceedings of the SIGCHI Conference on Human Factors in Computing Systems*. ACM, New York, NY, USA, 3481–3490.

[19] Anil K Jain, M Narasimha Murty, and Patrick J Flynn. 1999. Data clustering: a review. *ACM computing surveys (CSUR)* 31, 3 (1999), 264–323.

[20] Raja Jurdak, Kun Zhao, Jiajun Liu, Maurice AbouJaoude, Mark Cameron, and David Newth. 2015. Understanding human mobility from Twitter. *PloS one* 10, 7 (2015), e0131469.

[21] David Jurgens. 2013. That's What Friends Are For: Inferring Location in Online Social Media Platforms Based on Social Relationships. In *Seventh International AAAI Conference on Weblogs and Social Media*.

[22] David Jurgens, Tyler Finethy, James McCorriston, Yi Tian Xu, and Derek Ruths. 2015. Geolocation prediction in twitter using social networks: A critical analysis and review of current practice. In *Proceedings of the 9th International AAAI Conference on Weblogs and Social Media (ICWSM)*.

[23] Sheila Kinsella, Vanessa Murdock, and Neil O'Hare. 2011. I'm eating a sandwich in Glasgow: modeling locations with tweets. In *Proceedings of the 3rd international workshop on Search and mining user-generated contents*. ACM, 61–68.

[24] James MacQueen and others. 1967. Some methods for classification and analysis of multivariate observations. In *Proceedings of the fifth Berkeley symposium on*

mathematical statistics and probability, Vol. 1. Oakland, CA, USA., 281–297.

[25] Jalal Mahmud, Jeffrey Nichols, and Clemens Drews. 2012. Where Is This Tweet From? Inferring Home Locations of Twitter Users. In *Sixth International AAAI Conference on Weblogs and Social Media*.

[26] Jalal Mahmud, Jeffrey Nichols, and Clemens Drews. 2014. Home location identification of twitter users. *ACM Transactions on Intelligent Systems and Technology (TIST)* 5, 3 (2014), 47.

[27] S. McClendon and A. C. Robinson. 2013. Leveraging Geospatially-Oriented Social Media Communications in Disaster Response. *International Journal of Information Systems for Crisis Response and Management (IJISCRAM)* 5, 1 (2013), 22–40.

[28] Emily T. Metzgar, David D. Kurpius, and Karen M. Rowley. 2011. Defining hyperlocal media: Proposing a framework for discussion. *New Media and Society* 13, 5 (2011), 772–787.

[29] Ehsan Mohammady and Aron Culotta. 2014. Using county demographics to infer attributes of twitter users. *ACL 2014* (2014), 7.

[30] Alexander Pak and Patrick Paroubek. 2010. Twitter as a Corpus for Sentiment Analysis and Opinion Mining.. In *LREc*, Vol. 10. 1320–1326.

[31] Umashanthi Pavalanathan and Jacob Eisenstein. 2015. Confounds and consequences in geotagged twitter data. *arXiv preprint arXiv:1506.02275* (2015).

[32] F Pedregosa, G Varoquaux, A Gramfort, V Michel, B Thirion, O Grisel, M Blondel, P Prettenhofer, R Weiss, V Dubourg, J Vanderplas, A Passos, D Cournapeau, M Brucher, M Perrot, and E Duchesnay. 2011. Scikit-learn: Machine Learning in Python. *Journal of Machine Learning Research* 12 (2011), 2825–2830.

[33] Owen Phelan, Kevin McCarthy, and Barry Smyth. 2009. Using twitter to recommend real-time topical news. In *Proceedings of the third ACM conference on Recommender systems*. ACM, 385–388.

[34] Barbara Plank and Dirk Hovy. 2015. Personality Traits on Twitter - or - How to Get 1,500 Personality Tests in a Week. In *Proceedings of the 6th Workshop on Computational Approaches to Subjectivity, Sentiment and Social Media Analysis*. 92–98.

[35] Adam Poulston, Mark Stevenson, and Kalina Bontcheva. 2016. User profiling with geo-located posts and demographic data. In *Proceedings of the First Workshop on NLP and Computational Social Science*. Association for Computational Linguistics, Austin, Texas, 43–48.

[36] William H Press. 2007. Gaussian Mixture Models and k-Means Clustering. In *Numerical recipes (3rd edition): The art of scientific computing*. Cambridge university press.

[37] Afshin Rahimi, Trevor Cohn, and Timothy Baldwin. 2015. Twitter User Geolocation Using a Unified Text and Network Prediction Model. In *Proceedings of the 53rd Annual Meeting of the Association for Computational Linguistics and the 7th International Joint Conference on Natural Language Processing (Volume 2: Short Papers)*. Association for Computational Linguistics, 630–636.

[38] Afshin Rahimi, Duy Vu, Trevor Cohn, and Timothy Baldwin. 2015. Exploiting Text and Network Context for Geolocation of Social Media Users. In *Proceedings of the 2015 Conference of the North American Chapter of the Association for Computational Linguistics: Human Language Technologies*. Association for Computational Linguistics, 1362–1367.

[39] Stephen Roller, Michael Speriosu, Sarat Rallapalli, Benjamin Wing, and Jason Baldridge. 2012. Supervised text-based geolocation using language models on an adaptive grid. In *Proceedings of the 2012 Joint Conference on Empirical Methods in Natural Language Processing and Computational Natural Language Learning*. Association for Computational Linguistics, 1500–1510.

[40] Dominic Rout, Kalina Bontcheva, Daniel Preoţiuc-Pietro, and Trevor Cohn. 2013. Where's@ wally?: a classification approach to geolocating users based on their social ties. In *Proceedings of the 24th ACM Conference on Hypertext and Social Media*. ACM, 11–20.

[41] R. W. Sinnott. 1984. Virtues of the Haversine. *Sky and Telescope* 68, 2 (1984), 159.

[42] T. Vincenty. 1975. Direct and Inverse Solutions of Geodesics on the Ellipsoid with application of nested equations. *Survey Review* 23, 176 (1975), 88–93. DOI: http://dx.doi.org/10.1179/sre.1975.23.176.88

[43] Jianshu Weng and Bu-Sung Lee. 2011. Event Detection in Twitter. *ICWSM* 11 (2011), 401–408.

Estimating Relative User Expertise for Content Quality Prediction on Reddit

Wern Han Lim
Faculty of Information Technology
Monash University
lim.wern.han@monash.edu

Mark James Carman
Faculty of Information Technology
Monash University
mark.carman@monash.edu

Sze-Meng Jojo Wong
Faculty of Information Technology
Monash University
jojo.wong@monash.edu

ABSTRACT

Reddit as a social curation site relies on its users to curate content from the World Wide Web (WWW) for the consumption of other users. Content on the site is enriched through user comments, discussions and extensions. This additional content is of varying quality however – ranging from meaningful information to misleading content; depending on the reliability, expertise and intention of the authors. Reddit relies on the Wisdom of the Crowd (WotC) from its community as well as selected moderators to manage its content. We argue that this approach suffers from the cold start in collecting user votes and is at risk of user bias, particularly a group-think mentality. Besides that, managing the large collection of content on Reddit is expensive. In our study, we explore the estimation of relative user expertise through various content-agnostic approaches. We show that it is possible to infer information quality on Reddit using the expertise of the authors. This prediction of content quality could lead to an improved organisation of Reddit content (re-ranking) for user consumption and future information retrieval.

KEYWORDS

Reddit; User expertise; Information quality; Knowledge management; Information retrieval

1 INTRODUCTION

Content aggregation platforms are one-stop-fits-all destinations for information – where quality content from the World Wide Web (WWW) is identified and curated for the consumption of users. Such platforms have prospered since the beginning of the Internet (notably Slashdot[1], Digg[2] and Reddit[3]) commanding a large amount of internet traffic [30]. These platforms impact the WWW by:

- Identifying interesting content on the Web [30] that meets the information needs of the users. Popular and novel content [21, 33] often receives increased visibility [12].

[1] https://slashdot.org/
[2] http://digg.com/
[3] https://www.reddit.com/

HT '17, July 04–07, 2017, Prague, Czech Republic.
© 2017 ACM. 978-1-4503-4708-2/17/07...$15.00
DOI: http://dx.doi.org/10.1145/3078714.3078720

- Directing a large volume of user traffic to the shared content. This is termed as the "Slashdot Effect" – a Flash Crowd occurrence [4, 7] where sites linked from Slashdot's stories receive a sudden swell in traffic.
- Playing a role in disseminating of information [8, 12], especially through influential users [20] to great effect [19]. Influence spreads beyond individual platforms and linked sites; shaping how stories can be viewed, enhancing content and creating new viral content (aka memes) that are picked up by mainstream media.
- From a sociological perspective, collaborative news aggregators provide an understanding in regard to the interest and importance that users place on topics – this characterises the Internet Zeitgeist [7].

These platforms have evolved over the years particularly in loosening the responsibility from hired editors to the user community of the platforms. This shift towards social curation discussed in Section 2 poses new challenges in the organization of large and diverse content with varied quality. One important content aggregation platform is Reddit which has gained popularity [29] to the point where it is sometimes referred to as the "Front Page of the Internet". We conducted a study of Reddit in Section 3.

This research proposed content-agnostic approaches towards the estimation of user expertise in Section 4. By estimating the user expertise, one can infer the quality of content – users of higher expertise have a higher probability to produce content of higher quality. The prediction of content information quality could then be applied to the improve management of content on social curation platforms; validated through an experimentation setup in Section 5. We analyse the findings in Section 6.

2 SOCIAL CURATION

Over the years, content aggregation platforms have shifted the responsibilities of content curation and creation from expert editors onto users acting collaboratively as a community. Slashdot was one of the earliest content curation platforms. Slashdot editors would select, edit, summarize and aggregate news or stories from the WWW for the platform.

Digg experimented with giving its users more responsibility as contributors on the platform, allowing its users to submit content. The submitted content were moderated through peer-moderation where users vote for content – actions coined as *digging* with a up-vote known as a *dig* and a down-vote known as a *bury*. These votes indicate how interesting the users find a piece of content [18]. When a user votes for an item of content, the content is shared to the voter's followers as recommendations [13] sorted by temporal order. Content on the highly visible front-page of Digg is still however selected and managed by the editors of Digg; resulting in a competition between users for attention towards their contributed content.

Today, Reddit has built its reputation as one of the biggest websites with approximately 450 millions page views daily [30]. The growth in Reddit's adoption is through a large migration of users from Digg in 2010 following Digg $v4$, a phenomena known as the Great Digg Migration. The migration was largely motivated by the increased user empowerment offered by Reddit where users have the capability to create communities (*subreddits*), aggregate content and moderate the content with up-votes or down-votes. Users on Reddit are equals unlike the segregation of roles on Digg into editors, moderators, power users (who were perceived by Digg users as having too much power in $v4$ of the website) and anonymous users [20] – each with their own privileges including the number of votes possible and the magnitude of the votes. Without such roles, it is up to the user community to aggregate, curate and moderate the content including determining which content are pushed to the front-page.

2.1 Content on Social Curation Platforms

Often times, the lack of user contributions on social platforms can be of concern in order to achieve a good coverage of the Web. This is however not a challenge for many of the discussed social curation sites where we can observe a large amount of content which is very diverse in nature and topic domain [29]. Content threads are shared in the form of (1) a link to an external site such as news articles or image hosting services which define the platform role as a content aggregator; or (2) textual content written by the authors themselves as a curation platform like Reddit transitions towards a hybrid discussion board [29].

2.2 Organisation of Content

A very large amount of content exists on social curation sites. Over 60 million threads were submitted to Reddit between 2008 and 2012 [29] and we found that popular subreddits such as the *r/gaming* have an average of 1,257 threads submitted daily[4]. The volume of data creates a need for the management and ordering of content on these platforms for user consumption and peer-moderation.

The ordering of content matters. Users were found to have a positional bias for links [6], where users were observed to display consumption patterns from the top of a webpage or a list [15] before proceeding down to the bottom [21] – top items having greater visibility for user consumption. Thus, the content on the users' stream should be sorted to better direct the users' attention towards content of good quality [21]. We note that a thorough study of how best to rank content on a user's stream is currently lacking for Reddit [30].

2.2.1 Peer Recommendation. Prior works on social curation platforms mainly look into the recommendation of content (particularly on Digg) and focused on analyzing the visibility and attraction of shared content. All the content competes for the general users' attention to be on the front-page of the platform. In Digg, recommendations are fed directly to a user's followers' content stream

whenever the user votes for review of a content [13]. The items are sorted according to temporal order. The motivation for the feed is from the discovery that users do follow other users for content [19]. Researchers have looked to improve on the recommendation performance of Digg with user models [14] for identifying similar users. Users would then be pushed content that is highly rated by similar users as personalised recommendation [20], via a peer recommendation process [21] to better meet these information needs.

2.2.2 Content Popularity. A common approach in the ordering of content is to sort the content according to popularity. Studies have found that the popularity of items on Digg is largely influenced by quality [20], with content of high popularity found to be of higher quality than less popular ones [30]. It should however be noted that the novelty of the content degrades overtime [33] and that the popularity of Reddit content does not equate to quality. For example, studies have shown that popular image threads are often reposts of earlier threads with identical links often ignored by the community before achieving popularity [9].

Content popularity can be determined by looking at the number of votes garnered by the content [18]. It is however difficult to predict the future popularity of an item [31], particularly new content due to the cold start problem. The only available data initially comes from the content itself which are weak features for prediction [5].

2.3 Challenges in Social Curation

Social curation on Reddit faces multiple challenges which motivate our work in Section 4 for the estimation of user expertise.

2.3.1 Managing high amounts of unstructured content with varying quality. Users are of different expertise levels and produce or submit content based on their capabilities. This creates a diverse spread of content – some of which may not be suitable for consumption. If not properly managed, such misinformation could spiral out of control [8]. Thus, there is a need to infer the information quality of content for improved management of content.

2.3.2 Vulnerability to malicious users. As an open platform, users are welcomed to be a part of the communities – to contribute and help moderate the platform [21]. The existence of malicious users however can undo such efforts. For example, these users could game the system by creating proxy accounts for self promotion or coordinate attacks for propaganda [25]. By early identification of such users, social curation platforms could defend against such attacks.

2.3.3 Obtaining sufficient user interactions. Often, traditional social platforms rely on the user's personal motivation for contributing content [9] with the vast majority of users only consuming content without submitting any content on Reddit [26]. In our study of Reddit (Section 3), we see a high amount of user activities in creating threads and commenting on them. While large subreddits are immune to this, smaller subreddits and the community do suffer from the lack of user activities as the user interactions are centred around the larger subreddits [29]. We also note from the same study however that there is a lack of user votes for the moderation of content where the median score for threads and comments has the value 1 (Table 4 and Table 5). This deficiency in user review greatly affects the content moderation itself [18] on Reddit. Through the estimation of user expertise of content authors, it is possible to predict the information quality of the content despite the lack of user votes.

2.3.4 Vote bias. User bias does exist on social platforms, particularly in the judgment of content through their votes. Users tend to vote for the content which they have viewed early [32] and might not continue to browse the remaining content; resulting in the content not being judged well when the content is sorted by temporal order. Besides that, users can be biased by the "herding" effect – where the community's views on the content [28] such as the current votes gained by the content or an early swell in user votes that affect the decision of the users [27].

3 REDDIT

Reddit is a social curation platform that relies solely on User-Generated Content (UGC) which it provides for the consumption of its users – both the role as aggregators of content from the Web and also contributors of additional information to the discussions within threads. UGC has the information potential to enrich content especially on platforms like Reddit [30]. This research attempts to overcome the challenges presented in Section 2.3.

3.1 The Reddit Dataset

The study of Reddit is based on a publicly available dataset hosted on a Google BigData repository[5] from the *r/datasets* subreddit[6]. From this dataset, we made use of threads and comments for various subreddits between December 2015 and and July 2016; as downloaded on 27th September 2016[7].

3.2 Organization and Subreddits

Reddit introduces user-defined communities known as subreddits, $Z = \{z_1, z_2, ..., z_{|Z|}\}$. Users can create and manage the communities for content aggregation, sharing or consumption. Many of these subreddits are often topic-based. It is within the subreddit that threads are created for the sharing and discussion of content.

From the repository, this research investigated threads from the highly subscribed subreddits of rank 5th, 6th, 10th, 17th and 55th [8] – r/science, r/worldnews, r/gaming, r/explainlikeimfive (elifive) and r/politics. As we discuss below, user behaviour on these subreddits differ from one another; thus user expertise are estimated relative to that of the other users within the same subreddit.

The quantity of threads created daily differ between subreddits as shown in Figure 1. We note that the *r/science* subreddit recorded the lowest number of threads created daily and *r/gaming* the highest.

The number of threads created on these subreddits are relatively stable with the exception of the *r/politics* which fluctuates with regards to the political scene. Upon further inspection, we note that this subreddit despite its name is a subreddit only for the United States (US) political news. Thus, this contrasting behaviour would be an interesting exploration point against that of the global

[5]Compiled by Reddit user *u/Stuck_In_the_Matrix*
[6]https://www.reddit.com/r/datasets/comments/3bxlg7
[7]Leaving a temporal gap for the threads and comments to stabilise
[8]As of 2nd September 2016 with healthy number of threads

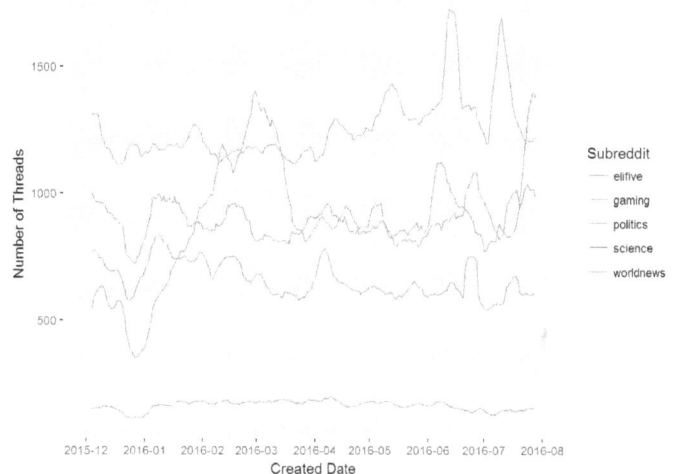

Figure 1: Moving Average (7 Days) of Reddit Threads Created

r/worldnews subreddit in future studies. The number of threads created is very stable for the *r/science* subreddit with little fluctuations when compared to the other subreddits.

From the plot, a consistent dip in the number of threads created towards the end of December 2015 and earlier January 2016 can be observed. Presumably, the holiday season has an effect on user activity – users are less active during such period with the exception of the *r/gaming* subreddit with holiday releases.

Such observations encourage the research to explore the possible performance difference between expertise estimation algorithms across these subreddits; each with varying amount of user activity and available information for estimation.

Table 1: Thread Density of Subreddits by Day

Subreddit	Number of Threads by Day						Total
	Minimum	1st Q	Median	Mean	3rd Q	Maximum	
elifive	446.0	593.0	648.0	663.2	717.8	1484.0	161827
gaming	973.0	1161.0	1227.0	1257.0	1328.0	2355.0	306735
politics	190.0	673.8	904.0	894.3	1061.8	1728.0	218210
science	65.0	118.8	174.0	164.8	199.0	263.0	40215
worldnews	503.0	774.8	922.0	892.8	1006.5	1567.0	217834

3.3 Reddit Threads

Reddit threads, $D = \{d_1, d_2, ..., d_{|D|}\}$ can be created by any users on any subreddit. These threads begin with a submission of an external link or self-written text [29]. Users including the thread starter can then interact with the thread by posting comments, critics and questions at any time point. Unlike many other UGC platforms, Reddit allows users to interact with other user comments in threads; creating a tree-like structure of various levels for the discussion. The structure of a Reddit thread is as shown in Figure 2.

The thread-based user interactions create a new challenge in estimating user expertise which differs from many other UGC platform such as community question-answering platforms [23]:

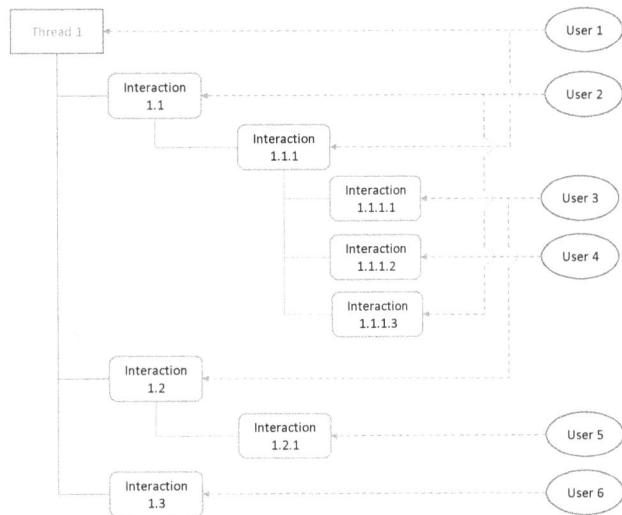

Figure 2: Structure of a Reddit Thread

- Multiple interactions from the same user.
- Not every comment in a thread directly respond to the content posted by the thread starter.
- Replies can both enhance, agree or disprove other comments.

3.4 Reddit Comments

Comments, $I = \{i_1, i_2, ..., i_{|I|}\}$ can provide additional meaningful information to the thread discussion. The distribution of user comments on threads do vary however and is very skewed to the right as we observed in Table 2. An interesting observation to be made here is that the threads in *r/explainlikeimfive* and *r/politics* would often receive at least 1 user comment; and on the other hand, at least half of the *r/gaming* threads have no user response.

Table 2: Comment Distribution of Reddit Threads

	Number of Comments on Reddit threads					
Subreddit	Minimum	1st Q	Median	Mean	3rd Q	Maximum
elifive	0.0	1.0	2.0	8.5	5.0	6105.0
gaming	0.0	0.0	0.0	9.9	2.0	9502.0
politics	0.0	1.8	3.0	43.8	15.0	47831.0
science	0.0	0.0	1.0	15.8	2.0	6370.0
worldnews	0.0	0.0	1.0	22.5	2.0	32901.0

Diving deeper by looking at the comment word count, it can be noted that the comments for *r/gaming* threads are usually short. The question-answering nature of threads in *r/explainlikeimfive* encourages more complete and elaborate responses which resulted in a higher word count for user comments.

3.4.1 Direct Comments. Direct comments are comments that respond directly to the thread. These comments could directly comment on, discuss or argue with the content shared by the thread starter. If the thread itself is a question, the comments would attempt to answer it. In Table 3, we observe that the comments in

r/politics and *r/worldnews* are often responses to other comments in a discussion thread unlike the other subreddits here.

Table 3: Comment Types of Reddit Threads

	Number of Comments		Correlation between Direct and All Comments in Threads	
Subreddit	Direct	All	Pearson's	P-value
elifive	502010 (34.29%)	1463800	0.8957	$< 2.2 \times 10^{-16}$
gaming	524804 (36.23%)	1448582	0.9178	$< 2.2 \times 10^{-16}$
politics	1842373 (18.17%)	10137258	0.8371	$< 2.2 \times 10^{-16}$
science	210202 (30.78%)	682810	0.9267	$< 2.2 \times 10^{-16}$
worldnews	969053 (18.41%)	5263228	0.9413	$< 2.2 \times 10^{-16}$

There is a strong correlation in the number of direct comments with the number of comments in every Reddit thread. An interesting observation here is that despite the threads in *r/worldnews* having a much lower number of direct comments when compared to the other subreddits, it does record the highest correlation here telling us that it is very discussion-focused with users replying to each other a lot more.

3.5 Reddit Votes and Vote Difference

Reddit facilitates the peer moderation of content through user votes which are often regarded as the community's long-term judgement on the quality of content on many UGC platforms [1] – Up-votes (positive votes) to indicate content which they deem to be good, and down-votes (negative votes) to be poor. Often, negative votes are abused particularly for cyberbullying and thus are removed from many platforms [11]. Earlier studies have concluded however that the existence of down-votes does not negatively affect Reddit [25].

As a prevention of vote abuse by malicious users, Reddit is no longer displaying the number of up-votes and down-votes gained by a content (since June 2014) [16]. Instead, content votes are calculated internally in Reddit according to the up-votes and down-votes received through a function they called Vote Fuzzing (VF). The VF mechanism artificially inflates the number of up and down-votes for a resource, while maintaining the true difference between them which is then attached to the content itself. In this paper we extract user vote difference, Vote(I), as a content-agnostic indicator to estimate user expertise.

Starting with the threads themselves in Table 4, it can be noticed that there are no Reddit threads with negative vote difference. The vote difference distribution for Reddit threads are heavily skewed to the right particularly for the *r/explainlikeimfive* and *r/gaming*. On the other hand, the *r/politics* has almost half of its threads without any vote difference whereas the voted threads have a higher vote difference when compared to the other subreddits.

Unlike the threads, we observed Reddit comments with negative vote differences (shown in Table 5). These negative votes are however not dominant as they account for less than a quarter of the comments. We look to extend and adapt the algorithms from earlier work done on community question-answering data [23] to account for the negative vote difference. In general, most of the comments tend to have a relatively low vote difference value within the region of 1 to 3.

Table 4: Vote Difference Distribution of Reddit threads

Subreddit	Scores of Reddit threads					
	Minimum	1st Q	Median	Mean	3rd Q	Maximum
elifive	0.0	1.0	1.0	17.5	1.0	7074.0
gaming	0.0	1.0	1.0	57.7	1.0	9942.0
politics	0.0	0.0	1.0	111.2	12.0	9605.0
science	0.0	1.0	1.0	108.6	5.0	10924.0
worldnews	0.0	1.0	1.0	62.5	4.0	11850.0

Table 5: Vote Difference Distribution of Reddit comments

Subreddit	Scores of Reddit comments					
	Minimum	1st Q	Median	Mean	3rd Q	Maximum
elifive	-3276.0	1.0	1.0	6.8	2.0	8537.0
gaming	-865.0	1.0	1.0	9.5	3.0	6243.0
politics	-1763.0	1.0	1.0	5.2	3.0	7098.0
science	-206.0	1.0	1.0	6.9	3.0	5313.0
worldnews	-3032.0	1.0	1.0	8.0	3.0	6917.0

3.6 Reddit Users

Reddit users are integral to Reddit as a social curation platform – users share external content via thread links or produce their own textual content through self texts and comments. There are healthy number of users for each subreddit seen here in Table 6.

We however observed that user behaviour differs between subreddits which motivates this research to investigate the estimation of user expertise for these diverse subreddits. Unlike the other subreddits, the users of *r/explainlikeimfive* and *r/gaming* are active thread contributors, with almost 20% of the users of *r/gaming* only contribute to threads without any comments. Most users are active commentors on these subreddits particularly the users of *r/politics*, *r/science* and *r/worldnews*. Only a small portion of users in *r/science* and *r/worldnews* are active contributors of threads and comments. It is interesting that despite the question-answering nature of *r/explainlikeimfive*, 12.72% of its users are both thread starters and commentors; a phenomena explainable through the assumption that the thread starter themselves would post comments to further seek information, such as clarification from the other comments.

Table 6: Activities of Reddit Users

SubReddit	Number of Users				
	Threads	Comments	Threads only	Comments only	Total
elifive	81965 (27.55%)	253324 (85.16%)	44139 (14.84%)	215499 (72.45%)	297464
gaming	124630 (29.84%)	335491 (80.32%)	82221 (19.68%)	293083 (70.16%)	417713
politics	37914 (11.82%)	304619 (94.99%)	16067 (5.01%)	282773 (88.18%)	320687
science	13387 (9.47%)	131269 (92.84%)	10126 (7.16%)	128009 (90.53%)	141396
worldnews	48566 (9.56%)	476480 (93.81%)	31453 (6.19%)	459368 (90.44%)	507934

The distribution in the amount of items contributed by the users is heavily skewed to the right, as we observe at least 60% of the users of the explored subreddits created only 1 thread or made only 1 comment. At the 90th user percentile, they only created between 2-6 threads and 3-4 comments.

4 ESTIMATION OF USER EXPERTISE

This research attempts to overcome the challenges discussed in Section 2.3 with the estimation of user expertise through content-agnostic approaches and then apply it to predict the information quality of user-generated content. To the best of our knowledge, there exists no research that aims to predict the contribution quality of Reddit users through their estimated user expertise and instead all prior work focuses on the processing of the content itself [17, 30]. It should be noted that our work here can be used to supplement content-based approaches. The contribution from this research includes:

- Improved management of content according to the content's information quality. As a content-agnostic approach, the content quality could be predicted despite its unstructured nature.
- Reduces the platform's vulnerability towards malicious users. The estimated user expertise could be used to detect potential malicious or unreliable users earlier and reduce their influence from the get-go.
- Provides an early indicator of content quality which overcomes the cold start problem in garnering user votes for content moderation. The organisation of content can then be adjusted to improve peer-moderation.

Thus, the quality content can be promoted in the list for the consumption of users (since users do consume content from the highly visible top of a list to the bottom [15, 21]). This is the alternative to the temporal sorting of content that does not overcome the cold-start and is instead susceptible to temporal bias [9].

4.1 User Expertise on Reddit

Users of higher expertise tend to produce content of higher information quality [16]. This observation has encouraged works into identifying users of high expertise within domains – a process known as expert search [35] in order to improve content quality [22]. For this research on Reddit, the estimated user expertise is:

- **A relative measure.** The user expertise is estimated relative to other users. Comparing the expertise between two users enables us to infer the odds that one user would produce a better content than another user.
- **Domain sensitive.** A user cannot be an expert in every domain. Thus the user expertise is estimated within the domains where the user is active – i.e. we compute a different value for each subreddit.

This research looks at the content-agnostic approach towards user expertise estimation. In the following sections, we discuss the explored approaches which revolves around the central theme of user expertise according to their contribution significance.

4.2 Contribution Count (C-Count)

This is the simplest approach. It makes the assumption that expert users are those users who make a large number of significant contributions as judged by the vote difference. Thus, the approach counts the number of good contributions made by the users as their estimated user expertise.

4.2.1 Identifying Good and Bad Contributions. The vote difference gained is used to measure the contribution of each comment. The contribution significance of each comment, Sig(I) can be judged within each thread according to:

- **Polarity.** A user comment is a "good contribution" if the vote difference gained by that comment is positive; and negative otherwise. This measure of polarity would however suffer from user voting bias where users are inclined to vote positively for good content but not negatively for poor content [28] – motivating us to explore the other variants.
- **Median.** The median vote difference over all comments in a thread can act as threshold to judge if a comment's contribution is significant. A contribution is good if it is "more significant" than half of the other contributions of the thread; consistent with the relative nature of our estimated user expertise. Moreover, this variant overcomes the imbalanced ratio of positive vs. negative vote difference in separating good and bad contributions.
- **Median Direct.** This variant is an extension of the median approach which uses the median vote difference of all direct comments instead.
- **Mean.** Similar to median variant, we adjust the threshold to consider the significance of the user comment. This approach could however punish the users when there is a non-uniform distribution over votes.
- **Mean Direct.** The threshold is adjusted according to the vote difference mean of direct user comments.

4.2.2 Punishing Bad Contributions? If a user produced a bad contribution Sig(I) < 0, the user could be punished. This research determines the effect from punishing users for their bad contributions by counting the following as the user's estimated expertise – (1) Only the number of good user contributions as in Function 1; or (2) The difference between the number of good vs. bad contributions as in Function 2.

$$\text{C-Count}(u) = |\text{Sig}(I_u) \geq 0| \tag{1}$$

$$\text{C-Count}(u) = |\text{Sig}(I_u) \geq 0| - |\text{Sig}(I_u) < 0| \tag{2}$$

4.2.3 Decay. User expertise changes overtime as users grow to become better experts in their area. Thus, the user's latest interactions would provide a better judgment for expertise estimation. We update a user's estimated expertise at temporal time t, C-Count$_t(u)$ by a power of the decay factor $\lambda = 1.0, 0.9, 0.5, 0.1$ on the earlier measure as shown in Function 3.

$$\text{C-Count}_{t+1}(u) = \text{C-Count}_t(u)^\lambda + |\text{Sig}_t(I_u) \geq 0| \tag{3}$$

4.2.4 Multiple Interactions. A Reddit user can contribute one or multiple comments in a thread. Here, this research takes into account all of these interactions. If a user is active, then it is up to the user to ensure that the comments made are "good contributions", or suffer the consequences otherwise. This research takes this stance as to not discourage user activity which is vital towards to generation of content on the platform. Besides that, this enabled the research to study the effect of user activity on user expertise estimation.

4.3 Contribution Z-Index (Z-Index)

The Contribution Z-Index is another baseline approach for this research as a possible improvement over the earlier Contribution Count approach. It is based on the Z-Index used in Community Question-Answering (CQA) platform [34] adapted for Reddit – it considers how many times more a user has made a good contribution rather than a bad one; based on the assumption that a random user is just as likely to make a good contribution as they are to make a negative one. Thus the count of positive vs negative contribution should follow a Binomial distribution. The Z-Index measure is used as the estimated user expertise. This approach also includes all the variants discussed earlier.

$$\text{Z-Index}(u) = \frac{|\text{Sig}(I_u) \geq 0| - |\text{Sig}(I_u) < 0|}{\sqrt{|\text{Sig}(I_u) \geq 0| + |\text{Sig}(I_u) < 0|}} \tag{4}$$

4.4 Contribution Scores (C-Score)

In this baseline, this research measures the significance of user contributions as a score. The vote difference of user contributions, Vote(I) in the range of $(-\inf, \inf)$ are used to infer contribution [24] and experts are users with high collected scores from their comments. In this paper, we utilize this additional information as a measure of how good or bad user interactions are in contributing towards the estimation of user expertise.

4.4.1 Scores as Expertise. From the collected contribution scores, the user expertise can be estimated. Here, this research look at 2 variants – (1) sum of contribution scores as shown in Function 5; and (2) average of contribution scores shown in Function 6. In the sum variant, users are rewarded for being active. Similar to the Contribution Count and Contribution Z-Index; we decay the contribution scores of the earlier user comments before including the newest user comments for the estimation of user expertise.

$$\text{C-Score}(u) = \sum_{k=0}^{|I_u|} \text{Vote}(i_k) \tag{5}$$

$$\text{C-Score}(u) = \frac{\sum_{k=0}^{|I_u|} \text{Vote}(i_k)}{|I_u|} \tag{6}$$

4.4.2 Contribution Adjustments. The implementation of contribution scores can be tricky due to the varying number of user comments and the number of votes within a Reddit thread. Thus, there would be a need to adjust the contribution scores according to the thread where the interaction is. The variants explored here are:

- **Raw.** The vote difference is taken as the user's contribution score without any adjustments, enabling us to explore the effect of popular threads[9] on the contribution scores for user expertise estimation.
- **Mean and Mean Direct.** The mean variant attempts to normalize the contribution scores gained for each user interaction according to the mean vote difference of all comments or direct comments only.
- **Median and Median Direct.** Similar to the mean adjustment, here we normalise the contribution scores by the median instead.

---

[9]High number of comments and user votes

4.5 Contribution Rating (C-Rating)

The C-rating approach is a pairwise comparison approach for user interactions, inspired from its success in answer quality prediction on CQA platforms [23]. Here, we model each thread as a competition between the users who comment on it. The performance of the users are measured according to the significance of their contribution. The estimated expertise are the user ratings updated according to the users' performance in each thread, compared to that of other users in the thread. A user of higher rating is expected to be more likely to contribute significant contributions than users of lower rating.

4.5.1 Comparison Pairs. Comparisons pairs are built within each Reddit thread for the pairwise comparison between each comment in the thread; given that the authors of the comments are not the same. This Round Robin comparison with other direct comments instead of all comments reduces the runtime complexity of the approach[10].

4.5.2 Glicko-2 Rating. The user ratings are updated according to the Glicko-2 rating model [10]. The outcomes of each comparison pair are collected if they lie within the same rating period[11] t and are then used to update the user rating μ_u as shown in Equation 7. Here $w_{u_2}^t$ denotes the (aggregated) outcome of all pairwise comparisons between user u_1 and user u_2 in period t.

$$\mu_{u_1}^{t+1} = \mu_{u_1}^t + (\sigma_{u_1}^{t+1})^2 \cdot \sum_{i=2}^{k} g(\sigma_{u_i}^t)(w_{u_i}^t - P(\mu_{u_1}^t, \mu_{u_i}^t, \sigma_{u_i}^t)) \quad (7)$$

The probability of user u_1 defeating opponent u_2 is modelled in Glicko using the logistic function of their score differences in Equation 8 where the uncertainty in the opponent's strength $\sigma_{u_2}^t$ is taken into accounted using the formula in 9.

$$P(\mu_{u_1}^t, \mu_{u_i}^t, \sigma_{u_2}^t)) = \frac{1}{1 + exp(-g(\sigma_{u_2}^t)(\mu_{u_1}^t - \mu_{u_2}^t))} \quad (8)$$

$$g(\sigma) = \frac{1}{\sqrt{1 + 3\sigma^2/\pi^2}} \quad (9)$$

The uncertainty in the estimated user ratings are also measured in Glicko-2 as the rating deviation σ_u based on δ^2 is the game outcome variance.. The third measure, the volatility ϕ is used during the rating updates to reduce the impact of a sudden user performance shift.

$$\sigma^{t+1} = \sqrt{\left(\frac{1}{(\sigma^t)^2 + (\phi^{t+1})^2} + \frac{1}{\delta^2}\right)^{-1}} \quad (10)$$

In this paper, we measure a user expertise according to the user's rating deducted by its uncertainty, $\mu_u - \sigma_u$.

4.5.3 Win-Margin. Traditionally, competitions including real world sports are only concerned with the outcome of a match-up and the winner takes all. Thus, pairwise comparison approaches are often scoreless without looking at the margin of victory and often disregard draws [2, 24]. The win-margin variant is inspired by the Bradley-Terry model which correlates the win probability of a player in a game with the player's real rating μ_1. This win

---

[10]This differs from our earlier work in building every comparison pairs[23].
[11]Daily on Reddit due to the high traffic.

probability is $\frac{\mu_1}{\mu_1+\mu_2}$ when the player is against an opponent with a rating of μ_2 [3]. Our earlier work on CQA platform [23] found improvements towards the estimation of user expertise if we were to consider the win-margin between the winner and the loser of a pairwise comparison. Since Reddit is a different platform (with negative vote difference) we once again explore the scoreless and the win-margin variant. To account for the negative vote difference in comments,modifications to the win-margin are required:

- If the vote difference for both comments is positive, there is no change to the win-margin approach.
- If there is a negative vote difference, then it is a total victory (win-margin of 1) for the comment with the higher vote difference.

5 EXPERIMENT

The performance of the approaches discussed in Section 4 are evaluated for the estimation of user expertise on the collected Reddit dataset detailed in Section 3.1. The user expertise estimated from the approaches are used to predict the information quality of comments (future vote difference gained) contributed by the users.

The evaluation process investigates the user expertise estimation performance on 4 subreddits – *r/explainlikeimfive*, *r/gaming*, *r/science* and *r/worldnews*. The *r/politics* is not evaluated pending more data collection for future work due to the volatility surrounding the US 2016 Presidential Elections; unlike the global *r/worldnews*.

5.1 Training and Testing Cycles

Unlike traditional Web platforms with static content, a social curation platform like Reddit expand rapidly with the constant flow of user content. Beside building high accuracy models for the estimation of user expertise, the approaches explored are fast and efficient in taking in new content for the estimation process. Thus, the performance evaluation is modelled as a continuous cycle, beginning with a training cycle according to the thread timestamp.

5.1.1 Testing Cycle. In the testing cycle, the threads and comments of the threads are used for evaluation. Here, the estimated user expertise from the explored approaches are used to predict the information quality of comments according to the evaluation measures discussed in Section 5.2. Only comments of known users (with expertise estimated from their prior interactions) are evaluated.

5.1.2 Training Cycle. Once the threads and the comments have been used for evaluation, they are added to the training data. New users will have their expertise estimated for the first time and existing users have their expertise updated with the additional new data. The updated user expertise are then used for prediction in the following testing cycle.

5.2 Evaluation Measure

The proposed algorithms are evaluated according to their capabilities in estimating user expertise that can be used to predict information quality of comments.

5.2.1 Ground Truth. The actual vote difference gained is used as the ground truth judgment of information quality for thread comments. User comments within each Reddit thread are ranked according to this judgment. The explored approaches attempt to rank the same comments according to the estimated expertise of comments' author; to match the ground truth rank order to predict the future community assessment of content quality. Our experiment looked at predicting the ordering of – (1) direct comments; and (2) all comments in a thread. We then measure the Kendall's Tau correlation between the ground truth and the predicted ordering.

5.2.2 Kendall's Tau Rank Coefficient, Tau-B Measure. This research selects up to the 10 best comments for each Reddit thread[12] according to the ground truth. Joint observation pairs are then formulated for each of these comments in a Reddit thread. We then measure the number of concordant and discordant pairs for the observation pairs between the ground truth and the explored approaches. As it is possible for two comments to have the same vote difference or two users to have the same estimated expertise, we handle these ties with the Kendall's Tau-B, τ_B statistic.

6 RESULTS AND DISCUSSION

As detailed in Section 5, the evaluation process is based on an online training-test cycle. From a total of $724,505$ threads, $333,175$ threads have at least 1 direct comment created by a user with prior contribution (for the expertise to be estimated) and $344,375$ threads with at least 1 comment. Thus, 45.99% and 47.53% of the threads are suitable for direct comments and all comments evaluation respectively. We note that this value is much smaller for the *r/gaming* subreddit with only 23.03% and 25.70% respectively; possibly due to the low number of comments per thread and also almost 20% of its users are thread contributors only (as noted in Section 3). On the other hand, the *r/explainlikeimfive* subreddit recorded a higher number of suitable threads for evaluation with 78.78% and 79.51% of threads for direct comments and all comments respectively; possibly due to a higher density of threads in the subreddit with at least one interaction (see Table 2). The high number of threads and the comments in each thread ensures the significance of the evaluation measure.

6.1 Differentiating Users

The estimated user expertise is a relative measure which allow us to compare the odds of quality contributions between two users. For example in Reddit threads, it would be ideal for the expertise of the authors of the comments to not be the same unless they are all contributing comments of the same quality, otherwise there would not be a possible ordering in the prediction of information quality. Due to space limitations we present in Table 7, the evaluated approaches at their best variant by not having an order according to the estimated user expertise when there is an order for the ground truth. Here, we observe that the C-Count approach is unable to differentiate user expertise well within an evaluated thread when compared to the other approaches. Upon further inspection, we note that the C-Rating (scored variant) has the highest number of ties in order when the ground truth is a tie as well with only 0.24% of the ties going undetected.

Table 7: Evaluated Approaches (Best Variant) with the Least Number of Orderless User Expertise in Reddit Thread Comments

Approach	Percentage of Thread	
	Direct Comments	All Comments
C-Count (mean threshold, no decay)	5.88%	5.12%
C-Score (averaged score, raw value, no decay)	5.31%	4.70%
Z-Index (mean threshold)	5.58%	4.88%
C-Rating (scoreless)	5.46%	4.77%

6.2 Prediction Performance

Table 8 summarises the comment quality prediction based on the estimated user expertise of the explored approaches at their best variant; measured with the Kendall's Tau-B Rank Coefficient against the ground truth. It can be observed that the best performing approach is the C-Rating approach followed by the C-Count, C-Score and finally the Z-Index.

Generally, the explored approaches perform well on all subreddits with the exception of the *r/gaming* subreddit where the threads lack user comments[13]. The C-Rating approach however performed very well in this subreddit as a robust approach.

6.3 Vote Difference as Contribution Measure

Similar to the earlier work on CQA platforms [23], the user vote information should not be directly used as an estimate of user expertise. The C-Score approach recorded a low performance measure with the average value variant outperforming the sum variant. Instead this information should be used as an indication of contribution significance – by counting the significance of a contribution using the C-Count or be used for pairwise comparison in the C-Rating. This is crucial for an environment with sparse user activity (a lower comment count in thread, a lower word count per comment) such as the *r/gaming* subreddit where we observe the largest performance gain.

6.3.1 Raw Values as Measures. Another interesting observation here is that the best performing variant for the C-Score uses the vote difference as a raw value; a value which we had feared would be inflated and thus should be normalised within the context of the thread itself. For example, popular threads tend to have higher number of user votes that inflate the vote difference of comments. What this finding suggests is that users who commented on such threads and recorded a high number of vote difference should be rewarded (for being able to make an impact on such a challenging thread in the first place). This is further supported by the C-Score having the average score value as its best variant, implying users should be providing consistently high quality content instead of more content of a lower quality.

6.3.2 Significance Threshold. The vote difference gained by a content is useful as an indicator of content contribution for a thread discussion. Often, the polarity of vote difference is used to differentiate contribution significance especially from the users' perspective. Our findings here showed that the best performing variant for both the C-Count and the Z-Index have the mean of vote difference for

---

[12]Computation are expensive for threads with very high number of comments

[13]Discussed in Section 3

Table 8: Kendall's Tau-B Rank Coefficient for Comments Ordering based on Quality Prediction with User Expertise Estimation with the Evaluated Approaches (Best Variant). Best performance in bold.

Approach	Direct Comments for Subreddit					All Comments for Subreddit				
	elifive	gaming	science	worldnews	All	elifive	gaming	science	worldnews	All
C-Count (mean threshold, no decay)	0.9164	0.7923	0.9148	0.8890	0.8797	0.8284	0.6923	0.8610	0.8512	0.8084
C-Score (average score, raw value, no decay)	0.7816	0.7014	0.8873	0.7810	0.7720	0.6423	0.5702	0.8098	0.6941	0.6566
Z-Index (mean threshold)	0.7400	0.6928	0.8710	0.7088	0.7280	0.6258	0.5709	0.7975	0.6265	0.6256
C-Rating (scoreless)	**0.9796**	**0.9298**	**0.9760**	**0.9867**	**0.9716**	**0.9472**	**0.8786**	**0.9469**	**0.9777**	**0.9434**

all comments in a thread as a threshold for content significance – a comment is considered significant for a thread if the vote difference of that comment is above the mean.

6.4 Vote Difference as a Relative User Performance Measure

The high performance of the C-Rating approach is consistent with our earlier findings on CQA platforms [23] that it is possible to apply rating systems in user expertise estimation through pairwise comparisons, even when comparing against direct comments of threads only. User votes on content can be used as a judgment of user performance including the negative vote difference. The existence of negative vote difference however does not benefit the successful win-margin (scored) variant [23] as the scoreless variant recorded a slightly better performance with the exception on the r/science and r/worldnews subreddit.

6.5 Penalising Bad Content

This research explored the possibility to ignore bad contributions by users which maybe caused by user bias and instead only reward good contributions. The findings however suggest otherwise where all of such variants in the C-Count and C-Score were outperformed by variants which takes the bad contribution into account. Besides that, the C-Rating which naturally account for bad contributions as a losing performance measure recorded the highest evaluation measure.

6.6 Decaying User Expertise

Literature suggests that the user expertise improves overtime and earlier contributions should be discounted. A decay factor is introduced to reduce the impact of earlier contributions towards the estimation of user expertise. Our findings do not agree with this notion where the variants with decay for the C-Count and C-Score were outperformed by the non-decay variants; possibly be due to:

- There is a lack of consistent user contribution or activity on Reddit as discussed in Section 3.
- There should be an impact from the earlier user interaction, rewarding the good and penalising the bad. Thus, the users would need to be making significant contributions in the present and future to atone for the earlier bad interactions.

7 CONCLUSION

Social curation platforms have a large impact on the World Wide Web (WWW) today as a content-rich platform enriched by their users. The large amount of user-generated content (UGC) of varying information quality however creates a challenge for community-based content management. A detailed study was conducted using data from Reddit, one of the largest social curation platforms in use today. Here, we analysed 5 large subreddits which provided us with an understanding on Reddit, its content management and the behaviour of its users.

This research proposed the content-agnostic estimation of user expertise by extracting the vote difference from prior generated content; which is then used to predict the information quality of future content generated by the users themselves. Four main approaches were proposed based on previous work in expertise estimation; with multiple variants each for further exploration. These approaches were evaluated according to their prediction performance in the ranking of Reddit thread comments.

The findings suggest that it is possible to estimate user expertise for the prediction of content quality, with an average Kendall's Tau-B rank correlation of 0.9434 using the proposed C-Rating approach (which is based on competitive pairwise comparisons) to rank thread comments in comparison against the ground truth of unseen actual user moderation. This performance is consistently better than the other explored baseline approaches even in subreddits with sparse amount of user comment interactions such as the r/gaming subreddit; showcasing the robustness of the approach for the unpredictable nature of UGC platforms.

The vote difference is a good feature to indicate prior content quality for the explored approaches. This research discovers however that the vote difference should not be used directly as an indication of user expertise as the C-Score approach performs poorly. Instead, the vote difference can be used to identify the content of significance contribution in a thread discussion using the mean vote difference of comments in a thread in the C-Count approach; or as a relative measure for the pairwise comparison of user performance in the C-Rating approach. Both approaches were able to estimate user expertise for the prediction of content quality.

Findings from the research also suggest that the despite raw vote difference values are inflated within the popular threads, the values should not be normalised as users should be rewarded for interacting and making an impact on such competitive threads. Besides that, this research discovers that the polarity of vote difference gained by content is not a suitable threshold in judging contribution significance of content. Instead, a content is deemed to be significant if it registered a vote difference above the average of vote difference of other content within the same scope.

7.1 Future Works

Next, the research aims to further develop approaches to better estimate user expertise for content management on social platforms; by accounting for the comment chain in Reddit threads and learning user behaviours. A possible extension from this work is to explore applying user expertise to weight a user's votes.

REFERENCES

[1] Ashton Anderson, Daniel Huttenlocher, Jon Kleinberg, and Jure Leskovec. 2012. Discovering Value from Community Activity on Focused Question Answering Sites: A Case Study of Stack Overflow. In *Proceedings of the 18th ACM SIGKDD International Conference on Knowledge Discovery and Data Mining (KDD '12)*. ACM, 850–858.

[2] Çiğdem Aslay, Neil O'Hare, Luca Maria Aiello, and Alejandro Jaimes. 2013. Competition-based Networks for Expert Finding. In *Proceedings of the 36th International ACM SIGIR Conference on Research and Development in Information Retrieval (SIGIR '13)*. ACM, 1033–1036.

[3] Ralph A. Bradley and Milton E. Terry. 1952. Rank Analysis of Incomplete Block Designs: I. The Method of Paired Comparisons. *Biometrika* 39, 3/4 (1952).

[4] Xuan Chen and John Heidemann. 2005. Flash Crowd Mitigation via Adaptive Admission Control Based on Application-level Observations. *ACM Trans. Internet Technol.* 5, 3 (Aug. 2005), 532–569.

[5] Justin Cheng, Lada Adamic, P. Alex Dow, Jon Michael Kleinberg, and Jure Leskovec. 2014. Can Cascades Be Predicted?. In *Proceedings of the 23rd International Conference on World Wide Web (WWW '14)*. ACM, New York, NY, USA, 925–936.

[6] Nick Craswell, Onno Zoeter, Michael Taylor, and Bill Ramsey. 2008. An experimental comparison of click position-bias models. In *WSDM '08: Proceedings of the international conference on Web search and web data mining*. ACM, New York, NY, USA, 87ﬁ?!94.

[7] Jeremy Elson and Jon Howell. 2008. Handling Flash Crowds from Your Garage. In *USENIX 2008 Annual Technical Conference (ATC'08)*. USENIX Association, Berkeley, CA, USA, 171–184.

[8] Adrien Friggeri, Lada Adamic, Dean Eckles, and Justin Cheng. 2014. Rumor Cascades. (2014).

[9] Eric Gilbert. 2013. Widespread Underprovision on Reddit. In *Proceedings of the 2013 Conference on Computer Supported Cooperative Work (CSCW '13)*. ACM, New York, NY, USA, 803–808.

[10] Mark Glickman. 2001. Dynamic paired comparison models with stochastic variances. *Journal of Applied Statistics* 28, 6 (2001).

[11] Joshua Guberman, Carol Schmitz, and Libby Hemphill. 2016. Quantifying Toxicity and Verbal Violence on Twitter. In *Proceedings of the 19th ACM Conference on Computer Supported Cooperative Work and Social Computing Companion (CSCW '16 Companion)*. ACM, New York, NY, USA, 277–280.

[12] Nathan Oken Hodas and Kristina Lerman. 2012. How Visibility and Divided Attention Constrain Social Contagion. In *Proceedings of the 2012 ASE/IEEE International Conference on Social Computing and 2012 ASE/IEEE International Conference on Privacy, Security, Risk and Trust (SOCIALCOM-PASSAT '12)*. IEEE Computer Society, Washington, DC, USA, 249–257.

[13] Nathan Oken Hodas and Kristina Lerman. 2013. The Simple Rules of Social Contagion. *CoRR* abs/1308.5015 (2013).

[14] Tad Hogg, Kristina Lerman, and Laura M. Smith. 2013. Stochastic Models Predict User Behavior in Social Media. *CoRR* abs/1308.2705 (2013).

[15] Jeon-Hyung Kang and Kristina Lerman. 2015. VIP: Incorporating Human Cognitive Biases in a Probabilistic Model of Retweeting. In *Social Computing, Behavioral-Cultural Modeling, and Prediction*, Nitin Agarwal, Kevin Xu, and Nathaniel Osgood (Eds.). Lecture Notes in Computer Science, Vol. 9021. Springer International Publishing, 101–110.

[16] Simon Kassing, Jasper Oosterman, Alessandro Bozzon, and Geert-Jan Houben. 2015. Locating Domain-specific Contents and Experts on Social Bookmarking Communities. In *Proceedings of the 30th Annual ACM Symposium on Applied Computing (SAC '15)*. ACM, New York, NY, USA, 747–752.

[17] Himabindu Lakkaraju, Julian McAuley, and Jure Leskovec. 2013. What's in a Name? Understanding the Interplay between Titles, Content, and Communities in Social Media. (2013).

[18] Kristina Lerman and Aram Galstyan. 2008. Analysis of Social Voting Patterns on Digg. In *Proceedings of the First Workshop on Online Social Networks (WOSN '08)*. ACM, New York, NY, USA, 7–12.

[19] Kristina Lerman and Tad Hogg. 2010. Using a Model of Social Dynamics to Predict Popularity of News. In *Proceedings of the 19th International Conference on World Wide Web (WWW '10)*. ACM, New York, NY, USA, 621–630.

[20] Kristina Lerman and Tad Hogg. 2012. Using Stochastic Models to Describe and Predict Social Dynamics of Web Users. *ACM Trans. Intell. Syst. Technol.* 3, 4, Article 62 (Sept. 2012), 33 pages.

[21] Kristina Lerman and Tad Hogg. 2014. Leveraging Position Bias to Improve Peer Recommendation. *PLoS ONE* 9, 6 (11 June 2014), e98914+.

[22] Baichuan Li and Irwin King. 2010. Routing Questions to Appropriate Answerers in Community Question Answering Services. In *Proceedings of the ACM Conference on Information & Knowledge Management (CIKM)*.

[23] Wern Han Lim, Mark James Carman, and Sze-Meng Jojo Wong. 2016. Estimating Domain-Specific User Expertise for Answer Retrieval in Community Question-Answering Platforms. In *Proceedings of the 21st Australasian Document Computing Symposium (ADCS '16)*. ACM, New York, NY, USA, 33–40.

[24] Jing Liu, Young-In Song, and Chin-Yew Lin. 2011. Competition-based User Expertise Score Estimation. In *Proceedings of the 34th International ACM SIGIR Conference on Research and Development in Information Retrieval (SIGIR '11)*. ACM, 425–434.

[25] Richard Mills. 2011. Researching Social News -ﬁ?! Is reddit.com a mouthpiece for the ﬁHive Mindﬁ, or a Collective Intelligence approach to Information Overload?. In *ETHICOMP 2011 Proceedings*. Sheffield Hallam University.

[26] Blair Nonnecke and Jenny Preece. 2000. Lurker Demographics: Counting the Silent. In *Proceedings of the SIGCHI Conference on Human Factors in Computing Systems (CHI '00)*. ACM, New York, NY, USA, 73–80.

[27] Henrique Pinto, Jussara M. Almeida, and Marcos A. Gonçalves. 2013. Using Early View Patterns to Predict the Popularity of Youtube Videos. In *Proceedings of the Sixth ACM International Conference on Web Search and Data Mining (WSDM '13)*. ACM, New York, NY, USA, 365–374.

[28] Maria Priestley and Alex Mesoudi. 2015. Do Online Voting Patterns Reflect Evolved Features of Human Cognition? An Exploratory Empirical Investigation. *PLoS ONE* 10, 6 (06 2015), e0129703.

[29] Philipp Singer, Fabian Flöck, Clemens Meinhart, Elias Zeitfogel, and Markus Strohmaier. 2014. Evolution of Reddit: From the Front Page of the Internet to a Self-referential Community?. In *Proceedings of the Companion Publication of the 23rd International Conference on World Wide Web Companion (WWW Companion '14)*. International World Wide Web Conferences Steering Committee, Republic and Canton of Geneva, Switzerland, 517–522.

[30] Greg Stoddard. 2015. Popularity and Quality in Social News Aggregators: A Study of Reddit and Hacker News. In *Proceedings of the 24th International Conference on World Wide Web (WWW '15 Companion)*. International World Wide Web Conferences Steering Committee, Republic and Canton of Geneva, Switzerland, 815–818.

[31] Gabor Szabo and Bernardo A. Huberman. 2010. Predicting the Popularity of Online Content. *Commun. ACM* 53, 8 (Aug. 2010), 80–88.

[32] Tim Weninger, Xihao Avi Zhu, and Jiawei Han. 2013. An Exploration of Discussion Threads in Social News Sites: A Case Study of the Reddit Community. In *Proceedings of the 2013 IEEE/ACM International Conference on Advances in Social Networks Analysis and Mining (ASONAM '13)*. ACM, New York, NY, USA, 579–583.

[33] Fang Wu and Bernardo A. Huberman. 2007. Novelty and collective attention. *Proceedings of the National Academy of Sciences* 104, 45 (2007), 17599–17601. arXiv:http://www.pnas.org/content/104/45/17599.full.pdf

[34] Jun Zhang, Mark S. Ackerman, and Lada Adamic. 2007. Expertise Networks in Online Communities: Structure and Algorithms. In *Proceedings of the 16th International Conference on World Wide Web (WWW '07)*. ACM, 221–230.

[35] Zhi-Min Zhou, Man Lan, Zheng-Yu Niu, and Yue Lu. 2012. Exploiting User Profile Information for Answer Ranking in cQA. In *Proceedings of the Conference Companion on World Wide Web (WWW)*.

Hate is not Binary:
Studying Abusive Behavior of #GamerGate on Twitter

Despoina Chatzakou[†], Nicolas Kourtellis[‡], Jeremy Blackburn[‡]
Emiliano De Cristofaro[♯], Gianluca Stringhini[♯], Athena Vakali[†]

[†]Aristotle University of Thessaloniki   [‡]Telefonica Research   [♯]University College London
deppych@csd.auth.gr, nicolas.kourtellis@telefonica.com, jeremy.blackburn@telefonica.com
e.decristofaro@ucl.ac.uk, g.stringhini@ucl.ac.uk, avakali@csd.auth.gr

ABSTRACT

Over the past few years, online bullying and aggression have become increasingly prominent, and manifested in many different forms on social media. However, there is little work analyzing the characteristics of abusive users and what distinguishes them from typical social media users. In this paper, we start addressing this gap by analyzing tweets containing a great amount of abusiveness. We focus on a Twitter dataset revolving around the Gamergate controversy, which led to many incidents of cyberbullying and cyberaggression on various gaming and social media platforms. We study the properties of the users tweeting about Gamergate, the content they post, and the differences in their behavior compared to typical Twitter users.

We find that while their tweets are often seemingly about aggressive and hateful subjects, "Gamergaters" do not exhibit common expressions of online anger, and in fact primarily differ from typical users in that their tweets are less joyful. They are also more engaged than typical Twitter users, which is an indication as to how and why this controversy is still ongoing. Surprisingly, we find that Gamergaters are less likely to be suspended by Twitter, thus we analyze their properties to identify differences from typical users and what may have led to their suspension. We perform an unsupervised machine learning analysis to detect clusters of users who, though currently active, could be considered for suspension since they exhibit similar behaviors with suspended users. Finally, we confirm the usefulness of our analyzed features by emulating the Twitter suspension mechanism with a supervised learning method, achieving very good precision and recall.

1 INTRODUCTION

Abuse on social media is becoming a pressing issue. Over the past few years, social networks have not only been targeted by bots and fraudsters [2, 31, 36], but have also been used as a platform for harassing and trolling other individuals [29]. Detecting and mitigating such activities presents important challenges since abuse performed by human-controlled accounts tends to be less homogeneous than the one performed by bots, making it hard to identify the characteristics that distinguish them from non-abusive attacks (and detect them). Recent work showed that human-controlled accounts involved in harassment actually present degrees of synchronized activity [16]. However, no systematic measurement has been performed to understand what distinguishes a social network account behaving in an abusive way from a typical one. Such an understanding is crucial to enable effective mitigation and help social network operators to detect and block these accounts.

Roadmap. In this paper, we start addressing this gap by performing a large-scale comparative study of abusive accounts on Twitter, aiming to understand their characteristics and how they differ from typical accounts. We collect a large dataset of tweets related to the Gamergate (GG) controversy [4], which after two years since its start has evolved into a fairly mature, pseudo-political movement that is thought to encompass semi-organized campaigns of hate and harassment by its adherents, known as Gamergaters (GGers), against women in particular. Then, we explore the differences between the GG-related accounts identified as abusive, and random Twitter accounts, investigate how these differences lead to disproportional suspension rates by Twitter, and discuss possible causes of these differences. We also look at accounts of users that were deleted by their owner and not by Twitter. Further, we cluster GG accounts that exhibit similar behavior, aiming to identify groups of similar accounts that should have been suspended by Twitter but are instead still active. Based on the findings of our clustering, we reason about what may have driven Twitter to not suspend them. Finally, we test the performance of a supervised method to automatically suspend Twitter users based on the various features analyzed.

Findings. In summary, we discover that users involved in Gamergate were already-existing Twitter users probably drawn to the controversy, which might be the reason why GG exploded on Twitter in the first place. While the subject of their tweets is seemingly aggressive and hateful, GGers do not exhibit common expressions of online anger, and in fact primarily differ from random users in that their tweets are less joyful. We find that despite their clearly anti-social behavior, GGers tend to have more friends and followers than random users and being more engaging in the platform may have allowed this controversy to continue until now. Surprisingly, we find that GGers are disproportionally *not suspended* from Twitter in comparison to random users, which is rather unexpected

HT'17, July 4-7, 2017, Prague, Czech Republic.
© 2017 ACM. 978-1-4503-4708-2/17/07...$15.00
DOI: http://dx.doi.org/10.1145/3078714.3078721

given their hateful and aggressive postings. Suspended GG users expressed more aggressive and repulsive emotions, offensive language, and interestingly, more joy than suspended random users, and their high posting and engaging activity may have delayed their suspension from Twitter. Also GGers who deleted their account demonstrated the most activity in comparison to other users (deleted or suspended), exhibited signs of distress, fear, and sadness. They have probably showed these emotions through their high posting activity filled with anger, reduced joy, and negative sentiment. Such users have small social ego-networks which may have been unsupportive or too small to help them before deleting their accounts.

Paper Organization. The rest of the paper is organized as follows. The next section reviews related work on measuring abusive behaviors on online platforms. Section 3 introduces our dataset and the steps taken for cleaning and preparing it for analysis, then, in Section 4, we analyze the behavioral patterns exhibited by GGers, and compare them to random Twitter users. In Section 5, we discuss how users get suspended on Twitter, differences observed between GGers and random users, reasons for deviating from the expected rates, and a basic effort to emulate Twitter's suspension mechanism. In Section 6 we discuss our findings and conclude.

2 RELATED WORK

We now review related work on studying/detecting offensive, abusive, aggressive or bullying content on social media sources. Chen et al. [7] aim to detect offensive content, as well as, potential offensive users based on YouTube comments. Both Yahoo Finance [10, 25] and Yahoo Answers [19] have been used as a source of information for detecting hate and/or abusive content. More specifically, [19] studied a Community-based Question-Answering (CQA) site and finds that users tend to flag abusive content in an overwhelmingly correct way.

Cyberbullying has also attracted a lot of attention lately, for instance [3], [17] and [18] focus on Twitter, Ask.fm, and Instagram, respectively, to detect existing bullying cases out of text sources. [3] considers a variety of features, i.e., user, text, and network-based, to distinguish bullies and aggressors from typical Twitter users. In addition to text sources, [18] also tries to associate an image's topic (e.g., drugs, celebrity, sports, etc) with cyberbullying events. In [9], the cyberbullying phenomenon is further decomposed to specific sensitive topics, i.e., race, culture, sexuality, and intelligence, by analyzing YouTube comments extracted from controversial videos. A study of specific cyberbullying cases, e.g., threats and insults, is also conducted in [35] by considering Dutch posts extracted from Ask.fm. Apart from cyberbullying, they also study specific user behaviors: harasser, victim, and bystander-defender or bystander-assistant who support the victim or the harasser, respectively. In follow-up work [29], the authors exploit Twitter messages to detect bullying cases which are specifically related to the gender bullying phenomenon. Finally, in [8], YouTube users are characterized based on a "bulliness" score. The rise of cyberbullying, and abusive incidents in general, is also evident in online game communities. Since these communities are widely used by people of all ages, such a phenomenon has attracted the interest of the research community. For instance, [20] studies cyberbullying and toxic behaviors

in team competition online games in an effort to detect, prevent, and counter-act toxic behavior. [12] investigates the prevalence of sexism in online game communities finding personality traits, demographic variables, and levels of game-play predicted sexist attitudes towards women who play video games. Overall, previous work considers various attributes to distinguish between normal and abusive behavior, like text-based attributes, e.g., URLs and Bag of Words (BoW), lexicon-based (offensive word dictionary), or user/activity based attributes, e.g., number of friends/followers and users' account age. Our work aims to use such attributes to study and understand the different behavioral patterns between random and Gamergate Twitter users, while shedding light on how such differences affect their suspension and deletion rates on Twitter.

Analysis of Gamergate. To create an abuse-related dataset, i.e., a dataset containing abusive behavior with high probability, previous works rely on a number of words (i.e., seed words) which are highly related with the manifestation of abusive/aggressive events. In this sense, a popular term that can serve as a seed word is the #GamerGate hashtag which is one of the most well documented large-scale instances of bullying/aggressive behavior we are aware of [22]. The Gamergate controversy stemmed from alleged improprieties in video game journalism, which quickly grew into a larger campaign centered around sexism and social justice. With individuals on both sides of the controversy using it, and extreme cases of bullying and aggressive behavior associated with it (e.g., direct threats of rape and murder), #GamerGate can serve as a relatively unambiguous hashtag associated with texts that are likely to involve abusive/aggressive behavior from a fairly mature, hateful online community. In [23], the author shows that #GamerGate can be likened to hooliganism, i.e., a leisure-centered aggression were fans are organized in groups to attack another group's members. Also, [13] aims to detect toxicity on Twitter, considering #Gamer-Gate to collect a sufficient number of harassment-related posts. In this paper, we also study a number of abusive users involved in this controversy via #GamerGate. However, we are the first to investigate the attributes characterizing these users with respect to their Twitter account status (active, suspended, deleted), and to perform an unsupervised and supervised analysis of suspicious users for possible suspension.

3 DATASET

In this section, we present the data used throughout the rest of the paper, as well as the two prepocessing steps: spam removal and dataset cleaning.

3.1 Data Collection

The data used in the next sections were collected between June and August 2016 using the Twitter Streaming API [34] which gives access to 1% of all tweets. Data returned from the Twitter API include either user-related info, e.g., users' follower/friends count, total number of posted, liked and favorited tweets, or text-related, e.g., the text itself, hashtags, mentions, etc. Here, two sets of tweets were gathered: (i) a *baseline* dataset with $1M$ random tweets, and (ii) a *Gamergate*-related dataset with $650k$ tweets.

Gamergate dataset. To build a dataset containing an adequate number of bullying / aggressive instances, we initially selected

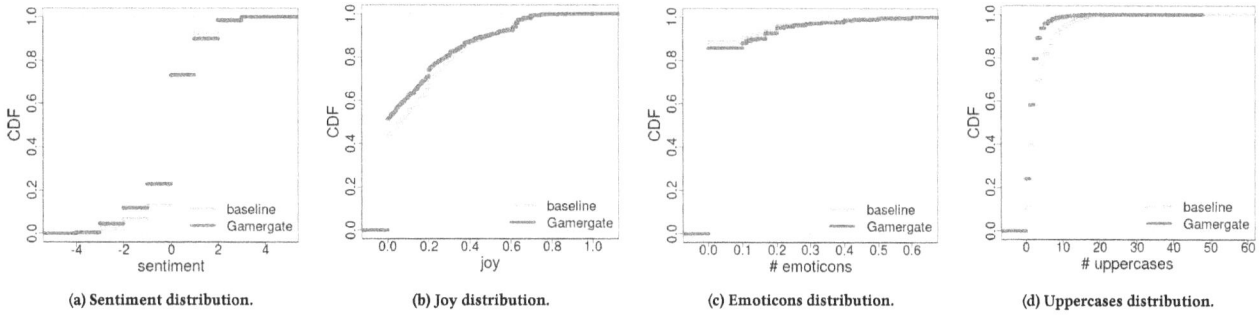

Figure 1: Average CDF distribution of (a) Sentiment, (b) Joy, (c) Emoticons, (d) Uppercases in baseline and Gamergate datasets.

#GamerGate as a seed word. From the 1% sample of public tweets, we selected only those containing this seed word and performed a snowball sampling of other hashtags likely associated with abusive behavior. Thus, we included tweets which contained hashtags that appeared in the same tweets as #GamerGate (the keywords list was updated on a daily basis - more details about the data collection process can be found in our previous work [4]). Overall, we collected 308 hashtags during the data collection period. After a manual examination of these hashtags, we verified that they indeed contain a number of abusive words or hashtags, e.g., #InternationalOffendAFeministDay, #IStandWithHateSpeech, and #KillAllNiggers.

Baseline (random) dataset. To compare the hate-related dataset with cases which are less prone to contain abusive content, and for the same time period, we also crawled a random sample of $1M$ tweets which serve as a baseline.

3.2 Preprocessing

Next, we focus on the tasks performed to make our data suitable for analysis, cleaning text, and removing noise, and dealing with other erroneous data.

Cleaning. We remove stop words, numbers, and punctuation marks. Also, we normalize text by eliminating repetitive characters which users often use to express their feelings with more intensity (e.g., the word 'hellooo' is converted to 'hello'). Users tend to add extra vowels in words to show emphasis or intense emotion. So, based on such an assumption, initially we remove all the duplicate vowels (only when they are above 2) of a word, if any. Then, we check for the existence of the "new" word in the Wikipedia database. Such process is repeated for all the possible combinations when more than one vowels is duplicate. If none of the "new" words is available in the Wikipedia database, we keep the initial one.

Spam removal. Even though extensive work has been done on spam detection in social media, e.g., [31, 36], Twitter is still plagued by spam accounts [6]. Two main indications of spam behavior are [36]: (i) the large number of hashtags within a user's posts, as it permits the broader broadcast of such posts, and (ii) the population of large amounts of (almost) similar posts. Based on the 2-month dataset collected from Twitter, the distributions of hashtags and duplications of posts are examined to detect the cutoff-limit above

which a user will be characterized as spammer and consequently will be removed from the dataset.

Hashtags. Studying the hashtags distribution, we observe that users use on average 0 to 17 hashtags. Building on this, we examine various cuttoffs to select a proper one above which we can characterize a user as spammer. In the end, after a manual inspection we observed that in most of the cases where the number of hashtags was 5 or more, the text was mostly related to inappropriate content. So, the limit of 5 hashtags is used, and consequently we remove those users that have more than 5 hashtags on average in their tweets.

Duplications. In many cases a user's texts are (almost) the same, with only the listed mentioned users modified. So, in addition to the previously mentioned cleaning processes, we also remove all mentions. Then, to estimate the similarity of a user's posts we proceed with the Levenshtein distance [24] which counts the minimum number of single-character edits needed to convert one string into another, averaging it out over all pairs of their tweets. Initially, for each user we calculate their intra-tweets similarity. Thus, for a user with x tweets, we arrive at a set of n similarity scores, where $n = x(x-1)/2$, and an average intra-tweet similarity per user. Then, all users with average intra-tweets similarity above 0.8 (about 5%) are excluded from the dataset.

4 COMPARING GAMERGATERS WITH TYPICAL USERS

In this section, we compare the baseline and GG-related dataset across two dimensions, considering emotional and activity attributes.

4.1 Emotional characteristics of Gamergaters

Sentiment. To detect sentiment, we use the SentiStrength tool [30], which estimates the positive and negative sentiment (on a [-4, 4] scale) in short texts. Figure 1a plots the CDF of sentiment of tweets for the two datasets. We note that around 25% of tweets are positive for both types of users. However, GGers post tweets with a generally more negative sentiment (a two-sample Kolmogorov-Smirnov test rejects the null hypothesis with $D = 0.101$, $p < 0.01$). In particular, around 25% of GG tweets are negative compared to only around 15% for baseline users. This observation is in line with the GG dataset containing a large number of offensive posts.

Emotions. We also extract the sentiment values for six emotions using a similar approach to [5]: anger, disgust, fear, joy, sadness,

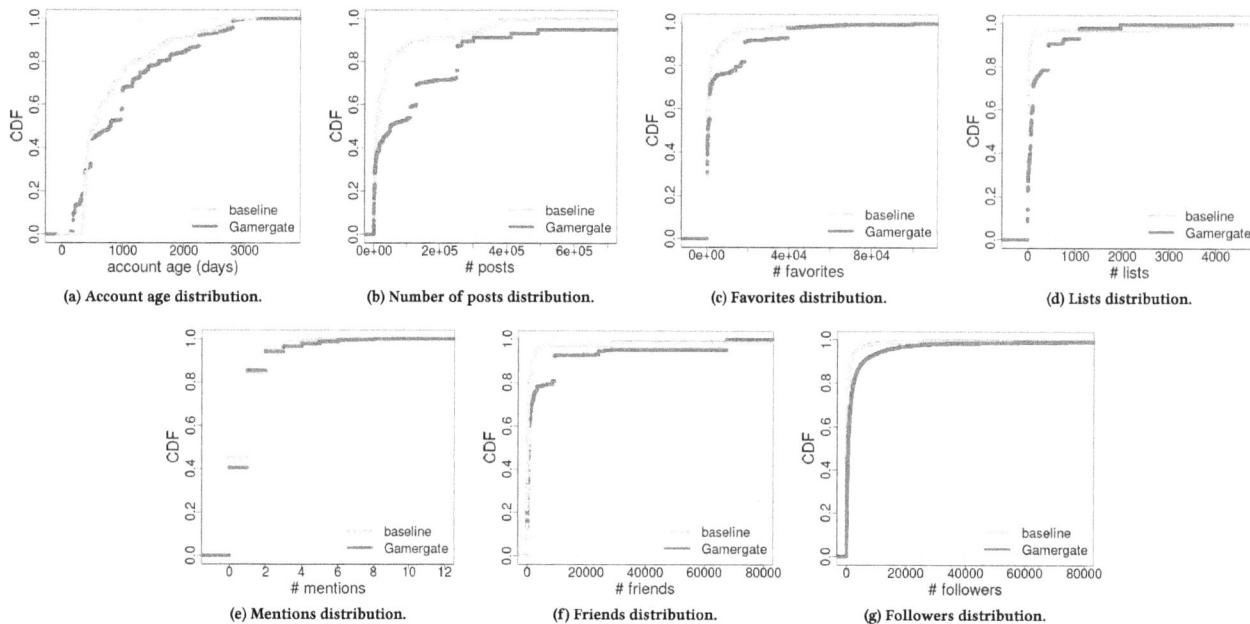

Figure 2: CDF distribution of (a) Account age, (b) Number of Posts, (c) Favorites, (d) Lists, (e) Mentions, (f) Friends, (g) Followers.

and surprise which, based on Ekman et al. [11], are considered as *primary* emotions. Also known as basic, they are a fixed number of emotions which we experience instantly as a response to a pleasant (or unpleasant) stimulus. Figure 1b shows the CDF of joy, where we reject the null hypothesis that the two distributions are the same ($D = 0.089$, $p < 0.01$). We are *unable* to reject the null hypothesis for the other five primary emotions. This is particularly interesting because it contradicts the narrative that GGers are posting virulent content out of anger. Instead, GGers appear to be less joyful. This is a subtle but important difference: GGers are not necessarily angry, but they are apparently less happy.

Offensive. Looking a bit deeper, we compare the offensiveness score that tweets have been marked with according to the hatebase (HB) [15] crowdsourced dictionary. Each word included in HB is scored on a [0, 100] scale which indicates how hateful it is. Though the visual difference is small, GGers use more hateful words than a baseline user ($D = 0.006$, $p < 0.01$).

Emoticons and Uppercase. Two common ways to express emotion in social media are emoticons and "shouting" by using all capital letters. Based on the nature of GG, we initially suspected that there would be a relatively small amount of emoticon usage, but many tweets that would be shouting in all uppercase letters. However, as we can see in Figures 1c and 1d, which plot the CDF of the average number (per user) of emoticon usage and all uppercase tweets, respectively, this is not the case. GG and baseline users tend to use emoticons similarly (we are unable to reject the null hypothesis with $D = 0.028$ and $p = 0.96$). However, GGers tend to use all uppercase *less* than baseline users ($D = 0.212$, $p < 0.01$). As seen previously, GGers are quite savvy Twitter users, and generally speaking, shouting tends to be ignored. Thus, one explanation is that GGers avoid such a simple "tell" as posting in all uppercase to ensure their message is not so easily dismissed.

4.2 Activity characteristics of Gamergaters

Account age. An underlying question about GG is what started first: participants' use of Twitter or their participation in the controversy. I.e., did Gamergate draw people to Twitter, or were Twitter users drawn to Gamergate? Figure 2a plots the distribution of account age for GG participants and baseline Twitter users. For the most part, GGers tend to have older accounts than baseline Twitter users ($D = 0.20142$, $p < 0.01$, $mean = 982.94$ days, $median = 788$ days, $STD = 772.49$ days). The mean, median, and STD values for the baseline users are 834.39, 522, and 652.42 days, respectively. Overall, the oldest account in our dataset belongs to a GG user, while only 26.64% of baseline users have account ages older than the mean value of the GGers. The figure indicates that GG users were existing Twitter users that were drawn to the controversy. In fact, their familiarity with Twitter could be the reason that GG exploded in the first place.

Posts, Favorites, and Lists. Figure 2b plots the distribution of the number of tweets made by GGers and baseline users. GGers are significantly more active than baseline Twitter users ($D = 0.352$, $p < 0.01$). The mean, median and STD values for the GG (random) users is 135, 618 (49, 342), 48, 587 (9, 429), and 185, 997 (97, 457) posts, respectively. Figures 2c and 2d show the CDFs of favorites and lists declared in users' profiles. We note that in the median case, GGers are similar to baseline users, but looking at the 30% of users in the tail of each distribution, GG users have more favorites and lists than baseline users.

Mentions. Figure 2e shows that GGers tend to make more mentions within their posts, which can be due to the higher number of direct attacks in contrast to the baseline users.

Followers and Friends. GGers are involved in what we would typically think of as anti-social behavior. However, this is somewhat at odds with the fact that their activity takes place primarily on social media. To get an idea of how "social" GGers are, Figures 2f and 2g plot the distribution of friends and followers for GGers and baseline users. We observe that GGers tend to have more friends and followers than baseline twitter users ($D = 0.34$ and 0.39, $p < 0.01$ for both). Although this result might be initially counter-intuitive, the truth of the matter is that GG was born on social media, and is a very clear "us vs. them" situation. This leads to easy identification of in-group membership, and thus heightens the likelihood of relationship formation.

5 SUSPENSION OF GAMERGATE ACCOUNTS BY TWITTER

In the previous section, we studied users involved in the GG controversy and identified attributes that distinguish them from random Twitter users, either regarding the way they write tweets and the sentiment they carry, or their embeddedness in the Twitter social network. In fact, we found that GGers post tweets that are more negative, less joyful, and more hateful or offensive. However, we also observed that such users have more friends and followers, more posting and dissemination activity (via hashtags and mentions). From this clearly distinctive behavior, what remains unclear is how these users are handled by Twitter.

To shed more light on this aspect, in the next sections, we examine further the GGers by introducing a new factor characterizing each one: their Twitter account status. In particular, we investigate the following questions:

- What is the twitter account status and how do we measure it? What does it imply for a user and what is the breakdown for different statuses between GGers and random users (§ 5.1)?
- What are the characteristics of suspended users and users who deleted their Twitter account (§ 5.2)?
- What are the characteristics of users who remain active on Twitter, but should have been suspended (§ 5.3)?
- Can we emulate the Twitter account suspension mechanism (§ 5.4)?

Methodology. To answer these questions, we analyze users on features presented in the previous section, under the following two general categories:

- *emotional attributes*: sentiment, 6 emotions (anger, disgust, fear, joy, sadness, surprise), offensive words, uppercases, emoticons;
- *activity attributes*: account age, number of posts, user participating lists, mentions, followers and friends count.

We apply unsupervised and supervised methods to validate that these features are useful to study and compare their distributions to identify differences between types of users and account statuses.

5.1 Status of Gamergate Accounts on Twitter

A Twitter user can be in one of the following three statuses: (i) *active*, (ii) *deleted*, or (iii) *suspended*. Typically, Twitter suspends an account (temporarily or even permanently, in some cases) if it has been hijacked/compromised, is considered spam/fake, or if it is *abusive* [1]. A user account is *deleted* if the user himself, for his own personal reasons, deactivates his account.

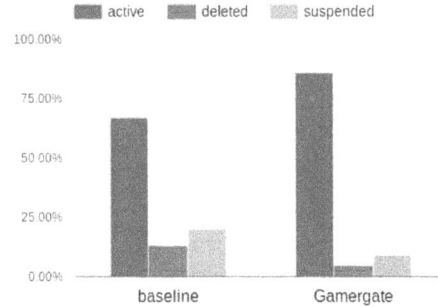

Figure 3: Distribution of baseline and GG users in Twitter statuses.

In order to examine the differences between these three statuses in relation to the GGers and baseline users, we selected a 10% random sample of $33k$ users from both the GG ($5k$) and baseline ($28k$) users to check their Twitter status, one month after the initial data collection. The status of each user's account was checked using a mechanism that queried the Twitter API for each user, and examined the error code responses returned: code 63 corresponds to a suspended user account and code 50 corresponds to a deleted one.

From Figure 3 we observe that both categories of users tend to be suspended rather than deleting their accounts by choice. However, baseline users are more prone to suspension (20%) and deletion (13%) of their accounts, in contrast to the GGers (9% and 5%, respectively). The higher number of the suspended and deleted accounts of the baseline users in comparison to GGers is in accordance with the behavior observed in Figure 2a which shows that the GGers have been in the platform for a longer period than baseline users, meaning they *appear* to be more compliant to Twitter rules.

Nevertheless, this disproportional rate of suspensions for random users with respect to GGers remains a surprising find. Given our previous observations on their posting behavior, it is unexpected that several of such users are allowed to continue posting tweets. Indeed, a small portion of these users may be spammers who are difficult to detect and filter out. That said, Twitter has made significant efforts in addressing spam accounts and we suspect there is a higher presence of such accounts in the baseline dataset, since the GG dataset is more hyper-focused around a somewhat niche topic.

These efforts are less apparent when it comes to the bullying and aggressive behavior phenomena observed on Twitter in general, e.g., [28, 33], and in our present study of GG users, in particular. However, recently, Twitter has increased its efforts to combat the existing harassment cases, for instance, by preventing suspended users from creating new accounts [26], or temporarily limiting users for abusive behavior [32]. Such efforts constitute initial steps to deal with the ongoing war among the abusers, their victims, and online bystanders. Next, we further analyze the available data to identify metrics that can provide explanations for understanding the Twitter suspension mechanism.

5.2 Who is suspended and who is deleted?

To understand how suspended and deleted users differ, here we compare each of these user statuses for both GG and baseline users considering the previously described dimensions, i.e., their emotional and activity based profiles.

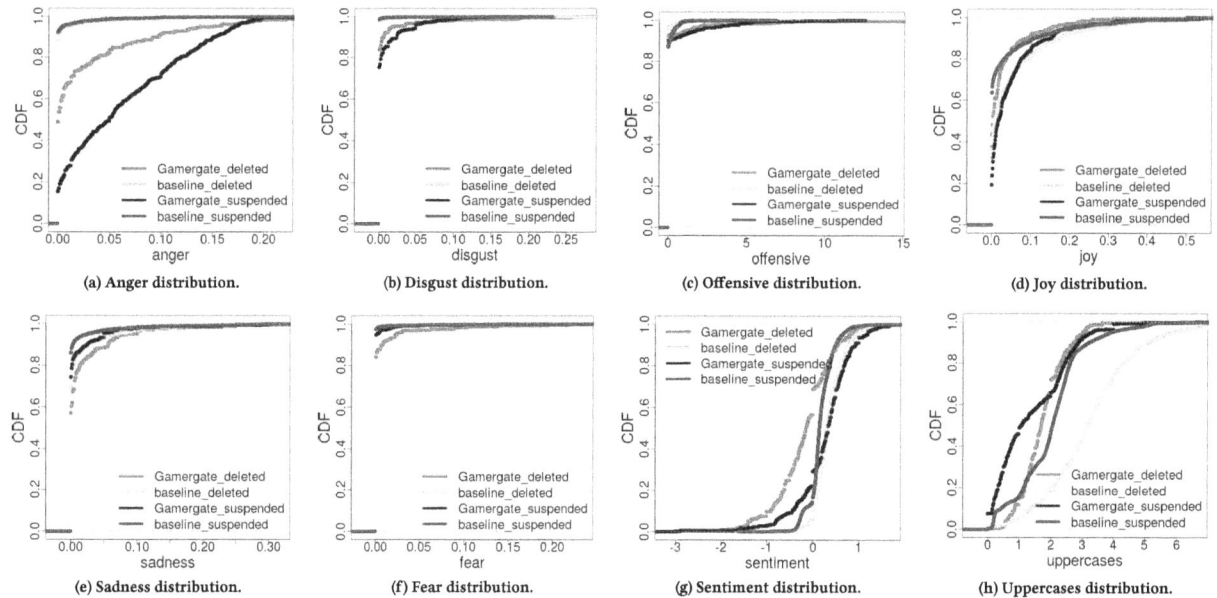

Figure 4: CDF plots for the suspended and deleted users considering the emotional attributes: (a) Anger, (b) Disgust, (c) Offensive, (d) Joy, (e) Sadness, (f) Fear, (g) Sentiment, (h) Uppercases.

Since users are suspended because their activity violates Twitter rules, and with the assumption that this detection system is consistent across users, we would expect GGers and baseline users to present similar behavior, or in some cases, we would expect GGers to be more extreme than baseline users. On the other hand, users who delete their accounts could present a variety of behavioral attributes, as this decision is *user-based*; i.e., there is a large number of confounding factors as to why the user decided to delete his account. Based on Figures 4 and 5, we observe that there are substantial differences among the suspended baseline users and GGers, and the deleted baseline and GGers.

Sentiment, Emotions, and Offensive language. Concerning the emotional and sentiment attributes, we observe different behaviors. For instance Figures 4a, 4b, and 4c show that suspended GGers are expressing more aggressive ($D = 0.76$, $p < 0.01$) and repulsive ($D = 0.23$, $p < 0.01$) emotions, and offensive language (use of hate words), in comparison to suspended baseline users. Interestingly, suspended GGers also post more joyful tweets (Figure 4d, $D = 0.44$ and $p < 0.01$), and even though 30% of them post more negative sentiment tweets than baseline users, the rest of the suspended GGers are more positive than baseline suspended users (Figure 4g, $D = 0.29$ and $p < 0.01$). The posting of more aggressive and joyful tweets from suspended GGers contradicts the behavior observed earlier when studying the overall dataset of GGers (i.e., regardless of account status) which implies that such a deviation from the norm could be a reason for suspension. Since extreme aggression, negative, and offensive language is abusive behavior, we would expect higher suspension rates for the GGers than baseline users.

In a similar fashion, we look at the deleted GGers and observe that they exhibit higher anger in their posted tweets than the deleted baseline users (Figure 4a, $D = 0.39$ and $p < 0.01$), but lower than the suspended GGers. They exhibit less joy (Figure 4d, $D = 0.14$

and $p < 0.01$), but more sadness (Figure 4e, $D = 0.15$, and $p < 0.01$) and fear (Figure 4f, $D = 0.13$ and $p < 0.01$) than the deleted baseline users and suspended GGers. On the other hand, they tweet with sentiment which is more negative than suspended GGers and deleted baseline users (Figure 4g, $D = 0.58$ and $p < 0.01$). Finally, they type less in all uppercase than deleted baseline users (Figure 4h, $D = 0.56$ and $p < 0.01$), but more than suspended GGers. Based on these observations and in accordance with the higher expression of fear, it seems that deleted GGers are more emotionally introverted users, and might be deleting their accounts to protect themselves from negative behaviors/attention.

Age, Followers, and Friends. As far as the activity patterns, Figure 5 shows that suspended and deleted GGers are more active overall than baseline users. In particular, we observe (Figure 5a) that users who delete their accounts (GGers or baseline), have been on the platform longer than suspended users ($D = 0.51$, $p < 0.01$). Surprisingly, for the limited amount of time their account was active, suspended GGers managed to become more popular and thus have more followers (Figures 5b) and friends (Figure 5c) than the suspended baseline users ($D = 0.64$ and 0.60, $p < 0.01$ for both comparisons) and deleted GGers and baseline users. The fact that the deleted users (GGers or baseline) have fewer friends and followers than suspended GGers, implies they have less support from their social network. On the contrary, high popularity for suspended GGers could have helped them attract and create additional activity on Twitter and could be a reason for delaying the suspension of such highly engaging, and even inflammatory, users.

Posts, Lists, and Favorites. Figures 5d, 5e, and 5f show the distribution of the number of posts, lists, and favorites, respectively, made by suspended GGers and baseline users, as well as deleted users. Overall, we observe suspended GGers to be more active than baseline users, with more posts, higher participation in lists, and

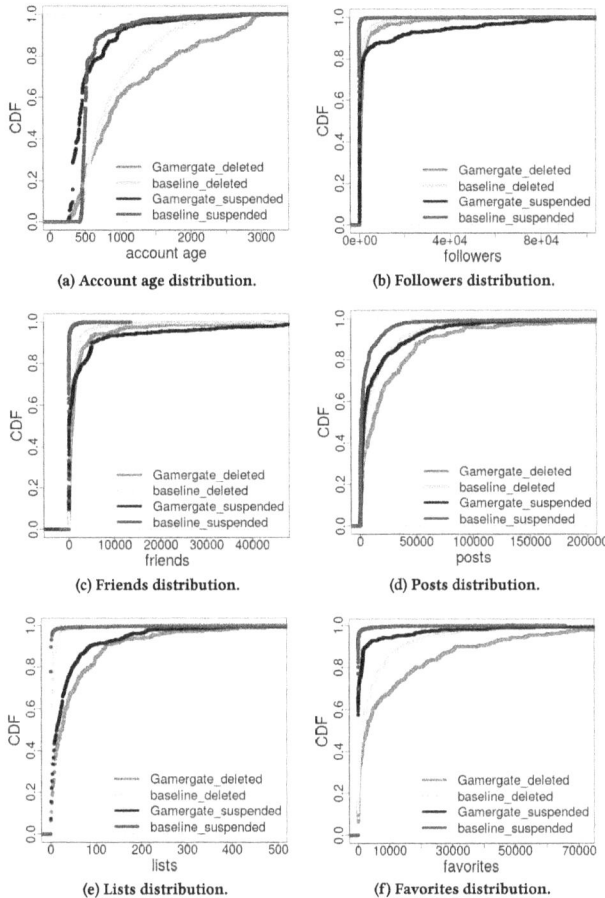

Figure 5: CDF plots for the suspended and deleted users considering activity attributes: (a) Account age, (b) Followers, (c) Friends, (d) Posts, (e) Lists, (f) Favorites.

more tweets favorited ($D = 0.24$, $D = 0.74$, $D = 0.27$, $p < 0.01$ for all comparisons). However, deleted GGers exhibit the highest activity in comparison to deleted baseline users ($D = 0.18$, $D = 0.58$, $D = 0.17$, $p < 0.01$ for all comparisons) as well as compared to suspended GGers.

Overall, deleted GGers appear to have been very active prior to their account deletion, have exhibited signs of distress and fear, and have shown, through their high posting activity, their anger, reduced joy, and negative sentiment. However, their social network (ego-network of friends and followers) was either unsupportive, or just too small to provide the emotional support needed to block verbal attacks and aggression by other users who were involved in the GG controversy, and this overall hostile environment may have led them to delete their accounts. Suspended users, however, managed to become highly popular in the platform in a short period of time and probably engaged in bullying and aggressive behaviors intense enough to lead to their suspension.

5.3 Who should be suspended?

In the previous paragraphs, we analyzed the behavior of GGers and baseline users, and compared them with respect to the status

of their accounts (active, deleted, and suspended). Furthermore, we observed that an important portion of the GGers remains active despite exhibiting, in some cases, abnormal behavior. Here, we organize users in groups to understand what homogeneity or commonalities users have, e.g., if they all tweet with many hate words, negative sentiment, or anger. By studying the heterogeneity of the identified groups, we then mark any diversity that users exhibit, and examine whether such a diversity could justify Twitter's tolerance against their abnormal behavior.

To group users who are highly similar over the available features studied, we use an unsupervised clustering method. After the clustering task, we label the top 3 groupings created that cover the majority of users under a specific status. We also investigate if the remaining clusters could be used to classify more users under the suspended status.

Clustering approach. Initially we extract both emotional and activity related attributes for the $33k$ users and proceed with a clustering process (separately on baseline and GG users, since we have seen a totally different behavior) in order to understand the commonalities behind Twitter's different statuses. We use K-means [21], an unsupervised learning algorithm, where each user in the dataset is associated to the nearest cluster centroid out of the K clusters in total. Each user x is assigned to a cluster considering its distance from the K cluster centroids C as follows: $\text{argmin}_{c_i \in C} \, dist(c_i, x)^2$. In our case, $dist$ is the standard squared Euclidean distance in the N-dimensions used. When all users are assigned to a cluster, the algorithm proceeds with a re-calculation of the K new cluster centroids and a new binding of users to the nearest new centroids is made. The re-calculation of the clusters' centroids is done by taking the mean value of the feature vector for users included in that centroid's cluster. This process is completed when no change in cluster membership is observed, or a maximum number of iterations is reached.

Detecting the optimal number of clusters. In K-means the number of clusters to be extracted should be known a priori. To find an appropriate number of clusters, one can run the K-means clustering algorithm for a range of K values and compare the results with respect to compactness of clusters and distance between centroids. A more sophisticated approach is to build upon the Expectation-maximization algorithm (EM) [14] which identifies naturally occurring clusters. The EM algorithm is an efficient method to estimate the maximum likelihood in the presence of missing or hidden data. Thus, given some observed data y, the EM algorithm attempts to find the parameters θ that maximize the probability:$\theta = \text{argmax}_\theta \, logp(y|\theta)$. Then, for the unobserved or missing data x, we estimate θ that maximizes the likelihood, l, of x: $l(\theta) = \sum_x p(x, y; \theta)$.

Clustering tendency of Gamergaters. Considering the GG users based on the EM algorithm, we ended up with 3 clusters for the emotional attributes and 8 clusters for the activity-related attributes. We see that some clusters are "easily" labeled due to the majority of users being one type of status. Table 1 (Table 2) shows the distribution of the GGers in the 3 (8) clusters which have been characterized as either active, deleted, or suspended using the Twitter status, and considering the emotional (activity)-based attributes. As the GG

Status ->	Cluster	# active	# deleted	# suspended
active	1	2,429	139	135
deleted	2	258	11	33
suspended	3	1,615	87	260

Table 1: Distribution of GG users in 3 clusters and the assigned label based on majority participation (emotional-related features).

Status ->	Cluster	# active	# deleted	# suspended
active	1	825	11	5
deleted	2	66	125	8
suspended	3	440	18	324
	4	57	0	1
	5	757	27	56
	6	692	11	5
	7	725	32	22
	8	740	13	7

Table 2: Distribution of GG users in 8 clusters and the assigned label based on majority participation (activity-related features).

Status->	Cluster	# active	# deleted	# suspended
active	1	4,999	1,501	658
deleted	2	1,984	392	439
suspended	3	4,200	690	3,832
	4	3,333	373	134
	5	1,308	358	120
	6	1,030	169	162
	7	1,525	133	257
	8	433	85	71

Table 3: Distribution of baseline users in 8 clusters and the assigned label based on majority participation (emotional-related features).

Status->	Cluster	# active	# deleted	# suspended
active	1	6,885	1,121	651
deleted	2	882	1,124	63
suspended	3	4,942	574	3,765
	4	1,580	156	74
	5	2,733	594	78
	6	858	51	51
	7	142	24	2
	8	787	57	989

Table 4: Distribution of baseline users in 8 clusters and the assigned label based on majority participation (activity-related features).

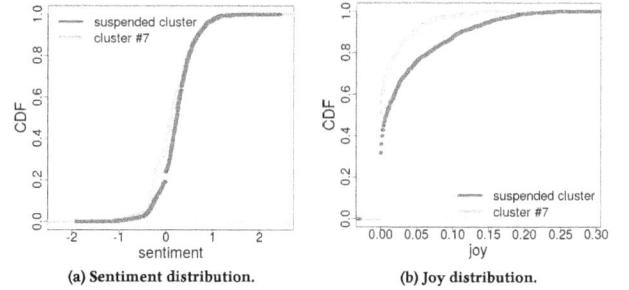

(a) Sentiment distribution.   (b) Joy distribution.

Figure 6: CDF plots of baseline users for the suspended and an unnamed cluster considering the emotional attributes: (a) Sentiment, (b) Joy.

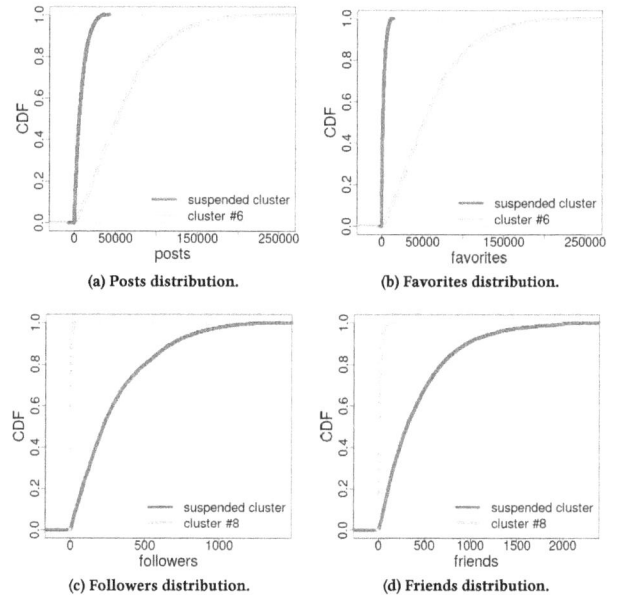

(a) Posts distribution.   (b) Favorites distribution.

(c) Followers distribution.   (d) Friends distribution.

Figure 7: CDF plots of baseline users for the suspended and an unnamed cluster considering the activity attributes: (a) Posts, (b) Favorites, (c) Followers, (d) Friends.

dataset tends to contain a larger proportion of bullying and aggressive behavior phenomena, one would expect that based on the emotional-related features, the clustering results would be in better accordance to the Twitter status labels. However, we observe that using the activity-related features results in those clusters better matching the Twitter applied status labels.

Clustering tendency for baseline users. We now perform the same analysis on the baseline users, looking for any differences of the suspension mechanism from GGers. Here, the EM algorithm converged on 8 clusters for *both* the emotional and activity-related attributes. Tables 3 and 4 show these distributions, respectively. We observe that for both feature sets, the cluster assigned the suspended label is clearly distinct, with substantially more users as members. Deleted users are harder to fit: they do not seem to be primarily present in a single cluster, however, the activity-based features do seem to better cluster them. This indicates that further analysis on deleted users should be conducted.

In general, and as expected, the clustering is not perfect in either of the two datasets: the clusters are fairly diverse with respect to users from the three statuses. This is mainly because of two reasons: (i) the majority of users are active and since they exhibit a wide range of behaviors, they would be included in various clusters, (ii) some of these active users should probably be suspended, but the suspension mechanism failed to detect them. Such users should

be placed under evaluation for possible suspension. To this end, we study the properties of the users included in each of the unnamed clusters (in emotional or activity-based clusterings), for baseline and GG users, and propose clusters which could be considered candidate for suspending users.

For instance, studying the unlabeled clusters of Table 2, there is the cluster #5 (with 757 active, 27 deleted, and 56 suspended users) where GGers show similar activity patterns to those of the suspended cluster indicating that there are active users who could be possible candidates for suspension. These users are similar to those of the suspended cluster: their accounts are pretty old and exhibit intense activity in terms of tweet posting (*mean* $= 23,664$, *median* $= 17,510$). Also, they show similar patterns in terms of the favorited tweets and lists with the GGers of the suspended cluster. Quite suspicious is the unlabeled cluster #7 with $1,525$ active, 133 deleted, and 257 suspended users in Table 3: the cluster members show signs of negative behavior by using offensive language and negativity in their tweets (Figure 6a) and lower levels of joy (Figure 6b).

Another unnamed cluster (#6) which could be flagged as suspicious for suspension is the one with 858 active, 51 deleted, and suspended users in Table 4. Here, both the suspended and #6 clusters show similar activity in terms of list participation. Quite interestingly, even though users in these clusters tend to have similar account age on Twitter, there are important differences in the number of their posted (Figure 7a) and favorited (Figure 7b) tweets. Such a disproportionality in the number of posted/favorited tweets (i.e., quite increased activity) and their lifetime on Twitter could be an indication of spam users. Finally, focusing again on the same set of clusters (Table 4), cluster #8 shows abnormal and consequently suspicious behavior. The majority of its users have been suspended, but it also includes a lot of active users. If we compare the popularity of users in cluster #8 with the users from the suspended cluster, we find the suspended cluster users being more popular in terms of their followers (Figure 7c) and friends (Figure 7d). However, the users in cluster #8 have posted a relatively large number of tweets (the mean and standard deviation values are 547.15 and 640.63, respectively), considering their short lifetime. Such "strange" behavior could be indicative of spammer accounts.

5.4 Emulating the suspension engine

Having gained an overview of the homogeneity or commonalities users have in accordance to their Twitter status, here we investigate if the features we have analyzed so far are meaningful and correlated with account statuses, and more importantly, if they can be used to automatically classify users. To this end, we perform a supervised classification task using the three statuses as labels in an attempt to emulate the Twitter suspension engine. We study the two types of users (GGers and baseline users) separately to understand if such features are more predictive of one or the other.

For the classification task, we test several tree-based algorithms as we find them to perform best (J48, LADTree, LMT, NBTree, Random Forest (RF), and Functional Tree). Overall, tree-based classifiers are built from three types of nodes: (i) the *root* node, with no incoming edges, (ii) the *internal* nodes, with just one incoming edge and two or more outgoing edges, and (iii) the *leaf* node, with one incoming edge and no outgoing edges. The root and internal nodes correspond to feature test conditions that separate data based on their characteristics, while the leaf nodes correspond to the available classes. In the end, we select RF [27], as it achieved the best results with respect to time for training without overfitting

	Prec.	Rec.	ROC		Prec.	Rec.	ROC
active	0.898	0.982	0.747	active	0.937	0.973	0.886
deleted	0.667	0.008	0.550	deleted	0.725	0.489	0.804
suspended	0.669	0.407	0.865	suspended	0.742	0.591	0.925
overall (avg.)	0.867	0.886	0.747	overall (avg.)	0.910	0.917	0.886
(a) Emotional-related features				(b) Activity-related features			

Table 5: Classification results based on the GG dataset.

	Prec.	Rec.	ROC		Prec.	Rec.	ROC
active	0.756	0.946	0.742	active	0.806	0.943	0.826
deleted	0.197	0.022	0.674	deleted	0.570	0.248	0.806
suspended	0.803	0.598	0.882	suspended	0.892	0.718	0.937
overall (avg.)	0.692	0.755	0.761	overall (avg.)	0.792	0.807	0.846
(a) Emotional-related features				(b) Activity-related features			

Table 6: Classification results based on baseline dataset.

the dataset. We test the two categories of features (emotional and activity-based) separately, as well as combined. Based on Tables 5 and 6 in both the GG and baseline datasets, we observe that by considering the activity-related features, the precision, recall, and ROC (weighted area under the ROC curve) values are always higher at both the class level and overall across classes. Adding all features together the scores are a little better than the emotional-related features (omitted due to space).

We remark that this classification task is not ideal for two main reasons: (i) we only use a subset of data and extract a subset of features from the ones that Twitter has available for making decisions with its status mechanism, and (ii) we only use a fairly simple, but robust, classification algorithm to attempt this task. We suspect that Twitter computes many more features per user to assess their behavior, as well as using highly sophisticated algorithms for user suspension. However, given these caveats, we show that it is possible to approximate the status mechanism, and perform very well with respect to standard machine learning metrics: we achieve $0.7 - 0.91$ precision, $0.76 - 0.92$ recall, and $0.75 - 0.89$ ROC. From these preliminary results, we conclude that our features are meaningful in studying such user behaviors, and probably useful in detecting what status a user should be given by Twitter.

6 DISCUSSION AND CONCLUSION

In this paper we have performed a large-scale comparative study of abusive accounts on Twitter, aiming to understand their characteristics and how they differ from regular accounts. Specifically, we focused on a Twitter dataset revolving around the Gamergate controversy which led to many incidents of cyberbullying and cyberaggression on various gaming and social media platforms. We studied the properties of users tweeting about GG, the content they post, and the differences in their behavior compared to typical Twitter users. We found that users involved in this controversy were existing Twitter users that were probably drawn to the controversy. In fact, their familiarity with Twitter could be the reason that GG exploded in the first place. We also discovered that while the subject of their tweets is seemingly aggressive and hateful, GGers do not exhibit common expressions of online anger, and in fact primarily differ from typical users in that their tweets are less joyful. This aligns with the viewpoint of the GG supporters who claim that they never agreed to the aggressive methods used in this campaign [23], which can result in a confusing expression of anger manifestation. GGers tend to be organized in groups, and in fact they participate also in face-to-face meetings to create stronger bonds, which also reflects on the higher number of followers and friends they have in relation to typical users, despite their seemingly anti-social behavior. Also, we discover that GGers are seemingly more engaged than typical Twitter users, which is an indication as to how and why this controversy is still ongoing.

To better understand how these abusive users are handled by Twitter, we performed an in-depth analysis of the status of accounts posting about GG and typical Twitter users. Surprisingly, we found that GGers are disproportionally *not suspended* with respect to random users, which is rather unexpected given their hateful and aggressive postings. Therefore, we investigated users' properties with respect to their account status to understand what may have led to suspension of some of them, but not all of them. Even though suspended GGers are expressing more aggressive and repulsive emotions, and offensive language than random users, they tend to become more popular and more active in terms of their posted tweets. This popularity could be the reason for the delayed suspension from the Twitter mechanism, a situation that seems to have changed lately, considering the new actions taken by Twitter itself, e.g., [26, 32].

We also studied the GG users who deleted their account. These users demonstrate the highest activity in comparison to other users (deleted or suspended). Overall, such deleted users exhibit signs of distress, fear, and sadness, and have probably showed these emotions through their high posting activity filled with anger, reduced joy, and negative sentiment. We also found that such users have small social ego-networks, which may have been unsupportive or too small to help them deal with aggressive attacks by other GGers before deleting their account.

Finally, we performed an unsupervised machine learning analysis to detect clusters of users who, though currently active, could be considered for suspension as they exhibit similar behaviors with already suspended users. Our findings are a first step towards understanding better, and at large-scale, the behavior of abusive users in online social media such as Twitter, their victims and what may have led them to delete their account, and propose supervised methods to detect suspicious users whose accounts should be evaluated for suspension. As part of future work, we plan to perform a more in-depth study of the Gamergate controversy and further compare it with other organized groups that exhibit online aggressive and abusive behaviors.

7 ACKNOWLEDGEMENT

This research has been fully funded by the European Commission as part of the ENCASE project (H2020-MSCA-RISE of the European Union under GA number 691025).

REFERENCES

[1] About suspended accounts 2017. goo.gl/byStB8. (2017).
[2] Fabricio Benevenuto, Gabriel Magno, Tiago Rodrigues, and Virgilio Almeida. 2010. Detecting spammers on Twitter. In *CEAS*, Vol. 6.
[3] Despoina Chatzakou, Nicolas Kourtellis, Jeremy Blackburn, Emiliano De Cristofaro, Gianluca Stringhini, and Athena Vakali. 2017. Mean Birds: Detecting Aggression and Bullying on Twitter. In *WebSci*.
[4] Despoina Chatzakou, Nicolas Kourtellis, Jeremy Blackburn, Emiliano De Cristofaro, Gianluca Stringhini, and Athena Vakali. 2017. Measuring #GamerGate: A Tale of Hate, Sexism, and Bullying. In *WWW Companion*.
[5] Despoina Chatzakou, Vassiliki Koutsonikola, Athena Vakali, and Konstantinos Kafetsios. 2013. Micro-blogging Content Analysis via Emotionally-Driven Clustering. In *ACII*.
[6] Chao Chen, Jun Zhang, Xiao Chen, Yang Xiang, and Wanlei Zhou. 2015. 6 million spam tweets: A large ground truth for timely Twitter spam detection. In *IEEE ICC*.
[7] Ying Chen, Yilu Zhou, Sencun Zhu, and Heng Xu. 2012. Detecting Offensive Language in Social Media to Protect Adolescent Online Safety. In *PASSAT and SocialCom*.
[8] Maral Dadvar, Dolf Trieschnigg, and Franciska Jong. 2014. Experts and machines against bullies: A hybrid approach to detect cyberbullies. In *Canadian AI*.
[9] Karthik Dinakar, Roi Reichart, and Henry Lieberman. 2011. Modeling the detection of Textual Cyberbullying. *The Social Mobile Web* 11 (2011).
[10] Nemanja Djuric, Jing Zhou, Robin Morris, Mihajlo Grbovic, Vladan Radosavljevic, and Narayan Bhamidipati. 2015. Hate Speech Detection with Comment Embeddings. In *WWW*.
[11] Paul Ekman, Wallace V. Friesen, and Phoebe Ellsworth. 1982. What emotion categories or dimensions can observers judge from facial behavior? *Emotion in the human face* (1982).
[12] Jesse Fox and Wai Yen Tang. 2014. Sexism in online video games: The role of conformity to masculine norms and social dominance orientation . *Computers in Human Behavior* 33 (2014).
[13] Joshua Guberman and Libby Hemphill. 2017. Challenges in Modifying Existing Scales for Detecting Harassment in Individual Tweets. In *System Sciences*.
[14] Maya R Gupta, and others. 2011. Theory and use of the EM algorithm. *Foundations and Trends® in Signal Processing* 4, 3 (2011).
[15] Hatebase database. 2017. (2017). https://www.hatebase.org/.
[16] Gabriel Emile Hine, Jeremiah Onaolapo, Emiliano De Cristofaro, Nicolas Kourtellis, Ilias Leontiadis, Riginos Samaras, Gianluca Stringhini, and Jeremy Blackburn. 2017. Kek, Cucks, and God Emperor Trump: A Measurement Study of 4chan's Politically Incorrect Forum and Its Effects on the Web. In *ICWSM*.
[17] Homa Hosseinmardi, Richard Han, Qin Lv, Shivakant Mishra, and Amir Ghasemianlangroodi. 2014. Towards understanding cyberbullying behavior in a semi-anonymous social network. In *IEEE/ACM ASONAM*.
[18] Homa Hosseinmardi, Sabrina Arredondo Mattson, Rahat Ibn Rafiq, Richard Han, Qin Lv, and Shivakant Mishra. 2015. Analyzing Labeled Cyberbullying Incidents on the Instagram Social Network. In *SocInfo*.
[19] Imrul Kayes, Nicolas Kourtellis, Daniele Quercia, Adriana Iamnitchi, and Francesco Bonchi. 2015. The Social World of Content Abusers in Community Question Answering. In *WWW*.
[20] Haewoon Kwak, Jeremy Blackburn, and Seungyeop Han. 2015. Exploring Cyberbullying and Other Toxic Behavior in Team Competition Online Games. In *CHI*.
[21] James MacQueen. 1967. Some methods for classification and analysis of multivariate observations. In *Mathematical Statistics and Probability*, Vol. 1.
[22] Adrienne Massanari. 2015. #Gamergate and The Fappening: How Reddit's algorithm, governance, and culture support toxic technocultures. *New Media & Society* (2015).
[23] Torill Elvira Mortensen. 2016. Anger, Fear, and Games. *Games and Culture* (2016).
[24] Gonzalo Navarro. 2001. A Guided Tour to Approximate String Matching. *ACM Comput. Surv.* 33, 1 (2001).
[25] Chikashi Nobata, Joel Tetreault, Achint Thomas, Yashar Mehdad, and Yi Chang. 2016. Abusive Language Detection in Online User Content. In *WWW*.
[26] Pham, Sherisse. 2017. Twitter tries new measures in crackdown on harassment. CNNtech. (7 February 2017). goo.gl/nMi4ZQ.
[27] Lior Rokach and Oded Maimon. 2014. *Data mining with decision trees: theory and applications*.
[28] Rozsa, Matthew 2016. Twitter trolls are now abusing the company's bottom line. goo.gl/Kb514G. (20 Oct 2016).
[29] Huascar Sanchez and Shreyas Kumar. 2011. Twitter bullying detection. *NSDI*.
[30] SentiStrength. 2010. https://goo.gl/FlpUYU. (2010).
[31] Gianluca Stringhini, Christopher Kruegel, and Giovanni Vigna. 2010. Detecting spammers on social networks. In *ACSAC*.
[32] Aatif Sulleyman. 2017. Twitter temporarily limiting users for abusive behaviour. Independent. (16 February 2017). goo.gl/yfJrZn.
[33] The Guardian. 2016. Did trolls cost Twitter 3.5bn and its sale? goo.gl/73h7jX. (18 Oct 2016).
[34] Twitter Streaming API. 2017. goo.gl/OLhKsR. (2017).
[35] Cynthia Van Hee, Els Lefever, Ben Verhoeven, Julie Mennes, Bart Desmet, Guy De Pauw, Walter Daelemans, and Véronique Hoste. 2015. Automatic detection and prevention of cyberbullying. In *HUSO*. 13–18.
[36] Alex Hai Wang. 2010. Don't Follow Me - Spam Detection in Twitter. In *SECRYPT*.

Place-Type Detection in Location-Based Social Networks

Mohammed Hasanuzzaman
ADAPT Centre
School of Computing, Dublin City University
Dublin 9, Ireland

Andy Way
ADAPT Centre
School of Computing, Dublin City University
Dublin 9, Ireland

ABSTRACT

While most prior studies in Location-Based Social Networks (LS-BNs) have mainly centered around areas such as Point-of-Interest (POI) recommendation and place tag annotation, there exists no works looking at the problem of associating place-type to venues in LBSNs. Determining the type of places in location-based social networks may contribute to the success of various downstream tasks such as Point-of-Interest recommendation, location search, automatic place name database creation, and data cleaning.

In this paper, we propose a multi-objective ensemble learning framework that (i) allows the accurate tagging of places into one of the three categories: *public, private,* or *virtual*, and (ii) identifying a set of solutions thus offering a wide range of possible applications. Based on the check-in records, we compute two types of place features from (i) specific patterns of individual places and (ii) latent relatedness among similar places. The features extracted from specific patterns (SP) are derived from all check-ins at a specific place. The features from latent relatedness (LR) are computed by building a graph of related places where similar types of places are connected by virtual edges. We conduct an experimental study based on a dataset of over 2.7M check-in records collected by crawling Foursquare-tagged tweets from Twitter. Experimental results demonstrate the effectiveness of our approach to this new problem and show the strength of taking various methods into account in feature extraction. Moreover, we demonstrate how place type tagging can be beneficial for place name recommendation services.

CCS CONCEPTS

•**Information systems →Information systems applications;** *Location based services;*

KEYWORDS

Location-Based Social Networks; Place-type tagging; POI recommendation

1   INTRODUCTION

Recently, with the rapid development of GPS-enabled smart phones and Web 2.0 technologies, location-based social networks (LB-SNs) have become very popular. Typical examples of LBSNs are Foursquare,[1] Facebook Places,[2] Yelp,[3] BrightKite, [4] and Gowalla,[5] etc.. In LBSNs, users can share their locations (e.g., tourist attractions, shops, cinemas, restaurants etc.) via check-in facilities, write reviews, connect with their friends, and upload photos among others.

Location or venue is one of the main concept in LBSNs, and the number of venues in LBSNs is growing continuously. For example, Foursquare had more than 10 million registered users with 1 billion check-ins in September 2011, and by April 2012 the number of check-ins doubled [19]. In LBSNs, a venue can be business, physical location, or virtual location. LBSNs allow registered users to explicitly record their presence at a venue. Users can choose to display their check-in information on their connected friends' Foursquare sites, and post the check-ins on their Twitter or Facebook accounts. Most of the LSBN services allow users to create new venues using various methods,[6] especially when they unable to find their current place during their check-in process. Apart from that, LBSNs users can add "tags" to venues or leave "tips" to venues, which are crucial for assisting users in searching and exploring new places as well as for developing recommendation services [1, 14, 36].

To support various business purposes, most LBSNs services grant users unique opportunities by allowing them to freely create venues, add tags, and leave tips. Although this represents incredible and unique business opportunities, it also presents important challenges by adding noise into the user-generated place records for many downstream tasks such as Point of Interest (POI) recommendation, place search, data filtering, and automatic place name database creation that can perform better with high quality data. In [36], authors observed that about 30% of created venues in Whrrl and Foursquare are lacking any meaningful textual descriptions. Based on our observation of data collected from Twitter, many of these place records are personal places (e.g. a user's private home) or entities without any physical location (e.g. online stores).

People in architecture, urban planning, philosophy, and geography have defined and categorized places mainly into four categories [22]:

- *public places*, *places that do not systematically limit the entry of people. Typical examples include public squares, parks, and beaches.*
- **semi-public places** such as restaurants, stores, and other commercial places where entry is not limited as long as one is engaging in the sanctioned activities such as eating, drinking, and shopping.

HT'17, July 4-7, 2017, Prague, Czech Republic.
© 2017 ACM. 978-1-4503-4708-2/17/07...$15.00
DOI: http://dx.doi.org/10.1145/3078714.3078722

---

[1] https://foursquare.com/
[2] https://www.facebook.com/places/
[3] https://www.yelp.com/
[4] https://brightkite.com/
[5] http://gowalla.com/
[6] For example, Foursquare allows users to create new venues via Foursquare website or mobile applications

- *private places*, that are not open to all. Typical examples are people's homes, gardens, bedrooms.
- *virtual places*, which do not have an actual physical location, e.g., online shopping stores, chat rooms.

In this work, we use public to also include semi-public places and tag all places in our dataset as one of the three categories: *public (+ semi-public), private,* or *virtual*. Please note that distinction between ***public places*** *and* **semi-public places** could have considerable relevance to some downstream tasks such as place recommendations. For example, public places are essentially free, visiting the other (semi-pubic) might involve a cost of some kind (admission fee, purchasing of items) that makes it less attractive to an unwitting visitor. For this current study, we merge these two categories into one to simplify the task of place-type detection.

Given the high volume of check-ins and existing businesses on LBSNs, even a low rate of private and virtual place creation results in a large number of private and virtual places. As a result, ***private*** and ***virtual*** places may bring irrelevant and ambiguous information to various downstream tasks, which makes automatic place-type detection an important research problem. Despite its practical importance, place type detection is a particularly challenging task for several reasons:

- *data diversity*– Check-in records contain diverse types of data including time, location, and text. Therefore, due to the heterogeneous nature LBSNs, methods that effectively take all these data types into consideration for place-type detection must be developed.
- *sparse information* – When creating a venue, a user is asked to provide a few attributes of the venue, such as the venue's name, address, location, category, zip code, cross street, and etc. However, in many cases attributes such as address, category, zip code, and country are not provided by the users. Moreover, users personal experiences (tips) associated with most of the check-in records are either contain a few words or just empty. Without enough context and background knowledge, it is difficult even for a human to determine whether a given place is public or private in the physical world.
- *overwhelming noise*– Almost 30% of the check-in records do not contain any meaningful textual descriptions.
- *ambiguity* – place names can be ambiguous. So, only relying on place names would be challenging to differentiate between place types. Fortunately, in our dataset we have user check-in activities at various places and times. Therefore, we propose to explore the user behaviours to extract useful pattern and features from check-in records in order to distinguish place types.

Whereas most prior computational studies have focused on place labels (e.g., restaurants food, shopping, hotel travel, arts entertainment) annotation [6, 16, 36], there has been a lack of work looking at place-type detection in LBSNs. To the best of our knowledge, this is the first attempt to solve the problem of place-type detection in LBSNs. For doing so, fundamental issue is identifying and extracting a number of descriptive features for each place type from the available check-in records. Following the idea of [36] for semantic annotation of places, we explore the set of user behaviours and

look for unique features of places recorded in the check-in data for the specific task of place-type classification. We know that human behaviours are not completely random [12] and so can be predicted [17]. For example, people often go for cinema on a Friday/at the weekend in the evening. Moreover, people exhibit patterns in their activities, e.g. various places visited by the same person at the same time may be similar (e.g. having the similar type).

Similar to [36], we compute two kind of features: (i) specific patterns (SP) at individual places; and (ii) latent relatedness (LR) among similar places. Features computed from SP, corresponding to a given place, can be derived from all check-ins at that place. We compute features from LR to determine the relatedness among similar places. Since we have only small number of places manually annotated with their type, we can make good use of LR by deriving descriptive features of a given place from its "related" places. To facilitate the extraction of LR features, we adapted a similar strategy proposed in [36] to build a graph of related places (GRP) by exploiting the regularity of user check-in records to similar places. In particular, we explore different graph representations: (i) visitors-place; and (ii) time-place relationship from the user check-in records. We employ different techniques to these graphs to measure their relatedness. Finally, we calculate the probability of the category tag for each place by leveraging the relatedness of places on the graph and treat them as LR features for supervised learning algorithms.

We then implement a supervised ensemble learning framework defined as a multi-objective optimization problem in order to i) obtain accurate classification results even when training evidences are limited; and ii) identify different solutions thus offering a wide range of possible application scenarios. Indeed, depending on the task at hand, precise classification may be required (e.g. filtering) or high recall may be preferred (e.g. ranking of places for recommendation).

Finally, we examine the usefulness of place-type tagging in the context of place name recommendation. In particular, we present a neural network framework to complete the place recommendation task and compare its performance in various scenarios.

2   RELATED WORK

Previous studies in LBSNs can broadly be divided into two different categories: recommendations and place labeling.

Recommendation in LBSNs is basically divided into four different categories [2] : i) location recommendations, which suggest locations (e.g., POIs) or sequential locations (such as travel routes) to a user; ii) user recommendations, which suggest popular users (like local experts), potential friends (i.e., who share similar interests and preferences), or communities, which a user may wish to join due to shared interests and activities; iii) activity recommendations, which refer to activities that a user may be interested taking; iv) content recommendations, which suggest media as photos, videos, and web contents, to the user. Depending on the working methodology and used data attributes, recommender systems in LBSNs can be divided into: a) content-based recommendation, which uses data from a userfis profile and the features of locations; b) link analysis-based recommendation, which applies link analysis models, e.g., hypertext induced topic search (HITS) and PageRank; and c) collaborative filtering (CF) recommendation, which infers a userfis preferences from historical behavior.

Venue recommendation has been the focus of research in LBSNs. Several recommendation systems have been proposed in the literature including [8, 37, 42]. In [8], authors developed GeoSocialDB–a recommender system for providing three services, namely, location-based news feed, location-based news ranking, and location-based recommendation. In particular GeoSocialDB implemented these services as query operators inside a database engine to optimize the query processing performance. An interesting strategy, namely, user-centered collaborative location and activity filtering (UCLAF) method is proposed in [42], to pull many users' data together and apply collaborative filtering to find like-minded users and like-patterned activities at different locations. Authors in [42] modeled the user-location-activity relations with a tensor representation, and proposed a regularized tensor and matrix decomposition solution which can better address the sparse data problem in mobile information retrieval. In line with [42], [37] analyzed location recommendation services for large-scale LBSNs, by exploiting the social and geographical characteristics of users and locations/places. Precisely, they proposed a variant of friend-based collaborative filtering (FCF) technique, namely Geo-Measured FCF (GM-FCF), based on heuristics derived from observed geospatial characteristics in the Foursquare dataset for location recommendation.

Recently, researchers started to explore the content information on LBSNs for POI recommendation. In [13], authors showed that content information in LBSNs can be useful for POI recommendations. In particular, authors studied three types of content information (namely POI properties, User Interests, and Sentiment Indications) and proposed a unified framework to model them to achieve better performance for POI recommendation.

Different from the above mentioned works, several works exist to study sequential location recommendations based on either users' social media post [20, 35] or users' GPS trajectories [5, 39]. A Large volume of works have also been proposed for other categories of recommendations: user recommendations [10, 28, 38], activity recommendations [43], and content recommendations [25, 30].

Place labeling is the process of attaching semantic labels to venues, such as home, work, and school [16]. Place labeling techniques can be categorized mainly into two types: i) Manual; and ii) automatic. There are several prototypes exist that allows end users to manually label the places they visit, such as Reno [31], Connecto [3], and IMBuddy [15]. Automatic place tagging techniques can be classified mainly into two categories: i) rule based; and ii) machine learning based approach. In [44], authors proposed a system that rely on manually designed classification rules to infer the semantic category of a place. Despite effectiveness, this kind of methods require substantial efforts in rule design.

One of the very first attempts to propose a machine learning model that deals with place labeling task is proposed by [21]. The authors developed a system that uses hierarchically structured conditional random fields to generate a model of a person's activities and places. The computational models are learned over features from the locations of nearby restaurants, grocery stores and bus stops as well as the timing of visits. In [6], authors proposed a Hidden Markov Model (HMM)-based Location Extraction algorithm called HLE, which adopts a supervised learning based method for extracting user's daily significant semantic locations using mobile phone data.

Recently, the introduction of Nokia Mobile Data Challenge (MDC) [18] has clearly established the importance of place labeling tasks. The MDC provided labeled data and cell phone logs for 114 people (80 for training, 34 for testing) with an average of 282 days of observation for each one. All of the participants for the place labeling task adopted machine learning techniques and used phone features, including the time and duration of visits, to infer place label.

One of the most influencing work in this direction is proposed by [36], who considered the problem as multi-label classification problem and used supervised classification strategy to tackle the problem. In order to learn the classifier, two groups of features are computed from the check-in records. First group of features are derived from the patterns observed in places with same tag. The second group of feature is computed by exploiting similarities among similar places. These feature sets are used as inputs for the place labeling phase to learn a binary SVM for each tag. Finally, output of all SVM classifiers are assembled to derive the final labels. They conducted a experimental study based on a dataset collected from Whrrl for a period of one month consisting of 5,892 users, 53,432 places and 199 types of tags. Based on Yelp tag hierarchy, they merge those 199 semantic tags into 21 categories to simplify the task of place label annotation. Although these works are valuable in the context of LBSNs, its scope differs from our specific goal of place-type detection.

3 PROBLEM FORMULATION

Let $P = \left\{ p_1, p_2, ..., p_{|p|} \right\}$ be the set of places in our dataset, where $|P|$ denotes the total number of places. Each place $p_i \in P$ can be represented as $p_i = \langle name_i, lat_i, lon_i, A_i \rangle$ that indicates its given name, latitude, longitude, and attributes such as address, location, zip, cross street, and country. Moreover, some additional information is also available in the form of total number of check-ins, time of check-ins etc.. Given all the information for each place p_i, our goal is to predict its place type $t \in \{public, private, virtual\}$.

3.1 Approach Overview

In this section we present an overview of the approach adopted for place-type detection problem. The first step of the algorithm takes care of feature extraction, while the second step deals with place type assignment. While we explore SP in the check-in records of individual place to extract first group of features, the LR between similar places is used to compute descriptive features of a given place compared to its similar places. Supervised learning strategy is used to learn several ternary (public, private, and virtual) classifiers over the two groups of features derived from SP and LR on a set of manually labeled data in the place-tagging phase. Finally, individual decisions of classifiers are combined using a multi-objective ensemble learning framework to achieve higher accuracy and offer robust solutions to the task at hand.

3.2 Features derived from SP

Our motivation is to extract discriminative features from places of similar type. One can expect that at different places, users conduct themselves in accordance with the accepted activities offered by these places. As a consequence, distinct patterns form in the aggregated behaviors of users at different place types. These patterns are embedded in the check-in activities of users in LBSNs.

- *Total Number of Check-ins*: We observed (shown in Figure 1(a)) from the collected dataset that public places (same as restaurants and universities) attract higher numbers of check-ins than private places (e.g. home, private luxury vehicles). Therefore, the number of check-ins is considered as an important feature for the classification of place type.
- *Total number of distinct users*: This feature aims to capture the total number of distinct users who checked-in or were tagged at a specific place.
- *Check-in time in a week*: We examine (as shown in Figure 1(b)) the check-in patterns for different categories of places over the day of a week. We find that users check-in at a university more often on weekdays than at weekends. In contrast, they checked-in to online shopping stores at weekends more frequently than during weekdays.
- *User check-in locations*: We find from our dataset that location distribution patterns of users checking-in at public places is different from those observed for virtual or private places; public places has often attract high volume of check-ins from various locations that are either near or far within same city or region from the place's physical address, while virtual places have check-ins scattered across much wider geographical areas. Therefore, we compute the minimum, maximum, as well as average distance of check-in users at a specific place and consider these values as discriminative features for the classification of places such as online chat rooms and restaurants. To measure the distance between longitude/latitude points, we use the Haversine formula [33] to calculate the great-circle distance between two points, i.e. the shortest distance over the earth's surface.
- *n-grams*: We use 1-3 token sequences. Features are encoded simply as binary indicators regarding whether the n-gram appears in the place names.
- *Place profile*: We observed that places with more complete profile are more likely to be public. We consider, two attributes, namely, 'contact", "cross street". Features are encoded simply as binary indicators regarding whether the entries are there or not.

3.3 Features derived from LR

The rationale behind extraction of features from LR is that people's activities are not completely irregular. For example, we usually go to places for food at lunch/dinner time, visit places for shopping in the late afternoon, and usually return to our home in the evening. Such patterns appear for certain users in our dataset and so we explored these to tag similar places. To record the relatedness among places and compute discriminative features, similar to [36] built a graph of related places (GRP), where places are linked based on their relatedness, as measured from the information embedded in the user check-ins using the Random Walk and Restart method [32] (RWR). On the GRP, we compute the label probability of each place leveraging the relatedness of places. The derived label probability

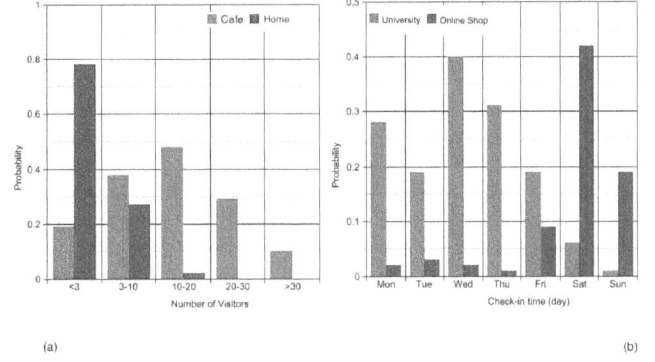

Figure 1: Check-in details at different place types: (a) Number of visitors at Cafe and Home, (b) Distribution of check-in time at University and Online Shop.

is used as a feature for classification. The details of our feature extraction from LR model are as follows.

Graph of Related Places: To facilitate the extraction of features from latent relatedness among similar places, following the idea of [36] we build two graphs: visitor-place and time-place graph. The underlying idea behind visitor-place is that the majority of users more often visit similar places. The motivation behind time-place graph is that the timing of check-ins at similar places may be similar. These graphs can be formally defined as:

- A **visitor-place Graph**, $G_u(V_u, E_u)$, is an undirected bipartite graph. Here, $V_u = U \cup P$, where U and P are the sets of all users and places, respectively, and $E_u = \{e_{i,j} | c(u_i, p_j, .) \in C\}$, where C is the collection of all check-in records and $c(u_i, p_j, .)$ denotes that user u_i has visited place p_i at some time. Each edge $e_{i,j} \in E_u$ is associated with a weight $w_{i,j}$, denoting how often user u_i has visited place p_i. Formally, $w_{i,j} = |\{c(u_i, p_j, h_s)\}|$, where h_s is the time stamp.
- A **time-place Graph**, $G_t(V_t, E_t)$, is an undirected bipartite graph. Here, $V_t = H \cup P$, where H and P are sets of all times (i.e. hours), and places, respectively, and $E_t = \{e_{j,s} | c(., p_j, h_s) \in C\}$, where C is the collection of all check-in records and $c(., p_j, h_s)$ denotes that a user has visited place p_j at time h_s. In this graph, each edge $e_{j,s} \in E_t$ is associated with a weight $w_{j,s}$, denoting how often p_j has been checked in at time h_s. Formally, $w_{j,s} = |\{c(u_i, p_j, h_s)\}|$.

Places are connected indirectly through visitors and times in the graphs described above. To construct the GRP, the relatedness of places from the *visitor-place* and *time-place* graphs needs to be derived. In this experiment, we calculate two relatedness values $r_{x,y}^u$ and $r_{x,y}^t$ for every pair of places p_x, p_y using RWR over the *visitor-place* and *time-place* graphs, respectively, and then merge them into one relatedness value between place nodes in the GRP. Below we only present how our RWR technique is applied on the *visitor-place* graph since the operation in *time-place* graph is similar.

Given a node x, RWR is carried out by randomly following one of its links to another node y in the *visitor-place* graph depending on the transition probabilities of these links, as well as on a probability

a to restart at node x. Our random walk transition matrix consists of two zero matrices, i.e. visitor-visitor matrix (VV) and place-place matrix (PP), and a visitor-place (UP) matrix and transpose UP^T, where the probability of transiting between a place p_j and a visitor u_i is proportional to $w_{i,j}$. The stationary (or steady-state) probabilities of each pair of nodes can be acquired by recursively processing RWR until convergence. The converged probabilities (i.e., relatedness values) give us the long-term visiting rates from any given node to any other node. In this way, we can calculate the relatedness of all pairs of location nodes, denoted by $r_{x,y}^p$ ($\forall p_x, p_y \in P$). Accordingly, we can derive two relatedness values $r_{x,y}^u$ and $r_{x,y}^t$ from *visitor-place* and *time-place* graph, respectively. Afterwards, we calculate the overall relatedness value for each pair of location as equation 1.

$$r_{x,y}^p = \eta r_{x,y}^u + (i - \eta) r_{x,y}^t, \forall p_x, p_y \in P \quad (1)$$

where η is a smoothing factor in the range 0 to 1. Finally, a graph of related place (GRP) is built where each place is connected to places with top-k relatedness values.

Place type label probability estimation: Our dataset contains millions of check-ins and it is challenging to create a sufficient amount of labeled data to cover various cases of *public, private*, and *virtual* places. Therefore, we build GRP which is able to make use of a large amount of unlabeled data to infer the label of a given place from its related places. In order to estimate the label probability of a place to be labeled, we derive the probability from the place tags of its neighbours recursively [23]. Assume N_i be the set of immediate neighbours with edges connecting place p_i, and y_i be a variable denoting a tag of place p_i. For all possible tags $t \in T$, we adopt a method similar to [36] for deriving the final $Pr(y_i = t|N_i)(t \in T)$ for each place p_i. The label probability of p_i is calculated by taking into account both the weighted average of the label probabilities of places in N_i, and the current label probability of p_i itself as equation (2).

$$Pr^{(n+1)}(y_i = t|N_i) = \beta^{(n+1)} \frac{1}{Z} \sum_{p_j \in N_i} r_{j,i}^p Pr^n(y_j = t|N_j)$$
$$+ (1 - \beta_t^{(n+1)}) Pr^{(n)}(y_i = t|N_i) \quad (2)$$

where $Z = \sum_{p_j \in N_i} r_{j,i}^p$ is a normalization term and $r_{j,i}^p$ is the relatedness between places p_j and p_i, and $Pr^{(n)}(y_i = t|N_i)$ denotes the estimation of $Pr(y_i = t|N_i)$ at round n. We also define $\beta_t^{(n+1)} = \beta_t^{(n)} \alpha$, where $\beta_t^{(0)}(t \in T)$ is a constant between 0 and 1, and α is a decay factor, i.e., $0 < \alpha < 1$.

We have initialized the label probability for each place $p_i \in P$ as follows.

$$Pr^{(0)}(y_i = t|N_i) = \begin{cases} 0.5, & \text{if } p_i \in p_{test} \\ 1, & \text{if } p_i \in P - P_{test} \text{ and } t \in T_i \\ 0, & \text{if } p_i \in P - P_{test} \text{ and } t \notin T_i \end{cases}$$

where p_{test} denotes the set of testing places, i.e., unlabeled data that do not have any place type tag. The label probability of a testing place is initialized as 0.5, while the label probability of a manually tagged place is set to 1 or 0 according to the labels. The label probability estimated for a place p_i is treated as the LR feature for supervised learning.

4 LEARNING FRAMEWORK

An ensemble of classifiers is a set of classifiers whose individual decisions are combined in some way (typically by weighted or binary voting) to classify new examples [11]. In particular, ensemble learning is known to obtain highly accurate classifiers by combining less accurate ones thus allowing to overcome the training data size problem. There are methods for constructing ensembles in the literature [11]. In this experiment, we propose ensemble learning as a multi-objective optimization (MOO) problem. Our motivations are two-fold. First, [27] showed that MOO strategies demonstrate improved results when compared to single objective solutions and state-of-the-art baselines. Second, MOO techniques propose a set of solutions rather than a single one. As place type tagging can be thought of as an intermediate module in some larger application (e.g. POI recommendation, place search, or database creation), offering different solutions can be a great value.

4.1 MOO Problem Defintion

A definition of multi-objective optimization can be stated as follows: find the vector $\overline{x} = [x_1, x_2, \ldots, x_n]^T$ of decision variables that optimizes O objective functions $\{O_1(\overline{x}), O_2(\overline{x}), \ldots, O_O(\overline{x})\}$ simultaneously which also satisfy user-defined constraints, if any. The concept of domination is also an important aspect of MOO. In case of maximization, a solution $\overline{x_i}$ is said to dominate $\overline{x_j}$ if both conditions (3) and (4) are satisfied.

$$\forall k \in 1, 2, \ldots, O, \quad O_k(\overline{x_i}) \geq O_k(\overline{x_j}) \quad (3)$$
$$\exists k \in 1, 2, \ldots, O, \quad O_k(\overline{x_i}) > O_k(\overline{x_j}) \quad (4)$$

Finally, the set of non-dominated solutions of the whole search space S is called the Pareto optimal front, from which a single solution may be selected based on any suitable criterion.

Ensemble learning can be seen as a vote-based problem. Suppose that one has a total number of N classifiers $\{C_1, C_2, \ldots, C_N\}$ trained for an M class problem. Then, the vote-based classifier ensemble problem can be defined as finding the combination of votes V per classifier C_i, which will optimize a quality function $F(V)$. V can either represent a binary matrix (binary vote-based ensemble) or a matrix containing real values (real/weighted vote-based ensemble) of size $N \times M$. In case of binary voting, $V(i, j)$ represents whether C_i is permitted to vote for class M_j. $V(i, j) = 1$ is interpreted as the ith classifier being permitted to vote for the jth class, else $V(i, j) = 0$ is interpreted as the ith classifier is not permitted to vote for the jth class. In case of real voting, $V(i, j) \in [0, 1]$ quantifies the weight of the vote of C_i for the class M_j. If a particular classifier is confident in determining a particular class, then more weight should be assigned to that particular pair, otherwise less weight should be attributed. In terms of MOO formulation, the classifier ensemble problem at hand is defined as determining the appropriate combination of votes V per classifier such that objectives $O_1(V)$ and $O_2(V)$ are simultaneously optimized where O_1 = recall and O_2 = precision.

4.2 Evolutionary Procedure

The multi-objective methods used here are based on the search capabilities of the non-dominated sorting genetic algorithm [9].

String Representation: In order to encode the classifier ensemble selection problem in terms of genetic algorithms, we propose to study three different representations.

(1) Simple Classifier Ensemble (SCE): each individual classifier is allowed to vote (or not). The chromosome is of length N and each position takes either 1 or 0 as value.

(2) Binary Vote-based Classifier Ensemble (BVCE): each individual classifier is allowed to vote (or not) for a specific class M_j. The chromosome is of length $N \times M$ and each position takes either 1 or 0 as value.

(3) Real/weighted Vote based Classifier Ensemble (RVCE): all classifiers are allowed to vote for a specific class M_j with a different weight for each class. The chromosome is of length $N \times M$ and each position takes a real value.

Fitness: Each individual chromosome corresponds to a possible ensemble solution V, which must be evaluated in terms of fitness. Let the number of available classifiers be N and their respective individual F-measure values by class F_{ij}, $i = 1 \ldots N, j = 1 \ldots M$ (i.e. F_{ij} is the F-measure of C_i for class M_j). For a given place p, receiving class M_j is weighted as in equation (5) where the output class assigned by C_i to p is given by $op(p, C_i)$. Note that in the case of SCE, $V(i, j)$ is redefined as $V(i, .)$ and F_{ij} as $F_{i.}$.

$$f(p, M_j) = \sum_{i=1:N \& op(p,C_i)=M_j} V(i,j) \times F_{ij}. \qquad (5)$$

Finally, the type of place p is given by $argmax_{M_j} f(p, M_j)$. As such, classifying all places from a development set gives rise to two fitness (or objective) values, which are, respectively, recall (O_1) and precision (O_2) and must be optimized simultaneously.

Optimization and Selection: The multi-objective optimization problem is solved by using the Non-dominated Sorting Genetic Algorithm (NSGA-II) [9]. The most important component of NSGA-II is its elitism operation, where the non-dominated solutions present in the parent and child populations are moved to the next generation. The chromosomes present in the final population provide the set of different solutions to the ensemble problem and represent the Pareto optimal front.

It is important to note that all the solutions are important, representing a different way of ensembling the set of classifiers. However, for the purpose of comparison with other methods, a single solution is required to be selected. For that purpose, we choose the solution that maximizes the F-measure based on its optimized sub-parts recall and precision as shown in equation (6):

$$F\text{-measure} = \frac{2 \times recall \times precision}{recall + precision}. \qquad (6)$$

5 CHECK-IN DATA COLLECTION AND LABELING

Since personal check-in information on location-sharing services like Foursquare, Gowalla, and Facebook Places is typically restricted to a user's immediate social circle (and hence unavailable for sampling), we take an approach similar to [7] to collect check-ins. In particular, we sampled location sharing (geo-tagged) Foursquare tagged tweets from Twitter Public Stream[7] for a month (from 1 March 2014 to 1 April 2014) and filtered out non-English tweets. Using this approach, we collected a dataset consisting of 155,27 users who performed 2,737,442 check-ins at 314,650 venues globally. In order to identify the language of a check-in message, we leverage the language detection library developed by Cybozu Lab [29].

Since no annotated place dataset exists, we designed our own annotation task using the crowdsourcing service of CrowdFlower platform.[8] We randomly sampled 10,000 venues and uploaded them to CrowdFlower. In particular, we represent each venue with details such as total number of check-ins, total number of unique users and their locations, tweet text, and asked crowdFlower annotators to decide whether the place is a *public, private,* or *virtual* place. There was a fourth option available to the annotators namely *"Unsure"*, when they are not confident about their decision. Each annotator was presented with detailed annotation instructions. Each venue was annotated by at least 4 annotators. Venues receiving a majority vote (at least 3 or more) for a particular class are considered as gold-standard, with the reminder rejected. The gold-standard data set contains 9,218 venues: *public*=6591; *private*=862; *virtual*=1765.

We follow standard rules of thumb for splitting a sample into a training set, a development set, and a test set. In particular, we divide instances of each place category from the gold-standard into the ratio of 3:1:1 for training, development, and testing, respectively. The final distributions are presented in Table 2.

6 EXPERIMENTS

Experiments for learning are run in a two-step process. First, $N = 10$ individual classifiers are learned over the features extracted from SP and LR on the training instances. For each classifier C_i, $F_i.$ (global F-measure) and F_{ij} (F-measure for class M_j) values are stored. All experiments were run over the Weka platform.[9] Following Weka's denomination, the list of the 10 classifiers is as follows: NaiveBayes, NBTree, MultilayerPerceptron, RandomForest, J48, LMT, RBFNetwork, Logistic, SimpleLogistics, and SMO. In order to assess the quality of each individual classifier, each one was tested on the test set containing 1844 venues. The results of the top-5 classifiers are given in Table 3.

The second step of the experiment is the optimization procedure. For that purpose, we used the development set consisting of 1844 venues. Based on the development set, the evolutionary optimization using NGSA-II is run for three representations (SCE, BVCE, RVCE) and the best solution is selected based on maximum F-measure as defined in equation (6). Performance results are presented in Table 1 and compared to two baseline ensemble techniques (BSL1, BSL2). BSL1 corresponds to Boosting with the single Logistic classifier, and BSL2 is a SVM solution with 10 features, each one corresponding to the output class (i.e., public, private, virtual) of each of the 10 classifiers.

As expected, our methodology significantly outperforms BSL1 and BSL2 in terms of F-measure for the RVCE representation. In particular, BSL1 suffers from the use of a single classifier family

---

[7]https://dev.twitter.com/docs/streaming-apis/streams/public
[8]http://www.crowdflower.com/
[9]http://www.cs.waikato.ac.nz/ml/weka/

Method	RVCE	BVCE	SCE	BSL1	BSL2
Public (p, r, f1)	(0.77,0.75,0.76)	(0.73,0.71,0.72)	(0.75,0.74,0.74)	(0.67,0.65,0.66)	(0.66,0.65,0.65)
Private (p, r, f1)	(0.79,0.77,0.78)	(0.74,0.71,0.72)	(0.78,0.75,0.76)	(0.68,0.66,0.67)	(0.67,0.67,0.67)
Virtual (p, r, f1)	(0.76,0.74,0.75)	(0.72,0.71,0.71)	(0.75,0.73,0.74)	(0.66,0.64,0.65)	(0.65,0.63,0.64)
Overall (p, r, f1)	**(0.76,0.74, 0.75)**	(0.73,0.71,0.72)	(0.73,0.73,0.73)	(0.68,0.65,0.66)	(0.66,0.65,0.65)

Table 1: Precision (p), recall (r), and f-measure (f1) achieved by different ensemble learning strategies for the place-type tagging task.

Dataset	Public	Private	Virtual	Total
Training	3955	516	1059	5530
Development	1318	173	353	1844
Test	1318	173	353	1844

Table 2: Distribution of places in training, development, and test sets.

Measures	Recall	Precision	F-measure
Max precision	0.69	**0.79**	0.73
Max recall	**0.78**	0.70	0.73
Max F-measure	0.74	0.76	**0.75**

Table 5: Precision and recall spectrum.

Classifiers	Precision	Recall	F-measure
Logistic	**0.65**	**0.64**	**0.64**
SMO	0.63	0.64	0.64
RandomForest	0.59	0.58	0.58
LMT	0.58	0.56	0.57
SimpleLogistics	0.56	0.55	0.56

Table 3: Results of single learning strategies.

while BSL2 cannot generalize over the small amount of training data. Moreover, the most fine-tuned strategy in terms of ensemble learning demonstrates improved results when compared to coarse-grain solutions. Improvements of 3% and 2% are shown against BVCE and SCE, respectively. In Table 4, we provide some examples of venues tagged as *public*, *private*, and *virtual* by the RCVE representation.

Public	Private	Virtual
CST Brands Corner Store	My Grand Villa	BlogtoRead
Central Park West, NYC	Kia Optima Ex.	MoneyGram
Astoria Plaza, HK	Static Caravan	TransferWise
CDG Airport	My Farm house	Boohoo
Wells Fargo	Apt. Home	Lavish Alice

Table 4: Examples of automatically tagged *public*, *private*, and *virtual* places.

In order to understand the spectrum of the different solutions on the Pareto front, we present in Table 5 three different situations: the solution that maximizes precision (line 1), the solution that maximizes recall (line 2) and the solution that maximizes F-measure (line 3). Results show that high overall performances are provided by every solution. However, depending on the application at hand, one may expect to find a better tuned configuration.

7 APPLICATION

We propose to test the usefulness of place-type tagging in the context of POI recommendation in LBSNs since it can be beneficial for many scenarios. including helping users explore attractive locations, as well as helping LBSNs to increase revenues by providing users with intelligent location services and location-aware advertisements. Note that our ultimate goal here is to examine whether place-tagging can improve the overall performance of a POI recommendation system.

With the available check-in records, existing recommendation approaches can be employed for POI recommendation in LBSNs by treating POIs as items. These approaches are mainly centred around collaborative filtering and matrix/tensor factorization [40]. In this experiment, we used neural networks to complete the task for several reasons: (i) it is natural to consider the POI recommendation problem as a sequential prediction problem since a user's visiting history can be considered as a sequence of venues, (ii) neural networks have been successfully applied to tackle sequence prediction problems [24, 41], and (iii) neural networks can learn richer representations compared to matrix factorization, and are more powerful in modeling complex relationships [4].

We formulate the POI recommendation problem as a sequential prediction problem [26]. Let $U=\{u_1, u_2, ..u_{|U|}\}$ be the user set and $P=\{p_1, p_2, ..p_{|P|}\}$ be the set of venues/places in our data set. For each user u, there is a sequence of places visited by the user represented as $S_u=(B_u^1, B_u^2, ..B_u^{t-1})$, where B_u^t is a set of venues/places visited by user at time t (we considered time t of granularity one day). The sequential prediction problem is to predict B_u^t for each user u, given S_u.

In this work, we propose to follow the work of [34] and introduce neural network-based recommender (NNR) framework consists of three layers: embedding, hidden, and output layers. The embedding layer takes a user id and the venues in the user's last k baskets. In the dataset, following the notion of item recommendation, *basket* is defined as a list of places visited by a user on one day. First, the inputs are transformed into a distributed representation where each user and place are represented as a vector $u \in \mathbb{R}^{d_u}$ and $v \in \mathbb{R}^{d_p}$, respectively. We obtain the user matrix $\mathbb{U} \in \mathbb{R}^{d_u*|U|}$ and place matrix $\mathbb{V} \in \mathbb{R}^{d_p * |P|}$ by putting all user and place vector together. Both $\mathbb{U}$ and $\mathbb{V}$ are learned during training. The output of the embedding layer is the concatenation of the user's and the place's representation and can be represented as $h_1 = \mathbb{R}^{d_u + k * d_p}$. It can be considered as representative of both the user's personal interest (what places the user likes) and sequential relatedness between places (the effect of places visited before compared to places visited next).

The next layer in the proposed neural network model is a non-linear hidden layer, which transforms h_1 to a hidden representation h_2 with dimensions l. Here $h_2 = tanh(W_1 h_1 + b_1)$, where $W_1 \in \mathbb{R}^{l * |h_1|}, b_1 = \mathbb{R}^{l * 1}$ are parameters to be learned. $tanh$, the most commonly used activation function in neural networks, is considered for this experiment. Finally, the output layer is a *softmax* layer, which produces the probabilities of the next places:

$$s = W_2 h_2 + b_2, \Pr(i_j \in B_t | u, B_{t-1}, .., B_{t-k}) = \frac{e^{s_{ij}}}{\sum_{n=1}^{|P|} e^{s_{in}}}$$

where $W_2 \in \mathbb{R}^{|P| * l}, b_2 \in \mathbb{R}^{|p| * 1}$ are parameters to be learned.

Our model has several advantages over existing state-of-the-art methods such as collaborative filtering and matrix/tensor factorization. Firstly, it can successfully model longer dependencies by varying the window size k (i.e. by taking a list of places visited by a user over a longer period of time) of the embedding layer, while other methods only capture the influence of recently visited places. Secondly, the embedding layer is flexible and capable of handling other features such as user and place attributes other from user ids and place ids. Finally, the hidden layer gives the freedom to model more complex relationships between users and places.

We conduct experiments to access the effectiveness of our approach on the check-in records collected for the period 1 March 2014 to 1 April 2014. Firstly, we split the dataset D into two non-overlapping sets: a training set D_{train} and a test set D_{test}. Again we followed standard procedure for splitting a sample into a training set, a development set, and a test set. In particular, the splitting is done by putting places visited by each user in the last week of our collection period into D_{test}, and the remaining ones into D_{train}. We used training data to create recommendations, and then we checked whether a user had followed the recommendation during the testing period, i.e. a fixed time period of one week. For each user we discarded all places from the test set (and corresponding predictions) that this user had already visited in the past, under the assumption that recommending to users new locations that they have never been to before is of greater importance recommending some already visited location. Note that this makes the prediction task much harder, as simply recommending already visited places is trivial.

Based on the test set, the dimensions of $h_2 (i.e., l)$, user vector (i.e.,d_u), and place vector (i.e.,d_p) are optimized. We recommend the top-C places for each user, denoted as $\hat{B}_u^t$, and use recall and precision over all test baskets using the top-5, -10 and -20 lists for evaluation. Precision (p) and recall (r) are defined as follows.

$$p = \frac{\sum_u |B_u^t \cap \hat{B}_u^t|}{|\mathbb{U}| * C}, r = \frac{\sum_u |B_u^t \cap \hat{B}_u^t|}{\sum_u |B_u^t|}$$

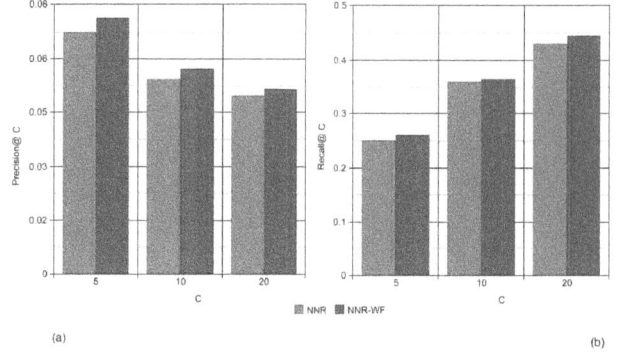

Figure 2: Precision and recall of neural networks based recommender with and without *private* place filtering. NNR represent model without *private* place filtering while the model, denoted as NNR-WF, includes *private* place filtering step.

In order to check the usefulness of place-type tagging in POI recommendation, an additional filtering step is introduced. Specifically, we removed places tagged as *private* from the dataset and measured the performance of NNR. Note that for filtering of *private* places, high precision is preferred over recall and so the solution presented in the first line of Table 5 is considered. Comparative precision and recall scores are presented in Figure 2(a) and (b), respectively. The figures show that the neural network recommender with the *private* place filtering step included (denoted as NNR-WF in the figures) is slightly better in terms of precision and recall than its counterpart. Note that only unvisited POIs are recommended for each user which explains the somewhat low performance of all methods. Results also indicate that place-type tagging can be utilized in the data preprocessing step to enhance the performance of POI recommendation.

8 CONCLUSIONS

To the best of our knowledge, we presented the first work on detection of place-type in location-based social networks. We adopted supervised machine learning strategy to tackled the problem of tagging places as *public*, *private*, or *virtual*. Due to the small amount of 'gold standard' training data, we proposed an ensemble learning solution, the underlying idea of which is to reduce bias by combining multiple classifiers instead of relying on a single one. In particular, recently developed multi-objective-based ensemble techniques have been applied to improve overall accuracy. By extracting effective features from check-in records and exploring large amounts of unlabeled data, our work achieves reasonable accuracies for all place types. Finally, we proposed to take a look at how recommender systems can benefit from this task. Precisely, we examined neural network-based POI recommendation and reported comparative results where place-type tagging is considered as an intermediate module. In future, we would like to consider other neural networks which can model longer sequential dependencies and use additional features such as user's immediate social circle and place attributes for POI recommendation.

ACKNOWLEDGMENTS

The ADAPT Centre for Digital Content Technology is funded under the SFI Research Centres Programme (Grant 13/RC/2106) and is co-funded under the European Regional Development Fund.

REFERENCES

[1] Jie Bao, Yu Zheng, David Wilkie, and Mohamed Mokbel. 2015. Recommendations in location-based social networks: a survey. *GeoInformatica* 19, 3 (2015), 525–565. DOI : https://doi.org/10.1007/s10707-014-0220-8

[2] Jie Bao, Yu Zheng, David Wilkie, and Mohamed Mokbel. 2015. Recommendations in location-based social networks: a survey. *GeoInformatica* 19, 3 (2015), 525–565.

[3] Louise Barkhuus, Barry Brown, Marek Bell, Scott Sherwood, Malcolm Hall, and Matthew Chalmers. 2008. From Awareness to Repartee: Sharing Location Within Social Groups. In *Proceedings of the SIGCHI Conference on Human Factors in Computing Systems (CHI '08)*. ACM, New York, NY, USA, 497–506. DOI : https://doi.org/10.1145/1357054.1357134

[4] Yoshua Bengio. 2009. Learning deep architectures for AI. *Foundations and trends® in Machine Learning* 2, 1 (2009), 1–127.

[5] Kai-Ping Chang, Ling-Yin Wei, Mi-Yeh Yeh, and Wen-Chih Peng. 2011. Discovering Personalized Routes from Trajectories. In *Proceedings of the 3rd ACM SIGSPATIAL International Workshop on Location-Based Social Networks (LBSN '11)*. ACM, New York, NY, USA, 33–40. DOI : https://doi.org/10.1145/2063212.2063218

[6] Z. Chen, Y. Chen, S. Wang, and Z. Zhao. 2012. A supervised learning based semantic location extraction method using mobile phone data. In *2012 IEEE International Conference on Computer Science and Automation Engineering (CSAE)*, Vol. 3. 548–551. DOI : https://doi.org/10.1109/CSAE.2012.6273012

[7] Zhiyuan Cheng, James Caverlee, Kyumin Lee, and Daniel Z Sui. 2011. Exploring Millions of Footprints in Location Sharing Services. *ICWSM* 2011 (2011), 81–88.

[8] Chi-Yin Chow, Jie Bao, and Mohamed F. Mokbel. 2010. Towards Location-based Social Networking Services. In *Proceedings of the 2Nd ACM SIGSPATIAL International Workshop on Location Based Social Networks (LBSN '10)*. ACM, New York, NY, USA, 31–38. DOI : https://doi.org/10.1145/1867699.1867706

[9] Kalyanmoy Deb, Amrit Pratap, Sameer Agarwal, and T. Meyarivan. 2002. A fast and elitist multiobjective genetic algorithm: NSGA-II. *IEEE Transactions on Evolutionary Computation* 6, 2 (2002), 181–197.

[10] Peter DeScioli, Robert Kurzban, Elizabeth N Koch, and David Liben-Nowell. 2011. Best friends: Alliances, friend ranking, and the MySpace social network. *Perspectives on Psychological Science* 6, 1 (2011), 6–8.

[11] Thomas G Dietterich. 2000. Ensemble Methods in Machine Learning. In *Multiple classifier systems*. Springer, 1–15.

[12] Nathan Eagle and Alex Sandy Pentland. 2009. Eigenbehaviors: identifying structure in routine. *Behavioral Ecology and Sociobiology* 63, 7 (2009), 1057–1066. DOI : https://doi.org/10.1007/s00265-009-0739-0

[13] Huiji Gao, Jiliang Tang, Xia Hu, and Huan Liu. 2015. Content-aware Point of Interest Recommendation on Location-based Social Networks. In *Proceedings of the Twenty-Ninth AAAI Conference on Artificial Intelligence (AAAI'15)*. AAAI Press, 1721–1727. http://dl.acm.org/citation.cfm?id=2886521.2886559

[14] Nevena Golubovic, Chandra Krintz, Rich Wolski, Sara Lafia, Thomas Hervey, and Werner Kuhn. 2016. Extracting Spatial Information from Social Media in Support of Agricultural Management Decisions. In *Proceedings of the 10th Workshop on Geographic Information Retrieval (GIR '16)*. ACM, New York, NY, USA, Article 4, 2 pages. DOI : https://doi.org/10.1145/3003464.3003468

[15] Gary Hsieh, Karen P. Tang, Wai Yong Low, and Jason I. Hong. 2007. *Field Deployment of IMBuddy: A Study of Privacy Control and Feedback Mechanisms for Contextual IM*. Springer Berlin Heidelberg, Berlin, Heidelberg, 91–108. DOI : https://doi.org/10.1007/978-3-540-74853-3_6

[16] John Krumm, Dany Rouhana, and Ming-Wei Chang. 2015. Placer++: Semantic place labels beyond the visit. In *Pervasive Computing and Communications (PerCom), 2015 IEEE International Conference on*. IEEE, 11–19.

[17] Nicholas D Lane, Ye Xu, Hong Lu, Andrew T Campbell, Tanzeem Choudhury, and Shane B Eisenman. 2011. Exploiting social networks for large-scale human behavior modeling. *IEEE Pervasive Computing* 10, 4 (2011), 45–53.

[18] Juha K Laurila, Daniel Gatica-Perez, Imad Aad, Olivier Bornet, Trinh-Minh-Tri Do, Olivier Dousse, Julien Eberle, Markus Miettinen, and others. 2012. The mobile data challenge: Big data for mobile computing research. In *Pervasive Computing*.

[19] Yanhua Li, Moritz Steiner, Limin Wang, Zhi-Li Zhang, and Jie Bao. 2013. Exploring venue popularity in foursquare. In *INFOCOM, 2013 Proceedings IEEE*. IEEE, 3357–3362.

[20] Defu Lian and Xing Xie. 2011. Learning Location Naming from User Check-in Histories. In *Proceedings of the 19th ACM SIGSPATIAL International Conference on Advances in Geographic Information Systems (GIS '11)*. ACM, New York, NY, USA, 112–121. DOI : https://doi.org/10.1145/2093973.2093990

[21] Lin Liao, Dieter Fox, and Henry Kautz. 2007. Extracting Places and Activities from GPS Traces Using Hierarchical Conditional Random Fields. *Int. J. Rob. Res.* 26, 1 (Jan. 2007), 119–134. DOI : https://doi.org/10.1177/0278364907073775

[22] David Lyon. 2006. *Theorizing surveillance*. Routledge.

[23] Sofus A Macskassy. 2007. Improving learning in networked data by combining explicit and mined links. In *Conference on Artificial Intelligence (AAAI)* (2007), 590–595.

[24] Tomas Mikolov, Martin Karafiát, Lukas Burget, Jan Cernocky, and Sanjeev Khudanpur. 2010. Recurrent neural network based language model.. In *Interspeech*, Vol. 2. 3.

[25] Mohamed Mokbel, Jie Bao, Ahmed Eldawy, Justin Levandoski, and Mohamed Sarwat. 2011. Personalization, socialization, and recommendations in location-based services 2.0.

[26] Steffen Rendle, Christoph Freudenthaler, and Lars Schmidt-Thieme. 2010. Factorizing personalized markov chains for next-basket recommendation. In *Proceedings of the 19th international conference on World wide web*. ACM, 811–820.

[27] Sriparna Saha and Asif Ekbal. 2013. Combining Multiple Classifiers Using Vote Based Classifier Ensemble Technique for Named Entity Recognition. *Data Knowledge Engineering* 85 (2013), 15–39.

[28] Salvatore Scellato, Anastasios Noulas, Renaud Lambiotte, and Cecilia Mascolo. 2011. Socio-spatial properties of online location-based social networks. (2011).

[29] Nakatani Shuyo. 2010. Language detection library for java. (2010).

[30] Ana Silva and Bruno Martins. 2011. Tag Recommendation for Georeferenced Photos. In *Proceedings of the 3rd ACM SIGSPATIAL International Workshop on Location-Based Social Networks (LBSN '11)*. ACM, New York, NY, USA, 57–64. DOI : https://doi.org/10.1145/2063212.2063229

[31] Ian Smith, Sunny Consolvo, Anthony Lamarca, Jeffrey Hightower, James Scott, Timothy Sohn, Jeff Hughes, Giovanni Iachello, and Gregory D. Abowd. 2005. *Social Disclosure of Place: From Location Technology to Communication Practices*. Springer Berlin Heidelberg, Berlin, Heidelberg, 134–151. DOI : https://doi.org/10.1007/11428572_9

[32] Hanghang Tong, Christos Faloutsos, and Jia-Yu Pan. 2008. Random walk with restart: fast solutions and applications. *Knowledge and Information Systems* 14, 3 (2008), 327–346. DOI : https://doi.org/10.1007/s10115-007-0094-2

[33] Chris Veness. 2011. Calculate distance and bearing between two Latitude/Longitude points using Haversine formula in JavaScript. *Movable Type Scripts* (2011).

[34] Shengxian Wan, Yanyan Lan, Pengfei Wang, Jiafeng Guo, Jun Xu, and Xueqi Cheng. 2015. Next Basket Recommendation with Neural Networks.

[35] Ling-Yin Wei, Yu Zheng, and Wen-Chih Peng. 2012. Constructing Popular Routes from Uncertain Trajectories. In *Proceedings of the 18th ACM SIGKDD International Conference on Knowledge Discovery and Data Mining (KDD '12)*. ACM, New York, NY, USA, 195–203. DOI : https://doi.org/10.1145/2339530.2339562

[36] Mao Ye, Dong Shou, Wang-Chien Lee, Peifeng Yin, and Krzysztof Janowicz. 2011. On the Semantic Annotation of Places in Location-based Social Networks. In *Proceedings of the 17th ACM SIGKDD International Conference on Knowledge Discovery and Data Mining (KDD '11)*. ACM, New York, NY, USA, 520–528. DOI : https://doi.org/10.1145/2020408.2020491

[37] Mao Ye, Peifeng Yin, and Wang-Chien Lee. 2010. Location Recommendation for Location-based Social Networks. In *Proceedings of the 18th SIGSPATIAL International Conference on Advances in Geographic Information Systems (GIS '10)*. ACM, New York, NY, USA, 458–461. DOI : https://doi.org/10.1145/1869790.1869861

[38] Josh Jia-Ching Ying, Eric Hsueh-Chan Lu, Wang-Chien Lee, Tz-Chiao Weng, and Vincent S. Tseng. 2010. Mining User Similarity from Semantic Trajectories. In *Proceedings of the 2Nd ACM SIGSPATIAL International Workshop on Location Based Social Networks (LBSN '10)*. ACM, New York, NY, USA, 19–26. DOI : https://doi.org/10.1145/1867699.1867703

[39] Hyoseok Yoon, Yu Zheng, Xing Xie, and Woontack Woo. 2012. Social itinerary recommendation from user-generated digital trails. *Personal and Ubiquitous Computing* 16, 5 (2012), 469–484. DOI : https://doi.org/10.1007/s00779-011-0419-8

[40] Yonghong Yu and Xingguo Chen. 2015. A Survey of Point-of-Interest Recommendation in Location-Based Social Networks. In *Workshops at the Twenty-Ninth AAAI Conference on Artificial Intelligence*.

[41] Yuyu Zhang, Hanjun Dai, Chang Xu, Jun Feng, Taifeng Wang, Jiang Bian, Bin Wang, and Tie-Yan Liu. 2014. Sequential Click Prediction for Sponsored Search with Recurrent Neural Networks. In *Twenty-Eighth AAAI Conference on Artificial Intelligence*.

[42] Vincent W. Zheng, Bin Cao, Yu Zheng, Xing Xie, and Qiang Yang. 2010. Collaborative Filtering Meets Mobile Recommendation: A User-centered Approach. In *Proceedings of the Twenty-Fourth AAAI Conference on Artificial Intelligence (AAAI'10)*. AAAI Press, 236–241. http://dl.acm.org/citation.cfm?id=2898607.2898645

[43] Vincent W. Zheng, Yu Zheng, Xing Xie, and Qiang Yang. 2010. Collaborative Location and Activity Recommendations with GPS History Data. In *Proceedings of the 19th International Conference on World Wide Web (WWW '10)*. ACM, New York, NY, USA, 1029–1038. DOI : https://doi.org/10.1145/1772690.1772795

[44] Yin Zhu, Erheng Zhong, Zhongqi Lu, and Qiang Yang. 2013. Feature Engineering for Semantic Place Prediction. *Pervasive Mob. Comput.* 9, 6 (Dec. 2013), 772–783. DOI : https://doi.org/10.1016/j.pmcj.2013.07.004

A Measurement Study of Hate Speech in Social Media

Mainack Mondal
MPI-SWS
Germany
mainack@mpi-sws.org

Leandro Araújo Silva
Universidade Federal de Minas Gerais
Belo Horizonte, Brazil
leandro@dcc.ufmg.br

Fabrício Benevenuto
Universidade Federal de Minas Gerais
Belo Horizonte, Brazil
fabricio@dcc.ufmg.br

ABSTRACT

Social media platforms provide an inexpensive communication medium that allows anyone to quickly reach millions of users. Consequently, in these platforms anyone can publish content and anyone interested in the content can obtain it, representing a transformative revolution in our society. However, this same potential of social media systems brings together an important challenge—these systems provide space for discourses that are harmful to certain groups of people. This challenge manifests itself with a number of variations, including bullying, offensive content, and hate speech. Specifically, authorities of many countries today are rapidly recognizing hate speech as a serious problem, specially because it is hard to create barriers on the Internet to prevent the dissemination of hate across countries or minorities. In this paper, we provide the first of a kind systematic large scale measurement and analysis study of hate speech in online social media. We aim to understand the abundance of hate speech in online social media, the most common hate expressions, the effect of anonymity on hate speech and the most hated groups across regions. In order to achieve our objectives, we gather traces from two social media systems: Whisper and Twitter. We then develop and validate a methodology to identify hate speech on both of these systems. Our results identify hate speech forms and unveil a set of important patterns, providing not only a broader understanding of online hate speech, but also offering directions for detection and prevention approaches.

CCS CONCEPTS

• **Information systems** → *Social networks*; • **Human-centered computing** → *Empirical studies in collaborative and social computing*;

KEYWORDS

hate speech; anonymity; social media; Whisper; Twitter; pattern recognition

ACM Reference format:
Mainack Mondal, Leandro Araújo Silva, and Fabrício Benevenuto. 2017. A Measurement Study of Hate Speech in Social Media. In *Proceedings of HT '17, Prague, Czech Republic, July 04-07, 2017*, 10 pages.
https://doi.org/http://dx.doi.org/10.1145/3078714.3078723

1 INTRODUCTION

Online social media sites today allow users to freely communicate at nearly marginal costs. Increasingly users leverage these platforms not only to interact with each other, but also to share news. While the open platform provided by these systems allow users to express themselves, there is also a dark side of these systems. Particularly, these social media sites have become a fertile ground for inflamed discussions, that usually polarize 'us' against 'them', resulting in many cases of insulting and offensive language usage.

Another important aspect that favors such behavior is the level of anonymity that some social media platforms grant to users. As example, "Secret" was created, in part, to promote free and anonymous speech but became a mean for people to defame others while remaining anonymous. Secret was banned in Brazil for this very reason and shut down in 2015 [1]. There are reports of cases of hateful messages in many other social media independently of the level in which the online identity is bonded to an offline identity – e.g., in Whisper [25], Twitter [24], Instagram [15], and Facebook [17].

With this context, it is not surprising that most existing efforts are motivated by the impulse to detect and eliminate hateful messages or hate speech [1, 2, 12, 26, 29]. These efforts mostly focus on specific manifestations of hate, like racism [3]. While these efforts are quite important, they do not attempt to provide a big picture of the problem of hate speech in the current popular social media systems. Specifically providing a broad understanding about the root causes of online hate speech was not main focus of these prior works. Consequently, these prior works also refrain from suggesting broad techniques to deal with the generic offline hate underlying online hate speech.

In this paper, we take a first step towards better understanding online hate speech. Our effort consists of characterizing how hate speech is spread in common social media, focusing on understanding how hate speech manifests itself under different dimensions such as its targets, the identity of the haters, geographic aspects of hate contexts. Particularly, we focus on the following research questions.

What is hate speech about? We want to understand not only which are the most common hated groups of people, but also what are the high-level categories of hate targets in online hate speech.

What role does anonymity play on hate speech? Is anonymity a feature that exacerbate hate speech or are social media users not worried about expressing their hate under their real names? What fraction of haters use their personal names in social media?

How does hate speech vary across geography? Does hate speech targets vary across countries? And within states of a country, like

---

[1] http://www.bbc.com/news/technology-32531175

US? Are there categories of hate speech that are uniformly hated and others that are hated only in specific regions?

Answering these questions is crucial to help authorities (including social media sites) for proposing interventions and effectively deal with hate speech. To find answers, we gathered one-year data from two social media sites: Whisper and Twitter. Then, we propose and validate a simple yet effective method to detect hate speech using sentence structure and using this method construct our hate speech datasets. Using this data, we conduct the first of a kind characterization study of hate speech along multiple different dimensions: hate targets, the identity of haters, geographic aspects of hate and hate context. Our results unveil a set of important patterns, providing not only a broader understanding of hate speech, but also offering directions for detection and prevention approaches.

The rest of the paper is organized as follows: Next, we briefly discuss related efforts in this field. Then, we present our whisper and Twitter datasets and our approach to identify and measure hate speech in them. The next sections provide a series of analysis results that answer our research questions stated before. We conclude the paper discussing some potential implications of our findings.

2 RELATED WORK

We review existing work on hate speech along three dimensions.

2.1 Understanding hate speech

Hate speech has been an active research area in the sociology community [9]. Particularly, [19] claims that some forms of hate speech are far from being solved in our society, specially those against black people and women. Hate speech originating from such prejudices are quite abundant and authorities have created standard policies to counter it. However, there has been a multitude of undesirable social consequences of these very policies (e.g., incivility, tension, censorship, and reverse discrimination) due to the suppression of haters and the protection of hate targets. Over time, this tension has driven the evolution of standard policies to regulate hate speech.

A very recent study [10], supported by UNESCO, reviews the growing problem of online hate speech with the advent of internet from a legal and social standpoint. They pointed out that platforms like Facebook and Twitter have primarily adopted only a reactive approach to deal with hatespeech reported by their users, but they could do much more. More specifically, their study reports *"These platforms have access to a tremendous amount of data that can be correlated, analyzed, and combined with real life events that would allow more nuanced understanding of the dynamics characterizing hate speech online"*. Our work is motivated by this vision.

Even before the popularity of social networks, the problem of racism and hate detection was already a research theme in computer science. Back in 2004, there has been efforts that attempt to identify hateful webpages, containing racism or extremism [13]. Nowadays, there has been a multitude of related problems under investigation in social media systems [5, 23]. However, these approaches does not give a data driven global view of hate speech in online media today, we aim to bridge this gap.

2.2 Detecting hate speech in online media

In recent years, there has been a number of studies which focus on computational methods to find hate speech in social media. [3] reviews three different recent studies that aim to detect the presence of racism or offensive words on Twitter. They point out that, while simple text searches for hate words in tweets represent a good strategy to collect hate speech data, it also creates a problem: the context of the tweets is lost. For instance, the word "Crow" or "Squinty" is a racial slur in United Kingdom, but it can also be used in multiple different non-hate related contexts. Multiple researchers try to solve this problem using manual inspection or a mix of crowdsource labeling and machine learning techniques [1, 2, 12, 26, 29, 31]. Their basic framework consists of creation of a corpus which contain a set of known hate keywords. This corpus is then manually annotated to construct a training dataset which contains positive and negative hate posts. Finally, they learn from this training dataset to build automated systems (via machine learning approaches) for detecting hate speech. Overall, these types of approaches have two shortcomings. Firstly, it is hard to detect new hate targets using hate keywords. Secondly, manual labeling, although useful, but is not scalable if we want to understand and detect hate speech at large scale. Aside from leveraging text based features researchers also explored other features like leveraging user history [8] or even community detection [6]; These techniques can be used in addition to the text based features. Although all these efforts offer advances in this field, it is safe to say that computational methods to detect hate speech currently are in a nascent stage.

Most of these prior efforts focus on detecting online hate speech. Differently, our research goal is to use computational techniques to *understand* the social phenomena of online hate speech. Our approach, based on sentence structure, provides a reasonably accurate data set to answer our research questions. Our strategy also allows us to identify a number of explicit hate speech targets (or communities), which directly complements (and benefits) the existing keyword search based semi-automated approaches.

2.3 Hate speech and anonymity

The problem of hate speech inspired a growing body of work in effectively detecting such speeches on various social media platforms. However so far these efforts focused on either non-anonymous social media platforms, like Twitter or Facebook [18, 29], or on radical forums and known hate groups [31]. However there is an interesting and unexplored middle ground in between—Anonymous social media like Whisper or Secret. These media sites are recently becoming quite popular within normal users. These platforms do not require any account or persistent identity to post on their sites. Recent efforts [7, 30] reviewed content posted on such forums in depth. They found that users post more sensitive content on such forums and a significant fraction of such posts are confessions about their personal lives. Existing efforts in sociology [22, 27] already pointed out that in the presence of anonymity, humans show a disinhibition complex. In other words, the posters might be much less inhibited and express their otherwise suppressed feeling or ideas on anonymous social media sites. Thus, intuitively, in the presence of anonymity one will expect to find the presence of hate speech from a diverse set of users who are not radicalized, but they have certain prejudices which otherwise they will not express in their posts. Based on this intuition we made an effort to investigate Whisper, an anonymous social media system, in our analysis. We hope to provide a more inclusive picture about hate speech in social media in that way.

In a preliminary short paper [25], we attempted to correlate hate crimes incident with hate speech in Whisper and Twitter. In this paper, we used the same methodology to gather data from Twitter and Whisper, but we provide a much wider and deeper understanding of hateful messages in these systems.

3 DATASETS

Now we briefly describe our methodology to gather data from two popular online social media sites: Whisper and Twitter.

3.1 Collecting data from Whisper

Whisper is a popular anonymous social media site, launched in March 2012 as a mobile application. Whisper users post short anonymous messages called "whispers" in this platform. In other words, whispers do not contain any identifiable information. An initial username is randomly assigned to users by Whisper, but it is not persistent i.e., users can change their usernames at any point of time. In addition, multiple users may choose to use the same username at the same time. Within a short span of time Whisper has become a very popular anonymous social media with more than 2.5 billion page views, higher than even some popular news websites like CNN [11]. Within 2013 Whisper reached more than 2 million users and 45% of these users post something every day [14]. Statistics published by Whisper mention that 70% of their users are women, 4% have age under 18 years, and most of the Whisper users belong to the age group 17-28.

Whisper represents a valuable venue for studying online hate speech. In fact, recent works [7, 30] suggest that Whisper offers an interesting environment for the study of online hate speech. These efforts show that users present a disinhibition complex in Whisper due to the anonymity. Since in an anonymous environment, people are more likely to shed their hesitation and disclose more personal information in their communications [16]. This anonymous nature of whispers combined with its popularity make Whisper an ideal candidate for our study.

Whisper users can only post messages via mobile phones, however Whisper has a read only web interface. In order to collect data from Whisper we employ a similar methodology as [30]. We gather our dataset for one year (from 6th June, 2014 to 6th June 2015) via the "Latest" section of the Whisper website which shows a stream of publicly posted latest whispers. Each downloaded whisper contains the text of the whisper, location, timestamp, number of hearts (favorites), number of replies and username.

Overall, our dataset contains 48.97 million whispers. We note that the majority (93%) of whispers are written in English. For the next sections we focus only on whispers in English as our approach to identify hate speech is designed for the English language. Moreover, we found that, 65% of these posts have a location associated to them. These locations are represented with unique place IDs (assigned by Whisper). We used the Whisper system to find a mapping between all possible values of latitude longitude (provided by us) and these

place IDs. Using this mapping we ascertain exact location of **27.55 million whispers**. This dataset of more than 27 million whispers constitutes our final Whisper dataset used in the next sections.

3.2 Collecting data from Twitter

Since we want to study general hate speech in the online world, along with Whisper we also collected and analyzed data from Twitter—one of the most popular social media sites today.The main difference between Whisper and Twitter is that users post in Twitter non-anonymously. The posts in Twitter are called tweets, and each tweet is associated with a persistent user profile which contains identifiable information. We found that, in spite of the non-anonymity, there are recent evidences of hate speech in Twitter [3] and decided that it is useful to include Twitter in our study for a more inclusive analysis.

We collected the 1% random sample of all publicly available Twitter data using the Twitter streaming API [28] for a period of 1 year—June 2014 to June 2015. In total, we collected 1.6 billion tweets (posts in Twitter) during this period. Some of the tweets also contained fine grained location information like whispers. However, one limitation for this Twitter dataset is that this addition of location is not enabled by default in Twitter. Thus, only a comparatively small fraction (1.67%) of Tweets have location information. Due to this limitation, we refrain from reporting results from Twitter in our location based analysis due to insufficient location information later in this paper. Just like Whisper, we also used only English tweets, resulting in a dataset containing **512 million tweets** (32% of our crawled dataset). This dataset of more than 512 million tweets constitute our final Twitter dataset.

4 MEASURING HATE SPEECH

Before presenting our approach to measure online hate speech, first we need to clarify what we mean by hate speech or hateful messages in this work. We note that, hate speech lies in a complex nexus with freedom of expression, group rights, as well as concepts of dignity, liberty, and equality [10]. For this reason, any objective definition (i.e. that can be easily implemented in a computer program) can be contested. In this work, we define hate speech as *an offensive post, motivated, in whole or in a part, by the writer's bias against an aspect of a group of people.*

Under our definition, all online hate speech might not necessarily be criminal offenses, but they can still harm people. The offended aspects can encompass offline hate crimes[2], based on race, religion, disability, sexual orientation, ethnicity, or gender. However, they might also include behavioral and physical aspects that are not necessarily crimes. We do not attempt to separate organized hate speech from a rant as it is hard to infer individual intentions and the extent to which a message will harm an individual.

4.1 Using sentence structure for hate speech detection

Most existing efforts require knowing the hate key words or hate targets apriori [18] for detecting hate speech. Differently, we propose a simple yet very effective method for identifying hate speech

---

[2]https://www.fbi.gov/about-us/investigate/civilrights/hate_crimes

in social media posts which is in agreement with our definition of hate speech and which properly allows us to answer our research questions. Our key idea is the following: If some user posts about their hateful emotions in a post, e.g. "I really hate black people", then there is little ambiguity that it is a hate speech. In other words, we can leverage the sentence structure to detect hate speeches with high precision very effectively. Although our strategy does not identify all the existing hate speech in social media (signifying possibly low recall), however it still provides us a good and diverse set of hate speeches to perform analysis presented in this study.

Our expression to find hate speech: Based on our key idea, we construct the following basic expression (i.e., a sentence template) to search in social media posts:

$$I < intensity >< user intent >< hate target >$$

The components of this expression are explained next. The subject "I" means that the social media post matching this expression is talking about the user's (i.e., post writer's) personal emotions. The verb, embodied by the <user intent> component specifies what the user's intent is, or in other word how he feels. Since we are interested in finding hate in social media posts, we set the <user intent> component as "hate" or one of the synonyms of hate collected from an online dictionary[3]. We enumerate our list of synonyms of hate in the appendix. Some users might try to amplify their emotions expressed in their intent by using qualifiers (e.g., adverbs), which is captured by the <intensity> component. Note that a user might decide to not amplify their emotions and this component might be blank. Further the intensity might be negative which might disqualify the expression as a hate speech, for e.g., "I don't hate X". To tackle these cases, we manually inspect the intent expressions found using our dataset and remove the negative ones. We list expressions and words used as the <intensity> component in appendix as well. The final part of the expression is related to the hate targets, i.e., who is on the receiving end of hate.

Twitter	% posts	Whisper	% posts
I hate	70.5	I hate	66.4
I can't stand	7.7	I don't like	9.1
I don't like	7.2	I can't stand	7.4
I really hate	4.9	I really hate	3.1
I fucking hate	1.8	I fucking hate	3.0
I'm sick of	0.8	I'm sick of	1.4
I cannot stand	0.7	I'm so sick of	1.0
I fuckin hate	0.6	I just hate	0.9
I just hate	0.6	I really don't like	0.8
I'm so sick of	0.6	I secretly hate	0.7

Table 1: Top ten hate intent in Twitter and Whisper.

Table 1 shows the top ten hate expressions formed due to the <intensity> component in conjunction with synonyms of hate. Although the simple expression "I hate" accounts for the majority of the matches, we note that the use of intensifiers was responsible for 29.5% of the matches in Twitter and for 33.6% in Whisper.

Determining hate targets: A simply strategy that searches for the sentence structure I <intensity> <user intent> <any word> results in a number of posts that do not actually contain hate speech against people, i.e. "I really hate owing people favors", which is not in agreement with our the definition of online hate speech. Thus, to focus on finding hate against groups of people, we additionally design two templates for filtering correct hate target tokens.

First template: The first template for our <hate target> token is simply "<one word> people". Thus, hate targets like "black people" or "mexican people" will match this template. This template for <hate target> captures the scenario when hate is directed towards a group of people. However, we observe that this template gives some false positives like "I hate following people". Thus, in order to reduce false positives we create a list of exclusion words for this particular hate target template. They include words like following, all, any or watching. The full list of such exclusion words is in the appendix.

Second template: Naturally, not all hate targets might not contain the term "people". To account for this general nature of hate speech we take the help of Hatebase [4]. It is world's largest online crowd-sourced repository of structured, multilingual, usage-based hate words. So, we crawled Hatebase on September 12, 2015 to create a comprehensive list of hate targets. There are 1,078 hate words in Hatebase spanning 8 categories: archaic, class, disability, ethnicity, gender, nationality, religion, and sexual orientation. However each word in Hatebase is associated with an offensivity score (provided by hatebase). The score varies from 0 (not offensive) to 100 (most offensive). We take only the hate words from Hatebase with offensivity score greater than fifty[5], and use those words as template for <hate target> tokens in our sentence pattern. Experimenting with other thresholds of offensivity score is part of our future work.

Twitter		Whisper	
Hate target	% posts	Hate target	% posts
Nigga	31.11	Black people	10.10
White people	9.76	Fake people	9.77
Fake people	5.07	Fat people	8.46
Black people	4.91	Stupid people	7.84
Stupid people	2.62	Gay people	7.06
Rude people	2.60	White people	5.62
Negative people	2.53	Racist people	3.35
Ignorant people	2.13	Ignorant people	3.10
Nigger	1.84	Rude people	2.45
Ungrateful people	1.80	Old people	2.18

Table 2: Top ten targets of hate in Twitter and Whisper.

Overall, our strategy identified **20,305 tweets** and **7,604 whispers** containing hate speech. We present the top hate targets (by% occurrence in posts) from Twitter and Whisper that we found using our methodology in Table 2. It shows racist hate words like "Black people", "White people" or "Nigga" are the most significant hate targets. We further checked how many of these hate messages are detected by our two different templates for hate target. Overall,

---

[3]http://www.thesaurus.com/browse/hate/verb

[4]http://www.hatebase.org/
[5]There are 116 such hate words in Hatebase

the template with "people" finds more hate speech than using the words from Hatebase, accounting for 65% of the Twitter dataset and 99% of the Whisper dataset. One possible explanation for this difference is that Whisper operators might already filtering out some of the offensive words from Hatebase [4].

Limitation of our detection methodology: We acknowledge that our methodology aims for high precision while collecting hate speech and thus misses hate speech which does not conform to our sentence structure (i.e., have possibly low recall). However we actually aimed to identify a diverse set of posts (not only race or gender based) which are truly spewing hate for further analysis, so we found our method acceptable. We also allowed a bit manual intervention to increase the precision further (e.g., exclusion keywords). Moreover, our work may suffer from the biases that any work that rely on gathering online social media data currently suffers [21].

4.2 Evaluating our detection method

Next, we evaluate the accuracy of hate speech detection for our approach. To that end, we performed a simple experiment: We randomly sampled 50 posts from each of Twitter and Whisper which matched our language structure based expression. Then one of the authors manually verified whether these 100 posts can be really classified as hate speech by human judgment. We found that that 100% of both the whispers and tweets can be classified as hate speech, where the poster expressed their hate against somebody.

It is important to highlight that our methodology was not designed to capture *all* of the hate speech that in social media. In fact, detecting online hate speech is still an open research problem. Our approach aimed at building a high precision dataset that allowed us to simply answer our research questions.

4.3 Categorizing hate targets

Categories	Example of hate targets
Race	nigga, nigger, black people, white people
Behavior	insecure people, slow people, sensitive people
Physical	obese people , short people, beautiful people
Sexual orientation	gay people, straight people
Class	ghetto people, rich people
Gender	pregnant people, cunt, sexist people
Ethnicity	chinese people, indian people, paki
Disability	retard, bipolar people
Religion	religious people, jewish people
Other	drunk people, shallow people

Table 3: Hate categories with example of hate targets.

For better understanding of the hate targets, two of the authors manually categorize them in hate categories (one author first categorized the targets and another author independently reviewed the categories and hate targets to ensure correctness of the categorization). For example, the term "black" should be categorized as race and "gay" as sexual orientation. In order to decide the hate

categories, we take inspiration from the hate categories of Hatebase (mentioned earlier). We also consider categories reported by FBI for hate crimes. We end up with nine hate categories. We also add an "other" category for any non-classified hate targets. The final hate categories and some examples of hate targets for each category is shown in Table 3.

Since manual classification of hate targets into categories are resource consuming, we aim to categorize only the top hate targets that cover most of the hate speech in our data. Our Twitter and Whisper datasets contain 264 and 242 unique hate targets respectively, and there is high overlap between the hate targets from Twitter and Whisper. We manually label the most popular 178 hate targets into categories, which accounts to more than 97% for both Twitter and Whisper hate speeches. We will explore these hate categories and associated hate speech further in the next section.

5 TYPES OF ONLINE HATE SPEECH

Twitter		Whisper	
Categories	% posts	Categories	% posts
Race	48.73	Behavior	35.81
Behavior	37.05	Race	19.27
Physical	3.38	Physical	14.06
Sexual orientation	1.86	Sexual orientation	9.32
Class	1.08	Class	3.63
Ethnicity	0.57	Ethnicity	1.96
Gender	0.56	Religion	1.89
Disability	0.19	Gender	0.82
Religion	0.07	Disability	0.41
Other	6.50	Other	12.84

Table 4: The hate categories observed in hate speech from Twitter and Whisper.

We start with observing which categories of hate are most prevalent in our experimental platforms—Twitter and Whisper. The results are shown in Table 4. The hate categories are sorted by the percentage of hate speech in these categories (except for the non-classified hate targets, which we put in the other category). We made two observations from Table 4. Firstly, for both Twitter and Whisper the top three hate categories (by percentage of hate targets, not counting "other" category) are the same – Race, behavior, and physical. However, in Twitter these categories cover 89% of the tweets, whereas in Whisper they cover only 69% of all the whispers related to hate. As mentioned earlier, one potential explanation for this difference may be that, Whisper already filters very aggressive hate words, like those from the hatabase [4]. We also note that, for these categories in both Twitter and Whisper, there is also hate speech as a response to hate, e.g., "I hate racist people". However such types of hate are not expressed in a high number of posts, and usage of "I hate" with negative connotation is much more common.

Secondly, we observe that out of the top 3 hate categories for both Twitter and Whisper, the categories "behavior" and "physical aspects" are more about *soft* hate targets, like fat people or stupid people. This observation suggests that perhaps many of the online hate speech are targeted towards groups of people, that are not generally captured by the documented offline hate speech (which considers hate speech based on race, nationality or religion).

6   ANONYMITY AND HATE SPEECH

Early social psychology research found a number of evidences that the feeling of anonymity strongly influences one's behavior. Particularly, people tend to be more aggressive in situations in which they feel they are anonymous [32]. Thus, in this section we aim to investigate the effects of anonymity on online hate speech. Specifically we investigate the amount of users that unveil personal names as part of their identities across different categories of online hate speech. Our hypothesis is that more sensitive categories of hate speech, like those associated to offline hate crimes, tend to be posted by a large fraction of users that do not use a personal name as part of their Twitter profiles (we exclude Whisper from this section as it is already anonymous).

Detecting personal names: Our approach consists of using a lexicon lookup approach to detect if the name provided by the Twitter account can be considered a common personal name. Since Facebook, another large social media site has a 'Real Name' policy, we exploit the names provided by Facebook users to build our personal name database. We use a Facebook dataset[6] containing 4.3 million unique first names and 5.3 million unique last names as lexicon. In order to reduce noise, we removed first/last names that appear lesser than five times in the Facebook dataset. We call a name provided by a Twitter account as personal if the name matches two or more tokens in our lexicon. In other words, we posit that a personal name must have at least two tokens as names used in the real world (equivalent to Facebook's first and last name policy). We ensure a clean matching by eliminating tokens from Twitter account names that contain stopwords or those that belong to WordNet [20], a database that contains common English words. We evaluate this system independently and discover the accuracy (F1 score) to be 78% for detecting names of real people. Using this method, we identify the fraction of hate speech that is posted by *not* using a personal name, i.e., anonymously.

Correlation between anonymity and hate speech: In Table 5 we show the percentage of tweets posted using anonymous accounts across top hate speech categories. We also consider a set of random tweets, unrelated to hate speech, which we use as baseline for comparison. We make two observations: Firstly, the percentage of users posting hate speech not using personal names i.e, anonymously is more than a random set of tweets. Secondly, more hate speech concerning race or sexual orientation is posted anonymous compare to when users post softer categories of hate, i.e., Behavior and Physical. Our findings suggest that weak forms of identity (i.e., anonymity) fuels more hate in online media systems and the use of anonymity varies with the type of hate speech.

7   THE GEOGRAPHY OF HATE SPEECH

Next we explore the correlation of geography and hate speech. For this analysis, we focus solely on whisper data as the amount of Twitter with geographic information is not significant. We start by comparing hate speech in different countries.

[6]https://blog.skullsecurity.org/2010/return-of-the-facebook-snatchers

Category	% Tweets posted anonymously (without personal names)
Random tweets	40%
Race	55%
Sexual Orientation	54%
Physical	49%
Behavior	46%
Other	46%

Table 5: Percentage of tweets posted through accounts without common personal names (i.e., anonymously) across categories of hate speech.

7.1   Hate speech across countries

Recall that our approach to measure hate speech only considered posts in English. Thus, unsurprisingly, US, Canada, and UK are top three countries in our Whisper dataset; they are responsible for 80%, 7%, and 5% of total hate speech in Whisper respectively. We focus our inter-nation comparative analysis on these three countries.

What are the top hate categories across countries? Table 6 shows the ranked breakdown of hate speech posted by users from these countries across hate speech categories. We make a few interesting observations from this breakdown. We note that, hate towards people based on behavior is the most dominant hate category in all three countries. Hate based on physical aspects of individuals also appear in the top three positions for the three countries. Interestingly hate based on race in US is higher (20%) in comparison with Canada (13%) and UK (13%). On the other hand, hate speech related to sexual orientation in UK (14%) is almost two times higher than in US (8%) and Canada (7%). We further checked the exact hate targets posted by users from these countries.

What are the top hate targets across countries? In Table 7, we notice country specific biases on the usage of hate targets, which helps to explain the observed differences in the hate categories across countries. In US, there is a clear bias towards hate against black people, as it is the most popular hate target in hate speeches from US, accounting alone for 11% of the hate speech. Hate speech against white people only ranked 6th in hate targets from US and accounts only for 5% of hate speech. This discrepancy tends to be smaller in Canada and UK, where both of hate targets, Black and White people appear around the ranks 4th to 6th and account for about 4% to 6% of the hate speech. Interestingly, we also observed hate against specific groups of haters in these countries. For instance, racist people are one of the top 10 hate targets in all of these three countries. Similar type of bias can be noted for sexual orientation. We note that, in UK, hate against gays appears in second place, whereas hate against homophobic people is ranked 11th in the list of hate targets of UK (nor shown in table). Furthermore, in hate based on physical aspects, Fat people appear with high frequency, being the most popular hate target for Canada and UK and on the behavior category, hate against fake, stupid, selfish, and rude people are quite common across countries.

These results not only highlight the different forms in which hate speech manifests itself in different countries, but it also identifies country specific biases in the hate speech. Our observation suggests

Rank	US		Canada		UK	
	Hate category	%	**Hate category**	%	**Hate category**	%
1	Behavior	36	Behavior	39	Behavior	26
2	Race	20	Physical	17	Physical	21
3	Physical	14	Other	15	Sexual orientation	14
4	Other	13	Race	13	Race	13
5	Sexual orientation	8	Sexual orientation	7	Other	12
6	Class	4	Class	3	Class	4
7	Religion	1	Ethnicity	3	Religion	4
8	Ethnicity	1	Religion	2	Ethnicity	4
9	Gender	1	Gender	1	Gender	1
10	Disability	0	Disability	1	Disability	0

Table 6: Top hate categories for the countries with most posts: US, Canada and United Kingdom.

Rank	US		Canada		UK	
	Hate target	%	**Hate target**	%	**Hate target**	%
1	Black people	11	Fat people	11	Fat people	17
2	Fake people	10	Stupid people	9	Gay people	10
3	Stupid people	8	Fake people	6	Stupid people	7
4	Fat people	8	Black people	6	Black people	5
5	Gay people	7	Gay people	5	White people	4
6	White people	5	White people	4	Rude people	4
7	Ignorant people	4	Rude people	4	Fake people	4
8	Racist people	4	Racist people	3	Ignorant people	4
9	Old people	2	Selfish people	3	Religious people	3
10	Rude people	2	Old people	3	Racist people	3

Table 7: Top hate targets in US, Canada and United Kingdom.

that, monitoring hate in online social media can help authorities to strategically detect and prevent different types of hate speech in different countries. Next, we analyze hate speech within US.

7.2 Hate speech within a country

We start with measuring the volume of hate speech in each US state. As whisper is a young social media platform with uneven adaptation within US, the raw volume of hate speech from a state might be biased by simply the total volume of posts uploaded from that state. Thus we measure the relative amount of hate speech contributed by each state by dividing the state level actual percentage of hate speech with a state level expected percentage of hate speech. The state level expected percentage of hate speech for a state is simply the state level percentage of Whisper messages from that state in our Whole Whisper dataset posted from US.

Comparison of volumes of hate speech posted by US states: Interestingly, Figure 1 shows that west and northeast state users tend to have less relative amount of online hate speech. To further explore this trend we divided US into regions and focus on hate speech at region level[7]. We calculate the relative amount of hate speech for each region (similar to that of each state). Notably users from west and northeast states tend to have less relative amount of hate speech (relative amount 0.91 and 0.93 respectively), compare

---
[7]We adopted the following division of US States across regions http://www2.census.gov/geo/pdfs/maps-data/maps/reference/us_regdiv.pdf

to the users from midwest and southern states (relative amount 1.07 and 1.05 respectively). To better understand these differences, we take three top categories of hate speech – race, physical, and sexual orientation. Then, we check what normalized volume of hate speech from these categories are posted from different US regions. Figure 2 shows the heat map of the volume of hate speech three hate categories across U.S. regions. The presented values are normalized by total volume of hate speech in each respective region. We can note that users from southern states post more hate speech based on race and sexual orientation. Whereas users from west post more hate speech based on physical features.

How concentrated are hate speech from different hate categories across US states? Finally, we focus on measuring the extent to which certain kinds of hate appear more or less spread across different U.S states. To do that, we define *hate entropy*, which is effectively the information entropy of the distribution of hate speech against a target category over the different regions. Hence, higher values of hate entropy denote target categories whose speeches are spread more uniformly across several US states, while lower entropy values signal hate speech more concentrated in a few regions.

Table 8 shows these entropy values for top hate categories in our US hate speech data. We note that categories that are related to crimes such as other, behavior, and physical features are more uniformity distributed across all the states. On the other hand, hate speech on crime related topics, such race, sexual orientation and

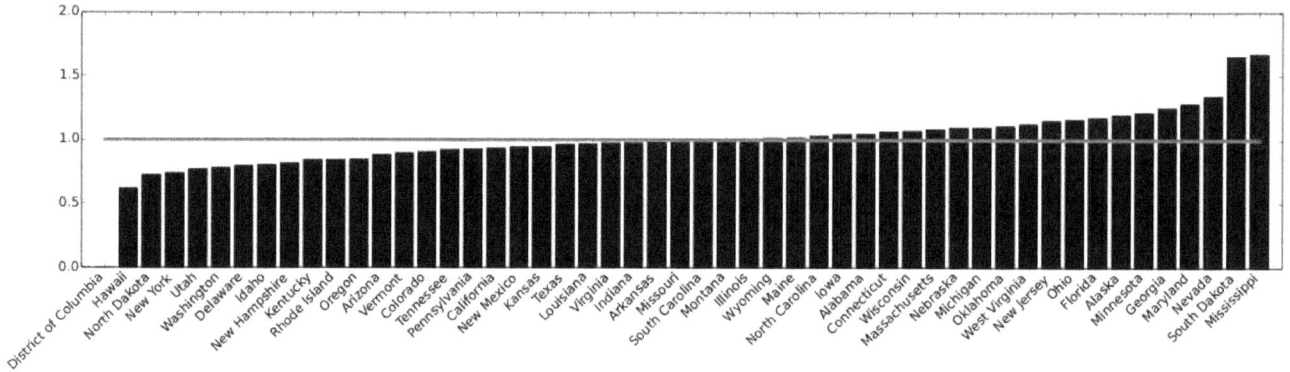

Figure 1: Relative amount of hate speech posted by users from different US states.

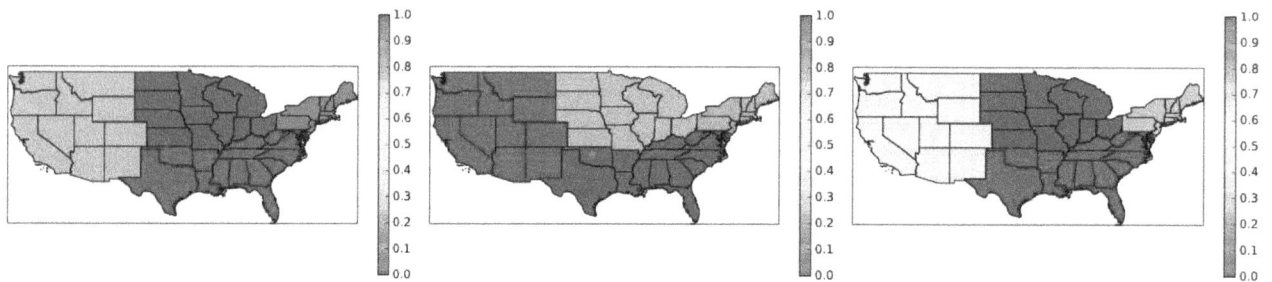

Figure 2: Heat map of US regions showing the distribution of normalized volume of hate speech for three hate categories: Race (left), Physical (center), and Sexual orientation (right).

Category	Hate entropy across US states
Other	5.1334
Behavior	5.0575
Physical	4.9550
Race	4.9313
Sexual orientation	4.8423
Class	4.4207

Table 8: Hate entropy across U.S. states for different hate categories.

class present lower values of entropy, indicating that the distribution of popularity of these forms of hate speech is more skewed across states. This observation further suggests that local actions and interventions for specific types of hate speech in specific locations (even within a country) is necessary.

8 THE CONTEXT OF HATE SPEECH

Finally, we investigate other sentences that appear together with hate speech. Our goal is to better understand the sentences associated with hate speech (which provide the context for hate speech). We noted that 65% of the messages in our whisper dataset and

80% in our Twitter dataset contains extra (part of) sentences following a detected hate pattern (i.e, the part that matched our hate expression).

Thus to filter out the context we take our detected hate speeches, and for each hate speech remove the parts of sentences that matched our hate expression (along with the hate target). The resulting sentence gives us the context for that hate speech. For example, in the hate speech "I hate black people, their point of view is subhuman", we extract the (partial) sentence "their point of view is subhuman" as context for this hate speech.

Figure 3 shows a WordTree [8] visualization built from our contexts for the root *I* and *they* (i.e. "I hate fat people, they..."), using as input our aforementioned analysis. The visualization shows phrases that branch off from this root expression (hate speech) across all hate speeches of our dataset. A larger font size means that the word occurs more often. We can note that the words *I, I, they, who, and, but* are quite popular. Among them, 'I' and 'they' emphasize personal nature of hate whereas 'but' soften the hate the users express in hate speech. Due to space limitations, next we chose the suffixes *I* and *they* to further analyze.

Figure 4 zooms on the WordTrees for these two suffixes. We can make two important observations from them. Firstly, we noted that part of these sentences simply attempt to intensify the hate expressed against a group of people. Second, and more interestingly,

---

[8]https://www.jasondavies.com/wordtree/

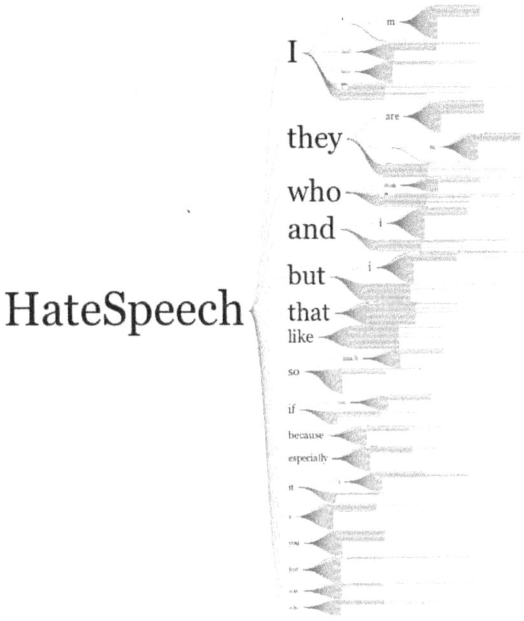

Figure 3: Word tree for our contexts of hate speeches.

these phrases provide evidence that many users tend to justify their hate against others, especially in Twitter. We believe that the analysis of these particular sentences might be a valuable source of information to better understanding the root causes of hate in some regions and places.

9 IMPLICATIONS

The fight against online hate speech is beginning to reach a number of concerned parties, ranging from governments, private companies and Internet Service Providers to a growing number of active organizations and affected individuals. Our measurement study on online hate speech provides an overview of how this important problem of spewing hate manifests online. Our effort consists of studying generic online hate speech according to four dimensions: the main targets of online hate speech, correlation with anonymity, the geography of hate speech and the context of hate speech. On a broad level our findings have three important implications:

Improving current keyword monitoring systems: A key aspect of a hate speech detection algorithm is that it must be able to classify messages in near real-time, as the longer the hateful message stays online, the larger is its damage to individuals. For example, Facebook, Google, and Twitter have recently agreed a deal with Germany under which they would remove hate speech posted on their websites within only 24 hours [9]. Moreover, recently, Google even promised marketers to find online hate speech to make sure advertisements are not shown alongside such content [10]. In this context, a key challenge is to identify new hate targets constantly. Our measurement methodology in this work is different from the

Figure 4: Word tree for context of hate speech starting with the words *I* and *They*.

ones used in previous efforts since we primarily used sentence structures to detect different types of hate speech instead of specific keywords. An interesting side effect is that our study is unique in the sense that it unveils a number of explicit hate targets (i.e. keywords associated to hate speech). Our effort even unveils new forms of online hate that are not necessarily crimes, but can still be harmful to people. We hope that our dataset and methodology can help monitoring systems and detection algorithms to identify novel keywords related to hate speech as well as inspire more elaborated mechanisms to identify online hate speech. To that end, building a hate speech detection system leveraging our findings is also part of our future work. In fact, such a system could be easily leveraged to notify the haters (users who post hate speech) and help them to better understand what harm they are causing.

[9]http://www.bbc.com/news/world-europe-35105003
[10]https://www.nytimes.com/2017/03/21/technology/google-advertising-apologizes-ad.html

Strong and weak online identities: Our findings quantitatively suggest that having a stronger notion of online identify may help individuals to better behave in the online world. This observation has interesting implications for system developers and researchers working in this space. For example, a social media platform could apply different hate speech monitoring strategies in their posts, i.e. heavily monitor the posts of those who do not use strong identities.

Leveraging online hatespeech to detect offline hate: We noted some tension related to racism in US as well as another tension related to sexual orientation in UK. These observations highlight the importance of monitoring hate speech in the online world in order to gain knowledge about hate in the offline world. Although there is no doubt that hate speech should be rapidly removed from social media platforms, the very removed data might provide a unique opportunity to identify the root causes of the offline hate.

APPENDIX

List of synonyms of "hate": *do not like, abhor, despise, detest, loathe, scorn, shun, abominate, anathematize, contemn, curse, deprecate, deride, disapprove, disdain, disfavor, disparage, execrate, nauseate, spurn, am allergic to, am disgusted with, am hostile to, am loath, am reluctant, am repelled by, am sick of, bear a grudge against, cannot stand, down on, feel malice to, have an aversion to, have enough of, have no use for, look down on, do not care for, object to, recoil from, shudder at, spit upon*

List of words used as <intensity> token: *absolute, absolutely, actually, already, also, always, bloody, completely, definitely, do, especially, extremely, f*cking, fckin, fkn, fr, freakin, freaking, fucken, fuckin, fucking, fuckn, generally, genuinely, honestly, honesty, jus, just, kinda, legitimately, literally, naturally, normally, now, officially, only, passively, personally, proper, really, realy, rlly, rly, secretly, seriously, simply, sincerely, so, sometimes, sorta, srsly, still, strongly, totally, truly, usually*

List of words to exclude from the first hate word pattern: *about, all, any, asking, disappointing, everyone, following, for, having, hearing, how, hurting, is, it, letting, liking, many, meeting, more, most, my, myself, on, other, seeing, sexting, some, telling, texting, that, the, them, these, this, those, watching, wen, what, when, when, whenever, why, with, you*

ACKNOWLEDGMENTS

This work was partially supported by the project FAPEMIG-PRONEX-MASWeb, Models, Algorithms and Systems for the Web, process number APQ-01400-1, and individual grants from CNPq, CAPES, Fapemig, and Humboldt Foundation.

REFERENCES

[1] Swati Agarwal and Ashish Sureka. 2015. Using KNN and SVM Based One-Class Classifier for Detecting Online Radicalization on Twitter. In *Proceedings of The 11th International Conference on Distributed Computing and Internet Technology (ICDCIT'15)*.

[2] J. Bartlett, J. Reffin, N. Rumball, and S. Williamson. 2014. *Anti-social media*. DEMOS.

[3] Irfan Chaudhry. 2015. #Hashtagging hate: Using Twitter to track racism online. *First Monday* 20, 2 (2015).

[4] Adrian Chen. 2014. The Laborers Who Keep Dick Pics and Beheadings Out of Your Facebook Feed. https://www.wired.com/2014/10/content-moderation/.

(2014). (Accessed on May 2017).

[5] Ying Chen, Yilu Zhou, Sencun Zhu, and Heng Xu. 2012. Detecting Offensive Language in Social Media to Protect Adolescent Online Safety. In *Proceedings of the 2012 ASE/IEEE International Conference on Social Computing and 2012 ASE/IEEE International Conference on Privacy, Security, Risk and Trust*.

[6] Justin Cheng, Cristian Danescu-Niculescu-Mizil, and Jure Leskovec. 2015. Anti-social Behavior in Online Discussion Communities. In *International Conference on Web and Social Media (ICWSM)*.

[7] Denzil Correa, Leandro Silva, Mainack Mondal, Fabricio Benevenuto, and Krishna P. Gummadi. 2015. The Many Shades of Anonymity: Characterizing Anonymous Social Media Content. In *Proceedings of The 9th International AAAI Conference on Weblogs and Social Media (ICWSM'15)*.

[8] Maral Dadvar, Dolf Trieschnigg, Roeland Ordelman, and Franciska de Jong. 2013. Improving Cyberbullying Detection with User Context. In *Proceedings of 35th European Conference on IR Research*.

[9] Richard Delgado and Jean Stefancic. 2004. *Understanding words that wound*. Westview Press.

[10] Iginio Gagliardone, Danit Gal, Thiago Alves, and Gabriela Martinez. 2015. *Countering online Hate Speech*. UNESCO.

[11] Liz Gannes. 2013. On Making Our Digital Lives More Real. http://allthingsd.com/20130802/im-so-over-oversharing-on-making-our-digital-lives-more-real/. (August 2013).

[12] Njagi Dennis Gitari, Zhang Zuping, Hanyurwimfura Damien, and Jun Long. 2015. A Lexicon-based Approach for Hate Speech Detection. *International Journal of Multimedia and Ubiquitous Engineering* 10, 4 (2015), 215–230.

[13] Edel Greevy and Alan F. Smeaton. 2004. Classifying Racist Texts Using a Support Vector Machine. In *Proceedings of the 27th Annual International ACM SIGIR Conference on Research and Development in Information Retrieval*.

[14] Erin Griffith. 2013. With 2 million users, "secrets app" Whisper launches on Android. http://pando.com/2013/05/16/with-2-million-users-secrets-app-whisper-launches-on-android/. (May 2013).

[15] Homa Hosseinmardi, Sabrina Arredondo Mattson, Rahat Ibn Rafiq, Richard Han, Qin Lv, and Shivakant Mishra. 2015. Detection of cyberbullying incidents on the instagram social network. *arXiv preprint arXiv:1503.03909* (2015).

[16] Adam N Joinson. 2001. Self-disclosure in computer-mediated communication: The role of self-awareness and visual anonymity. *European Journal of Social Psychology* 31, 2 (2001), 177–192.

[17] Grace Chi En Kwan and Marko M. Skoric. 2013. Facebook Bullying: An Extension of Battles in School. *Computers in Human Behavior* 29, 1 (2013), 16–25.

[18] I. Kwok and Y. Wang. 2013. Locate the hate: Detecting tweets against blacks. In *Proceedings of The AAAI Conference on Artificial Intelligence (AAAI'13)*.

[19] T. M. Massaro. 1990. Equality and freedom of expression: The hate speech dilemma. *William and Mary Law review* 32, 2 (1990), 211–265.

[20] George A Miller. 1995. WordNet: a lexical database for English. *Commun. ACM* 38, 11 (1995), 39–41.

[21] Fred Morstatter, Jürgen Pfeffer, and Huan Liu. 2014. When is It Biased?: Assessing the Representativeness of Twitter's Streaming API. In *Proceedings of the 23rd International Conference on World Wide Web*.

[22] Alain Pinsonneault and Nelson Heppel. 1997. Anonymity in group support systems research: A new conceptualization, measure, and contingency framework. *Journal of Management Information Systems* 14, 3 (1997), 89–108.

[23] Julio Reis, Fabrício Benevenuto, Pedro O.S. Vaz de Melo, Raquel Prates, Haewoon Kwak, and Jisun An. 2015. Breaking the News: First Impressions Matter on Online News. In *International Conference on Web and Social Media (ICWSM)*.

[24] Huascar Sanchez and Shreyas Kumar. 2011. Twitter bullying detection. *ser. NSDI* 12 (2011).

[25] Leandro Araújo Silva, Mainack Mondal, Denzil Correa, Fabrício Benevenuto, and Ingmar Weber. 2016. Analyzing the Targets of Hate in Online Social Media. In *International Conference on Web and Social Media (ICWSM)*.

[26] M. Stephens. 2013. The Geography of Hate Map. http://users.humboldt.edu/mstephens/hate/hate_map.html. (2013).

[27] John Suler. 2004. The online disinhibition effect. *Cyberpsychology & behavior* 7, 3 (2004), 321–326.

[28] Twitter team. 2017. The Streaming APIs. https://dev.twitter.com/streaming/overview. (2017).

[29] I-Hsien Ting, Hsing-Miao Chi, Jyun-Sing Wu, and Shyue-Liang Wang. 2013. An approach for hate groups detection in facebook. In *Proceedings of The 3rd International Workshop on Intelligent Data Analysis and Management (IADM'13)*.

[30] Gang Wang, Bolun Wang, Tianyi Wang, Ana Nika, Haitao Zheng, and Ben Y. Zhao. 2014. Whispers in the Dark: Analyzing an Anonymous Social Network. In *Proceedings of the 2014 Conference on Internet Measurement Conference (IMC'14)*.

[31] William Warner and Julia Hirschberg. 2012. Detecting hate speech on the world wide web. In *Proceedings of the 2nd Workshop on Language in Social Media (LSM'12)*.

[32] Philip G Zimbardo. 1969. The human choice: Individuation, reason, and order versus deindividuation, impulse, and chaos. *Nebraska Symposium on Motivation* 17 (1969), 237–307.

The Nature of Real and Perceived Bias in Chilean Media

Erick Elejalde*
Department of Computer Science
University of Concepcion
Concepción, Chile
eelejalde@udec.cl

Leo Ferres
Data Science Institute
Universidad del Desarrollo &
Telefónica R&D
Santiago, Chile
lferres@udd.cl

Eelco Herder
L3S Research Center
Leibniz-University
Hannover, Germany
herder@l3s.de

ABSTRACT

News consumers expect news outlets to be objective and balanced in their reports of events. However, there is a body of evidence of bias in the media caused by underlying political and socio-economic viewpoints. Previous studies have tried to classify the partiality of the media, sometimes giving a quantitative evaluation, but there is little reported on its nature. The vast amount of content in the social media enables us to quantify the inclination of the press to either side of the political spectrum. To describe such tendencies, we use tweets to automatically compute a news outlet's political and socio-economic orientation. We show that the media have a measurable bias, and illustrate this by showing the favoritism of Chilean media for the ruling political parties in this country. We also found that the nature of the bias is reflected in the vocabulary used and the entities mentioned by different news outlets. A survey conducted among news consumers confirms that media bias has an impact on the coverage of controversial topics and that this is perceivable by the general audience. Having a more accurate method to measure and characterize media bias will clarify to the readers where outlets stand within the socio-economic landscape, even when a self-declared position is stated. This will empower readers to better reflect on the content provided by their news outlets of choice.

KEYWORDS

Media bias; bias characterization; political quiz

1 INTRODUCTION

The media have a strong influence on how people perceive the world that surrounds them. More and more power has been ascribed to the modern press since its inception, even calling it the "Fourth State"[1] emphasizing its independence and its ability to provide strict limits to what governments may or may not do. There are well known examples of the press even toppling governments: the Washington Post in the Watergate scandal is perhaps the most resounding example.

---

*Funded by CONICYT doctoral scholarship (63130228)

[1]https://en.wikipedia.org/wiki/Fourth_Estate

However, as the media grows in power, the political and economic interests of news outlets and the ones who control it have grown as well, which has its impact on the news that the population of a territory gets served. Among others Herman and Chomsky [16] argue that political and doctrinal interests have penetrated the press at different stages of the news generation process, deliberately or accidental - for example through homophily effects. In certain cases the resulting bias is explicitly stated, in other cases – like FOX News – the bias is known but not communicated. People usually have some intuition of media bias. For average readers, though, it is very difficult and time-consuming to be aware or even find the bias of all media outlets, let alone quantify these biases and give them a total order in terms of the magnitude of the leaning.

Bias in the media is a global phenomenon, not exclusive to one kind of economy or particular political system. As such, there is now a quickly growing body of empirical evidence on its existence [7, 20, 24]. In previous work [29], we showed several types of bias in media coverage of ongoing news stories on crises in the world. What has not been studied as deeply, however, at least not quantitatively, is *how* outlets could be positioned in a socio-economic space. Knowing *the nature* of media bias will help individuals and organizations take actions that counteract bias. If, for example, a newspaper claims to be objective, but is in fact "right-wing, conservative" (as is the case with El Mercurio in Chile[2]), people should be able to recognize this and take this bias into account when reading its content. The case of El Mercurio is quite clear, and being a very old, traditional newspaper, the bias is actually known and arguably accepted. It is important to emphasize here that "bias" is not categorical, but comes embedded in a geopolitical news context determined by other outlets in the region [30]. In other, bolder words, some bias is inherent to the media, but how biased they are, depends, to an extent, upon a comparison to other media.

In this work, we automatically identify the (largely implicit) socio-economic "relative bias" of news outlets in the context of Chilean media. The value of our methodology and study here is to position those media outlets that do **not** state their socio-economic bias, or are not even aware of their bias. Socio-economic studies at this scale may help uncover patterns of editorial policies that show a systematic bias that favors governments' propaganda or private economic interests over social welfare. Operationalizing bias is a difficult task. It relies not only on linguistic information, but also on the actual geo-socio-economic, and even historical, context of the newspaper. We propose to automatically categorize news outlets by analyzing what they "think" about certain relevant, controversial topics using their tweet content and then map these worldviews

---

[2]https://en.wikipedia.org/wiki/El_Mercurio

onto a well-known political quiz: "The World's Smallest Political Quiz" (henceforth *PolQuiz*) [27].

The *PolQuiz* is a ten-question educational quiz for an American audience[3] designed by the Libertarian Advocates for Self Government[4], created by Marshall Fritz in 1985. The quiz is based on the one proposed by David Nolan Chart in 1971 [22][5], which in turn can be traced back to a 2D chart proposed in 1968 [4], representing variations in political and socio-economic orientation.

In short, we use what the media say on Twitter to position them in a Cartesian plane that tells us more about their orientation based on Fritz' PolQuiz. In turn, the PolQuiz results motivate a deeper investigation into the nature of the found bias, which we study through the vocabulary used and entities covered by the news outlets. Finally, we conducted a survey that confirm that media bias has a noticeable impact on how news related to controversial topics are presented.

2 RELATED WORK

There are several works related to the topic of media bias [7, 12, 14, 23, 31]. Some works do not try to identify bias directly, but instead try to identify and track events in order to present different points of view of the same affair to the readers in order to counteract these possible bias [23]. These are complemented by works like J. An *et.al.* [2], which create a so-called landscape of newspapers based on the similarity of their communities. They measure the exposure of Twitter users to politically diverse news. Other authors assume a certain leaning by contacts association [6]. In [24] the authors go deeper and try to identify different kinds of bias, what they term gatekeeping, coverage and statement bias, according to the stage at which the news acquire the alleged bias.

Most outlets identify themselves as unbiased free press, which makes the discussion on the direction and degree of media bias very controversial[6]. Media bias is usually found in the editorial policies that ultimately decide which stories are worth publishing and which amount and angle of coverage they get [23, 24, 26].

This bias reflects the political and socio-economic views of the institution, rather than the point of view of a particular reporter. For example, the authors in [16] use a few recent events to point out how the press applies the word "genocide" to cases of victimization in non-allied states, but almost never to similar or worse cases committed by the home state or allied regimes. In the latter case, they could use terms such as "repression of insurgency".

In [19], the authors defined a model to predict political preference among Twitter users. Through this model they calculate, for each user, a ranking of the likelihood that they prefer a political party over another. This model is based on the usage of *weighted words*. The words and their weights are extracted from tweets of candidates of certain political parties. Using these weights, in combination with Twitter specific features (retweets, following, etc.) the authors train classifiers that achieve a performance similar to that of human annotators. Similarly, in [12], the authors estimate the bias in newspapers according to how similar the language is to that used by congressmen for which a right/left stand is known. One interesting result is that bias in the news is found to be correlated to political inclinations of readers, showing a tendency in these news outlets to maximize profit by "catering" to a certain audience.

The topology of the social network on its own has also been shown to give enough information to create classifiers concerning a user's preference, even when the choices are very similar [11](e.g. Pepsi vs. CocaCola, Hertz vs. Avis or McDonalds vs. BurgerKing). Although we carefully select the dataset to use in our experiments to achieve extensible results [5], we notice here that in our dataset, news outlets (which may be considered the participants of our studies), regularly talk about these controversial topics, and thus, it is possible to use traditional methods to find a political stand.

Combining topological characteristics of the social networks with language features has also been tested [6], showing that users tend to interact more frequently with like-minded people. This phenomenon is known as *homophily*. As we mentioned before, our dataset is derived from a special type of users (news outlets Twitter accounts), and this method may not apply directly.

As an alternative approach, in [31] the authors propose a semi-supervised classifier for detecting political preference. They design a propagation method that, starting with a few labeled items and users, creates a graph representing the connections between users and items or even users with other users. Based on the same phenomena of homophily, they assume that users interacting with the same item, or with each other, most likely have the same political leaning. This way, they can propagate the labels from tagged users and tagged items to the rest of the graph. They report that the system achieves over 95% precision in cross-validation. In [14, 15], the authors also follow a propagation strategy to compute the political preference of Twitter users, but using Congress members as the initially tagged users.

In [18], the authors describe a framework to discover and track controversial topics that involve opposing views. They first use tags that represent each side (e.g. "#prolife" - "#prochoice") as seeds to find an expanded set of labels to represent each side. This may also help in cases where labels may change over time as the result of new arguments for either side. With these sets of labels they identify strong partisans (anchors) that have a clear lean to one side. Having these anchors and a graph representing relationships between users (based on tweet content-similarity or based on re-tweets), they propagate the classification through the graph inferring the opinion bias of "regular" users.

Yet another approach to quantifying political leaning is presented in [20]. They based their analysis on the number of tweets and re-tweets generated about different real-life political events associated with some predefined topics. The authors developed a model that takes into account both the sentiment analysis of the tweets and the number of time they are re-tweeted to calculate the political leaning score of each outlet.

In [30], the authors propose an unsupervised model based on how news outlets quoted president Barack Obama's speeches. The findings suggest that quotation patterns do reveal some underlying structure in the media, and that these may be evidence of bias. They

---

[3]Although we believe this does not imply a loss of generality wrt Latin American culture, at least in the topics chosen. It does, obviously, impact the polarity of attitudes towards those topics, but that is what we explore in these pages.

[4]https://www.theadvocates.org/

[5]Although widely cited in the literature, we could not find this manuscript online. We cite it for historical reasons here.

[6]To be fair, it is true that "bias" in journalism may arise naturally out of the interaction of reporters, rather than *a prior*, but this discussion is left for another paper.

found that one of the identified dimensions roughly aligns with the traditional left(liberal)-right(conservative) political classification and the other with a mainstream/independent one. This is a strong finding. Still, we believe this is to be somewhat expected, given the selected corpus; namely, presidential speeches in the strongly bipartisan system that dominates U.S. politics. Although this model helps classify and quantify bias in the media, it does not explain the causes and nature of this bias.

In this paper, we present a new methodology that quantifies the political leaning of news outlets based on the automation of a well known political quiz. The prediction of the answers for each question for each outlet is generated based on the polarity of their tweets on subjects related to the issues addressed in the quiz. The automation of a quiz has been used before to automatically classify mood [3] but, as far as we know, this is the first attempt to quantify media bias using this approach.

3 METHODOLOGY

In this section, we describe our dataset, followed by an overview of the *PolQuiz* and an explanation on how we applied this quiz to our data. In Section 3.4, we introduce the Rank Difference method for investigating the nature of bias. We conclude with an overview of the survey that we carried out to measure perceived bias.

3.1 Data

Every news outlet, from the smallest to the largest, has some presence on the web, which opens the possibility for the automatic collection of the news stream they produce. Twitter is a prime example of a web platform that allows this. Twitter is an online social network that enables users to send and read short messages called "tweets". Twitter offers an open API to automatically access the flow of tweets and query the system for user profiles, followers and tweeting history. This makes it possible to explore the behavior and interactions of personal and institutional accounts, developing and testing social theories at a scale never seen before. This is the closest thing we have to a record of the every-day life of over 300 million people[7]. We treat every tweet as an independent document from which we can extract a statement. We assume that these reflect the ideology of the news outlet as an entity. We use Twitter as our source documents because it provides us (and any news consumer) with a standardized way to access the daily events reported by the media. Technically, tweets are much easier to collect (as opposed to, for example, scraping the content of complete articles from a wide range of newspapers and formats). A tweet from a media outlet is a man-made summary of the news, usually in the form of a *headline*. It conveys the main idea, and hence the main editorial point of view. Headlines of online news articles have shown to be a reliable source for adequately providing a high-level overview of the news events [1, 8, 28]. These summaries are expected to be representative of the newspaper's bias, but with the advantage that bias is easier to detect than in a full articles (shorter, to the point). Tweets also contain features/annotations (e.g. hashtags (#) and mentions (@)) that help to give semantic to the text.

Chile ranks among the top-10 countries regarding the average number of Twitter users per 1000 individuals [21]. This allows experiments to be comparable with other countries where a larger number of studies have been performed, such as the UK and even the United States. We find this of particular interest, since many of the studies in the literature have been conducted only on English-speaking countries, which may bias the knowledge we posses in general about these issues.

To create our database of outlets, we used different sources, with Poderopedia's "influence" database as our baseline[8], manually adding other news outlets in Chile. Our database contains 399 *active* accounts[9]. The data set contains 1,916,709 tweets, spanning a period of 8 months - from October 6, 2015 to June 4, 2016. The accounts vary dramatically in tweet publication behavior, with some having published more than a hundred thousand tweets to others with less than a hundred in this timeframe. Out of the 399 active accounts, only 269 outlets published at least one document about the topics of interest.

3.2 PolQuiz

The *PolQuiz* has ten questions, divided into two groups: economic and personal issues, of five questions each. The answers to the questions may be *Agree*, *Maybe (or Don't Know)* or *Disagree*.
Personal issue questions:
  (1) Government should not censor speech, press, media or Internet.
  (2) Military service should be voluntary. There should be no draft.
  (3) There should be no laws regarding sex between consenting adults.
  (4) Repeal laws prohibiting adult possession and use of drugs.
  (5) There should be no National ID card.
Economic issue questions:
  (6) End corporate welfare. No government handouts to business.
  (7) End government barriers to international free trade.
  (8) Let people control their own retirement: privatize Social Security.
  (9) Replace government welfare with private charity.
  (10) Cut taxes and government spending by 50% or more.

Based on the answers to these questions, the quiz-taker is classified into one of five categories: left-liberal, libertarian, centrist, right-conservative, or statist. *Left-liberalism* is a political ideology that supports governments that take care of the welfare of vulnerable people and keeps a centralized economy, but at the same time, allows a great deal of liberties in personal matters. *Libertarians* seek freedom in both economic and personal issues, minimizing the role of the state in all matters. An extreme position in this direction would be anarchism. On the other side, *statists* - or supporters of a big government - want the state to regulate both personal and economic issues. Examples of this position would be totalitarian regimes, such as Kim Jong-Un in North Korea. *Right-wing conservatives* are more reluctant to accept changes in personal issues and want official standards on these matters (i.e. morality and family traditions), but demand economic freedom and a free market. Finally, *centrists* accept or even support a balance between the government reach and personal/economic freedom. They favor selective government interventions to current problems while avoiding drastic measures that may shift society to either side of the spectrum.

---

[7]Twitter reports 313 million active users, see https://about.twitter.com/company (accessed Aug. 2016)

[8]http://apps.poderopedia.org/mapademedios/index/
[9]An account is *active* if it tweets at least once a month

For each *Agree* answer, we increase the score of the quiz-taker in the corresponding dimension by 20 points. If the answer is *Maybe (or don't know)*, we only add 10 points. Finally, if the answer is *Disagree*, no points are added. This way, if the quiz taker agrees with all the issues in one dimension, it will be in one end of that axis. In the other extreme of the axis, we will have a quiz-taker who disagrees with all issues in that dimension. In our study, we assume that news outlets are (or strive to be) unbiased, so in an ideal world, most of their comments should have no polarity toward any side of the issue and, as such, they should score as a *Maybe*. Another expected behavior would be that news outlets report on both sides of the issue to cover different points of view. Both approaches would result in the news outlet being in the center of the graph.

3.3 Operationalizing the Quiz

We filtered the collected tweets to get only those with information regarding the issues referred to in the *PolQuiz*. For this, we created a seed query for each question, containing a set of preselected keywords (see Table 1).

With the subset of documents returned by the seed queries, we then analyzed the hash-tags to find an expanded set of labels that may represent related aspects of the same issues [18]. We removed hash-tags that contain the name of a news outlet, as it is common practice in news papers accounts to use hash-tags to refer to themselves or the original source of the news (regardless of the subject). We also remove hash-tags with names of politicians: even when these politicians could potentially provide some relevant documents, they also introduce a lot of noise, mostly due to the salience of politicians who appear regularly in the news for a wide variety of issues not necessarily related to the query in question. The new labels are added as keywords to the original query. Our enriched queries give us the final set of tweets used to evaluate any possible bias of each news outlet, see Table 2.

Having the set of tweets for each question, we classified their polarity *with respect to the corresponding question*. For example, for *question 7* (**q7**), a tweet classified as *Agree* is *"TPP abrira puertas a más de 1.600 productos chilenos no incluidos en acuerdos vigentes." (tr. TPP will open doors for more than 1.600 Chilean products not included in existing agreements)*. For that same question, the following tweet disagrees with it: *"El TPP: un misil contra la soberanía" (tr. TPP: a missile against our sovereignty)*. In other words, we classify the polarity of the tweet with respect to the corresponding issue. As the number of tweets is too large to label manually, we created and trained a supervised model for each question. This approach also allows us to scale in the presence of an even larger number of resulting documents.

To create a representative sample for the training set, we randomly select, where possible, two tweets from each question from each news outlet. We took care to not include duplicate tweets (tweets with the exact same text) published by the same outlet. The training set consisted of 1916 documents (an average of about 190 documents per question). We manually classified this training set in four groups: *Agree*, *Maybe*, *Disagree* and *Out of topic (Not relevant)*. The distribution of each training set is shown in Table 2.

For the automatic classification task, we used a "Randomized Trees" model[11] [13]. Decision trees are less susceptible to overfitting, considering that we have relatively small training sets. Given that the classes in our training set are not evenly populated, we decided to evaluate the model using a 10 iterations stratified shuffle-split cross validation. Each fold leaves out 20% for validation. The other 80% is selected while preserving the percentage of samples for each class. The accuracy values for each model is presented in Table 2.

After the classification stage, we scored each news outlet on each question. We removed those documents classified as *off-topic (Not relevant)*. We scored the remaining documents' polarity according to the *PolQuiz* scoring system and we found the average for each question/news-outlet pair. For simplicity, in the question/news-outlet pairs for which we have no associated documents, we assume a *Maybe (or don't know)* answer. This assumption is the least disruptive towards the default supposition of an unbiased media[12].

In order to find out how sensitive the observed bias is to noise, we repeated the scoring steps 20 times. Each time we leave out 5% of the tweets, selected at random while maintaining the original distribution of documents per question. Each time we measure the average score of the news outlets for which we were able to answer at least one question in the corresponding dimension. We did not go over 5%, because the smallest news outlets already have a small set of documents: removing too many entries would have resulted in the elimination of an entire outlet, affecting the results.

Finally, we tested how the entire system adapts to the local environment. For a proof of concept, we introduced the subject of abortion in the personal dimension. This topic appears among the personal issues in other political quizzes (e.g Political Compass[13]) In addition, abortion was a very relevant and controversial topic in the Chilean media during this period because of a new bill presented by the president and approved by the Chamber of Deputies to legalize the abortion on three grounds: pregnancy resulting from rape, lethal fetal infeasibility or danger to the life of the pregnant women. We formulated this new question as follows:

(0) All women should be free to choose whether she wants to terminate her pregnancy or not.

Notice that the question is formulated in the same "direction" as the rest of the questions. This is, agreeing with the statement will be an indicator of a more liberal tendency by the quiz taker.

We apply the same methodology described before to the original *PolQuiz*. We named this question **q0** and the query we applied (before injecting the hash-tags) is shown in Table 3. The enriched query returned 4891 documents from our corpus. We selected two random documents for each news outlets to create a training set containing 409 tweets. We had an average precision of 0.70 ($\pm$0.08) in the 10 iterations stratified shuffle-split cross validation.

3.4 Rank difference

Using the *PolQuiz*, we aim to show empirically that the news media in Chile have some socio-economic leaning. This means that news

---

[11]Implemented in the python library scikit-learn in the module `sklearn.tree.ExtraTreeClassifier`
[12]We are aware this is too conservative. However, for the sake of space, we leave a more detailed discussion for future research
[13]https://www.politicalcompass.org/

Table 1: Initial set of keywords for each query.

Question	Keywords
q1	(censura | libertad) & (prensa | discurso | expresion)
q2	(servicio | reclutamiento | entrenamiento | reserva) & (militar | ejercito | armada)
q3	(ley | legal | legislacion | regulacion | penalizacion) & (sexual | prostitucion | sexo | sodomia | gay) & ¬(infantil | menor | niño | acoso | abuso | agresion)
q4	(ley | legal | legislacion | regulacion | penalizacion) & (droga | marihuana | cannabis | psicotropico | cocaina)
q5	inmigracion | inmigrante | refugiado | xenofobia
q6	(subsidio | bienestar | ayuda) & (corporativa | empresa)
q7	(trato | tratado | convenio | negociacion | relacion) & (comercial | economica) & (internacional | bilateral | gobierno | libre | liberal | barrera | proteccion | bloque)
q8	("seguridad social" | afp[10] | pension | jubilado | prevision) & (privada | gobierno | estatal)
q9	("beneficio sociale" | bono | "ayuda sociale" | "programa social") & (gobierno)
q10	(reducion | recorte | aumento | incremento) & (impuesto | gasto) & (gobierno | gubernamental)

Our actual queries are designed so they can also find variations of the keywords (such as variations in gender and number)

Table 2: Tweets extracted from our corpus after applying the enriched queries.

Qs	# tweets	Training set (TS)	% Agr (TS)	% Mb (TS)	% Dis (TS)	% Not rel (TS)	Prc (±2 * *stdev*)
q1	374	179	0.486	0.167	0.178	0.167	0.76 (± 0.14)
q2	194	132	0.181	0.295	0.204	0.318	0.87 (± 0.11)
q3	144	78	0.576	0.051	0.243	0.128	0.83 (± 0.17)
q4	597	203	0.610	0.083	0.142	0.162	0.80 (± 0.10)
q5	746	219	0.351	0.127	0.159	0.360	0.73 (± 0.16)
q6	636	117	0.264	0.256	0.239	0.239	0.53 (± 0.20)
q7	1162	238	0.298	0.247	0.399	0.054	0.76 (± 0.09)
q8	251	117	0.213	0.094	0.418	0.273	0.76 (± 0.13)
q9	298	167	0.059	0.131	0.694	0.113	0.87 (± 0.09)
q10	8573	466	0.167	0.133	0.660	0.038	0.71 (± 0.06)

The last column indicates the average precision obtained by the model in cross-validation (See Section 3.3)

Table 3: Initial set of keywords for q0 query.

Question	Keywords
q0	(ley | legal | legislacion | regulacion | penalizacion | despenalizacion) & (aborto | interrupcion | embarazo)

Our actual queries are designed so they can also find variation of the keywords (such as variations in gender and number)

outlets tend to have a stand in at least some of the controversial topics that dominate the political landscape of the country. However, we are also interested in the *nature* of the bias regarding such controversial topics.

To do this, we use the *rank difference* method proposed in [17]. Rank difference is used to identify terms that characterize a specific domain. For example, the word *court* will be probably identified as a term if we are analyzing a corpus of legal documents. The method creates a ranking of words based on their frequency in a domain and a generic corpus. By comparing their relative position in both corpora, the algorithm identifies words that are significantly more used in a given domain. These unusual word frequencies are used as an indication of the importance of these words in the given domain. The formula for calculating rank difference is shown in Equation 1,

$$\tau(w) = \frac{r_D(w)}{\sum_{w' \in V_D} r_D(w')} - \frac{r_B(w)}{\sum_{w' \in V_B} r_B(w')} \quad (1)$$

where $r_D(w)$ and $r_B(w)$ are the ranks of word w in the domain and background corpus respectively. Rank normalization is done against the summation of all word rankings in the corresponding vocabulary (V_D and V_B).

3.5 Survey

To investigate to what extent the bias – as measured with the *PolQuiz* and investigated using the rank difference method – is perceived by the general audience, we conducted an online survey. We chose abortion as the topic of this survey, as this is (as explained in Section 3.3) a current and controversial item in Chile that has received an important amount of coverage in the local media. This means that most people in Chile are aware of the discussion and probably have their own criteria. We also restricted our survey to the subset of news outlets who had relevant tweets for at least four questions per dimension (see Section 4) since these are the ones that we were able to position in the chart with the highest confidence.

We calculated the bi-grams' rank difference (see Section 3.4) for each news outlet. We decided to present bi-grams to users in the survey instead of words, because bi-grams offer more context, so it was easier for people to assess the connotation of a word or set of words within the selected topic. We also decided to use bi-grams over named entities because people not always recognize all the names involved in the discussion, although they do have an intuition in the discourse and the arguments used on both sides.

For each survey we presented a randomly selected and anonymised list (each list represents a news outlet) with the top-20 ranked bi-grams in one column and the bottom-20 bi-grams in another column. The top-20 list was presented as the words used with a relatively high frequency by one outlet. The bottom-20 list was presented as words the outlet tried to avoid or used with a relatively low frequency. The user had to answer if, based on these lists, he or she considered the outlet to be "in favor" or "against" abortion. The user could also respond with an "I can't tell" option. A user could answer the survey more than once, but the random selection was always made from the remaining lists.

We scored the "perceived bias" for each news outlet based on the answers we received in the survey. For each outlet, we calculated the percentage of users that answered "in favor" and subtracted the percentage of "against" answers. These percentage include the users that answered "I can't tell". So, we consider outlets with a negative score to have a conservative "perceived bias". Equivalently, outlets with a positive score are considered as liberals in our "perceived bias". It is worth noticing that an unbiased news outlet should be expected to score close to zero (because it should have mixed signals and, either a proportional number of user labeled in each direction or most users were unable to classify it).

4 RESULTS AND DISCUSSION

In this section, we first show how the *PolQuiz* helps to measure the bias in the media. We verified that our results are stable to small changes in the dataset and investigated the benefit of contextualizing the quiz by including new questions that fit the current political landscape in Chile. In Section 4.2, we explore the nature of the bias showed by the media by using the rank difference method. We show the differences in the type of coverage between news outlets of various leanings when we deep in the analysis of one particular topic. Finally, in Section 4.3 we investigate, using a survey, to what extent this bias is perceived by the general audience.

4.1 Measuring Bias Using the PolQuiz

For our statistical analysis we will treat each axis independently, so we can work with values in only one dimension.

We aim to make a comparative analysis between outlets, so we only report quantifications relative to the other news outlets. For this, we normalize the scores on each axis in the range [0, 100].

Using our methodology, we find that the news media do have a political bias. This corresponds with previous findings studying this subject [7, 12, 24]. We conducted a one-sample Student t-test[14] (two-sided) for each dimension (economic and personal) to test if the mean score is significantly different from 50 (the assumed unbiased score). We used, for each dimension, only the scores of those news outlets for which we were able to answer at least one question on that dimension. For the economic dimension, there is a significant bias, $t(254) = -10.93, p < .001$, with a leaning to the left-wing ($M = 40.28, SD = 14.21$). In the personal issues the bias is lower, but still is statistically significant, $t(190) = -2.10, p < .05$, with a leaning to the conservative side ($M = 47.42, SD = 16.98$).

We found that the bias is more evident in economic issues than in personal issues. This can be seen in the number of news outlets that comment on those issues and the average score for that dimension. The slight left-wing bias in the economic issues might be explained by the political context of Chile during the observed period: the president, Michelle Bachelet, is affiliated to the socialist party. The ruling coalition is "Nueva Mayoría", which mainly consists of center-left to left-wing parties, but with a strong component of Christian democracy. Christian democracy is still a center-left party, but conservative, specially in personal issues. So, in this case,

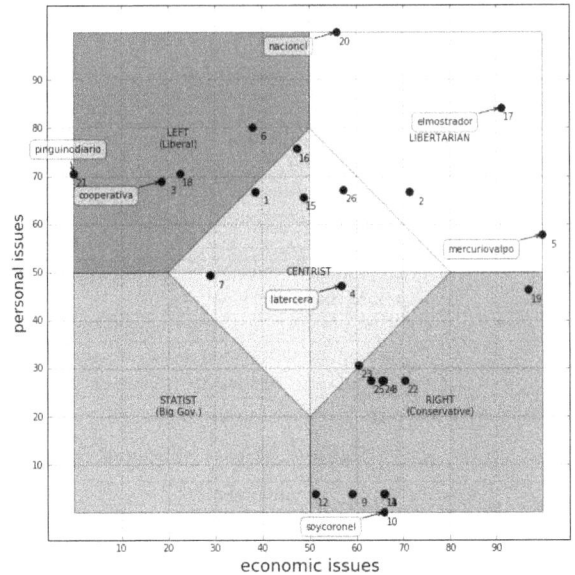

Figure 1: Relative position of the 26 news outlets who had relevant tweets for at least four questions per dimension (the *26ers*): 1. adnradiochile, 2. biobio, 3. cooperativa, 4. latercera, 5. mercuriovalpo, 6. publimetrochile, 7. emol, 8. soyarauco, 9 soyconcepcion, 10. soycoronel, 11. soyquillota, 12. soysanantonio, 13. soytalcahuano, 14 soytome, 15. dfinanciero, 16. el_ciudadano, 17. elmostrador, 18. tele13_radio, 19. el_dinamo, 20. nacioncl, 21. pinguinodiario, 22. soychillan, 23. soycopiapo, 24. soyvaldiviacl, 25. soyvalparaiso, 26. t13

the observed bias has a similar tendency to the political alignment of the ruling coalition. This result is also in correspondence with the theory postulated in the *Propaganda Model* [16]. On the personal issues dimension, we can also see some bias, although less prominent, tending to the conservative end of the spectrum.

We show in Figure 1 the 26 news outlets for which we were able to answer at least four questions on each dimension (we will call this subset of news outlets the *26ers*). This represents 10% of our database and 13% of those that regularly report on economics and politics. Even though we are showing relative values with respect to the other outlets, we show them on the original Nolan's chart, to give an intuition on their political tendencies. We tagged some of the most prominent ones to help to understand the landscape.

In the rightmost cell, we have mercuriovalpo[15] (*El Mercurio de Valparaíso*), one of the oldest newspapers in Chile currently in circulation. This newspaper is part of a big conglomerate (*El Mercurio S.A.P*) that owns more than 20 news papers and several radio stations, among other broadcast media (such as magazines, TV cable, etc.). The regional newspaper *Soy Coronel* (soycoronel), on the bottom, is also part of this group. In fact, 11 regional newspapers of *El Mercurio S.A.P* are within this 26 and are all clustered bottom-right, with scores under 31 on personal issues. As we mentioned earlier, the *El Mercurio*'s newspapers are popularly perceived as right-wing conservative, which coincides with the scores they received.

---

[14]The QQplot and the histogram suggested normality was a reasonable assumption.

[15]Tags in Figure 1 are the corresponding Twitter accounts (e.g. https://twitter.com/mercuriovalpo)

La Tercera (latercera), is owned by *Copesa S.A.*, which is *El Mercurio*'s closest competitor. These two companies have a so-called news media duopoly. *La Tercera*, also in the lower-right quadrant but closer to the center of the chart, is thought to be moderate-conservative[16]. *El Mostrador* (elmostrador) is an on-line newspaper with a perceived orientation to progressivism[17], which corresponds with its position in the chart.

Finally, *La Nación* (nacioncl) is a newspaper that currently only publishes its online edition and is partially controlled by the government. This newspaper appears in the topmost region of the *personal* dimension. Compared to the other 25 news outlets, this one appears as the most progressive on personal issues. This score is due to a series of populist reforms promoted by the government during the observed period (i.e. therapeutic marihuana legalization, decriminalization of abortion, anti-xenophobic campaigns, promote voluntary enlistment of women to the military service, etc.)

To summarize, using the PolQuiz we were able to position Chilean newspapers on a chart with respect to their bias with regard to economic and personal issues. In the next sections we will investigate the nature of the bias and to what extent these positions are in line with common perceptions. However, before doing so, we first need to know how stable the results are.

4.1.1 Stability of the results. In order to find out the stability of the observed bias with respect to changes in the obtained evidence (i.e. the collected tweets), we repeated the scoring steps 20 times. Each time we leave out 5% of the tweets selected at random, while maintaining the original distribution of documents per question. Each time, we measure the average score of the news outlets for which we were able to answer at least one question in the corresponding dimension. In the *economic* issues, we could observe a consistent bias to the left ($M = 40.45$, 95% $CI[36.91, 43.99]$). On the other hand, the *personal* dimension, although it is also leaning to one side, is much closer to the center of the spectrum ($M = 46.89$, 95% $CI[43.99, 49.79]$). Figure 2 shows a similar analysis, but at an individual level in the *26ers*. The mean for each individual score stays close to its original position, and each newspaper can be located in a relatively small neighborhood with high confidence, meaning that there are not any drastic changes in the previous classification.

The relatively low impact of leaving out data in the positioning process indicates that the results are not very sensitive to change and not influenced by only a small number of tweets.

4.1.2 Contextualizing the PolQuiz. We noticed that some of our queries, particularly in the personal issues dimension, returned only a small number of documents (e.i **q2** and **q3**). This is because of lack of interest or too few relevant events related to the corresponding topics during the observed period. We think that a way to counteract this environmental/circumstantial effect is to substitute the respective questions or to increase the number of questions.

We repeated our analysis using **q0** as a replacement for question **q3** (related to laws concerning sex between consenting adult, see Section 3.2). We replaced **q3**, because it was the one with the lowest number of retrieved documents. This substitution increased the

[16]https://en.wikipedia.org/wiki/La_Tercera
[17]https://es.wikipedia.org/wiki/El_Mostrador

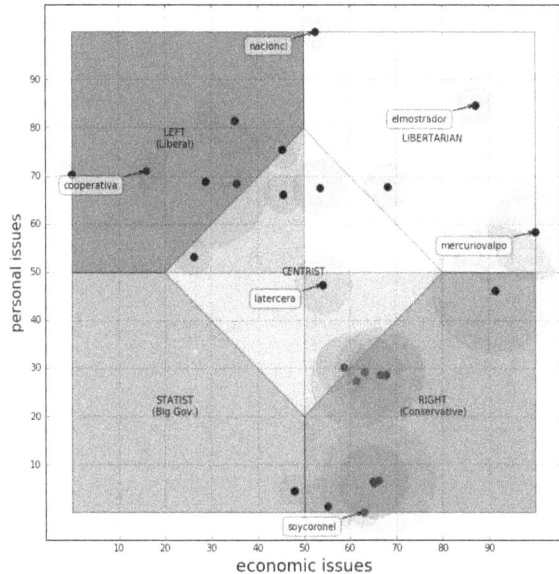

Figure 2: **Relative position of the *26ers*. The score on each dimension is the average over 20 repetitions, leaving out each time a random 5% of the documents. Gray shade around outlets is its 95% confidence interval.**

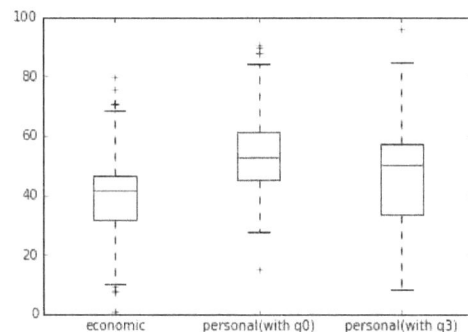

Figure 3: **New scores after replacing q3 by q0. These are the scores of news outlets for which we were able to answer at least one question in the corresponding dimension.**

number of news outlets with at least one answer. There is now a stronger statistical effect for the personal issues dimension, $t(239) = 3.54, p < .001$. Interestingly, this dimension now leans to the more liberal end of the spectrum ($M = 53.57, SD = 15.63$) (see Figure 3).

In Figure 4 we plot the scores of the *26ers* in the original quiz (dots) and the adapted quiz (diamonds). Note that the difference in scores between the quiz with **q3** and the quiz with **q0** is considerably larger (with a negative difference) for outlets in the right/conservative quadrant. This is expected and validates the model.

4.2 Investigating the nature of bias using rank difference

The PolQuiz showed the existence of bias in Chilean media. In this section, we investigate the nature of this bias in terms of vocabulary used and entities mentioned in the different newspapers' tweets (see Section 3.4). We focused on the *26ers* and the topic of abortion.

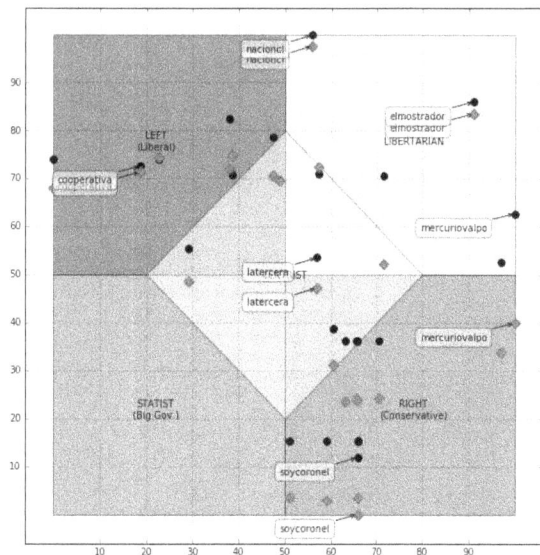

Figure 4: Relative position of the *26ers*. Dots represent the scores with q3. Diamonds represent the scores with q0.

4.2.1 Topic bias based on named entities. We used the Stanford's NE recognizer system [9] to extract the entities mentioned in the tweets related to the abortion issue. We compare the extracted entities against a list of politicians, public personalities and activist groups. For the list of politicians and their position in the abortion issue, we use the vote sessions in the house of representatives[18] and in the senate[19]. We manually labeled another 53 personalities and groups according to comments and events reported in the local news. The complete list L_E has 199 labeled entities. We labeled with −1 the politicians who voted against the abortion bill, and the public figures that were openly against the issue. Equivalently, we use +1 for politicians and personalities in favor of the subject. We assign a 0 to the entities not included in our list. We will refer to these labels as the leaning of the entities (e.g. *leaning(entity)*)

After applying the rank difference method to the NE mention counts, we calculated a score for each outlet in function of the $\tau(entity)$ and the leaning of *entity* in the issue (for every *entity* mentioned more than once in the news). This final score of the outlet o_i is found using the equation 2.

$$score(o_i) = \sum_{e \in L_E} \Big(\tau(e) * leaning(e) \Big) / size\_of(L_E)) \quad (2)$$

A low value in this score indicates that this outlet tends to mention with relatively high frequency entities with a conservative leaning and/or it tends to ignore those with a more liberal view.

As expected, the outlets tagged as independent, libertarians and classical liberalism are within the higher values. According to our scores, this means they have comparably more mentions of entities with a liberal leaning than the rest of the outlets. Interestingly, the lower values are occupied by the outlets linked to parties in the ruling coalition (Christian democracy and Left-Liberal(*nacioncl*)). Apparently these outlets focus their tweets in negative reports of

the opposition. For example, when we look at the rank-differnce results for *nacioncl*, within the top-20 entities, only two refer to entities with a liberal leaning ('President Michelle Bachelet' and 'Government'). To investigate more on this, we run a sentiment analysis on the most used bi-grams. The results are presented in the next section.

4.2.2 Topic bias based on bi-grams. We again apply the rank difference method, this time using the bi-gram counts in the tweets relevant to the subject of abortion. Following the same strategy as before, we calculated a score for each outlet in function of the $\tau(bigram)$ and the sentiment calculated for *bigram* (for every *bigram* mentioned more than once in the news). For determining the sentiment of words and bi-grams we use the Spanish lexicon from [25]. To calculate $\tau(bigram)$ we use a formula equivalent to that shown in Equation 2. Accordingly, we give a similar interpretation to these scores. That is, a high value indicates that this outlet tends to convey mostly positive sentiments with the bi-grams used with relatively high frequency and/or avoid using negative sentiments when referring to the issue of abortion. For example, *elmostrador*, with the highest score, has as a frequently use bi-gram "proyecto aprobado" (tr. "project approved" - referring to the bill). This bi-gram is classify as positive by the sentiment analyzer, so it will add to the score. On the other hand, this same outlet has "injusticia gobierno" (tr. "government injustice") as a totally ignored bi-gram. Since the bi-gram is assigned a negative sentiment and the rank-difference is also negative, the bi-gram will also add to the score of the outlet, pushing it to the liberal side. Following the same reasoning, an outlet with a very low score can be understood as an outlet that uses predominantly negative words with relatively high frequency.

When we analyze the scores of the *26ers*, we notice that *nacioncl* (controlled by the government) has the lowest score. This, together with the previous NE analysis, confirms the theory that this outlet focuses in tweeting negative reports of the opposition, at least for the abortion issue. Most of the others outlets show the expected behavior, with conservative in the lower half of the ranking (i.e. lower scores) and liberals in the higher positions.

4.3 Survey

For the survey described in Section 3.5, we collected 372 answers from 54 unique Chilean[20] users on how they perceive the bias on the topic of abortion in the different Chilean newspapers. We received between 11 and 19 answers for each of the *26ers* (M: 14.31, SD: 2.07). We carried out 10 Fleiss' kappa measurements; each time we selected 10 ratings at random per outlet (subject). This shows a fair agreement in the answers (M: 0.2253, SD: 0.0167). In Table 4 we show the *26ers* and their corresponding "Perceived bias" (see Section 3.5). The political alignment information shown in the table was extracted from Wikipedia[21], the official web site of the news outlet or the political alignment known for the owners. Note that the Christian Democracy party is part of the center-left coalition that was ruling in Chile during the observed period, so is generally in favor of the social changes promoted by the government.

[18]https://www.camara.cl/trabajamos/sala_votacion_detalle.aspx?prmID=23099
[19]http://www.senado.cl/appsenado/index.php?mo=sesionessala&ac=detalleVotacion&votaid=6668

[20]The IP addresses indicate we have representation of different regions of the country
[21]Since Wikipedia pages are a crowdsourced content, we consider the political alignment extracted from there as either self-declared or a popular perception

Table 4: Results from popular survey for the *26ers*.

Id	Name	Owner	Political alignment	Perceived bias	PolQuiz Personal issues
21	pinguinodiario	Patagónica Publicaciones	–	-66.67	39.18
24	soyvaldiviacl	El Mercurio	Right-wing, conservative	-66.67	-50.49
22	soychillan	El Mercurio	Right-wing, conservative	-57.14	-50.55
25	soyvalparaiso	El Mercurio	Right-wing, conservative	-43.75	-51.81
8	soyarauco	El Mercurio	Right-wing, conservative	-42.86	-51.27
12	soysanantonio	El Mercurio	Right-wing, conservative	-30.77	-92.98
13	soytalcahuano	El Mercurio	Right-wing, conservative	-30.77	-92.98
18	tele13_radio	Grupo Luksic & PUC	–	-28.57	52.42
9	soyconcepcion	El Mercurio	Right-wing, conservative	-25.00	-94.09
14	soytome	El Mercurio	Right-wing, conservative	-25.00	-92.92
7	emol	El Mercurio	Right-wing, conservative	-25.00	-0.59
10	soycoronel	El Mercurio	Right-wing, conservative	-23.53	-100
11	soyquillota	El Mercurio	Right-wing, conservative	-18.18	-92.92
15	dfinanciero	Grupo Claro	Right-wing, conservative	0.00	42.57
5	mercuriovalpo	El Mercurio	Right-wing, conservative	21.43	-51.81
2	biobio	BÁŋo-BÁŋo Comunicaciones	Independent	23.53	6.91
6	publimetrochile	Grupo metro	International	25.00	47.50
17	elmostrador	La Plaza	Libertarian	26.32	70.95
19	el_dinamo	Ediciones Giro Pais	Christian democracy	29.41	-30.79
4	latercera	Copesa	Classical liberalism	33.33	-3.38
1	adnradiochile	Grupo Prisa	International	37.50	52.98
16	el_ciudadano	Red de medios de los pueblos	Libertarian	37.50	44.54
23	soycopiapo	El Mercurio	Right-wing, conservative	38.46	-36.21
3	cooperativa	Co. Chilena de Comunicaciones	Christian democracy	57.14	46.04
26	t13	Grupo Luksic & PUC	–	57.14	48.45
20	nacioncl	Estado de Chile	Left, Liberal	63.64	100

The list is sorted by the perceived bias. Outlets with an unclear Political Alignment (shadowed rows in the table) were left out of the analysis.

Results show that there is a perceivable difference in the language used by the outlets in both sides of the spectrum. Note that, based on the rank difference of bi-grams, the users were able to collectively classify the outlets with over 90% precision[22]. Our positioning of these outlets in the adapted *PolQuiz* has also a high correspondence in the bias direction (90%) with the political alignment and a good agreement with the direction of the Perceived bias (80%).

To evaluate the relative positions of the outlets in our *PolQuiz*, we calculated the number of inversions with respect to the ranking of the outlets in the perceived bias. The Kendall's Tau-b coefficient between the two rankings is $\tau_b(21) = 0.4203$ ($z = 2.66, p < .01$). Even though the popular perception resulting from the survey can not be seen as ground-truth for the relative positioning of the outlets, it is important to notice that our results show a good correlation with the intuition of the public. As a future work, we aim to add some other content features (e.g. leaning of the named entities) to the polarity classification of the tweets as these may help to refine the relative positioning found by our model.

To summarize, we have shown that reported political alignment is highly correlated with the PolQuiz results as well as with the bias, as perceived by the general audience. This implies that existing bias has a noticeable influence on how controversial issues such as abortion are reported in the media.

5 CONCLUSIONS

In this paper, we presented an automatic approach for estimating the political bias of news outlets in Chile, exploiting the well-known and widely used "The World's Smallest Political Quiz". We empirically confirmed the estimation results and showed that they are stable with respect to evolving data. Furthermore, we have demonstrated the benefits of adapting questions to the local context. Building upon the PolQuiz results, we investigated the nature of this political bias and found this to exist in the chosen vocabulary and the entities covered by the newspaper. Finally, we conducted a survey, of which the results confirm that political bias in newspapers has an impact on how controversial topics are covered and that the general audience does notice this bias. Our methodology does not make too many assumptions about the underlying system. The way it is designed could be applied to any Western culture. Our system can deal with any number of outlets, can compare relative quantitive positions, can show empirical evidence of consistent bias, and can partially explain the source of these tendencies.

As a future work we are interested to see what is the most accurate way to score the missing answers. Since "coverage" is a form of bias [24], perhaps the outlet is not being *neutral* by not mentioning a specific subject. Even when the decision of which stories/events are newsworthy is subjective and depends on the editorial strategy [29], there are some events that are very relevant in the national context and are covered for the majority of the

---

[22]We are not taking into account those for which we could not find a political alignment or those that belong to international groups

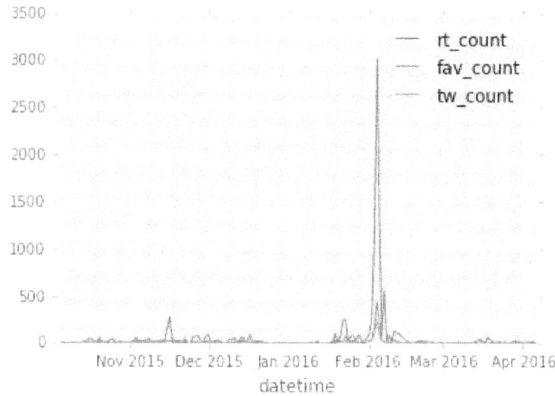

Figure 5: Counting tweets and re-tweets for q7.

media. So, a complete silence of a news outlet on such an event may be interpreted as something other than neutrality.

For example, question **q7** is about international free trade. Taking the number of tweets and re-tweet as an indicator of important events [20], we can see in Figure 5 that this topic has had at least one major event during this period. This event was the adscription of Chile to the Trans-Pacific Partnership (TPP) signed by the country on Feb 3th, 2016. Despite the magnitude of the event, only 135 out of 198 newspapers with a section on politics mentioned it. A plausible cause is that the other news outlets decided not to report about this event, in other words 'bias by omission'.

We show that a careful selection or update of the questions may lead to a significant improvement in the results. If we have an inside understanding of the socio-economic environment from where the news are being collected, then we could replace the questions to capture more relevant topics. In this sense, we could benefit from advances in systems that focus on identifying controversial topics in social media [10]. On the other hand, if we do not have any intuition on the news collected, then we can accumulate the new questions so we can widen the spectrum of topics and have a better chance of capturing relevant events/discussions with our queries.

For individuals as well as for society as a whole it is important to recognize and understand media bias that are shaped through underlying general political or socio-economic orientations. As we have shown in this paper, these general tendencies have a clear and noticeable effect on the way concrete topics are covered and commented upon, and therefore should be investigated and published.

REFERENCES

[1] Scott L. Althaus, Jill A. Edy, and Patricia F. Phalen. 2001. Using Substitutes for Full-Text News Stories in Content Analysis: Which Text Is Best? *American Journal of Political Science* 45, 3 (2001), 707–723. http://www.jstor.org/stable/2669247
[2] Jisun An, Meeyoung Cha, Krishna Gummadi, and Jon Crowcroft. 2011. Media Landscape in Twitter: A World of New Conventions and Political Diversity. In *Proceedings of the Fifth International Conference on Weblogs and Social Media*. AAAI, Menlo Park, CA, USA.
[3] Johan Bollen, Alberto Pepe, and Huina Mao. 2009. Modeling public mood and emotion: Twitter sentiment and socio-economic phenomena. *CoRR* abs/0911.1583 (2009). http://arxiv.org/abs/0911.1583
[4] Maurice Bryson and William McDill. 1968. The political spectrum: A bidimensional approach. *Rampart Journal of Individualist Thought* 4, 2 (1968), 19–26.
[5] Raviv Cohen and Derek Ruths. 2013. Classifying Political Orientation on Twitter: It's Not Easy!. In *ICWSM*, Emre Kiciman, Nicole B. Ellison, Bernie Hogan, Paul Resnick, and Ian Soboroff (Eds.). The AAAI Press. http://dblp.uni-trier.de/db/

conf/icwsm/icwsm2013.html#CohenR13
[6] M Conover, B Gonçalves, J Ratkiewicz, A Flammini, and F Menczer. Predicting the Political Alignment of Twitter Users. In *Proceedings of 3rd IEEE Conference on Social Computing (SocialCom)*.
[7] Alexander Dallmann, Florian Lemmerich, Daniel Zoller, and Andreas Hotho. 2015. Media Bias in German Online Newspapers. In *Proceedings of the 26th ACM Conference on Hypertext & Social Media (HT '15)*. ACM, 133–137.
[8] Daniel Dor. 2003. On newspaper headlines as relevance optimizers. *Journal of Pragmatics* 35, 5 (2003), 695 – 721. DOI:http://dx.doi.org/10.1016/S0378-2166(02)00134-0
[9] Jenny Rose Finkel, Trond Grenager, and Christopher Manning. 2005. Incorporating Non-local Information into Information Extraction Systems by Gibbs Sampling. In *Proceedings of the 43rd Annual Meeting on Association for Computational Linguistics (ACL '05)*. 363–370.
[10] Kiran Garimella, Gianmarco De Francisci Morales, Aristides Gionis, and Michael Mathioudakis. 2015. Quantifying Controversy in Social Media. *CoRR* abs/1507.05224 (2015). http://arxiv.org/abs/1507.05224
[11] Venkata Rama Kiran Garimella and Ingmar Weber. 2014. Co-following on Twitter. In *Proceedings of the 25th ACM Conference on Hypertext and Social Media (HT '14)*. 249–254.
[12] Matthew Gentzkow and Jesse M. Shapiro. 2010. What Drives Media Slant? Evidence From U.S. Daily Newspapers. *Econometrica* 78, 1 (2010), 35–71.
[13] Pierre Geurts, Damien Ernst, and Louis Wehenkel. 2006. Extremely randomized trees. *Machine Learning* 63, 1 (2006), 3–42.
[14] Jennifer Golbeck and Derek Hansen. 2011. Computing Political Preference Among Twitter Followers. In *Proceedings of the SIGCHI Conference on Human Factors in Computing Systems (CHI '11)*. ACM, 1105–1108.
[15] Y. Gu, T. Chen, Y. Sun, and B. Wang. 2016. Ideology Detection for Twitter Users with Heterogeneous Types of Links. *ArXiv e-prints* (Dec. 2016). arXiv:1612.08207
[16] E.S. Herman and N. Chomsky. 1988. *Manufacturing consent*. Pantheon Books. https://books.google.cl/books?id=Up5sAAAAIAAJ
[17] Chunyu Kit and Xiaoyue Liu. 2008. Measuring mono-word termhood by rank difference via corpus comparison. *Terminology. International Journal of Theoretical and Applied Issues in Specialized Communication* 14, 2 (2008), 204–229.
[18] Haokai Lu, James Caverlee, and Wei Niu. 2015. BiasWatch: A Lightweight System for Discovering and Tracking Topic-Sensitive Opinion Bias in Social Media. In *Proceedings of the 24th ACM International on Conference on Information and Knowledge Management*. 213–222.
[19] Aibek Makazhanov and Davood Rafiei. 2013. Predicting Political Preference of Twitter Users. In *Proceedings of the 2013 IEEE/ACM International Conference on Advances in Social Networks Analysis and Mining (ASONAM '13)*. ACM, 298–305.
[20] Felix Ming, Fai Wong, Chee Wei Tan, Soumya Sen, and Mung Chiang. 2013. Quantifying Political Leaning from Tweets and Retweets. In *Proceedings of the 7th International AAAI Conference on Web and Social Media*. AAAI Press, Boston, Massachusetts, USA.
[21] Delia Mocanu, Andrea Baronchelli, Nicola Perra, Bruno GonÃ§alves, Qian Zhang, and Alessandro Vespignani. 2013. The Twitter of Babel: Mapping World Languages through Microblogging Platforms. *PLoS ONE* 8, 4 (04 2013), e61981.
[22] DF Nolan. 1971. Classifying and Analysing Politico-Economic Systems. *The Individualist* (Jan. 1971), 5–11.
[23] Souneil Park, Seungwoo Kang, Sangyoung Chung, and Junehwa Song. 2012. A Computational Framework for Media Bias Mitigation. *ACM Trans. Interact. Intell. Syst.* 2, 2, Article 8 (2012), 32 pages.
[24] Diego Saez-Trumper, Carlos Castillo, and Mounia Lalmas. 2013. Social Media News Communities: Gatekeeping, Coverage, and Statement Bias. In *Proceedings of the 22Nd ACM International Conference on Information & Knowledge Management (CIKM '13)*. ACM, 1679–1684.
[25] Hans Stadthagen-Gonzalez, Constance Imbault, Miguel A. Pérez Sánchez, and Marc Brysbaert. 2016. Norms of valence and arousal for 14,031 Spanish words. *Behavior Research Methods* (2016), 1–13.
[26] Saatviga Sudharan, Thomas Lansdall-Welfare, Ilias Flaounas, and Nello Cristianini. 2012. ElectionWatch: Detecting Patterns in News Coverage of US Elections. In *Proceedings of the Demonstrations at the 13th Conference of the European Chapter of the Association for Computational Linguistics (EACL '12)*. 82–86.
[27] The Advocates for Self Government. 1985. The World's Smallest Political Quiz. (1985). [Online http://www.theadvocates.org/quiz/quiz.php; 12-August-2016].
[28] Giang Tran, Mohammad Alrifai, and Eelco Herder. 2015. *Timeline Summarization from Relevant Headlines*. Springer International Publishing, Cham, 245–256. DOI:http://dx.doi.org/10.1007/978-3-319-16354-3_26
[29] Giang Binh Tran and Eelco Herder. 2015. Detecting Filter Bubbles in Ongoing News Stories. In *UMAP Extended Proceedings*.
[30] Justine Zhang Cristian Danescu-Niculescu-Mizil Jure Leskovec Vlad Niculae, Caroline Suen. 2015. QUOTUS: The Structure of Political Media Coverage as Revealed by Quoting Patterns. In *Proceedings of WWW 2015*.
[31] Daniel Xiaodan Zhou, Paul Resnick, and Qiaozhu Mei. 2011. Classifying the Political Leaning of News Articles and Users from User Votes. In *Proceedings of the International AAAI Conference on Web and Social Media*.

Discovering Typical Histories of Entities by Multi-Timeline Summarization

Yijun Duan
Graduate School of Informatics,
Kyoto University, Japan
yijun@dl.kuis.kyoto-u.ac.jp

Adam Jatowt
Graduate School of Informatics,
Kyoto University, Japan
adam@dl.kuis.kyoto-u.ac.jp

Katsumi Tanaka
Graduate School of Informatics,
Kyoto University, Japan
tanaka@dl.kuis.kyoto-u.ac.jp

ABSTRACT

Categorization is a common solution used for organizing entities. For example, there are over 1.13 million categories in Wikipedia which group various types of entities such as persons, locations, etc. What is however often lacking when it comes to understanding categories is a clear information about the common aspects of the entities in a given category, for example, information on their shared histories. We propose in this paper a novel task of automatically creating summaries of typical histories of entities within their categories (e.g., a typical history of a Japanese city). The output summary is in the form of key representative events together with the information on their average dates. We introduce 4 methods for the aforementioned task and evaluate them on Wikipedia categories containing several types of cities and persons. The summaries we generate can provide information on the common evolution of entities falling into the same category as well as they can be compared with the summaries of related categories for providing contrastive type of knowledge.

CCS CONCEPTS

•Information systems → Digital libraries and archives;

KEYWORDS

entity summarization; digital history; typicality; Wikipedia

1 INTRODUCTION

Categorization is a common strategy applied for organizing and understanding entities. Wikipedia, which is considered these days to be the most comprehensive encyclopedia, contains over 1.13 million categories [3]. Each category typically consists of multiple related members that share some common traits (e.g., list of cities in Japan, list of American scientists active in the 19th century, etc.). To obtain a good understanding of a category, one needs to know well about its members, which is definitely a difficult task, especially, for larger categories. For example to fully understand the category of Japanese cities a user would need to read over 500 Wikipedia articles about different Japanese cities.

HT'17, July 4-7, 2017, Prague, Czech Republic.
© 2017 ACM. 978-1-4503-4708-2/17/07…$15.00
DOI: http://dx.doi.org/10.1145/3078714.3078725

In particular our interest is on historical knowledge. Wikipedia abounds in knowledge about the histories of entities or concepts. Many articles contain dedicated history sections. For instance, an article about a person typically contains his/her biography, and an article about a city usually includes extended section covering its history. In fact, most entities cannot be properly understood without the knowledge of their histories. The same can be said about their categories.

What is the history of Japanese cities? How is it different from, e.g., the history of Chinese or UK cities? Which events frequently occurred during the life of French scientists? How different was the life of a French scientist in the 19th century from that of an American scientist at that time? Questions of this type are not easy to be answered as they usually require substantial knowledge of history, or at least necessitate much effort. For an average user, to answer them he/she would need to read histories of many individual instances.

Straightforward approaches to automatically creating such historical knowledge would be to formulate it as a standard multi-document summarization task. However, traditional multi-document summarization techniques are not suitable for our scenario. The first problem is that input documents in multi-document summarization are assumed to be similar to each other (e.g., news articles about the same event). This assumption is not guaranteed in the case of the category history summarization as entity histories can be quite different from each other. For example, while we expect to find some common events and tendencies within Japanese cities, each individual city has many specific events in its history, which have varying degree of resemblance to the events of other cities. The second problem stems from the strong temporal character of input documents in our task. Entity histories (e.g., biographies) typically have a sequential character and abound in multiple dates used to mark important events in time, delineate key periods, support explanation of causal-effect relationships and, in general, to provide logical progression and coherent account of entity's history.

A uniting feature of traditional multi-document summarization techniques is an implicit assumption that the importance of a sentence can be estimated based on its similarity to other sentences within the input document set. For instance, in MEAD system [25] a sentence is judged important if it is similar to the centroid sentence, or if it is similar to many important sentences as in LexRank method [12]. Considering the unique characteristics of our task, it is clear that the common approach of sentence selection used in multi-document summarization is not appropriate. To provide effective means for capturing shared traits in entity histories we make use of the following observations: (1) *Histories of many types of entities (e.g., countries, persons) can be often divided into particular eras.* For example, the history of Japan as well as the one of Japanese cities covers several dynasties, while a person's life can be divided into stages such as childhood, early education, early career, etc. (2) *Documents describing histories of entities often contain underlying themes. These themes may be also correlated.* (3) *Themes as well as eras are usually not equally important.* An event contained in an important era and being part of important topics can be regarded more salient than one in less important era or belonging to trivial topics. (4) *Finally, some entities are better representatives of a category than others.* This is known as the *graded structure* [26] of a category. An event belonging to a typical entity is then deemed to be more salient than one of a trivial entity.

To reflect the above observations we rely on graph analysis. In particular, we adapt Markov Random Walk (MRW) [18] and Hyperlink-Induced Topic Search (HITS) [16] methods to our scenarios. To address the limitations of traditional techniques we propose 4 different models which are based on MRW and HITS and incorporate additional information about documents, eras, topics and topic correlation. The resulting summaries are in the form of timelines containing key events represented by set of words (Section 8.7 shows an example of output). Our experiments are performed on 7 Wikipedia category datasets (3 cities datasets and 4 persons datasets) with the results demonstrating higher effectiveness of our methods when compared to common multi-document summarization techniques.

To sum up, we make the following contributions in this paper:

(1) We introduce a new research problem of characterizing entity categories by generating typical histories of their entities.
(2) We propose 4 different models to discover typical histories of entities utilizing information about sentences, eras, topics and topic correlation. All our models work in an unsupervised way, which is important considering the lack of manually created summaries for most of the categories.
(3) The effectiveness of our methods is demonstrated in experiments on 7 Wikipedia category datasets.

The reminder of this paper is organized as follows. The related works are introduced in Section 2. We formulate our research problem and discuss different types of summaries in Section 3. Section 4 introduces the approach for event representation. Our summarization models are presented in Sections 5 and 6. Section 7 discusses the generalization of extracted events. In Section 8, we describe the experiments and evaluation results. Finally, we draw conclusions in Section 9.

2 RELATED WORK

Multi-Document Summarization. Multi-document summarization is the process of creating a summary that retains the most important information from multiple documents. Summarization methods can be coarsely divided into extractive summarization and abstractive summarization techniques. Extractive type of methods, to which our techniques belong, aims to select a subset of units (e.g. words, sentences) of original documents to form a summary. As an example of extractive methods, the centroid-based method MEAD [25] scores sentences based on sentence level and inter-sentence level features including cluster centroid, position, and TF-IDF, etc. Graph-based ranking methods, such as LexRank [12] and TextRank

[22], have been developed to estimate sentence importance using random walks and eigenvector centrality. In order to remove redundancy in final summaries, Maximal Marginal Relevance (MMR) technique [10] has been commonly used. Wan *et al.* have improved the graph-ranking algorithm by utilizing sentence-to-sentence and sentence-to-topic relationships [29], and intra-document and inter-document links between sentences [30]. In contrast, abstractive methods create summary containing words not explicitly present in the original documents. In this process, information fusion [5], sentence compression [17] and reformulation [21] may be applied.

Timeline Summarization. Timeline Summarization defined as the summarization of sequences of documents (typically, news articles about the same event) has been actively studied in the recent years. In [31], Yan *et al.* proposed the evolutionary timeline summarization (ETS) to compute evolution timelines consisting of a series of time-stamped summaries. David *et al.* presented a method for discovering biographical structure based on a probabilistic latent variable model [4]. Abdalghani *et al.* [2] addressed the problem of identifying important events in the past, present, and future from semantically-annotated large-scale document collections. Tuan *et al.* [28] presented a novel approach for timeline summarization of high-impact events, which uses entities instead of sentences for summarizing the events.

The above-mentioned methods can not be directly applied to our task. While documents are timestamped in the timeline summarization task, in the task of category summarization, each document spans over a certain range of time. Due to this, existing timeline summarization techniques are unable to estimate well the representativeness of a document and the correlation between sentences, which are important factors considered for generating summaries.

3 PROBLEM STATEMENT

3.1 Input

The input are documents containing histories of entities belonging to the same category. Each history-related document spans over a certain range of time and each sentence is assumed to refer to a historical event. The dates of events can be either explicitly mentioned in the sentence or could be estimated based on nearby sentences.

We note that sometimes categories can consist of entities with very diverse histories. Naturally, the summarization task becomes then more difficult in those cases.

3.2 Research Problem

Given a set of history-related documents $[d_1, d_2, ..., d_n]$ each about a particular entity within the same category and a time window $[t_{begin}, t_{end}]$, the task is to select k most typical historical events $[e_1, e_2, ..., e_k]$ to form a summarized timeline reflecting typical history of the entities within $[t_{begin}, t_{end}]$. Each event in the summary is represented by words $[w_1, w_2, ..., w_i]$.

The events selected for inclusion into the summary should be:

(1) **typical**: we want to retain typical information of the history of category entities;
(2) **diverse**: events contained in the summary should be both diverse in their contents and in terms of their occurring time;

(3) **comprehensible**: events contained in the summary should be understandable to users.

3.3 Types of Output Summary

Cognitive science studies suggest two modes in which people understand categories: *prototype view* [27] and *exemplar view* [9]. The first one posits that a category be represented by a constructed prototype (sometimes called centroid), such that entities closer to the prototype are considered better examples of the category. The exemplar view is an alternative to the prototype view that proposes using real entities as exemplars instead of abstract prototypes that might actually not exist. Based on this division, we propose two types of summarization approaches:

Prototype-based summarization. In the prototype-based summarization, events may come from the history of arbitrary entity within the category. The prototype-based summary represents the category by constructing an imaginary prototype.

Exemplar-based summarization. In the exemplar-based summarization, events are drawn from a relatively small set of typical representatives among all entities. The size of the set depends on the size of summary. The exemplar-based summary thus uses a few typical representative instances to describe the whole category.

3.4 System Overview

Fig. 1 provides an overview of our approach. We first pre-process input documents and extract events. For the prototype-based summarization, we additionally detect eras and topics. Then we compute event importance by MRW and HITS for both the prototype-based summarization and exemplar-based summarization. Lastly, we remove redundancy and generalize the events for constructing final summary.

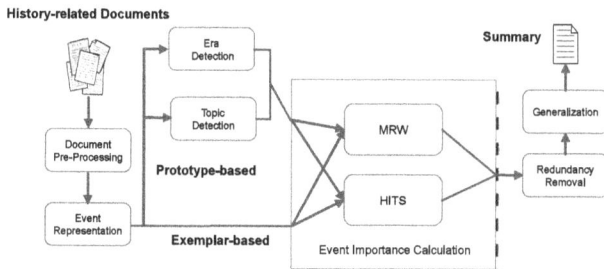

Figure 1: System Overview.

4 EVENT REPRESENTATION

A historical event is represented by a sentence and is associated with a date of its occurrence. As not all words of the original sentence are meaningful, each sentence is first normalized by pre-processing steps such as removing stopwords, stemming and retaining the most frequent 5,000 unigrams and bigrams. In the recent years, word2vec [23] was widely utilized for automatically learning the meaning behind words based on neural networks. We use word2vec to represent terms and events. The vector representation of an event is a weighted combination of the vectors of terms contained in the normalized sentence that represents the event. The weight of a term is its TF-IDF value calculated from the original corpus.

5 PROTOTYPE SUMMARY GENERATION

In this section we describe two methods which rely on prototype summarization strategy. Both use era and topic information. We start then with explaining the way to detect eras and themes underlying our datasets.

5.1 Eras Detection

Given a sequence of atomic time units $\xi = (t_1, t_2, ..., t_n)$, the task is to select a proper segmentation Θ containing m eras dividing the entire time span $[t_1, t_n]$, where each era T_i is expressed by two time points representing its beginning date τ_b^i and the ending date τ_e^i. Formally, let $\Theta = (T_1, T_2, ..., T_m)$, where $T_i = [\tau_b^i, \tau_e^i]$. In order to perform era detection we state two hypotheses:

Hypothesis 1 *A statistically significant increase or decrease in the number of events in two adjacent time units can be an indicator of the emergence of a new era.*

Hypothesis 2 *Events occurring in the same era tend to be more similar to each other than events occurring in other eras.*

Hypothesis 1 is similar to the one stated in [1] where authors utilized statistically significant changes in the frequencies of news articles in time segments in order to locate different stages of events.

The above hypotheses form the basis for the two stage process of era detection. We discuss both the steps below:

Chi-Square Test. The initial set of time units the category history is $\xi = (t_1, t_2, ..., t_n)$, where each time unit t_i represents a year. Based on Hypothesis 1, a chi-square test of independence is applied. We test for the independence of adjacent time units, and the lack of independence allows the adjacent time units to be combined. More concretely, the chi-square test is used to determine whether two neighboring time units exhibit a statistically significant association based on the number of contained events.

The default significance level is set to 0.05, thus a statistically significant change is defined where the χ^2 value exceeds the critical cut-off of 3.84. By this we obtain the intermediate set of segments $\varsigma = (\mu_1, \mu_2, ..., \mu_k)$, where $\mu_i = [\eta_b^i, \eta_e^i | \eta_b^i \in \xi, \eta_e^i \in \xi]$, is created after some of time units are combined.

Optimization. We next use an optimization formula to determine the final eras based on Hypothesis 2. Given the pre-set number of final periods, m, every possible combination Θ of segments from the intermediate set will be explored. Formally, let $\Theta = (T_1, T_2, ..., T_m)$ where $T_i = [\tau_b^i, \tau_e^i | \tau_b^i \in \varsigma, \tau_e^i \in \varsigma]$. In particular, we prefer the combination, in which the eras to be selected are characterized by high intra-similarity, low inter-similarity, and, in addition, they have high abundancy defined as the number of instances having their events in a given era. The era combination that has the highest score by applying Eq. (1) will be adopted.[1]

---

[1] We experimentally set weights for ω_1, ω_2 and ω_3 in Eq. (1) to be 0.4, 0.4 and 0.2, respectively.

$$\Theta \equiv \mathrm{argmax}[\omega_1 \sum_{i=1}^{m} IntraSimilarity(T_i)$$

$$- \omega_2 \sum_{i=1}^{m-1} InterSimilarity(T_i, T_{i+1}) \qquad (1)$$

$$+ (1 - \omega_1 - \omega_2) \cdot \sum_{i=1}^{m} Abundancy(T_i)]$$

Here, the intra-similarity measures the cosine similarity between events within a given era:

$$IntraSimilarity(T_i) = \sum_{e_i \in T_i} \sum_{e_j \in T_i} \frac{Sim_{cosine}(e_i, e_j)}{|T_i|^2} \qquad (2)$$

The inter-similarity measures the cosine similarity between the events of the neighboring eras:

$$InterSimilarity(T_i, T_{i+1}) = \sum_{e_i \in T_i} \sum_{e_j \in T_{i+1}} \frac{Sim_{cosine}(e_i, e_j)}{|T_i| \cdot |T_{i+1}|} \qquad (3)$$

Finally, the abundancy of an era indicates how many of the category instances have at least one event located in this era.

5.2 Topic Detection

Different entities may share similar historical events which however may not belong to the same eras. For instance, many Japanese cities were hit by earthquakes at different times throughout the last millennium. Thus, in addition to detecting eras we also conduct topic detection for better capturing event importance.

Clustering algorithms like K-means are popular techniques to detect topics. However, these are not appropriate as each event is expected to belong to only one topic. Latent Dirichlet Allocation (LDA) [7] allows for soft association of topics with events. However, LDA does not explicitly compute topic to topic association which could constitute another useful signal for estimating topic importance.

We then construct topics with Correlated Topic Model (CTM) [8] which captures both topic-event relations as well as topic-topic relations. Given a set of documents $D=[d_1, d_2, ..., d_N]$ and its vocabulary $W=[w_1, w_2, ..., w_M]$, CTM returns a set of latent topics $Z=[z_1, z_2, ..., z_K]$ (K is pre-specified). Each document d_j is considered as arising from the mixture of topics in Z, each of which is a distribution over the vocabulary W. In addition, the covariance structure among topics Z (which is a K-dimensional covariance matrix) is estimated via adopting the logistic normal distribution to model the latent topic proportions of a document.

Given CTM, we are able to obtain the per-document topic distributions $P(z_i|d_j)$, the per-topic word distributions $P(w_i|z_k)$ and the topic-topic correlations $Corr(z_i, z_j)$. We then incorporate this information to compute event importance as detailed next.

5.3 Prototype-based MRW

The Markov Random Walk Model (MRW) has been successfully exploited in multi-document summarization. MRW is a way of calculating the importance of a vertex within a graph based on global information recursively drawn from the entire graph. In MRW model, voting (or "recommendation") between two vertices is represented in the form of a link from one vertex to another, and the score associated with a vertex is determined by the votes received from adjacent vertices.

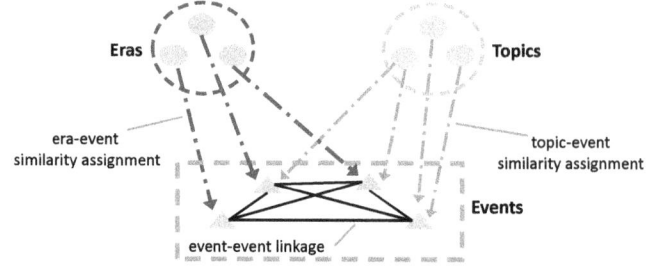

Figure 2: Illustration of Prototype-based MRW.

We use MRW for estimating the importance of events (see Fig. 2). In this process we make use of era and topic information. The underlying topics as well as eras are not equally important. An event contained in an important era and being part of important topics is deemed more salient than one in a less important era or belonging to trivial topics. Thus in order to calculate event importance with the prototype-based MRW, we state four hypotheses for determining important events as below:

Hypothesis 3 *An important event is contained in an important era and is similar to many events in this era.*
Hypothesis 4 *An important event is similar to important topics.*
Hypothesis 5 *An important event is similar to other important events.*
Hypothesis 6 *An important event is strongly correlated with other important events.*

Formally, let $G = (V_e, Q_{ee})$ be a graph (see Fig. 2) with the set of vertices V_e and the set of edges Q_{ee}. Let $V_e=E=\{e_i\}$, $T=\{T_j\}$, $Z=\{z_k\}$ denote the sets of events, detected eras and that of detected topics, respectively, and let $Q_{ee} = \{q_{ij}|e_i, e_j \in V_e\}$ represent the set of links between events. Below we are going to explain the way to assign initial scores to vertices in V_e and the way to compute edge weights.

First we compute the importance score of an era T_i denoted by $I(T_i)$ as follows:

$$I(T_i) = Sim(T_i, D) = \sum_{e_i \in T_i} \sum_{e_j \in D} \frac{Sim_{cosine}(e_i, e_j)}{|T_i| \cdot |D|} \qquad (4)$$

where D is the document set. We also compute the importance score of a topic z_i denoted as $I(z_i)$:

$$I(z_i) = \frac{\sum_{d \in D} P(z_i|d)}{|D|} \qquad (5)$$

$Sim(e_i, T_l)$ denotes the similarity between an event e_i and the era T_l that e_i is contained in. It is computed as follows:

$$Sim(e_i, T_l) = \frac{1}{|T_l|} \cdot \sum_{e_j \in T_l} Sim_{cosine}(e_i, e_j) \qquad (6)$$

$Sim(e_i, z_k)$ denotes the similarity between an event e_i and a topic z_k:

$$Sim(e_i, z_k) = \frac{\sum_{w \in e_i} P(w|z_k)}{|e_i|} \quad (7)$$

Let $Score(e_i)$ be the score of a vertex e_i. We then compute the initial score $Score^0(e_i)$ of e_i used for MRW as follows:

$$Score^0(e_i) = I(T_l|e_i \in T_l) \cdot Sim(e_i, T_l) \cdot \sum_{z_k \in Z} I(z_k) \cdot Sim(e_i, z_k) \quad (8)$$

In other words, we assign high initial score to a given event if it belongs to an important era (Hypothesis 3), it is similar to this era (Hypothesis 3) and it is similar to important topics (Hypothesis 4).

We also associate each edge q_{ij} in Q_{ee} with an affinity weight w_{ij} between events e_i and e_j. Considering Hypothesis 5 and Hypothesis 6, this weight is computed using both the similarity $Sim(e_i, e_j)$ and the correlation $Corr(e_i, e_j)$ between the two events:[2]

$$w_{ij} = \alpha \cdot Sim_{cosine}(e_i, e_j) + (1 - \alpha) \cdot Corr(e_i, e_j) \quad (9)$$

$$Corr(e_i, e_j) = \sum_{z_i \in Z} \sum_{z_j \in Z} \frac{Sim(e_i, z_i) \cdot Sim(e_j, z_j) \cdot Corr(z_i, z_j)}{|Z|^2} \quad (10)$$

The transition probability p_{ij} from e_i to e_j is then computed by normalizing the corresponding affinity weight to ensure convergence:

$$p_{ij} = \frac{w_{ij}}{\sum_{e_k \in V_e} w_{ik}} \quad (11)$$

Based on the transition probability, the importance score $Score(e_i)$ for an event e_i can be deduced from all other events in a way similar to PageRank [24] algorithm by iteratively computing the following formula until convergence:

$$Score(e_i) = (1 - d) + d \cdot \sum_{e_j \in V_e, e_j \neq e_i} p_{ji} \cdot Score(e_j) \quad (12)$$

where d is a damping factor set by default to 0.85. The computation ends when the difference between the scores computed at the two successive iterations for the events is less than 0.0001.

5.4 Prototype-based HITS

Hyperlink-Induced Topic Search (HITS) is a link analysis algorithm that has been successfully used to rate web pages. HITS algorithm defines two types of nodes in a network, hubs and authorities, and computes their ranking scores in a mutually reinforcing way.

We are going to apply HITS for estimating the importance of events (see Fig. 3). We state the following hypotheses for measuring event importance with the prototype-based HITS method:

Hypothesis 7 *An important event is similar to many important eras.*

Hypothesis 8 *An important era is similar to many important events.*

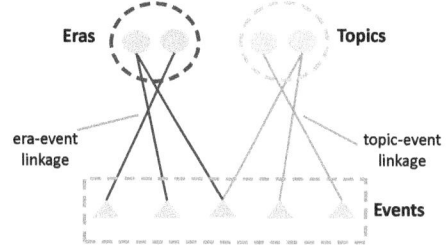

Figure 3: Illustration of the Prototype-based HITS.

Hypothesis 9 *An important event is similar to many important topics.*

Hypothesis 10 *An important topic is similar to many important events.*

Formally, we build a tripartite graph $G = (V_e, V_t, V_z, Q_{et}, Q_{ez})$ with three types of sets of vertices $\{V_e, V_t, V_z\}$ and two types of sets of edges $\{Q_{et}, Q_{ez}\}$. Let $V_e = E = \{e_i\}$, $V_t = T = \{T_j\}$, $V_z = Z = \{z_k\}$ denote the sets of events, detected eras and detected topics, respectively. Let $Q_{et} = \{q_{ij}|e_i \in V_e, T_j \in V_t\}$, $Q_{ez} = \{q_{ik}|e_i \in V_e, z_k \in V_z\}$ represent the set of links between an event and an era, and the set of the links between an event and a topic, respectively.

Era denoting vertices V_t and topic vertices V_z are regarded as hubs, while event vertices V_e are considered as authorities. Each edge q_{ij} in Q_{et} is associated with an affinity weight w_{ij} denoting the similarity between an event e_i and an era T_j, while each edge q_{ik} in Q_{ez} has an affinity weight w_{ik} representing the similarity between an event e_i and a topic z_k. Similarly, w_{ij} and w_{ik} are computed by Eqs. (6) and (7).

In the mutual reinforcement process, the authority scores of events (denoted as $Auth(e_i)$) and the hub scores of eras and topics (denoted as $Hub(T_j)$ and $Hub(z_k)$, respectively) are iteratively computed. The scores at the $(i + 1)^{th}$ iteration are calculated based on the scores at the $(i)^{th}$ iteration as follows:

$$Auth^{(i+1)}(e_i) = \sum_{T_j \in T} w_{ij} \cdot Hub^{(i)}(T_j) + \sum_{z_k \in Z} w_{ik} \cdot Hub^{(i)}(z_k) \quad (13)$$

$$Hub^{(i+1)}(T_j) = \sum_{e_i \in E} w_{ij} \cdot Auth^{(i)}(e_i) \quad (14)$$

$$Hub^{(i+1)}(z_k) = \sum_{e_i \in E} w_{ik} \cdot Auth^{(i)}(e_i) \quad (15)$$

Both the authority scores and hub scores are normalized after each iteration in order to achieve convergence. The initial scores of all hubs and the ones of authorities are set to 1. The computation terminates when the difference between the scores computed at the two successive iterations for the hubs and the authorities is less than 0.0001.

6 EXEMPLAR SUMMARY GENERATION

The second type of summarization, the exemplar based summarization approach, assumes selecting a small number of representative entities and constructing the summary upon them. In this section

---

[2]We empirically set the weight for α in Eq. (9) to be 0.6.

we describe two methods that rely on the selection of the most representative entities.

6.1 Exemplar-based MRW

In the first method we decide the importance of entities using MRW with the following hypothesis:

Hypothesis 11 *An entity is important if it shares history similar to that of other important entities.*

To incorporate this hypothesis into event scoring we again use MRW model. Formally, let $G = (V, Q)$ be an undirected graph, where $V=D=\{d_i\}$ and $Q = \{q_{ij}|d_i, d_j \in D\}$ denote the set of entities (actually, documents representing their histories) and the set of links between entities, respectively. In view of Hypothesis 11, the affinity weight w_{ij} of edge q_{ij} between entities d_i and d_j is computed using the similarity $Sim(d_i, d_j)$.

Since cosine similarity is not a proper similarity measure for sequences such as sequences of events, we propose to use Dynamic Time Warping (DTW) for measuring distances between entities' histories (Eq. (16)). DTW calculates an optimal match between two sequences. Hence, entities' histories can be "warped" non-linearly in the time dimension so as their similar events become aligned. The advantage of DTW is that the order of events is considered when computing the similarity. Thus, histories containing identical events yet, positioned in different order will not be judged identical.

$$w_{ij} = Sim_{DTW}(d_i, d_j)$$
$$= \frac{1}{DTW(d_i, d_j) + 1} \qquad (16)$$

The transition probability p_{ij} from d_i to d_j is computed using Eq. (11), and the importance score $Score(d_i)$ for an event d_i is found by iteratively computing Eq. (12) until convergence.

After computing the entity importance scores we select the top m important entities. Let the expected summary size be k events and the number of events in the history of the i-th ranked entity d_i be $size(d_i)$. m is then decided as follows:

$$\sum_{i=1}^{m-1} size(d_i) < k, \sum_{i=1}^{m} size(d_i) \geqslant k \qquad (17)$$

We next merge the histories of the selected m entities and pick up the top k important events from the merged history using MRW-based ranking method called LexRank [12].

6.2 Exemplar-based HITS

We now propose the last method that represents the exemplar based approach using a bipartite graph framework. In order to calculate document importance with the exemplar-based HITS, we state the following hypotheses:

Hypothesis 12 *An important document is similar to many important events.*
Hypothesis 13 *An important event is similar to many important documents.*

Formally, we build a bipartite graph $G = (V_e, V_d, Q_{ed})$ with two types of vertice sets $\{V_e, V_d\}$ and the set of edges $\{Q_{ed}\}$, where $V_e=E=\{e_i\}$, $V_d=D=\{d_j\}$ denote the set of events and the set of documents, respectively. $Q_{ed} = \{q_{ij}|e_i \in V_e, d_j \in V_d\}$ represents the set of links between events and documents representing entity histories.

Document vertices V_d are regarded as hubs, while event vertices V_e are regarded as authorities. Each edge q_{ij} in Q_{ed} is associated with an affinity weight w_{ij} denoting the similarity between an event e_i and a document d_j. It is is computed as follows.

$$w_{ij} = Sim(e_i, d_j) = maxSim_{cosine}(e_i, e_j|e_j \in d_j) \qquad (18)$$

In the mutual reinforcement process, the authority scores of events and the hub scores of documents are iteratively calculated by Equations (19) and (20). All scores are normalized after each iteration. The initial score of all hubs and authorities are set to 1.

$$Auth^{(i+1)}(e_i) = \sum_{d_j \in D} w_{ij} \cdot Hub^{(i)}(d_j) \qquad (19)$$

$$Hub^{(i+1)}(d_j) = \sum_{e_i \in E} w_{ij} \cdot Auth^{(i)}(e_i) \qquad (20)$$

After document importance scores are calculated, events from the top m important documents are merged (where m is decided by Eq. (17)). Finally, the top k important events from the merged history are chosen according to ranking by their authority scores.

7 POST-PROCESSING

7.1 Redundancy Removal

After the historical events of a certain category are ranked by importance, we apply a modified version of MMR (Maximal Marginal Relevance) [10] denoted as TMMR (Temporally enhanced Maximal Marginal Relevance) to minimize redundancy. TMMR tries to avoid extracting similar (both semantically similar and temporally close) events in a summary by considering penalty based on the similarity between a newly extracted event and the already extracted events. TMMR allows extracting events which have high importance scores, yet, at the same time, are not semantically similar neither temporally close to the already extracted events.

$$TMMR \equiv argmax[\alpha \cdot score(e_i) - \beta \cdot maxSim_{cosine}(e_i, e_j)$$
$$- (1 - \alpha - \beta) \cdot min\frac{1}{|t_i - t_j| + 1}] \qquad (21)$$

Here, e_i denotes an event in the set of the candidate events which have not been selected, while e_j represents an event in the set of the already selected events. t_i and t_j denote the occurrence dates of e_i and e_j. The values of α and β are experimentally assigned to be 0.5 and 0.4, respectively.

7.2 Generalization

Each event in the final summary should be represented by a set of meaningful words. However, our models produce summaries in which each event is in the form of a sentence from the history of particular entity. The sentence representation may then contain too specific details which might be true only for the instance from which the given sentence has been extracted. For example, many cities in Japan have suffered from earthquakes, and, so, the sentence "earthquake hits city" would be a good general description of this type of event, instead of sentences giving detailed descriptions of specific circumstances or effects of earthquakes in particular cities. Thus, we choose to generalize the top-scored sentences to produce the set of descriptive words representing in a general way a given event type (see Tab. 2 for an example).

More concretely, for each sentence indicating an event to be included into the summary, we seek m most similar sentences in the corpus and construct a cluster of $m+1$ sentences. Sentences within each cluster are semantically similar and each cluster represents the same event type. Then we compute Term Frequency-Inverse Cluster Frequency (TF-ICF) on the created clusters to extract the set of meaningful words describing each cluster (see Eq. (22)). Those sets of words are used as the final representation of events to be included into the output summary. We set the number m of events used for building the event clusters to be 10.

$$tficf_{i,j} = \frac{n_{i,j}}{\sum_k n_{k,j}} \cdot log \frac{|C|}{|c : c \ni t_i|} \qquad (22)$$

8 EXPERIMENTS

In this section, we describe the experiments conducted to evaluate the effectiveness of our proposed methods.

8.1 Datasets

We test our methods on entities separated by both time and space dimensions. In particular, we perform experiments on 7 Wikipedia categories including 3 city categories and 4 person categories. The city categories are Japanese cities, Chinese cities and English cities (denoted by C_1, C_2, C_3 respectively), while for the person categories we have selected American scientists, French scientists, Japanese Prime Ministers till 1945 (i.e., the end of WW2) and Japanese Prime Ministers after WW2 (denoted by P_1, P_2, P_3, P_4, respectively). Note that our methods are not bound to Wikipedia categories as any listing of entities can form an input, provided the historical data about each instance is made available. In this work, we just use Wikipedia categories as a convenient data source.

For preparing the city categories, each city history is extracted from the "History" section in the corresponding Wikipedia article. To capture historical events, we collect all sentences with dates. As further preprocessing, we reduce inflected words to their word stems and retain only the terms that are among the most frequent 5,000 unigrams, excluding stopwords and numbers. Each historical event is then represented by the bag of unigrams extracted from its sentence along with the corresponding date.

For the person categories, we utilize a dataset of 242,970 biographies publicly released by Bamman *et al.* [4]. Every biography consists of several life events, each represented by bag of unigrams with a date. Unlike in the city datasets, the date here is measured as the difference between the observed date in the event and the date of birth of the entity (i.e., relative date for a person when counting from its birth date). In other words, the date of an event is a relative date here instead of an absolute one as in the city datasets. The basic statistics about our datasets are shown in Tab. 1.

Table 1: Summary of datasets (the time range of datasets C_1, C_2, C_3 are based on absolute time, while that of datasets P_1, P_2, P_3, P_4 are based on relative time.)

Dataset	Category	# Entity	Time Range
C1	Japanese Cities	532	40 - 2016
C2	Chinese Cities	357	12 - 2016
C3	UK Cities	68	1 - 2016
P1	American Scientists	141	0 - 103
P2	French Scientists	41	0 - 101
P3	Japanese PMs (pre WW2)	32	0 - 98
P4	Japanese PMs (post WW2)	30	0 - 93

8.2 Analyzed Methods

We test 4 proposed methods: *Prototype-based MRW* (*P-MRW*, see Sec. 5.3), *Prototype-based HITS* (*P-HITS*, see Sec. 5.4), *Exemplar-based MRW* (*E-MRW*, see Sec. 6.1) and *Exemplar-based HITS* (*E-HITS*, see Sec. 6.2). In addition, we set up 2 baselines as follows:

(1) *LexRank + TMMR (LexRank)* LexRank [12] method has been widely adopted in multi-document summarization tasks such as [15] and [11]. It constructs a sentence connectivity matrix and computes sentence importance based on the algorithm similar to PageRank. Same as in our methods we also use TMMR to remove redundancy. Finally, selected events are generalized from sentences to the sets of words following the generalization procedure described in Sec. 7.2.

(2) *k-Means Clustering (K-Means)* K-Means clustering is a popular method used for cluster analysis. It partitions all events into k clusters in which each event belongs to the cluster with the nearest mean (given k as the size of summary). Then, within each cluster, we pick up 10 sentences which are closest to the cluster centroid in order to build an event cluster. Finally, TF-ICF is applied to extract meaningful words for each event cluster.

8.3 Experiment Settings

We set the parameters as follows:
(1) **size of summary**: we experimentally set the summary size of the city datasets to be 20 events, and of the person datasets to be 10 events considering the sizes of the corresponding categories.
(2) **parameters in the prototype-based methods**: we empirically let the number of eras for the city datasets to be 10, and for the person datasets to be 5 considering the lengths of entity histories. In addition, the number of topics K is set to be identical to the size of summary (K = 10 for person datasets and K = 20 for city datasets).

8.4 Evaluation Criteria

Manually creating summaries of typical histories of categories is a difficult task. We then ask users to evaluate summary quality. To test our methods we conduct evaluation based on five criteria which we believe are crucial for a high quality summary. Each event in the summary is graded in terms of:

- **Saliency** which measures how sound and important the extracted events are.
- **Comprehensibility** which measures how easily the output words can be associated with real events.

Besides, each summary is graded in terms of:

- **Diversity** which measures how diverse the events in the summary are (both semantically and temporally).
- **Coverage** that quantifies the extent to which important events in a category history are included in summary.
- **Interestingness** which measures how interesting the results are. Intuitively, it represents the degree to which the extracted events are novel to annotators.

We have 6 methods to be tested (4 proposed methods and 2 baseline methods). 5 annotators (4 males, 1 female) who have significant interest in history were asked to evaluate 42 different summaries (6 methods, each on 7 datasets). Each summary was ensured to be evaluated by 3 annotators. Thus, 4 annotators were assigned to evaluate 25 summaries and 1 annotator received 26 summaries to evaluate. During the assessment, the annotators were allowed to utilize any external resources including the Wikipedia, Web search engines, books, etc. All of the scores were given in the range from 1 to 5 (1: not at all, 2: rather not, 3: so so, 4: rather yes, 5: definitely yes). After the annotation scores have been completed we averaged saliency and comprehensibility scores per each summary. Lastly, we averaged the individual scores given by the annotators to obtain the final scores per each summary.

8.5 Evaluation Results

Below we discuss the key experimental results.

Average results. Fig. 4 shows the average scores of summaries generated from all the datasets in 5 criteria by all the compared methods. We first note that our proposed methods outperform the baselines based on almost all the criteria (the only exception is that *E-HITS* achieves worse performance than *LexRank* in terms of coverage by 1.8%). On average, our proposed methods outperform *LexRank* by 10.5% and *K-Means* by 14.3% across all the metrics. In particular, *P-MRW* outperforms *LexRank* by 14.6% and *K-Means* by 18.5%. Especially, in terms of saliency, the proposed methods are better than *LexRank* by 22.4% and than *K-Means* by 21.7%. This proves that *incorporating the importance of eras, topics and entities helps to improve the saliency of events contained in summary.*

Furthermore, we note that the two prototype-based methods *P-MRW* and *P-HITS* are superior to the two exemplar-based methods *E-MRW* and *E-HITS* by on average 2.9% across all the metrics. On the other hand, MRW-based methods *P-MRW* and *E-MRW* generate better results than the HITS-based methods *P-HITS* and *E-HITS* on average by 2.8%. This suggests that *adding information about eras and topics may play more important role than selecting a few representative entities.* Moreover, these results support the conclusion that *event-to-event relationships (utilized in the MRW-based methods) could be more crucial than event-to-entity relationships (used in the HITS-based methods).*

Per dataset results. Fig. 5 shows the summation of evaluation scores in 5 criteria of each method on every dataset. The proposed methods *P-MRW*, *P-HITS*, *E-MRW*, *E-HITS* and the two baselines *LexRank*, *K-Means* are denoted by $M_1, M_2, M_3, M_4, M_5, M_6$ in Fig. 5, respectively. We note that all our proposed methods outperform the baselines across all the datasets. In particular, on the Japanese city dataset (C1), the two MRW-based methods *P-MRW* and *E-MRW* achieve the best performance outperforming the two

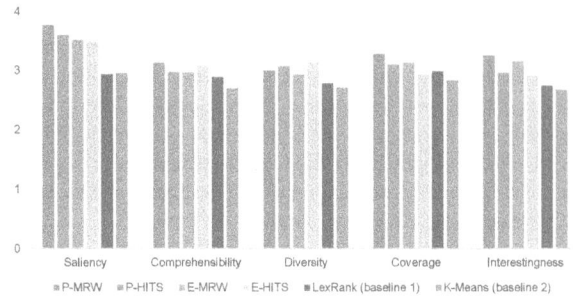

Figure 4: Average Results of All Datasets.

baselines by 47.8%, while all the proposed methods have better results by on average 40.0% on this dataset. The worst performance is on the French scientists dataset (P2) on which our methods manage to output results better by, on average, only 7.9%.

In addition, we note that the average summation scores of the three city datasets are higher than the ones for the four person datasets by 4.4%, which may support the observation that *the quality of summary could be influenced by the number of entities within the category.* Moreover, the average standard deviation of the summation scores by all methods of the city datasets is larger than the one for the person datasets by 16.9%. These both observations suggest that *person related datasets are more difficult and the performance is more uniform across all the methods including the baselines.*

8.6 Additional Observations

Diversity. The reason why the proposed methods work better on the city datasets than on the person datasets could be because city histories have longer time span, hence, their events may be characterized by higher diversity.

Coverage. The prototype-based methods achieve much better performance with regards to the coverage than the exemplar-based methods. It may be because events in exemplar-based summaries are extracted from a small set of typical representatives, which may miss some important information.

Interestingness. MRW-based methods in general outperform HITS-based methods in terms of interestingness. The reason can be due to MRW-based methods incorporating correlation between events and era information, which could make summary more coherent and consistent.

8.7 Example Summary

We present in Fig. 6 and Tab. 6 the summary of a typical history of Japanese cities generated by the prototype-based method *P-MRW*. The summary consists of a timeline containing 20 events ordered chronologically (see Fig. 6), followed by a table (see Tab. 2) which includes up to 15 top scored words representing each event. For every event, we manually create a label based on the words representing the event. In addition, each event is associated with two numbers indicating the median date and the standard deviation of occurrence dates of the corresponding events (these are computed from the event clusters that were discussed in Sec. 7.2).

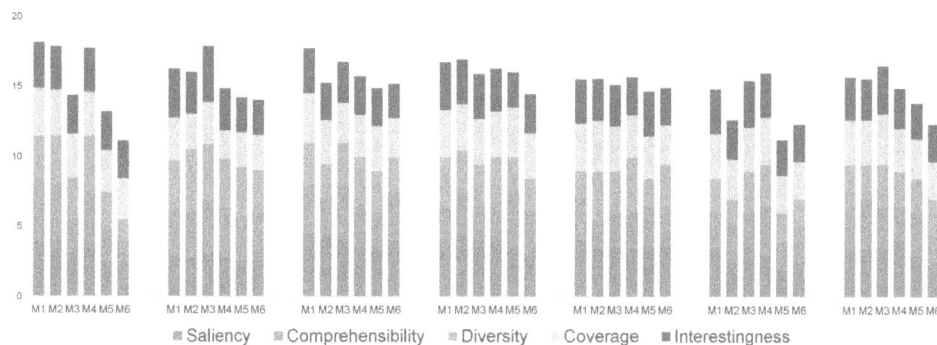

Figure 5: **Results on Each Dataset (M1: P-MRW; M2: P-HITS; M3: E-MRW; M4: E-HITS; M5: LexRank; M6: K-Means). The datasets from left to right are C1 (Japanese Cities), C2 (Chinese Cities), C3 (UK Cities), P1 (American Scientists), P2 (French Scientists), P3 (Pre-WW2 Japanese PMs) and P4 (Post-WW2 Japanese PMs).**

As we can notice, the ***Meiji Revolution*** is a key turning point in the history of Japanese cities, as most of the events occurred after it. Japanese cities were frequently at war, as reflected by the events: ***Battle*** with median date at around 1333, ***War*** at around 1876 and ***WW2*** at around 1939. The modern ***Education*** in Japan started from the early 20th century. After ***WW2***, Japanese cities enjoyed rapid economic and social development, embodied in the events of ***Population*** (which shows the rapid growth in population), ***Economics*** (which describes the economic boom of Japan in the late 20th century), ***Transportation*** (which reflects the advancement of transportation infrastructure) and ***Film*** (which shows the development of culture industry). Japan cities hosted many ***Sport*** events such as Summer Olympics in the 1960's and Winter Olympics in the 1970's and 1990's. In addition, it can be observed that Japanese cities frequently suffered from ***Natural Disasters*** such as earthquakes, tsunamis and typhoons (e.g. the *Hanshin Earthquake* in 1994), and Japan is paying particular attention to ***Nuclear*** issues (e.g. the *Fukushima Daichi Nuclear Disaster* in 2011). Many of these events can be found in books about Japan history [13] and [20].

9 CONCLUSIONS

It is natural for humans to categorize entities into meaningful groups based on their common traits. One way to better understand categories is by learning histories of their members. In this paper we have introduced a novel type of summarization task consisting in generating gists of histories of multiple entities. We then proposed 4 methods which utilize diverse kinds of signals such as information about documents, eras, topics and correlation between events, and incorporate them into graph-based ranking models. The output summary is in the form of key representative events represented by the sets of meaningful words and approximate event dates. The effectiveness of our models has been demonstrated by the experiments on 7 Wikipedia category datasets.

In the future, we plan to conduct more detailed evaluation on diverse types of entities as well as incorporate abstractive summarization strategies for increasing the readability of the generated summaries. The next step is to improve and extend methods for extracting and representing temporal information from input documents using techniques similar to the one presented in [14].

Acknowledgments This work was supported in part by MEXT Grant-in-Aid (#15H01718, #17H01828), and by the JST research promotion program Presto/Sakigake.

REFERENCES

[1] A. Abdulkareem, and H. Tchalian. Corpus Periodization Framework to Periodize a Temporally Ordered Text Corpus. (2016).

[2] A. Abujabal and K. Berberich. 2015. Important Events in the Past, Present, and Future. In Proceedings of the 24th International Conference on World Wide Web (WWW '15 Companion). ACM, New York, NY, USA, 1315-1320.

[3] R. B. Bairi, M. Carman, and G. Ramakrishnan. On the Evolution of Wikipedia: Dynamics of Categories and Articles. In Ninth International AAAI Conference on Web and Social Media, 2015.

[4] D. Bamman, and N. A. Smith. Unsupervised discovery of biographical structure from text. Transactions of the Association for Computational Linguistics 2 (2014): 363-376.

[5] R. Barzilay, K. R. McKeown, and M. Elhadad. Information fusion in the context of multi-document summarization. Proceedings of the 37th annual meeting of the Association for Computational Linguistics on Computational Linguistics. Association for Computational Linguistics, 1999.

[6] D. J. Berndt, and J. Clifford. Using Dynamic Time Warping to Find Patterns in Time Series. KDD workshop. Vol. 10. No. 16. 1994.

[7] D. M. Blei, A. Y. Ng, and M. I. Jordan. Latent dirichlet allocation. Journal of machine Learning research 3.Jan (2003): 993-1022.

[8] D. M. Blei, and J. Lafferty. Correlated topic models. Advances in neural information processing systems 18 (2006): 147.

[9] L. R. Brooks. Nonanalytic concept formation and memory for instances. In Cognition and categorization, 1973. Hillsdale.

[10] J. Carbonell, and J. Goldstein. The use of MMR, diversity-based reranking for reordering documents and producing summaries. Proceedings of the 21st annual international ACM SIGIR conference on Research and development in information retrieval. ACM, 1998.

[11] P. Flach, and E. T. Matsubara. A simple lexicographic ranker and probability estimator. European Conference on Machine Learning. Springer Berlin Heidelberg, 2007.

[12] E. Gnes, and D. R. Radev. LexRank: Graph-based lexical centrality as salience in text summarization. Journal of Artificial Intelligence Research 22 (2004): 457-479.

[13] K. Henshall. A History of Japan: From Stone Age to Superpower. ISBN = 9780230346628, Palgrave Macmillan, 2012.

[14] A. Jatowt, C. M. Au Yeung, and K. Tanaka. Estimating document focus time. In Proceedings of the 22nd ACM international conference on Conference on information & knowledge management (pp. 2273-2278). ACM, 2013.

[15] P. Kaustubh, and P. Brazdil. Text summarization: Using centrality in the pathfinder network. Int. J. Comput. Sci. Inform. Syst [online] 2 (2007): 18-32.

[16] J. M. Kleinberg. Authoritative sources in a hyperlinked environment. Journal of the ACM (JACM), 46(5), 604-632, 1999.

[17] K. Knight, and D. Marcu. Summarization beyond sentence extraction: A probabilistic approach to sentence compression. Artificial Intelligence 139.1 (2002): 91-107.

[18] L. Lovsz. Random walks on graphs. Combinatorics, Paul erdos is eighty, 2, 1-46, 1993

[19] R. Lowry. Concepts and applications of inferential statistics. (2014).

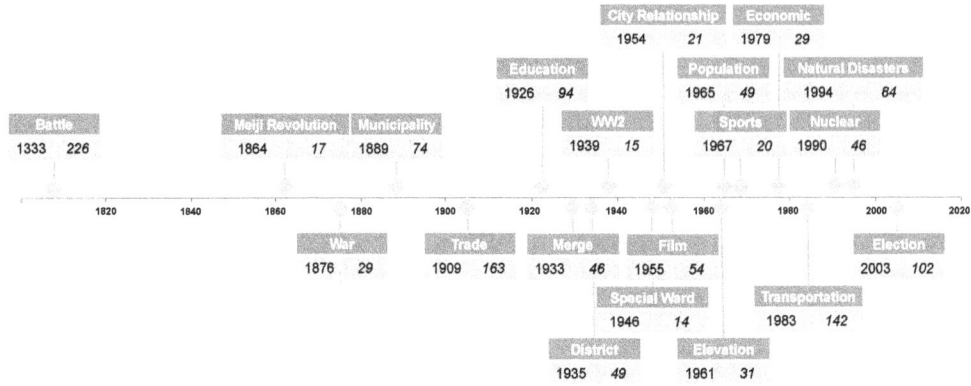

Figure 6: Typical history of a Japanese city learned from 532 instances presented in the form of a timeline. The timeline consists of 20 events ordered chronologically by their median occurrence time. Each event is illustrated by a manually created label along with its median (left value) and the standard deviation of occurrence time (right value).

Table 2: Events in the summary of Japanese cities (see Fig. 6). For each event we show up to top 15 words due to space limit.

Event	Terms
Battle	battle, kamakura, fought, took, kumegawa, area, komaki, period, site, place, war, zenkunen, yasutsune, ultimately, ujigawa
Meiji Revolution	people, peasant, escape, christianity, another, rebellion, damage, raid, air, war, yokkaichi, went, weakened, toyotomi, subsequent
War	war, naval, japan, school, russojapanese, kiyohara, fujiwara, japanese, rebellion, navy, english, end, meiji, major, period
Municipality	system, within, municipality, establishment, modern, created, district, saitama, prefecture, restoration, gunma, town, creation, meiji
Trade	first, tea, made, tsuen, shop, service, held, festival, completed, yoshimitsu, world, waraji, uji, telephone, still
Education	school, established, confucian, high, william, welfare, vories, university, ueshiba, tsujido, teacher, taught, taizen, studies, science
Merge	merged, district, form, create, village, town, tkamachi, numakuma, nakaminato, incorporated, both, neighboring, urasaki, toyosu
District	takikawa, ebeotsu, becomes, continued, tend, village, district, hekikai, town, domain, began, area, period, yamagata, utashinai
WW2	training, center, military, imperial, navy, naval, japanese, industry, facility, built, army, air, production, nagoya, development
Special Ward	ward, became, tokyo, special, founded, city, district, former, shinj, shinagawa, sanbu, sanbe, nine, minamiadachi, metropolis
City Relationship	founded, city, relationship, established, ueno, sister, yamatotakada, wales, tkai, takaishi, sistercity, raised, nanao, mitaka, lomita
Film	year, story, film, festival, shibuya, sakura, record, narita, master, mai, every, appear, place, name, one
Elevation	elevated, city, status, ska, seba, village, town, surrendered, sekigawa, sashima, neighoring, matsumoto, kunitachi, kitaadachi
Population	public, housing, population, real, estate, development, trading, revenue, rapidly, rapid, debt, bubble, large, koku, construction
Sports	olympics, summer, hosted, host, winter, walk, sport, played, park, marathon, events, event, athletics, part, national
Economic	toyota, line, city, opened, nagoya, largest, economic, detroit, aichi, expanded, local, aircraft, became, plant, new
Transportation	expressway, road, line, junction, connected, station, tokaihokoriku, thoku, kaid, highway, established, train, tokyo, opened
Nuclear	fukushima, school, nuclear, evacuee, accident, city, status, student, public, problem, high, caused, rapid, housing, population
Natural Disasters	damage, earthquake, tsunami, thoku, suffered, caused, due, typhoon, rain, flooding, city, isewan, fishing, extensive, although
Election	mayor, motomiya, former, elected, plan, hall, first, party, ochiai, mayoral, kitamura, harue, city, office, woman

[20] J. L. McClain. Japan: A Modern History. ISBN = 9780393041569, W. W. Norton & Company, 2012.

[21] K. McKeown, et al. Towards multidocument summarization by reformulation: Progress and prospects. AAAI/IAAI. 1999.

[22] R. Mihalcea, and P. Tarau. TextRank: Bringing order into texts. Association for Computational Linguistics, 2004.

[23] T. Mikolov, et al. Efficient estimation of word representations in vector space. arXiv preprint arXiv:1301.3781 (2013).

[24] L. Page, et al. The PageRank citation ranking: Bringing order to the web. Stanford InfoLab, 1999.

[25] D. R. Radev, H. Jing, M. Sty, and D. Tam. Centroid-based summarization of multiple documents. Information Processing & Management, 40(6), 919-938, 2004.

[26] E. Rosch. On the internal structure of perceptual and semantic categories. Cognitive Development and Acquisition of Language, pages 111-114, 1973.

[27] E. Rosch. Cognitive representations of semantic categories. Journal of Experimental Psychology: General, 104:192-233, 1975.

[28] T. A. Tran, C. Niederee, N. Kanhabua, U. Gadiraju, and A. Anand. 2015. Balancing Novelty and Salience: Adaptive Learning to Rank Entities for Timeline Summarization of High-impact Events. In Proceedings of the 24th ACM International on Conference on Information and Knowledge Management (CIKM '15). ACM, New York, NY, USA, 1201-1210.

[29] X. Wan, and J. Yang. Multi-document summarization using cluster-based link analysis. Proceedings of the 31st annual international ACM SIGIR conference on Research and development in information retrieval. ACM, 2008.

[30] X. Wan, J. Yang, and J. Xiao. Manifold-Ranking Based Topic-Focused Multi-Document Summarization. IJCAI. Vol. 7. 2007.

[31] R. Yan, et al. Evolutionary timeline summarization: a balanced optimization framework via iterative substitution. Proceedings of the 34th international ACM SIGIR conference on Research and development in Information Retrieval. ACM, 2011.

There and Here: Patterns of Content Transclusion in Wikipedia

Mark Anderson
Southampton University
Electronics and Computer Science
Southampton SO17 1BJ, UK
mwra1g13@soton.ac.uk

Leslie Carr
Southampton University
Electronics and Computer Science
Southampton SO17 1BJ, UK
lac@ecs.soton.ac.uk

David E. Millard
Southampton University
Electronics and Computer Science
Southampton SO17 1BJ, UK
dem@ecs.soton.ac.uk

ABSTRACT

As large, collaboratively authored hypertexts such as Wikipedia grow so does the requirement both for organisational principles and methods to provide sustainable consistency and to ease the task of contributing editors. Large numbers of (potential) editors are not necessarily a sufficient bulwark against loss of coherence amongst a corpus of many discrete articles. The longitudinal task of curation may benefit from deliberate curatorial roles and techniques.

A potentially beneficial technique for the development and maintenance of hypertext content at scale is hypertext transclusion, by offering controllable re-use of a canonical source. In considering issues of longitudinal support of web collaborative hypertexts, we investigated the current degree and manner of adoption of transclusion facilities by editors of Wikipedia articles. We sampled 20 million articles from ten discrete language wikis within Wikipedia to analyse behaviour both within and across the individual Wikipedia communities.

We show that Wikipedia makes limited, inconsistent of use of transclusion (as at February 2016). Use is localised to subject areas, which differ between sampled languages. A limited number of patterns were observed including: Lists from transclusion, Lists of Lists, Episodic Media Listings, Tangles, Articles as Macros, and Self-Transclusion. We find little indication of deliberate structural maintenance of the hypertext.

CCS CONCEPTS

• **Information systems** → **Wikis**; *Document structure*; • **Human-centered computing** → **Collaborative content creation**; *Computer supported cooperative work*;

KEYWORDS

Hypertext, Transclusion, Collaboration, Wikis, Wikipedia, Digital Curation

ACM Reference format:
Mark Anderson, Leslie Carr, and David E. Millard. 2017. There and Here: Patterns of Content Transclusion in Wikipedia. In *Proceedings of HT'17, Prague, Czech Republic, July 4-7, 2017,* 10 pages.
https://doi.org/10.1145/3078714.3078726

1 INTRODUCTION

A large public collaborative hypertext gives free access to allow any person both to read its content and to add to, or improve, the hypertext's data and structure. The hypertext may thus contain the work of many authors, spread across discrete pages. Their varying editing skills can pose a challenge for those trying to maintain the overall coherence and accuracy of the hypertext's content as a whole—as opposed to activity revising individual articles or generating new content. In wikis, where focus is on the rendered page, incremental edits can lead to unseen structural issues. For instance, under 50% of 'articles' in the English Wikipedia are actually content articles, the remainder are re-direction stubs (see Table 2).

The same information may need to be repeated within different articles across a large hypertext. If text is copied, potential exists for thematic drift between different articles through subsequent edits by different authors. Ideally, in order to retain coherence of the hypertext over time, what we call *longitudinal coherence*, content duplication needs to be identified and consistency maintained.

Transclusion [17] offers one means of avoiding duplication. Deliberate and considered transclusional re-use of canonical sources throughout the hypertext can potentially assist with maintaining coherence and avoiding divergent copy. For example, by re-using text summarising a subject in articles referring to that subject. Furthermore, transclusion—if identified up as such—also offers the potential to indicate provenance of re-used text.

It therefore follows that the use of transclusion within a large Web hypertext should increase longitudinal coherence, but it is unclear how widely and how effectively these techniques are used in existing examples such as Wikipedia. Wikipedia's MediaWiki software does support transclusion (see Section 3), but Wiki studies appear to ignore the implied linkage created by transclusion. Despite some analysis as to the functional nature of edits made in Wikipedia [5], no study has been made of the nature of editing as relating specifically to transclusional (re-)use of content. Built-in Wikipedia queries ('special' pages[1]) and API methods can give some indication of transclusion use, but the reports are opaque and do not lend themselves to further exploration, especially as to how or why editors implemented their ideas. Thus more focused study of transclusion is needed.

By analysing the occurrence and nature of Wikipedia content transclusion, the study set out to investigate these questions:

- *Does Wikipedia show evidence of deliberate use of transcluded article content?* If transclusion is used in Wikipedia, then at minimum transclusion mark-up should be detected

---

[1]See: https://en.wikipedia.org/wiki/Special:WhatLinksHere, on all article pages.

in article source code using transclusion, disparity in usage should become apparent, either within discrete per-language wikis, or between different wikis.

- *Does the nature of transclusion vary between discrete areas within per-language wikis, or between different languages?* By categorising the subject area of any transclusion activity, disparity in use of transclusion should become apparent, both within discrete per-language wikis and between different wikis.

- *Does article content show distinct patterns of transclusion?* If common, transclusion link patterns may be identified which aid those maintaining the hypertext.

2 BACKGROUND

Transclusion, as coined by Nelson in his *Literary Machines* [17], referred originally to a single hypermedia source occurring in multiple places "*Transclusion means that part of a document may be in several places—in other documents beside the original—without actually being copied there*" [18, preface footnote]². Subsequently, he re-defined transclusion as "*reuse with original context available, through embedded shared instancing*" [19, p32], tying it more closely to ideas expressed in his Xanadu system with its 'transpointing'³ windows.

Besides giving a canonical source, the inherent transclusion linkage can help establish provenance and copyright. Nelson held that indication of transclusion is a front-end function of the hypertext's reader (renderer) [18, footnote p2/37]. The technique does not preclude changes in transcluded sources, it is left to the user to select to which version to link: if the system holds past version(s) of the source these may be linked [18, p2/26]. Web transclusion, e.g for image placement, generally draws material directly from its source meaning that the transcluding document will reflect any change to the source, i.e. the current version. Thus a transcluded source can provide a single, up to date, canonical source for re-use in multiple other contexts.

For the general computer user, pure hypertext systems have largely been supplanted by the more versatile—albeit less rich—World Wide Web. With this move the general understanding of transclusion has broadened to a more general sense of content re-use. Glushko[7, p.231] defines transclusion as "*The inclusion, by hypertext, of a resource or part of a resource by another resource*". Missing from this is Nelson's concept of side-by-side, visually linked, display of source and calling contexts.

Currently, the pre-eminent form of transclusion of Web content occurs in the crafting of advertisements or sponsored content for just-in-time insertion (transclusion) into web pages; transcluded content is brokered in the blink of an eye. Besides the Web itself, this same form of transclusion is active in the 'walled gardens' of social networks such as Facebook where both ads and sponsored articles 'of interest' may be transcluded into a users feed.

There has been some discussion of transclusion of Web hypertext: in general [13], using hypertext [20][22], HTML transclusion [24][21][11][16][12] and XML/HTML transclusion[6]. However,

transclusion still remains atypical for hypertextual *writing* for the Web. Research interest tends to focus on either the technical implementation or the social aspect of use. Consideration of the writing of hypertext, in a non-fiction context, can fall between these stools.

Halasz's 'Reflections on "Seven Issues"' [8, p.112] noted that the versioning 'issue' was not fully resolved. In a wiki system [14], the default is to render the current edit of the requested page. All past edits can be rendered and by furnishing the UID of the desired edit. However links, including transclusions, are not tied to a target edit; thus rendered content may change if the transcluded source is edited. For a web-based hypertext wiki supporting transclusion this means, in simplest terms, that the rendered article content (the body copy) of a page is able dynamically to include content not present in the article's own source code. Further indication of transclusion, or ability to traverse such implied links is left to individual implementation.

Transclusion, applied appropriately, could help Wikipedia's many editors maintain cohesion. A precept of Wikipedia quality is the 'many eyes' theory [15]—that many people have looked at any given fact. However, Wikipedia's Manual of Style⁴ makes no mention of transclusion (or transcluding from Wikidata), effectively blinding the 'many eyes' to the concept.

Halfaker *et al.*[9] find that there is a plateauing in numbers of active editors of Wikipedia, with the suggestion that there may a natural equilibrium in levels of active editors in collaborative wikis.

Wikipedia has a very flat hierarchy of administrators and users although either of those may have extra roles [1]. There is a notion of a 'quality assurance' role but this seems to apply more to anti-vandalism than hypertextual coherence. For Wikipedia editors kudos is most easily acquired, and thus promoted, by concentration on the 'quality'⁵ of individual rendered articles. There appears to be no role or similar incentive for editors maintaining the hypertext's structure in support of its longitudinal coherence (and which may be seen as conflicting with per-article focus).

3 TRANSCLUSION MECHANISMS IN WIKIPEDIA

Wikipedia supports transclusion⁶ of the simplest form: all or part of one article may be transcluded into another. Transclusional links are one-way: content is transcluded *into* an article. The link is not locked to particular edit. Thus, regardless of the edit version of the transcluding page, the transcluded content is always from the current edit. A confusing factor for the study is that transclusion—of article content—is effected as a *subset* of general templating functionality. Transclusion markup assumes a target in the `Template`⁷ namespace but may target other namespaces, as explained below. Thus any analysis needs to separate out content transclusion from more general utility scripting activity.

A wiki page element (article, template, etc.) named somepage can be transcluded into another page via use of a series of general

---

²In the same footnote he records that in the book he actually mistakenly used the word 'inclusion' instead of 'transclusion'

³See: http://xanadu.com.au/ted/TN/PARALUNE/paraviz.html and [18, p2/34]

---

⁴See: https://en.wikipedia.org/wiki/Wikipedia:Manual_of_Style

⁵See: https://en.wikipedia.org/wiki/Wikipedia:Featured_articles.

⁶Since 30 May 2004. See: https://en.wikipedia.org/wiki/History_of_Wikipedia#Hardware_and_software.

⁷See: https://www.mediawiki.org/wiki/Help:Templates.

mark-up variations based on the target namespace[8]. The following basic variations occur (as documented[9] in Wikipedia):

- `{{somepage}}`: this transcludes the page `somepage` from the `Template` [sic] namespace, i.e. Template is the default namespace for transclusion assessment.
- `{{:somepage}}`: this transcludes the page `somepage` from the main namespace, i.e. a content article.

The second form above is therefore the canonical marker for *content* transclusion. Various tag forms based on the above interact to form a confusing and incompletely documented set of alternative transclusion pathways as shown at Figure 1 and described in more detail below.

3.1 Transclusion Mark-up

3.1.1 Tags Marking Transclusion. Incremental improvements to MediaWiki's codebase have resulted in multiple forms of transclusion mark-up. The method termed '*Labeled Section Transclude*' (LST) is a recent addition and allows partial transclusion of specified 'sections' of a called page. A 'section' is either text following a defined heading or ad hoc ranges of text as defined by mark-up in the called page using the `<section>` tag[10]. For transcluding articles there are five pertinent source code tags, some with aliases[11]:

- `{{:somepage}}`. Marker: '`{{:`'. Denotes full article transclusion from `somepage` unless modified by scope-resisting mark-up within the transcluded article.
- `{{:pagename|transcludesection=section_name}}`. Marker: '`|transcludesection=`'. Partial transclusion via '`<section>`' tags or ad hoc section definition in target article.
- `{{#lst:pagename|section_name}}`. Marker: '#lst'. LST partial transclude. Only `section_name` is transcluded from `pagename`. Aliased as #section:.
- `{{#lstx:pagename|section_name}}`. Marker: '#lstx'. This is an LST exclude. All of `pagename` is transcluded except `section_name`. Aliased as #section-x:.
- `{{#lsth:pagename|heading_name}}`. Marker: '#lsth'. This LST targets headings. Only the content below `heading_name` up to the next heading of same depth is transcluded from `pagename`. Aliased as #section-h:.

3.1.2 Tags Controlling Transclusion. Unless an LST or a '`transcludesection`' call is used in the transcluding mark-up, it is otherwise not possible to tell whether the article is wholly or partially transcluded. For transcluded articles there are 5 pertinent source code tags:

- `<noinclude></noinclude>`. Marks ad hoc sections of the called article which are not to be transcluded (but is still rendered for the article itself).
- `<onlyinclude></onlyinclude>`. Marks ad hoc sections of the called article which are the only parts of an article to transclude (and rendered for the article itself).
- `<includeonly></includeonly>`. Marks ad hoc sections of the called article which are not rendered *except when transcluded*.
- `<section begin="section_name">` `<section end="section_name">`. Marks ad hoc sections of the called article transcluded by 'transcludesection' calls or via LST.
- `<onlyinclude>{{#ifeq:{{{transcludesection| SECTIONNAME}}}|SECTIONNAME| }}</onlyinclude>`. Marks an ad hoc section of the called article to be treated, dynamically, as a named transcludable section by 'transcludesection' calls (bullet #2 in list above). The `#ifeq` method predates LST and the `<section>` tag.

3.1.3 Visible Indication of Transclusion. All editors, both human and automated, are allowed to use transclusion although it is not self-annotating. It is thus an editor's optional task. English Wikipedia documents allow template-based mark-up to indicate whole[12] or partial[13] transclusion, including a link to the source article.

3.1.4 Transclusion from Wikidata. The 'Phase 2' of the Wikidata[14] project was implemented for all Wikipedia languages in 2013[15], via the `{{#property:P_number}}` mark-up. However, the method is not yet documented in Wikipedia nor publicly recommended.

4 METHODOLOGY

Our approach deliberately concentrated on transclusion as it affects the task of editing the content of the hypertext rather than the technological aspects of transclusional article rendering. We took the perspective of an editor trying to use transclusion—perhaps for the first time—and having only the information provided *within Wikipedia's documentation* for guidance.

By article *content*, we refer specifically to the whole or partial re-use of copy from *articles*—pages in the main namespace[16] of Wikipedia wikis, i.e. the content as presented via Wikipedia's webpages. Although MediaWiki's transclusional method allows content to be drawn from any namespace in the current wiki, our data analysis focused only on use within the 'main' namespace of each single language wiki within Wikipedia; links to other namespaces were tabulated but not further analysed (except for Wikidata transclusion). 'Active' articles are all main namespace articles excluding redirection stubs.

To reflect the information available to a Wikipedia editor trying to employ transclusion, our understanding of Wikipedia's use

---

[8]Namespaces are described at https://www.mediawiki.org/wiki/Extension_default_namespaces.

[9]See 'Wikipedia:Transclusion': https://en.wikipedia.org/w/index.php?title=Wikipedia:Transclusion&oldid=693549756.

[10]See: https://www.mediawiki.org/wiki/Extension_talk:Labeled_Section_Transclusion. The introduction date is not documented. The `<section>` tag is a Wikipedia innovation that predates the HTML 5 `<section>` tag and there is no functional connection between the two same-named tags, although the MediaWiki tag's mandatory attributes make disambiguation easier. Wikipedia's documentation is ambiguous as to whether '#lst' and '|transcludesection=' are or are not (by design intent) full functional equivalents.

[11]LST Aliases were added to make the mark-up's intent less confusing for inexperienced editors. Wikis may optionally localise for their language.

[12]See: https://en.wikipedia.org/wiki/Template:Transcluding_article.

[13]See: https://en.wikipedia.org/wiki/Template:Transcluded_section.

[14]See: https://www.wikidata.org/.

[15]See: https://blog.wikimedia.de/2013/04/24/wikidata-all-around-the-world/.

[16]i.e. `<page>` elements in the 'main' XML namespace.

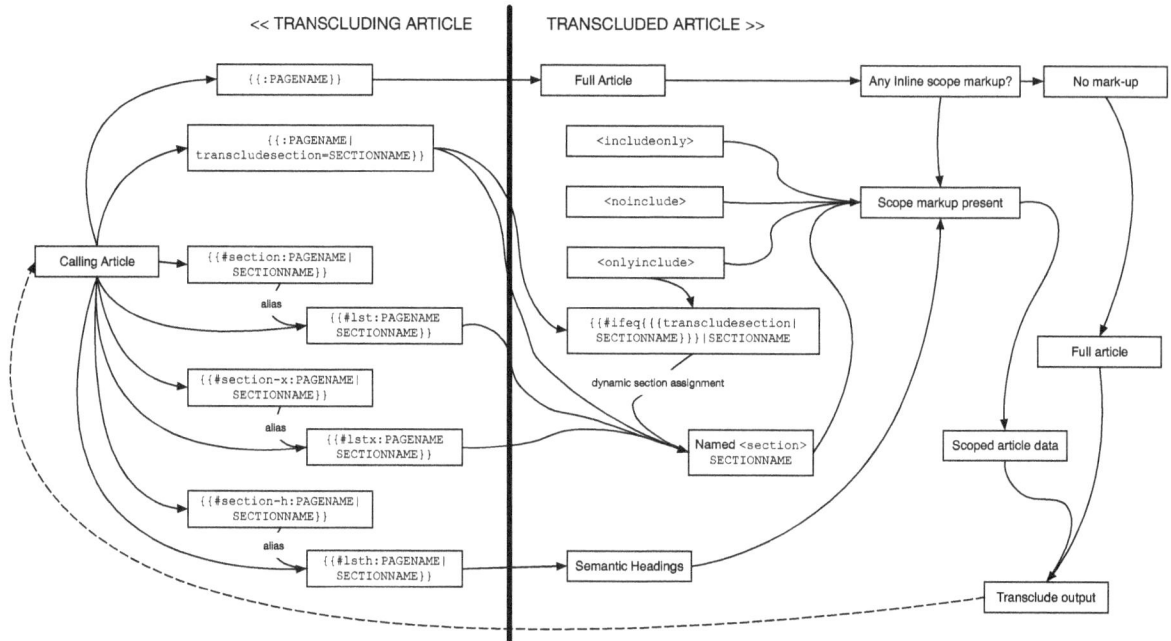

Figure 1: Transclusion pathways in Wikipedia (excluding Wikidata pathway, Section 3.1.4).

of transclusion has been derived from from its own documentation. The wikipedia.org domain serves content in many different languages[17] via per-language sub-domains. For the purposes of this study individual language wikis have been treated as discrete hypertexts.

Working with a static set of data ensured ongoing edits did not affect the transclusion network. Initial sampling tests of various static and live Wikipedia data sources also revealed that less ambiguity arose from directly analysing Wikipedia's static XML data dumps than from working with an API into a live wiki. Of the available types of Wikipedia data available for analysis, the monthly 'dumps' of wiki data in XML format were selected as the form of dataset for analysis (see Section 4.1).

To allow exploration of possible differences in transclusion behaviour across differing language communities, data from a number of wikis was collected. Of the languages used in the largest individual wikis, by article count, most are Northern European and use the Roman alphabet. The 10 different languages retrieved are at Table 1; all but Japanese fall within the top 10 wikis by article count Wikipedia. Russian, Japanese and Cebuano were included deliberately, to widen the sample to include wikis using non-Roman characters and non-European languages. English forms the largest wiki in the dataset, containing over 3 times the number of pages of the next largest wiki (Swedish).

URL references to Wikipedia examples have been added as footnotes. Where pertinent, the URLs point to the then-current edit as found in the dataset. In some cases checking details against edits on the live Wikipedia showed problems created by renaming or deletion of articles.

---

[17] 281 active discrete wikis as at 17 February 2016.

Language	Articles (M)	Pages (M)	Data (GB)	# Files
English (en)	5.06	12.18	56.01	27
Swedish (sv)	2.53	4.14	10.85	1
German (de)	1.90	3.20	10.03	4
Dutch (nl)	1.85	2.52	6.16	4
Cebuano (ceb)	1.81	2.96	7.53	1
French (fr)	1.71	3.11	14.66	4
Russian (ru)	1.28	2.81	16.20	4
Italian (it)	1.25	1.87	9.34	4
Spanish (es)	1.18	2.81	10.24	4
Japanese (ja)	0.99	1.60	9.35	4
Total	**19.57**	**37.22**	**150.37**	**60**

Table 1: Dataset. Wikipedia February 2016 XML dumps. Per-language wiki data, ordered by article count. The Article count includes both live ('active') articles and re-direct stubs. Data date is 13th February for English and 11th February for all other wikis.

4.1 Wikipedia Dataset

XML data from the February 2016 dumps was downloaded (see Table 1) for each of the 10 sampled languages. The dump version chosen was that labelled '*Articles, templates, media/files descriptions and primary meta-pages*', as it proved to have all article source code with a minimum of extraneous material. By comparison, larger dumps included data such as past article revisions and user pages which were not pertinent to the analysis and thus only added overhead to parsing the data.

The chosen dataset provides the content, in XML, of all current articles including re-direction stubs. However, the datasets are undocumented and provide no metadata as to the range and number of namespaces' data included. A complication during initial assessment of data was the lack of any consolidated documentation of namespace titles, including localisations thereof. A primary source used to identify namespace was the (partial) namespace table placed at the head of the XML data files. The XML contains data as `<page>` elements which list namespace, title, and text (source code) of the then-current edit with details of the edit UID and its editor.

4.2 Extraction & Processing

Instance of transclusion markers in source code (see Section 3) were identified via iterative development of a series of Python scripts using regular expressions to detect each of variations of article content transclusion mark-up. English data was used initially and then further localisation added as required, hampered by a lack of documentation of per-wiki namespace and tag localisation strings.

The scripts filtered out all non 'main' namespace XML data elements to interrogate only articles and further filtered active articles from re-direction stubs. The latter are article elements, but can be identified by the presence of an optional `<redirect>` XML element. Of note (Table 2) is the significant number of articles which prove to be simply (hidden) re-directs[18]. The script's namespace filtering design also allowed for re-configured use to look for markers in the Template namespace (the default transclusion namespace).

Of the 10 wiki datasets, 2 have localised[19] aliases defined for the LST hash-based mark-up. Because English versions are supported by default in all wikis regardless of and namespace or tag localisations, this required scripts to test for both mark-up forms.

Initially, extraction scripts generated a Unicode text file per source XML file to assist with resolving detection edge case, helping link detections to the relevant source XML file if extra detail extraction was required. In final form the text files listed the transcluding article's name and each discrete article content transclusion marker within the article; occurrence counts were recorded in a separate file. Items were given additional text delimiters to assist with later separation of articles names for transcluding and transcluded items. For transclusion-limiting tags, discrete start and end tag counts were recorded to indicate whether proper tag closure was being used. Occurrences of 12 discrete transclusional mark-up forms, as described in Section 3, were enumerated for each wiki.

Per-source file output was then aggregated to single file per wiki for each strand of extracted data before data analysis. The generally low occurrences of mark-up allowed analysis using regular expression pattern analysis—and further visual inspection as required. This process enabled identification of edge case detection errors. Besides actual human error in the original article source code, out-of-scope references were tabulated and set aside. Though more laborious, this process gave a richer picture than could be obtained using API query methods.

Further analysis was undertaken in Tinderbox[3], which was chosen for its support for incremental formalisation of emergent structure in the data [23]. Tinderbox data was used to create network data for Gephi analysis of transclusion patterns (as shown in Section 5.3).

5 RESULTS & ANALYSIS

5.1 Occurrence of Transclusion

Evidence of article transclusion was found in every wiki sampled except Cebuano, as shown in Table 2. Despite detection of transclusion, the incidence is very low in comparison to overall article counts. The German wiki showed the highest occurrence rate at 0.58% of all active articles. Aggregating data across all 10 sampled wikis, the averaged transclusion occurrence is 0.095%.

There is no consistency in level of use across the sampled languages. This is also reflected in the occurrence within transcluded articles of the three main mark-up tags used to control the scope of transclusion (as described in Section 3.1.2): see Table 3.

The two most-used scoping tags are actually functional equivalents, the German and Russian wikis using a different tag but to similar effect. The German (1.58%) and Russian (1.61%) wikis show similar levels of their most-used tag, although active articles in the Russian wiki represent a sample size 67% that of the German wiki. The German and English wikis favour delimiting source data to be *included* in transclusion whilst the Russian and Italian wikis favour delimiting data to be *excluded*. No annotation was discovered indicating the rationale of these choices, although copying existing within-wiki practice is a plausible cause.

The amount of articles containing multiple transclusions varied greatly across languages (Table 2). In addition, only 3 wikis were were found to contain articles that both transcluded content and were themselves transcluded: German 614 (5.498% of transcluding articles), English 241 (11.091%), and Russian 34 (2.214%).

The lower occurrence of LST mark-up (see Table 2) must in part reflect its relative newness. Added to MediWikia c.2006, it was cited as unavailable in (English) Wikipedia in mid-2008 and was not added to the Transclusion documentation until early 2014[20] although use of LST has been found as far back as August 2013[21].

The complete absence of content transclusion in the Cebuano wiki, the fourth largest wiki by article count, likely reflects the high degree of bot edits. Many of this wiki's articles are stubs created automatically by the activity of bots, such as 'lsjbot'[10]. Absence does not necessarily imply bots cannot program content transclusion as shown by the incidence of Wikidata transclusion in the Cebuano wiki (see Table 2). Where found, edits adding Wikidata transclusions are generally not given explanatory edit comments.

In some cases, every use of a particular tag type can be linked to a single editor. For example, all instances of `#lsth` in the German wiki were first added by the same editor—again, usually without explicit edit comment.

The possibility that a significant amount of transclusion is hidden within templates is discounted. Supplementary sampling of non-main namespaces found `Template` had 7 instances (all English) of content transclusion called from outside the main namespace. The

---

[18]These arise due to actions like article renaming or (non) use of underscores in URLs.

[19]As described in https://www.mediawiki.org/wiki/Extension:Labeled_Section_Transclusion#Localisation from c.2007. English offers #section and German #Abschnitt (although the latter doesn't localise #lsth).

[20]See: https://en.wikipedia.org/w/index.php?title=Wikipedia:Transclusion&diff=595137158&oldid=586910323

[21]See: https://en.wikipedia.org/w/index.php?title=2013_FIBA_Asia_Championship&diff=567549313&oldid=567548989.

	ceb	de	en	es	fr	it	ja	nl	ru	sv	Total
All 'main' namespace Articles	2,963,362	3,200,021	12,188,486	2,807,709	3,115,027	1,873,355	1,602,047	2,516,924	2,807,922	4,140,672	37,215,525
'Active' (i.e. non re-direct) Articles	1,811,648	1,895,965	5,055,811	1,184,099	1,713,868	1,246,493	998,908	1,850,771	1,281,320	2,533,120	19,572,003
Re-directs as % All Articles	61%	59%	41%	42%	55%	67%	62%	74%	46%	61%	53%
TA Transcluding other Articles.	0	11,167	2,173	70	175	3,046	47	141	1,536	304	18,659
TA as % Active Arts.	0.000%	0.589%	0.043%	0.006%	0.010%	0.244%	0.005%	0.008%	0.120%	0.012%	0.095%
TA Using Multiple Transcludes	0	3,659	933	8	7	2,260	25	103	83	121	7,199
Multiple TA as % TA	0.000%	32.766%	42.936%	11.429%	4.000%	74.196%	53.191%	73.050%	5.404%	39.803%	38.582%
LST Transcludes as % TA	0.000%	0.690%	5.861%	0.000%	0.000%	0.000%	21.277%	0.000%	0.326%	0.658%	1.189%
Wikidata Transclusions as % Active	0.083%	0.000%	0.021%	0.001%	0.087%	0.004%	0.001%	0.020%	0.001%	0.035%	0.026%

Table 2: Per-language occurrence of transcluding articles (TA) in the main namespace.

Language	{{: and LST	onlyinclude	noinclude	includeonly
ceb	0.000%	0.000%	0.000%	0.000%
de	0.589%	1.582%	0.043%	0.008%
en	0.043%	0.225%	0.050%	0.019%
es	0.006%	0.013%	0.116%	0.028%
fr	0.012%	0.007%	0.011%	0.012%
it	0.244%	0.007%	0.595%	0.004%
ja	0.004%	0.022%	0.038%	0.007%
nl	0.008%	0.058%	0.001%	0.000%
ru	0.120%	0.061%	1.615%	0.019%
sv	0.012%	0.046%	0.013%	0.001%
Aggregate	0.095%	0.230%	0.172%	0.010%

Table 3: Per-language transclude mark-up occurrence. Column 2: transclusion calls. Columns 3-5: scope-restriction in transcluded pages.

Portal namespace contained 29 main namespace transclusions (German 10, English 6, Dutch 1, Russian 12). Nothing was found in the Module namespace.

In general, it is hard to assess editors' transclusion intent because where it occurs it is often implemented without any explanation—in either edit comments or talk pages. Unhelpfully, such opaque use informs neither later editors nor a less experienced editor who as yet may not understand the concept of, or rationale for, transclusion. This is reflected in talk page comment from July 2014: "*The word "transclusion," the concepts of transclusion, and code to adeptly accomplish transclusion are not general knowledge. Transclusion is a computer science concept, so little known as to be marked as a spelling error by my dictionary as I work in Wikipedia...*"[22].

Visual marking of transclusion (Section 3.1.3) was not detected, suggesting that the lack of both examples and documentation means editors are unaware of these useful transclusion indicators.

In summary, the fragmented and incomplete documentation, and lack of coherent worked examples obfuscate the transclusion technique for those who might employ it.

5.2 Variation in Purpose of Transclusion

Occurrence counts alone only give part of the picture. Articles in Wikipedia vary in size and scope. Transclusion may simply be more pertinent in some contexts than in others. To investigate this, the transcluding and transcluded articles were reviewed and assigned to broad groupings ('topics') based on their subject (see Table 4). Transclusions to other namespaces or wikis were assessed as 'out of context'. Articles with code errors or unresolvable transclusion targets were assessed as errors.

Across the 9 wikis with transclusions, this required assessment of 20,901 articles; in many cases the title and transclusion targets (translated to English as needed) gave sufficient indication of topic. Where necessary, a smaller number of articles were assessed by direct inspection of the then-current edit. Although the topic choices were subjective, clear groupings did emerge. This is perhaps because some topics do indeed lend themselves naturally to transclusion use. For example, sports articles often include team and competition listings. Such tabular data might reasonably be expected to be re-used in multiple contexts, in which context transclusion would aid the process.

Although some groupings were necessarily broad, so as to ensure aggregation of otherwise small discrete topics, the picture that emerged was unexpectedly diverse (see Table 4). The most common topic in aggregate is disambiguation, but it was the most common per-wiki topic in only 3 of the 9 wikis. Though grouped separately, the use of a pair of 'died on' and 'born on' topics in the Italian wiki might also be considered a case of indexing akin to disambiguation.

Whilst each wiki had a predominant transclusion topic, they showed no overall consistency (see Table 4). The most popular topic in each discrete wiki represented over 50% of transclusions, with the exception of Japanese (that also had the fewest total transclusions). The second-most popular topic represents at maximum 26.2% (Dutch), but in most cases is lower, as shown in Table 5.

In the English wiki, the most popular 'Episodic Media' topic covered listings of series and episodes for TV shows or film franchises as well as a smaller amount of printed media such as series of anime magazines and graphic novels. The same topic was seen in only 4 other wikis (see Table 4) and at generally much lower levels.

Combining the English wiki's category listings of US and of UK TV shows gives 3,974 discrete articles (Wikipedia's categories are a folksonomy, thus not necessarily an accurate listing of relevant articles). The intersection with transcluding articles in the Episodic Media topic is only 74 (17%) articles. This indicates transclusion occurrence is low within all possible articles in the overall grouping of Episodic Media. It also illustrates that at least 951 articles relating to episodic media are under-categorised within Wikipedia.

---

[22]See: https://en.wikipedia.org/wiki/Wikipedia_talk:Transclusion#Please_add_clearer_real_example_text.

Topic:	ceb	de	en	es	fr	it	ja	nl	ru	sv	Aggregate	Agg. %	Rank
Disambiguation		9,820			8				1,284	200	11,312	60.62%	1
Born/Died						2,901					2,901	15.55%	2
Episodic Media			1,125	51			2		129	20	1,327	7.11%	3
Sport		416	251	8	150		17	37		76	955	5.12%	4
Music		602					3				605	3.24%	5
Astronomy			243					100			343	1.84%	6
Political			152	4							156	0.84%	7
Computer Games						132					132	0.71%	8
Administrative			85								85	0.46%	9
Film							5				5	0.03%	10
Nature							3				3	0.02%	11
Other Topics <3% ea.		324	271	3	12	4	4	4	99	6	727	3.90%	-
- Other language			5	1	1				3	2	12	0.06%	-
- Other namespace		5	9			9	3		21		47	0.25%	-
- Errors			32	3	4		10				49	0.26%	-
Total	0	11,167	2,173	70	175	3,046	47	141	1,536	304	18,659	-	-

Table 4: Per-language occurrence of transclusion by subject group, topics ranked by aggregate totals. (Zero % values omitted.)

In the German wiki alone, the Music topic showed a consistent pattern of transclusion—that of a discography into a musician's article. As with the Episodic Media case, the articles which use transclusion are only some of those articles that might do the same. However, creating a separate discography article for artists with an as-yet limited discography, arguably represents limited return on extra work.

Other emergent topics were Sport (in all but Italian and Russian), and Astronomy (English, Dutch). Sporting transclusions show the greatest re-use of tabulated data and listings, and made the greatest use of LST-style transclusion. Sport being a subject likely to have entries in all wikis for some articles and thus useful to compare per-wiki transclusion. Two sports teams' articles were analysed for transclusion and template use: the Boston Bruins ice hockey team ('Bruins') and Manchester United Football Club ('MUFC'). Both subjects had a page in 9 of the sampled wikis (all except Cebuano).

The Bruins articles were found to have a team roster table in 5 of 9 articles, the others being stub pages. Of those 5, only 3 used transclusion and of the 3 only the French[23] wiki transcluded another article[24]: the German and English[25] wikis transcluded a Template namespace page. Cross-checking other ice hockey teams' articles, the per-language choice of namespace for defining the team sheet was consistent.

MUFC had articles in all but Cebuano with 4 of the 9 articles had Wikipedia 'featured article' status. No pages directly transcluded content but 6 of 9 used 'navbox' type[26] indexes at page foot. The articles use many tables but, unlike the Ice Hockey pages, these tables are not transcluded. Similarly other UK Premier League club articles (in English) show the same lack of content transclusion.

Though visual style is similar, use of (table) templates shows some variation.

In summary, as with general transclusion occurrence, a clear feature of the analysis was a *lack* of consistent practice. Small groupings of similar transclusion use suggest either copying of source mark-up or off-wiki discussion by editors. Edit comments annotating use of transclusion, or intent thereof, were conspicuously absent.

5.3 Transclusional Patterns

Link patterns in various types of hypertext have been documented in the past (Bernstein [2][4]). This task tested if such repeating patterns may be discerned in transclusion linkage within Wikipedia. Due to the volume of data for manual review, only data from the English wiki was fully mapped to identify patterns (9,774 articles). The full tracing of the English wiki also showed that of 2,127 transcluding articles 2,119 (99.624%) used a partial transclude of some form. 241 articles both transcluded other articles and were themselves transcluded. A number of distinct patterns were seen. Note that most patterns—though distinct when seen—do not occur in great numbers, reflecting the limited overall occurrence of transclusion.

5.3.1 Lists: lists from transclusions. These articles create lists, with some or all items being created from transcluded material. Each item is normally a section of the called articles, the degree of transclusion constrained by mark-up. This first pattern is most prevalent in the German and Italian wikis, but found in most languages. In the German (Disambiguation) and Italian (Births/Deaths lists[27]) wikis the main topics make greater use of the mixing inline data with transcluded listings. Again, the transcluded articles' own mark-up limits the degree of content re-used in the main listing.

In a few cases, the lists could be large and built entirely from transclusion such as the English wiki's listing of UK diplomatic

---

[23] See: https://fr.wikipedia.org/w/index.php?title=Bruins_de_Boston&oldid=122040311.

[24] See: https://fr.wikipedia.org/w/index.php?title=Effectif_actuel_des_Bruins_de_Boston&oldid=120808444.

[25] See: https://en.wikipedia.org/w/index.php?title=Boston_Bruins&oldid=699243091.

[26] See: https://en.wikipedia.org/w/index.php?title=Manchester_United_F.C.&oldid=699017841.

[27] See: https://it.wikipedia.org/w/index.php?title=1798&oldid=70628770.

Topic ranking	DE	EN	ES	FR	IT	JA	NL	RU	SV
1	87.938%	51.772%	72.857%	85.714%	95.240%	36.170%	70.922%	83.594%	65.789%
2	5.391%	11.551%	11.429%	4.571%	4.334%	10.638%	26.241%	8.398%	25.000%
3	3.725%	11.183%	5.714%			6.383%			6.579%
4		6.995%				6.383%			
5		3.912%				4.255%			
Other (<3% ea.)	2.901%	12.471%	4.286%	6.857%	0.131%	8.511%	2.837%	6.445%	1.974%
Out of scope	0.045%	0.644%	1.429%	0.571%	0.259%	6.383%	0%	1.563%	0%
Errors	0%	1.473%	4.286%	2.286%	0.000%	21.277%	0%	0%	0%

Table 5: Per-topic contribution to overall transclusion occurrence, by language.

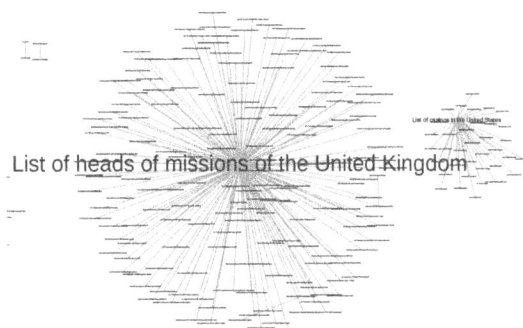

Figure 2: List of UK diplomatic reps: English wiki.

representatives[28] (see Figure 2): this article uses 205 discrete transclusions drawn from 160 discrete sources[29]. The article is also unusual in the care taken to add HTML comments to the source of both calling and called pages to ensure editors understand the process.

The Japanese wiki has a listing of film box office figures[30] using 145 transclusions of (between 1 and 5 instances of) 65 discrete source articles, each representing per-year data. This was also the largest instance found of transclusion that used only LST mark-up.

5.3.2 Lists: lists of lists. This form is best seen in the listings of minor planets, as found in the English[31] and Dutch[32] wikis. In this pattern for structured data, summaries of lower-level listings are transcluded into a more abstracted listing in the level above. The pattern is easily extended, encompassing large numbers of articles (see Table 4, Astronomy data).

5.3.3 Lists: Episodic Media listings. This is similar to the last but specifically reflects the structure of a show/publication article's listings by season/series summaries and then per-season articles listing episode synopses. In some cases all 3 levels are connected by transclusion (see Figure 3), or else just two; some shows also

transclude in character lists. While newer shows may lack content, and older ones verifiable data, there is no clear sign as to why some editors only connect two levels.

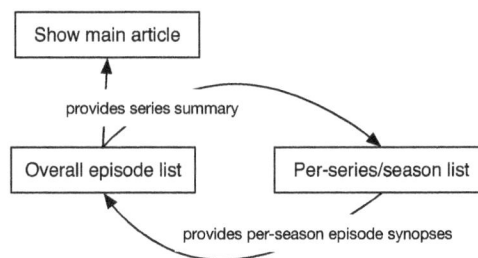

Figure 3: Episodic media listing structure.

Summaries, for upward transclusion of synopses, are consistently defined using scope-limited mark-up. However, choice of scope-limiting tag (Section 3.1.2) varies, with no documented rationale for differing use. It is likely current practice represents initial rote copying of early examples with subsequent divergence through error or further customisation. The English wiki does have some code examples that, *if* found by a user, can assist with consistent practice but the degree of variation (as seen at source code level) does point to a lack of coherent practice. For instance, the Episodic Media topic appears as many small clusters of 2-3 levels, the overall cluster size reflecting the number of series (see Figure 4).

There are remarkably few instances of linking between these clusters, one such is shown at Figure 5 (note also a 3-level cluster bottom right). The centre of this largest small tangle is the article "List of longest-running U.S. primetime television series"[33], transcluding articles for shows such a *The Simpsons* and *South Park*.

Cross-cluster linking is most seen in the 'Sport' topic area. Some competitions have many rounds (clusters) forming the route to major championships (Figure 6).

5.3.4 Tangles. If list groupings are interconnected, a 'tangle' can form, with no obvious linear structure[34]. The more closely interconnected the different lists the more complex the result. In Figure

---

[28] See: https://en.wikipedia.org/w/index.php?title=List_of_heads_of_missions_of_the_United_Kingdom&oldid=690855670.
[29] This is because some people hold multiple posts.
[30] See:https://ja.wikipedia.org/w/index.php?title=%E5%B9%B4%E5%BA%A6%E5%88%A5%E6%98%A0%E7%94%BB%E8%88%88%88%E8%A1%8C%E6%88%90&oldid=58063614.
[31] See: https://en.wikipedia.org/w/index.php?title=List_of_minor_planets:_86001âÄ\$87000&oldid=656043730.
[32] See: https://nl.wikipedia.org/w/index.php?title=Lijst_van_planetoÄ́den_11001-12000&oldid=38287749.

[33] See: https://en.wikipedia.org/w/index.php?title=List_of_longest-running_U.S._primetime_television_series&oldid=699285724.
[34] This echoes the unstructured 'Tangle' pattern in general hypertext patterns [2, p.24].

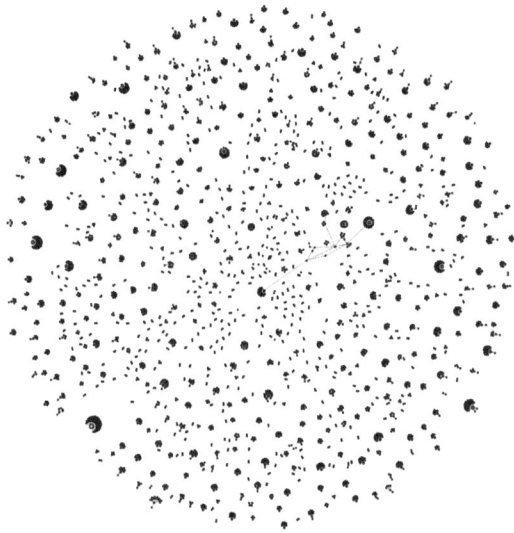

Figure 4: Episodic Media topic transcludes, English wiki. (orange=transcluder, purple=transcluded, green=both)

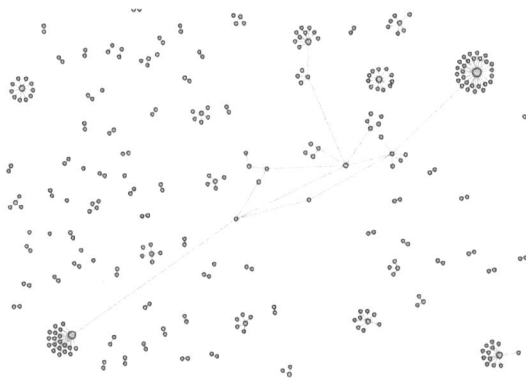

Figure 5: Detail of listing of episodic media (from Fig. 4).

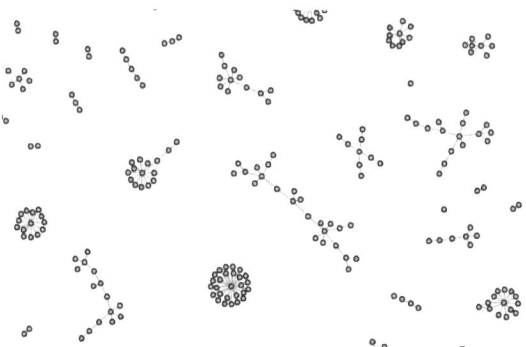

Figure 6: Inter-subject linking, (part of) 'Sport' topic, English wiki.

7, eight discrete listings of villages, towns and cities in Canada, and some per-State listings of communities are co-mingled.

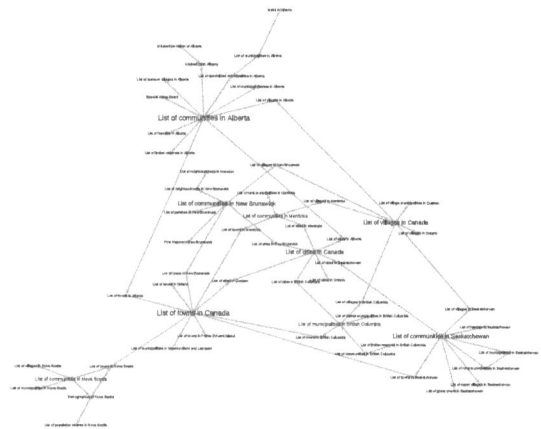

Figure 7: Canadian communities, English wiki.

5.3.5 Articles as macros. An unusual form, seen in Episodic Media in the English Wiki, is where scope control mark-up excludes all data but the current number of aired episodes. Though the article is transcluded, essentially it functions as a metadata macro. The article on The Simpsons[35] is transcluded for this purpose by 10 other articles. Although this pattern emerged (without edit comment) in October 2015, by February 2016 another 49 Episodic Media articles used the same mechanism to show article count suggesting editors were simply copying a new 'technique'. English wiki 'Portal' namespace articles also transclude counts from 3 different media shows, doing so 5 times in the case of 'The Simpsons'.

5.3.6 Self-transclusion. An article may transclude itself so as to re-use internal structural content such as list headings. For example, a page on Mediatek tablet processors[36] LST-transcludes a <section>-defined heading to the first table in the page into all the other 15 table headings on the page.

To summarise, some transclusion patterns were detected. Were there a means to easily visualise these patterns, it could assist with identifying consistent use of transclusion is suitable subject areas.

6 CONCLUSIONS

The analysis undertaken shows that whilst content transclusion definitely occurs in Wikipedia, it does so at very low levels. Moreover, in subject areas where transclusion might reasonably be applied, it still occurs inconsistently. The current lack of clear documentation, examples and tools to identify transclusion use should be considered a contributory factor. For example, there is no detected use of available templates specifically designed for visibly indicating transclusion (see Section 3.1.3): these assist editors to discern the transcluded material and edit it at source. In addition, although support for transclusion of data from Wikidata was added in 2013 it has yet (as of February 2016) to be added to Wikipedia documentation of transclusion, or to style guides.

---

[35]See: https://en.wikipedia.org/w/index.php?title=The_Simpsons&oldid=699225461.
[36]See: https://en.wikipedia.org/w/index.php?title=List_of_devices_using_Mediatek_tablet_processors&oldid=691189367.

Tools available to editors to detect transclusion, if not explicitly marked by the originator, are also limited[37] making it difficult even for a diligent editor to detect with ease any transclusions created by other editors (especially if they make no relevant edit comment).

Transclusion is thus found in Wikipedia but appears to be used in a fragmented manner. Whilst MediaWiki software allows for quite nuanced use of transclusion, the full range of capability is not employed. Editors would be better served if transclusion was referenced explicitly in existing style and writing guides. These should explain what sort of topics do or do not suit transclusion and why, along with worked examples to explain the necessary markup and the sort of signposting that should be left for other editors. If it were possible to add an option to version-link transclusions (or have a method to record the erstwhile edit UIDs of calling and called pages) this would also benefit long-term maintenance.

With better identification of areas—or categories—suitable for transclusion there is also scope for bots to check on transclusion presence and indicate article clusters that might be improved by transclusion. Such additional structure would also be of use to Semantic Web and data interfaces to the hypertext.

Highlighting apparent weaknesses in documentation is not disparagement of the general efforts of Wikipedia's editors. Rather, it points to a lack of a support role that considers the hypertext as a whole. Transclusion patterns can help both as usage examples and as markers which hypertext maintainers might exploit to identify subject areas where transclusion is ineffectively used. The existing roles available to Wikipedia editors do not, as yet, have a niche for those focussed on maintaining the hypertext as a whole. The page 'Wikipedia:Transclusion costs and benefits'[38] states: "*There is a social cost of transclusion, the total expectation over time of the risk that a transcluded template page may be vandalized*". This indicates a possible misalignment of interests between article-centric editors and those looking to maintain the hypertext as a whole. Having a more clearly defined role of this type would make it easier to identify and mediate conflicts between editors (and automated bots) operating in narrow versus broad scope.

The WikiProjects[39] initiative focuses volunteers' effort on specific subject areas within Wikipedia. Recent analysis of WikiProjects found that "*WikiProjects has reconfigured the article production and improvement process*"[25, p.9], suggesting they may be a possible catalyst area for some more deliberate structural wiki maintenance for the long term. Future work plans include both conducting interviews with WikiProject volunteers assessing whether their editing intent considers aiding longitudinal curation of Wikipedia and, separately, looking at the possibility of identifying patterns marking clusters of articles where deliberate transclusion may be of benefit.

As the the web matures the effort to support large hypertexts such as Wikipedia will shift from growth to maintenance - with an emphasis on what we have called longitudinal coherence. The infrequent and inconsistent use of transclusions in Wikipedia indicates that approaches that could make this maintenance more manageable have yet to be embraced, although the presence of particular patterns of transclusion do demonstrate potential usefulness. More broadly, a challenge for collaborative hypertexts is to consider long term structure and not just the individual pages of visible content.

7 ACKNOWLEDGMENTS

This work was supported by the Web Science Centre for Doctoral Training at the University of Southampton, funded by the UK Engineering and Physical Sciences Research Council (EPSRC) under grant number EP/L016117/1.

REFERENCES

[1] Ofer Arazy, Felipe Ortega, Oded Nov, Lisa Yeo, and Adam Balila. 2015. Functional Roles and Career Paths in Wikipedia. Proceedings of the 18th ACM Conference on Computer Supported Cooperative Work & Social Computing (2015), 1092–1105.

[2] Mark Bernstein. 1998. Patterns of Hypertext. Proceedings of the ninth ACM conference on Hypertext and hypermedia (1998), 21–29.

[3] Mark Bernstein. 2009. Shadows in The Cave: Hypertext Transformations. *Journal of digital information* 10, 3 (2009), 1–8.

[4] Mark Bernstein. 2011. Can We Talk About Spatial Hypertext? Proceedings of the 22nd ACM Conference on Hypertext and Hypermedia (2011), 103–112.

[5] Philip Boulain, Nigel Shadbolt, and Nicholas Gibbins. 2009. Studies on Editing Patterns in Large-scale Wikis. In *Weaving Services and People on the World Wide Web*. Springer, 325–349.

[6] Angelo Di Iorio and John Lumley. 2009. From XML Inclusions to XML Transclusions. Proceedings of the 20th ACM Conference on Hypertext and Hypermedia (2009), 147–156.

[7] Robert J. Glushko. 2013. *The Discipline of Organizing*. MIT Press. 752 pages.

[8] Frank G Halasz. 2001. Reflections on "Seven Issues": Hypertext in the Era of the Web. *ACM Journal of Computer Documentation (JCD)* 25, 3 (2001), 109–114.

[9] Aaron Halfaker, R. Stuart Geiger, Jonathan T. Morgan, and John Riedl. 2013. The Rise and Decline of an Open Collaboration System. *American Behavioral Scientist* 57, 5 (2013), 664–688.

[10] E.E. Jervell. 2014. For This Author, 10,000 Wikipedia Articles Is a Good Day's Work. (2014). Retrieved 20 July, 2016 from http://www.wsj.com/articles/for-this-author-10-000-wikipedia-articles-is-a-good-days-work-1405305001

[11] Clemens N. Klokmose, James Eagan, Siemen Baader, Wendy Mackay, and Michel Beaudouin-Lafon. 2016. Webstrates: Demonstrating the Potential of Shareable Dynamic Media. Proceedings of the 19th ACM Conference on Computer Supported Cooperative Work and Social Computing Companion (2016), 61–64.

[12] Josef Kolbitsch. 2005. Fine-Grained Transclusions of Multimedia Documents in HTML. *J. UCS* 11, 6 (2005), 926–943.

[13] Harald Krottmaier and Denis Helic. 2002. Issues of transclusions. Proceedings of E-Learn (E-Learn 2002) (2002), 1730–1733.

[14] Bo Leuf and Ward Cunningham. 2001. *The Wiki way Quick Collaboration on the Web*. Addison-Wesley Boston, MA.

[15] Andrew Lih. 2004. Wikipedia as participatory journalism: Reliable sources? metrics for evaluating collaborative media as a news resource. *Nature* 3, 1 (2004).

[16] Hermann Maurer and Josef Kolbitsch. 2006. Transclusions in an HTML-Based Environment. *CIT. Journal of Computing and Information Technology* 14, 2 (2006), 161–173.

[17] Theodor Holm Nelson. 1965. Complex Information Processing: A File Structure for the Complex, the Changing and the Indeterminate. Proceedings of the 1965 20th National Conference (1965), 84–100.

[18] Theodor Holm Nelson. 1982. *Literary Machines*. Mindful Press.

[19] Theodor Holm Nelson. 1995. The Heart of Connection: Hypermedia Unified by Transclusion. *Commun. ACM* 38, 8 (1995), 31–33.

[20] Hartmut Obendorf. 2004. The Indirect Authoring Paradigm – Bringing Hypertext into the Web. *Journal of Digital Information* 5, 1 (2004).

[21] Andrew Pam. 1997. Fine-Grained Transclusion in the Hypertext Markup Language. *Project Xanadu Memo* 2 (1997).

[22] m. c. schraefel, Leslie Carr, David De Roure, and Wendy Hall. 2004. You've Got Hypertext. *Journal of Digital Information (JoDI)* 5, 1.253 (2004).

[23] Frank M Shipman III and Catherine C Marshall. 1999. Formality Considered Harmful: Experiences, Emerging Themes, and Directions on the Use of Formal Representations in Interactive Systems. *Computer Supported Cooperative Work (CSCW)* 8, 4 (1999), 333–352.

[24] Giuseppe Sindoni. 1999. Incremental Maintenance of Hypertext Views. In *The World Wide Web and Databases*, Paolo Atzeni, , Alberto Mendelzon, , and Giansalvatore Mecca (Eds.). Springer Berlin Heidelberg, Berlin, Heidelberg, 98–117.

[25] Ramine Tinati and Markus Luczak-Roesch. 2017. Wikipedia: A Complex Social Machine. *SIGWEB Newsletter* Winter (2017), 6:1–6:10.

---

[37]For example,'what links here' queries that list inbound links, redirections and transclusions.

[38]See: https://en.wikipedia.org/wiki/Wikipedia:Transclusion_costs_and_benefits.

[39]See; https://en.wikipedia.org/wiki/Wikipedia:WikiProject.

Negative Link Prediction and Its Applications in Online Political Networks

Mert Ozer, Mehmet Yigit Yildirim, Hasan Davulcu
School of Computing, Informatics, and
Decision Systems Engineering
Arizona State University
Tempe, US
{mozer,yigityildirim,hdavulcu}@asu.edu

ABSTRACT

Disagreements, oppositions and negative opinions are indispensable parts of online political debates. In social media, people express their beliefs and attitudes not only on issues but also about each other through both their conversations and platform-specific interactions such as like, share in Facebook and retweet in Twitter. While there are explicit "like" features in these platforms, there is no explicit "dislike" feature. Many network analysis tasks, such as detecting communities and monitoring their dynamics (i.e. polarization patterns) require information about both positive and negative linkages. Hence, predicting negative links between users is an important task and a challenging problem. In this study, we propose an unsupervised framework to predict the negative links between users by utilizing explicit positive interactions and sentiment cues in conversations. We show the effectiveness of the proposed framework on a political Twitter dataset annotated through Amazon MTurk crowdsourcing platform. Our experimental results show that the proposed framework outperforms other well-known methods and proposed baselines. To illustrate the contribution of the predicted negative links, we compare the community detection accuracies using signed and unsigned user networks. Experimental results using predicted negative links show superiority on three political datasets where the camps are known a priori. We also present qualitative evaluations related to the polarization patterns (i.e. rivalries and coalitions) between the detected communities which is only possible in the presence of negative links.

KEYWORDS

Negative Link Prediction; Online Political Networks; Social Media Mining; Sentiment Analysis

1 INTRODUCTION

Beyond any doubt, social media has become a prominent platform for people to express their political stances and opinions for more than a decade. It developed into a medium for politicians and political organizations to interact with the public [22]. While 44th President of the United States, Barack Obama makes an appearance on a Reddit Ask Me Anything, 45th President Donald Trump tweets about how hypocrite he thinks the mainstream media is. While many protesters mobilize their political movements, online social networks more and more start to show the characteristics of public sphere in the online world [1].

Many researchers have extensively studied the nature of online political networks [2], [3], [12], [24]. Most of the existing works utilize platform-specific positive interactions between users such as share and like in Facebook or retweet and like in Twitter to infer insights from and model political activities in such social media platforms. In [2], Conover et al. presents how platform-specific positive interactions in Twitter shows a polarized behaviour in which one side does not retweet or like the other side's contents.

Major online social media platforms, however, do not provide its users options to state negative opinions in the form of a simple click such as "dislike" which might convey opposition or disagreement towards each other. Nonetheless, many political analysis tasks need the information of rivalries, resentments between political actors to get a complete picture of the online political landscape. This very nature of major social media platforms limit the capabilities of researchers studying online political networks. For that reason many researchers usually choose to study the online social networks where explicit negative links are available to them such as Epinions, Slashdot or Wikipedia instead [5], [16], [28]. Certainly, these online platforms are not the hotspots where people participate to express their political views through.

Therefore, we focus on inferring the negative links between users of online political networks. We aim to predict the link's negative nature, when any form of an overall disagreement, opposition or hostility is present between two social media users. It is a challenging problem due to the two main reasons. First, there is no readily available online political network dataset in which negative links are explicitly present between its users. Therefore, the developed model must be unsupervised. Second, there is no simple predictor of negative links such as "dislike" in major social media platforms where the main body of the online political activity resides. However, opportunities are unequivocally present as well. Recent works in the social media mining research [25], [20] show that negative sentiment in the textual interaction between users is a good predictor of the negative link of those two users. Moreover, certain social psychology phenomenons such as social balance and status theory are proven to be helpful in predicting negative links in certain network configurations[17].

HT'17, July 4-7, 2017, Prague, Czech Republic.
© 2017 ACM. 978-1-4503-4708-2/17/07...$15.00
DOI: http://dx.doi.org/10.1145/3078714.3078727

In this work, we first propose a nonnegative matrix factorization framework SocLS-Fact that combines signals from sentiment lexicon of words, platform-specific positive interactions and social balance theory to predict negative and positive links in online political networks. We do not focus on the accuracy of the positive links since it is already a well studied problem and simple good predictors are already available. Then, we discuss two applications where predicted negative links can be employed to give a better understanding of the underlying political configuration of the target dataset. The first application is presented to show the added value of the predicted negative links in community detection tasks. The second application is proposed to show the informativeness of the predicted negative links related to polarization patterns between political groups. The main contributions of the paper are,

- Proposing an unsupervised model for negative link prediction in social media platforms where platform-specific negative interactions or negative links between users are not present.
- Showing the added value of the negative links in community detection tasks for online political networks.
- Presenting the effectiveness of negative links in describing the rivalries, coalitions between groups and its temporal dynamics qualitatively.

2   RELATED WORK

We survey link prediction and sentiment classification methods proposed for similar line of research in social media mining literature.

Link prediction in social media is an extensively studied problem. Its precedings can be traced back to the structuralist social psychology studies [8] that became popular in early 20th century. Link prediction studies standing out as most related to our problem definition are [13], [16], [25], [28]. In [16], Leskovec et al. propose a framework that predicts the sign of links in user networks in social media. They train classifiers using certain triad configuration and graph features to learn from existing data in which both explicit positive and negative links are present. In [28], Yang et al. make use of explicit negative links through items that users comment to rather than using direct negative links between users. Signed bipartite graph of users and items is used to infer connectivity patterns among users. In their prediction model, they accommodate the principles of balance and status from social psychology theory.

However, these methods are not capable of being trained for major social media platforms (i.e. Twitter, Facebook) due to the nonexistence of explicit negative links or platform-specific negative interaction capabilities of users in those platforms. To address this limitation, in [13], Kunegis et al. present an approach to predict negative links when only positive links are available explicitly. They further investigate the added value of negative links when they are predictable to a certain extent by using only properties of the positive links and not using any additional information such as textual content. However, they experiment only with Slashdot and Epinions datasets in which negative links or interactions between users are explicitly available. How generalizable their approach for other major social media platforms such as Facebook or Twitter, in which no platform-specific negative interaction is available, is not

discussed. In [25], Tang et al. introduce a supervised classification scheme to predict the negative links among missing links assuming that in many social media platforms, negative links are indirect and implicit. They use negative sentiment polarity of textual interactions between user pairs to synthetically generate the negative labeled links. This method also relies on experiments conducted only on Slashdot and Epinions datasets. On the other hand, our framework stands out as it is proposed for the online settings that does not provide any platform-specific negative interaction capabilities to its users. Moreover, it is experimented by utilizing political Twitter datasets, which does not include any platform-specific negative interactions.

Second line of research related to our work is sentiment classification in social media. Hu et al., in [11], propose a supervised sentiment classification model which takes advantage of connected text messages having similar sentiment labels. Hu et al., in [10], further investigate whether emotional signals such as emoticons can be incorporated in order to infer the sentiment classes of the tweets in Twitter. To credit the informative value of the overall sentiment of the textual interactions between users for predicting the polarity of the user link, Hassan et al., in [7], propose a supervised classification framework. It considers all textual interactions of the user pairs' and learn relevant sentiment features from human annotated prior user link polarities. However, it does not use any platform-specific interaction types which are vastly available on many social media platforms. West et al., in [27], develop a model that combinatorially optimizes the agreement between the sentiment class of user pairs' textual interaction and the polarity label of the explicit user link. They make use of Wikipedia, and U.S. Congress dataset, in which explicit negative links or platform specific negative interactions are available. Our work differentiates itself, from aforementioned others in the literature by using platform-specific positive interactions, and a sentiment lexicon of words to predict the negative link between users.

3   PROPOSED FRAMEWORK

In this section, we first present the notation used throughout the paper, formally define the problem and then propose the SocLS-Fact optimization solution. Finally, we provide the details of how to build the prior knowledge that the SocLS-Fact requires.

Before going into the details of the framework, the notation that is used throughout the paper can be seen in Table 1. Let m be the number of interacting user pairs, and n be the number of unique sentiment words. An example with 3 interacting user pairs and 8 unique sentiment words can be seen in Figure 1a and 1b. All textual interaction happening between two users are represented as rows of X. X encodes how many times each sentiment word occurs in textual interactions of two users. In Figure 1b, when user a and b interacts they use 2nd, 3rd, 5th and 6th words while user b and c interacts they use 1st, 3rd and 8th and so on. Initial user link polarities are embedded in matrix S_{u0}. Initial sentiment lexicon is embedded in S_{w0}. Positive and negative polarities are represented as two latent dimensions in matrix S_{u0}, and S_{w0}. Which user links should have the same polarity following the social balance theory is governed by matrix M. Further details of how matrices S_{u0}, S_{w0}, M are derived is given later in this section.

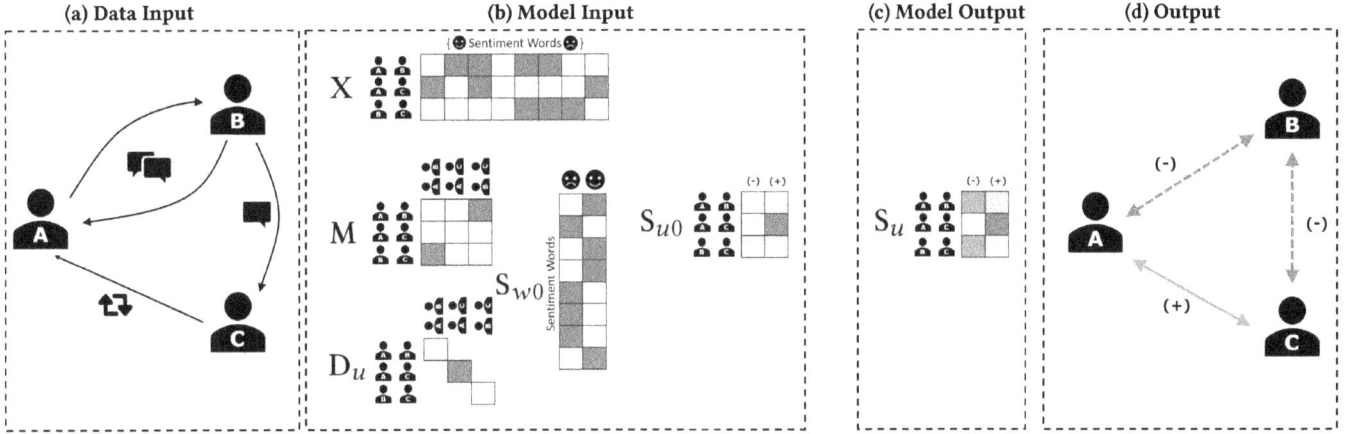

Figure 1: Modeling of social media data and interpretation of output.

Table 1: Notation

Symbol	Size	Explanation
m		Number of interacting user pairs
n		Number of sentiment words
I_k	$k \times k$	Identity matrix of size k
$\mathbf{X}$	$[m \times n]$	Matrix of occurrences of sentiment words in textual interactions of user pairs
$\mathbf{S}_u$	$[m \times 2]$	User link polarity
$\mathbf{S}_{u0}$	$[m \times 2]$	Initial user link polarity
$\mathbf{D}_u$	$[m \times m]$	Binary diagonal matrix of user pairs with positive interaction
$\mathbf{S}_w$	$[n \times 2]$	Sentiment word polarity
$\mathbf{S}_{w0}$	$[n \times 2]$	Initial sentiment lexicon
$\mathbf{M}$	$[m \times m]$	Social balance matrix

As we discuss earlier, sentiment of words used in user interactions are proven to be good predictors of the polarity of user links. Moreover, built-in positive interactions (i.e. retweet, like, share) are good predictors of positive user links by their nature. As referred in Section 1, how user links form triangles with each other is also a decisive factor of their polarities since they tend to follow social balance theory. To factorize all textual interactions between users into two latent dimensions as positive and negative and enjoy aforementioned three predictors of polarity of user links at the same time, we propose the following optimization problem;

$$\min_{\mathbf{S}_u, H, \mathbf{S}_w} \quad ||\mathbf{X} - \mathbf{S}_u H \mathbf{S}_w^T||_F^2 \tag{0}$$

$$+ \alpha ||\mathbf{S}_w - \mathbf{S}_{w0}||_F^2 \tag{1}$$

$$+ \beta Tr\left((\mathbf{S}_u - \mathbf{S}_{u0})^T \mathbf{D}_u (\mathbf{S}_u - \mathbf{S}_{u0})\right) \tag{2}$$

$$+ \gamma ||\mathbf{M} - \mathbf{S}_u \mathbf{S}_u^T||_F^2 \tag{3}$$

$$\text{subject to} \quad \mathbf{S}_u > 0, \mathbf{S}_w > 0, H > 0$$

Optimization formulation consists of 4 terms. $(0)^{th}$ term factorizes user pair textual interactions into three matrices. $\mathbf{S}_u \in \mathbb{R}_+^{m \times 2}$ is the lower-rank projection of matrix $\mathbf{X}$. The first column of $\mathbf{S}_u$ is the latent negative and second column is the latent positive dimension. $\mathbf{S}_w$ is the lower-rank projection of columns of matrix $\mathbf{X}$. Note that each column of $\mathbf{X}$ represents a sentiment word. Projection matrix $\mathbf{S}_w$ corresponds to distributed polarity representation of each sentiment word. As in $\mathbf{S}_u$, first column of $\mathbf{S}_w$ is the latent negative and the second column is the latent positive dimension.

$(1)^{st}$ term in the optimization formulation penalizes the meaning change of the sentiment words compared their initial lexicon meaning. Parameter α governs the relaxation on the penalty.

$(2)^{nd}$ term governs how much the polarity prediction of links diverges from their initial inferred labels. Initial labels are inferred as positive if there is any platform-specific positive interaction between users that the link connecting to. Diagonal matrix D_u helps to penalize divergences of links which have platform-specific positive interactions only.

$(3)^{rd}$ term in the optimization formulation penalizes the triangles in the user network that do not follow social balance theory. $\mathbf{M}$ encodes the information of pair of links that should have the same polarity if they are forming a triangle with another positive link.

3.1 Constructing $\mathbf{S}_{w0}$

A well-known off-the-shelf sentiment word lexicon is utilized[1] to populate the initial sentiment polarities of words. A word is represented as $[1, 0]$ if it has negative sentiment meaning. It is represented as $[0, 1]$ if it has positive sentiment meaning. In Figure 1b, initial sentiment lexicon is embedded in $\mathbf{S}_{w0}$ such that 1st, 3rd, 4th and 8th words as positive sentiment words and 2nd, 5th, 6th and 7th words as negative sentiment words.

3.2 Constructing $\mathbf{S}_{u0}$ and $\mathbf{D}_u$

Each row of the initial user link polarity matrix $\mathbf{S}_{u0}$ encodes the information of the prior inference of the polarity of user link. First

---

[1] http://www.cs.uic.edu/~liub/FBS/opinion-lexicon-English.rar

column of the polarity matrix S_{u0} is the latent negative dimension, while the second column is the latent positive dimension. For the links that connect user pairs having previous platform-specific positive interaction, we infer the initial polarity of them as positive and embed it as $[0, 1]$ in the corresponding row of S_{u0} and as 1 in the corresponding diagonal entry of D_u. For the links that connect user pairs having no previous platform-specific positive interaction, we do not infer any initial polarity and represent them as $[0.5, 0, 5]$ in S_{u0} and as 0 in the corresponding diagonal entry of D_u. To illustrate in Figure 1b, the positive interaction between user A and C is represented as $[0, 1]$ in the second row of S_{u0} and as 1 in the second diagonal entry of D_u.

3.3 Incorporating Social Balance Theory

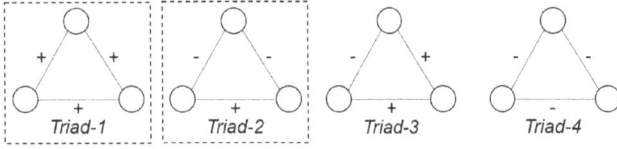

Figure 2: All possible configurations of undirected signed links in a triad. Balanced ones are framed with dashed rectangles.

The theory of social balance of signed links in triads is extensively studied since its introduction by Heider et al. in [8] as structural balance of signed links. It suggests that for a signed triad to be balanced, it has to have an odd number of positive links (i.e. one or three positive links), otherwise it is not balanced. The balanced configurations among all possible configurations are presented with dashed frames in Figure 2. The definition of structural balance is analogous to common daily phrase of "enemy of my enemy is my friend" and "friend of my friend is my friend" in social settings.

To encode the social balance theory, we utilize the prior knowledge of positive links inferred from platform-specific positive interactions. Our intuition is that if two users have any prior platform-specific positive interaction, the polarity of their interaction with any other third user should be similar. They can connect to third user either with both negative or positive links (i.e. Triad-1 and Triad-2 in Figure 2). The cases which they connect to a third user with different polarities are not socially balanced configurations (i.e. Triad-3 in Figure 2).

The matrix $M \in \{0, 1\}^{m \times m}$ encodes the link pairs that are needed to have the same polarity to follow social balance theory by having 1 in the related row and column of M and 0 for the rest. In Figure 1a, link between user A and B should have the same polarity with link between user B and C. It is because they are forming a triad with link between user A and C which has prior platform-specific positive interaction. In Figure 1b, it is encoded as 1 in the $M(1, 3)$ and $M(3, 1)$. Eventually, minimizing the squared frobenious norm of the difference between M and $S_u S_u^T$ forces triads to have odd number of positive links in the whole network.

3.4 Algorithm

The objective function proposed in Section 3 is not convex for all variables of S_u, S_w, H. We introduce an alternating optimization

solution for our problem similar to [18]. We update each variable S_u, S_w, H iteratively while fixing others to find a local minimum in the solution space. The update rules for each variable is given as;

$$S_u \leftarrow S_u \odot \sqrt{\frac{XS_wH^T + \gamma(M + M^T)S_u + \beta D_u S_{u0}}{S_u HS_w^T S_w H^T + \gamma S_u S_u^T S_u + \beta D_u S_u}} \quad (1)$$

$$H \leftarrow H \odot \sqrt{\frac{S_u^T X S_w}{S_u^T S_u H S_w^T S_w}} \quad (2)$$

$$S_w \leftarrow S_w \odot \sqrt{\frac{X^T S_u H + \alpha S_{w0}}{S_w H^T S_u^T S_u H + \alpha S_w}} \quad (3)$$

Derivation of the update rules is presented in Appendix A,B and C. The proposed algorithm employs an iterative scheme of the above rules until convergence. Each step of the algorithm is shown in Algorithm 1.

Algorithm 1: Proposed Algorithm for the Optimization Problem

Input: X, S_{u0}, S_{w0}, M.
Output: S_u, S_w.
1 Initialize $S_u \leftarrow S_{u0}, H \leftarrow I_2, S_w \leftarrow S_{w0}$.
2 **while** *not convergent* **do**
3   Update S_u using Equation 1.
4   Update H using Equation 2.
5   Update S_w using Equation 3.

Finally, the polarity of the latent dimension with higher numerical value in the ith row of S_u is assigned as the polarity output of the link i. To illustrate in Figure 1c and 1d, it can be seen that the value in the first column is greater than the second column for the first and the third rows of S_u. Therefore, the polarity of the link between user A and B and the link between user B and C are inferred as negative. Since the value in the second column is greater than the first column for the second row of S_u the polarity of the link between user A and C is inferred as positive.

The most computationally costly operations of the update rules are matrix multiplications since matrix summation, matrix hadamard product and element-wise division can be handled in linear time. Complexity of the update rule in Equation 1 is $O(mn + m^2 + m + n^2 m)$. Complexity of the update rule in 2 is $O(mn + m + n)$. Complexity of update rule in 3 is $O(mn + m^2 n)$. Therefore, overall time complexity of the Algorithm 1 complexity is $O(i(m^2 n + n^2 m + m^2 + mn + m + n))$ where i is the iteration count that algorithm takes until update rules converges to a local minima. Experiments empirically show that convergence takes usually less than 20 iterations.

The proof of the convergence of the algorithm is omitted here due to space constraints which can be followed in similar works using the auxilary function approach, such as presented in [4]. The source code for the whole running pipeline presented in this section can be reached at www.public.asu.edu/~mozer/HT2017Code.tar.gz.

Table 2: Dataset Statistics

	UK	UK-annotated	US	Canada
Textual interactions	4,217	18,903	31,276	5,001
Users	400	260	596	136
Interacting pair of users	3,367	1,074	6,114	1,291
Positive/negative links	N/A	948/126	N/A	N/A
Baseline communities	5	5	2	5

4 EXPERIMENTS

In this section, we present three experiments we design to demonstrate our method's effectiveness and different use-cases. In the first experiment, we investigate the effectiveness of SocLS-Fact for negative link prediction. In the second experiment, we explore how these predicted negative links contribute to community detection performance. In the third experiment, we qualitatively analyze the added value of predicted negative links in revealing polarization patterns of political party members in social media.

4.1 Dataset

We work with politician Twitter networks from United Kingdom, United States and Canada. Each politician account in the dataset either self declares her political party membership in her user profiles or has the abbreviation of the political party in her user name as suffix or prefix. Baseline communities are constructed according to each account's self-identification of political party memberships.

- **UK Dataset** covers 421 prominent political figures' twitter accounts from 5 major political parties, namely, Conservative Party (Cons), Labour Party (Lab), Scottish Nationalist Party(SNP), Liberal Democrat Party (LibDem), and United Kingdom Independence Party (UKIP).
- **UK-Annotated Dataset** covers 1,074 user pairs sampled from aforementioned UK dataset and polarity of each user interaction is annotated using crowdsourcing. Details is explained in Section 4.1.1.
- **US Dataset** covers 603 prominent political figures' twitter accounts from Republican (Rep) and Democrat (Dem) Party.
- **Canada Dataset** covers twitter accounts of 192 parliament members from 5 major political parties, namely, Liberal Party of Canada (Lib), Green Party (Green) of Canada, Conservative Party of Canada (Cons), New Democratic Party (NDP), and Bloc Quebecois (BLOC).

Latest 3,200 tweets of each identified account are crawled by using Twitter's REST API. Users who do not participate in any textual user interaction are removed from the dataset. An overview of the preprocessed data can be seen in Table 2.

For the first experiment, it is essential to obtain labels for user links to (1) test the effectiveness of our algorithm (2) have a grasp on the effect of the parameters. In [29], crowdsourcing is acknowledged as a good approach for gathering labels in social media, thus we have created a categorization task in the crowdsourcing platform, Amazon Mechanical Turk (MTurk). Details are explained in the Section 4.1.1.

For the second experiment, we directly make use of UK, US and Canada datasets.

For the third experiment, we utilize UK dataset to create 3 datasets as a representation of political environment in different time frames.

4.1.1 Labeling Through Crowdsourcing. First, we extracted user pairs that interact with each other at least three times. Then, all the textual interactions (i.e. tweets identified as mentions and reply to's) of these user pairs were aggregated. While aggregating, we filtered the data to include textual interactions which contains a single user mentioned to avoid the confusion as it is ambiguous which user is addressed in the multiple mentions case.

We requested 3 Mechanical Turk Masters (elite workers demonstrated high accuracy in the previous tasks) who had knowledge of UK politics to rate the polarity of given all textual interactions between two politicians. We have also provided users' political party affiliations and retweet counts between them to help the labelers assess the polarity of the link better.

After retrieving all the answers from 3 labelers, we assigned the polarity labels using majority voting. Then, we analyzed the labelers inter-rater agreement using Cohen's Kappa [15] and Fleiss' Kappa [6]. Two-way inter-rater agreement is nearly perfect according to [15] with Cohen's Kappa scores calculated as 0.810, 0.898 and 0.911. Fleiss' kappa is reported as 0.731.

Finally, we remove the neutral user links as they are not covered by our problem formulation.

4.2 Negative Link Prediction

Our first experiment aims to demonstrate the negative link prediction performance of SocLS-Fact in political Twitter networks.

To assess the performance of our method, we explain and compare with two existing state-of-the-art matrix factorization approaches along with three other baseline predictors we define as follows:

- **Random**: Motivated by [19], this method predicts user links randomly.
- **Only Sentiment**: This predictor infers the polarity of user pairs' links using only textual interaction. Sum of the inverse distance weighted sentiment values (+1, -1) of words in textual interactions is given as the polarity of the link between user pairs. Note that the predictor can simply be modeled as XS_{w0}, thanks to our initialization scheme we provide for S_{w0} and X in Section 3.
- **Only Link**: This predictor infers user pairs' links as positive if there is any historical platform-specific positive interaction between them and negative otherwise.
- **NMTF[4]**: This predictor is a simple non-negative matrix tri-factorization method without any regularizers of sentiment lexicon, link prior or social balance.
- **SSMFLK[18]**: Proposed as sentiment classification method, it is a semi-supervised matrix factorization framework utilizing prior sentiment lexicon knowledge. This method is similar to SocLS-Fact method, however, it does not encode platform-specific positive interaction between users or social balance theory.

- **LS-Fact**: This predictor is a variant of the proposed method but it does not embed social balance theory. It is introduced as a baseline to show the effect of social balance regularizer.

Methods using regularizer coefficients (i.e. SSMFLK, LS-Fact, SocLS-Fact) are experimented with all powers of ten from -6 to 2 and the best performance is reported.

4.2.1 Evaluation Metrics. We use three gold-standard metrics, namely; accuracy, precision and F-measure to evaluate our method. Scores are reported in terms of our method's prediction performance on the negative links. We do not report recall explicitly as we emphasize quality over quantity; retrieving meaningful negative links is the most important task in this work as suggested for many tasks in [26]. The change in recall can be indirectly observed through F-measure. Although we present the accuracy for reader convenience it may be misleading considering the imbalanced nature of our dataset. Hence, we focus mainly on precision and F-measure throughout the discussion of our results.

4.2.2 Negative Link Prediction Results. An overview of the negative link prediction performance of the proposed and baseline methods can be found in Table 3. As can be clearly observed through the table, performance increase is consistent among all three metrics: precision, F-measure and accuracy. Important findings are reported below:

- Encoding the sentiment information using SSMFLK improves the performance over the random classifier.
- An interesting finding can be observed when "only sentiment" predictor is used. It yields better results than SSMFLK due to its deterministic nature; whereas SSMFLK may be highly affected by the random starting conditions.
- Only link predictor gives much better results than using just the sentiment information. A steep increase in all three metrics is evident that prior platform specific positive interaction is a very strong signal that the link between users is not negative.
- Co-optimizing the link information with sentiment information in LS-Fact framework results in superior performance compared to both only link and only sentiment predictors. It may be reasonable to think that our encoding strategy for starting conditions contributes to this result marginally.
- Finally, our framework, SocLS-Fact obtains the best results by incorporating the social balance theory into the framework. SocLS-Fact performs slightly better than LS-Fact thanks to the user link triads following social balance theory in formation.

4.2.3 Parameter Analysis. It is essential that our framework performs effectively under different parameter settings. So, we experiment with various values of α, β, and γ then report the performance in terms of F-measure scores. Best performance was obtained using the parameters $\alpha = 10^{-2}$, $\beta = 100$, and $\gamma = 10^{-1}$.

Figure 3 demonstrates the effect of prior platform-specific positive interaction parameter α and sentiment lexicon parameter β when the social balance regularizer γ is fixed at optimal value, 10^{-1}. α and β are tweaked as powers of ten between -6 to 2. Parameters out of this range gives very low F-measure scores thus excluded.

Table 3: SocLS-Fact negative link prediction performance on UK data

	Precision	F-Measure	Accuracy
Random	0.1450	0.2344	0.5317
SSMFLK[18]	0.3143	0.4490	0.7737
Only Sentiment	0.4010	0.4892	0.8464
Only Link	0.6032	0.6726	0.9062
NMTF[4]	0.6741	0.6973	0.9264
LS-Fact	0.6976	0.7059	0.9302
SocLS-Fact	**0.7236**	**0.7149**	**0.9339**

- SocLS-Fact is robust to changes of α and β as F-measure does not differ more than 0.07 ranging from 0.65 to 0.72.
- Lower values of α yield the lowest F-measure scores. Performance sharply increases when α is incremented from 10^{-6} to 10^{-2}. After $\alpha = 10^{-2}$, a decrease can be observed at $\alpha = 0$; then F-measure stays fairly stable until α becomes 100.
- Change of β creates rather stable results for any given α. When $\alpha = 10^{-2}$, there is an increasing pattern between β values 10^{-3} and 1. Finally, a very slight rise can be observed between β values 1 and 100, hence maximal F-measure 0.7149 is observed when $\beta = 100$.

Figure 4 shows how social balance regularizer γ affects the performance when the other parameters are fixed at optimal values, 10^{-2} and 100 respectively. γ is supplied incrementally as powers of ten between -5 to 1. As the chart shows, SocLS-Fact is robust also to changes of γ performing in a F-measure margin of 0.025. F-measure is minimally constant around 0.69 for lower values γ. There is a significant performance gain between γ values 10^{-3} and 10^{-1}. After reaching the optimal score, a decreasing pattern is observed for larger γ values. For our UK dataset, maximal F-measure is obtained when $\gamma = 10^{-1}$.

4.3 Added Value of Negative Links

4.3.1 Community Detection. To evaluate the added value of negative links we test the contribution of negative links in detecting the underlying political communities in the dataset. To that end, we employ a simple spectral clustering algorithm. We feed both unsigned links of the given dataset and predicted signed links by our framework SocLS-Fact separately. We employ UK, Canada and US datasets to evaluate the performance of our method. Parameters for SocLS-Fact are set to be the ones which minimizes the residual error of the objective function.

Spectral Clustering. As proposed by [14], we define the laplacian matrix $\bar{L}$ of an adjacency matrix A of signed network as;

$$\bar{L} = \bar{D} - A \qquad (4)$$

where

$$\bar{D}_{ii} = \sum_{j \sim i} |A_{ij}| \qquad (5)$$

The rest of the clustering framework follows the standard spectral clustering as given in Algorithm 2.

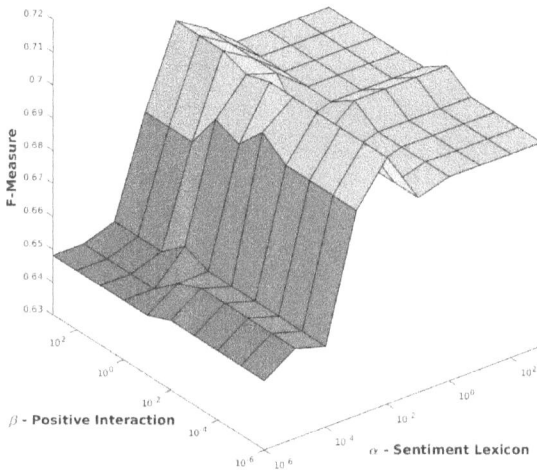

Figure 3: Effect of Regularizer Coefficients

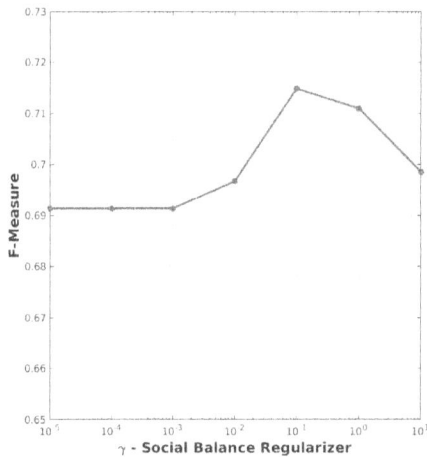

Figure 4: Effect of Social Balance Regularizer

Evaluation Metrics. To evaluate the contribution of predicted negative links in community detection tasks, we make use of three well known clustering quality metrics, namely; purity, adjusted rand index and normalized mutual information.

Community Detection Results. Table 4 shows the community detection results for UK, US and Canada datasets. Inclusion of the predicted negative links of our framework consistently contributes to the performance of community detection tasks. The ground-truth community counts for UK is 5, Canada is 5 and US is 2 as described in 4.1.

Algorithm 2: Spectral Clustering Algorithm for Signed and Unsigned Networks

Input: $\bar{L}$ (signed) or L (unsigned).
Output: Clusters $C_1, C_2, ..., C_k$.
1　Find the smallest k eigenvalues of $\bar{L}$ (or L).
2　Form matrix U as $[v_1, v_2, ..., v_k]$ with corresponding k eigenvectors as columns.
3　Cluster the rows of U into $C_1, C_2, ..., C_k$ by applying k-means.;

For experiments having matching k's with number of ground-truth communities of datasets, following observations is made. Significant improvement in all three metrics can be observed in the results of UK and Canada datasets. US dataset reveals even more intriguing results: purity increases by %25, ARI by %208, and NMI by %241. This finding suggests that addition of negative links does not only boost the performance but can be of very critical importance for community detection.

Another observation we make is the higher contribution of the predicted negative links in community detection tasks when the number of clusters k given to spectral clustering algorithm is equal to the ground-truth community count of the datasets. Most increase by percentage in all three metrics is achieved when k = 5 in UK and Canada, and k = 2 in US dataset. This further suggests the informativeness of the predicted negative links in implying the underlying communities.

4.3.2　Group Polarization. To show a use-case of our framework SocLS-Fact, we set up an experiment that quantifies the group polarization patterns over time among UK politicians who interact with each other in Twitter. We demonstrate how our method and predicted negative links can be used to represent political dynamics such as emerging and diminishing rivalries or coalitions among political party members. We visualize and qualitatively analyze the predicted polarities of links among groups and their change over time.

We sample UK dataset and create three dataset spanning different time intervals to represent political climate change in an online setting. First dataset covers the whole timespan which we treat as the overall political climate among members. This dataset constitutes our baseline for detecting divergences from conventional behaviours of political party members in the sampled representative data. The second dataset spans the all tweets in 2015. General election held on May, 5 2015 is considered to be the major political event of the year. We refer to the second dataset as general election dataset for future references. The third dataset spans the time interval of first 6 months of the year 2016. Brexit unequivocally being the major political event of that time interval, we refer to the third dataset as Brexit sample for future references.

After sampling these three datasets, we run SocLS-Fact algorithm and predict the polarity of each user link. Links that connect users are aggregated with users' affiliated political parties. Aggregation yields the polarization scores among and within political parties. Positive scores are mapped to hues of greens while negative scores are mapped to reds. Darker color means higher polarity. White color stands for the non-existence or very few links between groups,

Table 4: Contribution of negative links in community detection tasks with different k's.

k		United Kingdom			Canada			United States		
		Purity	ARI	NMI	Purity	ARI	NMI	Purity	ARI	NMI
2	Unsigned Links	0.4818	0.1195	0.3829	**0.8013**	**0.4915**	**0.5485**	0.7445	0.2412	0.1863
	SocLS-Fact Links	**0.4844**	**0.1213**	**0.4052**	0.7947	0.4749	0.5057	**0.9294**	**0.7429**	**0.6364**
3	Unsigned Links	0.8333	0.6572	0.6770	**0.9338**	0.8237	**0.7481**	0.8622	0.4566	0.3962
	SocLS-Fact Links	**0.8411**	**0.6814**	**0.6854**	**0.9338**	**0.8247**	0.7473	**0.8807**	**0.5494**	**0.4709**
4	Unsigned Links	**0.9167**	0.8074	0.7838	0.9338	0.7522	0.7026	0.8605	0.4288	0.3770
	SocLS-Fact Links	**0.9167**	**0.8120**	**0.7859**	**0.9470**	**0.7924**	**0.7424**	**0.8773**	**0.4597**	**0.4268**
5	Unsigned Links	0.9167	0.8070	0.7794	0.9272	0.7185	0.6803	0.8706	0.4411	0.3935
	SocLS-Fact Links	**0.9427**	**0.8587**	**0.8041**	**0.9536**	**0.8015**	**0.7456**	**0.8790**	**0.4735**	**0.4304**

thus omitted. The overview of the resulting polarity among and within groups for each of the three datasets is presented in Figure 5.

Table 5: Popular hashtags in the textual interactions of two samples from UK dataset.

Sampled Datasets	Popular Hashtags
General Election	#GE2015, #labourdoorstep, #GE15, #VoteSNP, #Labour, #VoteLabour, #bedroomtax, #NHS, #PMQs, #voteSNP
Brexit	#StrongerIn, #Brexit, #EUref, #VoteLeave, #labourdoorstep, #Remain, #LabourInForBritain, #BackZac2016, #BothVotesSNP, #EU

General Election Dataset. Major event of the 2015 which this dataset covers is the United Kingdom general election 2015 as implied by the popular hashtags presented in Table 5. It took place on May, 5 2015. Conservative Party and Labour Party was the prominent candidates of winning the election. Government before the election was a coalition between Conservative Party and Liberal Democrat Party. Further background information about UK politics can be obtained from [21].

Brexit Dataset. The biggest political event of the first 6 months of the year 2016 that Brexit Dataset covers, is clearly the European Union (EU) Referendum [9] that took place on June, 23 2016. UKIP and some politicians from Conservative party supported leaving the EU. On the opposite side of leave campaign, SNP, Labour Party, Liberal Democrats and part of the Consertavite Party were for staying in the EU. UKIP was a prominent political actor in the campaign. As implied by the popular hashtags used in the textual interactions between users, the dataset also covers London mayoral election (i.e. #BackZac2016) and Scottish Parliament Election (#BothVotesSNP). The election in Scotland resulted as a victory for SNP.

4.3.3 Tracking the Divergence of Political Parties From Overall Behaviour. In this section, we elaborate on how much polarization

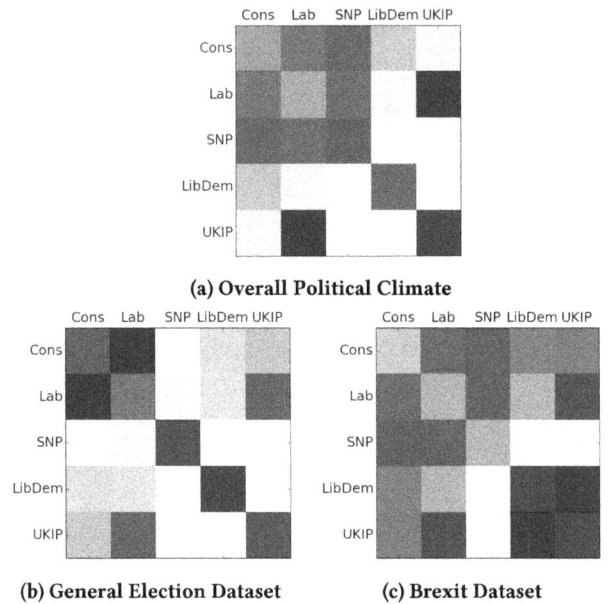

(a) Overall Political Climate

(b) General Election Dataset   (c) Brexit Dataset

Figure 5: United Kingdom link prediction results for political parties for different time frames. Predicted polarities of user links are aggregated according to users' political party affiliation. Red color implies negative links while green color implies positive links. The darker the color is the higher the polarity is between two parties.

between groups deviate from their overall representation in the full dataset. The findings can be summarized as;

- Comparing Figure 5a and Figure 5b shows the increasing positive link ratio in inner-party links. De Nooy et al., in [23], suggests that if two politicians belong to the same political party, they are more likely to support each other in an election season as the partisanship increases. The behavior can be justified with the existence of the general election.

4.3.4 Tracking the Temporal Dynamics of Polarization among Political Parties. To evaluate the performance of the tracking the temporal dynamics of polarization between groups, we qualitatively analyze the polarity shifts from 2015 to 2016 between groups.

- Inner group positive link ratio of Conservative Party members decrease from 2015 (Figure 5b) to 2016 (Figure 5c) which can be explained by the members of the party diverging apart by having different point of views for EU Referandum.
- The rivalry between Conservative Party and Labour Party members dissolves slightly in 2016, because they were the two most prominent competiters in the general election.
- The coalition in 2015 between Conservative Party and Liberal Democrats shifts to rivalry in 2016. It may be due to the coalition government that still existed in 2015 but were not formed again after the election.
- Rivalry increases between UKIP and other parties in Brexit dataset compared to General Election dataset. It can be explained by the EU Referandum in which UKIP was a leading figure.

5 CONCLUSION

In this paper, we propose a negative link prediction framework that performs well on online political networks in which no platform-specific negative interactions or explicit negative links between users are present. We further show two relevant applications of our framework that may help researchers to better make sense with their political social media data. For future work, we plan to experiment with more annotated datasets from different platforms to evaluate the generalizability of the SocLS-Fact framework.

ACKNOWLEDGMENTS

This work is supported by the Office of Naval Research under Grant No.: N00014-16-1-2015, and N00014-15-1-2722.

Appendices

A DERIVATION OF S_U'S UPDATE RULE

By rewriting the optimization formulation as;

$$
\begin{aligned}
\min_{S_u, H, S_w} \quad & Tr((X - S_u H S_w^T)(X - S_u H S_w^T)^T) \\
& + \alpha Tr((S_w - S_{w0})(S_w - S_{w0})^T) \\
& + \beta Tr\left((S_u - S_{u0})^T D_u (S_u - S_{u0})\right) \\
& + \gamma Tr((M - S_u S_u^T)(M - S_u S_u^T)^T) \\
\text{subject to} \quad & S_u \geq 0, H \geq 0, S_w \geq 0
\end{aligned}
$$

Objective function with respect to S_u of the rewritten optimization formulation is;

$$
\begin{aligned}
\min_{S_u} \quad & - 2Tr(X S_w H^T S_u^T) + Tr(S_u H S_w^{\ T} S_w H S_u^T) \\
& + \beta Tr(S_u^T D_u S_u) - 2\beta Tr(S_u^T D_u S_{u0}) - \gamma Tr(M S_u S_u^T) \\
& - \gamma Tr(M^T S_u S_u^T) + \gamma Tr(S_u S_u^T S_u S_u^T) - Tr(\Gamma S_u^T)
\end{aligned}
$$

where Γ is the Lagrange multiplier for the constraint of $S_u \geq 0$. The derivative of the objective function with respect to S_u is;

$$
\begin{aligned}
\frac{\partial \mathcal{L}_{S_u}}{\partial S_u} = & - 2X S_w H^T + 2S_u H S_w^{\ T} S_w H + 2\beta D_u S_u - 2\beta D_u S_{u0} \\
& + \gamma (M + M^T) S_u - 2\gamma S_u S_u^T S_u - \Gamma
\end{aligned}
$$

By setting the derivative to 0, we get;

$$
\begin{aligned}
\Gamma = & - 2X S_w H^T + 2S_u H S_w^{\ T} S_w H + 2\beta D_u S_u - 2\beta D_u S_{u0} \\
& + \gamma (M + M^T) S_u - 2\gamma S_u S_u^T S_u
\end{aligned}
$$

Having Karush Kuhn Tucker (KKT) complementary condition of the nonnegativity of S_u as $\Gamma_{ij}(S_u)_{ij} = 0$ gives;

$$
\begin{aligned}
& \left(S_u H S_w^{\ T} S_w H + \beta D_u S_u + \gamma(M + M^T)\right)_{ij} (S_u)_{ij} \\
& - \left(X S_w H^T + \beta D_u S_{u0} + \gamma S_u S_u^T S_u\right)_{ij} (S_u)_{ij} = 0
\end{aligned}
$$

which leads to the update rule of S_u;

$$
S_u \leftarrow S_u \odot \sqrt{\frac{X S_w H^T + \gamma(M + M^T) S_u + \beta D_u S_{u0}}{S_u H S_w^T S_w H^T + \gamma S_u S_u^T S_u + \beta D_u S_u}}
$$

B DERIVATION OF S_W'S UPDATE RULE

Objective function with respect to S_w of the rewritten optimization formulation in Appendix A is;

$$
\begin{aligned}
\min_{S_w} \quad & - 2Tr(X S_w H^T S_u^T) + Tr(S_u H S_w^{\ T} S_w H S_u^T) \\
& + \alpha Tr(S_w S_w^T) - 2\alpha Tr(S_w S_{w0}^T) - Tr(\Theta S_w^T)
\end{aligned}
$$

where Θ is the Lagrange multiplier for the constraint of $S_w \geq 0$. The derivative of the objective function with respect to S_w is;

$$
\frac{\partial \mathcal{L}_{S_w}}{\partial S_w} = - 2X^T S_u H + 2S_w H^T S_u^T S_u H + 2\alpha S_w - 2\alpha S_{w0} - \Theta
$$

By setting the derivative to 0, we get;

$$
\Theta = -2X^T S_u H + 2S_w H^T S_u^T S_u H + 2\alpha S_w - 2\alpha S_{w0}
$$

By employing the KKT complentary condition of the nonnegativity of S_w as $\Theta_{ij}(S_w)_{ij} = 0$ it yields;

$$
\left((S_w H^T S_u^T S_u H + \alpha S_w) - (X^T S_u H + \alpha S_{w0})\right)_{ij} (S_w)_{ij} = 0
$$

which leads to the update rule of S_w;

$$
S_w \leftarrow S_w \odot \sqrt{\frac{X^T S_u H + \alpha S_{w0}}{S_w H^T S_u^T S_u H + \alpha S_w}}
$$

C DERIVATION OF H'S UPDATE RULE

Objective function with respect to H of the rewritten optimization formulation in Appendix A is;

$$
\min_{H} \quad - 2Tr(X S_w H^T S_u^T) + Tr(S_u H S_w^{\ T} S_w H S_u^T) + Tr(\Phi H^T)
$$

where Φ is the Lagrange multiplier for the constraint of $H \geq 0$. The derivative of the objective function with respect to H is;

$$
\frac{\partial \mathcal{L}_H}{\partial H} = - 2S_u^T X S_w + 2S_u^T S_u H S_w^T S_w - \Phi
$$

By setting the derivative to 0, we get;

$$
\Phi = -2S_u^T X S_w + 2S_u^T S_u H S_w^T S_w
$$

Employing the KKT complentary condition of the nonnegativity of H as $\Phi_{ij}H_{ij} = 0$ yields;

$$\left(S_u^T S_u H S_w^T S_w - S_u^T X S_w\right)_{ij} H_{ij} = 0$$

leading to the update rule of H;

$$H \leftarrow H \odot \sqrt{\frac{S_u^T X S_w}{S_u^T S_u H S_w^T S_w}}$$

REFERENCES

[1] Julian Ausserhofer and Axel Maireder. 2013. NATIONAL POLITICS ON TWITTER. *Information, Communication & Society* 16, 3 (2013), 291–314. https://doi.org/10.1080/1369118X.2012.756050 arXiv:http://dx.doi.org/10.1080/1369118X.2012.756050

[2] Michael Conover, Jacob Ratkiewicz, Matthew Francisco, Bruno Goncalves, Filippo Menczer, and Alessandro Flammini. 2011. Political Polarization on Twitter. (2011). http://www.aaai.org/ocs/index.php/ICWSM/ICWSM11/paper/view/2847

[3] M. D. Conover, B. Goncalves, J. Ratkiewicz, A. Flammini, and F. Menczer. 2011. Predicting the Political Alignment of Twitter Users. In *2011 IEEE Third International Conference on Privacy, Security, Risk and Trust and 2011 IEEE Third International Conference on Social Computing*. 192–199. https://doi.org/10.1109/PASSAT/SocialCom.2011.34

[4] Chris Ding, Tao Li, Wei Peng, and Haesun Park. 2006. Orthogonal nonnegative matrix t-factorizations for clustering. In *Proceedings of the 12th ACM SIGKDD international conference on Knowledge discovery and data mining*. ACM, 126–135.

[5] T. DuBois, J. Golbeck, and A. Srinivasan. 2011. Predicting Trust and Distrust in Social Networks. In *2011 IEEE Third International Conference on Privacy, Security, Risk and Trust and 2011 IEEE Third International Conference on Social Computing*. 418–424. https://doi.org/10.1109/PASSAT/SocialCom.2011.56

[6] J. L. Fleiss. 1971. Measuring nominal scale agreement among many raters. *Psychological Bulletin* 76, 5 (1971), 378–382.

[7] Ahmed Hassan, Amjad Abu-Jbara, and Dragomir Radev. 2012. Extracting Signed Social Networks from Text. In *Workshop Proceedings of TextGraphs-7 on Graph-based Methods for Natural Language Processing (TextGraphs-7 '12)*. Association for Computational Linguistics, Stroudsburg, PA, USA, 6–14. http://dl.acm.org/citation.cfm?id=2392954.2392956

[8] F. Heider. 1958. *The psychology of interpersonal relations*. Wiley, New York.

[9] Sara B. Hobolt. 2016. The Brexit vote: a divided nation, a divided continent. *Journal of European Public Policy* 23, 9 (2016), 1259–1277. https://doi.org/10.1080/13501763.2016.1225785 arXiv:http://dx.doi.org/10.1080/13501763.2016.1225785

[10] Xia Hu, Jiliang Tang, Huiji Gao, and Huan Liu. 2013. Unsupervised Sentiment Analysis with Emotional Signals. In *Proceedings of the 22Nd International Conference on World Wide Web (WWW '13)*. ACM, New York, NY, USA, 607–618. https://doi.org/10.1145/2488388.2488442

[11] Xia Hu, Lei Tang, Jiliang Tang, and Huan Liu. 2013. Exploiting Social Relations for Sentiment Analysis in Microblogging. In *Proceedings of the Sixth ACM International Conference on Web Search and Data Mining (WSDM '13)*. ACM, New York, NY, USA, 537–546. https://doi.org/10.1145/2433396.2433465

[12] Kristen Johnson and Dan Goldwasser. 2016. "All I know about politics is what I read in Twitter": Weakly Supervised Models for Extracting Politicians' Stances From Twitter. In *COLING*.

[13] Jérôme Kunegis, Julia Preusse, and Felix Schwagereit. 2013. What is the Added Value of Negative Links in Online Social Networks?. In *Proceedings of the 22Nd International Conference on World Wide Web (WWW '13)*. ACM, New York, NY, USA, 727–736. https://doi.org/10.1145/2488388.2488452

[14] Jérôme Kunegis, Stephan Schmidt, Andreas Lommatzsch, Jürgen Lerner, Ernesto W De Luca, and Sahin Albayrak. 2010. Spectral analysis of signed graphs for clustering, prediction and visualization. In *Proceedings of the 2010 SIAM International Conference on Data Mining*. SIAM, 559–570.

[15] J. Richard Landis and Gary G. Koch. 1977. The Measurement of Observer Agreement for Categorical Data. *Biometrics* 33, 1 (1977), 159–174. http://www.jstor.org/stable/2529310

[16] Jure Leskovec, Daniel Huttenlocher, and Jon Kleinberg. 2010. Predicting Positive and Negative Links in Online Social Networks. In *Proceedings of the 19th International Conference on World Wide Web (WWW '10)*. ACM, New York, NY, USA, 641–650. https://doi.org/10.1145/1772690.1772756

[17] Jure Leskovec, Daniel Huttenlocher, and Jon Kleinberg. 2010. Signed Networks in Social Media. In *Proceedings of the SIGCHI Conference on Human Factors in Computing Systems (CHI '10)*. ACM, New York, NY, USA, 1361–1370. https://doi.org/10.1145/1753326.1753532

[18] Tao Li, Yi Zhang, and Vikas Sindhwani. 2009. A non-negative matrix tri-factorization approach to sentiment classification with lexical prior knowledge. In *Proceedings of the Joint Conference of the 47th Annual Meeting of the ACL and the 4th International Joint Conference on Natural Language Processing of the AFNLP: Volume 1-Volume 1*. Association for Computational Linguistics, 244–252.

[19] David Liben-Nowell and Jon Kleinberg. 2003. The Link Prediction Problem for Social Networks. In *Proceedings of the Twelfth International Conference on Information and Knowledge Management (CIKM '03)*. ACM, New York, NY, USA, 556–559. https://doi.org/10.1145/956863.956972

[20] Huan Liu, Fred Morstatter, Jiliang Tang, and Reza Zafarani. 2016. The good, the bad, and the ugly: uncovering novel research opportunities in social media mining. *International Journal of Data Science and Analytics* 1, 3-4 (2016), 137–143.

[21] M. Moran. 2015. *Politics and Governance in the UK*. Palgrave Macmillan.

[22] BRIGITTE L. NACOS. 2013. Politics and the Twitter Revolution: How Tweets Influence the Relationship between Political Leaders and the Public by John H. Pamelee and Shannon L. Bichard. Lanham, MD, Lexington Books, 2011. 256 pp. $75.00. *Political Science Quarterly* 128, 1 (2013), 178–179. https://doi.org/10.1002/polq.12021

[23] Wouter De Nooy and Jan Kleinnijenhuis. 2013. Polarization in the Media During an Election Campaign: A Dynamic Network Model Predicting Support and Attack Among Political Actors. *Political Communication* 30, 1 (2013), 117–138. https://doi.org/10.1080/10584609.2012.737417

[24] M. Ozer, N. Kim, and H. Davulcu. 2016. Community detection in political Twitter networks using Nonnegative Matrix Factorization methods. In *2016 IEEE/ACM International Conference on Advances in Social Networks Analysis and Mining (ASONAM)*. 81–88. https://doi.org/10.1109/ASONAM.2016.7752217

[25] Jiliang Tang, Shiyu Chang, Charu Aggarwal, and Huan Liu. 2015. Negative Link Prediction in Social Media. In *Proceedings of the Eighth ACM International Conference on Web Search and Data Mining (WSDM '15)*. ACM, New York, NY, USA, 87–96. https://doi.org/10.1145/2684822.2685295

[26] Dashun Wang, Dino Pedreschi, Chaoming Song, Fosca Giannotti, and Albert-Laszlo Barabasi. 2011. Human Mobility, Social Ties, and Link Prediction. In *Proceedings of the 17th ACM SIGKDD International Conference on Knowledge Discovery and Data Mining (KDD '11)*. ACM, New York, NY, USA, 1100–1108. https://doi.org/10.1145/2020408.2020581

[27] Robert West, Hristo Paskov, Jure Leskovec, and Christopher Potts. 2014. Exploiting Social Network Structure for Person-to-Person Sentiment Analysis. *Transactions of the Association for Computational Linguistics* 2 (2014), 297–310. https://transacl.org/ojs/index.php/tacl/article/view/396

[28] Shuang-Hong Yang, Alexander J. Smola, Bo Long, Hongyuan Zha, and Yi Chang. 2012. Friend or Frenemy?: Predicting Signed Ties in Social Networks. In *Proceedings of the 35th International ACM SIGIR Conference on Research and Development in Information Retrieval (SIGIR '12)*. ACM, New York, NY, USA, 555–564. https://doi.org/10.1145/2348283.2348359

[29] Reza Zafarani and Huan Liu. 2015. Evaluation Without Ground Truth in Social Media Research. *Commun. ACM* 58, 6 (May 2015), 54–60. https://doi.org/10.1145/2666680

Multiple Images of the City

Unveiling Group-Specific Urban Perceptions through a Crowdsourcing Game

David Candeia
Universidade Federal de Campina Grande
Campina Grande, Paraíba, Brazil
david.maia@ifpb.edu.br

Flavio Figueiredo
Universidade Federal de Minas Gerais
Belo Horizonte, Minas Gerais, Brazil
flaviovdf@dcc.ufmg.br

Nazareno Andrade
Universidade Federal de Campina Grande
Campina Grande, Paraíba, Brazil
nazareno@computacao.ufcg.edu.br

Daniele Quercia
Bell Labs
Cambridge, UK
daniele.quercia@gmail.com

ABSTRACT

Our perceptions of public spaces are central for our experience in the city. Understanding which factors shape this perception informs both urban planners, that aim at improving city life, as well as computational models that help us navigate in urban spaces. To understand cities at scale, crowdsourcing games have been employed successfully to evaluate citizens' opinions about cities and urban scenes. By analyzing human perceptions from residents of a mid-sized Brazilian city, this work brings three novel contributions. First, we consider theories from urban design to explore through crowdsourcing which high and low level features in an urban space are linked to perceptions of safety and pleasantness. Secondly, this paper leverages theory from urban sociology and anthropology to show how the sociodemographic profile of the citizens significantly mediate their perception of safeness and pleasantness of places. Finally, we show that features of the urban form proposed by urbanists can be combined with sociodemographics to improve the accuracy of machine learning models that predict which scene a person will find more safe or pleasant. This last result paves the road for more personalized recommendations in cold-start scenarios.

KEYWORDS

Urban Informatics; Urban Perception; Crowdsourcing

1 INTRODUCTION

In order to better understand the relationship between humans and urban environments, researchers have investigated urban perception through the years [3, 21, 24, 34], pointing that such perceptions influence our behavior, decisions and day to day lives [11, 16, 21] and how these perceptions vary across individuals [5, 8, 12, 17, 19, 36]. For instance, Lynch [21] demonstrates that different people depend on different urban elements (paths, edges, etc.) to guide themselves in cities. These past efforts, however, are usually unable to gather perceptions and perform studies at city scale, missing to reach large and diverse sociodemographic groups and understand the differences between these groups.

To offer broader insights at a large scale, crowdsourcing has been more recently employed as a tool to enlarge the participant pool [10, 18, 29, 31, 35]. One of the alternatives being used by crowdsourcing studies to gather perceptions is by designing web games that present urban scenes to the crowd [10, 29, 31, 35]. One of such studies [31] explores a method that translates preferences stated through pairwise comparison of urban scenes into an overall ranking, and other [29] investigates the influence of visual cues (e.g., image colors and texture) on the perception of urban scenes.

Nevertheless, two important factors were started to be investigated by [10, 35] and guide this paper. First, can we link the differences in the perception of how pleasant and how safe a urban scene is to high-level elements that are actionable by urban designers, such as the presence of trees, street width, or building height? Second, do people of different sociodemographic backgrounds (e.g., males versus females and/or people from different economic classes) differ in the ways they perceive the city [32]?

These two questions are considered in turn, with data collected through two crowdsourcing applications. The first is a game that captures perceptions about 108 urban scenes and sociodemographics of game players, based on previous work [10, 29, 31]. The second is a crowdsourcing task that makes use of human judgments to extract from urban scenes a set of high-level features that are linked with urban design (in this paper we will refer to them as urban design elements). Finally, our study is also conducted using scenes from a Brazilian mid-sized city, the city of Campina Grande, a city in a context which has received much less attention in the literature than economically more developed cities in the Northern hemisphere and, so, with markedly different characteristics.

In this context, our main results are:

- The analysis of perceptions collected in Campina Grande highlights similarities with previous work, such as green places being perceived as more pleasant;
- Our analysis points that urban design elements can help explain pleasantness and safety scores. Understanding such elements is interesting since they are measurable components that can be used to improve city life as more trees and fewer cars;

HT'17, July 4-7, 2017, Prague, Czech Republic.
© 2017 ACM. 978-1-4503-4708-2/17/07...$15.00
DOI: http://dx.doi.org/10.1145/3078714.3078728

- The study on how urban perceptions differ across different sociodemographic groups points that while much scenes raise similar perceptions between participants, others raise perception differences. We've built a method that gathers collected perception, urban elements and sociodemographics to evaluate such differences. Gender, age and income were highlighted as important sociodemographic variables that mediate perception differences;
- We evaluate the novelty of urban elements combined with sociodemographic variables to predict scenes preferences in cold-start recommender settings. Classifiers achieved about 0.62 precision, around a 9.6% mean increase when compared to models that only explore urban elements.

Before continuing, in line with [10, 35] we point out that our work supports the possibility of evaluating divergences of different sociodemographic groups in terms of crowdsourced perception of city images. Also, our work provides evidences that these perception divergences are related to high-level urban elements. By uncovering these differences, we highlight the importance of residents background when results from crowdsourced games are used to motivate the decisions of urban planners.

2 RELATED WORK

The study of environment perception has been conducted over the years [3, 5, 10, 21, 31, 34, 35] in order to better understand the relation between humans and their environments. The psychological definition of perception [30] highlights that perception is built based on the individual, with his/her experiences, needs and emotions, on the thing being perceived and on the context. Over the years, evidences have pointed that the way we perceive our environments is influenced by our past experiences and way of life [3, 24] and by the aesthetics of different places [39]. Also, the way we perceive our environments influence our daily decisions [16, 21].

Regarding the effect of the individual, a large set of studies have investigated similarities [2, 10, 31, 35, 41] and differences [2, 5, 8, 10, 12, 17, 19, 32, 35, 36] in urban environment perceptions mediated by different sociodemographic aspects. Age [5, 19, 32, 35, 41], income [17, 19], gender [8, 12, 19, 32, 36], education levels [2, 5], social roles [41], hometown [35], nationality and culture [2, 12, 32, 36] are aspects that may influence urban perception.

Past studies were conducted using *small samples of* city images/photos [33, 34], personal interviews [32], as well as pen-and-paper questionnaires [19, 26]. Such methods used by previous researchers made it possible to understand perceptions of city environments and raised our knowledge on urban perceptions. However, such methods are mostly non-scalable when we consider medium to larger cities. In this direction, the recent development of computational technologies and crowdsourcing, combined with quantitative analysis, have created the opportunity to repeat and continue perception studies in a scalable way, at lower cost, higher speed and with larger pools of participants [10, 18, 20, 29, 31, 35]. With such tools there is the opportunity to capture perceptions using web games [10, 29, 31, 35] or even analyzing data from social media [18, 20]. This development has also created the opportunity to train machine learning models on perception data [9, 25] to learn

urban preferences and then predict preferences for places not yet studied, producing perception data even faster.

Recent studies aiming at larger scale data collection developed the Place Pulse [31], UrbanGems [29] and Street Seen [10] applications. Such applications pick geotagged images from different cities (e.g., New York, London), present pairs of images and ask perception questions such as "Which place looks safer?". Place Pulse [31] demonstrates the possibility of creating a quantitative measure, named Q-Score, that translates user votes on preferred urban scenes to a score of urban perception. UrbanGems [29] investigates the influence of visual cues (i.e., image colors, texture and visual words) on perception. Evans and Akar [10] relates cyclability perceptions with features of the urban form. Also, authors in [35] evaluate safety perception variations according to characteristics of people present in images (e.g., gender, ethnicity and facing). All such studies demonstrate the potential of crowdsourcing applications to capture urban perceptions, but only Evans and Akar [10] and Traunmueller, Marshall and Capra [35] focused on investigating, respectively, cyclability and safety perceptions through different groups of people. This is the focus of this study.

As a further step, the PlacePulse team has investigated the use of PlacePulse data [9, 25] to train machine learning models and predict urban preferences, with promising results. Such studies [9, 25] have investigated the use of low-level features of images, such as color histograms, to predict scenes preferences. We investigate if using high-level features, urban design elements that are closer to urbanists, combined with participants profile can achieve good prediction results. Also, considering our focus on a smaller city of Brazil, a less studied and underdeveloped country, we also deal with a different culture and habits when compared to such studies.

3 METHODS

To investigate how Campina Grande is perceived, we collected data in three steps: (1) Crowdsourcing the perceptions of urban scenes; (2) Crowdsourcing the extraction of urban design elements from the scenes; and (3) Extracting color patterns from the same scenes.

3.1 Crowdsourcing Urban Perceptions

We collected perceptions of participants who live in the city of Campina Grande, Brazil. The collection was enabled by the creation of a crowdsourcing application called "*Como é Campina?*" (How is Campina like?, in Portuguese).

Building a crowdsourcing platform. Our platform is based on other platforms such as UrbanGems [29], Place Pulse [31] and StreetSeen [10]. Each participant is asked to compare urban scenes randomly selected from a pool of scenes extracted from Google Street View. Each time, the user is asked to select two scenes (Figure 1): the most and least pleasant (or safe) scenes. The participant can also choose a "Can't tell" option. Each 4-image comparison provides information about six pairwise comparisons: the most pleasant (safest) scene outperforms the other three, which, in turn, outperform the least pleasant (safe) scene. After ten 4-image comparisons, the user is asked to answer sociodemographic questions about their age, gender, income, education level and marital status.

We evaluate scenes based on safety and pleasantness. This is aligned with previous studies that explored urban security [25, 26,

Figure 1: *Como é Campina?* **crowdsourcing application.**

33] and beauty [29, 31, 33]. The main difference in the design of our application compared to previous work [10, 29, 31] is the use of this 4-image comparison instead of pairwise comparisons. The use of four images provides considerable more data per task, and is inspired by MaxDiff [23] design, common in marketing studies, and known to have a comfortable cognitive load for participants[1].

Collecting urban scenes. Campina Grande is a city of 593.026 km^2 in the northeast of Brazil, with 49 neighborhoods and 385, 213 inhabitants [15]. To allow for the study of diverse socioeconomic conditions and land uses, we focus on three diverse neighborhoods: *Catolé* is residential and high-income; *Liberdade* is residential, has mostly low-/medium-income inhabitants, and a diverse land use, including commerce and residences; and *downtown* is mostly commercial and highly iconic. For each neighborhood, we selected two census areas (defined by the Brazilian Institute of Spatial Geography) such that one area would include main streets and commercial places, and the other area would include a residential portion of the neighborhood. In each area, we then select 10 random geographic points (latitude and longitude) that are at least 50 meters apart from each other. For each latitude and longitude point, we collect Google Street views in four headings (i.e., $0°$, $90°$, $180°$ and $270°$), so as to create a comprehensive view of each place. After filtering the scenes that do not allow for a view of the public space (e.g., obstructed by walls and buildings), we were left with 108 urban scenes. It is important to note that using Google Street views helps making meaningful scenes comparison, as its methodology for data collection controls for weather and time of the day in order to publish images of a city under similar conditions and quality.

Recruiting participants. After publicizing our crowdsourcing platform, 304 participants answered a total of more than 5, 400 4-image comparisons, resulting in votes for a total of 32, 723 pairwise comparisons of scenes. The platform was advertised using Facebook campaigns focused on residents of Campina Grande. At times, the campaign was targeted to ensure the participation of less represented groups such as older women. The encouragement for participants to contribute aimed at tapping into intrinsic motivations, highlighting, for example, the enjoyment of a task and improvement of available information about the city.

Comparing urban scenes. Using scenes comparisons data, we analyze preferences for scenes in two ways. First, we follow the same steps as Salesses, Schechtner and Hidalgo [31] to derive Q-Scores for the scenes, which allow us to identify those evaluated as most and least pleasant or safe. Next, we consider the comparisons where participants preferred one scene over others to analyze what urban elements are associated with preferred scenes and whether sociodemographic variables moderate such preferences.

The Q-Score metric works as follows [31]. Each urban scene goes through a series of pairwise disputes extracted from a 4-way comparison. Each dispute has three possible outcomes: the scene is selected as the best and wins the dispute; it is selected as the worst and loses the dispute; or there is a draw. For each scene i, its win (W) and loss (L) ratios are computed, and then i's Q-Score is function of all the other scenes' (against which i has been compared) win and loss ratios. More formally, we computed i's win (W) and loss (L) ratios for each of our two questions q (one about safety and the other about pleasantness):

$$W_{i,q} = \frac{w_{i,q}}{w_{i,q} + l_{i,q} + t_{i,q}} ; L_{i,q} = \frac{l_{i,q}}{w_{i,q} + l_{i,q} + t_{i,q}}$$

where $w_{i,q}$ is the number of times scene i won a dispute, l is the number of times the scene lost a dispute, and t is the number of times that the scene ended in a draw. Then, we compute i's Q-Score:

$$Q_{i,q} = \frac{10}{3}(W_{i,q} + \frac{1}{n_i^w} \sum_{j1=1}^{n_i^w} W_{j1,q} - \frac{1}{n_i^l} \sum_{j2=1}^{n_i^l} L_{j2,q} + 1)$$

where n_i^w is the total number of scenes i was preferred over, n_i^l is the total number of scenes i was not preferred over. As a result, a value in the range $[0, 10]$ is obtained, where 10 represents the best evaluation of a scene (i.e., the scene was preferred over scenes that were also preferred in their disputes) and 0 represents the worst evaluation of a scene (i.e., the scene was not preferred over scenes that were also not preferred in their disputes). This way of scoring urban scenes circumvents the need to perform all possible pairwise comparisons of scenes. Experimentally, it has been shown that each scene needs to go through $22 - 32$ disputes to obtain a stable Q-Score [31]. Each of our scenes went through 25 disputes, and each dispute had answers from at least 3 application users of diverse sociodemographic conditions.

3.2 Crowdsourcing Urban Elements

Our second data source aims at informing us about high-level urban design elements in the scenes, such as street width or number of trees in the scene. Such elements were extracted from the *Como é Campina?* scenes using the CrowdFlower[2] crowdsourcing platform. To identify an expressive and comprehensive list of visible urban elements, we resorted to the most authoritative study in the field. In their "Measuring Urban Design" book, Ewing and Clemente [11] summarized decades of research on the identification of desirable urban design qualities, which include imageability, complexity, and human scale, and their relation to walkability and urban elements. As walkable places may relate to pleasant and safe places, we devised a series of human computation tasks to extract

---

[1]We have validated the 4-way comparison by comparing the Kendall correlation of the Q-Scores produced with this strategy with Q-Scores obtained from another version of our application that uses pairwise comparisons only. The correlation of two waves of participants using only pairwise comparisons and between participants using pairwise and 4-way comparison was very similar, and always greater than 0.78

[2]http://www.crowdflower.com/

31 relevant urban elements from our scenes, based on [11]: **mean building height**; **street width**; **number of trees**; **number of moving cars**; **number of parked cars**; **number of moving cyclists**; **number of buildings with identifiers**; **number of different buildings**; **number of people on streets**; **presence of graffiti**; **maintenance**, debris and pavement conditions, which are grades from 1 to 5; sidewalk width; number of major landscape features; number of non-rectangular buildings; number of basic building colors; number of accent building colors; number of long sight lines; presence of outside dining; number of public lights; number of street furniture; number of courtyards/plazas/parks; number of pieces of public art; number of small planters; presence of buildings with different ages; proportion of sky; proportion of street wall; proportion of active use buildings; proportion of street-level facade that is covered by windows; proportion of historic buildings. To control for accuracy and reliability of our estimates of such elements, two approaches were used:

i) throughout the execution of tasks, a worker is presented to test questions already answered by authors, and worker's answers accuracy is calculated from these test questions. A reliable worker has to achieve at least a 70% accuracy and only answers of reliable workers are considered;

ii) Krippendorff's alpha coefficients were calculated to filter urban elements whose estimations presented agreement rates of at least 0.6. Other four elements (a grade, street width, presence of graffiti and number of buildings), were also considered in spite of lower agreement rates, following a manual inspection of estimates that revealed reasonable values.

After controlling for accuracy and reliability we were able to extract estimates for the 11 elements highlighted in bold above.

3.3 Extracting Image Colors

In addition to extracting visual elements related to urban planning, we are also interested in investigating the relation of colors with pleasantness and safety perceptions. To do so, we extracted color information from our scenes in a way similar to Quercia, O'Hare and Cramer [29]. Each scene was associated with its average RGB triplet (r,g,b) and 64-bin color histograms. The OpenCV[3] library was used to calculate all color features.

4 OVERALL PERCEPTIONS

Our first analysis uses the same method as previous work [10, 29, 31] to evaluate the overall perception of our participants. We then link this perception with high-level urban design elements.

As one expects, perceptions of safety and pleasantness are related (Figure 2), but do not match perfectly. The corresponding linear regression (*pleasantness* = 0.81 + 0.83 · *safety* + *error*) results in an R^2 of 0.55. Our values are somewhat larger than some values found in previous studies. Previous work found $R^2 = 0.35$ between perceptions of safety and uniqueness [31], $R^2 = 0.37$ between uniqueness and economic-class [31], and $r = 0.64$ between beauty and happiness [29]. Although this small increase may simply be a consequence of the different questions asked, we also conjecture that it may stem from the reality of some Brazilian cities. Segregated areas tend to be both those with less urban development [4] as well

[3]http://opencv.org/

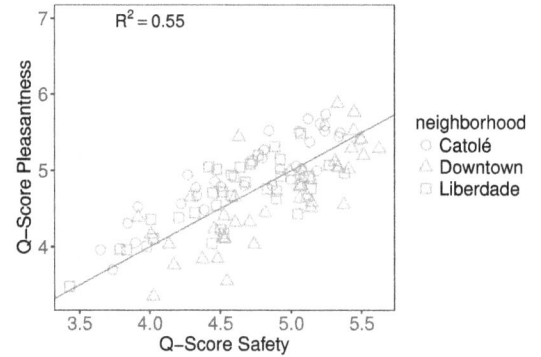

Figure 2: Q-Scores: Pleasantness versus Safety.

as more criminality [28, 38]. Crowdsourced urban perceptions can thus be used by urban planners to tackle and understand segregation issues.

4.1 Best and Worst Scenes Evaluations

To make evaluations concrete, we inspect in Figure 3 the 3 most and least pleasant urban scenes. The most pleasant places are well-maintained and have vegetation, while the least pleasant present physical disorder (e.g., dirty, wastelands, lack of maintenance). Figure 4 shows the 3 safest and least safe urban scenes. The safest places are well-maintained and have people, while the least safe show signs of physical disorder. Those findings are in line with previous work in which pleasantness (or beauty) has been related to greenery [2, 29, 33] and well-maintained places [2, 33], and in which safety has been related to physical order [26, 32, 33, 40, 41].

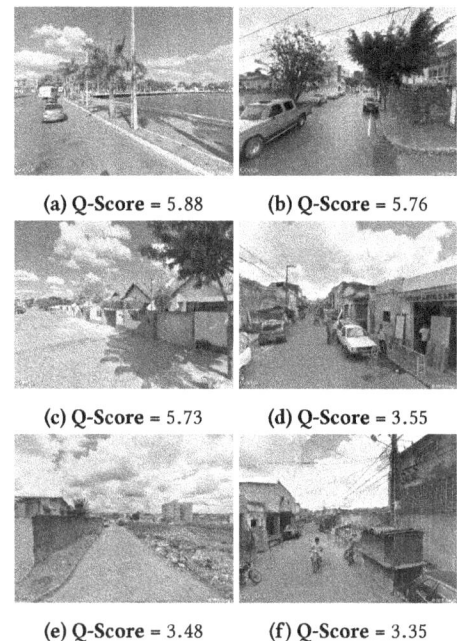

(a) Q-Score = 5.88   **(b) Q-Score = 5.76**

(c) Q-Score = 5.73   **(d) Q-Score = 3.55**

(e) Q-Score = 3.48   **(f) Q-Score = 3.35**

Figure 3: The three most and least pleasant urban scenes.

(a) Q-Score = 5.62   (b) Q-Score = 5.51

(c) Q-Score = 5.49   (d) Q-Score = 3.73

(e) Q-Score = 3.64   (f) Q-Score = 3.42

Figure 4: The three safest and least safe urban scenes.

4.2 Perceptions and Colors

To then determine which colors tend to be present in safe and pleasant urban scenes, we computed linear regressions between safety (pleasantness) Q-Scores and RGB values of colors. To compute a percent importance of each color [29], we divide each color's β coefficient by the sum of the absolute values of all the β coefficients. Very much in line with previous work [29], pleasantness was associated with less red (−40.4%) and more green (48.8%) in scenes. Safety was also associated with less red (−53.9%). Similar results are found when regressing safety (pleasantness) with the color histograms: pleasantness was associated with variations of green and red, and safety with variations of yellow.

The confirmation of previous findings on a Brazilian city serves as evidence that the relation of colors with pleasantness (and also safety to some extent) is universal. Though outside of the scope of our study, we notice that novel datasets [9] that cover perceptions of multiples cities can be used to further validate these findings.

4.3 Perceptions and Urban Design Elements

We now turn to investigate the relation between the crowdsourced perceptions of safety and pleasantness in each scene and urban elements extracted through CrowdFlower. A similar first effort was done by Evans and Akar [10] by relating urban elements and cyclability perception. Different from colors, urban elements capture simple and measurable entities (e.g., more trees or less cars) that can be explored to improve city life for urban dwellers. Our results here can thus be viewed from a practical perspective on how to improve urban settings. More importantly, our findings in this section will be complemented by a study on how sociodemographic variables moderate the perceptions of some urban elements in Section 5.

To perform our analysis, a new dependent variable called **rank evaluation** was created for this task by first applying a rank transformation to the scenes according to their Q-Scores for pleasantness and safety, and then inverting the sign of such ranks. Such transformations make linear models more readily applicable, and result in a configuration where the best evaluated scene has the highest value of the dependent variable.

Table 1 shows regression models relating **rank evaluation** for safety and pleasantness, urban elements and the neighborhood where each picture was taken. Positive coefficients indicate that a better image ranking is positively related to the predictor value.

As expected, there is a significant positive relation between pleasantness and trees (vegetation) and good maintenance condition in a scene. Also, there is a positive relation between perception of safety and the presence of more people (number of people, number of parked cars) and good maintenance conditions. The importance of people on streets and good maintenance for walkability was demonstrated by Ewing and Clemente [11], and walkable places may relate with more pleasant and safe places. As pointed before, the relation of greenery [2, 29, 33] and well-maintained places [2, 33] with beauty/pleasantness, and the link of visual signs of physical order [26, 32, 33, 40, 41] with perception of safety were demonstrated. Regarding safety, the positive relation with proximity to human elements in parks [33] was also highlighted and may indicate that presence of cars may be interpreted as presence of people. Such results and ours supports the intuition that places where there are eyes on the street are perceived as safer.

Also, a few unexpected results were found. First, such high values for R^2 are not expected, since perceptions deal with past experiences and personal background, and our models consider only objective features from images of places. Second, indicators of people presence are associated with safe scenes but not necessarily with pleasant scenes. Finally, the presence of graffiti is not strongly associated with pleasantness or safety [8, 33]. This may happen because graffiti is typically present in places with poor maintenance conditions in our sample, and so the effect of graffiti may be indistinguishable in this data.

The positive evaluation of cars in terms of safety may point a divergent perception of Brazilian culture compared to developed countries. Brazil has a markedly car-oriented culture, and the car is seen as an object associated with wealth, social status, greater sense of security and avoidance of poor public transport systems [7]. Also, there is a predominant culture in government city planning that typically focuses on enlarging streets for cars instead of investing in public transportation systems or pedestrian streets [37].

5 GROUP DIFFERENCES IN URBAN PERCEPTION

After evaluating the overall perception of the city, we now investigate perception differences. Initially we note that from the set of 304 participants who contributed in our experiment, 211 of them (69%) answered the sociodemographic questions. Considering the groups with largest numbers of participants, we divided them in terms of: gender, age, and income. The percentage of participants in each of these groups are: i) 66.89% men and 33.11% women; ii) 45.89% young (below 25 years), and 54.11% adult (25 − 62 years);

Table 1: Linear regression models of scene ranking for pleasantness and safety controlling for neighborhood. β and standard error values are shown.

	Pleas.	Saf.
(Intercept)	−39.40˙	−56.48**
	(19.99)	(20.09)
Street width (ft)	0.00	0.07
	(0.38)	(0.38)
Number of moving cars	−1.24	2.68
	(1.74)	(1.75)
Number of parked cars	1.01	1.98*
	(0.76)	(0.77)
Number of moving cyclists	1.39	−0.90
	(4.06)	(4.08)
Maintenance condition	23.38***	20.74***
	(3.46)	(3.48)
Number of building with identifiers	−1.84˙	−1.35
	(0.99)	(0.99)
Number of trees	2.66*	1.53
	(1.17)	(1.18)
Log of mean building height (feet)	0.62	2.96
	(3.37)	(3.39)
Number of people	0.00	2.50*
	(1.14)	(1.14)
Image is in downtown	0.72	8.26
	(7.57)	(7.61)
Image is in Catolé	11.41˙	7.77
	(6.18)	(6.21)
Number of different buildings	1.00	2.01
	(1.51)	(1.52)
Presence of graffiti	−8.14	−15.51˙
	(8.39)	(8.43)
R^2	0.51	0.51
Adj. R^2	0.45	0.44

*** $p < 0.001$, ** $p < 0.01$, * $p < 0.05$, ˙ $p < 0.1$

iii) 45.05% low income (classes E and D according to the Brazilian census authority, IBGE), and 54.95% high income (classes A, B and C in the same classification).

First, we examine whether there are striking differences in rankings created from preferences of different groups. For that, we calculate Q-Scores for the scenes according only to answers from each sociodemographic group. Overall, there is a high correlation in the ranking of scenes as evaluated by the different groups. In general, we found Kendall correlation values ranging from 0.60 (in the case of Low vs High income for safety) to 0.72 (in the case of Men vs Women for pleasantness).

Given that the overall perception of the city is similar across groups, we now turn to pinpoint the situations where differences occur and to examine which urban elements are associated with such differences. All 11 urban elements extracted reliably from Crowdflower are considered in this analysis since they are related to walkability. Also, although only some of them were significantly related to pleasantness and safety overall ranking of scenes (Table 1), different elements may be related to specific groups differences.

5.1 Group-Specific Perceptions and Urban Design Elements

We now focus on determining the effect of sociodemographic variables and urban elements on safety and pleasantness perceptions. To achieve our goal, we focus on situations where there are a marked preference for one scene over another. That is, we resort to pairwise disputes instead of evaluating rankings. This approach allows us to more accurately model and isolate multiple moderation effects, as building a ranking implies in aggregating scenes preferences from people with diverse backgrounds without controlling for the inherent variation that can be attributed to the different individuals. Thus, we can analyze better the relation of the visual content of scenes and participants backgrounds using the pairwise comparisons.

More specifically, we first filter the pairwise scenes disputes (scene A x scene B) to consider only disputes in which our participants indicated a preference (they picked either A or B as the most pleasant/safe scene). In other words, we removed draws from our disputes. For each selected dispute we compute the differences in each urban element between both scenes. For example, we calculate the number of trees for scene A minus the quantity of trees for scene B. As a result, there is for each dispute a preferred scene A or B, the differences in urban elements between A and B, and the sociodemographic profile of the participant. It is important to note that, while the decision of which picture is A or B is arbitrary (we choose so randomly and our findings do not change with multiple executions of our experiments), our evaluations will be interpreted in relation to the difference between urban elements from A to B, being A the reference scene, as we now describe.

Our models consider the selected scene as our dependent variable (i.e., a binary variable indicating that selecting A over B is the positive class, the opposite is the negative class), urban elements differences (i.e., elements in A minus those in B) as independent variables, and age, gender and income as moderators. We model the sociodemographic group as moderators in order to capture how a certain group, say men, potentially moderates (or perceives) an element such as trees. This moderation is used to compare the perception of trees between men and women. Finally, we also consider the neighborhoods of each image as explanatory variables. Here, we encode the neighborhood of both scenes in the comparison as a single indicator variable that captures the different pairs of *distinct neighborhoods*. With this variable we can investigate if there are inherent preferences of one neighborhood over another.

We resort to logistic regression models [14] to investigate the impact of sociodemographic variables on choosing A over B. We shall validate these results with more advanced machine learning models later on. With this consideration, two logistic regression models were built, one for pleasantness and another for safety.

Positive coefficients (β) in the logistic regression models will indicate that higher number of urban elements (e.g., trees) in scene A (our reference scene) will bias participants to preferring A over B. That is, if A has more trees, for instance, and β is positive, the model indicates that an increase in trees will lead to a higher chance of preferring A. In contrast, negative coefficients indicate that the higher number of urban elements in scene A will bias to choosing

Table 2: Logistic regression of the preference towards scene A for pleasantness. Relevant predictors are sorted according to their coefficients, which are each in the scale of the independent variable. Neighborhood comparison coefficients and intercepts are shown in the bottom rows of the table.

Term	β	std. error
1. Maintenance diff.	0.51***	0.05
2. Cyclists diff. x adult	−0.11*	0.05
3. Maintenance diff. x men	0.10*	0.04
4. Maintenance diff. x high inc.	0.08*	0.04
5. Moving cars diff. x high inc.	−0.08***	0.01
6. People diff. x adult	0.05***	0.01
7. Trees diff. x adult	0.04**	0.01
8. Trees diff.	0.04**	0.01
9. Buildings identifiers diff. x adult	−0.02*	0.01
10. Parked cars diff.	0.02*	0.01
11. Street width diff.	0.01*	0.00
12. Street width diff x adult	−0.01*	0.00
(Intercept)	−0.18***	0.03
Catolé x Downtown	0.71***	0.06
Catolé x Liberdade	0.52***	0.06
Liberdade x Downtown	0.17**	0.06
Num. groups: participant 282		

***$p < 0.001$, **$p < 0.01$, *$p < 0.05$, ˙$p < 0.1$

Table 3: Logistic regression of the preference towards scene A for safety. Relevant predictors are sorted according to their coefficients, which are each in the scale of the independent variable. Neighborhood comparison coefficients and intercepts are shown in the bottom rows of the table.

Term	β	std. error
1. Maintenance condition	0.39***	0.04
2. Moving cars diff.	0.20***	0.02
3. Maintenance diff. x men	0.13**	0.04
4. Maintenance diff. x high inc.	0.11**	0.04
5. Moving cars diff. x men	−0.08***	0.02
6. Buildings diff. x adult	0.08***	0.01
7. Moving cars diff. x adult	−0.06**	0.02
8. Buildings diff. x high inc.	−0.05***	0.01
9. People diff. x high inc.	0.05***	0.01
10. People diff.	0.05***	0.01
11. Trees diff.	0.04**	0.01
12. Parked cars diff.	0.04***	0.01
13. Trees diff. x high inc.	0.03*	0.01
14. Trees diff. x adult	−0.03*	0.01
15. Street width diff. x adult	0.01***	0.00
(Intercept)	−0.15***	0.03
Catolé x Downtown	0.36***	0.06
Downtown x Catolé	0.34***	0.07
Liberdade x Catolé	−0.16**	0.06
Downtown x Liberdade	0.16*	0.06
Num. groups: participants 279		

***$p < 0.001$, **$p < 0.01$, *$p < 0.05$, ˙$p < 0.1$

image B as their preferred image. That is, a positive coefficient indicates a preference towards an urban element, whereas a negative one represent a rejection.

It is also important to point out that we present our results considering a random effects approach related to each participant. We account for the fact that participants provided answers to multiple comparisons by adding the participant as a random effect in the models. In our setting, random effects will relate to the expected variability across participants. This random effect contributed to significantly varying the intercept for pleasantness ($p < .001$) and was marginally significant for safety ($p < .1$). Finally, results without random effects lead to similar qualitative findings but less accurate models (greater AIC and BIC scores [14])[4]. The logistic regression models considering random effects are shown in Tables 2 and 3, which we now discuss. For clarity, our tables only present coefficients deemed statistically significant ($p < .05$ at least) and moderations are represented with an x symbol indicating the preferences of a certain group (i.e., men) for a certain urban element in comparison to the other corresponding group (i.e., women).

Some of our previous results are confirmed by analyzing non-moderated predictors in Tables 2 and 3. Better maintenance condition and amount of trees lead to scenes being preferred for pleasantness. Moreover, better maintenance, greater numbers of parked cars and people bias the safety perception (also positively). In addition to such predictors, some neighborhoods comparison, in contrast to places in the same neighborhood, were also highlighted as important predictors. Wider streets also impact pleasantness and more moving cars and trees impact safety. These last new effects are expected according to the culture of cars previously discussed,

as well as the idea that wider streets may be related with more comfortable streets and that a positive relation between vegetation and safety was already highlighted [22].

Regarding groups differences, it's important to highlight that the majority of significant predictors, and 7 of the top 10 predictors (i.e., greater β values) in our models were moderated by age, gender or income. Figure 5 summarizes the moderations presented on the tables. Age was the most influential sociodemographic variable perceived for pleasantness in our data, while age and income were equally important for safety and gender was the least important one for both pleasantness and safety. These moderations increase or decrease the impact of urban elements in scenes evaluation for some groups, and in some cases turn some elements as relevant. For example, the number of people in streets was not relevant for pleasantness in general, but for adults (line 6 of Table 2) this element was important to prefer a scene as more pleasant. The same can be observed for the number of moving cyclists (line 2 of Table 2). Maintenance condition, on the other hand, is a relevant element in both pleasantness and safety general evaluation, but it's effect is increased for men and high income groups.

We can also evaluate the coefficients in Tables 2 and 3 in light of the "divide by 4" rule [14]. This rule indicates that dividing the β by 4 we have an estimate of the maximum difference in probability corresponding to a unit difference in the predictor. For example, considering Table 2 we can point that more trees (line 8) are associated with a greater chance of a scene being preferred, and one more tree increases this probability by a maximum of 1%. In Table 3 we can point that more moving cars (line 2) are associated

[4]AIC and BIC capture the trade-off between accurate (log likelihood) and complex models. Lower values indicate a good accuracy with fewer complexity [14].

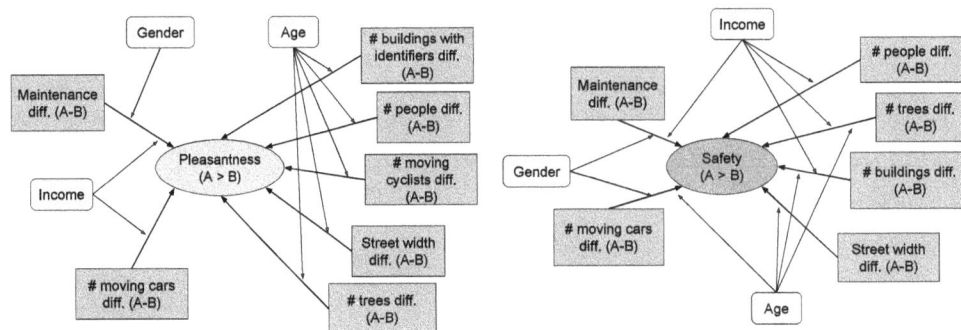

Figure 5: Significant moderations of predictors in logistic models. Moderators are shown in yellow.

with a greater chance of a scene being preferred, and one more car increases this probability by a maximum of 5%.

It is important to note that, given that moderator variables are binary (e.g., 1 will indicate men while 0 will indicate women), to interpret the effect of a sociodemographic group the β value of the urban element must be added to the value of the same element moderated by a group. In addition to general preference of more trees (including young people) for pleasantness (line 8 of Table 2), adults prefer trees even more (positive β in the moderation, line 7). So, one more tree increases the adult probability of preferring a scene in 1% more than young people by maximum. Another additive example is that, for safety (Table 3), better maintenance is preferred by the whole group of participants (line 1). In addition to this preference, men place a higher value to maintenance condition of places than women (line 3). A greater number of moving cars is preferred for safety by the whole group of participants (line 2), but men do not prefer more cars as women (line 5).

It's also important to notice that some moderations are present both for pleasantness and safety, this is expected since pleasantness and safety scores were related (Section 4). Maintenance condition is moderated by gender and income, while number of trees and street width are moderated by age for both perceptions. While gender and income influence both perceptions in the same way, age impacts both perceptions differently. Regarding gender and income, better maintained places are generally preferred for pleasantness and safety, but men and high income people prefer even more well maintained places. Regarding age, trees are generally preferred for pleasantness and safety, but adults evaluate places with more trees as even more pleasant than young people do, but not safe. Wider streets are generally preferred for pleasant places and its effect was not significant for safety perception, however, adults do not prefer wider streets as young people do for pleasantness and for safety the relation is exactly the opposite, with adults preferring wider streets more than young people.

Finally, analyzing significant coefficients, moderated or not, and their association with urban qualities [11] we can point Human Scale and Complexity as the most important urban qualities for both pleasantness and safety. This importance is expected since these qualities describe, respectively, proportions and visual richness of spaces, which can be related to pleasantness, and they are also related to intimidation and pedestrians stimulation, which can be

related to safety. Although the qualities are the same, the most impacting elements associated with these qualities are number of trees for pleasantness and number of moving cars for safety.

5.2 Predicting Scene Preferences

Once relevant effects of user profiles are established through logistic models, our next step is an experiment to evaluate the predictive capability of using urban elements and participant profile information to predict scenes preferences.

Our experiment here is motivated by a recommendation scenario. For example, on a navigational system a recommender can predict pairwise preferences of urban places to create rankings of places for a user to visit or pass through. Motivated by this setting, we look into how sociodemographic variables can be explored in cold-start settings [1]. In a cold-start setting, previous evaluations of participants are not available. Once these evaluations are present, classic approaches as collaborative filtering [1] may be able to capture user preferences. When not present, the cold-start case, classifiers will usually rely on other user features as the sociodemographic groups.

To represent the cold-start, we remove each participant from the training dataset in a turn (and we also remove the scenes evaluated by him/her). This single participant's answers become our test set. We trained multiple classifiers with the votes of other participants and then tested the prediction on the removed participant. By removing the participant and every pair with a scene s/he evaluated, we filter out the possibility of the classifier learning users' latent preferences or factors related to individual scenes. So, the classifier will only explore sociodemographics and urban elements.

We evaluated four classifiers using the scikit-learn framework [27]: KNN, RBF SVM, Naive Bayes and Extra Trees. For each pair of scenes, classifiers were trained considering the urban elements (of each scene in the pair) as real numbers and sociodemographic information as indicator variables. In order to tune classifiers, a grid-search on hyperparameters, in a 3-fold cross validation, was performed by further breaking the training set into training and validation. Overall, Extra Trees led to the best results and we focus our analysis on this classifier in isolation (our goal is not to compare different classifiers).

We resort to accuracy, precision, recall and F1 scores to gain a better understanding of the classifier ability to perform correct predictions in both positive and negative classes. In Figure 6 we show such metrics for a classifier that consider sociodemographic variables (participant profile) and for other that explores only urban elements. By comparing both, we unveil the impact of sociodemographic variables in cold-start settings. The figure presents the average of each score (one per left-out user) and corresponding 95% confidence intervals, and, also, a random classifier for comparison.

Firstly, the use of urban elements and participant profile improves scores in comparison to a random classifier (our baseline model), with mean gains of 22.9% for pleasantness scores and 18.9% for safety scores. Then, we compare the use of both participant and urban elements information to the scenario in which only urban elements are used. In these scenarios, the mean accuracy gains were about of 7.2% and 8.2% for pleasantness and safety, respectively. For precision, the mean gains were of 10.2% and 8.9%, respectively.

The gains in precision and accuracy further validate our previous find that the sociodemographic background of participants impact their perceptions of urban scenes. Statistically speaking (i.e., considering the confidence intervals), it is also important to point that using only urban elements information was not sufficient to improve recall values. Nevertheless, there are small gains in average. This last result stems from the fact that many other social and cognitive factors, as well as other urban elements, impact participants perceptions. Because of this, our classifiers will not correctly predict every possible evaluation, we only explore a small number of complex human background features. Investigating other factors that impact perceptions is left as future work.

6 IMPLICATIONS

Our results lead to implications for researchers, practitioners, and for theory. First, and in line with [10], some of our results link citizens' pleasantness and safety perceptions to urban elements that can be used by urban planners to understand what interventions may be applied to areas perceived as less pleasant or safe. Moreover, using crowdsourcing, this evaluation can be done at scale.

A second important aspect is the comparison of urban elements that are most related to safety and pleasantness in Campina Grande and in previous work. On the one hand, this examination contributes to a body of results that can lead us to understand invariants affecting how people perceive safety and pleasantness in the city. On the other hand, the fact that moving and/or parked cars are positively associated with these perceptions in Campina Grande calls for further study of this phenomenon in Brazil.

Our main result with implications for both theory and practice is the significant moderation that age, income and – to a lesser extent – gender exert on how different groups perceive urban elements in terms of pleasantness and safety perceptions. This results calls for attention to planning the city for diversity. Moreover, unveiling which elements lead to discordance seems to us as a promising pointer for future work that leverages this discordance for productive debates about the city. It is also relevant that these sociodemographic characteristics can be used to improve the accuracy of predictive models that help one navigate in the city. Future work providing recommendation methods for more pleasant routes or routes perceived as safer may take these results into account.

Finally, this work provides to methodological contributions for researchers. First, the design of our crowdsourcing game shows that it is feasible to compare scenes four at a time, instead of the commonly used pairwise comparisons [10, 29, 31]. This design speeds up data production, and should be considered by researchers. Second, our method for modeling the effect of moderators on pairwise scene preferences may be relevant for further research, as it provides an intuitive and tractable framework for the analysis considering both the effects of urban elements in individual scenes, and the multilevel modeling of random effects in participant preferences.

7 LIMITATIONS

The way we captured urban perceptions is partly biased for five main reasons. First, perceptions depend on our participants' past experiences, and we have no systematic way of capturing those experiences. However, the higher the number of participants, the more randomized such effects become. Second, we have elicited perceptions from images. But a place's image does not fully capture the place - for example, how it smells, sounds, and changes over time. Third, the perceptions of a place might drastically change over the course of a day. This study has investigated relations between urban design elements and scenes preferences captured from crowdsourcing solutions. For finer-grained analyses and the development of a robust recommendation system, future work should capture additional information to further stratify perceptions across, for example, times of the day. Also, as opposed to other images of urban scenes, Google Street views tend to control for factors such as time of the day, presence of people, and weather conditions. So, using images from other sources that help to capture such variations is necessary. Fourth, it is unclear whether our findings generalize to other cities. To ascertain that, again, additional data has to be collected. Nevertheless, the methodology presented in this paper can be readily applied to different cities for further comparisons if need be. Finally, although considering residents of Campina Grande may incur in biases of recognizing places of the city, residents know the particularities of their city, how it works, how safe and pleasant places are like. We try to minimize individual bias by capturing data from at least 3 participants for each 4-image comparison task.

8 CONCLUSION

Considering the growth of urban population, local authorities need to evaluate and implement solutions to manage the complexity, problems and expectations that come with larger cities in order to improve their citizens well-being. This work contributes towards this goal in the emerging theme of urban informatics [13], in particular associated with social computing and urban dynamics [6].

Our aim has been to test whether urban perceptions of safety and pleasantness change across different "classes" of people. In order to do so we developed a crowdsourcing web game based on [10, 29, 31] to gather urban scenes perception of residents of the city of Campina Grande, Brazil. We compared the overall perception of our participants with previous crowdsourcing [29, 31] and urbanism works in order to validate our findings. Then, we evaluated collected perceptions considering different sociodemographic groups (age, gender and income) and found that different groups perceived about 60% to 72% of scenes in similar ways, but other scenes raised perception differences. A few urban elements were related with perception differences being mediated by income, age and gender.

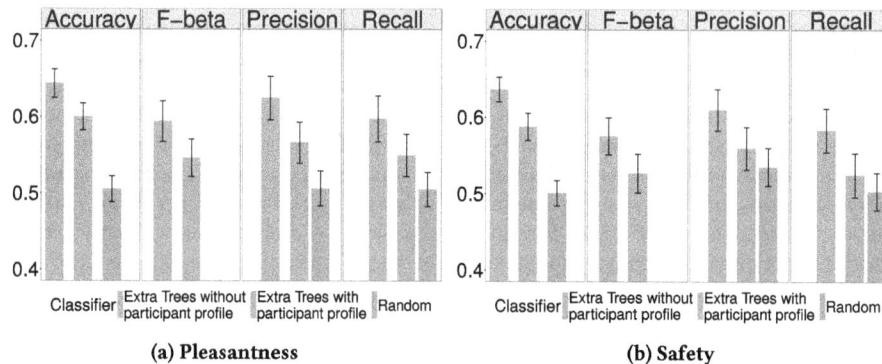

(a) Pleasantness (b) Safety

Figure 6: Confidence intervals for classifiers Accuracy, Precision, Recall and F-beta scores

The maintenance condition is an important one since it contributes to explain differences in pleasantness and safety perceptions.

ACKNOWLEDGMENTS

This research is supported by EU-BR BigSea project (MCTI/RNP 3rd Coordinated Call).

REFERENCES
[1] Charu C Aggarwal. 2016. *Recommender Systems: The Textbook*. Springer.
[2] Tarik M Al-Soliman. 1990. The impact of the surrounding environment on people's perception of major urban environmental attributes. *Journal of King Saud University* (1990).
[3] Donald Appleyard. 1973. *Notes on urban perception and knowledge*.
[4] Florine Bos and Rivke Jaffe. 2015. A rejuvenated approach to urban development and inequality: Young people's perceptions and experiences in Rio de Janeiro. *Habitat International* 48 (2015), 106–112.
[5] Xinyu Jason Cao. 2015. How does neighborhood design affect life satisfaction? Evidence from Twin Cities. *Travel Behaviour and Society* (2015).
[6] Justin Cranshaw, Raz Schwartz, Jason I Hong, and Norman Sadeh. 2012. The livehoods project: Utilizing social media to understand the dynamics of a city. In *International AAAI Conference on Weblogs and Social Media*. 58.
[7] Roberto DaMatta. 2012. *Fé em Deus e pé na tábua: ou como e por que o trânsito enlouquece no Brasil*. Editora Rocco.
[8] Kristen Day, Cheryl Stump, and Daisy Carreon. 2003. Confrontation and loss of control: Masculinity and men's fear in public space. *Journal of Environmental Psychology* 23, 3 (2003), 311–322.
[9] Abhimanyu Dubey, Nikhil Naik, Devi Parikh, Ramesh Raskar, and César A Hidalgo. 2016. Deep learning the city: Quantifying urban perception at a global scale. In *European Conference on Computer Vision*. Springer, 196–212.
[10] Jennifer S Evans-Cowley and Gulsah Akar. 2014. Streetseen: factors influencing the desirability of a street for bicycling. In *Forthcoming in 93rd Annual Meeting of the Transportation Research Board*.
[11] Reid Ewing and Otto Clemente. 2013. *Measuring urban design: Metrics for livable places*. Island Press.
[12] S Farrell, J Bannister, J Ditton, and E Gilchrist. 2000. Social psychology and the fear of crime: Re-examining a speculative model. *British Journal of Criminology* 40 (2000), 399–413.
[13] Marcus Foth, Jaz Hee-jeong Choi, and Christine Satchell. 2011. Urban informatics. In *Proceedings of the ACM 2011 conference on Computer supported cooperative work*. ACM, 1–8.
[14] Andrew Gelman and Jennifer Hill. 2006. *Data analysis using regression and multilevel/hierarchical models*. Cambridge University Press.
[15] Instituto Brasileiro de Geografia e Estatística IBGE. 2011. Sinopse do censo demográfico 2010. (2011).
[16] William H Ittelson, Harold M Proshansky, Leanne G Rivlin, and Gary H Winkel. 1974. *An introduction to environmental psychology*. Holt, Rinehart & Winston.
[17] Haydea Izazola, Carolina Martínez, and Catherine Marquette. 1998. Environmental perceptions, social class and demographic change in Mexico City: a comparative approach. *Environment and Urbanization* 10, 1 (1998), 107–118.
[18] Andrew Jenkins, Arie Croitoru, Andrew T Crooks, and Anthony Stefanidis. 2016. Crowdsourcing a Collective Sense of Place. *PloS one* 11, 4 (2016), e0152932.
[19] CY Jim and Xizhang Shan. 2013. Socioeconomic effect on perception of urban green spaces in Guangzhou, China. *Cities* 31 (2013), 123–131.
[20] Matthew James Kelley. 2013. The emergent urban imaginaries of geosocial media. *GeoJournal* 78, 1 (2013), 181–203.

[21] Kevin Lynch. 1960. *The image of the city*. Vol. 11. MIT press.
[22] Jolanda Maas, Peter Spreeuwenberg, Marijke Van Winsum-Westra, Robert A Verheij, Sjerp de Vries, and Peter P Groenewegen. 2009. Is green space in the living environment associated with people's feelings of social safety? *Environment and planning. A* 41, 7 (2009), 1763.
[23] Anthony AJ Marley and Jordan J Louviere. 2005. Some probabilistic models of best, worst, and best-worst choices. *Journal of Mathematical Psychology* 49, 6 (2005), 464–480.
[24] Stanley Milgram. 1974. The experience of living in cities. *Crowding and behavior* 167 (1974), 41.
[25] Naren Naik, Jade Philipoom, Ramesh Raskar, and Cesar Hidalgo. 2014. Streetscore-Predicting the Perceived Safety of One Million Streetscapes. In *Computer Vision and Pattern Recognition Workshops (CVPRW), 2014 IEEE Conference on*. IEEE, 793–799.
[26] Segun Okunola and Dolapo Amole. 2012. Perception of safety, social participation and vulnerability in an urban neighbourhood, Lagos, Nigeria. *Procedia-Social and Behavioral Sciences* 35 (2012), 505–513.
[27] F. Pedregosa, G. Varoquaux, A. Gramfort, V. Michel, B. Thirion, O. Grisel, M. Blondel, P. Prettenhofer, R. Weiss, V. Dubourg, J. Vanderplas, A. Passos, D. Cournapeau, M. Brucher, M. Perrot, and E. Duchesnay. 2011. Scikit-learn: Machine Learning in Python. *Journal of Machine Learning Research* 12 (2011), 2825–2830.
[28] Jennifer Peirce. 2008. Divided cities: crime and inequality in urban Brazil. *Paterson Review* 9 (2008), 85–98.
[29] Daniele Quercia, Neil Keith O'Hare, and Henriette Cramer. 2014. Aesthetic capital: what makes london look beautiful, quiet, and happy?. In *Proceedings of the 17th ACM conference on Computer supported cooperative work & social computing*. ACM, 945–955.
[30] Alan Saks and Gary Johns. 2011. Perception, attribution, and judgment of others. *Organizational Behaviour: Understanding and Managing Life at Work* 7 (2011), 72–114.
[31] Philip Salesses, Katja Schechtner, and César A Hidalgo. 2013. The collaborative image of the city: mapping the inequality of urban perception. *PloS one* 8, 7 (2013), e68400.
[32] Robert J. Sampson and Stephen W. Raudenbush. 2004. Seeing Disorder: Neighborhood Stigma and the Social Construction of Broken Windows. *Social Psychology Quarterly* 67, 4 (2004).
[33] Herbert W Schroeder, LM Anderson, et al. 1984. Perception of personal safety in urban recreation sites. *Journal of Leisure Research* 16, 2 (1984), 178–194.
[34] WC Sullivan. 1994. Perceptions of the rural-urban fringe: citizen preferences for natural and developed settings. *Landscape and Urban Planning* 29, 2 (1994), 85–101.
[35] Martin Traunmueller, Paul Marshall, and Licia Capra. 2015. Crowdsourcing Safety Perceptions of People: Opportunities and Limitations. In *International Conference on Social Informatics*. Springer, 120–135.
[36] Adri Van der Wurff, Leendert Van Staalduinen, and Peter Stringer. 1989. Fear of crime in residential environments: Testing a social psychological model. *The Journal of social psychology* 129, 2 (1989), 141–160.
[37] Eduardo Alcântara Vasconcellos. 2014. *Urban Transport Environment and Equity: The case for developing countries*. Routledge.
[38] Julio Jacobo Waiselfiz. 2013. Mapa da Violência 2013: mortes matadas por armas de fogo. (2013).
[39] Ralf Weber, Jörg Schnier, and Thomas Jacobsen. 2008. Aesthetics of streetscapes: Influence of fundamental properties on aesthetic judgments of urban space 1, 2. *Perceptual and motor skills* 106, 1 (2008), 128–146.
[40] James Q Wilson and George L Kelling. 1982. Broken windows. *Atlantic monthly* 249, 3 (1982), 29–38.
[41] Sue-Ming Yang and Chih-Chao Pao. 2015. Do We "See" the Same Thing? An Experimental Look into the Black Box of Disorder Perception. *Journal of Research in Crime and Delinquency* 52, 4 (2015), 534–566.

Quantifying Location Sociality

Jun Pang
FSTC & SnT
University of Luxembourg
jun.pang@uni.lu

Yang Zhang
CISPA, Saarland University
Saarland Informatics Campus
yang.zhang@cispa.saarland

ABSTRACT

The emergence of location-based social networks provides an unprecedented chance to study the interaction between human mobility and social relations. This work is a step towards quantifying whether a location is suitable for conducting social activities, and the notion is named location sociality. Being able to quantify location sociality creates practical opportunities such as urban planning and location recommendation. To quantify a location's sociality, we propose a mixture model of HITS and PageRank on a heterogeneous network linking users and locations. By exploiting millions of check-in data generated by Instagram users in New York and Los Angeles, we investigate the relation between location sociality and several location properties, including location categories, rating and popularity. We further perform two case studies, i.e., friendship prediction and location recommendation, experimental results demonstrate the usefulness of our quantification.

CCS CONCEPTS

• **Human-centered computing** → **Social networking sites**; **Ubiquitous computing**;

KEYWORDS

Online social networks; location-based social networks; data mining; friendship prediction; location recommendation

1 INTRODUCTION

Online social networks (OSNs) have been the most successful web applications during the past decade. Leading companies, including Facebook,[1] Twitter[2] and Instagram,[3] have gained a large number of users. More recently, with the development of positioning technology on mobile devices, OSNs have been extended to geographical space. Nowadays, it is quite common for OSN users to share their geographical locations, i.e., check-ins. Moreover, a special type of OSNs dedicated to location sharing are created, namely location-based social networks (LBSNs). Foursquare and Yelp are two representative companies. With the emergence of LBSNs, a large quantity of data concerning human mobility become available. This gives us

[1] https://www.facebook.com/
[2] https://twitter.com/
[3] https://www.instagram.com/

HT'17, July 4-7, 2017, Prague, Czech Republic.
© 2017 ACM. 978-1-4503-4708-2/17/07...$15.00
DOI: http://dx.doi.org/10.1145/3078714.3078779

an unprecedented opportunity to understand human mobility and moreover to study the interaction between social relations and mobility. Some previous works have been focused on inferring social relationships from mobility, such as [13, 28, 32, 37, 41], others exploit users' social information to predict their future locations, such as [1, 3]. More recently, researchers propose new understandings of locations by using user generated data such as happiness [30] and walkability [29].

Location has been recognized as an important factor for social activities back in 1950s. In his seminal work [10], Erving Goffman described social interactions as a series of performance given by social actors, and physical setting, i.e., location, is an important aspect of a social actor's performance. In [10], Goffman stated that "*A setting tends to stay put, geographically speaking, so that those who would use a particular setting as a part of their performance cannot begin their act until they have brought themselves to the appropriate place*". Based on Goffmann's study, Milligan [21] further proposed that "*physical sites (however defined by the participants) become the stages for social interaction, stages that are both physically and socially constructed*". She explained that not only being physically constructed (by architects, facility managers, property owners and others), a location will also be socially constructed by people who conduct social interactions there. Following this theory, we argue that social construction will make some locations more suitable for social activities than others.

In the current work, we aim to quantify whether a location is a suitable for conducting social activities. The notion we quantify is named *location sociality*. We define a location's sociality as *the degree to which individuals tend to conduct social activities at that location*. A location is considered social if friends frequently visit, especially for the purpose of socializing or recreation, and vice versa. Studying location sociality could advance the boundary of our understanding on the interaction between social relations and mobility. It can also help us to solve challenging problems such as urban planning and traffic control. In practice, location sociality can be also used to build appealing applications such as location recommendation.

Contributions. In the current work, we make the following contributions:

- We propose a framework to quantify location sociality (Section 2). Our framework is based on the assumption that a location's sociality and its visitors' social influence are mutually reinforced. To model this assumption, we construct a heterogeneous network consisting of users (in a social network) and locations (a user-location network). Then, we propose a mixture model of HITS [16] and PageRank to quantify location sociality on this heterogeneous network.

- Following our solution, we exploit millions of check-in data from Instagram in New York and Los Angeles to quantify location sociality (Section 3). We then study the relation between location sociality and several location properties including location categories, rating and popularity. Our discoveries include: certain types of locations (music venues and nightclubs) are more social than others; location sociality shares a positive relation with location rating given by users; social locations distribute more uniformly w.r.t. geographical space than popular locations.
- To demonstrate the usefulness of our quantification of location sociality, we perform a case study on friendship prediction in Section 4.1. We extract two users' common locations and define features based on these common locations' sociality for machine learning classification. Experimental results show that with very simple location sociality features, we are able to achieve a strong prediction. Moreover, adding location sociality into a state-of-the-art prediction model achieves a 5% performance gain.
- We perform another case study on using location sociality for location recommendation in Section 4.2. We integrate our quantification into a random walk with restart framework. Experimental results show that the recommender based on location sociality achieves a better recommendation performance (at least 5%) than the baseline recommender that does not consider location sociality.

We discuss some implications and limitations of the current work in Section 5. Related works are discussed in Section 6 and Section 7 concludes the paper.

2 PROPOSED SOLUTION

In this section, we first discuss the intuition of our solution on quantifying location sociality (Section 2.1), then we formally describe the solution (Section 2.2).

2.1 Intuition

Our intuition on quantifying location sociality in this paper is based on the assumption that a location's sociality and its visitors' social influence are mutually reinforced. To explain this intuition, we start by addressing socially influential users. In the society, if a person is considered socially influential, he must visit different social places frequently to organize or participate in different social activities and events. On the other hand, if a location is frequently visited by influential users, then it must be suitable for conducting social activities, i.e., it is a social place. Following this, we establish a mutual reinforcement relation between user influence and location sociality, i.e., more social a location is, more socially influential users visit it, and vice versa. In addition to visiting many social places, an influential user should also occupy an important position in the social network, e.g., he should have many friends who are also socially influential. Following the above discussion, our intuition on quantifying location sociality can be summarized as the following two assumptions.

Assumption 1. Location sociality and users' social influence are mutually reinforced.

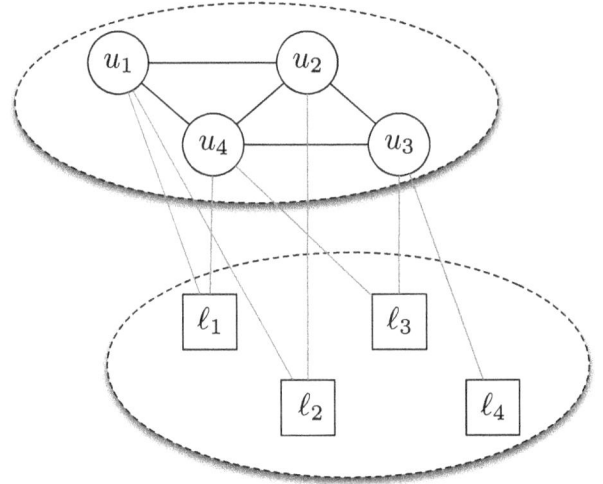

Figure 1: A model of the network.

Assumption 2. Users' social influence can be quantified from the social network.

The first intuition can be naturally formulated into a HITS-style framework [16]. For the second intuition, we apply PageRank on the social graph to quantify each user's influence. In the rest of the paper, we use location sociality and sociality interchangeably.

2.2 Our framework

We start by modeling users, locations and their relationships into two types of networks including social network and user-location network.

Social network. A *social network*, denoted as $G_{\mathcal{U}} = (\mathcal{U}, \mathcal{E}_{\mathcal{U}})$, is an unweighted graph with nodes in set $\mathcal{U}$ representing all users. $\mathcal{E}_{\mathcal{U}} \subseteq \mathcal{U} \times \mathcal{U}$ is a symmetric relation containing the edges in $G_{\mathcal{U}}$. If u_i and u_j are friends, then $(u_i, u_j) \in \mathcal{E}_{\mathcal{U}}$ and $(u_j, u_i) \in \mathcal{E}_{\mathcal{U}}$. We use matrix X to represent $G_{\mathcal{U}}$ where $X_{i,j} = 1$ if $(u_i, u_j) \in \mathcal{E}_{\mathcal{U}}$ and $X_{i,j} = 0$ otherwise. It is easy to see that X is symmetric. We further use $\overline{X}$ to denote the column stochastic matrix of X where $\overline{X}_{i,j} = \frac{X_{i,j}}{\sum_k X_{k,j}}$.

User-location network. A *user-location network*, denoted as $G_{\mathcal{U},\mathcal{L}} = (\mathcal{U}, \mathcal{L}, \mathcal{E}_{\mathcal{U},\mathcal{L}})$, is a weighted bipartite graph. $\mathcal{E}_{\mathcal{U},\mathcal{L}} \subseteq \mathcal{U} \times \mathcal{L}$ consists of the edges in $G_{\mathcal{U},\mathcal{L}}$. Each edge $(u_i, \ell_j) \in \mathcal{E}_{\mathcal{U},\mathcal{L}}$, also written as $e_{i,j}^{\mathcal{U},\mathcal{L}}$, is associated with a weight $w_{i,j}^{\mathcal{U},\mathcal{L}}$ defined as the number of times that the user u_i has visited (checked in) the location ℓ_j (denoted by $|ci(u_i, \ell_j)|$). We use matrix Y to represent $G_{\mathcal{U},\mathcal{L}}$ with $Y_{i,j} = w_{i,j}^{\mathcal{U},\mathcal{L}}$. The transpose of Y is further denoted by Y^T. In the end, we use $\overline{Y}$ and $\overline{Y^T}$ to denote the column stochastic matrices of Y and Y^T, respectively.

Figure 1 shows an example of the heterogeneous graph. Within our framework two sets of values, locations' sociality and users' social influence, can be obtained. Each location ℓ's sociality is defined as $\kappa(\ell)$ and $\eta(u)$ for each user's social influence. Following the intuition in Section 2.1, our model is formulated into the following equations:

$$\eta(u_i) = \sum_j \overline{X}_{i,j} \cdot \eta(u_j) \qquad (1)$$

$$\eta(u_i) = \sum_j \overline{Y}_{i,j} \cdot \kappa(\ell_j) \qquad (2)$$

$$\kappa(\ell_j) = \sum_i \overline{Y^T}_{j,i} \cdot \eta(u_i) \qquad (3)$$

Equations 1 is the PageRank implementation for quantifying users' social influence from $G_{\mathcal{U}}$. Equations 2 and 3 are an instance of the HITS framework which establishes the mutual reinforcement relationship between locations and users. We then linearly combine the above equations as

$$\eta(u_i) = \alpha \cdot \sum_j \overline{X}_{i,j} \cdot \eta(u_j) + (1-\alpha) \cdot \sum_j \overline{Y}_{i,j} \cdot \kappa(\ell_j) \quad (4)$$

$$\kappa(\ell_j) = \sum_i \overline{Y^T}_{j,i} \cdot \eta(u_i) \qquad (5)$$

where α specifies the contributions of each component to users' social influence. In our experiments, α is set to 0.5 which indicates the social network structure and user mobility are equally important on quantifying users' social influence. Note that $\alpha = 0.5$ is a typical setting in many fields such as [36] where the authors aim to discover salient sentences for document summarization.

We further use two vectors η and κ to denote users' social influence and locations' sociality. Then the above equations can be written into the following matrix form.

$$\eta = \alpha \cdot \overline{X} \cdot \eta + (1-\alpha) \cdot \overline{Y} \cdot \kappa \qquad (6)$$

$$\kappa = \overline{Y^T} \cdot \eta \qquad (7)$$

Equations 6 and 7 can be computed through an iterative updating process. We set all locations' (users') initial sociality (social influence) to be $\frac{1}{|\mathcal{L}|}$ ($\frac{1}{|\mathcal{U}|}$). According to our experiments, the computation stops after around 10 iterations, when the maximal difference between κs of two consecutive iterations is less than 0.00001.

3 EXPERIMENTS

In this section, we first introduce the dataset used for our experiments. Then, we present the results of our quantification: we start by discussing the top social locations and location categories; then we focus on the relation between location sociality and location rating; in the end, the correlation between location sociality and popularity is discussed.

3.1 Dataset description

Instagram is a photo-sharing social network with a fast growing user number. By now, it has 400M monthly active users and with 75M photos published everyday. Similar to other social network services such as Facebook and Twitter, Instagram allows users to share their locations when publishing photos. Moreover, unlike Twitter where only a small amount of tweets are geo-tagged, the authors of [19] have shown that Instagram users are much more willing to share their locations (31 times more than Twitter users), which makes Instagram a suitable platform to study the interaction between mobility and social relations.

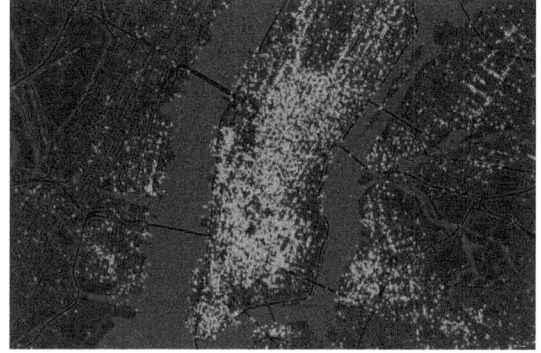

Figure 2: Check-ins in New York.

	New York	Los Angeles
# check-ins	6,181,169	4,705,079
# active users	12,280	8,643
# edges (active users)	74,230	44,994
# locations	8,683	6,908

Table 1: Dataset summary.

We collect the geo-tagged photos, i.e., check-ins, in New York and Los Angeles from Instagram through its public API[4]. Since locations' category information is an important aspect of our analysis, and fortunately the API of Instagram is linked with the API of Foursquare, a leading location-based social network with resourceful information about each place, thus we exploit the following methodology to collect our data. We first resort to Foursquare to extract all location ids within each city, meanwhile we collect each location's category information together with its rating (number of tips and number of likes). Then for each Foursquare's location id, we query Instagram's API to get its corresponding location id in Instagram. After this, we query each location's recent check-ins in Instagram several times a day from August 1st, 2015 until March 15th, 2016. In the end, more than 6M check-ins have been collected in New York and 4.7M in Los Angeles[5]. To resolve the data sparseness issue, we focus on users with at least 20 check-ins (considered as active users) and locations with at least 10 check-ins. Figure 2 depicts a sample check-in distribution in New York. Since Foursquare organizes location categories into a tree structure[6], we take its second level categories to label each location.

To obtain users' social networks, we exploit Instagram's API to query each active user's follower/followee list[7]. We consider two users as friends if they mutually follow each other in Instagram. To further guarantee that users we have collected are not celebrities or business accounts, we filter out the top 5% of users with most followers. Also, only the relations among active users (users with

---

[4]https://www.instagram.com/developer/
[5]It is worth noticing that the authors of [20] has applied a similar methodology.
[6]https://developer.foursquare.com/categorytree
[7]Since Instagram's API only provides one page with 50 follower/followees per query, we perform multiple queries until all follower/followees of each user are obtained.

(a) New York

(b) Los Angeles

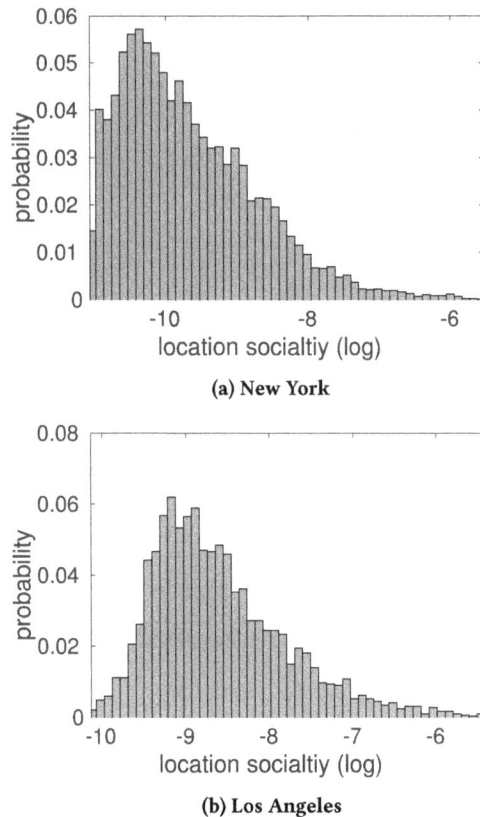

Figure 3: Distributions of log-transformed location sociality.

New York	
Top Social	Top Unsocial
Webster Hall	Staples
Madison Square Park	17 Frost Gallery
Rockwood Music Hall	China Institute
Washington Square Park	Manhattan Theatre Club
Baby's All Right	El Rey Del Taco II
Los Angeles	
Top Social	Top Unsocial
The Fonda Theatre	Panda Express
Avalon Hollywood	Gap
The Echo	Ebar
Hermosa Beach Pier	Palms Super Market
Exchange LA	7-Eleven

Table 2: The most and least social locations in New York and Los Angeles.

New York	
Social Categories	Unsocial Categories
Music Venue	Laundry Service
Nightclub	Convenience Store
Harbor	Post Office
Museum	Pharmacy
Park	Fast Food Restaurant
Los Angeles	
Social Categories	Unsocial Categories
Concert Hall	Convenience Store
Nightclub	Vintage Store
Music Venue	Fast Food Restaurant
Mall	Pet Service
Beach	Automotive Shop

Table 3: Top 5 location categories with highest and lowest average location sociality in New York and Los Angeles.

at least 20 check-ins) are kept. In the end, the social network contains 74,230 edges for New York and 44,994 edges for Los Angeles. Table 1 summarizes the dataset. For the sake of experimental result reproducibility, our dataset is available upon request.

3.2 Location sociality vs. location category

Figure 3 depicts the log transformed distributions of location sociality, both of which indicate that most locations have a middle value of sociality while only a few locations are very social or unsocial. This is different from other location measurement, for instance, the number of mobility transitions from or to each location follows a power law distribution [24].

Table 2 presents the top five locations with highest and lowest sociality. For New York, Webster Hall (music venue) is the most social place followed by Madison Square Park (park). On the other hand, the least social place is one Staples store (convenience store) in midtown. For Los Angeles, The Fonda Theatre (concert hall) has the highest sociality. Meanwhile, one Panda Express (fast food restaurant) is the least social place. From Table 2, we can see a clear distinction between social and unsocial places w.r.t. their categories. Next, we take a deeper look at the relation between sociality and location category.

Table 3 lists the top five location categories with the highest and lowest average location sociality. Nightclub and music venue are

in the top 3 in both cities. On the other hand, convenience store seems to be less attractive to friends. Besides, we also observe some interesting difference between the two cities. For example, beach is the No. 5 social choice for people living in Los Angeles while it is not New Yorkers' choice since there are no beaches in Manhattan.

As music venue and nightclub have high rankings in both cities, we further list the top 5 music venues and nightclubs in Table 4. Although the ranking of music venues and nightclubs are rather subjective, we have checked several blogs and articles (listed in the additional material) and most of our top-social nightclubs and music venues have received positive reviews and been recommended by these blogs and articles. We conclude that a location's sociality is related to its category. Normally, location category itself is not sufficient to judge whether a location is social or not. Next, we study

New York	
Social Music Venues	Social Nightclubs
Webster Hall	Stage 48
Rockwood Music Hall	Marquee
Baby's All Right	Pacha NYC
Bowery Ballroom	1 OAK
Music Hall of Williamsburg	VIP Room NYC

Los Angeles	
Social Music Venus	Social Nightclubs
Avalon Hollywood	Exchange LA
The Echo	OHM Nightclub
The Roxy	Sound Nightclub
The Troubadour	Club Los Globos
The Hollywood Bowl	Create Nightclubs

Table 4: Top 5 music venues and nightclubs with highest location sociality in New York and Los Angeles.

other properties of locations and their relationship with location sociality.

3.3 Location sociality vs. rating, tips and likes

For each location, Foursquare provides us with not only its category information, but also other properties including rating[8], number of tips and number of likes generated by Foursquare users. Next, we study whether it is possible to use these properties to explain location sociality. To proceed, we build a linear regression model with rating, number of tips and number of likes as explanatory variables while location sociality as the dependent variable. By fitting the model with ordinary least square method, we obtain a coefficient of determination (R^2) of 0.192 in New York and 0.280 in Los Angeles, meaning that 19.2% (28.0%) of the variability of location sociality in New York (Los Angeles) can be explained by these properties. By checking the parameters of our linear model, we discover that the major predictive power is driven by location rating.

We further plot the average location sociality as a function of rating in Figure 4: the two variables share a positive relation. Especially when location rating is high (≥ 8), location sociality increases sharply for both cities. This indicates that social places are assigned with high ratings by users.

3.4 Location sociality vs. location popularity

A social location is often popular in the sense that it attracts many people. On the other hand, to conduct social activities, everyone has his own preference on choosing locations. For example, one may prefer to go to a bar near his home, which might not be well-known at the city level. The relationship between a location's sociality and its popularity is worth investigation: a location's sociality should be correlated with its popularity, while the two notions should exhibit difference.

---

[8]In Foursquare, rating is in the range from 1 to 10.

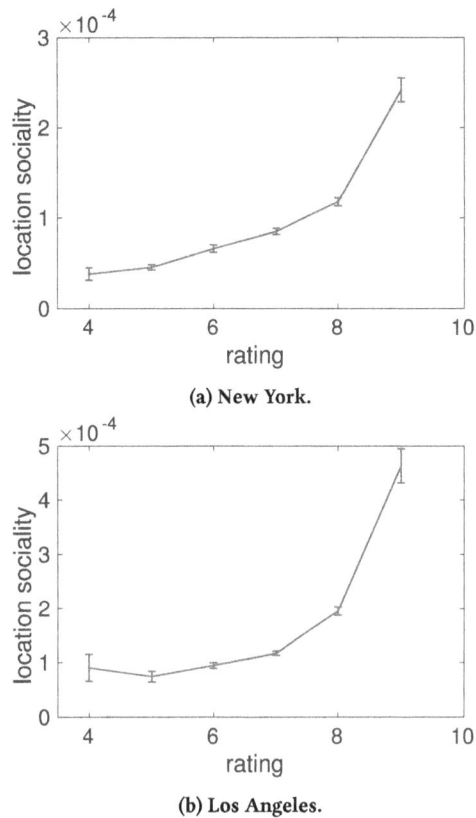

(a) New York.

(b) Los Angeles.

Figure 4: Location sociality vs. location rating.

By far, the most common notion for quantifying a location's popularity is location entropy [4], it is formally defined as

$$le(\ell) = - \sum \frac{|ci(u,\ell)|}{|ci(\ell)|} \log \frac{|ci(u,\ell)|}{|ci(\ell)|},$$

where $|ci(u,\ell)|$ is user u's number of check-ins at location ℓ (Section 2) and $|ci(\ell)|$ is the total number of check-ins of location ℓ. More popular a location is, higher location entropy it has.

To check the difference between the two measurements, we plot the heatmaps w.r.t. location entropy and sociality of New York. As expected, midtown and downtown New York are "hot" areas in both maps. On the other hand, we observe that location sociality is more uniformly distributed than location entropy. For example, the areas marked by green circles in Figure 5a are obviously lighter than those in Figure 5b. After having a close look, we discover that bars and restaurants are the "hot" locations inside these areas. Data in Los Angeles exhibits a similar result and is not shown.

We further extract the top 20 popular locations in both cities (listed in the additional material). In New York, the most popular locations are parks and museums (e.g., The MET, MoMA and Guggenheim). On the other hand, in Los Angeles, the most popular locations concentrate on malls followed by museums. Moreover, in both cities, famous landmarks have high location entropy, such as Rockefeller Center in New York and Hollywood Walk of Fame in Los Angeles. This is quite different from the ranking in Table 2 and Table 3: social locations are mainly music venues and nightclubs

(a) Location entropy

(b) Location sociality

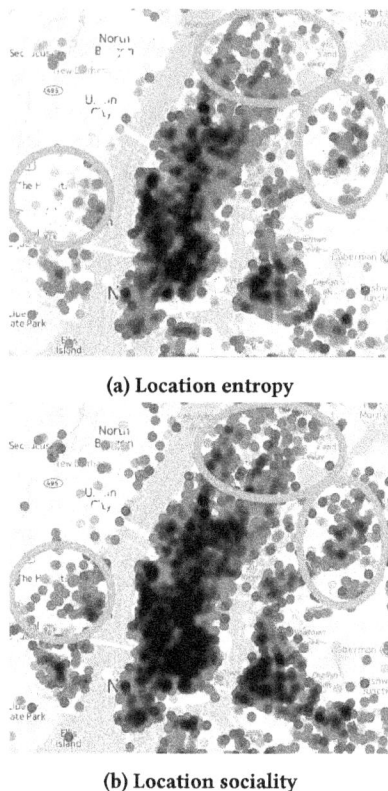

Figure 5: Heatmaps in New York.

(a) New York

(b) Los Angeles

Figure 6: Evaluation results on our model w.r.t. four classification algorithms.

while popular locations are mainly tourist attractions. In the end, we conclude that there exists a large difference between social and popular locations.

4 CASE STUDIES

In this section, we perform two case studies to show how location sociality can be used to build real world applications. The applications we focus on are friendship prediction and new location recommendation, both of which are essential for social network services.

4.1 Friendship prediction

Following the seminal work of Liben-Nowell and Kleinberg, friendship prediction has been extensively studied [17], resulting in appealing applications such as friendship recommendation which is essential for OSNs to increase user engagement. During the past five years, with the development of LBSNs, many researchers start to exploit users' location data as a new source of information for friendship prediction.

Model. In our case study, we consider friendship prediction as a binary classification problem. Each pair of friends is treated positive if they are friends (mutually following each other in Instagram) and negative otherwise. We extract the common locations of two users and construct the feature space based on these common locations. Here, two users' common locations are the intersection of the places they have checked in, regardless of time. For two users u_i and u_j,

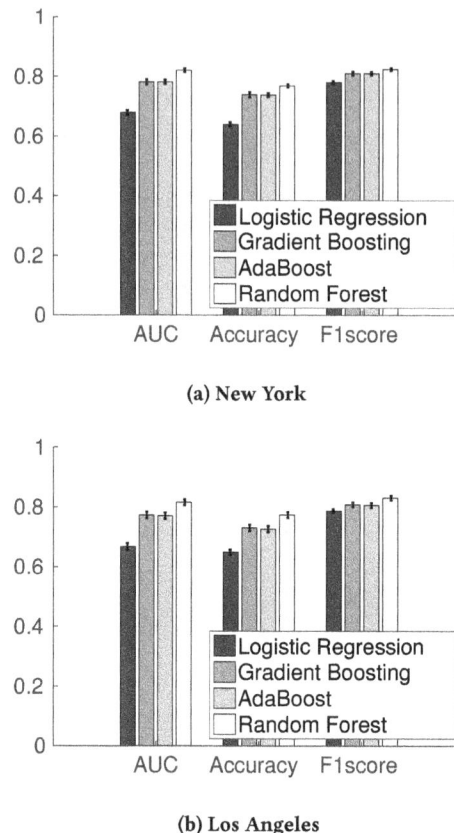

we find their common locations' sociality and utilize the average, maximal, minimal and standard deviation of theses sociality as features for classification.

Experiment setup. To resolve the data sparseness issue, we filter out pairs of users who have only one or zero common location. This leaves us 7,525 pairs of friends, i.e., positive cases, in New York and 3,961 pairs of friends in Los Angeles. For negative case, we randomly sample the same number of non-friend pairs – each pair of them has at least two common places as well. It is worth noticing that this way of sampling negative cases increases the hardness of classification since a non-friend pair also has at least two common locations. Therefore, we can further evaluate the usefulness of location sociality. We have adopted four classification algorithms in our experiments including logistic regression, gradient boosting, AdaBoost and random forest. Accuracy, F1score and AUC (area under the ROC curve) are used as our metrics. We randomly split the dataset with 70% for training and 30% for testing, this random split is repeated for 10 times and we report the average result.

Results. Figure 6 depicts the performance of our classifications. Among all the classifiers, random forest performs the best with AUC = 0.82 and Accuracy = 0.77 in the two cities. Meanwhile, we have F1score = 0.82 in New York and F1score = 0.83 in Los Angeles.

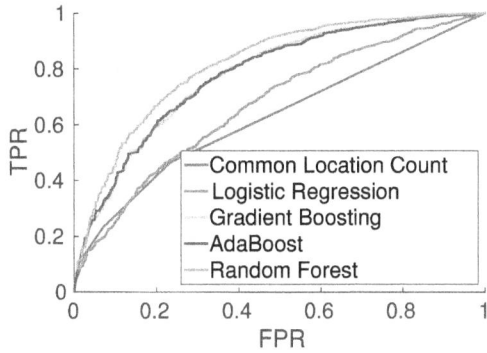

(a) New York

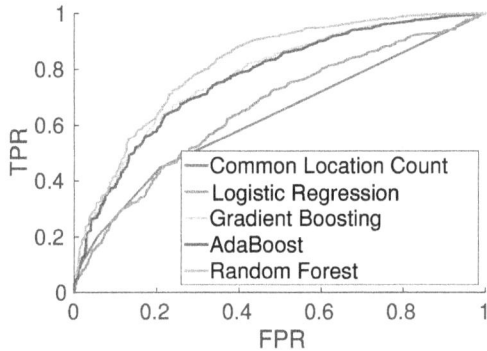

(b) Los Angeles

Figure 7: ROC curves for our classification and the number of common locations.

AdaBoost and gradient boosting have a comparable performance. On the other hand, logistic regression performs the worst.

The number of common locations is further adopted as a naive baseline model for comparison, i.e., we tune the threshold (the number of common locations) for classification to obtain the ROC curve. Figure 7 plots the results. As we can see, all our classifiers based on location sociality outperform this naive baseline.

Next, we check whether adding location sociality into a state-of-the-art model as proposed in [32] [9] can increase prediction performance. The model in [32] (location feature setting) extracts two users' common locations and design features mainly with these common locations' entropies (see Section 3.4 for location entropy), such as the minimal location entropy. In our experiments, we combine our four location sociality features with the features in [32] and fit them into our best performing classifier random forest. The results in Table 5 show that the classification with location sociality improves [32] by around 5% among all three metrics in both New York and Los Angeles. This further demonstrates that location sociality is useful for friendship prediction.

New York	AUC	Accuracy	F1score
[32]	0.83	0.77	0.82
sociality+[32]	**0.87**	**0.81**	**0.85**

Los Angeles	AUC	Accuracy	F1score
[32]	0.82	0.77	0.82
sociality+[32]	**0.86**	**0.80**	**0.85**

Table 5: Evaluation result on [32] and location sociality+[32] .

Indeed, there exist other solutions for friendship prediction such as considering two users' meeting events [13, 28, 37]. However, the main issue for this method is that meeting events (reflected in OSNs) are rare, for example, with 6M check-ins in New York, we only observe around 100 meeting events. Moreover, we want to emphasize that friendship prediction is not the focus of the current work. Therefore, we choose the most straightforward features for training our classifiers. Nevertheless, our prediction still achieves a strong performance showing that location sociality is a good indicator for recommending friends. Further investigation on integrating location sociality into the state-of-the-art friendship prediction models is worth studying and we leave it as a future work.

4.2 Location recommendation

The second case study we perform is recommending new locations for users to visit. Location recommendation has a great potential to build appealing applications. During the past five years, it has attracted academia a lot of attention (e.g. [2, 6, 7, 42]). Our goal here is to demonstrate the usefulness of location sociality in recommending new locations. In order to integrate location sociality into a location recommender, we adopt a classical approach, namely random walk with restart [34].

Model. In a typical setting of random walk with restart for recommendation, in the beginning we define a matrix Q as

$$Q = \begin{pmatrix} 0 & Y \\ Y^T & 0 \end{pmatrix}$$

where Y and Y^T represent user-location network (location-user network) (Section 2). Meanwhile, $\bar{Q}$ denotes the column stochastic version of Q [39]. Then to recommend locations to a user u_i, we modify $\bar{Q}$ to allow every node in the graph having a certain probability (15% in the experiments) to jump to the node representing u_i. Formally, for every $Q_{a,b} \in Q$, $\bar{Q}_{a,b}$ is defined as

$$\bar{Q}_{a,b} = \begin{cases} (1-c) \cdot \frac{Q_{a,b}}{\sum_j Q_{j,b}} + c \cdot 1 & \text{if the } a\text{th row represents } u_i \\ (1-c) \cdot \frac{Q_{a,b}}{\sum_j Q_{j,b}} & \text{otherwise} \end{cases}$$

where $c = 0.15$. By applying the same method of solving PageRank, e.g., power method, we can obtain the steady state distribution over $\bar{Q}$, which is the relevance score of all nodes (both locations and users) to u_i. Locations with high relevance scores are recommended to u_i. Noulas et al. [23] have exploited this approach for location recommendation[10], where the weight on an edge between a user u_i and a location ℓ_j is simply the user's number of visits to that location, i.e., $Y_{i,j} = w_{i,j}^{\mathcal{U},\mathcal{L}} = |ci(u_i, \ell_j)|$ in Section 2.

To integrate location sociality into the edge weight for location recommendation, we change Y to T, i.e., Q is modified to:

$$Q = \left(\begin{array}{cc} 0 & T \\ \mathcal{T} & 0 \end{array} \right)$$

where $T_{i,j}$ is defined as

$$T_{i,j} = |ci(u_i, \ell_j)| \cdot \frac{1}{-\log(\kappa(\ell_j))}. \qquad (8)$$

Here, $\kappa(\ell_j)$ is the location sociality of ℓ_j, meanwhile $\mathcal{T}$ is the transpose of T. Under this formulation, Equation 8 assigns higher weight to locations with high sociality, which will bias the recommended locations to be more social. In the end, by performing power method on the column stochastic version of the modified Q, we obtain the recommended locations for each user.

Experiment setup. The check-in dataset is partitioned temporally with each one covers consecutively 60 days [23]. For each partition, we use the data of the first 30 days to train the model while the left 30 days for testing. Since our aim is to perform new location recommendation, for each user we further filter out his locations in the testing set that he has already been to in the training set. In the end, we perform random walk with restart with location sociality (rwr-ls) to recommend locations for each user, and exploit rwr without location sociality (rwr), i.e., the one in [23], as the baseline model. Two metrics including precision@10 and recall@10 are adopted for evaluation.

Results. Table 6 presents the results for location recommendation in both cities. As we can see, rwr-ls outperforms rwr in all months. For precision@10, rwr-ls outperforms rwr by 10%, while for recall@10, even in the worst case in New York, rwr-ls still has 3.4% improvement on rwr. Even though the absolute precision and recall of our recommendation is not high, it is worth noticing that the similar performances of location recommendation have been obtained by [7, 18, 38], thus our results are reasonable. Similar to Gao et al. [7], we emphasize that the focus here is to compare the relative performance, in order to demonstrate the usefulness of our quantification.

Many state-of-the-art algorithms exploit other factors for location recommendation such as geographical distance and users' published contents, one of our future works is to integrate location sociality into these algorithms to further improve recommendation.

5 IMPLICATIONS AND LIMITATIONS

We discuss implications and limitations of the current work.

Implications. Location sociality as a measurement can characterize a social map for a city. The applications based on it, including the friendship prediction and location recommendation addressed in Section 4, can benefit several parties.

For city administrator, understanding where people prefer to socialize can help them make better city plans. For example, during conventional social time such as Friday nights, the city government

could make specific transportation plans, such as more buses and taxis, or security plans such as deploying more policemen, for areas with high sociality. Moreover, location sociality can be a good reference for the government to plan future city development. For city residents, location sociality provides a good reference for them to find or discover new places to socialize with their friends. In addition, location sociality can be used as an important factor for location recommendation services for social network services, such as Yelp and Foursquare. For visitors, visiting high sociality places is a good way to engage local people's social life. This can help visitors understand the city's culture in a better way. For business owners, knowing where people like to go to conduct social activities is an important factor for them to determine where to open new business.

Limitations. We point out the following limitations of the current work. First, we only focus on the data from Instagram which cannot reflect the general population both socially and geographically. Socially, the authors of [22, 33] have shown that most of Instagram users are center around a younger age (25 yeas old); geographically, most of the check-ins concentrate on the city center (Figure 2).

Second, our quantification does not take into account the temporal factor which could also be important for understanding locations. One approach for considering time would be concentrating on users' meeting events, i.e., users check in at the same location at the same time, however, as we have discussed previously, meeting events are rare even in large datasets as ours. In the future, we plan to incorporate data with rich temporal information from other sources to further improve our quantification.

Third, we quantify a location's sociality based on its visitors' information. In some cases, a location's own property can also contribute to its sociality. For example, it is pointed out that the decoration, the space allocation and even the bicycle parking design can result in different number of visitors to a cafe located in a university campus [21]. However, we argue that data of this kind is hard and expensive to obtain at a large scale.

6 RELATED WORK

The emergence of LBSNs has brought us an unprecedented opportunity to study human mobility and its interaction with social relationships. Many works have been done on understanding human mobility and its interaction with social relations. There mainly exist two research directions: one is to exploit users' location information to understand social relations, e.g., see [13, 28, 32, 37, 41]; the other is to use social relations to understand mobility and locations, including the current work.

Backstrom et al. [1] present one of the pioneer works on friendship-based location prediction. They analyze Facebook users' home location and discover that friends tend to live closer to each other than strangers. Then they build a maximal likelihood estimator to predict a user's home location. They have shown that their model outperforms significantly the method based on IP addresses. Cho et al. [3] study a general problem: instead of predicting home location, they aim to predict where a user is at a certain time. They construct a dynamic Gaussian mixture model with the assumption that each user's mobility is centered around two states, such as home and work. The experimental results show that their model

---

[10]They [23] also consider social network in Q, here we ignore it for better demonstrating location sociality's usefulness.

New York					
15.8-15.10	Precision@10	Recall@10	15.11-16.1	Precision@10	Recall@10
rwr	0.009	0.021	rwr	0.009	0.028
rwr-ls	**0.010**	**0.024**	rwr-ls	**0.010**	**0.031**
15.9-2015.11	Precision@10	Recall@10	15.12-16.2	Precision@10	Recall@10
rwr	0.010	0.032	rwr	0.009	0.026
rwr-ls	**0.011**	**0.034**	rwr-ls	**0.010**	**0.028**
15.10-15.12	Precision@10	Recall@10	16.1-16.3	Precision@10	Recall@10
rwr	0.009	0.028	rwr	0.008	0.027
rwr-ls	**0.010**	**0.029**	rwr-ls	**0.009**	**0.029**
Los Angeles					
15.8-15.10	Precision@10	Recall@10	15.11-16.1	Precision@10	Recall@10
rwr	0.010	0.028	rwr	0.008	0.024
rwr-ls	**0.011**	**0.030**	rwr-ls	**0.009**	**0.026**
15.9-2015.11	Precision@10	Recall@10	15.12-16.2	Precision@10	Recall@10
rwr	0.013	0.038	rwr	0.012	0.047
rwr-ls	**0.015**	**0.042**	rwr-ls	**0.013**	**0.048**
15.10-15.12	Precision@10	Recall@10	16.1-16.3	Precision@10	Recall@10
rwr	0.010	0.025	rwr	0.007	0.035
rwr-ls	**0.012**	**0.029**	rwr-ls	**0.009**	**0.044**

Table 6: Precision@10 and recall@10 for location recommendation.

achieves a promising accuracy. Other works include [8, 14, 26, 27]. More recently, Jurgens et al. [15] perform a comprehensive study on most of the existing works in the field and points out some future directions.

Besides predicting a user's location, researchers begin to advance our understandings of locations based on the data from social networks. In [30], the authors focus on recommending pleasant paths between two locations in a city. Unlike the traditional shortest path recommendation, they assign three values to describe whether a street is quiet, beautiful and happy, respectively. Then they adjust the path recommendation algorithm with these factors and recommend the most pleasant path for users. In [29], the authors quantify whether a street is suitable for walk, namely walkability. To assess their results, they propose to use concurrent validity. Their discoveries, to mention a few, include walkable streets tend to be tagged with walk-related words on Flickr and can be identified by location types on those streets. The authors of [5] exploit the data from Foursquare to analyze different neighborhoods in a city. They extract some signature features to profile each neighborhood and propose an algorithm to match similar neighborhoods across different cities. Experimental results show that they are able to match tourists areas across Paris and Barcelona, and expensive residential areas in Washington D.C. and New York. More recently, Hristova et al. [11] propose four location measurements, including brokerage, serendipity, entropy and homogeneity, under a heterogenous social and location network model. Their experiments are conducted with a Foursquare dataset collected in London, and the authors show

that their proposed measurements can be used to describe dynamics that is hard to capture including gentrification and deprivation. Other recent works include [9, 12, 25, 31].

The current work also falls into the field of urban informatics [43], a newly emerging field where researchers tend to use the ubiquitous data to understand and improve the city where we live. Besides the research literature, several open projects have been established as well. To mention a few examples, Yuan et al. [40] focus on discovering the function of each region in a city; Venerandi et al. [35] measure the socio-economic deprivation of a city. Another excellent example is the goodcitylife project[11], where the team members try to imitate human beings' five senses on food to understand cities.

7   CONCLUSION

In this paper, we have proposed a new notion namely location sociality to describe whether a location is suitable for conducting social activities. We constructed a heterogenous network linking locations and users and proposed a mixture model of HITS and PageRank to quantify location sociality. Experimental results on millions of Instagram check-in data validate location sociality with some in-depth discoveries. Two case studies including friendship prediction and location recommendation demonstrate the usefulness of our quantification.

---

[11]http://goodcitylife.org/

Location data do not only come from LBSNs, but many other sources, such as GPS traces and WIFI points. In the future, we are interested in establishing more connections between LBSN data and other sources to gain a deep understanding of cities.

REFERENCES

[1] Lars Backstrom, Eric Sun, and Cameron Marlow. 2010. Find me if you can: improving geographical prediction with social and spatial proximity. In *Proc. 19th International Conference on World Wide Web (WWW)*. ACM, 61–70.

[2] Jie Bao, Yu Zheng, David Wilkie, and Mohamed Mokbel. 2015. Recommendations in location-based social networks: a survey. *GeoInformatica* 19, 3 (2015), 525–565.

[3] Eunjoon Cho, Seth A. Myers, and Jure Leskovec. 2011. Friendship and mobility: user movement in location-based social networks. In *Proc. 17th ACM Conference on Knowledge Discovery and Data Mining (KDD)*. ACM, 1082–1090.

[4] Justin Cranshaw, Eran Toch, Jason Hone, Ankiet Kittur, and Norma Sadeh. 2010. Bridging the gap between physical location and online social networks. In *Proc. 12th ACM International Conference on Ubiquitous Computing (UbiComp)*. ACM, 119–128.

[5] Geraud Le Falher, Aristides Gionis, and Michael Mathioudakis. 2015. Where Is the soho of Rome? Measures and algorithms for finding similar neighborhoods in cities. In *Proc. 9th AAAI Conference on Weblogs and Social Media (ICWSM)*. The AAAI Press, 228–237.

[6] Huiji Gao, Jiliang Tang, Xia Hu, and Huan Liu. 2013. Exploring temporal effects for location recommendation on location-based social networks. In *Proc. 7th ACM Conference on Recommender Systems (RecSys)*. ACM, 93–100.

[7] Huiji Gao, Jiliang Tang, Xia Hu, and Huan Liu. 2015. Content-Aware Point of Interest Recommendation on Location-Based Social Networks. In *Proc. 29th AAAI Conference on Artificial Intelligence (AAAI)*. The AAAI Press, 1721–1727.

[8] Huiji Gao, Jiliang Tang, and Huan Liu. 2012. Exploring social-historical ties on location-based social networks. In *Proc. 6th AAAI Conference on Weblogs and Social Media (ICWSM)*. The AAAI Press, 114–121.

[9] Petko Georgiev, Anastasios Noulas, and Cecilia Mascolo. 2014. Where businesses thrive: predicting the impact of the Olympic games on local retailers through location-based services data. In *Proc. 8th AAAI Conference on Weblogs and Social Media (ICWSM)*. The AAAI Press, 151–160.

[10] Erving Goffman. 1959. *The Presentation of Self in Everyday Life*. Random House.

[11] Desislava Hristova, Matthew J. Williams, Mirco Musolesi, Pietro Panzarasa, and Cecilia Mascolo. 2016. Measuring Urban Social Diversity Using Interconnected Geo-Social Networks. In *Proc. 25th International Conference on World Wide Web (WWW)*. ACM, 21–30.

[12] Hsun-Ping Hsieh, Cheng-Te Li, and Shou-De Lin. 2015. Estimating Potential Customers Anywhere and Anytime Based on Location-Based Social Networks. In *Proc. 2015 European Conference on Machine Learning and Principles and Practice of Knowledge Discovery in Databases (ECML/PKDD)*. Springer, 576–592.

[13] Hsun-Ping Hsieh, Rui Yan, and Cheng-Te Li. 2014. Where You Go Reveals Who You Know: Analyzing Social Ties from Millions of Footprints. In *Proc. 24th ACM International Conference on Information and Knowledge Management (CIKM)*. ACM, 1839–1862.

[14] David Jurgens. 2013. That's what friends are for: Inferring location in online social media platforms based on social relationships. In *Proc. 7th AAAI Conference on Weblogs and Social Media (ICWSM)*. The AAAI Press.

[15] David Jurgens, Tyler Finethy, James McCorriston, Yi Tian Xu, and Derek Ruths. 2015. Geolocation prediction in Twitter using social networks: a critical analysis and review of current practice. In *Proc. 9th AAAI Conference on Weblogs and Social Media (ICWSM)*. The AAAI Press, 188–197.

[16] Jon Kleinberg. 1999. Authoritative sources in a hyperlinked environment. *J. ACM* 46, 5 (1999), 604–632.

[17] David Liben-Nowell and Jon Kleinberg. 2007. The link-prediction problem for social networks. *Journal of the American Society for Information Science and Technology* 58, 7 (2007), 1019–1031.

[18] Bin Liu and Hui Xiong. 2013. Point-of-interest recommendation in location based social networks with topic and location awareness. In *Proc. 13th SIAM International Conference on Data Mining (SDM)*. SIAM, 396–404.

[19] Lydia Manikonda, Yuheng Hu, and Subbarao Kambhampati. 2014. Analyzing user activities, demographics, social network structure and user-generated content on Instagram. *CoRR* abs/1410.8099 (2014).

[20] Yelena Mejova, Hamed Haddadi, Anastasios Noulas, and Ingmar Weber. 2015. #FoodPorn: obesity patterns in culinary interactions. In *Proc. the 5th International Conference on Digital Health (DH)*. ACM, 51–58.

[21] Melinda J Milligan. 1998. Interactional past and potential: The social construction of place attachment. *Symbolic Interaction* 21, 1 (1998), 1–33.

[22] Minyue Ni, Yang Zhang, Weili Han, and Jun Pang. 2016. An Empirical Study on User Access Control in Online Social Networks. In *Proc. 21st ACM Symposium on Access Control Models and Technologies (SACMAT)*. ACM, 13–23.

[23] Anastasios Noulas, Salvatore Scellato, Neal Lathia, and Cecilia Mascolo. 2012. A Random Walk around the City: New Venue Recommendation in Location-Based Social Networks. In *Proc. 2012 International Confernece on Social Computing (SocialCom)*. IEEE, 144–153.

[24] Anastasios Noulas, Blake Shaw, Renaud Lambiotte, and Cecilia Mascolo. 2015. Topological properties and temporal dynamics of place networks in urban environments. In *Proc. 24th International Conference on World Wide Web (WWW Companion)*. ACM, 431–441.

[25] Alexandra-Mihaela Olteanu, Kévin Huguenin, Reza Shokri, Mathias Humbert, and Jean-Pierre Hubaux. 2017. Quantifying interdependent privacy risks with location data. *IEEE Transactions on Mobile Computing* 3 (2017), 829–842.

[26] Jun Pang and Yang Zhang. 2015. Exploring communities for effective location prediction (poster paper). In *Proc. 24th International Conference on World Wide Web Conference (Companion Volume) (WWW)*. ACM, 87–88.

[27] Jun Pang and Yang Zhang. 2015. Location prediction: Communities speak louder than friends. In *Proc. 3rd ACM Conference on Online Social Networks (COSN)*. ACM, 161–171.

[28] Huy Pham, Cyrus Shahabi, and Yan Liu. 2013. EBM: an entropy-based model to infer social strength from spatiotemporal data. In *Proc. 2013 ACM International Conference on Management of Data (SIGMOD)*. ACM, 265–276.

[29] Daniele Quercia, Luca Maria Aiello, Rossano Schifanella, and Adam Davies. 2015. The digital life of walkable streets. In *Proc. 24th International Conference on World Wide Web (WWW)*. ACM, 875–884.

[30] Daniele Quercia, Rossano Schifanella, and Luca Maria Aiello. 2014. The shortest path to happiness: recommending beautiful, quiet, and happy routes in the city. In *Proc. 25th ACM Conference on Hypertext and Social Media (HT)*. ACM, 116–125.

[31] Daniele Quercia, Rossano Schifanella, Luca Maria Aiello, and Kate McLean. 2015. Smelly maps: the digital life of urban smellscapes. In *Proc. 9th AAAI Conference on Weblogs and Social Media (ICWSM)*. The AAAI Press, 237–236.

[32] Salvatore Scellato, Anastasios Noulas, and Cecilia Mascolo. 2011. Exploiting place features in link prediction on location-based social networks. In *Proc. 17th ACM Conference on Knowledge Discovery and Data Mining (KDD)*. ACM, 1046–1054.

[33] Flavio Souza, Diego de Las Casas, Vinicius Flores, SunBum Youn, Meeyoung Cha, Daniele Quercia, and Virgilio Almeida. 2015. Dawn of the selfie era: the whos, wheres, and hows of selfies on Instagram. In *Proc. 3rd ACM on Conference on Online Social Networks (COSN)*. ACM, 221–231.

[34] Hanghang Tong, Christos Faloutsos, and Jia yu Pan. 2006. Community detection in networks with node attributes. In *Proc. 6th IEEE International Conference on Data Mining (ICDM)*. IEEE CS, 613–622.

[35] Alessandro Venerandi, Giovanni Quattrone, Licia Capra, Daniele Quercia, and Diego Saez-Trumper. 2015. Measuring urban deprivation from user generated content. In *Proc. 18th ACM Conference on Computer Supported Cooperative Work & Social Computing (CSCW)*. ACM, 254–264.

[36] Xiaojun Wan, Jianwu Yang, and Jianguo Xiao. 2007. Towards an iterative reinforcement approach for simultaneous document summarization and keyword extraction. In *Proc. 45th Annual Meeting of the Association of Computational Linguistics (ACL)*. 552–559.

[37] Hongjian Wang, Zhenhui Li, and Wang-Chien Lee. 2014. PGT: Measuring mobility relationship using personal, global and temporal factors. In *Proc. 14th IEEE International Conference on Data Mining (ICDM)*. IEEE, 570–579.

[38] Mao Ye, Xingjie Liu, and Wang-Chien Lee. 2012. Exploring social influence for recommendation: a generative model approach. In *Proc. 35th ACM SIGIR conference on Research and Development in Information Retrieval (SIGIR)*. ACM, 671–680.

[39] Mao Ye, Dong Shou, Wang-Chien Lee, Peifeng Yin, and Krzysztof Janowicz. 2011. On the semantic annotation of places in location-based social networks. In *Proc. 17th ACM Conference on Knowledge Discovery and Data Mining (KDD)*. ACM, 520–528.

[40] Jing Yuan, Yu Zheng, and Xing Xie. 2012. Discovering regions of different functions in a city using human mobility and POIs. In *Proc. 18th ACM Conference on Knowledge Discovery and Data Mining (KDD)*. ACM, 186–194.

[41] Yang Zhang and Jun Pang. 2015. Distance and friendship: A distance-based model for link prediction in social networks. In *Proc. 17th Asia-Pacific Web Conference (APWeb)*. Springer, 55–66.

[42] Vincent W. Zheng, Yu Zheng, Xing Xie, and Qiang Yang. 2010. Collaborative location and activity recommendations with GPS history data. In *Proc. 19th International Conference on World Wide Web (WWW)*. ACM, 1029–1038.

[43] Yu Zheng, Licia Capra, Ouri Wolfson, and Hai Yang. 2014. Urban computing: concepts, methodologies, and applications. *ACM Transactions on Intelligent Systems and Technology* 5, 3 (2014), 1–55.

Leveraging Followee List Memberships for Inferring User Interests for Passive Users on Twitter

Guangyuan Piao
Insight Centre for Data Analytics
National University of Ireland, Galway
IDA Business Park
Galway, Ireland
guangyuan.piao@insight-centre.org

John G. Breslin
Insight Centre for Data Analytics
National University of Ireland, Galway
IDA Business Park
Galway, Ireland
john.breslin@nuigalway.ie

ABSTRACT

User modeling for inferring user interests from Online Social Networks (OSNs) such as Twitter has received great attention in the user modeling community with the growing popularity of OSNs. The focus of previous works has been on analyzing user-generated content such as tweets to infer user interests. Therefore, these previous studies were limited to *active users* who have been actively generating content. On the other hand, with the percentage of passive use of OSNs on the rise, some researchers investigated different types of information about followees (i.e., people that a user is following) such as *tweets*, *usernames*, and *biographies* to infer user interests for *passive users* who use OSNs for consuming information from followees but who do not produce any content. Although different types of information about followees have been exploited, *list memberships* (a topical list which other Twitter users can freely add a user into) of followees have not yet been investigated extensively for inferring user interests.

In this paper, we investigate *list memberships* of followees, to infer interest profiles for passive users. To this end, we propose user modeling strategies with two different weighting schemes as well as a refined interest propagation strategy based on previous work. In addition, we investigate whether the information from *biographies* and *list memberships* of followees can complement each other, and thus improve the quality of inferred interest profiles for passive users. Results show that leveraging *list memberships* of followees is useful for inferring user interests when the number of followees is relatively small compared to using *biographies* of followees. In addition, we found that combining the two different types of information (*list memberships* and *biographies*) of followees can improve the quality of user interest profiles significantly compared to a state-of-art method in the context of link recommendations on Twitter.

CCS CONCEPTS

•**Information systems → Personalization; Social recommendation;**

HT'17, July 4-7, 2017, Prague, Czech Republic.
© 2017 ACM. 978-1-4503-4708-2/17/07…$15.00
DOI: http://dx.doi.org/10.1145/3078714.3078730

KEYWORDS

User modeling; Personalization; Twitter; Passive users;

1 INTRODUCTION

With the rapid growth of Online Social Networks (OSNs), people can now consume rich, diverse information that previously was not available. According to a survey, one in three Web users seeks medical information using OSNs, and over 50 percent of users consume news in OSNs [27]. On the other hand, the huge volume of user-generated content causes an information overload problem for users consuming relevant information that they might be interested in. It has been reported that users follow 80 people on average on Twitter[1][26], which results in hundreds or even thousands of tweets posted to each user every day. In this regard, it is important to infer user interest profiles based on user activities in OSNs such as Twitter to support personalized recommendations for content. Researchers have focused on *active users* who actively generate content on Twitter, and addressed the problem by exploiting user-generated content such as tweets to build user interest profiles. However, there is also an increasing number of *passive users* in OSNs[2]. For example, 44% of Twitter users have never sent a tweet according to a research done by Twopcharts[3]. Therefore, it is important to infer user interest profiles for those *passive users* who are only consuming information on Twitter and not generating any content. To this end, different types of information such as *tweets*, *usernames*, and *biographies* of followees have been exploited to infer user interest profiles for *passive users* on Twitter. **Biographies (*bios*)** on Twitter are *self-descriptions* of users, and it has been shown that exploiting *bios* of followees can provide improved user interest profiles of passive users compared to exploiting usernames or tweets of followees in a recent study [25]. For example, we can assume a user might be interested in "*Pokémon Go*" if the user is following another user who describes himself/herself as a "*Pokémon Go player*" in his/her biography on Twitter. In this paper, we investigate another type of information - **list memberships** of followees to infer user interests for passive users. *List memberships* for a user on Twitter denote a topical list which the user has been added into by the list owners. Figure 1 shows an example of some *list memberships* that a Twitter user *@alice* has been added to by other users on Twitter. Different from *bios* (*self-descriptions*), *list memberships* can be seen as *others-descriptions* about *@alice*, which

---

[1]https://twitter.com/
[2]http://www.corporate-eye.com/main/facebooks-growing-problem-passive-users/
[3]http://guardianlv.com/2014/04/twitter-users-are-not-tweeting/

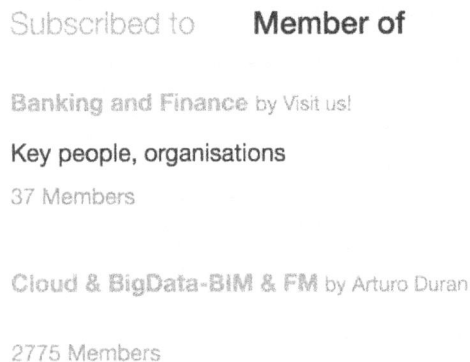

Figure 1: An example of list memberships for a Twitter user.

provide some third-party indications about what kind of topics @alice has been tweeting about on Twitter.

In this paper, we first propose a user modeling strategy leveraging *list memberships* of followees. In addition, we also explore whether the two different views (*self-descriptions* and *others-descriptions*) of followees can complement each other to improve the quality of inferred user interest profiles for *passive users* in the context of a link recommender system on Twitter. The contributions of this work are summarized as follows.

- We investigate whether *list memberships* of followees can provide sufficient and qualitative information for inferring user interests for *passive users* by applying two different weighting schemes and a refined interest propagation strategy.
- We combine the two different views (*self-descriptions* and *others-descriptions*) of followees to infer user interest profiles for *passive users* to study the synergetic effect of combining the two views.
- We evaluate our user modeling strategies for *passive users* in the context of link recommendations on Twitter compared to a state-of-art approach.

The organization of the rest of the paper is as follows. In Section 2, we give some related work. Section 3 describes our user modeling strategy which leverages the list memberships of users' followees to infer user interest profiles. In section 4, we present the experimental setup for our study. The results of our experiment are presented in Sections 5 and 6. Finally, Section 7 concludes the paper with some future work.

2   RELATED WORK

The first and fundamental step for user modeling is the representation of user interests. In order to represent user interest profiles, various approaches have been proposed in the literature [2, 3, 11, 12, 15, 18–20]. For example, Mislove et al. [18] proposed using *Bag of Words*, and Harvey et al. [12] proposed using a *Topic Modeling* approach to represent user interest profiles. Some previous studies also explored list memberships to build word-based user profiles. Kim et al. [15] explored the tweets published by the

users in the same list to model the characteristics of the target user. Hannon et al. [11] exploited human-annotated tags of list memberships from third-party services such as Listorious to construct user interest profiles. However, these approaches focused on words, and the semantic information and relationships among words cannot be incorporated. Furthermore, the *Topic Modeling* approach based on the assumption that a single document contains rich information, which is not the case on Twitter. Some previous studies have shown that *Topic Modeling* approaches did not work well on Twitter [14, 17, 29].

To overcome the limitation of *word-based* approaches, researchers proposed using *Bag of Concepts* to represent user interest profiles. Here, a concept denotes an entity such as Steve_Jobs or a corresponding category of the entity such as Apple_Inc._executives based on the background knowledge from a knowledge base such as DBpedia [16]. For example, Abel et al. [2] compared three different representations of user interest profiles, and found that *entity-based* user profiles outperform *hashtag-* and *topic-based* user profiles on Twitter in the context of news recommendations. Some previous studies further exploited background knowledge linked to the concepts to enrich user interest profiles [14, 20, 21] with the *Bag of Concepts* approach e.g., using Wikipedia[4] entities or categories for representing user interests. For instance, Siehndel et al. [28] proposed constructing user interest profiles leveraging 23 top-level Wikipedia categories, which linked from the extracted entities from the tweets of a target user. Similarly, Kapanipathi et al. [14] first extracted Wikipedia entities from the tweets of a target user, and set those entities as activated nodes. Afterwards, they applied various spreading activation functions by exploiting refined Wikipedia categories to build *category-based* user interest profiles. Different from using Wikipedia categories, DBpedia has been used for propagating user interest profiles in some recent studies [20, 22] as it provides rich background knowledge about entities (e.g., related entities via different properties in addition to the categories of them). For example, Piao et al. [22] showed that considering different structures of background knowledge, i.e., categories and related entities, can improve the quality of user modeling on Twitter compared to exploiting categories only.

On top of a fixed representation of user interests, there are also some works studying temporal dynamics of user interests on Twitter based on the hypothesis that the interests of users change over time [1, 2, 5, 8, 20, 22, 23], which is not the focus on our work. In this study, we also use the *Bag of Concepts* approach for representing user interests, and use DBpedia as our background knowledge base. Although those previous works presented interesting results on user modeling in OSNs, most of them focused on *active users* who actively post tweets, to infer user interest profiles by analyzing users' tweets. Our work differs in that we focus on *passive users* who do not generate content on Twitter, but keep following other users to receive information they might be interested in.

Some authors from previous studies [6, 7, 25, 28] also pointed out the needs to investigating other types of information beyond tweets for inferring user interest profiles. This line of work focuses on inferring interests for *passive users* who do not generate content (tweets), but mostly consume content from their followees. For example,

---

[4]http://www.wikipedia.org

Faralli et al. [10] and Besel et al. [6] proposed linking followees' accounts to Wikipedia entities based on followees' full names, and then propagate user interests leveraging Wikipedia categories. For instance, the entity `Cristiano_Ronaldo` would be found as a user's interest if the user was following `Cristiano_Ronaldo` on Twitter. Afterwards, the corresponding Wikipedia categories of the entity were leveraged to construct *category-based* user interest profiles by applying different propagation strategies. Faralli et al. [10] pointed out that the user interest profiles built by leveraging followee profiles are more stable and scalable compared to analyzing the tweets of followees. However, they also pointed out that linking Twitter accounts to Wikipedia entities is limited to a small percentage of famous users such as celebrities (e.g., less than 13% of followees can be linked to Wikipedia entities in [10]). To overcome this, the authors from [25] studied whether the *biographies* of followees can be exploited to provide useful information for user modeling for *passive users*. To this end, they fetched all of the followees of a target user first and then extracted DBpedia entities from the biographies of those followees. For example, the entity `Pokémon_GO` can be extracted based on a followee's bio *"Pokémon Go player"*. Afterwards, the extracted entities were further used for propagating user interests based on background knowledge from DBpedia by exploiting their related entities as well as corresponding categories. The results from [25] showed that exploiting biographies of followees can provide quantitative and qualitative information for inferring user interests for passive users compared to the approach linking followees' accounts to Wikipedia entities. In this regard, we use this approach [25] as our baseline for evaluating our proposed user modeling strategies.

3 USER MODELING LEVERAGING LIST MEMBERSHIPS OF FOLLOWEES

In the same way as previous studies, user interest profiles in this work are represented using DBpedia concepts and corresponding weights. We use the same definition from [22] as follows.

Definition 3.1. The interest profile of a user $u \in U$ is a set of weighted DBpedia concepts. The weight with respect to u for a concept $c \in C$ is computed by a weighting scheme $w(u, c)$.

$$P_u = \left\{ \left(c, w(u, c) \right) \mid c \in C \right\} \tag{1}$$

Here, C and U denote the set of concepts in DBpedia and set of users respectively. Concepts can be either *entities* or *categories* in DBpedia.

The general process of building user interest profiles based on *list memberships* of followees is shown in Figure 2. Given a Twitter user, we go through five main steps to construct an interest profile for the user.

(1) Fetch all of the user's followees.
(2) Fetch all *list memberships* of followees.
(3) Extract DBpedia entities from the *list memberships*.
(4) Construct *primary interests* based on the extracted entities by applying a weighting scheme.
(5) Apply an interest propagation strategy to *primary interests*.

First, for a given user u, the followees of u and their *list memberships* can be fetched (steps 1 and 2) using the Twitter API[5]. Afterwards, DBpedia entities are extracted using the TAG.ME API[6] based on the full names of *list memberships*. For example, entities such as `Middle_East` and `Celebrity` can be extracted from *list memberships* with full names *"Middle East"* and *"Celebs"*. Afterwards, these extracted entities are used to construct u's **primary interests**. Although the Aylien API[7] has been used for extracting entities for tweets and news articles in the literature [23, 25], we found the Aylien API is not the optimal choice for extracting entities from the names of *list memberships* due to the short nature of those names. Therefore, we use the TAG.ME API instead for extracting entities from *list memberships*.

3.1 Constructing Primary Interests

In this subsection, we introduce two different weighting schemes for weighting extracted entities in order to construct a user's *primary interests*.

- **Weighting Scheme 1 (WS1).** The intuitive way of weighting extracted entities from *list memberships* of followees is based on the the number of occurrences of these entities. However, directly summing the number of occurrences might be biased by followees who have a great number of *list memberships*. In this regard, we use a normalized sum of occurrences of entities from followees as a weighting scheme for constructing the *primary interests* of a target user u. For example, an interest profile of a followee $f \in F_u$ can be normalized as follows.

$$P_f = \left\{ \left(c, w(f, c) \right) \mid c \in C \right\} \tag{2}$$

where $\sum_{c_i \in C} w(f, c_i) = 1$, and F_u denotes all the followees of a user u. Finally, the weight of an entity c_j with respect to u is measured as below:

$$w(u, c_j) = \sum_{f \in F_u} w(f, c_j). \tag{3}$$

- **Weighting Scheme 2 (WS2).** For a target user u, Chen et al. [9] aggregated the weight of each word from followees' tweets by excluding the words mentioned only in a single followee. Similarly, we aggregate the weight of each entity from followees' *list memberships* by excluding entities extracted only in a single followee. The weight of each entity in u's profile $w(u, c_j)$ is calculated as $w(u, c_j) = $ *the number of followees who have c_j in their list memberships*. Note that this weighting scheme does not care about the number of occurrences of an entity in a single followee's *list memberships*, but only counts the number of followees who have the entity in their profile. For example, the weight of an entity c_j equals 5 if there are five followees of u having the entity in their *list memberships*.

---

[5]https://dev.twitter.com/
[6]https://tagme.d4science.org/tagme/
[7]http://aylien.com/text-api

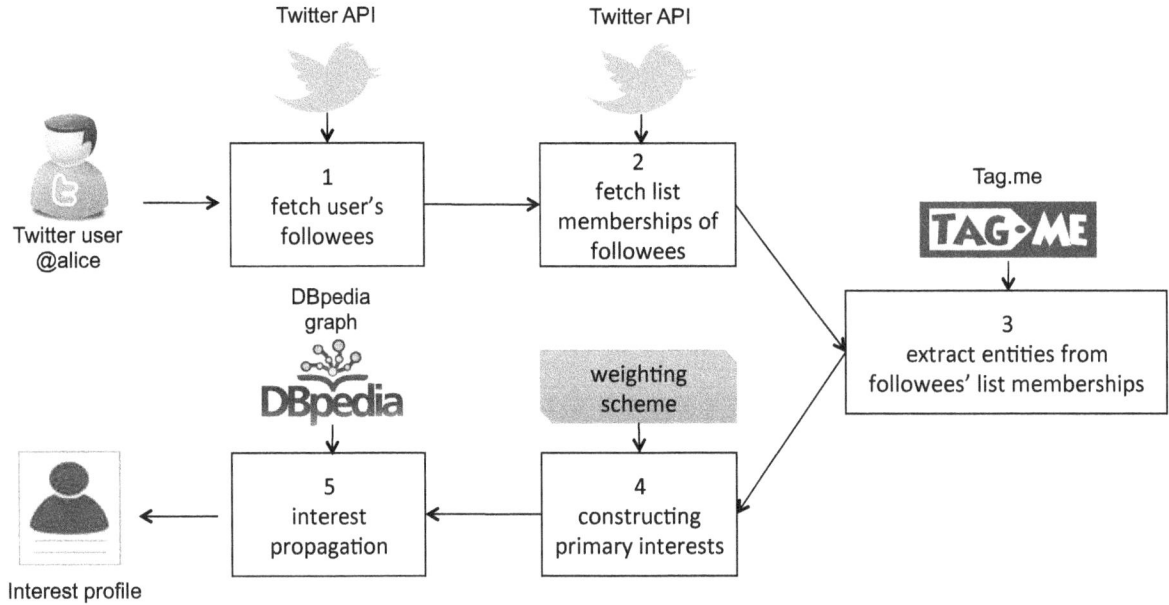

Figure 2: Overview of user modeling strategy based on followees' list memberships.

3.2 Interest Propagation Strategy

Based on the *primary interests* constructed in previous steps, background knowledge from DBpedia can be exploited to propagate user interests. For instance, we can assume that a user might be interested in Apple_Inc. if the user is interested in Steve_Jobs based on the corresponding categories of the entity Steve_Jobs from DBpedia.

Some *discounting strategies* can be used to discount the weights of propagated user interests based on the *primary interests* [14, 22]. We adopt the propagation method from [22] as the method showed overall better performance compared to the approach applying a spreading activation function from [14] in the previous study [25]. The proposed method [22] discounts a propagated category using the log scale of the numbers of sub-pages (SP) and sub-categories (SC, see Algorithm 4) of the category. The intuition behind this is that general categories, which have many sub-pages and sub-categories, should be discounted heavily.

$$CategoryDiscount = \frac{1}{\alpha} \times \frac{1}{\log(SP)} \times \frac{1}{\log(SC)} \qquad (4)$$

Also, a propagated entity via a property is discounted based on the log scale of the number of occurrences of the property in the DBpedia graph (P, see Algorithm 5), i.e., if the property appears frequently in the graph, the entities extended through this property should be discounted heavily. In addition, α is a decay factor for the propagation from directly extracted entities to related categories or entities ($\alpha = 2$ as in the study [22]).

$$PropertyDiscount = \frac{1}{\alpha} \times \frac{1}{\log(P)} \qquad (5)$$

Extracting subset of DBpedia categories. We consider leveraging all DBpedia categories of entities might be noisy since many Wikipedia categories are created for Wikipedia administration. Similar to the approach from [14], we extract a subset of all DBpedia categories which we use for our interest propagation. The subset consists of all inferred sub-categories of dbc[8]:Main_topic_classifications. However, different to [14] which requires the Wikipedia dump for extracting a hierarchical category graph, we connect directly to DBpedia to extract the subset of categories by using Algorithm 1. Therefore, it can be directly extracted via the DBpedia SPARQL Endpoint[9], and can be reproduced easily. In addition, we do not remove all administration categories (inferred sub-categories of dbc:Wikipedia_administration) as in [14] since we found that many useful categories are in the inferred sub-categories of the administration category as well as the main topic classification. This process results in 957,963 categories for our consideration while propagating user interests.

Merging categories and entities with same title. In DBpedia, many entities and categories have same title (name), e.g., dbr[10]:Apple_Inc. and dbc:Apple_Inc.. Considering these concepts separately as entities and categories might decrease the quality of propagated user interests or unnecessarily increase the size of user interest profiles. In this regard, we do not treat entities and categories differently in our propagation strategy, i.e, if there is a category which has same name with an entity that has been propagated, the category and entity will be merged into a single concept, and the weights will be accumulated. For example, in Figure 3(a), the propagated category dbc:Apple_Inc. has its own weight based

---

[8]The prefix dbc denotes http://dbpedia.org/resource/Category:
[9]http://dbpedia.org/sparql
[10]The prefix dbr denotes http://dbpedia.org/resource/

Algorithm 1 GetSubsetOfDBpediaCategories

1: **procedure** GETSUBSETOFDBPEDIACATEGORIES(topCategory)
2:     category_dictionary = {topCategory:0}   ▷ 0 denotes unprocessed
3:     **while** $size$(unprocessed categories in category_dictionary) > 0 **do**
4:         **for** category in unprocessed categories **do**
5:             **if** category $not\ in$ category_dictionary **then**
6:                 add category:0 to category_dictionary
7:     **return** keys of category_dictionary ▷ return all inferred sub-categories

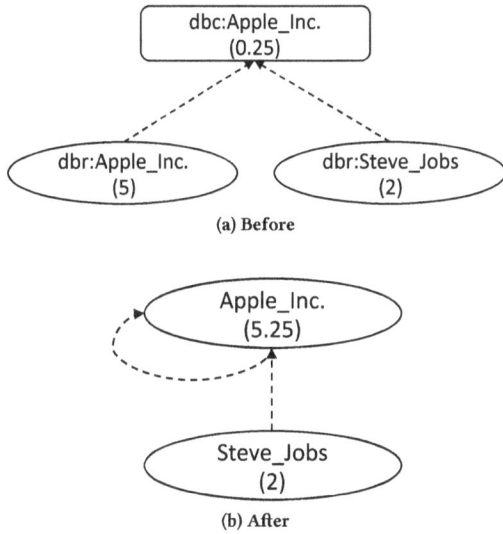

(a) Before

(b) After

Figure 3: Before and after merging categories and entities with the same title.

on two entities dbr:Apple_Inc. and dbr:Steve_Jobs by considering categories and entities separately. On the other hand, Figure 3(b) shows that Apple_Inc. is considered as a single concept and its weight has been accumulated. In Section 5.2, we will show how these trimmed categories using Algorithm 1, and the strategy merging categories and entities with same title, positively affect the quality of inferred user interest profiles.

Finally, we apply Inverse Document Frequency (IDF) on the user interest profile P_u, and then normalize P_u in order to make the sum of all concept weights equal to 1: $\sum_{c_i \in C} w(u, c_i) = 1$.

4 EXPERIMENTAL SETUP

In this section, we describe the evaluation methodology for evaluating constructed user interest profiles (Section 4.1), and the dataset used in our experiment (Section 4.2).

4.1 Evaluation Methodology

In the literature, user interest profiles have been evaluated in terms of recommendation performance for content-based recommendation systems by inputting different user interest profiles generated by different user modeling strategies [1, 2, 25, 31, 32]. In the same

way, we evaluate different user interest profiles constructed based on different types of information (e.g, *bios* and *list memberships*) of followees in terms of a link (URL) recommendation system on Twitter. To this end, for a target user u, we construct the ground truth as the links shared via u's tweets within the last two weeks. Afterwards, as our focus here is exploring different types of information of followees for inferring user interest profiles, we blind out all of u's tweets, and use only different types information from followees of u to build user interest profiles for u.

A link (URL) profile is constructed with the same representation model (i.e., Bag of Concepts) based on its content. For instance, DBpedia entities can be extracted based on the content of a link l, and the propagation strategy mentioned in Section 3.2 is then applied to those entities to build the link profile P_l. As our focus is not optimizing recommendation quality, we compare the quality of different user interest profiles with a lightweight recommendation algorithm when inputting different types of user interest profiles, similar to the one used in the previous studies [1, 2, 25].

Recommendation Algorithm: given a user interest profile P_u and a set of candidate links $N = \{P_{l1}, ..., P_{ln}\}$, which are represented via profiles using the same vector representation, the recommendation algorithm ranks the candidate links according to their *cosine similarity* to P_u.

Therefore, the link recommender system provides the top-N recommendations based on the cosine similarity scores between user and link profiles. Four evaluation metrics, namely *MRR* (Mean Reciprocal Rank), the success rate at rank N, recall at rank N, and precision at rank N were used for evaluating the recommendation performance in the same way as previous studies [2, 4, 20, 22, 24]. We focus on $N = 10$ as our recommender system provides 10 link recommendations.

- **MRR** The *MRR* (Mean Reciprocal Rank) indicates at which rank the first link *relevant* to the user occurs (denoted by $rank_k$) on average.

$$MRR = \frac{1}{|U|} \sum_{k=1}^{|U|} \frac{1}{rank_k} \quad (6)$$

- **S@N** The Success at rank N (S@N) stands for the mean probability that a relevant link occurs within the top-N ranked.

$$S@N = \begin{cases} 1, & if\ a\ relevant\ link\ in \\ & retrieved\ links\ at\ N \\ 0, & otherwise \end{cases} \quad (7)$$

- **R@N** The Recall at rank N (R@N) represents the mean probability that *relevant* links are successfully retrieved within the top-N recommendations.

$$R@N = \frac{|\{relevant\ links\}| \cap |\{retrieved\ links\ at\ N\}|}{|\{relevant\ links\}|} \quad (8)$$

Table 1: Dataset statistics

# of passive users	avg. # of considered followees	avg. # of list memberships of followees
439	170	173

- **P@N** The Precision at rank N (P@N) represents the mean probability that retrieved links within the top-N recommendations are *relevant* to the user.

$$P@N = \frac{|\{relevant\ links\}| \cap |\{retrieved\ links\ at\ N\}|}{|\{retrieved\ links\}|} \quad (9)$$

We set the significance level of alpha as 5% for all statistical tests, and used the *bootstrapped paired t-test*[11] to test the significance.

4.2 Dataset

The Twitter dataset used in this study is from [21], which consists of 480 randomly chosen users on Twitter with their tweets and followees. We selected 439 users who have topical links (URLs which have at least four entities based on their content) in their tweets from last two weeks. All of the links shared by each user in the last two weeks of their timelines were used to build the set of candidate links for recommendations. On average, each user has 2,771 followees. As the rate limits of the Twitter API for retrieving followees and *list memberships* are 15 and 75 for a 15-minute window, we only consider up to 200 followees for each user, and crawled all *list memberships* of those followees for this study. The main details of our dataset are presented in Table 1. Finally, the dataset corresponds to 74,488 followees for 439 users with 170 followees on average, and the candidate set of links consists of 15,053 distinct links.

5 COMPARISON BETWEEN USING LIST MEMBERSHIPS AND BIOGRAPHIES OF FOLLOWEES FOR INFERRING USER INTERESTS

We use the recent approach which exploits *bios* of followees for inferring user interests [25] as a baseline to evaluate our user modeling strategies since the approach performs better than other approaches such as linking followee accounts to Wikipedia/DBpedia entities or leveraging the tweets of followees for inferring user interests.

5.1 Quantitative analysis

We first look at how many list memberships a followee has been added into. The Cumulative Distribution Function (CDF) of the number of *list memberships* for 74,488 followees is shown in Figure 4. The figure shows that 90% of followees have less than 492

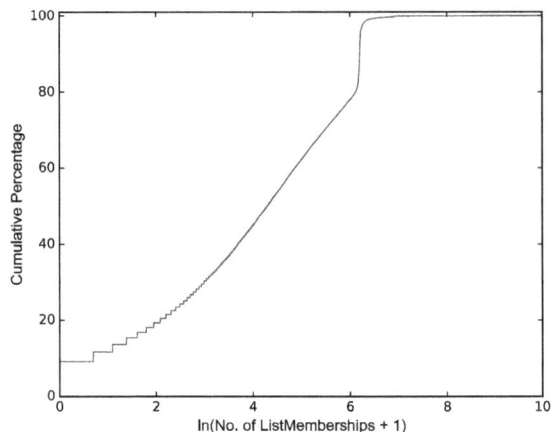

Figure 4: Cumulative distribution of the number of list memberships of followees in the dataset.

(ln(492+1)=6.2) *list memberships*. 6,871 (9.2%) out of 74,488 followees have no *list membership*, i.e., over 90% of followees have at least one *list membership*. On average, each followee belongs to 173 *list memberships*, which might be a useful information source of "descriptions" about a followee compared to the bio provided by him/her. For example, 3,047 entities can be extracted from the *list memberships* of followees on average when we consider up to 50 followees for each target user in our dataset. On the other hand, 23 entities can be extracted from the *bios* of followees on average. Given this quantified information from *list memberships* of followees, we move on to investigate whether it can be leveraged for building *qualified* user interest profiles in the context of link recommendations.

5.2 Qualitative analysis

Table 2 shows the link recommendation performance using three different user modeling strategies in terms of MRR, R@10, P@10, and S@10 respectively.

Comparison between the baseline and our approach. As we can see from the table, the user modeling strategy which exploits *list memberships* of followees using weighting scheme 1 ($UM(f\_listmemberships, WS1)$) performs better than $UM(f\_listmemberships, WS2)$ and the baseline method $UM(f\_bios)$. For example, when a passive user has less than 50 users, a significant improvement of $UM(f\_listmemberships, WS1)$ over $UM(f\_bios)$ in MRR (+17%, $p < 0.01$), P@10 (+12%, $p < 0.05$), and S@10 (+14%, $p < 0.05$) can be noticed. However, we can also observe that with the number of followees of a user increasing, the difference between using $UM(f\_listmemberships, WS1)$ and $UM(f\_bios)$ becomes smaller. This shows that exploiting *list memberships* of followees can help with inferring user interest profiles in the case of a user having a small number of followees, which would be typical of "new" passive users.

Comparison between two weighting schemes in our approach. Table 2 also shows that the weighting scheme WS1 always

Table 2: Recommendation performance of different user modeling strategies in terms of four different evaluation metrics and numbers of followees. The best performing user modeling strategy is in bold. ** denotes $p < 0.01$, and * denotes $p < 0.05$.

# of followees	Evaluation metric	UM(f_bios) [baseline]	UM(f_list memberships, WS1)	UM(f_list memberships, WS2)
50	MRR	0.2243	**0.2622** **	0.2584 *
	R@10	0.0473	**0.0532**	0.0471
	P@10	0.1226	**0.1371** *	0.1223
	S@10	0.3690	**0.4191** *	0.4169 *
100	MRR	0.258	**0.2792**	0.2613
	R@10	0.0532	**0.0584**	0.0550
	P@10	0.1428	**0.1481**	0.1337
	S@10	0.4146	**0.4579** *	0.4442
150	MRR	0.2871	**0.2995**	0.2643
	R@10	0.0579	**0.0635**	0.0609
	P@10	**0.1535**	0.1508	0.1358
	S@10	0.4579	**0.4852**	0.4738
200	MRR	0.2952	**0.3065**	0.2638
	R@10	0.0627	**0.0653**	0.0575
	P@10	**0.1615**	0.1526	0.1353
	S@10	0.4715	**0.4920**	0.4784

outperforms WS2 in terms of four different evaluation metrics and different numbers of followees. The result indicates that WS1, which applies the normalized sum of occurrences of an entity from *list memberships* of followees, reflects the importance of the entity to passive users better when compared to the second weighting scheme which uses the number of followees having the entity in their *list memberships* (WS2).

Effects of DBpedia refinement. In Section 3.2, we introduced an interest propagation strategy by refining DBpedia categories and entities. Figure 5 shows the numbers of entities with/without refinement in terms of different numbers of followees. We found that the refinement of trimming DBpedia categories as well as merging categories and entities with the same name can compress the size of user interest profiles by around 9% compared to the user modeling strategy without the refinement, while remaining at a similar performance level in the context of link recommendations.

Another observation we noticed is that the recommendation results using *biographies* and *list memberships* might complement each other. For different users, we found that using *biographies* provides better performance while using *list memberships* does not and vice versa. To test the hypothesis whether combining two different views about followees can improve the quality of user modeling or not, we use an approach used in the literature in the next section.

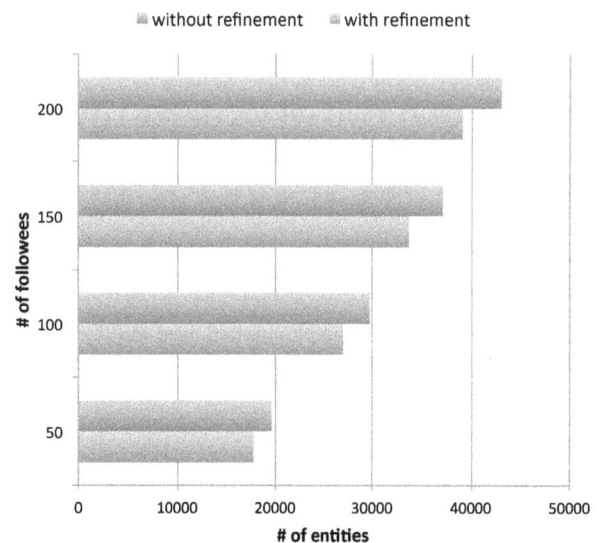

Figure 5: Number of entities in terms of different number of followees of a user using WS1 with/without refinement.

Table 3: Recommendation performance of combining two views (from bios and list memberships) of followees compared to the baseline in terms of four different evaluation metrics and numbers of followees. The best performing user modeling strategy is in bold. ** denotes $p < 0.01$, and * denotes $p < 0.05$.

# of followees	Evaluation metric	UM(f_bios) [baseline]	Combined
50	MRR	0.2243	**0.2777 **
	R@10	0.0473	**0.0475**
	P@10	0.1226	**0.1396 **
	S@10	0.3690	**0.4305 **
100	MRR	0.258	**0.2946 **
	R@10	0.0532	**0.0584 ***
	P@10	0.1428	**0.1615 **
	S@10	0.4146	**0.4784 **
150	MRR	0.2871	**0.3303 **
	R@10	0.0579	**0.0639 ***
	P@10	0.1535	**0.1745 **
	S@10	0.4579	**0.5194 **
200	MRR	0.2952	**0.3397 **
	R@10	0.0627	**0.0654**
	P@10	0.1615	**0.1779 **
	S@10	0.4715	**0.5125 ***

6 COMBINING TWO VIEWS OF FOLLOWEES

As we mentioned in Section 1, the *bio* of a followee f can be seen as a *self-description* of himself / herself, while the *list memberships* of f can be seen as *others-descriptions* about f. In this section, we investigate whether combining these two different views of followees can complement each other in terms of the recommendation performance.

To this end, we apply a simple method used in [30], which is based on the principle of *polyrepresentation* [13]. The approach [30] combined different views of a user for predicting user interests in the context of a search engine. The final rank of an item is determined by the average rank position of each rank based on $UM(f\_bios)$ and $UM(f\_listmemberships, WS1)$. For example, if an item i is ranked in x-th and y-th position based on $UM(f\_bios)$ and $UM(f\_listmemberships, WS1)$, the combined score for the item i is $1/(x + y)$. The higher the value is, the higher the item will be ranked. We also evaluated an alternative approach for combining the two views which puts them into a single vector for building user interest profiles. However, the simple approach used in [30]

provides better performance than the alternative. Therefore, we report the results based on [30] in this section.

The recommendation performance of user modeling strategy combining two different views (*self-descriptions* and *others-descriptions*) of followees compared to the baseline user modeling strategy using bios (*self-descriptions* only) of followees is displayed in Table 3. As we can see from the table, combining two different views with a simple approach clearly outperforms the baseline method significantly in terms of four different evaluation metrics. Also, while using *list memberships* of followees only has a significant difference compared to the baseline when the number of followees is small (i.e., # of followees = 50, 100, see Table 2), the combined approach has a higher significant difference ($p < 0.01$) compared to the baseline method even when the number of followees becomes larger (i.e., # of followees = 100, 150, 200, see Table 3).

The aforementioned combination of the two views considers the importance of each view equally [30]. To better understand which view of followees has higher importance in different situations, we change the combined score as $1/(\beta \times x + (1 - \beta) \times y)$, where β controls the importance of the first view, i.e., *bios* (*self-descriptions*) of followees. As one might expect, $\beta = 0$ denotes that we only consider *list memberships* (*other-descriptions*) of followees, while $\beta = 1$ denotes that we only consider *bios*(*self-descriptions*) of followees. $\beta = 0.5$ denotes that we treat two different views of followees equally as we already discussed earlier in this section.

Figure 6 shows the link recommendation performance in terms of four evaluation metrics by setting β between 0 and 1 in steps of 0.1. As depicted in Figure 6, the recommendation performance is better with smaller values of β for combining the two different views (i.e., *self-descriptions* and *others-descriptions*) of followees for inferring user interest profiles in terms of R@10, P@10 and S@10. The best performance is achieved with $\beta = 0.1$, and the performance starts decreasing with increasing β. This denotes *others-descriptions* of followees plays more important role for combining the two views. Similar results can be observed in terms of MRR with a small number of followees, i.e., # of followees = 50 or 100. However, as we can see from Figure 6 (a) that, with a big number of followees, i.e., # of followees = 150 or 200, the difference with different β values are tending towards being stable in terms of MRR.

Thus we conclude that *bios* (*self-descriptions*) and *list memberships* (*others-descriptions*) can complement each other and improve the quality of user modeling in terms of link recommendations. Also, *list memberships* plays a more important role for combining the two different views especially in the case of a small number of followees being discovering available.

7 CONCLUSIONS

In this paper, we were interested in whether leveraging *list memberships* of followees can provide quantitative and qualitative information for inferring user interests for *passive users*, which has not been studied before. In addition, we further investigated whether the two different views, *biographies* (*self-descriptions*) and *list memberships* (*others-descriptions*) of followees, can complement each other to improve the quality of inferred user interest profiles. A series of offline experiments were performed to evaluate the inferred user interest profiles built by different user modeling strategies in terms

(a) MRR

(b) R@10

(c) P@10

(d) S@10

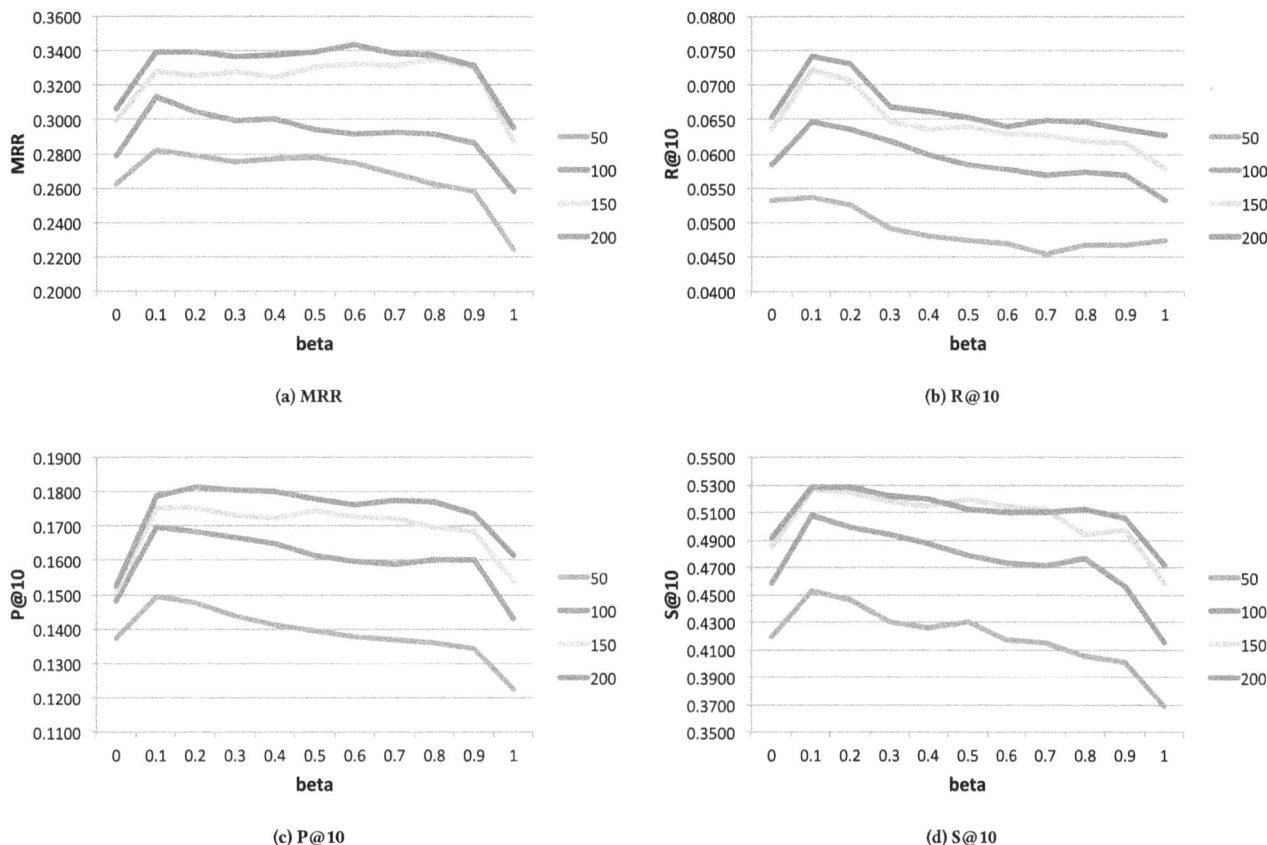

Figure 6: The quality of user modeling with different β values for combining two different views (*self-descriptions* and *others-descriptions*) of followees in terms of link recommendations on Twitter.

of a link (URL) recommender system on Twitter using four different evaluation metrics. The study results indicate that: (1) leveraging *list memberships* of followees performs better than exploiting *biographies* especially in the case of a user having a small number of followees, (2) combining the two different views of followees can improve the quality of user modeling significantly compared to the baseline method which exploits *biographies* of followees only, and the *list memberships* of followees play a more important role in the combination. As a further step, we plan to study whether combining other views of followees, such as their generated content, can also have a synergetic effect on user modeling to improve the inferred user interest profiles for passive users.

8 ACKNOWLEDGMENTS

This publication has emanated from research conducted with the financial support of Science Foundation Ireland (SFI) under Grant Number SFI/12/RC/2289 (Insight Centre for Data Analytics).

REFERENCES

[1] Fabian Abel, Qi Gao, Geert-Jan Houben, and Ke Tao. 2011. Analyzing Temporal Dynamics in Twitter Profiles for Personalized Recommendations in the Social Web. In *Proceedings of the 3rd International Web Science Conference*. ACM, 2.
[2] Fabian Abel, Qi Gao, Geert-Jan Houben, and Ke Tao. 2011. Analyzing User Modeling on Twitter for Personalized News Recommendations. In *User Modeling,*
Adaption and Personalization. Springer, 1–12.
[3] Fabian Abel, Qi Gao, Geert-Jan Houben, and Ke Tao. 2011. Semantic Enrichment of Twitter Posts for User Profile Construction on the Social Web. In *The Semantic Web: Research and Applications*. Springer, 375–389.
[4] Fabian Abel, Claudia Hauff, Geert-Jan Houben, and Ke Tao. 2012. Leveraging User Modeling on the Social Web with Linked Data. In *Web Engineering SE - 31*. Springer, 378–385.
[5] Amr Ahmed, Yucheng Low, Mohamed Aly, Vanja Josifovski, and Alexander J Smola. 2011. Scalable distributed inference of dynamic user interests for behavioral targeting. In *Proceedings of the 17th International Conference on Knowledge Discovery and Data Mining*. ACM, 114–122.
[6] Christoph Besel, Jörg Schlötterer, and Michael Granitzer. 2016. Inferring Semantic Interest Profiles from Twitter Followees: Does Twitter Know Better Than Your Friends?. In *Proceedings of the 31st Annual ACM Symposium on Applied Computing (SAC '16)*. ACM, New York, NY, USA, 1152–1157. https://doi.org/10.1145/2851613.2851819
[7] Christoph Besel, Jörg Schlötterer, and Michael Granitzer. 2016. On the Quality of Semantic Interest Profiles for Onine Social Network Consumers. *SIGAPP Appl. Comput. Rev.* 16, 3 (nov 2016), 5–14. https://doi.org/10.1145/3015297.3015298
[8] Ceren Budak, Anitha Kannan, Rakesh Agrawal, and Jan Pedersen. 2014. *Inferring User Interests from Microblogs*. Technical Report. Microsoft.
[9] Jilin Chen, Rowan Nairn, Les Nelson, Michael Bernstein, and Ed Chi. 2010. Short and Tweet: Experiments on Recommending Content from Information Streams. In *Proceedings of the SIGCHI Conference on Human Factors in Computing Systems*. ACM, 1185–1194.
[10] Stefano Faralli, Giovanni Stilo, and Paola Velardi. 2015. Recommendation of Microblog Users based on Hierarchical Interest Profiles. *Social Network Analysis and Mining* 5, 1 (2015), 1–23.
[11] John Hannon, Kevin McCarthy, Michael P O'Mahony, and Barry Smyth. 2012. A multi-faceted user model for twitter. In *International Conference on User Modeling,*

Adaptation, and Personalization. Springer, 303–309.

[12] Morgan Harvey, Fabio Crestani, and Mark J Carman. 2013. Building User Profiles from Topic Models for Personalised Search. In *Proceedings of the 22nd ACM international conference on Information & Knowledge Management*. 2309–2314. https://doi.org/10.1145/2505515.2505642

[13] Peter Ingwersen. 1994. Polyrepresentation of information needs and semantic entities elements of a cognitive theory for information retrieval interaction. In *SIGIR'94*. Springer, 101–110.

[14] Pavan Kapanipathi, Prateek Jain, Chitra Venkataramani, and Amit Sheth. 2014. User Interests Identification on Twitter Using a Hierarchical Knowledge Base. In *The Semantic Web: Trends and Challenges*. Springer, 99–113. https://doi.org/10.1007/978-3-319-07443-6_8

[15] Dongwoo Kim, Yohan Jo, Il-Chul Moon, and Alice Oh. 2010. Analysis of twitter lists as a potential source for discovering latent characteristics of users. In *ACM CHI Workshop on Microblogging*. Citeseer, 4.

[16] Jens Lehmann, Robert Isele, Max Jakob, Anja Jentzsch, Dimitris Kontokostas, Pablo N Mendes, Sebastian Hellmann, Mohamed Morsey, Patrick van Kleef, and Sören Auer. 2013. Dbpedia-a Large-scale, Multilingual Knowledge Base Extracted from Wikipedia. *Semantic Web Journal* (2013).

[17] Matthew Michelson and Sofus A Macskassy. 2010. Discovering Users' Topics of Interest on Twitter: A First Look. In *Proceedings of the 4th Workshop on Analytics for Noisy Unstructured Text Data*. ACM, 73–80.

[18] Alan Mislove, Bimal Viswanath, Krishna P Gummadi, and Peter Druschel. 2010. You are Who You Know: Inferring User Profiles in Online Social Networks. In *Proceedings of the third ACM International Conference on Web Search and Data Mining*. ACM, 251–260.

[19] Fedelucio Narducci, Cataldo Musto, Giovanni Semeraro, Pasquale Lops, and Marco Gemmis. 2013. Leveraging Encyclopedic Knowledge for Transparent and Serendipitous User Profiles. In *User Modeling, Adaptation, and Personalization: 21th International Conference*. Springer Berlin Heidelberg, Berlin, Heidelberg, 350–352.

[20] Fabrizio Orlandi, John Breslin, and Alexandre Passant. 2012. Aggregated, Interoperable and Multi-domain User Profiles for the Social Web. In *Proceedings of the 8th International Conference on Semantic Systems*. ACM, 41–48. https://doi.org/10.1145/2362499.2362506

[21] Guangyuan Piao and John G. Breslin. 2016. Analyzing Aggregated Semantics-enabled User Modeling on Google+ and Twitter for Personalized Link Recommendations. In *User Modeling, Adaptation, and Personalization*. ACM, 105–109.

[22] Guangyuan Piao and John G Breslin. 2016. Exploring Dynamics and Semantics of User Interests for User Modeling on Twitter for Link Recommendations. In

12th International Conference on Semantic Systems. ACM, 81–88.

[23] Guangyuan Piao and John G Breslin. 2016. Interest Representation, Enrichment, Dynamics, and Propagation: A Study of the Synergetic Effect of Different User Modeling Dimensions for Personalized Recommendations on Twitter. In *Knowledge Engineering and Knowledge Management: 20th International Conference*. Springer International Publishing, 496–510.

[24] Guangyuan Piao and John G. Breslin. 2016. User Modeling on Twitter with WordNet Synsets and DBpedia Concepts for Personalized Recommendations. In *The 25th ACM International Conference on Information and Knowledge Management*. ACM, 2057–2060.

[25] Guangyuan Piao and John G. Breslin. 2017. Inferring User Interests for Passive Users on Twitter by Leveraging Followee Biographies. In *39th European Conference on Information Retrieval*. Springer.

[26] Zhonghua Qu and Yang Liu. 2011. Interactive group suggesting for Twitter. In *Proceedings of the 49th Annual Meeting of the Association for Computational Linguistics: Human Language Technologies: short papers-Volume 2*. Association for Computational Linguistics, 519–523.

[27] Amit Sheth and Pavan Kapanipathi. 2016. Semantic Filtering for Social Data. *IEEE Internet Computing* 20, 4 (2016), 74–78.

[28] Patrick Siehndel and Ricardo Kawase. 2012. TwikiMe!: user profiles that make sense. In *Proceedings of the 2012th International Conference on Posters & Demonstrations Track-Volume 914*. CEUR-WS. org, 61–64.

[29] Bharath Sriram, Dave Fuhry, Engin Demir, Hakan Ferhatosmanoglu, and Murat Demirbas. 2010. Short Text Classification in Twitter to Improve Information Filtering. In *Proceedings of the 33rd International ACM SIGIR Conference on Research and Development in Information Retrieval*. ACM, 841–842.

[30] Ryen W White, Peter Bailey, and Liwei Chen. 2009. Predicting User Interests from Contextual Information. In *Proceedings of the 32Nd International ACM SIGIR Conference on Research and Development in Information Retrieval (SIGIR '09)*. ACM, New York, NY, USA, 363–370. https://doi.org/10.1145/1571941.1572005

[31] Fattane Zarrinkalam. 2015. Semantics-Enabled User Interest Mining. In *The Semantic Web. Latest Advances and New Domains SE - 54*, Fabien Gandon, Marta Sabou, Harald Sack, Claudia D'Amato, Philippe Cudré-Mauroux, and Antoine Zimmermann (Eds.). Lecture Notes in Computer Science, Vol. 9088. Springer International Publishing, 817–828. https://doi.org/10.1007/978-3-319-18818-8_54

[32] Fattane Zarrinkalam and Mohsen Kahani. 2015. Semantics-enabled User Interest Detection from Twitter. In *2015 IEEE/WIC/ACM International Conference on Web Intelligence and Intelligent Agent Technology*. 469–476.

Evaluating Navigational RDF Queries over the Web

Jorge Baier, Dietrich Daroch, Juan L. Reutter, Domagoj Vrgoč

Pontifica Universidad Católica de Chile and Center for Semantic Web Research

ABSTRACT

Semantic Web, and its underlying data format RDF, lend themselves naturally to navigational querying due to their graph-like structure. This is particularly evident when considering RDF data on the Web, where various separately published datasets reference each other and form a giant graph known as the Web of Linked Data. And while navigational queries over singular RDF datasets are supported through SPARQL property paths, not much is known about evaluating them over Linked Data. In this paper we propose a method for evaluating property path queries over the Web based on the classical AI search algorithm A*, show its optimality in the open world setting of the Web, and test it using real world queries which access a variety of RDF datasets available online and that are not necessarily known in advance.

KEYWORDS

RDF; Linked Data; property paths; evaluation algorithms

1 INTRODUCTION

Background. The Resource Description Framework (RDF) is the World Wide Web consortium (W3C) standard for representing Semantic Web data. In essence, an RDF graph is a set of triples of internationalised resource identifiers (IRIs), where the first and last of them represent entity resources, and the middle one relates these resources, just as is it done in graph databases [4]. The official query language for RDF databases is SPARQL [15].

To answer the need for including navigational features into SPARQL, the latest version of the language includes *property paths*, a set of queries that can be seen as the analogues of established graph database languages such as regular path queries and two-way regular path queries [11]. Consequently, property paths are already supported by the vast majority of existing SPARQL engines (e.g., [10, 24, 36]). The inclusion of navigational queries is also present in most other graph database models (see e.g. [4, 7]).

Besides the traditional approach where one issues a query over a (set of) graph databases, the community has further raised the need for a fundamentally different way of querying RDF data: to obtain answers of queries over the whole corpus of RDF data present on the Web and linked together into what is known as the *Web of Linked Data*, in a distributed way and without assuming any mediation nor centralised organisation in control of the data, following the *Linked Data Principles* [9].

HT'17, July 4-7, 2017, Prague, Czech Republic.
© 2017 ACM. 978-1-4503-4708-2/17/07...$15.00
DOI: http://dx.doi.org/10.1145/3078714.3078731

The fundamental property of RDF data that makes this querying possible is that the IRIs in RDF documents published online should be *dereferenceable*. This basically means that by accessing any given IRI, we obtain a new RDF document describing its neighbourhood (or a part of it) in the Linked Data graph. Let us explain how this works using the online RDF documents published by DBLP, one of the simplest datasets now forming part of the Web of Linked Data. In the RDF representation of DBLP, each researcher is given a unique IRI, as well as each paper. The authorship relation indicating that an author A wrote a paper P is then represented by the triple $\{P, \texttt{dc:creator}, A\}$. The IRI for each author, then serves as a good starting point for investigating the DBLP dataset, as dereferencing their IRI will intuitively give us all the papers written by this author. For example, if we dereference the IRI M.Stonebraker, representing Michael Stonebraker, we obtain a document containing, amongst other things, the following triples

M.Stonebraker	foaf:name	"M.Stonebraker"
inTods:StonebrakerWKH76	dc:creator	M.Stonebraker
inSigmod:PavloPRADMS09	dc:creator	M.Stonebraker

These triples indicate that M.Stonebraker is the author of the papers represented by IRIs inTods:StonebrakerWKH76 and inSigmod:PavloPRADMS09, and that the name of the entity represented by M.Stonebraker is indeed "Michael Stonebraker". Suppose now that we need to retrieve the names of all the co-authors of Michael Stonebraker. It is very easy to do this using the linked data infrastructure: We first dereference the IRI M.Stonebraker, obtaining an RDF document that contains, in particular, a triple $\{P, \texttt{dc:creator}, \texttt{M.Stonebraker}\}$ for each paper P authored by M. Stonebraker. Then we just need to dereference each of the IRIs of these papers: dereferencing each of these IRIs P gives us triples of the form $\{P, \texttt{dc:creator}, A\}$, and now we know that A is a coauthor of M. Stonebraker. The last step is to further dereference the IRI of each of these researchers, to look for a triple $\{A, \texttt{foaf:name}, N\}$ that indicates the name of the researcher (in this case N).

Problem statement. Of course, the query looking for co-authors of Michael Stonebraker can be seen as a fixed pattern: namely, it is a path of length two, starting in the IRI M.Stonebraker and traversing the edge dc:creator backwards (thus reaching a paper written by Michael Stonebraker), and then traversing the dc:creator edge forwards to reach one of his co-authors. But what happens when we want to generalise this query and obtain the collaboration reach of Michael Stonebraker, that is, his co-authors, the co-authors of his co-authors, their co-authors, etc? This is similar to the popular notion of Erdős number, but this time starting with a different author. To answer such a query a fixed length path will no longer suffice, since we do not know the distance between the starting node and the ending node in advance. We therefore need to use property paths; in this case this would be done using the query

    M.Stonebraker   (^dc:creator/dc:creator)*   ?x,

which repeats the simple path from one author to a paper (using ^dc:creator to follow an edge labelled dc:creator in a reverse direction) and then to another author (using dc:creator) an arbitrary number of times, as signified by the star operator ⋆. The idea is as before, but now once a co-author is retrieved, search does not stop, but continues with this (co-)author as the starting node.

When evaluating these queries we have only dereferenced and fetched the documents that we needed in order to answer the query, and thus we are taking full advantage of the nature of Linked Data. There is another fundamental advantage of this approach: we can cross between different domains without any effort by using the infrastructure of the Web, which happens when a dereferenced IRI links to another IRI residing on a different server. This is in contrast with, for instance, issuing a single distributed query to a centralised endpoint, since we can access an arbitrary number of different sources. Furthermore, we can access data that is not published on dedicated endpoints; all that we need is data published on the standard Web architecture. Up to our best knowledge, this framework of distributed, decentralised and ungoverned querying has not been considered before the advent of Linked Data.

The advantages of these approaches have led the Semantic Web community to investigate the fundamentals of querying over the Web [18], and developing algorithms for answering SPARQL queries over Linked Data [19, 34]. Unfortunately, despite the potential that property paths could have in Web querying, most of the algorithms developed in this context focus on the pattern matching features of SPARQL, and do not consider property paths. Indeed, the majority of studies about property paths only consider how they work over a single centralised dataset [5, 14, 26, 37]. And while the need for understanding how property paths might work over the Web has repeatedly been raised by the research community [8, 20, 21], previous studies have mostly focused on understanding appropriate semantics and/or proposing new languages to help users navigate the Web, instead of describing the algorithms computing these answers. The only exception is [13], suggesting a basic depth-first search algorithm in the context of NautiLOD queries: a language proposal that extends property paths. Therefore, the main objective of this paper is to answer the question: *How can one efficiently evaluate property path queries over the Web of Linked Data?*

Contributions. Our main contribution is an algorithm for efficiently retrieving answers to property path queries over Linked Data. Our solution is based on the observation that evaluating property paths can be seen as a search problem over an initially unknown graph. Indeed, in the examples above we start from one known IRI (M.Stonebraker) and begin exploring its neighbours guided by the query we are trying to answer. But this problem has been well studied by the Artificial Intelligence community, and it is generally agreed that the most appropriate solution here is an heuristic-search algorithm such as A⋆ [16, 30]. In this paper we propose a variant of A⋆ for the setting of Linked Data by using the property path we are trying to answer as a heuristic to guide our search. The main advantages of this approach are the following:

- It allows to overcome shortcomings of basic graph traversal algorithms such as depth-first search (DFS) and breadth-first search (BFS). In fact, we show that A⋆ dominates BFS and DFS, and that it is optimal with respect to the part of the graph that became available during the search. This, in some sense, is the best we can hope for in the open-world setting of the Web.

- It does not only allow to find pairs of nodes connected by a property path, but it can also return (one of the) shortest paths which witness this connection: a feature that existing SPARQL engines are currently lacking.

- It is very robust when evaluating property paths live over the Web infrastructure, and can often answer queries which fail even on SPARQL implementations executed over a local dataset.

Apart from describing the basic implementation of the A⋆ algorithm and proving its optimality, we also develop several optimisations geared towards query answering in the Linked Data setting. Most notably, we show that dereferencing multiple IRIs in parallel can speed up the computation of property paths significantly. Finally, we describe how our implementation runs over the Web of Linked data using a number of real-world queries which utilise different RDF datasets. We compare our approach to BFS and DFS-based algorithms and their parallel versions, showing that A⋆ is superior when it comes to querying over the Web.

Outline. We formalise Linked Data and property paths in Section 2. In Section 3 we describe how DFS and BFS can be used to answer property path queries and what are their shortcomings. In Section 4 we introduce the A⋆ algorithm and show its optimality. Optimisations are presented in Section 5, and real-world experiments in Section 6. We conclude in Section 7.

2 PRELIMINARIES

RDF graphs. Let $\mathcal{I}$ and $\mathcal{L}$ be countably infinite disjoint sets of *IRIs* and *literals*, respectively. An *RDF triple* is a triple (s, p, o) from $(\mathcal{I} \cup \mathcal{L}) \times \mathcal{I} \times (\mathcal{I} \cup \mathcal{L})$, where s is called *subject*, p *predicate*, and o *object*. An *(RDF) graph* is a finite set of RDF triples. For simplicity we only deal with RDF documents that do not contain blank nodes.

Linked Data. We are interested in computing navigational queries over the wide body of RDF documents published on the Web that comprise what is known as the Web of Linked Data. As customary in the literature (see e.g. [3, 17]), we treat this corpus of documents as a tuple $W = (\mathcal{G}, adoc)$, where $\mathcal{G}$ is a set of RDF graphs and $adoc : \mathcal{I} \rightarrow \mathcal{G} \cup \{\emptyset\}$ is a function that assigns graphs in $\mathcal{G}$ to some IRIs, and the empty graph to the rest of the IRIs. Note that previous work (e.g. [17]) usually defines *adoc* as a partial function. We adopt instead the convention that $adoc(u) = \emptyset$ whenever *adoc* is not defined for u, as it simplifies the presentation.

The intuition behind this definition is that $\mathcal{G}$ represents the set of documents on the Web of Linked data, and *adoc* captures dereferencing; that is, $adoc(u)$ gives us the neighbours of u in $\mathcal{G}$. Note that $\mathcal{G}$ is usually not available and has to be retrieved by looking up IRIs with *adoc*.

Example 2.1. We can now formalise the operations performed in the introduction over the linked data architecture of DBLP. Starting with the IRI M.Stonebraker, we can invoke *adoc* on this IRI to fetch its associated graph obtaining the following:

$$adoc(\text{M.Stonebraker}) =$$

$$\left\{ \begin{array}{ccc} \text{M.Stonebraker} & \text{foaf:name} & \text{"M. Stonebraker"} \\ \text{inSigmod:PavloPRADMS09} & \text{dc:creator} & \text{M.Stonebraker} \\ \vdots & \vdots & \vdots \end{array} \right.$$

When looking for the coauthors of M. Stonebraker, we might want to fetch *adoc*(inSigmod:PavloPRADMS09), which will give us a graph containing, amongst other things, triples of the form (inSigmod:PavloPRADMS09, dc:creator, A), with A being the IRI of the authors of the paper. To get the name of A we fetch the graph *adoc*(A) and look for the triple with foaf:name as the predicate.

Property Paths. Navigational queries over graph databases commonly ask for paths that satisfy certain properties. The most simple of them correspond to *regular path queries*, or *RPQs* [2, 12], which select pairs of nodes connected by a path conforming to a regular expression, and *2-way* regular path queries, or *2RPQs* [11], which extend RPQ with the ability to traverse an edge backwards. SPARQL features a class of navigational queries known as *property paths*, which are themselves an extension of the well known class of 2RPQs. For readability we assume we deal only with 2RPQs, adopting the formalisation in [26]. Note however that our algorithms (and our implementation) work for all property path expressions.

Formally, we define property paths by the grammar

$$e := u \mid e^- \mid e_1 \cdot e_2 \mid e_1 + e_2 \mid e^* \mid e?,$$

where u is an IRI in $\mathcal{I}$. The semantics of property paths, denoted by $[\![e]\!]_G$, for a property path e and an RDF graph G, is shown below.

$$[\![a]\!]_G = \{(s, o) \mid (s, a, o) \in G\},$$
$$[\![e^-]\!]_G = \{(s, o) \mid (o, s) \in [\![e]\!]_G\},$$
$$[\![e_1 \cdot e_2]\!]_G = [\![e_1]\!]_G \circ [\![e_2]\!]_G,$$
$$[\![e_1 + e_2]\!]_G = [\![e_1]\!]_G \cup [\![e_2]\!]_G,$$
$$[\![e^*]\!]_G = \bigcup_{i \geq 1} [\![e^i]\!]_G \cup \{(a, a) \mid a \text{ is a term in } G\},$$
$$[\![e?]\!]_G = [\![e]\!]_G \cup \{(a, a) \mid a \text{ is a term in } G\}.$$

Here $\circ$ is the usual composition of binary relations, and e^i is the concatenation of i copies of e.

2.1 Evaluating Property Paths via Automata

As in the case of the query computing the coauthor reach of M. Stonebraker, one is usually interested in computing all the IRIs that can be reached from a starting IRI u by means of a property path expression. Formally, we study the following problem.

Problem:	PPCOMPUTATION
Input:	Property Path e, RDF graph G, starting IRI u
Output:	All IRIs v such that $(u, v) \in [\![e]\!]_G$

Alternatively, one may wish to compute the full evaluation $[\![e]\!]_G$ of pairs connected via a path conforming to e. However, this operation is seldom used in practice: it is not an intuitive query to ask, and when using property paths in SPARQL one usually obtains starting points from other patterns or joins of patterns. Also, computing the full $[\![e]\!]_G$ is not even supported in all SPARQL systems (for instance Virtuoso allows only property paths with a starting point). Furthermore, as we will see in the following sections, in the open world setting of Linked Data it is only natural to have a starting point for our search, since it is unrealistic to expect the computation to traverse and manipulate the entire Web graph. This is why we chose to focus on PPCOMPUTATION.

To solve the PPCOMPUTATION problem, the theoretical literature proposed a simple algorithm based on automata theory. To present

this algorithm, note first that our property paths are nothing more than regular expressions over the alphabet $\mathcal{I}^\pm = \mathcal{I} \cup \{u^- \mid u \in \mathcal{I}\}$ that contains all IRIs and their inverses. Thus, for each property path e we can construct a nondeterministic finite state automaton (NFA) A_e over $\mathcal{I}^\pm$ that accepts the same language as e, when viewed as a regular expression. We can now show:

PROPOSITION 2.2 ([11, 12, 26]). *PPCOMPUTATION can be solved in* $O(|G| \cdot |e|)$ *(thus linear in both the size of the graph and the query).*

The idea is as follows. Let G be an RDF graph, e a property path expression and u an IRI. First, we construct the automaton $A_e = (Q_e, \mathcal{I}^\pm, q_e^0, F_e, \delta_e)$ equivalent to the query e, where Q_e is the set of states, q_e^0 is the initial state, F is the set of final states and $\delta_e \subseteq Q_e \times \mathcal{I}^\pm \times Q_e$ is the transition relation. Next, from G and A_e we construct the labelled product graph $G \times A_e$ whose nodes come from $\mathcal{I} \times Q_e$, and there is an edge from a node (u_1, q_1) to a node (u_2, q_2) labelled with $a \in \mathcal{I}$ if and only if (i) G contains a triple (u_1, a, u_2) and (ii) the transition relation δ_e contains the triple (q_1, a, q_2), that is, if in A_e one can advance from q_1 to q_2 while reading a. Similarly, there is an edge between (u_1, q_1) and (u_2, q_2) labelled with $a^- \in \mathcal{I}^-$ if (i) $(u_2, a, u_1) \in G$ and (ii) $(q_1, a^-, q_2) \in \delta_e$. It is now not difficult to show the following property:

LEMMA 2.3 ([12]). *A pair (u, v) belongs to $[\![e]\!]_G$ if and only if there is a path from (u, q_e^0) to (v, q_e^f) in the labelled graph $G \times A_e$, where $q_e^f \in F_e$ is a final state of A_e.*

We can now solve the PPCOMPUTATION problem by traversing the product graph $G \times A_e$ starting in (u, q_e^0) and returning all the IRIs v such that we encounter a node (v, q_e^f), with $q_e^f \in F_e$, during our traversal. Thus, in a sense, one can recast the problem of query computation (in a single graph) as the problem of searching for all connected final nodes in the product graph. This duality between evaluation and search is a crucial component of our approach for querying multiple graphs on the Web of Linked Data.

3 COMPUTING PROPERTY PATHS OVER THE WEB

When computing the answer of a property path over the Web, we cannot simply rely on the algorithm outlined in Section 2.1, because this assumes that we have our entire graph in memory, which is not a feasible option for the case of the Web. Having a starting IRI u comes in handy here, as we can emulate the algorithm from Section 2.1 by dereferencing u, retrieving its neighbours in *adoc*(u), and continuing from there, thus building a local copy of a portion of the Web graph needed to answer the query.

To formalise this, let us define the *Web graph* G_{Web} as the RDF graph consisting of the union $\bigcup_{u \in \mathcal{I}} adoc(u)$ of all the graphs resulting by dereferencing an IRI in $\mathcal{I}$ (i.e. the complete Web of Linked Data). From here onwards we assume that *adoc*(u) gives us the neighbours of u in the Web graph (see Section 5.2 for a discussion of how to deal with the shortcomings of the current Linked Data infrastructure). The problem we are now interested in is solving PPCOMPUTATION above for the graph G_{Web}, i.e. the problem:

Problem:	PP_OVER_THE_WEB
Input:	Property Path e, starting IRI u
Output:	All IRIs v such that $(u, v) \in [\![e]\!]_{G_{\text{Web}}}$

Now, although the approach of Section 2.1 would require us to do our search over $G_{\text{Web}} \times A_e$, we can recast PP_OVER_THE_WEB as finding paths inside a subgraph $G_P \subset G_{\text{Web}} \times A_e$ which is constructed dynamically by dereferencing IRIs starting at u. And although the graph G_P might be much smaller (in fact, we can stop constructing it when we desire), selecting the best algorithm for producing this graph and doing path searching over it is not an obvious task, due to the following issues not occurring in the classical path-finding setting.

First, path-finding algorithms are designed to work with graphs that can be either stored in memory or generated efficiently. In contrast, graph G_P is generated by dereferencing IRIs which involves resolving a number of HTTP requests. The time required to complete a request dominates significantly the time required to carry out any operation performed in memory. Efficient algorithms for this problem should therefore aim at reducing network requests, a factor that is usually not considered when solving path-finding problems. The second issue is that here we are interested in more than one solution. As such, an algorithm that returns answers incrementally seems to be a more sensible option than one that computes *all* answers prior to returning any.

Next, we discuss how classical path-finding algorithms can be modified to return answers to property path queries over the Web and pinpoint some of their shortcomings in this setting.

3.1 Depth-First Search

Depth-First Search (DFS) is an easy-to-implement path-finding algorithm that can be used to solve the PP_OVER_THE_WEB problem. On input a starting IRI u and an automaton A_e over $\mathcal{I}^{\pm}$, the algorithm begins a search over the graph $G_{\text{Web}} \times A_e$ starting with the node $init = (u, q_e^0)$, where q_e^0 is the initial node of A_e. The goal of the algorithm is to look for nodes of the form (v, q_f), with v an IRI and q_f a final state of A_e; this is commonly known as the *goal* condition of the algorithm. At every moment during execution, the algorithm maintains a *search frontier* (or *Open* list) implemented as a stack. At initialisation, the frontier is set to only contain the start node *init*. In the main loop, a node s is extracted from the frontier and *expanded* by computing its neighbours in $G_{\text{Web}} \times A_e$, by means of the function *Neighbours*. All neighbouring goal nodes are returned, and then all neighbours that have not been previously added to the frontier are now inserted at the top of the frontier. The algorithm terminates unsuccessfully if the frontier empties.

A pseudo code for DFS is presented in Algorithm 1. Note that we need *Open* to be a stack for DFS (Line 7). Observe additionally that the algorithm does not return a path but rather a node from which a path can be obtained by following the so-called parent pointers (set in Line 11). Finally, observe that in the context of navigational query answering, computing the neighbours of a node (function *Neighbours*) needs IRI dereferencing (set in Line 16) which in turn requires network communication, an operation that may take significantly more time than others carried out by the algorithm, such as data management.

There are three properties of DFS that are important for query answering. First, DFS can be easily modified to return paths incrementally instead of only one path. Indeed, instead of returning in Line 12, the node just found to be a goal node can be added to a list

---

Algorithm 1: Breadth/Depth-First Search

1   **function** *Search*(u, A_e)
2    $init \leftarrow (u, q_e^0)$
3    $init.parent \leftarrow null$
4   **if** $q_e^0 \in F_e$ **then** return *init* or add *init* to solutions
5   Initialise *Open* as an empty stack (DFS) or queue (BFS)
6   Initialise *Seen* as an empty set
7   Insert *init* into both *Open* and *Seen*
8   **while** *Open* is not empty **do**
9   Extract node $s = (v, q)$ from *Open* and compute *Neighbours*(s)
10   **for each** $t = (v', q')$ in *Neighbours*(s) that is not in *Seen* **do**
11      $t.parent \leftarrow s$
12   **if** $q' \in F_e$ **then** return t or add t to solutions
13   Insert t into both *Open* and *Seen*

14   **function** *Neighbours*$((v, q))$
15   Initialise *Succ* as an empty set and RDF graph G_{temp} as an empty graph
16    $G_{temp} \leftarrow adoc(v)$
17   **for each** IRI $a \in \mathcal{I}$ and state q' s.t. (q, a, q') is in δ_e **do**
18   **for each** *triple* (v, a, v') in G_{temp} **do** Insert (q', v') into *Succ*
19   **for each** IRI $a^- \in \mathcal{I}^-$ and state q' s.t. (q, a^-, q') is in δ_e **do**
20   **for each** *triple* (v', a, v) in G_{temp} **do** Insert (q', v') into *Succ*
21   **return** *Succ*

---

of solutions. In the same spirit, one can easily adapt DFS to return the first k solutions by introducing k as an additional parameter. Second, DFS is complete for finite graphs: if a goal node is reachable from *init* then the algorithm eventually retrieves this node. This is important because it guarantees that all solutions to a query are eventually returned. Third, the memory footprint of DFS is relatively low. Actually, if the depth of the node on top of the stack is k and the maximum branching factor (number of neighbours of a node) is b, then the size of *Open* is $O(kb)$.

To see how DFS works when solving PP_OVER_THE_WEB, let us consider the first steps taken when processing the property path (dc:creator$^-$ · dc:creator)*, with the starting IRI M.Stonebraker, which was presented in the introduction. First, let A_e be the following NFA:

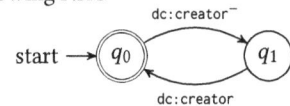

As explained in Lemma 2.3, the starting node for our search is (M.Stonebraker, q_0). In the first iteration we extract this node from *Open*, dereference the IRI M.Stonebraker, obtaining, amongst others, the triple (inTods:StonebrakerWKH76, dc:creator, M.Stonebraker). This will allow us to add to our frontier the node (inTods:StonebrakerWKH76, q_1) and we proceed similarly for other triples in *adoc*(M.Stonebraker). For the second iteration, let us assume (inTods:StonebrakerWKH76, q_1) is at the top of the stack. When expanded, DFS will lookup *adoc*(inTods:StonebrakerWKH76) and retrieve, amongst other things, all nodes connected to inTods:StonebrakerWKH76 by means of a label dc:creator. This, in particular, yields all 4 authors of this paper, but (M.Stonebraker, q_0) is not added to *Open* because it was already in *Seen*. For the next iteration DFS takes one of these nodes, say (G.Held, q_0), expands them again, obtaining all papers of G. Held; the next iteration expands one of these papers, adds all the authors to the list of answers; and so on.

Algorithm 1 implements a *loop detection* by preventing the insertion of a previously seen node to *Open*. This is important to guarantee that the algorithm terminates over a finite graph and that the answers are complete. In our case this implies that we are looking for simple paths, albeit not in the RDF graph but in the product graph $G_{\text{Web}} \times A_e$. In practice this implies that our algorithm looks for paths where the same IRI may be repeated at most a number of times equivalent to the states of the expression automata A_e. Completeness of DFS in our context follows from a simple pumping argument and the fact that property paths are regular expressions over $I^{\pm}$.

The most notable drawback of DFS is that there is no guarantee on solution quality, and solutions with much shortest paths may be missed. For instance, in the query above it will return the co-authors of G. Held, which are at distance two or more from M. Stonebraker, before returning the other authors of the paper in `Tods:StonebrakerWKH76`. In practice this means that we would need many more HTTP requests to retrieve subsequent solutions, which in turn means more time to compute answers.

3.2 Breadth-First Search

To alleviate the drawbacks of DFS, one could consider instead using *Breadth-First Search* (BFS), another complete search algorithm that is guaranteed to find shortest paths. BFS is similar to DFS in most aspects: it keeps a search frontier (i.e. the *Open* list) during execution and in each iteration it extracts a node from the frontier and then expands it. The most important difference is that BFS, instead of always expanding the deepest node in the frontier, it always expands the shallowest one. At the algorithmic level, BFS can be obtained from DFS by simply changing underlying data structure for *Open* to a FIFO queue instead of a stack. As such, successors of a node are always added at the end of the queue, and therefore a shallow node is always selected for expansion.

However, BFS also suffers from an important drawback in our context: BFS has the potential of needing many iterations to find a first solution to the problem. Indeed, assume once again that a node has at most b neighbours, and imagine that the shortest path in the search graph has k edges. Then, *all* nodes that are reachable in less than k edges are added to *Open* which means that $O(b^k)$ iterations are needed before such a path is found.

3.3 Issues with BFS and DFS

Both BFS and DFS have issues with some queries. Consider for example the following query, starting with M. Stonebraker:

$$(\text{dc:creator}^- \cdot \text{dc:creator})^* \cdot \text{dc:creator}^- \cdot \text{rdfs:label},$$

that is, intuitively we want to retrieve the papers written by a co-author of M. Stonebraker, or by a co-author of some of his co-authors, and so on. Furthermore, take the realistic assumption that there are hundreds of IRIs connected via `dc:creator`⁻ with M. Stonebraker (indeed, Stonebraker's DBLP entry, as of the writing of this paper, contains 298 papers).

Let us now focus on what BFS does with this query. It will first dereference the IRI for Stonebraker, adding the IRI of each of his 298 papers to *Open*. Then, it will dereference each of these IRIs, which requires 298 requests over the network. When each of these IRIs are expanded, we add to *Open* the co-authors of Stonebraker. Only after all the IRIs for Stonebraker's papers are expanded, it will

expand the IRI of one Stonebraker's coauthors, and, immediately will find a solution path.

Waiting for 298 HTTP requests before obtaining the first answer is not sensible: in this case only three requests are needed to find the first answer. Indeed, starting from Stonebraker's IRI, we just choose the IRI for *one* of Stonebraker's papers, we expand such an IRI, from where we choose the IRI of *one* of his co-author's. After dereferencing the latter IRI we find the first solution.

DFS has different yet important issue with this very same query. To find a first solution, DFS actually does the minimum amount of effort, dereferencing the minimum number of IRIs, as described above. The issue appears when looking for the answers that follow the first. Because the focus of DFS is depth, when executed over DBLP, the 5th answer of our query has length 6, the next 4 answers have length 12, and the following ones 32 and up. This implies that DFS will incur in more computation time to retrieve these answers, as well as more http requests. Moreover, returning these lengthy paths first does not seem intuitively right, as we normally want to display simpler, shorter paths first. Indeed, it is not hard to contrive examples in which the length of solutions increases much faster than in our examples, even when many shorter solutions exist.

What we need is a good balance between execution time and solution quality. In our example, a sensible way to proceed would be to take the IRI for the first paper, look at its authors, list them, and then proceed likewise with the second paper. This balance has been studied in the area of Heuristic Search, for many years, producing algorithms that are guided by a heuristic function h, that is such that $h(s)$ estimates the cost of a path from s to a goal node. Expansions are significantly (usually, exponentially) reduced as one improves the "quality" of h. Next we discuss the challenges of using of using heuristic search over Linked Data.

4 AI SEARCH TO THE RESCUE

A* is one of the most simple and well-studied heuristic algorithms capable of solving path search problems like the one we described in the previous sections. In this section we study how to apply it to the problem of answering property paths over the Web.

The main difference between A* and the algorithms described earlier is that the search frontier is a priority queue where the priority is given by $f(s)$, a function that estimates the cost of a solution that passes through s [16]. A high-level description of A* is as follows. At initialisation, the initial node is added to the *Open* queue. A* now repeats the following loop: first, it extracts a node with the highest priority from *Open*. It returns s if it is a goal state; otherwise, it expands s to obtain its neighbours, adds them to *Open* and continues execution. Next we give a formal description of A*.

The search graph of A* is *implicitly* described by (1) a start node s_{start}; (2) a set of actions *Act*; (3) a partial successor function *Succ*, such that $Succ(a, s)$, if defined, returns a set S of successor nodes; (4) a goal condition, which is a boolean function over nodes—*goal nodes* are those nodes for which this function returns true; (5) a non-negative cost function c between successor nodes. The objective of the algorithm is to find a path from s_{start} to a goal node.

An additional argument required by A* is a heuristic function h, which is a non-negative function over nodes such that $h(s)$ is an estimate of the cost of a path that starts in s and reaches a goal

Algorithm 2: The A* Algorithm

```
1  procedure A*
2  │  Closed ← empty set
3  │  Open ← empty priority queue ordered by f attribute
4  │  g(s_start) ← 0
5  │  f(s_start) ← h(s_start)
6  │  Insert s_start into Open
7  │  while Open ≠ ∅ do
8  │  │  Extract s from Open
9  │  │  if s is a goal node then
10 │  │  │  return s or add s to list of solutions
11 │  └  Expand(s)

12 procedure Expand (s)
13 │  Insert s into Closed
14 │  for each a in Act such that Succ(a, s) is defined do
15 │  │  for each s' in Succ(a, s) do
16 │  │  │  t ← s'
17 │  │  │  if t is not in Seen then
18 │  │  │  │  Add t to Seen
19 │  │  │  └  g(t) ← ∞
20 │  │  │  cost ← g(s) + c(s, t)
21 │  │  │  if cost < g(t) then
22 │  │  │  │  g(t) ← cost
23 │  │  │  │  f(t) ← g(t) + h(t)
24 │  │  │  │  parent(t) ← ⟨s, a⟩
25 │  │  │  │  if t is a goal and f(t) ≤ f(top(Open)) then
26 │  │  │  │  │  return t or add t to list of solutions
27 │  │  │  │  if t ∉ Open then Insert t in Open
28 │  │  └  └  else Update priority of t in Open
```

node. The heuristic is key to the performance of A*. An empirically well-known fact is that as h is more accurate, time savings can be very big because expansions are significantly reduced. It can be proven that when h is *admissible*, that is, for every s it holds that $h(s)$ does not overestimate the cost of any path from s to a goal node, then A* finds a minimum-cost path from s_{start} to a goal node.

Algorithm 2 shows a pseudo-code for A*. The priority function is defined as $f(s) = g(s) + h(s)$, where h is the heuristic function defined above and $g(s)$ is the cost of the best path found so far towards s. In an implementation of A*, a hash table is used to store nodes that have been generated in an expansion (cf. Line 18), and *parent*-, g-, h-, and f- values are stored as properties of s.

A final and important observation is that A* can be easily modified to return a sequence of answers, instead of a single one. In this case, we simply modify the return statement in Line 10 by something that adds s to a list.

Using A* for computing property paths. Let us show how we use A* to solve PP_over_the_Web. That is, given as inputs a property path e and a starting IRI u, we look for all v such that $(u, v) \in \llbracket e \rrbracket_{G_{Web}}$. Let $A_e = (Q_e, \mathcal{I}^\pm, q_e^0, F_e, \delta_e)$ be the automata over $\mathcal{I}^\pm$ that is equivalent to e. Recall that (see Lemma 2.3 and Section 3) we can reduce this problem to searching for all nodes (v, q_f), for an IRI v and a state $q_f \in F_e$, over the graph $G_P \subset G_{Web} \times A_e$ such that there is a path from (u, q_e^0) to (v, q_f). In turn, this problem can be seen as an A* description where *(1)* the start node s_{start} is (u, q_e^0); *(2)* the set Act of actions corresponds to IRIs in $\mathcal{I}^\pm$; *(3)* the partial successor function $Succ$ corresponds to the edges of $G_{Web} \times A_e$, that is, if $s = (u, q)$, we say $(u', q') \in Succ(a, s)$ if both $(u, a, u') \in adoc(u)$, and (q, a, q') is a transition in A_e, or if both $(u', a, u) \in adoc(u)$, and (q, a^-, q') is a transition in A_e; *(4)* a node

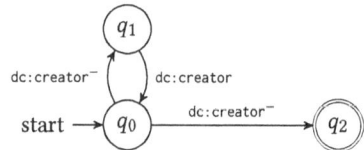

Figure 1: An automaton finding papers of the co-authors of M. Stonebraker.

$s = (v, q)$ is a goal if $q \in F_e$; and *(5)* the cost function is 1 for each pair of nodes connected by $Succ$.

There is an important subtlety that distinguishes our algorithm from classical A* applications. Just as in the case of BFS and DFS, the successors of (u, q) must be obtained by dereferencing an IRI (using, for example, the function *Neighbours* from Algorithm 1). This again means that the most costly operation is the expansion of new successor nodes, and as such any implementation of A* must try their best to find a way of reducing this bottleneck. We explain how to do this in Section 5.1. But before, let us see how to choose a good heuristic function in our scenario.

4.1 A Heuristic for Navigational Queries

Heuristic functions are essential for the performance of A*. We also want A* to be optimal, so our heuristic must be admissible, that is, it should not overestimate the cost of path to a goal node.

Let A be an automaton over $\mathcal{I}^\pm$. Our heuristic for this problem is defined as follows: for all nodes (v, q) over $\mathcal{I} \times Q_e$, where Q_e are the states of A_e, we define $h((v, q))$ as the minimum distance from q to a final state of A_e (and as ∞ if no path from q to a final state exists). To illustrate our heuristic consider Figure 1, corresponding to the automaton of the query for papers of the coauthor reach of M. Stonebraker introduced in Section 3.3. Then we define $h(u, q_1) = 2$, $h(u, q_0) = 1$, and $h(u, q_2) = 0$, for every $u \in \mathcal{I}$. Usually $h(u, q)$ is implemented as a simple lookup in a table. Given an automaton A we denote the heuristic defined as described above by h_A.

Our heuristic h_{A_e} is admissible for each property path e, as long as A_e is the minimum NFA for e. To see this, note that the minimum number of actions required to reach a goal node from node (u, q) cannot exceed the number of edges of a shortest path between the automaton state q and a final state. This is because each successor (u', q') of node (u, q) must be such that there is an edge between q and q' in the automaton's graph.

4.2 Theoretical Guarantees

A well-known property of A* is that is finds cost-optimal (i.e., shortest) paths. Here we provide an optimality result of the same sort. Now, because the function $adoc(u)$ is not necessarily guaranteed to return all triples containing u, we cannot show optimality over the entire Web, but rather only over the graph we have already discovered, that we denote by G_{A^*}.

Formally, given an execution of A*, the graph $G_{A^*} \subset G_{Web} \times A_e$ contains the edge (s, a, s') iff *(1)* $s \in Closed$, and *(2)* $s' \in Succ(a, s)$. This corresponds to the product of A_e with the graph containing all triples present in any of the documents that have been retrieved so far in our computation. The following is an optimality result both for BFS and A* run with our property-path heuristic.

THEOREM4.1. *Let G_{A^*} be defined as above from a run of A^* that has returned N answers with either $h = h_{A_e}$ or $h = 0$. Let π_k be path found to the k-th solution found by A^*, for any $k \in \{1, \dots, N\}$. Furthermore, let c_k be the length of the k-th shortest path from s_{start} to any goal state over G_{A^*}. Then the cost of π_k is c_k.*

SKETCH. Let $G_{A^*}^i$ denote G_{A^*} right after the i-th solution has been returned. We prove by induction that the i-th solution found by A^* would be thefi rst solution found by A^* if we were to mark as non-goals all solutions found prior to the i-th solution. Now we use the fact that the heuristic is admissible and thus the solution found is the i-th optimal over $G_{A^*}^i$. □

In practice, as we see later on, BFS runs slower than A^* with our heuristic. Interestingly, we can prove that A^* is better in the sense that BFS has to expand at least as many nodes as A^*.

THEOREM4.2. *Let (u, e) be an IRI and a property path. Then every node expanded by A^*, used with h_{A_e}, is also expanded by BFS.*

PROOF. We observe that $h_{A_e}(s) > 0$ for every non-goal state s. The result now follows from Theorem 7 in [30]. □

5 OPTIMISING QUERY EXECUTION

In this section we provide several optimisations to the base algorithms presented in Section 3 and Section 4. Wefi rst describe how parallel expansions can be used to reduce the execution times of our algorithms. We then explain how to overcome the current shortcomings of the Linked Data infrastructure. Finally, we discuss a way of tweaking the heuristic used in A^* in order to both avoid unnecessary network requests andfi nd answers sooner.

5.1 Parallel Expansions

All of our search algorithms function in such a way that they select a set of nodes which will serve as the starting point in the next iteration, and then start the search from these nodes one by one. An issue with this is that a request over the network—which on average takes more than a second— is needed per each dereference.

Instead of expanding one node at a time, our algorithms can benefit greatly from expanding multiple ones in parallel. More specifically, we modify the algorithm to extract up to k of nodes that could be at the top of the *Open*, and expand them in parallel. k is now a parameter of the algorithms which can be understood as a *degree of parallelism*. To obtain k-BFS and k-DFS, we modify Algorithm 1 such that Line 16 deals with up to k top-valued nodes from *Open*, and neighbours are computed for them in paralell. Similarly, k-A^* is obtained by extracting up to k nodes with the highest f-values from *Open* in Line 8 of Algorithm 2, and expanding them all in parallel in line 11. In all 3 algorithms, after all successors are computed, we add them all together to *Open*, in the same order that we would have, had the nodes been expanded sequentially. It is then not hard to see that optimality (Theorem 4.1) still holds for k-A^* (and k-BFS).

In Section 6 we show that, depending on the degree of parallelism, the computation is sped up tenfold in some instances.

5.2 Using The Endpoint Infrastructure

The evaluation algorithms presented in previous sections rely on the dereferencing mechanism of Linked Data and work under the assumption that when a specific IRI is dereferenced, we obtain all the triples mentioning such an IRI which reside on the server we are using. Unfortunately, it was shown repeatedly that this is generally not the case when working with Linked Data [22, 23], which can lead to incomplete answers since many triples containing the dereferenced IRI might not be returned. This is particularly problematic when working with inverse links, as it is estimated that publishers include only about a half of the triples where the requested IRI appears as the object [23].

Many Linked Data providers also set up public SPARQL endpoints where users can query the dataset, so we can partially alleviate the lack of Linked Data infrastructure by relying on public SPARQL endpoints together with Linked Data. When evaluating property paths over Linked Data, we combine the two approaches and, each time we dereference an IRI, we also query the appropriate endpoint in order to obtain the triples mentioning the said IRI. Furthermore, we query the endpoint only asking for links in the appropriate direction. For instance, if our property paths needs to traverse the author edge forwards starting from an IRI start, we ask the query SELECT ?x WHERE {start author ?x} to the appropriate endpoint and similarly for the backwards edges.

5.3 Minimising Network Requests

We have argued above that dereferencing is an expensive operation. When A^* is modified tofi nd multiple answers, as we proposed above (i.e., by simply adding solutions to a list), some expansions may be carried out sooner than we would want, leading to unnecessary dereferencing. Indeed, our heuristic assigns the value 0 to any node of the form (u, q_f) with q_f afi nal state (because the distance to a final state is 0). Assuming q_f has outgoing transitions, the standard A^* algorithm would prioritise the expansions of those nodes over any other node with the same f value, an operation that intuitively would take us farther from the goal.

We can postpone these expansions by using a slightly different heuristic, defined as follows. Let $A = (Q, \Sigma, q_o, F, \delta)$ be an NFA. The *pathmax* distance $\hat{d}(q, q')$ between two states is defined as $\hat{d}(q, q') = 1 + \min_{q | \delta(q, a) \text{ is defined}} d(q, q')$, if $\delta(q, a)$ is defined for at least some $a \in \Sigma$, or $\hat{d}(q, q') = \infty$ otherwise; and where d is the usual graph distance between q and q'. Then the pathmax heuristic $\hat{h}_A$ with respect to A is defined as $\hat{h}_A((u, q)) = \min_{q_f \in F} \hat{d}(q, q_f)$, that is, the minimum pathmax distance from q to anyfi nal state of A. This is a standard technique used by search algorithms in which a node may have to be re-expanded [25, 32]. Interestingly, one can see that the pathmax distance $\hat{d}$ coincides with the usual distance in all states of the automata except for thefi nal states. We avoid early re-expansion of nodes withfi nal states because the heuristic for them now corresponds to 1 plus the minimum of the heuristic value of the neighbours of this state.

6 EXPERIMENTAL EVALUATION

In this section we evaluate how an implementation of A^* algorithm performs when executing property path queries over a real Web environment. To establish a baseline, we compare A^* with BFS and DFS. We begin by presenting our experimental setup, the queries, and then compare how A^* fares against BFS and DFS, showing that A^* outperforms the other two algorithms on a regular basis. Next

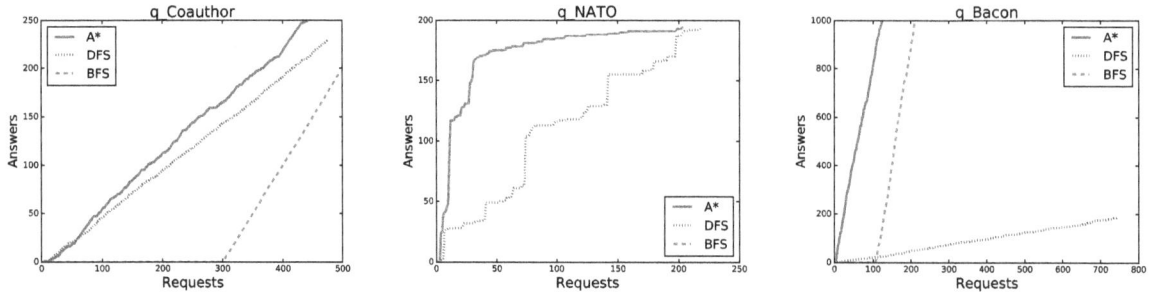

Figure 2: A* minimises the requests needed to obtain answers of q_Coauthor, q_NATO and q_Bacon

we investigate the impact of parallel requests on our algorithms. As we see, adding parallelism reduces total runtime for all three algorithms, with A* remaining the most consistent. Interestingly, all algorithms tend to look more alike as more and more parallel requests are allowed. Finally, we discuss some real-world examples of the paths retrieved by our algorithms.

6.1 Experimental Setup

We selected 11 navigational queries that are inspired by previous benchmarks (see e.g. [14, 31]). These queries are representative of several different features of property paths, ranging from easy, fixed-depth ones to queries using multiple star operations which are much harder to evaluate. Our queries target one or more of the following Linked Data domains: YAGO, a huge knowledge base extracting data from Wikipedia and various other sources [29]; DBPedia [6], one of the central datasets of the Linked Data initiative that also originates from Wikipedia; Linked Movie Database, the best known semantic database for movie information [27]; and the Linked Data domain of DBLP. Our implementations will always use the optimisation techniques presented in Section 5.2 and Section 5.3, while we assess the benefits of parallelism (Section 5.1) separately. As an example, below are 3 of the 11 queries we use. For complete details of the queries, results of all our runs, and implementation of our algorithms, please refer to our online appendix [1].

q_Coauthor: This property path looks for the IRI of all authors that are related to M. Stonebraker on DBLP, by a co-authorship path of arbitrary length, as discussed in the Introduction.

q_NATO: A property path that selects all places that host an entity dealing with a NATO member state, according to YAGO.

q_Bacon: A property path that looks for the IRIs of actors having a finite Bacon-number[1], and that navigates using links and/or IRIs present in any of YAGO, DBPedia or Linked Movie Database. This is an interesting query, as currently the only way to evaluate it is by means of our Linked Data approach (see [8] for a discussion).

To assess our algorithm we use two indicators: the number of HTTP requests made to compute a fraction of the answers, and the time needed to compute them. In both cases we want to minimise the number of requests, or the amount of time needed to produce the answers. We note that the number of requests is a much better indicator on how the algorithm works: because HTTP requests take considerably more time than all the other operations, the total

time of computing our queries is essentially given by the number of requests performed by the algorithm. This also rules out the dependence on parameters which we have no control over, such as the Internet traffic, or the availability of servers providing us with data. Thus, by focusing on requests we ignore latency differences that may persist even after taking several runs of the same query.

All experiments were run without an access to the data locally, relying solely on the Web infrastructure to retrieve the data needed at each step of the computation. The experiments were run on a Manjaro Linux machine with a i5-4670 quad-core processor and 4GB of RAM. To avoid flooding servers with requests we only ran our search until we either found 1 000 answers, retrieved more than 100 000 triples from the server, or reached a 10-minute time limit. Each experiment was ran 10 times, and since the results were largely equivalent, we report the numbers of the latest execution. The source code for running the experiments is available at [1].

6.2 Heuristic Search Against BFS and DFS

The general conclusion of our experiments is that A* both requires fewer requests and is faster than BFS and DFS. Before reporting our results in full, let us examine the runs of queries **q_Coauthor**, **q_Bacon** and **q_NATO** presented above. Figure 2 shows the number of requests needed to compute a fraction of the total answers available for these queries. In particular, we see that both A* and DFS are the best choice for the query **q_Coauthor**, because they produce more answers using fewer HTTP requests (even though the quality of the answers produced by A* is arguably better – see below). On the other hand, BFS requires around 300 expansions to start producing answers, which results in a much slower throughput altogether. Next, both A* and BFS are the best choice for the query **q_NATO**. This is again expected, because this query requires less navigation and more shallow exploration. It is interesting to see that in this case A* really simulates the optimal BFS search. On the other hand, DFS wastes a lot of time exploring long paths and obtaining "deep" answers. Finally, for **q_Bacon**, A* is shown to strictly beat both BFS and DFS. In the case of BFS, this is mostly because A*'s heuristic allows a finer control on which links to explore, and the main detractor for DFS is that it starts exploring initial links which often require many requests before encountering a solution.

Full results. For reasons of space, we cannot report the remaining 8 experiments with the same detail, so instead we do the following. For each query, we analyse the complete behaviour of the answers vs. request and answers vs. time curves. We say that an algorithm

---

[1]An actress has Bacon number 1 if she acted in the same movie as Kevin Bacon, and Bacon number n if she acted with someone with Bacon number $n - 1$.

dominates the others if it is such that it returns at least as many answers as any other for 80% of the range of requests (or time) for which we evaluate them. For example, in Figure 2 we see that A^* dominates the other algorithms for queries **q_Coauthor** and **q_Bacon**, while in the case of **q_NATO** both A^* and BFS dominate. The total number of times each algorithm dominates (out of 11 queries) is shown below, for both the answers vs. request and answers vs. time curves (full details are found in our online appendix [1]). Once again, A^* remains the most consistent option.

Measure	A^*	BFS	DFS
Requests v/s Answers	11	3	4
Time v/s Answers	11	3	4

6.3 The Effect of Parallel Requests

Next, we test the effect of allowing parallel requests in our algorithms, as presented in Section 5.1. This optimisation goes a long way into tackling the slow latency of Web requests, one of the main problems of querying over the HTTP protocol. Indeed, HTTP requests are such an important bottleneck in our algorithm that allowing parallel requests essentially means parallelising the entire algorithm. Issuing parallel requests also soften up high latency pockets or temporary network problems. Moreover, we can also expect the algorithms to be accelerated even further when the number of allowed requests is increased, simply because more requests essentially means more parallel instances of our algorithm and even more softening power. The other interesting observation is that, as we allow more parallel requests in our algorithms, all of A^*, BFS and DFS start to look alike, and in fact it is easy to see that all three algorithms are essentially equivalent in the limit where we issue an infinite number of requests at the same time.

To empirically test these observations, we issued new live runs of the 11 queries described in the previous sections, but this time using parallel versions of A^*, BFS and DFS. To see the impact on the number of parallel threads allowed, we report experiments with a maximum of 10, 20, and 40 parallel threads. Before reporting the full results, let us start with comparing the results of the algorithm with no parallelism against the one with 20 parallel threads. Figure 3 shows the time needed to compute the answers of query **q_Coauthor**, for all three algorithms on their non-parallel version and on their parallel version with a maximum of 20 threads. As we see, the time needed to compute the same amount of answers decreases by almost tenfold in all three cases. Moreover, the parallel version of BFS now behaves almost as A^* and DFS when computing the first 300 answers (it then reaches a stalemate because all shallow answers have already been discovered).

Full results. As expected, the time taken to compute answers decreases drastically (the behaviour is the same as for **q_Coauthor**). Perhaps more interestingly, we focus on how algorithms change when more parallel threads are allowed. In order to do this, we repeat the same reports made in the previous subsection, but this time for different levels of parallelism. More precisely, for each of our 11 queries and 4 different thread counts we report which of A^*, BFS or DFS dominates in the time needed to compute the answers. As we see as more parallelism is allowed into the algorithms, both BFS and DFS start becoming more competitive compared to A^*.

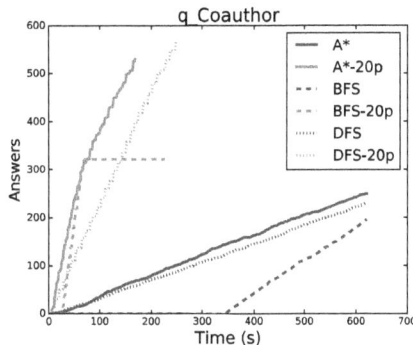

Figure 3: Answers over time on q_Coauthor. The parallel versions (in red) are much faster than the non-parallel ones.

```
dblpAuthor:Michael_Stonebraker
  ^dc:creator   dblpPub:conf/acm/MuthuswamyKZSPJ85
   dc:creator   dblpAuthor:Matthias_Jarke
   rdfs:label"  Matthias Jarke"
dblpAuthor:Michael_Stonebraker
  ^dc:creator   dblpPub:conf/dbvis/AikenCLSSW95
   dc:creator   dblpAuthor:Mybrid_Spalding
   rdfs:label"  Mybrid Spalding"
dblpAuthor:Michael_Stonebraker
  ^dc:creator   dblpPub:conf/vldb/StonebrakerABCCFLLMOORTZ05
   dc:creator   dblpAuthors:Adam_Batkin
   rdfs:label"  Adam Batkin"
```

Figure 4: Paths for the 10th, 50th, and 200th answers found by A^* on q_Coauthor.

Max parallel calls	A^*	BFS	DFS
1	11	3	4
10	7	3	3
20	7	3	3
40	6	4	5

6.4 Returning paths

As already mentioned, our algorithms can not only find pairs of nodes connected by a property path query, but can also compute the entire *path* between two nodes. In fact, this can be achieved at marginal cost: we already keep track of all the expansions, so we can produce paths simply by returning the IRIs corresponding to each of the requests made by our algorithm.

Paths can be used as a justification for the answers, or to continue extracting more information afterwards. For these reasons returning paths is a very sought-after functionality of graph query languages, and is present for example in the popular Neo4j engine [33]. Unfortunately, a language capable of returning (all) paths, or even (all) simple paths, is bound to be very complicated to evaluate [5, 28], and this is the reason why the SPARQL standard does not include such a functionality. In our case we have a natural workaround for this issue, as our search focuses on shortest paths, which are known to be easier to evaluate than simple paths.

As an example of the usefulness of paths, it was by analysing paths that we inferred that A^* normally produces better answers than DFS (because the paths are shorter). As an illustration, Figure 4 presents paths witnessing the answers 10, 50, and 200 of a run of the query **q_Coauthor** with A^*. From the query itself all that we can say is that these three researchers are connected to M. Stonebraker by a coauthorship path of arbitrary length. However, by looking at the paths we now know that they are direct coauthors. On the other hand, the length of paths retrieved by DFS are going to be much higher. For one run of **q_Coauthor** with DFS the lengths of the answers 10, 50 and 200 were respectively 14, 74, 312.

7 CONCLUSIONS AND FUTURE WORK

This paper presents the first fundamental study of the problem of computing property paths over the Web. We showed how to cast query answering as an AI search problem, and provided an optimal algorithm based on the classical A* algorithm. We provide strong theoretical and practical evidence that A* is a better alternative than both BFS and DFS in the context of Linked Data, and this can be sped up even further by allowing parallel execution threads.

Using triple pattern fragments. As noted in Section 5, there are some issues with the Linked Data infrastructure; most notably, it does not provide all the information one would expect when dereferencing IRIs. While it is possible to alleviate this issue by using endpoints, since their uptime can be erratic, it was recently suggested that a more lightweight infrastructure of triple pattern fragments [35] would be more appropriate for the task. In the future we plan to test how using triple pattern fragments affects the performance and accuracy of our algorithms when compared to the standard endpoint infrastructure.

Answering NautiLOD and LDQL queries with A*. NautiLOD [13] is a traversal-based language proposed as an option to SPARLQ when querying Linked Data, in which one has more finer control on how is the Web going to be traversed. In the same spirit, LDQL [20] is another language aimed at controlling how data is to be retrieved, albeit much less powerful than NautiLOD. The interesting observation is that we can also cast the query evaluation problem for these languages as a search problem, and thus A* should also provide optimal query answering algorithms. In fact, the algorithm proposed in [13] is essentially what we define here as k-DFS, so one can naturally suspect that A* should provide a better behaviour.

A* in local computations. Although we based our investigation in the context of Linked Data, there is some evidence that our approach might have potential in the classical setting where data is available locally. The main reason is the fact that the currently available property path evaluation algorithms demand a lot of resources, especially when dealing with property paths that use the Kleene star operator, and current systems cannot easily cope with these requirements [8]. On the other hand, we have seen that the memory usage of an A*-based algorithm is directly dependant on the amount of answers that need to be computed, and each answer requires an almost negligible amount of additional memory. This suggests that, in those cases when we do not need all the answers, an approach based on A* might be a better option.

Acknowledgements. The authors were funded by the Millennium Nucleus Center for Semantic Web Research under Grant NC120004. Vrgoč was also partially funded by the STIC AMSUD project Foundations of Graph Structured Data (Fog) and FONDECYT project N11160383.

REFERENCES

[1] 2016. http://dvrgoc.ing.puc.cl/navigation/. (2016).
[2] S. Abiteboul, P. Buneman, and D. Suciu. 1999. *Data on the Web: From Relations to Semistructured Data and XML*. Morgan Kauffman.
[3] Serge Abiteboul and Victor Vianu. 1997. Queries and Computation on the Web. In *ICDT '97*. 262–275.
[4] Renzo Angles and Claudio Gutiérrez. 2008. Survey of graph database models. *ACM Comput. Surv.* 40, 1 (2008).
[5] Marcelo Arenas, Sebastián Conca, and Jorge Pérez. 2012. Counting beyond a Yottabyte, or how SPARQL 1.1 property paths will prevent adoption of the standard. In *WWW*.
[6] Sören Auer, Christian Bizer, Georgi Kobilarov, Jens Lehmann, Richard Cyganiak, and Zachary Ives. 2007. *Dbpedia: A nucleus for a web of open data*. Springer.
[7] Pablo Barceló Baeza. 2013. Querying graph databases. In *PODS 2013*. 175–188.
[8] Jorge Baier, Dietrich Daroch, Juan L. Reutter, and Domagoj Vrgoč. 2016. Property Paths over Linked Data: Can It Be Done and How To Start?. In *COLD@ISWC*.
[9] Tim Berners-Lee, Christian Bizer, and Tom Heath. 2009. Linked data-the story so far. *Int. Journal on Semantic Web and Information Systems* 5, 3 (2009), 1–22.
[10] Blazegraph 2016. Blazegraph. https://www.blazegraph.com/. (2016).
[11] D. Calvanese, G. De Giacomo, M. Lenzerini, and M.Y. Vardi. 2000. Containment of conjunctive regular path queries with inverse. In *KR 2000*. 176–185.
[12] I. Cruz, A.O. Mendelzon, and P. Wood. 1987. A graphical query language supporting recursion. In *SIGMOD '87*. 323–330.
[13] Valeria Fionda, Giuseppe Pirrò, and Claudio Gutierrez. 2015. NautiLOD: A Formal Language for the Web of Data Graph. *TWEB* 9, 1 (2015), 5:1–5:43.
[14] Andrey Gubichev, Srikanta J. Bedathur, and Stephan Seufert. 2013. Sparqling kleene: fast property paths in RDF-3X. In *GRADES 2013*. 14.
[15] Steve Harris and Andy Seaborne. 2013. SPARQL 1.1 query language. *W3C* (2013).
[16] Peter E. Hart, Nils Nilsson, and B. Raphael. 1968. A formal basis for the heuristic determination of minimal cost paths. *IEEE Transactions on Systems Science and Cybernetics* 4, 2 (1968).
[17] Olaf Hartig. 2012. SPARQL for a Web of Linked Data: Semantics and computability. In *The Semantic Web: Research and Applications*. Springer, 8–23.
[18] Olaf Hartig, Christian Bizer, and Johann-Christoph Freytag. 2009. *Executing SPARQL queries over the web of linked data*. Springer.
[19] Olaf Hartig and M. Tamer Özsu. 2016. Walking Without a Map: Ranking-Based Traversal for Querying Linked Data. In *ISWC 2016*. 305–324.
[20] Olaf Hartig and Jorge Pérez. 2015. LDQL: A Query Language for the Web of Linked Data. In *ISWC 2015*. Springer, 73–91.
[21] Olaf Hartig and Giuseppe Pirrò. 2015. A Context-Based Semantics for SPARQL Property Paths Over the Web. In *ESWC 2015*. 71–87.
[22] Aidan Hogan and Claudio Gutierrez. 2014. Paths towards the Sustainable Consumption of Semantic Data on the Web. In *AMW 2014*.
[23] Aidan Hogan, Jürgen Umbrich, Andreas Harth, Richard Cyganiak, Axel Polleres, and Stefan Decker. 2012. An empirical survey of Linked Data conformance. *J. Web Sem.* 14 (2012), 14–44.
[24] Jena 2015. Apache Jena Manual. http://jena.apache.org. (2015).
[25] Richard E. Korf. 1993. Linear-Space Best-First Search. *Artificial Intelligence* 62, 1 (1993), 41–78. DOI:http://dx.doi.org/10.1016/0004-3702(93)90045-D
[26] Egor V Kostylev, Juan L Reutter, Miguel Romero, and Domagoj Vrgoč. 2015. SPARQL with Property Paths. In *ISWC 2015*. Springer, 3–18.
[27] LMDB 2008. Linked movie database. http://linkedmdb.org/. (2008).
[28] Katja Losemann and Wim Martens. 2012. The complexity of evaluating path expressions in SPARQL. In *PODS 2012*. 101–112.
[29] Farzaneh Mahdisoltani, Joanna Biega, and Fabian Suchanek. 2014. Yago3: A knowledge base from multilingual wikipedias. In *CIDR*.
[30] Judea Pearl. 1984. *Heuristics: Intelligent Search Strategies for Computer Problem Solving*. Addison-Wesley Longman Publishing Co., Inc., Boston, MA, USA.
[31] Juan L. Reutter, Adrián Soto, and Domagoj Vrgoč. 2015. Recursion in SPARQL. In *ISWC 2015*.
[32] Stuart J. Russell. 1992. Efficient Memory-Bounded Search Methods. In *ECAI'92*.
[33] The Neo4j Team. 2016. The Neo4j Manual v3.0. http://neo4j.com. (2016).
[34] Jürgen Umbrich, Aidan Hogan, Axel Polleres, and Stefan Decker. 2015. Link traversal querying for a diverse Web of Data. *Semantic Web* 6, 6 (2015), 585–624.
[35] Ruben Verborgh, Olaf Hartig, Ben De Meester, Gerald Haesendonck, Laurens De Vocht, Miel Vander Sande, Richard Cyganiak, Pieter Colpaert, Erik Mannens, and Rik Van de Walle. 2014. Querying Datasets on the Web with High Availability. In *ISWC 2014*. 180–196.
[36] Virtuoso 2015. Open Link Virtuoso. http://virtuoso.openlinksw.com/. (2015).
[37] Nikolay Yakovets, Parke Godfrey, and Jarek Gryz. 2016. Query Planning for Evaluating SPARQL Property Paths. In *SIGMOD 2016*. 1875–1889.

Linking Content Information with Bayesian Personalized Ranking via Multiple Content Alignments

Ladislav Peska
Department of Software Engineering
Faculty of Mathematics and Physics, Charles University, Prague
Czech Republic
peska@ksi.mff.cuni.cz

ABSTRACT

In many application domains of recommender systems, content-based information are available for users, objects or both. Such information can be processed during recommendation and significantly decrease the cold-start problem. However, content information may come from several, possibly external, sources. Some sources may be incomplete, less reliable or less relevant for the purpose of recommendation. Thus, each content source or attribute possess different level of informativeness, which should be taken into consideration during the process of recommendation.

In this paper, we propose a multiple content alignments extension to the Bayesian Personalized Ranking Matrix Factorization (BPR-MCA). The proposed method incorporates multiple sources of content information in the form of user-to-user or object-to-object similarity matrices and aligns users' and items' latent factors according to these similarities. During the training phase, BPR-MCA also learns the relevance weight of each similarity matrix.

BPR-MCA was evaluated on the MovieLens 1M dataset, extended by the content information from IMDB, DBTropes and ZIP code statistics. The experiment shows that BPR-MCA can help to significantly improve recommendation w.r.t. nDCG and AUPR over standard BPR under several cold-start scenarios.

KEYWORDS

Recommender systems; BPR; content alignment; Cold-start problem

1 INTRODUCTION

Recommender systems belongs to the class of automated content-processing tools, aiming to provide users with unknown, surprising, yet relevant objects without the necessity of explicitly

HT '17, July 04-07, 2017, Prague, Czech Republic
© 2017 Association for Computing Machinery.
ACM ISBN 978-1-4503-4708-2/17/07...$15.00
http://dx.doi.org/10.1145/3078714.3078732

query for them. As such, they are complementary to both keyword and attribute-based search engines, because the user does not have to provide detailed queries and recommendations can be provided implicitly, without his/her conscious cooperation. The core of recommender systems are machine learning algorithms applied on the matrix of user to object preferences. So far, the majority of research effort was spent on the collaborative filtering (CF) algorithms and explicit user rating. Collaborative recommender systems were shown to be more accurate than content-based (CB) algorithms if sufficient amount of data is available [1], [19].

Various matrix factorization (MF) approaches, e.g., SVD++ [13], PMF [21], BPR [20], Logistic MF [8] etc. gain in prominence after the NetFlix Challenge and are still considered as state-of-the-art in collaborative filtering. The core idea of applying matrix factorization techniques in recommender systems is to map both users and objects into a shared low-dimensional latent feature space and use this representation to calculate the score of any user-object pair. Matrix factorization techniques differ from one another especially in the optimization criteria, the choice of iterative optimization method and the exact inference of user-object score.

The explicit user rating is rich and reliable source of user preferences, however it is not numerous enough or completely unavailable on many application domains [7], [18]. Thus, more realistic approaches use *implicit feedback* as a source of user preferences. Although there is some recent research on diversification of *implicit feedback*, e.g., [14], [18], [24], positive-only unary feedback is often the only available information.

Several matrix decomposition techniques were designed to handle positive-only implicit feedback (also referred as one-class matrix factorization). One of the first such approaches (WRMF) was proposed by Hu et al. [7]. WRMF decompose positive-only implicit feedback into the binary polarity attribute and confidence, non-decreasing w.r.t. the feedback value. WRMF learns the latent representation of users and objects effectively via Altering Least Squares (ALS) algorithm. In the following years, further one-class matrix factorization techniques were proposed, e.g., Logistic MF [8], Maximum Margin MF [23] or Bayesian Probabilistic Ranking MF (BPR) [20].

BPR was designed to optimize AUC-like ranking criterion with positive-only feedback information. Unlike other MF approaches, e.g., SVD++ or WRMS, BPR uses pairwise preferences of positive and unknown object and directly optimizes a ranking criterion, whereas SVD++ and WRMS aim to minimize squared prediction error.

So far, the described MF techniques were purely collaborative, using only user feedback to provide recommendations. However, CF methods' performance greatly decreases in case of insufficient data (referred as a *cold start problem*) [11]. Furthermore, purely collaborative recommender systems cannot make any predictions for new users or new objects.

In order to overcome the cold-start problem, recommendations can be based on content-based attributes of users or objects. Also, some hybrid techniques combining content-based and collaborative learning are plausible. Several hybrid techniques using content-based attributes in matrix factorization were proposed recently. Forbes and Zhu proposed a factorization model, where objects were defined through the latent factors of its attributes [5]. Nguyen et al. [16] and Zheng et al. [26] proposed SVD++ extensions incorporating similarity of latent factors driven by the content-based similarity of objects or users respectively. Another related approach was proposed by Zheng et al. [25] for drug-target interaction prediction problem (MSCMF). MSCMF method extends WRMF by adding several drug and target similarity matrices in order to better predict interacting drug-target pairs.

In our work, we aim on extending BPR method by incorporating content-based information in form of arbitrary many similarity matrices for both users and objects. Such an arrangement enables us to learn or define importance of each type of content information and thus contribute to the improved recommendation, especially in the cold-start scenarios.

Our approach extends the work of Nguyen et al. [16] and Zheng et al. [26] by using multiple similarity matrices and learning its weights. We also significantly differ from the MSCMF method [25], e.g., in incorporation of content-based similarity into the optimization criterion, learning algorithm and ability to predict also for novel users and objects. For more information, please refer to the Sections 2.3 and 2.4. Also, to the best of our knowledge, this is the first method providing content-based extension of BPR.

Main contributions of this paper are:

- Proposing extension to the BPR matrix factorization incorporating multiple (content-based) similarity matrices.
- Evaluation of the proposed BPR-MCA method on the extended MovieLens 1M dataset under several cold-start scenarios.
- Content-based extensions to the MovieLens 1M dataset available for future work.

2 MATERIALS AND METHODS

2.1 Notation and Problem Formalization

In this paper, we denote the set of users as $U = \{u_1, ..., u_n\}$ and the set of objects as $O = \{o_1, ..., o_m\}$, where n and m are the number of users and objects respectively. The $n \times m$ matrix $\mathbf{R}$ represents known user-object interactions. In the current scenario, $\mathbf{R}$ is a binary matrix with $r_{i,j} = 1$ denoting that a user

u_i positively preferred an object o_j and $r_{i,j} = 0$ otherwise, i.e., we have no information about their interaction. Matrices $\mathbf{S}_p^U \in \mathbb{R}^{(n \times n)}, p \in \{1, ..., n_s\}$ represent user similarities. Each element $s_{p,i,k}^U$ contains the similarity between users u_i and u_k. Analogically, matrices $\mathbf{S}_q^O \in \mathbb{R}^{(m \times m)}, q \in \{1, ..., m_s\}$ represent objects similarities. Variables ω_p and ω_q represents weight of each similarity matrix $\mathbf{S}_p^U$ and $\mathbf{S}_q^O$ respectively.

We further define the set of novel users U^N and objects O^N as the users (objects) without any known interaction: $U^N := \{u_i \in U; \sum_{j=1}^m r_{i,j} = 0\}$, $O^N = \{o_j \in O; \sum_{i=1}^n r_{i,j} = 0\}$ and sets of objects O_i^N, novel for user u_i: $O_i^N = \{o_j \in O; r_{i,j} = 0\}$.

Matrix factorization methods aim to map both users and objects into a shared latent space, where f denotes its dimension (number of latent factors), $\boldsymbol{\mu}_i \in \mathbb{R}^f$ denotes latent factors of user u_i and $\mathbf{v}_j \in \mathbb{R}^f$ denotes latent factors of object o_j. We will further define $\mathbf{U} \in \mathbb{R}^{(n \times f)}$ as the matrix of all users' latent factors and $\mathbf{V} \in \mathbb{R}^{(m \times f)}$ as the matrix of all objects' latent factors. The predicted probability of positive preference $\hat{r}_{i,j}$ in unknown pair of user u_i and object o_j is defined as the dot product of its latent factors $\hat{r}_{i,j} := \boldsymbol{\mu}_i \times \mathbf{v}_j^T$. Last, we define the train set of the BPR method as the set of triples $T_s \subset U \times O \times O$; $T_s := \{(u_i, o_j, o_k): r_{i,j} = 1 \wedge r_{i,k} = 0\}$.

Under this notation, our task is to calculate unknown preferences $\hat{r}_{i,j}$ of the current user u_i. Interaction matrix $\mathbf{R}$ and similarity matrices $\mathbf{S}_p^U, \mathbf{S}_q^O$ can be utilized in this task. Afterwards, the objects $o_j \in O_i^N$ are ranked according to the $\hat{r}_{i,j}$ and top-k best ranked objects are recommended to the user.

2.2 Bayesian Personalized Ranking

In order to make this paper self-contained, let us briefly describe the original BPR method by Rendle et al. [20]. BPR is based on the ranking optimization and the idea of reducing ranking of objects to the correctness of its pairwise classification. As a common feature of matrix factorization techniques, BPR projects both users and objects on a shared latent space. The projection is based on an optimization criterion BPR-OPT, derived from the maximum posterior estimator for optimal targets ranking.

The Bayesian formulation of finding the correct ranking of all objects $o \in O$ is to maximize posterior probability:

$$p(\Theta \mid >_u) \propto p(>_u \mid \Theta) \, p(\Theta)$$

where Θ represents parameters of the model and $>_u$ is desired, but latent ordering, specific for the user u. BPR method further assumes independency of users on each other, independency of ordering pairs of objects on any other pair, totality and antisymmetry of the ordering. Hence, the user-specific likelihood function $p(\Theta \mid >_u)$ can be combined for all users as follows:

$$\prod_{u \in U} p(>_u \mid \Theta) = \prod_{(u_i, o_j, o_k) \in T_s} p(o_j >_u o_k \mid \Theta)$$

In order to establish total ordering of objects for each user, the individual probability that user u interacts with object o_j rather than with o_k is defined as follows:

$$p\left(o_j >_u o_k | \Theta\right) \coloneqq \sigma(\hat{r}_{u,j,k}(\Theta))$$

where σ is the logistic sigmoid function $\sigma(x) \coloneqq 1/(1+e^{-x})$ and $\hat{r}_{u,j,k}(\Theta)$ is a real-valued evaluation function, capturing the relationship between user u, object o_j and object o_k. BPR method further assumes the prior density of model parameters to be of normal distribution with zero mean $p(\Theta) \sim N(0, \lambda_\theta I)$, where λ_θ are model specific regularization parameters. Thus the optimization criterion BPR-OPT can be derived as follows:

$$
\begin{aligned}
\text{BPR-OPT} &\coloneqq \ln p(\Theta \mid >_u) \\
&= \ln p(>_u | \Theta) \, p(\Theta) \\
&= \ln \prod_{(u_i, o_j, o_k) \in T_s} p(o_j >_u o_k | \Theta) \, p(\Theta) \\
&= \sum_{(u_i, o_j, o_k) \in T_s} \ln \sigma(\hat{r}_{u,j,k}(\Theta)) + \ln p(\Theta) \\
&= \sum_{(u_i, o_j, o_k) \in T_s} \ln \sigma(\hat{r}_{u,j,k}(\Theta)) - \lambda_\theta \|\Theta\|^2
\end{aligned}
$$

So far, the derivation of BPR-OPT criterion was general, without consideration of a specific model. In case of matrix factorization, the natural definition of $\hat{r}_{u,j,k}$ is to substract predicted ratings of known and unknown interaction:

$$\hat{r}_{u,j,k} \coloneqq \hat{r}_{u,j} - \hat{r}_{u,k}$$

The matrix factorization model parameters Θ are the latent factors of users and objects $\Theta = (\mathbf{U}, \mathbf{V})$, so the optimization criterion specific for matrix factorization, can be rewritten as follows:

$$
\begin{aligned}
\text{BPR\_OPT}_{\text{MF}} &= \sum_{(u_i, o_j, o_k) \in T_s} \ln \sigma(\hat{r}_{i,j} - \hat{r}_{i,k}) \\
&\quad - \lambda_R \big(\|\mathbf{U}\|^2 + \|\mathbf{V}\|^2\big)
\end{aligned}
\tag{1}
$$

The BPR_OPT criterion is maximized via stochastic gradient ascend with bootstrap sampling of training points. In our implementation, we slightly deviate from the original BPR, as we uniformly sample users and for each sampled user, uniformly sample interacting and non-interacting objects. The bold driver heuristics is applied after each iteration, with iteration i defined as the sequence of samples T_i from T_s with the same size as the total volume of positive interaction:

$$T_i \subset T_s : |T_i| = \big|\{(i,j) : r_{i,j} = 1\}\big|$$

2.3 Content Alignments for BPR

We propose content alignments to the BPR method to overcome one of the main limitation of all CF methods – poor performance in cold-start settings. Our proposal suppose relaxing of the objects and users independence by precomputed similarity matrices $\mathbf{S}_p^U$ and $\mathbf{S}_q^O$. An intuition behind our proposal is that high similarity of users or objects (w.r.t some of the $\mathbf{S}_p^U$, resp. $\mathbf{S}_q^O$ matrices) should be reflected in similarity of its latent factors. Thus, differences in highly similar users' and objects' latent factors should be penalized in BPR-OPT criterion (1). Furthermore, suppose that we can define the level of trust or relevance of the content-based information, resp. the similarity matrices $\mathbf{S}_p^U, \mathbf{S}_q^O$. The relevance of similarity matrices can be explicit, based on some external evaluation, or latent, learned from the data. Naturally, the amount

of penalization for latent factor differences should reflect also the relevance of the base similarity matrix.

To be more specific, we base our work on the approach of Nguyen and Zhu [16]. Authors defined additional content-based regularization term in SVD++ optimization criterion as a squared norm of the latent factors distance for similar users. Applying such regularization on BPR's ternary train set $(u_i, o_j, o_k) \in T_s$ and supposing to have only two similarity matrices $\mathbf{S}^U$ and $\mathbf{S}^O$, the content alignment regularization term should looks as follows:

$$
CA = \lambda_C \left(
\begin{aligned}
&\sum_{i=1}^{n} \sum_{\bar{i}=1}^{n} s_{i,\bar{i}}^{U} \|\boldsymbol{\mu}_i - \boldsymbol{\mu}_{\bar{i}}\|^2 + \\
&\sum_{j=1}^{m} \sum_{\bar{j}=1}^{m} s_{j,\bar{j}}^{O} \|\mathbf{v}_j - \mathbf{v}_{\bar{j}}\|^2 + \\
&\sum_{k=1}^{m} \sum_{\bar{k}=1}^{m} s_{k,\bar{k}}^{O} \|\mathbf{v}_k - \mathbf{v}_{\bar{k}}\|^2
\end{aligned}
\right)
$$

Now, suppose that we have multiple similarity matrices $\mathbf{S}_p^U, \mathbf{S}_q^O$ for users and objects respectively and weight ω_S for each similarity matrix $\mathbf{S}$ represents its level of trust. If the ω_S weights are static, externally defined, we can simply sum all $\mathbf{S}_p^U, \mathbf{S}_q^O$ similarity matrices into $\mathbf{S}^U$ and $\mathbf{S}^O$ and use the previous approach.

$$
\mathbf{S}^U \coloneqq \sum_{p=1}^{n_s} \omega_p \mathbf{S}_p^U, \quad \mathbf{S}^O \coloneqq \sum_{q=1}^{m_s} \omega_q \mathbf{S}_q^O
$$

If the ω_S weights are latent, they need to be inferred from the data. Let us suppose that a hyperparameter λ_c reflects the total amount of trust in content-based information. Then the following condition should hold.

$$
\sum_{s \in \{\mathbf{S}_p^U, \mathbf{S}_q^O\}} |\omega_s| = \lambda_c
\tag{2}
$$

Furthermore, as we prefer simpler weighting models, we impose squared regularization penalty on the ω_s weights: $\sum_{S \in \{\mathbf{S}_p^U, \mathbf{S}_q^O\}} (\omega_S - \omega_0)^2$, where ω_0 corresponds with an uniform weighting scheme $\omega_0 = \frac{1}{|\{\mathbf{S}_p^U, \mathbf{S}_q^O\}|} \lambda_c$. With these assumptions, the multiple content alignments regularization term looks as follows:

$$
MCA =
\begin{aligned}
&\sum_{p=1}^{n_s} \sum_{i=1}^{n} \sum_{\bar{i}=1}^{n} \omega_p s_{p,i,\bar{i}}^{U} \|\boldsymbol{\mu}_i - \boldsymbol{\mu}_{\bar{i}}\|^2 + \\
&\sum_{q=1}^{m_s} \sum_{j=1}^{m} \sum_{\bar{j}=1}^{m} \omega_q s_{q,j,\bar{j}}^{O} \|\mathbf{v}_j - \mathbf{v}_{\bar{j}}\|^2 + \\
&\sum_{q=1}^{m_s} \sum_{k=1}^{m} \sum_{\bar{k}=1}^{m} \omega_q s_{q,k,\bar{k}}^{O} \|\mathbf{v}_k - \mathbf{v}_{\bar{k}}\|^2 + \\
&\lambda_w \sum_{s \in \{\mathbf{S}_p^U, \mathbf{S}_q^O\}} (\omega_S - \omega_0)^2
\end{aligned}
\tag{3}
$$

However, our intention was to impose the latent factors similarity only on highly similar users or objects. In real-world applications, there are large volumes of users and objects with only a negligible similarity to each other, approximately following the power law distribution. These low similarities could introduce unnecessary noise into the optimization. In order to cope with this problem, all

SCHEMA OF MOVIELENS1M DATASET EXTENSION

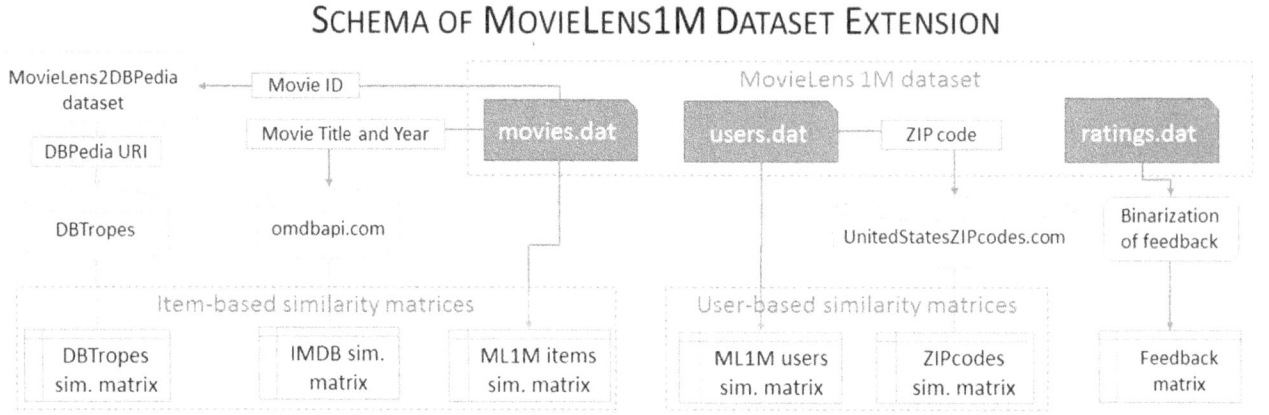

Figure 1: Schema of the extensions made on the MovieLens 1M dataset.

similarity matrices $\mathbf{S}_p^U$ and $\mathbf{S}_q^O$ are altered to contain only the top-k most similar neighbors to each user and object respectively; similarity to all other users (objects) is defined as 0. Such approach effectively remove noise coming from the low-similar entries and also significantly decrease the computation complexity. In order to keep the model simple, we empirically define $k = 10$ in the evaluation.

Note that although MCA criterion contains triple sum, the outer sum is evaluated over (supposedly low number of) similarity matrices and the inner sum can be evaluated only for the non-zero entries of each similarity matrix (i.e. ten entries per user / object in our current model).

Removal of low-similar entries is one key difference to the MSCMF approach [25], where penalty is imposed on the whole similarity matrix, e.g., for users as follows:

$$CA_{MSCMF} = \lambda_C \left\| \sum_{\bar{p}=1}^{n_s} \omega_p \mathbf{S}_p^U - \mathbf{U}\mathbf{U}^T \right\|$$

Note that due to the MSCMF optimization procedure, direct removal of low-similar entries from its optimization criterion is not applicable.

2.4 Content Smoothing for BPR

In case of the novel objects $o_k \in O^N$, its latent factors can be constructed from negative examples $(u_i, o_j, o_k) \in T_s$ in standard BPR. However, for novel users $u_i \in U^N$, standard BPR algorithm cannot learn anything (i.e. there are no triples containing u_i in the train set T_s). Common solution of this "*new user*" problem is to use some non-personalized recommender system [11], [12]. However, the existence of user similarity matrices $\mathbf{S}_p^U$ provides us with further options. After the training phase, the latent factors $\boldsymbol{\mu}_i$ of new user $u_i \in U^N$ can be redefined through their similarity to the other users as follows.

$$\boldsymbol{\mu}_i = \frac{\sum_{\bar{i} \neq i} \sum_{p=1}^{n_s} \omega_p s_{p,i,\bar{i}}^U \, \boldsymbol{\mu}_{\bar{i}}}{\sum_{\bar{i} \neq i} \sum_{p=1}^{n_s} \omega_p s_{p,i,\bar{i}}^U} \tag{4}$$

The proposed approach is an extension of Liu et al. [15] applied on multiple similarity matrices. According to (4), the latent factors of user u_i are smoothed by the weighted average of its neighbors'

latent factors. Similar approach can be defined also for users with too few known interactions. In order to be consistent with the rest of our approach, we applied content smoothing on the same restricted $\mathbf{S}_p^U$ matrices as content alignments, i.e. each $\mathbf{S}_p^U$ matrix contains only top-10 most similar neighbors of each user.

2.5 BPR-MCA Method

Finally, the Bayesian Ranking Prediction with Multiple Content Alignments method is assembled as follows. The original BPR-OPT criterion (1) is extended by MCA term:

$$BPR\text{-}MCA\_OPT = \sum_{(u_i, o_j, o_k) \in T_s} \ln \sigma\left(\hat{r}_{i,j} - \hat{r}_{i,k}\right)$$
$$-\lambda_R \left(\|\mathbf{U}\|^2 + \|\mathbf{V}\|^2 + MCA \right)$$

Bootstrapped stochastic gradient ascent is used to maximize the BPR-MCA_OPT criterion. Update rules for each parameter are as follows:

$$\boldsymbol{\mu}_i = \boldsymbol{\mu}_i + \eta \left(x \cdot (\mathbf{v}_j - \mathbf{v}_k) - \lambda_R \left(\boldsymbol{\mu}_i + \sum_{p=1}^{n_s} \sum_{\bar{i}=1}^{n} \omega_p \mathbf{S}_{p,i,\bar{i}}^U (\boldsymbol{\mu}_i - \boldsymbol{\mu}_{\bar{i}}) \right) \right)$$

$$\mathbf{v}_j = \mathbf{v}_j + \eta \left(x \cdot \boldsymbol{\mu}_i - \lambda_R \left(\mathbf{v}_j + \sum_{q=1}^{m_s} \sum_{\bar{j}=1}^{m} \omega_q \mathbf{S}_{q,j,\bar{j}}^O (\mathbf{v}_j - \mathbf{v}_{\bar{j}}) \right) \right)$$

$$\mathbf{v}_k = \mathbf{v}_k + \eta \left(x \cdot (-\boldsymbol{\mu}_i) - \lambda_R \left(\mathbf{v}_j + \sum_{q=1}^{m_s} \sum_{\bar{k}=1}^{m} \omega_q \mathbf{S}_{q,k,\bar{k}}^O (\mathbf{v}_k - \mathbf{v}_{\bar{k}}) \right) \right) \tag{5}$$

$$\omega_p = \omega_p - \eta \left(\sum_{\bar{i}=1}^{n} \mathbf{S}_{p,i,\bar{i}}^U \|\boldsymbol{\mu}_i - \boldsymbol{\mu}_{\bar{i}}\|^2 + \lambda_w (\omega_p - \omega_0) \right)$$

$$\omega_q = \omega_q -$$
$$\eta \left(\sum_{\bar{j}=1}^{m} \left(\mathbf{S}_{q,j,\bar{j}}^O \|\mathbf{v}_j - \mathbf{v}_{\bar{j}}\|^2 + \mathbf{S}_{q,k,\bar{j}}^O \|\mathbf{v}_k - \mathbf{v}_{\bar{j}}\|^2 \right) + 2\lambda_w (\omega_p - \omega_0) \right)$$

where $x = \sigma\left(\hat{r}_{i,j} - \hat{r}_{i,k}\right)$ and hyperparameters η, λ_R and λ_w are learning rate, general regularization and content weight regularization respectively. Algorithm 1 contains the pseudocode of the proposed optimization method.

Function Optimize_BPR-MCA

Input: $f, \eta, \lambda_R, \lambda_C, \lambda_w, max\_iterations, k, \mathbf{R}, \mathbf{S}_p^U, \mathbf{S}_q^O$

Output: $\hat{\mathbf{R}}$

1: **Initialize** $\mathbf{U}, \mathbf{V}$
2: **Alter** $\mathbf{S}_p^U, \mathbf{S}_q^O$ to contain only top-k neighbors for each item
3: **Repeat** until $max\_iterations$ is reached:
4:     **Repeat** $\left|\{r_{a,b} \in \mathbf{R}: r_{a,b} = 1\}\right|$ times:
5:         Draw random $u_i \in U \backslash U^N$
6:         Draw random o_i, o_j: $r_{i,j} = 1$ & $r_{i,k} = 0$
7:         **Update** $\boldsymbol{\mu}_i, \mathbf{v}_j, \mathbf{v}_k, \omega_p, \omega_q$ according to (5)
8:         Linearly scale all ω_p, ω_q so that (2) holds
9:     **Update** η by bold driver heuristics
10: **Foreach** $u_i \in U^N$:
11:     Redefine $\boldsymbol{\mu}_i$ as in (4)

Algorithm 1: Optimization of BPR-MCA method.

2.6 Dataset

To evaluate the proposed method, we extended the well-known MovieLens 1M (ML1M) dataset [6]. The original dataset contains over one million ratings on 1 to 5 scale from 6041 users and in total 3883 movies. Furthermore, the dataset contains some basic user statistics, such as gender, occupation, age group and a ZIP code. Title, year of publication and genres are available for the movies. As the input of BPR method is a binary user rating, the original graded feedback was binarized as follows: all known interactions with user rating ≥ 3 were considered as positive, i.e., $r_{u,o} = 1$, all other interactions (unrated and those with rating < 3) were considered as unknown, i.e., $r_{u,o} = 0$.

Thereafter, the resulting dataset was extended by content-based information from three sources:

- User profiles were extended via ZIP code statistics.

- Item profiles were extended via IMDB movie features.

- Item profiles were extended via DBTropes features.

Figure 1 depicts the general schema of the dataset extensions. First, we hypothesize that some factors influencing user's preference can be attributed to the influence of his/her surroundings. The closest "*influential groups*" such as friends or family are not possible to track from the original ML1M user profile. However, we suppose that also the area in which the user lives can partially determine him/her and his/her preferences. In order to collect features describing user's neighborhood, we employ a wrapper to the *UnitedStatesZipCodes.org* website, with the user's ZIP code serving as a query. The website provides statistical information such as housing types, age and ethnical picture, several economic indicators etc. The collected features aims to distinguish between urban and countryside areas (*total population, density*), social picture (*median age, singles ratio*), economical situation (*vacant houses ratio*) and ethnicity of the inhabitants. In total, we were able to collect ZIP code statistics about 5875 out of 6041 users. The rest of the users filled-in incorrect or non-US ZIP codes. All collected features are described in Table 1. Note that although ZIP codes are not commonly

Table 1: User-based features collected via ZIP codes.

Feature	Description
population	log_2(total population)
density	log_2(population density)
medAge	Median of age
vacant	Ratio of vacant households
singles	Ratio of single-inhabitant households
Ratios of *black*, *white*, *native* and *asian* inhabitants	

Table 2: Item-based features collected via IMDB API.

Feature	Description
Year	Publication year
Rating	Average IMDB rating
Country	Country(s) of origin
Language	Spoken language(s)
Genre	Movie genre(s)
Persons	List of director(s), writer(s) and actors

provided by the users, similar information can be obtained based on their IP addresses.

The original ML1M dataset provides merely some basic information about the movies, allowing us to define a very rough movie similarity at best. In order to define some finer grained similarity metrics, we collected further movie attributes available through IMDB API[1]. Movie title and the year of production served as the query to the API. In total, we were able to match 3085 movies of the original ML1M dataset. Collected features foremost link movies through the contributing persons (*actors, director, writer*) and provide further general description (*language, country of origin, average rating*). All collected features are described in Table 2.

Although the IMDB metadata already provide relevant features of the movies, these features are mostly "external" (i.e., providing contributing persons and circumstances rather than describing relevant plot features). In order to bridge this semantic gap, we also collected plot characteristics available from DBTropes [10], a linked open data (LOD) extension of TvTropes[2]. TvTropes community focus on identifying and describing behavior archetypes, typical story lines and common character types that occurs across the movies. As such, TvTropes represents ideal source of information for an "intrinsic" movie similarity metric. In order to link TvTropes to the ML1M dataset, we used DBTropes *owl:SameAs* link to DBPedia[3], which is available for a subset of the movies. There is also existing mapping of ML1M movies to DBPedia [4], so we match ML1M and DBTropes objects through the same DBPedia URI. In total, we were able to match 589 movies of the original ML1M dataset.

BPR-MCA method requires user-to-user and object-to-object similarity matrices as its input, so the collected users' and objects' features need to be further processed. There are numerous methods to derive similarity from content-based information. However, as the similarity computation is not the core of our work, we opted for a rather simple approach. Each ML1M dataset

---

[1] http://www.omdbapi.com
[2] http://tvtropes.org/
[3] http://www.dbpedia.org

Table 3: Overall results of the evaluation on extended ML1M dataset. Best results are in bold, baseline method is in grey, italic. Results with significantly lower performance than the best method (p<0.001 according to the paired t-test) are marked with an asterisk (*).

Method	nDCG				AUPR			
	p75	*p90*	*p95*	*p98*	*p75*	*p90*	*p95*	*p98*
Graph-based	*0.4863	*0.4930	*0.4913	*0.4853	*0.0681	*0.0641	*0.0605	*0.0560
WRMF	*0.6634	*0.5854	*0.5421	*0.5124	*0.2443	*0.1553	*0.1485*	*0.2132*
BPR	*0.6848	*0.6351	*0.5739	*0.5490	*0.2607	*0.1976	*0.1147	*0.0895
BPR-MCA2	**0.6872**	*0.6361	*0.5732	*0.5510	**0.2618**	*0.1974	*0.1199	*0.0906
BPR-MCA5	*0.6836	**0.6425**	**0.6016**	**0.5645**	*0.2589	**0.2045**	**0.1485**	*0.1030
BPR-MCA5uniform	*0.6846	*0.6336	*0.5757	*0.5516	*0.2604	*0.1922	*0.1284	*0.0909

extension, as well as the original ML1M user and object profiles induce one similarity matrix. All collected features were binarized and similarity of two users (items) was computed as a *cosine similarity* of vectors of features' TF-IDF score. This results in total of five similarity matrices, two user-based and three item-based. Another alternative is to derive just one user-based and item-based matrix. This option is less computationally expensive, but prevent us from assessing relevance of the data sources.

3 EVALUATION AND RESULTS

In this section, we would like to provide details of the evaluation procedure. It was shown that collaborative techniques need support of content-based or non-personalized recommendations especially in cold-start scenarios [11], [19], which are however quite common in the real-world applications [9], [17], [18]. So, our main goal in evaluation was to measure BPR-MCA performance under the various cold-start settings. Following method variants were evaluated:

- Original BPR method [20] (denoted as *BPR*).
- BPR-MCA method with two ML1M-based similarity matrices (*BPR-MCA2*).
- BPR-MCA employing all similarity matrices and learning ω_p, ω_q weights (*BPR-MCA5*).
- BPR-MCA employing all similarity matrices and uniform ω_p, ω_q weights (*BPR-MCA5uniform*).

Apart from the variants of BPR-MCA method, we also evaluated two further baselines:

- *WRMF* matrix factorization [7] (collaborative).
- *Graph-based* recommender (content-based).

The graph-based recommender first builds user profile as a list of visited objects and the visited objects of similar users. Each object is weighted by the sum of user-user similarities $\mathbf{S}_p^U$. Thereafter, the method recommends most similar objects to the ones in the user profile via the sum of $\mathbf{S}_q^O$ matrices. The same neighborhood reduction parameter $k = 10$ as in the *BPR-MCA* method is applied on $\mathbf{S}_p^U$ and $\mathbf{S}_q^O$ matrices.

Comparison of *BPR* against *WRMF* should indicate, whether we choose suitable matrix factorization technique for this particular task, while comparison of *BPR-MCA5uniform* against *Graph-based*

approach indicates whether the additional collaborative information can provide some improvement over purely content-based recommendations.

Hyperparameters of BPR-based methods were learned via grid-search and internal bootstrap sampling as follows. The number of latent factors was fixed $f = 20$, initial learning rate was fixed $\eta = 0.1$, regularization λ_R was selected from $\{0.01, 0.05\}$ and the number of iterations was selected from $\{5, 10, 15, ..., 30\}$. Furthermore for BPR-MCA, total content weight λ_C was selected from $\{0.001, 0.01, 0.05\}$ and content regularization λ_w from $\{0.01, 0.05, 0.2\}$.

For *WRMF*, hyperparameters were learned via grid-search as follows. The number of latent factors was fixed $f = 20$, regularization r was selected from $\{5, 10, 50\}$, confidence of positive examples c was selected from $\{r \times 0.1, r, r \times 10\}$ and the number of iterations was selected from $\{5, 10, 15, ..., 30\}$.

As the ML1M dataset is known to be extremely dense, we opted for Monte Carlo cross-validation with low train/test ratios to simulate the cold-start problem. In total four scenarios were evaluated, with 75%, 90%, 95% and 98% of the interactions randomly removed from the interaction matrix **R** for training. These scenarios are denoted as *p75*, *p90*, *p95* and *p98* in the results. Each training scenario was repeated 5-times, while the hidden interactions were used for per-user evaluation. We used normalized discounted cumulative gain (nDCG) and area under precision-recall curve (AUPR) as evaluation metrics. NDCG logarithmically penalizes relevant objects appeared too low in the recommended list. Also AUPR is considered to reflect algorithm's performance well in case of highly imbalanced data [3], so both metrics seems to be a reasonable approximation of top-k ranking evaluation problem[4]. Both metrics were evaluated for each user and averaged results over all users and CV runs are provided.

3.1 Results

The overall results are depicted in Table 3. As can be seen from the results, *BPR-MCA5* method significantly outperform original *BPR* method on three more difficult cold-start scenarios (*p90*, *p95* and *p98*). As for *p75*, we hypothesize that in this scenario, the

---

[4] In this paper, we used only a binary relevance as a measure of recommendation quality. We plan to consider also other aspects, such as diversity or novelty in the future work.

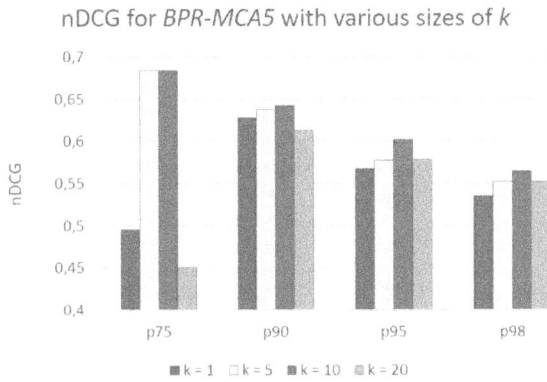

Figure 2: Evaluation of *BPR-MCA5* w.r.t. nDCG for various values of hyperparameter *k*.

amount of data for collaborative filtering (sparsity of 99.1%) is already sufficient to suppress content-based component of *BPR-MCA* method. Note that BPR-MCA method based solely on ML1M data (*BPR-MCA2*) provided only marginal improvement on all scenarios compared to the BPR-MCA based on all available data (*BPR-MCA5*).

Furthermore, the comparison of *BPR-MCA5* and *BPR-MCA5uniform* results indicate the importance of assigning proper weights to similarity matrices as well as the ability of BPR-MCA method to learn them. Also note that the improvement of *BPR-MCA5* over *BPR* cannot be attributed solely to improvement of recommendations to the new users. There were only a few novel users even in the *p98* scenario and both *BPR-MCA2* and *BPR-MCA5uniform* methods contained the same content smoothing extension as *BPR-MCA5* method, yet performed significantly inferior.

The *graph-based* recommender was clearly inferior compared to the *BPR-MCA5uniform* method indicating the significant contribution of collaborative component of *BPR-MCA* method. The results of *WRMF* were significantly inferior to *BPR* in all scenarios w.r.t. nDCG. Results w.r.t. AUPR were rather inconclusive (*BPR* was better in *p75* and *p90*, *WRMF* was better in *p95* and *p98* scenarios), but overall we can still conclude that *BPR*-based methods are suitable for the task.

The Role of *k* Parameter

The hyperparameter *k* defines the number of considered nearest neighbors in the content-based similarity matrices so it is worth to show how it affects the results of the *BPR-MCA* method. Thus, we performed some additional experiments with *BPR-MCA5* method and various settings of *k* hyperparameter ($k \in \{1, 5, 10, 20\}$). The results w.r.t. nDCG indicate (see Figure 2) that *BPR-MCA5* method performs best with *k* parameter around 10 for all scenarios. However, the results also indicates increasing relative performance of $k = 5$ variant for larger scenarios (*p90*, *p75*), so we can suppose that less neighbors are needed while more collaborative information is available. This observation seems to be a consequence of [19] stating that even if only a few ratings are known per user, collaborative filtering is more effective than content-based techniques. In order to further examine this effect, we performed additional analysis of the results based on the size of user's train set.

The Role of User's Train Set Size

Although the *BPR-MCA* methods significantly improved results of standard *BPR* in all but *p75* scenario, we wanted to further evaluate its performance w.r.t the size of user's train set. Thus, we split the set of users according to the size of their train sets and evaluate each group of users separately. The subsets were defined as follows.

- Users with *no objects* in the train set
- Users with small train set (*1-2 objects*)
- Users with medium train set (*3-9 objects*)
- Users with large train set (*10+ objects*)

The results according to the train set size are depicted on Figure 3. It can be seen that even in *p75* scenario *BPR-MCA5* outperforms *BPR* on the subset of users with small and empty train sets. Furthermore, in *p90*, *p95* and *p98* scenarios, *BPR-MCA5* outperforms *BPR* also on the subset of users with medium and large train sets with gradually increasing difference. Based on these observations, we can conclude that BPR-MCA method can be used also as a content-based component of an alternating or weighted hybrid together with some purely collaborative method. Weight of each prediction method should depend on both the overall sparsity of the dataset and the train set size of the particular user.

3.2 Discussion

During the analysis of the results, we observed several interesting points, which we would like to remark.

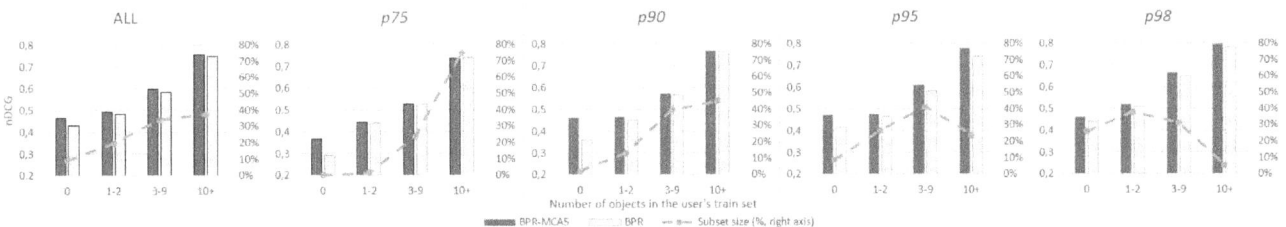

Figure 3: Evaluation w.r.t. nDCG grouped by the user's train set size. First graph depicts overall results, other graphs depicts results of *p75*, *p90*, *p95* and *p98* scenarios respectively. Grey dotted line indicates the volume of users in each group.

Figure 4: Histograms of similarity matrices' weights ω_p for *BPR-MCA5* method. In average, the highest weights were learned for DBTropes-based similarity matrix, the lowest weights were learned for IMDB-based similarity.

As for the weights of the similarity matrices, we were surprised by the large differences in the learned weights ω_p, ω_q. Similarity matrix based on DBTropes data received the highest weights in average despite the low coverage of the movies. We suppose this can be attributed to the high relevance of the intrinsic information contained in the DBTropes dataset. Also, both user-based similarity matrices were evaluated quite positively (see Figure 4 for details). On the other hand, ML1M object similarity received consistently lower weights than the three previously mentioned similarity matrices. Similar weight distribution was also observed for *BPR-MCA2* method, so we can tentatively conclude on the higher relevance of ML1M user attributes over ML1M item attributes. Furthermore, the weight of IMDB-based similarity matrix was often significantly negative. The reason could be simply low information value of the IMDB-based matrix, however it could also be an aspect of intrinsic diversity of user preferences. We would like to focus on this problem more in the future. Nonetheless, the highly differentiated weights learned by *BPR-MCA5* together with the superiority of *BPR-MCA5* over the uniform weighting model are key observations supporting the mechanism of learning content weights.

Furthermore, we observed an interesting trend in learned values of the total content relevance λ_c hyperparameter. Whereas in the *p75* scenario, the total content weight λ_c was almost uniformly learned at the lowest possible level ($\lambda_c = 0.001$), larger λ_c values were selected for more difficult cold-start scenarios. Similar trend was shown for the content-based neighborhood size k and similar trend with the opposite direction was seen also for content regularization hyperparameter λ_w. These observation supports and extends previous research on cold-start recommendation [11], [12], [17], [19] such that the importance of content-based learning and also content weighting gradually decreases with the amount of interactions. Although this observation should be validated on more datasets and over further variables, we believe that it could lead into some generally-applicable rules or thresholds defining the necessity/importance of using content-based or hybrid preference learning in specific applications.

In this scenario, we did not consider diversity of the recommended list, user context, preference shift or graded feedback. However, please note that the proposed method can be naturally combined,

e.g., with BPR++ [14] to incorporate graded feedback, xQUAD [22] to enhance diversity etc.

We would also like to make some remarks on the difficulty of the "cold-start" settings. Although hiding up to 98% of the interactions might seem as a rather extreme use-case, please note that MovieLens is one of the densest available dataset with the sparsity of 96%. By removing 98% of the interactions, there is still approx. 16700 interactions left (i.e. in average 2.8 interactions per user and 99.93% sparsity). Such dataset parameters are similar to some known e-commerce datasets, e.g., [18] with the average volume of interactions per user 1.9 and 99.9% sparsity. From this perspective, using content-based or hybrid techniques such as BPR-MCA instead of purely collaborative might be inevitable on some domains[5].

4 CONCLUSIONS

In this paper, we proposed an extension of BPR matrix factorization. The proposed method incorporates content alignments based on multiple similarity matrices into the BPR's optimization criterion and is able to learn the weight of each similarity matrix.

An extended MovieLens 1M dataset was used to evaluate the proposed BPR-MCA method. BPR-MCA provided significant improvements over standard BPR in three cold-start settings w.r.t nDCG and AUPR. Furthermore, evaluation also pointed out the importance of using informative content-based attributes contained in the extended ML1M dataset as well as proper weights for similarity matrices derived from them.

Evaluation also raised several questions, which we would like to address in the future. Negative weights were often learned for some similarity matrices and further research should clarify, whether this is an attribute of low information value, or rather an aspect of diversity in user preferences. Similarly, it would be interesting to find some generally-applicable relationship between the amount of interactions and the need for content-based learning.

Thus, a substantial part of the future work should focus on evaluating BPR-MCA on further datasets, with different content-based similarities and also compare it with other state-of-the-art approaches. The results of DBTropes extension pointed out the importance of using intrinsic data bridging the semantic gap. A

---

[5] Given the fluctuation of both objects and users, there might never be enough data to employ purely collaborative approaches.

promising direction extending this work would be to enhance relevant dataset with the similarity based on visual or multimedia data, e.g., in the form of descriptors of convolutional neural networks [2].

Furthermore, there is definitely some space for incorporating diversity, temporality, graded feedback or negative implicit feedback [18] into the BPR-MCA method. Another branch of the future work involves on-line evaluation of the proposed approach on some real-world application or through a controlled user-study.

ACKNOWLEDGMENTS

The work on this paper was supported by Czech grants P46 and GACR-17-22224S. Some additional materials are available online:

- Extensions to the MovieLens 1M dataset are available on: *http://www.ksi.mff.cuni.cz/~peska/BPR_MCA/*.

- BPR-MCA source codes are available on GitHub: *http://github.com/lpeska/BPR_MCA*.

REFERENCES

[1] de Campos, L. M.; Fernandez-Luna, J. M.; Huete, J. F. & Rueda-Morales, M. A. Combining content-based and collaborative recommendations: A hybrid approach based on Bayesian networks. *International Journal of Approximate Reasoning* , **2010**, 51, 785 - 799

[2] Covington, P.; Adams, J. & Sargin, E. Deep Neural Networks for YouTube Recommendations. *Proceedings of the 10th ACM Conference on Recommender Systems, ACM*, **2016**, 191-198

[3] Davis, J. & Goadrich, M. The relationship between Precision-Recall and ROC curves. *In Proceedings of the 23rd international conference on Machine learning (ICML '06). ACM*, **2006**, 233-240.

[4] Di Noia, T.; Ostuni, V.C.; Tomeo, P & Di Sciascio, E. SPrank: Semantic Path-Based Ranking for Top-N Recommendations Using Linked Open Data. *ACM Trans. Intell. Syst. Technol. 8, 1, Article 9*, **2016**, 34 pages

[5] Forbes, P. & Zhu, M. Content-boosted matrix factorization for recommender systems: experiments with recipe recommendation. *In RecSys 2011, ACM*, **2011**, 261-264

[6] Harper, F.M. & Konstan, J.A. The MovieLens Datasets: History and Context. *ACM Transactions on Interactive Intelligent Systems (TiiS) 5, 4, Article 19*, **2015**, 19 pages.

[7] Hu, Y.; Koren, Y. & Volinsky, C. Collaborative Filtering for Implicit Feedback Datasets. *Proceedings of the 2008 Eighth IEEE International Conference on Data Mining, IEEE Computer Society*, **2008**, 263-272

[8] Johnson, CC. Logistic matrix factorization for implicit feedback data. *NIPS 2014 Workshop on Distributed Machine Learning and Matrix Computations*, **2014**, 1-9

[9] Kaminskas, M.; Bridge, D.; Foping, F. & Roche, D. Product Recommendation for Small-Scale Retailers. *In Proceedings of EC-WEB 2015, Springer, LNBIP 239*, **2015**, 17-29

[10] Kiesel, M.; & Grimnes, G.A. DBTropes - a linked data wrapper approach incorporating community feedback. In International Conference on Knowledge Engineering and Knowledge Management (EKAW2010), CEUR-WS, **2010**

[11] Kluver, D. & Konstan, J. A. Evaluating Recommender Behavior for New Users. *Proceedings of the 8th ACM Conference on Recommender Systems, ACM*, **2014**, 121-128

[12] Knijnenburg, B. P.; Reijmer, N. J. & Willemsen, M. C. Each to His Own: How Different Users Call for Different Interaction Methods in Recommender Systems. *Proceedings of the Fifth ACM Conference on Recommender Systems, ACM*, **2011**, 141-148

[13] Koren, Y.; Bell, R. & Volinsky, C. Matrix Factorization Techniques for Recommender Systems. *Computer, IEEE Computer Society Press*, **2009**, 42, 30-37

[14] Lerche, L. & Jannach, D. Using Graded Implicit Feedback for Bayesian Personalized Ranking. *Proceedings of the 8th ACM Conference on Recommender Systems, ACM*, **2014**, 353-356

[15] Liu, Y.; Wu, M.; Miao, C.; Zhao, P. & Li, X. L. Neighborhood Regularized Logistic Matrix Factorization for Drug-Target Interaction Prediction. *PLoS Comput Biol 12(2): e1004760*, **2016**, 1-26.

[16] Nguyen, J. & Zhu, M. Content-boosted matrix factorization techniques for recommender systems. *Statistical Analysis and Data Mining, Wiley Subscription Services*, **2013**, 6, 286-301

[17] Peska, L. & Vojtas, P. Recommending for Disloyal Customers with Low Consumption Rate. *SOFSEM 2014: Theory and Practice of Computer Science, Springer International Publishing*, **2014**, 8327, 455-465

[18] Peska, L. & Vojtas, P. Using Implicit Preference Relations to Improve Recommender Systems. *Journal on Data Semantics, Springer*, **2016**, 16 pages

[19] Pilászy, I. & Tikk, D. Recommending New Movies: Even a Few Ratings Are More Valuable Than Metadata. *Proceedings of the Third ACM Conference on Recommender Systems, ACM*, **2009**, 93-100

[20] Rendle, S.; Freudenthaler, C.; Gantner, Z. & Schmidt-Thieme, L. BPR: Bayesian Personalized Ranking from Implicit Feedback. *Proceedings of the Twenty-Fifth Conference on Uncertainty in Artificial Intelligence, AUAI Press*, **2009**, 452-461

[21] Salakhutdinov, R. & Mnih, A. Probabilistic Matrix Factorization. *Advances in Neural Information Processing Systems 20 (NIPS 2007)*, **2007**, 1-8

[22] Santos, R.; Macdonald, C. & Ounis, I. Exploiting query reformulations for web search result diversification. *In Proceedings of the 19th international conference on World wide web (WWW '10). ACM*, **2010**, 881-890.

[23] Weimer, M.; Karatzoglou, A. & Smola, A. Improving maximum margin matrix factorization. *Machine Learning, 72(3)*, **2008**, 263-276.

[24] Yi, X.; Hong, L.; Zhong, E.; Liu, N. N. & Rajan, S. Beyond Clicks: Dwell Time for Personalization. *Proceedings of the 8th ACM Conference on Recommender Systems, ACM*, **2014**, 113-120

[25] Zheng, X.; Ding, H.; Mamitsuka, H. & Zhu, S. Collaborative matrix factorization with multiple similarities for predicting drug-target interactions. *KDD'13: Proceedings of the 19th ACM SIGKDD International Conference on Knowledge Discovery and Data Mining, ACM*, **2013**, 1025–1033.

[26] Zhen, Y.; Li, W. J. & Yeung, D.Y. TagiCoFi: Tag informed collaborative filtering. *In Proceedings of the 3rd ACM Conference on Recommender Systems, ACM*, **2009**, 69–76

Does Personality Matter? A Study of Personality and Situational Effects on Consumer Behavior

Zhe Liu, Anbang Xu, Yi Wang, Jerald Schoudt, Jalal Mahmud, Rama Akkiraju

IBM Research - Almaden

San Jose, CA, USA

{liuzh, anbangxu, wangyi, jschoudt, jumahmud, akkiraju}@us.ibm.com

ABSTRACT

Personality traits[1] have long been shown to contribute to consumer behaviors. Besides the main effect of personality, it seems also plausible that other factors may impact this relationship. To understand such situational effects, in this study we analyze two possible variables, namely, income and needs. We conduct extensive analysis on a large industry dataset across over 100 product categories. For each category, we build a prediction model for consumption decision based on the derived personality features. We experiment with our prediction models under different conditions segmented by both situational factors. Our results suggest that personality's decisive power on consumer behavior varies significantly among different income levels, but non-significantly between consumer needs. Together, income and needs also have significant effect on the association between individual's personality and consumption behavior. We conclude this work by discussing the implications of our experiments and how our finding can benefit the design of more personalized recommender systems in real-world settings.

CCS CONCEPTS

• **Human-centered computing** → **Human computer interaction (HCI)** → **HCI design and evaluation methods** → User models

KEYWORDS

Consumption behavior; Personality traits; Big five personality; Income; Needs

1 INTRODUCTION

Consumer behavior study focuses on consumer activities including consumption analysis about how individuals make

HT'17, July 4-7, 2017, Prague, Czech Republic.
© 2017 ACM. ISBN 978-1-4503-4708-2/17/07...$15.00
DOI: http://dx.doi.org/10.1145/3078714.3078733

decisions on how to spend their available resources on items to satisfy their varied needs [1]. Studies in this area encompass knowledge from a wide variety of domains, such as psychology, sociology, anthropology, marketing, and economics. Consumer behavior research can be conducted from both the consumer and the product perspectives, analyzing dimensions such as age, gender, price, and quality, etc. Among consumer related factors, individual's personality has been addressed by many literature, due to its special characteristics. According to Kassarjian [2], human personality can be linked to any sub-area that one can think of within a consumption process, for instance, purchasing behavior, decision, media choice, product choice, and brand preference. Many studies, using either theory or modeling, have proved the existence of such linkage between personality and consumer behavior.

Although the correlation between individual personality and consumer behavior has been well-established, little is known about the situational impacts of this association. Some argued that the decisive role of personality in making consumption decisions can be influenced when exposing to certain degree of external stimuli, such as social norm [3], consumer attitude [4], and brand personality [5]. To examine this proposition, in this paper we focus mainly on two situational factors that have received relatively little attention in the literature, namely consumer income and needs.

Even though income has not been formally evaluated as a situational effect of the relationship between personality and consumer behavior, it has long been considered as an effective stimulus in the marketing domain. Theories have been developed to hypothesize income's effect on individual's attitude towards consumption [6]. In addition to consumer income, consumer needs have also been analyzed as a direct effect on individual's purchasing behaviors [7]. Needs are defined as the physiological or psychological deficiencies that arouse behavior [8]. According to Maslow [8], individual needs can be formed into five different dimensions, which can be further merged into two higher-level categories, deficiency needs and growth needs. Both needs have been proved to have direct effect on individual's consumption preferences [9].

Given the limited literature on this subject, in this study we want to systematically investigate the situational effects of both income and needs, as well as their interaction, on the relationship between personality and consumer behavior. Specifically, we want to answer the questions: Whether different income levels will affect the decisive power of one's personality on his/her consumption behavior? Will the decisive power of one's personality change when making purchases satisfying his/her deficiency needs versus growth needs? How will income and needs interact and impact one's consumption behavior motivated by personality? By answering these questions through a large-scale data analysis, our work can provide some theoretical foundations for later psychology or marketing studies on human personality and their purchasing behaviors. In addition, in terms of more practical contributions, we hope that the findings from this study can be used to guide the design and developed of more personalized recommender systems which takes individual's personality, income and needs into consideration.

To achieve our research goals, we perform extensive analysis on a large industry dataset, which contains 188,654 individual level purchasing records. We build a large amount of prediction models on consumer behaviors across over 100 product categories using the big five personality traits. We test our prediction accuracies under different conditions segmented by income, needs and income × needs.

We believe that our study offers significant contributions by providing a more dynamic view of the relationship between personality and income and needs in predicting consumer behavior:

1. It is one of the first studies that investigate the situational effects of income and needs on consumer behavior prediction using personality traits. Our current investigation incorporates the various relationship dimensions that have not been studied in the previous literature.

2. Compared with the previous studies, this study first adopts derived personality in predicting individual's consumption behaviors. Traditionally, to evaluate one's personality, individuals are required to take the long psychometric tests. Without sufficient incentives, it is difficult to expand such method to a large number of audiences. In contrast, the derived personality using social media analytics [10] enables us to perform larger scale consumer analysis as compared to the traditional survey-based method.

3. Unlike most of the existing studies on consumer behavior analysis, our study uses a large industry dataset from a real-world company, containing almost 190,000 purchasing records across over 100 product categories. Compared with the survey based methods, or even studies on some self-collected dataset, the scale of our analysis provides us the benefit to understand the consumer behavior on a more detailed manner. In addition, analysis on the industry dataset will enable us to provide more practical implication insights for the design and development future personalization systems.

2 LITERATURE REVIEW

2.1 Big five Personality Model

Personality is defined as individual's distinctive and enduring dispositions that cause characteristic patterns of interaction with environment [11]. A variety of personality taxonomies have

been proposed in the past [12, 13]. However, among these different models, the big five factor constructs is the most established and used model of normal personality traits [14]. The big five personality model consists of five personality factors, namely, openness, conscientiousness, extraversion, agreeableness, and neuroticism [15]. All 5 factors of the big five personality model are thought to contain several correlated but distinct lower level dimensions, called facets. In order to map individual's personality into the corresponding 5 dimensions, a number of measurement have been proposed including the 60-item NEO Five-Factor Inventory (NEO-FFI) [14], the 300-item International Personality Item Pool (IPIP-300) [15], the 50-item International Personality Item Pool (IPIP-50) [16], and the 44-item Big five Inventory (BFI) [17], etc. Among them, the IPIP-50 is the most widely used due to its high validity and shorter length. In Table 1 we summarize the big five personality traits, their corresponding facets, as well as the high/low example items from the IPIP.

Table 1: Big five Personalities, Facets, and IPIP Examples

Big five Personality	Facets	High/low example items from IPIP
Openness	• Adventurousness • Artistic Interests • Emotionality • Imagination • Intellect • Liberalism	• Have a vivid imagination/seldom daydream • Experience emotions intensely/seldom get emotional
Conscientiousness	• Achievement Striving • Cautiousness • Dutifulness • Orderliness • Self-discipline • Self-efficacy	• Prefer variety to routine/dislike changes • Like order/leave a mess • Follow rules/break rules
Extraversion	• Activity Level • Assertiveness • Cheerfulness • Excitement • Seeking • Friendliness • Gregariousness	• Make friends easily/hard to get to know • Love large parties / prefer to be alone • Take charge/wait for others to lead the way
Agreeableness	• Altruism • Cooperation • Modesty • Morality • Sympathy • Trust	• Trust others/distrust people • Easy to satisfy/have a sharp tongue
Neuroticism	• Anger • Anxiety • Depression • Immoderation • Self-consciousness • Vulnerability	• Worry about things/relaxed most time • Get angry easily/rarely get irritated • Often feel blue/feel comfortable with self

2.2 Predicting Personality Traits from Social Media

The traditional measurements of human personality traits rely heavily on self-report questionnaires. For instance, in order to measure an individual's personality, one has to ask the subject to finish a long survey containing at least 50 items from the IPIP which could be very time and effort intensive. To avoid such costly process, a number of recent studies attempted to identify individual's personality traits from their social media fingerprints in an automatically way.

Given that psychologists have demonstrated the existence of correlations between the linguistic variables, such as lexical categories [18], n-grams [19] and personality traits, a majority of the existing studies used textual features as their main source of information to predict individual's personality traits from social posts. Yarkoni [20] reported in his work the results of a large-scale analysis on the correlation between personality and word used in blogs. Golbeck, Robles, and Turner [21], Qiu, Lin, Ramsay, and Yang [22], and Gou, Zhou and Yang [23] used Linguistic Inquiry and Word Count (LIWC) dictionary [24] categories to build classifiers that identify individual's personality from Facebook and Twitter. Other than the usage of LIWC-related features, researchers also showed the benefits of the open-vocabulary approach in personality prediction. By extracting words, phrases and topics from Facebook messages, Schwartz et al. [25] built a model with higher prediction accuracy on individual's personality traits.

In addition to the works relying on lexical features, there are other studies predicting human personality traits using behavioral and social patterns. With individual's follow relationship on Twitter, Quercia et al. [26] accurately predict a user's personality. Bachrach et al. [27] correlated the user's personality with a number of behavioral features, such as the number of uploaded photos, number of events attended, number of group memberships, and number of times user has been tagged in photos. Their results showed significant relationships between personality traits and those features. Kosinski, Stillwell, and Graepel [28] in their recent work showed that social behaviors such as Facebook likes can be successfully used to predict human personality traits, especially individual's agreeableness. With the aim of inferring individual's personality from their interactions on Facebook, Ortigosa, Carro, and Quiroga [29] developed classifiers that are able to predict user personality using parameters related to social interactions, such as number of posts the user has in his wall, number of different friends that have written in the user's wall, etc.

2.3 Personality Traits and Purchasing Behaviors

Personality traits have long been shown to successfully contribute to human behaviors [30-32], especially in the field of consumption of goods and services. Verplanken and Herabadi [33] investigated how impulse buying tendency is influenced by personality. They found that the impulse buying behavior is correlated with extraversion, negatively with conscientiousness. Agreeableness and neuroticism were unrelated to impulse buying tendency. Barkhi, Reza, and Wallace [34] studied online purchase intent using personality traits. They found that 3 of the big five factors, neuroticism, openness and agreeableness, have significant influences on the willingness to buy online. Their results implied that people tend to make shopping decision with emotion rather than reasoning. Boudreaux and Palmer [35] also indicated that individual personality types have great influence on determining consumer attitudes and intentions to purchase. Matzler, Bidmon and Grabner-Kräuter [36] specifically studied two personality traits openness and extraversion. They empirically confirm the link between these two traits and perceived hedonic values of products (which is related to brand effect).

The relationship of personality and purchasing behavior has been studied across a variety of products and services. While testing individual's preferences concerning organic foods, Chen, Mei-Fang [37] indicated that an individual's personality traits play an important role in establishing personal food choice criteria. Several studies have suggested that food-related personality traits play an important role when predict the likelihood of future food consumption [38, 39]. Schlegelmilch, Bohlen, and Diamantopoulos [40] explored the relationship between personality variables and pro-environmental purchasing behavior. He showed that consumers' overall environmental consciousness has a positive impact on green purchasing decision. For products with strongly symbolic meanings, such as wine, consumer's purchasing decision will be strongly affected by specifically perceptions of personality [35]. Among all the survey-based studies, Yang et al. [41] proposed one of the very few studies relying on derived personality to predict brand preferences. They showed that personality traits have played a very important role in brand preference prediction. Liu et al. [42] proved personality's impact on consumer behaviors across different product categories, and suggested the use of derived personality traits, as an alternative to traditional demographic factors, in consumption predictions.

3 DEVELOPMENT OF RESEARCH QUESTIONS

Although many studies have assessed the association between personality traits and individual behavior, it has been argued that the relationship between the two could be influenced by a number of situational factors [43, 44]. In other words, the predictive power of an individual's personality traits on behavior "is hypothesized to differ depending on the degree to which the external environment inhibits a person's freedom to behave in idiosyncratic ways" [45]. To examine this proposition, in this paper we focus mainly on two variables that have received relatively little attention in the literature, namely consumer income and needs. Due to the lack of literature in this area, we formulate no hypothesis concerning income and needs' effect as situational variables, but will examine them exploratively.

3

3.1 Consumer Income as a Situational Variable

Consumer income has long been considered as an affective stimulus that influences consumer behavior. On a macro-level, economists introduced many theories about individual's attitude to consumption, such as the absolute income hypothesis [46], the relative income hypothesis [6], the permanent income hypothesis [47], and the life cycle permanent income hypothesis [48], etc. All of these theories hypothesized that income, to some extent, affects an individual's attitude towards consumption and saving. On a micro-level, more detailed examination of the income's impact on individual's consumption behavior have been conducted. By combining email data with demographic information, Kooti et al. [49] characterized and modelled consumer behavior using a number of profile features. They showed significant correlation between income and the number of purchases users make, average price of products purchased, and total money spent. Abeliotis, Koniari, and Sardianou [50] concluded that high-income consumers are more willing to purchase eco-friendly products than others. Wakefield and Inman [51] in their study showed that higher income leads to less price sensitivity for hedonic consumption occasions, such as purchasing of sporting goods and movies. Ricciuto, Tarasuk, and Yatchew [52] demonstrated that higher income was associated with greater consumption of vegetables and fruit. The authors claimed that this was due to the relatively higher price of the vegetables and fruits, and price has less of an influence on purchase decisions at higher incomes. Given its main effect on purchasing behaviors, we in this study would like to know how income, as a situational variable, influences the association between personality traits and consumer behavior. This leads us to the following research question:

RQ1: *How does income affect the decisive influence of personality on consumer behavior prediction?*

3.2 Consumer Needs as a Situational Variable

In addition to income's effect, researchers have taken an interest in learning about the influence of consumer needs on individual's purchasing behaviors. Park, Jaworski, and MacInnis [53] developed a framework containing three basic consumer needs to reflect value dimensions, including: functional needs, symbolic needs, and experiential needs. Using Park's framework of consumer needs, Kim, Forsythe, Gu, and Jae Moon [54] showed that individuals with higher social and experiential needs tend to purchase more apparels. While investigating people's motivations for shopping, Tauber [7] exhibited that shopping may occur not only for acquiring functional goods, but also for satisfying one's social and experiential needs. Besides Park's framework, there is another well-adapted consumer needs model proposed by Maslow [8]. As discussed in the literature review section, Maslow's hierarchy of needs are of five types, which he further merged into two higher-level categories, deficiency needs and growth needs. Deficiency needs consist of physical needs, safety needs, and belonging needs, while growth needs consist of self-esteem needs and self-actualization needs.

Compared with the deficiency needs, the growth needs have been proved to be more related to people's subjective well-beings[35, 40]. Adopting Maslow's hierarchy of needs as a theoretical framework, we offer the following research question:

RQ2: *How is the influence of personality on consumer behavior affected by different types of individual needs, namely deficiency needs and growth needs?*

3.3 Interaction of Consumer Income and Needs as a Situational Variable

Next to these main research questions on consumer income and needs as situational variable, we also examined the possible interaction effects between them. We are interested in testing the interaction effect of income and needs (income × needs) on the association relationship between personality traits and consumer behavior. We propose this research question because the interaction effect between income and needs has been observed in a number of previous studies. Kim, Forsythe, Gu, and Jae Moon [54] noticed that with the rising income, Chinese consumers pursued more products that could attain their experiential needs, rather than functional needs. Roth [55] indicated that when resources are limited, consumers tend to purchase the products that satisfy their most basic and functional needs. Based on above presented findings from prior researches, we propose our third research question:

RQ3: *What are the interaction effects between income and needs on the decisive influence of personality on consumer behavior prediction?*

4 DATA PREPARATION

4.1 Consumer Behavior Data Preparation

The data that we used in this study is obtained from Acxiom Corporation [2], which is an industry-leading supplier of demographic data for clients' marketing needs. By collecting, parsing and analyzing customer and business information, Acxiom helps its clients to accurately identify relevant audience and to conduct targeted advertising campaigns. Their main product, InfoBase, is the nation's largest repository of customer intelligence, contains hundreds of millions of records which covers information including: individual demographics (age, gender, education), household characteristics (household size, number of children), financial situations (income ranges, net worth) and a number of purchasing activities (products bought, method of payment), etc. Our dataset contains a subset from InfoBase, which covers over 250 million household-level records on 1,048 dimensions over a 24 months' period. Regarding individual's consumption behaviors, we manually selected 287 fields out of the 1,048 dimensions indicating if a household has made any purchase across a variety of product categories, ranging from apparel, books, housewares, to charity donations.

---

[2] https://www.acxiom.com/

To avoid gender and age's bias on purchasing behaviors, we further removed a set of gender and age-specific product categories (e.g. women's apparel, children's books, men's footwear), and a number of inferred variables (e.g. vacation travel to Canada-would enjoy, casino-would enjoy, which were inferred from survey data), as well as duplicated categories (e.g. Books and Music-Super Category, Books and Music-Category, Books and Music-General). This left us with a total of 169 purchasing categories.

4.2 Personality Traits Data Preparation

To derive the personality traits of each input individual from Acxiom's dataset, we adopted the Personality Insights[3] service from IBM Watson [56]. The Personality Insights API can automatically infer, from personal writings, portraits of individuals that reflect their personality traits, including big five personalities, needs, and values. Ever since its release, the Personality Insights service has received high intention and has been adopted in a number of research studies [57-59]. However, the major restrictions of directly applying Personality Insights service to the consumer data is that, first, we have no writing samples from the input individuals within the consumption dataset; second, most of the consumption behaviors in the consumer dataset are at the household level, instead of the individual level.

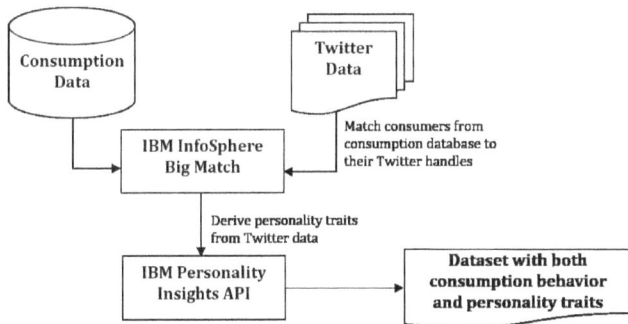

Figure 1: Calculating individual personality traits from Acxiom's dataset using IBM InfoSphere Big Match and Personality Insights.

To solve the first restriction, we rely on the help of IBM InfoSphere Big Match[4], an industry-leading Probabilistic Matching Engine, that helps organizations to match customer identities across unstructured and structured data in a Hadoop environment. In [60], authors discuss the architecture and accuracy of IBM Big Match product. They reported the accuracy of IBM Match by conducting experiments on a real-world dataset from a public-safety scenario. Authors report 91% precision and 73% recall for their match on this dataset as compared to a naive

approach of matching using person's names alone, which was recorded as only 48% recall at 91% precision.

By correlating the individual's characteristics, such as first name, last name, email, and address, from the consumption data to the unstructured personal twitter data, Big Match returns us the corresponding Twitter accounts of the input individuals from the consumption dataset. After collecting all individual tweets using Twitter API, we then use these tweets as input to the Personality Insights service and calculated the personality score for each input individual. We deleted those individuals that Big Match cannot identify or match with very low confidence, and this left us with 784,971 records. A record is considered a match when the probability of the match between the given two identity profiles was above 80%. Figure 1 depicts the matching process in more details. All information is kept confidentially and only used for purposes of this research.

Regarding the second restriction, the mismatch between household level consumption attributes and individual level personality traits, we came up with the solution of focusing on household with one person only. This type of households only has one single individual, so it is reasonable to assume that such individual performs all the consumption behaviors. In our consumption dataset, 188,654 out of 784,971 records are on the single person household level. By matching these 188,654 individual's purchasing records from the consumption data with their personality traits returned from the Personality Insights service, we derived the dataset used in this study.

5 DATA ANALYSIS

5.1 Analysis of the Situational Effects

We categorized individuals into groups according to their income levels as indicated from the consumption dataset. As categorization criteria, we adopt the predefined intervals of a) $25,000 and under (low-income), b) $25,000 to $75,000 (middle-income), and c) $75,000 and over (upper-income), from the US Census Bureau on "Money Income of Households — Percent Distribution by Income Level in Constant (2009) Dollars" (Table 690) [61]. The same categorization has been validated and used in previous studies [48, 49]. After the categorization, we have 66,923 low-income, 64,188 middle-income, and 55,543 upper-income individuals in our dataset.

Similarly, we further grouped the 169 purchasing categories from the consumption dataset into two types based on Maslow's hierarchy of needs [8]: products that can fulfill individual's deficiency needs and products that can fulfill individual's growth needs. We recruited three annotators, showed them the annotation criteria and asked them to label the 169 purchasing categories into the two types. Their annotation results yielded a 0.79 inter-rater agreement rate, indicating a reasonable inter-rater reliability. In total, all three annotators reached their agreement on 113 out of 169 product categories. 51 out of the 113 are for fulfilling one's deficiency need and 62 are for growth needs.

We split our data into multiple blocks based on a) income, b) needs, c) income × needs, so that we could compare the

---

[3] https://www.ibm.com/watson/developercloud/personality-insights.html
[4] http://www-03.ibm.com/software/products/en/infosphere-big-match-for-hadoop

5

prediction accuracies across conditions and investigate both the main and interaction effects of each variable. We experimented with the above mentioned 113 product categories for all of our analyses. ANOVA and t-tests are used to determine the statistical significance.

5.2 Prediction Model Building

Overall, for the task of modeling purchasing behaviors using personality, we implement a number of supervised binary classifiers with the 35 personality traits as features, as shown in Table 1 (5 personalities features + 30 facet features), and each of the purchasing behavior (e.g. whether or not a purchase of any book has occurred within the last 24 months, whether or not a purchase of any consumer electronics has occurred within the last 24 months) as labels. For each purchasing behavior, we build a classifier using Weka's logistic regression. Due to the existence of possible collinearities between personality traits measurements, such as between the high level big five features and the underlying facets, we penalize our model with a ridge estimator. We experiment with a number of values for the ridge estimator, ranging from 10^{-8} to 10^{50}. Our classification models are evaluated using 10-fold cross validation.

More specifically, while only looking at the data split by income levels, we noticed higher purchasing power from the middle and upper-income groups. So, to avoid the prediction bias caused by the larger training size, we further balanced our training sets across income categories. For each purchasing class, we kept all positive instances from the lower-income group and randomly sampled the same number of positive instances for both the middle and upper-income collections. In other words, in each income group, an equal number of purchasing instances are presented. The same balancing procedure were also performed to the subsets of data grouped by needs, as well as income × consumer needs. In addition, as we also identified many more negative than positive instances, we balanced the data by taking all positive instances and an equal number of randomly selected negative samples.

6 RESULTS

6.1 Research Question 1: Main Effect of Income

To answer our research question 1, we performed ANOVA to determine if there were any statistically significant differences among the prediction accuracies across income levels. Like expected, the ANOVA returned a significant main effect for income levels ($F_{(2, 333)} = 50.19$; $p < 0.05$). Post-hoc analysis using Tukey HSD were then conducted to further determine which groups significantly differed from one another. The results showed significant differences between the low-income group and the other two groups ($p < 0.05$), whereas such difference was not found between the middle-income and the upper- income groups ($p = 0.69$). This means that comparing with people with middle and upper-income levels, lower-income individual's

personality plays a more decisive role when making purchasing decisions.

In Figure 2, to better examine the cross-income differences, we presented the prediction results for all three income groups as empirical cumulative distribution functions (ECDF) of the classification accuracy. We found that in general the prediction models with income as situational effects achieved accuracies ranging from 51.75% to 66.23%. Personality's effect on purchasing decisions is significantly more decisive among the low-income individuals (with the mean prediction accuracy equals 59.12% and standard deviation equals 2.41%) than the middle-income (with the mean prediction accuracy equals 57.02% and standard deviation equals 2.40%) and high-income ones (with the mean prediction accuracy equals 56.82% and standard deviation equals 2.11%). For the lower-income individuals, about 36% of their purchasing activities can be predicted with an above 60% accuracy, whereas such percentage rate decreased to 13% and 6% to middle-income and upper-income individuals.

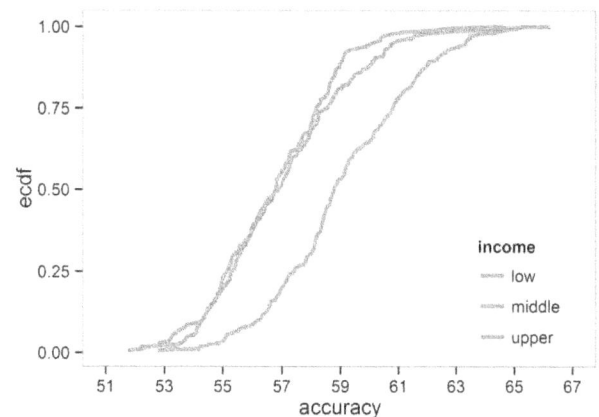

Figure 2: Empirical cumulative distributions of prediction accuracies for consumer behaviors across low, middle, and upper-income individuals.

6.2 Research Question 2: Main Effect of Needs

To answer research question 2, we applied two sample Welch's t-test on the dataset with annotated consumer needs. The results enable us to compare the mean prediction accuracy between purchases of goods satisfying one's deficiency needs and goods satisfying growth needs. Surprisingly, the differences revealed by the Welch's t-test was not significant between the two kinds of needs (t = 1.4874, p = 0.14).

Again, for better illustration purpose, we plotted the ECDF of the classification accuracy across two types of consumer needs in Figure 3. Unlike the patterns shown in Figure 2, the distribution functions for prediction accuracies on both needs showed no significant differences, as the two lines are not clearly separated in the plot. However, while taking a more in-depth look at the plot, we noticed that the green line (growth needs, with the mean prediction accuracy equals 56.00% and standard deviation equals 10.38%) is almost always above the red

6

line (deficiency needs, with the mean prediction accuracy equals 57.97% and standard deviation equals 2.16%). This means that in general, individual's personality is more decisive when making purchasing decisions on goods fulfilling deficiency needs than growth needs, even though such difference is non-significant. About 20% of the purchases on goods satisfying deficiency needs can be predicted with an above 60% accuracy, compared to 18% of the prediction rate on purchases of goods with growth needs.

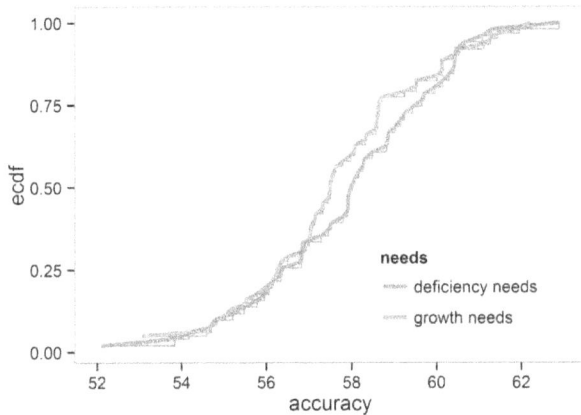

Figure 3: Empirical cumulative distributions of prediction accuracies for consumer behaviors across deficiency and growth needs.

6.3 Research Question 3: Interaction Effect between Income and Needs

To answer our research question 3, in Figure 4 we presented the interaction plot of income and needs for consumption prediction. We performed two-way ANOVA (3 income × 2 needs) conditions for significant test. Post-hoc analysis with Tamhane's T2 tests were also conducted for pairwise comparisons.

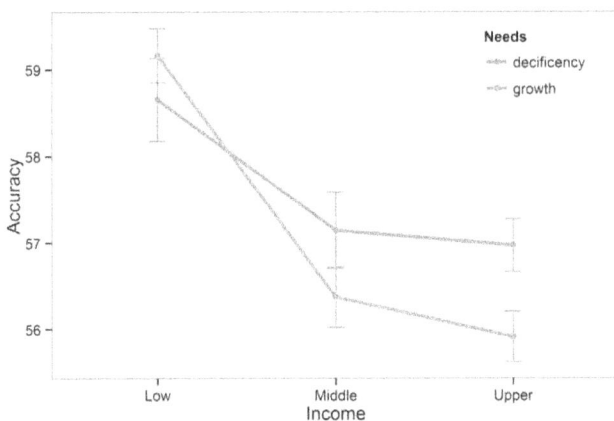

Figure 4: Interaction plot of income and needs on the prediction accuracies for consumer behavior.

7 DISCUSSION

We found that the effect of people's personality on their product purchase is more predominant when they have less income. It is evident that consumer purchase behavior is an extremely complex phenomenon. This complexity is increased as individual purchase decisions are aggregated and these decisions vary among persons faced with the same purchase decision [62]. One possible explanation is that people with higher income already possess a larger number of products and these aggregated effects could substantially mitigate the effect of people's personality on their purchase decisions.

The effect of people's personality was consistently observed across both deficiency and growth product purchases. According to the instrumental-symbolic framework [63], people's perceptions of products can be associated with two types of attributes: symbolic and instrumental. Marketing literature suggests that personality effects on purchase behavior are often evoked by symbolic images of products. For example, researchers argued that the product or brand image is a symbol of the buyer's personality. One explanation is that both deficiency and growth products are associated with a variety of symbolic meanings.

Although main effects of needs categories were not detected, significant interaction effects were observed between needs categories and income levels. Specifically, the predictive power of personality was greatly reduced in subgroups of growth products purchased by middle-income and high-income people. Growth needs, by nature, will increase when these need are met, and these needs can never be satisfied completely [8]. In other words, the more growth needs are satisfied, the more people want to pursue them. Compared with low-income people, middle-income and high-income people have relatively more resources to satisfy their growth needs, but these needs may evoke additional needs. While people's growth needs keep increasing, at certain point their personality is no longer domain in affecting their purchase behavior.

Prior research in consumer behavior often emphasizes that consumers with lower income may focus more heavily on price and performance attributes in making product evaluations and purchase decisions [54]. Because low-income people often lack of mobility. This typically limits people learning about the more symbolic meanings of consumption, resulting in greater reliance on performance and functional attributes of consumer goods. However, our results suggest that people with limited resources are able to greatly consider symbolic aspects of products. It is possible that, with the development of social media, people have sufficient exposure to symbolic-oriented consumption. This exposure may already overcome the mobility limitation in low-income people. One implication for developing successful marketing strategies is to consider people's personality in market segmentation rather than just focusing on their incomes.

Another implication is to enhance product recommender systems. Various personalized systems have been designed to fit users' human attributes. Our results show that the effect of personality can be significantly influenced by various situational factors such as needs categories and income. System designers should be aware of the situational factors to better meet people product needs. For example, additional weight can be placed on personality, when low-income users are looking for products to satisfy their growth needs. In contrast, when users have purchased a larger number of growth products, recommendation systems may provide more diverse stimulus to enhance users' purchase experiences.

The present research only considers the population in U.S. It would be interesting to examine how the effect of personality can be influenced by income and needs categories in different cultures and countries. For example, comparatively rich counties often witness more hedonistic consumer behavior than comparatively poor countries. Also, we only consider people's income in the current study, future studies can future examine additional demographic variables such gender, age, location, city size, and education levels. Another limitation of the current work is that individual's personality has been examined on an aggregated level. It would be interesting to see after decomposing personality into various trait-level dimensions, or even facet-level dimensions, how the situational factors would impact the decisive power of each of the lower-level personality measurements.

8 CONCLUSION

We studied the situational effect of income and needs on the relationship between derived personality and consumption behavior. Leveraging a large industry dataset containing almost 190,000 individual level records, we first built a number of category-specific prediction models on consumption decision based on derived personality features. We then experimented our classifiers across different income and needs, and through a two-way ANOVA, we found significant situational effect of income on the relationship between personality and consumption behavior, as well as significant effect of the income and need interaction. We claimed that our results can be beneficial for the design and development of more personalized product recommender systems.

ACKNOWLEDGMENTS

We thank Bryan Donovan from Acxiom Corporation for providing the Acxiom data set without which we could not have conducted this research.

REFERENCES

[1] Armstrong, Gary, Adam, Stewart, Denize, Sara and Kotler, Philip *Principles of marketing*. Pearson Australia, 2014.

[2] Kassarjian, Harold H Personality and consumer behavior: A review. *Journal of marketing Research* (1971), 409-418.

[3] Cialdini, Robert B and Trost, Melanie R Social influence: Social norms, conformity and compliance (1998).

[4] Balderjahn, Ingo Personality variables and environmental attitudes as predictors of ecologically responsible consumption patterns. *Journal of business Research*, 17, 1 (1988), 51-56.

[5] Xu, Anbang, Liu, Haibin, Gou, Liang, Akkiraju, Rama, Mahmud, Jalal, Sinha, Vibha, Hu, Yuheng and Qiao, Mu *Predicting Perceived Brand Personality with Social Media*. City, 2016.

[6] Duesenberry, James Stemble Income, saving, and the theory of consumer behavior (1949).

[7] Tauber, Edward M Why do people shop? *The Journal of Marketing* (1972), 46-49.

[8] Maslow, Abraham Harold A theory of human motivation. *Psychological review*, 50, 4 (1943), 370.

[9] Sun, Tao and Wu, Guohua Consumption patterns of Chinese urban and rural consumers. *Journal of Consumer Marketing*, 21, 4 (2004), 245-253.

[10] Gou, Liang, Zhou, Michelle X and Yang, Huahai *Knowme and shareme: Understanding automatically discovered personality traits from social media and user sharing preferences*. ACM, City, 2014.

[11] Goldberg, Lewis R The structure of phenotypic personality traits. *American psychologist*, 48, 1 (1993), 26.

[12] Eysenck, Hans Jürgen *The scientific study of personality*. Routledge & K. Paul, 1952.

[13] Briggs, Katharine C *Myers-Briggs type indicator*. Consulting Psychologists Press Palo Alto, CA, 1976.

[14] Costa, Paul T and Maccrae, Robert R *Revised NEO personality inventory (NEO PI-R) and NEO five-factor inventory (NEO FFI): Professional manual*. Psychological Assessment Resources, 1992.

[15] Goldberg, Lewis R The development of markers for the Big-Five factor structure. *Psychological assessment*, 4, 1 (1992), 26.

[16] Goldberg, Lewis R A broad-bandwidth, public domain, personality inventory measuring the lower-level facets of several five-factor models. *Personality psychology in Europe*, 7, 1 (1999), 7-28.

[17] John, Oliver P, Donahue, Eileen M and Kentle, Robert L *The big five inventory—versions 4a and 54*. Berkeley, CA: University of California, Berkeley, Institute of Personality and Social Research, City, 1991.

[18] Pennebaker, James W and King, Laura A Linguistic styles: language use as an individual difference. *Journal of personality and social psychology*, 77, 6 (1999), 1296.

[19] Oberlander, Jon and Gill, Alastair J Language with character: A stratified corpus comparison of individual differences in e-mail communication. *Discourse Processes*, 42, 3 (2006), 239-270.

[20] Yarkoni, Tal Personality in 100,000 words: A large-scale analysis of personality and word use among bloggers. *Journal of research in personality*, 44, 3 (2010), 363-373.

[21] Golbeck, Jennifer, Robles, Cristina and Turner, Karen *Predicting personality with social media*. ACM, City, 2011.

[22] Qiu, Lin, Lin, Han, Ramsay, Jonathan and Yang, Fang You are what you tweet: Personality expression and perception on Twitter. *Journal of Research in Personality*, 46, 6 (2012), 710-718.

[23] Gou, Liang, Zhou, Michelle X and Yang, Huahai *KnowMe and ShareMe: understanding automatically discovered personality traits from social media and user sharing preferences*. ACM, City, 2014.

[24] Pennebaker, James W, Francis, Martha E and Booth, Roger J Linguistic inquiry and word count: LIWC 2001. *Mahway: Lawrence Erlbaum Associates*, 71 (2001), 2001.

[25] Schwartz, H Andrew, Eichstaedt, Johannes C, Kern, Margaret L, Dziurzynski, Lukasz, Ramones, Stephanie M, Agrawal, Megha, Shah, Achal, Kosinski, Michal, Stillwell, David and Seligman, Martin Ep Personality, gender, and age in the language of social media: The open-vocabulary approach. *PloS one*, 8, 9 (2013), e73791.

[26] Quercia, Daniele, Kosinski, Michal, Stillwell, David and Crowcroft, Jon *Our Twitter profiles, our selves: Predicting personality with Twitter*. IEEE, City, 2011.

[27] Bachrach, Yoram, Kosinski, Michal, Graepel, Thore, Kohli, Pushmeet and Stillwell, David *Personality and patterns of Facebook usage*. ACM, City, 2012.

[28] Kosinski, Michal, Stillwell, David and Graepel, Thore Private traits and attributes are predictable from digital records of human behavior. *Proceedings of the National Academy of Sciences*, 110, 15 (2013), 5802-5805.

[29] Ortigosa, Alvaro, Carro, Rosa M and Quiroga, José Ignacio Predicting user personality by mining social interactions in Facebook. *Journal of computer and System Sciences*, 80, 1 (2014), 57-71.

[30] Chen, Jilin, Haber, Eben, Kang, Ruogu, Hsieh, Gary and Mahmud, Jalal *Making use of derived personality: The case of social media ad targeting*. City, 2015.

[31] Higgins, E Tory Does personality provide unique explanations for behavior? Personality as cross-person variability in general principles. *European Journal of Personality*, 14, 5 (2000), 391-406.

[32] Ajzen, Icek *Attitudes, personality, and behavior*. McGraw-Hill Education (UK), 2005.

[33] Verplanken, Bas and Herabadi, Astrid Individual differences in impulse buying tendency: Feeling and no thinking. *European Journal of personality*, 15, S1 (2001), S71-S83.

8

[34] Barkhi, Reza and Wallace, Linda The impact of personality type on purchasing decisions in virtual stores. *Information Technology and Management*, 8, 4 (2007), 313-330.

[35] Boudreaux, Claire A and Palmer, Stephen E A charming little Cabernet: Effects of wine label design on purchase intent and brand personality. *International Journal of Wine Business Research*, 19, 3 (2007), 170-186.

[36] Matzler, Kurt, Bidmon, Sonja and Grabner-Kräuter, Sonja Individual determinants of brand affect: the role of the personality traits of extraversion and openness to experience. *Journal of Product & Brand Management*, 15, 7 (2006), 427-434.

[37] Chen, Mei-Fang Consumer attitudes and purchase intentions in relation to organic foods in Taiwan: Moderating effects of food-related personality traits. *Food Quality and Preference*, 18, 7 (2007), 1008-1021.

[38] Cohen, Erik and Avieli, Nir Food in tourism: Attraction and impediment. *Annals of tourism Research*, 31, 4 (2004), 755-778.

[39] Brown, Graham P, Havitz, Mark E and Getz, Donald Relationship between wine involvement and wine-related travel. *Journal of Travel & Tourism Marketing*, 21, 1 (2007), 31-46.

[40] Schlegelmilch, Bodo B, Bohlen, Greg M and Diamantopoulos, Adamantios The link between green purchasing decisions and measures of environmental consciousness. *European Journal of Marketing*, 30, 5 (1996), 35-55.

[41] Yang, Chao, Pan, Shimei, Mahmud, Jalal, Yang, Huahai and Srinivasan, Padmini Using Personal Traits For Brand Preference Prediction (

[42] Liu, Zhe, Wang, Yi, Mahmud, Jalal, Akkiraju, Rama, Schoudt, Jerald, Xu, Anbang and Donovan, Bryan *To Buy or Not to Buy? Understanding the Role of Personality Traits in Predicting Consumer Behaviors*. Springer, City, 2016.

[43] Bem, David J and Funder, David C Predicting more of the people more of the time: Assessing the personality of situations. *Psychological Review*, 85, 6 (1978), 485.

[44] Monson, Thomas C, Hesley, John W and Chernick, Linda Specifying when personality traits can and cannot predict behavior: An alternative to abandoning the attempt to predict single-act criteria. *Journal of Personality and Social Psychology*, 43, 2 (1982), 385.

[45] Barrick, Murray R and Mount, Michael K Autonomy as a moderator of the relationships between the Big Five personality dimensions and job performance. *Journal of applied Psychology*, 78, 1 (1993), 111.

[46] Keynes, John Maynard *General theory of employment, interest and money*. Atlantic Publishers & Dist, 2006.

[47] Friedman, Milton *The permanent income hypothesis*. Princeton University Press, City, 1957.

[48] Hall, Robert E Stochastic implications of the life cycle-permanent income hypothesis: theory and evidence. *NBER working paper*, R0015 (1979).

[49] Kooti, Farshad, Lerman, Kristina, Aiello, Luca Maria, Grbovic, Mihajlo, Djuric, Nemanja and Radosavljevic, Vladan Portrait of an Online Shopper: Understanding and Predicting Consumer Behavior. *arXiv preprint arXiv:1512.04912* (2015).

[50] Abeliotis, Konstadinos, Koniari, Christina and Sardianou, Eleni The profile of the green consumer in Greece. *International Journal of Consumer Studies*, 34, 2 (2010), 153-160.

[51] Wakefield, Kirk L and Inman, J Jeffrey Situational price sensitivity: the role of consumption occasion, social context and income. *Journal of Retailing*, 79, 4 (2003), 199-212.

[52] Ricciuto, Laurie, Tarasuk, Valerie and Yatchew, A Socio-demographic influences on food purchasing among Canadian households. *European Journal of Clinical Nutrition*, 60, 6 (2006), 778-790.

[53] Park, C Whan, Jaworski, Bernard J and MacInnis, Deborah J Strategic brand concept-image management. *The Journal of Marketing* (1986), 135-145.

[54] Kim, Jai-Ok, Forsythe, Sandra, Gu, Qingliang and Jae Moon, Sook Cross-cultural consumer values, needs and purchase behavior. *Journal of Consumer marketing*, 19, 6 (2002), 481-502.

[55] Roth, Martin S The effects of culture and socioeconomics on the performance of global brand image strategies. *Journal of Marketing Research* (1995), 163-175.

[56] Badenes, Hernan, Bengualid, Mateo N, Chen, Jilin, Gou, Liang, Haber, Eben, Mahmud, Jalal, Nichols, Jeffrey W, Pal, Aditya, Schoudt, Jerald and Smith, Barton A *System U: automatically deriving personality traits from social media for people recommendation*. ACM, City, 2014.

[57] Hu, Tianran, Xiao, Haoyuan, Luo, Jiebo and Nguyen, Thuy-Vy Thi *What the Language You Tweet Says About Your Occupation*. City, 2016.

[58] Appel, Ana Paula, Candello, Heloisa, De Souza, Beatriz Sr and Andrade, Bruna D *Destiny: A Cognitive Mobile Guide for the Olympics*. International World Wide Web Conferences Steering Committee, City, 2016.

[59] Adamopoulos, Panagiotis and Todri, Vilma Personality-Based Recommendations: Evidence from Amazon. com (

[60] Murthy, Karin, Deshpande, Prasad M, Dey, Atreyee, Halasipuram, Ramanujam, Mohania, Mukesh, Deepak, P, Reed, Jennifer and Schumacher, Scott Exploiting evidence from unstructured data to enhance master data management. *Proceedings of the VLDB Endowment*, 5, 12 (2012), 1862-1873.

[61] Us Census Bureau *Money Income of Households - Percent Distribution by Income Level in Constant (2009) Dollars (Table 690)*. . City, 2009.

[62] Brody, Robert P and Cunningham, Scott M Personality variables and the consumer decision process. *Journal of Marketing Research* (1968), 50-57.

[63] Lievens, Filip and Highhouse, Scott The relation of instrumental and symbolic attributes to a company's attractiveness as an employer. *Personnel Psychology*, 56, 1 (2003), 75-102.

9

Demographics of News Sharing in the U.S. Twittersphere

Julio C. S. Reis
Universidade Federal de Minas Gerais
Belo Horizonte, Brazil
julio.reis@dcc.ufmg.br

Haewoon Kwak
Qatar Computing Research Institute
Doha, Qatar
haewoon@acm.org

Jisun An
Qatar Computing Research Institute
Doha, Qatar
jan@hbku.edu.qa

Johnnatan Messias
Universidade Federal de Minas Gerais
Belo Horizonte, Brazil
johnnatan@dcc.ufmg.br

Fabrício Benevenuto
Universidade Federal de Minas Gerais
Belo Horizonte, Brazil
fabricio@dcc.ufmg.br

ABSTRACT

The widespread adoption and dissemination of online news through social media systems have been revolutionizing many segments of our society and ultimately our daily lives. In these systems, users can play a central role as they share content to their friends. Despite that, little is known about news spreaders in social media. In this paper, we provide the first of its kind in-depth characterization of news spreaders in social media. In particular, we investigate their demographics, what kind of content they share, and the audience they reach. Among our main findings, we show that males and white users tend to be more active in terms of sharing news, biasing the news audience to the interests of these demographic groups. Our results also quantify differences in interests of news sharing across demographics, which has implications for personalized news digests.

CCS CONCEPTS

•Human-centered computing →Social media; •Applied computing →Sociology;

KEYWORDS

Online News; Demographics; News Sharing; Social Media; Twitter

1 INTRODUCTION

In recent years, with the huge success of Twitter and Facebook, social media has become one of the most important channels in news diffusion. In particular, Twitter's unique concepts of asymmetric "follow" and "retweet", which were later adopted by Facebook, allow users to follow each other's updates and propagate interesting pieces of information quickly and broadly [24]. Such great power to disseminate information embedded in social media naturally has attracted the news media. As a result, a majority of U.S. adults (62%) get news mostly on social media, according to a new survey by Pew Research Center [10].

HT'17, July 4-7, 2017, Prague, Czech Republic.
© 2017 Copyright held by the owner/author(s). Publication rights licensed to ACM.
978-1-4503-4708-2/17/07...$15.00
DOI: http://dx.doi.org/10.1145/3078714.3078734

Along with their traditional channels, news media manage their presence in social media by creating Twitter accounts and publishing tweets containing URLs that link their news media sites. For those accounts, it is clearly visible who the audience is – their followers. Furthermore, as any Twitter user can share URLs to news media web sites, Twitter users exposed to news media's tweets through retweets can also be visible and accounted as audience. We call these users *news spreaders* in the rest of this paper. This form of sharing of news URLs has long been a pervasive practice in social media, but its role and impact are relatively unexplored.

In this work, we characterize news spreaders in Twitter along three dimensions: 1) their demographics (who they are), 2) their news shared (what they share), and 3) their impact (why they are important). To this end, the inference of demographics of Twitter users is essential. Among various techniques that have been proposed [27], we use state-of-the-art techniques to locate Twitter users and infer their demographics based on profile photos.

Through a longitudinal data collection of news spreaders and their URL sharing behavior of five popular global news media, we test how similar news URL sharing is to typical URL sharing in terms of demographics of spreaders. We find a statistically significant trend that white males participate more in news URL sharing than other race-gender groups. This suggests that news spreaders have unique characteristics, which cannot be easily perceived for typical URL spreaders in Twitter. Thus, our work is essential to understand news spreaders correctly.

We then answer the above research questions. First, we examine demographics of news spreaders. By comparing the followers of news media accounts, we discover huge differences in terms of race-gender demographics. This suggests that we need to have a broader definition of the exposure of the news media on social media that are not only a set of followers [1] but also news spreaders. Second, we examine what kinds of news are shared by news spreaders. The properties of the pieces of news are defined along three dimensions: topics, author's (journalist's) gender and race, and linguistic analysis [33] of news headlines. These three dimensions have been discovered as important factors in news reading/sharing behavior [34, 38]. Finally, we answer how important news spreaders are for news media from the perspective of audience expansion: 1) about 59% of news spreaders do not follow news media accounts in Twitter; 2) the audience brought by the spreaders is much bigger than that of the original followers of the news media; 3) in addition to that the demographics of the spreaders and those of the followers are quite different, the followers of the spreaders are also substantially different from the followers of the news sources in terms of demographics. In other words, the spreaders play an important role in expanding the audience of news in Twitter, which would otherwise be very limited. Lastly, we find that the demographics of news spreaders are related to the popularity of news.

Our contributions are three-fold: 1) by using a combination of state-of-the-art techniques, we investigate in details aspects of the audience of news media in Twitter, which has been considered as in-house data so far; 2) we suggest a robust statistical framework to test the news URL sharing behavior by comparing it with typical URL sharing behavior; and 3) Our findings show that news media should understand spreaders and their followers to capture the complete picture of their presence in news media. News media's direct followers are only the tip of the iceberg of their audience in Twitter in terms of volume and demographics.

The rest of the paper is organized as follows. Section 2 briefly surveys related efforts. Then, we present our experiment methodology and the data gathered. The next three sections cover our results. We conclude the paper by discussing implications from our findings as well as presenting directions for future work.

2 RELATED WORK

In this Section, we review existing work related to news sharing along two main dimensions.

2.1 News Sharing and Propagation

Social media services have made personal contacts and relationships more visible and quantifiable than ever before. Users interact by following each others' updates and passing along interesting pieces of information to their friends. This kind of word-of-mouth propagation occurs whenever a user forwards a piece of information to her friends, making users a key element in this process. Not surprisingly, a number of efforts have attempted to quantify and characterize information spread in social networks as well as the role users play in such propagation [11, 12, 36, 37, 42]. For example, Rodrigues et al. [36] showed that retweets are responsible for increasing the audience of URLs by about 2 orders of magnitude. As social media became an important channel in news diffusion, some recent research efforts attempted to investigate how news are shared in these systems. Next, we detail a few approaches that provides news sharing and propagation.

Naveed et al. [29] showed that bad news tends to spread faster in systems like Twitter. In this same year, also with the use of this same social media, Armstrong et al. [5] analyzed how online media companies employ men and women in Twitter feeds and how it connects to portrayals in news. In particular, the authors looked at how mentions of men and women on Twitter may influence mentions in news stories (e.g. newspaper, television). Through the content analysis of newspaper and television tweets at different granularity (i.e. local, regional and national), they found that male mentions were more likely to appear in national news than in regional or local news and more often than female mentions in the print media than on television.

A recent effort [7] has tackled the question "Why are some news articles shared more than others?". They showed that story importance cues are relevant in driving social sharing and that certain topics (i.e. stories about politics, accidents, disasters, and crime) were less shared. Some topics can be shared in order to improve the users' reputation. This dynamic media attention has inspired other recent studies [3]. Bright et al. [7], compare different social networks platforms and showed that some kind of news are shared more in one network than the others (e.g. economy news on LinkedIn).

Unlike previous works, our effort focuses on understanding the dynamics of news sharing on Twitter of each demographic group. Thus, to the best of our knowledge, this is the first effort that investigates intersection between news sharing and demographic information of users, including how these aspects are related.

2.2 Demographics in Social Media

Mislove et al. [27] was one of the first researchers that analyze demographic characteristics of Twitter users considering a geographical perspective (i.e. how the demographics vary across different U.S states). After that, several efforts have arisen that investigate demographic information, in various social media, using different strategies for distinct purposes [6, 8, 22]. Particularly, researchers are jointly applying computer science and statistical techniques to support sociological studies using large-scale social media datasets. These studies can range from a simple characterization of to the investigation of more complex causes, including to raising attention to the different levels at which gender biases can manifest themselves on the web [41].

In [16] the authors used Twitter data to analyze the difference between men and women behavior in terms of dynamics in free tagging environments. The results obtained present gender distinctions in the use of Twitter hashtags, emphasizing it as a social factor influencing the user's choice of specific hashtags on a specific topic. Still about tags (or hashtags), recently, the work presented in [4] explored their use by different demographic groups. The demographic characteristics of each user were obtained using *Face++* and the Twitter user's profile picture. The results showed that, although there are more popular hashtags that are commonly used, there are also many group-specific hashtags with non-negligible popularity. Besides that, the researchers show that the strategy of getting demographic data from *Face++* is reliable and provides accurate demographic information for gender and race, encouraging the application of this strategy in other recent efforts [13]. We use a similar strategy to gather demographic information.

Nilizadeh et al. [31] explore gender inequalities in Twitter, showing that gender may allow inequality to persist in terms of online visibility. Looking at Pinterest, Gilbert et al. [20] investigated what role gender plays in the website's social connections. The results highlight a major difference between female and male users regarding their motivations for using this social media. They found that being female means more repins (i.e., more shared content), but fewer followers in comparison with Twitter. Gender differences has also been explored in terms of social media disclosures of mental illness [17].

More recently, An et al. [2] examined the news consumption in South Korea (from Daum News portal). The authors analyzed on a large scale the differences in news consumption from a demographic

News Media	#Shares	#Authors	Screen name	#Followers
New York Times	14,505	1,165	@nytimes	1,141
Reuters	4,712	485	@Reuters	1,259
The Guardian	4,457	844	@guardian	1,620
Wall Street Journal	1,379	313	@WSJ	1,445
BBC News	1,144	190	@BBCBreaking	1,130

Table 1: Data collection by news source.

Race (%)	Gender (%)		Total:
	Male	Female	
Asian	5.29	6.05	11.34
AF-AM	6.09	3.80	9.89
White	43.46	35.31	78.77
Total:	54.84	45.16	100.00

Table 2: Demographic distribution of news spreaders.

perspective. Through a multidimensional analysis of gender and age differences in news consumption, they quantify such differences along four distinct dimensions: actual news items, topic, issue, and angle. The top 30 news items for each gender and age group in Daum News were used and the demographics information were obtained through the website itself. Overall, focus mainly on quantifying and explaining differences in news consumption.

More broadly, most of the previous efforts attempt to quantify differences in gender behavior and inequalities in different social media or news systems. Our effort is the first of its kind to provide a characterization of news sharing across different demographic groups. Thus our effort is complementary to the existing ones.

3 METHODOLOGY

In order to understand demographics of news sharing in Twitter, first we define our strategy for data collection. Then, we define our strategies for inference of demographic information of each individual Twitter user and collection of information such as category and authors of the news, and followers of each of the news media on Twitter. Our ultimate goal, in this section, consists of reporting our baseline for comparison in order to verify the statistical significance of the results. Next, we briefly describe the methodology adopted for this work, including a discussion of its main limitations.

3.1 Gathering Twitter

For this work, we gathered the 1% random sample of all tweets, through the Twitter Streaming API [1], along a 3 months period, from July to September, 2016. Specifically, we considered only tweets (and retweets) that contain at least one URL and have been shared by U.S. users. We understand that users who share URLs may present a slight difference in behavior compared to others, so, considering our research objective, we only select this set of American users. Besides that, as we are interested in analyzing demographic characteristics, it is important to study users from the same place. For this reason, we consider only U.S. users, filtered by timezone. In total, we retrieved 11,790,679 tweets posted by 11,770,273 U.S. users. From this initial dataset, we infer demographics information about users and build: (i) our news sharing dataset, used in the execution of our experiments, and (ii) our baseline dataset.

3.2 Inferring Demographics Information

In the literature, several studies present strategies for inference of gender, race, and age. Some efforts attempt to infer the gender of a user from her name [22, 25, 27], or the age from Twitter profile descriptions [39], by using patterns like 'like 25 yr old' or 'born in 1990'. However, in some cases the number of unrealized inferences

(e.g. for lack of information) is high (Liu and Ruths [25] reported 66% users in their dataset did not have a proper name).

To overcome such limitation, in this work, we use the profile picture's URLs of all users in our dataset and use the Face++ API [2], a face recognition platform based on deep learning [43], to infer the gender (i.e., male or female), race (limited to Asian, Black[3], and White) and age information from the recognized faces in the profile images. We discarded users whose profile pictures do not have a recognizable face or have more than one face, according to Face++. Our final dataset contains 937,308 unique users located in U.S. with identified demographic information, which are gender, race, and age by Face++.

3.3 Shared News Dataset

To focus on news sharing in Twitter, we filtered only tweets that shared news URLs from important and different news sources (i.e. BBC News[4], The New York Times[5], Reuters Online[6], The Wall Street Journal[7], The Guardian[8] and BBC News[9]), known worldwide. All these news sites appear among the most popular ones in the world, according to Alexa.com.[10] Simultaneously, we gathered information from users who posted each of the tweets including demographic information from Face++, as detailed above. From news URLs, we crawled information about them including, title, text, principal image (link - when there is one), authors (when there is one) and date. Lastly, Table 1 shows the dataset used in this work containing 26,211 unique news articles shared by 16,382 unique users. We note that The New York Times is the most widely shared news media in Twitter, in comparison with those news sites considered. Table 2 shows the demographic decomposition of those 16,382 users who shared news URLs.

3.4 Inferring News Category

In order to infer the categories of the news articles, we use meta information embedded in the news URLs. News media usually have several news sections, such as Politics, Sports, or World News, and group their news articles by these sections. By looking at which section a news article belongs to, we can infer a topical category of the news articles. The section information is often embedded in news URL. For example, the URL http://www.nytimes.com/2016/07/

---

[1] https://dev.twitter.com/streaming/public

[2] https://www.faceplusplus.com
[3] We called African-American (AF-AM) in the rest of this paper.
[4] http://www.bbc.com
[5] http://www.nytimes.com
[6] http://www.reuters.com
[7] http://www.wsj.com/
[8] https://www.theguardian.com
[9] http://www.bbc.com
[10] http://www.alexa.com/topsites/category/News

02/us/politics/loretta-lynch-hillary-clinton-email-server.html represents that the news article is about "Politics". We parsed all News URLs and extracted the topic information. The New York Times, The Guardian, and BBC adopt the above mentioned strategy for their URLs, and thus we simply parse their URL and infer the topic of a given news article. Reuters and The Wall Street Journal do not have category information in their URLs, however, the news articles have the category information. Thus, we collected news articles and extracted category information by parsing HTML files. We successfully inferred the topical categories of 93.3% (24,466) of news articles. Figure 1 shows the proportion of the top 10 most significant news categories. We find that "World" is the most "shared" category (21.16%), similar to the results in [34].

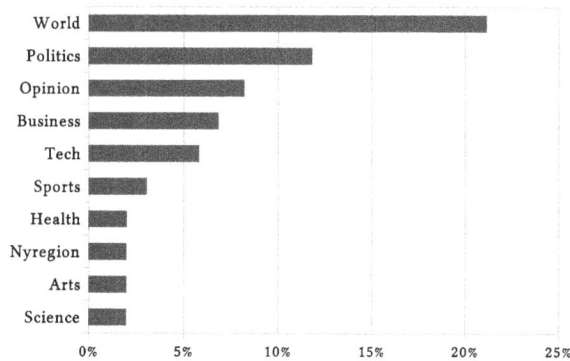

Figure 1: Top 10 most significant news categories.

3.5 Finding Journalists in Twitter

We aim to collect demographics of the authors of news articles in our dataset. Figure 2 shows the procedure for creating an author dataset. For each news URL, we collect its title, text, principal image, authors, and date by parsing the original web page. Then, we search and collect the Twitter profiles of the authors if they have Twitter accounts. Then, we infer those authors' demographic characteristics using *Face++* (see Section 3.2). Table 1 shows the number of authors for each news media. As expected, the largest number of names of distinguished authors we have gathered are from the The New York Times news media, which had the largest number of news shared in Twitter in our dataset.

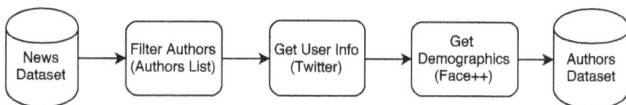

Figure 2: Strategy for collecting news authors.

3.6 Collecting Followers of News Media in Twitter

For each news source, we collected their followers in Twitter. Again, we infer their demographics by *Face++*. Table 1 presents the total of gathered news media followers in Twitter, including the screen name used for collection. On average, we retrieved 1,319 followers by news source.

Race (%)	Gender (%)		Total:
	Male	Female	
Asian	7.07	10.33	17.40
AF-AM	8.52	6.93	15.45
White	31.97	35.18	67.15
Total:	47.56	52.44	100.00

Table 3: Demographic distribution of users in the Baseline dataset.

3.7 Baseline Dataset

A null model is widely used to estimate the statistical significance of the observed trend in given data. As the null model is randomly generated data that preserve some properties of the original data (e.g., the degree distribution in complex networks), the same trend observed from the null model captures its occurrence by chance. Then, by comparing the trend in the original data with that in the null model, the statistical significance of the observed trend in the original data can be measured. Table 3 shows the breakdown of ethnicity and gender of the $\approx$ 1 million users who shared URLs in Twitter between July and September 2016. We present a detailed description of the comparison with null models.

In this work, whenever we report the number of users with certain properties who share URLs on particular news media, we report Z-score by comparing the number of those users in the actual data with that in null models.

Consider that we are interested in users who are Asian and share BBC News. In this case, we denote by $|U_{BBC}|$ the number of users who share BBC News and $|U_{BBC}^{Asian}|$ by the number of Asian among them. To construct a null model, we create k random samples from a separate huge set of users, which is called Population, where each sample has exactly $|U_{BBC}|$ users. The demographic information of users in Population is inferred by *Face++*. For each sample, we count how many Asians are included, $|S_{BBC}^{Asian}|$. Then, the Z_{BBC}^{Asian} is computed as following:

$$Z_{BBC}^{Asian} = \frac{|U_{BBC}^{Asian}| - mean(|S_{BBC}^{Asian}|)}{std(|S_{BBC}^{Asian}|)} \quad (1)$$

where $mean(\cdot)$ is the mean and $std(\cdot)$ is the standard deviation of the values from multiple samples. Intuitively, when the absolute value of Z value becomes bigger (either positive or negative), the trend (more number or less number, respectively) is less likely observed by chance. In this work, the size of Population is $\approx$ 1 million, and k=100.

3.8 Potential Limitations

There are a few limitations of our data, discussed next.

Accuracy of the inference by *Face++*. First, *(i)* we are limited by accuracy of *Face++* in the inference. *Face++* itself returns confidence levels for the inferred gender and race attributes and returns an error range for inferred age. In our data, the average confidence level reported by *Face++* is 95.24 ± 0.020% for gender and 86.12 ± 0.032% for race, with a confidence interval of 95%. Besides that, as the performance of deep learning systems continues to improve, the inferred demographic attributes should become more accurate.

Also, recent efforts have used *Face++* for similar tasks and reported high confidence in manual inspections of small samples [4, 44]; Another limitation, is that *(ii) Face++* reports race of recognizable faces from images but not the *ethnicity* (e.g. *Hispanic*); Finally, though *(iii)* we had discarded about 70% of the crawled users (i.e. those users whose profile pictures do not have a recognizable face or have profile pictures in which *Face++* recognized with low confidence). However, we note that the remaining final dataset is still representative and we only provide results that are statistically significant based on well known statistical tests.

Data. *(iv)* Our approach to identify users in U.S. may contain users located in the same time zone, but not in the U.S. We, however, believe that these users represent a small fraction of the users, given the predominance of active U.S. users in Twitter [14]; *(v)* We are using the 1% random sample off all tweets. Although the 1% random sample is not the best data to capture all the dynamics happening in Twitter, its limitations are known [28] and it is the best available option at our disposal.

Even with limitations, we believe that our dataset and methods can provide interesting insights on demographics and news sharing behaviors. In the following sections, we present and discuss the main results from characterizing news spreaders in Twitter along three dimensions: 1) their demographics (who they are), 2) their news shared (what they share), and 3) their impact (why they are important).

4 WHO ARE THE NEWS SPREADERS?

Our first research question is to understand who the spreaders are. We compare the demographics of news spreaders with 1) the spreaders of typical URLs in Twitter and 2) the Twitter followers of news media to see whether and to what extent they differ.

4.1 Typical URL Sharing Vs. News Sharing

Table 4 shows, for each news media, the proportion of news URL shares by different demographic groups. For example, for The New York Times, 54.1% of news shares are made by men and 79.2% of news shares are by Whites. The numbers in the parenthesis correspond to the Z-values, detailed in Section 3.7. We note that the Z-value indicates how news URL sharing behavior is similar or dissimilar from typical URL sharing behavior in terms of demographic composition.

By comparing between the news sources, we see some obvious patterns: 1) The Wall Street Journal is favored by Male (62.3%) more than Female (37.7%); 2) The New York Times has the most balanced gender distribution among spreaders (54.1% vs 45.9%); and 3) for The New York Times, The Guardian, and BBC News, the proportion of shares by Asians is greater than by AF-AM.

From a simple comparison to Table 2 which shows the demographic compositions of typical URL sharing behavior, we observed the following trends for all five news sources. First, Males share more news URLs than Female do. Male (54.84% of news spreaders) issue 54.1% to 62.3% of news URL shares. Secondly, Whites share more news URLs than other race groups–White (78.77% of total users) cover 78.2% to 82.2% of news URL shares.

News media	Race (%)	Gender (%)		Total:
		Male	Female	
The New York Times	Asian	5.1 (-9.22)	5.9 (-18.02)	11.0 (-19.96)
	AF-AM	6.1 (-13.95)	3.7 (-15.01)	9.8 (-21.75)
	White	42.8 (26.24)	36.4 (2.86)	79.2 (31.32)
	Total:	54.1 (15.30)	45.9 (-15.30)	100.0
Reuters	Asian	3.6 (-8.06)	6.8 (-7.62)	10.4 (-12.09)
	AF-AM	7.3 (-3.02)	3.7 (-8.70)	10.9 (-9.03)
	White	47.0 (23.21)	31.7 (-4.89)	78.7 (16.38)
	Total:	57.9 (14.00)	42.1 (-14.00)	100.0
The Guardian	Asian	4.9 (-6.11)	5.9 (-9.75)	10.7 (-12.75)
	AF-AM	5.5 (-7.63)	3.3 (-9.77)	8.8 (-12.11)
	White	46.9 (23.03)	33.6 (-2.39)	80.5 (18.41)
	Total:	57.2 (13.24)	42.8 (-13.24)	100.0
The Wall Street Journal	Asian	4.9 (-3.91)	3.6 (-8.60)	8.5 (-9.43)
	AF-AM	6.1 (-3.41)	3.3 (-5.86)	9.4 (-6.68)
	White	51.3 (15.70)	30.8 (-3.35)	82.2 (12.23)
	Total:	62.3 (10.77)	37.7 (-10.77)	100.0
BBC News	Asian	5.3 (-2.64)	6.6 (-4.49)	12.0 (-5.11)
	AF-AM	7.1 (-1.91)	2.7 (-6.01)	9.8 (-5.76)
	White	46.2 (11.00)	32.1 (-2.36)	78.2 (8.04)
	Total:	58.6 (7.97)	41.4 (-7.97)	100.0

Table 4: Proportion of news shares by different demographic groups for each news source.

News media	Race (%)	Gender (%)		Total:
		Male	Female	
The New York Times	Asian	12.7 (6.69)	10.5 (0.28)	23.2 (5.28)
	AF-AM	11.4 (3.71)	3.9 (-4.35)	15.2 (-0.36)
	White	35.0 (2.41)	26.6 (-6.12)	61.5 (-4.08)
	Total:	59.1 (7.97)	40.9 (-7.97)	100.0
Reuters	Asian	11.3 (5.83)	7.9 (-2.97)	19.2 (1.71)
	AF-AM	16.9 (9.97)	3.6 (-4.64)	20.5 (3.98)
	White	39.5 (5.74)	20.8 (-10.31)	60.3 (-4.52)
	Total:	67.7 (15.81)	32.3 (-15.81)	100.0
The Guardian	Asian	8.5 (2.22)	7.8 (-3.34)	16.4 (-1.30)
	AF-AM	10.5 (2.79)	3.8 (-4.58)	14.3 (-1.04)
	White	41.4 (8.99)	27.9 (-5.82)	69.3 (1.80)
	Total:	60.4 (10.45)	39.6 (-10.45)	100.0
The Wall Street Journal	Asian	9.9 (4.13)	8.0 (-3.20)	17.9 (0.54)
	AF-AM	14.5 (8.55)	4.2 (-4.06)	18.8 (3.64)
	White	41.6 (6.97)	21.7 (-11.70)	63.3 (-3.28)
	Total:	66.0 (13.93)	34.0 (-13.93)	100.0
BBC News	Asian	12.5 (5.85)	11.3 (0.92)	23.8 (4.67)
	AF-AM	12.5 (4.58)	2.2 (-6.30)	14.7 (-0.59)
	White	34.6 (1.92)	26.9 (-5.13)	61.5 (-3.25)
	Total:	59.6 (7.57)	40.4 (-7.57)	100.0

Table 5: Proportion of distinct followers by different demographic groups for each news source.

The Z-values in Table 4 tell whether the differences between news spreaders and typical URL spreaders are statistically significant or not. The most strong tendency is observed for White-Male. White-Male share more news URLs than they share typical URLs and this tendency is strong (Z > 11[11]). Then, another observations is that White-Female are less likely to share news URLs than typical URLs (Z < 0) except for The New York Times. On average, White-Male make 46.8% and White-Female make 32.9% of news URL shares. From the two proportions, one may think this is because White-Female are less active than White-Male in Twitter. However, our method of comparing the news URL sharing behavior with typical URL sharing behavior can effectively tell that the difference is not because of the activity level, but of the type of URLs. White-Female do share a significant number of typical URLs.

---

[11]Z-value is minimum for BBC News, the largest Z-value is 26.24 for The New York Times.

4.2 Are Spreaders Similar to Followers of Media Sources?

In the previous analysis, we observed that White-Male are dominant in sharing news URLs. Then, would such pattern find for the Twitter followers of news sources?

Table 5 presents the demographics of Twitter followers of each news source. Again, the number in the parenthesis is Z-value, reporting how it differs from typical news sharing behavior. Compared to those users who share typical URLs, we observe two main differences of news media followers: 1) there are more male users ($Z > 0$); 2) except The Guardian, all the other four news sources have fewer White users ($Z < 0$). The New York Times and BBC News have more Asian followers and Reuters and The Wall Street Journal have more Asian and AF-AM users. This results in that the following three groups, Asian-Male, AF-AM-Male, and White-Male, are prominent in the followers of media sources ($Z > 0$). In addition, we observe that two news sources, The New York Times and BBC News, have positive Z-values for Asian Female followers.

For both type of users the followers and the spreaders we observe a "Male dominant" pattern, confirming that Male are more interested in news for consumption and spread. However, we find significant differences in demographic compositions between the followers and the spreaders of news. While the followers have a certain degree of racial equality, the spreaders are biased towards one particular race, White. This result is particularly important because so far it was known that individuals affiliated with news media play a large part in breaking the news [21]. Our observation indicates that breaking news is from not only those followers, but also from these news spreaders who are not necessarily following the news sources in Twitter.

5 WHAT NEWS SPREADERS SHARE

We study what news spreaders share along three distinct dimensions: the topical category of news, the demographic trait of the authors (journalist) of a news article, and the linguistic properties of news headlines.

5.1 By News Category

We firstly examine which categories of news are shared more by particular demographic groups. To this end, we standardized the names of topical categories for the analysis. For example, we grouped news categories relating to health and life and named "Health and Life" and grouped news categories relating to science and named "Science and Tech.".

Table 6 shows the proportion of news shares by each demographic group for each topical category. We consider only topics that were present in all news sources for this analysis. Foremost in Science and Tech, Business, and Politics, we can see the great gender differences. On average, 61.2% of news URLs of these three topics are shared by Male. In the others two categories, World and Health and Life, Female make more contributions (48.6% of shares).

When compared to typical URL sharing behavior, we observe the tendency of White-Male sharing news URLs for all categories ($Z > 0$), but the tendency is stronger for Science and Tech, Business, and Politics ($Z > 9.76$) than World ($Z = 4.55$) and Health and Life ($Z = 1.89$). One interesting observation is that White-Female do

Category	Race (%)	Gender (%)		Total:
		Male	Female	
World	Asian	4.3 (-6.96)	7.8 (-6.32)	12.1 (-9.84)
	AF-AM	6.1 (-6.47)	3.2 (-9.35)	9.3 (-12.53)
	White	40.4 (13.71)	38.3 (4.62)	78.6 (17.67)
	Total:	50.8 (4.55)	49.2 (-4.55)	100.0
Health and Life	Asian	6.8 (-0.18)	7.0 (-2.76)	13.8 (-2.25)
	AF-AM	3.3 (-3.82)	3.7 (-2.94)	7.0 (-5.54)
	White	41.9 (4.77)	37.3 (0.93)	79.2 (5.97)
	Total:	52.0 (1.89)	48.0 (-1.89)	100.0
Science and Tech	Asian	5.2 (-3.55)	5.4 (-6.98)	10.5 (-7.61)
	AF-AM	6.3 (-3.25)	1.7 (-10.12)	8.0 (-9.17)
	White	52.6 (19.17)	28.8 (-5.95)	81.4 (12.34)
	Total:	64.1 (15.74)	35.9 (-15.74)	100.0
Business	Asian	4.0 (-4.95)	5.3 (-6.93)	9.3 (-8.13)
	AF-AM	7.0 (-2.54)	3.1 (-5.69)	10.0 (-6.30)
	White	49.4 (15.59)	31.3 (-3.48)	80.7 (10.45)
	Total:	60.3 (9.76)	39.7 (-9.76)	100.0
Politics	Asian	5.5 (-3.06)	4.6 (-9.52)	10.1 (-9.94)
	AF-AM	6.3 (-4.01)	3.2 (-7.53)	9.5 (-8.18)
	White	47.3 (16.91)	33.1 (-2.58)	80.4 (14.20)
	Total:	59.1 (13.23)	40.9 (-13.23)	100.0

Table 6: Number of shares by category.

share more news URLs of World and Health and Life categories than the typical URLs ($Z > 0$).

To understand better how demographic traits relate to topical preferences, we compute the relative preferences of each demographic group to ten topical categories (see Figure 1). News articles about Tech are more likely to be shared by Male than Female. We then see White are more likely to share news about Health and Tech while Asian and AF-AM participate more in sharing news about Sports and Arts. Lastly, Science is favored by Asian but Business is favored by AF-AM. Our analysis shows that demographic groups have different topical tastes in sharing. This guides us how news media publish their contents to target appropriate user segments.

5.2 By Author's Demographics

In this section, we study how the gender of a journalist who wrote a news article influences its shares. While some differences in topics written [26] or sources used [45] between male and female journalists have been reported [26] , its appealing to each demographic group has not been fully explored.

Table 7 shows the demographics of the authors for each news source. Overall, the proportion of Male authors are higher than that of Female authors–on average, 60.04% of the authors are Male. Reuters and BBC News have more skewed gender distributions than the other three sources. In terms of race, most of the authors are White (83.8% on average across five media sources), followed by Asian authors (10.5%). We observe only 5.7% of the authors are AF-AM and strikingly low fraction of AF-AM Female authors (1.42%).

Table 8 shows the proportion of the spreaders who shared any news URLs written by a certain author demographic group for each news source.

5.2.1 Author's Gender. Does the gender of an author affect the spreading behavior? For The New York Times and Reuters, the proportion of Male spreaders is not significantly different ($< 2\%$) no matter the gender of the author is. However, in the rest three others sources, Male tend to share more news URLs written by Male–the difference is 12.4% for BBC News, 7.4% for The Wall Street Journal,

| News Media | Race (%) | Gender (%) | | Total: |
		Male	Female	
The New York Times	Asian	4.9	5.8	10.7
	AF-AM	3.9	0.9	4.8
	White	49.4	35.1	84.5
	Total:	58.1	41.9	100.0
Reuters	Asian	6.8	6.0	12.8
	AF-AM	4.3	2.3	6.6
	White	51.3	29.3	80.6
	Total:	62.5	37.5	100.0
The Guardian	Asian	3.4	4.6	8.1
	AF-AM	3.8	1.2	5.0
	White	50.4	36.6	87.0
	Total:	57.6	42.4	100.0
The Wall Street Journal	Asian	7.0	6.1	13.1
	AF-AM	2.9	1.6	4.5
	White	47.9	34.5	82.4
	Total:	57.8	42.2	100.0
BBC News	Asian	3.2	4.7	7.9
	AF-AM	6.3	1.1	7.4
	White	54.7	30.0	84.7
	Total:	64.2	35.8	100.0

Table 7: Demographic characteristics of the collected authors by news source.

and 5.3% for The Guardian. While the effect of the gender of the authors on spreading behavior exists, this might be a mere effect of biological differences in topical tastes–Male and Female journalists write only the topics that readers of the same gender are interested in.

To control the effect of the topics, we use a Chi-square test [9] to find which topics are written significantly more by Female (or Male) journalists and which topics are significantly more shared by Female (or Male) spreaders. Table 9 shows the graphical presentation of the statistically significant results by Chi-square test statistics ($p < 0.05$). In the table, an upward pointing arrow represents a higher tendency in writing or sharing. For example, Male authors write news significantly more about Sport and Opinion, and Female authors write about Health. There are no topics that authors and spreaders have the same gender differences except for Health. Therefore, the gender difference in spreading behavior is unlikely driven by that in journalists' choice of the topics. We bring the potential explanation in later section based on linguistic component of news.

5.2.2 Author's Race. Does the race of an author affect the spreading behavior? We observe that the proportion of Asian spreaders are significantly difference across different race of the authors in all news sources except The New York Times. For Reuters, The Guardian, and The Wall Street Journal, Asian spreaders are more likely to share news URLs written by Asian or AF-AM authors. Compared to the proportion of shares by Asian (Table 4) which are 10.4%, 10.7%, and 8.5% for those three news sources, respectively, the proportion of the news URLs shares written by Asian authors are increased by 26.9%, 23.4%, and 47.1%, respectively. For AF-AM users, we did not find the same pattern. Lastly, BBC News has a strong tendency that AF-AM share extensively news URLs written by AF-AM and Asian.

Table 9(b) shows the discriminative topics for each racial group of authors and spreaders. Asian authors are writing more about World and Tech than White. White authors write more opinionated news articles than Asian. For spreaders, Asian and AF-AM share

(a) The New York Times

Authors (%)	Spreaders (%)		
		Male	Female
	Male	54.8	45.2
	Female	53.1	46.9
		Asian	AF-AM	White
	Asian	11.0	10.7	78.3
	AF-AM	11.3	11.6	77.1
	White	10.7	10.3	79.1

(b) Reuters

Authors (%)	Spreaders (%)		
		Male	Female
	Male	58.7	41.3
	Female	57.5	42.5
		Asian	AF-AM	White
	Asian	13.2	10.4	76.5
	AF-AM	14.0	9.6	76.3
	White	9.5	10.9	79.6

(c) The Guardian

Authors (%)	Spreaders (%)		
		Male	Female
	Male	59.7	40.3
	Female	54.4	45.6
		Asian	AF-AM	White
	Asian	13.2	10.0	76.8
	AF-AM	14.1	11.1	74.8
	White	10.5	9.7	79.8

(d) The Wall Street Journal

Authors (%)	Spreaders (%)		
		Male	Female
	Male	66.9	33.1
	Female	59.6	40.4
		Asian	AF-AM	White
	Asian	12.5	9.2	78.4
	AF-AM	12.3	9.9	77.8
	White	9.3	9.8	80.9

(e) BBC News

Authors (%)	Spreaders (%)		
		Male	Female
	Male	62.4	37.6
	Female	50.0	50.0
		Asian	AF-AM	White
	Asian	3.4	6.9	89.7
	AF-AM	13.3	40.0	46.7
	White	11.3	9.1	79.6

Table 8: Confusion matrixes for news authors and spreaders by news source.

(a) Gender

Topic	Author		Spreader	
	Female	Male	Female	Male
Sport	↓	↑		
Opinion	↓	↑		
Health	↑	↓	↑	↓
Tech			↓	↑
Business			↓	↑

(b) Race

Topic	Author			Spreader		
	Asian	AF-AM	White	Asian	AF-AM	White
World	↑		↓			
Tech	↑		↓			
Opinion	↓		↑			
Sports				↑	↑	↓
Art				↑		↓

Table 9: Discriminative topics for gender and race groups by authors and spreaders.

more Sports news than White. News about Arts is favored by Asian more than White. Once again, we do not find any relationship between the topical interests of a certain racial author group and those of a certain racial spreaders group.

5.3 By LIWC Analysis

Linguistic Inquiry and Word Count (LIWC) [33] is a dictionary-based text mining software. Since it has been proposed, it has been widely used for a number of different tasks, including sentiment analysis [35] and discourse characterization in social media platforms [15]. Next, we use LIWC to characterize differences in the content shared by different demographic groups. Its latest version, LIWC 2015 (used in this work), defines about 90 linguistic categories and classifies more than 6,400 words into those categories [32]. For example, the word 'cried' falls into the sadness, negative emotion, overall affect, verbs, and past focus categories. Then, in a given text, the LIWC software finds the occurrence of the words in each category. The output is the proportion of the words in each category to the total words in the text.

LIWC Dimension	Our data	Newman et al. [30]
Pronouns		
First-person singular	M<F	M<F
Third-person	M<F	M<F
Linguistic dimensions		
Negations	M<F	M<F
Current concerns		
Money	M>F	M>F
Biological process		
Ingestion	M<F	-
Spoken categories		
Assent	M<F	-
Swear words	M>F	M>F
Female references	M<F	-

Table 10: LIWC analysis of ours and [30].

Table 10 presents the result of LIWC analysis of headlines shared by Male spreaders and Female spreaders. For comparison purposes, we also show the result of effects of gender on language use [30]. We show only LIWC dimensions that have more than 20% differences between Male and Female and omit the rest because the number of the whole dimensions is more than 90.

In our data, we find exactly the same trend as [30]: Female share headlines including more first-person singular pronouns, third-person pronouns, negations, words about ingestion (e.g., dish, eat, or pizza), assent (e.g., agree, yes, or ok), and female references (e.g., girl, her, or mom), and Male share headlines including more words about money (e.g., audit, cash, or owe), and swear words (e.g., damn, or shit). Considering that [30] observed those language usage patterns in the texts Male or Female *write*, finding the same patterns in the texts he or she *shares* is surprising and interesting. The spreaders are likely to share the news that is aligned with the language usage of their own. While many research have focused on attracting more clicks by tweaking headlines, such as including named-entities in headlines [23], we show that those studies can be extended to target specific user segments.

In addition, we find some results that are aligned with some stereotypes of races (e.g. Asian share headlines including more words related to family). However, we omit the result of LIWC by race of the spreaders because there have been no available references for a systematic comparison.

6 IMPORTANCE OF SPREADERS

Finally, we study the impact of understanding news spreaders in two ways: 1) extended readership by news spreaders and 2) understanding news popularity and demographics of news spreaders.

For the first, we compare the original followers and followers of spreaders by the number and the demographics. That is, we analyzed how spreaders extend news media's readers. For example, if followers of the The New York Times are usually white male but spreaders of The New York Times URLs have a lot of Asian followers, then, the role of spreaders is really important not only because it increases the number of audience but also because it brings "different" audiences. The results are shown below in detail.

6.1 Extended Readership by Spreaders

Ideally, to study the audience size reached by spreaders that is not reached directly by news sources profiles, we would like to have at our disposal the followers and friends of all users from our dataset. However, the number of followers and friends of these users surpasses a billion users, which is unfeasible to be crawled given our resources. As an attempt to provide evidence that spreaders can largely benefit audience of news papers in social media systems, Table 11 contrasts the number of followers of the news media profiles and the sum of the number of followers of the spreaders of each news source. Although these results do not quantify exactly the extent to which spreaders are able to increase the audience size of news sources, it clearly shows that they play a very important role in many news source audiences. For example, the number of followers in our sample of spreaders from NYTimes contains more than double the number of followers of The New York Times.

News Media	#Followers (news media)	# Followers (spreaders)
The New York Times	32,626,611	67,458,732
Reuters	15,946,449	11,119,453
The Guardian	6,154,465	21,120,210
The Wall Street Journal	12,563,525	6,193,775
BBC News	27,871,624	4,713,614

Table 11: Total/Real number of followers of the news sources in Twitter and number of followers of the spreaders that shared news of the news source.

We move onto demographic of the followers of news spreaders. First, we collected followers from a sample of 25% of spreaders from our dataset. For this data sample, the average confidence level for the number of the followers of the spreaders is 6111.154 ± 66396.94, with a confidence interval of 95%. After that, we analyze the demographic characteristics of the followers of the spreaders.

Table 12 shows the demographics of the followers of news spreaders. Compared with the demographics of the followers of news sources (Table 5), we observe the increase in the percentage of Female–the average increase is 9%. Besides that, for race, the percentage of White is higher–the average increase is 16%. We tried to test whether this difference in demographics of spreaders' followers and those of the original followers is statistically significant. We define the demographic distribution of the audience for each news media as a six-long vector whose element is a proportion of each demographic group (e.g., Male-Asian, Female-Asian, ..., and Female-White), respectively. With these vectors, we use the Kolmogorov-Smirnov test, which is a widely used statistical test to check whether two distributions are generated from an identical reference distribution. However, the difference is not statistically significant (for The New York Times, D = 0.5, p-value = 0.1641). The main reason is that the length of the vector, six, is too short to get statistical evidence. In future work, we will build demographic vectors for multiple snapshots and compute the statistical significance by concatenating those vectors.

6.2 News Popularity and Demographics

In the previous section, we show that understanding news spreaders is important as they extend the readership of news media. Another important aspect is whether the demographic traits of news spreaders are relating to the popularity of news. To this end, we collect the number clicks for each news URL using the Bit.ly API[12]. Then, we compare the popularity of news articles shared by different demographic groups to know whether a certain demographic group share news URLs likely to be more popular.

For gender group, we observe that the news items shared by Female are more clicked that those shared by Male. The differences are statistically significant by Kruskal-Wallis H-test ($H = 7.719, p < 0.005$). For race, the news articles shared by Asians are more clicked ($H = 6.659, p < 0.005$). The results show that the demographic information of news spreaders can potentially help in predicting the popularity of news articles.

---

[12]https://dev.bitly.com/

News Media	Race (%)	Gender (%) Male	Gender (%) Female	Total:
The New York Times	Asian	4.8	5.6	10.4
	AF-AM	6.3	4.2	10.5
	White	41.5	37.5	79.1
	Total:	52.7	47.3	100.0
Reuters	Asian	4.8	5.4	10.2
	AF-AM	6.3	4.0	10.4
	White	42.3	37.1	79.4
	Total:	53.4	46.6	100.0
The Guardian	Asian	4.8	5.3	10.1
	AF-AM	6.1	3.8	9.9
	White	42.7	37.2	80.0
	Total:	53.6	46.4	100.0
The Wall Street Journal	Asian	4.8	5.3	10.1
	AF-AM	6.1	3.9	10.0
	White	43.0	36.9	79.9
	Total:	54.0	46.0	100.0
BBC News	Asian	4.8	5.3	10.1
	AF-AM	6.1	3.8	9.8
	White	42.9	37.2	80.1
	Total:	53.7	46.3	100.0

Table 12: Demographic characteristics of each the followers of the spreaders by news source.

7 CONCLUDING DISCUSSION

The increasing diffusion of news in social media systems, associated with the great power provided to users along the dissemination process, are making these platforms a fertile ground for misleading or fake news propagation. The growing use of Twitter as a news' channel highlights the importance of characterizing news spreaders to understand who they are, what they share and their impact. Next, we briefly discuss implications of our main findings and discuss directions we aim to explore next.

Bias on breaking news stories: A widely used tool that users use to find breaking news-stories in online social networks is the Trending stories (or topics) [19, 40]. Recently, Facebook has been involved in many controversies related to trending stories [18]. First, Facebook involved human curators as part of its process to identify trending stories. A main criticism was that human curators could bias the final list of stories. Then, Facebook removed the human intervention and followed the popular perception that data-driven algorithms would not be biased as they simply process data. Our results, however, shows the data itself is biased, at least in terms of the demographic groups considered. We show that demographic groups of white and male users tend to share more news in Twitter. Our results also quantify the existing bias on Twitter shares towards specific demographic groups across news categories and other dimensions. Thus, our work contributes with a new and important perspective to the emerging debate in the community centered around concerns about bias and transparency of decisions taken by algorithms operating over user-generated data. Finally, we believe that the increasing availability of information about demographics will help the development of systems that promote more diversity and less inequality to users. Thus, as a final contribution of our effort, we intend to release our demographic dataset to the research community by the time of publication of this study.

Personalized news recommendations: Our analysis shows different user behaviors in terms of news sharing and also highlight demographic differents in terms of user interests. Identifying intrinsic characteristics of the users who spread the news in the online world and identifying how users interest across demographics is a key step towards the development of a framework that can promote the customization of the user experience using social media for news digest. We aim at further exploring this topic as part of our future work by investigating the discriminative power of demographic, linguistic, and network features in predicting a user's interest in specific news and news topics.

ACKNOWLEDGMENTS

This work was partially supported by the project FAPEMIG-PRONEX-MASWeb, Models, Algorithms and Systems for the Web, process number APQ-01400-1 and grants from CNPq, CAPES, Fapemig, and Humboldt Foundation.

REFERENCES

[1] Jisun An, Meeyoung Cha, Krishna Gummadi, and Jon Crowcroft. 2011. Media landscape in Twitter: A world of new conventions and political diversity. In *ICWSM*.

[2] Jisun An and Haewoon Kwak. 2016. Multidimensional Analysis of Gender and Age Differences in News Consumption. In *Computation + Journalism Symposium*.

[3] Jisun An and Haewoon Kwak. 2017. What Gets Media Attention and How Media Attention Evolves Over Time - Large-scale Empirical Evidence from 196 Countries. In *ICWSM*.

[4] Jisun An and Ingmar Weber. 2016. # greysanatomy vs.# yankees: Demographics and Hashtag Use on Twitter. In *ICWSM*.

[5] Cory L Armstrong and Fangfang Gao. 2011. Gender, Twitter and news content: An examination across platforms and coverage areas. *Journalism Studies* 12, 4 (2011), 490–505.

[6] Cameron Blevins and Lincoln Mullen. 2015. Jane, John... Leslie? a historical method for algorithmic gender prediction. *Digital Humanities Quarterly* 9, 3 (2015).

[7] Jonathan Bright. 2016. The Social News Gap: How News Reading and News Sharing Diverge. *Journal of Communication* 66, 3 (2016), 343–365.

[8] John D Burger, John Henderson, George Kim, and Guido Zarrella. 2011. Discriminating gender on Twitter. In *EMNLP*.

[9] George Casella and Roger L Berger. 2002. *Statistical inference*. Vol. 2. Duxbury Pacific Grove, CA.

[10] Pew Research Center. 2016. News Use Across Social Media Platforms 2016. (2016).

[11] Meeyoung Cha, Fabrício Benevenuto, Hamed Haddadi, and Krishna Gummadi. 2012. The world of connections and information flow in twitter. *IEEE Transactions on Systems, Man, and Cybernetics-Part A: Systems and Humans* 42, 4 (2012), 991–998.

[12] Meeyoung Cha, Hamed Haddadi, Fabricio Benevenuto, and Krishna P. Gummadi. 2010. Measuring User Influence in Twitter: The Million Follower Fallacy. In *ICWSM*.

[13] Abhijnan Chakraborty, Johnnatan Messias, Fabricio Benevenuto, Saptarshi Ghosh, Niloy Ganguly, and Krishna P. Gummadi. 2017. Who Makes Trends? Understanding Demographic Biases in Crowdsourced Recommendations. In *ICWSM*.

[14] Alex Cheng, Mark Evans, and Harshdeep Singh. 2009. Inside Twitter: An in-depth look inside the Twitter world. *Report of Sysomos, June, Toronto, Canada* (2009).

[15] Denzil Correa, Leandro Araújo Silva, Mainack Mondal, Fabrício Benevenuto, and Krishna P. Gummadi. 2015. The Many Shades of Anonymity: Characterizing Anonymous Social Media Content. In *ICWSM*.

[16] Evandro Cunha, Gabriel Magno, Virgilio Almeida, Marcos André Gonçalves, and Fabricio Benevenuto. 2012. A gender based study of tagging behavior in twitter. In *HT*.

[17] Munmun De Choudhury, Sanket S Sharma, Tomaz Logar, Wouter Eekhout, and René Clausen Nielsen. 2017. Gender and Cross-Cultural Differences in Social Media Disclosures of Mental Illness. In *CSCW*.

[18] Caitlin Dewey. 2016. What we really see when Facebook Trending picks stories for us. washingtonpost.com/news/ the-intersect/wp/2016/05/20/what-we-really-see-when- facebook-trending-picks-stories-for-us. (May 2016).

[19] Facebook. 2016. Search FYI: An Update to Trending. newsroom.fb.com/news/2016/08/search-fyi-an-update-to-trending/. (2016).

[20] Eric Gilbert, Saeideh Bakhshi, Shuo Chang, and Loren Terveen. 2013. I need to try this?: a statistical overview of pinterest. In *SIGCHI*.

[21] Mengdie Hu, Shixia Liu, Furu Wei, Yingcai Wu, John Stasko, and Kwan-Liu Ma. 2012. Breaking news on twitter. In *SIGCHI*.

[22] Fariba Karimi, Claudia Wagner, Florian Lemmerich, Mohsen Jadidi, and Markus Strohmaier. 2016. Inferring gender from names on the web: A comparative evaluation of gender detection methods. In *WWW(Companion Volume)*.

[23] Joon Hee Kim, Amin Mantrach, Alejandro Jaimes, and Alice Oh. 2016. How to Compete Online for News Audience: Modeling Words that Attract Clicks. In *SIGKDD*.

[24] Haewoon Kwak, Changhyun Lee, Hosung Park, and Sue Moon. 2010. What is Twitter, a social network or a news media?. In *WWW*.

[25] Wendy Liu and Derek Ruths. 2013. What's in a Name? Using First Names as Features for Gender Inference in Twitter.. In *AAAI spring symposium: Analyzing Microtext*, Vol. 13.

[26] Dianne Lynch. 1993. Catch 22?: Washington Newswomen and Their News Sources. *Newspaper Research Journal* 14, 3-4 (1993), 82–92.

[27] Alan Mislove, Sune Lehmann, Yong-Yeol Ahn, Jukka-Pekka Onnela, and J Niels Rosenquist. 2011. Understanding the Demographics of Twitter Users.. In *ICWSM*.

[28] Fred Morstatter, Jürgen Pfeffer, and Huan Liu. 2014. When is it biased?: assessing the representativeness of twitter's streaming API. In *WWW*.

[29] Nasir Naveed, Thomas Gottron, Jérôme Kunegis, and Arifah Che Alhadi. 2011. Bad news travel fast: A content-based analysis of interestingness on twitter. In *WebScience*.

[30] Matthew L Newman, Carla J Groom, Lori D Handelman, and James W Pennebaker. 2008. Gender differences in language use: An analysis of 14,000 text samples. *Discourse Processes* 45, 3 (2008), 211–236.

[31] Shirin Nilizadeh, Anne Groggel, Peter Lista, Srijita Das, Yong-Yeol Ahn, Apu Kapadia, and Fabio Rojas. 2016. Twitter's Glass Ceiling: The Effect of Perceived Gender on Online Visibility. In *ICWSM*.

[32] James W Pennebaker, Ryan L Boyd, Kayla Jordan, and Kate Blackburn. 2015. *The development and psychometric properties of LIWC2015*. Technical Report.

[33] James W Pennebaker, Martha E Francis, and Roger J Booth. 2001. Linguistic inquiry and word count: LIWC 2001. *Mahway: Lawrence Erlbaum Associates* 71 (2001).

[34] Julio Reis, Fabricio Benevenuto, Pedro OS de Melo, Raquel Prates, Haewoon Kwak, and Jisun An. 2015. Breaking the news: First impressions matter on online news. In *ICWSM*.

[35] Filipe N. Ribeiro, Matheus Araújo, Pollyanna Gonçalves, Marcos André Gonçalves, and Fabrício Benevenuto. 2016. SentiBench - a benchmark comparison of state-of-the-practice sentiment analysis methods. *EPJ Data Science* 5, 1 (2016).

[36] Tiago Rodrigues, Fabrício Benevenuto, Meeyoung Cha, Krishna P. Gummadi, and Virgílio Almeida. 2011. On Word-of-Mouth Based Discovery of the Web. In *SIGCOMM(IMC)*.

[37] Daniel M Romero, Wojciech Galuba, Sitaram Asur, and Bernardo A Huberman. 2011. Influence and passivity in social media. In *Joint European Conference on Machine Learning and Knowledge Discovery in Databases*.

[38] Dhavan V Shah, Joseph N Cappella, W Russell Neuman, Stuart Soroka, Lori Young, and Meital Balmas. 2015. Bad news or mad news? Sentiment scoring of negativity, fear, and anger in news content. *The ANNALS of the American Academy of Political and Social Science* 659, 1 (2015), 108–121.

[39] Luke Sloan, Jeffrey Morgan, Pete Burnap, and Matthew Williams. 2015. Who tweets? Deriving the demographic characteristics of age, occupation and social class from Twitter user meta-data. *PloS one* 10 (2015).

[40] Twitter. 2010. To Trend or Not to Trend. blog.twitter.com/2010/to-trend-or-not-to-trend. (2010).

[41] Claudia Wagner, David Garcia, Mohsen Jadidi, and Markus Strohmaier. 2015. It's a man's wikipedia? Assessing gender inequality in an online encyclopedia. In *ICWSM*.

[42] Shaomei Wu, Jake M Hofman, Winter A Mason, and Duncan J Watts. 2011. Who says what to whom on twitter. In *WWW*.

[43] Qi Yin, Zhimin Cao, Yuning Jiang, and Haoqiang Fan. 2016. Learning deep face representation. (July 26 2016). US Patent 9,400,919.

[44] Emilio Zagheni, Venkata Rama Kiran Garimella, Ingmar Weber, and others. 2014. Inferring international and internal migration patterns from twitter data. In *WWW*.

[45] Geri Alumit Zeldes, Frederick Fico, and Arvind Diddi. 2007. Race and gender: An analysis of the sources and reporters in local television coverage of the 2002 Michigan gubernatorial campaign. *Mass Communication & Society* 10, 3 (2007), 345–363.

Detection of Trending Topic Communities:
Bridging Content Creators and Distributors

Lorena Recalde, David F. Nettleton,
Ricardo Baeza-Yates
Web Research Group, DTIC, Universitat Pompeu Fabra
Roc Boronat, 138
Barcelona, Spain 08018
{lorena.recalde,david.nettleton,ricardo.baeza}@upf.edu

Ludovico Boratto
Digital Humanities
EURECAT
Av. Diagonal 177
Barcelona, Spain 08018
ludovico.boratto@acm.org

ABSTRACT

The rise of a trending topic on Twitter or Facebook leads to the temporal emergence of a set of users currently interested in that topic. Given the temporary nature of the links between these users, being able to dynamically identify communities of users related to this trending topic would allow for a rapid spread of information. Indeed, individual users inside a community might receive recommendations of content generated by the other users, or the community as a whole could receive group recommendations, with new content related to that trending topic. In this paper, we tackle this challenge, by identifying coherent topic-dependent user groups, linking those who generate the content (*creators*) and those who spread this content, *e.g.*, by retweeting/reposting it (*distributors*). This is a novel problem on group-to-group interactions in the context of recommender systems. Analysis on real-world Twitter data compare our proposal with a baseline approach that considers the retweeting activity, and validate it with standard metrics. Results show the effectiveness of our approach to identify communities interested in a topic where each includes content creators and content distributors, facilitating users' interactions and the spread of new information.

CCS CONCEPTS

• Information systems → Social networking sites; Recommender systems; Clustering and classification;

KEYWORDS

Trending topics; community detection; content creators; content distributors, Twitter.

ACM Reference format:
Lorena Recalde, David F. Nettleton,
Ricardo Baeza-Yates and Ludovico Boratto. 2017. Detection of Trending Topic Communities: Bridging Content Creators and Distributors. In *Proceedings of HT '17, Prague, Czech Republic, July 04-07, 2017,* 9 pages.
https://doi.org/http://dx.doi.org/10.1145/3078714.3078735

1 INTRODUCTION

Once we belong to an online social network (OSN) we can share content, add people to our network, access interesting information streams created by relevant users, and express our likes and comments about items shared by other users. Personalization is a key feature in OSNs because not all the content generated by our connections may be of our interest, regardless of its quality. Likewise, not all of our connections generate content that we might consider adequate, even if it fits into our topics of interest.

In order to enhance personalization, social recommender systems as part of OSNs are in charge of filtering content streams based on each user's interests model, their trusted social connections activity, and content authority. To do this, one way of finding relevant items to recommend to a user would be to discover their meaningful connections. For instance, the degree of significance could be measured in terms of the impact of the resources the user shares and the links the user has with those inside a topic-dependent community.

When a word, a phrase, or a hashtag is used with a high frequency, it is said to be associated to a *trending topic*. With the rise of a trending topic, a set of users interested in it also emerges. However, multiple points of view might be associated to it (*e.g.*, the #donaldtrump hashtag, related to the recently-elected US president, is used by people with opposing political views). Being able to manage these users and detect communities associated to a given trending topic is a problem of central interest in social recommender systems. Indeed, having a community of users who are linked and have the same interests would allow a system to generate suggestions at multiple granularities, *i.e.*, (*i*) for individual users, by providing recommendations of content related to the trending topic and generated by the other users in the community (thus allowing a quick and effective spread of information); or (*ii*) for the community as a whole, by providing group recommendations with new content related to the trending topic. At the same time, the problem is challenging, since trending topics are characterized by their temporary nature and evolve quickly; therefore, an approach that detects communities in this context should run quickly (*i.e.*, have a fast processing time), in order to dynamically adapt to the evolution of the trending topic (for example, by considering new users interested in it).

In order to tackle the problem of detecting communities related to a trending topic, in this paper we focus on Twitter, the widely-known microblogging platform. The activity of Twitter is depicted by tweets, retweets, replies, likes and shares, and its structure is defined by *follower* and *followee* unidirectional relationships. A key characteristic of Twitter, and of our approach, in order to enable the desired spread of information, is following and being followed by other users. Follower users are interested in tracking down significant users to follow, whereas the followed (leader) users wish to accumulate a lot of followers. However, to create significant content and be a topic influential user it is necessary to obtain interesting, trendy, and relevant information to generate a tweet. One way of doing this is to form a "collusion" with other content creators or influencers in the domain. As a result, the influential group is able to share and filter key news before they become widely known, and then potentiate its diffusion through the group of users interested in that topic (who may have the role of distributors or consumers of the given topic). Accordingly, we present a method to identify groups of topic-dependent "content creators" (CCs) in Twitter. Another key element of our proposal is the identification of their matching spreader groups or topic-dependent "content distributors" (CDs). After the identification of these two categories of users, both CCs and CDs are linked by our approach in a unique community, which represents the user base for the different forms of recommendation previously mentioned.

In summary, given this real-world application scenario, our objective is to detect communities of users who (i) are associated to a given trending topic, (ii) are interested in the same content, (iii) are linked among themselves (i.e., they follow each other), and (iv) can be either identified as content creators or content distributors.

Formally, the problem statement is the following:

PROBLEM 1. *Let H be the set of trending topics at a given time. For each topic $h \in H$, let T_h be the set of tweets that contain h (i.e., those associated to the trending topic), and U_h be the set of users who posted a tweet that belongs to T_h. The first goal is to identify a set of content creators $CCs \subseteq U_h$, who generated tweets that have been retweeted multiple times. The second goal is the identification of a set of content distributors $CDs \subseteq U_h$, who retweeted content generated by a CC. The final goal is building a graph G that contains the CCs and CDs as vertices, connected by edges that represent the "following" and "who-retweeted-who" relationships, which will allow us to detect communities that contain both CCs and CDs.*

To the best of our knowledge, our work represents the first attempt to detect several communities interested in a given topic, where each community integrates both a content creator group and the corresponding distributor group. The proposed method would improve the interaction and communication among the members of the community, and may be used to generate more personalized recommendations based on the structure of the topic-based community and levels of social influence. To summarize, our contributions are:

- We define a social model that detects topic-dependent content creator and content distributor groups on Twitter;
- The model can be embedded in an individual or group recommender system to suggest social entities;
- We validate our proposal on a real-world dataset extracted from Twitter, by employing standard metrics and by comparing it with a baseline approach that only requires the retweeting activity.

The remainder of the paper is organized as follows: Section 2 summarizes the context of the present work and the related state of the art; Section 3 describes our approach; in Section 4 we present the analytical framework built to validate our proposal and the obtained results; finally, in Section 5, we conclude and propose future work.

2 BACKGROUND AND RELATED WORK

The Social Web has shown to be one of the richest sources for mining people's interests, personality, and social interactions [21]. Therefore, recommender systems extended the traditional methods like Collaborative [16] and Content-based Filtering [13] to include users' information extracted from their OSNs. In this way, Social Recommender Systems make more personalized suggestions based on an improved user preferences model [9]. Several relevant works related to the present paper are discussed next.

2.1 OSN Analysis to Discover User's Interests

It has been shown that friends are able to make suggestions in a different number of domains and also share some similar interests [3]. Therefore, recommender systems might make suggestions for the target user based on her/his friends' preferences. Thus, *social recommender systems* have emerged with the aim of modeling the user's preferences by using the information s/he and their friends have published in OSNs. For instance, the study done in [17] demonstrated that friends of the target user provided more useful and better recommendations than recommender systems. Ma *et al.* [14] also modeled the preferences of the user in a social recommender system. They took into account that some of the user's friends might have different interests. The premise is that people tend to look for their friends recommendations; hence, this work establishes the difference between trust relationships and social friendships. The authors represent the diversity of tastes among the user's social connections using matrix factorization to improve the accuracy of the recommendations.

In our paper we also consider the exploration of users' connections in the Social Web. However, our approach differs from [17] and [14], since the item recommendation for the user may be not only based on his/her direct friends, but also on a community to which the user belongs and which is related to a topic of interest.

2.2 Social Entity Recommendation on Twitter

There are two important concerns about information stream personalization (Twitter activity feeds): (i) items or news feed filtering of what is to be considered of interest, and (ii) relevant content discovery that comes from friends of friends [5]. In [6], the authors present a framework that merges a traditional collaborative ranking approach with Twitter features such as content information and social relations data, so the model can generate better personalized tweet recommendations. In [1], the authors make a proposal to solve the news feed filtering problem in OSNs by presenting a method that automatically reorganizes the feeds and filters out irrelevant posts. The authors in [10] propose a "users to follow" recommender, implemented by using real time data from Twitter. The details about profiling algorithms and recommending strategies used in their recommender system are presented in http://twittomender.ucd.ie. Each user is modeled considering their recent Twitter activity and their social graph.

Other social entities to recommend to Twitter users are hashtags. Users can add some words prefixed by the symbol # to their tweets and they are identified as hashtags. The hashtags give some relevant meaning and structure to the users' posts as a folksonomy. In [12], a method that recommends hashtags is presented. It is based on finding similar user-tweet pairs to the target user-tweet pair, so the hashtags used by the neighbors may be recommended.

Compared to the state of the art, our approach may also be used to generate recommendations of news feeds, users to follow, hashtags, and other social entities. However, the novelty of our method is to employ a trending topic of interest to a set of users; consequently, the recommendations that can be generated are topic-dependent and are different for users who are content creators and for those who are distributors.

2.3 Social Influence and Grouping

In general, people do not make decisions in a completely rational way; instead they are usually influenced by many factors [3]. Marketing and e-commerce have exploited data in social network sites to propagate knowledge about products faster and collect users' opinions about them. Depending on these connections, consumer groups or communities are then detected. Dholakia *et al.* [8] present a model that structures the role of social influence by the community on its members to define its effect at the moment a user makes a choice, participates in collaboration activities, adopts certain behavior or goes into an engagement process. In the model, they set decision making as a direct function of social influence and as an indirect function of worth judgment.

In [19], the study shows the identification of influential tweeters based on their social and commercial importance. The authors propose a method in which the influential users are classified and ranked by topic of interest, and every topic has a small set of representative words associated with it. In [4], the researchers analyze three measures of influence in Twitter: indegree, retweets, and mentions per user in their dataset, as well as how influence varies across topics. They found that the most influential accounts were authoritative news sources and content trackers (topic independent results).

Some researchers in the field of group recommender systems (which suggest items for a group of friends, a family or a team) have seen that social factors, inherent in human behaviour, influence the recommendation and adoption phases. In [7, 15, 20], the authors study social influence inside groups to evaluate how this can be used to improve group recommender systems design. The work in [18] explains the *two-step flow model of influence* [11] where it is said that a small number of people act as influential individuals transmitting information with their own view of mass media to the rest of society. The first step refers to the transmission from the mass media to a group of influential people, and the second step comprises the diffusion of information from the influential group to a bigger audience. Those are the two steps in which a group of leaders may accelerate or prevent an item adoption. From this comes the motivation of our current work to identify influential groups involved in a specific domain of interest in an OSN, where those groups are formed by joining content creators and detecting their corresponding set of distributors. The result may be used to

build or improve users' preference models and then formulate social item recommendation. This social model has not been proposed before in the related state of the art.

3 APPROACH

This section provides the details of our approach, named *TreToC* (which stands for "*Trending Topic Communities*"), able to identify content creators and content distributors, as well as detect topic dependent communities related to a trending topic. The approach works in three steps:

(1) **Identification of** *CCs*. Analyzing the activity of the users who tweeted about a given trending topic, this step identifies the *content creators, i.e.,* those who generate content that is subsequently retweeted by other users.
(2) **Identification of** *CDs*. Analyzing the activity of the users who tweeted about a given trending topic, this step identifies the *content distributors, i.e.,* those who retweet content generated by the creators.
(3) **Detection of Trending Topic Communities.** Given the sets of users detected in the previous two steps, we first generate a graph G that connects them, and then apply a community detection algorithm to detect communities associated to the considered trending topic.

What follows is a systematic account of how the tasks performed by our approach have been implemented.

3.1 Identification of CCs

Users with a certain number of followers, whose tweets are quickly propagated or retweeted because of their content, and who are experts or somehow represent a specific domain, may be considered creators of significant content.

Given a trending topic $h \in H$, we collect the set of tweets T_h that contain h and consider the set of users U_h associated to these tweets (*i.e.,* those that either tweeted or retweeted content in T_h). Out of all the collected tweets, let T'_h denote the set of tweets that do not represent retweets (*i.e.,* those tweets that contain original content).

Every tweet $t \in T'_h$ is created by users who promote the content amplification over the social network. However, not all the users who generate content can be seen as topic propagators. Indeed, it is essential that the content is considered as interesting by other users, who retweeted a given tweet $t \in T'_h$ at least once. For this reason, we build a set $\hat{T}'_h \subseteq T'_h$, which contains these tweets:

$$\hat{T}'_h = \{t \in T'_h : retweets(t) > 0\}$$

where $retweets()$ is a function that returns the number of times a given tweet was retweeted by other users.

Given the previously defined set, we designate as $CCs \subseteq U_h$ the collection of *content creators*, who favor the content generation. More formally, the set of content creators is defined as follows:

$$CCs = \{u \in U_h : \exists t \in \hat{T}'_h \ s.t. \ author(t) = u\}$$

where $author()$ is a function that returns the author of a given tweet.

3.2 Identification of CDs

A user who follows another is probably interested in knowing the content s/he posts, but if the user retweets that content as it is, s/he is showing an agreement with it. Moreover, considering the diffusion of a topic, some particular level of interest arises, since many people retweet the emerging tweets. Therefore, the fact that a user *retweets* the tweets of another user is an important source of information to identify the content distributors of a trending topic. Consider that every user $u \in CCs$ posts a tweet $t \in \hat{T}'_h$. Let R_t be the set of tweets that represent a retweet of t:

$$R_t = \{t' \in T_h \setminus \hat{T}'_h : rt(t', t) = true\}$$

where $rt()$ is a function that returns true if a tweet t' is originated by a tweet t (*i.e.*, if it is a retweet of t).

We define as *content distributors* (*CDs*) the set of users who retweet content in $\hat{T}'_h$ and act as propagators. More specifically, the set is defined as follows:

$$CDs = \{u \in U_h : \exists t' \in \cup_{t \in \hat{T}'_h} R_t \; s.t. \; author(t') = u\}$$

It is worth highlighting that in our approach replies to a tweet are not considered, as they cannot be treated as forms of agreement. It should also be noted that, unlike the *retweeted* content of users, their *favorited* content is not shown in their followers' timelines; thus, favorite activity does not promote the spread of a topic and it is not considered as part of our study.

3.3 Detection of Trending Topic Communities

Given the set of users who generated topic-dependent content (*CCs*) and those who retweeted this content (*CDs*), the first goal is to find an effective way to link them. Indeed, in order to allow a rapid spread of information, users should follow each other. Moreover, we have to ensure that an explicit connection between a *CC* and her/his *CDs* is present.

In order to detect the communities related to a trending topic $h \in H$, it is first necessary to build a graph $G = (V, E)$ that represents the previously mentioned connections. The set V of vertices is represented as the union of the two sets of users identified in the previous two steps:

$$V = CCs \cup CDs$$

In order to build the set E of edges that represent the connections among the users, we consider three types of relationships. The first is the following relationship between two topic-dependent content creators:

$$F_C = \{(u_x, u_y) : follow(u_x, u_y) = true, u_x, u_y \in CCs\}$$

where $follow()$ is a function that returns true if the first user follows the second.

The second type of connection we consider is the following relationship between two topic-dependent content distributors:

$$F_D = \{(u_x, u_y) : follow(u_x, u_y) = true, u_x, u_y \in CDs\}$$

In the third type of connection we link a *CC* to a *CD* only if the *CD* retweeted content generated by the *CC*. Note that we avoid adding in the graph the following relationships between *CCs* and *CDs* because, in this context, this kind of link would be too generic and too weak to relate two users. Indeed, even if a user follows

another, it cannot be taken for granted that these two users agree on everything.

Saying that a Twitter following relationship does not explicitly show dependency to a given topic may sound arbitrary. However, if a user retweets another but does not follow her, and the following relationship would represent the link between two users, there would be no connection between them (even if, with respect to the trending topic, an important connection between the two users exists). Moreover, our focus is to detect communities in which the consumers get in touch with agreeable content with respect to the considered trending topic. Then, the connection between a *CC* and a *CD* is well represented by a retweeting link. More formally, the set can be defined as follows:

$$Ret = \{(u_x, u_y) : \exists (t', t) \in T_h \; s.t. \; rt(t', t) = true \; \wedge$$
$$author(t') = u_x \; \wedge \; author(t) = u_y\}$$

Finally, the set E of edges in the graph is represented as:

$$E = F_C \cup F_D \cup Ret$$

At this point, the Louvain method [2] is applied to detect topic-dependent communities of interest in the graph G. The choice of employing a community detection algorithm was made since it can easily handle networks with millions of nodes in a very short time. This characteristic of the algorithm fits with our need to detect communities that rapidly evolve and are characterized by a temporary nature. Given the evolution of a trending topic over time (*e.g.*, the appearance of new users that generate new content related to the trending topic), being able to detect communities in a matter of seconds allows the algorithm to work in a real-time scenario like the one we are considering.

Another interesting feature of the Louvain method is its capability to generate communities at different granularities (the structure returned by the algorithm is a dendrogram). Therefore, if a trending topic is emerging, our approach would be able to consider communities at higher granularities to make sure that each community contains both content creators and distributors, and if a topic has existed for a longer amount of time and more users are participating in it, communities at lower granularities might be considered.

As previously mentioned, this capability of the Louvain algorithm to rapidly detect communities would allow to capture a snapshot of the evolution of a trending topic (*e.g.*, at fixed time intervals, it would be possible to re-run the algorithm). However, since our proposal was conceived to provide effective recommendations to the users (both individuals and groups) there would be no need to recompute the communities too many times, to avoid "flooding" the users interested in the trending topic with excessive information.

4 ANALYTICAL FRAMEWORK

This section presents the analytical framework and gives our results. We first present the analytical strategy and setup (Section 4.1), followed by a description of the employed dataset (Section 4.2) and metrics (Section 4.3). Finally, we present the analytical results (Section 4.4).

4.1 Analytical Setup and Strategy

The environment for this work is based on the Python language. To build and manipulate the graph, as well as to calculate the metrics presented next, we used the *NetworkX* module[1]. However, the clustering coefficient of nodes for directed graphs is not part of the functions. Then, we implemented it following its formal definition. To run the Louvain community detection algorithm and measure the graph modularity we used the *community* module[2]. In order to ensure the repeatability of the analyses, some parameters need to be considered:

- By construction, the graph is *directed* and *unweighted*;
- To define the communities the function employed was *community.best_partition()* where the *resolution* parameter is set to 1. The resolution in modularity is used to adjust the optimization in partitioning. If this value is bigger than 1 it leads to the merging of two communities that share one or more edges, independently of the communities' features. We did not alter the resolution to avoid bias. Because of the properties of Louvain, the directed graph needs to be transformed into undirected when calling the function[3].

The dataset employed in the analyses is the only one existing in the literature containing trending topics on Twitter and the tweets associated to them, which we enriched with the *following* relationships between the users, collected thanks to the Twitter API.

To validate our proposal, five sets of analyses were performed:

(1) **Characterization of the trending topics.** Given a trending topic, we analyze the number of content creators and distributors that characterize it. This will allow us to understand the dynamics that characterize the activity on Twitter, even before communities are detected.

(2) **Analysis of the disconnected users.** In this case, we analyze the percentage of disconnected users from the graph (which would not be involved in the community detection[4] and thus would not benefit of the information spreading).

(3) **Analysis of the cohesion among the users.** For each community, we evaluate its quality by measuring the cohesion between the users in it, using standard metrics such as modularity, ratio between the number of communities and the number of users, and density.

(4) **Analysis of the community structure.** For each community, we analyze its composition, by measuring the ratio of content creators and distributors in it, and their clustering coefficient. This allows us to evaluate the effectiveness of our approach to connect those who generate the content to those who make use of it.

(5) **Analysis of the relationships between the users.** On Twitter, there are some kinds of relationships that connect people together. Our assumption was that users in a social

network might be connected at a given time because of a common topic of interest. However, these users might be associated to a topic because of previous relationships between them (*e.g.*, friendship). In order to validate that our communities are topic-based and do not appear together because of previous relationships, for each set of trending topics that share at least one user in common we analyze the percentage of users who take part in the intersection by measuring the Jaccard index.

In order to verify the choices made in our approach to consider the three previously presented types of connections in the graph, we compare our proposal with a baseline approach named *Retweeting-Based Communities* (*RBC*). In the *RBC* method, the set of edges in the graph connects two users only if one retweeted the other. It is worth mentioning that a graph built on the *following* relationship only would represent a community detection performed on the original Twitter graph, and this is completely unrelated to the trending topic dependency, so we discarded a baseline that considered only this type of connection.

4.2 Dataset

The analyses were performed on a dataset specifically built to collect information about trending topics on Twitter, which was presented in [22] and is available online[5]. The dataset contains 1,036 trending topics, which are associated to 567,452 tweets from 348,757 different users. However, in order to form the graph and detect the trending topic communities, the information about the tweets and the users who posted them is not enough. Indeed, we need to have the following relationship between the content creators, and the following relationship between the content distributors (Section 3.3). This was collected by querying the Twitter API, for the first 368 topics (due to the limitations imposed by the API on the number of calls that could be made). The final dataset contains 67,607 tweets, which correspond to the content retweeted at least once and the retweets found during collection, 15,918 unique creators, and 36,890 unique distributors. Of these, 673 were found to be creators of one topic and distributors of another. If a creator retweeted a tweet in the same topic, s/he was considered only as creator, in order to keep the topic graph structure proper. In conclusion, the total number of users in our study was 52,135, having 29.24% of them as creators, 69.46% as distributors, and 1.3% acting as both (in different topics).

4.3 Metrics

The method we propose produces a graph for a trending topic being analyzed. The graph is then divided into communities of interest. Both the graph and its communities can be evaluated by using the following metrics.

4.3.1 Ratio of disconnected users. The *ratio of users disconnected from the graph* measures the fraction of users, either content creators or distributors, who are not present in the graph because of the lack of linkage. Let $\overline{V} \subseteq V$ be the subset of users for which there is no edge $e \in E$ that connects them to the graph G. The ratio is calculated as follows:

$$|\overline{V}|/|V|$$

---

[1]https://networkx.github.io

[2]http://perso.crans.org/aynaud/communities/api.html

[3]Note that, even though the communities were detected on the undirected graph, the metrics to evaluate their quality were measured on the original directed graph, as described in Section 3.3.

[4]Community detection algorithms work on the largest connected component of a graph.

[5]http://nlp.uned.es/~damiano/datasets/TT-classification.html

4.3.2 Cohesion among the users. After executing the community detection, every node in the graph is going to be assigned to a community. The *modularity* is a value that represents the strength of division of a network into communities. High modularity means the connections between the nodes within communities are dense and the connections between nodes in different communities are sparse. The algorithm returns this metric after the community detection process is finished. Readers can refer to [2] for further details.

The *ratio between the number of communities and the number of users* allows us to evaluate the ability of an approach to group the individual users into communities. Indeed, higher values represent a low cohesion among the users (they are not added to the same community), while lower values indicate a smaller number of communities and higher cohesion among the users.

The *density* is the ratio between the number of edges per node to the number of possible edges. The density of a directed graph $G = (V, E)$ can be calculated as:

$$|E|/(|V| * (|V| - 1))$$

4.3.3 Community structure. Every community is expected to have several content creators in order to have newly generated content that can be spread through the community. The *number of creators per community* quantifies how many creators we can find in a community.

The *number of content distributors per community* measures how many distributors we can find in a community.

The last metric we are going to use, the *community clustering coefficient*, quantifies the extent to which nodes in the graph tend to cluster together. The clustering coefficient for nodes in a directed graph is defined by:

$$C_i = |\{e_{jk} : v_j, v_k \in N_i, e_{jk} \in E\}|/k_i(k_i - 1)$$

where k_i is the number of neighbors of a vertex $v_i \in G = (V, E)$ and N_i is defined by the neighborhood for the vertex:

$$N_i = \{v_j : e_{ij} \in E \vee e_{ji} \in E\}$$

4.4 Analytical Results

In the following subsections, we provide a detailed evaluation of our proposal.

4.4.1 Characterization of the trending topics. In the following, we analyze what characterizes the trending topics in the dataset. Each boxplot in Figure 1 represents the number of tweets found per trending topic, the number of creators who posted those tweets, the number of retweets found per trending topic, and the number of distributors who made those retweets. From the distributions obtained as results, we see that content generation and content propagation behave differently. Indeed, the data related to tweets presents a normal distribution (very few outliers) for which the average number of tweets per trending topic is 55.51, while the number of creators per trending topic is 46.20. In contrast, with respect to the content propagation, the distribution is skewed to the right, showing that few trending topics reached a high incidence of retweets/distributors. The median value for the retweets per trending topic is 84.5 and the median number of distributors per trending topic is 69.

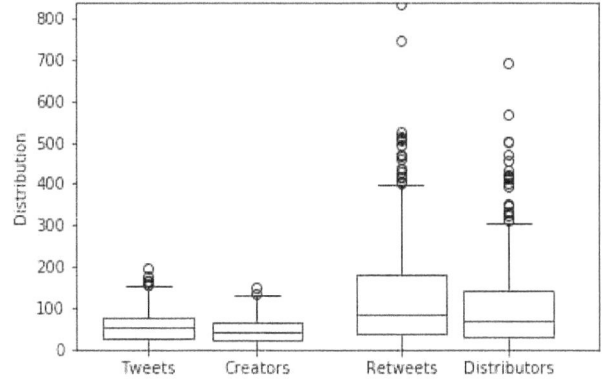

Figure 1: Distribution of the number of tweets, creators, retweets and distributors for the Trending Topics.

4.4.2 Analysis of the disconnected users. When a user has a connection with another, it is going to be considered in a graph (as a source or destination node, depending on the relationship). Accordingly, the average number of disconnected users for the trending topics was analyzed. Non-linked users are detected once the trending topic graph is obtained by following the corresponding approach, *RBC* or *TreToC*, while the rest of the users shape the main connected component.

The results show that the trending topic graphs generated with our approach (*TreToC*) cover 85% of the users who take part of the topic. The *RBC* baseline loses 23.6% of the user base of the dataset. These results demonstrate that our graph construction approach (presented in Section 3.3) includes more users in the community detection process. Indeed, if only the retweets (*RBC* baseline) are considered, more users are left out of the detected communities with respect to our approach, thus reducing the information spreading.

4.4.3 Analysis of the cohesion among the users. In order to analyze the level of cohesion between the users in a community, in Table 1 we report the average values of *modularity, ratio between the number of communities and the number of users*, and *density*, for our approach *TreToC* and the baseline *RBC*.

The corresponding metric values obtained are presented in Figure 2. A lower *modularity*, as that obtained in the *TreToC* method, shows that the communities in the graph maintain certain level of interaction or connection between them. This is not seen in *RBC* graph where the distributors behave only as source nodes, causing the modules partitioning being well defined. In this case, if we would like to adjust the resolution to get fewer communities it would not be possible because the *RBC* communities are not connected between them. Furthermore, the *density* is influenced by this fact, since the users in *TreToC* share two links (*i.e.*, following as well as retweeting) and act as source or destination nodes, resulting in a bigger value compared to density for *RBC*. Note that a higher modularity does not necessarily mean 'better', it is better just when we want smaller communities (in terms of number of vertices) or non-connected communities (as the *RBC* baseline

Table 1: Cohesion among the users (average).

Method	Modularity	Ratio of Communities/Nodes	Density
RBC	0.780	0.278	0.021
TreToC	0.622	0.183	0.027

Table 2: Community structure (average).

Method	% of Creators	% of Distributors	Clustering Coefficient
RBC	4.54	6.76	0.000
TreToC	7.76	9.05	0.077

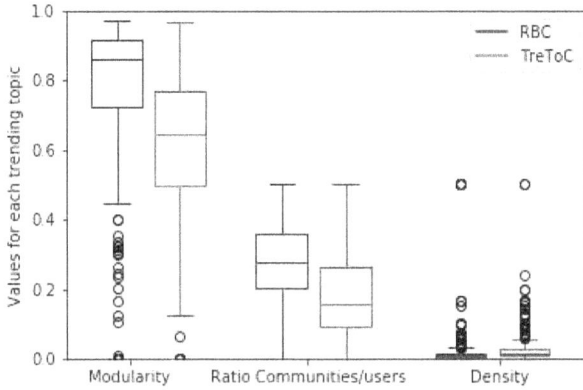

Figure 2: Cohesion among the users: Distribution of the metric values.

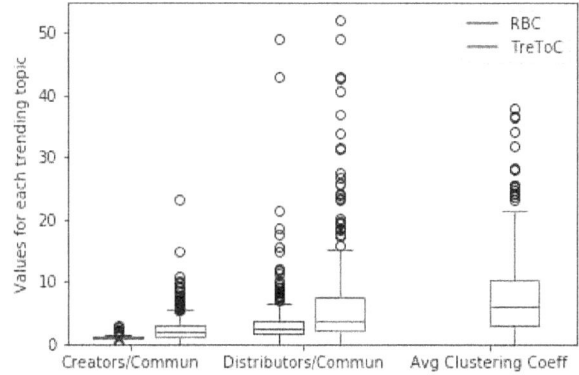

Figure 3: Community structure: Distribution of the metric values.

produces). Nevertheless, the purpose of our work is to get fewer communities, which are highly associated units composed by a suitable number of content creators and distributors. For example, more linked content creators in a community would cause diversity in future recommendations.

The average number of communities found in *RBC* graphs is 26.05, that exceeds the average amount of communities found in the *TreToC* graphs (16.22 communities per trending topic) which is what our method looks for (*i.e.*, our approach obtains larger communities).

4.4.4 Analysis of the community structure. Table 2 shows a summary of the analysis of the community structure obtained for the set of trending topics in our study. More specifically, this analysis measures the *average percentage of content creators*, the *average percentage of content distributors*, and the *average clustering coefficient* for a given community.

The *RBC* method relates two content creators only if a suitable number of distributors retweeted both of them; just then, we are going to be able to find few creators in a community (in average). In the *TreToC* method, the following relationship joins content creators making it more likely to find them as close neighbors. Consequently, their individual distributors come together too. We can observe this in the percentage of content distributors in a community in *TreToC* method, which is bigger too.

As a consequence of being able to have more content creators and distributors linked together in a *TreToC* community, the *clustering coefficient* increases as well compared to the *RBC* graph.

The boxplots in Figure 3, report the results of the three metrics found over the trending topics and compare the two approaches.

From the results, we notice that the *TreToC* method creates proper communities where we can find groups of content creators and the corresponding distributors groups. Notice that to represent the average clustering coefficient in the same figure, the values were multiplied by 100. As the clustering coefficients obtained for the *RBC* communities had a value of zero, they are not plotted in the figure.

4.4.5 Analysis of the relationship between the users. Considering the users who participated in more than one trending topic (3,599 users) and either appear (*i*) as distributors in a given topic and also as creators in other topics (18.7% of the mentioned 3,599), (*ii*) only as creators in more than one topic (22%), or (*iii*) only as distributors in more than one topic (59.3%), we evaluated to which extent those trending topics that share one or more users are overlapped, in order to find out if our communities are topic-dependent or exist because of previous relationships. To do so, we calculated the Jaccard index considering all the users of the set of *possible* overlapped trending topics. We obtained 1,894 different combinations of trending topics that had users in common and the basic statistics show an average Jaccard index of 0.008, having 0.0004 as the minimum value found and 0.65 as the maximum value.

The results validate our approach, whose main focus is to find topic-dependent communities where the users are related to a topic and then linked. The users are gathered together because of the topic and not because of previous relationships between them (indeed, the Jaccard index is very low). As an example, consider the two trending topics '#dealwithit' and 'Vernon Gholston', both related to sports and sharing users in common. The hashtag #dealwithit was used by fans of the American football team Buckeyes, who posted tweets like 'Go Buckeyes! 93-65 #dealwithit Wisconsin'. On

Figure 4: Two trending topics graph based on following relationships.

the other hand, the proper name 'Vernon Gholston' belongs to an American football player (who played in Buckeyes). Indeed, the two trending topics are connected between them, hence the overlap between the users. The graph obtained by taking the *CCs* and *CDs* for both topics and relating them according to the proposed method (Section 3.3) is shown in Figure 4. However, despite the shared users, the graph presents two separated groups of participants that are actually dependent of their respective topic, being the #dealwithit group the smallest one.

4.5 Discussion

We now summarize the results obtained in our analysis. When working with trending topics, Section 4.4.1 showed us that while content generation keeps stable (normal distribution) content propagation is maximized for few trending topics that reach more retweets and distributors than the average. As the analysis of the disconnected users showed (Section 4.4.2), in order to detect communities that are related to a trending topic and involve most of the users, it is necessary to link the users both with the "following" and "who-retweeted-who" relationships. Indeed, the retweeting relationship alone leaves around 24% of the users out of the graph, while the other around 15%. The analysis of the cohesion among the users (Section 4.4.3) showed that the communities we created are large (the number of communities is very low if compared to the number of users), that the users in a community are well connected (density is high) and that the communities themselves are connected (modularity is not high); this means that the evolution of a trending topic over time would allow a user to be moved from one community to another, to better fit with her/his current interests and the evolution of the trending topic itself. The third analysis, which studied the structure of the communities (Section 4.4.4) showed us that each community contains both a proper number of content creators and distributors (this would allow the distributors to get in touch with diverse content, generated by their content creators counterpart); moreover, the clustering coefficient confirmed that the nodes in the communities tend to cluster well together (the values are high), thus enabling the desired spread of information. The last analysis showed that, even though some topics are related and share users in common, they do not overlap, because the users participating

in a given topic depend on it (*i.e.*, the communities formed around a trending topic are topic-dependent and do not exist because of other types of relationships).

The results summarized above were monitored while the number of analyzed trending topics increased and they maintained the same tendency for the values obtained in the different metrics. From this we can infer that the captured phenomena are generalizable as trending topic behavior in Twitter.

5 CONCLUSIONS AND FUTURE WORK

In this work, we have proposed a framework to bring together topic-dependent content creator and distributor groups and identify relations between them.[6] This approach is new with respect to the state of the art, in which there is a lack of study of *N* group to *N* group relationships. Our validation showed the effectiveness of our approach at identifying the proper links between the users who participate in the evolution of a trending topic and then to detect suitable communities, which contain both creators and distributors.

The last stage of information diffusion is given when the content is presented to the *consumers*. They are the end users who have visibility of the trending topic and related content and are those who follow the creators and distributors. However, a *cold start* problem is evident for "first time" consumers given that we cannot know if a consumer is really interested in a topic until s/he retweets/favorites a post. In order to mitigate this, text mining can be applied over their historical tweets and content in their Twitter lists where they are subscribed. This is proposed for future work.

In the context of recommendations, we propose for future work to generate suggestions of social items for groups of Twitter users by leveraging information about their corresponding topic-based creator groups. For instance, the *CDs* can be supplied with a recommendation list of new and relevant users to follow, or a set of the latest tweets corresponding to those users and that fit into their topics of interest. We believe that the recommended items will be optimal for a given time frame, that is, an item is recommended at the time the related topic of interest is actually a current interest for a group. However, the recommendation framework must overcome some of the challenges presented by working with Twitter. For example, Twitter provides relevant information about the topics of interest of a user but it is difficult to quantify the user-to-topic tie strength when the user activity on the social network is very dynamic. That is, a topic may be a trend in a given city for no more than one hour and the number of followers and followees may vary every minute.

In order to implement a group recommender system based on the current work, our next goal will be to understand the correlation between *CCs* and Twitter influential users. Another challenge is to filter robot accounts that are created to propagate certain kinds of information and give them a top position in trending topics. This could lead to the identification of non-connected distributors as well as isolated content creators. We propose using machine learning techniques to identify these robots and filter them out.

[6]Our solution including datasets, code, and results are provided in https://github.com/lore10/Detection-of-Trending-Topic-Communities_Datasets-Code.

REFERENCES

[1] S. Berkovsky and J. Freyne. 2015. Personalised Network Activity Feeds: Finding Needles in the Haystacks. In *Mining, Modeling, and Recommending 'Things' in Social Media*, Martin Atzmueller, Alvin Chin, Christoph Scholz, and Christoph Trattner (Eds.). Lecture Notes in Computer Science, Vol. 8940. Springer International Publishing, 21–34. https://doi.org/10.1007/978-3-319-14723-9_2

[2] V. D. Blondel, J. L. Guillaume, R. Lambiotte, and E. Lefebvre. 2008. Fast unfolding of communities in large networks. *Journal of Statistical Mechanics: Theory and Experiment* 2008, 10 (2008), P10008.

[3] P. Bonhard and M. A. Sasse. 2006. 'Knowing Me, Knowing You' – Using Profiles and Social Networking to Improve Recommender Systems. *BT Technology Journal* 24, 3 (July 2006), 84–98.

[4] M. Cha, H. Haddadi, F. Benevenuto, and K.P. Gummadi. 2010. Measuring user influence in Twitter: The million follower fallacy. In *4th International AAAI Conference on Weblogs and Social Media (ICWSM)*.

[5] J. Chen, R. Nairn, L. Nelson, M. Bernstein, and E. Chi. 2010. Short and Tweet: Experiments on Recommending Content from Information Streams. In *Proceedings of the SIGCHI Conference on Human Factors in Computing Systems (CHI '10)*. ACM, New York, NY, USA, 1185–1194. https://doi.org/10.1145/1753326.1753503

[6] K. Chen, T. Chen, G. Zheng, O. Jin, E. Yao, and Y. Yu. 2012. Collaborative Personalized Tweet Recommendation. In *Proceedings of the 35th International ACM SIGIR Conference on Research and Development in Information Retrieval (SIGIR '12)*. ACM, New York, NY, USA, 661–670. https://doi.org/10.1145/2348283.2348372

[7] Y. Chen, L. Cheng, and Ch. Chuang. 2008. A group recommendation system with consideration of interactions among group members. *Expert Systems with Applications* 34, 3 (2008), 2082 – 2090.

[8] U. M. Dholakia, R. P. Bagozzi, and L. K. Pearo. 2004. A social influence model of consumer participation in network- and small-group-based virtual communities. *International Journal of Research in Marketing* 21, 3 (2004), 241 – 263.

[9] I. Guy, N. Zwerdling, D. Carmel, I. Ronen, E. Uziel, S. Yogev, and S. Ofek-Koifman. 2009. Personalized Recommendation of Social Software Items Based on Social Relations. In *Proceedings of the Third ACM Conference on Recommender Systems (RecSys '09)*. ACM, New York, NY, USA, 53–60. https://doi.org/10.1145/1639714.1639725

[10] J. Hannon, M. Bennett, and B. Smyth. 2010. Recommending Twitter Users to Follow Using Content and Collaborative Filtering Approaches. In *Proceedings of the Fourth ACM Conference on Recommender Systems (RecSys '10)*. ACM, New York, NY, USA, 199–206.

[11] E. Katz and P. F. Lazarsfeld. 1955. *Personal Influence, the Part Played by People in the Flow of Mass Communications*. The Free Press, Chicago, USA.

[12] S. M. Kywe, T. A. Hoang, E. P. Lim, and F. Zhu. 2012. On Recommending Hashtags in Twitter Networks. In *Proceedings of the 4th International Conference on Social Informatics (SocInfo'12)*. Springer-Verlag, Berlin, Heidelberg, 337–350. https://doi.org/10.1007/978-3-642-35386-4_25

[13] P. Lops, M. de Gemmis, and G. Semeraro. 2011. Content-based Recommender Systems: State of the Art and Trends. In *Recommender Systems Handbook*, Francesco Ricci, Lior Rokach, Bracha Shapira, and Paul B. Kantor (Eds.). Springer US, 73–105. https://doi.org/10.1007/978-0-387-85820-3_3

[14] H. Ma, D. Zhou, Ch. Liu, M. Lyu, and I. King. 2011. Recommender Systems with Social Regularization. In *Proceedings of the Fourth ACM International Conference on Web Search and Data Mining (WSDM '11)*. New York, USA, 287–296. https://doi.org/10.1145/1935826.1935877

[15] L. Quijano-Sanchez, J. Recio-Garcia, B. Diaz-Agudo, and G. Jimenez-Diaz. 2013. Social Factors in Group Recommender Systems. *ACM Transactions on Intelligent Systems and Technology* 4, 1, Article 8 (Feb. 2013), 30 pages.

[16] J. B. Schafer, D. Frankowski, J. Herlocker, and S. Sen. 2007. Collaborative Filtering Recommender Systems. In *The Adaptive Web*, Peter Brusilovsky, Alfred Kobsa, and Wolfgang Nejdl (Eds.). Lecture Notes in Computer Science, Vol. 4321. Springer Berlin Heidelberg, 291–324. https://doi.org/10.1007/978-3-540-72079-9_9

[17] R. R. Sinha and K. Swearingen. 2001. Comparing Recommendations Made by Online Systems and Friends. In *DELOS Workshop: Personalisation and Recommender Systems in Digital Libraries*.

[18] D. J. Watts and P. S. Dodds. 2007. Influentials, Networks, and Public Opinion Formation. *Journal of Consumer Research* 34, 4 (2007), 441–458. https://doi.org/10.1086/518527

[19] J. Weng, E. P. Lim, J. Jiang, and Q. He. 2010. TwitterRank: Finding Topic-sensitive Influential Twitterers. In *Proceedings of the Third ACM International Conference on Web Search and Data Mining (WSDM '10)*. ACM, New York, NY, USA, 261–270. https://doi.org/10.1145/1718487.1718520

[20] M. Ye, X. Liu, and W. Lee. 2012. Exploring Social Influence for Recommendation: A Generative Model Approach. In *Proceedings of the 35th International ACM SIGIR Conference on Research and Development in Information Retrieval (SIGIR '12)*. ACM, New York, NY, USA, 671–680.

[21] X. Zhou, Y. Xu, Y. Li, A. Josang, and C. Cox. 2012. The state-of-the-art in personalized recommender systems for social networking. *Artificial Intelligence Review* 37, 2 (2012), 119–132. https://doi.org/10.1007/s10462-011-9222-1

[22] Arkaitz Zubiaga, Damiano Spina, Raquel Martínez-Unanue, and Víctor Fresno. 2015. Real-time classification of Twitter trends. *JASIST* 66, 3 (2015), 462–473. https://doi.org/10.1002/asi.23186

Bumps and Bruises:
Mining Presidential Campaign Announcements on Twitter

Huyen Le
The University of Iowa, USA
huyen-t-le@uiowa.edu

G.R. Boynton
The University of Iowa, USA
bob-boynton@uiowa.edu

Yelena Mejova
Qatar Computing Research Institute,
Qatar
ymejova@qf.org.qa

Zubair Shafiq
The University of Iowa, USA
zubair-shafiq@uiowa.edu

Padmini Srinivasan
The University of Iowa, USA
padmini-srinivasan@uiowa.edu

ABSTRACT

Online social media plays an increasingly significant role in shaping the political discourse during elections worldwide. In the 2016 U.S. presidential election, political campaigns strategically designed candidacy announcements on Twitter to produce a significant increase in online social media attention. We use large-scale online social media communications to study the factors of party, personality, and policy in the Twitter discourse following six major presidential campaign announcements for the 2016 U.S. presidential election. We observe that all campaign announcements result in an instant *bump* in attention, with up to several orders of magnitude increase in tweets. However, we find that Twitter discourse as a result of this bump in attention has overwhelmingly negative sentiment. The *bruising* criticism, driven by crosstalk from Twitter users of opposite party affiliations, is organized by hashtags such as #NoMoreBushes and #WhyImNotVotingForHillary. We analyze how people take to Twitter to criticize specific personality traits and policy positions of presidential candidates.

KEYWORDS

Sentiment Analysis; Social Media Analysis; Twitter

1 INTRODUCTION

Election campaigns are complex socio-political processes that conclude with the vote on election day. An election campaign's evolution – with its varied attention 'bumps' and 'bruises' – is critical to understand the outcomes. For the U.S. presidential elections, the campaign season now typically extends 18 to 20 months prior to the election day [3]. Election outcomes are sometimes very difficult to foresee during the early and sometimes even at the late stages of campaigns. In 2008, for example, most analysts did not expect Barack Obama to be elected president at the beginning of the election campaign. In 2016, Donald Trump's win was unexpected even just a few days prior to the vote. Irrespective of whether it is possible to predict the outcome of an election, a longitudinal analysis of election data can provide important insights for our understanding of election campaigns.

A presidential election campaign starts with the candidacy announcement. Candidacy announcements are important because these are the time points when the candidates start to seriously introduce themselves to the electorate and invest significant resources into garnering favorable public opinions. Traditionally these announcements were made in mainstream media followed by a 'bump' in public attention. In recent elections, and especially during the 2016 U.S. presidential election, candidates leveraged online social media to launch their campaigns. For example, Ted Cruz was the first mainstream politician to officially announce his candidacy with a tweet. His announcement tweet received a big bump in attention for the candidate with approximately 12.3K retweets and 10.5K likes within one day [2]. Hillary Clinton followed just a few weeks later and also took advantage of Twitter in announcing that she was running. Her announcement tweet received an even higher attention bump with 95.7K retweets and 91.5K likes within one day [1]. Although political insiders knew that both were running before their announcement, Ted Cruz needed attention as did most of the other Democratic and Republican candidates. While announcements and consequent attention bumps were seen in mainstream media in earlier elections, present-day candidacy announcements appear carefully designed to also garner maximum attention on online social media.

In this paper, we focus on these crucial candidacy announcements on online social media and analyze the extent and kinds of public reactions they elicit. Since it is the start of the election process, our aim is not to predict the election outcome but rather to conduct a rich analysis – going beyond simple counts and sentiment analysis – of the tweets about the candidates from around the time of the announcement. We conduct this analysis within the framework of *The American Voter* [10], a seminal work in political science which demonstrated that the most important factors for voters were *party affiliation*, *policy considerations*, and *personality* of the person seeking the office. First, being a Democrat or a Republican, in the context of U.S. politics, was an important factor for individual voters. Second, voters' perception of importance of specific policies such as immigration and national security was also a key factor. Third, candidates' personality or character perception was also important for voters. Among these three factors, only party affiliation seemed to consistently impact voters' choices

HT'17, July 4-7, 2017, Prague, Czech Republic.
© 2017 ACM. 978-1-4503-4708-2/17/07...$15.00
DOI: http://dx.doi.org/10.1145/3078714.3078736

across multiple election cycles. While policies and personality perceptions are important, the specific policies and traits emphasized varied from one election to the next. *The American Voter*, now more than five decades old, set a research tradition that has extended to this point [26]. It is noteworthy that the classic paper and almost all of the follow-up research relied on survey research to analyze these three factors. In contrast, we use the same framework but apply it to online social media data related to these campaigns.

There is little doubt that online social media has played a significant role in elections in the U.S. and elsewhere [21, 38]. Recent elections, and especially the 2016 U.S. presidential election, amply demonstrate the importance of online social media in enabling candidates to directly reach the electorate. First, candidates are routinely active in promoting themselves on online social media. Second, many voters not only discuss political news but also post opinions about candidates and election events on social media [36]. Because of the nature of the medium, there is more opportunity for crosstalk as compared to traditional broadcast media – Democrats can post about Republican candidates and Republicans can post about Democratic candidates. Also in the mix we have journalists, who not only exchange opinions on online social media but also frame communications in traditional broadcast media.

Previously, we adopted *The American Voter* framework to analyze Twitter discourse in the 2012 and 2016 U.S. presidential elections [8, 25]. In [8], we demonstrated the importance of perceptions of personality traits of Obama and Romney during the 2012 U.S. presidential election. In [25], we showed the relevance of all three factors when analyzing Twitter conversations about candidates during the 2016 primaries and several debates. In contrast to our prior work, in this paper we focus on analyzing these three factors at beginning of presidential election campaigns. To the best of our knowledge, an in-depth characterization of carefully design online campaign announcements and the followup public discourse is lacking in prior literature. We summarize our key contributions and findings as follows:

(1) We study Twitter communications around candidacy announcements, an early milestone in the 2016 U.S. election campaign, for six major candidates from both parties. Specifically, we analyze Twitter communications from a week before to a week after these announcements. Of note is that all candidates analyzed announced their run on Twitter that resulted in an instant **bump** in attention, with orders of magnitude increase in tweets.

(2) Our sentiment analysis indicates that an overwhelming majority of tweets about candidates are negative. As soon as the candidates announce, we note a sharp increase in negative tweets – **bruises** – for all candidates. The ratio of negative to positive tweets is very high for some candidates (e.g., 19× for Jeb Bush and 10× for Ted Cruz) and relatively low for others (e.g., 2.8× for Hillary Clinton and 2.6× for Scott Walker).

(3) **Party.** We find that Twitter users of opposite party affiliation dominate the Twitter communication about a candidate. For example, almost 3× more Democrats tweeted about Jeb Bush than Republicans. Such communication is typically organized by hashtags such as #NoMoreBushes and #WhyImNotVotingForHillary.

(4) **Personality.** Personality perceptions also vary across candidates. For example, we find that Jeb Bush, Hillary Clinton, and Rand Paul are considered to be intellectually brilliant whereas Scott Walker and Marco Rubio are perceived as lacking intellectual brilliance. Hillary Clinton and Rand Paul are considered to be machiavellian whereas Marco Rubio and Ted Cruz are perceived as lacking machiavellianism.

(5) **Policy.** We notice that certain policy issues are disproportionately discussed for specific candidates. For example, Marco Rubio leads other candidates on immigration and Hillary Clinton leads others on gay rights. Overall, we find that health care and foreign policy dominates other policy issues.

2 RELATED WORK

We first discuss our previous work on analyzing political communications on Twitter [8, 25] during the 2012 and 2016 U.S. presidential elections. We then discuss prior literature related to analyzing online social media to predict elections. Finally, we discuss prior literature related to analyzing online social media to characterize political affiliation, personality perceptions, and policy issues.

In [8], we proposed a method to systematically track public perception of personality using a core set of 110 traits identified by Simonton [34]. We employed high-precision search templates on an 18-month tweet collection about Obama and Rommney collected during the 2012 U.S. presidential election. Our results showed interesting differences in public perceptions of their personalities. For instance, Romney was perceived as more of an achiever while Obama was perceived as more friendly. We further aggregated the 110 personality traits into 14 broad personality dimensions [34]. Our results showed, for example, that Obama rated far higher than Romney on the moderation dimension and lower on the machiavellianism dimension. We also made observations consistent with party ideology. For example, during time periods when mentions of Obama being conservative increased his Gallup support went down (-0.48 correlation). But when mentions of Romney as conservative increased his Gallup support went up (+0.40 correlation).

In [25], we adopted *The American Voter* and its three factors (party, personality, and policy) as an analysis framework for the 2016 U.S. presidential election. By employing state-of-the-art techniques in political affiliation detection, personality perception measurement, and policy analysis, we analyzed Twitter communications around 10 presidential candidates during multiple 2016 caucuses, primaries, and debates. Including in the data analysis were models built to regress on opinion poll data using a variety of features extracted from Twitter. These models demonstrated, independent of candidate party affiliation, the continuing importance of these three factors. These results further motivate our analysis using *The American Voter* framework in the current paper.

In contrast to our prior work, here we focus on analyzing the beginning of presidential election campaigns. As we discuss next, there is a plethora of prior research on analyzing political discourse as a whole during elections. However, an in-depth characterization of carefully designed campaign announcements on online social media is lacking in prior literature. We aim to fill this gap by analyzing campaign announcements and the public discourse that follows on online social media.

2.1 Election prediction

Using online social media communications to track public opinion and specifically to predict presidential elections is a hot research topic. However, there are conflicting results reported in prior literature. Some researchers [29, 38] found that there is a correlation between public opinion measured from traditional polls and sentiment measured from Twitter. Some researchers [18] claimed that Twitter sentiment analysis cannot accurately predict electoral outcomes, and its performance is only slightly better than a random classifier. Other researchers [17, 23, 32, 35] have also highlighted issues with using Twitter to predict elections such as the need of methodological justification in terms of accuracy, the need to produce a true forecast (i.e. issued prior to the election), and the need to control for biases. Some researchers [7, 9, 11, 16] have tried to address these issues, albeit with limited success. In this paper, we measure and analyze tweets collected around candidate announcements but we do not focus on election prediction due to the well-known issues raised in prior literature.

2.2 Party, personality, and policy

Prior work on inferring political affiliation in online social media can be broadly divided into two categories: content-based methods and audience-based methods. Content-based methods (e.g., [14, 30, 43]), as the name implies, address the problem more *directly* by analyzing users' own characteristics such as profile features (e.g., name, location), linguistic features (e.g., tweet text, hashtags), and network features (e.g., followers, retweets, replies). Audience-based methods (e.g., [19, 45]), in contrast, rely on the idea that users have their own ideological biases which are reflected in their sharing and networking behavior [33]. These methods *indirectly* measure political affiliation of users based on whether they post about well-known conservative/liberal issues or follow well-known conservative/liberal users. As we discuss later, our method [24] to infer political affiliation of Twitter users falls in the latter category.

Prior work on analyzing personality perceptions of presidential candidates have relied on broad categorization of sentiment such as positive, negative, and neutral [7, 23, 27, 40]. Tumasjan et al. [38] looked at more detailed sentiment aspects such as anxiety, anger, and sadness for different candidates in the 2009 German national election. More recently, in [8], we proposed a method to systematically measure public perceptions of a candidate's personality using a template-driven approach that measures such perceptions on a continuum for each of 110 personality traits. At one end the continuum represents the perceived absence of a trait and at the other its presence. We use this method in this paper as well.

Public policy issues have been examined at both the macro-level (nation or public as a unit of analysis) [6, 12] and the micro-level (how individuals define issues) [41, 42]. In order to track policy-related discussions on online social media, researchers typically create a lexicon of relevant terms of each policy and track their occurrences within the content [37, 44]. For instance, Zhang et al.

[44] manually identified relevant keywords, phrases, and hashtags related to same-sex marriage on Twitter, community wikis, and news articles to predict policy changes on the issue. We follow a similar high-precision approach, utlizing political scientists' domain expertise to build vocabularies for each topic.

3 METHODS

3.1 Party

We estimate Twitter users' political affiliations based on their connectivity patterns on Twitter with a set of landmark Democrat and Republican accounts. Our method [24] is founded on selective exposure theory [33] which in the context of American politics implies that a user following more Republicans than Democrats is likely to be affiliated with Republicans and vice versa [15, 28]. Thus, by carefully consulting with political scientists we manually curate a set of 30 well recognized Democrats (e.g., Rachel Maddow) and 30 well recognized Republicans (e.g., Sean Hannity) on Twitter as our "landmarks." Generally these landmarks have many followers which help to infer political affiliations for a large number of users. In fact, on average each Democratic landmark has 223,656 followers and each Republican landmark has 277,671 followers. Then, we estimate political affiliation as a function of the number of landmark Democrats and Republicans that each user follows on Twitter: $\frac{\#Republicans - \#Democrats}{\#Republicans + \#Democrats}$. The output is in the range of [-1,1], where -1 indicates Democratic affiliation, +1 indicates Republican affiliation, and 0 indicates Other (independent or alternative).

3.2 Personality

We measure the personality perceptions for the 2016 presidential candidates with the high-precision search template method proposed in [8]. This method has two main components. The first is the Adjective Check List (ACL) (consisting of 300 'personality trait' adjectives such as honest and strong) proposed by [20]. Simonton [34] identified a core subset of 110 traits/adjectives and further consolidated these 110 traits into 14 non-orthogonal personality dimensions. Bhattacharya et al. [8] built tweet search templates around these 110 trait adjectives augmented with synonyms and antonyms. This set of forty high-precision search templates is the second component of the method. In general there are two types of templates, one to retrieve tweets stating that a trait is present and the other to retrieve tweets saying that a trait is absent. For instance, "[P] is [A]? [T]" is a template where [P] represents a person name (e.g. Hillary Clinton), [A] represents a class of high certainty words (e.g., definitely, very), [T] is a specific trait (e.g., honest or its synonyms), and '?' designates optional. This template retrieves statements such as 'Hillary Clinton is certainly smart' and 'Hillary Clinton is intelligent'. Negation is considered in statements such as 'Hillary Clinton is not decisive', and trait antonyms are also considered such as in 'Hillary Clinton is somewhat unfriendly'. The method calculates a score for each trait using the tweets retrieved by these search templates. Scores are normalized for the number of tweets discussing the trait since individuals may accumulate varying numbers of tweets. These scores allow us to compare candidates

Candidate	Announce Date	Week Before Announce	Announce Day	Week After Announce	Total
Hillary Clinton	April 12	213,021	342,745	684,721	1,240,487
Ted Cruz	March 23	112,846	269,441	412,460	794,747
Rand Paul	April 7	29,535	227,437	334,134	591,106
Jeb Bush	June 15	95,040	103,710	205,648	404,398
Scott Walker	July 13	57,215	94,640	143,197	295,052
Marco Rubio	April 13	18,659	90,643	177,125	286,427

Table 1: Candidate announcement dates in 2015 and size of tweet collections on the announcement days, the week before, and the week after the announcements. The rows are sorted in the decreasing order of the total number of tweets.

in terms of personality perceptions from Twitter users. Further details are in [8].

3.3 Policy

Since public assessments on candidates are also shaped by the candidates' policy preferences, we track Twitter discussions on different policies for each candidate. The list of six policies analyzed include abortion, gay rights, climate change, foreign policy, health care, and immigration. Although not a complete list by any means, these are some of the key issues discussed in our data and in fact were heavily discussed for candidates on Twitter [31]. To identify the list of keywords for each policy, we started with a few well recognized keywords for each policy (e.g., "pro-life" and "pro-choice" for abortion). We then identified other related keywords that co-occurred (e.g., "planned parenthood" was frequently mentioned for abortion). Given the set of keywords for a policy, we extracted all tweets that contain at least one of the keywords.

3.4 Sentiment

In addition to the three factors from *The American Voter*, we also gauge sentiment of the tweets about each candidate, using the more common text mining strategy of sentiment analysis. Given the limited size of tweets (140 characters), we can safely assume that the sentiment detected in political tweets concern some aspect of the entities (in this case, the candidates) mentioned therein [29]. Among several dictionaries for sentiment analysis, we rely on the SENTIWORDNET lexicon [5], which assigns positive and negative scores to each *synset* (set of synonyms) of WORDNET (containing around 117K synsets). To this end, we split a tweet's text as separate sentences, remove symbols such as "< [>]* >", tokenize, and stem before matching to the SENTIWORDNET lexicon. To quantify the overall sentiment of each tweet, we use the common approach which is to sum up positive and negative sentiment scores of the matched tokens. If the positive sentiment score is larger than the negative sentiment score, we label the tweet as positive, and similarly for negative. In case both scores are equal, we label the tweet as neutral.

4 CANDIDACY ANNOUNCEMENTS

4.1 Data Collection

Based on our anticipation of potential candidates, we decided to monitor Twitter communications for several individuals starting

early 2015. Unfortunately, we did not anticipate all individuals who later announced their candidacy. For example, we did not anticipate Bernie Sanders or Donald Trump in early 2015. Therefore, we do not have data for their candidacy announcements. We anticipated other individuals such as Joe Biden and Elizabeth Warren who eventually decided not to run. Table 1 lists six candidates that we study in this work: Hillary Clinton, Ted Cruz, Rand Paul, Jeb Bush, Scott Walker, and Marco Rubio. Note that we excluded some candidates such as Bobby Jindal, Mike Huckabee, and Rick Perry who received very few tweets around their announcements.

We collected tweets concerning each individual posted during the time span of one week before and one week after the announcement. The data were collected using Twitter's streaming API with filter keywords (statuses/filter) for each candidate, such as "hillary clinton" for Hillary Clinton. The API tries to provide all tweets related to the filter keywords but caps the tweets at 1% of all public tweets. Since more than 500 million tweets per day are posted on Twitter, we are set to capture up to five million tweets per day for each candidate. Note that the highest daily tweet count (for Hillary Clinton) is less than 350K, thus we can safely assume that we are capturing a vast majority of tweets for all candidates. It is also noteworthy that a non-trivial amount of the collected tweets may come from bot accounts on Twitter [39]. In this paper, however, we do not attempt to distinguish between human and bot accounts and leave it as future work. For estimating Twitter users' political affiliations, we also used Twitter's REST API to crawl the follower lists for the Democratic and Republican landmarks.

4.2 Pre and Post Announcement

We note in Table 1 that users tweet more about candidates during the week after their announcement than the week prior. While it is not surprising that the day of the announcement has a big "bump" in the number of tweets, it is noteworthy that this number is larger than the total number received during the entire previous week. For Ted Cruz the number on the day of announcement is more than double for the previous week, while for Rand Paul it goes up by an order of magnitude. Candidate differences in bumps of tweet counts can be explained in part by their popularity. This may also be due to the surprise factor for certain candidates. For example, Ted Cruz (the first major 2016 presidential candidate) was expected to announce his candidacy several days before the announcement day.

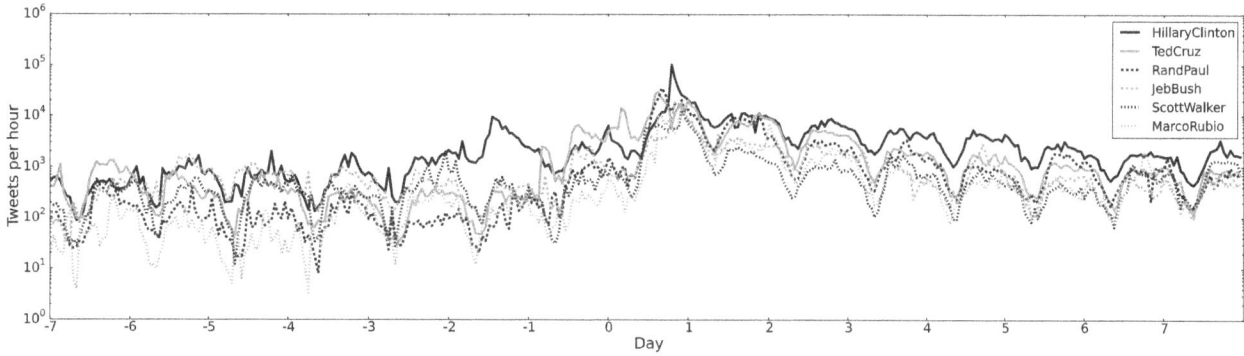

Figure 1: Time series of tweets for candidates a week before and after their candidacy announcements.

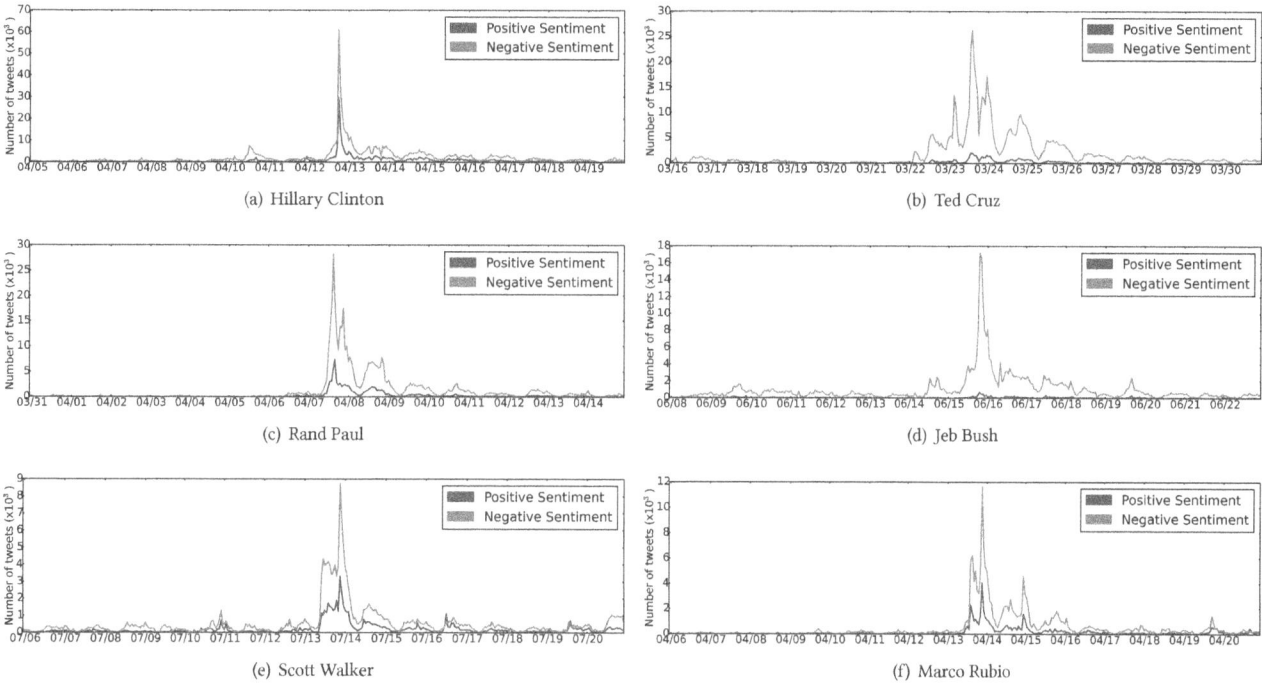

Figure 2: Time series of positive and negative sentiment for the presidential candidates a week before and after their candidacy announcement. We use the SentiWordNet lexicon to classify tweets as positive or negative based on their overall sentiment scores. The y-axis represents the count of tweets labeled as positive or negative.

Figure 1 shows the hourly tweet distribution for the candidates around their announcement dates (note the log scale of the y-axis). The plot confirms that tweet volume peaks at the announcement date (signified as 1 in the Figure). We note sharp bumps most notably for Clinton. A large fraction of bumps comprise of retweets of the candidacy announcement tweets. For example, Hillary Clinton's tweet ("I'm running for president. Everyday Americans need a champion, and I want to be that champion.") was retweeted by more than 100K users. Such retweets for others range from 13K for Ted Cruz, 6K for Jeb Bush, and around 2K for Rand Paul and Scott Walker. The ramp up in tweets to the announcement day (e.g., for

Ted Cruz and Hillary Clinton) indicates that announcements were not entirely un-anticipated.

4.3 Sentiment Analysis

We dissect the time series of tweets by applying the sentiment classifier to the captured tweets. Figure 2 shows the resulting volumes of tweets with negative and positive sentiment (excluding neutral, i.e., neither positive nor negative tweets). Interestingly, negative tweets significantly outnumber positive tweets for all candidates, but to a different extent for each. The announcement of Jeb Bush especially prompted a large spike in negative sentiment. Specifically, the ratio of negative to positive tweets was 19.0 for Jeb Bush,

10.9 for Ted Cruz, 4.4 for Rand Paul, 3.4 for Marco Rubio, 2.8 for Hillary Clinton, and 2.6 for Scott Walker. A majority of negative tweets were organized by hashtags. For example, we find 13,743 mentions of #NoMoreBushes for Jeb Bush, 33,458 mentions of #You-CruzYouLose for Ted Cruz, 28,372 mentions of #CantStandRand for Rand Paul, and 9,395 mentions of #WhyImNotVotingForHillary for Hillary Clinton. Overall sentiment analysis indicates bruising negative reactions on Twitter for most candidates.

5 PARTY, PERSONALITY, AND POLICY

5.1 Party

The importance of political affiliation is widely recognized in prior literature [10, 26]. This serves as a key factor in that only a small fraction of people vote against their political affiliations. According to the 2014 Gallup Daily tracking interviews with more than 177K U.S. adults [22], 26% Americans identify as Republicans, 30% Americans identify as Democrats, and 43% American identify as independents. As shown in Table 2, we identify 15.4% of users as Republicans, 20.0% of users as Democrats, and 64.6% of users as Others. Note that while the order of our numbers matches the ordering by Gallup, our method to infer political affiliation of Twitter users based on whether they follow well-recognized Democratic and Republican landmarks offers high precision but low recall. Therefore, the "Other" category may include politically inactive Twitter users whose political affiliation cannot be inferred by our method [13].

Table 2 also lists the party breakdown of users who tweet about different candidates. It is interesting to note that the percentage of users from the opposite party significantly outweighs users from the affiliated party for all candidates. For example, 11.9% users who talk about Hillary Clinton are identified as Democrats and 15.0% users are identified as Republicans. As another example, 8.7% users who talk about Jeb Bush are identified as Republicans and 22.0% users are identified as Democrats.

Our findings for political party affiliation help explain the sentiment trends we observed earlier in Figure 2. Recall that the number of negative sentiment tweets clearly outweighed positive sentiment tweets during candidate announcements. Thus, we can conclude that more users negatively talk about the candidates of the opposite party than in support of the candidates of their party. For example, soon after Hillary Clinton's announcement, #WhyImNotVoting-ForHillary and other negative hashtags started trending on Twitter and it outnumbered #ReadyForHillary and other positive hashtags. Similarly, #NoMoreBushes trended for Jeb Bush and #TedCruz-CampaignSlogans trended for Ted Cruz. To mitigate such negative crosstalk at announcements, a possible counter-strategy for campaigns would be to engage their supporters with positive messaging beforehand.

In the following discussion of results for personality and policy, we enrich the analysis by adding the breakdown of results with respect to user party affiliation.

5.2 Personality

Table 3 tabulates the tweet distribution for candidates for the 15 most mentioned traits (of 110 total traits). First, we note that the total number of trait-relevant tweets differs widely across candidates; Cruz has the highest number of tweets and Rubio the lowest.

Candidate	Democrat (%)	Republican (%)	Other (%)
Hillary Clinton	11.9	15.0	73.1
Ted Cruz	26.1	19.4	54.5
Rand Paul	23.5	14.6	61.9
Jeb Bush	22.0	8.7	69.3
Scott Walker	31.4	16.2	52.4
Marco Rubio	18.9	13.0	68.1
All	20.0	15.4	64.6

Table 2: The party affiliation breakdown of users tweeting for each candidate in percentage.

To avoid bias, tweet distribution in Table 3 is shown as percentages instead of counts. The top 15 traits include 9 positive, 3 negative, and 3 neutral traits. The table also breaks down the percentages by traits that are perceived as "present" or "absent" for each candidate. Note that the perceived presence of a positive trait or the absence of a negative trait may be regarded as a *strength*. Similarly, the perceived presence of a negative trait or the absence of a positive one may be regarded as a *weakness*. The top three traits mentioned overall are "easy going" (83.42%), "conservative" (62.68%), and "dull" (38.50%). In fact, easy-going ranks high for three candidates (consistently on the absence side) and conservative for two candidates on the present side. The remaining traits are dominant (10% or greater) for individual candidates. For example, Clinton alone is perceived as deceitful while the tweet percentages of this trait are less than 1% for other candidates.

Figure 3 displays the top ranking 15 traits calculated for each candidate and summary trait scores. The number of tweets matching a trait is listed alongside the trait name. The counts range from a low of 23 (is 'confused' for Walker) to a high of 2,577 (is not 'healthy' for Cruz) and 1,477 (is not 'easy going' for Paul). Scores are from -1 to +1, with -1 (+1) indicating the trait is viewed as absent (present) with high confidence. Puzzled by the "not healthy" perception for Cruz, our further investigation noted some level of noise. For example, we observed tweets such as *Ted Cruz is 'absolutely unfit' for office* and *Ted Cruz is 'sick'*. Clearly unfit and sick are used in a context that is different from physical health.

We focus first on those positive and negative trait bars that touch or cross the 0.5 point in magnitude interpreting these as perceived strengths or weaknesses as described earlier. For Clinton, her top two perceived strengths are that she is poised and persistent. Her top two weaknesses are that she is not seen as natural or handsome. Cruz's top two perceived strengths are that he is not meek and he is equally humorous and aggressive. His leading weaknesses are in not being perceived as moderate or healthy. Discounting healthy because of the noise described earlier, his second weakness is that he is not perceived as being wise. As strengths, Paul is perceived as assertive and not greedy. As weaknesses, he is perceived as rude and not mannerly. Bush's top two strengths are equal; he is not perceived as cold or unscrupulous. His two top weaknesses are that he is perceived as silent and not easy going. Walker's top two strengths are in coming across as dominant and not meek. But he is also perceived as not pleasant and equally not easy going or shrewd. As strengths, Rubio is not perceived as meek or greedy. But then

#	Trait	Clinton		Cruz		Paul		Bush		Walker		Rubio		Total
		pre	abs	pre	abs	pre	abs	pre	abs	pre	abs	pre	abs	
1	easy going(+)	0.91	**15.42**	0.05	**13.01**	0.10	**37.71**	0.06	5.47	0.11	7.20	0.14	3.25	**83.42**
2	conservative (=)	4.48	0.37	5.87	0.19	**10.13**	0.32	3.76	1.03	5.86	0.33	**30.12**	0.21	**62.68**
3	dull (-)	0.05	4.07	0.15	3.18	0.42	0.42	0.80	6.33	**16.52**	3.24	2.56	0.76	**38.50**
4	healthy (+)	0.12	2.48	0.86	**23.98**	0.29	0.69	0.06	0.17	0.11	0.28	0.76	0.21	**30.01**
5	shrewd (+)	4.03	0.30	3.86	1.21	0.64	0.42	1.43	1.25	0.78	6.98	0.69	3.67	**25.26**
6	intelligent (+)	4.09	0.25	4.52	0.74	0.74	0.44	1.60	2.28	0.73	3.91	0.69	3.19	**23.16**
7	dissatisfied (=)	0.00	0.14	0.07	0.02	0.00	0.00	**20.52**	0.17	0.28	0.22	0.07	0.00	**21.50**
8	moderate (+)	0.05	0.04	0.09	5.91	3.85	1.37	0.46	0.80	0.22	5.69	0.00	0.00	**18.48**
9	spontaneous (=)	0.04	9.53	0.00	5.73	0.00	0.22	0.00	0.29	0.00	0.50	0.00	0.48	**16.79**
10	deceitful (-)	**12.42**	0.21	0.06	0.25	0.34	0.17	0.23	0.17	0.56	0.00	0.00	0.35	**14.25**
11	cold (-)	0.05	0.27	0.07	0.16	0.00	0.44	0.06	**10.21**	0.06	0.28	0.00	1.18	**12.77**
12	dominant (+)	0.00	0.02	0.07	0.00	0.07	0.00	0.00	0.06	**11.72**	0.00	0.07	0.00	**12.00**
13	pleasant (+)	0.07	1.55	0.02	0.52	1.72	2.23	0.74	1.03	0.00	3.68	0.35	0.07	**11.98**
14	poised (+)	**10.31**	0.00	0.02	0.00	0.17	0.00	0.06	0.00	1.00	0.00	0.35	0.00	**11.91**
15	honest (+)	0.36	8.28	0.88	0.11	0.22	0.32	0.06	0.34	0.28	0.17	0.48	0.00	**11.49**
	#total trait-relevant tweets	5,604		10,376		4,079		1,754		1,792		1,444		

Table 3: Tweet distribution for candidates for 15 most frequently discussed traits (by %). Note that (+) represents a positive trait, (-) represents a negative trait, and (=) represents a neutral trait. The values exceeding 10% are in highlighted in bold.

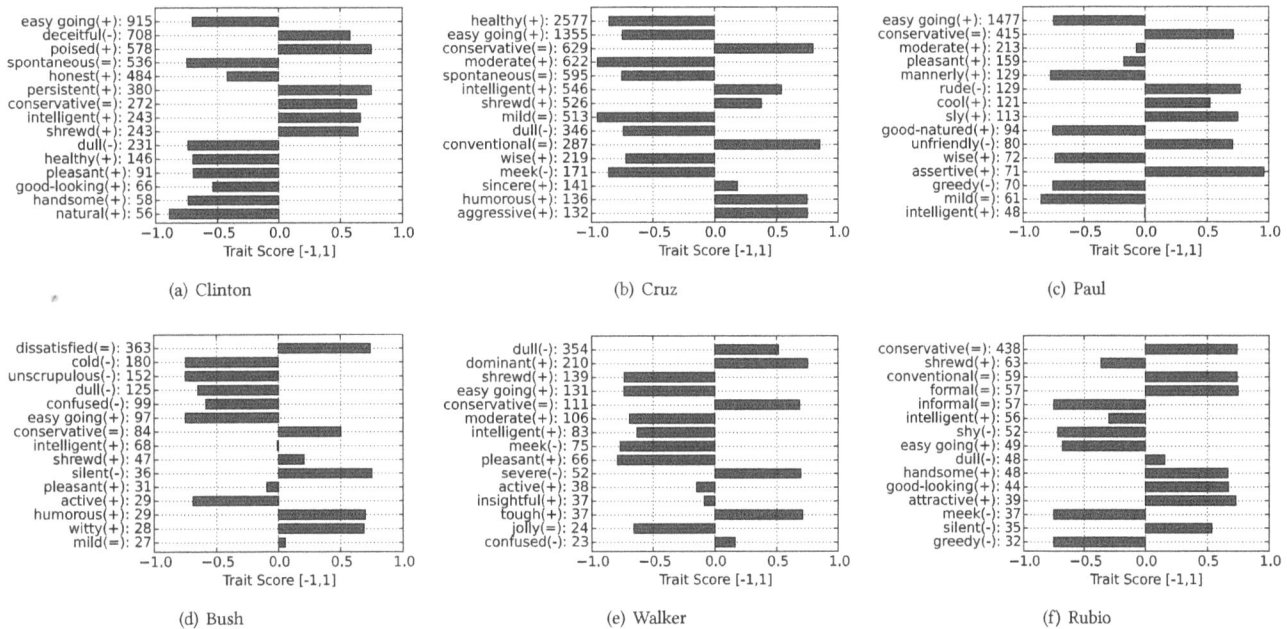

(a) Clinton

(b) Cruz

(c) Paul

(d) Bush

(e) Walker

(f) Rubio

Figure 3: Summary trait scores of top 15 (ranked in the descending order of tweet frequency) personality traits for each candidate. Scores are in the range -1 to +1; -1 (+1) indicates the trait is viewed as absent (present) with high confidence.

he is perceived as silent and not easy going. Overall the perceived strengths and weaknesses are distinct for each candidate.

Figure 4 plots the six most discussed personality dimensions (aggregated from relevant traits) for each candidate. The dimensions are refined with respect to party affiliation and their presence and absence. Scores are in the range [-1,+1]; -1 (+1) indicates the

personality is viewed as absent (present) with high confidence. For succinct analysis, we consider personality dimensions whose net scores cross the 0.5 threshold. We note that no candidate stands out in 'Moderation' or 'Friendliness'. Only Walker is seen as lacking in 'Intellectual Brilliance' while only Rubio is seen as lacking

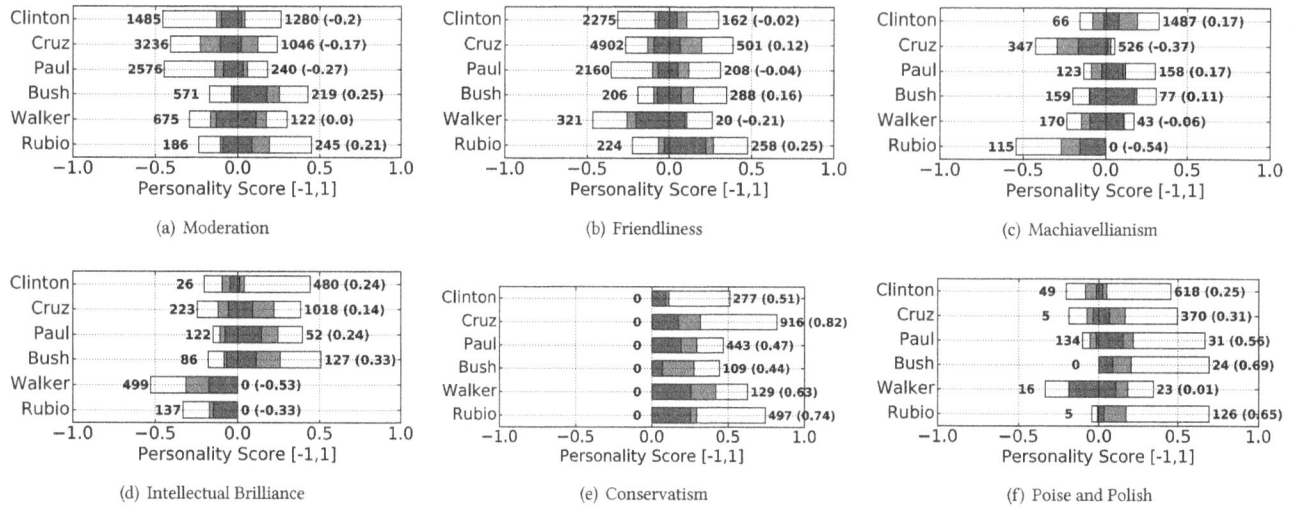

(a) Moderation

(b) Friendliness

(c) Machiavellianism

(d) Intellectual Brilliance

(e) Conservatism

(f) Poise and Polish

Figure 4: Personality scores with party breakdown. Scores are in the range -1 to +1; -1 (+1) indicates the personality is viewed as absent (present) with high confidence. The number of tweets for absence (presence) of each personality dimension are provided on the left (right) of the bar plot. The net score is included in the parenthesis. The blue, red, white regions indicate tweets from Democrats, Republicans, and Others, respectively.

'Machiavellianism'. Multiple candidates stand out in the remaining dimensions. For example, Paul, Bush, and Rubio are perceived as having 'Poise and Polish'. All candidates are also perceived as conservative but interestingly Bush and Paul do not cross the threshold. Combining party affiliations and personality scores, we note that most candidates received more tweets from Democratic-leaning users than Republican-leaning users. This is most obvious for Walker and Rubio who received about three times more tweets from Democratic-leaning users than from Republic-leaning users. In contrast, Clinton and Paul received about the same numbers of tweets from users affiliated with both parties: around 4% from each group for both candidates.

5.3 Policy

The policies advocated by candidates are an important consideration in their public assessment. Out of the policies that we considered, the ones most frequently mentioned in the data are: health care (also known as Obamacare), foreign policy, gay rights (particularly same sex marriage), immigration, climate change, and abortion. We find that about 22.9% of all tweets match at least one of these policies. More specifically, 7.4% of all tweets mention health care, 6.9% tweets mention foreign policy, 2.8% tweets mention gay rights, 2.2% tweets mention climate change, 1.9% tweets mention immigration, and 1.7% of tweets mention abortion. We noticed a mix of partisan perspectives for each candidate on different policies, due to the partisan crosstalk on online social media. Based on our identification of party affiliation, we were able to get a clear picture of how users from both parties are communicating about the policies of the candidates.

Figures 5(a) through (f) compare the breakdown of tweets for different policies. Overall, we note that the blue area is mostly larger than the red area, which means there were more Democratic tweets

from those we could identify as Democrats or Republicans. We observed that criticisms are generally more frequent than support for all candidate, with foreign policy being the most popular. That is an unexpected finding as generally foreign policy has not been important in elections [4, 31]. The spike of mentions of health care or Obamacare when tweeting about Cruz is also striking. Clinton leads the way on gay rights and gay marriage. Her position is well-known and it is generally supported. Paul and Walker stand out as most frequently mentioned for their policies on abortion. Rubio is the most frequently mentioned of the candidates about immigration. We next separately discuss our observations for different candidates, achieved via a manual expert analysis of the most frequent tweets.

Hillary Clinton: Foreign policy was one of the two most frequently mentioned, as Clinton's tenure as the Secretary of State as well as other current stances drove the conversation. It was overwhelmingly negative, with the ratio of mentions by Republicans to Democrats at 5 to 3. Her support for the Iran nuclear deal was most frequently mentioned, Republicans being uniformly critical of it. We also observed tweets about other issues such as ISIS, email scandal related to the 2012 Benghazi attack, Iraq, Israel, Cuba. Other international relations, such as those involving Europe and Russia, were not as prevalent. This contrasts with the other most prominent policy area of gay rights and especially her commitment on gay marriage, where Democratic mentions were double the mentions by Republicans, setting an overall positive tone. Most frequently mentioned stance was "same-sex marriage should be a constitutional right," and it was even a part of her announcement: e.g., "Hillary Clinton featured an engaged gay couple in her Presidential campaign announcement."

Ted Cruz: The major focus of tweets about Ted Cruz was about ObamaCare; two-thirds were about health care. This was largely due to the incident in which Ted Cruz, a noted critic of Obamacare,

(a) Health care

(b) Foreign policy

(c) Gay rights

(d) Immigration

(e) Climate change

(f) Abortion

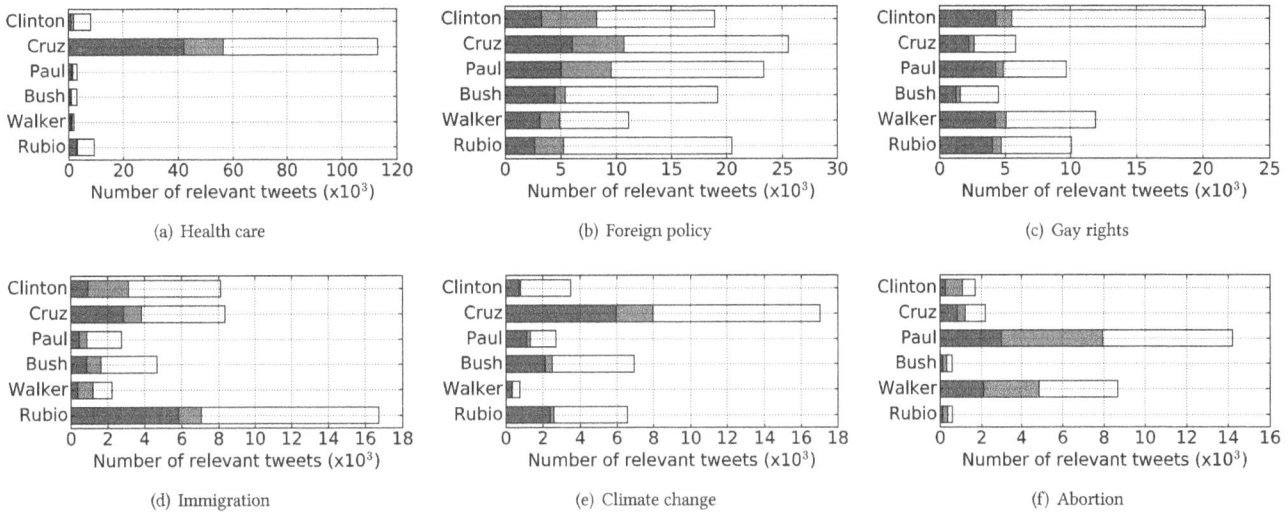

Figure 5: Number of mentioned tweets for different policies with party affiliation breakdown. The blue, red, white regions indicate tweets from Democrats, Republicans, and Others, respectively.

used it to buy health insurance for his wife, producing a large spike of derision such as: "Ted Cruz signs up for #Obamacare after vowing to repeal every word of it." Interestingly, he was criticized on this issue by both Democrats and Republicans. Cruz was also a critic of various Obama policies involving relationships with Iran and Cuba, climate change, immigration, women's health care and abortion, often garnering Democratic attention at 2 to 1 compared to his Republican supporters.

Rand Paul: As with the other candidates, foreign policy was mentioned more frequently for Rand Paul than other policy areas. Besides, his position on abortion provoked much criticism from Democrats, making the issue most prominent for Paul compared to other Republican candidates. Health care or Obamacare, climate change, gay rights, and abortion were all mentioned much more frequently by Democrats than by Republicans. The Democrats were critical of his positions for each of these policy areas.

Jeb Bush: Democrats' criticism of Bush's foreign polices concerning Israel, Iran, ISIS, and Cuba (by a 10 to 1 ratio compared to Republican tweeting) made it the most frequent. He was the only candidate for whom Putin was mentioned frequently, and it was negative by more than 2 to 1. Similarly, pungent criticism extended to his positions on climate change, gay rights, and gay marriage.

Scott Walker: Walker's stance on gay rights garnered an overwhelmingly negative discussion, with Democrats tweeting five times more than Republicans about the issue. Further, Democratic critique extended to his positions on the arrangements with Iran, his conception about how to deal with ISIS, and foreign policy in general. Although the mentions of his position on women's health care and abortion were about even between the parties, the opinions were again divided along the partisan lines with Republican support and Democratic opposition.

Marco Rubio: The attention to Rubio's policy positions was overwhelmingly critical. Democrats outnumbered Republicans on his policies on immigration, health care, climate change, and gay rights.

Tweets about his positions on foreign policy were almost equally distributed between Democrats, who were critical, and Republicans, who were supportive. Only on policy on abortion was there a substantial number of mentions by Republicans, and that was the least frequently mentioned of the policy areas.

6 CONCLUDING REMARKS

In this paper, we studied Twitter communications of six major presidential campaign announcements, an early milestone in the process of presidential elections in the U.S. We studied how party, personality, and policy impact the discourse on Twitter after candidacy announcements. Our study was designed with two objectives in mind.

Our first objective was to move from traditional survey research to online social media. Specifically, we wanted to characterize online social media communications about the candidates in terms of party, policy, and personality. To this end, we employed text mining techniques to explicate views on candidate personalities and their stance on different policy issues. We were further able to characterize policy issues and personality traits of the candidates by analyzing partisanship. Our methods to measure party, policy, and personality aspects in online social media communications are reusable in the context of different elections.

Our second objective was to establish a starting baseline from which we can track changes in public view of the candidates. The public view of the candidates is expected to change as the campaigns evolve over time. To illustrate this change, we compare our results from the announcement period to a later period that covers several debates and primaries [25]. In terms of personality, for example, our comparative analysis shows that Clinton was perceived as not moderate (moderation personality score of -0.2) when she announced her candidacy but this perception changed to moderate (score of 0.28) afterwards. As another example, Rubio was perceived as not intellectually brilliant (intellectual brilliance personality score of -0.54) when he announced his candidacy but this perception changed (score of 0.04) later. In terms of policy, gay rights were mostly mentioned for Clinton during the announcement period but they were mostly mentioned for Cruz later. While some of our findings may not generalize for other elections, we envision that our results would serve as a baseline for future election campaigns.

REFERENCES

[1] Hillary Clinton on Twitter: "I'm running for president. Everyday Americans need a champion, and I want to be that champion. -H https://t.co/w8Hoe1pbtC". https://twitter.com/hillaryclinton/status/587336319321407488, April 2015.

[2] Ted Cruz on Twitter: "I'm running for President and I hope to earn your support! http://t.co/0UTqaIoytP". https://twitter.com/tedcruz/status/579857596191899648, March 2015.

[3] US presidential candidate announcements: A history of hat throwing. The Economist. http://www.economist.com/blogs/graphicdetail/2015/06/us-presidential-candidate-announcements, March 2015.

[4] J. Aldrich, C. Gelpi, P. D. Feaver, J. Reifler, and K. T. Sharp. Foreign Policy and the Electoral Connection. Annual Review of Political Science, 9:477–502, 2006.

[5] S. Baccianella, A. Esuli, and F. Sebastiani. Sentiwordnet 3.0: An enhanced lexical resource for sentiment analysis and opinion mining. In LREC, volume 10, pages 2200–2204, 2010.

[6] F. R. Baumgartner, F. R.tner and B. D. Jones. Agendas and Instability in American Politics. Chicago : University of Chicago Press, 1993.

[7] A. Bermingham and A. F. Smeaton. On Using Twitter to Monitor Political Sentiment and Predict Election Results. In Sentiment Analysis where AI meets Psychology, 2011.

[8] S. Bhattacharya, C. Yang, P. Srinivasan, and B. Boynton. Perceptions of Presidential Candidates' Personality in Twitter. Journal of the Association for Information Science and Technology, 2015.

[9] P. Burnap, R. Gibson, L. Sloan, R. Southern, and M. Williams. 140 characters to victory?: Using Twitter to predict the UK 2015 General Election. Electoral Studies, 41:230–233, March 2016.

[10] A. Campbell, C. Philip, M. Warren, and S. Donald. The American Voter. University of Chicago Press, 1960.

[11] A. Ceron, L. Curini, and S. M. Iacus. Every tweet counts? How sentiment analysis of social media can improve our knowledge of citizens' political preferences with an application to Italy and France. New Media & Society, 16(2):340–358, 2014.

[12] R. W. Cobb and C. D. Elder. Participation in American Politics: The Dynamics of Agenda Building. Johns Hopkins University Press, 1972.

[13] R. Cohen and D. Ruths. Classifying Political Orientation on Twitter: It's Not Easy! In Proceedings of the Seventh International AAAI Conference on Weblogs and Social Media (ICWSM), 2013.

[14] M. D. Conover, B. Goncalves, J. Ratkiewicz, A. Flammini, and F. Menczer. Predicting the political alignment of twitter users. Proceedings of the International Conference on Social Computing, 2011.

[15] M. D. Conover, J. Ratkiewicz, M. Francisco, B. Goncalves, F. Menczer, and A. Flammini. Political Polarization on Twitter. In AAAI International Conference on Weblogs and Social Media, 2011.

[16] J. DiGrazia, K. McKelvey, J. Bollen, and F. Rojas. More tweets, more votes: Social media as a quantitative indicator of political behavior. PLOS ONE, 11(8), 2013.

[17] D. Gayo-Avello. "I Wanted to Predict Elections with Twitter and all I got was this Lousy Paper" – A Balanced Survey on Election Prediction using Twitter Data. arXiv: 12046441, 2012.

[18] D. Gayo-Avello, P. T. Metaxas, and E. Mustafaraj. Limits of electoral predictions using twitter. In AAAI International Conference on Weblogs and Social Media (ICWSM), 2011.

[19] J. Golbeck and D. Hansen. A method for computing political preference among twitter followers. Social Networks, 2014.

[20] H. G. Gough and A. B. Heilbrun. The Adjective Check List Manual. Consulting Psychologists Press, 1983.

[21] S. Hong and D. Nadler. Which candidates do the public discuss online in an election campaign? The use of social media by 2012 presidential candidates and

its impact on candidate salience. Government Information Quarterly, 29(4):455–461, 2012.

[22] J. M. Jones. In U.S., New Record 43% Are Political Independents. Gallup. http://bit.ly/17uCqDC, January 2015.

[23] A. Jungherr, P. Jrgens, and H. Schoen. Why the Pirate Party Won the German Election of 2009 or The Trouble With Predictions. Social Science Computer Review, 2(30):229–234, 2012.

[24] H. Le, Z. Shafiq, and P. Srinivasan. Scalable News Slant Measurement Using Twitter. In AAAI International Conference on Weblogs and Social Media (ICWSM), 2017.

[25] H. T. Le, G. Boynton, Y. Mejova, Z. Shafiq, and P. Srinivasan. Revisiting The American Voter on Twitter. ACM Conference on Human Factors in Computing Systems (CHI), 2017.

[26] M. Lewis-Beck, J. G. William, N. Helmut, and W. F. Herbert. The American Voter Revisited. University of Michigan Press, 2008.

[27] Y. Mejova, P. Srinivasan, and B. Boynton. GOP Primary Season on Twitter: "Popular" Political Sentiment in Social Media. In WSDM, 2013.

[28] J. S. Morgan, C. Lampe, and M. Z. Shafiq. Is News Sharing on Twitter Ideologically Biased? In ACM Conference on Computer-Supported Cooperative Work (CSCW), 2013.

[29] B. O'Connor, R. Balasubramanyan, B. R. Routledge, and N. A. Smith. From Tweets to Polls: Linking Text Sentiment to Public Opinion Time Series. In AAAI International Conference on Weblogs and Social Media (ICWSM), 2010.

[30] M. Pennacchiotti and A.-M. Popescu. A machine learning approach to twitter user classification. AAAI International Conference on Weblogs and Social Media (ICWSM), 2011.

[31] T. Rupar, A. Blake, and S. Granados. The ever-changing issues of the 2016 campaign, as seen on Twitter. http://wapo.st/1OgbJ45, December 2015.

[32] E. T. K. Sang and J. Bos. Predicting the 2011 Dutch senate election results with Twitter. In Workshop on Semantic Analysis in Social Media (SASN), 2012.

[33] D. O. Sears and J. L. Freedman. Selective Exposure to Information: A Critical Review. Public Opinion Quarterly, 31(2):194–213, 1967.

[34] D. K. Simonton. Presidential Personality: Biographical Use of the Gough Adjective Check List. Journal of Personality and Social Psychology, 51(1):149–160, 1986.

[35] M. Skoric and N. Poor. Tweets and Votes: A Study of the 2011 Singapore General Election. In Hawaii International Conference on System Sciences (HICSS), 2012.

[36] A. Smith. Cell Phones, Social Media and Campaign 2014. Pew Research Center, November 2014.

[37] S. Stieglitz and L. X. Dang. Social media and political communication: a social media analytics framework. Social Network Analysis and Mining, 4(4):1277–1291, December 2013.

[38] A. Tumasjan, T. O. Sprenger, P. G. Sandner, and I. M. Welpe. Predicting elections with twitter: What 140 characters reveal about political sentiment. In AAAI International Conference on Weblogs and Social Media (ICWSM), 2010.

[39] O. Varol, E. Ferrara, C. A. Davis, F. Menczer, and A. Flammini. Online Human-Bot Interactions: Detection, Estimation, and Characterization. In AAAI International Conference on Weblogs and Social Media (ICWSM), 2017.

[40] H. Wang, D. Can, A. Kazemzadeh, F. Bar, and S. Narayanan. A System for Realtime Twitter Sentiment Analysis of 2012 U.S. Presidential Election Cycle. In 50th Annual Meeting of the Association for Computational Linguistics, pages 115–120, July 2012.

[41] D. B. Wood and A. Doan. The politics of problem definition: A theory and application to sexual harassment. American Journal of Political Science, 47(4):640–653, October 2003.

[42] D. B. Wood and A. Vedlitz. Issue definition, information processing, and the politics of global warming. American Journal of Political Science, 51(3):552–568, July 2007.

[43] F. A. Zamal, W. Liu, and D. Ruths. Homophily and latent attribute inference: Inferring latent attributes of twitter users from neighbors. AAAI International Conference on Weblogs and Social Media (ICWSM), 2012.

[44] A. X. Zhang and S. Counts. Modeling ideology and predicting policy change with social media: Case of same-sex marriage. ACM Conference on Human Factors in Computing Systems (CHI), 2015.

[45] D. X. Zhou, P. Resnick, and Q. Mei. Classifying the Political Leaning of News Articles and Users from User Votes. In AAAI International Conference on Weblogs and Social Media (ICWSM), 2011.

Eatery – A Multi-Aspect Restaurant Rating System

Rrubaa Panchendrarajan, Nazick Ahamed, Prakhash Sivakumar, Brunthavan Murugaiah,
Surangika Ranathunga and Akila Pemasiri
Department of Computer Science and Engineering
University of Moratuwa
Katubedda 10400, Sri Lanka
{ruba.11, nazick.11, prakhash.11, bruntha.11, surangika, akila.10}@cse.mrt.ac.lk

ABSTRACT

This paper presents Eatery, a multi-aspect restaurant rating system that identifies rating values for different aspects of a restaurant by means of aspect-level sentiment analysis. Eatery uses a hierarchical taxonomy that represents relationships between various aspects of the restaurant domain that enables finding the sentiment score of an aspect as a composite sentiment score of its sub-aspects. The system consists of a word co-occurrence based technique to identify multiple implicit aspects appearing in a sentence of a review. An improved version of Analytic Hierarchy Process (AHP) is used to obtain weights specific to a restaurant by utilizing the relationships between aspects, which allows finding the composite sentiment score for each aspect in the taxonomy. The system also has the ability to rate individual food items and food categories. An improved version of Single Pass Partition Method (SPPM) is used to categorise food names to obtain food categories.

KEYWORDS

Rating system, aspect-level opinion mining, implicit aspect detection, text categorisation.

1 INTRODUCTION

Entities in a restaurant refer to products (e.g. food), services, individuals (i.e. staff), events, etc. Aspects are the attributes or components of these entities [1]. For example, in the review "food tasted great", *food* is the entity, and *taste* is its aspect. When considering the relationships between different entities, an entity may become an aspect of another entity. For example, *food* is a main aspect of *restaurant* entity. Therefore here

HT '17, July 04-07, 2017, Prague, Czech Republic
© 2017 Association for Computing Machinery.
ACM ISBN 978-1-4503-4708-2/17/07...$15.00
http://dx.doi.org/10.1145/3078714.3078737

onwards we refer both entities and aspects with the term 'aspects'.

In the modern era, customers rely on restaurant reviews to choose a better restaurant to dine in. However, reading a lot of reviews and making a conclusion is a tedious process. Therefore it is desirable to process customer reviews and automatically find rating values for restaurants. Nowadays, customers visit a restaurant with different intentions such as having meetings and parties. Therefore they are interested in the ratings for different aspects that are related to their intention of the visit. For example, a set of professionals who wish to select a restaurant for a meeting would be interested in the rating for the aspect *parking*. However, manually going through customer reviews to pick a restaurant based on few of these aspects is a daunting task. Aspect-level sentiment analysis (or opinion mining) has been proposed as a solution for this [2].

The process of aspect-level sentiment analysis includes the identification of different aspects mentioned in the reviews, and sentiment analysis to find the level of polarity of these aspects. An aspect in a review can be categorised as explicit or implicit. Aspects that are literally mentioned in the text are called explicit aspects, whereas the implicit aspects are implied by the review but are not literally mentioned [3]. For example, consider the sentences "Taste of food in that restaurant is great", and "Food is delicious in that restaurant". In the first sentence, aspect *taste* is explicitly mentioned. In the second one, we can infer that the review refers to the aspect *taste*, thus it is an implicit aspect.

In the restaurant domain, aspects exhibit hierarchical relationships. For example, *staff* with sub-aspects *appearance*, *behaviour* and *availability* can be considered as an aspect of *service*, which in turn is one of the major aspects of *restaurant*. Therefore, when calculating the sentiment score for a particular aspect, contribution of its sub-aspects should also be considered. However, this contribution is not uniform across all sub-aspects. For example, a composite sentiment score for a restaurant can be calculated using the rating values of its sub-aspects, *food, service, ambiance*, etc. However, some aspects can be considered more important than others. For example, if the aspect *food* is more important compared to other aspects, it should be given a higher weight when calculating the composite score for the restaurant. This gives rise to the need of capturing these hierarchical relationships among aspects and the identification of a proper weighting scheme to compute the composite score for each aspect in the hierarchy using the sentiment scores of corresponding sub-aspects.

Similar to the rating value for different aspects of a restaurant, food lovers are usually interested in the ratings for different types of food. However identifying rating values for individual food items may not always be useful. For example, a customer who would like to eat Pizza will be interested in the rating value for the food category Pizza. In contrast, a customer who had tasted a specific type of Pizza is more inclined to refer to that specific type of Pizza in his review. This leads to the problem of categorizing individual food items and identifying rating values for the generic food categories as well, similar to the rating value of other aspects of a restaurant.

This paper presents Eatery, a multi-aspect restaurant rating system as a continuous research of our previous work [4] - [6]. Eatery is based on a hierarchical taxonomy of aspects for the restaurant domain, the first of its kind, according to the best of our knowledge. An improved weighting model using the Analytic Hierarchy Process (AHP) [7] is used to find weights for the aspects in the upper levels of the taxonomy by utilizing the hierarchical relationships between aspects [4]. This allows calculating the ratings for aspects at different levels as a weighted composite score of their sub-aspects, whereas the previous research disregarded these multi-level relationships between aspects and focused only on calculating r1)atings for few aspects such as *food, service, ambience,* and *worthiness* [8] - [13]. Further, this paper discusses an improved method for identifying multiple implicit aspects appearing in a sentence of a review using co-occurrence of words [5], a capability not provided in the related research [14] - [16]. This is a domain-independent technique, which can be used to identify multiple implicit aspects appearing in a sentence that inclines any domain. Our system also includes a new approach for categorising food names in restaurant reviews using an improved version of single pass partitioning method (SPPM) [6]. This allows calculating ratings for individual food items and different food categories, instead of only calculating ratings for individual food items as done in previous research [17], [18].

Rest of the paper is organized as follows. Section 2 presents related work and section 3 describes the data collection process. Section 4 describes the implemented system. Evaluations are given in section 5 and finally, section 6 concludes the paper.

2 RELATED WORK

Currently, many well-known restaurant recommendation and rating systems such as Yelp [19] are available. Swant and Pai [20] have presented a recommendation system that is capable of calculating the rating for a restaurant based on the actual numerical rankings given by customers and recommending a suitable restaurant for a user using clustering algorithms.

A research by Kang et al. [21] introduced a system to predict the level of hygiene of restaurants using customer reviews. It provides a single rating per restaurant based only on the hygiene factor. Ahiladas et al. [17] and Trevisiol et al. [18] have presented approaches that rate individual food items based on the customer reviews. Gupta et al. [8] have focused on

summarizing restaurant reviews by attaching the sentiment polarity of a review to three main aspects *food, service,* and *ambience.* An approach by Lu et al. [9] rates main aspects *food, service, ambience* and *prices* using the topic modeling technique. Another approach by Mittal et al. [10] finds ratings for a similar set of aspects. Snyder and Barzilay [11] have used the good grief algorithm to rate multiple aspects in restaurants. In their approach, they consider only the main aspects *food, service, ambience, value,* and o*verall experience.* Similarly, Govindarajan [12] has focused on finding rating values for *food, service, ambience, deals/discounts* and *worthiness* using a hybrid classification method. A regression-based approach to finding sentiment polarities is introduced by Ganu et al. [13], which focuses on the categories *food, service, price, ambiance, anecdotes,* and *miscellaneous.* It identifies four overall sentiment polarity labels (positive, negative, conflict, neutral) for a given sentence and assigns one or more aspects together with a polarity label for each aspect. However, none of the above research has focused on identifying rating values for all the hierarchically related aspects of a restaurant.

Pontiki et al. [22] have experimented on identifying different aspects expressed in reviews towards a target entity and the sentiment expressed in each aspect. They have evaluated their system for restaurant reviews and laptop reviews. They have separately considered aspect-terms (lower level aspects such as waiter) and aspect categories (higher level aspects such as service) and do the sentiment analysis and find sentiment polarity independently. Therefore the relationship between aspect-term and aspect-category is not utilized here. Pavlopoulos [23] has focused on a similar research that identifies aspect-terms and aggregates them by clustering similar aspect-terms and identifying sentiment polarity for both cluster and individual aspect-term. For example, the aspects *money, price,* and *cost* are clustered together and sentiment polarity is identified for that cluster. Later, Pontiki et al. [24], [25] have extended their work to identify different entities and their aspects and carried out aspect-level sentiment analysis to find the sentiment polarity of each aspect. However, this research does not utilize entity-aspect relationships to identify composite sentiment score for an entity. Cena et al. [26] considered a hierarchy of aspects of a restaurant for extracting opinions on those aspects by means of a tagging framework, where tags are enriched with structure and expressivity. However they do not consider all the possible aspects of a restaurant.

In summary, all this research considers few high-level aspects or low-level aspects only, or both independently while performing aspect-level sentiment analysis in restaurant reviews. Very little research considers even a sub set of the hierarchy of aspects to process structured tags given by users to express opinions on social context. None has focused on utilizing the entity-aspect or entity-entity relationships that can be modeled as a hierarchy of aspects thus enabling sentiment score calculation of an aspect as a composite score of its sub-aspects by performing aspect-level sentiment analysis in restaurant reviews.

3 DATA COLLECTION

3.1 Food Names Collection

A list of more than 200,000 food names extracted from restaurant menus (under a different project) served as the main source. Apart from that, 1400 food names were collected from the A-Z of Food and Drink dictionary [27], and 1300 food names were collected from the Food timeline [28]. As described in section 4.1, these food names were used to obtain food categories.

3.2 Review Collection, Pre-processing, and Annotation

Review Collection & Pre-processing. 990627 restaurant reviews were extracted from the Yelp data challenge [29]. From this set, reviews written in languages other than English were removed with the help of a language detection library [30]. An automatic spell corrector [31] was used to correct language errors in the reviews. The spell corrector algorithm requires a dictionary file that contains the correctly spelled words that are taken as the reference to predict the correct words for the given inputs. This allows the inclusion of domain-specific words in this dictionary file to obtain high accuracy for a specific domain. In Eatery, the dictionary file contains words that are related to the restaurant domain and the words that are frequently cited in the restaurant reviews. We also included many food names that are used in the training data set. This allows correcting spelling mistakes in food names. Apart from these domain-specific words, we also added stop words, adjectives, and adverbs. Spam identification was not considered as the Yelp dataset has already been spam filtered.

Annotation. Previous research [32] suggests that a dataset to train a model to identify aspects in the text should contain at least 15000 sentences for that model to perform well. From the Yelp dataset, 1500 reviews were randomly picked to create the annotated dataset to be used for training and testing. In the training dataset, each review had an average of 10 sentences to ensure that the entire training data set has 15000 sentences. In these 1500 reviews, aspects (both explicit and implicit) were manually labeled. For example, in the sentence "Pizza was small in that big restaurant", *pizza* and *restaurant* are identified as explicit aspects and are labeled as *Food_item* and *Restaurant*, respectively. *small* and *big* are opinion words that identify implicit aspects. Therefore each opinion word that identifies an implicit aspect is labeled with the aspect it implies. For example, in the above sentence, *small* and *big* are labeled as *Food_item_size* and *Environment_size*, respectively. Finally, the annotated sentence appears as follows in the training data set:

<Start: Food_item> Pizza <End> was <Start: Food_item_size> small <End> in that <Start: Environment_size> big <End> <Start: Restaurant> restaurant <End>

Food names are labeled automatically by doing string matching with the collected food names.

4 EATERY SYSTEM

Figure 1 shows the workflow of Eatery that rates different aspects of a restaurant. Categorised food names, trained models to identify explicit and implicit aspects, and weighting model are input to the system. Eatery taxonomy contains the hierarchical relationships among different aspects of a restaurant. A new set

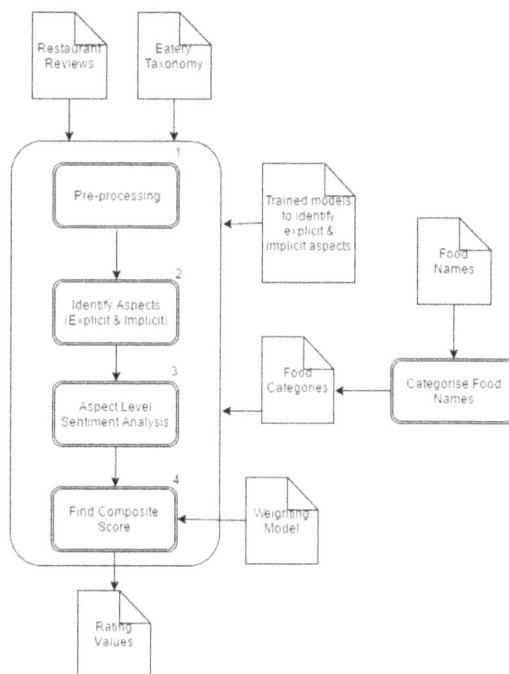

Figure 1: Eatery Flow

of reviews is first pre-processed as described in section 3.2, and the next step identifies explicit and implicit aspects. Individual food items and food categories in the reviews are also identified as explicit aspects.

Once the aspects are identified, sentiment analysis is carried out to find the sentiment polarities of opinion phrases of identified aspects. Scores given by sentiment classification are aggregated to find the rating value for each aspect in the Eatery taxonomy. Using a weighting model, the composite score for each aspect is calculated as a weighted score of its sub-aspects. An improved version of AHP that utilizes the relationship between the aspects is used to obtain the weight for each aspect in the taxonomy. As food items and food categories are considered as a part of the Eatery taxonomy, the composite score for each food category is also calculated as a weighted score of food items that come under that category.

4.1 Food Names Categorisation

Work by Sawant and Pai [20] is the only existing work that categorises food names in restaurants. As we collected only the food names, the data for the food categorisation component in our system is one dimensional. Therefore clustering using algorithms such as k-means as done by Sawant and Pai [20] is not a possible option. Therefore the single pass partitioning (SPPM) [33] text clustering approach was considered as an initial option to categorise food names. SPPM randomly picks an element (food names from the list of food names in our case) as the centroid of a cluster and adds elements to the cluster by measuring the surface similarity between the centroid element and other elements. Jaro [34] distance was used to measure the similarity between two food names. The threshold for the acceptable similarity between two food names to be categorised was decided by manually increasing the threshold till an optimum level of accuracy was achieved.

However, it could be seen that SPPM did not perform well in case of food name categorisation as it considers the entire food name as a single string. For example, consider "Vegetable Burger" and "Chicken Burger". Both food items should be categorized under the food category "Burger". However, since the Jaro distance between "Vegetable" and "Chicken" is large, "Vegetable Burger" and "Chicken Burger" may not get clustered together unless the similarity between these two items exceeded the threshold.

Therefore rather than considering the similarity between entire food names, a set of cluster elements for each food name was created by splitting a food name into multiple words [6]. For example, the food name *Tandoori chicken pizza* is broken into three words *Tandoori, chicken,* and *pizza* to create three cluster elements. SPPM was applied for these cluster elements. This allows clustering similar names that refer to the same food item. For example, different users may mention the food *pizza* as *piza, pizaa* or *pizzza* in reviews. These similar words are clustered together so that finally a cluster of words represents a food category. As the final step, individual food items are assigned to one of the clusters (food categories) using simple string matching. It is worth to note that in improved SPPM, each cluster element plays the role of a food category whereas a food category cannot be identified in original SPPM without manual effort. Moreover, a very high threshold for an acceptable similarity between two cluster elements is used to avoid clustering of different food names that have high similarity. For example, *pizza* and *pasta* will be clustered together unless a higher threshold is used.

However, due to this modification, the resulting categories had several food category names that do not refer to food names. For example, the food name, *Pizza with cheese* results in a redundant category *with*. Therefore a wiki API[1] was used to determine whether a category name refers to food or not. Each cluster element is given as an input to the wiki API and words in the response are checked against a manually created list of words related to the food domain. For example, if we consider *Chicken pizza*, it is categorised under both *chicken* and *pizza*. When validating the *chicken* cluster by giving the word *chicken* as an input to the wiki API, we get response lines including *chicken, broiler, meat, skin, cooked* and *stewed*. Since the word *cooked* is there in the response, *chicken* is considered as a word related to food and is accepted as a food category. Moreover, it can be noticed that *Pizza with cheese* results in a food category "cheese", which is related to food domain so that it will not be removed by our verification process. However, this is not going to be a useful category. Moreover, the semantic similarity between words is not considered when measuring the similarity between two cluster elements. These are the two limitations that our improved SPPM has at the moment. After completing the categorisation, newly encountered food names in restaurant reviews containing the words in a particular category can be added to that category using simple string matching.

---

[1] https://www.mediawiki.org/wiki/API:Main_page

4.2 Eatery Taxonomy

Figure 2 shows the taxonomy that was developed to represent hierarchical relationships between different aspects. This taxonomy was developed using a random sample of 400 reviews from the preprocessed reviews. It was again validated and refined using another set of 400 reviews obtained randomly. This process was carried out with 6 human participants. Level 1 is *restaurant*, which has five main categories: *food, service, ambience, discount/offer,* and worthiness in the second level. Level 2 is further categorized and the final level contains the sub-aspects of Level 3 aspects. In addition to the main sub-aspects of *restaurant*, aspects that cannot be categorised under any of the sub-aspects of the *restaurant* are considered as *others*. For example, *overall experience* of a customer cannot be categorised under any of the sub-aspects of *restaurant*. However, since this is one of the important aspects of a *restaurant*, it is categorised under *others*.

Aspects in the Eatery taxonomy pose three different relations, parent-child, siblings, and grandparent-grandchild. Following are examples of these three different relationships:

Food_item_taste <parent-child> Food_item

Food_item_taste <grandparent-grandchild> Food

Food_item_taste <sibling> Food_item_size

These different relationships between aspects are used by different components of our system.

4.3 Aspect Identification

In order to identify explicit and implicit aspects, two models *M1* and *M2* are created using the annotated 1500 reviews. These annotated reviews serve as the training data set for the aspect identification component.

Explicit Aspect Identification. A standard maximum entropy classifier [35] is used to train the model *M1* to identify explicit aspects. Bigrams is used as the feature of the classifier.

Implicit Aspect Identification. This approach is an extended version of Schouten et al.'s [3] approach, which did not have the capability of identifying multiple implicit aspects appearing in a sentence. It also could not successfully identify implicit aspects of a large number of different aspects.

A model *M2* is created to identify the implicit aspects in reviews. Initially, training data is scanned and opinion words that are labeled as implicit aspects are extracted to create the list of opinion words *O*. In the second iteration of scanning, only the sentences with one or more implicit aspects are extracted. Each sentence is stored under each opinion word identified in that sentence, along with the aspect that it is related to. This stored structure defines the model *M2* that gives information of the list of opinion words and the list of aspects that can be implicitly mentioned by a particular opinion word (candidate aspects for an opinion word). For example, consider the sentences "The restaurant was large enough to have a birthday party" and "We had a large pizza". Both sentences appear in the training dataset with an annotated label. They are indexed under the opinion word *large* in the model *M2* as follows:

4

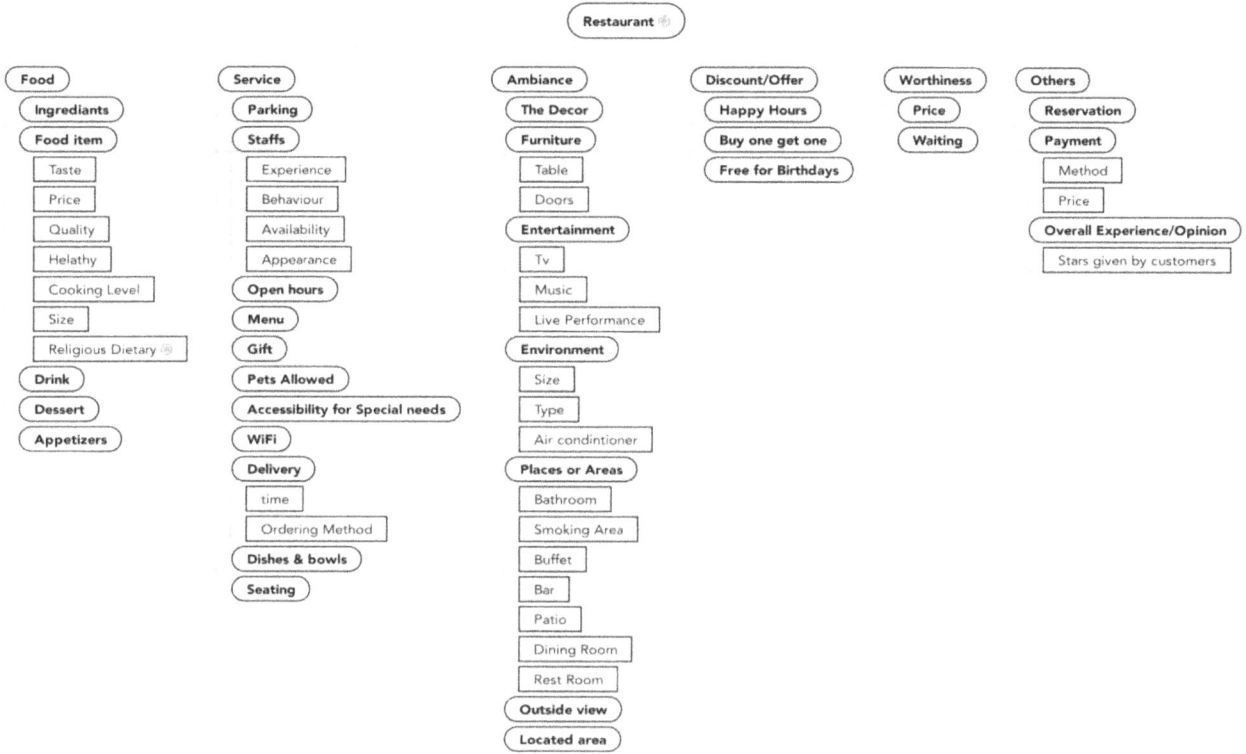

Figure 2: Eatery Taxonomy

large:

Environment_size - The <Start: Restaurant> restaurant <End> was <Start: Environment_size> large <End> enough to have a birthday party

Food_item_size - We had a <Start: Food_item_size> large <End> <Start: Food_item> pizza <End>

When a new review is given, each of its sentences is processed word by word for opinion words available in the opinion list O. Processing a sentence word by word allows to identify multiple implicit aspects in a given sentence whereas Schouten et al.'s [3] approach carries out similar approach by processing an entire sentence to identify a single implicit aspect implied by a sentence. For each identified opinion word in a sentence, the list of candidate aspects A is extracted using the model M1. For example, if the opinion word *large* is encountered while processing a review sentence, *Environment_size* and *Food_item_size* are listed as candidate aspects. If there is only one candidate aspect, it is chosen as the potential candidate aspect. Otherwise, the score for each candidate aspect is calculated using equation (1). This equation considers the co-occurrence between the opinion word and other words appearing in the input sentence. In equation (1), n is the number of words in the given sentence, A_i is the ith candidate aspect in A for which the score is computed, j represents the jth word in the sentence, C_{ij} is the co-occurrence frequency of aspect A_i and the jth word, f_j is the frequency of the jth word, and d_j is the distance between the jth word and the opinion word which is calculated by counting the number of words that lie between the two strings. $1/d_j$ operates as weight.

$$\text{Score } A_i = 1/n * \Sigma(C_{ij}/f_j * 1/d_j) \qquad (1)$$

This equation is a modified version of the score calculation presented by Schouten et al. [3], where we normalize the co-occurrence by the distance between the opinion word and other words in the sentence, thus removing the impact of faraway words on the sum of co-occurrence. The aspect with the highest score is chosen as the potential candidate aspect. The highest scoring aspect that exceeds the threshold becomes the potential aspect for the next step. If the highest score is lower than the threshold, identified opinion word is discarded. The optimal threshold is identified based on the training data using a simple linear search. The threshold is increased from 0 by a step size of 0.01 until the optimum value for F1-measure is obtained.

Once the potential candidate aspect is chosen, a validation process is carried out to identify one implicit aspect in a given sentence. This, is an addition to the approach suggested by Schouten et al. [8]. Here, opinion target of the potential candidate aspect (aspect on which the opinion is expressed) is extracted to carry out the validation process. For example, in the sentence "Lunch was very expensive", opinion target of the opinion word *expensive* is *lunch*. Opinion targets are extracted using double propagation approach proposed by Qiu et al [7], which propagates information back and forth between opinion words and targets using grammar rules. Extracted target is checked against the Eatery taxonomy to see whether it has any relationship (out of the three relationships) with the potential candidate aspect or not. If the target is the parent aspect, then

5

the potential candidate aspect is chosen as the winning implicit aspect. Otherwise, it is discarded.

The double propagation technique [7] uses the dependency relations mod, pnmod, subj, s, obj, obj2 and desc to define the grammar rules. Dependency between the words in the sentence "The restaurant has good parking" can be explained using the dependency relations as

The restaurant -> *subj* -> has <- *obj* <- parking <- *mod* <- good

The grammar rules are used to carry out the verification process in a sequence as follows:

Verification 1 – Given an opinion word, the target is extracted using grammar rules and is validated to check whether it is the parent or grandparent (only for food hierarchy) aspect of a potential candidate or not in the Eatery taxonomy. Example: in the sentence "Food was delicious", *Food* is identified as the target using the rule *delicious -> mod -> Food*. If *Food_item_taste* is the potential candidate, it is accepted as *Food* is the grandparent of *Food_item_taste*.

Verification 2 – If verification 1 fails, target extracted in verification 1 is used to extract further targets using grammar rules. For example, consider the sentence "Food and dessert are very cheap in that restaurant". When verifying the potential candidate aspect *Food_item_price* for the opinion word *cheap*, dessert is extracted as the opinion target during verification 1. However, it is discarded as it has no relationship with *Food_item_price* in the taxonomy. During verification 2, Food is extracted using the grammar rule *dessert -> conj -> Food* and is verified whether it is the parent/grandparent of the potential candidate aspect.

Verification 3 – This step allows finding further opinion words using grammar rules. For the extracted opinion word, a new potential candidate aspect is identified using model *M2* and it is verified to see whether the earlier winning potential candidate and current candidate are same or are siblings in Eatery taxonomy. For example, consider the sentence "That restaurant was very big and peaceful". When processing the opinion word *big* for the potential candidate aspect *Environment_size*, it is verified in verification 1 and accepted. Using the grammar rule *big -> conj -> peaceful*, *peaceful* is extracted as an opinion word, and model *M2* is used to extract the potential candidate for the opinion word *peaceful* as explained earlier. If *Environment_type* is selected as the potential candidate aspect, it is verified against the earlier winning candidate *Environment_size* and is accepted as both aspects are siblings in the Eatery taxonomy.

This validation process is required since we deal with many aspects at different levels, which leads to ambiguity in identifying the opinion target. For example, consider the sentence "I am a big fan of that restaurant". Here, "I" is identified as the opinion target of the opinion word *big* with the prediction of either *Food_item_size* or *Environment_size*. If *Environment_size* or *Food_item_size* is chosen as the potential candidate aspect with the highest score, it is discarded as its opinion target "I" has no relationships with the potential candidate aspect in Eatery taxonomy.

4.4 Sentiment Analysis

Once both explicit and implicit aspects are identified, the system calculates the sentiment scores related to those aspects by doing sentiment analysis at aspect-level where the sentiment score for each individual aspect is calculated.

In restaurant reviews, most of the sentences contain more than one aspect. Therefore the sentences are split in such a way that each phrase contains one aspect and the related opinion phrase, using the typed dependency engine designed by Ahiladas et al. [17]. This approach uses the grammatical relationships of words to extract the opinion words and the other related words for each and every aspect identified in a sentence. Once the opinion phrases are identified, sentiment orientation that the corresponding aspects have in the sentences is analyzed using a recursive neural sensor network [36]. A sentence is classified into 5 polarity classes: very negative (1), negative (2), neutral (3), positive (4) and very positive (5).

Every time when an aspect occurs in the review, the sentiment score for that aspect is calculated for that review and is accumulated with the previous scores. In order to accumulate the scores, the lower bound on normal confidence interval method [37] is used with 95% of confidence level. This method considers both the rating value and the number of occurrences to calculate the aggregate ratings. This characteristic is significant in restaurant reviews since it is preferred to have a higher rating for an aspect that has more number of positive ratings and similarly, lower rating for an aspect that has more negative ratings.

4.5 Composition of Scores Using the Weighting Model

At the end of the sentiment analysis process, the system contains individual ratings for each and every aspect in the aspect hierarchy. Next process is to calculate a composite score for the parent aspects using their individual scores and the scores of the corresponding sub-aspects. For this, an improved version of the AHP method [38] was used by improving the creation of pairwise matrix of AHP that utilizes the relationships between aspects [6].

Analytic Hierarchy Process (AHP). Analytic Hierarchy Process (AHP) [38], proposed by Saaty is one of the well-known methods for weight estimation. AHP works as follows. When calculating the weights for n attributes, an $n \times n$ pairwise matrix A is created as the initial step. Each entry a_{ij} in the pairwise matrix A represents the relative importance of the ith attribute compared to the jth attribute that satisfies the following condition:

$$a_{ij} = 1/a_{ij} \qquad (2)$$

Identifying the relative importance between two attributes is a manual task using Saaty's scale definition as given in Table 1. Upper triangular part of the pairwise matrix is filled using Saaty's scale definition and the rest of the matrix is filled using the condition given in equation (2). It is obvious that $a_{ii} = 1$. Once the pairwise matrix is created, it is normalized through the columns as shown in equation (3):

$$a'_{ij} = a_{ij} \Sigma a_{kj} \qquad (3)$$

6

where k = 1, 2, 3 .... n. Finally, the weight for each attribute is calculated by taking the average of the normalized values using the normalized matrix as shown in equation (4):

$$W_i = (\Sigma a'_{ik})/n \qquad (4)$$

Table 1: The Saaty Scale Definition

Insensitivity of Importance	Definition
1	Equal Importance
3	Moderate Importance
5	Strong Importance
7	Very Strong Importance
9	Extreme Importance
2, 4, 6, 8	Can be used to express intermediate values

As computing the relative importance between two aspects in AHP is a manual task, there can be inconsistencies between two relative importance values. For example, consider the following pairwise matrix,

$$A = \begin{bmatrix} 1 & 3 & 1/3 \\ 1/3 & 1 & 3 \\ 3 & 1/3 & 1 \end{bmatrix}$$

Here, the first attribute is 3 times important than the second attribute, and 1/3 times important than the third attribute. Thus relative importance of the third attribute compared to the second attribute should be nearly 9 in order to maintain the consistency of the pairwise matrix. However, the relative importance of the third attribute compared to the second attribute is 1/3 in the above example, which is not consistent. Therefore it is essential to measure the consistency of a pairwise comparison matrix. For that, Consistency Ratio (CR) [38] of a pairwise matrix is calculated as follows:

$$CR = CI/RCI \qquad (5)$$

Here, *CI* is the Consistency Index and *RCI* is Random Consistency Index, which is the average CI of randomly generated reciprocal matrices with dimension n [38]. Consistency Index of a pairwise matrix is defined as follows:

$$CI = (\lambda_{max} - n)/(n-1) \qquad (6)$$

Where λ_{max} is the highest Eigenvalue for the pairwise comparison matrix and n is the dimension of the pairwise matrix. The pairwise comparison matrix is accepted if the consistency ratio *CR* is less than 10%. Otherwise, we can conclude that the in-consistency is too large so the pairwise comparison matrix values should be revised.

Improved AHP. Original AHP requires manual work to identify the relative importance of a set of attributes, thus it does not utilize any relationship between those attributes to obtain the relative importance. Therefore we introduced an improved version of AHP that utilizes the relationship between aspects to obtain the weights for the set of aspects [4]. This improved AHP

is applied to each non-leaf node in the hierarchy to obtain the weights for its sub-aspects. Along with the sub-aspects, weight is obtained for the parent as well. Finally, each non-leaf aspect gets two weights: one as a parent and one as a child. Each leaf aspect gets a single weight. For example, composite rating for *staff* is obtained as follows,

Composite score for staff = $W_{experience}*R_{experience} + W_{behaviour}*R_{behaviour} + W_{appearance}*R_{appearance} + W_{availability}*R_{availability} + W'_{staff}*R_{staff}$ (7)

where W represents the weight of an aspect as a child node, W' represents the weight of an aspect as a parent, and R represents the rating value of an aspect obtained using aspect level sentiment analysis.

Improved AHP works as follows. For a particular non-leaf aspect, a pairwise comparison matrix A is created with the dimensions of nxn where n is the total number of sub-aspects + 1 for the parent aspect. For each aspect, the occurrence of an aspect in the training data set is counted. If an aspect is a parent for which the pairwise comparison matrix is created, the occurrence of an aspect is simply the number of explicit and implicit aspect labels in the training data set. If the aspect is a sub-aspect, the occurrence of an aspect is obtained by adding up the occurrences of that aspect and all its sub-aspects (both direct and indirect sub-aspects). This enables to utilize the relationship between aspects in such a way that the occurrence of an aspect is obtained by considering the occurrence of all its direct and indirect sub-aspects.

Relative importance between two aspects is obtained as the ratio of occurrence of aspects and is used as an element in the pairwise comparison matrix. Rest of the AHP processes as the usual flow [38] with this improved pairwise comparison matrix to obtain the weights for n + 1 aspects. It is worth to note that AHP is applied to each non-leaf aspect in the Taxonomy separately for different restaurants so that the resulting weights are specific to a particular restaurant. Moreover, this improved AHP can be applied to any domain where the aspects of that particular domain can be modeled as a hierarchy.

5 EVALUATION

5.1 Preprocessing

Spell correction. Evaluation for spell correction of the pre-processing step was carried out with 800 manually misspelled words related to restaurant domain. With the default dictionary file that is used by the Peter Norvig algorithm [30], we obtained an accuracy of 57.35%. With the inclusion of restaurant domain-specific words to the dictionary as explained in section 4.1, the accuracy was increased up to 85.25%.

5.2 Aspect Identification

This component of the system was evaluated with the annotated 1500 reviews as the training data set using 10 fold cross validation. For each instance of the algorithm, 1400 reviews are used as the training dataset and remaining 100 reviews are used for testing. Figure 3 shows the distribution of aspects in 1000 reviews randomly picked from the training data set. The

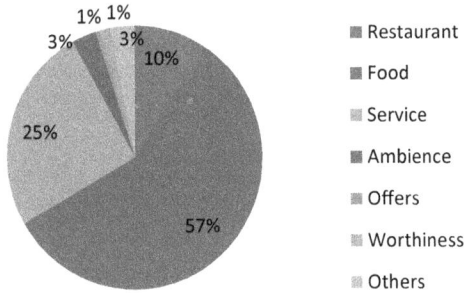

Figure 3: Distribution of Level 1 and Level 2 aspects in 1000 reviews

occurrence of level 3 and level 4 aspects are counted as the occurrence of level 2 aspect to show the distribution up to 2 levels. It can be observed that the aspects *food* and *ambience* are highly mentioned in restaurant reviews both directly and indirectly.

Explicit Aspect Identification. Model $M1$ explained in section 4.3 was evaluated and a precision and recall of 0.9317 and 0.8348 (respectively) were obtained for this evaluation. Thus this gave an F1-measure of 0.88 for model $M1$.

The evaluation of individual aspect identification figures out how the above evaluation result is distributed among individual aspects. This evaluation is done for all the aspects in the Eatery taxonomy, and Table 2 shows the results for the main aspects *Food*, *Service*, *Ambience*, *Worthiness* and *Others*. These evaluations consider the identification of that particular aspect (not their sub-aspects). Apart from these, we evaluated for the restaurant aspect as well.

It can be observed that the identification of three main popular aspects *food*, *service* and *ambience* give similar evaluation results as model $M1$ (F1-meausre of model $M1$ and F1-measure of the three main aspects). Here the results for the *Worthiness* and *Others* deviate from other aspects since the number of occurrences of these aspects in the reviews is much lower compared to other aspect verticals.

Table 2: Evaluation results for the individual aspects in explicit aspect extraction

Aspect	Precision	Recall	F1- measure
Restaurant	0.6493	0.9615	0.7751
Food	0.7369	0.9533	0.8312
Service	0.7245	0.9890	0.8364
Ambience	0.7241	0.9292	0.8139
Worthiness	0.0625	0.3333	0.1052
Others	0.9189	1.0000	0.9577

Implicit Aspect Identification. Even though restaurant domain deals with many aspects, not all the sentences contain implicit aspects. In 1000 reviews (each review contains an average of 10 sentences) picked randomly from the training data set, 15.6% of the sentences contain one or more implicit aspects. However, it is essential to identify that small fraction of implicit aspects as some of the important aspects are most likely to appear implicitly in customer reviews. For example, 92% of each sub-aspects (behavior, experience, appearance and availability) of staff aspect were found to be implicit in a randomly picked set of 1000 reviews from the training data set.

Table 3 shows the evaluation results of 10-fold-cross validation for several methods. Methods 1 to 3 use the annotated explicit aspects so that the accuracy of model $M1$ does not impact model $M2$. Method 4 shows the results when both $M1$ and $M2$ are used to obtain the explicit and implicit aspects, respectively. Method 2 extends Schouten et al.'s [3] approach to identify multiple implicit aspects in a sentence. This extended approach does not have a validation process. Method 3 extends Method 2 by validating the potential candidate using opinion target extraction as explained in section 4.3.

It can be seen in Table 3 that our approach gives the best result. Moreover, extending the approach suggested by Schouten et al. [3] (Method 2) fails in the case of identifying a large number of interrelated implicit aspects. Therefore adding potential candidate validation to that method improves precision from 0.49 to 0.91. The result for our approach is slightly higher than this (Method 3), as our approach considers the distance between opinion words and other words in the sentence.

Table 3: Evaluation results for implicit aspect extraction

	Method	Precision	Recall	F1 Measure
1	Our solution	0.947	0.758	0.842
2	Method 2	0.495	0.929	0.645
3	Method 3 - Method 2 with validation process	0.916	0.752	0.826
4	Our solution with trained model $M1$	0.886	0.694	0.779

Table 4 shows the evaluation results for 10-fold-cross validation of the model $M2$ for sentences with more than one aspect. It can be observed that the F1-Measure is above 0.82.

Table 4: Evaluation results for sentences with multiple implicit aspects

	Method	Precision	Recall	F1-Measure
1.	Sentences with two	0.978	0.709	0.822
2.	Sentences with more than two	0.975	0.725	0.832

5.3 Sentiment Analysis

A separate set of 400 random reviews from the Yelp dataset was used as the test set for this component and two types of evaluations were carried out.

Evaluation of Aspect-Opinion relationship in opinion phrases: In this evaluation, it is checked whether the relevant opinion words are correctly associated with the aspects in the opinion phrase. An average accuracy of 71.82% was obtained for this evaluation.

Evaluation of sentiment analysis: Reviews in the test data set were split into small phrases and are manually marked as (P)/ neutral (O)/ negative (N) in the sentiment polarity. The output of the sentiment analysis tool was compared against the manually given polarity. An average accuracy of 72.55 was obtained for this evaluation. Here the training data set used for sentiment analysis is a general corpus associated with the sentiment analysis tool [36]. This accounts for the drop in the accuracy in this system since it does not contain any opinions specific to restaurant domain.

5.4 Weighting Model

Improved AHP approach explained in section 4.5 is executed by giving 1500 annotated reviews as the input, and weights for all the aspects in our Eatery taxonomy is calculated. Table 5 shows the consistency ratio for three pairwise matrices of a random restaurant. It can be seen that all values are very close to zero so that all three pairwise comparison matrices are acceptable. Weights obtained for the sub-aspects of that restaurant using our approach are shown in Table 6.

Table 5: Consistency ratio for three different levels of pair wise matrices

Parent Aspect	Consistency Ratio (CR)
Restaurant	$2.2428 \times 10{-}14$
Service	0.0
Staff	0.0

Table 6: Weights for sub-aspects of restaurant

Aspect	Weight
Restaurant	0.0943
Food	0.5734
Service	0.2534
Ambience	0.0308
Offers/Discount	0.0048
Worthiness	0.0135
Others	0.0296

5.4 Food Name Categorisation

Evaluating improved SPPM: 5 sets of random samples, each with 100 food names were selected from the dataset and were manually categorized to be used as the test data set. An average accuracy of 90% was obtained for the evaluation of the food categorisation component. However, it was taking high execution time as the individual word processing is done with wiki API to identify the actual food names.

Another drawback of this approach is the resulting categorisation containing redundant categories (i.e. same word falling into multiple categories. E.g. "Tandoori chicken pizza" categorized under both *chicken* and *pizza*). In order to evaluate the level of redundancy in every category, another 5 random samples of 500 food names were used. Those samples were again categorized manually and also by the improved SPPM method, and then the redundancy test was done. It is found that the average redundancy is around 25%.

Categorizing food names appearing in restaurant reviews: Annotated 1500 reviews were used as the test data set, which contained the food names annotated as explicit aspects. An average accuracy of 82.6% was obtained for this evaluation.

5.5 Evaluation of the overall system

For the overall system evaluation, two restaurants were randomly picked and 400 reviews for each restaurant were randomly obtained from Yelp reviews as test data. For the selected restaurants, ratings were given manually by human judges for four aspects from four different levels of the taxonomy. At the end of the manual scoring, these four aspects had their individual scores, which are then compared with the corresponding score calculated by the system. The evaluation results are shown in Figure 4 and Figure 5. It can be seen that the results from the system are relatively similar to the actual values given by manual judges with small variations. The main reason for the system values being low compared to the manual values is the accuracy drop caused by the general corpus used for sentiment analysis.

In order to measure the consistency among the annotators, three data sets, each with 100 reviews were used. Each set was tagged by two different annotators. Two types of measure of consistency were computed, absolute agreement, and the Kappa coefficient [39]. Result for the former is 0.917, and the result for the latter is 0.834 (a fair agreement).

6 CONCLUSION

This paper presented Eatery, a multi-aspect restaurant rating system. This research introduced a new taxonomy to the restaurant domain that captures the hierarchical relationships among entities and aspects. It also contains a novel approach to find multiple implicit aspects appearing in a sentence, a new food categorisation technique, and a weighting model that helps calculate the sentiment score of an aspect as a composite of the sentiment scores of its sub-aspects. However, the entire system can be applied to other domains as well, where the aspects of those domains are modeled as a hierarchy.

As future work, sentiment analysis component should be enhanced by using a corpus specific to the restaurant domain and identifying implicit opinion which is a limitation in current sentiment analysis approach. It would be interesting to extend this work dynamically to improve the Eatery taxonomy, as new aspects are found while processing reviews.

9

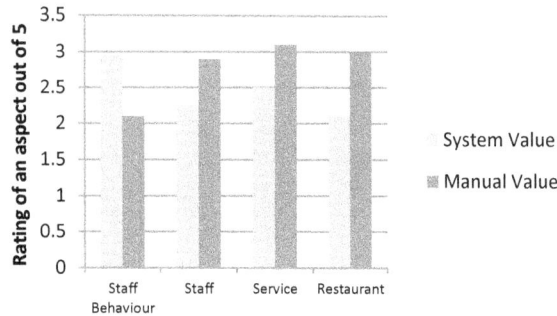

Figure 4: Results for Restaurant 1

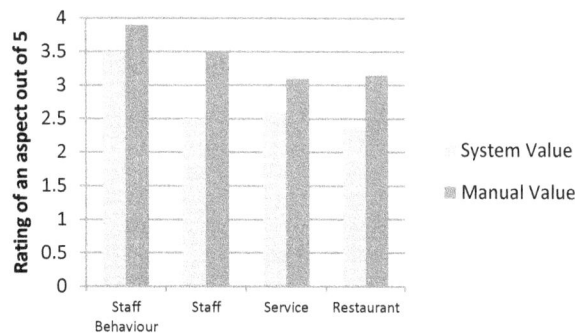

Figure 5: Results for Restaurant 2

REFERENCES

[1] Zhang, L. and Liu, B. Aspect and entity extraction for opinion mining. In *Data mining and knowledge discovery for big data*, (2014), Springer, 1-40.

[2] Sharma, R., Nigam, S. and Jain, R. Mining of product reviews at aspect level. *International Journal in Foundations of Computer Science and Technology*, 4(3). (2014).

[3] Schouten, K., de Boer, N., Lam, T., van Leeuwen, M., van Luijk and R., Frasincar, F. Semantics-driven implicit aspect detection in consumer reviews. In *24th International Conference on World Wide Web Companion*, (2015), 109-110.

[4] Panchendrarajan R., Murugaiah, B., Sivakumar, S., Ahamed, M.N.N., Ranathunga and S., Pemasiri, A. Cheap food or friendly staff? Weighting hierarchical aspects in the restaurant domain. In *2nd Moratuwa Engineering Research Conference*, (IEEE, 2016), 24-49.

[5] Panchendrarajan R., Ahamed, N., Murugaiah, B., Sivakumar, S., Ranathunga, S. and Pemasiri, A. Implicit Aspect Detection in Restaurant Reviews using Cooccurence of Words. In *7th Workshop on Computational Approaches to Subjectivity, Sentiment and Social Media Analysis*, (ACL, 2016), 128-136.

[6] Sivakumar, P., Ahamed, N., Panchendrarajan, R., Murugaiah, B.,Ranathunga and S., and Pemasiri, A. Categorizing food names in restaurant reviews. In *2nd Moratuwa Engineering Research Conference*, (IEEE, 2016), 1-5.

[7] Qiu, G., Liu, B., Bu, J. and Chen, C. Opinion word expansion and target extraction through double propagation. *Computational linguistics* 37(1), 9-27, (2011).

[8] Gupta, A., Tenneti, T. and Gupta A., Sentiment based Summarization of Restaurant Reviews. *Final Year Project*. (2009).

[9] Lu, B., Ott, M., Cardie, C. and Tsou, B. K. Multi-aspect sentiment analysis with topic models. In *11th IEEE International Conference on Data Mining Workshops*, (IEEE, 2011). 81-88.

[10] Mittal, N., Agarwal, B., Laddha, S. and Sharma, M. Aspect Based Analysis for Rating Prediction of the Restaurant Reviews. In *International Journal of Computer Systems*, 59-62. (2015).

[11] Snyder, B. and Barzilay, R. Multiple aspect ranking using the good grief algorithm. In *Joint Human Language Technology/North American Chapter of the ACL*, (ACL, 2007). 300-307.

[12] Govindarajan, M. Sentiment Analysis of Restaurant Reviews using Hybrid Classification Method. In *International Journal of Soft Computing and Artificial Intelligence*, 2(1). (2014).

[13] Ganu, G., Elhadad, N. and Marian, A. Beyond the Stars: Improving Rating Predictions using Review Text Content. In *12th International Workshop on the Web and Databases*, (2009). 1-6.

[14] Schouten, K.. and Frasincar, F. Finding implicit features in consumer reviews for sentiment analysis. In *Web Engineering*, (Springer, 2014). 130-144.

[15] Wang, W., Xu, H. and Wan, W. Implicit feature identification via hybrid association rule mining. In *Expert Systems with Applications*, 40(9), 3518-3531 (2013).

[16] Zhang, Y. and Zhu, W. Extracting implicit features in online customer reviews for opinion mining. In *22nd international conference on World Wide Web companion*, (2013). 103-104.

[17] Ahiladas, B., Saravanaperumal, P., Balachandran, S., Sripalan, T. and Ranathunga, S. Ruchi: Rating individual food items in restaurant reviews. In *12th International Conference on Natural Language Processing*, (2015).

[18] Trevisiol, M., Chiarandini, L. and Baeza-Yates, R. Buon appetito: recommending personalized menus. In *25th ACM conference on Hypertext and social media*, (ACM, 2014). 327-329.

[19] Yelp Inc. Yelp. http://www.yelp.com/, 2017. Web. 17 Feb. 2017

[20] Sawant, S. and Pai, G. Yelp food recommendation system. http://cs229.stanford.edu/proj2013/SawantPai-YelpFoodRecommendationSystem.pdf (2016).

[21] Kang, J. S., Kuznetsova, P., Luca, M. and Choi, Y. Where Not to Eat? Improving Public Policy by Predicting Hygiene Inspections Using Online Reviews. In *Empirical Methods in Natural Language Processing*, (2013). 58-77.

[22] Pontiki, M., Galanis, D., Pavlopoulos, J., Papageorgiou, H., Androutsopoulos, I., and Manandhar, S. Semeval-2014 task 4: Aspect based sentiment analysis. In *8th International Workshop on Semantic Evaluation*, (SemEval 2014), 27–35.

[23] Pavlopoulos, J. Aspect based sentiment analysis. Ph.D. thesis, Dept. of Informatics, Athens University of Economics and Business, Greece. (2014).

[24] Pontiki, M., Galanis, D., Papageorgiou, H., Manandhar, S., and Androutsopoulos, I. Semeval-2015 task 12: Aspect based sentiment analysis. In *9th International Workshop on Semantic Evaluation*, (SemEval 2015).

[25] Pontiki, M., Galanis D., Papageorgiou, H., Androutsopoulos, I., Manandhar, S., AL-Smadi, M., Al-Ayyoub, M., Zhao., Y., Qin, B., Clercq, O., Hoste, V., Apidianaki, M., Tannier, X., Loukachevitch, N., Kotelnikov, E., Bel, N., Jiménez-Zafra, S. M., Eryigit, G., . Semeval-2016 task 5: Aspect based sentiment analysis. In *10th International Workshop on Semantic Evaluation*, (SemEval 2016).

[26] Cena, F., Likavec, S., Lombardi, I. and Picardi, C., Synthesis of Collective Tag-Based Opinions in the Social Web. In *XIIth International Conference on AI*IA 2011: Artificial Intelligence Around Man and Beyond*, (ACM, 2011), 286-298.

[27] Ayto, J. An AZ of food and drink. Oxford University Press (2004)

[28] Food timeline: Food timeline food list. http://www.foodtimeline.org/foodfaqindex.html, 2017. Web. 17 Feb. 2017

[29] Yelp Inc.: Yelp data challenge. https://www.yelp.com/dataset_challenge/dataset, 2017. Web. 17 Feb. 2017

[30] GitHub, optimaize/language-detector, https://github.com/optimaize/language-detector, 2017. Web. 17 Feb. 2017

[31] Norvig, P.: How to write a spelling corrector. http://norvig.com/spell-correct, 2017. Web. 17 Feb. 2017

[32] Apache OpenNLP Developer Documentation: opennlp. https://opennlp.apache.org/documentation/manual/opennlp.html, 2017. Web. 17 Feb. 2017

[33] Gupta, R. and Satsangi, C. An efficient range partitioning method for finding frequent patterns from huge database. In *International Journal of Advanced Computer Research*, 2(2), 62-69. (2012).

[34] M Pilar. An Espino Comparison of methods Hamming Distance, Jaro, and Monge-Elkan. In 7th International Conference on Advances in Databases, Knowledge, and Data Applications , (2015).

[35] Apache Software Foundation.: Opennlp. https://opennlp.apache.org/, 2017. Web. 17 Feb. 2017

[36] Socher, R., Perelygin, A., Wu, J.Y., Chuang, J., Manning, C. D., Ng, A.Y. and Potts, C. Recursive deep models for semantic compositionality over a sentiment treebank. In *Empirical methods in natural language processing*, (2013).

[37] McGlohon, M., Glance, N. and Reiter, Z. Star Quality: Aggregating Reviews to Rank Products and Merchants. In *Fourth International Conference on Weblogs and Social Media (ICWSM)*, (2010).

[38] Saaty, T.L. What is the analytic hierarchy process?. *Mathematical Models for Decision Support*, (Springer, 1988). 48, 109-121.

[39] Carletta, J. Assessing agreement on classification tasks: The Kappa statistic. *Computational Linguistics*, 22(2), 249-254. (1996)

SENA: Preserving Social Structure for Network Embedding

Sanghyun Hong[*]
University of Maryland
College Park, Maryland, USA
shhong@umd.edu

Tanmoy Chakraborty[†]
University of Maryland
College Park, Maryland, USA
tanchak@umd.edu

Sungjin Ahn
University of Montreal
Montreal, Canada
ahnsungj@umontreal.ca

Ghaith Husari
University of North Carolina
Charlotte, North Carolina, USA
ghusari@uncc.edu

Noseong Park[‡]
University of North Carolina
Charlotte, North Carolina, USA
npark2@uncc.edu

ABSTRACT

Network embedding transforms a network into a continuous feature space where inherent properties of the network are preserved. Network augmentation, on the other hand, leverages this feature representation to obtain a more informative network by adding potentially plausible edges while removing noisy edges. Traditional network embedding methods are often inefficient in capturing – (i) the latent relationship when the network is sparse (the *network sparsity* problem), and (ii) the local and global neighborhood structure of vertices unique to the network (*structure preserving* problem).

In this paper, we propose SENA, a structural embedding and network augmentation framework for social network analysis. Unlike existing social embedding methods which only generate vertex features, SENA generates features for both vertices and relations (edges) after solving the aforementioned two problems.

We compare SENA with four baseline network embedding methods, namely DeepWalk, SE, SME and TransE. We demonstrate the efficacy of SENA through a task-based evaluation setting on different real-world networks. We achieve up to 13.67% higher accuracy for community detection and link prediction.

CCS CONCEPTS

•**Information systems →Social networks**; •**Computing methodologies →Knowledge representation and reasoning**;

KEYWORDS

Network Embedding; Community Detection; Link Prediction

1 INTRODUCTION

One of the fundamental problems in social network analysis is how to represent a network into a low-dimensional feature space. An efficient way to reconstruct the network is to learn the vector

---

[*][†]Equally Contributed; [‡]Corresponding Author

HT'17, July 4-7, 2017, Prague, Czech Republic.
© 2017 ACM. 978-1-4503-4708-2/17/07...$15.00
DOI: http://dx.doi.org/10.1145/3078714.3078738

representation of vertices and relations[1] while keeping the intrinsic properties of the network. Many network-related applications, such as clustering, classification, and prediction, can directly be conducted on the feature representation of the network. Moreover, such learned representative features can alleviate the problem of tedious hand-crafted feature engineering for supervised learning models.

Recently, there have been few attempts to learn the latent features of a network [8–10, 28]. However, there are multiple challenges to achieve reasonably good latent representation of a network: (i) **network sparsity**: most of the real networks are too sparse to obtain meaningful information; (ii) **application independence**: objective functions used in an embedding method should be independent of applications in hand, and the latent representation should be learned in a completely unsupervised way; (iii) **structure preserving**: embedding methods should retain structural properties of the original network in the feature space, e.g., neighborhood patterns of vertices should be preserved; (iv) **heterogeneity**: embedding methods should capture diverse relationships among vertices that are often present in real (heterogeneous) networks, e.g., a person is connected with another person via a "friendship" relation and with a company via an "employee" relation.

Once the network is represented into a feature space, there are two ways to utilize the learned features: (i) perform classifications or predictions only with the learned features, or (ii) construct a more informative network by removing noisy edges and augmenting informative edges, and run applications on the augmented network. We will test both approaches in our experiments. An important issue pertaining to the second approach is how to reconstruct the network from its feature representation. Note that the augmented network might not be exactly similar to the original network; rather one can expect to get a richer and more informative representation in the augmented network compared to the original network. However the existing methods addressed only the "network embedding" problem, and tended to ignore the "network augmentation" problem.

Contributions. We propose SENA, a **S**tructural **E**mbedding and **N**etwork **A**ugmentation framework for social network analysis. One fundamental difference of SENA from existing social network embedding methods is that *we learn both vertex and relation (edge)*

---

[1]In homogeneous social networks, relations between all pair of vertices are same. For example, in Facebook friendship network, all relations among vertices are "friendship".

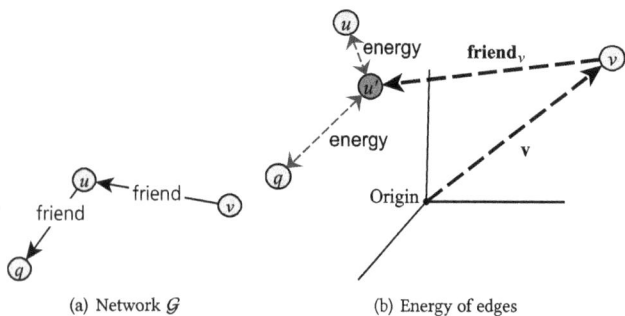

(a) Network $\mathcal{G}$ (b) Energy of edges

Figure 1: A schematic representation of *feature operator* and *energy function*. Assume a toy network in (a) and *vector addition* as a feature operator. Feature operator takes v (the feature vector of the source vertex v) and friend$_v$ (a source-dependent feature of the relation "friend") and returns the blue point u', which is the expected location of v's friends in the embedding space (see (b)). The *energy* of the true edge $(v, friend, u)$ is defined as the gap between u (the position of u in the embedding space in (b)) and u' (the predicted point of u by the feature operator in (b)) in the embedding space. Note that the energy of the false edge $(v, friend, q)$ is higher than the true edge $(v, friend, u)$.

features simultaneously whereas other methods only generate vertex features. Moreover, we are the first to propose an augmentation algorithm to generate a new network from the feature representation of the original network.

SENA minimizes an objective function that consists of ***application independent*** loss function and regularization terms (whereas many embedding algorithms focus only on loss functions [8–10]). The proposed loss function is defined based on an *energy function* (a popular term to denote *error function* in Machine Learning). The less energy value of an edge, the more plausible the edge is. The loss function aims at imposing more energy on implausible edges and less energy on plausible edges. For measuring the energy of an edge, we adopt a concept of *feature operator*. Given a source vertex v, its feature **v** and the source-dependent feature $\mathbf{r}_v$ of a certain relation r (thus capturing the **heterogeneity**), the feature operator computes a vector operation (such as vector addition, dot product, projection, etc.) to return an expected location of v's neighbors in the feature space, which are connected with v via the relation r in the original network. For example, let us consider a toy network in Figure 1(a). In the feature space, the expected location of vertices connected with v through the relation "friend" is u' (Figure 1(b)). The energy gap between u' and u is lower than that between u' and q. It indicates that u is a true friend of v; whereas q is a false friend. The proposed loss function indeed reduces the **network sparsity** problem by learning from both true and false relationships[2] (Section 4).

The **structure preserving** is another critical factor for any network embedding method. It essentially indicates that neighborhood structures of vertices and edges present in the original network should be preserved in the embedding space. We propose two

regularization terms to handle this factor (Section 4). The first regularization method is a combination of *locally linear embedding* (LLE) and random walk. LLE requires that a vertex feature should be a linear combination of the features of its adjacent vertices [33]. Random walk is performed from each vertex in order to know co-occurrence of visited vertices and their frequency of visits. Inspired by the previous literature [18, 28], we first calculate the probability distribution of h-hop random walks. A vertex feature should then be a linear combination of the features of its h-hop neighbors, weighted by the random walk probabilities (i.e., the more the random walk passes through a neighbor, the greater the contribution of its features in the linear combination).

The second regularization term follows other popular embedding methods that use a symmetric matrix representation of the original network (e.g., adjacency matrix, Laplacian matrix, distance matrix, etc.) [25]. The usual approach is to use the top-k largest eigenvectors of the adjacency matrix or the top-k non-zero smallest eigenvectors of the Laplacian matrix. Here we force the learned features, while minimizing the loss function, to capture the *eigen-structure*[3] of the network. We prove that this regularization term is so general that it works with any symmetric matrix and any of its eigenvectors (see Theorem 4.2).

Moreover, SENA provides a network augmentation algorithm which removes existing high-energy noisy edges and adds low energy undiscovered edges to generate more informative network structure (Section 6).

In Section 8, we introduce experiment results with various baseline methods. We compare the performance of SENA framework with four baseline embedding methods, namely DeepWalk, SE, SME and TransE. However since these baseline methods did not provide any network augmentation method, we incorporate our augmentation method into the baselines to generate the modified networks from the embedding result, if needed. The proposed method outperforms baseline methods by atmost 13.6%.

2 RELATED WORKS

Network embedding methods encode a network into a d-dimensional feature space such that each entity of the network can be uniquely represented by a vector (or sometimes matrix) in the embedding space [8–11, 19, 20, 28].

One traditional visualization embedding is to map vertices onto a surface with no cross edge.

Among all the embedding methods, spectral embedding is widely used, which takes k largest eigenvectors of adjacency matrix or k smallest non-zero eigenvectors of Laplacian matrix. There are many other matrix factorization methods, all of which rely on the symmetric matrix representation of the network. They use Singular Value Decomposition (SVD) or Principle Component Analysis (PCA) in order to have a low-rank embedding. In a graph-based dimensionality reduction, a set of data points in the original feature space are represented by a symmetry matrix — each element of which is the distance between two points. In [4], data points are mapped onto a line while preserving neighborhood relationships.

---

[2]Note, the sparsity problem arises when we learn from only true relationships.

[3]Eigenvalues and eigenvectors of adjacency (or Laplacian) matrix are called *network spectra* or *eigen-structure*.

A popular method proposed for network embedding in Natural Language Processing is the Skip-gram model [26]. Inspired by this model, recent research considered a network as a "document" [35]. DeepWalk [28] further adopted this idea to discover latent features of vertices. DeepWalk first runs truncated random walks from each vertex, and each random walk result is treated as a sentence, i.e., each visited vertex becomes a word. It was shown that DeepWalk works well for community detection, one of the tasks we consider here as well.

On the other hand, there have been series of attempts on network embedding for knowledge graphs (*aka* Resource Description Framework graphs); three of them are SE [10], SME [8], and TransE [9]. The major aim of these approaches is to retrieve knowledge, given a certain user query. A detailed description of these methods can be found in Section 3.

Our framework is different from existing network embedding methods in at least four different ways: (i) unlike other methods which only learn vertex features, we learn both vertex and relation features, (ii) we design a loss function and two regularization terms by considering many aspects of social networks, such as reciprocity, adaptive margin, local neighborhood, eigen-structures, etc., (iii) we consider both true and false edges for learning features, and (iv) we are the first to propose a network augmentation method based on latent features.

3 PRELIMINARIES: ENERGY FUNCTION AND MARGIN-BASED (HINGE) LOSS FUNCTION

In this section, we will introduce two fundamental concepts of our framework: *energy function* (or *error function*) and *margin-based loss function*. These two concepts are actively used in knowledge graph embedding [8–10]. We adopt these concepts and suitably redesign them for social network embedding.

Notation: We use **bold** characters to denote feature vector throughout the paper. For instance, $\mathbf{v}$ is the feature vector of vertex v, $\mathbf{r}$ is the feature vector of relation r.

Let $\mathcal{G} = (\mathcal{V}, \mathcal{E})$ be a network. The energy (or error) function $e(\ell)$ measures how plausible an edge $\ell = (s, r, t)$ is in $\mathcal{G}$, where $s \in \mathcal{V}$ is a source vertex, $t \in \mathcal{V}$ is an target vertex, and r is a relationship between s and t. Note that it is not necessary that $\ell \in \mathcal{E}$. Instead, true (plausible) edges are assumed to have a low energy value while a high energy value is expected for false (implausible) edges.

Among many possible ways of defining energy functions, SE [10], SME [8], and TransE [9] proposed the three most popular definitions, based on which we define our energy functions (Equations 4–6). The general idea of these approaches is to use *feature operator* that outputs the feature of other vertex given one vertex feature and one relation feature as inputs. For example, in TransE [9], the feature operator is defined in such a way that the energy of an edge (s, r, t) becomes the L_1 or L_2 norm of the distance vector between the sum of the source feature and the relation feature and the target feature as follows (see Figure 1).

$$e(s, r, t) = ||\mathbf{s} + \mathbf{r} - \mathbf{t}||_{L_1 \text{ or } L_2} \tag{1}$$

The energy function is then used to define a margin-based hinge loss function [31], which maintains that the energy of a true edge

is small than the energy of a false edge by at least γ as in:

$$\mathcal{L} = \sum_{\ell^+ \in \mathcal{E}} \sum_{\ell^- \in \mathcal{N}(\ell^+)} \max(0, \gamma + e(\ell^+) - e(\ell^-)) \tag{2}$$

where $\mathcal{N}(\ell^+)$ is a set of false edges generated from a true edge ℓ^+. A false edge ℓ^- is obtained by replacing either the source s or the target t of the true edge by one random vertex such that $\ell^- \notin \mathcal{E}$. Based on this equation, we build our own loss function mentioned in Equation 7.

Example 3.1. In Figure 1 (b), the energy of the true edge $(v, friend, u)$ is defined as the gap between u and u'; and the energy of the false edge $(v, friend, q)$ is the gap between q and u'. The energy of the true edge should be smaller than that of the false edge by at least γ according to the hinge loss function.

In general, the network embedding problem can be formulated as an optimization problem:

$$\arg\min_{\mathsf{M}} \mathcal{L}(\mathsf{M}) + \lambda \mathcal{R}(\mathsf{M}) \tag{3}$$

where $\mathsf{M} \in \mathbb{R}^{d \times n}$ is the feature matrix, each column of which is a d-dimension feature vector of a vertex in the network. $\mathcal{L}(\mathsf{M})$ and $\mathcal{R}(\mathsf{M})$ are the loss and regularization functions, respectively. The coefficient λ is a hyper-parameter that controls the strength of the regularization term.

4 PROPOSED LOSS FUNCTION AND REGULARIZATIONS

Social networks exhibit unique properties which are significantly different from other types of networks. In many cases, social relationships are reciprocal and have different strength. To the best of our knowledge, no one considered both these factors together. For example, existing social network and knowledge graph embedding methods [8–10, 28] assume equal relational strength for all edges even though there exist stable methods to measure the relation strength (or similarity that can be used to calculate the strength) [1, 21, 24]. We propose an improved hinge loss function specially designed for social network embedding. One important feature of the proposed loss function is that the required minimum margin dynamically varies from one edge to another depending on the relational strength.

Designing a good regularization method is a standalone research topic. For graph embedding, however, dedicated research on designing regularizers are rare. Here we design two different regularizers particularly designed for graph embedding. In the first regularizer, we extend the popular concept of "locally linear embedding" (LLE), i.e., a feature vector of a vertex is a linear combination of its neighbors' feature vectors, in order to consider multi-hop connectivity and random walks. Thus, the extended LLE considers each multi-hop neighbor as a weight value proportional to the probability that the neighbor will be visited during random walks. Note that we do not perform random walks, but calculate only the probabilities.

Eigen-structure is the fundamental unit in spectral graph theory [34] and in fact, utilizing eigenvectors as latent features is one of the most classical embedding methods [25]. Our second regularizer is inspired by this idea. We propose an additional condition which, if satisfied, can guarantee that the learned features will preserve the eigen-structure.

In summary, we propose one adaptive hinge loss function and two regularization terms, particularly considering the social network characteristics. The novelty of our contribution comes from the fact that that it requires (i) careful customization and combination of existing methods and (ii) a generalized eigen-structure preserving regularization method involving spectral graph analysis.

4.1 Loss Function

In Equation (1), one may notice that $\mathbf{r}$ is fixed for all s and t, which may be a problem in social networks with reciprocal relationships. For example, assume a relation "friendship" and its fixed feature vector **friend**. Given that a and b are friends to each other, i.e., $(a, friend, b) \in \mathcal{E}$ and $(b, friend, a) \in \mathcal{E}$, we cannot minimize the energy of $||\mathbf{a} + \mathbf{friend} - \mathbf{b}||$ and $||\mathbf{b} + \mathbf{friend} - \mathbf{a}||$ at the same time if the feature vector **friend** of the "friendship" relation is fixed.

In order to overcome this problem, we propose to use the **source-dependent relation** embedding, i.e., we define a feature of the friendship relation $\mathbf{friend}_s$ for each source s. In the above example, the direction of two vectors $\mathbf{friend}_a$ and $\mathbf{friend}_b$ can be opposite such that both energy values can be minimized simultaneously. While this resolves the problem mentioned in the above example, one might suffer from the "sparsity problem" in the training dataset because some vertices may have only a small number of neighbors. However, since our optimization function considers both true (existing) and false (non-existing) edges, we can generate $O(|\mathcal{V}|)$ observations even for a low-degree vertex.

Therefore, we can still maintain a training dataset which is large enough to learn with the source-dependent relation at a reasonable quality. In the experiments, we particularly test the following three most popular energy functions with source-dependent relations.

(i) *Vector addition* [9]: $\quad\quad ||\mathbf{s} + \mathbf{r}_s - \mathbf{t}||_{L_1 \text{ or } L_2}$ (4)

(ii) *Dot product* [8]: $\quad\quad g_u(\mathbf{r}_s, \mathbf{s})^{\mathrm{T}} \cdot g_v(\mathbf{r}_s, \mathbf{t})$ (5)

where g_u and g_v are linear or bilinear functions.

(iii) *Projection* [10]: $\quad\quad ||\mathbf{r}_s^u \mathbf{s} - \mathbf{r}_s^v \mathbf{t}||_{L_1 \text{ or } L_2}$ (6)

where $\mathbf{r}_s^u \in \mathbb{R}^{d \times d}$ and $\mathbf{r}_s^v \in \mathbb{R}^{d \times d}$ are projection matrices.

Example 4.1. In Figure 1 (b) where we use *vector addition*, the energy of the true edge $(v, friend, u)$ is defined as the L_1 or L_2 norm of $\mathbf{v} + \mathbf{friend}_v - \mathbf{u}$ which is same as the gap between u and u'. Note that the position of u' in the embedding space is same as $\mathbf{v} + \mathbf{friend}_v$.

SENA_{va}, SENA_{dp}, and SENA_{pr} denote the SENA framework with *vector addition*, *dot product*, and *projection*, respectively.

In addition to the source-dependent relation, we also propose to use the **similarity-dependent margin** in the loss function. In Equation (2), a value γ is fixed regardless of the similarity between a true and a false edge. However, in social networks we observe that a high (*resp.* low) margin is required if two edges are very different (*resp.* similar).

This adaptive margin should be inversely proportional to the similarity between a true edge ℓ^+ and its false edge sample ℓ^-. We

define the edge similarity as:

$$\delta_\ell(\ell^+, \ell^-) = \begin{cases} \mu(\delta(s, t'), \delta(t', t)), & \text{if } t \text{ is replaced by } t' \\ \mu(\delta(s, s'), \delta(s', t)), & \text{if } s \text{ is replaced by } s' \end{cases}$$

where δ is a vertex similarity metric and μ is a mean function[4], and $t', s' \in \mathcal{V}$ $(t' \neq t, s' \neq s)$. Remember that a false edge ℓ^- is created by replacing either the source s or the target t of a true edge ℓ^+.

For our experiments, we choose the following two vertex similarity metrics that have been proved to be effective for various social network analysis [1, 24]:

4.1.1 Resistance Distance. The resistance distance [1] considers each edge as a unit electrical resistor and measures the total resistance between two vertices (assuming a battery attached across them) in a given network $\mathcal{G}$. This can be regarded as information flow between two vertices. The resistance distance $\delta_{\text{res}}(v, u)$ between two vertices v and u is defined as:

$$\delta_{\text{res}}(v, u) = \Gamma_{v,v}^{-1} + \Gamma_{u,u}^{-1} - 2\Gamma_{v,u}^{-1}$$

where

$$\Gamma = \mathsf{L} + \frac{1}{|\mathcal{V}|},$$

and L is the Laplacian matrix of $\mathcal{G}$.

4.1.2 Adamic-Adar Similarity. The Adamic-Adar similarity considers the number of shared neighbors:

$$\delta_{\text{aa}}(v, u) = \sum_{z \in Neigh(v) \cap Neigh(u)} \frac{1}{\log(|Neigh(z)|)}$$

where $Neigh(v)$ denotes the neighbors of v. It has been shown to be very effective for link prediction [24].

Merging all together, we propose our loss function as:

$$\mathcal{L}_{\text{SENA}} = \sum_{\ell^+ \in \mathcal{E}} \sum_{\ell^- \in \mathcal{N}(\ell^+)} \max(0, \tau(\ell^+, \ell^-) + e(\ell^+) - e(\ell^-)) \quad (7)$$

where $\tau(\ell^+, \ell^-) = \gamma(1 - \delta_\ell(\ell^+, \ell^-))$.

4.2 Structure Preserving Regularization: Multi-hop Locally Linear Embedding with Random Walk

Social network embedding is similar to the idea of manifold learning [12] in the sense that we look for a low dimensional feature representation where the intrinsic structural/geometrical properties of the original data is preserved. In particular, the locally linear embedding (LLE) [33] finds the low-dimensional representation such that each feature is regenerated as a linear combination of its neighbors' features. In other words, $\mathsf{T}\mathsf{M}_\mathcal{V}^{\mathrm{T}} \approx \mathsf{M}_\mathcal{V}^{\mathrm{T}}$, where T is a transition matrix which we obtain by normalizing the rows of the adjacency matrix, $\mathsf{M}_\mathcal{V}$ is a partial matrix of M that contains vertex features, and $\mathsf{M}_\mathcal{V}^{\mathrm{T}}$ is the transpose of M.

Note that all 1-hop neighbors have equal weights in the LLE. This definition, however, lacks its ability to weight neighbors differently according to the importance. Thus, we propose the h-hop locally linear embedding (h-LLE) with random walk. In h-LLE, a vertex feature is represented by the weighted combination of its h-hop

---

[4]We can use any of arithmetic, geometric, and harmonic mean. In our experiments, arithmetic mean produces the best results.

neighbors' features: $T^h M_\mathcal{V}^T \approx M_\mathcal{V}^T$. The h-hop transition matrix T^h can be pre-computed and thus the computational complexity remains the same as that of LLE. This h-LLE can be written using the following regularization form:

$$\mathcal{R}_h = \sum_{v \in \mathcal{V}} ||\mathbf{v} - \sum_{u \in Neigh(v)} w_{v,u} \mathbf{u}||^2 \qquad (8)$$

where $Neigh(v)$ is a set of v's neighbors and $w_{v,u}$ is (v, u) element of the matrix T^h.

The proposed h-LLE is closely related to the random walk on the network. We can consider $w_{i,j} \in T^h$ as the probability that a h-hop random walk starting from vertex i ends at vertex j. As opposed to the multiple random walks proposed by Hassan et al. [18], here we consider the h-hop transition matrix T^h (multiply T with itself h times) in order to capture exact probability distribution of all random walks[5].

4.3 Structure Preserving Regularization: Eigen-Structure Preserving Embedding

In traditional social network analysis, it is well-known that the eigen-structure of a network preserves important properties of the network. It is popular to construct a symmetric matrix representing the network and use some of its eigenvectors selectively. For example, it has been shown that the eigenvectors of the Laplacian matrix L, especially the largest and the smallest eigenvectors, are closely related to several network problems [27], and the largest eigenvectors of the adjacency matrix A is used to obtain the spectral embedding. Also, the distance matrices are used for network embedding with its largest eigenvectors. Likewise, the largest or the smallest eigenvalues are preferred in various social network analysis.

Inspired by these, we hypothesize that it would provide a better structural embedding if we preserve such eigen-structures while minimizing the loss function. To do so, we propose the eigen-structure preserving regularization. For a given symmetric matrix Q, we show that minimizing the following function is equivalent to enforcing the learned feature matrix $M_\mathcal{V}$ to be close to the i-th eigenvector of Q,

$$\mathcal{R}_{eigen} = \left(tr(KQ) - \lambda_{Q,1} \lambda_{Q,i} \right)^2 \qquad (9)$$

where $K = M_\mathcal{V}^T M_\mathcal{V}$, $tr(\cdot)$ is trace, and $\lambda_{Q,1} > \lambda_{Q,2} > \cdots$ are eigenvalues of Q. We use the projected stochastic gradient descent method to optimize this function. We need to compute the eigenvalues of Q only at the initial step, instead of computing it in every iteration. There are many efficient parallel computation and approximation methods to calculate eigenvalues [5]. Especially, the two most preferred eigenvalues, the largest and the smallest ones, can be very efficiently calculated with the power iteration or the inverse power iteration [15] method that can be easily parallelized.

The matrix K is a gram matrix and it is positive semi-definite whose eigenvalues are all non-negatives. The trace of a square matrix S is defined as $tr(S) = \sum s_{i,i} = \sum \lambda_{S,i}$, where $s_{i,i}$ is a

diagonal element of S, and $\lambda_{S,i}$ is the i-th eigenvalue of S^6. Especially for K, $tr(K)$ is the same as the square of the Frobenius norm of $M_\mathcal{V}$ (denoted by $||M_\mathcal{V}||_F$). Note that K is a $n \times n$ square matrix, and $tr(KQ) = \lambda_K^T \lambda_Q$ where λ_K is a vector containing K's eigenvalues and λ_Q containing eigenvalues of Q. After having eigen-decomposition of K $= U\Lambda U^{-1}$ (resp. Q), the diagonals of Λ constitute λ_K (resp. λ_Q). Importantly, the number of diagonal elements is the same for both eigen-decompositions, and eigenvalues are sorted in descending order. The value of λ_K keeps changing as $M_\mathcal{V}$ changes during the training phase. Thus, $tr(KQ)$ (resp. $tr(K)$) is essentially a linear combination (resp. simple sum) of eigenvalues in λ_K.

THEOREM 4.2. *For a given symmetric matrix* Q *representing* $\mathcal{G}$ *and an embedding method that uses the i-th eigenvector of* Q, $M_\mathcal{V}$ *regenerates the i-th eigenvector of* Q *if* $\mathcal{R}_{eigen}$ *is minimized.*

PROOF. We set $M_\mathcal{V} = \frac{v_{Q,i}}{||v_{Q,i}||_F} \times \sqrt{\lambda_{Q,i}}$, where $v_{Q,i}$ is the eigenvector corresponding to the eigenvalue $\lambda_{Q,i}$ and K is created by the outer product of the scaled i-th eigenvector of Q. There are two interesting properties: (i) K always becomes a rank-1 positive semidefinite matrix which has only one positive eigenvalue and many other zero eigenvalues, and (ii) $tr(K) = \sum \lambda_{K,i} = \lambda_{K,1} = ||M_\mathcal{V}||_F^2 = \lambda_{Q,i}$ because $M_\mathcal{V}$ is scaled to have the norm of $\sqrt{\lambda_{Q,i}}$. All these properties imply that $tr(KQ) = \lambda_{Q,1} \lambda_{Q,i}$. Therefore, $\mathcal{R}_{eigen} = 0$ when $M_\mathcal{V} = \frac{v_{Q,i}}{||v_{Q,i}||_F} * \sqrt{\lambda_{Q,i}}$, a scaled version of the i-th eigenvector of Q^7. □

4.4 Visualizing Results of Network Embedding Methods

We pictorially show the differences among the results obtained from different embedding methods in Figure 2. We take Football network containing 115 vertices and 12 ground-truth communities as a test case (see Section 8.1). Each diagonal block in Figures 2 (b)-(d) corresponds to a community; and in each block we show the pair-wise energy (*resp.* Euclidean distance) of all constituent vertices by TransE and SENA$_{pr}$ (*resp.* DeepWalk). We expect that the best embedding method should return low energy for the intra-community edges because these edges are plausible. As expected, we observe that for SENA$_{pr}$, intra-community energy is no larger than the median energy of all the edges in the network, which means that intra-community edges are considered as more plausible than inter-community edges. This shows the efficacy of the proposed loss function and regularizers.

5 EMBEDDING ALGORITHM

We propose an embedding algorithm (Algorithm 1) based on the projected stochastic gradient descent method to optimize the proposed loss and regularization terms. We construct the following

---

[5]Owing to today's GPU technology advancement, matrix multiplication can be computed efficiently.

[6]This further implies that the sum of diagonals is equal to the sum of eigenvalues for a square matrix.

[7]Strictly speaking, $M_\mathcal{V}$ should be a d-dimensional embedding matrix. Thus, we do not directly compare $M_\mathcal{V}$ and $v_{Q,i}$ but compare K and Q because their dimensions are same after the outer product. Note that this is a regularization to prevent the main hinge loss function to be optimized for a certain area of the network (i.e., over-fitting for a certain area of the network). Thus, we hope this regularizer shows a positive effect even with the dimensional mismatch, and our experiments support it.

Feature Operator	Similarity of $\mathcal{L}_{\text{SENA}}$	Objective Function	Energy Function of an edge (s, r, t)
Vector addition	Resistance Distance or Adamic-Adar	$\mathcal{L}_{\text{SENA}} + \alpha \mathcal{R}_{h \in \{1,2,3\}}$ or $\mathcal{L}_{\text{SENA}} + \beta \mathcal{R}_{\text{eigen}}$	$\|\mathbf{s} + \mathbf{r}_s - \mathbf{t}\|_{L_1 \text{ or } L_2}$
Dot product	Resistance Distance or Adamic-Adar	$\mathcal{L}_{\text{SENA}} + \alpha \mathcal{R}_{h \in \{1,2,3\}}$ or $\mathcal{L}_{\text{SENA}} + \beta \mathcal{R}_{\text{eigen}}$	$g_u(\mathbf{r}_s, \mathbf{s})^{\mathsf{T}} \cdot g_v(\mathbf{r}_s, \mathbf{t})$
Projection	Resistance Distance or Adamic-Adar	$\mathcal{L}_{\text{SENA}} + \alpha \mathcal{R}_{h \in \{1,2,3\}}$ or $\mathcal{L}_{\text{SENA}} + \beta \mathcal{R}_{\text{eigen}}$	$\|\mathbf{r}_s^u \mathbf{s} - \mathbf{r}_s^v \mathbf{t}\|_{L_1 \text{ or } L_2}$

Table 1: Tested setups for the proposed embedding method. We compare the listed settings with other baseline methods including DeepWalk [28], SE [10], SME [8], and TransE [9].

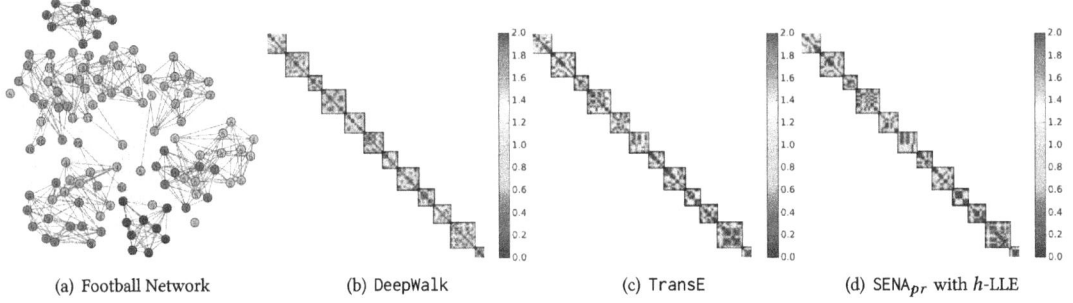

(a) Football Network   (b) DeepWalk   (c) TransE   (d) SENA$_{pr}$ with h-LLE

Figure 2: Football network with 115 vertices (see the description of the dataset in Section 8.1) and its embedding results. For fair comparison, we scale all embedding results such that the median distance/energy of all 115×115 pairs in each embedding method becomes 1. (a) The visualization of Football network. (b) - (d) The visualization of the energy values within communities of Football network. The diagonal blocks represent ground-truth communities. We show the pair-wise distance of vertices in each community (relative to the median distance) in the embedding space by (b) DeepWalk, (c) TransE, and (d) SENA$_{pr}$. We notice that the energy of vertex pairs belonging to the same communities is lower for SENA$_{pr}$ than that of others (each block for SENA$_{pr}$ is mostly colored with blue and green).

objective function:

$$\underset{M}{\arg\min} \; \mathcal{L}_{\text{SENA}} + \alpha \mathcal{R}_h + \beta \mathcal{R}_{\text{eigen}} \quad (10)$$

where either α or β is non-zero because we do not use two regularization terms simultaneously (line 2). All possible variations of the objective functions we tested for experiments are summarized in Table 1. In order to create a training set, we randomly sample a mini-batch training set T_{mini} by merging a set $\mathcal{E}_{mini}$ of random true edges and a set F_{mini} of false edges (derived from selected true edges) (line 8). The feature matrix M is updated only for the selected mini-batch training set (line 9). We calculate the gradients w.r.t. T_{mini} only.

THEOREM 5.1. *The gradient of the h-LLE is calculated as:*

$$\nabla_{M_{\mathcal{V}}} \mathcal{R}_h = 2 M_{\mathcal{V}} (I - T^h)^T (I - T^h) \quad (11)$$

PROOF. $\mathcal{R}_h$ can be re-written as the matrix sum of the following $\mathcal{R}_h'$, i.e., $\mathcal{R}_h = \sum_i \sum_j a_{i,j}$, where $a_{i,j} \in \mathcal{R}_h'$.

$$\mathcal{R}_h' = (M_{\mathcal{V}} - T^h M_{\mathcal{V}})^T (M_{\mathcal{V}} - T^h M_{\mathcal{V}})$$
$$= M_{\mathcal{V}} (I - T^h)^T M_{\mathcal{V}} (I - T^h)$$
$$= M_{\mathcal{V}}^2 (I - T^h)^T (I - T^h)$$

Thus, its gradient w.r.t $M_{\mathcal{V}}$ becomes $2 M_{\mathcal{V}} (I - T^h)^T (I - T^h)$ after partial derivation. □

THEOREM 5.2. *The gradient of the eigen-structure preserving regularizer is calculated as:*

$$\nabla_{M_{\mathcal{V}}} \mathcal{R}_{eigen} = 4 \big(tr(KQ) - \lambda_{Q,1} \lambda_{Q,i} \big) M_{\mathcal{V}} Q \quad (12)$$

PROOF. Let us re-write the regularization term as follows.

$$\mathcal{R}_{eigen} = \big(tr(KQ) - \lambda_{Q,1} \lambda_{Q,i} \big)^2$$
$$= tr(KQ)^2 - 2 \lambda_{Q,1} \lambda_{Q,i} tr(KQ) + (\lambda_{Q,1} \lambda_{Q,i})^2$$

Next, we substitute $tr(KQ)$ with $g(M_{\mathcal{V}})$. This substitution is valid because Q is fixed; and $g(M_{\mathcal{V}}) = tr(KQ) = tr(M_{\mathcal{V}}^{\mathsf{T}} M_{\mathcal{V}} Q) = \sum_i \sum_j \sum_k m_{i,j}^2 q_{j,k}$, where $m_{i,j} \in M_{\mathcal{V}}$ and $q_{j,k} \in Q$. After the substitution, the regularization term will be changed as follows.

$$\mathcal{R}_{eigen} = g(M_{\mathcal{V}})^2 - 2 \lambda_{Q,1} \lambda_{Q,i} g(M_{\mathcal{V}}) + (\lambda_{Q,1} \lambda_{Q,i})^2$$

First, $\nabla_{M_{\mathcal{V}}} g(M_{\mathcal{V}})^2 = 2 g(M_{\mathcal{V}}) \nabla_{M_{\mathcal{V}}} g(M_{\mathcal{V}}) = 4 tr(KQ) M_{\mathcal{V}} Q$ because the derivative of a composite function $f(g(x)) = f'(g(x)) \cdot g'(x)$, where $f(x) = x^2$ in our case. Second, $\nabla_{M_{\mathcal{V}}} g(M_{\mathcal{V}}) = 2 M_{\mathcal{V}} Q$ from the definition of the matrix trace. Therefore, the gradient of the regularization term w.r.t. $M_{\mathcal{V}}$ is proved. □

From $\nabla_{M_{\mathcal{V}}} \mathcal{R}_h$ and $\nabla_{M_{\mathcal{V}}} \mathcal{R}_{eigen}$, we choose columns related to T_{batch} and it becomes the gradient matrix of T_{batch}.

Last, we project the updated embedding onto a sphere at line 10. The purposes of the projection are two-fold. First, it prevents M becoming arbitrarily large in order to minimize the objective function [22]. Second, M should be scaled according to the proof of Theorem 4.2.

Input: Social Network $G = (\mathcal{V}, \mathcal{E})$, Max Iteration max_iter,
Regularization Parameters α and β
Output: Feature Matrix M
1 M $\leftarrow$ $d \times n$ matrix with random initialization
2 $f = \mathcal{L}_{\text{SENA}} + \alpha \mathcal{R}_h + \beta \mathcal{R}_{\text{eigen}}$
3 **while** $iter \leq max\_iter$ **do**
4 | Randomly permute $\mathcal{E}$
5 | $\mathcal{E}_{batch} \leftarrow$ mini-batch chunks of $\mathcal{E}$
6 | **while** $\mathcal{E}_{mini} \in \mathcal{E}_{batch}$ **do**
7 | | $F_{mini} \leftarrow$ false edges by randomly replacing either source or
   | | target of each true edge
8 | | $T_{mini} = \mathcal{E}_{mini} \cup F_{mini}$
9 | | Update M w.r.t T_{mini}
10 | | Project M
11 | **end**
12 **end**
13 **return** M

Algorithm 1: The network embedding algorithm in SENA

Runtime Analysis: The runtime of the proposed embedding algorithm mostly depends on how quickly it calculates the gradient of the objective function. The time for the random permutation of $\mathcal{E}$ and the mini-batch construction is not a critical part. There exists $O(n)$ random permutation algorithm [16] with an efficient random number generator; and the mini-batch construction is to cut the permuted edge list evenly. For two regularization terms, there exist explicit gradient formulas; but this is not the case for the loss function. We leverage the state-of-the-art Deep Learning platform [3] based on symbolic execution to calculate the gradient of the loss function. It internally tests with $M_\mathcal{V}$ and numerically calculates the required gradient. In [8–10, 28], it had been already shown that this method is fast for knowledge graph embedding. The last projection operation in each iteration can also be done efficiently because it divides the feature matrix M by a scalar value.

6 NETWORK AUGMENTATION ALGORITHM

With the learned features M, we can enrich G and create an augmented network G'. For instance, assume two vertices v and u that do not have any relationship in G. After embedding, if we discover that the vertex features **v** and **u** have low energy with a certain relation feature **r**, we then add an edge (v, r, u). Note that DeepWalk uses Euclidean distance between vertices in the embedding space in order to calculate the plausibility of an edge; however SE, SME, and TransE use their own definition of energy. We remove true edges having high energy from G if these edges contradict other edges such that the loss function cannot be minimized for all. In Section 8, we show that this augmented network G' constantly gives better performance for various applications than G.

In Algorithm 2, we first calculate energies of all existing edges in G (line 1), sort them in ascending order of energy, and take per_h percentile of energy values as threshold ths_h (line 2). We remove all edges whose energy is greater than ths_h from G (line 3) because they do not conform to the learned latent features.

In order to augment G with latent edges, we repeat the similar process. For each vertex $v \in \mathcal{V}$, we calculate energies of all the non-existing edges (line 5), sort them in ascending order, and take

Input: Feature Matrix M, Network $G = (\mathcal{V}, \mathcal{E})$, Removal Threshold
per_h, Addition Threshold per_l
Output: Augmented Network G'
1 $D \leftarrow \{energy(s, r, t) | (s, r, t) \in \mathcal{E}\}$
2 $ths_h \leftarrow Percentile(D, per_h)$
3 Remove edges $(s, r, t) \in \mathcal{E}$ if $energy(s, r, t) \geq ths_h$
4 **foreach** $v \in \mathcal{V}$ **do**
5 | $U \leftarrow \{energy(v, r, u) | u \neq v \wedge (v, u) \notin \mathcal{E}\}$
6 | $ths_l \leftarrow Percentile(U, per_l)$
7 | Add edges (v, r, u) to G if $energy(v, r, u) \leq ths_l$
8 **end**
9 **return** G

Algorithm 2: The network augmentation algorithm in SENA

per_l percentile of energy values as threshold ths_l (line 6). Finally, We add new edges whose energy is no larger than ths_l (line 7).
Runtime Analysis: The runtime of the network augmentation algorithm is $O(|\mathcal{E}|)$ to remove high energy existing edges and $O(|\mathcal{V}|^2)$ to add low energy non-existing edges because calculating a percentile value does not require sorting with selection algorithms [7]. Fortunately, all these procedures can easily be parallelized with existing distributed graph processing platforms [36].

7 EXPERIMENTAL SETUP

The objective of SENA described here is independent of any application, and the flexibility of exploring the latent representation of a network can widely be used in any network analysis setting. Here we describe three such applications to show the efficacy of SENA – (i) community detection, and (ii) link prediction. In this section, we start with explaining other baseline methods for network embedding with which we compare SENA, which is followed by the parameter settings. In Section 8, we will describe the experimental results.

7.1 Baseline Network Embedding Methods

Throughout the experiments, we will compare SENA with four state-of-the-art network embedding methods: (i) DeepWalk (DW), a recently proposed neural network based embedding method [28], and three other graph embedding methods, namely (ii) SE [10], (iii) SME [8], and (iv) TransE [9][8]. Since none of them propose network augmentation methods, we apply our augmentation method with their embedding results, if needed.

7.2 Parameter Settings

There are a number of parameter combinations used in competing network embedding methods. We conducted initial small experiments for each task and decided a candidate range for each parameter used by the methods. For regularization weights, $\alpha \in \{0.1, 0.01, 0.001\}$ and $\beta \in \{0.1, 0.01, 0.001\}$. Note, α and β are never set to non-zero simultaneously because using two different regularizations together may hinder each other and leads to performance degradation. We tested both adjacency and Laplacian matrices for Q of $\mathcal{R}_{\text{eigen}}$, and $h \in \{1, 2, 3\}$ for $\mathcal{R}_h$. We found that the performance with $h = 2$ is the best. In general, the best performance was

---

[8]Note that although SE, SME and TransE are successful in knowledge graph embedding, we use them for the first time for social network embedding.

obtained with $\alpha \in \{0.1, 0.01\}$ or $\beta \in \{0.1, 0.01\}$, and $\gamma \in \{1, 5\}$. For network augmentation, we vary per_h and per_l from 1% to 5%.

8 TASK-BASED EVALUATION

There is no direct way of evaluating how efficiently a given network is mapped into a low-dimensional space by an embedding method. Instead a common practice is to show the efficacy of the embedding method through a task based evaluation framework [9, 10, 28]. Here we present three well-studied tasks in social networks – community detection, link prediction and knowledge graph query answering, to show the performance of the competing network embedding methods. Note that for community detection we use the network augmentation method to create the latent network, and for link prediction and network query answering we use network embedding method for feature generation.

8.1 Community Detection

The problem of community detection is to group the vertices such that vertices are strongly connected internally and sparsely connected externally [13]. The challenge is that in most cases, the network is incomplete due to problems in data acquisition (such as privacy constraint, noise during crawling etc.). Moreover, the lack of representative features for vertices and edges limits the appropriate understanding of the relations among nodes. We hypothesize that the latent network generated by the augmentation method will compensate this incompleteness, and further enhance the performance of community detection algorithms.

Datasets. We perform the community detection on following five networks with known ground-truth communities (first three networks have disjoint community structure, and last two networks have overlapping community structure):

• *Football network* [17] has 115 vertices and 613 edges.

• *Railway network* [14] consists of 301 vertices (representing stations in India) and 1, 224 edges.

• *Coauthorship network* [14] contains 103, 677 vertices representing scientific authors in Computer Science and 352, 183 edges representing the coauthorship relationship among authors via publishing at least one paper.

• *Amazon network* [2] represents the 925, 872 co-purchase activities (edges) of 334, 863 users (vertices). Each product category provided by Amazon defines the ground-truth overlapping community (5, 000 communities).

• *DBLP network* [2] represents 949, 665 coauthor relationships (edges) among 227, 080 authors (vertices) where the vertices are grouped into 5, 000 overlapping communities based on the publication venues (conferences/journals).

Community Detection Algorithms. We consider four state-of-the-art disjoint community detection algorithms, namely Louvain (LOU) [6], Infomap (INFO) [32], Walktrap (WT) [29] and Label Propagation (LP) [30], and two overlapping community detection algorithms, namely OSLOM (OS) [23] and BIGCLAM (BC) [37].

Validation Metric. To compare the results obtained from community detection algorithms with the ground-truth communities, we use (i) Normalized Mutual Information (NMI) and Adjusted Rand Index (ARI) for disjoint communities, and (ii) Overlapping Normalized Mutual Information (ONMI) and Omega (Ω) index for overlapping communities [14].

Experimental Results. We first run the community detection algorithms on the respective networks (considering the original network structure) and detect the communities. Subsequently, we construct the augmented networks individually using DeepWalk, SE, SME, TransE and SENA. Following this, we run the community detection algorithms again on the augmented networks to detect the communities. We anticipate that the latter would produce better community structure than the former if the embedding methods appropriately unfold the latent structure of the network, and the one with which the community detection algorithms produce the best results would be the best embedding method.

Following [37], we show the composite performance of the embedding methods as follows. Considering the disjoint case, for each community detection algorithm (LOU, INFO, WT and LP), we separately scale the scores of the embedding methods so that the best embedding method has the score of 1. Finally, we compute the composite performance by summing up the 4 normalized scores for 4 community detection algorithms. If an embedding method outperforms all the other methods in all the scores, then its composite performance is 4. Similarly, for overlapping case, since there are two algorithms (OS and BC), the composite performance of the best embedding method is 2.

Figure 3 displays the composite performance (over all the community detection algorithms w.r.t. NMI and ONMI[9]) of the embedding methods for disjoint and overlapping community detection on different networks. Among three of our embedding methods, $SENA_{pr}$ turns out to be the best one. On an average for disjoint (overlapping) case, the composite performance of $SENA_{pr}$ is 3.86 (1.98) which significantly outperforms other baseline algorithms: 9.23% (6.43%) higher than that of DeepWalk, 12.33% (16.22%) higher than that of TransE, 13.56% (20.75%) higher than that of SME, 18.64% (21.19%) higher than that of SE, and 28.44% (32.22%) higher than that of the original network. However, one can see that DeepWalk is quite competitive in case of the University network. Table 2 presents the absolute values of the validation measures for different datasets averaged over all the community detection algorithms. In general, for disjoint community detection $SENA_{pr}$ achieves the average NMI of 0.67 (average ARI of 0.91) which is 13.67% (11.98%) higher than the best baseline embedding method. Similarly for the overlapping case, $SENA_{pr}$ achieves the average ONMI of 0.057 (average Ω index of 0.192) which is 10.27% (14.21%) higher than the best baseline embedding method.

8.2 Link Prediction

Given a network with a certain fraction of links removed, the problem of link prediction is to predict the removed links as accurately as possible. In our case, we perform our experiments by removing 20% of edges randomly (act as test set), but ensuring that it does not create a new component (i.e., the original network and the resultant network after random removal should have same set of vertices). The rest 80% edges are used to train the models. The state-of-the-art link prediction algorithms rely on the real vertex and edge features (such as age, gender, salary, common friends,

---

[9]The patterns are almost same for the other validation measures.

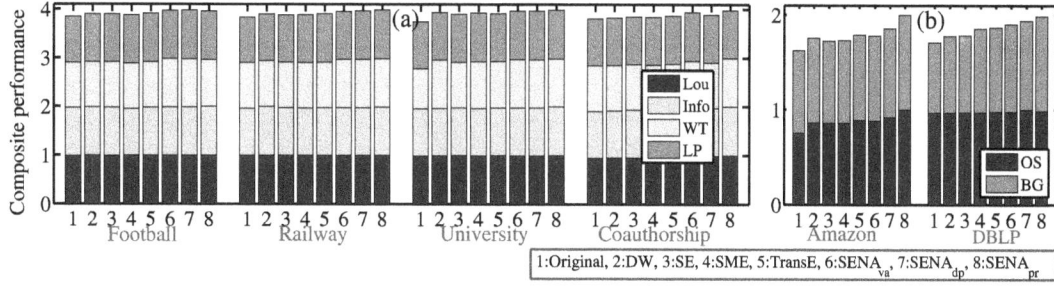

Figure 3: Composite performance of the network embedding methods ((a) disjoint: composite NMI scores ranging from 0-4, (b) overlapping: composite ONMI scores ranging from 0-2) based on the outputs obtained from CD algorithms. We also show the performance of the algorithms with the original networks.

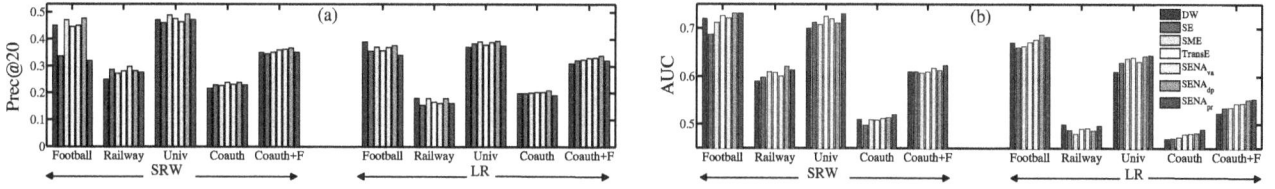

Figure 4: Performance (in terms of (a) Prec@20 and (b) AUC) of the link prediction algorithms on the different networks. The vertex features are generated from different embedding methods. Additionally, the results are shown by concatenating the generated features with the real features in Coauthorship network (Coauth+F).

Table 2: Average performance of the community detection algorithms on the original networks and the augmented networks obtained from the best baseline embedding method and $SENA_{pr}$.

	Dataset	Original Network		Best Baseline		$SENA_{pr}$	
		NMI	ARI	NMI	ARI	NMI	ARI
Disjoint	Football	0.871	0.963	0.882	0.967	0.889	0.978
	Railway	0.624	0.895	0.631	0.899	0.645	0.906
	University	0.801	0.913	0.802	0.915	0.805	0.919
	Coauthorship	0.352	0.812	0.357	0.823	0.371	0.838

	Dataset	Original Network		Best Baseline		$SENA_{pr}$	
		ONMI	Ω	ONMI	Ω	NMI	Ω
Overlapping	Amazon	0.011	0.167	0.013	0.172	0.016	0.187
	DBLP	0.082	0.145	0.097	0.176	0.101	0.198

etc.) and train the systems on the resultant network to predict the removed links. However, the real features are often unavailable due to the privacy constraints or inefficient data crawling. Here we will show that the latent features of vertices and edges extracted by the embedding methods can be leveraged to predict the missing links.
Datasets. We use four real networks – Football, Railway, University and Coauthorship (discussed in Section 8.1) for this experiment. Additionally, we consider the real features of vertices in Coauthorship network (mentioned in Section 8.1) and concatenate them with the latent features to show the change in performance.
Link Prediction Algorithms. We choose two standard supervised learning models for link prediction: Linear Regression (LR) [2] and Supervised Random Walks (SRW) [2].
Validation Metrics. We evaluate the methods on the test set by considering two performance metrics: (i) Precision at top 20

(Prec@20), i.e., for each vertex s, what fraction of top 20 vertices suggested by the method actually receive links from s in the test set, (ii) the Area under the ROC curve (AUC).
Experimental Results. We generate the *latent vertex features* using different network embedding methods separately and run two link prediction algorithms. In Figure 4, we observe that SENA once again outperforms other baseline methods. Irrespective of any link prediction algorithm and used dataset, $SENA_{pr}$ achieves an AUC (Prec@20) of 0.608 (0.455), which is 2.728% (2.43%) higher than that of $SENA_{dp}$, 3.41% (3.96%) higher than that of $SENA_{va}$, 4.52% (6.68%) higher than that of DeepWalk, 4.71% (7.23%) higher than that of TransE, 6.01% (9.24%) higher than that of SE and 9.13% (12.49%) higher than that of SME. Moreover for Coauthorship network, if we concatenate the latent features with the real features, the improvement is significantly high in comparison with the models using only real features (see the results for Coauth+F in Figure 4) – the performance gains based on Prec@20 for $SENA_{pr}$, $SENA_{dp}$ and $SENA_{va}$ are 9.43%, 8.72% and 6.18% respectively.

Note that the above experiments are conducted only based on the vertex features generated by the embedding methods. As we mentioned earlier, unlike other embedding methods, SENA can also generate the edge features. To this end, we extract the edge features using SENA and concatenate with vertex features. Table 3 shows that with the edge features along with vertex features SENA can perform even better than only with vertex features.

9 CONCLUSION

We presented SENA, a social structure preserving framework for network embedding and augmentation. To our knowledge, SENA is the first attempt to generate relation (edge) features for social networks. Moreover, it overcomes the network sparsity problem by learning from both true and false edges and considers the issues

Table 3: Performance improvement (in %) of SENA **w.r.t.** Deepwalk **after concatenating the edge features obtained from** SENA **along with vertex features for different networks.**

Network	$SENA_{pr}$		$SENA_{dp}$		$SENA_{va}$	
	Prec@20	AUC	Prec@20	AUC	Prec@20	AUC
Football	8.67	10.87	7.98	7.34	7.01	6.98
Railway	9.21	8.89	7.90	7.33	7.45	7.11
University	10.11	10.45	8.32	8.45	7.98	7.15
Coauthorship	8.33	9.10	7.31	7.22	6.98	6.22

related to structure preserving, application independent objective function, heterogeneity, etc. In conjunction with the loss function, we proposed two regularization terms to preserve the structural properties of the networks. The presented augmentation method in SENA removes existing high-energy edges and adds non-existing low-energy edges to generate more informative networks. Experimental results showed the superiority of SENA in comparison with other embedding methods for two applications on different datasets. In particular, with SENA's representation, the state-of-the-art community detection algorithms achieved up to 13.67% improvement in comparison to the representation of the best baseline embedding method. Similar result was obtained for the link prediction task where SENA's representation beats the best baseline with 9% higher accuracy.

In future, we will extend SENA for other information networks (such as biological networks, enterprise networks). We are keen to conduct more rigorous study on knowledge graph query answering task where we observed remarkably high performance improvement. We are also interested to see the performance of SENA for other tasks, such as edge and node classification, information diffusion, etc.

REFERENCES

[1] D. Babić, D. J. Klein, I. Lukovits, S. Nikolić, and N. Trinajstić. 2002. Resistance-Distance Matrix: a Computational Algorithm and its Application. *International Journal of Quantum Chemistry* 90, 1 (2002), 166–176. DOI:http://dx.doi.org/10.1002/qua.10057

[2] Lars Backstrom and Jure Leskovec. 2011. Supervised Random Walks: Predicting and Recommending Links in Social Networks. In *WSDM*. Hong Kong, China, 635–644.

[3] Frédéric Bastien, Pascal Lamblin, Razvan Pascanu, James Bergstra, Ian J. Goodfellow, Arnaud Bergeron, Nicolas Bouchard, and Yoshua Bengio. 2012. Theano: new features and speed improvements. Deep Learning and Unsupervised Feature Learning NIPS 2012 Workshop. (2012).

[4] Mikhail Belkin and Partha Niyogi. 2001. Laplacian Eigenmaps and Spectral Techniques for Embedding and Clustering. In *NIPS*. MIT Press, Granada, Spain, 585–591.

[5] Paolo Bientinesi, Inderjit S. Dhillon, and Robert A. van de Geijn. 2005. A Parallel Eigensolver for Dense Symmetric Matrices based on Multiple Relatively Robust Representations. *SIAM Journal on Scientific Computing* 27 (sep 2005). Issue 1.

[6] Vincent D Blondel, Jean-Loup Guillaume, Renaud Lambiotte, and Etienne Lefebvre. 2008. Fast unfolding of communities in large networks. *JSTAT* (2008), P10008.

[7] Manuel Blum, Robert W. Floyd, Vaughan Pratt, Ronald L. Rivest, and Robert E. Tarjan. 1973. Time Bounds for Selection. *J. Comput. Syst. Sci.* 7, 4 (Aug. 1973), 448–461. DOI:http://dx.doi.org/10.1016/S0022-0000(73)80033-9

[8] Antoine Bordes, Xavier Glorot, Jason Weston, and Yoshua Bengio. 2014. A semantic matching energy function for learning with multi-relational data - Application to word-sense disambiguation. *Machine Learning* 94, 2 (2014), 233–259.

[9] Antoine Bordes, Nicolas Usunier, Alberto García-Durán, Jason Weston, and Oksana Yakhnenko. 2013. Translating Embeddings for Modeling Multi-relational Data.. In *NIPS*. 2787–2795.

[10] Antoine Bordes, Jason Weston, Ronan Collobert, and Yoshua Bengio. 2011. Learning Structured Embeddings of Knowledge Bases.. In *AAAI*. AAAI Press, San Francisco, USA.

[11] Matthew Brand. 2003. Continuous Nonlinear Dimensionality Reduction by Kernel Eigenmaps. In *IJCAI*. Morgan Kaufmann Publishers Inc., San Francisco, CA, USA, 547–552. http://dl.acm.org/citation.cfm?id=1630659.1630740

[12] Lawrence Cayton. 2005. Algorithms for manifold learning. *Univ. of California at San Diego Tech. Rep* (2005), 1–17.

[13] Tanmoy Chakraborty, Ayushi Dalmia, Animesh Mukherjee, and Niloy Ganguly. 2016. Metrics for Community Analysis: A Survey. *arXiv preprint arXiv:1604.03512* (2016).

[14] Tanmoy Chakraborty, Sriram Srinivasan, Niloy Ganguly, Animesh Mukherjee, and Sanjukta Bhowmick. 2014. On the Permanence of Vertices in Network Communities. In *SIGKDD*. New York, USA, 1396–1405.

[15] James W. Demmel. 1997. *Applied Numerical Linear Algebra*. Society for Industrial and Applied Mathematics, Philadelphia, PA, USA.

[16] Richard Durstenfeld. 1964. Algorithm 235: Random Permutation. *Commun. ACM* 7, 7 (July 1964), 420–. DOI:http://dx.doi.org/10.1145/364520.364540

[17] M. Girvan and M. E. Newman. 2002. Community structure in social and biological networks. *PNAS* 99, 12 (June 2002), 7821–7826.

[18] Samer Hassan, Rada Mihalcea, and Carmen Banea. 2007. Random-Walk Term Weighting for Improved Text Classification.. In *ICSC*. IEEE Computer Society, 242–249.

[19] Xiaofei He, Deng Cai, Shuicheng Yan, and Hong-Jiang Zhang. 2005. Neighborhood Preserving Embedding. In *ICCV*. IEEE Computer Society, Washington, DC, USA, 1208–1213. DOI:http://dx.doi.org/10.1109/ICCV.2005.167

[20] ML. Huang, P. Eades, and J. Wang. 1998. On-line animated visualisation of huge graphs using a modified spring algorithm. *IEEE Transactions on Computers* 9 (1998), 623–645.

[21] Paul Jaccard. 1912. The Distribution of the Flora in the Alpine Zone. *New Phytologist* 11, 2 (Feb. 1912), 37–50. http://www.jstor.org/stable/2427226?seq=3

[22] Rodolphe Jenatton, Nicolas Le Roux, Antoine Bordes, and Guillaume Obozinski. 2012. A latent factor model for highly multi-relational data. In *NIPS*. Lake Tahoe, Nevada, USA, 3176–3184.

[23] A. Lancichinetti, F. Radicchi, J. J. Ramasco, and S. Fortunato. 2011. Finding statistically significant communities in networks. *PLoS ONE* 6, 4 (2011), e18961.

[24] David Liben-Nowell and Jon Kleinberg. 2003. The Link Prediction Problem for Social Networks. In *CIKM*. ACM, New York, USA, 556–559. DOI:http://dx.doi.org/10.1145/956863.956972

[25] Ulrike Luxburg. 2007. A Tutorial on Spectral Clustering. *Statistics and Computing* 17, 4 (Dec. 2007), 395–416. DOI:http://dx.doi.org/10.1007/s11222-007-9033-z

[26] Tomas Mikolov, Kai Chen, Greg Corrado, and Jeffrey Dean. 2013. Efficient Estimation of Word Representations in Vector Space. *CoRR* abs/1301.3781 (2013).

[27] Bojan Mohar. 1991. The Laplacian spectrum of graphs. In *Graph Theory, Combinatorics, and Applications*. Wiley, 871–898.

[28] Bryan Perozzi, Rami Al-Rfou', and Steven Skiena. 2014. DeepWalk: online learning of social representations.. In *KDD*. ACM, 701–710.

[29] Pascal Pons and Matthieu Latapy. 2006. Computing Communities in Large Networks Using Random Walks. *J. Graph Algorithms Appl.* 10, 2 (2006), 191–218.

[30] U. N. Raghavan, R. Albert, and S. Kumara. 2007. Near linear time algorithm to detect community structures in large-scale networks. *Phy. Rev. E.* 76, 3 (2007).

[31] Lorenzo Rosasco, Ernesto De Vito, Andrea Caponnetto, Michele Piana, and Alessandro Verri. 2004. Are Loss Functions All the Same? *Neural Comput.* 16, 5 (May 2004), 1063–1076. DOI:http://dx.doi.org/10.1162/089976604773135104

[32] Martin Rosvall and Carl T. Bergstrom. 2008. Maps of random walks on complex networks reveal community structure. *PNAS* 105, 4 (2008), 1118–1123.

[33] S.T. Roweis and L.K. Saul. 2000. Nonlinear dimensionality reduction by locally linear embedding. *Science* 290, 5500 (2000), 2323–2326.

[34] Daniel A. Spielman. 2007. Spectral Graph Theory and its Applications. In *FOCS*. IEEE Computer Society, 29–38. DOI:http://dx.doi.org/10.1109/FOCS.2007.56

[35] Jian Tang, Meng Qu, Mingzhe Wang, Ming Zhang, Jun Yan, and Qiaozhu Mei. 2015. LINE: Large-scale Information Network Embedding. In *WWW*. ACM, Florence, Italy, 1067–1077.

[36] Reynold S. Xin, Joseph E. Gonzalez, Michael J. Franklin, and Ion Stoica. 2013. GraphX: A Resilient Distributed Graph System on Spark. In *First International Workshop on Graph Data Management Experiences and Systems (GRADES '13)*. ACM, New York, NY, USA, Article 2, 6 pages. DOI:http://dx.doi.org/10.1145/2484425.2484427

[37] Jaewon Yang and Jure Leskovec. 2013. Overlapping Community Detection at Scale: A Nonnegative Matrix Factorization Approach. In *WSDM*. ACM, New York, USA, 587–596.

A Hypervideo Model for Learning Objects

Antonio José G. Busson
Federal University of Maranhão
São Luis, MA, Brazil
busson@laws.deinf.ufma.br

André Luiz de B. Damasceno
PUC-Rio
Rio de Janeiro, RJ, Brazil
andre@telemidia.puc-rio.br

Roberto G. de A. Azevedo
PUC-Rio
Rio de Janeiro, RJ, Brazil
razevedo@inf.puc-rio.br

Carlos de Salles Soares Neto
Federal University of Maranhão
São Luis, MA, Brazil
csalles@deinf.ufma.br

Thacyla de Sousa Lima
Federal University of Maranhão
São Luis, MA, Brazil
thacyla@laws.deinf.ufma.br

Sérgio Colcher
PUC-Rio
Rio de Janeiro, RJ, Brazil
colcher@inf.puc-rio.br

ABSTRACT

Learning Objects (LOs) are entities that can be used, reused, or referred during the teaching process. They are commonly embedded
into documents that establish spatial and temporal relationships
on their contents. Hypervideos LOs allow students to individualize
their learning experience with non-linear browsing mechanisms
and content adaptation. This paper presents a survey of features
for a set of documents representing such LOs as well as desirable
aspects that should be expressed during the authoring phase. Also,
this paper presents a conceptual model that fits such requirements.
The model is implemented by SceneSync, a domain specific language focused on the synchronization and temporal behavior of
LOs. As a result of the work, we present a set of LOs specified in
SceneSync and a discussion about the identified features, which
confirm the expressiveness and applicability of the model.

CCS CONCEPTS

•Human-centered computing → Hypertext / hypermedia;

KEYWORDS

Hypervideos; Learning Objects; SceneSync

1 INTRODUCTION

Learning Objects (LOs) are digital entities that can be used, reused,
or referred during the learning process with technological support [1, 2]. LOs can be seen as multimedia documents composed
of different synchronized media objects, such as images, texts,
and videos. A specific, and nowadays popular, type of LO is the
hypervideo-based LO, or *hypervideo LO*. Hypervideos are non-linear
videos whose playback can be influenced by hyperlinks embedded
in elements contained within the video stream [3, 4]. Using these
additional elements thus one can specify complex behaviors to LOs
such as playing video lectures in sequence, synchronizing lecture

HT'17, July 4-7, 2017, Prague, Czech Republic.
© 2017 ACM. 978-1-4503-4708-2/17/07...$15.00
DOI: http://dx.doi.org/10.1145/3078714.3078739

videos and additional elements through temporal and spatiotemporal links, and providing different user navigation modes over video
lectures [5].

Although general-purpose multimedia authoring languages (such
as HTML, SMIL, and NCL) have been used to specify hypervideo
LOs (more details on Section 4), there are some advantages on defining a domain-specific language (DSL [6]) for such a purpose. A DSL
offers a higher abstraction level to authors, closer to its application
domain. This way, LOs can be created similar to how the teacher
structures its lectures. Also, DSLs are small languages that do not
have as many elements as general purpose languages so that the
complexity in the development of authoring tools and exhibition
players (or formatters [7]) is usually less time consuming.

This paper presents SceneSync, a DSL for authoring hypervideo
LOs. SceneSync is based on a concise and straightforward conceptual model that structures LOs in scenes and provides simple
declarative concepts for defining the temporal behavior of LOs. SceneSync was created specifically for the domain of LOs authoring.
Therefore, it has a restricted and specific semantics. SceneSync documents represent the concept of interoperable learning objects [8],
as the same document can be used to run on both web browsers or
iDTV (Interactive Digital Television) plataforms.

The temporal features of SceneSync documents are specified
by a timeline-based synchronization model (instead of a structure-
based [9] one) that can be easily used by non-programmers, and
that can be coupled to different authoring tools. This project decision simplifies the implementation of graphical representation for
the SceneSync document model in authoring tools. It also eases the
implementation of formatters that maintain the temporal relationships during the document exhibition.

The remainder of this paper is structured as follows. Section 2
presents a study to identify the requirements observed in different hypervideo LOs. Section 3 presents hypermedia authoring
languages that are currently used to develop hypermedia LOs. Section 4 contains the core of the proposal, with the construction of a
model for hypervideo LOs. The viability of applying SceneSync is
discussed in Section 5. Finally, Section 6 brings our final considerations and discusses the results and future work.

2 REQUIREMENTS FOR MODELING HYPERVIDEO-BASED LEARNING OBJECTS

Table 1 summarizes the functional and non-functional requirements
we have gathered for the creation of hypervideo-based LOs. These

requirements were gathered through design techniques performed with stakeholders (as detailed in [10]) and by surveying the LO literature for works that have identified similar requirements or preferential features of users when using hypervideo LOs. As discussed in the next sections, those requirements were used as the basis for the creation of the SceneSync conceptual model.

Interactivity and multimedia content have long been seen as ways of supporting and enhance the teaching-learning process. For instance, Vieira *et al.* [11] highlight the importance of the students' interaction and the promotion of their participation in e-learning environments that use videos. Vieira *et al.*'s work compares different e-learning environment patterns and identifies fundamental requirements that should be taken into account when developing such environments. The analyzed patterns were: *Lecture Capture* (recording of a class or lecture); *Talking Head* (top recording of the instructor talking to the camera); *Voice Over Presentation* (slides presentation complemented with narration); and *Interactive Video* (video presentation enriched with multimedia content and interaction features). The main identified requirements were: the usage of short videos, soft transitions, hyperlinks support, and content summarization (for selective viewers).

Zhang *et al.* [12] and Dotta *et al.* [13] studied the preferences of the students and their learning satisfaction on e-learning environments. Zhang *et al.* [12] analyzed four different environments. The first environment uses interactive videos. The second one uses non-interactive videos. The third one does not use any video. And, the fourth environment is a traditional classroom. They concluded that students are significantly better satisfied and they have better learning performances in the first environment, i.e., the one that uses interactive videos. Based on Zhan *et al.* studies, interactivity is an important way to improve learning effectiveness in e-learning environments. Indeed, by providing an individualized control for content access through an organized content index, the student can learn at his pace. Dotta *et al.* [13] surveyed the predilection of students for the use of animations in videos. They found that, according to the majority of the students, the use of animations eases the learning process.

Brecht [16] measured the benefits of using video lectures to complement face-to-face classes. For that, he analyzed three different LO designs. The first design is characterized by the lack of attention to relief and change-of-pace elements (this is similar to the previously mentioned *Lecture Capture* from [11]). The second one included graphics/cartoons and sound/music clips, which were used to provide relief from fatigue during the class. Finally, the third design uses a significantly reduced number of graphics and sounds that were subtly presented in a way that they did not call too much of the students' attention. By comparing those designs, Brecht found that the second design (which uses graphics/cartoons and sound/music clips) had presented the best performance (i.e., the best learning rate and the lowest dropout rate of the students) in comparison to the other two.

Mujacic *et al.* [5] evaluate the performance of students in e-learning environments using hypervideo LOs. For this purpose, they analyzed two groups of students. The first group undertook the course using the traditional model of lectures, while the second group used the hypervideo LOs. By interviewing the students,

Table 1: Requirements for a hypervideo model for designing LOs.

FR# - Functional requirements
FR1 - Use multiple short videos instead of a single video (split into scenes) [5, 10, 11];
FR2 - Support for internal and external hyperlinks [10-12, 14, 15];
FR3 - Additional information: video enriched with images, texts, animations, other videos, audios, etc. [10, 13-17];
FR4 - Clickable areas, button panels, questions or quizzes. [10-12] [14, 15];
FR5 - Non-linear structure: no predefined course of playback, but a graph-structure of scenes [10-12, 14];
FR6- Timeline-based synchronism paradigm: media items are placed along a time axis, but possibly on different tracks [5, 10];
FR7 - Temporal links: jump labels on a timeline of a scene [5, 10].

NF# - Non-functional requirements
NF1 - Transition effects: presentation effect used when the formatter starts or finishes displaying a media [11];
NF2 - Interoperability: run on the Web, Mobile, iDTV [10, 15, 18];
NF3 - Adaptability: adaptation to different contexts [12, 15];
NF4 - Accessibility [15];
NF5 - Durability: resist technological changes without the need for recoding [15];
NF6 - Reusability: reuse of components [10, 15];
NF7 - Reliability: reliable and without errors [10].

it was verified that the introduction of the hypervideo LOs, provided for the second group, gave them better insight into the activities, and enabled a higher level of interaction and control over the contents. The LO model features used by Mujacic *et al.* include scenes composition, timeline-based synchronism, and spatiotemporal links.

Interactivity and multimedia content are also important for including impaired children and improving their learning experience. Focused on mathematics and pre-calculus, Munoz-Soto *et al.* [14] present a LO model for children diagnosed with autism spectrum disorders (ASD). By a preliminary validation of the proposed model, Munoz-Soto *et al.* have verified that the ASD children approved the interaction features and the use of multimedia content to add learning value. Becerra *et al.* [17] present a LO for children with language impairments that uses multiple sounds synchronized with other multimedia. The goal of the proposal is to use sound elements to stimulate children's phonological awareness.

Besides the Web, the iDTV is another important platform for diffusing educational applications. The interactive support and the processing capacity of TV sets and set-top boxes, however, does not enable the execution of complex applications [18]. Gadelha *et al.* [15] present OAF-TV, a scheme for the description of functional LOs for iDTV that can be adapted and reused to meet different teaching contexts and methodologies. OAF-TV is defined as a digital artifact that can have components to be reused in different learning contexts supporting interactivity, which allows the provision of exclusive content tuned to specific user needs and profiles.

3   HYPERMEDIA AUTHORING LANGUAGES

It is possible to develop hypervideo LOs using declarative languages such as SMIL, HTML, XMT, and NCL. However, those languages are designed for general purpose hypermedia applications and do not implement specific features of the educational domain.

SMIL (Synchronized Multimedia Integration Language) [19] is an XML-based declarative language for the specification of interactive multimedia presentations for the Web. SMIL provides temporal behavior constructions, and it allows authors to associate hyperlinks to media objects and to specify spatial layouts. The SMIL specification is organized into modules [20], which makes it possible to reuse parts of the language. However, in April 2012, W3C has extinguished the committee responsible for the language evolution, defining HTML5 [21] as a related topic [22].

HTML (together with some package format, such as SCORM [23], which will be discussed in the next section) is currently the most used language for developing LOs. Using HTML has the big advantages of being supported on many platforms. HTML5 provided multimedia features such as <video> and <audio> elements, which were a big advancement in the language towards a more multimedia environment. However, even today, the main features of LOs using HTML are usually developed using Javascript. Differently, we are more interested in high-level declarative features for hypervideo LOs. As discussed later in this paper, to take advantage of the high-availability of HTML5 the SceneSync model can also be converted to it (plus some Javascript code).

XMT (eXtensible MPEG-4 Textual Format) [24] is the MPEG-4 standard for interactive multimedia content representation. XMT has two representation levels: XMT-A and XMT-O. XMT-A is a direct textual (XML-based) representation of the MPEG-4 binary format used for transmission, named BIFS (BInary Format for Scenes) [25]. This way, XMT-A has the same expressiveness of BIFS. XMT-O, on the other hand, is an attempt of simplifying the authoring process, by providing higher-level language (based on SMIL elements). The XMT-O elements are temporarily arranged and synchronized with the SMIL time containers (<par>, <seq>, and <excl>). This simple set of temporal compositions hinders the definition of complex temporal relationships. Thus, in such cases, it is necessary to define compositions with several nested levels. Moreover, those compositions force authors to structure the document according to the temporal presentation specification [26]. Some modules of SMIL and XMT also incorporates characteristics from the X3D language [27], which allows content interchange between XMT, SMIL and X3D users, respecting the compatibility limit between the languages.

NCL (Nested Context Language) [28] is a declarative language for the authoring of hypermedia documents based on the NCM (Nested Context Model) [29] conceptual model. Initially, the language was designed for the Web, but today its main usage is as the declarative language of the Brazilian Digital Television System (SBTVD) and the H.761 recommendation of International Telecommunications Union for IPTV services [30]. In both cases, NCL supports the development of interactive multimedia applications for Digital TV. Similar to SMIL and XMT, NCL is also designed as a set of modules, which can be combined to produce different language profiles. The modules can also be reused by other languages. The latest NCL

version, 3.0 [31], reviewed some features contained in older versions. In special, the new version introduces two new features: navigation using keys and support for animations. Also, it introduces changes in the composite node template functionality and restructures the specification of hypermedia connectors in order to have a more concise notation. NCL, however, has several elements that are used to facilitate the reuse structuring of certain elements, and which does not have a direct influence on the application's semantic [32]. Hypervideo LOs can also be specified with NCL, but NCM is a broad-spectrum model so that teachers must rationalize all the complexity of the model to be able to define new LOs.

In contrast to the general purpose hypermedia languages above, this paper proposes a declarative language to specify hypervideo documents in the educational domain. Moreover, SceneSync does not take into account human aspects such as expressiveness and usability, which would be essential when designing multimedia authoring tools. Indeed, SceneSync is not designed to be used directly by end users, but to be used by authoring tools and players, or converted to one of the languages discussed in this section.

4   THE SCENESYNC MODEL

This section presents the *SceneSync Model* (SSM), a model for creating hypervideo LOs. SSM has been designed taking into account the requirements described in Section 2. Figure 1 shows the model entities.

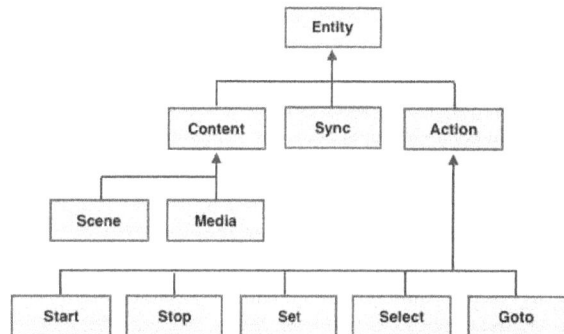

Figure 1: Class hierarchy of the SSM entities.

A *Content* entity can be a *Scene* or a *Media* object. The *Scene* entity is used as an abstraction for representing multimedia compositions (FR1 and FR3 requirements). A *Scene* entity instance has, as its content, a collection of *Media objects* and *Synchronization anchors* (*Sync*). For simplifying the LOs modeling, a *Scene* entity cannot contain others scene objects, i.e., SSM does not allow nesting compositions.

The timeline abstraction is used for providing synchronism among *Media objects* (FR6 requirement) in the same *Scene*. Every *Content* object (*Scene* or *Media*) has an internal clock that can be used as a reference for defining temporal anchors on the scene. An anchor is defined by the *Sync* entity, and has, as its content, a collection of *Action* objects.

An *Action* defines the relationships between the *Anchor* and *Content* objects, and can be of one of the following five types: *Start*, which starts the presentation of a media object; *Stop*, which stops the presentation of a media object; *Set*, which sets the properties of a media object; and *Select* and *Goto*, which redirect the presentation to another time point or scene node. The difference between the *Select* and *Goto* actions is that the *Select* action is triggered via the user interaction (requirements FR2, FR4 and FR7), whereas the *Goto* action is triggered when the scene reaches a specific time point. In special, these actions enable modeling non-linear LOs (FR5 requirement).

4.1 The SceneSync Language

LOs specified in SceneSync are compliant with the SCORM (Sharable Content Object Reference Model) [23] standard specifications, as they can be encapsulated into a Shareable Content Object (SCO) package (Figure 2). Besides the SceneSync document (c), an SCO package should contain three additional files: a manifest file SCORM (a), which informs AVA systems how, when, and where the SceneSync document should be executed; a LOM [33] metadata file (b), used to facilitate the searching of LOs; and the media files (d).

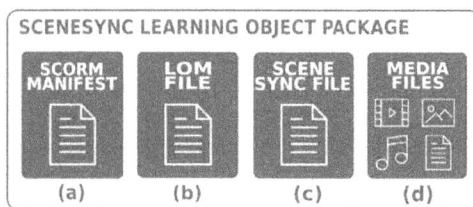

Figure 2: SceneSync Learning Objects Package

The SSM model is instantiated in XML by the SceneSync language. Similar to SMIL and NCL, the SceneSync language is specified using a modular approach in XML Schema [34]. Table 2 details the three modules of the language: *Structural*, *Content*, and *Synchronization*.

4.1.1 Structure module.
The structure module defines three main elements: <scenesync>, <head>, and <body>. The <scenesync> is the root element of the language, and it has the <head> and <body> elements as children. It also has the *id* and *xmls* attributes, which identify the application and the standard scheme, respectively. The <head> element may have an optional <meta> element that allows authors to specify metadata about the document. The <body> element has as children the elements that describe the presentation content, such as media and synchronism objects.

4.1.2 Content module.
A SceneSync presentation is composed of one or more scene nodes, represented by the <scene> element. Besides the identifier, a <scene> has a collection of media objects and synchronization elements as children. Each media object type is represented by a different first class element with their proper attributes: <image>, <text>, <audio>, or <video>. Media objects have as attributes: *id*, a unique identifier of the media object; *src*, which defines the media object contents *URI*; and others attributes that define presentation characteristics, such as *top*, *left*, *width*, *height*, and *transparency*. Media objects also contain a list of synchronism objects (<sync> elements, discussed next).

4.1.3 Synchronization module.
The synchronization among the media objects and scenes are defined by the <sync> element. The <sync> element has the *id* and *time* attributes. The *id* attribute identifies a <sync> element unambiguously in the document. The *time* attribute defines a temporal anchor in its parent element timeline (a <scene> or a media object). The children actions of the <sync> element will be fired when the parent element presentation reaches the time specified by the *time* attribute.

In the SceneSync language, every possible action over a <scene> or media object is represented by a different element. The <start> and <stop> elements represent actions that, respectively, starts or stops the presentation of a <scene> or media object. The <set> element represents an action that changes the property of a media object. The <goto> and <select> elements represent actions to redirect the multimedia presentation to another moment in time or to another <scene>. The difference between the <goto> and <select> actions is that the former is always triggered when the presentation reaches the specified time, whereas the latter is only triggered by a user interaction (such as a key press or mouse click).

Besides their identifiers, action objects have also the *target* attribute, which defines the target object of the action. In particular, the <set> element has a list of <property> elements. A <property> element specifies the property that will be modified (*name* attribute) and the new value to be defined (*value* attribute). The <select> element has the *key* attribute, which defines a key that triggers the action. The *timeEvent* attribute, which may be specified in a <select> and <goto>, defines the time anchor the scene node will be redirected to.

4.2 Modeling a LO using SceneSync

To help the understanding of the SceneSync language, this subsection presents a step-by-step development of a simple hypervideo LO, the "Sorting Algorithms" LO. This LO begins with the video of a teacher introducing general concepts related to sorting algorithms. At some point during his lecture, the teacher asks the viewer to choose whether he wants to learn more about the *InsertSort* or the *QuickSort* sorting algorithm. The LO then presents a specific lecture (about *InsertSort* or *QuickSort*) based on the user choice.

To implement the "Sorting Algorithms" LO, we divide it into three <scene> elements:

(1) *IntroductoryScene*, which contains:
    (a) one introductory video about sorting algorithms;
    (b) one image that represents the *InsertSort* option; and
    (c) one image that represents the *QuickSort* option.
(2) *InsertSortScene*, which contains:
    (a) one background image;
    (b) one video about the *InsertSort* algorithm; and
    (c) one image that illustrates an example of the *InsertSort* algorithm.
(3) *QuickSortScene*, which contains:
    (a) one background image;
    (b) one video about the *QuickSort* algorithm; and
    (c) one image that illustrates an example of the *QuickSort* algorithm.

Table 2: SceneSync language modules, elements, and attributes.

Element	Attributes	Child Elements
Structure module		
scenesync	id, xmls	(head?, body)
head	-	meta?
body	-	(scene - media - sync)*
Content module		
scene	id	(image, text, audio, video, sync)*
audio	id, src, volume	sync*
image	id, src, left, top, width, height, transparency, layer	sync*
video	id, src, left, top, width, height, transparency, volume, layer	sync*
text	id, src, left, top, style, align, color, fontfamily, fontsize, transparency, layer	sync*
Synchronization module		
sync	id, time	(start, stop, set, select, goto)*
start	id, target	-
stop	id, target	-
set	id, target	property*
goto	id, target, timeevent	-
select	id, target, timeevent, key	-
property	id, name, value	-

Listing 1 shows part of the "Sorting algorithm" source code, highlighting the <scene> and media objects, organized as above. Next, we discuss the behavior specification of each of the <scene>s.

The *IntroductoryScene* starts with the "vid_alg" video. This can be modeled with a <sync> element containing a child object of action <start> pointing to a video object (as shown in lines 3–5 of Listing 2). Note that we do not need to provide the value of the *time* attribute, which by default is 0.

Moreover, when the teacher invites the viewer to choose the next lecture (*InsertSortScene* or *QuickSortScene*) two images are displayed, illustrating those options to the viewer. It is also necessary to enable the user interactions that will lead to the selection of the respective scenes. To do this, we create a new <sync> element (lines 6–11 of Listing 2) with the *time* attribute set to "45s" (the time the teacher asks the user to interact). Inside this <sync> we define two <start> actions, the first one created to start the "img_insert" object, and the second one created to start the "img_quick" object. To enable user interaction, we define two <select> actions, which enable the key interaction feature.

Finally, when the main video of the *IntroductoryScene* ends (65s), the scene presentation should go back to 45s, and stay in a loop until the user chooses an option. We use the <goto> element to implement such behavior (lines 12–14 of Listing 2). The <goto> element is used with *target* and *timeEvent* attributes set as "IntroductoryScene" and "45s", respectively. Figure 3 shows the preview and temporal view of the *IntroductoryScene*.

Listing 1: Scenes and media objects of the "Sorting Algorithm" LO.

```
1   <scene id="IntroductoryScene">
2     <video id="vid_alg" src="intro.mp4"
          width="100%" height="100%" />
3     <image id="img_insert" src="img1.png"
          left="30%" top="80%" width="30%"
          height="20%" />
4     <image id="img_quick" src="img2.png" left="65%"
          top="80%" width="30%" height="20%" />
5     ...
6   </scene>
7   <scene id="InsertSortScene">
8     <video id="vid_insert" src="video1.mp4"
          width="100%" height="100%" />
9     <image id="back_insert" src="back.png"
          width="100%" height="100%" />
10    <image id="img_alg_insert" src="img2.png"
          left="65%" width="80%" width="30%"
          height="20%" />
11    ...
12  </scene>
13  <scene id="QuickSortScene">
14    <video id="vid_quick" src="video1.mp4"
          width="100%" height="100%" />
15    <image id="back_quick" src="back.png"
          width="100%" height="100%" />
16    <image id="img_alg_quick" src="img2.png"
          left="65%" width="80%" width="30%"
          height="20%" />
17    ...
18  </scene>
```

Listing 2: Source code defining the temporal behavior of *IntroductoryScene* of the "Sorting Algorithm" LO.

```
1   <scene id="IntroductoryScene">
2   ...
3    <sync>
4     <start target="vid_intro" />
5    </sync>
6    <sync time="45">
7     <start target="img_insert" />
8     <start target="img_quick" />
9     <select key="1" target="InsertSortScene"/>
10    <select key="2" target="QuickSortScene"/>
11   </sync>
12   <sync time="65s">
13    <goto target="IntroductoryScene"
            timeEvent="45s"/>
14   </sync>
15  </scene>
```

Listing 3: Source code defining the temporal behavior of *InsertSortScene* of the "Sorting Algorithm" LO.

```
1   <scene id="InsertSortScene">
2   ...
3    <sync>
4     <start target="vid_insert" />
5    </sync>
6    <sync time="5s">
7     <start target="img_back_insert" />
8     <start target="img_alg_insert" />
9     <set target="vid_insert">
10     <property name="left" value="5%" />
11     <property name="top" value="5%" />
12     <property name="width" value="17%" />
13     <property name="height" value="10%" />
14    </set>
15   </sync>
16  </scene>
```

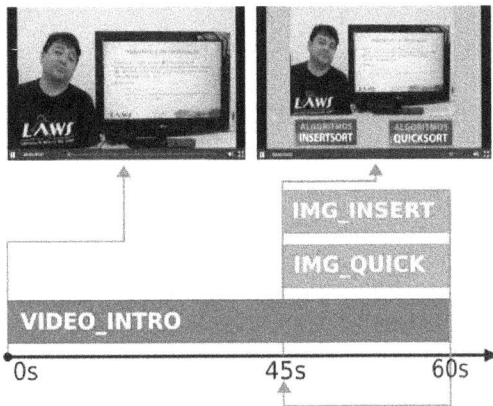

Figure 3: Preview (top) and temporal view (bottom) of *IntroductoryScene*.

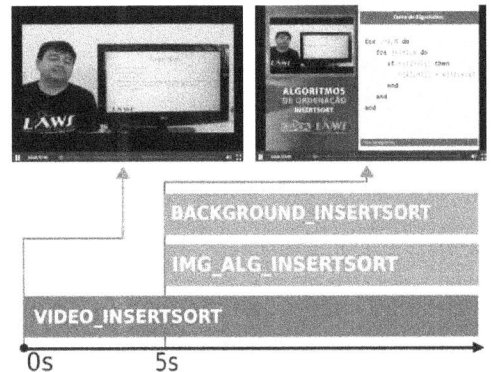

Figure 4: Preview (top) and temporal view (bottom) of *InsertSortScene*.

The second (*InsertSortScene*) and the third (*QuickSortScene*) scenes have a similar behavior. Therefore, we will discuss only the second scene here. The *InsertSortScene* starts by displaying the video about the *InsertSort* algorithm. For that, a <sync> element is defined containing a <start> action referring the video presentation "vid_insert" (Listing 3, lines 3–5). As an additional behavior of this scene, at 5 seconds: (1) the main video must be resized and moved to the upper left corner; (2) a background image must be started (behind the video and occupying the entire scene); and (3) the image containing an example of the *InsertSort* algorithm must be displayed on the right side of the screen. To implement that, we used the <sync> element defined in Listing 3, lines 6–15. Figure 4 shows the preview and temporal view of the *InsertSortScene*.

5 ANALYSIS

In order to show the viability of using the SceneSync model we have asked for 142 stakeholders (teachers and educational content creators) to develop LOs using the concepts provided by SceneSync. To allow them to use the SceneSync concepts and create an executable LO, we have used the Cacuriá [35], which is an authoring tool that graphically implements the SSM concepts. The LOs were created as part of 7 workshops and 1 technical session held in 5 Brazilian cities during three years of a research project. A complete description of the evaluation of the Cacuriá authoring tool can be found in [36]. Here, we summarize and analyze those results with regards to the underlying SceneSync model.

Both in the workshops and in the technical session, first, the participants were presented to the process of authoring LOs using SceneSync concepts and the Cacuriá authoring tool. Then, they were asked to develop a LO about some topic of their interest (in the workshops) or a predefined LO (in the technical session). In total, 32 LOs [1] (Figure 5) were specified in SceneSync using the Cacuriá tool.

Table 3 shows the developed LOs, with their respective disciplines and identified functional requirements. As can be seen, all the functional requirements that guided us in the development of SceneSync could be successfully explored by the authors of LOs.

All the LO authors were able to use the following features successfully: multimedia compositions (FR1) through the <scene> element; additional video information such as images, texts, animations, another videos, and audio (FR3); timeline-based synchronism (FR6), through the <sync> and action elements; clickable areas (FR4) and non-linear narrative structures (FR5), through the <sync> and <select> elements; temporal links, spatial-temporal links (FR7), <sync>, <goto>, and <select> elements.

Cacuriá supported the external hyperlinks (FR2) feature only in the last workshop. Thus, only three LOs ("05-Citation", "08-Scientific Work", and "15 - Game of Thrones quiz") have used it. Probably, if that functionality had been provided before, more LOs would have been created using this feature.

6 CONCLUSION

This paper presents the SceneSync model (SSM), a hypervideo model for LOs, and its instantiation as an XML-based language. Compared to other approaches to implementing hypervideo LOs, such as using a general-purpose multimedia languages directly, SSM provides abstractions close to the hypervideo LOs domain, so that it simplifies the authoring process (which is now in a proper abstraction level), the development of authoring tools on a similar domain (such as the Cacuriá authoring tool), and the development of players for hypervideo LOs. Moreover, the final artifact created using SSM can be converted to other lower-level languages, such as HTML (to run on the Web) to NCL (to run in iDTV platforms). Indeed, the Cacuriá authoring tool can export to both of those formats.

In the process of developing SSM, an additional contribution of the paper is the set of requirements defined in Section 2. Aiming at characterizing the hypervideo LOs domain, we present a survey of features for hypervideo LOs documents gathered through design techniques performed with stakeholders and from a literature review, focused on functional features and users' preferences when using hypervideo LOs. The SSM supports all the gathered requirements. Also, to show the viability of our proposal, we analyzed 32 LOs created by 142 stakeholders, showing that most of the features were indeed used by them when creating hypervideo LOs.

Based on the results presented in Section 5 we have good confidence that SSM is useful for a broad range of hypervideo LOs. So far, however, SSM was not designed to be directly used by teachers. In future work, we plan to perform a qualitative study of the communicability and usability of the model without the interposing of a visual authoring tool. We also want to investigate the reusability degree that we can achieve when using SSM together with the SCORM standard.

Still focused on reusability, we plan to extend the SSM features by providing native support for defining new concepts in the model

through templates. Templates can improve the reuse of the specification of LOs and help to create a visual identity among sets of LOs.

Finally, another future work is related to the identification and analysis of design patterns that could be useful in the scope of hypervideo LOs. In such a future work, the focus is on finding recurrent code structures and best practices that authors can reuse when creating new LOs. Researching design patterns can be useful in at least two ways: for defining authoring guidelines and ii) for providing new concepts, which can be used to extend SSM.

ACKNOWLEDGMENTS

This work was supported by RNP, the National Research and Educational Network from Brazil, and was developed in the context of the RNP Working Groups program, during the cycles 2012–2013, 2013–2014, and 2015. The authors also thank CAPES, FAPEMA, and CNPq for their additional support.

REFERENCES

[1] IEEE Learning Technology Standards Committee et al. Draft standard for learning object metadata. *Accessed July*, 14:2002, 2002.
[2] David A Wiley. *Connecting learning objects to instructional design theory: A definition, a metaphor, and a taxonomy.* 2003.
[3] Britta Meixner, Katarzyna Matusik, Christoph Grill, and Harald Kosch. Towards an easy to use authoring tool for interactive non-linear video. *Multimedia Tools and Applications*, 70(2):1251–1276, 2014.
[4] Nitin Sawhney, David Balcom, and Ian Smith. Hypercafe: narrative and aesthetic properties of hypervideo. In *Proceedings of the the seventh ACM conference on Hypertext*, pages 1–10. ACM, 1996.
[5] Samra Mujacic, Matjaz Debevc, Primoz Kosec, Marcus Bloice, and Andreas Holzinger. Modeling, design, development and evaluation of a hypervideo presentation for digital systems teaching and learning. *Multimedia Tools and Applications*, 58(2):435–452, 2012.
[6] Marjan Mernik, Jan Heering, and Anthony M Sloane. When and how to develop domain-specific languages. *ACM Computing Surveys (CSUR)*, pages 316–344, 2005.
[7] Luiz Fernando G Soares, Rogério F Rodrigues, and Débora C Muchaluat Saade. Modeling, authoring and formatting hypermedia documents in the hyperprop system. *Multimedia Systems*, 8(2):118–134, 2000.
[8] Norm Friesen. Interoperability and learning objects: An overview of e-learning standardization. *Interdisciplinary Journal of Knowledge and Learning Objects*, 1 (1):23–31, 2005.
[9] Lynda Hardman, Guido Van Rossum, and Dick CA Bulterman. Structured multimedia authoring. In *Proceedings of the first ACM international conference on Multimedia*, pages 283–289. ACM, 1993.
[10] André Luiz de Brandão Damasceno, Carlos Salles Soares Neto, and Simone Diniz Junqueira Barbosa. Integrating participatory and interaction design of an authoring tool for learning objects involving a multidisciplinary team. In *Proceedings of the International Conference on Human-Computer Interaction*, 2017.
[11] Isabel Vieira, Ana Paula Lopes, and Filomena Soares. The potential benefits of using videos in higher education. In *Proceedings of EDULEARN14 Conference*, pages 0750–0756. IATED Publications, 2014.
[12] Dongsong Zhang, Lina Zhou, Robert O Briggs, and Jay F Nunamaker. Instructional video in e-learning: Assessing the impact of interactive video on learning effectiveness. *Information & management*, 43(1):15–27, 2006.
[13] Silvia C Dotta, Erica FC Jorge, Edson P Pimentel, and Juliana C Braga. Análise das preferências dos estudantes no uso de videoaulas: Uma experiência na educação a distância. In *Anais do Workshop de Informática na Escola*, volume 1, page 21, 2013.
[14] Roberto Munoz-Soto, Carlos Becerra, René Noël, Thiago Barcelos, Rodolfo Villarroel, Sandra Kreisel, and Matías Camblor. Proyect@ matemáticas: A learning object for supporting the practitioners in autism spectrum disorders. In *Learning Objects and Technology (LACLO), Latin American Conference on*, pages 1–6. IEEE, 2016.
[15] Bruno Freitas Gadelha, Alberto Nogueira CASTRO-JR, and Hugo Fuks. Representando objetos de aprendizagem funcionais para tvdi. In *SET2007–Congresso da Sociedade Brasileira de Engenharia de Televisão, São Paulo*, 2007.
[16] H David Brecht. Learning from online video lectures. *Journal of Information Technology Education*, 11:227–250, 2012.

---

[1] Available at https://goo.gl/I6SyKu

Figure 5: LOs developed by stakeholders.

Table 3: Functional requirements used by every LO's authors

#	Title	Discipline	FR1	FR2	FR3	FR4	FR5	FR6	FR7
01	Nephrology	medicine	Yes	No	Yes	Yes	Yes	Yes	Yes
02	Plagiarism	education	Yes	No	Yes	Yes	Yes	Yes	Yes
03	Scientific methodology	philosophy	Yes	No	Yes	Yes	Yes	Yes	Yes
04	LIBRAS (Brazilian Sign Language)	accessibility	Yes	No	Yes	Yes	Yes	Yes	Yes
05	Citation	education	Yes	Yes	Yes	Yes	Yes	Yes	Yes
06	Cupcake recipe	culinary	Yes	No	Yes	Yes	Yes	Yes	Yes
07	Thyroid	medicine	Yes	No	Yes	Yes	Yes	Yes	Yes
08	Scientific Work	education	Yes	Yes	Yes	Yes	Yes	Yes	Yes
09	Recycling actions	recycling	Yes	No	Yes	Yes	Yes	Yes	Yes
10	Tourist points of "Urbano Santos"	turism	Yes	No	Yes	Yes	Yes	Yes	Yes
11	Knowledge	philosophy	Yes	No	Yes	Yes	Yes	Yes	Yes
12	Importance of bees	biology	Yes	No	Yes	Yes	Yes	Yes	Yes
13	"Boa Hora" river	geography	Yes	No	Yes	Yes	Yes	Yes	Yes
14	PGASS Elaboration	management	Yes	No	Yes	Yes	Yes	Yes	Yes
15	"Game of Thrones" quiz	entertainment	Yes	Yes	Yes	Yes	Yes	Yes	Yes
16	Social control in SUS	health	Yes	No	Yes	Yes	Yes	Yes	Yes
17	Princess abduction	entertainment	Yes	No	Yes	Yes	Yes	Yes	Yes
18	Sucupira platform	technology	Yes	No	Yes	Yes	Yes	Yes	Yes
19	Aedes aegypti	biology	Yes	No	Yes	Yes	Yes	Yes	Yes
20	Geometry in the square	mathematics	Yes	No	Yes	Yes	Yes	Yes	Yes
21	Elderly health	health	Yes	No	Yes	Yes	Yes	Yes	Yes
22	Sedentary Lifestyle	health	Yes	No	Yes	Yes	Yes	Yes	Yes
23	IHC	design	Yes	No	Yes	Yes	Yes	Yes	Yes
24	Communicability	design	Yes	No	Yes	Yes	Yes	Yes	Yes
25	Dishes	culinary	Yes	No	Yes	Yes	Yes	Yes	Yes
26	Route of the day	turism	Yes	No	Yes	Yes	Yes	Yes	Yes
27	Life cycle of bryophytes	biology	Yes	No	Yes	Yes	Yes	Yes	Yes
28	Empiricism	philosophy	Yes	No	Yes	Yes	Yes	Yes	Yes
29	Physical education	health	Yes	No	Yes	Yes	Yes	Yes	Yes
30	Scientific text	education	Yes	No	Yes	Yes	Yes	Yes	Yes
31	Cybersecurity	technology	Yes	No	Yes	Yes	Yes	Yes	Yes
32	Wifi help	technology	Yes	No	Yes	Yes	Yes	Yes	Yes

[17] Carlos Becerra, René Noel, Roberto Munoz, and Ian Quiroga. Explorando aprendo: Learning object to enhance language development in children with specific language impairment. In *Learning Objects and Technology (LACLO), Latin American Conference on*, pages 1–5. IEEE, 2016.

[18] Júlia Marques Carvalho da Silva and Rosa Maria Vicari. Relacionando a televisão digital interativa com o conceito de objetos de aprendizagem: conceitos, aspectos históricos, e perspectivas. In *Anais do Simpósio Brasileiro de Informática na Educação*, volume 1, 2009.

[19] P Vuorimaa, D Bulterman, and P Cesar. Smil timesheets 1.0. *W3C Working Draft*, 2008.

[20] Y Ayers, A Cohen, Dick Bulterman, et al. Synchronized multimedia integration language (smil) 2.0. *W3C Recommendations*, 2001.

[21] Ian Hickson and David Hyatt. Html5: A vocabulary and associated apis for html and xhtml. *W3C Working Draft, May*, 25, 2011.

[22] W3C. The symm wg is closed since 01 april 2012. http://www.w3.org/AudioVideo/. [Acessado em 20/05/2016].

[23] Oliver Bohl, Jörg Scheuhase, Ruth Sengler, and Udo Winand. The sharable content object reference model (scorm)-a critical review. In *Computers in education, 2002. proceedings. international conference on*, pages 950–951. IEEE, 2002.

[24] Michelle Kim, Steve Wood, and Lai-Tee Cheok. Extensible mpeg-4 textual format (xmt). In *Proceedings of the 2000 ACM workshops on Multimedia*, pages 71–74. ACM, 2000.

[25] Julien Signes. Binary format for scene (bifs): Combining mpeg-4 media to build rich multimedia services. In *Electronic Imaging'99*, pages 1506–1517. International Society for Optics and Photonics, 1998.

[26] Débora Christina Muchaluat Saade. *Relações em Linguagens de Autoria Hipermídia: Aumentando Reuso e Expressividade*. PhD thesis, Tese de Doutorado, Departamento de Informática, PUC-Rio, Rio de Janeiro, Brasil, 2003.

[27] Leonard Daly and Don Brutzman. X3d: extensible 3d graphics standard. *IEEE Signal Processing Magazine*, 24(6):130, 2007.

[28] Luiz Fernando Gomes Soares, Marcio Ferreira Moreno, Carlos de Salles Soares Neto, and Marcelo Ferreira Moreno. Ginga-ncl: declarative middleware for multimedia iptv services. *IEEE Communications Magazine*, 48(6):74–81, 2010.

[29] Luiz Fernando Gomes Soares and Rogério Ferreira Rodrigues. Nested context model 3.0: Part 1–ncm core. *Monografias em Ciência da Computação do Departamento de Informática, PUC-Rio*, (18/05), 2005.

[30] ITU-T. Recommendation h.761 - nested context language (ncl) and ginga-ncl for iptv services. ITU-T, Geneva, Switzerland, 2009.

[31] Luiz Fernando Gomes Soares and Rogério Ferreira Rodrigues. Nested context language 3.0 part 8–ncl digital tv profiles. *Monografias em Ciência da Computação do Departamento de Informática da PUC-Rio*, 1200(35):06, 2006.

[32] Luiz Fernando Soares, Guilherme Augusto Lima, and Carlos Soares Neto. Ncl 3.1 enhanced dtv profile. *III Workshop de TV Digital Interativa (WTVDI) - Colocated with ACM WebMedia'10*, 2010.

[33] IEEE Learning Technology Standards Committee et al. Draft standard for learning object metadata (lom) ieee 1484.12. 1, 2002.

[34] XML Schema Part. 0: Primer. *W3C Recommendation*, 2, 2001.

[35] André Luiz de Brandão Damasceno, Rosendy Jess Galabo, and Carlos Salles Soares Neto. Cacuriá: Authoring tool for multimedia learning objects. In *Proceedings of the 20th Brazilian Symposium on Multimedia and the Web*, pages 59–66. ACM, 2014.

[36] André Luiz de Brandão Damasceno, Carlos Salles Soares Neto, and Simone Diniz Junqueira Barbosa. Lessons learned from evaluating an authoring tool for learning objects. In *Proceedings of the International Conference on Human-Computer Interaction*, 2017.

Engaging Neighbors: The Double-Edged Sword of Mobilization Messaging in Hyper-Local Online Forums

Claudia López
Universidad Técnica F. Santa María
Av. Espana 1680
Valparaíso, Chile
claudia@inf.utfsm.cl

Rosta Farzan
University of Pittsburgh
North Belliefield Av. 135
Pittsburgh, PA
rfarzan@pitt.edu

Yu-Ru Lin
University of Pittsburgh
North Belliefield Av. 135
Pittsburgh, PA
yrlin@pitt.edu

ABSTRACT

Information technologies for local communities can augment the relationships among neighbors and reduce barriers for collective action, thus increasing social capital. However, the benefits arise only if enough residents are engaged with the technology. Based on a six-year dataset of messages among neighbors on 35 online discussion forums, we examined the relationship of different kinds of content shared on the forums and user engagement. We leveraged text analysis to automatically classify over 32,000 posts shared in these hyper-local forums. Our findings suggest that neighbors use the forums largely for social capital mobilization, requesting both active and passive actions. Nevertheless, a balance between these two kinds of content is crucial for attracting new users and retaining current ones in order to keep a thriving stream of content. These results advance the understanding of the role of content on sustainability and impact of hyper-local technologies.

KEYWORDS

social capital; mobilizations; neighborhoods; hyper-local

1 INTRODUCTION

Social technologies such as NextDoor,[1] a private social network for connecting neighbors, are revitalizing the interest in information technologies for communities of place, such as neighborhoods and cities. A number of such platforms have been built over the last decade with the focus on strengthening local communities. The concept of "hyper-local" media has recently emerged to signal the goal of some media to focus on geographically-bounded communities [25]. Similarly, the term hyper-local social technologies have been getting traction to refer to technologies focusing on communities of place [4].

Many hyper-local social technologies aim to increase connections among neighbors and/or to enable their collective action, which were also the goals of older technologies often known as community information systems [23].

[1]https://nextdoor.com/

The social capital framework has been useful to investigate the achievement of these goals in a number of studies (see literature reviews in [26, 29]). Social capital, as defined by Lin [18], refers to "*resources embedded in a social structure which are accessed and/or mobilized in purposive actions.*" It denotes the potential value that comes from people's connections to others. This value can range from small favours, such as a ride to an airport, to higher reputation or to better physical and mental health [18].

Prior research provides evidence that community information systems that rely on neighbors to gather content can positively affect social capital. Initial studies argued that these technologies can prompt new instances that encourage local interactions [10]. The argument was confirmed through cross-sectional and longitudinal user surveys. Participation in local technologies was associated with more social connections to other neighbors [11, 12, 16]. Further, an ethnographic study concluded that these technologies can reduce barriers for collective action to achieve a shared goal [12].

A necessary condition to achieve such goals is that the technology can sustain over time; however, achieving critical mass remains a challenge for hyper-local technologies [8, 14]. A review of technologies for neighborhoods concludes that new local information appears infrequently (few new items per day) and it generates little further community interaction online [2]. Unfortunately, replicating designs from highly adopted social media might not solve the problem. There are mismatches between neighbors' expectations about what a community information system ought to be and the affordances of mainstream social media [14]. Mismatches range from digital inclusion issues to the kinds of content that people see as appropriate to be shared with neighbors [14].

In this work, we aim to unpack the relationships between shared content, social capital, and sustainability in hyper-local technologies. Using a six-year dataset of citizen participation on 35 online discussion forums [20, 21], we automatically classify more than 32,000 posts shared in these online forums in regard to whether or not they represent any kind of mobilizations of social capital. Then, we conduct a longitudinal study of the relationship between the proportion of social capital mobilizations and three collective (i.e., forum-level) aspects of sustainability: attraction of new contributors of content, retention of current contributors, and generation of more content. In our analysis, we control for key contextual variables (such as neighborhood demographics and the forums' tenure and time of creation) that have been often dismissed in previous quantitative studies of hyper-local technologies, but had been suggested as critical factors on sustainability [13, 16, 29].

This work's contributions are: (1) to characterize the linguistic features of mobilizations of social capital in hyper-local online forums, (2) to reveal how the prevalence of different kinds of mobilizations relate to the forums' sustainability in the future, and (3) to offer new empirical evidence regarding how different uses of hyper-local technologies support social capital. By combining text mining and longitudinal data analyses of the content shared in the same hyper-local technology across multiple communities of place, our findings complement previous findings that have often arisen from self-reported and participant observation methods investigating technologies that served a single geographical community [6] (e.g., [11, 12, 16]).

The paper describes the related work and states our research questions in Section 2. Section 3 introduces our research method. Section 4 details the results of the content classification in regard to social capital mobilization. Section 5 examines the relationship between content and sustainability. We discuss implications of the results in Section 6.

2   PRIOR WORK AND RESEARCH QUESTIONS

Several studies of community information systems have used "ad-hoc" categories to describe the content shared by their members. Reviews of local businesses, goods for sale and housing data were the kinds of information found in the earliest systems [5]; event announcements, restaurant reviews, and personal topics were mentioned in another study [3]; information about local businesses, services, events, and classifieds were available in another one [11]. The most systematic content analysis, so far, explored the content of three community information systems in the US and compiled a 20-item categorization that included the categories mentioned above and added others, such as volunteerism and local news [24].

Our goal is to complement this strand of work by drawing from research connecting social media content and social capital [7, 17]. We examine the existence of social capital mobilizations in hyper-local technologies as evidence of their potential to utilize and accumulate social capital in communities of place. Following Lin's definition of social capital [18], we conceptualize a hyper-local social technology as an instance where a local community's social structure is available to the neighbors. Thus, a user's online request for information, a favor, or support for a collective action would represent an attempt to mobilize social capital in the community.

Related research provided a categorization of social capital mobilizations [7] and our own prior work used it to manually classify a small sample of posts (n=516) in hyper-local technologies [20]. This manual annotation achieved a reliable inter-coder agreement score, thus indicating that the categorization scheme was useful for content shared in community information systems. A question that remains open is whether this content annotation can be scaled-up by identifying textual features that allow an automatic content classification. Therefore, our first research questions is:

RQ1: *To what extent textual features enable reliable automatic content classification of posts in hyper-local social technologies with respect to mobilization attempts?*

Our prior work's results revealed that more than 80% of the annotated posts were requests for social capital mobilizations [20], which is significantly larger than the 4.4% share of posts found in Facebook [7]. Given this high prevalence of mobilization requests,

it is important to better understand the implications that this kind of content has on the sustainability of the hyper-local technologies.

There is evidence that content drives particular measures of sustainability in topic-centered online groups [1, 28] as well as in ego-centered groups in Twitter [27] and Facebook [17]. This effect has been studied at individual [17, 28] and collective levels [1, 27]. At the individual level, users who contribute and seek social support instead of informational content are more likely to return to health-related online discussion forums [28]. In Facebook, requests for recommendations and factual knowledge were more likely than other kinds of social capital mobilizations to get a response and to obtain a response faster [17]. In hyper-local technologies, the same mobilization requests were more likely than non-mobilizations to obtain an online response, but were negatively related to user retention in the future [20]. Additionally, requests for social coordination, invitations and offers were less likely than non-mobilizations to obtain a response.

At the collective level, email-based online groups with higher content diversity retained fewer contributors in a subsequent period of time [1]. Similarly, lower content diversity was associated with a larger and more connected group of followers (i.e. readers) in Twitter [27]. On the other hand, content diversity was positively associated with higher frequency of posts in Facebook groups related to neighborhoods [19]. Digging deeper into the kinds of content in hyper-local technologies, researchers have found that discussion of politics and local issues related to danger and novelty generated more participation in local discussion forums [22]. Furthermore, while community characteristics have been mentioned as potential factors on sustainability of local technologies [13, 16, 29], prior work revealed that content diversity and length of discussions do not vary across neighborhoods with different poverty levels [9].

Considering that different kinds of social capital mobilizations have opposing relationships to sustainability at the individual level [20], we pose a new research question regarding the collective (aggregated) effect of mobilization requests:

RQ2: *What is the relationship between social capital mobilizations and the collective measures of sustainability of hyper-local social technologies, after controlling for the neighborhood effect?*

3   RESEARCH METHOD

To answer our research questions, we examined data provided to us by the E-Democracy.org platform. Active since 1994, E-Democracy hosts online discussion forums for cities and neighborhoods. The neighborhood discussion forums are the focus of this study. These forums aim to be a virtual space to discuss the "neighborhood life". For example, the stated goal of one of the neighborhood forums is to: "share announcements and discuss neighborhood issues, life, and events specific to the neighborhood."[2]

As we have argued in our prior work [20, 21], several characteristics of the neighborhood forums make them appropriate for studying a hyper-local technology across several communities. All forums have used the same interface, have followed a similar process of creation, and have enacted similar moderation rules.

Our current dataset includes all the posts that were exchanged in 35 online forums for neighborhoods or districts in the cities

---

[2] http://forums.e-democracy.org/groups/mpls-poho Last retrieved on Jan. 9th 2017

of Minneapolis and St. Paul in the US state of Minnesota. This archival dataset includes 75,374 posts that were organized into 32,903 threads of discussion and posted by 5,207 unique users. These posts were collected during the whole lifecycles of the forums until the second quarter of 2014. We segmented the data into calendar quarters as the observation period for our longitudinal analysis.[3] Given that not all forums have been active since the same year, our panel dataset was unbalanced. By the end of our observation period, the neighborhood forums' tenure ranged from one to six years. Additionally, we had the membership data of the forums; i.e. the timestamp of when a member joined. However, this data was only available since last quarter of 2010, not for the whole lifecycle of all forums. While we had data about active contributions (i.e., messages) to the forums and the act of joining a given forum, we did not have data about user reading behavior or explicit requests to unsubscribe a forum. Therefore, our study could not investigate the last two kinds of user actions.

Overall, we had 481 observations in our longitudinal data of posts and 402 observations with membership data. Each observation consist of data of a forum within one quarter.

3.1 Machine classification of content as mobilizations

Content categorization and ground-truth annotation. To learn about the content shared in the forums, we followed a procedure to automatically annotate their posts. We adopted a coding scheme from prior research [7, 17] that characterizes posts according to their intention to mobilize social capital into five kinds of requests:

- Recommendation,
- Factual knowledge,
- Opinion/poll,
- Favor/request/ collective action, and
- Social coordination/invitation/offer.

To test this coding scheme in our data and define a ground truth for the automatic classification, we manually annotated a sample of 516 posts that initiated a new discussion thread in the forums, as reported in [20]. The posts were randomly chosen within three subsets of threads: threads with zero answers, threads with one or two answers, and threads with three or more answers. Each post was coded by three annotators to indicate if it was a request to mobilize social capital (i.e., a mobilization) or no (i.e., a non-mobilization). A majority vote was used to decide the corresponding label for each post. Posts coded as mobilizations were also classified into the five categories listed above. The inter-coder agreement score for this categorization was 0.67 and was considered sufficient. Further discrepancies were discussed until reaching agreement.

Machine classification The results of the manual coding were used as a ground truth for training the machine classifiers. The goal was to classify all posts that initiated a new thread of conversation in the neighborhood forums.

To build the automatic classifiers, we first processed the text by extracting N-grams (unigrams, bigrams and trigrams) and the count of various linguistic features in the posts, after stemming the text. Linguistic features, such as pronouns and verbs in past tense,

were retrieved by reusing the Linguistic Inquiry and Word Count (LIWC)[4] dictionary and functions.

We tested different classification methods such as k-nearest-neighborhoods, decision trees, and support vector machine (SVM). Given the uneven distribution of different kinds of mobilizations, all classification algorithms achieved low levels of performance when we trained them to identify all categories. For example, the best results from decision trees had an error rate equal to 0.38. The performance improved considerably when the most infrequent kinds of mobilizations were grouped together. Therefore, we decided to train classifiers to categorize content into three labels:

- *"active mobilization"* which consists of posts coded as *social coordination/invitation/offer* and represents mobilization requests with a strong tendency to request offline actions that are harder to satisfy;
- *"passive mobilization"* which comprises *recommendation, factual knowledge, opinion/poll* and *favor/request/collective action* that more often request online answers and, therefore, are considered easier to meet; and,
- *"non-mobilization"*, which includes posts that do not explicitly request any kind of mobilization.

This distinction was still considered useful for our analysis as it could distinguish between the most popular category of social capital mobilization from other mobilizations and non-mobilizations. This new categorization is also useful to reason about the level of social capital that is accumulated when a mobilization is successfully satisfied. Active mobilizations seek to create opportunities for offline interactions and such interactions can help accumulate stronger social capital in the communities, but might not be reflected on further interaction in the online space. In turn, passive mobilizations might make the online space more dynamic by getting online responses; however, it might have a lower impact of accumulation of social capital in the community as it requires less effort to meet the requests. The results of the machine categorization of these labels will be reported in a later section.

After obtaining the automatically-classified posts, we defined variables of *Prevalence of mobilizations* for the statistical data analysis. *Prevalence of mobilizations* is defined as the ratio of a forum's threads that started in a quarter and whose initial post was classified as a particular kind of mobilization to the total number of new threads in the forum at the same quarter. Given that the kinds of content are often significantly related to the chance of obtaining an online response [1, 17, 20, 27, 28], we also defined *% online responsiveness* as the proportion of new threads in a quarter with at least one response to the total number of new threads in the quarter.

3.2 Neighborhood context as proper control

To control for a potential neighborhood effect that has been suggested in prior work [13, 16, 29], we identified major demographic features of the local communities served by the E-Democracy forums. We used a public dataset[5] that has 166 demographic features of the neighborhoods located in St. Paul and Minneapolis. The dataset comprises data from the 2010 US Census, the 2009 Local

---

[3]We conducted analyses using alternative observation periods, such as semesters, and the results were qualitatively similar.

[4]http://liwc.wpengine.com/

[5] http://www.mncompass.org/profiles/neighborhoods/minneapolis-saint-paul#!areas

Employment Dynamics study, and the 2005-2009 American Community Survey. As in a prior study [21], we conducted principal component analysis to reduce dimensions of the neighborhood features. The results indicate that 81.15% of the variance in the data is explained by the first three components. After removing redundant demographic features, the main three components revealed groups of variables that we conceptualized as follows:

- *Size* of the neighborhood includes total population, housing, number of employed residents, and number of jobs.
- *Diversity* of the neighborhood includes the percentage of the population that is people of color, the percentage of the population that is seventeen or younger, and the percentage of the population that is 25 and over whose education level is less than high school graduate.
- *Instability* represents how transient a neighborhood's population is and contains the percentage of rented occupied households, the ratio of occupied households that moved into the neighborhood in 2005 or later, and the percentage of households with an annual income of less than $35,000.

To simplify the interpretation of the results, we chose the most representative variable to characterize each component in our statistical analyses. Size is represented by the total population of the neighborhood. Diversity is measured as the proportion of the population that is people of color. Instability is characterized by the ratio of residents who had moved into the neighborhood since 2005.

3.3 Measuring sustainability

To assess the relationship between content and sustainability of the hyper-local forums at a collective level, we operationalized sustainability in terms of attraction, retention and performance [21]. For each quarter in a forum, we computed the following dependent variables:

- *Attraction* comprises two variables: (a) number of new users who joined the forum in the quarter; and (b) number of users who posted for the first time to the forum (i.e., new contributors).
- *Retention* is represented by the number of contributors from the previous quarter who continued to post in the current quarter.
- *Performance* is measured by the number of posts in the quarter.

All of them were count measures and had right-skewed distributions. Therefore, we used Poisson regressions to model their relationship to the independent and control variables. We used *xt commands* in Stata 14 to analyze our longitudinal data while properly controlling for the correlation of measures within forums.

4 RQ1: AUTOMATIC CONTENT CLASSIFICATION IN HYPER-LOCAL FORUMS

To answer our first research question, we followed the method reported in Section 3.1. Overall, the SVM classification model consistently out-performed alternative classification methods such as k-nearest neighbors and decision trees. We used the tuning methods with 10-fold cross-validation in order to train the model and

find the most appropriate SVM classifier parameters for our data. To compare results, we use accuracy, precision and recall measures. N-grams and LIWC-based features, hereafter called linguistic, were used as potential features. To reduce the dimensionality of text features, we used principal component analysis on the N-grams and linguistic features data and explored different strategies to achieve high levels of performance in the automatic classification. We considered all features in isolation and in conjunction. We tested different thresholds to filter out very common and uncommon N-grams and to keep the most important components from the principal component analyses.

The best classification results were obtained with 19 components that explain 95% of variance of the linguistic features. Adding the main components of the unigrams and trigrams harmed the performance. The main components from the bigrams performed almost as well as the linguistic features alone. Bigrams generally helped to improve the classification of non-mobilizations, but made the classification of passive mobilizations slightly worse. Therefore, we chose the classifiers that use linguistic components only.

Overall, the classifier has an accuracy level of 0.70. An examination of the predicted values by label (see Table 1) reveals that the classifier achieves very high performance at classifying *active mobilizations* (high recall and precision) and a good performance for *passive mobilizations*. However, it fails more often at classifying *non-mobilizations*. Table 2 shows the confusion matrix of predicted and true labels for the testing set. Given that we have more confidence in the classification of *mobilizations*, we focus our data analysis on them.

Table 1: Performance of the automatic classification

Predicted labels	Active mobilization	Passive mobilization	Non-mobilization
Recall	0.8600	0.5952	0.50000
Precision	0.8113	0.6944	0.42105
Balanced accuracy	0.8438	0.7143	0.69022

Table 2: Confusion matrix of the automatic classification

Predicted labels	True labels		
	Active mobiliz.	Passive mobiliz.	Non-mobiliz.
Active mobilization	43	9	1
Passive mobilization	4	25	7
Non-mobilization	3	8	8

Given that linguistic-based components are the only input of our classifier, we present here a description of the most distinctive linguistic features according to our ground truth. Figure 1[6] shows

---

[6]In Figure 1, observations are the number posts in the ground truth. The next columns show average count of linguistic features as follows. sentcnt: sentences, wc: words, dic_wc: LIWC dictionary words, funct: function words, social: words about social processes, affect: words about affective processes; cogmech: words about cognitive

Label	observations	sentcnt	wc	dic_wc	funct	social	affect	cogmech	percept
Non mobilizations	119	10.50	206.70	159.37	0.61	0.12	0.05	0.17	0.02
Passive mobilizations	190	8.36	147.56	114.10	0.61	0.14	0.06	0.20	0.02
Active mobilizations	240	8.75	170.60	122.94	0.53	0.14	0.06	0.17	0.02

Label	posemo	negemo	tentat	p1	p2	p3	past	present	future
Non mobilizations	0.04	0.01	0.03	0.05	0.01	0.01	0.04	0.07	0.01
Passive mobilizations	0.04	0.01	0.04	0.04	0.02	0.02	0.03	0.09	0.01
Active mobilizations	0.05	0.01	0.03	0.03	0.02	0.01	0.01	0.07	0.02

Label	motion	space	time	work	achieve	leisure	home	money	death
Non mobilizations	0.03	0.10	0.07	0.04	0.02	0.01	0.02	0.01	0.00
Passive mobilizations	0.02	0.09	0.06	0.03	0.02	0.02	0.03	0.01	0.00
Active mobilizations	0.03	0.11	0.08	0.06	0.03	0.03	0.02	0.01	0.00

Figure 1: Linguistic features by the three kinds of mobilizations

the average prevalence of each linguistic feature in each of the three human-defined content labels and reveals the following patterns:

- *Active mobilizations* have the smallest proportions of function words (which includes pronouns, articles and adverbs) and verbs in past tense. They also have the largest proportions of positive emotions, verbs in future tense, and words related to space, time, work and leisure.
- *Passive mobilizations* have the largest ratio of words associated with home, cognitive processes (especially tentative words), and verbs in present tense.
- *Non-mobilizations* tend to be the longest posts and have the smallest proportions of words that represent affective processes, second person pronouns, and leisure-related words. They also have the maximum ratios of first person pronouns and verbs in past tense.

Across all kinds of content, there were larger proportions of positive than negative emotions. A closer look at the sub-categories of passive mobilizations revealed that *recommendations* and *factual knowledge* tended to include more tentative words such as maybe, perhaps and guess. They also had larger proportions of verbs in present tense. These kinds of content and *opinion/poll* used more first person pronouns. Once we collapsed all infrequent kinds of mobilizations into *passive mobilizations*, the majority of the trends of these features were preserved. One exception is that requests for *factual knowledge* had a more distinctive pattern of features than other passive mobilizations, and this distinction was lost (averaged up/down) when we included *factual knowledge* in a larger category. This is a limitation of our automatic classification.

The automatic classifier was used to predict the kind of content of 32,362 posts that initiated a new thread of conversation in an E-Democracy neighborhood forum. A total of 541 posts could not be automatically classified because they had paragraphs written in a language other than English or had no words that were identified by our algorithm. Table 3 details the number and proportion of

posts that were categorized into each kind of content by the human annotators and the machine classifiers, respectively. Table 4 shows examples of posts for each kind of automatically-coded label.

Table 3: Ground-truth vs. machine classification

Human-labeled categories	Posts (%)	Machine-classified categories	Posts (%)
Social coordination/ invitation/offer	240 (47%)	Active mobilization	15,272 (47.19%)
Recommendation Factual knowledge Opinion/poll Favor/request/ collective action	35 (7%) 24 (5%) 28 (5%) 103 (20%)	Passive mobilization	10,926 (33.76%)
Non-mobilization	86 (17%)	Non-mobilization	6,164 (19.05%)

The predicted values estimate the prevalence of *active mobilizations* to be 47.19% of the content, which is very similar to the ratio found in the human-annotated categorization (47%). Among the other kinds of content, the proportion of *passive mobilizations* in the full set of tests is 33.76%, slightly smaller than the ratio in the manually-coded posts. The remaining 19.05% are classified as *non-mobilizations*, which is a somewhat higher than the proportion of this kind in our ground truth.

The predicted labels were later used to obtain the average proportion of each kind of content in the neighborhood forums across their lifecycle (in quarters). Table 5 shows the descriptive statistics of such measure. The average neighborhood forum has 53.89% of posts requesting *active mobilizations*, such as events or offers that require social coordination (range: 14% - 100%). The mean percentage of *passive mobilizations* and *non-mobilizations* are about 30% and 20%, respectively. Note that these figures are different to the overall prevalence of the same kinds of content in the complete dataset (shown in Table 3). The difference means that, in most of

processes, percept: words about perceptual processes, posemo: positive emotions, negemo: negative emotions, tentat: tentative words, p1: first personal pronouns, p2: second personal pronouns, p3: third personal pronouns, past: past tense, present: present tense, future: future tense. The remaining columns show the mean count of words related to motion, space, time, work, achievement, leisure, money and death.

Table 4: Examples of posts and their categorizations

Active mobilization: "*NNO event on Hoyt street between Rice and Marion. 4:30-7:30. Block party and everyone is welcome. Free food and fun. Come join us and the theme this year is wear blue. Hope to see you as we come together for community*" [**human-labeled category: Social coordination/invitation/offer**]
Passive mobilization: "*I am looking for a 'no-Jobs-too-small' handyman, replacing a screen under a porch where I can no longer crawl, etc.. Anyone have a referral or recommendation? Thanks*" [**human-labeled category: recommendation**]
Non-Mobilization: "*Our bottom front door glass was smashed and the store was broken into last night around midnight. Nothing appears to have been taken.*" [**human-labeled category: Non-mobilization**]

our observations (i.e. forums in a quarter), *active mobilizations* are overrepresented and *passive mobilizations* are underrepresented in regard to the overall trend.

Table 5 also includes the average level of responsiveness in the forums and this reveals that approximately 30% of the posts starting a new thread receive at least one response. Thus, on average, most new threads in a local forum do not receive any response.

Table 5: Content measures of local forums by quarter

Independent variable	Mean	Std. Dev.	Min	Max
% active mobilizations	53.89	16.44	14.29	100
% passive mobilizations	29.93	13.20	5.56	100
% non-mobilizations	19.68	11.28	2.70	100
% responded new threads	29.38	15.55	0	100

5 RQ2: IMPACT OF CONTENT ON SUSTAINABILITY

To answer our second research question, we considered the demographic characteristics of the local communities that were served by the E-Democracy forums. Table 6 shows the mean, dispersion and range of the variables considered in this study. The forums target areas with population sizes ranging from 2,833 to 36,255 inhabitants. Out of the total population in an area, the percentage of people of color ranges from 10.2% to 86.3%. The percentage of households with new residents (those who moved into the neighborhood in 2005 or later) varies from 16% to 60.2%. These variations allow us to account for variability of community demographics when assessing the relationship between content and sustainability.

Table 6: Demographics of the forums' local communities

Independent variable	Mean	St.Dev.	Min	Max
Size: Population	12,412	8.527	2,833	36,255
Diversity: % people of color	42.89	22.31	10.2	86.3
Instability: % moved in 2005+	35.53	10.82	16	60.2

On average, a forum attracts 34 new members and 9 new contributors in a quarter (see Table 7). The maximum number of users who have joined a forum in a quarter is 345 people. The most active forum has attracted 60 new contributors in a single quarter. From

one quarter to the next, neighborhood forums on average retain 23 of its contributors. In a quarter, the forums garner a mean number of 152 posts. The range of this measure goes from a single post to 1,180 posts in a quarter.

We used longitudinal models to estimate the association between aggregated content measures at a given quarter (time t) and the measures of attraction, retention and performance at the following quarter (time $t+1$) while controlling for the potential neighborhood effect, the forum's time of creation and tenure at each observation period. We also controlled for the same dependent variable as measured in the prior quarter. We made this decision as a way to control for the effect of hidden variables that could affect the dependent variable in every quarter, but we could not measure. Table 8 reports the results of the four dependent variables. For each dependent variable, it includes the results of two alternative analyses using either the ratio of active mobilizations or the ratio of passive mobilizations.

Table 7: Dependent variables that represent sustainability

Dependent variable	Mean	Std. Dev.	Min	Max
# new members	34.308	39.381	1	345
# new contributors	9.593	11.638	0	60
# retained contributors	23.519	34.932	0	171
# posts	152.645	215.039	1	1180

5.1 Attraction

Larger proportions of passive mobilizations are significantly associated with more new members and new contributors in the next quarter (see Table 8, columns 1-4). The relationship between the proportion of active mobilization and attraction measures is positive but not statistically significant. These results provide support for a positive association between mobilization requests and attraction.

While the ratio of posts that received at least one response is negatively related to attraction of new members, it is positively associated with the number of new contributors. It is possible that responsiveness is perceived negatively (e.g., as controversial, heated arguments) by outsiders and thus discourages people from joining the forums. However, once people are part of the forums, the interpretation of responsiveness is more positive and encourages further active participation.

We controlled for the time of creation of each forum and the tenure of the forum at the observation period. Forums that were

Table 8: Attraction, retention and performance of hyper-local forums

	(1) # new members	(2) # new members	(3) # new contributors	(4) # new contributors	(5) # retained contributors	(6) # retained contributors	(7) # posts	(8) # posts
L.% active mob.	1.001		1.001		0.999		1.006***	
L.% passive mob.		1.011***		1.006*		1.008***		0.999
L.% responded	0.995***	0.993***	1.006**	1.005*	1.014***	1.012***	1.007***	1.005***
Created 2011+	0.379***	0.378***	0.363***	0.367***	0.424***	0.430***	0.404***	0.420***
F. tenure	0.957***	0.957***	0.999	0.998	1.023***	1.023***	1.020***	1.021***
log population	3.056**	3.897***	2.805*	2.967*	1.422	1.469	1.782	1.834
% of color	0.999	1.003	1.002	1.003	1.013*	1.014*	1.012*	1.013*
% moved 2005+	0.974**	0.967***	0.958**	0.959**	0.960**	0.961**	0.952***	0.953***
L.# new members	0.999***	0.998***						
L.# new contrib.			1.010***	1.009***				
L.# retained contrib.					1.006***	1.006***		
L.# posts							1.001***	1.001***
Observations	407	383	375	373	342	340	383	381
AIC	10251.0	9576.2	2887.1	2875.3	2552.5	2525.2	12605.8	12688.0
BIC	10291.0	9615.7	2926.3	2914.5	2590.9	2563.5	12645.3	12727.5

Exponentiated coefficients

* $p < 0.05$, ** $p < 0.01$, *** $p < 0.001$

created in 2011 or later are less likely to engage new users and new contributors. This indicates that forums created more recently struggle more than older forums to attract neighbors as users. This can be due to the larger number of alternative hyper-local social technologies that have become available for local communities in the past few years. Tenure has a negative relationship to attraction of new members. This behavior hints that more new members are engaged in early phases of the forums' lifecycle.

Among the community demographics, size and instability of the neighborhoods are related to both attraction measures. Forums that serve larger neighborhoods attract more people as new members and new contributors. Instability of the neighborhoods' populations is negatively associated with the same variables; i.e. forums belonging to neighborhoods with larger proportions of new residents attract fewer neighbors as users. Population diversity was not a significant factor on any of the measures of forum attraction.

5.2 Retention

Both the proportion of passive mobilizations and responsiveness have a significant relationship to retention (see Table 8, columns 5-6). Larger proportions of passive mobilizations are expected to increase the number of contributors that remain active from one quarter to the next. In turn, more responsiveness positively affects the number of retained contributors in the next quarter.

Time is a significant aspect on retention. Forums that were created in 2011 or later are expected to retain significantly fewer contributors. Over time, and after controlling for other measures, the neighborhoods forums are expected to maintain more of their contributors from one quarter to the next.

Neighborhoods' population size has a less relevant impact on retention as compared to attraction measures. Neighborhood diversity and instability are related to contributor retention. Forums

belonging to more diverse neighborhoods retain significantly more of their contributors. On the contrary, forums of neighborhoods with larger proportions of new residents keep fewer contributors active from one quarter to the next one.

5.3 Performance

Different to prior measures of sustainability, higher prevalence of active mobilizations (instead of passive ones) are related to larger number of posts in the following quarter (Table 8, columns 7-8). Higher responsiveness is also positively associated with future content creation in hyper-local forums.

Time, again, plays a significant role. Newer forums are associated with lower volume of posts than older forums. Altogether, newer forums have more difficulty becoming sustainable in terms of attraction and performance, but not retention. Tenure has a positive relationship to performance. Over time, forums are likely to garner more posts.

Similar to retention, neighborhood diversity and instability have significant relationships to forum performance. Compared to homogeneous neighborhoods, more diverse neighborhoods are expected to have forums with higher volume of posts. On the contrary, forums belonging to neighborhoods with high population instability have worse performance. The more newly-arrived residents a neighborhood has, the fewer posts its forum gather.

5.4 Where is the balance point?

To find out what is a good balance between passive and active mobilizations, we categorized the neighborhood forums into more active and less active forums. To do so, we studied the trends of number of contributors over time and computed the coefficient of variation of the number of contributors by quarter. Using these data, we classified forums into five subcategories: *up* includes forums with increasing numbers of contributors over time; *stable* comprises forums with stable numbers of contributors over time, always fourteen people or greater; *inverted U* contains forums that show curvilinear trends with an increasing trend at the beginning followed by a consistent decreasing pattern in more recent quarters; *unstable* covers forums with high variability on the numbers of contributors over time; and *stable-neg* consists of forums that have stable numbers of contributors fewer than fourteen people. While the categories *up* and *stable* tend to have low coefficients of variance, the categories *unstable* and *inverted U* often present higher coefficients of variance. To simplify our analysis, we grouped these categories into two groups: *more active* includes the categories *up* and *stable*, and *less active* comprises the remaining categories.

Beyond having a larger number of contributors, the forums that were categorized as *more active* have on average more new members, more new contributors, more retained contributors, and more posts. These differences are statistically significant. Table 9 shows the mean and standard deviation (in parentheses) of each sustainability measure.

Compared to less active forums, more active forums have smaller proportions of active mobilizations, higher shares of passive mobilizations, and higher ratios of responsiveness to posts that create a new thread of conversation (see Table 10). In an average active forum, slightly less than half of posts are active mobilizations and more than 30% are passive mobilizations. This combination is accompanied by a response rate of a third of all new threads created in a quarter.

Table 9: Sustainability measures by activity level

	# new members	# new contributors	# retained contributors	# posts
Less active	26.52 (40.91)	3.61 (5.48)	5.40 (5.35)	42.01 (49.68)
More active	43.63 (35.37)	15.91 (13.01)	42.37 (42.01)	269.43 (256.87)

Table 10: Content measures by activity level

	% active	% passive	% non-mob.	% responded
Less active	58.43 (18.12)	28.62 (17.04)	20.83 (14.12)	25.46 (17.94)
More active	47.18 (10.65)	32.52 (10.91)	19.28 (6.17)	34.34 (12.73)

6 DISCUSSION

To assess the relationship between shared content and collective measures of sustainability of hyper-local online forums, we conducted an automatic classification of all posts that started a new thread in the 35 neighborhood forums.

Exploring our first research question, our study shows that ***textual features can enable an automatic classification of requests for social capital mobilization***. We found that simple linguistic features are enough to distinguish between active and passive mobilizations with reasonable accuracy. *Active mobilizations* include social coordinations, invitations and offers that generally request offline actions such as going somewhere. *Passive mobilizations* comprise other kinds of requests that often ask for on-site actions, such as recommendations and questions about factual knowledge. A key difference lies in the verbs in different tenses. While *passive mobilizations* use verbs in present tense, *active mobilizations* are characterized by verbs in future tense. Another important difference relates to places. While *passive mobilizations* often include words related to home concepts, *active mobilizations* are more associated to work and leisure concepts. These linguistic differences hint the conceptual differences between these kinds of content. Active mobilizations are often invitations to undertake activities somewhere outside the home and at a time in the future. Indeed, these posts are also more prone to include words related to space and time, which can be characterizing location and timing of local events and working hours of local services. The higher use of emotional words also connect to the idea of trying to candidly encourage people to do things. On the other hand, passive mobilizations are about more immediate needs (present tense). The higher prevalence of words related to home might be indicating that these needs are often associated with various home issues (see an example in Table 4). These posts are also more likely to have tentative words, which can be revealing the question-like style of passive mobilizations. Finally, and even though the automatic classification of *non-mobilizations* is less reliable, the linguistic features of the human-annotated non-mobilizations also seem to connect to the conceptual meaning of this label. *Non-mobilizations* have more verbs in past tense and first person pronouns while have fewer second person pronouns and leisure-related words. This goes along with the concept of a post's author reporting a fact without asking the reader to do something about it. Together, these linguistic patterns allowed the machine classifiers to perform well enough to conduct further analysis on a significantly larger-scale dataset, thus confirming the potential of machine content classification

Most content aims to mobilize the local community: As many community information systems aim to increase social capital, they have often been assessed regarding their impact on the neighbors' social ties. Based on self-reporting research methods, researchers have found that hyper-local technologies have a positive influence on social capital. To complement this evidence, we have taken another research approach. We analyzed the content shared in 35 community information systems to find out whether it reveals a connection with social capital. Our approach shows that about 80% of the posts that initiate a new thread in a quarter are mobilization requests. These represent user attempts to mobilize the social connections —and associated resources— that are available through the hyper-local information system. This proportion is significantly larger than the 4.4% of posts that were categorized as mobilization requests in a study of Facebook [7], where users draw resources from their ego-centric social networks. We interpret this high occurrence rate of mobilization requests as additional evidence that local online systems are closely related to exercising social capital within the neighborhoods. Further research can consolidate the connection between different kinds of mobilization requests and self-reported assessments of social capital.

Beyond the high prevalence of mobilization requests, *different kinds of mobilizations have divergent consequences on sustainability*. Considering the two kinds of mobilizations that we were able to distinguish using an automatic content classification, active mobilizations such as event announcements or requests to meet up account for a majority of the posts in the neighborhood forums. Moreover, larger proportions of this kind of mobilizations are positively associated with more posts in a subsequent period of time. This might indicate that certain users frequently use the forums to post active mobilizations (thus influencing performance over time). However, the ratio of active mobilizations is not significantly related to attraction or retention. In turn, passive mobilizations positively are associated with attraction and retention, but have no role on performance at the collective level. We conclude that a good balance between active and passive mobilization requests is needed to maintain an active stream of content in the forums without allowing the forums to become a one-way information dissemination tool. Active E-Democracy forums had on average 47% active mobilizations and 32% of passive mobilizations (std. dev. of 10% for both). These proportions are indicators of a trade-off that works well for the E-Democracy neighborhood forums. Further research can automatically classify content to monitor the proportions of different kinds of mobilization requests and encourage corrective actions when some of these proportion deviates significantly from a healthy balance.

Once we account for content, *the level of overall responsiveness in the forums has mixed effects*. Responsiveness is associated with more new contributors and more posts. This means that once people are involved in the forums, responsiveness helps sustainability. However, responsiveness reduces the attraction of new members. The positive effect of making people contribute do not extend to broaden the forums' audience. It is possible that outsiders do not perceive responsiveness as a major benefit of the forums, but as a burden. Responsiveness might be seen as information overload that can discourage people from joining. Mechanisms to avoid this negative effect of responsiveness in attraction need to be tested in further work.

Finally, all of our control variables have significant associations with sustainability. The results confirm that there is a neighborhood effect on sustainability of hyper-local technologies. Neighborhoods with larger populations attract more new members and new contributors; however, this effect does not extend to other key sustainability measures. Neighborhood diversity is related to more contributor retention and content generation. Instability of the neighborhoods' populations is negatively associated with all measures of sustainability. A potential explanation for the latter result can be also connected to social capital. Residential instability is associated with lower levels of neighborhood social capital [15]; therefore, this result might be indicating that neighborhoods with low social capital to start with struggle to sustain hyper-local social technologies as one of their communication media.

Further, timing variables are also important. More recently created forums were associated with lower sustainability. As forums become older, attraction of new members declines while forums'

retention and performance improve. We speculate that these results reflect that newer forums face more competition as more hyper-local social technologies have become available recently. Nevertheless, the effect of this competition weakens as time goes by and the forums engage enough users to survive. Overall, these findings confirm that contextual variables are critical to understand when and how hyper-local social technologies thrive.

This work has limitations proper of any research endeavor. We have used the archival data of a sample of local forums in a specific state in the US, which might not be representative of hyper-local technologies for local communities in different cultural and social contexts. While we strove to control for neighborhood demographics, we could not control for other variables that could have affected the results, such as the average level of civic engagement in the neighborhood. Further, we were not able to control for the number of contributors due to multicollinearity with the neighborhood's population size. Additionally, our classifier performed better at identifying active mobilizations than any other content label. This characteristic could have led to results that under-estimate the prevalence of passive mobilizations and non-mobilizations in the forums. In spite of these limitations, we believe that our results contribute to deepen the understanding of how hyper-local technologies function by providing new evidence of the connection between content, social capital, and sustainability of hyper-local social technologies through a longitudinal study of the same platform across several local communities.

7 CONCLUSIONS

In this work, we presented the results of an automatic classification of all posts shared in 35 long-tenure hyper-local discussion forums in the US. The results show that linguistic characteristics of the posts enable automatic classifiers to distinguish between requests for active and passive actions. We interpret these requests as attempts to mobilize the community social capital available through the hyper-local technology. Together, these mobilization requests account for about 80% of the content shared in the forums every quarter, thus providing further evidence of the connection between community information technologies and social capital development. We also report on a longitudinal data analysis of the association between content and sustainability measures. We found that while passive mobilizations drive measures of user participation, active mobilizations play a key role on content creation in the future. Based on this empirical findings, a balance between these two kinds of mobilizations is recommended.

8 ACKNOWLEDGMENTS

The authors would like to thank E-Democracy.org for providing its data and domain knowledge. This work was partially funded by CONICYT Chile, under grant Conicyt-Fondecyt Iniciación 11161026, and a Google Research Faculty Award.

REFERENCES

[1] Brian S. Butler. 2001. Membership Size, Communication Activity, and Sustainability: A Resource-Based Model of Online Social Structures. *Info. Sys. Research* 12, 4 (2001), 346–362.
[2] John M. Carroll. 2012. *The Neighborhood in the Internet*. Routledge, Chapter What are community networks?, 23–47.

[3] John M. Carroll and Mary Beth Rosson. 1996. Developing the Blacksburg electronic village. *Commun. ACM* 39, 12 (1996), 69–74.

[4] John M Carroll, Patrick C Shih, Jess Kropczynski, Guoray Cai, Mary Beth Rosson, and Kyungsik Han. 2016. The Internet of Places at Community-Scale: Design Scenarios for Hyperlocal. *Enriching Urban Spaces with Ambient Computing, the Internet of Things, and Smart City Design* (2016), 1.

[5] Ken Colstad and Efrem Lipkin. 1975. Community memory: a public information network. *SIGCAS Comput. Soc.* 6, 4 (1975), 6–7.

[6] Aldo de Moor. 2009. Moving community informatics research forward. *The Journal of Community Informatics* 5, 1 (2009).

[7] Nicole B Ellison, Rebecca Gray, Jessica Vitak, Cliff Lampe, and Andrew T Fiore. 2013. Calling All Facebook Friends: Exploring Requests for Help on Facebook. In *Proceedings of the International Conference on Weblogs and Social Media (ICWSM '13)*.

[8] Marcus Foth. 2006. Analyzing the factors influencing the successful design and uptake of interactive systems to support social networks in urban neighborhoods. *International Journal of Technology and Human Interaction* 2, 2 (2006), 65–79.

[9] Samah Gad, Naren Ramakrishnan, Keith N. Hampton, and Andrea Kavanaugh. 2012. Bridging the Divide in Democratic Engagement: Studying Conversation Patterns in Advantaged and Disadvantaged Communities. In *Proceedings of the 2012 International Conference on Social Informatics*. 165–176.

[10] Keith N. Hampton. 2002. Place-Based and IT Mediated "Community". *Planning Theory & Practice* 3, 2 (2002), 228–231.

[11] Keith N. Hampton. 2007. Neighborhoods in the Network Society the e-Neighbors study. *Information, Communication & Society* 10, 5 (2007), 714–748.

[12] Keith N. Hampton and Barry Wellman. 2003. Neighboring in Netville: How the Internet Supports Community and Social Capital in a Wired Suburb. *City & Community* 2, 4 (2003), 277–311.

[13] Nicholas W Jankowski, Martine Van Selm, and Ed Hollander. 2001. On crafting a study of digital community networks. *Community informatics: Shaping computer-mediated social relations* (2001), 101–117.

[14] Bonnie J Johnson and Germaine R Halegoua. 2014. Potential and challenges for social media in the neighborhood context. *Journal of Urban Technology* 21, 4 (2014), 51–75.

[15] Naewon Kang and Nojin Kwak. 2003. A Multilevel Approach to Civic Participation Individual Length of Residence, Neighborhood Residential Stability, and Their Interactive Effects With Media Use. *Communication Research* 30, 1 (2003), 80–106.

[16] Andrea L Kavanaugh and Scott J Patterson. 2001. The Impact of Community Computer Networks on Social Capital and Community Involvement. *American Behavioral Scientist* 45, 3 (2001), 496–509.

[17] Cliff Lampe, Rebecca Gray, Andrew T. Fiore, and Nicole Ellison. 2014. Help is on the Way: Patterns of Responses to Resource Requests on Facebook. In *Proceedings of the 17th ACM Conference on Computer Supported Cooperative Work & Social Computing (CSCW '14)*. 3–15.

[18] Nan Lin. 1999. Building a Network Theory of Social Capital. *Connections* 22, 1 (1999), 28–51.

[19] Claudia López and Brian S Butler. 2013. Consequences of content diversity for online public spaces for local communities. In *Proceedings of the 2013 Conference on Computer Supported Cooperative Work (CSCW '13)*. 673–682.

[20] Claudia López and Rosta Farzan. 2015. Lend Me Sugar, I Am Your Neighbor!: A Content Analysis of Online Forums for Local Communities. In *Proceedings of the 7th International Conference on Communities and Technologies (C&T '15)*. 59–67.

[21] Claudia López, Yu-Ru Lin, and Rosta Farzan. 2015. What Makes Hyper-local Online Discussion Forums Sustainable?. In *Proceedings of the 48th Hawaii International Conference on System Sciences (HICSS '15)*. 2445–2454.

[22] David R. Millen and John F. Patterson. 2002. Stimulating social engagement in a community network. In *Proceedings of the 2002 ACM Conference on Computer Supported Cooperative Work (CSCW '02)*. 306–313.

[23] Dara O'Neil. 2002. Assessing community informatics: a review of methodological approaches for evaluating community networks and community technology centers. *Internet Research* 12, 1 (2002), 76–102.

[24] Karen E Pettigrew, Joan C Durrance, and Kenton T Unruh. 2002. Facilitating community information seeking using the Internet: Findings from three public library–community network systems. *Journal of the American Society for Information Science and Technology* 53, 11 (2002), 894–903.

[25] Damian Radcliffe. 2012. *Here and Now UK Hyperlocal media today*. Technical Report. Nesta.

[26] Lyn Simpson. 2005. Community Informatics and Sustainability: Why Social Capital Matters. *The Journal of Community Informatics* 1, 2 (2005), 102–119.

[27] Yi-Chia Wang and Robert Kraut. 2012. Twitter and the development of an audience: those who stay on topic thrive!. In *Proceedings of the 2012 ACM Annual Conference on Human Factors in Computing Systems (CHI '12)*. 1515–1518.

[28] Yi-Chia Wang, Robert Kraut, and John M. Levine. 2012. To stay or leave?: the relationship of emotional and informational support to commitment in online health support groups. In *Proceedings of the ACM 2012 Conference on Computer Supported Cooperative Work (CSCW '12)*. 833–842.

[29] Kate Williams and Joan C Durrance. 2008. Social Networks and Social Capital : Rethinking Theory in Community Informatics. *The Journal of Community Informatics* 4, 3 (2008), 1–20.

Tags, Titles or Q&As? Choosing Content Descriptors for Visual Recommender Systems

Belgin Mutlu	Eduardo Veas	Christoph Trattner
Know-Center GmbH	Know-Center GmbH	MODUL University Vienna
bmutlu@know-center.at	eveas@know-center.at	christoph.trattner@modul.ac.at

ABSTRACT

In today's digital age with an increasing number of websites, social/learning platforms, and different computer-mediated communication systems, finding valuable information is a challenging and tedious task, regardless from which discipline a person is. However, visualizations have shown to be effective in dealing with huge datasets: because they are grounded on visual cognition, people understand them and can naturally perform visual operations such as clustering, filtering and comparing quantities. But, creating appropriate visual representations of data is also challenging: it requires domain knowledge, understanding of the data, and knowledge about task and user preferences. To tackle this issue, we have developed a recommender system that generates visualizations based on (i) a set of visual cognition rules/guidelines, and (ii) filters a subset considering user preferences. A user places interests on several aspects of a visualization, the task or problem it helps to solve, the operations it permits, or the features of the dataset it represents. This paper concentrates on characterizing user preferences, in particular: i) the sources of information used to describe the visualizations, the content descriptors respectively, and ii) the methods to produce the most suitable recommendations thereby. We consider three sources corresponding to different aspects of interest: a title that describes the chart, a question that can be answered with the chart (and the answer), and a collection of tags describing features of the chart. We investigate user-provided input based on these sources collected with a crowd-sourced study. Firstly, information-theoretic measures are applied to each source to determine the efficiency of the input in describing user preferences and visualization contents (user and item models). Secondly, the practicability of each input is evaluated with content-based recommender system. The overall methodology and results contribute methods for design and analysis of visual recommender systems. The findings in this paper highlight the inputs which can (i) effectively encode the content of the visualizations and user's visual preferences/interest, and (ii) are more valuable for recommending personalized visualizations.

CCS CONCEPTS

•**Information systems → Recommender systems;**

HT'17, July 4-7, 2017, Prague, Czech Republic.
© 2017 ACM. 978-1-4503-4708-2/17/07...$15.00
DOI: http://dx.doi.org/10.1145/3078714.3078741

KEYWORDS

Recommending visualizations; information theory; user modeling; personalization

1 INTRODUCTION

The effectiveness of personalized recommender systems (RS) highly depends on user and item profile completeness and accuracy [17]. Hence, regardless of the approach, the key factor in personalized recommendations is the decision about how to exploit the relevant information about the user and items, and more important, which information better describes the properties of items and the preferences/needs of a user. Collaborative filtering approaches for instance use ratings, while content based approaches build on user-provided input, typically in form of tags and comments. Rating is fast, simple, and effective in communicating user preferences also in the context of visualizations [16], but it does not indicate much about goals or intentions of the user regarding the item. Annotating visualizations with tags brings extra benefits, as a user indicates her insights and interpretation of the data being visualized, i.e., issuing details with keywords pulled from a personal vocabulary [15, 27, 28]. Hereby, visualizations are organized for later retrieval.

There are two caveats in these approaches to personalizing visualizations: 1) people are often reluctant to give a feedback, 2) ratings and tags forego information about the context where the item was used. Unless the benefit is evident, users rarely engage in tagging or rating items. This is true in the context [4, 27] and can be more acute for visualizations where the user is possibly engaged in a thought process that would be interrupted by rating/tagging. More importantly, a single rating does not tell much about goals or intentions of the user. Whereas tags encode features of the item, it is not evident that users will include their task or intentions when tagging a chart. Our working question is: can we use alternative sources to derive item descriptions suitable for recommendation?

In the context of visualizations, user's provided input (annotations) can take other forms. For instance, it is common for user to pose a question that is answered with a visualization, or to define a title and description for the visualization in form of a caption. We consider these two alternative sources of information (titles, questions&answers (Q&As)) as potential descriptors both of item and user intentions. To investigate how effectively they encode information, each information source (tags, titles, Q&As) is characterized using information-theoretic measures, such as entropy, conditional entropy and mutual information, as suggested in Chi et al. [3, 11]. Finally, using each of these sources separately, we build models for user and item profiles to recommend personalized visualizations applying a content based recommender. This allows us to obtain insights and draw general conclusions about the drawbacks and benefits for each source as input for the visual recommender systems. The input data for our studies was obtained with a crowd-sourced experiment involving 47 participants that had to provide accurate description of each visualization in forms of tags, a title and a question it may answer.

In a nutshell this paper makes the following contributions. We propose a framework to assess the encoding power of different textual information sources in describing user preferences and visualizations. The framework is used in a thorough analysis of different kinds of user-provided input characterizing data models for user and visualizations. We derive insights on how their nature impacts the generation of personalized visualization recommendations.

2 RELATED WORK

One of the key concerns in personalizing recommendations is building personalized profiles of individual users and candidate items. These profiles constitute models of (i) individual user characteristics describing what the user needs and prefers— user model, and (ii) item characteristics describing what the items represent, their content respectively— item model. Yet content-based recommender systems try to define personalized recommendations by matching up the attributes of the user model with the attributes of the item model. However the following questions arise: (i) which source of information is most effective at encoding user preferences and item characteristics, (ii) which source of information yields the more accurate recommendations, and finally (iii) how to acquire this information from the user.

In traditional content based recommendation approaches, systems collect user preferences by explicitly asking users to share their interest and needs, typically in form of tags. Although partially successful, these approaches often suffer on the missing motivation of the user for annotations [5, 13]. However, recent studies on this topic show that user's motivation to annotate resources increases if this provides a navigational aid to the resources [25]. Ricci et al [22], for instance, present a recommender system to help user with searching for travel products. To define recommendations that are closer to user's needs the system asks user to provide critiques in form of textual feedback when one feature of the recommended product is not satisfactory or very important. The authors prove the effectiveness of their system with an empirical study. This also applies for visualizations. When user annotates visualizations, she provides her insights and her interpretation on the data being visualized. Hence, the annotations serve as analysis finding records and personal reminder for later data discovering and analysis tasks [4].

The process of annotating can be considered as an encoding process where the annotations encode the information (facts, features etc.) about the items [25]. However, it depends on the encoding quality of the used annotation type (tags, titles, Q&As) how good a recommender performs. Chi et al. [3] use information-theoretic measures (entropy, conditional entropy, mutual information) to evaluate the encoding power of tags collected from the social tagging site del.icio.us. Using these measures Chi et al. quantify the diversity in tags and documents and the amount of shared information between them. The obtained results finally provide insight into how effective the tags are at encoding documents. Strohmaier

et al. [25] use conditional entropy and orphan ratio for measuring and detecting the tacit nature of tagging motivation by analyzing the tag sets produces by 8 different tagging systems regarding to their encoding and descriptive power. The results of their study show that (i) tagging motivation of individuals varies within and across tagging systems, and (ii) user's motivation for tagging has an influence on produced tags and folksonomies. Yi-ling Lin et al. [11] analyze the tags they collected for images in two different tagging conditions (with and without description) on perspectives such as diversity, specificity, quality, similarity and descriptiveness. The analysis mainly covers common text-quality metrics, such as number of unique- and common words of each content and so far.

Regarding to the research question "which source of information defines the more accurate recommendations" the most notable research is provided by Bellogín [1] et al., who try to identify the sources of information (ratings, tags, social contacts, etc.) most valuable for a recommender in a social music service. To do so Bellogín et al. evaluate a number of content based, collaborative filtering and social recommenders on heterogeneous datasets obtained from Last.fm with well-known metrics precision, recall and ranking based matrix. Next, they compare the characteristics of the generated recommendations using non-performance metrics such as coverage, overlap, diversity and novelty between different set of recommendations.

Our paper extends the research on evaluating the power of annotations (tags, ratings etc.) at encoding documents, music tracks and users' interests in these resources into encoding visualizations and users' visualization preferences. Similar to the relevant works we suggest for this purpose information-theoretic measures entropy, conditional entropy and mutual information as these measures have been proposed in many field to assess the diversity of textual content [8, 14, 29]. Furthermore, we address the question of how valuable different source of information are for recommending visualizations by applying a content based filtering approach as this recommendation approach builds on the content features.

3 APPROACH

We developed a recommender system, called *VizRec*, with the purpose to generate personalized visualizations [15, 16]. The schematic overview of the approach is depicted in Figure 1. VizRec responds to a query with a list of personalized visualizations ordered in a top-n sorted manner. The query is a typical free-form text common in search engines (e.g., "most popular movies 2006-2016"). The response to the query is a dataset compiled by a federated system from various associated sources, each with its proprietary data model. Before passing to VizRec, the data are structured after a common data model with a predefined schema. Within VizRec, two recommendation stages take place. First, a rule-based system applies visual encoding guidelines to generate a collection of visualizations appropriate for the data. Second, the collection is sorted and filtered according to user preferences using a content-based recommender system (CB-RS).

Visual encoding guidelines are generic principles that establish relations between visual components of a visualization (e.g., x-axis of a bar chart) and elements of the data (e.g., whether a field is numeric, categorical, or a location, see Section 3.1). A preprocessing

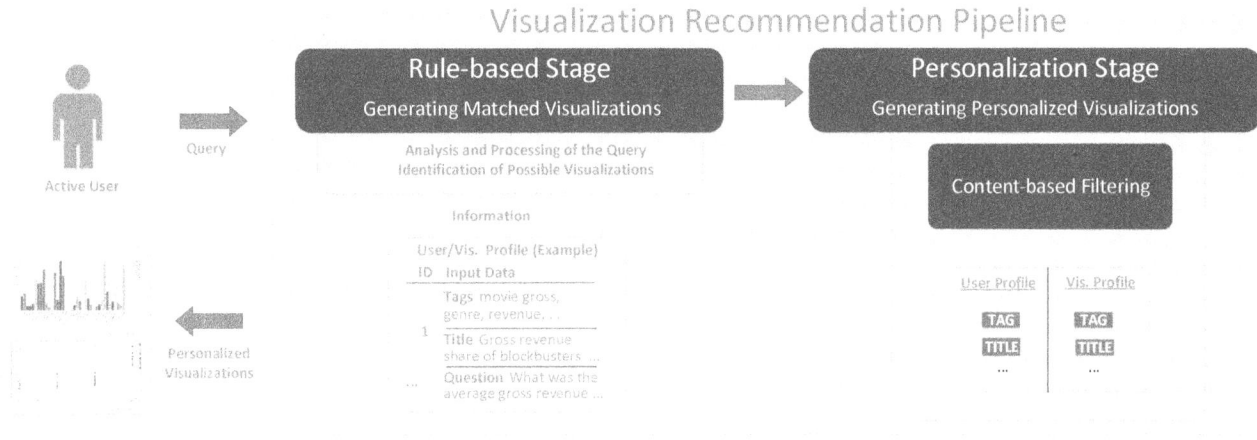

Figure 1: Schematic representation of the visualization recommender: The rule-based stage applies visual encoding guidelines to generate a collection of visualizations appropriate for the data. The personalization stage applies user preferences/profiles (content terms such as tags and titles) and filters the visualizations according to users' needs and interests. This stage also maintains repositories for user preferences/profiles.

unit analyzes the data to structure them in terms of interesting data elements so visual encoding can take place. The three steps to generate personalized visualization recommendations are: (1) preprocessing, (2) visual mapping, and (3) user preference filtering. In the following subsections, we briefly describe each of these units.

3.1 Preprocessing

The preprocessing unit is responsible for extracting and annotating data attributes appropriate for mapping. The input data for VizRec are structured following the specification of the data model described in [18]. The defined specification, concretely, focuses on organizing the different kind of data attributes (content information) extracted from the original sources (ACM digital Library, DBpedia, Mendeley, Europeana etc.). To define the set of appropriate visualizations *VizRec*, first, extracts and analyzes the attributes of the data set being visualized and then categorizes them into standard and/or specific datatypes. The data are categorized into standard datatypes, such as categorical, temporal and numerical – represented by primitive data types string, date and number, respectively. This categorization into primitive datatypes is basically performed by analyzing values of the individual attributes. To do so, the analysis employs a top-down approach, i.e., for a given value it is first decided to which of the aforementioned standard datatypes it belongs. Next, by using gazetteer lists more specialized datatypes are derived, e.g., for spatial information.

Furthermore, the preprocessing unit addresses the task of prior organization of the visualizations into visual patterns each describing one possible combination of visual components of a visualization and data types supported. For instance, two possible patterns for the bar chart are (1) $\{x - axis : string, y - axis : number\}$, and (2) $\{x - axis : date, y - axis : number\}$. These patterns specify the types of data required for a bar chart to be instantiated. Note that the pattern definition is based on so called Visual Analytics (VA) Vocabulary. For more details about the used vocabulary we refer to our previous paper [15].

3.2 Visual Mapping

The visual mapping process can be considered as a schema matching problem [20]. The basic idea behind schema matching is to figure out a semantic relevance between two objects in schemes under consideration. The result is a mapping comprising a set of elements, each of which indicates that certain elements of schema S1 are related to certain elements of schema S2. In our case, the schemes we deal with are on the one hand the data model which describes the input data, and on the other hand the VA Vocabulary which describes the semantics of the visualizations. Hence, the schema matching in our context produces mappings (possible configurations of a visualization) each of which describes the correspondence between a data attribute of user's current data and a visual component of a visualization. Concretely, the relation from a data attribute to a visual component is valid only if we can establish syntactic correspondences between them. One possibility to identify this is to verify the data type compatibility. The preprocessing unit provides visual patterns for visualizations and the data attributes both including the data types of their elements. Thus, to define a valid mapping the mapping operator simply compares the data types of the visual components and data attributes and builds so the list of plausible mappings. For more details about the mapping algorithm we refer to our previous paper [15].

3.3 User Preference Filtering

To finally filter the generated mapping combinations according to the user's preferences, we employ a content based recommender system (CB-RS). In a nutshell, the CB-RS generates recommendations by analyzing the relevant content, concretely, the information we know about the active user and the information we extracted from the items (visualizations). The item specific information might be (i) features describing the item, (ii) annotations user applied to the item, or (iii) both features and annotations. Yet, if the visualization is e.g., a bar chart showing the budget per genre (see Figure 2 top left), the features describing this visualization would be the data fields *genre* and *budget* plotted on the $x - axis$-and $y - axis$. Note that these data fields are extracted from the current dataset they therefore not only represent the content of the visualization but also of the dataset.

Following the basic principles of CB-RS, the recommendations are produced based on the content similarity, in our case between the interests of the active user i.e., her profile, and the content information of the candidate items, item profile respectively. An excerpt of these both profiles is given in Figure 1, in the "User/Vis. Profile" block. Generally, a profile is a collection of terms provided to characterize user or items. Thus, for each user in user profile, there is a set of terms describing interests of that particular user. Yet, a user annotates a visualization with terms which describe its content and thus serve as information sources to profile that particular visualization [2, 11]. To take this into account, our recommender defines the item (=visualization) profiles with the aggregated terms supplied by the current user in the past. Note, before we build the profiles we perform a normalization process on the keywords, which involves, (i) removing of commoner morphological and inflectional endings from English words using the Porter stemmer algorithm [9], (ii) removing of stop words (what, how, some, many, etc.) and punctuations (keyword tokenizer), and finally (iii) the lowercase filtering. This step helps to avoid that the words represented in various language forms are interpreted differently [12]. As mentioned, we address in this paper three types of input data models: tags, title and Q&As. So, for each entry in our user profile, we have normalized terms categorized either to tags, titles or question. However, in our item profile we have normalized terms categorized either to tags, titles or answers.

Similarity Estimation and Item Ranking: To determine the correlation between visualizations and users, we transform the content of the user profiles and item profiles into the Vector Space Model (VSM) with the TF-IDF (Term Frequency-Inverse Document Frequency) weighting schema. VSM is a common technique to vectorize the content and in this way to enable analysis tasks, such as classification and clustering for example. In our case, VSM consists of user profile (the current tags, titles or questions) and item profile (tags, titles or answers user applied to the visualizations in the past), both represented in form of vectors. Concretely, using this scheme, each visualization is defined as an n-dimensional vector, where each dimension corresponds to a term, or more precisely, to the TF-IDF weight of that particular term. To clarify this, let $M = \{m_1, m_2, m_3, ..., m_N\}$ be a set of visualizations and $T = \{t_1, t_2, t_3, ..., t_n\}$ a set of terms in M. Each visualization m_i is represented as a vector in a n-dimensional vector space, i.e., $m_i = w_{1,i}, w_{2,i}, w_{3,i}, ..., w_{n,i}$, where $w_{k,i}$ denotes the weight for the term t_k applied a visualization m_i, i.e.:

$$w_{k,i} = tf_{t_k, m_i} \times idf_t = tf_{t_k, m_i} \times \left[log_e \left(\frac{N}{df_t + 1} \right) + 1 \right] \quad (1)$$

where the former factor of the product is an occurrence frequency of the term t_k applied a visualization m_i, and the later indicates the distribution of the term among the both profiles (i.e., so that particular and commonly occurring terms can be discriminated from each other). We apply the same weighting scheme to define the user profile. Having defined the profiles, it is now possible to

estimate their similarity. To do so, we use the weighting information in the vectors and apply the *cosine similarity* measure [12], defined as follows:

$$sim(m_i, m_j) = \frac{\sum_k \mathbf{w}_{k,i} \mathbf{w}_{k,j}}{\sqrt{\sum_k (\mathbf{w}_{k,i})^2} \sqrt{\sum_k (\mathbf{w}_{k,j})^2}} \quad (2)$$

where m_j denotes the tag (or title, question) collection of the current user. The result of this measure is a cosine value of the angle between two vectors, in our case between the mapping combination and e.g., the tag collection. The retrieved values are then used as scores to rank the relevant visualizations following the Equation:

$$pred_{cb}(m_i, m_j) = \sum_{m_i, m_j \in M} sim(m_i, m_j) \quad (3)$$

Note that the approach of our recommender system is described in detail in our previous paper and is beyond the scope of this paper. For more details please refer to [15].

4 EXPERIMENT SETUP

The goal of the study is to investigate the characteristics of tags, titles, and Q&As and their impact on recommending personalized visualizations. To collect these different kinds of annotations we designed a crowd-sourced study where we asked the user to annotate and rate the visualizations according to the different data sources. In Section 4.1, we provide details about how we collected the annotations (tags, titles, Q&As). In our previous work [16], we have already investigated the characteristics of the collected ratings and their impact on the recommendation quality— on our CF-RS respectively. Thus, here we put focus on tags, titles and Q&As. To that end, we proceed with the experiment as follows:

- First, we analyse how good these three types of input data models encode both user and visualizations (see Section 5). The observations from this part of the experiment shall reveal us some important facts about why some of the inputs are better than the other. Based on those observations, we build a list of candidate inputs for each data set (i.e., which descriptors accurately describe user, and which ones the visualizations). Those are in the end our assumptions that we want to confirm using the offline study.

- Next, we execute our content-based recommender on candidate input data models to see if their encoding power can be confirmed. The results of this study are presented in Section 6.

4.1 Datasets

Visualizations were generated for three open source datasets (see below) using a rule-based visualization recommendation system [15]. Note that the rule-based recommendation system uses heuristic rules that produce visually correct charts, but they are not always useful. Some examples of such charts are given in Figure 2, in the right column. They generally received low ratings since either they were visually useless or do not reveal much about the underlying data (cf. chart for the EU dataset) or they do reveal something, but not enough. For instance, the geo chart on bottom shows countries, but it actually hides all data about book publishers, which is essential to understand what is being visualized. Finally, there were also charts which show enough information, but have in fact

USEFUL VISUALIZATIONS — NOT USEFUL VISUALIZATIONS

Figure 2: Examples of (in average) highest (left) and lowest (right) rated visualizations for all three datasets.

received low ratings. These are typical cases where user expressed their subjective opinions (cf. stacked bar chart on top).

The following datasets have been used for the experiment:
MovieLens dataset (Movies): Top-ranked movies for the years 1960, 1970, 1980, and 1990. The rule based recommender produced for this dataset four types of visualizations (bar chart, line chart, timeline and geo chart) using the method described in [16] with the following frequencies: 32 bar charts, 9 line charts, 13 timelines and 1 geo-chart combinations. Hence, a total of 55 visualizations were generated.
EU Open Linked Data Portal dataset (EU): The percentage of the population looking for educational information online in the years 2009-2011 for 28 EU countries. The rule based recommender suggested 30 possible visualizations, concretely 15 bar charts, 6 line charts, 8 timelines and 1 geo chart.
Book-Crossing dataset (Books): 41 randomly chosen books published between 1960 and 2003. The rule based recommender suggested 3 visualization types: bar chart with 3 combinations, geo chart with 1 combination and timeline with 3 combinations, the total of 7 visualizations respectively.

4.2 Procedure

A crowd-sourced experiment was carefully designed to obtain user preferences in different formats for each chart. While using a crowd-sourced platform, it is important to design the study so that participants do not blindly click through the options. Our datasources require ratings tags, titles, and Q&As for each chart. Following the suggestion of Kittur et al. [10], a cognitively demanding preparatory tasks should bring participants to accurately study the chart and prevent a random or rash answer. Therefore, the task (Human Intelligent Task, HIT) was designed as follows: a participant was given a one line description of a dataset originating the visualization, looking at the visualization she had to: 1) write tags (at most five), 2) write a title, 3) rate it, and finally 4) write a question the chart can answer. Figure 3 shows an example of a HIT. Rating a visualization with a single score would be rather unrealistic. Instead, a multidimensional rating scale lets the user consider various aspects of a visualization. We adapted a multidimensional scale from a list of usability factors presented in [24] and [30]. It included the following factors: (1) cluttered, (2) organized, (3) confusing, (4) easy to understand, (5) boring, (6) exciting, (7) useful, (8) effective and (9) satisfying. Note that dimensions 1-6 are duplicated with opposing sentiment (e.g., cluttered vs. organized). Opposing dimensions were used to ensure meaningful ratings for scales with complex meaning. Dimensions were rated on a 7-point Likert scale (1=not applicable 7=very applicable). After a pilot study, we decided to collect 3 charts per HIT, which makes for sensible task duration (5 min). Charts were distributed in 32 HITs, each with 3 randomly chosen charts. The procedure was as follows: After accepting a HIT, the participant (worker or turker) received a tour to complete a task, which showed a visualization and corresponding tags, title, ratings and Q&As in the exact same format as the subsequent study. The worker started the first task in the HIT by pressing a button. Workers were allowed to write not applicable (NA) for tags, title and Q&As, but were alerted if they failed to write any of these. The rating dimensions were not assigned a score until the worker did it. Workers could only proceed if they wrote the tags, a title, rated all dimensions and provided a question with the corresponding answer. A HIT with three charts was compensated with $1.00. A worker evaluated a minimum of three visualizations and was allowed to perform more than one HIT. Only expert workers who consistently achieved a high degree of accuracy by completing HITs were allowed to take part in the study. To make sure that the quality of collected data is satisfying, all entries have been manually verified. To that end, 10% of workers was rejected from the experiment, since they provided either incomplete or invalid inputs.

4.3 Participants

Each HIT was completed by ten workers. Note, this was the minimum required number on workers per visualization to train our recommender (see Section 6). In total, 47 workers (some of them were assigned to more than one HIT) completed our study. Workers completed on average 4.8 HITs. For 92 visualizations, we collected 8280 ratings across 9 dimensions, 4483 tags, 3881 titles and 4387 Q&As. The experiment started on November 26, 2014 and ended on December 3, 2014. The allotted working time per HIT was 900 sec and the average working time was 570 sec.

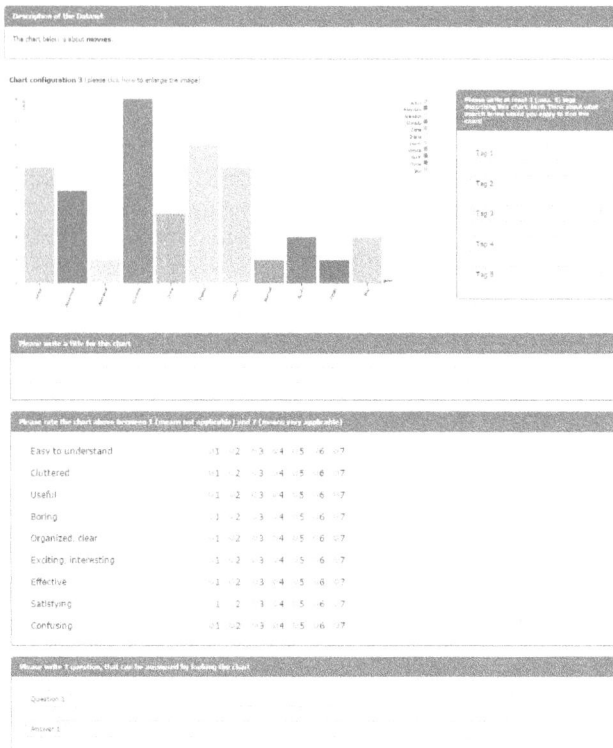

Figure 3: Example of a HIT for our crowd-sourcing experiment. Participants were motivated to carefully observe the visualization with the study task, in terms of writing tags and a title. Thereafter, they had to rate it in a multidimensional scale and pose a question that is answered with the visualization.

5 ENCODING POWER OF USER-PROVIDED INPUT

In this study we aim to explore the characteristics of different user-provided input (annotations) in terms of encoding users and visualizations. Information-theoretic measures are used to characterize the tags, titles, and Q&As.

5.1 Methodology

For the analysis of tags, titles and Q&As we employ information-theoretic measures: entropy, conditional entropy and mutual information. Using information-theoretic measures, we are able to (i) quantify the diversity in annotations (terms in further text), their encoding power respectively, and (ii) the amount of shared information between terms describing users and items (visualizations). With this information, we expect to answer why one input might be more suitable for recommending visualizations than the others.

In information theory, entropy measures the amount of uncertainty in a single random variable [6]. Given a random variable (X), which consist of occurrences $\{x_1 \cdots x_N\}$, each of which occurs with the probability $p(x)$, the entropy $H(X)$ is defined as:

$$H(X) = - \sum_{x \in X} p(x) log(p(x))$$

Table 1: Basic statistical properties of the datasets collected via Amazon Mechanical Turk. Column "User/Vis" shows the average number of user assigned to a visualization; "Vis/User" is the average number of visualizations assigned to a user. Note that the values in brackets indicate number of unique terms.

Dataset	#Vis	#User	Users/Vis	Vis/User	#Tags	#Titles	#Q&As
Movies	55	36	10	15.27	2731 (292)	2217 (295)	2638 (822)
EU	30	19	10	15.79	1403 (166)	1394 (234)	1354 (514)
Books	7	15	10	4.67	349 (87)	270 (92)	395 (188)

Conditional entropy [6], on the other side, measures the uncertainty in a random variable given the value of another random variable. Given two discrete random variables X = $\{x_1 \cdots x_N\}$ and Y = $\{y_1 \cdots y_N\}$ so that the event (x, y) occurs with the joint probability $p(x, y)$, the joint entropy is defined as:

$$H(Y, X) = - \sum_{\{y, x\} \in \{Y, X\}} p(y, x) log(p(y, x))$$

Using this value, conditional entropy is defined as $H(Y|X)$ [3]:

$$H(Y|X) = H(Y, X) - H(X)$$

Concretely, conditional entropy quantifies the amount of information needed to describe the variable X (e.g., user or visualization) when the value of the variable Y (e.g., tags, titles, Q&As) is known. If $H(Y|X)$ is minimized, each tag (or title, Q&A) uniquely refers to an individual user (or visualization) [3]. In contrast, when $H(Y|X)$ is maximized, each tag (or title, Q&A) is as likely as all others.

Finally, mutual information [6] is a measure of independence between two random variables. In other words, it quantifies the amount of data (information) shared (mutual) between variables. Given two discrete random variables X = $\{x_1 \cdots x_N\}$ and Y = $\{y_1 \cdots y_N\}$ so that the event (x, y) occurs with the joint probability $p(x, y)$, the mutual information $I(X; Y)$ is defined as:

$$I(X; Y) = H(Y) - H(Y|X)$$

High mutual information indicates a large dependency between two variables. In contrast, if the mutual information is minimized the variables are independent.

5.2 Results

Table 1 summarizes basic statistics for tags, titles and Q&As and shows the distribution of the entire terms [1] over user and visualizations. As introduced earlier, each of the visualizations in a particular dataset was individually evaluated regarding to tags, titles, and Q&As, i.e., 55 visualizations in Movies dataset, 30 and 7 in EU and Books respectively (cf. the second column in Table 1). For this configuration, user involved in the study have provided overall 4483 tags, 3881 titles, and 4387 Q&As (2% yes/no Q&As). The average worth length (char) was 5.2 for tags and questions, 5.3 for titles, and 4.7 for answers. An excerpt of the most popular terms for EU is shown in Table 2. Some important differences between collected data could already be identified when considering this distribution in conjunction with unique terms (Note that unique terms are enclosed with brackets, see Table 1). According to descriptive

---

[1]A term is considered here as a single word e.g., in a tag input data model, a term corresponds to a single tag.

Table 2: Example distributions of top-5 terms for the EU dataset. Note, the terms are stemmed using Porter stemmer [9].

Tags	Count	
	# of visualizations	# of users
chart	20	4
countri	17	13
govern	14	8
onlin	14	8
valu	22	13
Titles		
constit	15	8
countri	22	5
european	14	8
popul	21	8
valu	17	8
Q&As		
inform	14	10
larg	16	9
onlin	13	9
republ	13	10
type	13	10

Table 3: Information-theoretic measures for tags, titles and questions used for user profiles. Note that the measures have been calculated among all three datasets.

Datasets	Term	User Model		
		Entropy	Conditional Entropy	Mutual Inf.
Movies, EU, Books	Tags	5.9376	3.0381	2.8995
	Titles	6.1421	2.9815	3.1606
	Questions	6.8898	3.1436	3.7462

data from the table, 10.69% of the tags, 13.31% of titles and 31.16% of Q&As were unique, i.e., not globally repeated. The fact that a question typically associates with only one specific visualization may explain this phenomenon. Taking this cue, we can assume that the varied number on different type of terms directly affects the recommendation quality. In brief, the more unique terms are applied to a visualization the easier it should become to discriminate this visualization in the finding process from others. Subsequently, the more individual terms a user provides, the higher the ability should be to accurately direct this user to the preferred visualizations [25]. However, the more accurate way to measure how good a term is in discriminating a resource from others is measuring the value of the information it provides about a resource and about the user. For this purposes we investigate in the following, first, the power of users' terms at encoding users' visual preferences, and, next, at encoding the content of visualizations.

5.2.1 Power of user-provided input at encoding users. To investigate the quality of extracted terms at encoding users' visual preferences we applied the information-theoretic measures among all three datasets. Considering all three datasets in our analysis helps us to achieve more objective results, compared to analyzing each dataset individually.

In this experiment, X is users and Y is either tags, titles or Q&As. The analysis intends to determine which of $H(Tags)$, $H(Titles)$, $H(Q\&As)$ indicates more diversity, which of $H(User|Tags)$, $H(User|Titles)$, $H(User|Q\&As)$ has more power in describing users, and which of $I(User; Tags)$, $I(User; Titles)$, $I(User; Q\&As)$ has higher value and can specify users better. Table 3 summarizes the results of this study. Note, to follow a common design principle of interactive (question-answering) systems, we suggest to split the Q&As input so that questions are used for the user- and answers for the item model.

When considering the results in Table 3, at the first look we can observe that the entropy ($H(Questions)$) is higher than ($H(Titles)$) and ($H(Tags)$). This suggests, users provided more diverse and specific questions than titles and tags. Given this fact, we hypothesize that questions have a strong encoding power. Yet, entropy measures the amount of uncertainty. Conditional entropy, however, quantifies the amount of uncertainty in a random variable (i.e., user) given the value of another random variable (i.e., tags, titles or questions).

We therefore consider next the entropy of users conditional on tags (or titles, questions), i.e., $H(User|Tags)$, $H(User|Titles)$ and $H(User|Questions)$ (see Table 3 second column). Looking at the results, $H(User|Questions) > H(User|Tags) > H(User|Titles)$. What that means is, that tags and titles have a strong power in describing user than questions.

Yet, conditional entropy is a relative measure and tells little about the independence between tags (or titles, questions) and user [3]. The independence, however, matters in recommender systems when it comes to defining a link between user and resources. Thus, to complete the analysis on tags (or titles, questions) in specifying user, we next, analyze the amount of information shared between tags (or titles, questions) and a user, mutual information ($I(User; Tags)$, $I(User; Titles)$, $I(User; Questions)$) respectively. The results show that $I(User; Questions)$ is the highest compared to $I(User; Tags)$ and $I(User; Titles)$ (see Table 3 last column). Yet, these results finally suggest, questions are more effective in specifying user than tags and titles.

5.2.2 Power of user-provided input at encoding visualizations. Similar to our previous study, to investigate the general quality of the user-provided input at encoding visualizations we applied the information-theoretic measures among all three datasets. In this case, X are visualizations and Y are either tags, titles or answers. The analysis intends to determine which of $H(Tags)$, $H(Titles)$, $H(Answers)$ indicates more diversity across visualizations, which of $H(Vis|Tags)$, $H(Vis|Titles)$, $H(Vis|Answers)$ has more power in describing visualizations, and which of $I(Vis; Tags)$, $I(Vis; Titles)$, $I(Vis; Answers)$ has higher value and can specify visualizations better. Table 4 summarizes the results of this study. The entropy of answers is higher than of tags and titles. At a first glance, this indicates, the visualizations have been annotated with more specific and unique answers than tags and titles. However, as we noted in the previous study, entropy just measures the amount of uncertainty in a random variable (i.e., visualization) given the value of another random variable (i.e., tags, titles or answers). When

Table 4: Information-theoretic measures for tags, titles and answers used for item profiles. Note that the measures have been calculated among all three datasets.

Datasets	Term	Item Model		
		Entropy	Conditional Entropy	Mutual Inf.
Movies, EU, Books	Tags	5.9376	4.1429	1.7947
	Titles	6.1421	4.1384	2.0037
	Answers	6.6371	2.7405	3.8966

considering $H(Vis|Tags)$, $H(Vis|Titles)$, $H(Vis|Answers)$, we observe that answers are more unique and special than tags and titles ($H(Vis|Answers) < H(Vis|Tags)$, $H(Vis|Answers) < H(Vis|Titles)$) (see Table 4 second column). Thus, it might be more difficult for the system to retrieve a visualization that has been annotated with a certain tag or title than with a certain answer. To validate this we finally measure the degree of independence between tags (or titles, answers) and a visualization– the amount of information shared (mutual) $I(Vis; Tags)$, $I(Vis; Titles)$, $I(Vis; Answers)$. Remember, full independence is reached when e.g., $I(Vis; Tags)$ is zero.

Table 4 (last column) shows the mutual information $I(Vis; Answers)$ is higher than of $I(Vis; Tags)$ and $I(Vis; Titles)$. These results, finally, suggest a high quality of answers at encoding visualizations. Taking this cue, we can assume the answers are powerful to direct the user to the corresponding visualizations than tags and titles.

5.2.3 Summary. Using information-theoretic measures we aimed to characterize tags, titles and Q&As in describing user and items (visualizations). To that end we performed two studies where we analyzed the power of (i) tags, titles and questions at encoding user, and (ii) tags, titles and answers at encoding visualizations. The findings of the studies should help in predicting performance of the potential candidates for the user- and item models being used for our visual recommender.

Results suggest a strong link (dependency) between user and her questions and items and their (assigned) answers. This assumption is made regarding to the shared information between (i) user & questions, and (ii) item & answers, $I(User; Questions)$, $I(Vis; Answers)$ respectively. Namely, the results of $I(User; Questions)$, $I(Vis; Answers)$ show that a set of specific terms from questions refers to an individual user and each answer to a specific item. Yet, this is an essential finding for designer of content-based recommender systems. It suggests using questions for user modeling and answers for the item modeling.

To verify this assumption, we build, in the following, user and item models using user's questions and answers and explore the quality of the generated recommendations in an offline study employing our CB based recommender system. We applied this recommender technique since it is traditionally used for user-provided input, such as tags, comments, etc. We measured the quality of the recommendations by their closeness to what user prefers and needs.

Note, for the sake of completeness, we also included additional setting where tags are taken for user- and item models. Considering the results in Section 5.2.1, the quality of the generated recommendations should be lower when using this combinations, since tags

have a lower mutual information than Q&As. Moreover, to verify the low performance of titles, settings with titles are reported too.

In the following we describe the method and metrics used to validate our approach in detail and present the results of the offline study.

6 RECOMMENDATION QUALITY

6.1 Methodology

Following the method described in [26], we split the preference model including either users' tags, titles or questions into the two distinct sets, one for training the recommender (training-set), and another one for testing (test-set). The test-set acts here as a reference value that, in an ideal case, has to be fully predicted for the given training-set. From each of the datasets in the preference model, we randomly select 80% of user's data and enter them into the training-set performing 5-fold cross validation. The recommendations produced out of the training-set are further used to evaluate the performance of our recommender. The performance of the recommender depends generally on how good it predicts the test-set. We compared the generated recommendations (prediction-set) and the test-set by applying a variety of well-known evaluation metrics in information retrieval [7]: Recall (R), Precision (P), F-Measure (F), Mean Average Precision (MAP) and the Normalized Discounted Cumulative Gain (nDCG). The first three metrics basically express the quantity of relevant recommended results, whereas MAP and nDCG quantify the concrete ordering of the results (i.e., penalizing results which are not on the top but are relevant for the user). We refer to the research papers [19, 21, 23] for more detailed definitions of the evaluation metrics. Note, the tests are performed for each user- and item model combination independently.

6.2 Results

To measure the improvements in terms of recommender quality (=accuracy, relevance), we compared the individual CBs ($CB_{Tags,Tags}$, $CB_{Titles,Titles}$, $CB_{Q,A}$) with the baseline filtering algorithm Random (RD). The RD method simulates the recommender behavior providing a random rating for each visualization. Note, for the Q&As based CB approach ($CB_{Q,A}$) we used user's questions in user- and user's answers in item model.

For the comparison, we analyzed the top 3 recommendations (k=3), since our datasets are relatively smaller than some commonly used datasets, such as CiteULike and BibSonomy. Table 5 shows the quality metrics values F@3, MAP@3, nDCG@3 estimated for the three datasets.

Yet, when considering the recommendation accuracy (F@3), at a first glance, we can observe that tags based CB ($CB_{Tags,Tags}$) outperforms for all three datasets the baseline algorithms RD (cf. F@3($CB_{Tags,Tags}$) = 0.0740, F@3(RD) = 0.0055 for Movies). So, we hypothesize that the experimentation with individual user- and item models has had some effect among all three datasets. To discover what the effect was and how significant it is, we performed statistical tests which we report in the following.

The results for F@3, MAP@3, nDCG@3 have been analyzed independently for each dataset applying Friedman's ANOVA. Note, we used this test since our data were not normally distributed and (per dataset) the same participants have been used for each

Table 5: The performance of our individual content based filtering approaches (CB), compared with baseline algorithm RD: quality metric values considering the first three recommendations in the list (k=3). ***Significant at p<0.001.

Dataset	Algorithms	Metric		
		F@3	MAP@3	nDCG@3
Movies	RD	0.0055	0.0020	0.0048
	$CB_{Tags,Tags}$	0.0740***	0.0545***	0.0830***
	$CB_{Titles,Titles}$	0.0650***	0.0500***	0.0743***
	$CB_{Q,A}$	0.0547***	0.0450***	0.0643***
EU	RD	0.0150	0.0044	0.0103
	$CB_{Tags,Tags}$	0.1862***	0.1120***	0.1801***
	$CB_{Titles,Titles}$	0.1726***	0.1030***	0.1663***
	$CB_{Q,A}$	0.1505***	0.1014***	0.1642***
Books	RD	0.0333	0.0333	0.0420
	$CB_{Tags,Tags}$	0.2360***	0.2077***	0.2700***
	$CB_{Titles,Titles}$	0.2310***	0.2133***	0.2720***
	$CB_{Q,A}$	0.2267***	0.2233***	0.2720***

individual CB approach. The results for all three datasets show a significant effect of the used type of item- and user models on the recommendation accuracy (F@3), with $\chi^2(4) = 25.10$ for Movies, $\chi^2(4) = 19.80$ for EU, and $\chi^2(4) = 20.14$ for Books, p<0.001. To explore where the differences lie we applied *Post hoc* tests with Bonferroni correction. The results for all three datasets reveal a significant difference between the values of the individual CB approaches ($CB_{Tags,Tags}$, $CB_{Titles,Titles}$, $CB_{Q,A}$) and baseline algorithm. Note, the critical difference ($\alpha = 0.05$ corrected for the number of tests) was 28.10 for Movies, 20.10 for EU and 18.65 for Books. However, there were no significant differences between the values of individual recommenders ($CB_{Tags,Tags}$, $CB_{Titles,Titles}$, $CB_{Q,A}$), p>0.05.

Looking at the results for MAP@3 and nDCG@3 measures which examine the ranking of the recommended visualizations we observe similar results. Concretely, the results show a significant effect of the used type of item- and user models on the ranking of the recommendations, with $\chi^2(4) = 23.56$ for Movies, $\chi^2(4) = 20.10$ for EU, and $\chi^2(4) = 18.65$ for Books, p<0.001. Similar to the previous analysis, to explore where the differences lie we applied *Post hoc* tests with Bonferroni correction. The results of *Post hoc* tests shown for all three datasets, when tags, title and Q&As based models are used, the visual recommender can sort the recommendations according to their relevance better than baseline algorithm. The critical difference ($\alpha = 0.05$ corrected for the number of tests) was 28.10 for Movies, 20.10 for EU and 18.65 for Books. The results for nDCG confirmed the results we obtained for MAP@3 measures showing a significant improvement by ranking of recommendations when using either (i) tags, (ii) titles or (ii) Q&As based models compared to the random baseline algorithm.

7 DISCUSSION

The main outcome of our study is that all three inputs (tags, title, and Q&As) show a comparable quality in recommending visualizations. This result is important because it gives the designer freedom in choosing the method for preference elicitation. Besides, it makes the

suggested approach applicable in domains in which only particular types of inputs can be supported (e.g., question-answering systems).

We could confirm this result for all datasets, as illustrated in Table 5. Moreover, all three inputs are, as expected, significantly better at encoding visualizations than the baseline algorithm RD. Also, when considering the results in more detail, i.e., the quality F@3, and the sorting accuracy (*MAP@3* and *nDCG@3*), it does not matter which of the inputs to use. (Note that there are negligible differences in means, which are statistically not significant). This would, in the end, mean that characteristics of the individual inputs are very close to each other. In fact, providing a title would be nothing else but providing a set of tags (in terms of how many and which words have been provided). We analyzed these characteristics in the first part of our study.

Using information-theoretic measures we found that some inputs better encode user/visualizations than the other. In particular, questions and answers have been identified to show distinctive characteristics compared to tags and titles. It turned out that they more precisely address a particular user/visualization, since, as results reveal, they have terms which are less common (shared) than in the case of tags and titles. This, in fact, comes from the nature on how questions/answers are built. For instance, it is more likely that similar or same words are provided when describing visualizations via tags rather than using complex sentences. Generally, users are familiar when describing resources in form of tags, as tagging approach is quite intuitive and straightforward. Using question/answers, instead, is more subjective. One aspect here is building a sequence of words (a sentence), and another is using proper adjectives in that sequence. These terms also contribute to the user/item model. Nevertheless, as shown later in the offline experiment, these differences were not significant enough to be manifested by the content-based recommender (at least with the cosine similarity metric we chose).

8 CONCLUSIONS

In this paper we investigated the power of different kinds of user-provided input to effectively encode user's visual preferences and the content of visualizations. To do so we employed information-theoretic measures including entropy, conditional entropy and mutual information. Using these measures, we were able to quantify the diversity in individual inputs, their encoding power respectively, and also the amount of shared information between them and users/visualizations. The outcome of the study should suggest a list of potential candidates to build user models defining users' interest/needs and item models describing the content of the visualization— both crucial for content-based recommender systems. Finally, we executed our content-based recommender on candidate models to see if their encoding power could be confirmed. In other words, we performed an offline study to assess the practicability of the individual models in recommending personalized visualizations. The data we used in this paper was collected in the scope of the empirical study, where we involved 47 participants to annotate different types of visualizations using tags, titles, questions and answers.

Regarding to our first study, we found that the best user- item model combination is guaranteed when using questions for the user- and answers for the item models (considering their mutual information values). The offline study has confirmed the good quality of this combination as it produced better recommendations than the baseline algorithm. However, the quality of this combination was not significantly better or different than that of the tags and titles. Although differences at encoding power between the individual inputs could be manifested, those differences were negligible and not crucial for the content-based recommender system we employed. Nevertheless, the fact that the recommendation quality and accuracy were still high using the alternative inputs, titles and Q&As respectively, demonstrated the capability of these inputs being used for visual recommender systems.

In summary, this paper shows the good quality of alternative input types (titles, Q&As) to derive high quality visualization recommendations. It further emphasizes the relevance of annotations for the users as they directly link them to the items which might be closer to what they need and prefer.

Our research so far did not concentrate how a hybrid recommender would perform when using user's ratings with titles or Q&As. This is planned for the near future. In the current work, we used each information sources separately. In the future, we will investigate how our CB performs when using a combination of multiple information sources as data model. Furthermore, we plan to investigate interfaces to elicit such information with minimal effort making it part of the analysis process whenever possible.

9 ACKNOWLEDGMENTS

This work is funded by the European Horizon 2020 research project AFEL (grant nr. 687916) and CONICET. The Know-Center GmbH is funded within the Austrian COMET Program - managed by the Austrian Research Promotion Agency (FFG).

REFERENCES

[1] Alejandro Bellogín, Iván Cantador, and Pablo Castells. 2010. A Study of Heterogeneity in Recommendations for a Social Music Service. In *Proceedings of the 1st International Workshop on Information Heterogeneity and Fusion in Recommender Systems*. ACM, 1–8.
[2] Toine Bogers and Antal Van den Bosch. 2009. Collaborative and content-based filtering for item recommendation on social bookmarking websites. In *Proceedings of the ACM Recommender Systems workshop on Recommender Systems and the Social Web*, Vol. 9. 9–16.
[3] Ed H. Chi and Todd Mytkowicz. 2008. Understanding the Efficiency of Social Tagging Systems Using Information Theory. In *Proceedings of the Nineteenth ACM Conference on Hypertext and Hypermedia*. ACM, 81–88.
[4] Micheline Elias and Anastasia Bezerianos. 2012. Annotating BI Visualization Dashboards: Needs & Challenges. In *Proceedings of the SIGCHI Conference on Human Factors in Computing Systems*. ACM, 1641–1650.
[5] Umer Farooq, Yang Song, John M. Carroll, and C. Lee Giles. 2007. Social Bookmarking for Scholarly Digital Libraries. *Internet Computing, IEEE* 11, 6 (05 Nov. 2007), 29–35.
[6] Robert M. Gray. 1990. *Entropy and Information Theory*. Springer-Verlag New York, Inc.
[7] Jonathan L. Herlocker, Joseph A. Konstan, Loren G. Terveen, and John T. Riedl. 2004. Evaluating Collaborative Filtering Recommender Systems. *ACM Transactions on Information Systems* 22, 1 (Jan. 2004), 5–53.
[8] Jiwoon Jeon and R. Manmatha. 2004. *Using Maximum Entropy for Automatic Image Annotation*. Springer Berlin Heidelberg, 24–32.
[9] Wahiba Ben Abdessalem Karaa and Nidhal Gribâa. 2013. Information Retrieval with Porter Stemmer: A New Version for English. In *Advances in Computational Science, Engineering and Information Technology*. Vol. 225. Springer International Publishing, 243–254.
[10] Aniket Kittur, Ed H. Chi, and Bongwon Suh. 2008. Crowdsourcing User Studies with Mechanical Turk. In *Proceedings of the SIGCHI Conference on Human Factors in Computing Systems*. ACM, 453–456.
[11] Yi-Ling Lin, Christoph Trattner, Peter Brusilovsky, and Daqing He. 2015. The impact of image descriptions on user tagging behavior: A study of the nature and functionality of crowdsourced tags. *Journal of the Association for Information Science and Technology* 66, 9 (2015), 1785–1798.
[12] Pasquale Lops, Marco de Gemmis, and Giovanni Semeraro. 2011. Content-based Recommender Systems: State of the Art and Trends. In *Recommender Systems Handbook*. Springer US, 73–105.
[13] Jared Lorince, Sam Zorowitz, Jaimie Murdock, and Peter M. Todd. 2015. The Wisdom of the Few? "Supertaggers" in Collaborative Tagging Systems. *Journal of Web Science* 1, 1 (2015), 16–32.
[14] Qiaozhu Mei and Kenneth Church. 2008. Entropy of Search Logs: How Hard is Search? With Personalization? With Backoff?. In *Proceedings of the International Conference on Web Search and Data Mining*. ACM, 45–54.
[15] Belgin Mutlu, Eduardo Veas, and Christoph Trattner. 2016. VizRec: Recommending Personalized Visualizations. *ACM Transactions on Interactive Intelligent Systems* 6, 4, Article 31 (Nov. 2016), 31:1–31:39 pages.
[16] Belgin Mutlu, Eduardo Veas, Christoph Trattner, and Vedran Sabol. 2015. Towards a Recommender Engine for Personalized Visualizations. In *User Modeling, Adaptation and Personalization*. Vol. 9146. Springer International Publishing, 169–182.
[17] F. Matsatsinis Nikolaos, Lakiotaki Kleanthi, and Tsoukiás Alexis. 2011. Multicriteria User Modeling in Recommender Systems. *IEEE Intelligent Systems* 26 (2011), 64–76.
[18] Thomas Orgel, Martin Höffernig, Werner Bailer, and Silvia Russegger. 2015. A metadata model and mapping approach for facilitating access to heterogeneous cultural heritage assets. *International Journal on Digital Libraries* 15, 2-4 (2015), 189–207.
[19] Denis Parra and Shaghayegh Sahebi. 2013. Recommender Systems: Sources of Knowledge and Evaluation Metrics. In *Advanced Techniques in Web Intelligence-2*. Vol. 452. Springer Berlin Heidelberg, 149–175.
[20] Erhard Rahm and Philip A. Bernstein. 2001. A Survey of Approaches to Automatic Schema Matching. *The VLDB Journal* 10, 4 (Dec. 2001), 334–350.
[21] Majdi Rawashdeh, Heung-Nam Kim, JihadMohamad Alja'am, and Abdulmotaleb El Saddik. 2013. Folksonomy link prediction based on a tripartite graph for tag recommendation. *Journal of Intelligent Information Systems* 40, 2 (2013), 307–325.
[22] Francesco Ricci and Quang Nhat Nguyen. 2007. Acquiring and Revising Preferences in a Critique-Based Mobile Recommender System. *IEEE Intelligent Systems* 22, 3 (May 2007), 22–29.
[23] C.J. Van Rijsbergen. 1974. Foundation of Evaluation. *Journal of Documentation* 30, 4 (1974), 365–373.
[24] Ahmed Seffah, Mohammad Donyaee, Rex B. Kline, and Harkirat K. Padda. 2006. Usability Measurement and Metrics: A Consolidated Model. *Software Quality Control* 14, 2 (June 2006), 159–178.
[25] Markus Strohmaier, Christian Koerner, and Roman Kern. 2010. Why Do Users Tag? Detecting Users' Motivation for Tagging in Social Tagging Systems. In *Proceedings of the Twenty-Fourth AAAI Conference on Artificial Intelligence*.
[26] Christoph Trattner, Dominik Kowald, and Emanuel Lacic. 2015. TagRec: Towards a Toolkit for Reproducible Evaluation and Development of Tag-based Recommender Algorithms. *ACM Special Interest Group on Hypertext and the Web, SIGWEB Newsl.* Winter, Article 3 (Feb. 2015), 3:1–3:10 pages.
[27] Fernanda B. Viegas, Martin Wattenberg, Frank van Ham, Jesse Kriss, and Matt McKeon. 2007. ManyEyes: A Site for Visualization at Internet Scale. *IEEE Transactions on Visualization and Computer Graphics* 13, 6 (Nov. 2007), 1121–1128.
[28] William Wright, David Schroh, Pascale Proulx, Alex Skaburskis, and Brian Cort. 2006. The Sandbox for Analysis: Concepts and Methods. In *Proceedings of the SIGCHI Conference on Human Factors in Computing Systems*. ACM, 801–810.
[29] Y. Y. Yao. 2003. *Information-Theoretic Measures for Knowledge Discovery and Data Mining*. Springer Berlin Heidelberg, 115–136.
[30] Xianjun Sam Zheng, James j W. Lin, Salome Zapf, and Claus Knapheide. 2007. Visualizing User Experience Through "Perceptual Maps": Concurrent Assessment of Perceived Usability and Subjective Appearance in Car Infotainment Systems. In *Proceedings of the 1st International Conference on Digital Human Modeling*. Springer-Verlag, 536–545.

Linguistic Diversities of Demographic Groups in Twitter

Pantelis Vikatos
University of Patras
Rio, Greece
vikatos@ceid.upatras.gr

Johnnatan Messias
Universidade Federal de Minas Gerais (UFMG)
Belo Horizonte, Brazil
johnnatan@dcc.ufmg.br

Manoel Miranda
Universidade Federal de Minas Gerais (UFMG)
Belo Horizonte, Brazil
manoelrmj@dcc.ufmg.br

Fabrício Benevenuto
Universidade Federal de Minas Gerais (UFMG)
Belo Horizonte, Brazil
fabricio@dcc.ufmg.br

ABSTRACT

The massive popularity of online social media provides a unique opportunity for researchers to study the linguistic characteristics and patterns of user's interactions. In this paper, we provide an in-depth characterization of language usage across demographic groups in Twitter. In particular, we extract the gender and race of Twitter users located in the U.S. using advanced image processing algorithms from Face++. Then, we investigate how demographic groups (i.e. male/female, Asian/Black/White) differ in terms of linguistic styles and also their interests. We extract linguistic features from 6 categories (affective attributes, cognitive attributes, lexical density and awareness, temporal references, social and personal concerns, and interpersonal focus), in order to identify the similarities and differences in particular writing set of attributes. In addition, we extract the absolute ranking difference of top phrases between demographic groups. As a dimension of diversity, we also use the topics of interest that we retrieve from each user. Our analysis unveils clear differences in the writing styles (and the topics of interest) of different demographic groups, with variation seen across both gender and race lines. We hope our effort can stimulate the development of new studies related to demographic information in the online space.

CCS CONCEPTS

•Human-centered computing →Social media; •Applied computing →*Sociology;*

KEYWORDS

Demographic Aspects; Linguistics; Twitter Analysis

1 INTRODUCTION

The number of users in online social networking sites, such as Facebook and Twitter increases each day. As of the third quarter

of 2016, Facebook and Twitter have 1.79 billion[1] and 317 million[2] monthly active users, respectively, sharing content about their daily lives and things that happen around them. This massive popularity of online social media provides the opportunity to detect useful characteristics and patterns about users and their interconnections. For instance, patterns are valuable for marketing and advertisement companies which capture users' behavior and needs in order to promote products, specifically on a target group. In terms of group, demographics constitute a significant factor to cluster people and understand their behavior. Twitter provides a plethora of different information, e.g. posts, social connections. However, it lacks data about demographics such as gender, race, or age. We deal with this absence of this information using profile image as an input of deep learning algorithms on image processing. We are interested in extracting demographic status in a large scale and correlate it with available information on the social media. Twitter is a micro-blogging platform so the main way of communication and action is by posting texts (tweets). The use of natural language processing in these type of data can extract many features describing cognitive and user' personal concerns.

Many studies have used text analysis to study the user behavior in the online space [2, 6, 7, 11]. Our work provides a complementary perspective to these efforts, by providing a characterization of language usage (i.e. common phrases and topics of interest), but grouping users according to their gender and race. Our effort is motivated by previous studies that uses computational linguistics in order to extract patterns about demographic information [14], but our effort further explores race as a new demographic dimension. Our findings reveal significant differences between the linguistic content shared by female and male users as well as Asian, Black, and White and can be used for automatically categorization of Twitter users through their texts.

The main challenge is that users in Twitter are prone not to provide information about demographics. In our work, we crawled a large scale sample of active Twitter users and then we identify the gender and race of about 1.6 million users located in U.S by using Face++[3] [15, 30], a face recognition software able to recognize gender and race of identifiable faces in the user's profile pictures. Actually, the state of the art algorithms, for pattern recognition

[1] https://www.statista.com/statistics/264810/number-of-monthly-active-facebook-users-worldwide/
[2] https://www.statista.com/statistics/282087/number-of-monthly-active-twitter-users/
[3] http://www.faceplusplus.com

and image processing, can provide with high accuracy the gender, race, and even the age of an individual via his/her image. From the demographic recognized users, we gathered tweets of $304,477$ users to characterize linguistic patterns. Particularly, we extract the absolute ranking difference of top phrases between demographic groups. As a dimension of diversity, we also use the topics of interest that we retrieve from each user. Our analysis concludes that there are clear differences in the way of writing across different demographic groups in both gender and race domains as well as in the topic of interest.

The rest of the paper is organized as follow. Section 2 provides a review of the relevant literature. Then, Section 3 presents the Twitter and demographic dataset. After that, the analysis and discussion of linguistic differences and topic of interests are presented. Finally, the last section summarizes our results and offers some concluding remarks.

2 RELATED WORK

In this section, we review the related literature along two axes. First, we discuss the methodology used by efforts that measure demographic factors in Twitter. Then, we refer to studies that combine linguistic with demographic status.

2.1 Demographics in Social Media

One of the first efforts to extract and analyze demographic information presents a comparative study between the demographic distribution of gender/race of Twitter users and U.S. population [23]. After that, several efforts have arisen that investigate demographic information, in various social media, using different strategies for distinct purposes [4, 5, 18, 19, 29]. Particularly, in terms of text analysis, Cunha et al. [13] used Twitter data to analyze the difference between males and females in terms of generation of hashtags. Their results emphasize gender as factor able to influence the user's choice of specific hashtags to a specific topic.

Recent studies focused on demographics [4, 19, 21, 24, 25] present methodologies to extract the necessary data through analysis and pattern matching of screen/full name as well as descriptions of user profiles and image in the profile status. Particularly, Chen et al. [9] focus on demographic inference using namely profile self-descriptions and profile images. They categorize demographic status using as signals users' names, self-descriptions, tweets, social networks, and profile images to infer attributes as ethnicity, gender, and age. An alternative approach, Culotta et al. [12] declare that the demographic profiles of visitors to a website are correlated with the demographic profiles of followers of that website on the social network and propose a regression model to predict demographic attributes such as gender, age, ethnicity, education, income, and child status. More recently, An et al. [1] provide an accurate scheme in order to predict gender and race using the correlation of hashtags that are used in different demographic groups.

Finally, our effort uses the similar strategy to gather demographic information as Chakraborty et al. [8], but we investigate very different research questions as we focus on the linguistic analysis of demographic groups.

2.2 Demographics and linguistic analysis

In the field of demographics, most studies use linguistic analysis in order to extract useful features for predicting demographic information as gender, race, and age. Burger et al. [5] produce n-grams from users' tweets, description, screen name, and full name, in order to predict Twitter user gender. They conclude that the training of an SVM classifier with the combination of all factors can create an efficient and accurate prediction scheme (92% acc) for gender classification. Also, Chen et al. [9] introduce a similar methodology for predicting gender, ethnicity, and age. However, using n-grams from the social neighbors, including followers and friends, and the distribution of 100 generated topics of LDA algorithm as the input of SVM classifier. Their results present that the performance of classification is much lower in terms of ethnicity and age. Gilbert et al. [17] present an interesting statistical overview in Twitter and Pinterest using textual analysis and comparing what users text on Pinterest to what they text on Twitter.

We mainly motivate our research based on Choudhury et al. [14] study which discover gender and cultural differences in Twitter. They correlate several linguistic features to mental illness. Our findings reinforce their observations about linguistic and topical differences against male and female users in Twitter and also contribute with a new analysis of race.

3 DEMOGRAPHIC INFORMATION DATASET

This section focuses on the procedure of data collection in order to extract useful inference about the discrimination of demographic status of a Twitter user. Our ultimate goal consists of gather demographic characteristics as gender and race as well as attributes about social behavior and tweet activity of active U.S. Twitter users. Next, we describe our steps to create this dataset and also discuss its main limitations.

3.1 Twitter dataset gathered

Our procedure uses the provided information from Twitter Stream API [4] in order to identify active Twitter users. We use a time window of three complete months from July to September 2016, collecting $341,457,982$ tweets posted by $50,270,310$ users.

Due to the fact that geographic coordinates are available on Twitter only for a limited number of users (i.e. $< 2\%$) [7], our strategy to identify U.S. Twitter users is based on the time zone information to retrieve users which are actually from the US as the methodology in previous efforts [8, 20] presented.

We filtered users that provided free text location indicating they are not U.S. (i.e. Montreal, Vancouver, Canada). We end up with a dataset containing $6,286,477$ users likely located in the United States.

3.2 Crawling Demographic Information

The field of demographic status is not mandatory when a user registers in Twitter and, thus, the direct retrieval of gender, race, or even age is not feasible. There are several studies related to demographic information in Twitter that attempt to infer the user's gender from the user name [4, 19, 21, 23]. Also, some works use

---
[4]https://dev.twitter.com/streaming/public

pattern based methodology to identify age [27] in Twitter profile description using regular expressions '25 yr old' or 'born in 1990'.

Here, we use a different strategy that allows us to extract the demographic dimension using the profile picture of each user. To do that, we needed to gather the profile picture web link of all Twitter users identified as located within the United States. In December 2016, we crawled the profile picture's URLs of about 6 million users, discarding 4, 317, 834 (68.68%) of them. We discarded users in two situations, first when the user does not have a profile picture and second when the user has changed her picture since our first crawl. When users change their picture, their profile picture URL changes as well, making it impossible for us to gather these users in a second crawl.

From the remaining 1, 968, 643 users, we submitted the profile picture web links into the *Face++ API*. Face++ is a face recognition platform based on deep learning [15, 30] able to identify the gender (i.e. male and female) and race (limited to Asian, Black, and White) from recognized faces in images.

Table 1: Dataset construction

Phase	Number of Users
Crawling 3 months of Tweets	50 million
Filtering U.S. users	6 million
U.S. users with profile image	2 million
U.S. users with one face (Baseline)	1.6 million
U.S. users with crawled tweets	304 thousand

We have also discarded those users whose profile pictures do not have a recognizable face or have more than one recognizable face, according to Face++. Our final dataset contains 1, 670, 863 users located in U.S. with identified demographic information. The phases of our data crawling and the amount of data discarded on each step are summarized in Table 1.

3.3 Baseline Dataset

In this section, we use the null model as our approach to estimate the statistical significance of the observed trend in given data. We compare the distribution of random samples created by the null model with the one of the original dataset and we measure the statistical significance.

Table 2 shows the distribution of gender and race in the dataset of the $\approx$ 1.6 million Twitter users between July and September 2016. To construct a null model, we create k random samples from the entire dataset (our crawled dataset containing 1.6 million users with demographic attributes), where each sample has exactly 304, 477 users. We choose this value for each sample size as it corresponds to the number of users we were able to gather tweets. For each sample, we count how many Whites are included. Then, the Z_{White} is computed as following:

$$Z_{White} = \frac{|U_{White}| - mean(|S_{White}|)}{std(|S_{White}|)} \quad (1)$$

where $mean(\cdot)$ is the mean and $std(\cdot)$ is the standard deviation of the values from multiple samples. We use the same equation for the other gender and race attributes. Table 3 presents the demographic

Table 2: Demographic distribution of 1.6 million users, our Baseline dataset.

Race (%)	Gender (%)		Total (%)
	Male	Female	
Asian	7.24	10.61	17.85
Black	7.84	6.45	14.29
White	32.23	35.63	67.86
Total	47.31	52.69	100.00

Table 3: Demographic distribution of 304, 477 users with linguistic attributes. The numbers in the parenthesis correspond the Z-values.

Race (%)	Gender (%)		Total (%)
	Male	Female	
Asian	7.07 (−3.85)	10.05 (−11.28)	17.12 (−10.90)
Black	8.17 (8.53)	6.74 (7.68)	14.91 (11.69)
White	32.88 (8.49)	35.09 (−7.69)	67.97 (1.20)
Total	48.12 (10.91)	51.88 (−10.91)	100.00

Table 4: Basic statistical descriptions of number of tweets with confidence intervals of 95% confidence level.

Demographic	Mean	Median	Max
Male	11, 624.76 ± 109.40	3, 874	1, 683, 948
Female	12, 933.40 ± 105.89	4, 885	1, 132, 964
Asian	14, 020.92 ± 183.73	5, 544	1, 108, 525
Black	18, 949.91 ± 248.46	8, 245	973, 225
White	10, 432.49 ± 85.28	3, 637	1, 683, 948

distribution of 304, 477 users with linguistic attributes. The numbers in the parenthesis correspond the Z-values.

Intuitively, when the absolute value of Z-value becomes bigger (either positive or negative), the trend (more number or less number, respectively) is less likely observed by chance. In this work, we use k=100.

3.4 Gathering Tweets

We are interested in correlating linguistic features of Twitter users with demographic information. We crawled the recent 3, 200 tweets of 304, 477 users for the purpose of linguistic analysis. Table 3 shows the demographic breakdown of users in our dataset across the different demographic groups. We can note a prevalence of females (51.88%) in comparison to males (48.12%) and a predominance of Whites (67.97%) in comparison to Blacks (14.91%) and Asians (17.12%). This means if we pick users randomly in our dataset, we would expect demographic groups with these proportions. Table 4 shows the statistical descriptions of number of tweets with 95% confidence level for each demographic group.

3.5 Extraction of Topics

We extracted the information about topics of interests for active users using the *Who Likes What*[5] web service [3]. The produced topics are derived from the list of the friends (other users the user is following) of each user. Then, we sort the produced topics based on their frequency to conclude the 20 most common topics from the Twitter users, including them as Binary variables. We manually cleaned several top topic labels following the same procedure as [24]. Therefore, we merged topics like *businesses* and *biz*, group topics into similarity (e.g. *celebrities* and *famous*, *actors* and *actor*), and remove some topics like *best, br, bro, new*. Table 5 presents a list of the 20-top topics and the merged sub-topics in each one as well as the number of users that belong to them.

3.6 Linguistic Measures

To quantify gender and race dimensions in the language of Twitter users, we use the 2015 version of the psycholinguistic lexicon Linguistic Inquiry and Word Count (LIWC) [28]. Since LIWC has been proposed, it has been widely used for a number of different tasks, including sentiment analysis [26] and discourse characterization in social media platforms [11]. The features are categorized into 3 main categories, (1) affective attributes, (2) cognitive attributes, and (3) linguistic style attribute as Choudhury *et al.* [14] propose. For this work, we considered 36 features from LIWC categorized into 6 groups in order to find the main differences across each demographic group.

The affective attributes contemplate features that show how strong is the expression of feelings like anger, anxiety, sadness, and swear. Cognitive attributes are related to the process of knowledge acquisition through perception. The lexical density and awareness group gather features related to the language itself and its structure. Temporal references are related to the tense expressed in the writing, while interpersonal focuses in present features related to the speech. The social/personal concerns group comprises features that express characteristics inherent to the individual as well his/her relation to the environment where he/she lives.

3.7 Data Limitations

The gender and race inference are challenge tasks, and as other existing strategies have limitations and the accuracy of Face++ inferences is an obvious concern in our effort. Face++ itself returns the confidence levels for the inferred gender and race attributes, and it returns an error range for inferred age. In our data, the average confidence level reported by Face++ is 95.22 ± 0.015% for gender and 85.97±0.024% for race, with a confidence interval of 95%. Recent efforts have used Face++ for similar tasks and reported fairly well confidence in manual inspections [1, 8, 31]. Our dataset may contain fake accounts and bots as previous studies provide evidence for a non-negligible rate of fake accounts [16, 22] in Twitter.

Finally, we note that our approach to identify users located in U.S. may bring together some users located in the same time zone, but from different countries. We, however, believe that these users might represent a small fraction of the users, given the predominance of active U.S. users in Twitter [10].

[5]http://twitter-app.mpi-sws.org/who-likes-what

4 LINGUISTIC DIFFERENCES

In order to show how demographic groups differ from each other in both gender and race domains, this section presents the difference between demographic groups across various linguistic categories. Table 6 shows the linguistic features extracted from LIWC into 6 categories (affective attributes, cognitive attributes, lexical density and awareness, temporal references, social and personal concerns, and interpersonal focus).

Figure 1 shows the mean absolute differences between male and female users across each linguistic category. The difference for a specific group of features is calculated by taking the average ratio of the difference between the values for male and female to the values of the measure among male. The mean difference in the first group (affective attributes) for instance is calculated as the average of the absolute difference of each feature that comprises this group. This shows in which linguistic categories the analyzed users differ the most. The amount of users considered in each group were the same.

Figure 1 also shows that interpersonal focus, which contemplates features like family, friends, health, religion, body, achievement, home, and sexual as the most prominent linguistic difference among males and females. In counterpart, from the race domain, the differences tend to be higher in affective attributes.

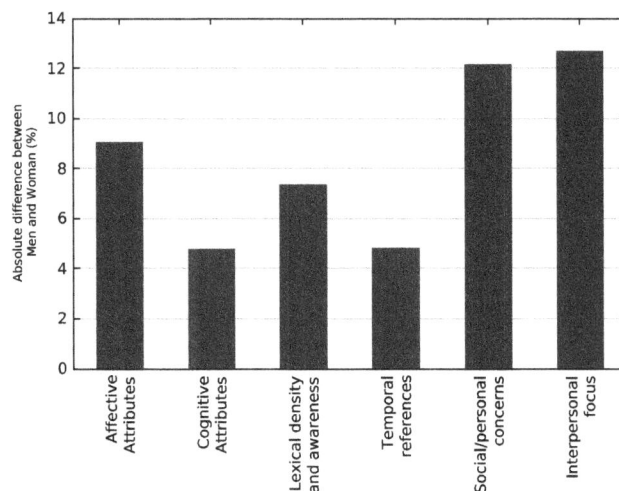

Figure 1: Mean absolute differences between male and female users per the various categories of linguistic measures

In the race domain, the analysis of the linguistic difference for each race was performed in the same way as gender, but considering the other two races combined. Figure 2 shows the mean absolute differences between White and Black/Asians combined. As we can see, there is a stronger difference in affective attributes, which comprises the expression of anger, anxiety, sadness, and swear. Other linguistic aspects such as social/personal concerns and interpersonal focus showed to be relevant when comparing the writing of White users against the Black and Asian group.

Respectively, the linguistic difference among Black users was compared against White and Asian users combined. Again, affective

Table 5: 20-top Topics of user's interests

Topic	Sub-Topics	Total
Celebrities	celebrities, famous, stars, celebs, celebrity, star, celeb	1, 319, 765
Artists	musicians, singers, artist, singer, musician, rappers, bands	731, 370
World	world, earth, hollywood, usa, canada, texas, international, nyc, country, city, boston, san francisco, france, america, los angeles, brasil, london, india	654, 555
Music	music, pop, hip hop, rap, gospel, hiphop	463, 451
Fun	fun, funny, humor, lol, laugh	415, 113
Entertainment	entertainment	371, 503
TV	tv, television	369, 440
Info	info, information	297, 705
Sports	sports, football, basketball, baseball, soccer, futbol, basket, martial arts, sport, mma, golf, cricket, boxing, motorsports, f1, racing	296, 652
Media	sports news, tech news, newspapers, music news, breaking news, world news, news media, radio, internet, social media, youtube, sports media, magazines, magazine	293, 206
Life	life, lifestyle, health, healthcare, fitness, food, style, smile, drink	278, 348
Actors	actors, actresses, actress, actor	267, 626
Bloggers	bloggers, blogs, blog	230, 347
Technology	technology, tech, iphone, digital, geek, software, computer, electronic, android, xbox, mac, gadgets, programming, geeks	208, 739
Movie	movie, movies, film, films	203, 577
Writers	writers	189526
Organizations	organizations, nfl, nba, mlb, nhl, ufc, lfc, lgbt	178, 030
Business	business, biz, businesses	171, 759
Politics	politics, government, political, politicians, politician	110, 367
Companies	companies, apple, company, microsoft, google	79, 528

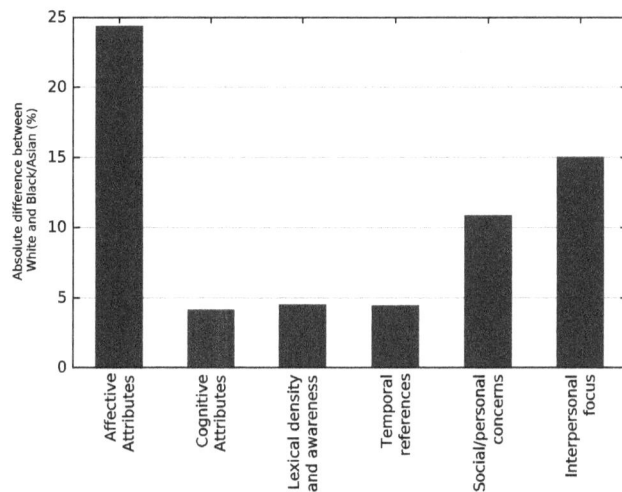

Figure 2: Mean absolute differences between White and Black/Asian users combined per the various categories of linguistic measures

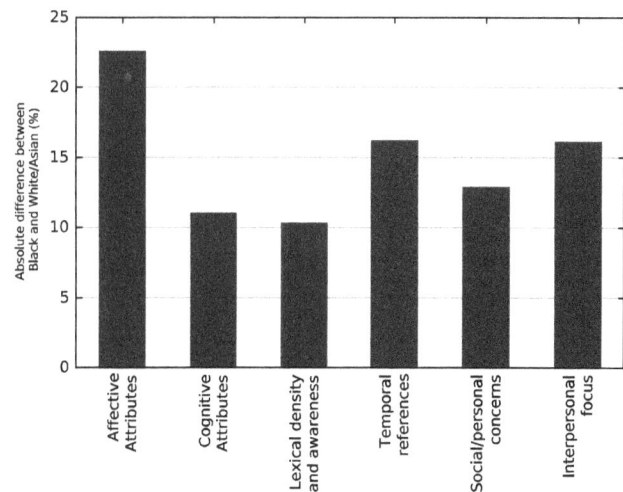

Figure 3: Mean absolute differences between Black and White/Asian users combined per the various categories of linguistic measures

attributes are the linguistic group with the features that most differ from one ethnicity to the others.

When it comes to comparing the Asian linguistic to that in White and Black users, some group of features that did not present higher absolute differences when comparing Black and White groups, now

tend to be higher such as lexical density and awareness and temporal references, which reveal some differences reflected by such different cultures especially in their way of writing.

Additionally, we correlate the produced linguistic features with gender based on Wilcoxon rank sum significance tests. p-values are

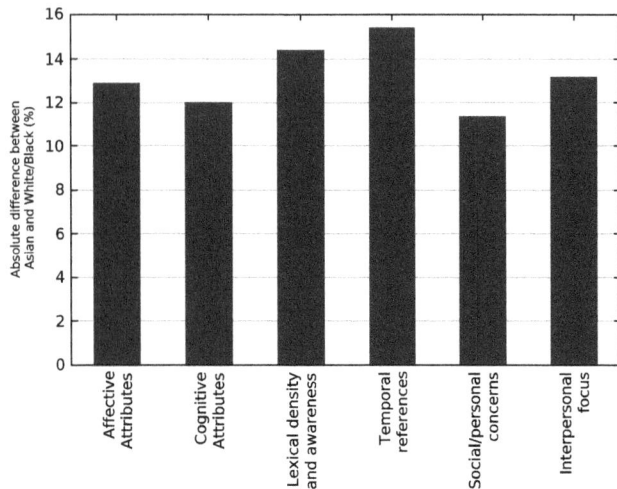

Figure 4: Mean absolute differences between Asian and White/Black users combined per the various categories of linguistic measures

represented in asterisks scale using * as significant ($0.1 < p \leq 0.5$), ** very significant($0.001 < p \leq 0.01$), ***($0.0001 < p \leq 0.001$) and ****($p < 0.001$) extremely significant. As Table 6 presents, females tend to use anxiety ($z = -74.534$) and sadness ($z = -74.394$) terms and phrases. On the other hand, males express with anger ($z = 4.733$) in their tweets.

In terms of cognitive attributes, females are more likely to write phrases that express cognition and perception. From this group of features, two stand out: certainty ($z = -60.593$) and feel ($z = -70.766$) showing how females express more confidence and feelings in their writing.

In Lexical Density and Awareness, we can see that females make more use of verbs ($z = -45.808$), auxiliary verbs ($z = -46.441$), conjunctions ($z = -72.098$), and adverbs ($z = -66.915$), while males use more articles ($z = 77.303$) and prepositions ($z = 32.596$).

The temporal references attributes are more present in the females writing, as we can see from the values for present tense ($z = -62.110$) and future tense ($z = -15.118$)

From Social/Personal Concerns perspective there is a clear trend on the usage of these features by females more than by males. Among the most notorious values shown in Table 6, are family ($z = -93.252$), bio ($z = -102.681$). Also, the predominance of features like friends, social, health, and body show that females express more social and personal concerns in their writing than males. The only feature in this group that is more present in males' writing is achievement ($z = 65.265$)

Noticeably, females also have a higher tendency to write in the first person singular ($z = -97.329$) and in the second person ($z = -88.482$) than males, while there is a slight trend towards males using the first person plural in detriment of females ($z = 4.309$).

Also, from the race perspective, the difference of values between each race shows some particularities in the way of writing for each race. In this analysis, one race is compared with the other two combined (e.g. White users are compared with Blacks and Asians).

From affective attributes, it is possible to see that Black users tend to express more anger ($z = 94.610$) and swear ($z = 107.344$) than White/Asian.

From cognitive attributes, almost all features were more present in Black users' texts than in the other races, with higher values for certainty ($z = 62.239$), hear ($z = 62.137$), and feel ($z = 63.963$).

In terms of lexical density and awareness, Black users have more presence in features like verbs, auxiliary verbs, conjunctions, and adverbs, while prepositions are more present among White users.

When talking about Social/Personal concerns, there is a higher presence of Black people in the features from this class, noticeably in family ($z = 86.721$), social ($z = 90.830$), religion ($z = 85.163$), and body ($z = 86.903$).

The Interpersonal Focus feature set reveal that there is a predominance in the use of first person plural for White ($z = 77.425$) while first person singular ($z = 63.492$), second person ($z = 95.495$) and third person ($z = 87.717$) are more prominent in the Black group.

Table 8 & Table 9 present the ranking difference for the 20 most common phrases for gender and races respectively. To find these differences, we randomly selected $1,000$ users from each group (male, female, Asian, Black and White). Their tweets were used to create ngrams for each group. With this subset of our dataset, we extracted the top 100 phrases for each demographic group and the top 20 are shown in these Tables.

As we can see in Table 8 phrases expressing negation are in the top positions for both males and females. It is also clear to see that females are more into signs than males since phrases with this kind of content present higher differences in the gender ranking.

Due to the informal nature of Twitter, the top phrases also reveal that it is common the usage of slangs like "do n't", "ca n't" and "wan na" for both genders.

When analyzing the ranking of race top phrases in Table 9, the trend of using negation phrases also repeat here. Phrases containing expressions like "i don't", "i can't" and "i'm not" appear in the top positions for all the racial groups. Another interesting result is the position of the expression "i love you" in the writing of different races. White and Asian users seem to be more likely to tweet contents with this expression than Black users. Also, the expression "i want to" appears more often in the writing of White and Asian users than in the Blacks. Table 8 and Table 9 show differences regarding the way of writing of each demographic group and reveal interesting characteristics about the difference from one to another.

5 DIFFERENCES IN TOPIC INTERESTS

Males and females may have differences in preferences and interests in digest information. In order to understand which topic is preferable to females than males, we analyze the differences in the topic interest of users in our dataset. The Figure 5 shows the gender distribution for the 20-top topics that we extracted, with log-ratio of perceived male to female. It shows the topic interest for users based on gender in our dataset. On the right side, we see topics related to males' interests while on the left side we see the topics that females are more interested than males. The 3-top topics for males are sports, organizations, and technology. In other words, males tend to interest more in these topics than females. However, females interest more for life, actors, and movie than males. More

Table 6: Differences between tweets from male and female users based on linguistic measures. $\mu(male)$ and $\mu(female)$ are the median values of feature for male and female, respectively. Statistical significance is count based on Wilcoxon rank sum tests. p-values are represented in asterisks scale using * as significant ($0.1 < p \leq 0.5$), ** very significant ($0.001 < p \leq 0.01$), ***($0.0001 < p \leq 0.001$) and ****($p < 0.001$) extremely significant.

	$\mu(male)$	$\mu(female)$	z
Affective attributes			
anger	0.0055	0.0056	4.733
anxiety	0.0016	0.0019	-74.534
sadness	0.0029	0.0034	-74.394
swear	0.0023	0.0026	-7.411
Cognitive attributes			
Cognition			
causation	0.0101	0.0104	-18.627
certainty	0.0101	0.0111	-60.593
tentativeness	0.0136	0.0141	-14.641
Perception			
see	0.00957	0.0099	-24.538
hear	0.0055	0.0056	-0.033*
feel	0.0035	0.0041	-70.766
percepts	0.0207	0.0218	-41.373
insight	0.0115	0.0125	-46.806
relative	0.1014	0.0999	18.026
Lexical Density and Awareness			
verbs	0.1103	0.1170	-45.808
auxiliary verbs	0.0539	0.0583	-46.441
articles	0.0370	0.0340	77.303
prepositions	0.0843	0.0817	32.596
conjunctions	0.0279	0.0314	-72.098
adverbs	0.0317	0.0355	-66.915
Temporal references			
present tense	0.0802	0.0871	-62.110
future tense	0.0103	0.0106	-15.118
Social/Personal Concerns			
family	0.0026	0.0034	-93.252
friends	0.0028	0.0033	-66.168
social	0.0938	0.1021	-77.896
health	0.0037	0.0044	-76.446
religion	0.0024	0.0025	-26.485
bio	0.0157	0.0203	-102.681
body	0.0045	0.0056	-58.386
achievement	0.0116	0.0105	65.265
home	0.0022	0.0026	-74.049
sexual	0.0011	0.0012	-18.691
death	0.0014	0.0013	29.463
Interpersonal focus			
1st p. singular	0.0245	0.0340	-97.329
1st p. plural	0.0046	0.0045	4.309
2nd p.	0.0160	0.0198	-88.482
3rd p.	0.0030	0.0031	-3.371***

specifically, the gender difference between topics varies among males and females.

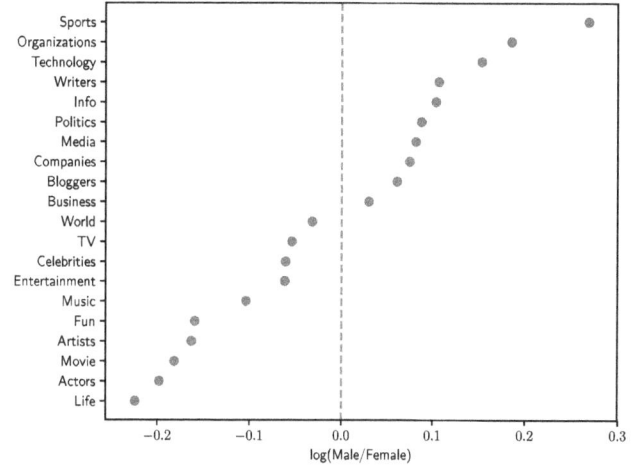

Figure 5: Gender interests: Blue dots represent the gender interests for the 20-top popular topics.

In a similar way, we present the race distribution for the 20-top topics of Asian, Black, and White users in Figure 6. In order to show results regarding race, for this specific analysis, we have normalized the dataset by the number of Black users once they are the minority amount of users in our dataset, as shown in Table 3. Therefore, we have randomly selected 45,398 users for each race to study their topic interests. Users from different races may also vary in interests and preferences. Figure 6-a shows that White users have more interest in politics, writers, and organizations than Asians. However, Asians prefer more artists, actors, and music topics than Whites. Figure 6-b compares the differences in topic interests for White and Blacks. We see that White users are interested in technology, movie, and politics more than Blacks. Nonetheless, Blacks prefer more artists, life, and music topics. Finally, when we look at Figure 6-c, Asians interest more for movie, companies, and technology topics than Blacks. On other hand, Blacks prefer more business, sports, and organizations than Asians.

6 CONCLUSION

The results presented in this paper allow us to conclude that there are clear differences in the way of writing across different demographic groups in both gender and race domains. Our main contribution relies on characterizing the differences in the way of writing for each group pointing the most important linguistic aspects for a specific gender and race. Through the analysis of mean absolute differences amongst linguistic features between each demographic group, we were able to identify those which affective attributes were more present in their writing. In the same way, features based on cognitive attributes, temporal references, social and personal concerns, and interpersonal focus showed to have different weights throughout different demographic domains.

Another interesting conclusion is based on the most common phrases encountered on each group and their position ranking when

Table 7: Differences between tweets from White, Black, and Asian users based on linguistic measures. $\mu(White)$, $\mu(Black)$ and $\mu(Black)$ is the median value of features for each demographic group respectively. Statistical significance is count based on Wilcoxon rank sum tests. The p-values present extremely significant for all linguistic features. We test the correlation of each unique demographic group with the others.

	$\mu(White)$	$\mu(Black)$	$\mu(Asian)$	$z_{W/B-A}$	$z_{B/W-A}$	$z_{A/W-B}$
Affective attributes						
anger	0.0051	0.0081	0.0056	-67.261	94.610	-5.236
anxiety	0.0017	0.0019	0.0016	-0.696	33.789	-30.517
sadness	0.0031	0.0034	0.0032	-20.814	28.205	-0.625
swear	0.0021	0.0064	0.0027	-90.375	107.344	11.329
Cognitive attributes						
Cognition						
causation	0.0104	0.0105	0.0096	29.931	19.465	-54.832
certainty	0.0105	0.0116	0.0101	-19.404	62.239	-33.955
tentativeness	0.0138	0.0152	0.0130	-8.958	55.174	-40.226
Perception						
see	0.0098	0.0098	0.0095	18.756	6.970	-29.506
hear	0.0055	0.0062	0.0054	-26.349	62.137	-25.331
feel	0.0037	0.0044	0.0039	-44.180	63.963	-5.128
percepts	0.0212	0.0223	0.0210	-14.067	43.711	-23.308
insight	0.0122	0.0128	0.0112	11.133	40.420	-51.201
relative	0.1020	0.1012	0.0936	50.614	15.841	-76.870
Lexical Density and Awareness						
verbs	0.1125	0.1222	0.1082	-16.435	64.214	-39.436
auxiliary verbs	0.0554	0.0612	0.0529	-12.202	58.285	-39.130
articles	0.0366	0.0339	0.0314	96.532	-26.056	-94.363
prepositions	0.0851	0.0817	0.0743	77.024	1.032	-95.556
conjunctions	0.0291	0.0319	0.0286	-11.852	43.571	-25.898
adverbs	0.0329	0.0363	0.0325	-17.239	48.159	-23.542
Temporal references						
present tense	0.0825	0.0912	0.0798	-21.972	69.126	-37.196
future tense	0.0103	0.0119	0.0099	-28.333	79.181	-38.719
Social/Personal Concerns						
family	0.0029	0.0040	0.0032	-74.318	86.721	10.755
friend	0.0031	0.0033	0.0033	-26.248	25.332	8.717
social	0.0956	0.1101	0.0971	-60.389	90.830	-10.166
health	0.0040	0.0044	0.0039	-9.579	45.973	-30.920
religion	0.0024	0.0031	0.0024	-53.672	85.163	-13.154
bio	0.0176	0.0204	0.0179	-32.215	53.914	-10.492
body	0.0048	0.0067	0.0052	-62.906	86.903	-3.428
achievement	0.0114	0.0109	0.0097	69.227	-1.632	-83.506
home	0.0025	0.0024	0.0022	50.362	-4.554	-57.624
sexual	0.0011	0.0019	0.0012	-51.768	71.799	-3.084
death	0.0014	0.0015	0.0013	4.356	31.454	-34.554
Interpersonal focus						
1st p. singular	0.0268	0.0355	0.0296	-51.874	63.492	4.760
1st p. plural	0.0048	0.0042	0.0039	77.425	-28.107	-68.994
2nd p.	0.0169	0.0227	0.0177	-63.930	95.495	-10.148
3rd p.	0.0030	0.0039	0.0028	-36.070	87.717	-37.143

compared to different demographic groups. The analysis of these most common phrases led us to conclude that phrases expressing negation figure as one of the most frequent for all domains. Also, the usage of slangs, which is common in an environment like Twitter, appears in these frequent phrases too. When we compare the difference between the groups, we find interesting trends, like the higher interest in signs by females than by males.

By analyzing topic interests, we found that each demographic group tends to have its own preferences over the information they share. For instance, we found that males are more into sports,

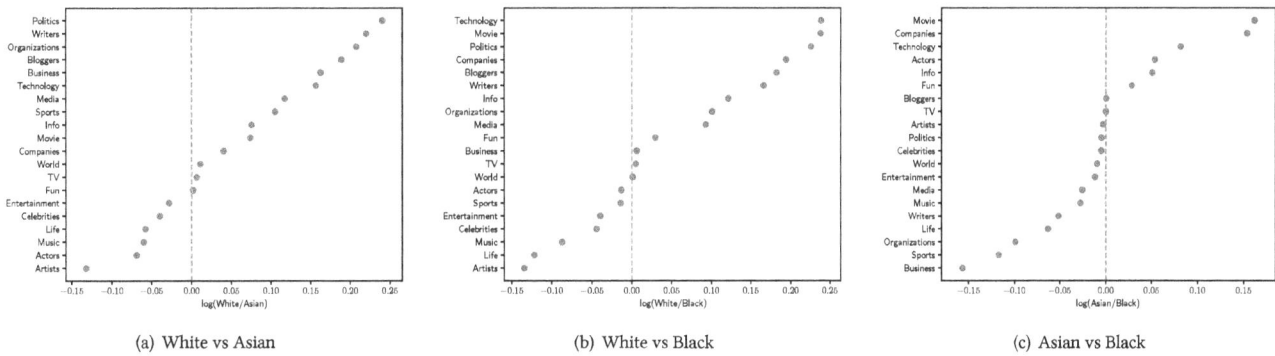

(a) White vs Asian   (b) White vs Black   (c) Asian vs Black

Figure 6: Race interests: Blue dots represent the race interests of (a) White against Asians, (b) White against Blacks, and (c) Asian against Blacks for the 20-top popular topics. The dataset is normalized by the number of Blacks as shown in Table 3.

Table 8: Ranking Differences of Gender Top Phrases. We use *ne* for no existing phrases in a group.

	Rank(Female)	Rank(Male)	DifF(F-M)
i do n't	1	1	0
i ca n't	2	2	0
you do n't	3	3	0
i 'm not	4	4	0
ca n't wait	5	8	3
i 'm so	6	19	13
i love you	7	15	8
do n't know	8	11	3
i want to	9	24	15
more for virgo	10	55	45
more for cancer	11	29	18
i wan na	12	28	16
! i 'm	13	25	12
you ca n't	14	16	2
more for libra	15	39	24
it 's a	16	10	6
and i 'm	17	33	16
more for pisces	18	ne	-
i need to	19	34	15
do n't have	20	27	7

organizations, and technology while females have more interest in topics related to life, actors, and movie. In the same way, users from different races are also likely to have different interests and preferences. White users are more interested in politics, writers, and organizations when compared to Asians, and technology, movie, and politics when compared to Black users. On the other hand, Black users are more into artists, life, and music topics. When we look into Asians, they are more interested in artists, actors, and music than Whites and tend to have higher interest for movie, companies, and technology when compared to Blacks.

There are some future directions we would like to pursue next. First, we plan to study the correlation of linguistic differences with other demographic factors e.g. age. We plan to use our extracted linguistic characteristics as a feature vector for prediction of gender and race. Also, our will is to extend this work correlating demographic aspects with the social behavior, e.g. number of followers, listed, etc. In addition, we plan to examine the speed of tweets that are propagated through a specific demographic group.

ACKNOWLEDGMENTS

This work was partially supported by the project FAPEMIG-PRONEX-MASWeb, Models, Algorithms and Systems for the Web, process number APQ-01400-1 and grants from CNPq, CAPES, Fapemig, and Humboldt Foundation.

REFERENCES

[1] Jisun An and Ingmar Weber. 2016. #greysanatomy vs. #yankees: Demographics and Hashtag Use on Twitte. In *Proceedings of the 10th International AAAI Conference on Web and Social Media*. 523–526.

[2] Fabrício Benevenuto, Tiago Rodrigues, Meeyoung Cha, and Virgílio Almeida. 2009. Characterizing user behavior in online social networks. In *IMC '09: Proceedings of the 9th ACM SIGCOMM conference on Internet measurement conference*. ACM, New York, NY, USA, 49–62. DOI:http://dx.doi.org/10.1145/1644893.1644900

[3] Parantapa Bhattacharya, Muhammad Bilal Zafar, Niloy Ganguly, Saptarshi Ghosh, and Krishna P. Gummadi. 2014. Inferring User Interests in the Twitter Social Network. In *Proceedings of the 8th ACM Conference on Recommender Systems (RecSys '14)*. ACM, New York, NY, USA, 357–360.

[4] Cameron Blevins and Lincoln Mullen. 2015. Jane, John... Leslie? a historical method for algorithmic gender prediction. *Digital Humanities Quarterly* 9, 3 (2015).

[5] John D Burger, John Henderson, George Kim, and Guido Zarrella. 2011. Discriminating gender on Twitter. In *Proceedings of the Conference on Empirical Methods in Natural Language Processing*. Association for Computational Linguistics, 1301–1309.

[6] Meeyoung Cha, Fabrício Benevenuto, Hamed Haddadi, and Krishna P. Gummadi. 2012. The world of connections and information flow in Twitter. *IEEE Transactions on Systems, Man and Cybernetics - Part A* 42, 4 (2012), 991–998.

[7] Meeyoung Cha, Hamed Haddadi, Fabricio Benevenuto, and Krishna P. Gummadi. 2010. Measuring User Influence in Twitter: The Million Follower Fallacy. In *Proceedings of the 4th International AAAI Conference on Weblogs and Social Media (ICWSM'10)*. Washington DC, USA.

[8] Abhijnan Chakraborty, Johnnatan Messias, Fabricio Benevenuto, Saptarshi Ghosh, Niloy Ganguly, and Krishna P. Gummadi. 2017. Who Makes Trends? Understanding Demographic Biases in Crowdsourced Recommendations. In *Proceedings of the 11th International AAAI Conference on Web and Social Media (ICWSM'17)*. Montreal, Canada.

[9] Xin Chen, Yu Wang, Eugene Agichtein, and Fusheng Wang. 2015. A comparative study of demographic attribute inference in twitter. In *In Proceedings of the 9th International AAAI Conference on Weblogs and Social Media*.

[10] Alex Cheng and Mark Evans. 2009. Inside Twitter: An In-Depth Look Inside the Twitter World. (2009).

Table 9: Ranking Differences of Race Top Phrases. We use *ne* for no existing phrases in a group.

	Rank(White)	Rank(Black)	Rank(Asian)	Diff(W-B)	Diff(W-A)	Diff(B-A)
i do n't	1	1	1	0	0	0
i ca n't	2	2	2	0	0	0
ca n't wait	3	18	7	15	4	11
you do n't	4	4	3	0	1	1
i 'm not	5	8	6	3	1	2
i love you	6	33	4	27	2	29
i 'm so	7	16	6	9	1	10
do n't know	8	19	11	11	3	8
it 's a	9	26	16	17	7	10
one of the	10	48	20	38	10	28
i want to	11	47	10	36	1	37
! i 'm	12	46	29	34	17	17
if you 're	13	28	19	15	6	9
thank you for	14	126	28	112	14	98
it 's not	15	34	32	19	17	2
and i 'm	16	58	21	42	5	37
you ca n't	17	17	17	0	0	0
i 'm at	18	53	26	35	8	27
n't wait to	19	100	51	81	32	49
i liked a	20	7	ne	13	-	-

[11] Denzil Correa, Leandro Araújo Silva, Mainack Mondal, Fabrício Benevenuto, and Krishna P. Gummadi. 2015. The Many Shades of Anonymity: Characterizing Anonymous Social Media Content. In *In Proceedings of the 4th International AAAI Conference on Weblogs and Social Media (ICWSM'10)*.

[12] Aron Culotta, Nirmal Ravi Kumar, and Jennifer Cutler. 2015. Predicting the Demographics of Twitter Users from Website Traffic Data.. In *Proceedings of the 29th AAAI Conference on Artificial Intelligence*. 72–78.

[13] Evandro Cunha, Gabriel Magno, Virgilio Almeida, Marcos André Gonçalves, and Fabricio Benevenuto. 2012. A Gender Based Study of Tagging Behavior in Twitter. In *Proceedings of the 23rd ACM Conference on Hypertext and Social Media (HT '12)*. ACM, New York, NY, USA, 323–324. DOI:http://dx.doi.org/10.1145/2309996.2310055

[14] Munmun De Choudhury, Sanket S. Sharma, Tomaz Logar, Wouter Eekhout, and René Clausen Nielsen. 2017. Gender and Cross-Cultural Differences in Social Media Disclosures of Mental Illness. In *Proceedings of the 2017 ACM Conference on Computer Supported Cooperative Work and Social Computing (CSCW '17)*. ACM, New York, NY, USA, 353–369.

[15] Haoqiang Fan, Zhimin Cao, Yuning Jiang, Qi Yin, and Chinchilla Doudou. 2014. Learning deep face representation. *arXiv preprint arXiv:1403.2802* (2014).

[16] Carlos Freitas, Fabricio Benevenuto, Saptarshi Ghosh, and Adriano Veloso. 2015. Reverse Engineering Socialbot Infiltration Strategies in Twitter. In *Proceedings of the 2015 IEEEACM International Conference on Advances in Social Networks Analysis and Mining*.

[17] Eric Gilbert, Saeideh Bakhshi, Shuo Chang, and Loren Terveen. 2013. "I Need to Try This"?: A Statistical Overview of Pinterest. In *Proceedings of the SIGCHI Conference on Human Factors in Computing Systems*. ACM, New York, NY, USA, 2427–2436.

[18] Aniko Hannak, Claudia Wagner, David Garcia, Alan Mislove, Markus Strohmaier, and Christo Wilson. 2017. Bias in Online Freelance Marketplaces: Evidence from TaskRabbit and Fiverr. In *20th ACM Conference on Computer-Supported Cooperative Work and Social Computing (CSCW 2017)*. Portland, OR.

[19] Fariba Karimi, Claudia Wagner, Florian Lemmerich, Mohsen Jadidi, and Markus Strohmaier. 2016. Inferring Gender from Names on the Web: A Comparative Evaluation of Gender Detection Methods. In *Proceedings of the 25th International Conference on World Wide Web*. 53–54.

[20] Juhi Kulshrestha, Farshad Kooti, Ashkan Nikravesh, and P Krishna Gummadi. 2012. Geographic Dissection of the Twitter Network.. In *In Proceedings of the 6th International AAAI Conference on Weblogs and Social Media*.

[21] Wendy Liu and Derek Ruths. 2013. What's in a Name? Using First Names as Features for Gender Inference in Twitter.. In *AAAI Spring Symposium Series*, Vol. 13. 01.

[22] Johnnatan Messias, Lucas Schmidt, Ricardo Rabelo, and Fabrício Benevenuto. 2013. You followed my bot! Transforming robots into influential users in Twitter. *First Monday* 18, 7 (July 2013).

[23] Alan Mislove, Sune Lehmann, Yong-Yeol Ahn, Jukka-Pekka Onnela, and J Niels Rosenquist. 2011. Understanding the Demographics of Twitter Users.. In *In Proceedings of the 5th International AAAI Conference on Weblogs and Social Media*, Vol. 11. 5th.

[24] Shirin Nilizadeh, Anne Groggel, Peter Lista, Srijita Das, Yong-Yeol Ahn, Apu Kapadia, and Fabio Rojas. 2016. Twitter's Glass Ceiling: The Effect of Perceived Gender on Online Visibility. In *In Proceedings of the 10th International AAAI Conference on Weblogs and Social Media*.

[25] Julio C. S. Reis, Haewoon Kwak, Jisun An, Johnnatan Messias, and Fabricio Benevenuto. 2017. Demographics of News Sharing in the U.S. Twittersphere. In *Proceedings of the 28th ACM Conference on Hypertext and Social Media (HT '17)*. ACM, New York, NY, USA.

[26] Filipe N. Ribeiro, Matheus Araújo, Pollyanna Gonçalves, Marcos André Gonçalves, and Fabrício Benevenuto. 2016. SentiBench - a benchmark comparison of state-of-the-practice sentiment analysis methods. *EPJ Data Science* 5, 1 (2016), 1–29.

[27] Luke Sloan, Jeffrey Morgan, Pete Burnap, and Matthew Williams. 2015. Who tweets? Deriving the demographic characteristics of age, occupation and social class from Twitter user meta-data. *PloS one* 10, 3 (2015), e0115545.

[28] Yla R Tausczik and James W Pennebaker. 2010. The psychological meaning of words: LIWC and computerized text analysis methods. *Journal of language and social psychology* 29, 1 (2010), 24–54.

[29] Johannes Wachs, Aniko Hannak, Andras Voros, and Balint Daroczy. 2017. Why Do Men Get More Attention? Exploring Factors Behind Success in an Online Design Community. In *Proceedings of the 11th International AAAI Conference on Web and Social Media (ICWSM'17)*. Montreal, Canada.

[30] Qi Yin, Zhimin Cao, Yuning Jiang, and Haoqiang Fan. 2015. Learning Deep Face Representation. (Dec. 3 2015). US Patent 20,150,347,820.

[31] Emilio Zagheni, Venkata Rama Kiran Garimella, Ingmar Weber, and Bogdan State. 2014. Inferring International and Internal Migration Patterns from Twitter Data. In *Proceedings of the 23rd International Conference on World Wide Web*.

Interactive Concert Programs for Live Performances

A Presentation Software Integrating Slideshow and Hypertext Concepts

Raffaele Cipriano
University of Kansas
1350 Naismith Drive
Lawrence, Kansas 66045
rcipriano@ku.edu

ABSTRACT

Concerts and live shows are usually better appreciated when additional information about the exhibition and the performers are provided. For centuries, printed pamphlets or booklets have been the common way to provide the audiences with this information. Unfortunately, printed programs are not always the most efficient solution: they typically contain too much data to be read in a few minutes preceding the show, and after the performance they are usually thrown away. More crucial, printed information cannot be synchronized with the ongoing show, and the spectator has to constantly connect the data on the paper with what is happening on the stage. Technology can overcome this problem. *Interactive Concert Programs* (ICP) is a software that allows the streaming of digital information (such as text, images, or links) to the mobile devices of an audience in real time. Data can be triggered at a specific moment, according to what is performed. Moreover, any spectator can autonomously navigate the information streamed, using his/her device. ICP combines the characteristics of a *slideshow software* such as PowerPoint, and of a *hypertext*, such as HTML pages. There are several advantages of using ICP instead of printed programs. The listening experience can be guided with relevant information through all the duration of the show. Multilingual translations can be easily provided, as well as explaining texts for the Deaf. Users can save and share on social media the most interesting information, thus engaging new potential public. Lastly, the editing process of concert programs would be drastically simplified, and with a remarkable saving of printed paper. In this historical moment when performing arts can be difficult to understand and be appreciated, ICP can easily and inexpensively turn any theater or stage into a big lecture room, providing a new effective way for artists to tell the audience their artistic vision and the story behind the artwork performed. The audience would assimilate information more easily, with a better understanding and appreciation of the shows.

KEYWORDS

presentation; slideshow; hypertext; interaction; augmented performance; theater; concert

HT'17, July 4-7, 2017, Prague, Czech Republic.
© 2017 ACM. 978-1-4503-4708-2/17/07...$15.00
DOI: http://dx.doi.org/10.1145/3078714.3078743

1 INTRODUCTION

One of the biggest challenges for a theater or an orchestra company is to engage the audience and make sure that the public enjoys the shows and keeps coming to every concert of the current and following season. Recent research from the National Endowment for the Arts [ ] highlighted that the audience of performative arts has significantly decreased in the decade 2002-2012. The percentage of U.S. adults attending a performing art activity at least once in the past 12 months dropped in every genre.[1] Moreover, from the demographic distribution of the audience observed in that study, it is clear that performative arts lack in engaging important segments of their potential audience, such as people of non-white ethnicities or people of ages 18-24. If this trend remains, many concert halls and theaters will be facing financial crisis and risk closure. As a consequence, attending performative art shows would become even more difficult, with an alarming impact on society. In fact, the arts play an important role in connecting people with their souls and emotions: as William Bennett[2] said, the arts "are an essential element of education, just like reading, writing, and arithmetic... music, dance, painting, and theater are all keys that unlock profound human understanding and accomplishment"[ ].

One of the reasons for this decreasing interest in performative arts, is that they require a deeper focus and comprehension than other lighter forms of entertainment. Quoting Julian Johnson [ ]: "A piece of music is no different than a poem or a painting. To understand a poem, one has to be literate not only in language, but also in the formal conventions of the poetic genre and the broader tradition of poetry." According to him, "the goal of our relationship with music-as-art is understanding". As a consequence, if we want the performative arts to return being a regular part of people's entertainment and personal growth, it is crucial to give people easy and efficient ways to understand the artworks, the artists, as well as the history and the ideas beyond the creative process. One common way to help the audience understand a live show is to provide printed information about the work performed and the artists involved. As society has become very technologically-oriented in the last decade, some modern approaches could be more effective than the traditional printed paper.

The goal of the current work is to develop a software able to enrich any performance in theaters or concert halls, streaming real-time information on the audience's devices. The information provided should help the participants to better understand and

---

[1] The percentages recorded in the U.S. in 2002 and 2012 for the different genres are: jazz (10.8%-8.1%); classical music (11.6%-8.8%); opera (3.2%-2.1%); musical plays (17.1%-15.2%); non musical plays (12.3%-8.3%); ballet (3.9%-2.7%); other dances (6.3%-5.6%).
[2] Former US Secretary of Education.

enjoy the performances, leading to further engagement of the audience. *Interactive Concert Programs* (ICP) software has been developed to this aim. It has been tested in a few pilot studies, which helped tune the technology and led to an experiment at the University of Kansas that involved the use of ICP during a symphonic concert. In that experiment, ICP received very positive feedback from the participants. ICP is in a beta version and it is available to the HT2017 participants for testing (see section 3.5). One of the main advantages of ICP is its full compatibility with all the modern and future devices, since its technology is based on HTML and Javascript. Hopefully, a few years from now, wearable technologies for augmented reality, such as Google Glasses and Virtual Reality headsets, will become more accessible and common. At that point, ICP will be immediately available to be used on these devices. This could open the doors to the concept of *augmented live performances*, i.e. live shows where additional layers of information are digitally provided to the viewers in real time.

This article explains the reasons behind ICP, its design principles, the experiment performed, as well as its possible applications and improvements. In section 2 we first present some traditional and modern ways to provide the audience with information about a show and its performers; then, we briefly discuss some key features of slideshow and hypertext software, addressing their relation to the task of providing effective concert programs. Section 3 illustrates the ICP software, from its general principles to a more detailed explanation of its components and technologies; the links to access and try this technology are provided at the end of the section. Section 4 describes and discusses an experiment performed at the University of Kansas that used ICP during a symphonic concert. In section 5, some major applications of ICP are examined. Section 6 addresses some ideas that would improve ICP and some additional experiments that need to be performed to measure its effectiveness. Section 7 draws the conclusions of the present work.

2 STATE OF THE ART

Concert programs are traditionally provided in theaters as pamphlets incorporating information about the music to be performed, the ensemble, the conductor, and the soloists. Renowned concert halls may provide big booklets containing extensive information, such as state-of-the-art musicology studies, broad listening guides, and commented excerpts of the music (see for example [,]). In the case of opera houses, the concert program includes the libretto of the opera, usually both in the original language and in English. Moreover, opera houses provide supertitles with translations on the top of the stage or small screens in the backs of the seats [,]. These supertitles are synchronized with the music, but they only address the translations of the words. The use of supertitles during opera performances is sometimes questioned, as it could "take our minds and focus away from the music and all its richness" [ ]. Nevertheless, all the major opera houses provide them.

Currently, information about the music and the performers is mainly provided in printed concert programs, thus limiting the possibilities of guiding the listening experience throughout the performance, as in the dark of the ongoing show reading becomes difficult. Moreover, a study by Margulis points out that in some

cases, "prefacing an excerpt with a text description reduces enjoyment of the music" [ ]. A different, more technology-based approach, could challenge this results and lead to more enjoyment when attending live music.

A technological approach has been attempted in 2004 with the Concert Companion [ ], a personal digital assistant (PDA) provided to participants wishing to use it for receiving commentary and images during a live performance. This technology has not become popular as hoped, likely for the cost of the PDAs, that were expected to be rented by the users at every concert. Other technological approaches have been tried. For example, in more informal settings, such as family concerts, educational projects or avant-guard exhibitions, the performances are sometimes enriched with texts and photos projected on a screen on stage (for a more detailed discussion, see [ ]). A slideshow presentation software is commonly used in these situations, with a person following the show and triggering the slides accordingly. This approach adds some interesting features to the performance, such as the ability to guide the listening experience and the possibility of counterbalancing sounds with words or images. However, some disadvantages still take place: the projector could not be clearly visible from all the seats of the hall; the light of the projector could interfere with the lights designed for the show; people not interested in the visual information are forced to receive it; also, people cannot stop the presentation to focus on or examine a specific slide.

This last aspect is common to all the *slideshow* presentation software: the presenter typically sets the time for each slide, which are presented one after another, in a linear fashion. Of course, in the last twenty years presentation software have evolved, trying to overcome their linear, static nature. For example, PowerPoint and Keynote can include hyperlinks to other presentations or to external resources, such as web pages or videos, that could be activated by the presenter, thus breaking the linearity of a presentation. Prezi [ ] is a recent presentation software that breaks the sequentiality of the slides, placing them in a big bi-dimensional (or even tri-dimensional) space. In this way, the viewers can see how the individual slides fit together to form a larger picture. Even with these innovations, two main disadvantages remain: 1) from the viewer's perspective, the slides are always received in a linear order; 2) there is no possibility to break this uni-directional flow of information as decided by the presenter.

In a situation where people are properly engaged and sincerely interested in what they are attending, they would typically prefer to look autonomously for specific information, investigating in more depth what touches their curiosity. This possibility is typical of the *hypertext* (and of the whole Web, which is a huge hypertext): the users navigate links following a stream of related information, in order to increase their knowledge on a subject. Hypertexts provide the freedom of browsing information autonomously, but their navigation cannot be easily synchronized to a live performance.

Developing a new concept for digital concert programs should address theaters' and audiences' needs by incorporating the benefits of both the slideshow and the hypertext paradigms. The new concert programs should trigger real-time show-related information like in a slideshow, still giving every single person the chance to investigate what interests him/her more, like in a hypertext. As mobile devices have become more popular in the last two decades [ ], they could be the best tool for achieving this goal. In fact, they can deliver easy to navigate real-time information to the audience. Moreover, concert halls and theaters would not need to cover any additional cost on equipment to provide this service, since it would rely on the devices already owned by the audience.

3 INTERACTIVE CONCERT PROGRAMS SOFTWARE

The *Interactive Concert Programs* (ICP) software is a web application that allows venues to simultaneously stream visual information (texts or images) to multiple devices, such as mobile phones, tablets, and computers. The concept is similar to a PowerPoint presentation, where viewers are shown a series of information and images in a linear fashion. In this case, the slides are triggered by a person from a web back-end, and the information get projected on the screen of every device connected to the application[3]. All the devices are simultaneously updated, roughly within half a second from the moment the person triggers a new slide.

The user can passively follow the information streamed or actively interact with them: he/she can go back and forth between the slides streamed so far, and can surf the links provided in the slides. The links can bring the user to pages designed for that specific presentation or to external websites (such as Wikipedia pages or personal/companies websites). Independently from the slide or web page visualized, there is always the possibility to instantly return to the presentation, right to the slide currently streamed.

Thanks to the possibility of navigating the slides and the links, the user can break the linear path of a traditional presentation and potentially surf the whole web. For this reason, the ICP system embeds the characteristics of both a *presentation software* (information are shown in linear slides, triggered by a guide) and a *hypertext* (the user can follow the links, looking for the information in which he/she is more interested).

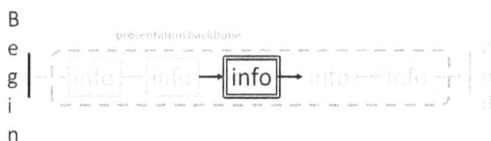

Figure 1: Information accessed by the user of a traditional presentation

Figure 1 and 2 show how a user accesses information during a traditional presentation or an ICP presentation. The double-line

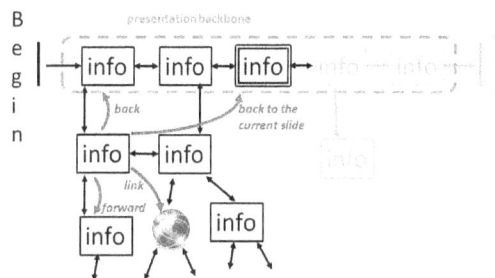

Figure 2: Information accessed by the user of a ICP presentation

square represents the slides currently projected while the gray squares represent the nonaccessible slides. The black straight arrows represent the directions the user can navigate to, while the red curved arrows represent the slides that can be reached by the user with an atomic action. In a traditional presentation, the slides are presented to the user one by one, and at a given time the user can visualize only the slide selected by the presenter. The previous slides are hidden, as well as the following ones. The scenario is different for an ICP presentation: all the slides previous to the current one are still accessible, with the black arrows allowing to move backward and forward. The links allow moving from the presentation backbone, thus obtaining additional information. The slides following the current one have not been unlocked yet, so they are not accessible. In this way, the viewer cannot anticipate (thus spoiling) the contents that are about to come. The red curved arrows show how the user can move from any slide: going back, going forward, following a link, returning to the current slide. Comparing figure 1 and 2, it is easy to notice that at any given time ICP allows the user to access more information than a traditional slideshow software.

3.1 ICP principles

The goal of ICP is to enrich a live performance with real-time information. This information should be:

(1) easy to produce;
(2) easy to access;
(3) minimally distracting for anyone else who wants to follow the show without using ICP.

In order to reach these expectations, the following characteristics have been guaranteed while developing the ICP software:

- producing ICP slides should be an easy and fast process; the possibility of reusing text already available is extremely encouraged, for example through cut-and-paste operations (principle 1);
- the interaction of the user is not required (principle 2 and 3); the user can simply look at the device and will still receive all the information necessary to enjoy the show;
- the interaction of the user would be limited to a few simple actions (principle 2 and 3); these actions include going back and forth, as well as navigating the links;

---

[3]Since ICP is intended to be used in live performances requiring synchronization, the slides are intentionally designed to be triggered manually. In fact, during live performances, many factors can suddenly change the timing of the show: an actor forgetting a line, a soloist taking more or less time than usual on a cadenza, a conductor taking a piece at a faster or slower tempo than expected. In the theater world, all the timing-sensitive tasks of a show (e.g., curtain, light cues, stage rotation, change of scenes, supertitles) are always handled live by a specific person. It could be interesting to create a software able to track the progression of the show, and to trigger specific events at the right moment. This software could be very challenging to develop, as it would involve complex speech recognition (on different actors, with different accents) and frequency recognition (on multiple and simultaneous pitches and timbres). Such a project goes beyond the goals of the current work.

- whatever part of the presentation (or web) the user is browsing, there should always be a 'safe' button that immediately brings him/her to the most recent triggered slide (principle 2);
- the size of the words in a slide should auto-adjust, to be as big as possible and to fit the screen size; this would both maximize the readability and release the user from resizing/scrolling the page (principle 2);
- colors used in the slides should maximize the readability (principle 2), without distracting other people in the hall (principle 3); to this aim, the application has followed the precautions pointed out in [, ,]. For example, the background color of the screen is set to black, to minimize the brightness of the multiple screens active in a concert hall. Also, the color of the words is ivory, which has a yellow/beige quality assuring high readability, without too much brightness.

3.2   ICP design

ICP is made of three components:

(1) an *editor*, to create the slides;
(2) a *control-room*, to start a presentation and trigger the slides;
(3) a *viewer*, to visualize and navigate the slides.

The control-room runs the slides on a specific web address, shared with the viewers. The viewers can navigate the ICP presentation browsing that web address with any browser, without any need of authentication or downloading an application. A control-room can have multiple viewers, while a viewer (i.e., a single page of a browser) can access only one presentation at a time. The communication between the control-room and the viewers happens through the shared web address. Once connected to the specific address, the screen of the viewer visualizes texts or images triggered as the live performance goes on.

The main goal of ICP is to give the user both the ability to follow the slides as streamed in traditional presentation, and the chance to interact with the information as in a hypertext. To this aim it is crucial to clearly define the responsibilities of the control-room and the viewer. *The control-room notifies the viewer the progress of the slides. The viewer decides to either follow the progress of the slides (with the times set by the control-room), or to autonomously navigate the information.* Let's analyze these components more in depth.

Control-room. The main actions of a control-room are to *load a presentation* and to *trigger the slides*. These actions are performed by a person operating on the control-room backend. Slides can be triggered by either selecting a desired slide or invoking a *nextslide* command. When this happens, the control-room *notifies all the viewers* connected to the presentation that a new slide has been triggered.

Viewer. Once connected to the web address, the viewer waits for notification from the control-room. The viewer has two main **statuses**: *live*, meaning that it is visualizing the latest slide and wants to be updated as soon as the next slides is triggered by the control-room; *surfing*, meaning that it is freely browsing the slides or the links and it is not interested in instant updates.

Figure 3: The interface of a smartphone running an ICP slide

Whenever the viewer receives the notification that a new slide has been triggered, it has two options, according to his status:

(1) if *live*, it fetches the new slide triggered and visualizes it;
(2) if *surfing*, it memorizes the information about the new slide, but it stays on the page currently visualized;

In this way, if the user decides to navigate the slides, his/her activity is not interrupted by a new slide triggered. As the new slide is memorized, the user can jump to it with a single action at any time.

The user can interact with the information streamed using one of the following **actions**:

(1) *backward*: it visualizes the previous slide;
(2) *forward*: it visualizes the following slide, but cannot access slides that have not yet been triggered by the control-room;
(3) *click-on-link*: if a slide contains a link, the user can click on it and the corresponding page will open, letting him/her out from the presentation backbone. To return to the presentation backbone, the user can use either the "backward" action or the "go-to-the-current-slide" action;
(4) *go-to-the-current-slide*: it visualizes the latest slide triggered by the control-room, bringing the user to the most advanced point on the presentation backbone.

Figure 3 shows the screen of a smartphone visualizing an ICP slide. The four actions that the user can perform are highlighted by the numbers in parenthesis.

The viewer starts with a *live* status, which can be changed during the presentation, according to the viewer's actions: *back*, *forward* and *click-on-link* typically switch the status to *surf*; *go-to-the-current-slide* restores the *live* status. If, after a few *back* actions, enough *forward* actions are performed to bring the viewer to the most recent slide, then the *live* status is also restored.

Editor. This component provides an easy and fast way to generate ICP slides. It mainly consists in a text-box where the user can type or cut-and-paste the text of the slides. To separate the text into different slides, the user has to add an empty line in the text. *An empty line means a new slide, so the text between two empty lines will belong to the same slide.* Thus, even generating a slide from a long text (such as the lyrics of an opera) is as easy as cutting and pasting the whole text and add some empty lines. It is also possible to add some editing to the text, such as the standard underlined, italicized or bold options. Inserting an external link in the text is performed in three steps: the user 1) selects the word that will contain the link, 2) types the link address in an input box, and 3) confirms with a click.

A preview of the slides is visualized on the side of the textbox and is updated every time some new text is typed or pasted. Once the slides appear as desired, a save button will generate them and store them in the specified directory.

3.3 Technology at work

Each module of the ICP software has been realized following the Model-View-Controller paradigm, using state-of-the-art web technologies, such as HTML 5, CSS 3, and Javascript. The server side of the web application has been developed using the Node.js platform. The key idea beyond ICP is that every 'slide' that will be streamed on the mobile devices is an HTML page. The editor generates the HTML files, the control-room sets which slide is currently on air, the viewer decides which slide will be visualized and fetches the corresponding HTML file.

The *editor* parses the text inserted in its textbox and generates multiple HTML pages. The HTML pages are saved using names with the form $[prefix][index][extension]$: $[prefix]$ is usually the string p (but it could be arbitrarily chosen); $[index]$ is an incremental number of four digits, starting from 0000; $[extension]$ is typically the string .html (but it could be a different string[4]). For example, if the editor generates 5 slides, it will generate the files p0000.html, p0001.html, p0002.html, p0003.html, and p0004.html. Every HTML page contains part of the text typed in the textbox (according to slide subdivision policy explained in the previous section) and a reference to a common CSS file. This CSS file stores information such as the color of the background, the color and the size of the the text, and so on.

The duty of the *control-room* is to determine which slide is triggered, and notify it to the viewers. The information about the triggered (or current) slide is contained in an *integer variable*. This variable can be read and written by the control-room and can be read (and only read) by the viewers.

The *viewers*, knowing the integer value of the current slide, build the name of the corresponding HTML file (adding the prefix, some 0 digits and the extension), fetch the page and visualize it. A viewer can also fetch and visualize pages with a smaller index than the current slide (going into the *surfing* status, as explained in the previous section).

With this design, the HTML pages are stored in a single place, the information about the current slide is managed only in the control-room, and every viewer can autonomously decide to visualize either the current slide or the previous ones. The action of jumping to the current slide is performed by reading the value of the integer variable for the current slide, building the name of the HTML file, and accessing that file.

3.4 Compatibility

ICP has been build on *standard technologies* (HTML 5, CSS 3 and Javascript), *using only tags and features that are fully supported by major browsers* (e.g., Internet Explorer, Firefox, Chrome, Safari,

Opera). This guarantees a high level of compatibility with all the possible devices that will use ICP. In fact, ICP works on any browser able to visualize HTML pages and run Javascript code. Any device with such a browser is able to run any ICP component, regardless of the operating system (MAC, PC, Linux, Android are fully compatible). The software has been successfully tested on Chrome, Internet Explorer, Edge, Safari, Firefox, and Opera, on laptops and smartphones running Windows, IOS or Android.

Moreover, the full compatibility with the web standards puts ICP in a good position for being compatible with any (even future) device. For example any wearable technology (such as Apple Watch [ ], Google Glasses [ ] or other devices for augmented reality) commonly supports HTML, CSS and Javascript, thus being ICP compatible.

3.5 Try ICP

ICP has not been officially released, since it is still in beta version. However, it has been made available for testing to the HT2017 participants. Here are the links to the components:

http://interactiveconcertprograms.azurewebsites.net/editor
http://interactiveconcertprograms.azurewebsites.net/control-room
http://interactiveconcertprograms.azurewebsites.net/viewer

The *editor* and the *control-room* pages require credentials to login; please, use username *ht2017* and password *ht2017*.

4 EXPERIMENT: ICP FOR A SYMPHONIC CONCERT

The ICP software has been preliminarily tested in pilot studies, like chamber music performances, with an audience limited to 20-35 people. These tests had the main goal of tuning the technology, fixing some technical issues, and having an initial feedback on the appreciation of the software. Once the ICP technology was considered mature, a bigger experiment was set up at the University of Kansas. The purpose of the experiment was to test the ICP technology in a real concert setting (concert hall with almost 2000 seats, orchestra of almost 80 players), through observation of audience technology use and collection of feedback about this service, to determine if audience prefers this technology to traditional printed concert programs. The feedback, collected with an electronic questionnaire, included rating the usefulness of ICP and traditional concert programs. The analysis of variances and the paired t-test has been performed to compare the responses. The results obtained from this study indicate that the audience prefers this new technology to traditional program notes and would like to have ICP software available in future concerts. The experiment took place in a concert hall with a real orchestra and a real audience. The concert happened on September 28th, 2016, when the Kansas University Symphony Orchestra performed a symphonic concert at the Lied Center of Arts, as part of the 2016-2017 concert season[5]. Before the concert, Maestro Jung-Ho Pak, guest conductor of the orchestra, kindly agreed on trying the ICP software during the performance. The concert took place in the main auditorium, which has almost

---

[4]The extension can be changed to allow compatibility with presentation software like PowerPoint. For example, it is possible to export a PowerPoint presentation into several image files, usually named Slide1.jpg, Slide2.jpg and so on. Changing *prefix* to 'Slide' and *extension* to '.jpg' allows to stream these files instead of HTML pages. Even if ICP works better with HTML pages, providing compatibility with PowerPoint presentations is a desirable feature.

[5]The Kansas University Symphony Orchestra (KUSO) is composed of 70-80 players from University of Kansas, who are mainly music majors from the School of Music. It performs standard symphonic repertoire, with at least three performances per semester. The Lied Center for Performing Arts is a big complex for concerts and conferences in Lawrence, KS.

2000 seats. The ICP software provided live textual information on the last piece of the concert, a selection from the ballet *Romeo and Juliet* by Prokofiev, including *Montagues and Capulets, Young Juliet, Masks, Death of Tybalt,* and *Romeo at the Juliet's Grave.* The experiment had two parts: first, the audience listened to the selection from *Romeo and Juliet,* with the option of following the live notes via the ICP software; then, at the end of the piece, they were asked to fill out an online questionnaire on their experience with ICP.

4.1 Setting up the experiment

Participants. The participants in this study were a subset of the people attending the concert. According to the ticket office, 607 tickets were sold for the show, and around 100 of them used the ICP software, as tracked by the software connection log. Among them, 28 completed the survey. Software use and survey completion were voluntary.

Materials. A set of 88 textual slides was prepared: the first two introduced the ensemble and the piece, while the other 86 followed the music. These 86 slides addressed the plot of the pieces, the connection between the music and the plot, and the musical choices of the composer (such as musical form, instrumentation, harmonic language). The selection from *Romeo and Juliet* was 25 minutes long, thus every slide was triggered on average every 17 seconds. The questionnaire was built on the Survey Monkey website and had ten questions. The first three questions inquired about the user's background, while the other seven questions focused on the specific experience with ICP during the concert. There were three types of questions: multiple-choice questions, rating questions, and one open-ended question. In addition to the survey, some feedback were received from a post-concert email sent by the Lied Center communication office to the subscribers, as some people provided feedback on the use of ICP. Questions 3 and 5 were the key questions of this study: question 3 asked to rate the usefulness of traditional concert programs on the base of participants' past experience, while question 5 asked to rate the usefulness of the ICP software during that show.

Procedure. The audience entering the hall received both the traditional booklet with information about the concert as well as a piece of paper with a brief explanation of the ICP software and the QR code containing the link to the ICP slides. Before starting the selection from *Romeo and Juliet,* the conductor introduced the technology and encouraged the audience to grab their phones, scan the QR code and follow the ICP slides while listening to the orchestra. After the last slide, the software visualized a link that directed the user to the questionnaire about the experience with ICP. A visual message thanked the user and encouraged him/her to take the questionnaire.

4.2 Results

Thanks to the ICP connection log, it was possible to know how many users were connected to the system while the slides were triggered. Figure 4 shows the number of active connections per slide. At the first slide (containing the ensemble's and conductor's name) the number of connections was low (only 11). After the introduction to ICP made by the conductor, the number of connections rapidly

increased to 84 (for the second slide, containing the title of the piece). For the whole performance, it stayed stable on an average of 104 connections. Considering 607 persons in the audience, it means that 17.1% of them used ICP throughout the whole *Romeo and Juliet* execution. Among these users, 28 filled out the questionnaire, i.e. the 26.9% of the ICP users.

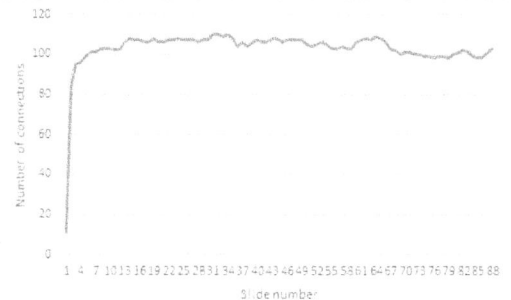

Figure 4: Number of connections to ICP for each slide

The information gained can be categorized in users' background information, technical feedback, overall ICP experience, additional feedback.

Users' background information. General information collected by survey questions 1, 2, and 3 indicated that the majority of the respondents (78.6%) looks for information about the music and the performers, either with personal research (10.7%), or reading the program notes provided in the hall (50%), or using both these methods (17.9%). Only a minority of them (24.4%) are not interested in getting additional information. The respondents show a general interest in reading program notes, with 89.3% of them reading program notes 'Usually' or 'Always'. When asked to rate the usefulness of traditional program notes from 0 (totally useless) to 100 (very useful), the average rate obtained was 71 (number of participants $N = 28$, mean $\overline{X} = 71.39$, standard deviation $\sigma = 26.4$). The analysis of variance showed that the answers varyed widely.

Technical feedback. Two questions were asked to obtain technical feedback on the technology used. Question 6 asked if the respondent were distracted by other people using their phones. 96.3% were 'not distracted at all', 3.7% were a 'little bit distracted', and no one (0%) was 'very distracted'. Question 7 was meant to verify if the live notes fitted the screen properly: it happened 'always' in the 39.3% of the cases and 'most of the time' in the 60.7% of the cases (other possibilities were 'occasionally', 'almost never' and 'never', which all got 0%).

Overall ICP experience. The remaining questions investigated the ICP experience. Question 4 verified that respondents followed the live notes. The 80% of the respondent followed 'all the notes', while the 12% followed 'almost all the notes' and the 8% 'some of the notes'. Question 5 asked to rate from 0 to 100 how much the live notes were useful to enjoy the show better (0 meaning totally useless, 100 very useful). The average rate obtained was 89 ($N = 28$, $\overline{X} = 89.93$, $\sigma = 16.85$). The analysis of variance showed that the shape of the curve for this answer was more compact than the one for question 3. The test for equality of variances was performed: the F value of the two variances is 2.45, above the critical value 2.13 (two-tailed test, $\alpha = 0.05$), thus the two variances are not comparable (as we can also see from Figure 5). To compare the ratings between the use of traditional progam notes (group 1) and live notes (group 2) a t-test was conducted. Results showed differences between groups, where group 1 had $\overline{X} = 71.39$, $\sigma = 26.4$, and group 2 had $\overline{X} = 89.93$, $\sigma = 16.85$. The paired t-test revealed a significant statistical difference between the two groups ($\alpha = 0.05$, $t(27) = 3.67$, $p = 0.43$).

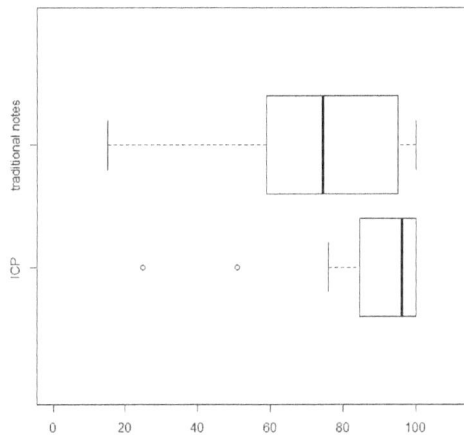

Figure 5: Comparison between the rates for the traditional notes and the ICP live notes

Question 8 asked to judge the overall experience with ICP, and question 9 addressed the desire to have the techonolgy available in future concerts. 96.43% of the respondents rated the ICP experience either 'Very positive' or 'Positive', and 92.85% of them answered that they would like to have this technology available in future performances either 'Always' or 'In some performace'. In the last question, respondents were free to leave any feedback on the live program notes experience. Apart from entusiastic comments (like "Excellent work!") and quick criticisms (such as "Do on projector above orchestra"), some feedback addressed very crucial issues. One participant stated that it is a great idea, but not for every concert, as "Getting lost in the music is part of the joy of a going to a concert...reading notes can prevent that escape." Someone else suggested multiple sets of live notes, to address different levels of musical background in the audience: "Maybe have two different ones going if possible. One for people with theory background to talk more about the theory based notes vs the one presented the concert hall." A few respondents showed interest in having information about "chord progression," "themes" "instruments,' "music forms". One person also suggested the use of pictures in addition to plain text.

Additional feedback. Some feedback arrived from the Lied Center in post-concert emails. Below two of them are reported, representing opposite sides of the spectrum. The first one was very critical: *"I think the idea of receiving texts during a performance is frankly, ridiculous. Before the concert suggest that attendees either read the program notes or perhaps hold a pre-conference talk. I do not enjoy being distracted by the glow. Raise up, don't dumb down. Other than that it was a most enjoyable performance."* The second one was very supportive: *"My wife and I were thrilled with the KU Orchestra program last night. It was so exciting to hear the fine musicians that KU has attracted. [...] My main reason for sending this note, however, is to express our appreciation of the Live Interactive Streaming during Prokofiev's* Romeo and Juliet *selection. Please let the conductor know of our appreciation of his including this new concert technology. I hope this experiment will be continued in future concerts."*

4.3 Discussion

As this experiment did not have a controlled set of participants, we cannot state scientific conclusions from the quantitative data collected, but we can draw some meaningful considerations. First of all, the audience was interested in trying the ICP technology. From Figure 4 it is clear that once people started using the live notes, they remained connected for the entire performance. Second, the audience cared about the music and the performers and was familiar with the traditional program notes. This means that our respondents were appropriate to judge the new ICP software, as they were familiar with the traditional concert programs and ICP software represented the modern version of concert programs. It is interesting that on two similar questions (question 3 and 5) asking to rate from 0 to 100 the usefulness of traditional program notes and live notes, the ICP live notes outperformed traditional program notes, as shown in figure 5.

This encouraging result was confirmed by the general level of appreciation of the ICP technology, with respondents clearly giving a positive feedback for the technology and expressing the desire to have it in future concerts. One of the common critics to this experiment was that following the notes on the phones, people might lose the connection with the music and the performers. It is a legitimate criticism that needs to be considered. First of all, it is important to ensure that people are not using the service are not distracted by other people's phones. According to the present study, the software performed well on this issue, with only 3.7% of the respondents being a little bit distracted by other phones. The part of the audience not using the phone did not participate in the survey, so we need to make sure in a future experiment that also people not using ICP will enjoy the concert without being distracted. The ideal setting that will ensure the best result will be with the use of modern devices like Google Glasses, special glasses able to projects textual information on the lenses. People wearing them and connecting them to the ICP web application could watch the show traditionally and have ICP live notes streamed directly on their lenses. This device would allow keeping the focus on the performer and the music, as well as receiving information without distracting other people.

5 APPLICATIONS

Improving the audience experience during *live performances* is the natural goal of the ICP software. This includes: program notes for concert halls; multi-language lyrics and texts for opera houses and theaters; description for the Deaf in theaters and movie theaters; live comments and audience interaction in any type of show, ranging from avant-guard music concerts, to improvised theatrical plays. It is important to notice that ICP also works well with shows that are web-streamed; anyone with the address of the ICP notes can receive the slides, even if not physically present in the theater.

ICP can also be a very powerful *educational tool*. As a presentation tool, it could be used during a lecture to simultaneously stream the slides on a projector and on the participants' devices, with the additional possibility of navigating the slides, zooming the images, browsing the web, and so on. Moreover, ICP allows streaming the presentation to participants not in the room, providing an easy tool for online classes or video conferences, where students or participants are spread in different places. One key characteristic of ICP presentations is that there is no limit on the audience dimension and location, allowing the presenter to provide live notes for worldwide live events. Consider a music concert which is broadcasted on TV in different states or countries; a musicologist could prepare live notes for this show, share the ICP address of the presentation, and reach all the people that are watching the concert on TV.

Of course, the use of ICP will be more natural and smooth as *wearable technology* will become available. With the right glasses or headsets, people could read the ICP notes without any need to look down to a screen. Google Glasses will probably be the best device for using ICP: Yacob in [ ], analyzing the potential applications of these glasses, reported that they could make "mainstream theater accessible to people who are deaf or hard of hearing by providing real-time subtitles through the display."

In a broader perspective, ICP can address an extended concept of augmented reality, which we may call *augmented performance*. Augmented reality provides additional information about the world that surrounds us, according to where we move in the space; similarly, augmented performance provides additional information about the imaginative world we hear/see on stage, according to the progression of the timeline of the live show.

6 FUTURE WORKS

In order to improve the ICP technology, two main tracks of development are necessary: 1) adding functionality to the ICP software, and 2) testing the software in real settings, setting up both controlled and noncontrolled experiments.

6.1 Adding functionality to ICP

The following features will be added to ICP and will improve the interactive experience during live performances.

- *Multi-language support*: each slide could embed the same information in several languages. ICP could detect the language of the device, or ask the users' preferred language, and trigger the text accordingly.
- *Adaptive slides*: each user could choose between different sets of slides, according to his/her musical background and

the type of information he/she would prefer to get during the show.

- *Slide templates*: some templates could be added in the *editor* component to facilitate the creation of slides containing both text and images.
- *Transition effects*: the transition from one slide to another (i.e., the way the old text disappears and the new text appears on the screen) could be performed in many ways. The editing process of the slides could offer several transition options.
- *Saving/sharing buttons*: when navigating the ICP slides, the user will have the possibility of saving/sharing a single slide or the entire presentation. These options can include: saving on a device or cloud, sending as an email or message, sharing on social media, such as Facebook, Twitter or Google+.
- *Real-time pool*: some slides could incorporate questions to the users. In this way, during a show, the performers could have immediate feedback from the audience that could drive the live performance.
- *Users' profiles*: every user, either an ICP *viewer* or an ICP *provider*, could set up his/her profile and interact with other users. Providers could advertise upcoming shows which will feature ICP notes, trying to reach new viewers. Viewers could subscribe to providers to receive notifications about upcoming interactive shows, rate the service, and give feedback. Viewers could share preferences and interests with other viewers or providers.

All these functionalities can be easily added, as the ICP software is based on web technologies, such as HTML, CSS, and Javascript, which are already able to manage these concepts.

6.2 More experiments

The case study reported in section 4 showed interest and appreciation on live notes during a symphonic concert, but a controlled experiment seems necessary to assess the effectiveness of this new technology scientifically. It would be ideal to perform a two-group pretest-posttest analysis, to compare traditional program notes and live notes on two factors: 1) the level of enjoyment of the show; 2) the amount of information that people remember after the show. A set of participants would be randomly selected and divided into two groups (group A and B). All participants would attend the same concert, with group A receiving information about the music and performers via traditional program notes, while group B would receive the same information via live notes on their phones. Questions about the appreciation of the show will be asked to all participants at the end of the performance. Questions certifying the participants' knowledge about the music and the performers would be asked before the show (thus, before giving them program notes or live notes) and after the show. This experiment should clearly determine if the ICP live notes are more effective than traditional program notes. Future experiments also need to measure the following aspects: disturbance on other audience members (both using and not using ICP); number of actions performed by the users on the viewer component (i.e., backward, forward, click-on-link, go-to-the-current-slide); time spent on each slide.

In addition to a proper controlled experiment like the one described above, we are performing several noncontrolled experiments, using ICP during concerts at the School of Music of the University of Kansas. These experiments include: providing program notes for the concert of the Ensemble Improptu Percussion Quartet (January 18th, 2017); providing a real-time full translation of *Carmina Burana* by Carl Orff, performed by KUSO and KU Choirs (February 18th, 2017); accompanying the presentation by astrophysicist Gregory Rudnick on the Hubble telescope at the Lied Center (April 18th, 2017); providing live program notes to premiered works by composition students of the KU School of Music. These experiments will help adjusting the technology and its new features, and will provide informal feedback from a wide range of users.

7 CONCLUSION

Noting the current lack of audience engagement in the performative arts, the present work uses new technologies as a powerful tool for helping people in better understanding and appreciating live performances. The long term goal is to strengthen interest in performative arts. To this aim, the Interactive Concert Programs software has been developed, a web application that can be easily used in any performative setting to provide live and interactive information on the audience's devices. ICP follows principles of simplicity, usability, effectiveness and cheapness. An experiment performed at the University of Kansas during a symphonic concert with a real audience collected feedback from the people using the software. The results of the experiment clearly showed that the software is effective, that it was well received and that people want to see this technology used in future concerts. Using web technologies already available, the software can be enriched with new features that would make it more interactive and easy to use. Lastly, ICP is compatible with any device supporting HTML and Javascript browsers, including wearable technology not yet released (e.g., Google Glasses).

The experiment performed with ICP also underlined possible disadvantages on its use that should be carefully taken into consideration. First of all, it is important *not to overwhelm the audience* with too much information. The ICP slides should be designed with a right balance between adding meaningful information and letting the audience enjoying the show freely. An average of a slide every 17 seconds (86 slides for 25 minutes of music) seemed a good compromise in the experiment, but the rhythm of the slides should be decided on a case by cases basis: the type of show and audience, as well as the type of learning/entertaining experience desired for that show should be considered.

It is also not effective that ICP provide *textual information simultaneously to other textual or oral information* delivered from the stage (spoken or sung). This is acceptable (and encouraged) if the ICP slides reinforce the live show, for example with translations or short summaries of the speech. The human brain can easily follow only one text at the time (written or spoken): thus, having to focus on different information from the stage and from the slides will likely result only in confusing the audience. A successful approach would be using text on ICP when the live show provides images/sound and using images/links on ICP when the live show provides text or speech.

More generally, it is important to determine in which shows it is appropriate to use this technology. For example, many concert goers worship the experience of a live concert as a moment of pure art, where nothing else than the music should matter. The use of technology in a concert hall might be seen as a despicable intrusion in a sanctuary of the art. For this reason, special occasions like opening nights and premieres could preserve the purity of the concert experience, without allowing the use of technology. Similarly, technology could be banned from being used in the central (and most expensive) seats of a concert hall (e.g., orchestra or parterre seats), which are usually taken by authorities and old-fashioned subscribers.

However, even recognizing the needs of the conservative segments of an audience, ICP technology can be successfully exploited in a lot of situations. For examples, theaters could reserve *interactive-friendly seating* for people that want to receive ICP information, without disturbing other people. Moreover, a concert season could schedule specific *learning nights*, (such as open dress rehearsals or closing nights), where the audience is allowed or even encouraged to use the devices for receiving live information via ICP. As an audience is made of people with different backgrounds, needs and expectations, it is always better to give them different modalities to enjoy a performance, and let them choose in which way they want to experience the show. In the future, with wearable technology like Google Glasses, ICP can be used without our seat neighbor noticing it.

Of course, avant-garde shows, performances in foreign languages and learning-oriented concerts will naturally benefit from the ICP software. This new technology will help the audience understanding and appreciating performing arts, engaging their curiosity and interaction. An entertainment setting like a live performance could easily become a friendly learning environment, leading to an *Edutainment* activity[6]. In this context, new layers of information will be delivered on top of the entertaining experience and will be hopefully understood and memorized more effectively.

ICP software can be used by anyone, as it does not require any coding skill or HTML knowledge in order to create and run the slides. A massive use of ICP can actually mitigate the editing process of printed concert programs, saving time, money and trees. Ideally, in the future, every concert hall will adopt the ICP technology and hire a musicologist. He/she would have the responsibility to tailor ICP notes for every concert, according to the specific show, the audience, and the type of entertaining/learning path that has been designed for that specific season or concert cycle.

The performative arts are going through a moment of crisis and demand new ideas to engage audiences, bring people to the theaters, and connect people with the artists and their artworks. ICP is a modern tool that anyone can easily access, and if broadly used, can give a substantial contribution to these goals.

---

[6]The term *Edutainment* originated in the 1970s, blending the words 'entertainment' and 'education'. According to the Merriem-Webster dictionary, it refers to 'entertainment that is designed to be educational.'

Acknowledgments

A special thanks to Maestro Jung-Ho Pak, guest conductor of the University of Kansas Symphony Orchestra, for kindly agreeing on trying the Interactive Concert Programs software during a public concert, and to the Lied Center staff for allowing and facilitating the use of live program notes at the Lied Center.

REFERENCES

[1] Anthony. 2011. When to use white text on a dark background. (April 2011). http://uxmovement.com/content/when-to-use-white-text-on-a-dark-background/

[2] A. Brown. 2004. Smart concerts: Orchestras in the Age of Edutainment. *Issues Brief* 5 (December 2004), 16 pages.

[3] J. Hooker and C. Perron. 2003. Colour choices on web pages: Contrast vs readability. (2003). http://www.writer2001.com/colwebcontrast.htm

[4] J. Johnson. 2002. *Who Needs Classical Music?: Cultural Choice and Musical Value.* Oxford University Press, New York.

[5] E. H. Margulis. 2010. When program notes donfit help: Music descriptions and enjoyment. *Psychology of Music* 38, 3 (2010), 285–302. DOI : http://dx.doi.org/10.1177/0305735609351921 arXiv:http://dx.doi.org/10.1177/0305735609351921

[6] The Metropolitan Opera. 2017. The Metropolitan Opera. (2017). http://www.metopera.org/

[7] NPAC Staff. 2012. National Performing Art Convention - Useful Quotes for Arts Advocates. (Spring 2012). http://www.performingartsconvention.org/advocacy/id=28

[8] C. Phililps. 2014. How smartphones revolutionized society in less than a decade. (November 2014). http://www.govtech.com/products/How-Smartphones-Revolutionized-Society-in-Less-than-a-Decade.html

[9] F. Plotkin. 2015. Have projected titles really been good for opera? (May 2015). http://www.wqxr.org/story/have-projected-titles-really-been-good-opera/

[10] A. H. Safar. 2015. Educating with Prezi: a New Presentation Paradigm for Teaching, Learning, and Leading in the Digital Age. *College Student Journal* 49, 4 (December 2015), 491–512.

[11] B. Silber and T. Triplett. 2015. A Decade of Arts Engagement: Findings from the Survey of Public Participation in the Arts, 2002-2012. *NEA Research Report* 58 (January 2015).

[12] P. Smith. 1997. Met-Titles: Two years later. *Opera News* 62, 6 (December 1997), 6.

[13] Teatro La Fenice. 2017. Libretti. (2017). http://www.teatrolafenice.it/site/index.php?pag=21871&lingua=eng

[14] A. Tommasini. 1995. Reinventing supertitles: How the Met Did It. *The New York Times* (October 2nd 1995). http://www.nytimes.com/1995/10/02/arts/reinventing-supertitles-how-the-met-did-it.html

[15] R. Valliere and E. Latzky. 2004. Wireless Offers More for Orchestras. *International Musician* 102, 8 (August 2004), 21.

[16] WebdesignerDepot Staff. 2016. The dos and donfits of ark web design. (August 2016). http://www.webdesignerdepot.com/2009/08/the-dos-and-donts-of-dark-web-design/

[17] R. Weber. 2015. DT* Phone Home: The Apple Watch. *Journal of Financial Service* 69, 4 (July 2015), 49–52.

[18] R. Yakob. 2012. Are Google's glasses the future for the web? *Campaign* (August 2012), 15.

Review Recommendation for Points of Interest's Owners

Thiago R. P. Prado and Mirella M. Moro
Universidade Federal de Minas Gerais
Belo Horizonte, MG, Brazil
thiagorpp@dcc.ufmg.br,mirella@dcc.ufmg.br

ABSTRACT

Websites that provide reviews for services and products deal with big volumes of data (many users writing many reviews for many items). Then, recommendation algorithms come to the rescue in matching reviews to the consumers who are reading them. Such online review applications usually recommend the most useful reviews for consumers to read. In this work, we propose a new perspective to this problem: how to evaluate the helpfulness of a review from the business owner's perspective. Our solution uses the review's aspects and sentiments, and ranks the most helpful ones seeking to assist establishment owners improve their businesses. Our experimental evaluations consider experts opinion and show that our solution is very close to the ideal ranking.

CCS CONCEPTS

•**Information systems** → **Social networks;** •**Human-centered computing** → **Social recommendation;**

KEYWORDS

Review Recommendation, Social Networks

1   INTRODUCTION

Online reviews have become a powerful way for users to make their opinions available to everyone. Indeed, the number of online reviews at many specialized websites, such as TripAdvisor and Yelp, has been growing significantly. Such reviews are extremely valuable for consumers when they are looking for information before acquiring a product or service. Analyzing review textual data (which represents the thoughts and communication between users) enables to understand the public needs and concerns about what constitutes valuable information from an academic, marketing, and policy-making perspective. For example, Lacic et al. aim to predict the satisfaction of air travelers by analyzing their reviews [14] and Rossetti et al. propose a new model to decision support and recommendation for online tourists [28].

A specific scenario is when the items being reviewed are locations. Specially, location based social networks, such as TripAdvisor[1] and FourSquare[2], are important tools for users to choose hotels, restaurants and attractions – also known as *points of interest* (POI). Their contents are generated by users, thus providing access to the opinions of many individuals. A user may: contribute with an opinion, evaluate a POI by a rating or indicating whether liked or not, and write a review. Then, the problem with big volumes of data persists: as of April 2017, TripAdvisor handles 500 million reviews from 7 million places in more than 135,000 destinations; whereas FourSquare handles data of more than 93 million places. With so many reviews, how can a user find a proper one?

In an attempt to help consumers identify useful reviews, many sites allow users to vote if a review is helpful. While most websites just show the percentage of positive votes or the average of received votes, some of them provide the grade that each user gave to a review. However, this evaluation tends to be sparse with many reviews without any feedback [25]. This problem is due to the rich-get-richer effect, in which reviews on top tend to receive more feedback, while recent reviews are rarely read [16]. Even if the grades given to reviews are too sparse to help users identify relevant reviews, they can provide important data to create a model to automatically predict the quality of a review [12].

Regarding each POI review, several aspects may affect the users while writing them, including: noise level, quality of products or services, weather, season and existing expectations. In this context, identifying and managing these factors can provide customers and owners with valuable information through the interpretation of large amounts of reviews [21]. Nonetheless, how to manage is different for each role. Specifically, for the establishment's owner (or administrator, manager, etc), it is important to have a fast and reliable way to identify the reviews with relevant information for improving the services provided. Then for the client, it is important to identify reviews with details about the place that will help to decide where to go, eat, visit or stay.

Indeed, consumer online reviews have become a major factor in business reputation and brand image due to the popularity of TripAdvisor, Yelp and online review websites. A negative review can really damage the reputation of a business. The problem is so serious that an industry of reputation management has arisen: companies, such as *Reviewsthatstick*[3], attempt to remove or hide bad reviews such that more favorable content is found when potential customers look for products and services.

In this paper, we introduce a new problem: identifying the helpfulness of a review for the *owner* of an establishment. The relevance of a review to the establishment differs from the relevance

HT'17, July 4-7, 2017, Prague, Czech Republic.
© 2017 ACM. 978-1-4503-4708-2/17/07...$15.00
DOI: http://dx.doi.org/10.1145/3078714.3078744

[1]TripAdvisor: http://www.TripAdvisor.com
[2]FourSquare: https://www.FourSquare.com
[3]ReviewsThatStick: http://reviewsthatstick.com

to the customer because now the goal is not to help decide which product to buy or which place to go to. For example, considering two reviews: (*a*) complains about the distance to the nearby train station; and (*b*) complains about the hotel staff. A traveler may find (*a*) more important than (*b*), but surely the hotel owner will be more concerned about (*b*), as not much can be done about (*a*). Following such an example, the focus here is to identify comments on important issues, especially those regarding the establishment, which can be improved to increase customer satisfaction and help in making strategic and administrative decisions.

Also, providing a calculated average of the received rates (grades) or a summary of all comments to the owner is not enough, because: (*i*) the average is just a number for a global view of a set of aggregated users; (*ii*) the summary will potentially present complains and compliments for all aspects at the same time; (*iii*) and none of them provides a way for the owner to answer individual critics. In other words, a major goal here is to point out *textual* and *individual* reviews that qualify existing problems, so that the owner can properly answer and address them.

Hence, we propose creating a ranking of reviews according to their relevance for POI decision making, i.e. targeting owners and not clients. Our ranking considers aspects described and sentiments present in the reviews, a weight function that gives more importance to negative aspects, and the review's writer reputation. To evaluate it, we build a ground truth dataset formed by expert opinions on the relevance of a set of reviews to a set of POI owners. Likewise, as there is no similar work to use as baseline, we build one from scratch based on the similarity between reviews and their answers. Overall, our main contribution is a algorithm to recommend reviews for POIs *owners* and a through experimental evaluation on big volume of data.

The rest of the paper is organized as follows. Section 2 overviews basic concepts, and Section 3 goes over related work. In Section 4, we formalize the problem of recommending reviews for a POI owner. In Section 5, we describe how to measure the helpfulness of a review. Then, Section 6 presents our experimental evaluation and its results, and Section 7 concludes this work.

2 BASIC CONCEPTS

We first introduce basic concepts, both for generic and review recommendation, and then state the problem.

2.1 Location Based Social Networks

Location based social networks (LBSN) are web platforms that reflect the social networking structures of real world [35]. In recent years, the study of LBSNs has attracted attention because they consider interaction information among users along with their geographic location for a period of time. Such information is useful for developing applications as recommendation systems of places, reviews, travel planning, among others [25, 36].

2.2 Recommendation Systems

Recommendation systems combine several computational techniques to select custom items based on the interests of users and the context in which they are inserted [20]. Such items may take

varied forms, including reviews, places, books, movies, news, music, videos, ads, people and products from a virtual store [3]. One common form of recommendation is to order these items in a rank according to their relevance to the target user [4, 17, 27, 32].

A recommendation system is traditionally divided into two types. First, *collaborative filtering* is a domain-independent prediction technique that cannot easily and adequately be described by metadata, e.g. movies. Such techniques work by building a database (user-item matrix) of preferences for items by users, and then matching users with relevant interest and preferences by calculating similarities between their profiles to make recommendations [9]. Those users build a group called neighborhood. A user gets recommendations to those items that he has not rated but were already positively rated by users in his neighborhood.

Second, *content-based* is a domain-dependent method and emphasizes the analysis of the attributes of items in order to generate predictions. When documents (such as web pages, publications and news) are to be recommended, content-based filtering technique is the most successful. In content-based filtering techniques, recommendation is made based on the user profiles by using features extracted from the content of the items the user has evaluated in the past [3]. Items that are mostly related to the positively rated ones are recommended to the user.

2.3 Review Recommendation Problem

A review refers to an evaluation written by a user or consumer for a product or a service based on an opinion and/or experience as a user of the reviewed item. Reviews are in the form of several lines of texts accompanied by a numerical rating. This text aims to help in shopping decision of a possible buyer, for example. A consumer review of a product usually evaluates how well the product measures up to expectations based on the specifications provided by the manufacturer or seller. It focuses on performance, reliability, quality, defects if any, and value for money. Often it includes comparative evaluations against competing products. Observations are factual as well as subjective in nature.

Considering a website in which users may give feedback about the consumed services or products, the user can act in three different ways: (*i*) writer - user writes a review about the consumed item; (*ii*) reader - user reads reviews looking for important information about a target item; (*iii*) voter - user gives a note to an existing review indicating how useful it is [21].

Ideally, a review recommendation system provides a review ranking in descending order of helpfulness for a given pair of user and item. Thereafter, whenever a reader accesses a product, the most helpful reviews are on top, eliminating the problem of manually looking for a needle in a haystack.

3 BACKGROUND AND RELATED WORK

We now discuss work related to our problem and solutions.

3.1 Sentiment Analysis

Besides quality, sentiment analysis is widely used to obtain relevant information about reviews. Previous work studying aspects and sentiments of reviews can be classified as *opinion mining*, which operates on text portions of any size and shape, such as web pages, comments, tweets, etc. Every opinion is composed of at least two elements: a target (topic, product, person, etc.) and a feeling (attitude, opinion, emotion) about this target [15]. The process of mining temporal opinions involves defining the average opinion on a particular topic in two or more different points in time. Changes in opinion can then be identified and used to find patterns or summarize the opinion regarding a specific aspect [5].

For example, Lourenco et. al [19] studied an efficient way to analyze opinions about topics and entities on social networks like Twitter. However, changes in opinions are not necessarily useful by themselves, as they need some factor of comparison. Hence, the utility of opinion change detection becomes more evident when combined with the understanding of why such a change occurred.

Sentiment (and opinions) analysis requires to differentiate between statements of fact and opinions, and to detect the polarity of the sentiment expressed. For example, Turney [31] ranked the polarity of feeling reviews on document level, and Yu and Hatzivassiloglou [33] identified the polarity of sentences opinions using semantically oriented words.

These techniques have been applied and examined in different fields, such as user reviews and news articles. In our proposed solution, the sentiment analysis serves to identify opinions about topics and the polarity of the sentiment expressed in the reviews. Knowing what customers are talking about and if they like or not allows to identify the most relevant aspects of service or product, and to determine if they should be improved by POIs owners.

3.2 Spam, Fake Review Detection

Online reviews have become a valuable resource for decision making, but this importance of reviews also encourages spam. There are generally two types of spam reviews: (i) those that deliberately mislead readers or automated opinion mining systems that give undeserving positive opinions to some target product in order to promote it, or give unjust or malicious negative reviews to some product in order to damage its reputation; (ii) non-reviews (e.g. ads) that contain no opinion on the product.

Jindal et. al [11] propose to perform spam detection based on duplicate finding and classification, then applying Logistic regression to learn a predictive model. Mukherjee et. al [24] study how well existing research methods work in detecting real-life fake reviews in a commercial website, and compare them to Yelp's filtered/unfiltered reviews. Filtering ads and detecting spam reviews are important steps before recommending reviews for owners: ads have no value for a manager, and spam reviews could lead to wrong decisions and analysis about services and products.

3.3 Influence of Reviews on Sales

The creation of online consumer communities to provide product reviews and advice has been touted as an important (although somewhat expensive) component of Internet retail strategies. For example, Chevalier and Mayzlin[6] examine the effect of consumer reviews on relative sales of books at Amazon[4] and BarnesAndNoble[5] and find that positive reviews and book sales positively correlate. Dellarocas et. al [7] propose concrete models for decision

support in a specific business context and provide quantitative assessments of the information value of online review metrics relative to more traditional metrics. Hence, it is crucial for a POI owner to have an efficient way to know the most important problems that clients are complaining about, making it possible to propose solutions and fix them shortly.

3.4 Predicting Review Helpfulness/Quality

The problem of automatically determining the quality of content generated by online social networking users has attracted much attention [10, 26, 31]. For instance, Bigonha et. al [2] defined quality metrics for influential users on Twitter. Pang e Lee [26] studied products reviews prediction, which can be significant due to the correlation between a product evaluation and the usefulness of a review. However, the overall assessment of a product is known.

Other previous works [8, 13, 16, 30, 34] have focused on automatically determining the quality of reviews through textual attributes and social aspects [22, 29]. Textual attributes include text statistics, such as the text size, average size of the sentences and percentage of adjectives. Social attributes relate to the reviews authors and are extracted from their social context, as the number of evaluations made by the author, author connection degree in the social network, average grades given, among others.

Another direction is to formulate it as a classification or regression problem with users votes serving as ground truth. These approaches consider that all users have a common perception of helpfulness and are limited to discovering helpfulness for an average person. For example, Zhang e Varadarajan [34] discovered that syntactical features of review text are most useful, whereas review size seems poorly related with its quality. Only a few works [23, 29] deal with the problem in a personalized fashion, considering users idiosyncrasy, then exploring the hypothesis that users do not perceive helpfulness in the same way (what is useful for one, is not for another) by incorporating relevant personalized information for review recommendation.

In addition to textual attributes, Kim et. al [13] included metadata information (such as notes given to an item under evaluation) and concluded that review size and the number of stars in product ratings are more useful to their regression model. Ghose e Ipeirotis [8], based on subjective analysis of the text, showed evidence that reviews addressing extreme aspects are considered more useful. In [18], Liu et. al considered user experience as reviewer and the frequency they create reviews in addition to writing style in a non-linear regression model.

Despite their differences, all these previous works consider the problem of evaluating the quality of reviews and classify them as best as possible from the user's point of view (e.g., product buyer in an e-commerce system). Here, we introduce a new problem: identifying the usefulness of a review for the *business owner*. To address this problem, we propose using aspects and sentiments of reviews, and creating a rank with reviews that can be most useful for the management and development of establishment at the top. For the owner of an establishment, the quality of a review can help identify negative aspects and problems of products and services. Moreover, it is possible to determine the most successful products to expand their production as well.

---

[4]Amazon: http://www.amazon.com
[5]Barnesandnoble: http://www.barnesandnoble.com

4 PROBLEM DEFINITION

A recent survey shows that all current works on review quality prediction identify the relevance of a review for clients (users) only [21], i.e., not to business owners. However, the relevance of a review to a establishment differs from the relevance to the customer because now the goal is not to help decide which product to buy or which place to visit. The focus is to identify comments that address important issues, especially those related to the establishment that can be improved to increase customer satisfaction and help in making strategic and administrative decisions. It is important to note that an unsatisfied user can cause considerable damage, since comments on the Internet can spread quickly and influence other potential customers.

Motivating Example. Assume that three travelers, who have joined an online reviewing website, have written a review about the hotel they booked in different dates. The first one covered the aspects about location, the second detailed the quality of breakfast, and the third enjoyed bedroom size. The clients made important and different compliments about hotel, but all off them also complained about room service. Service quality is one key point to make customers happy. If the hotel manager had an easy and efficient way to detect the problem with room service, such manager would be able to propose solutions and avoid more clients dissatisfaction after the first client review. Once again, providing the owner an averaged rate or summary of all complains is also not as useful as the individual and textual ones, as the owner may want to not only address and solve such issues but also properly give answers to the three users who complained about room service.

In the previous example, helpfulness of users review can be evaluated by focusing on the problems they mention. We argue that a personalized review quality for POIs owner may be more accurate than a user review recommendation approach and introduce the problem of *owner-oriented review ranking*. As exemplified in the introduction, a business owner cannot change the distance to the nearest train station, but can surely improve its staff.

Problem Statement. Given a set of reviews $R = r_1, r_2, ..., r_x$ about a POI, a set of reviewers $V = v_1, v_2, ..., v_y$ who have written R and a set of owners of POIs $O = o_1, o_2, ..., o_z$ who manage the POIs and are responsible to get clients feedback. The task is to rank R according to the quality rating (helpfulness) of each $r \in R$ for a given owner o_j.

5 IDENTIFYING HELPFUL REVIEWS FOR POI'S OWNER

We treat the task of finding helpful reviews as a ranking problem where the goal is to obtain a scoring function that gives higher scores to helpful reviews in a given set of reviews. Our strategy is to rank the reviews based on their aspects and sentiments. Knowing what clients are talking about and how they feel allows to detect important reviews, but we must consider the opinion of as many clients as possible to identify main problematic topics.

Overall, our solution to rank reviews according to the helpfulness for the business owner is composed of three steps. First, we describe our strategy to extract aspects and their sentiment from

a set of reviews of a given POI (Section 5.1). We then measure the weight of each aspect by considering its relevance for the whole set (Section 5.2). Finally, we score the helpfulness of a target review by using its aspects relevance (Section 5.3).

5.1 Sentiment Analysis and Aspects Extraction

We now turn to aspect extraction, which can also be seen as an information extraction task. In the context of sentiment analysis, some specific characteristics of the problem can facilitate the extraction. The key characteristic is that an opinion always has a target. The target is often the aspect or topic to be extracted from a sentence. Thus, it is important to recognize each opinion expression and its target from a sentence. Also, we should note that some opinion expressions can play two roles, i.e., indicating a positive or negative sentiment, and implying an (implicit) aspect (target). For example, in *this car is expensive*, the word *expensive* indicates both a sentiment and the aspect price.

The steps of identifying aspects and analyzing sentiment are complex data processing tasks. Luckily, there are many solutions available such as the whole framework described in [12]. There is also publicly available tools, as the services provided by *HPE HEAVEN OnDemand*[6]. For practical reasons and good overall performance, we use the latter as explained next.

HPE HEAVEN OnDemand is a platform for building cognitive computing solutions using text analysis, speech recognition, image analysis, indexing and search APIs. The sentiment analysis API processes reviews and returns a list of aspects mentioned in the review along with the sentiment and the score associated to them. The API returns the sentiment as positive, negative, neutral or mixed. It contains a dictionary of positive and negative words of different types, and defines patterns that describe how to combine these words to form positive and negative phrases. Automatically classifying text by sentiment allows to easily find out the general opinions of people in an area of interest. For example, a manager might want to analyze reviews from a restaurant to help improving services provided, food quality, menu choices or to enhance customer experience.

The API splits the input text into entities, which describe a part of the text with a particular sentiment. The API returns details of the extracted entities, including the length and the detected sentiment. Each sentiment extracted contains valuable information. For example, Figure 1 shows the text of a real review and its aspects as extracted by HPE tool. Specifically:

- **sentiment** is the qualifier for the sentiment or opinion, in this case the adjective *clean*;
- **aspect** indicates what the positive or negative sentiment is about, in this case *room*; and
- **score** is a value between 0 and 1 (0 and -1 in the negative case), which indicates the strength and confidence of the sentiment.

5.2 Calculating Aspect Weight

Using the sentiment and aspect identification API (described in 5.1) enables to extract all necessary knowledge to calculate the weight

---

[6]HPE HEAVEN OnDemand: http://www.havenondemand.com

Review	Sentiment	Aspect	Score
"The air conditioning unit was very noisy and there was also a lot of noise from the lift at night, not only noise but vibrations in the room. Saying that the room although small was clean as was the rest of the hotel. Staff were friendly"	clean	room	0.62
	friendly	staff	0.79
	very noisy	air conditioning unit	-0.778

Figure 1: Example of review and its aspects (total score: 0.21)

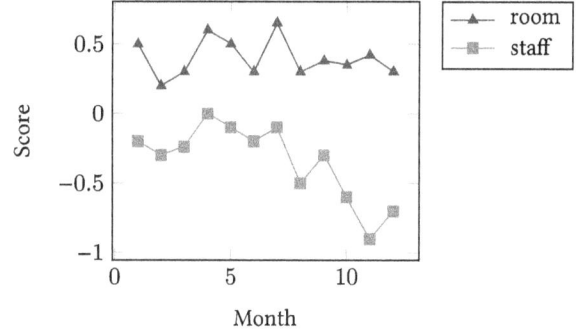

Figure 2: Aspect scores along a year for the same hotel

of each aspect considering the set of reviews of a POI. The sentiment of an aspect may be positive or negative, and both are useful:

- **positive** aspects help identify reviews with compliments about features or services. This kind of review allows to identify for example what clients like, and if a given promotion or service had the expected impact; and
- **negative** aspects help to find reviews with possible problems or features that clients do not like. It is probably more important than a positive aspect since it may lead to losses to the POI in a short amount of time, as it may spread quickly on social networks.

Analyzing POI reviews in the owners perspective is important to discover how the place is being evaluated by clients. Not identifying how the opinion of clients is varying, mainly when it is negative, may damage the POI. This kind of problem could be avoided if POIs owners had an efficient way to identify what aspects are not pleasing their clients. However, having just the rates given by clients or their average is not enough, as argued in Section 1. By knowing the specific problems, it should be simpler to take faster decisions to address them.

Considering a hotel as POI, an example of how the sentiment about *room* and *staff* (from a real hotel) varies through 2016 is shown in Figure 2. It presents the aggregated sentiment for each aspect considering all reviews from each month in that year. In this case, room sentiment varies, but is always positive. On the other hand, the opinion about the hotel staff is bad over the whole year, with some oscillation in the first semester and getting sour in the second one. Had the manager properly answered and solved such staff problems over the first months, its score curve could have been in the positive number by the end of the year.

There are two options when considering the relevance of an aspect: (*i*) ignore review date - useful to identify the main reviews and discover general aspects of POI over a set of reviews; and (*ii*) consider review date - useful to monitor the variation of customer opinion over time. Our assumption is that when considering the relevance of an aspect, we must also use the date of the review to weigh its importance. In a real case scenario, the manager is most worried about recent reviews than from last year. Having this in mind, the process of assigning a weight to an aspect is described in Algorithm 1. When evaluating review aspects, our solution treats negative and positive sentiments separately (lines 10,15 and 12,17) to emphasize that there are two perspectives of the same aspect. We also apply a log function (line 5) to give more relevance for recent reviews.

Algorithm 1 Aspect weight algorithm

Input R: a set of reviews from a POI processed by sentiment analysis API (Section 5.1).

Output: a list of aspects and their processed weights.

1: **procedure** WEIGHT(R)
2:     $lastDate \leftarrow S.getLastReviewDate()$
3:     $aspects \leftarrow \{\}$ ▷ Each aspect is a record with two counters: negative (n) and positive (p)
4:     **for** r in R **do** ▷ For each review
5:         $d \leftarrow 1/\log(lastDate - review.getDate())$ ▷ date score of the review **r**
6:         **for** a in $r.getAspects()$ **do** ▷ **a** is an aspect of r
7:             **if** a in $aspects$ **then**
8:                 $v \leftarrow a.getSentimentVal()$
9:                 **if** $v < 0$ **then** ▷ negative sentiment
10:                     $aspects[a].n \leftarrow aspects[a].n + v * d.$
11:                 **else** ▷ positive sentiment
12:                     $aspects[a].p \leftarrow aspects[a].p + v * d.$
13:             **else** ▷ initialize aspect values neg. and pos.
14:                 **if** $v < 0$ **then**
15:                     $aspects[a] \leftarrow \{n = v * d, p = 0\}$
16:                 **else**
17:                     $aspects[a] \leftarrow \{n = 0, p = v * d\}$
18:     **return** $aspects$

5.3 Review Score

Characterizing the helpfulness of a review for a POI owner (administrator, manager, etc) requires analyzing the topics and opinions expressed by a client in each review. Positive and negative comments are important feedback to POI owner, as they help to identify main problems and qualify good services. Evaluating such reviews by considering the perspective of all clients is also important to avoid biased decisions. Automatically identifying helpful reviews is a complex task, since a POI usually has access to thousands of comments. To solve such a problem, we introduce Algorithm 2 for measuring the helpfulness of a review by aggregating the importance of each aspect computed by Algorithm 1.

One challenge is how to aggregate all aspect scores to maximize the level of helpfulness agreement of a review for a POI owner. There are two main challenges that lead to different scores: (*i*) how

---

Algorithm 2 Review score algorithm

Input A, R, O, V: A - a set of aspects (each aspect with two counters: negative (n) and positive (p)) from a POI and their relevance obtained from Algorithm 1; R - a set of reviews from a POI processed by the sentiment analysis API (section 5.1); O - option to consider negative, positive, or negative and positive aspects; V - aspect sentiment value;

Output: a list of reviews ordered by the most helpful.

1: **procedure** SCOREHELPER(A, O)
2:     ▷ A.n and A.p represent neg. and pos. values of aspect A
3:     **if** $O =$ "*negative*" **then**
4:         **return** $A.n$
5:     **if** $O =$ "*positive*" **then**
6:         **return** $A.p$
7:     **if** $O =$ "*both*" **then**
8:         **return** $9.75 * A.n + A.p$
9:
10: **procedure** USER(U)
11:     **return** $1 + (U.helpfulVotes/U.numberOfReviews)$
12:
13: **procedure** SCORE(A, R, O)
14:     $rank \leftarrow \{\}$
15:     **for** r in R **do**   ▷ For each review
16:         **for** a in $r.getAspects()$ **do**   ▷ For each of its aspects
17:             **if** r in $rank$ **then**
18:                     ▷ increment review score with aspect score
19:                 $rank[r] \leftarrow rank[r] + ScoreHelper(a, O)$
20:             **else**
21:                     ▷ initialize review score with aspect score
22:                 $rank[r] \leftarrow ScoreHelper(a, O)$
23:         $rank[r] \leftarrow rank[r] * User(r.user)$ ▷ Reputation
24:     **return** $rank.sort("descending")$

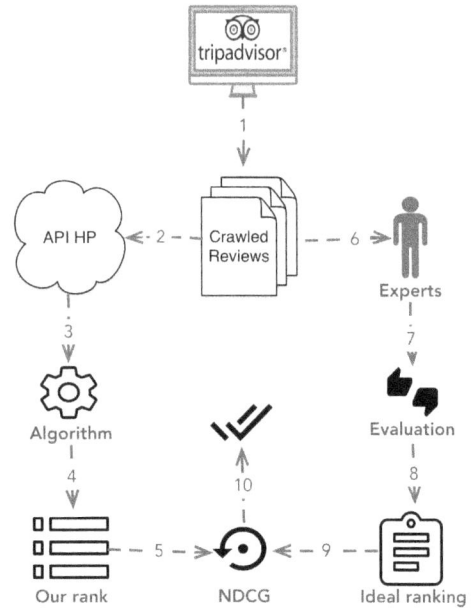

Figure 3: Ranking evaluation steps

6 EXPERIMENTAL EVALUATION

Overall, Figure 3 illustrates the process for our whole experimental evaluation. It also serves as a guide for this section as follows.

Our method is evaluated over real TripAdvisor review data, whose collecting and pre-processing are detailed in Section 6.1. We evaluate our solution against ground truth dataset built from scratch in Section 6.2. We note that our solution may be applied over any review dataset, not being limited by TripAdvisor or a POI category. The baseline for experimental comparisons is described in Section 6.3. Then, Section 6.4 presents the evaluation metrics, whereas Section 6.5 has the results and discussions.

6.1 Data and Pre-processing

Evaluating the helpfulness of reviews requires a dataset built from a social network that allows (*i*) users to write reviews for POIs, and (*ii*) POIs' owners to answer such reviews. The first restriction is easily satisfied by most POI-related social networks (e.g. FourSquare and TripAdvisor), but the second is not a common feature. TripAdvisor satisfies both and is the world's largest travel site, offering advice from millions of travelers: with 435 million reviews and opinions covering 6.8 million accommodations, restaurants and attractions. Although it allows POIs owners to answer their reviews, such feature is not present for all POI categories. Indeed, we have empirically evaluated TripAdvisor POIs categories and discovered that *hotel* is the category with largest answer rate. Therefore, we use TripAdvisor hotel category to construct our evaluation dataset.

Our experimental evaluation considers a dataset consisting of 72,876 reviews from 9,676 hotels, which were randomly selected from 55,238 hotels in the United States. The data were collected from TripAdvisor in July 2016, representing all reviews from the

to consider positive and negative aspects; and (*ii*) how to weight the review by the writer's reputation. The first one is solved by procedure *ScoreHelper()*: it allows the algorithm to use only negative, only positive or a combination of both sentiments about an aspect (the formula was empirically obtained by testing values from 1 to 20 with step 0.05; and the value 9.75 produced better results). The second uses valuable information about the writer: the number of reviews he/she has written and the number of positive votes received. It is calculated by procedure *User()*, and a user who always receives positive votes should be more reliable. This step helps to avoid fake users or spammers, since the reputation was evaluated by other users.

Having both challenges solved allows to calculate review score by procedure *Score()*: it loops through its aspects and invokes *ScoreHelper()* and *User()* procedures passing the desired tuning options. After calculating a score for each POI review, the algorithm sorts them in descending order and returns a rank. Such a rank is oriented towards the owner and not the client of a POI. Therefore, the most helpful reviews for the owners are at the top.

Table 1: Dataset statistics with number of aspects in one review, number of positive/negative reviews and answers.

#Aspects	# pos.rev.	# neg.rev.	# pos.ans.	# neg.ans.
0	490	3,900	96	5,468
1	685	1,508	435	945
2	953	783	840	537
3	1,165	424	1,222	181
4	1,147	244	1,374	80
5	859	147	1,123	35
6	663	90	892	12
7	416	57	530	5
8	273	38	344	4
9	195	23	201	2
10	143	16	86	-

Table 2: Ground Truth statistics with score, number of evaluations and percentage representation.

Score	# of evaluations	%
5/5	2,041	10.2%
4/5	3,917	19.6%
3/5	5,130	25.6%
2/5	4,099	20.5%
1/5	4,813	24.0%

6.2 Ground Truth

Evaluating a recommendation or ranking algorithm requires to compare the generated output with a ranking from a ground truth dataset (a ground truth represents the ideal ranking order). Then, the goal of the experimental evaluation is to check whether the proposed algorithm ranks a given collection as close as the ideal one. Therefore, evaluating our solution required to build (from scratch) a ground truth dataset from experts' evaluations. This dataset represents the *ideal* ranking of reviews for a POI owner.

For the ground truth evaluation, we randomly selected 25 hotels (from the United States) and the last 200 reviews from each hotel, giving a total of 5,000 reviews. To rate how helpful those reviews are, we defined a simple web interface to allow experts to evaluate them. Overall, we asked more than 100 experts to score the reviews from 1 to 5 – where 1 means the review is useless for a POI owner and 5 otherwise. Each review was evaluated five times, and then computed the average. With such experts evaluations,

selected hotels on the collecting date. A pre-processing is also necessary to eliminate incomplete and noisy data. We do so by filtering out: repeated reviews from a hotel, reviews with less than ten words, reviews with non English words (more than 10%), and meaningless words such as URLs. Such step reduced the number of reviews by about 16%, thus obtaining a final set of 61,815 reviews.[7] Finally, the API (Section 5.1) was applied to the final set of reviews and POIs answers.

Each review has the following data: writer's username, number of reviews made by the writer, number of positive votes[8] received by the writer, review date, and POI's owner answer (optionally a POI administrator may answer a review). We have also analyzed the dataset by focusing on the data necessary to identify helpful reviews (e.g., review text and answer). Table 1 presents the number of positive and negative aspects obtained after processing it with the API described in Section 5.1.

We notice that there are more positive than negative reviews, and negative reviews usually have between zero and three negative aspects. The distribution of the number of positive and negative aspects and answers has a clear trend: the concentration of positive aspects are between three and five, and negative aspects between zero and two. Such analysis points to a possible relation in the way a POI owner answers a user, as discussed in Section 6.3.

Another interesting fact is that only 1,673 from 9,676 POI owners answer user reviews, representing 17% of the dataset hotels. Such POIs owners answered 7,271 reviews, representing almost 12% of answered reviews. Despite such a small fraction of answers, POI owners are consistent, as when answering one, they usually answer almost all received reviews.

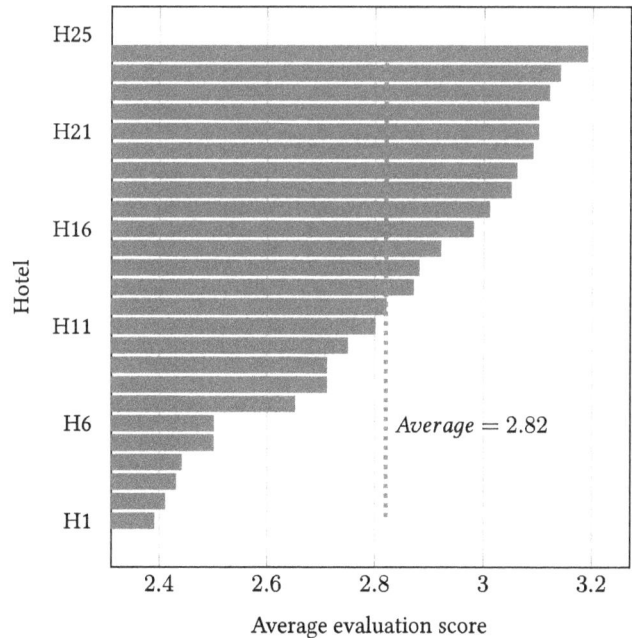

Figure 4: Hotels average evaluation score by experts

---

[7] The final dataset is available at http://www.dcc.ufmg.br/~mirella/projs/apoena
[8] Positive vote: a writer receives a positive vote when another user marks one of his/her reviews as useful

	regular (average)	+write's rep. (average)
pos. aspects	0.627	0.757
neg. aspects	0.239	0.258
pos. + neg.	0.662	0.792

Considering writer's reputation
Positive aspects
Negative aspects
Positive and negative aspects

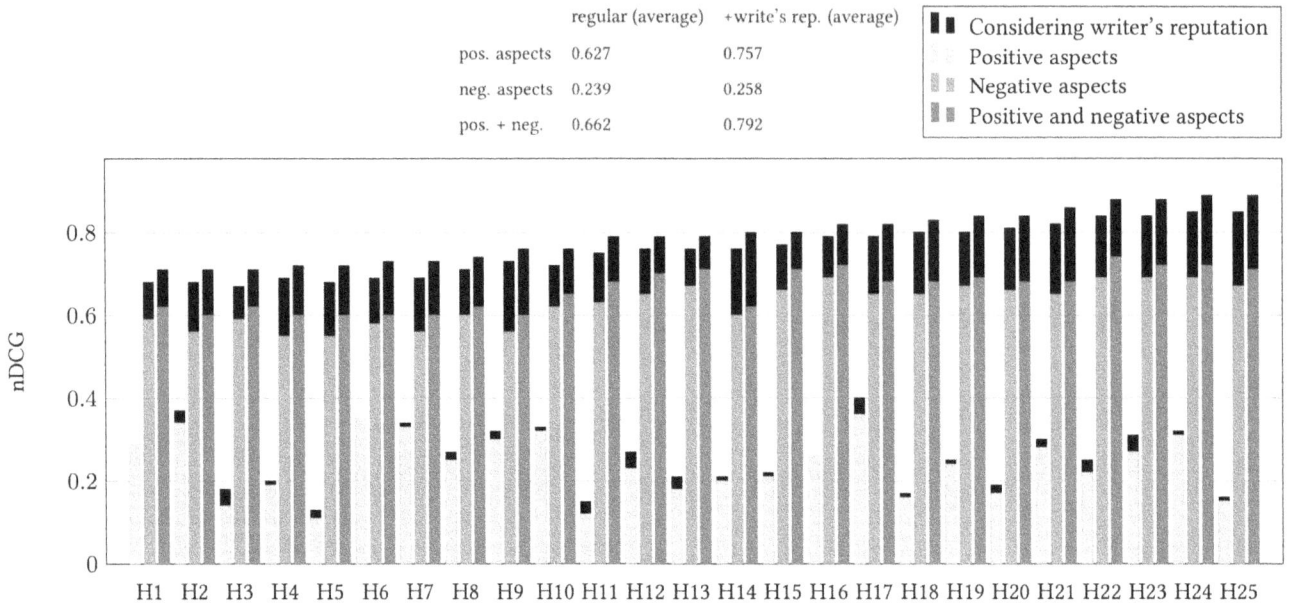

Figure 5: Algorithm evaluation scenarios

we built 25 test collections to use as ground truth. Despite being a small collection, we believe it to be highly reliable, once it was constructed by considering experts opinion.

Table 2 shows the average experts scores of each hotel, and Figure 4 shows the distribution of reviews score (average) given by experts. One may notice that average evaluation for each hotel is close or below 3. Considering all reviews, about 70% evaluations were indeed 3 or less. This means that most reviews were not rated as helpful. Considering this scenario, a hotel has hundreds of reviews and only a few give relevant information, making it even harder for a POI owner to identify the important ones.

6.3 Methods for Comparison

In our POI owner-oriented context, there is also no baseline to compare our solution against. After analyzing the reviews in Section 6.1, we define a hypothesis that there could be a relation between review quality (helpfulness) and the answer given by the POI owner. If such a relation exists, the POI owners may *explicitly* mention the important aspects in the reviews. Therefore, we propose to analyze such a relation to build (again from scratch) a ranking baseline.

Specifically, a user writes a review mentioning aspects with positive and negative opinions. The negative reviews usually point out problems and dissatisfaction on the establishment and its surroundings. The POI owner may answer such a review by (usually) thanking the positive compliments, and making excuses, explaining or even informing that solution is on the way for the negative aspects. Either positive or negative, the owner usually mentions again the aspect being answered, e.g., "the *room size* will be improved in the upcoming restoration" and "we are planing regular meetings with the *staff* regarding how to properly treat our guests". Then, such feedback allows to determine the relevance of a review

based on the cosine similarity between its aspects and the response given by the establishment. High similarity means the establishment took time in answering the points addressed in the review, i.e., this is a relevant review for the establishment. On the other hand, low similarity may indicate generic responses of establishments (e.g., "thanks for pointing it out, we will solve it soon").

We note that it is in the interest of an establishment to answer to a customer's complaints as informative as possible to prevent loosing clients and reputation. Thus, based on the similarity between review and response, our baseline considers a review ranking for each hotel, in descendant order of similarity.

6.4 Evaluation Metrics

We evaluate our ranking method by computing the Normalized Discounted Cumulative Gain [1] of the top-k reviews in the ranking produced by it (i.e, NDCG@k). NDCG is one of the existing metrics to compare rankings, and is our choice because it is simple, easy and produces good results. NDCG ranges from 0 to 1 indicating greater agreement between the ranking produced by the method and an ideal ranking determined by experts evaluations of hotels reviews. This metric is based on two rules:

- Extremely relevant documents are more important (valuable) than documents with marginal relevance; and
- The lower the position of the document in the ranking, the lower the value of this document for the user.

NDCG@k is built from DCG@k, the discounted cumulative gain in the top-k reviews, which is computed as:

$$DCG_k = \sum_{i=1}^{K} \frac{2^{rel_i} - 1}{\log(i+1)} \qquad (1)$$

where rel_i is the score given by the ranking algorithm to the review at position i. Then, the $IDCG_k$ is the ideal value of DCG@k obtained when the reviews are sorted in decreasing order of their actual helpfulness.

$$nDCG_k = \sum_{i=1}^{K} \frac{DCG_k}{IDCG_k} \quad (2)$$

6.5 Experimental results

We start by validating our method against the ground truth dataset to evaluate the quality of the rank produced by our algorithm. Then we compare the baseline versus the ground truth to verify our hypothesis that there is a relation between review and POI answer. When comparing against the ground truth, it is important to show each hotel evaluation to avoid bias data. Aggregating all data could lead to a satisfactory result on average, but could hide bad evaluations. We also evaluate our method against the baseline.

Validation against the Ground Truth. We start by evaluating which set of aspects and tuning options presents better results for our algorithm. There are three configurations for the aspects: (*i*) only positive aspects, (*ii*) only negative aspects, and (*iii*) both positive and negative aspects combined (ScoreHelper() from Section 5.3). Besides the aspects, we also need to evaluate if considering the review writers reputation score improves the ranking. All cases are evaluated by the nDCG metric described in Section 6.4.

Figure 5 shows the results of all evaluated configurations. The worst results are by considering *only* positive aspects, with nDCG lower than 0.4. In contrast, when considering only negative aspects, the nDCG is close or higher than 0.6. The combined option (empirically obtained by tuning *ScoreHelper()*) improves a little the ranking quality, by increasing nDCG in 0.035 on average and keeping all values greater than 0.6. Finally, we evaluate the review writers' reputation allied to both positive and negative aspects. Such combination provides considerable improvement on the ranking, by increasing nDCG in 0.1 on average.

This last configuration is also the best one, giving average nDCG around 0.8, implying that it produces ranking close to the ideal one. Overall, such results confirm our hypothesis that negative aspects are indeed more relevant to POI owners, and giving higher weight to them on our ranking algorithm is a distinct strategy.

Baseline Validation against the Ground Truth. Our baseline was built by considering the hypothesis that there is a relation between the review and its answer from the POI owner. Before considering it as a valid baseline ranking, we must evaluate if such hypothesis holds.

Figure 6 shows the nDCG results for all hotels in the ground truth dataset. These results are very promising, as the lowest nDCG value is 0.76 and the greatest is 0.9. The average nDCG is 0.82, indicating that the baseline produces ranking close to the ideal one. In other words, we may use it as baseline to evaluate big data volumes without asking for expert evaluations. Then, we solve the problem of automatic obtaining a large dataset to use as a comparison ranking.

Our Method against the Baseline. We now present the comparison between our proposed method and the baseline on a large

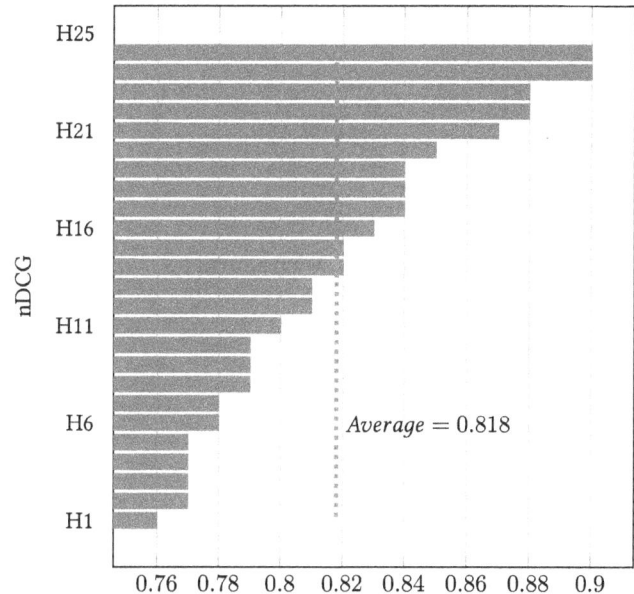

Figure 6: Baseline validation against the ground truth

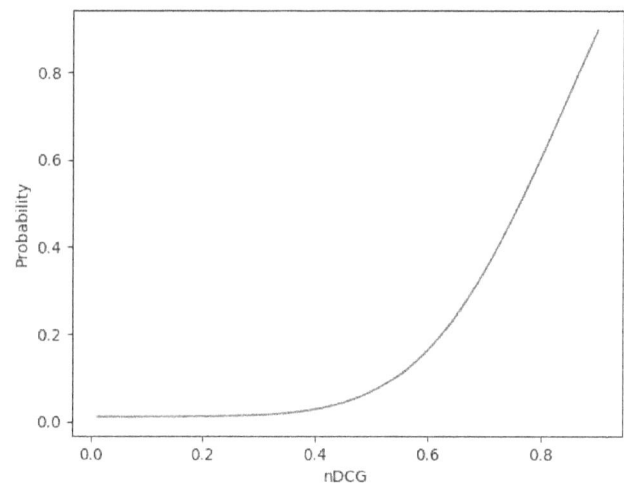

Figure 7: Cumulative Distribution Function on nDCG - Algorithm against the baseline

dataset (Section 6.1). We rank the reviews with both methods and then compare the results by using nDCG to show how close our algorithm is to the baseline. Figure 7 shows the Cumulative Distribution Function on nDCG value obtained for all 9,676 hotels. Both rankings are tied, and the set of reviews from a hotel has a chance larger than 20% of having a nDCG greater than 0.6. It is important to mention that the set of reviews used is different for each test case, since each is built based on the responses of one establishment at a time.

Overall, our technique obtains great results for most test cases and medium results for just a few. Investigating the reason for such a discrepancy, we found that the hotels with worst results were those that provided generic or vague answers to the reviews, without focusing on the complaints of the users.

7 CONCLUSION

In this paper, we defined a new twist to a known problem: how to rank reviews according to their helpfulness to the business owner, instead of to the client (which has been the only way, so far). Indeed, we have empirically showed that most reviews are not helpful at all to the owners, as evaluated by experts.

Regarding our solution, we proposed that positive and negative aspects of the review be considered, with more weight to the negative ones. Then, we have empirically showed that reviews on the negative aspects of a POI are more relevant to its owner. Hence, our solution of giving more weight to negative aspects holds. Furthermore, we proposed that not only positive and negative aspects of the review be considered, but also the reputation of its writer. Our experimental evaluation has indeed showed that considering such reputation is paramount for obtaining better ranking results.

As ranking reviews useful for owners (and not clients) is a new problem (as fully argued), there is no current state-of-the-art to compare our solution against. Therefore, our contributions also include creating two datasets: one ground truth built based on experts' evaluation, and one baseline built by the similarity between reviews and their answers. Both are publicly available for download and further exploration.

Given its complexity, there are different directions to keep pursuing a solution for proposing a owner-oriented review ranking. For example, we plan to investigate the benefits of adding new features to our method, for example geographic ones. We also plan to further analyze the temporal dynamics of the reviewing process and its correlation to POI popularity.

ACKNOWLEDGMENTS

This work is supported by the National Council of Scientific and Technological Development - CNPq, Brazil under Grants No.: 310715/2015-6 and 458400/2014-9 (Apoena Project), as well as the Minas Gerais State Agency for Research and Development - FAPEMIG, Brazil under Grant No.: CEX-PPM-00317-16.

REFERENCES

[1] Suhrid Balakrishnan and Sumit Chopra. 2012. Collaborative Ranking. In *WSDM*. Washington, USA, 143–152.
[2] Carolina Bigonha, Thiago N. C. Cardoso, Mirella M. Moro, Marcos A. Gonçalves, and Virgílio A. F. Almeida. 2012. Sentiment-based influence detection on Twitter. *JBCS* 18, 3 (2012), 169–183.
[3] J. Bobadilla, F. Ortega, A. Hernando, and A. Gutiérrez. 2013. Recommender Systems Survey. *Know.-Based Syst.* 46 (July 2013), 109–132.
[4] Michele A. Brandão and Mirella M. Moro. 2017. Social professional networks: A survey and taxonomy. *Computer Communications* 100 (2017), 20–31.
[5] Li-Chen Cheng, Zhi-Han Ke, and Bang-Min Shiue. 2011. Detecting changes of opinion from customer reviews. In *FSKD*. Shanghai, China, 1798–1802.
[6] Judith A. Chevalier and Dina Mayzlin. 2003. The Effect of Word of Mouth on Sales: Online Book Reviews. *Journal of Marketing Research* 43, 3 (2003), 345–354.
[7] Chrysanthos Dellarocas, Xiaoquan (Michael) Zhang, and Neveen F. Awad. 2007. Exploring the value of online product reviews in forecasting sales: The case of motion pictures. *Journal of Interactive Marketing* 21, 4 (2007), 23 – 45.
[8] Anindya Ghose and Panagiotis G. Ipeirotis. 2011. Estimating the Helpfulness and Economic Impact of Product Reviews: Mining Text and Reviewer Characteristics. *TKDE* 23, 10 (2011), 1498–1512.
[9] Jonathan L. Herlocker, Joseph A. Konstan, Loren G. Terveen, and John T. Riedl. 2004. Evaluating Collaborative Filtering Recommender Systems. *TOIS* 22, 1 (2004), 5–53.
[10] Minqing Hu and Bing Liu. 2004. Mining and summarizing customer reviews. In *SIGKDD*. Seattle, Washington, 168–177.
[11] Nitin Jindal and Bing Liu. 2007. Review Spam Detection. In *WWW*. Calgary, Canada, 1189–1190.
[12] Yohan Jo and Alice H. Oh. 2011. Aspect and Sentiment Unification Model for Online Review Analysis. In *WSDM*. Hong Kong, China, 815–824.
[13] Soo-Min Kim, Patrick Pantel, Tim Chklovski, and Marco Pennacchiotti. 2006. Automatically Assessing Review Helpfulness. In *EMNLP*. Sydney, Australia, 423–430.
[14] Emanuel Lacic, Dominik Kowald, and Elisabeth Lex. 2016. High Enough?: Explaining and Predicting Traveler Satisfaction Using Airline Reviews. In *ACM Hypertext and Social Media*. Halifax, Canada, 249–254.
[15] Bing Liu and Lei Zhang. 2012. A Survey of Opinion Mining and Sentiment Analysis. In *Mining Text Data*. Amsterdam, The Netherlands, 415–463.
[16] Jingjing Liu, Chin-Yew Lin, and Ming Zhou. 2007. Low-Quality Product Review Detection in Opinion Summarization. In *EMNLP-CoNLL*. Prague, Czech Republic, 334–342.
[17] Xin Liu and Karl Aberer. 2014. Towards a Dynamic top-N Recommendation Framework. In *RecSys*. San Francisco, 217–224.
[18] Yang Liu, Xiangji Huang, Aijun An, and Xiaohui Yu. 2008. Modeling and Predicting the Helpfulness of Online Reviews. In *ICDM*. Pisa, Italy, 443–452.
[19] Roberto Lourenco Jr. et al. 2014. Economically-efficient Sentiment Stream Analysis. In *SIGIR*. Gold Coast, Australia, 637–646.
[20] Augusto Q. Macedo, Leandro B. Marinho, and Rodrygo L.T. Santos. 2015. Context-Aware Event Recommendation in Event-based Social Networks. In *RecSys*. Vienna, Autria, 123–130.
[21] Luciana B. Maroun, Mirella M. Moro, Jussara M. Almeida, and Ana Paula C. Silva. 2016. Assessing Review Recommendation Techniques Under a Ranking Perspective. In *ACM Hypertext*. Halifax, Canada, 113–123.
[22] Julian McAuley and Jure Leskovec. 2013. Hidden Factors and Hidden Topics: Understanding Rating Dimensions with Review Text. In *RecSys*. Hong Kong, China, 165–172.
[23] Samaneh Moghaddam, Mohsen Jamali, and Martin Ester. 2012. ETF: Extended Tensor Factorization Model for Personalizing Prediction of Review Helpfulness. In *WSDM*. Seattle, Washington, 163–172.
[24] Arjun Mukherjee, Vivek Venkataraman, Bing Liu, and Natalie S. Glance. 2013. What Yelp Fake Review Filter Might Be Doing?. In *ICWSM*. Michigan, USA, 409–418.
[25] Michael P. O'Mahony and Barry Smyth. 2009. Learning to Recommend Helpful Hotel Reviews. In *RecSys*. New York, USA, 305–308.
[26] Bo Pang and Lillian Lee. 2005. Seeing Stars: Exploiting Class Relationships for Sentiment Categorization with Respect to Rating Scales. In *ACL*. Michigan, USA, 115–124.
[27] Sindhu Raghavan, Suriya Gunasekar, and Joydeep Ghosh. 2012. Review Quality Aware Collaborative Filtering. In *RecSys*. Dublin, Ireland, 123–130.
[28] Marco Rossetti, Fabio Stella, and Markus Zanker. 2016. Analyzing user reviews in tourism with topic models. *J. of IT & Tourism* (2016), 5–21.
[29] Jiliang Tang, Huiji Gao, Xia Hu, and Huan Liu. 2013. Context-aware Review Helpfulness Rating Prediction. In *RecSys*. Hong Kong, China, 1–8.
[30] Oren Tsur and Ari Rappoport. 2009. RevRank: A Fully Unsupervised Algorithm for Selecting the Most Helpful Book Reviews.. In *ICWSM*. San Jose, USA, 154–161.
[31] Peter D. Turney. 2002. Thumbs Up or Thumbs Down? Semantic Orientation Applied to Unsupervised Classification of Reviews. In *ACL*. Philadelphia, USA, 417 – 424.
[32] Saúl Vargas, Linas Baltrunas, Alexandros Karatzoglou, and Pablo Castells. 2014. Coverage, Redundancy and Size-awareness in Genre Diversity for Recommender Systems. In *RecSys*. San Francisco, USA, 209–216.
[33] Hong Yu and Vasileios Hatzivassiloglou. 2003. Towards Answering Opinion Questions: Separating Facts from Opinions and Identifying the Polarity of Opinion Sentences. In *EMNLP*. Stroudsburg, PA, USA, 129–136.
[34] Zhu Zhang and Balaji Varadarajan. 2006. Utility Scoring of Product Reviews. In *CIKM*. Arlington, Virginia, USA, 51–57.
[35] Yu Zheng. 2012. Tutorial on Location-Based Social Networks. In *WWW*. Lyon, France, 679–688.
[36] Yu Zheng, Lizhu Zhang, Zhengxin Ma, Xing Xie, and Wei-Ying Ma. 2011. Recommending Friends and Locations Based on Individual Location History. *TWEB* 5, 1 (2011), 5:1–5:44.

Multi-part Representation Learning For Cross-domain Web Content Classification using Neural Networks

Ganesh J[*]
IIIT, Hyderabad, India
Ganesh.J@Research.iiit.ac.in

Manjira Sinha
Conduent Labs India
Manjira.Sinha@Conduent.Com

Himanshu Sharad Bhatt[†]
American Express Big Data Labs
Himanshu.S.Bhatt@Aexp.Com

Shourya Roy[‡]
American Express Big Data Labs
Shourya.Roy@Aexp.Com

ABSTRACT

Owing to the tremendous increase in the volume and variety of user generated content, *train–once–apply–forever* models are insufficient for supervised learning tasks. The need is to develop algorithms that can adapt across domains by leveraging labeled data from source domain(s) and efficiently perform the task in the unlabeled target domain. Towards this, we present a novel two-stage neural network learning algorithm for domain adaptation which learns a multi-part hidden layer where individual parts contribute differently to the tasks in source and target domains. The multiple parts of the representation (i.e. hidden layer) are learned while being cognizant of what characteristics to transfer across domains and what to preserve within domains for enhanced performance. The first stage embroils around learning a two-part representation i.e. source specific and common representations in a manner such that the former do not detract the ability of the later to represent the target domain. In the second stage, the generalized common representation is further iteratively extended with discriminating target specific characteristics to adapt to the target domain. We empirically demonstrate that the learned representations, in different arrangements, outperform existing domain adaptation algorithms in the source classification as well as the cross-domain classification tasks on the user generated content from different domains on the web.

CCS CONCEPTS

•**Computing methodologies** → **Machine learning**; **Artificial intelligence**;

---

[*]Work done while working for Xerox Research Centre India during an internship from May-August 2016.
[†]Work done while working for Conduent Labs India till February 2017.
[‡]Work done while working for Xerox Research Centre India till December 2016.

HT'17, July 4-7, 2017, Prague, Czech Republic.
© 2017 ACM. 978-1-4503-4708-2/17/07...$15.00
DOI: http://dx.doi.org/10.1145/3078714.3078745

KEYWORDS

Domain Adaptation; Transfer Learning; Neural Networks; Text Classification

1 INTRODUCTION

As online social networks become popular, there has been tremendous growth of user generated content. Analysis on such huge volumes of data can help businesses to understand the brand perception and customers' opinion about their products and services. Supervised machine learning algorithms such as text classification have played a key enabler role to categorize user generated content, for e.g. sentiment categorization of reviews/posts, to gain insights. A fundamental assumption in supervised statistical learning is that training and test data are independently and identically distributed (i.i.d.) samples drawn from a distribution. These algorithms perform well when the training (source domain) and test (target domain) data are from the same domain and follow similar distributions. Otherwise, good performance on test data cannot be guaranteed even if the training error is low. Therefore, directly applying an algorithm, trained using labeled data from one domain, on a different domain often results in poor performance. Generally, such supervised algorithms need to be trained from scratch for every new domain. Since the data in new (target) domain is unlabeled, this often requires expensive and time consuming human efforts to annotate a fraction of data as labeled training data and hence, not pragmatic in real applications.

On the other hand, transfer learning (domain adaptation) [28] techniques allow domains, tasks, and distributions in training and testing to be different, but related. It works in contrast to traditional supervised techniques on the principle of transferring learned knowledge across domains. As discussed by Pan *et al.* [28], transfer can be performed at instance, feature, parameter or relational level; however, feature representation based adaptation has been the most successful direction in the domain adaptation literature. A feature representation based domain adaptation algorithm utilizes labeled data from the source and unlabeled data from the target domain to learn a "representation" such that the source and target data distributions appear as similar as possible using the learned representation [28]. A model trained on this learned representation using the labeled source data generalizes well for the target domain, this is known as *generalization*. Most existing domain adaptation algorithms emphasize on generalization and learn such common

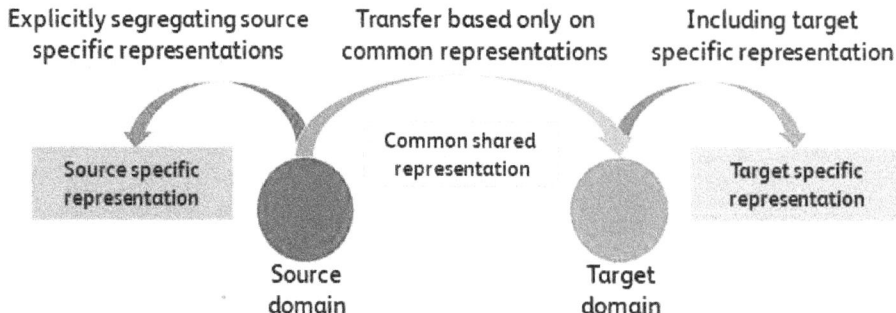

Figure 1: Illustrates the fundamental idea underlying the paper i.e. generalization from source domain and adaptation to the target domain. Generalization includes learning a common shared representation from the labeled source and unlabeled target domain such that the divergence between the two domain is minimized by explicitly limiting source specific representations. Adaptation focuses on learning discriminating target specific representations beyond common representations, that further enhances the cross-domain performance.

representations to act as a bridge to transfer the knowledge from the source to the target domain. However, a brute force transfer across domains often results in *negative transfer* if we do not account for a fundamental question about "what to transfer" [28].

Since each domain, both the source and target, has specific features that are highly discriminating for tasks only within the domain, therefore, these specific features should be preserved. Traditional domain adaptation algorithms, being oblivious to any such domain specific characteristics, learn common shared representations which suffer from transfer loss as the source specific characteristics limit their transferability to the target domain. Moreover, the common representations may not be optimal for target domain task as they do not posses any target specific characteristics. This exposes two major limitations of traditional methods of learning common representations between domains:

(1) They do not account for the negative influence of source specific characteristics on the generalization capabilities of the common representations.
(2) They do not adapt to the target domain by learning the discriminating target specific characteristics.

It is also observed that domain adaptation methods, which are based on generalization, solely optimize for target domain performance often at the cost of classification performance in the source. While this goes well along with the domain adaptation objective of maximizing the target performance, a technique like ours simultaneously sustains the performance in the source domain as well.

Contributions: This paper presents a method to learn transferable representations that address the above mentioned challenges and satisfy the fundamental principles of domain adaptation i.e. generalizing from source domain(s) and adapting to the target domain, as illustrated in Figure 1. Our primary contribution is a novel two-stage neural network learning algorithm based on the principle of learning a multi-part hidden layer where individual parts (or units, feature representations) can be disentangled or combined for different tasks in different domains. It learns the following parts of the hidden layer, 1) common shared representations between the source and target domains, 2) source specific representations, and

3) target specific representations. Firstly, common representations are learned between the source and target domains by explicitly excluding source specific characteristics so as to not detract from their ability to represent the target domain. Secondly, the learned common representations are dynamically extended to include target specific characteristics in an iterative manner to further enhance the performance in the target domain. Multiple parts of the representation behave differently for different learning objectives. For the source learning task, the source specific and common parts jointly contribute for the source domain performance where the performance of most domain adaptation algorithms is compromised. For the cross-domain task, the learned common representations along with the additional target specific representations contribute towards the target domain performance.

Organization: The paper is organized as follows: Section 2 presents the problem formulation, Section 3 summarizes the related work. Section 4 presents the proposed two-stage algorithm to learn the multi-part representation. Section 5 presents the dataset and the experimental results. Finally, we conclude in Section 6.

2 PROBLEM FORMULATION

Let us consider a binary classification task where $X \subseteq \mathbf{R}^n$ is the input space and $\mathcal{Y} = \{0, 1\}$ is the label space. We have two different distributions over $X \times \mathcal{Y}$, called the source domain $\mathcal{D}_S$ and the target domain $\mathcal{D}_T$. We have labeled samples from source S drawn i.i.d from $\mathcal{D}_S$ and unlabeled samples from target T drawn i.i.d. from $\mathcal{D}_T$.

$$S = \{(x_i^s, y_i^s)\}_{i=1}^m \sim (D_S)^m;$$
$$T = \{x_i^t\}_{i=1}^{m'} \sim (D_T)^{m'}$$

where m and m' are the number of labeled source and unlabeled target samples. Our objective here is two-fold: 1) *generalization*: learn a common shared representation from labeled source and unlabeled target domain samples while explicitly keeping away the source specific characteristics and 2) *adaptation*: extend the learned common shared representation using unlabeled samples from the target domain so as to learn target specific characteristics for enhanced classification performance.

3 RELATED WORK

Feature representation based domain adaptation methods aim to learn a 'representation' where the source and target data distributions appear as similar as possible. It includes learning non-linear mappings [6, 14, 26], mappings to mitigate domain divergence [27], common features [13, 15], and ensemble based approaches [4]. A large body of work exists on training both a classifier and a representation that are linear [2, 8, 12, 18]; subspace based approaches [16, 20–22]. A recent work on CORelation ALignment (CORAL) [29] aligns the distributions by re-coloring the source distribution with the covariance of the target distribution.

Approaches using non-linear neural network architectures [19], adaptive deep neural networks namely interpolating between domains (DLID) [11], ReverseGrad [17], Deep Adaptation Networks [23] and Deep Domain Confusion networks [31] have shown promising results. Residual transfer networks [24] which explicitly model the residual function for unsupervised domain adaptation is one of the popular methods. Unsupervised models such as denoising autoencoders [32] has demonstrated state-of-the-art performance on this problem. A variant of this architecture, known as marginalized stacked denoising autoencoders (mSDA) [9] learns robust representation to input corruption noise, which is stable across changes in domains, thus allowing cross-domain transfer. Bi-transferring deep neural networks (BTDNNs) [33] transfer the source examples to target and vice versa to handle the domain discrepancy issue using linear transfer, reconstruction of data, and effective modeling of the domain specifics and commonalities of domains.

Our work is inspired from the recent model, Domain Adversarial Neural Network (DANN) [1] which learns a single representation by using an adversarial gradient reversal component for domain divergence. However, we propose to learn a multi-part representation where every individual part contributes differently to task across domains. Other work, similar in principle to ours, is the domain separation networks (DSN) [7] which explicitly and jointly models the private (domain specific) and shared components of domain representation. DSN concepts differ from our approach in the following manner: (1) DSN is based on CNN while our approach is based on auto-encoders, (2) the learning model for DSN includes separate losses for difference, similarity, reconstruction and task-specificities, while our paper focuses on domain discrimination by incorporating domain divergence and source risk minimization into a single objective function. Zhou et. al. [34] proposed an algorithm for incremental learning of neural network with in-domain data; however, our approach proposes to extend the hidden layer of a pre-trained network for cross-domain learning from unlabeled target data.

4 PROPOSED ALGORITHM

We present a novel two-stage neural network algorithm that goes beyond the traditional "generalization" stage for domain adaptation and "adapts" to the target domain, as shown in Figure 2. The novelty of the proposed algorithm is learning a multi-part hidden layer where each part of the representation is optimized for different tasks. In the first generalization stage, the proposed neural network learns a two-part hidden layer (representation), namely, 1) source specific and 2) common representations. While learning the two-part representation, the source specific representations are explicitly kept away from the common shared representations so as to not detract their ability to generalize to the target domain. In the second stage of adaptation, the common part of the hidden layer is iteratively extended with additional hidden units to include the discriminating target specific representations for enhanced performance. The generalization stage uses labeled data from the source and unlabeled data from the target domains; whereas in the adaptation stage, unlabeled target domain instances are transformed into pseudo-labeled instances for tuning the weights of the additional target specific hidden units. Different stages of the proposed algorithm are further elaborated next.

4.1 Stage-1: Generalization from Source

As shown in Figure 2, the network has full connections among input, hidden, and output layers. In generalization stage, the neural network learns a two-part hidden representation for which it uses two objective functions: 1) classification in source and 2) domain divergence between two domains. The neural network architecture segregates the hidden layer as source specific and common parts where each part contributes differently for different objectives. Both the source specific and common units contribute positively[1] for classification in the source; whereas, for the domain regressor output, the source specific part contributes negatively while the common part contributes positively.

4.1.1 Classification in Source. A neural network architecture with one hidden layer learns the function $h : X \rightarrow \mathbb{R}^D$ to map the input to a D-dimensional representation:

$$h(x) = sigm(\mathbf{W}x + \mathbf{b}), \quad (1)$$

which is parameterized by a matrix-vector pair $(\mathbf{W}, \mathbf{b}) \in \mathbb{R}^{D \times n} \times \mathbb{R}^D$ and where:

$$sigm(a) = \left[\frac{1}{1 + \exp(-a_i)} \right]_{i=1}^{|a|} \quad (2)$$

. The neural network architecture proposed in this work segregates this internal representation as source specific and common parts; represented as:

$$h(x) = \{h_{ss}(x) \bigoplus h_c(x)\} \quad (3)$$

For the source classification task, both $h_{ss}(\cdot)$ and $h_c(\cdot)$ behave in exactly same manner; hence, it follows the objective of any standard neural network architecture where the output function $f : \mathbb{R}^D \rightarrow [0, 1]^L$ is represented as:

$$f(x) = softmax(\mathbf{V}h(x) + (c)) \quad (4)$$

---

[1] The positive contribution implies that while updating the weights using the gradient descent algorithm, the update occurs in negative direction of the gradient while the negative contributions implies updates in the direction of the gradient.

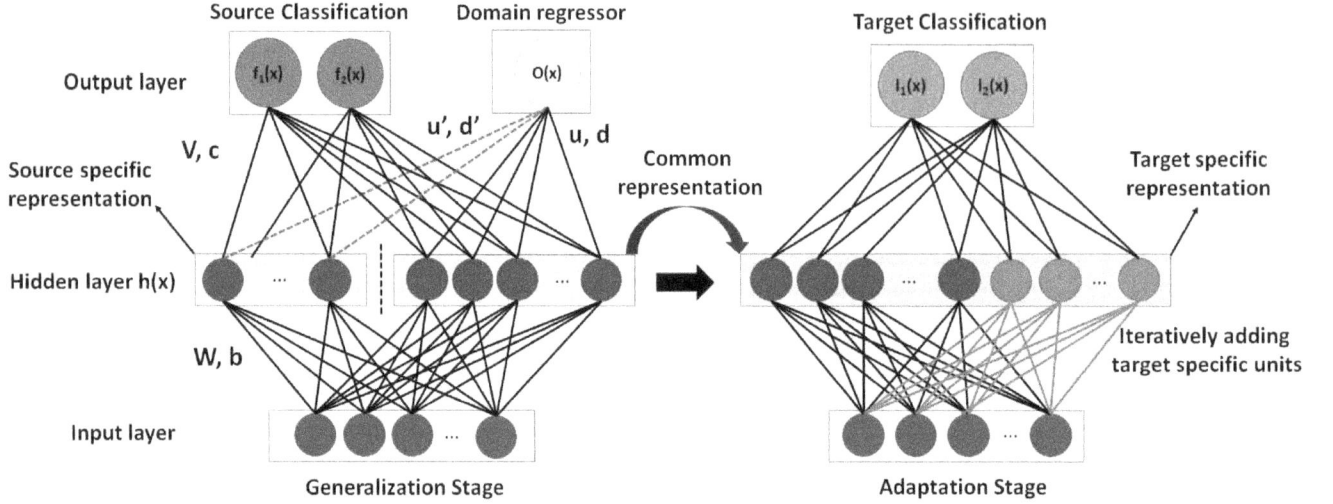

Figure 2: Illustrates the two stages of the the proposed algorithm i.e. 1) generalization where the algorithm learns common representations while explicitly keeping them away from source specific characteristics and 2) adaptation to the target domain where the algorithm iteratively extends the common representations with target specific representations for enhanced performance.

which is parameterized by a matrix-vector pair $(\mathbf{V}, \mathbf{c}) \in \mathbb{R}^{D \times L} \times \mathbb{R}^L$ and $L = |y|$ and where:

$$soft max(a) = \left[\frac{\exp(a_i)}{\sum_{j=1}^{|a|} \exp(a_j)} \right]_{i=1}^{|a|} \qquad (5)$$

Given training source examples $S = \{(x_i^s, y_i^s)\}_{i=1}^m$, the classification loss is given by the negative log-probability of the correct label:

$$\ell(f(x), y) = \log \frac{1}{f_y(x)}$$

and the objective function for the learning problem on the source domain is represented as:

$$\min_{\mathbf{W}, \mathbf{V}, \mathbf{b}, \mathbf{c}} \left[\frac{1}{m} \sum_{i=1}^m \ell(f(x_i^s), y_i^s) + \lambda R(\mathbf{W}, \mathbf{b}) \right] \qquad (6)$$

4.2 Domain Divergence

Theoretical results in transfer learning literature [3] show that adapting to a target domain by learning a classifier on a source domain depends on the similarity between the two. A formal measure used in this context is known as $\mathcal{H}$-*divergence*. Intuitively, it is based on the capacity of a hypothesis class $\mathcal{H}$ to distinguish between examples generated by a pair of source-target tasks. Higher the similarity between the tasks, less is $\mathcal{H}$-*divergence* between them and vice versa.

DEFINITION 1. *Given feature distributions of two domains, $\mathcal{D}_s$ & $\mathcal{D}_t$ and a hypothesis class $\mathcal{H}$, the $\mathcal{H}$-divergence between $\mathcal{D}_s$ and $\mathcal{D}_t$ is defined as:*

$$d_{\mathcal{H}}(\mathcal{D}_s, \mathcal{D}_t) = 2 \sup_{\eta \in \mathcal{H}} \left| \Pr_{\mathbf{x}^s \sim \mathcal{D}_s} \left[\eta(\mathbf{x}^s) = 1 \right] - \Pr_{\mathbf{x}^t \sim \mathcal{D}_t} \left[\eta(\mathbf{x}^t) = 1 \right] \right|$$

We reuse a result from Ben-David et al. [2010] where they proved that for a symmetric hypothesis class $\mathcal{H}$, one can compute an approximate empirical $\mathcal{H}$-*divergence* by running a learning algorithm on the problem of discriminating between source and target examples. For this, we construct a new dataset:

$$\{(\mathbf{x}_i^s, 1)\}_{i=1}^m \cup \{(\mathbf{x}_j^t, 0)\}_{j=1}^{m'}$$

where the target and source samples are labeled as 0 and 1 respectively. Then the error (ϵ) of the classifier trained on the above dataset can be used as an approximation of $\mathcal{H}$-*divergence* as following:

$$\hat{d}_A = 2(1 - 2\epsilon) \qquad (7)$$

The underlying idea here is to learn common representation such that it minimizes the divergence between the source and target domains while the source specific representation should (ideally) increase the divergence between two domains. Let the common representation for the source and target samples be $h_c(S) \overset{\text{def}}{=} \{h_c(x_i^s)\}_{i=1}^m$ and $h_c(T) \overset{\text{def}}{=} \{h_c(x_i^t)\}_{i=1}^{m'}$ respectively. Let $\hat{d}_{\mathcal{H}}^c(h_c(S), h_c(T))$ be the empirical $\mathcal{H}$-divergence on the common representation, given as:

$$\hat{d}_{\mathcal{H}}^c(h_c(S), h_c(T)) = 2 \left(1 - \min_{\eta \in \mathcal{H}} \left[\frac{1}{m} \sum_{i=1}^m [\eta(h_c(x_i^s)) = 1] \right. \right.$$
$$\left. \left. + \frac{1}{m'} \sum_{i=1}^{m'} [\eta(h_c(x_i^t)) = 0] \right] \right)$$

To estimate the "min" part of the above equation, we use a logistic regression model that predicts the probability that a given input (using the common representation) is from the source domain D_S^x (denoted by $z = 1$) or the target domain D_T^x (denoted by $z = 0$):

$$p(z = 1|\phi) = o(\phi) \overset{\text{def}}{=} sigm(d + u^T \phi)$$

Algorithm 1 : Learning Multi-part Representations

Input: Samples $S = \{(x_i^s, y_i^s)\}_{i=1}^m$ and $T = \{x_i^t\}_{i=1}^{m'}$, hidden layer l with n_s source specific nodes and n_c common hidden nodes, adaptation parameter λ, learning rate α.
Output: neural network $\{W, V, b, c\}$.
Initialization: $W, V \leftarrow random\_init(l)$
$b, c, u, d, u', d' \leftarrow 0$
while stopping criteria is not met **do**
  for i from 1 to m **do**
    #Forward Propagation
    $h(x_i^s) \leftarrow \sigma(b + Wx_i^s)$
    $f(x_i^s) \leftarrow softmax(c + Vh(x_i^s))$
    # where $h(x_i^s) = h_c(x_i^s) + h_{ss}(x_i^s)$
    #Backpropagation
    $\Delta_c \leftarrow -(e(y_i^s) - f(x_i^s))$
    $\Delta_V \leftarrow \Delta_c h(x_i^s)^\mathsf{T}$
    $\Delta_b \leftarrow (V^\mathsf{T}\Delta_c) \odot h(x_i^s) \odot (1 - h(x_i^s))$
    $\Delta_w \leftarrow \Delta_b \cdot (x_i^s)^\mathsf{T}$
    # where $h(x_i^s) = h_c(x_i^s) + h_{ss}(x_i^s)$
    #Domain adaptation regularizer...
    #...from current domain - common representation
    $o(x_i^s) \leftarrow \sigma(d + u^\mathsf{T} h_c(x_i^s))$
    $\Delta_d \leftarrow \lambda(1 - o(x_i^s)); \Delta_u \leftarrow \lambda(1 - o(x_i^s))h_c(x_i^s)$
    $tmp \leftarrow \lambda(1 - o(x_i^s))u \odot h_c(x_i^s) \odot (1 - h_c(x_i^s))$
    $\Delta_b \leftarrow \Delta_b + tmp; \Delta_w \leftarrow \Delta_w + tmp \cdot (x_i^s)^\mathsf{T}$
    #...from current domain - source specific representation
    $o'(x_i^s) \leftarrow \sigma(d' + u'^\mathsf{T} h_{ss}(x_i^s))$
    $\Delta_{d'} \leftarrow \lambda(1 - o'(x_i^s))$
    $\Delta_{u'} \leftarrow \lambda(1 - o'(x_i^s))h_{ss}(x_i^s)$

    $tmp \leftarrow \lambda(1 - o'(x_i^s))u \odot h_{ss}(x_i^s) \odot (1 - h_{ss}(x_i^s))$
    $\Delta_b \leftarrow \Delta_b + tmp; \Delta_w \leftarrow \Delta_w + tmp \cdot (x_i^s)^\mathsf{T}$
    #...from other domain - common representation
    $j \Leftarrow uniform\_integer(1, ..., m')$
    $h_c(x_j^t) \Leftarrow \sigma(b + Wx_j^t)$
    $o(x_j^t) \leftarrow \sigma(d + u^\mathsf{T} h_c(x_j^t))$
    $\Delta_d \leftarrow \Delta_d - \lambda o(x_j^t); \Delta_u \leftarrow \Delta_u - \lambda o(x_j^t)h_c(x_j^t)$
    $tmp \leftarrow -\lambda o(x_j^t)u \odot h_c(x_j^t) \odot (1 - h_c(x_j^t))$
    $\Delta_b \leftarrow \Delta_b + tmp; \Delta_w \leftarrow \Delta_w + tmp \cdot (x_j^t)^\mathsf{T}$
    #...from other domain - source specific representation
    $j \Leftarrow uniform\_integer(1, ..., m')$
    $h_{ss}(x_j^t) \Leftarrow \sigma(b + Wx_j^t)$
    $o'(x_j^t) \leftarrow \sigma(d' + u'^\mathsf{T} h_{ss}(x_j^t))$
    $\Delta_{d'} \leftarrow \Delta_{d'} + \lambda o'(x_j^t)$
    $\Delta_{u'} \leftarrow \Delta_{u'} + \lambda o'(x_j^t)h_{ss}(x_j^t)$
    $tmp \leftarrow \lambda o'(x_j^t)u' \odot h_{ss}(x_j^t) \odot (1 - h_{ss}(x_j^t))$
    $\Delta_b \leftarrow \Delta_b + tmp; \Delta_w \leftarrow \Delta_w + tmp \cdot (x_j^t)^\mathsf{T}$
    #Update neural network parameters
    $W \leftarrow W - \alpha\Delta_w; V \leftarrow V - \alpha\Delta_v$
    $b \leftarrow b - \alpha\Delta_b; c \Leftarrow c - \alpha\Delta_c$
    #Update domain classifier parameters
    $u \leftarrow u + \alpha\Delta_u; d \leftarrow d + \alpha\Delta_d$
    $u' \leftarrow u' + \alpha\Delta_{u'}; d' \leftarrow d' + \alpha\Delta_{d'}$
  end for
end while

---

where ϕ is either $h_c(x^s)$ or $h_c(x^t)$ and function $o(\cdot)$ is the domain regressor on the common representation of the source and target samples and its loss $\ell^d(\cdot, \cdot)$ defined as:

$$\ell^d(o(\cdot), z) = -z \log(o(\cdot)) - (1 - z) \log(1 - o(\cdot))$$

Similarly, $\hat{d}_{\mathcal{H}}^{ss}(h_{ss}(S), h_{ss}(T))$ id the divergence on the source specific representation which is represented as:

$$\hat{d}_{\mathcal{H}}^{ss}(h_{ss}(S), h_{ss}(T)) = 2\left(1 - \min_{\eta \in \mathcal{H}}\left[\frac{1}{m}\sum_{i=1}^m [\eta(h_{ss}(x_i^s)) = 1]\right.\right.$$

$$\left.\left. + \frac{1}{m'}\sum_{i=1}^{m'}[\eta(h_{ss}(x_i^t)) = 0]\right]\right)$$

The domain regressor on the source specific representation of source and target samples be $o'(\phi') \stackrel{def}{=} sigm(d' + u'^T \phi')$ where ϕ' is either $h_{ss}(x^s)$ or $h_{ss}(x^t)$ and $\ell^{d'}(\cdot, \cdot)$ is its loss represented as:

$$\ell^{d'}(o'(\cdot), z) = -z \log(o'(\cdot)) - (1 - z) \log(1 - o'(\cdot))$$

The algorithm is detailed in Algorithm 1 where $e(y)$ represents a fione-hotfi vector, consisting of all 0s except for a 1 at position y and $\odot$ represents the element-wise product. The minimization of the source risk and maximization of the domain divergence contribute to the adversarial nature. Also, W' refers to the weights of the common representation while W'' refers to the weights of the source specific representation. The parameter λ controls the trade-off between the source risk and domain divergence. We empirically set it to 0.1 for all our experiments. To optimize the objective above, we use a Stochastic Gradient Descent (SGD) algorithm which samples a pair of source and target examples x_i^s, x_i^t and updates all the parameters of the neural network. It is to be noted that updates for all parameters associated with the source classification function $f(\cdot)$ and domain regressor $o(\cdot)$ on common representation follow the opposite direction of the gradient. Whereas, updates for all parameters associated with the domain regressor $o'(\cdot)$ on source specific representation moves in the direction of gradient. This act as an adversarial for the source specific part which in turn strengthens the generalizability of the common representations.

4.3 Stage 2: Adaptation to Target Domain

The learned common representations, as described in the stage-1, allow to generalize well on the target domain. However, as there are source specific characteristics which are discriminative for the source domain, there are target specific characteristics that should be learned to adapt to the target domain. Most of the existing approaches are restricted only to the generalization stage and do not benefit from incorporating target specific representations. Our algorithm extends beyond generalization and attempts to learn the target specific representations by iteratively extending the common part of the hidden layer with additional units to capture the target specific characteristics.

4.3.1 Pseudo-labeled Target Instances. In several applications (such as cross-domain sentiment categorization), the labeled data from the target is not available. Therefore, we propose to iteratively transform unlabeled target samples into pseudo-labeled data which is used to learn weights of the additional target specific hidden units. In the first iteration, the neural network trained using the common representations is used to predict labels for the target examples. Examples which are predicted with a confidence greater than a predefined threshold (α) are used as pseudo-labeled target instances. We append new hidden units to the network and train them using the pseudo-labeled instances obtained in this round (process explained later). In successive iterations, we use the latest representation learned with additional target specific units and train the model using pseudo-labeled target domain instances. Each iteration produces a set of pseudo-labeled instances which are used to extend the hidden representation to include target specific units.

4.3.2 Extending the Hidden Layer. Let C and $\mathcal{T}$ denote the common units from stage-1 and target specific units respectively. Let $\theta_C = \{\mathbf{W}_C, \mathbf{b}_C, \mathbf{V}_C, \mathbf{c}\}$ and $\theta_{\mathcal{T}} = \{\mathbf{W}_{\mathcal{T}}, \mathbf{b}_{\mathcal{T}}, \mathbf{V}_{\mathcal{T}}, \mathbf{c}\}$ indicate the corresponding parameters. The functions of the hidden layer corresponding to the common hidden units and the new target units are represented as:

$$h_C^l(x^t) = \sigma(b_C^l + \mathbf{W}_C^l x_t) \in [0,1]^C, \tag{8}$$

$$h_{\mathcal{T}}^{\mathcal{P}}(x^t) = \sigma(b_{\mathcal{T}}^l + \mathbf{W}_{\mathcal{T}}^l x_t) \in [0,1]^{\Delta N}, \tag{9}$$

where l represents the last input batch consisting of the target domain instances and their pseudo-labels, ΔN represents the number of target specific units in the last iteration t. The output function for the network with extended hidden units is represented as:

$$f^l(x^t) = softmax\left(c + \mathbf{V}_C^l h_C^l(x^t) + \mathbf{V}_{\mathcal{T}}^l h_{\mathcal{T}}^l(x^t)\right) \tag{10}$$

Given the lth batch of pseudo-labeled target domain instances as n_l^t, the objective function for the learning problem on the target domain becomes:

$$\min_{\theta_C, \theta_{\mathcal{T}}} \frac{1}{n_l^t}\left[\sum_{i=1}^{n_l^t} \mathcal{L}(x_i^t, \hat{y}_i)\right] \tag{11}$$

where $\mathcal{L}$ represents the cross-entropy loss function and $\{x^t, \hat{y}\}$ represents the target domain instances and their pseudo-labels. Different sub tasks involved in extending the hidden layer of the network are elaborated below.

Adding New Features In an iteration, we add ΔN new target specific units and optimize the following objective function:

Algorithm 2 : Adaptation to Target

Input: n_l^t (l^{th} batch of labeled target domain instances in the iteration t), classifier f, ΔN and ΔM
    (1) Identify $2\Delta M$ candidate features and merge them into ΔM features (Section 4.3.2).
    (2) Add ΔN new features by greedy optimization (Section 4.3.2).
    (3) Optimize all the features (except θ_C) by gradient descent (Eq. 11).
    (4) Update ΔN and ΔM (Section 4.3.2).
Output: f.

$$\min_{\theta_{\mathcal{T}}} \frac{1}{n_l^t}\left[\sum_{i=1}^{n_l^t} \mathcal{L}(x_i^t, \hat{y}_i)\right] \tag{12}$$

Notice that we keep θ_C to be constant and focus on optimizing only the parameters corresponding to the new target specific units. This step allows us to rewrite the output function as:

$$f^l(x^t) = softmax\left(\mathbf{V}_{\mathcal{T}}^l h_{\mathcal{T}}^l(x^t) + c_d(h_C^l(x^t))\right) \tag{13}$$

where $c_d(h_C^l(x^t)) = \mathbf{V}_C^l h_C^l(x^t) + c$ can be viewed as a *dynamic decoding bias.*

Merging Redundant Features After each iteration, we merge redundant features to get compact representation which prevents the model from over-fitting which generally happens if we only perform addition of new features. Essentially, we select ΔM pairs of candidate features and merge each of them into a single feature as explained below:

- Identify a set of candidate features to be merged, $\mathcal{M} = \{m_1, m_2\} \subset C \cup \mathcal{T}$. We solve it by finding a pair of features whose cosine distance is maximal:

$$\hat{\mathcal{M}} = arg\,max_{\{m_1, m_2\}} cos(\mathbf{W}_{m_1}, \mathbf{W}_{m_2}) \tag{14}$$

- Remove the m_1^{th} and m_2^{th} feature
- Add and initialize the new feature as a linear combination of two candidate feature parameters for faster convergence as:

$$\theta_{\mathcal{T}} = \frac{\sum_{x \in n_i^t} \mathcal{P}(h_{m_1}|\mathbf{x}; \theta_{m_1})\theta_{m_1} + \mathcal{P}(h_{m_2}|\mathbf{x}; \theta_{m_2})\theta_{m_2}}{\sum_{x \in n_i^t} \mathcal{P}(h_{m_1}|\mathbf{x}; \theta_{m_1}) + \mathcal{P}(h_{m_2}|\mathbf{x}; \theta_{m_2})} \tag{15}$$

- Solve the following objective function to compute the new feature mapping:

$$\min_{\theta_{\mathcal{T}}, \mathcal{M}} \frac{1}{n_l^t}\left[\sum_{i=1}^{n_l^t} \mathcal{L}(x_i^t, \hat{y}_i)\right] \tag{16}$$

Updating Feature Increments/ Decrements For every iteration, we follow an update rule to compute ΔN and ΔM. Intuitively, we increase the number of feature increments when the performance improves (i.e. the model still improves), and decrease the number of feature increments when there is minimal or no performance

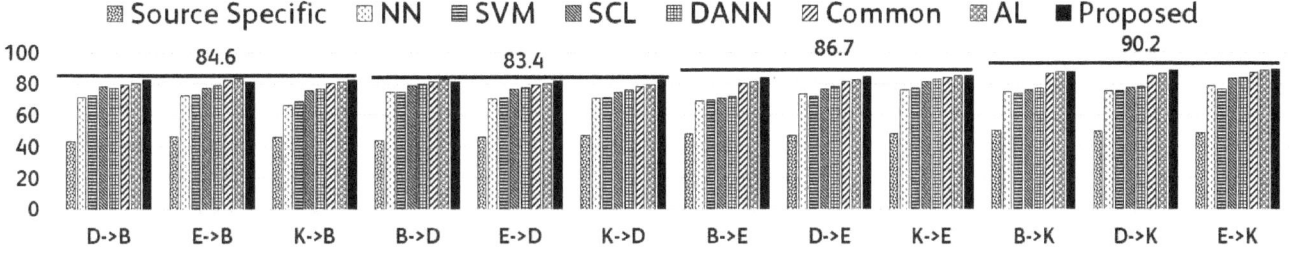

Figure 3: Comparing the performance of different method on the target domains. For example, D→B represent the performance of an algorithm with *D* as labeled source and *B* as unlabeled target domain. For the target task, the proposed algorithm leverages both the common representation and the target specific representations learned in the iterative manner. Horizontal black lines represent the in-domain (Skyline) performance.

improvement (i.e. the model has converged). Precisely, the update rule can be formulated as:

$$\Delta N_{l+1} = \begin{cases} \Delta N_l + 1, \frac{e_l}{e_{l-1}} < (1 - \epsilon_1) \\ \lfloor \Delta N_l / 2 \rfloor, \frac{e_l}{e_{l-1}} > (1 - \epsilon_2) \; ; \; \Delta M_l = \lceil \gamma \Delta N_l \rceil \\ \Delta N_l, otherwise \end{cases} \quad (17)$$

where ΔN_l and ΔM_l is the number of units added and merged in iteration l respectively. e_l is the average objective function value for the iteration l. The hyper-parameters ϵ_1, ϵ_2 control the pace of feature increments, where we accelerate by decreasing ϵ_1 or increasing ϵ_2, and vice-versa. The rate of convergence can be controlled by tuning γ and ΔN_0. We empirically set γ, ΔN_0, ϵ_1, ϵ_2 to 0.5, 20, 0.05 and 0.02 respectively. The algorithm for incremental extension of hidden layer to adapt to the target domain is summarized in Algorithm 2.

5 EXPERIMENTAL EVALUATION

The efficacy of the proposed two-stage technique for learning the multi-part representation across domains is evaluated for the cross-domain sentiment classification task on user reviews about different products from Amazon.com (a popular e-commerce website). We evaluate and examine different parts of the representation for classification tasks in different domains.

5.1 Dataset & Experimental Protocol

The dataset used in this research is the Amazon review dataset [5] which is a benchmark dataset for cross-domain sentiment classification task. It has four domains each comprising user provided reviews about Books (**B**), DVDs (**D**), Kitchen appliances (**K**) and Electronics (**E**) respectively from the Amazon.com. Each domain has 2000 reviews with equal number of positive and negative reviews. In our experiments, each review is encoded in 5000 dimensional feature vectors of unigrams and bigrams. A review is considered positive if the reviewer rated the product as 4 stars or above, otherwise, the review is considered negative if the reviewer rated the product with less than 3 stars[2]. The performance is compared on 12 different cross-domain tasks and is reported in terms of accuracy for

binary classification. For each task, 1400 labeled reviews from one domain constitute the source and 1400 unlabeled reviews from a different domain constitute the target. Unseen non-overlapping 200 and 400 reviews from the target domain are used as the validation set for parameter selection and the test set respectively.

The performance of the proposed algorithm is compared with a standard neural network architecture with one hidden layer (as described in Eq. 6), a support vector machine (SVM) [10] with linear kernel, structural correspondence learning (SCL) [5] and DANN [1]. SCL [5] one of the widely used domain adaptation algorithm used on the benchmark Amazon review dataset. Domain adversarial neural networks (DANN) is one of the recent approaches of representation learning for domain adaptation using neural network architecture. The skyline performance refers to one hidden layer neural network trained and tested on the same domain i.e. in-domain performance. The performance improvements due to the iterative extension of hidden layer using pseudo-labeled target instances is also compared with a traditional active learning approach (AL) [25, 30] where informative examples are queried to an oracle for actual labels.

5.2 Results & Analysis

Experimental results demonstrate the efficacy of the proposed algorithm for cross-domain classification as it clearly outperforms all existing algorithms. These improvements are primarily due to two factors: 1) learning common representation while keeping away the source specific characteristics facilitates in transferring truly common characteristics and 2) learning target specific characteristics enhances the discriminating ability of the learned representation in the target domain. The performance of the proposed technique that iteratively transforms unlabeled target instances to pseudo-labeled instances for extending hidden layer to include target specific characteristics is also compared with an active learning technique which requires an expensive oracle to provide the labels for target domain instances. Results in Figure 3 and Table 1 show that the proposed technique break-evens or outperforms active learning method without incurring any expenses for obtaining labels for the target domain instances.

5.2.1 Analyzing Target Specific Units. We analyze the benefits of extending the hidden layer of the network with target specific units for enhanced cross-domain performance. Figure 3 shows that

---

[2]This is a standard process to convert reviews with star ratings into positive and negative classes for the Amazon review dataset.

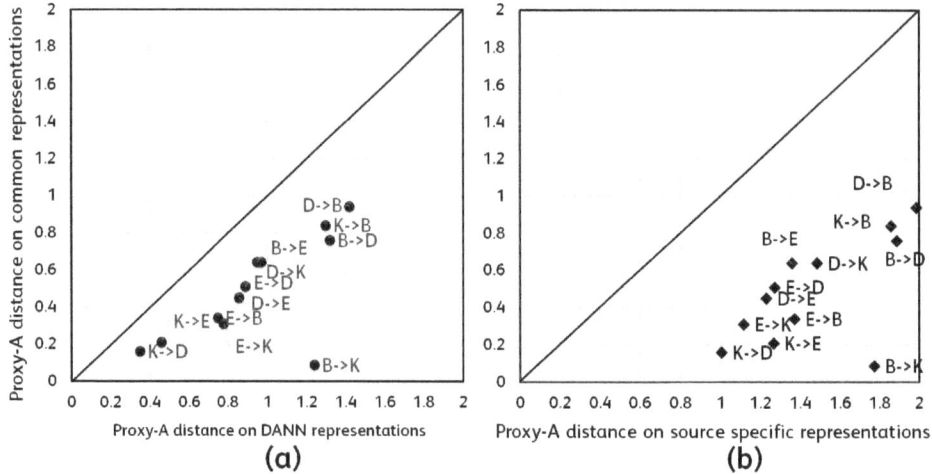

Figure 4: Compares proxy-$\mathcal{A}$ distance (PAD) between (a) the learned common representations v/s the DANN representations and (b) the learned common representations v/s the source specific representations.

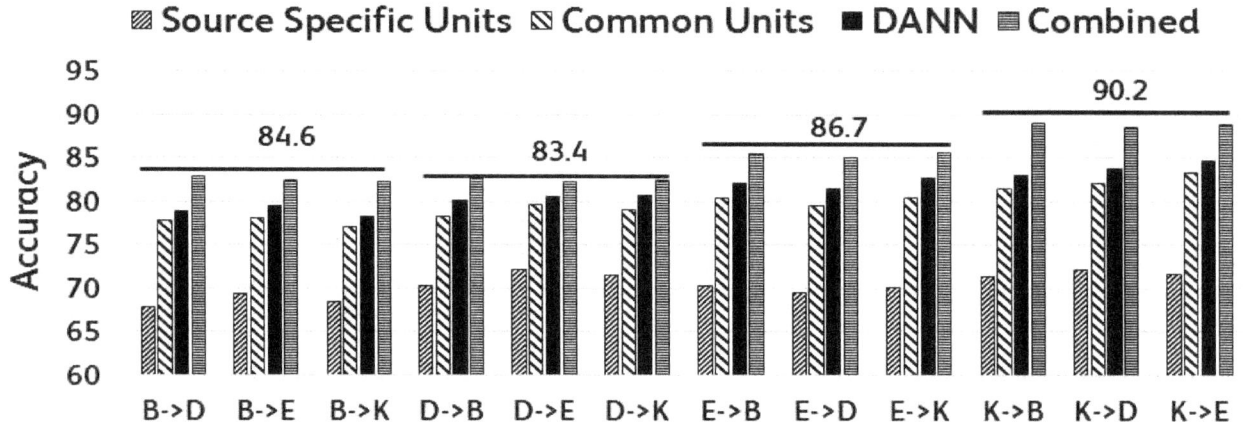

Figure 5: Comparing the performance of different representations on the source classification task. Combined here represent the source specific and common representations for the source classification task.

by iteratively extending the learned common representations with target specific representations results in at least 0.9% and 2.1% improvements over the performance of our common representations and the representations learned using DANN.

5.2.2 Analyzing Common Units. The idea adhered in this paper is to learn common representations such that it makes the source and target domains appear as similar as possible. While it is hard to actually measure $\mathcal{H}$-divergence, it can be closely approximated using proxy-$\mathcal{A}$ distance (PAD) where error (ϵ) of the model is used to compute the PAD as $d_A = 2(1 - 2\epsilon)$, as shown in Eq. 7.

Figure 4(a) shows the PAD computed between domains on the representations learned by DANN [1] and the common representations learned by the proposed algorithm. Since, the proposed algorithm explicitly eliminates any influence of source specific characteristics from the common representations, it yields a lower PAD between domains suggesting that the domains appear more

similar in this representation. Similarly, Figure 4(b) shows PAD between the learned common shared representations and source specific representations for different domains.

5.2.3 Analyzing Source Specific Units. Most of the existing domain adaptation algorithms focus on optimizing the target domain performance while the source domain performance is often compromised. However, the multi-part representation learned by the proposed algorithm alleviates such situation and sustains its performance in the source domains as well.

Results in Figure 5 and Table 2 compares the performance of the source specific and common parts of the learned representations and their combination (referred to as "Combined") with the representations learned using DANN [1] and the in-domain source performance. Results suggest that while the individual parts of the learned representation have low performance, the concatenation of

Table 1: Comparing the performance of the proposed method with existing techniques on the unlabeled target domains for the 12 transfer learning tasks. For example, D → B represents the task where D is used as the labeled source domain and the performance is reported on the unlabeled target domain B.

S → T	Source Specific	NN	SVM	SCL	DANN	Common	AL	Proposed
D→B	43.2	71.2	72.4	78.4	77.3	79.4	80.4	**82.4**
E→B	46.5	72.5	72.6	77.2	78.6	82.3	**83.3**	81.6
K→B	45.7	65.8	68.8	75.6	76.8	80.4	81.4	**82.5**
B→D	43.8	74.4	74.5	78.5	79.9	81.6	**82.6**	81.7
E→D	45.9	70.3	70.8	76.5	77.7	79.2	80.2	**81.8**
K→D	47.2	70.7	71.4	74.4	75.9	78.4	79.4	**82.2**
B→E	48.3	69.2	69.5	70.7	72.0	80.2	81.2	**84.1**
D→E	47.2	73.2	71.9	76.8	78.3	81.4	82.4	**84.7**
K→E	48.1	76.2	77.2	81.4	82.9	84.1	85.2	**85.0**
B→K	50.2	75.1	74.0	76.1	77.0	86.7	**87.8**	87.6
D→K	49.6	75.6	75.7	77.6	78.3	85.3	86.4	**88.7**
E→K	48.4	78.6	76.5	83.3	84.2	87.4	88.5	**89.1**

Table 2: Comparing the performance of different methods on the source classification task. For example, B→D represents the task where B and D are used as the source and target domains respectively and the performance is reported for the classification in the source domain B.

S → T	Source Specific	Common	DANN	Combined
B→D	67.8	77.8	78.9	**82.9**
B→E	69.4	78.1	79.5	**82.4**
B→K	68.4	77	78.3	**82.2**
D→B	70.3	78.3	80.2	**82.9**
D→E	72.1	79.7	80.6	**82.3**
D→K	71.5	79.0	80.8	**82.5**
E→B	70.3	80.4	82.2	**85.5**
E→D	69.6	79.6	81.5	**85.1**
E→K	70.2	80.5	82.7	**85.6**
K→B	71.3	81.6	83.1	**89.1**
K→D	72.1	82.1	83.8	**88.6**
K→E	71.7	83.3	84.7	**88.8**

Table 3: Lists various parameters used in the paper along with their possible value range.

Parameter	Range
Hidden layer size	$\{100, 200\}$
Common units size	100: $\{100, 90, 80, 70, 60\}$, 200: $\{200, 175, 150, 125, 100\}$
Source specific units size	60: $\{60, 50, 40, 30, 20, 10\}$
Batch size	50
Epochs	25
Learning Rate	$0.1, 0.01, 0.001, 0.0001$
λ: the regularization	0.1
ΔN_0: # feature increments	$\{5\text{-}20\}$
ΔM_0: # merged features	$\{5\text{-}20\}$

source specific and common parts outperforms the DANN performance on the source domain and is pretty close to the in-domain source performance. The performance of the common representations is significantly enhanced for the source domain when concatenated with the source specific representations as both the parts learn complementary information, one learning source discriminating features and the other learning the common generalizable characteristics. Both these complimentary pieces of information are useful of classification in the source domain.

5.2.4 Size of Different Parts. We observed that when the source and target domains are similar (as measured by PAD), hidden layer with a higher portion of common v/s source specific units results in better cross-domain performance as compared to when the source and target domains are dissimilar. This intuitively suggests that for similar domains there are more commonalities than domain

specific characteristics and hence a higher number of common units are required to capture this commonality. We keep increasing the number of target specific units with the number of iterations till adding more target specific units saturates the performance. Range of other selected hyper-parameters is mentioned in Table 3. The hyper-parameter λ is varied from 0 to 1. Decreasing λ less than 0.0001 degrades performance and is empirically set to 0.1. The learning rate is varied in log scale and is optimally set to 0.001. Mini-batch size is varied from 30 to 50 and finally set to 50. Epochs is varied between 25, 50, and 100 and set to 25, above which gradients are found to saturate. The common hidden size and source specific hidden size is varied empirically and the best performing model is chosen.

5.2.5 Pseudo-labeled data v/s Active Learning: We compare the performance of the proposed technique that obtains pseudo-labeled training instances from the target domain with an active learning approach that seeks labels for the informative samples from an oracle. Results suggest that the proposed technique is comparable to the active learning method which incurs a cost for querying the true label of an instance to the oracle. We assert that the proposed algorithm has better applicability as there are numerous domains in practice and obtaining labeled data for every domain using an oracle is expensive and time consuming. Moreover, the proposed technique can easily utilize any available labeled data whenever available from the target domain. We also observed that the performance of the proposed algorithm monotonically increases with iterative addition of target units and converges within $5 - 7$ iterations for all the 12 cross-domain learning tasks.

6 CONCLUSION & FUTURE WORK

This paper presented first-of-its-kind approach to learn a multi-part representation for cross-domain transfer learning using a novel neural network architecture. Multiple parts of the learned representation contribute differently for generalization from source and adaptation to the target domain. In the generalization stage, it learns a common shared representation between domains by explicitly keeping the source specific characteristics away from adversely influencing the abilities of common representation to represent the target domain. In the adaptation stage, the learned common representation is iteratively extended to include target specific characteristics for enhanced cross-domain performance. Experimental results on a benchmark dataset demonstrate the efficacy of the proposed algorithm as compared to other existing algorithms.

As a future work, we plan to extend the principle of learning multi-part representations for deep learning architectures for different applications. The proposed algorithm can also be extended for multi-source adaptation, as opposed to single source, where complementary information from more than one sources can be leveraged to perform the target task efficiently.

REFERENCES

[1] Hana Ajakan, Pascal Germain, Hugo Larochelle, François Laviolette, and Mario Marchand. 2014. Domain-adversarial neural networks. *arXiv preprint arXiv:1412.4446* (2014).
[2] Mahsa Baktashmotlagh, Mehrtash T. Harandi, Brian C. Lovell, and Mathieu Salzmann. 2013. Unsupervised Domain Adaptation by Domain Invariant Projection. In *The IEEE International Conference on Computer Vision (ICCV)*.
[3] Shai Ben-David, John Blitzer, Koby Crammer, Alex Kulesza, Fernando Pereira, and Jennifer Wortman Vaughan. 2010. A theory of learning from different domains. *Machine learning* 79, 1-2 (2010), 151–175.
[4] Himanshu Sharad Bhatt, Deepali Semwal, and Shourya Roy. 2015. An Iterative Similarity based Adaptation Technique for Cross-domain Text Classification. In *Proceedings of Conference on Natural Language Learning.* 52–61.
[5] John Blitzer, Mark Dredze, and Fernando Pereira. 2007. Biographies, bollywood, boom-boxes and blenders: Domain adaptation for sentiment classification. In *Proceedings of Association for Computational Linguistics.* 440–447.
[6] D. Bollegala, T. Mu, and J. Y. Goulermas. 2016. Cross-Domain Sentiment Classification Using Sentiment Sensitive Embeddings. *IEEE Transactions on Knowledge and Data Engineering* 28, 2 (2016), 398–410.
[7] Konstantinos Bousmalis, George Trigeorgis, Nathan Silberman, Dilip Krishnan, and Dumitru Erhan. 2016. Domain Separation Networks. *arXiv preprint arXiv:1608.06019* (2016).
[8] Lorenzo Bruzzone and Mattia Marconcini. 2010. Domain Adaptation Problems: A DASVM Classification Technique and a Circular Validation Strategy. *IEEE Transactions on Pattern Analysis and Machine Intelligence* 32, 5 (2010), 770–787.
[9] Minmin Chen, Zhixiang Xu, Kilian Weinberger, and Fei Sha. 2012. Marginalized denoising autoencoders for domain adaptation. (2012).
[10] Chih-Chung Chang Chih-Wei Hsu and Chih-Jen Lin. 2003. *A practical guide to support vector classification.* Technical Report. Department of Computer Science, National Taiwan University.
[11] Sumit Chopra, Suhrid Balakrishnan, and Raghuraman Gopalan. 2013. DLID: Deep Learning for Domain Adaptation by Interpolating between Domains. *ICML Workshop on Challenges in Representation Learning* (2013).
[12] Corinna Cortes and Mehryar Mohri. 2014. Domain adaptation and sample bias correction theory and algorithm for regression. *Theor. Comput. Sci.* 519 (2014), 103–126.
[13] Wenyuan Dai, Gui-Rong Xue, Qiang Yang, and Yong Yu. 2007. Co-clustering Based Classification for Out-of-domain Documents. In *Proceedings of International Conference on Knowledge Discovery and Data Mining.* 210–219.
[14] Hal Daumé III. 2009. Frustratingly easy domain adaptation. *arXiv preprint arXiv:0907.1815* (2009).
[15] Inderjit S. Dhillon, Subramanyam Mallela, and Dharmendra S. Modha. 2003. Information-theoretic Co-clustering. In *Proceedings of International Conference on Knowledge Discovery and Data Mining.* 89–98.
[16] Basura Fernando, Amaury Habrard, Marc Sebban, and Tinne Tuytelaars. 2013. Unsupervised visual domain adaptation using subspace alignment. In *Proceedings of the IEEE International Conference on Computer Vision.* 2960–2967.
[17] Yaroslav Ganin and Victor Lempitsky. 2014. Unsupervised domain adaptation by backpropagation. *arXiv preprint arXiv:1409.7495* (2014).
[18] Pascal Germain, Alexandre Lacasse, François Laviolette, and Mario Marchand. 2009. PAC-Bayesian Learning of Linear Classifiers. In *Proceedings of the 26th Annual International Conference on Machine Learning.* ACM, 353–360.
[19] Xavier Glorot, Antoine Bordes, and Yoshua Bengio. 2011. Domain adaptation for large-scale sentiment classification: A deep learning approach. In *In Proceedings of the International Conference on Machine Learning.*
[20] Boqing Gong, Yuan Shi, Fei Sha, and Kristen Grauman. 2012. Geodesic flow kernel for unsupervised domain adaptation. In *Computer Vision and Pattern Recognition (CVPR), 2012 IEEE Conference on.* IEEE, 2066–2073.
[21] Raghuraman Gopalan, Ruonan Li, and Rama Chellappa. 2011. Domain adaptation for object recognition: An unsupervised approach. In *2011 international conference on computer vision.* IEEE, 999–1006.
[22] Maayan Harel and Shie Mannor. 2010. Learning from multiple outlooks. *arXiv preprint arXiv:1005.0027* (2010).
[23] Mingsheng Long and Jianmin Wang. 2015. Learning transferable features with deep adaptation networks. *arXiv preprint arXiv:1502.02791* (2015).
[24] Mingsheng Long, Jianmin Wang, and Michael I Jordan. 2016. Unsupervised Domain Adaptation with Residual Transfer Networks. *arXiv preprint arXiv:1602.04433* (2016).
[25] Chunyong Luo, Yangsheng Ji, Xinyu Dai, and Jiajun Chen. 2012. Active learning with transfer learning. In *Proceedings of Association for Computational Linguistics Student Research Workshop.* Association for Computational Linguistics, 13–18.
[26] Sinno Jialin Pan, , Ivor W. Tsang, James T. Kwok, and Qiang Yang. 2011. Domain adaptation via transfer component analysis. *IEEE Transactions on Neural Networks* 22, 2 (2011), 199–210.
[27] Sinno Jialin Pan, Xiaochuan Ni, Jian-Tao Sun, Qiang Yang, and Zheng Chen. 2010. Cross-domain Sentiment Classification via Spectral Feature Alignment. In *Proceedings of International Conference on World Wide Web.* 751–760.
[28] Sinno Jialin Pan and Qiang Yang. 2010. A Survey on Transfer Learning. *IEEE Transactions on Knowledge and Data Engineering* 22, 10 (2010), 1345–1359.
[29] Baochen Sun, Jiashi Feng, and Kate Saenko. 2015. Return of frustratingly easy domain adaptation. *arXiv preprint arXiv:1511.05547* (2015).
[30] Devis Tuia, Michele Volpi, Loris Copa, Mikhail Kanevski, and Jordi Munoz-Mari. 2011. A Survey of Active Learning Algorithms for Supervised Remote Sensing Image Classification. , *IEEE Journal of Selected Topics in Signal Processing* 5, 3 (2011), 606–617.
[31] Eric Tzeng, Judy Hoffman, Ning Zhang, Kate Saenko, and Trevor Darrell. 2014. Deep domain confusion: Maximizing for domain invariance. *arXiv preprint arXiv:1412.3474* (2014).
[32] Pascal Vincent, Hugo Larochelle, Yoshua Bengio, and Pierre-Antoine Manzagol. 2008. Extracting and Composing Robust Features with Denoising Autoencoders. In *Proceedings of the International Conference on Machine Learning.* 1096–1103.
[33] Guangyou Zhou, Jimmy Xiangji Huang, and Tingting He. 2016. Bi-Transferring Deep Neural Networks for Domain Adaptation. (2016).
[34] Guanyu Zhou, Kihyuk Sohn, and Honglak Lee. 2012. Online Incremental Feature Learning with Denoising Autoencoders. In *AISTATS.*

Crowdsourcing the Verification of Fake News and Alternative Facts

Ricky J. Sethi
Fitchburg State University
160 Pearl St
Fichburg, MA 01420
rickys@sethiorg

ABSTRACT

Fake news and alternative facts have dominated the news cycle of late. In this paper, we present a prototype system that uses social argumentation to verify the validity of proposed alternative facts and help in the detection of fake news. We utilize fundamental argumentation ideas in a graph-theoretic framework that also incorporates semantic web and linked data principles. The argumentation structure is crowdsourced and mediated by expert moderators in a virtual community.

CCS CONCEPTS

• **Information systems** → *Social networking sites*;

1 MOTIVATION

The phenomenon of fake news and the rise of "alternative facts" have dominated the news cycle of late. Although these terms are new, reliance upon propaganda and misinformation predates the Internet, not just in politics but in communication exchange in general [4]. Critical thinking and evidence-based reasoning are essential for countering propaganda and misinformation intended to manipulate public opinion [9, 10].

Computational approaches for addressing fake news have so far focused mainly on automated tools. These tools flag previously identified hoaxes; or automatically detect fake news articles using natural language processing techniques with pre-existing ground truth; or track the viral-like transmission of hoaxes [2, 6, 8, 11]. None of the existing approaches, however, deal with verification of the alternative facts which constitute the semantic content of such articles.

In such cases, argumentation has been shown to be a natural, substantiated approach for analyzing the veracity and reliability of assertions and claims [3, 7]. In fact, in considering how to assess critical thinking, [3] asserts the need to identify conclusions, reasons, and assumptions as well as judging the quality of arguments and developing positions on an issue. Using this sort of evidence based reasoning not only has the potential to identify fake news to a greater extent but also to imbibe users with the critical thinking ability to navigate future fake news articles.

HT '17, July 04-07, 2017, Prague, Czech Republic
© 2017 Copyright held by the owner/author(s).
ACM ISBN 978-1-4503-4708-2/17/07...$15.00
https://doi.org/10.1145/3078714.3078746

In this paper, we present a prototype system that uses social argumentation to verify the validity of proposed alternative facts and help with fake news detection. We utilize fundamental argumentation principles in a graph-theoretic framework that also incorporates semantic web and linked open data principles [1, 5]. The argumentation structure is crowdsourced and mediated by expert moderators in a virtual community. To the best of our knowledge, our novel computational approach is the only one to address the verification of alternative facts and fake news.

2 SYSTEM ARCHITECTURE

In our argumentation framework, a Stance is the final conclusion composed of Claims and Evidence, and their associated Sources. Stances are fundamental stands on a topic and can be mutually exclusive, should have cohesive sub-structures, and are composed of atomic argumentation components (Claims, Evidence, and Sources). A Claim can be directly supported by a Source or have multiple Evidence components, each supported by its own Source. Multiple Sources can support multiple Evidence nodes.

The Sources themselves have their own properties. A Source can be fully described using the Dublin Core metadata[1]. In this way, users could query the system for assertions from certain sources or from sources with specified properties (e.g., government institutions).

Our methodology also incorporates Ratings for each Source and user in the system. Different trust, authority, and other attribute dimensions are amalgamated and weighted in a Summary Rating; these compound ratings reveal their constituent components (SourceRating, ContentRating, QuestionRating, etc.) on a

---

[1]http://dublincore.org

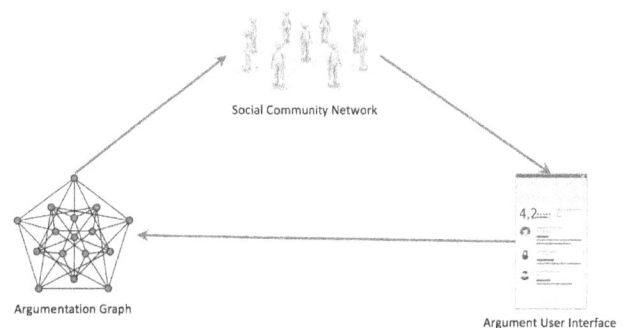

Figure 1: Overview of our System Architecture.

Figure 2: Screenshot of main proposition screen.

MouseOver event, displaying details of Users' Ratings, Source Ratings, Expert Ratings, etc.

2.1 Graph-Theoretic Framework

We create an *Argumentation Graph*, $G_A = (V, E, f)$, composed of a set of vertices, V, edges, E, and a function, f, which maps each element of E to an unordered pair of vertices in V. Each fundamental Claim, Evidence, or Source in an argument thus constitutes an atomic argumentation component, v_a, and is embedded as a vertex in the graph such that $v_a \in V$. The vertices contain not just the component's semantic content, but also the ratings, authority, trust, and other attribute dimensions of each atomic argumentation component. The edges $e \in E$ contain weights along the various dimensions of trust and authority as well as pro/con positions, while the function f maps how they're connected. Depending on the context of the argument, this graph can be undirected or directed, where the temporal component gives the direction to the directed graph.

In terms of a graph, we therefore see the set of vertices V as the set of Claims, Evidence, and Sources; the set of edges E as a set of links that may connect any two vertices. Each subgraph or path traversal that can be obtained from a graph results in a Stance. There are two ways to represent the stances: one way is by making the Stance another node in G_A that is added by the moderators in a top-down manner. The other is to designate each sub-graph as a different Stance. Once he G_A is formed, we can form sub-graphs which represent the different stances we can infer from the argumentation graph where each sub-graph would be a separate Stance. Our approach supports both ways of determining the various stances (what we call top-down vs bottom-up).

2.2 User Interface Component

Our fake news detection system was developed as a web-based application with a responsive interface that allows for viewing on desktops, tablets or mobile phones. The front-end component was developed using HTML, CSS, Bootstrap, jQuery and JavaScript, while the back-end was developed using C# and Asp.net MVC 5 framework. Our front-end connects to the graph-theoretic framework using JSON objects and to the backend using an Object Relational Mapping (ORM) framework. It uses MS SQL as its relational database management system.

2.3 Virtual Community for Crowdsourcing

Our framework is not just a system for argumentation structure; instead, we organize the community and system to work together synergistically to support learning via critical thinking. Members of this virtual community can take three major roles: 1) Users, who are the information seekers submitting the queries; 2) Responders, who have some degree of expertise or background to add Claim, Evidence, and Source nodes; and 3) Moderators, who are contributors that guide the question and answer flow, including triaging incoming questions, matching experts to new questions, evaluating answers for quality assurance, etc. These roles are dynamic as they may evolve over time, and may be multi-faceted with different functions and capabilities.

ACKNOWLEDGMENTS

We would like to gratefully acknowledge support from the Amazon AWS Research Grant program.

REFERENCES

[1] Christian Bizer, T Heath, and T Berners-Lee. 2009. Linked data-the story so far. *International journal on Semantic Web and Information Systems* 5, 3 (2009), 1–22. https://doi.org/10.4018/jswis.2009081901 arXiv:1011.1669

[2] Niall J Conroy, Niall J Conroy, Victoria L Rubin, and Yimin Chen. 2015. Automatic Deception Detection: Methods for Finding Fake News. In *ASIS&T*. http://onlinelibrary.wiley.com/doi/10.1002/pra2.2015.145052010082/full

[3] Robert H. Ennis. 1993. Critical thinking assessment. (1993), 179–186 pages. https://doi.org/10.1080/00405849309543594

[4] Stuart Ewen. 1996. *PR!: a social history of spin*. BasicBooks.

[5] Tom Heath and Christian Bizer. 2011. *Linked data: Evolving the Web into a global data space (1st edition)*. Vol. 1. 1–136 pages. https://doi.org/10.2200/S00334ED1V01Y201102WBE001 arXiv:arXiv:1011.1669v3

[6] Zhiwei Jin, Juan Cao, Yu-Gang Jiang, and Yongdong Zhang. 2014. News Credibility Evaluation on Microblog with a Hierarchical Propagation Model. *2014 IEEE International Conference on Data Mining* (2014), 230–239. https://doi.org/10.1109/ICDM.2014.91

[7] Ralph Johnson. 1996. *The Rise of Informal Logic*. Windsor Studies in Argumentation. https://doi.org/10.22329/10.22329/wsia.02.2014

[8] Adam Kucharski. 2016. Post-truth: Study epidemiology of fake news. *Nature* 540, 7634 (2016), 525–525. https://doi.org/10.1038/540525a

[9] Megan Barnhart Sethi. 2012. Information, Education, and Indoctrination: The Federation of American Scientists and Public Communication Strategies in the Atomic Age. *Historical Studies in the Natural Sciences* 42, 1 (2012), 1–29. https://doi.org/10.1525/hsns.2012.42.1.1 arXiv:http://hsns.ucpress.edu/content/42/1/1.full.pdf

[10] Michael J Sproule. 1997. *Propaganda and democracy : the American experience of media and mass persuasion*. Cambridge University Press, Cambridge, U.K. New York, NY.

[11] M. Tambuscio, G. Ruffo, A. Flammini, and F. Menczer. 2015. Fact-checking effect on viral hoaxes: A model of misinformation spread in social networks. *WWW* (2015), 977–982. https://doi.org/10.1145/2740908.2742572

OnToMap - Semantic Community Maps for Knowledge Sharing

Liliana Ardissono
Maurizio Lucenteforte
University of Torino
Computer Science Department
Torino, Italy 10149
liliana.ardissono@unito.it,maurizio.
lucenteforte@unito.it

Noemi Mauro
Adriano Savoca
University of Torino
Computer Science Department
Torino, Italy 10149
noemi.mauro@unito.it,savoca@di.
unito.it

Angioletta Voghera
Luigi La Riccia
DIST Politecnico di Torino
Torino, Italy 10125
angioletta.voghera@polito.it,luigi.
lariccia@polito.it

ABSTRACT

We present the information retrieval model adopted in the On-ToMap Participatory GIS. The model addresses the limitations of keyword-based and category-based search by semantically interpreting the information needs specified in free-text search queries. The model is based on an ontological representation of linguistic and encyclopaedic knowledge, which makes it possible to exploit terms and synonyms occurring in the definitions of concepts to flexibly match the user's and system's terminologies. This feature enables users to query the application using their own vocabulary.

CCS CONCEPTS

•**Information systems** → **Geographic information systems;** *Ontologies;* **Search interfaces;** *Presentation of retrieval results;*

KEYWORDS

Participatory GIS, Information search, Ontologies, Linked Data

1 INTRODUCTION

Web-GIS are increasingly used to support geographical information sharing, but they challenge information retrieval by imposing a fixed terminology for the specification of information the user is interested in. Starting from the GeoSpatial Semantic Web vision [2], we investigate the usefulness of semantics for enhancing not only data management and integration, but also multi-faceted information search and data visualization. Specifically, we propose an ontology-based model that integrates linguistic and encyclopaedic knowledge to enhance information search. This model is applied in the OnToMap Participatory GIS, described in the following.

This work is partially funded by project MIMOSA (MultIModal Ontology-driven query system for the heterogeneous data of a SmArtcity, "Progetto di Ateneo Torino_call2014_L2_157", 2015-17).

2 SEARCH QUERY INTERPRETATION

OnToMap [3] supports the management of interactive geographic maps for information sharing and participatory decision-making. The development of this application started with project "Mappe di Comunità 3.0" (https://ontomap.ontomap.eu), that investigated

the possibility of a new representation of community maps, using digital media and a semantic representation of spatial knowledge. OnToMap supports both the consultation of spatial data and the creation of public and private maps, which reflect individual information needs and can be enriched with crowdsourced content to help project design and group collaboration.

The application offers two information search modes, and different granularity levels in the specification of the relevant data.

- The former mode enables the user to enter free-text search queries; see [1]. Starting from the limitations of keyword-based and category-based search, that are offered by most Web GIS and location-based social networks, we investigated the potential of integrating semantic and linguistic knowledge for improving information retrieval. For this purpose, we defined an ontological representation of geographical information that allows the categorization of heterogeneous data, defining semantic relations among concepts, and is enriched with linguistic and encyclopaedic knowledge to define the meaning of concepts and the terms that can be used to refer to them. The ontology has a central role in supporting multi-faceted information retrieval because it offers a bridge between the domain conceptualization adopted by the system and the user's vocabulary: starting from the words occurring in the queries, and applying word sense disambiguation and synonym recognition, the system can identify the relevant concepts and provide the corresponding results, letting the user free to express her/himself in a natural way.

  Search queries are interpreted in three steps:
  (1) Recognition of geographical constraints and identification of the bounding box for data retrieval.
  (2) Semantic concept identification, by matching a semantically expanded query to the domain ontology in order to identify the referenced concepts. This enables the retrieval of a set of information items belonging to the general topics of the search query; e.g., hospitals.
  (3) Filtering of results to take the qualifiers specified in the query into account; e.g., *pediatric* hospitals. This is done by projecting the retrieved data on the items having in their own description attributes that coincide, or are semantically similar to those qualifiers (considering synonyms for flexibility).

  E.g., the query in Figure 1 ("nosocomi a Torino") is aimed at finding the hospitals in Torino, but it is expressed using a different name from the ontology concept ("Ospedali"). The

HT '17, July 4–7, 2017, Prague, Czech Republic.
© 2017 Copyright held by the owner/author(s). 978-1-4503-4708-2/17/07.
DOI: http://dx.doi.org/10.1145/3078714.3078747

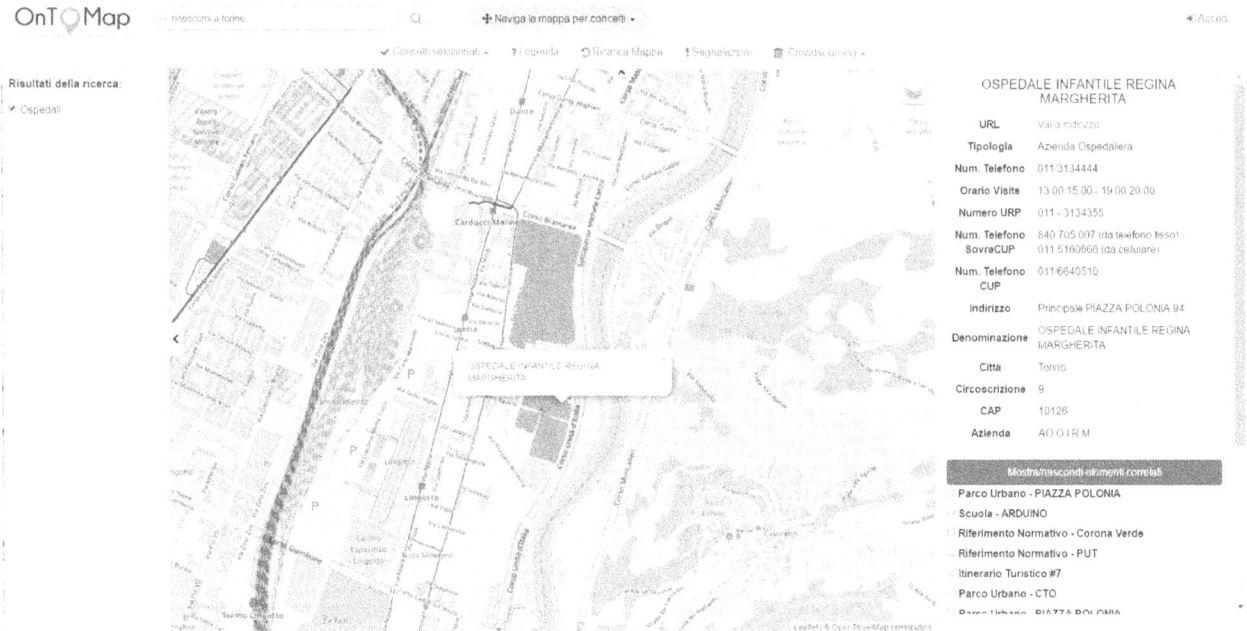

Figure 1: Search results for "nosocomi (hospitals) in Torino" and visualization of the data concerning a specific hospital.

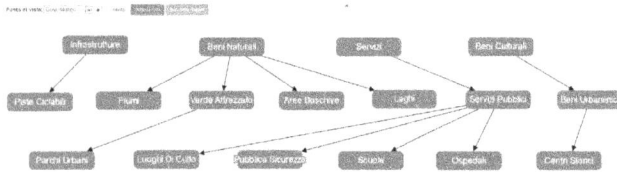

Figure 2: Generalist concept graph.

system has recognized the term as a synonym of "ospedale" and visualizes the results in the map. If the query included any qualifiers (e.g., *pediatric* hospitals), the application would filter the instances of "Ospedali" by matching the qualifiers to their descriptions. The result would be a single instance, "Ospedale Infantile Regina Margherita", having recognized that "Infantile" is a synonym of pediatric.

Semantic query expansion is also used to suggest other related concepts, guiding her/him towards types of information that can satisfy her/his needs in a more comprehensive way (not shown in the figure).

- The graph-based information search mode enables the user to explore concepts and relations in a direct way, by browsing a graph that represents a thematic view on the domain conceptualization. For instance, Figure 2 shows a generalist concept graph, which includes data categories relevant to non-expert users and displays subclass relations among concepts. This interaction mode enables the user to explore other possibly interesting concepts, by navigating the semantic relations that link the graph concepts to the rest of the ontology; e.g., the norms regulating the usage of infrastructures ("Infrastrutture") in the city.

The semantic knowledge representation helps the exploration of the information space in several ways, thanks to the structured representation of Linked Data; see [4]. For instance, the user can inspect the details of a geographical object by clicking on its icon; see the sticky note in Figure 1. In that case, a table reporting the main information about the item is displayed in the right portion of the page. Moreover, by clicking on button "Mostra/Nascondi elementi correlati" (*show/hide related items*), the user can visualize other information, related to the item in focus via semantic and geographic relations. For instance, the right portion of Figure 1 provides links to some official documents on land usage relevant for the area of the geographical item ("Riferimento normativo - ..."), to a school ("Arduino") and to a park adjacent to the hospital.

OnToMap was designed to manage participatory processes but it has supported other activities, outperforming other Web-GIS thanks to the semantic interpretation of search queries (w.r.t. keyword-based search) and map management functions. E.g., we collected positive feedback by comparing it with OpenStreetMap (openstreetmap.org) in an experiment in which a group of secondary level students used both applications to organize a sport event.

REFERENCES

[1] L. Ardissono, M. Lucenteforte, N. Mauro, A. Savoca, A. Voghera, and L. Lariccia. 2016. Exploration of Cultural Heritage Information via Textual Search Queries. In *MobileHCI '16 Proceedings Adjunct*. ACM, 992–1001.
[2] K. Janowicz, S. Scheider, T. Pehle, and G. Ha. 2012. Geospatial Semantics and Linked Spatiotemporal Data – Past, Present, and Future. *Semantic Web - On linked spatiotemporal data and geo-ontologies* 3, 4 (2012), 321–332.
[3] A. Voghera, R. Crivello, L.Ardissono, M. Lucenteforte, A. Savoca, and L. Lariccia. 2016. Production of spatial representations through collaborative mapping. An experiment. In *Proc. of INPUT 2016*. 356–361.
[4] W3C. 2017. Geospatial Semantic Web Community Group. https://www.w3.org/community/geosemweb/.

Stolperwege*

An App for a Digital Public History of the Holocaust

Alexander Mehler, Giuseppe Abrami, Steffen Bruendel,
Lisa Felder, Thomas Ostertag, Christian Spiekermann
Goethe-University Frankfurt

ABSTRACT

We present the Stolperwege app, a web-based framework for ubiquitous modeling of historical processes. Starting from the art project *Stolpersteine* of Gunter Demnig, it allows for virtually connecting these stumbling blocks with information about the biographies of victims of Nazism. According to the practice of *public history*, the aim of Stolperwege is to deepen public knowledge of the Holocaust in the context of our everyday environment. Stolperwege uses an information model that allows for modeling social networks of agents starting from information about portions of their life. The paper exemplifies how Stolperwege is informationally enriched by means of historical maps and 3D animations of (historical) buildings.

CCS CONCEPTS

•**Information systems → Multimedia information systems;** •**Applied computing → Hypertext / hypermedia creation;** *Interactive learning environments; Collaborative learning;*

KEYWORDS

Public History of the Holocaust, Historical Processes, Ubiquitous Computing, Geotagging, Geocaching, Historical Maps, 3D

1 INTRODUCTION

History is a public issue. It shapes the identity of social groups and communities. Hence, history does not exist as such, but is *made*. Further, historical knowledge and practice is not limited to academic settings. Rather, it is also produced by the non-professional public. It is not easy to precisely define public history for it incorporates a wide range of practices. The U.S.-based *National Council on Public History*, established in 1979 as the professional organization of people who practice interdisciplinary historical scholarship and thus transgress the boundaries of academia, defines public history as promoting "the utility of history" in society "through professional practice." [7] Generally speaking, this practice is characterized by the use of historical methods, an emphasis on professional training, and the aim to deepen public knowledge of the past.

---

*Contact author: Alexander Mehler (mehler@em.uni-frankfurt.de)

HT '17, July 04–07, 2017, Prague, Czech Republic
© 2017 Copyright held by the owner/author(s). 978-1-4503-4708-2/17/07.
DOI: http://dx.doi.org/10.1145/3078714.3078748

A public cultural artifact of large-scale relevance is Gunter Demnig's art project *Stolpersteine*. A *Stolperstein* dedicated to a person informs about the last place where the corresponding victim of Nazism has lived by her or his own choice (http://www.stolpersteine.eu/). We take this project as a starting point to model the biographies of victims of Nazism. To this end, we developed the Stolperwege app, a web-based framework for ubiquitous modeling of historical processes. This has been done by means of a series of students practicums lead by computer scientists and historians. In contrast to general purpose websites, Stolperwege allows for ubiquitously documenting portions of the life of persons also *on site*. It enables the public to document various aspects of the life of persons in a multimodal manner by integrating textual material as well as pictures, maps, videos and interactive animations. In this paper, we briefly describe how Stolperwege integrates interactive information units in support of its goals.

2 RELATED WORK

Though there exist several mobile applications for documenting and informing about *Stolpersteine*, not many of them are able to connect information about these stumbling blocks or to document larger biographical contexts. Some apps rather function as text-oriented mobile webpages (e.g., *Stolpersteine* in Berlin). Some of them are developed as applications to display *Stolpersteine* in conjunction with textual biographical information linked with maps for navigational issues.[1] Beyond that, the literature documents interesting projects in the field of *geocaching* and *geotagging* [2, 9, 11, 12] as well as of *urban computing* [4, 5] and *ubiquitous learning* [10]. None of these applications addresses *public history* according to the characteristics enumerated above. Further, none of the *Stolpersteine* apps supports entity linking or reasoning about biographical concepts. The Stolperwege app is developed to fill these gaps.

3 STOLPERWEGE APP

Stolperwege's front-end is split into two parts comprising its core navigational maps (see below) and 3D animations. Stolperwege's back-end consists of the Stolperwege webservice and the so-called OWLnotator [1]. OWLnotator is a web-based tool that allows for modeling ontologies for annotating humanities data (texts, lexica, pictures, their intermedia relations etc.). In our case, OWLnotator serves to integrate an OWL-based model of biographies that is extended by multimodal information units which are finally used to informationally enrich biographical entities. Currently, associations of biographical entities are represented by means of the *Biography* ontology of *TrendMiner* [8]. The so-called *ResourceManager* [3] is additionally used by Stolperwege to handle multimodal

---

[1]E.g., *Stolpersteine* app in Wiesbaden, Bochum or Bad Homburg. SWR2 *Stolpersteine* additionally provides audio files.

data units (pictures, videos, audio files etc.) while the *Authority-Manager* is used to adhere to copyright and to allow the formation of social networks of users who cooperate in documenting the same persons, events, places etc. Stolperwege uses free Android libraries as, for example, *OpenStreetMap* (https://www.openstreetmap.org/) to display geolocated entities (see Fig. 1). Depictable entities such as Stolpersteine, persons, places, buildings, their attributes, labels and connections to each other (displayed by means of polygons) are represented as so-called *StolperwegeElements*. *StolperwegeElements* are defined as informationally extensible elements which can be displayed on calculated positions on Stolperwege's map (see Fig. 2). They can be interrelated (as networks of persons, events or places) in order to manifest event-related portions of the biographies of the corresponding persons (see Fig. 3). In this way, Stolperwege even allows for modeling crossing points of the biographies of different persons taking part at the same events. Note that colors and geometrical means used to display such information units can be configured and managed by means of Stolperwege's webservice.

Figure 1: Event-related information about a person.
Figure 2: Information about a person as part of the event.
Figure 3: Road of life linking Amsterdam and Frankfurt.

Using maps of varying resolution, the public can trace the biographies of (groups of) persons between cities, within a city, a district or a neighborhood (see Fig. 1-3). Depending on the resolution of the map selected by the user, Stolperwege informs about nearby geotags relating to documented events or persons. The same can be done by focusing on a certain context (by reference to a person or an event) in order to be informed about related, nearby geotags. Clustering ensures an overseeable view and improves performance.

The "historical" part of Stolperwege opens the door to views of the past. To this end, Stolperwege synchronizes present-day maps with their historical counterparts to allow for tracing the locations of historical (possibly destroyed) places and buildings (see Fig. 4 and 5). OpenStreetMap overlays are managed by means of MapTiler (https://www.maptiler.com/). Further, interactive 3D animations of buildings are developed by means of *Blender* (https://www.blender.org/). This includes 3D reconstructions of the now destroyed "Palais Rothschild" and of the so called "Ghettohaus" [6] (see Fig. 5) both located at Frankfurt. Their models have been created after obtaining various historical maps, floor plans and photographs, made accessible and animated with *Unity3d* (https://unity3d.com/de). In this way, various interactions can be realised, e.g., tours through the building, displaying information about former inhabitants, playback of audio and video files. This makes it possible to convey information about historical events, places and people in an interactive manner. The generation of these 3D models is quite laborious which is one of the reasons why the build-up of Stolperwege is a long-term project.

Figure 4: Aligned historical map of Frankfurt from 1852 (Foltz-Eberle, Public Domain) integrated into Stolperwege.
Figure 5: Interactive 3D animation of the so-called "Ghettohaus" [6].

4 FUTURE WORK

Future work aims at instantiating Stolperwege by means of biographical information about persons for which *Stolpersteine* exist in Frankfurt am Main and to make it open source.

5 ACKNOWLEDGEMENTS

We thank all students and volunteers who worked on Stolperwege including Mevlüt Bagci, Lars Biroth, Emre Cümbüs, Joschua Fink, Simon Fleig, Giovanni Ilestro, Matthias Jostock, Markus Klötzl, Fabian Knöller, Nicolas Lupp and Angelo Mereu.

REFERENCES

[1] Giuseppe Abrami, Alexander Mehler, and Dietmar Pravida. 2015. Fusing Text and Image Data with the Help of the OWLnotator. In *Human Interface and the Management of Information. Information and Knowledge Design*, Sakae Yamamoto (Ed.). LNCS, Vol. 9172. Springer, 261–272.

[2] Martin Becker, Philipp Singer, Florian Lemmerich, Andreas Hotho, Denis Helic, and Markus Strohmaier. 2015. VizTrails: An Information Visualization Tool for Exploring Geographic Movement Trajectories. In *Proc. of the 26th ACM Conference on Hypertext & Social Media (HT '15)*. ACM, New York, NY, 319–320.

[3] Rüdiger Gleim, Alexander Mehler, and Alexandra Ernst. 2012. SOA implementation of the eHumanities Desktop. In *Proc. of DH 2012*.

[4] Frank Allan Hansen and Kaj Grønbæk. 2008. Social Web Applications in the City: A Lightweight Infrastructure for Urban Computing. In *Proc. of HT '08*. New York, NY, 175–180.

[5] Frank Allan Hansen and Kaj Grønbæk. 2010. UrbanWeb: A Platform for Mobile Context-aware social Computing. In *Proc. of HT '10*. ACM, New York, NY, 195–200.

[6] Renate Hebauf. 1999. Frankfurt am Main, Gaußstraße 14. Ein Haus und seine jüdischen Bewohner zwischen 1911 und 1945. In *"Nach der Kristallnacht": jüdisches Leben und antijüdische Politik in Frankfurt am Main 1938-1945*, Monica Kingreen (Ed.). Campus, Frankfurt/New York.

[7] Barbara J Howe. 1989. Reflections on an idea: NCPH's first decade. *The Public Historian* 11, 3 (1989), 69–85.

[8] Hans-Ulrich Krieger and Thierry Declerck. 2014. TMO – The Federated Ontology of the TrendMiner Project. In *Proc. of LREC'14*. Reykjavik, 4164–4171.

[9] Vanessa Lopez, Spyros Kotoulas, Marco Luca Sbodio, and Raymond Lloyd. 2013. Guided Exploration and Integration of Urban Data. In *Proc. of the 24th ACM Conference on Hypertext and Social Media (HT '13)*. ACM, New York, NY, 242–247.

[10] Hiroaki Ogata and Yoneo Yano. 2004. Context-aware support for computer-supported ubiquitous learning. In *Proc. of 2nd IEEE International Workshop on Wireless and Mobile Technologies in Education*. IEEE, 27–34.

[11] Kenton O'Hara. 2008. Understanding Geocaching Practices and Motivations. In *Proc. of SIGCHI (CHI '08)*. ACM, New York, NY, 1177–1186.

[12] Gianluca Tursi, Martina Deplano, and Giancarlo Ruffo. 2014. AIRCacher: Virtual Geocaching Powered with Augmented Reality. In *Proc. of HT'14*. ACM, New York, 330–332.

Exploring Cross-cultural Crowd Sentiments on Twitter

Yuanyuan Wang
Yamaguchi University
Ube, Yamaguchi, 755-8611 Japan
y.wang@yamaguchi-u.ac.jp

Muhammad Syafiq Mohd Pozi
Kyoto Sangyo University
Kyoto, 603-8555 Japan
syafiq@cc.kyoto-su.ac.jp

Yukiko Kawai
Kyoto Sangyo University
Kyoto, 603-8555 Japan
kawai@cc.kyoto-su.ac.jp

Adam Jatowt
Kyoto University
Kyoto, 606-8501 Japan
adam@dl.kuis.kyoto-u.ac.jp

Toyokazu Akiyama
Kyoto Sangyo University
Kyoto, 603-8555 Japan
akiyama@cc.kyoto-su.ac.jp

ABSTRACT

Twitter is frequently used to express personal opinions and sentiments. This work presents a novel crowd sentiment analysis of Twitter for exploring cross-cultural differences. We aim to find similar meanings but different sentiments between Twitter data collected over diverse geographic places. For this, we detect sentiments and topics of each tweet and assign sentiments to each topic based on the sentiments of the corresponding tweets. This permits finding interesting cross-cultural patterns. We demonstrate a visualization system that supports the interactive analysis of two countries: France and Italy.

CCS CONCEPTS

• Theory of computation → Semantics and reasoning; • Networks → Location based services;

KEYWORDS

crowd sentiment analysis; Twitter; cross-cultural study

1 INTRODUCTION

Despite the widespread utilization of social media internationally, still relatively little is known about cross-cultural differences in social media. Park and his colleagues [7] attempted to demonstrate cultural differences in the use of emoticons on Twitter. Other researches focused on cultural differences related to user multilingualism in Twitter [5, 6].

In this context, sentiment analysis has become a popular tool for data analysts, especially those that deal with social media data. It is common to find public opinions and reviews of services, events, and products on social media. As most of the existing sentiment analysis methods were designed for generic purposes, it is crucial to develop new technologies to leverage sentiment analysis for a wide number of cultures and languages [1].

In this work, we provide a novel crowd sentiment analysis to find semantically similar content characterized by different sentiments based on Twitter data collected from different countries. We then explore cross-cultural differences based on similar semantics but different sentiments in different geographical areas. Note that

HT '17, July 4–7, 2017, Prague, Czech Republic.
© 2017 Copyright held by the owner/author(s).
ACM ISBN 978-1-4503-4708-2/17/07.
http://dx.doi.org/10.1145/3078714.3078749

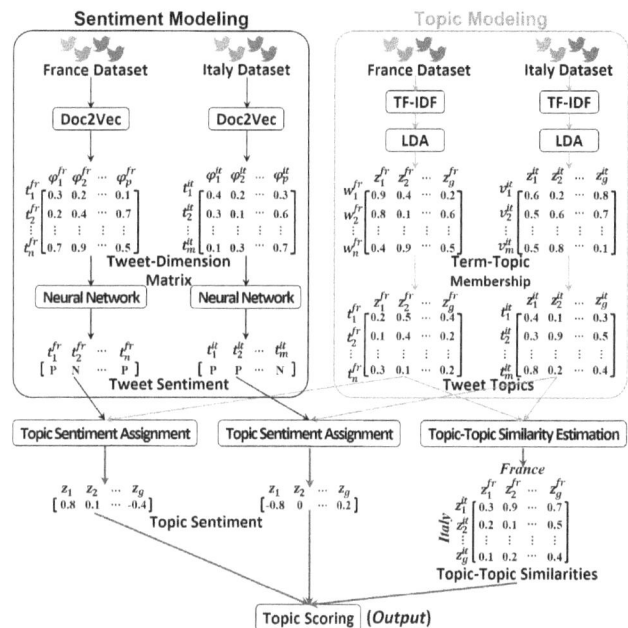

Figure 1: Crowd sentiment analysis.

although we focus on Twitter, our cross-cultural sentiment analysis can accept any datasets, e.g., services, products, or facilities, for discovering sentiments of topics over tweets. This should be useful to recommend particular activities, products, services, events, or places to visit for a given segment of users.

2 CROWD SENTIMENT ANALYSIS

The processing flow of our method is shown in Fig. 1. It has 3 main stages: sentiment modeling for categorizing tweets into Pos and Neg by applying neural networks, topic modeling for detecting tweet topics through the LDA model, and topic-topic similarity estimation for finding similar topics on two datasets derived from Twitter which are related to two different countries (e.g., France and Italy).

2.1 Sentiment Modeling

In order to identify each tweet's sentiment, we developed a sentiment classification model from existing labeled tweets dataset used in [2]. The dataset consists of 1,600K tweets used as the training set and 498 tweets used as the testing set. Re-tweets and any tweets that contain URLs were removed. We used the deep learning approach to implement the classification model.

Table 1: Dataset statistics

	France	Italy	Total
#Tweets	484,450	470,916	955,366
#Total unique words	44,970	39,762	84,732
#Ave. unique words per tweet	9.78	9.58	—

Next, every tweet was transformed into a feature vector. Representing a single instance of user vocabulary usage over a set of universal vocabulary will always result in a sparse vector. We then limit the dimensionality into 300 features using Doc2Vec algorithm. Each tweet has its own vector representation to be fed into a fully connected neural network model for supervised learning.

2.2 Topic Modeling

In the next stage, we perform a topic modeling based on tweets by using Latent Dirichlet allocation (LDA) algorithm with *TF-IDF* scored words of each dataset. LDA is a generative model in which the topic distribution is assumed to have a Dirichlet prior. After learning is completed, the probability of a word w to belong to a topic z_g ($g \in [1, G]$), $P(w|z_g)$, is known, where G denotes the topic number (set to 300 in our implementation). Then, the probability of a topic z_g given a word w can be easily inferred by applying Bayes' rule, $P(z_g|w) \propto P(w|z_g)P(z_g)$, where $P(z_g)$ is approximated by the exponential of the expected value of its logarithm under the variational distribution. Through the LDA model, we can obtain the probabilistic distribution of topics given a word in each dataset.

2.3 Topic-Topic Similarity Estimation

Since we have two separate tweet datasets, we need to synchronize topics from these datasets. In the next stage, we then measure the similarities between topics in the two datasets based on the probability distributions by computing the topic distributions of each dataset using the LDA model, and then computing Kullback-Leibler (KL) divergence [3] between the topic distributions of a pair of topics in two datasets:

$$D_{KL}(P||Q) = \sum_w P(w) \log \frac{P(w)}{Q(w)}$$

We consider a topic z_i to be similar to z_j if $D_{KL}(P||Q) \leq 0.0002$ for this topic pair. Hence, tweets that belong to such topics are assumed to be semantically similar. Note that we use joint vocabulary from the two datasets for computing KL divergence.

Finally, we assign sentiment to each topic based on the number of positive and negative tweets covered by given topics by computing the weighted average sentiment score over topics. Based on the computed sentiment scores of topics and the similarities of topics, we can then find semantically similar topics that have different sentiments. Pairs of similar topics where each comes from a different dataset are then ranked by the Euclidean distance such as $dist(z_i, z_j) = \sqrt{(\#pos(z_i) - \#pos(z_j))^2 + (\#neg(z_i) - \#neg(z_j))^2}$. Here, $\#pos(z_i)$ returns the number of positive tweets about a topic z_i, and $\#neg(z_i)$ returns the number of negative tweets about z_i.

3 DEMONSTRATION

With our visualization system similar to [4], users can find similar meaning but semantically different topics in Twitter from diverse geographical areas (currently, countries) in order to explore cross-cultural differences. We use the datasets derived from Twitter which

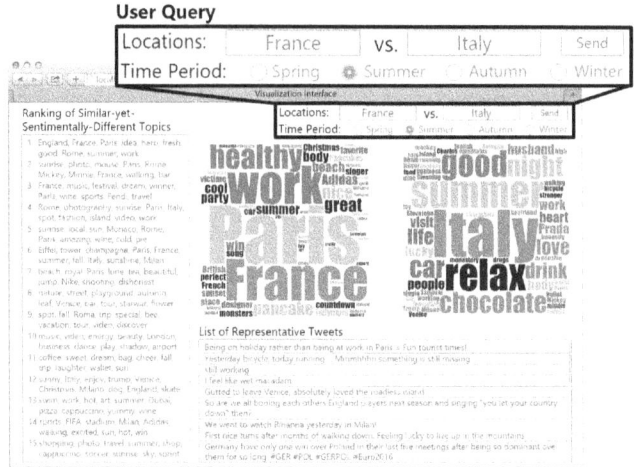

Figure 2: The user interface of our visualization system.

are related to two countries: France and Italy. Table 1 shows the statistics of both datasets.

3.1 Interaction

To use our visualization system, user needs to select two locations (countries). The system then returns the ranked list of similar-yet-sentimentally-different topics in the form of term clouds, as well as the list of representative tweets for the extracted topics in both the locations (see Figure 2). User can also select a time period (e.g., one of seasons) and by this the ranked topic list, the term clouds, and the tweet list can be updated according to the user's specified time period. When a user clicks a given term, the system presents the list of its most related tweets.

4 CONCLUSION

Twitter offers unique opportunities for conducting large scale cultural studies. In this research, we have proposed methodology for finding similar topics that are subject to different sentiments as a part of wider cross-cultural study. Future work will expand the current analysis method to recommend particular activities, products, services, events, or places to visit for a given segment of users. We will also experiment with Twitter data in other countries.

ACKNOWLEDGMENTS

This work was partially supported by MIC SCOPE (171507010), and JSPS KAKENHI Grant Numbers 15K00162, 16H01722, 17K12686, 17H01822.

REFERENCES

[1] Matheus Araújo, Julio Reis, Adriano Pereira, and Fabrício Benevenuto. 2016. An Evaluation of Machine Translation for Multilingual Sentence-level Sentiment Analysis. In *Proc. of SAC 2016*. 1140–1145.

[2] Alec Go, Richa Bhayani, and Lei Huang. 2009. Twitter sentiment classification using distant supervision. *CS224N Project Report, Stanford* 1 (2009), 12.

[3] S. Kullback and R. A. Leibler. 1951. On Information and Sufficiency. *The Annals of Mathematical Statistics* 22, 1 (1951), 79–86.

[4] Guy Lansley and Paul A. Longley. 2016. The geography of Twitter topics in London. *Computers, Environment and Urban Systems* 58 (2016), 85–96.

[5] Caitlin McCollister. 2016. *Predicting Author Traits Through Topic Modeling of Multilingual Social Media Text*. Ph.D. Dissertation. University of Kansas.

[6] Muhammad Syafiq Mohd Pozi, Yukiko Kawai, Adam Jatowt, and Toyokazu Akiyama. 2017. Sketching Linguistic Borders: Mobility Analysis on Multilingual Microbloggers. In *Proc. of WWW 2017 Companion*. 825–826.

[7] Jaram Park, Young Min Baek, and Meeyoung Cha. 2014. Cross-Cultural Comparison of Nonverbal Cues in Emoticons on Twitter: Evidence from Big Data Analysis. *Journal of Communication* 64, 2 (2014), 333–354.

Author Index

NOTES

www.ingramcontent.com/pod-product-compliance
Lightning Source LLC
Chambersburg PA
CBHW080919220326
41598CB00034B/5625